D0984729

The Letters of John Addington Symonds

VOLUME III

1885–1893

DAS

KONTRÄRE
GESCHLECHTSGEFÜHL

VON

HAVELOCK ELLIS

UND

J. A. SYMONDS

DEUTSCHE ORIGINAL AUSGABE

BESORGT UNTER MITWIRKUNG

VON

DR. HANS KURELLA

LEIPZIG
GEORG H. WIGAND'S VERLAG
1896

1. Title page of Havelock Ellis and J. A. Symonds, Das Konträre Geschlechtsgefühl *(1896). The first publication on sex by Ellis and (posthumously) by Symonds.*

The Letters of
John Addington Symonds

Volume III

1885–1893

edited by

Herbert M. Schueller

Wayne State University

&

Robert L. Peters

University of California, Irvine

Wayne State University Press, Detroit, 1969

For
Andrew, Janine, and Peggy Dakyns

Contents

Illustrations

1. Frontispiece—Title page of Havelock Ellis and J. A. Symonds, *Das Konträre Geschlechtsgefühl* (1896): the first publication on sex by Ellis and Symonds.

The following illustrations will be found grouped together after page 192.

2. The four Symonds daughters, ca. 1886; Davos in the background.
3. Margaret, Lotta, and Katharine Symonds, 1893.
4. Mr. and Mrs. J. A. Symonds with their daughter Katharine and the dog Ciò, taken at Davos, ca. 1886.
5. Poggio Gherardo, home of Janet Ross near Florence.
6. Countess Almorò Pisani.
7. The pulpit given by Symonds in memory of his daughter Janet to the English Church of St. Luke, Davos.
8, 9. Two works by Marianne North.
10. Samuel Richards, "Evangeline Discovering her Affianced in the Hospital."
11. H. H. Gilchrist, "Whitman."
12. Symonds and two unidentified friends.
13. Symonds' study at Am Hof.
14. Symonds in his study.
15. Tea time at Am Hof.
16. G. Plüschow, "Boy with Spear," from R. W. Schufeldt, *Studies of the Human Form for Artists* . . . (1908).
17. Edward Carpenter (1844–1929).
18. Charlotte Symonds Green, age 84.
19. Henry Graham Dakyns at Inchnadamff, Loch Assynt, 1903.
20. Title page of *Sexual Inversion,* second and final publication on sex by Ellis and Symonds (1897).
21, 22. Two ink drawings by Margaret Symonds illustrating two of Symonds' favorite poems.

Opposite page 839

23. The last letter: To Catherine Symonds written on Symonds' deathbed.

Preface

This is the third and final volume of the letters of John Addington Symonds. It covers the period 1885–1893, from a few months after Symonds' 44th birthday until his death in Rome 6 months after his 52nd. It includes 660 letters, 4 of which, designated by an "a," were added after the numbering for this volume was complete, and 6 of which are in an appendix. (The short notes, fairly common in the 2 preceding volumes, have ceased.) The final letter is 2113, a number somewhat higher than the 2000 we mentioned in the Biographical Introduction to Volume I. Since Volume II has 10 letters not numbered in the usual way (1254a, 1258a, and so forth), the total is actually 2127.

The letters of the present volume continue to reflect the mind and activity of a man involved in literary production. Symonds' primary interest, that of publishing his own poetry, though it was to die only with his own death, was suppressed. His energies were expended in completing the final 2 volumes of *The Renaissance in Italy* (1886), translating Gozzi (1890) and Cellini (1887), compiling materials for his 2 small books on Ben Jonson (1886, in the "English Worthies" series) and Sidney (1886, in the "English Men of Letters" series), writing and collecting his essays on art and literature (in *Essays Speculative and Suggestive,* 1890, and in *In the Key of Blue,* 1893), writing on Swiss life (*Our Life in the Swiss Highlands,* with his daughter Margaret, 1892), and doing research for his lives of Michelangelo (1893) and Walt Whitman (1893).

A good share of his energies was also devoted to work on homosexuality (*A Problem in Modern Ethics,* 1891) and to his work with Havelock Ellis (printed after his death, 1896 and 1897). When Symonds' contribution to an analysis of what Mrs. Symonds called "the great question" was, as it were, swallowed up, when Symonds' name no longer appeared on the title page of what eventually became Ellis' *Studies in the Psychology of Sex* (7 vols., 1898–1928), some of his most promising work went underground, and one must come to the conclusion that the real disappointment of Symonds' life (and the real disappointment of his readers and followers) was that, despite his quick intelligence, his powers of observation, his facility in writing, and his enormous industry (not to mention his frequent enjoyment of the physical aspects of life, which of course had little to do with the writing for which he is best known), his real talents were never used. From the first he should have been a worker like Havelock Ellis in the area of sexual physiology, pathology, and psychology. Most of his writing is a romantic and apparently self-indulgent substitute for biological and psychological scientific work which he was eminently fitted to do and which, being consistent with his own nature and primary interests, would have inspirited him as most of his writing dispirited and fatigued him.

The editorial practices of Volumes I and II are continued in III. For details the reader may consult the 2 earlier prefaces. The reader will find footnotes fewer in this volume than in previous ones. Also, places of publication are not always given in this volume even for non-English books. Furthermore, a skeleton index, as given in Volumes I and II is absent. Since the present volume carries an index for all 3, it seemed unnecessary to repeat notes or always to refer back to previous volumes (an example is Smith, Elder and Co., or "the Elder," as Symonds, following the practice of George Smith himself, sometimes called that firm).

A source important to us in this volume is the *Davos Courier*. Since its material is interesting for various reasons, especially to people familiar with Davos and its milieu, we have been tempted to quote from it extensively, to quote pieces from it in toto. But prudence has forced us to control ourselves, and it is with regret that we have often only listed news items and their publication dates. The library of the University of California, Riverside, has a microfilm copy of the *Courier* from November 1, 1888, when it began, into 1893, when Symonds died. It may be consulted by the reader.

To list all of the persons who deserve our thanks in preparing this volume would be to repeat some of the names in the preface to Volume I. It is, however, necessary to add to these names the following: Professor John P. Anton of the University of New York at Buffalo; Mrs. George S. Cunningham of the Carnegie Library at Pittsburgh; Mrs. Rebecca Dixon of the Institute for Sex Research at Indiana University; Mrs. Linda R. de Grand of the Center for Research Libraries, Chicago, Illinois; Robert H.

Land, Reference Department, the Library of Congress; A. C. C. Peebles, secretary of *The Athenaeum,* London; Douglas V. Steere of Traverse City, Michigan; the late Professor Leo Stoller of the English Department, Wayne State University. Anthony Ugolnik, now of Brown University, began as an assistant in the preparation of this volume. Mrs. Karen Oberstein completed what he had begun. She has also helped compile the Index. We are grateful also for a grant-in-aid from the Graduate Division of Wayne State University, Henry Bohm, Vice President.

This volume concludes with a list of corrections and additions to Volumes I and II. We are grateful to all persons who have pointed out errors, especially Alexander Brede, Janine Dakyns, Ernest J. Mehew, Ralph Nash, Dorothy L. Tyler, and Gail Weinberg. All instances of errors in the texts of the letters have been checked against the photographs and the manuscripts. When the errors are Symonds', they are not noted here; in the Preface to Volume I we indicated our intention to reproduce the letters as they are. Therefore the errors in the manuscripts stand unless we have misread or have been in error ourselves. Footnote errors are of course ours and are noted.

There is one moot question: the dating of L 1. When it was first shown us, we were told that the date is 1844; Mrs. Grosskurth interpreted the number in the manuscript as 1849; we thought the 1844 date closer to correct; to give evidence to the reader, we reproduced the manuscript opposite the letter in our collection. This minor point may never perhaps be settled. That L 1 is Symonds' first is, however, quite beyond question.

The most regrettable of the errors in Volume I are those in the Chronology which have been corrected in Volume II. They occur in the years 1886–88 and were originally caused by vagaries of book-dating. Note 2 to L 1617 explains the relevance to the changes in the Chronology to Symonds' translation of Cellini's autobiography. The practice of post-dating books puts in question the dates of most 19th century publications. To check every book date on every title-page does not make for any more certainty about dates of issue than does searching in the British Museum or the Library of Congress catalogs.

Herbert M. Schueller
Robert L. Peters

Detroit, Michigan
Irvine, California

Abbreviations

The following abbreviations are used throughout these volumes:

Babington — Percy L. Babington, *Bibliography of the Writings of John Addington Symonds.* London, 1925.

Biography — Horatio F. Brown, *John Addington Symonds: A Biography.* 2d. ed., 1903.

E S & S — John Addington Symonds, *Essays Speculative and Suggestive.* 2 vols., London, 1890.

Grosskurth — Phyllis Grosskurth, *John Addington Symonds.* London, 1964.

H & P — Katharine (Symonds) Furse, *Hearts and Pomegranates.* London, 1940.

HFB — Horatio Forbes Brown

HGD — Henry Graham Dakyns

KF — Katharine (Symonds) Furse

L or Ls — Letter or Letters

L & P — Horatio F. Brown, ed., *Letters and Papers of John Addington Symonds.* New York, 1923.

Michelangelo — John Addington Symonds, *The Life of Michelangelo Buonarroti.* 2 vols., London, 1893.

OLSH — John Addington Symonds and Margaret Symonds, *Our Life in the Swiss Highlands.* London and Edinburgh, 1892.

OOP — Margaret (Symonds) Vaughan, *Out of the Past.* London, 1925.

*Chronology**

No reference is made to periodical or posthumous publications; nor, except in one instance, are any editions after the first mentioned for each book.

1834		Marriage of Harriet Sykes and Dr. John Addington Symonds
18–		Edith Harriet Symonds (later Cave) born
1837		Mary Isabella (Maribella) Symonds (later Strachey) born
1839		[John Abdy Stephenson Symonds born and died]
1840	Oct. 5	John Addington Symonds born at 7 Berkeley Square, Bristol
1842		Charlotte Symonds (later Green) born
1844		Harriet Sykes Symonds, Symonds' mother, dies
1848		Symonds at day-school of the Rev. William Knight
1851	June	The Symonds family moves to Clifton Hill House, Clifton
1854	May	Symonds enters Harrow School
1856		Meets George and Josephine Butler
1858	Summer	Visits in Scotland
	Autumn	Enters Balliol College, Oxford University
1859	Summer	On reading party to Whitby with T. H. Green, A. O. Rutson, C. Puller, and John Conington
1860	June 20	Wins Newdigate prize for English Verse with essay on the Escorial
	Summer	On reading party to Coniston with Conington, Green, and others

* This table is to serve as a handy guide. It should be noted, however, that for the last few years of Symonds' life it is inadequate. He lived at Davos most of each year but took an annual journey to Venice to stay in Horatio F. Brown's house at 560 Zattere. But he took many other trips, either according to plan or spontaneously, throughout Switzerland. These have not been recorded here. One cannot be sure that a complete account of them is even possible. If it were, it would be less a guide than a successful piece of pedantry. Nor have we recorded every trip Symonds made from Switzerland to England.

	Autumn	On Belgian tour with the Caves and his sister Charlotte; in Berlin, Prague, Vienna, Salzburg, Munich, with his father
1861	March 25–April 6	With Miss Mary Ann Sykes (his aunt) and Charlotte in Amiens and Paris
	June–July	At Chamonix and in Lombardy with father: the first visit to Italy
	August	In North Wales (Bangor) with reading party with Rawlinson (as coach) and W. R. W. Stephens
	September	On visit to Wiltshire with Charlotte
	November	Introduced to Clough's poetry by Jowett
1862	April	At Great Malvern for reading party with Stephens
	June–July	In Munich, Innsbruck, and Venice with father and Charlotte
	July 20	Ill at Visp
	October	Elected fellow of Magdalen College
	October 27	Admitted as probationary fellow at Magdalen (1862–64)
	October–November	Personal attacks by G. H. Shorting
	December 28	Acquitted of Shorting's charges
1863	Late March	In Belgium with W. R. W. Stephens
	April	First breakdown; goes to Malvern with Charlotte
	June 17	Receives Chancellor's prize for essay on the Renaissance; leaves Oxford
	June 25–July	Sent to Switzerland by father; travels with Cecil Bosanquet: Strassburg, Basel, Lucerne, Pilatus, Engelberg, Interlaken, Mürren; meets Rosa Engel
	July	Meets Frederick North and his daughters Marianne and Catherine
	August–September	Meets T. H. Green in Zurich and travels with him to Mürren, to Munich, Dresden, Leipzig
	Early October	At Clifton Hill House; elected full fellow at Magdalen; meets Henry Graham Dakyns
	November–December	In Italy: Pisa, Florence, Rome, with A. O. Rutson
1864	January	In Rome; joined by W. R. W. Stephens
	February	In Naples, Sorrento, and (on the 11th) back to Rome; then Perugia, Assisi, Leghorn, Genoa, Marseilles, Paris
	April	Takes rooms at 7 Half Moon Street, London, to study law
	Early August	Pursues the Norths to Pontresina

	August 14	Proposes to Catherine North at Pontresina, is accepted two days later, and travels with the North family to Venice and then to Dover
	November 10	Marries Catherine North at St. Clement's Church, Hastings
1865	January	Lives first in London at 13 Albion Street, near Hyde Park, and then at 47 Norfolk Square
	February	In lawyer's chambers at 5 Paper Buildings, the Temple
	October 22	The Symonds' first child, Janet, born
1866	February 24	The Symondses, at father's advice, start out for the Riviera, a legal career for Symonds being abandoned: at Cannes, San Remo, Genoa, Pisa, Florence, Siena, Bologna, Ravenna, Parma, Pavia, Milan; to Switzerland: Macugnaga and Mürren
	August 24	Back at 47 Norfolk Square
1867	May–June (1st half)	With sister Charlotte in Normandy: Rouen, Caen, Bayeux, Avranches, Chartres
	July 30	Lotta (Charlotte Mary), the Symonds' second daughter, born (later Mrs. Walter Leaf)
	September 4	Symonds family goes to Melun, Dijon
	September 7	Enters Switzerland
	October 10	At Genoa; slowly travels to Cannes
	October 24	Cannes
1868	January	At Cannes with Henry Sidgwick and Edward Lear; undergoes second breakdown
	February	Goes to Nice and Monaco
	April	Goes to Corsica
	May–June	Bologna, Padua, Venice; then Switzerland
	July	At Clifton; London house abandoned
	November 17	Family moves to 7 Victoria Square, Clifton
	December	Proposal that Symonds lecture on Greek literature to sixth form at Clifton College accepted
1869	January	Lectures at Clifton College and for the Society for Higher Education for Women
	January 15	Margaret, the Symonds' third daughter, born (later Mrs. W. W. Vaughan)
	January 27	Friendship with Norman Moor begins in earnest
	April 10–17	Assists father-in-law Frederick North, whose election as M.P. from Hastings is challenged
	July	With Norman Moor in France and Switzerland
1870	May–June	In Switzerland, Italy, and Munich

	July 10	Back at Clifton
1871	January	Blocks out first chapter of a book on Italian literature
	February 25	Dr. John Addington Symonds dies, age 64
	March	Symonds writes introduction to his edition of his father's literary remains (*Verses* and *Miscellanies,* 1871)
	July 1	Charlotte Symonds marries T. H. Green
	July–August	With the Greens in Switzerland
	September	Moves into Clifton Hill House
	October	Writes to Whitman for the first time
1872	Publishes:	*An Introduction to the Study of Dante*
	July–August	In Switzerland and Italy with Norman Moor
1873	Publishes:	*Studies of the Greek Poets [First Series]*
	Spring	The Symondses in Sicily and Athens
	From October to	Travels with servant to Malta, Tunis, Sicily, Naples,
	January, 1874	Rome, Perugia, Florence, Cannes
1874	Publishes:	*Sketches in Italy and Greece*
1875	Publishes:	*The Age of the Despots* (Vol. I of *The Renaissance in Italy*)
	Spring	The Symondses go to Rome, Amalfi, Capri
	Summer	Symonds and Mr. & Mrs. H. G. Dakyns (married in 1872) go to the Rhone Valley, Bel Alp, and Chamonix
	November 23	Katharine, the Symonds' fourth daughter, born (later Mrs. Charles W. Furse)
1876	Publishes:	*Studies of the Greek Poets, Second Series*
	February	The Symondses in San Remo
	End of summer	With H. F. Brown and J. E. Pearson at the Valais
	From autumn to March, 1877	Campaigns for Professorship of Poetry at Oxford
1877	Publishes:	*The Revival of Learning* and *The Fine Arts* (Vols. II and III of *The Renaissance in Italy*)
	April	Leaves for Greece with Frank Tuckett, but at Cannes goes north to Lombardy
	May	Principal Shairp of St. Andrews elected Professor of Poetry at Oxford. Symonds returns to Clifton.
	August 7	Sees Davos for the first time (at the Greens' invitation) and remains there for the winter
1878	Publishes:	*The Sonnets of Michael Angelo Buonarroti and Tommaso Campanella*
		Many Moods, a volume of verse
		Shelley
	April–May	The Symondses in Italy (Milan and Venice)

	Mid–summer	Return to Davos
1879	Publishes:	*Sketches and Studies in Italy*
1880	Publishes:	*New and Old,* a volume of verse
	Summer	Varese, Florence, Tuscany, Rome, and Umbria; breaks up home at Clifton Hill House
	September	Moves permanently to Davos
	November 4	The R. L. Stevensons reach Davos
1881	Publishes:	*Italian Literature,* 2 vols. (Vols. IV and V of *The Renaissance in Italy*)
	May	In Venice, meets Angelo Fusato
	June–September	"Am Hof" at Davos built
1882	Publishes:	*Animi Figura,* verse
	March	Death of T. H. Green, his brother-in-law
	May	Goes to London for medical attention and to make his will
	September 25	Moves into "Am Hof"
1883	Publishes:	*Italian Byways*
		A Problem in Greek Ethics (privately)
	April–May	In Venice
	October 5	Mary Isabella (Maribella) Symonds Strachey dies of tuberculosis
		Organizes first international toboggan race at Davos
1884	Publishes:	*Wine, Women, and Song* (goliardic songs translated)
		Vagabunduli Libellus, verse
		Shakespere's Predecessors in the English Drama
	Spring	At San Remo; then Venice and Monte Generoso
1885	May	In Venice
1886	Publishes:	*Sir Philip Sidney*
		The Catholic Reaction, 2 vols. (Vols. VI and VII of *The Renaissance in Italy*)
		Ben Jonson ("English Worthies" series)
	Sept.–Nov.	Translates Cellini's *Life*
		Excursions throughout Switzerland
1887	Publishes:	Translation of *The Life of Benvenuto Cellini*
	April 7	Janet Symonds dies of tuberculosis
	May–June	In England
	Middle of July	At Davos
	October	In Venice with daughter Margaret
1888	Publishes:	Second edition, translation of *The Life of Benvenuto Cellini*
	Spring	In Venice

1889	March	Completes translation of the *Memoirs of Carlo Gozzi,* a year's labor
	April	In Venice
		Begins to write his autobiography
1890	Publishes:	Translation of *The Memoirs of Count Carlo Gozzi* (issued 1889)
		Essays Speculative and Suggestive
	April	In Venice
	November	In Venice; Nimmo the publisher requests a life of Michelangelo
1891	Publishes:	*A Problem in Modern Ethics* (privately)
	October	In Orvieto, Aquila, Rome, in search of materials for his biography of Michelangelo
1892	Publishes:	(with Margaret Symonds) *Our Life in the Swiss Highlands*
	July–August	In England, lectures at Oxford and visits various friends
1893	Publishes:	*The Life of Michelangelo Buonarroti* (issued 1892)
		In the Key of Blue and Other Essays
		and
	April 19	{ *Walt Whitman*
		{ Symonds dies in Rome

I

The Culmination of The Renaissance

1885–1886

1448. *To Eugene Lee-Hamilton*[1]

Am Hof, Davos Platz, Switzerland. Jan: 7 1884 [1885][2]

Dear Mr Lee Hamilton

I have just finished a rather elaborate review of your "Apollo & Marsyas" for the Academy[3]—with some difficulty, for I have sprained my right wrist & am ill with bronchitis.

I have made it the occasion of saying what I think about your work in general. And I wish I could have alluded to the great trial of your life, which seems to me to explain what a philistine public is sure to define as morbid in your work. But I thought you would rather be treated solely & simply as an artist.

It is borne in upon me very strongly that you should serve Apollo more in the future than you have yet done in your published work. Marsyas owns a very large share—too large, I venture to think, to be quite good for yourself, & entirely too large to allow you the popularity you merit as a poet.

But Quisque suos pacem manes [peace to his ashes].

I am being gibbetted & pilloried by the English press at the present moment for my Sonnets Stella Maris.[4] So I ought not to speak words of counsel to another. Physician heal thyself! Why, why do we speak in the marketplace & not keep silence, when speech brings us of profit in the world's wealth nothing, & for fame neglect or insult?

With kindest regards to your sister [Violet Paget] I am very sincerely yours

J A Symonds.

When I have dictated a fair copy of my article it will go to Cotton,[5] & you will I hope read in print what I should otherwise have written to you in a letter on your book.

---

1. See L 1182.
2. Symonds obviously meant 1885, habit having caused him to write 1884.

25

3. A review of *Apollo and Marsyas, and other Poems* in *The Academy,* XXVII (Jan. 31, 1885), 71; later reprinted, in part, in A. H. Miles, ed., *The Poets and the Poetry of the Century* (1891), pp. 223 ff.

4. Sixty-seven sonnets, published in *Vagabunduli Libellus* (1884), which were inspired by Angelo Fusato, the word "she" being substituted for "he" throughout.

T. Hall Caine, "*Vagabunduli Libellus.* By John Addington Symonds," *The Academy,* XXVI (Nov. 29, 1884), 349–50, found "the entire process and development of mind described by Symonds to be morbid and unhealthy in the last degree" and thought "Stella" to be a lovely courtesan. Two letters followed in *ibid.* (Dec. 6, 1884), 376, one by Samuel Waddington defending Symonds' use of the 11-syllable line in the sonnet, the other by John F. Rolph taking the same position, both in support of Symonds mentioning precedents in the English sonnet. In *ibid.* (Dec. 13, 1884), 395, Caine in a letter admitted to the correctness of Waddington's and Rolph's views. Later in *The Athenaeum,* No. 2986 (Jan. 17, 1885), 82–83, an anonymous reviewer was fairly noncommittal, though he said that Symonds lays "bare the miseries attendant upon hedonism [which have] a universal and not a satirical application" and takes advantage of solitude and nature for poetical discourse. Still later, in *The Spectator,* LVIII (March 21, 1885), 392–93, another anonymous reviewer found Symonds of all contemporary poets "of real intellectual culture, imaginative sensibility, and literary facility [the most] . . . disappointing and even irritating . . ." and commented on the vagueness, the sentimentality, and the morbidity of "Stella Maris."

5. James Sutherland Cotton (1847–1918), editor of *The Academy.*

1449. *To Mary Robinson*

Am Hof, Davos Platz, Switzerland. Jan: 7 1885

My dear Miss Robinson

I have just finished an article on "Apollo & Marsyas,"[1] which I shall send to the Academy.

I am rather sorry that I undertook the book, because in treating of Mr Lee Hamilton's work at large I feel that I have ascribed to it more than I believe its ultimate value really is. It is certainly interesting & powerful. But it is not quite true to human nature. The aegri somnia [hallucinations] are too predominant.

But I hope that he will like the attentive study I have given it, & I am nearly certain that I have said nothing to cause him pain.

I get more & more to feel that criticism should not inflict pain. Books (unless published by men of great authority, whose authority when used for evil has to be resisted) should be passed in silence, if we object to them.

This it is principally which makes me now so shy about undertaking reviews. If I write, I must write them genially toward the authors.

You will grieve to hear that we are very anxious about Madge.[2] Our doctor here tells us that her lungs show signs of weakness & that she must be treated like an invalid. As yet it is only "precautionary." But I know what that means at fifteen years of age.

I too am ill again, dragged low with bronchitis.

We had a bright & restful summer but for Janet's[3] illness & absence. So I do not mean to complain. Yet life, as it advances, narrows in a fatal circle round us. One after another of our children exhibits the same terrible tendency.

It was very good of you to remember us at Christmas. With best wishes I am yours always

J A Symonds

---

1. Eugene Lee-Hamilton's poems. See L 1448.
2. They feared his daughter Margaret had typhoid fever.
3. His daughter Janet was ill of consumption and was in San Remo. She died in 1887.

1450. *To Henry Graham Dakyns*

Am Hof, Davos Platz, Switzerland. Jan: 12. 1885

My dear Graham

We have plenty of room here for you & Maggie if you like to come to us.

Yesterday on receipt of your telegram we went to Buol's [Hotel] & found they had already provided for & telegraphed to you. Catherine did not like to seem to cut them out of their expectation.

So we have left it for you to decide.—I never thought you would really come! Benedicti!

Yours ever

JASymonds

We dine at 6.30.

1451. *To Bertram Dobell*[1]

Am Hof, Davos Platz, Switzerland. Jan: 17. 1885.

Dear Mr Dobell

I received your kind letter of the 14th here tonight. I should have earlier responded to your previous letter about [James] Thomson, which (instead of being "incoherent & not very sensible") gave me great pleasure & added to my personal apprehension of that most remarkable man. I was in the first place delighted to find that you accepted what I had ventured to write about him to you, & that you did not think my remarks upon his polemical work presumptuous or out of place.

I could not write earlier, because I sprained my right wrist on a tobogganning excursion over the snowfields here. And I am still unable to use my hand freely.

Thank you very heartily for the specimens of Thomson's handwriting wh you forward. I shall place them in the copy of the Shelley volume.[2]

I thought it was to you that I owed the gift of the newspaper containing the first part of Mr Maccoll's article.[3] I read that with interest, & I look forward to the sequel. There is no ordinary literary power in the opening paragraphs. The critical appreciation of Heine struck me at once, as also the attempt to fix the several places of Byron & Shelley & Leopardi in correlation to that extraordinary modern Mephistophiles of a mixed generation.

It will be very interesting to see how Mr Maccoll works from his exordium into the heart of his subject, & how he tackles the personality, literary philosophical & human, of a man like Thomson.

Your own intimation that, in spite of friendly intercourse with Thomson, you found it difficult to grasp him in his entirety, was very helpful to me. It made me feel that possibly one might venture to approach him critically without making some blunder of appreciation that would seem egregious to those who knew him. I want much to form such a conception as I could formulate, & could present to a wide reading public, of so exceptional & hitherto so inadequately recognized a genius as Thomson was.

Thank you for your kind wishes with regard to myself. In these Alpine regions we have an austere but a wonderfully healthful climate—37° Fahr of frost at night, but fine skies in the daytime. I am able to live here with greater sense of moderate enjoyment than I can have in any other climate. Yet I am nothing better than a man far gone in consumption. Great indeed are my privileges, when it is open to me to choose a place of residence that prolongs existence not without mental activity.

Believe me to be sincerely yours

John Addington Symonds.

If I come to England next summer, which I rather hope to do, I shall give myself the pleasure of calling on you.

---

1. See L 1442.

2. Bertram Dobell edited, with a prefatory note, Thomson's *Shelley: A Poem: with other writings relating to Shelley . . .* (1884).

3. William Maccoll, *A Nirvana Trilogy: Three Essays on the Career and the Literary Labours of James Thomson* (1886). Symonds refers to one of these essays, published separately. See William D. Schaefer, *James Thomson (B.V.): Beyond "The City"* (1965), pp. 154–55, for the relationship between Maccoll and Thomson.

1452. *To Margaret Symonds*

Have you heard that I have bought a farm & the white house before [Johannes] Ammann's[1] on the Lake?

Am Hof, Davos Platz, Switzerland. Jan: 28. 1885

My dearest Madge

I am still unable to write well & wish I had you to act as my amanuensis. By the way, you will be glad to hear that when the proof of your article reached me there was only the mistake of one word—wh shows that the printers found your writing clear.

Your mother & I are both delighted with your letters from San Remo which show, I may tell you, no little vigour of expression thought & feeling. Some day you may become one of those best of all writers, a remarkable epistolary woman.

I think you will gradually come to enjoy San Remo in spite of those monotonous daisy bushes etc. The glory of the sunrise you describe is worth in itself alone a long journey.

We had a very successful day for the Intern: Tob. Races yesterday.[2] Brown & I tobogginned down in a lovely clear Graubünden sunset blent with rising moonlight on Monday over a smooth swift snowpath; slept at Klosters & were at it all day from 9 a.m.

Keeping the course clear, taking the time, giving out the list at the window, arranging the luncheon, making speeches, entertaining the natives, afterwards, kept me hard at work till 4, when we left again for Davos. At home we found the little Duke of Newcastle,[3] Mr Watson[4] & a nice boy called England who are staying here. The Duke & his servant are in your mother's room & the red room opposite; Watson in your & Lotta's room, & England in [Peter] Minsch's[5] room.

Then we had a dinner party (Gore Langton[6] & Mr Horne[7] coming in) & I did not get to bed till midnight.

Mr [G.] Dale won the first prize and my cup in min. 6.35. Minsch was second in 6.36. Freeman Buol's [Hotel] 3rd 6.40. [F.] Henderson of [Hotel] Belvedere 4th 6.41. P. Netsch of Klosters 5th 6.42. Austin[8] of Belv. 6.47. None of the Engadiners [citizens of the region around Davos] had prizes.

Please thank Janet for her last letter. I will write to her soon. Ever with best love to you both yr most affe father

J A Symonds

1. A Davoser. This "young and handsome peasant" had proposed to Symonds' daughter Margaret (*H & P*, p. 58). In sports competitions he represented the Turnverein of Davos. He won the Symonds Cup in 1891 and was runner-up in 1890. Symonds negotiated for other farms later. See Ls 1464 and 1590.

2. International toboggan races. For an account of their growth see *H & P*, p. 62 *et passim*.

3. Henry Pelham Archibald Douglas, 7th Duke of Newcastle (1864–1928), succeeded to the title in 1879 at age 15. In 1880, his mother married the Rev. F. W. Thomas T. Hohler, a rector living in Gloucestershire.

4. Robert Spence Watson (1837–1911), political, social, and educational reformer, was a member of the Alpine Club at Davos to witness the races.

5. A close friend of the Symonds family; he became a post conductor at Klosters. See Ls 1748 and 1756.

6. Edward Grenville Gore Langton, third son of William Henry Powell Gore, of London; matriculated at Christ Church, 1878, age 19.

7. Herbert P. Horne (1864–1916), writer, architect, connoisseur, and editor of *The Century Guild Hobby Horse*.

8. We know nothing about G. Dale except that on Jan. 18, 1890, the *Davos Courier* reported that he was then working as a missionary in Central Africa. For Minsch see note 5 above; he placed among the winners in all the competitions from 1883–1889 and in 1891. Harold Freeman, Buol Hotel, competed and placed among the winners for the next 5 competitions; he tied for a first in 1891. Henderson cannot further be identified. Netsch was a Swiss bobsledder; he was among the winners in 1886, 1887, 1890, and 1891. Charles Austin came from Wickham Market, Suffolk; he was to tie for a second place in 1888.

1453. *To Henry Sidgwick*

Davos, Feb. 5, 1885

[Dear Henry]

It is true that we are here rather severely tried, but not more, nay, rather far less, than many, how many, better people than ourselves. I do not lose the light that guides me, and this light is a submissive belief in the order of the world, for which I am not responsible. I know that I sin daily against my belief; but I think that my will is to obey its judgment, whatever that may be.

Madge has gone off, ill, to join her sister at San Remo. I hope and trust it will go well with her. I do not give the game up. But I am weary of things that seem to me infinitely nugatory, face to face with mere human suffering. And so far as any energy is left in me, I strive now to spend my force (of will, and thought, and purse), in smoothing paths for happier people than myself. I have many opportunities here.

You see I cannot write well. So *Addio.* I love to hear about your life and all that it contains.

[Incomplete]

1454. *To Edmund Gosse*

Am Hof, Davos Platz, Switzerland. Feb: 9. 1885

My dear Gosse

Only one word to say that of course I am not so churlish or so foolish as to want to have both Jonson & Sidney!

I promised Morley[1] to do Sidney for him. But on looking into the materials which I could collect for it, I found that I should not be able to do more than condense previous biographies & add criticism. So I have always hung fire. If you will take Sidney & let me have Jonson, we shall divide & rule!

I rather wish I were about Jonson in a more literary series than the "English Worthies"[2] ought to be. Now that I approach the subject practically, I see that the book will have to be mainly critical.

Sir Philip Sidney is really a better choice. But you have the opportunities in London for doing it so far better than I could, that I am sincerely glad to renounce any slight hold I may still be supposed to retain on him (as advertised to write his life in the "Men of Letters" Series) in favour of your abler pen.

I hope you enjoyed your time in America.[3] I suppose it was a succession of social delights & oratorical triumphs!

With kind regards to Mrs Gosse, believe me very sincerely

Yours

JASymonds

---

1. John Morley (1838–1923), in whose "English Men of Letters" series appeared Symonds' *Sir Philip Sidney* (1886).
2. Symonds' *Ben Jonson* (1886) appeared in this series ed. by Andrew Lang (see L 1033).
3. Gosse had spent part of the winter of 1884–85 on a lecture tour in America.

1455. *To Horatio Forbes Brown*

Davos, Feb. 20, 1885

[Dear Horatio]

We have been having very bad weather—strong Föhn, snowstorms, torrents of rain. It is very depressing to health and spirits. Inside and outside all is gloomy with me, and life does not become easier to live. If I could do it, I should like to go into a cloister, and spend the rest of my days in literary labour appointed by a superior. What a contrast there is between the man as he knows himself, and the man as he appears to the world.

I have seen more of Clyde D. Cobham,[1] a profoundly gloomy man— nursed in the most terrible literature, the *fleur de mal* of which he lends me —awful books. If Heine's[2] was Lazaretto-literature, this is madhouse ditto. Good-bye. *Coraggio, amico* [Have courage, friend].

Going to St. Moritz, we crossed the Julier by starlight in open sleighs. Most impressive. Such stars. And long into the night, a fan sent up from the buried sun aloft among the constellations.

[Incomplete]

---

1. See L 247.
2. Heinrich Heine (1797–1856), German poet.

1456. *To Charlotte Symonds Green*

Am Hof, Davos Platz, Switzerland. Feb: 21, 1885

My dearest Charlotte

Yours of the 18th has come tonight, & as you ask me to reply by return, I must give you my first thoughts upon the subject.

My own personal bias is against your taking the matronship[1] of any hospital. And your last letter to Catherine on the subject of your life at the Infirmary makes me feel that you are not exactly adapted for it.

I do not see how you could be. You have been trained to so different an existence. Your opportunities of usefulness in a sphere for wh your previous education & habits, present circumstances & connections, fortune etc, specially qualify you are sufficient in my opinion to render the opening afforded by a matronship secondary to other more natural lines of work.

I should not say this if I saw that you had a strong personal leaning toward the hospital. Then I should consider that it was for your happiness to accept a duty for wh you felt a decided inclination & vocation.

As regards our children, I will tell you frankly that both Catherine & I feel you could be of the greatest comfort to us, & that at no great interval of time.

The girls are much attached to you, enjoy your company, & speak of you with enthusiasm. In the certainty of Mrs White's[2] leaving our service (she knows now that the present arrangement will come to an end in the summer) we have regarded the future as a blank of doubtfulness. Your intervention would make the future schemes for them quite simple & connect you closely with us in a way that would be most beneficial to us & to our children.

But I should never have told you this unless you had distinctly challenged me to speak upon the topic.

As it is, I feel I cannot leave it out of the account. I only fear, for your sake, lest you should afterwards (supposing you throw up the matronship) discover that you had abandoned a definite & busy sphere of useful work for one which looks in doing it like dawdling about. I therefore resume the points of my present opinion on the subject thus:

1) I have always been averse to your exchanging the wider & more indefinite sphere for which position, fortune, education & your work with Tom [Green] qualify you, in order to take the distinct & prescribed duty of a matron. Though I believe that you would make a good matron, & I understand Dr Bright's[3] wanting you.

33

2) Insofar as family ties go, I believe that you could be eminently useful to us, who will sorely need help, with regard to our invalid girls. Only I cannot record this without repeating that there is nothing heroic, nothing occupying, nothing strenuous in that sort of charge. And I beseech you not to let our needs weigh too much with you in your choice. It is impossible, situated as we are, to predict what will be the best for either Janet or Madge. I have decided to bring them both back to Davos this summer. But I do not think, for Janet at all events, Davos will do in the winter. How we should manage about her on the Riviera next year, I do not now know:—you would make that no longer a matter for uneasiness, if you do not take the matronship & remain in the same mind as when you wrote.

I have tried to state my points as simply as I can, knowing that this is the only thing to do, but emphatically adding that our necessities are by no means of the nature to demand a sacrifice from you.

I am glad to write instead of talking about these things. It is easier to be calm & clear.

But I cannot write more, for my hand is still very weak. Goodbye, dearest. You will certainly be guided to choose the right, & whatever you choose will be approved by your most loving brother

J A Symonds.

---

1. A supervisory and administrative position over workers in the hospital. See L 1441 to Charlotte.
2. The children's nurse.
3. James Frank Bright, dean of University College and master (1881–1906). Perhaps because he had been a friend of T. H. Green he urged Charlotte to accept the position as matron of Radcliffe Infirmary, Oxford.

1457. *To Robert Louis Stevenson*

Am Hof, Davos Platz, Switzerland. Feb: 27 1885

My dear Louis

It is terribly long since I wrote to you, and it seems long since I heard of you. There are a good many English people here who remember you and ask me about you. But I can only give them vague answers.

I hope it is not going altogether badly with you, for I still see the announcements of several literary works, some of wh I suppose to have been recently finished.

I am very idle, partly because I have sprained my hand and can only write a few lines at a time—partly because the present public miseries of England deaden me.[1] It is like the brewing of an abcess in some not acutely sensitive part of the body, always felt and always portending a crisis, yet never yielding the satisfaction of heroic suffering.

The affairs of my family are also depressing. Besides my eldest daughter, who is a confirmed invalid, the third [Margaret] has now shown signs of pulmonary weakness. They are both at San Remo. The youngest [Katharine], who was also threatened with chest troubles, has got through this winter well thanks to her mother's devoted care and to the help of an invaluable young Scotch lady [Mrs. White] who is our governess.

We have had a tiresome winter of changeable weather. It has come to an end now—the snow nearly gone—and the most intense sunlight. There is truly something gorgeous in such flaming skies by day and night. I crossed the Julier [Pass] last week in total darkness under the stars, in a sledge that had no driver and the horse had no reins! It was a very singular and splendid experience, more like a dream than anything except some nights at sea that I have ever undergone.

Lungs rather worse than they used to be. Brain decidedly weaker and wearier. No morale left, in the sense of having come to feel that there is nothing worth a red cent except the possession of a quiet conscience and submissive will.

Goodby to you both, if this finds you. I do not beg for news, only send you the love of your true friend

JASymonds.

Have you read a Russian novel (tr into German) called Raskolinkow?[2] Worth reading.

---

1. The Gladstone government was exceedingly unpopular, Prince Bismarck was evidently controlling world affairs in a way repugnant to British interests, the Irish represented by Parnell were both in trouble and troublesome, and there was opposition from all sides to a proposed graduated income tax.

2. Dostoyevsky's *Crime and Punishment*, published in Russia in 1866, appeared in an English translation published by Vizitelley in 1886. Symonds read it in a German translation by W. Henkel (3 vols., 1882). See L 1481.

1458. *To Henry Austin Bruce*[1]

Am Hof, Davos Platz, Switzerland. March 12, 1885

Dear Lord Aberdare

I have sprained my hand & have not been able to write well lately, else I should have thanked you sooner for your kind & reassuring letter about the Tass Vale Ry. A friend of mine, the nephew of Mr James the member of Merthyr,[2] had made me uneasy on the subject just before our friend [A.O.] Rutson[3] came to see me here. In course of conversation I asked him whether he could obtain any information from you. I am very much obliged to you for taking the trouble to write to me yourself.

Thank you also for what you say about my literary work. I am obliged to suspend my book upon the Elizabethan Drama, just when I had gotten through the monotonous period of all the origins. It has not sold, owing partly I believe to the ridiculously expensive form in which Mesrs Smith & Elder insisted against my wishes on publishing it; & they will not venture another volume. I am sorry, for I wanted to have my say about men like Fletcher Webster etc. whose plays have always interested me deeply.

I have been engaged during the last six months on a continuation of my Renaissance in Italy. It will cover the period 1530–1600, taking in the Council of Trent & showing the influence of the Counter Reformation on Italian literature thought manners etc. The subject is fascinating but tragically sad, since it involves the history of Italian decline. But such personalities as Tasso, Sarpi, Bruno, Campanella, throw a glory over the time; & the very copious & minute confirmation we possess about Italian society in the last half of the 16th century, enables me to animate criticism with picturesque details.

I have ventured to gossip thus about my work because you kindly expressed a hope that I should not abandon "le case Italiane". Of course I have as yet made only a beginning. And I find it difficult to do this kind of work in a place like Davos. Even reckless expenditure on books will not procure me what I require. Nothing can make up to me for my enforced absence from great libraries & archives.

Since I have embarked on this egotistical posing, I think I shall go on & have the boldness to call your attention to an article I wrote this winter for the Encyclopaedia Britannica on "Renaissance." I have endeavoured to epitomize a survey of that phase of modern evolution in Europe at large, & to deal with the relation of what we call Renaissance to what we call Reformation. The vol wh will contain it is not yet published.

Foster Alleyne[4] sent me a few days since his sister's book of poems[5] They are very touching as a vivid revelation of her fine intellect & nature. From a purely literary point of view also some of them strike me as excellent. The months which have elapsed since Fanny's death only make me feel her loss more deeply.

With kind regards to Lady Aberdare, in which my wife begs to join, believe me very sincerely yours

John Addington Symonds

---

1. Henry Austin Bruce, Lord Aberdare, 1st Baron (1815–95), raised to the peerage August 23, 1873; in 1846 married Annabella Reardon of Clifton, daughter of Richard Reardon, who became bishop of Bath and Wells, and Annabella A' Court (Heytesbury). His letters, in 2 vols., were privately printed at Oxford in 1902. He was M.P., under-secretary for the Home Department (1862–64), vice-president of the Education Board (1864–66), secretary of state for the Home Department (1868–73), and lord president of the Council (1873–74).

2. Charles Herbert James (1817–90); educated in part at Goulstone's boarding school, Bristol; a civic worker in Merthyr, Wales; became M.P. in 1880; published 3 small vols. in 1892, one of them titled *What I Remember About Myself and Old Merthyr*. His nephew we have not been able to identify.

3. See L 111.

4. Forster McGeachy Alleyne. See L 1034.

5. Sarah Frances ("Fanny") Alleyne died in August, 1884. See L 814. The book of poems was probably in manuscript; we find no evidence of its publication.

1459. *To Margaret Symonds*

Am Hof, Davos Platz, Switzerland. March 13. 1885

My dearest Madge

One line to you tonight to tell you that I am arranging plans for Janet & you to go with me at the end of April to Venice. Mrs White[1] will come of course. I hope that your Aunt Charlotte [Green] will also come to chaper-one you. [Dr.] Lionel [Kay-Shuttleworth] does not object to Janet's going.

All this has entailed some correspondence. But the thing seems as settled now as any project for the future can be.

I am extremely glad; for I believe that both you & Janet will enjoy it & I shall immensely enjoy having you together with me there.

I have written several letters already to Venice about suitable apartments. I want to get them on the Zattere, & if possible near the Calcina.[2] You remember the old dog, the birds & the pergola of vines in the little court there where one dines.

I shall probably try to go alone to Venice some time before you two & your Aunt will arrive, so as to secure what I think desirable!

Angelo will of course be our gondolier in chief; & I do not mean to set old Hop[3] up.

You must be enjoying the burst of lovely spring with those pathetic fruit trees in flower among the olives & all the bulbs & violets beneath. All you send of tokens in the way of flowers is immensely appreciated.

We have an odd spring of cold N.E. winds. Your mother has had a bad attack of influenza, but is better now—not well—yet she recovers very quickly when the fever is out of her.

Ever yours most loving

J A Symonds

From Venice I shall hope to bring you back by the Bremen, Innsbruck, Voralberg railway into Rheinthal.

I picked two gentians today on my own field above the Lake! The lake is healing up already.

———————

1. The children's nurse.
2. Horatio F. Brown lived on the Zattere. The Calcina was a hotel there.
3. Angelo Fusato's uncle.

1460. *To Horatio Forbes Brown*

Davos Platz, March 18 [1885]

[Dear Horatio]

It seems long since I heard from you. But I believe I am in debt to you for a letter. The bother in my hand goes on,[1] and this makes writing troublesome; I have also been very hard at work. After finishing a chapter on the social conditions of the latter half of the XVIth Century, I plunged into Bruno.[2] Berti[3] has printed the process in the Venetian Inquisition against Bruno. As usual, Venetian archives are in his case decisive. The lucidity of Venice is a remarkable fact.

I have arranged now to bring both Janet and Madge to Venice in

April. I should like to get quite into the *Calcina,*[4] in order to have no fuss about kitchens. Will you kindly tell me what is the most convenient hotel at Innsbruck and at Trento? I like old-fashioned inns best, if I can get them. But it is difficult to be sure one does not hit upon some musty haunt of rheumatism, pleurisy, and mouldy wine.

[Incomplete]

---

1. He had injured his hand tobogganing. See L 1451.

2. Filippo Giordano Bruno (1548–1600), Italian philosopher, burned by the Inquisition Feb. 17, 1600. Symonds focussed attention on him in *The Renaissance in Italy: The Catholic Reaction* (2 vols., 1886), Chap. IX.

3. Domenico Berti (1820–97), Italian scholar and statesman who wrote on the Italian philosophers of the Renaissance. His *Vita di Giordano Bruno* was published in 1868.

4. See L 1459.

1461. *To Robert Louis Stevenson*

Am Hof, Davos Platz, Switzerland. March 28 1885

My dear Louis

I was glad to get your last letter. It was good of you to write to me. The account on the whole seemed to be reassuring as to your intellectual condition:—& the physical, though so puzzling, may perhaps be better than "cough o' the lungs."[1] [If you remember, Webster's Duchess of Malfi told Bosola that *that* uncertain thing could kill as well as his cord.][2]

I should have liked to talk & take issue with you on some of your points. Why is Cole[3] a hero? I am charmed to hear that you dedicate your next book to him. Probably you have learned to respect his excellent qualities in private life. But a man who has been wounded upon duty is hardly a hero. At least, I hope England is not sunk so low that we have to call the common discharge of paid for obligations to the State heroic.

Then I should like to ask you why you burn for piety so much. Do you mean the piety of my snuffling Puritan ancestors & the piety of your Scotch dissenting ancestors; or the piety of Calvinist Geneva, wh burned Servetus;[4] or the piety of Lutheran Germany; or the piety of reactionary Rome, wh burned Bruno;[5]—or do you mean the *pietas* of ancient Rome,[6] devotion to principle, patriotic pride, & obstinacy combined with sharp business faculty (the *pietas* of Bismarck,[7] as things go)?

Which do you mean? It is not good to fall into the mood of Carlyle's or Ruskin's rout—the rout of men who dyspeptically belch forth undigested gobbets of the Minor Prophets or the French Socialists.

For heaven's sake, let us keep ourselves pure from the abominations of those bold bad men, pampered in intellectual egotism—the one a Stoic by nature, but jaundiced—the other a Sybarite by nature, but jangled.

See you not that Opalstein[8] would like to talk to you tonight—to you quick shining Firefly?

I am very considerably ill just now with lung inflammation. I won't say more. But this may explain the tone of my letter—a tone which you who live in sprite regions will not take amiss from an old friend.

Addio. My bookseller sends me tonight your verses.[9] I am just going to peep into the book. Love to Mrs Stevenson. Your ever

J.A.Symonds—

---

1. *The Duchess of Malfi,* IV, ii. The duchess forgives her executioners:
   The apoplexy, catarrh, or cough o' the lungs,
   Would do as much as they do.
2. The brackets are Symonds'.
3. In his letter to Symonds (February 1885) Stevenson wrote of his and Symonds' scepticism and of the lack of true national heroes:
   See, for example, if England has shown (I put it hypothetically) one spark of manly sensibility, they have been shamed into it by the spectacle of [General] Gordon. Police-Officer Cole is the only man that I see to admire. I dedicate my *New Arabs* [*More New Arabian Nights*] to him and Cox, in default of other great public characters.
   —*The Letters of Robert Louis Stevenson,* ed. by Sidney Colvin (new ed., 4 vols., 1923), II, 269.
On January 24, 1885, upon hearing of a suspicious package in the chapel of the Houses of Parliament, police constable William Cole rushed in, seized the package, and dropped it when he reached Westminster Hall. The ensuing explosion blew a hole in the pavement 6 feet in breadth, another in the roof, and shattered glass. A few minutes later there were other serious explosions in the House of Commons itself and in the Tower of London. On January 27 the Queen conferred the Albert Order upon the constable. On March 26, Sir William Harcourt, the House secretary, presented the medal to Cole and commended Sergeant Cox, who had come to Cole's aid, for his bravery at the time.
4. Michael Servetus (1511–53) opposed the doctrine of the Trinity. He was arrested in 1553 after the publication of *Christianismi restitutio;* he escaped, was apprehended by Calvin, tried for heresy, and burned at Geneva, October 27, 1553.
5. Giordano Bruno denied the possibility of absolute truth. He was arrested at Naples by order of the Inquisition and burned at the stake Feb. 17, 1600, in Rome.
6. Typical Roman attitude of dutiful respect toward gods, fatherland, parents, and other kinsmen, commemorated in a temple at Rome.
7. A reference to the views of Prince Otto Eduard Leopold von Bismarck (1815–98), known as the creator and first chancellor of the German Empire; a reactionary supporter of the Prussian monarchy and nationalist aims.

8. Stevenson's nickname for Symonds, in the essay "Talk and Talkers."
9. *A Child's Garden of Verses* (1885).

1462. *To Mary Robinson*

Am Hof, Davos Platz, Switzerland. March 30 1885

My dear Miss Robinson

It is so pleasant to get a letter from you tonight that I shall indulge myself by responding to it at once. I think you would have heard from me before in Florence but a slight accident (a sprain of my right wrist) which has made the use of the pen very irksome since Christmas last. You will see that I do not write plainly yet. Coming to Florence is always a vision for me. This winter I dreamed of it—of Castagnolo at least. But now that I have two invalid daughters to think of for the spring (Janet & Madge) I doubt whether I shall get there. I hate hotels; & much as I like Florence, I judge its climate one of quite the worst in Europe for delicate people of almost every kind.

It is probable that we shall therefore meet—I mean my two daughters & I—at Venice in some private apartment, next April. And an excursion to Florence might be made in May. I want these girls to see it if they can.

I am ill, however, now again, & the doctor menaces me with great mischief if I attempt to leave home with my lungs in so wretched a state.

All therefore hangs in the air. But my will is bent on Venice, wh I like, much better for many reasons than Florence, & wh I believe to be a healthier place.

I am so sorry to hear that you are suffering again from neuralgia at Florence. What a frightful drawback. But I cannot wonder. There is something singularly treacherous, according to the nerve & muscle of a human being, in that fine Florentine air that is supposed to have made the folk of the Trecento so acute.

Mr Pater's Marius[1] will of course be read by me—I hope in a gondola. My brain is so badly made that I cannot easily bear the sustained monotonous refinement in his style. To that exquisite instrument of expression I daresay that I shall do justice in the languor & the largeness of the lagoons —better than I can in this eager air of mountains, where everything is jagged & up & down & horribly *natural*.

I cannot sympathize with Pater's theory of life; & as this book seems to give it elaborate utterance, I do not want to study it in discordant circumstances:—for I want at least to respect it. But I have always thought it the theory of one who has not lived & loved—of a Pagan, not a Papal soprano [castrato].

Recently my mind has been in close contact with Bruno & Sarpi,[2] two very diverse natures, but both of them nearer to me than Mr Pater is. I am working at my Italy & the Council of Trent. Have written five chapters for it this winter. Please tell Miss [Violet] Paget that the book she once gave me on "Lucrezia Buonvisi"[3] has been very helpful for my present period. It is a sound documento storico. When I first read it, some four years ago, I left it to occupy a niche in the projected work upon the end of the 16th Century wh is now engaging me.

I seem to be writing a very stupid letter. Stupider than usual.

You don't say when you leave Florence. Please let me hear. You ought to come to Venice on your way back—or to Ravenna—or to Bologna— places to wh I think my studies will be calling me this spring, if the lungs get right. If they don't do so in the next 3 weeks, I must stay up here. I have been here since last June already. But on the whole I like it—interest myself in people, & buy land. Italy lives in my memory & heart enough to be now that better thing than a heard melody—an unheard one.

I look forward to your sister's novel.[4] Good indeed of her to send it me! You can hardly tell how much I value such kindness in my Alpine solitude, or with what eagerness a friend's book is perused by Catherine & me—she reading, I listening. With your letter tonight, comes an invitation to the Academy dinner in London. I should like to be there.

But enough. Please remember me to Mr [Eugene] Lee Hamilton & to Miss Paget. Ever yours

J A Symonds.

Much love to you from mine, who have all been charmed with the impertinent [section cut off].

---

1. *Marius the Epicurean* (1885). In L 1463 Symonds states that Pater's style had the "effect upon my nerves . . . of a civet cat."

2. Giordano Bruno and Fra Paolo Sarpi (see L 1218) figure in *The Renaissance in Italy: The Catholic Reaction* (2 vols., 1886), Chaps. IX and X. Symonds apparently felt that these men were activists in the sense that Pater was not; both were directly involved in intellectual and political struggles in Venice during the Reformation. Following Sarpi's advice, Venetian authorities banished the Jesuits.

3. Salvatore Bonghi, *Storia di Lucrezia Buonvisi* (Lucca, 1864). Symonds retold the course of this tragic woman's life in *The Renaissance in Italy: The Catholic Reaction*, Chap. V.

4. Frances Mabel Robinson (?–?), *Mr. Butler's Ward* (1885). See also L 1530.

1463. *To Henry Sidgwick*

Davos, April 5, 1885

[Dear Henry]

The post has brought me to-night your month's diary, which is a particularly interesting number to me. It makes me, as usual, rather wistful —this window opened for me by your friendship into a life so full of human interests, so active, so well-filled. I would not miss it now for the world. It has been, the last year, of real value to me. If I am ever self-satisfied, it is in a reckless, fierce, defiant way. I am improved by seeing how a man can be actually superior, calm in survey, conscious of the length and breadth and depth of himself, and kept in healthful equilibrium by frequent contact with the best of his own kind. This does me good, and monthly you keep alive in me the dying spark of mental life. It is rather bitter this fate.

"Marius"[1] I have not read. I suppose I must. But I shrink from approaching Pater's style, which has a peculiarly disagreeable effect upon my nerves—like the presence of a civet cat. Still, I believe I must read it.

My studies have, as usual, been chiefly in the past. I have taken much pleasure since September last in working at the counter Reformation period in Italy; and have got six chapters of my "Italy and the Council of Trent" roughly committed to paper. This book will form a sequel, if I can produce it, to "Renaissance in Italy."

But [Dr.] Ruedi informs me that I have broken down again in health. The old wound in the lung is active again for mischief. A chronic invalid cannot work in right conditions. Climate is good; but solitude from all society congenial to my work is pernicious. The work detaches itself against too vacant a background, which I am impelled to fill up by stupid distractions. Machiavelli's account of his life in banishment at San Casciano[2] represents mine. And I am too weak to bear the isolation of absorbing intellectual occupations mitigated by peasants.

[Incomplete]

---

1. Walter Pater, *Marius the Epicurean* (1885).
2. On leaving prison in March 1513, Machiavelli retired to a farm near San

Casciano where he completed the *Prince* before the end of that year. For his reaction to his banishment see his letters to Vettori in *Lettere familiari di N. Machiavelli pubblicata per cura di Edoardo Alvisa* (Florence, 1883).

1464. *To Horatio Forbes Brown*

Davos, April 8, 1885

[Dear Horatio]

I am astonished, when I now regard it, at the amount of work produced since the end of last September. Six respectable chapters of "Italy and the Council of Trent" are ranged before me. The book has been organised, and the main positions have been attacked. Of course these chapters are only in the rough; but the design is there, and of course there is about as much still to produce; and then there will be the whole to go over, filing and filling in. But I always find that to organise a big book drills the holes in my lung. The other part of the business bores the body, but does not destroy tissue. A good holiday would do me worlds of good now, if I could take it without serious risk.

I am sure you are right to take the minute pains you do about your house. I feel frequently how much I have lost in mine here by leaving the details—as my health compelled—to architect and builder. It is not merely that I disbursed 15 or 20 per cent. more than the just cost, but my work was not properly carried out. *L' occhio del padrone* [the watchful eye] is the thing. And you can give it. But then you have an Antonio. There is no such functionary in these parts to be had for love or money, or both combined.

I am carrying on land speculation on the lake here. Have taken a large farm[1] on mortgage, in addition to the one I bought just before you came to Davos last.[2] This mortgage is of a nature to make me the owner when the farm comes to sale. Altogether I have spent a good deal of money this spring.

Good-bye. I want to see Venice and you; but I harden my soul for a not improbable disappointment.

[Incomplete]

---

1. The farm of the Bätschi family at Meierhof. See L 1590.
2. See L 1452.

1465. *To Mary Robinson*

Am Hof, Davos Platz, Switzerland. April 11, 1885

Dear Miss Robinson

Thank you for writing on the 7th: I am always so glad to hear what you are doing.

I believe that I shall be allowed to go into Venice after all. I have had a bad three weeks & the weather here is all that is detestable. I will not tell you how bad. It would make you hate Davos more than you already do.

I wonder whether there would be any chance of your coming to Venice on your way home—if you leave for England in May? You would not find any cosmopolitan society—only Janet Madge myself & my sister Mrs T. H. Green.

I have taken rooms for them at the Calcina [Hotel] on the Zattere & for myself next door in a Casa Lombardini. One great object was to get a very open situation & to be near a good restaurant (wh the Calcina is) so as to have no bother about cooks. The last time I was in Venice my own French chef threatened to throw himself from the Campanile & had to be sent home. The Italian I took in his place turned out a dipsomaniac, & though he cooked well was incapable at times, so that I had to supplement him with a female cook who made things march.

It would be very nice if you could pay us a visit. Mrs Green would be chaperone enough in all conscience.

I should like to have the exact title of Ademollo's Le Giustize di Roma;[1] or if that is the title, the date & impress. I must clearly possess the book.

I am seriously thinking of building a large appendix to my house here, to hold books. They accumulate so atrociously.

I will tell you when I am in Italy, if I get there. Also what I shall be about. I think staying quiet at Venice. But I ought to go to Bologna in order to make myself familiar once more with those dreary productions of the Caracci Academy.[2] They come into my present period. I wish I could have come to know your friend M. Bourget.[3]

Ever yours

J A Symonds

---

1. Mary Robinson had probably seen an advance notice. Alessandro Ademollo (1826–91) edited and wrote an introduction to Giovanni Battista Bugatti, *Le Annota-*

45

*zioni, di Mastro Titto Carnefice Romano. Supplizi e Suppliziati. Giustize esquite da G. B.
Bugatti, e dal Sun succesore (V. Balducci). 1796–1870 (1886).*

2. A reference to the impact of 3 late 16th cent. Bolognese painters: Agostino
Carracci (or Caracci) (1557–1602), his brother Annibale (1560–1609), and their cousin
Lodovico (1555–1619). They are said to have revitalized art by their keen observations
of nature, studies from life, and bold draftsmanship.

3. Paul Bourget (1852–1935), French psychologist, critic, and novelist.

1466. *To Mary Robinson*

Alla Calcina Zattere Venezia May 1 1885

Dear Miss Robinson

I waited till I had been here a week to write to you.

It has given us all much delight to think that you will pay us a visit.

But I must tell you that we have no very fine room to offer you. I had
to take an apartment at this house for a great many reasons of convenience
for Janet. And when we came to it, I found it not so roomy as I like. I am
living out in spacious rooms. But you could not be my guest alone I fear.
Mrs Green invites you to the only small room she can give you with hearty
welcome, & will write if you let me hear that you really mean to come. I
believe you will not be uncomfortable though certainly not in grandeur.

Ever yours,

J A Symonds

1467. *To Mrs. R. L. Stevenson*

Alla Calcina Le Zattere Venezia May 20 1885

My dear friend

I have been thinking very much of you & Louis lately, & have often
been upon the point of writing. But two things kept me off it. One is that I
have got something the matter with my right hand (I call it not Scrivener's
Palsy or some other sort of palsy, though I begin to fear it may be that) wh
makes the pen immeasureably irksome. The other is that chronic inability
to say any thing veritably brave or hopeful, & the sense that if I cannot say
that I had better hold my tongue.

Physical health goes well enough with me, thank God. That is to say, I have only had one serious lung affair this past winter, & am now in Venice enjoying things fairly.

But mental & moral health are both in a speckly sinisterly bizarre state. I don't find the issue of life in any work wh satisfies me or wh I quite believe in; & growing older seems to make me internally more lawless.

The long monotony of life in that very exciting climate of Davos produces some peculiar differentiation of the man's quality wh is only partly beneficial.

A man (Lord Lytton,[1] who is interesting & amusing & is here) asked me last night how Davos agreed with me. I replied in two words that it made me "quarrelsome & conceited." He said he wished he could be made conceited, but that the only thing wh produced that desirable change in him was too dangerous to indulge in—Morphine. I wonder whether the common verdict would be that nothing made Lord Lytton conceited save Morphine!

How glad I am to hear that you & Louis have found a friend in Henry James! You ask me whether I have made any since you saw me. Well: I think I may decidedly answer—I have made none. Acquaintances, I have made wh brighten life; but no friend except among the Grisons peasants. And you know they cannot be exactly friends. There is an interesting German, Prince Emil von Carolath,[2] who comes to Davos, & who may grow into a friend. But it is difficult to get on really friendly terms with Germans.

It seems to me that Louis does a marvellous amount of work. His long and obscure illness has not diminished his mental vigour. I enjoyed his Children's Songs[3] immensely, & am looking forward to the Dynamiter.[4] When people ask me whether you really had any part in that book, I tell them that you suggest some half a dozen motifs for stories, out of wh Louis selects those he writes, & that he considers nothing written till it has obtained your Imprimatur.[5] Have you noticed the Amateur Emigrant in the PMG?[6] It gives me an odd echo-sense of Louis's book, the non-publication of wh I always regret.

Two of my girls, Janet & Madge, are with me here. They are both delicate, & Janet is seriously ill indeed. My wife & the other two are in England—engaged in dividing a two months' space of time into as many country-house visits as can be effected.

H. F. Brown has made himself into a Venetian & has bought a fine house here. He works at history a great deal, & is slowly developing into a man really learned in the past of Venice.

What do you think of Marius the Epicurean?[7] I wish I could talk to both of you about that book & some others. I have been reading [George] Meredith's "Modern Love"[8] here for the first time. Some of these poems are first rate.

My own work on hand is a sequel to the Renaissance in Italy. I do nothing for it here.

Goodbye. Ever yours

J A Symonds

---

1. Edward Robert Bulwer-Lytton (1831–91), poet, statesman, only son of the novelist Bulwer-Lytton, known under the pseudonym Owen Meredith; educated at Harrow and at Bonn. After a varied career in the diplomatic service in Washington, Florence, Paris, the Hague, Madrid, Vienna, and Lisbon, in 1876 he was appointed viceroy of India. He resigned in 1880, returned to England, and was made Earl of Lytton in 1885. He published romances in verse: *Lucile* (1860) and *Glenaveril* (1885).

2. Prince Émile Rudolphe Osman zu Schönaich-Carolath (1852–99), married July 1, 1887, Catherine Marguerite Sophie Anne de Knorring; had 6 children, the eldest 2 of whom were born at Davos-Dorf: Princess Marguerite, June 5, 1888; Prince Georges Jules Rodolphe, May 24, 1891. Margaret Symonds translated his novel *Melting Snows* (1895).

3. *A Child's Garden of Verses* (1885).

4. *The Dynamiter* (1885) by Robert Louis and Fanny Van de Grift Stevenson.

5. Mrs. Stevenson improvised stories with her husband, some of which she wrote down. One was the basis for *The Dynamiter.*

6. " 'Diary of an Amateur Immigrant' (From our Special Correspondent)," *Pall Mall Gazette,* XLI (1885), I: April 30, 1–2; II: May 5, 4–5; III: May 13, 4–5; IV: May 15, 4–5.

7. See L 1463.

8. *Modern Love and Poems of the English Roadside* (1862).

1468. *To Horatio Forbes Brown*

Innsbruck, June 3 [1885]

[Dear Horatio]

I scarcely think it needful to acquaint you with our progress so far. But the feeling of Venice still lingers with me—I think some of the salt of it still remains on my moustache. I am very glad to be in the mountains again. I feel physically better here. But the many charming things we saw together there: the white sail of the "Waring";[1] the dunes of Tre Porte;[2] the long-drawn melodies of Istria,[3] and Udine,[4] and San Daniele[5]—all are a golden chain of many links which will not break. The heart is happy to be going to its home. It remembers its *diverticulum* with joy. Man thirsts for clarity of vision. The sensual desires it in some body. The moral in some law. The intellectual in some definition. The religious in some creed or beatific insight. How shall beings, as complex as we, expect to find this clarity in the mixed quantities that make our wandering life? For myself, I am too tired to be more than grateful for what I have had, have, and childishly hope to have.

[Incomplete]

---

1. Brown's note: "An Ancona-built sailing-boat."

2. A town near the mouth of the Gresle, 45 miles northeast of Rouen, France, noted as a bathing resort.

3. A peninsula projecting into the northeast part of the Adriatic Sea. In 1797, at the time of the extinction of the Venetian Republic, the whole of Istria became an Austrian possession. It now belongs to Italy.

4. A town in Italy, capital of the province of Udine, 84 rail miles northeast of Venice.

5. San Daniele di Fruili, a small town united with Udine, 18 miles away, by a steam tramway and situated in a pleasant hill-district. Its cathedral has an altar-piece of the Trinity by Pordenone (1534) and its Gothic church of Sant' Antonio has a cycle of frescoes by Pellegrino da San Daniele (1497–1522).

1469. *To Charlotte Symonds Green*

[Ragatz, June, 1885]

[Dear Charlotte]

. . . for a journey through Tuscany with Lotta and Madge, to show them pictures & the rest of it.

What you write about the gravity of the situation in England[1] is well said & moderate. I quite agree. Everything indicates, in my opinion, the preparation for a vast change; & all will depend upon slight circumstances, whether the change takes place violently with disruption & ruin, or quietly by slower processes of metamorphosis. In either case the "fleur à sa boutonnière" (to use your phrase) will come out considerably draggled. I only pray that it may not be trampled in mud & blood.

My apprehension has been so serious for more than a year past that I have been investing money in land here rather than in any English securities; & I feel inclined to continue doing this. All the last winter Lotta & Madge have practised cookery in our kitchen. I think it would be just possible for us to live in one of my farm-houses here, if the worst came to the worst. I must also try to revive the failing vigour of my pen; for nothing in this life is safe, as property, except a trade that pays.

I began to read this morning Miss Paget's "Countess of Albany,"[2] wh, as usual with her work, takes a strong hold on my fancy. I cannot help sighing when I think of my Dryasdust Ben Jonson,[3] with no sparkle in it. An Elizn Dramatist is not a good subject for a popular book. Dramatic criticism is the heaviest to write & least attractive to the reader. I too have got into a bad style for the sort of production by writing Encycl: Brit: articles, & aiming at accurate brevity in my chapters upon Tasso, Bruno, Sarpi, Marino, & such folk.

To me there is deep interest in the tragedy of the Catholic Revival. But I doubt whether I have made it interesting. By the way I ought to have told you that I found *Felsina Pittrice*[4] adequate to my needs, about the Bolognese Painters. It is a very curious miscellany. Pity that we have not such a mass of anecdotes about men like Donatello Botticelli Mantegna & Signorelli!

[Incomplete]

---

1. Because of difficulties in the Sudan—General Gordon was killed at Khartoum in January, 1885—Gladstone's government resigned in June, 1885. The tone of Symonds' letter suggests that it was written just prior to the change.

2. Vernon Lee (Violet Paget), *Countess of Albany* ("Eminent Women" series, 1884). Her subject was Louise Maximilliane Caroline Emmanuele, Princess of Stolberg (1752–1824), who called herself the Countess of Albany.

3. Symonds was writing his *Ben Jonson*, which appeared in the "English Worthies" series the following year.

4. Symonds supplies the following note to *The Renaissance in Italy: The Catholic Reaction,* Chap. XIII:

I have mainly used the encyclopaedic work entitled *Felsina Pittrice* (2 vols., Bologna, 1841) for my study of the Eclectics [Bolognese painters]. This is based upon the voluminous writings of the Count C. C. Malvasia, who, having been born in 1616, and having enjoyed personal intercourse with the later survivors of the Bolognese Academy, was able to bequeath a vast mass of anecdotical and other material to posterity. The collection contains critical annotations and additions by the hand of Zanotti and later art students, together with many illustrative documents of the highest value.

1470. *To Henry Sidgwick*

Ragatz,[1] June 17 [7] 1885[2]

[Dear Henry]

We left Venice last Monday, driven away at length by the great heat. It is hardly cooler here; and I shall be glad to get into the mountains again. I suppose there is about ten months of Davos now ahead; though the state of my family, as usual, is so confusing that I can form no plans on which to depend with even human approximation to probability. The main fact about me internally is that I am doing the sequel to my "Renaissance." This is practically an inquiry into the methods used by the Catholic Powers to check the Renaissance and the Reformation. I wonder whether you have paid attention to Sarpi's[3] writings, and what you think of him in the history of political speculation?

Have you read Amiel's "Journal"?[4] I have just got it, and am looking through it with a curious sense of being stifled and sickened—in spite of its stylistic charm.

[Incomplete]

---

1. Bad Ragatz, a watering place in east Switzerland, 70 miles northwest of Davos-Platz; known for its hot mineral baths.
2. H. F. Brown clearly misdated this letter in *L & P* because in L 1471 of June 9 Symonds is back in Davos.
3. See L 1218.
4. Henri Frédéric Amiel (1821–81), Swiss essayist, poet, and professor of aesthetics. His *Journal intime* was published in part in 1883–84, and in 1889 was translated into English by Mrs. Humphry Ward. The tone of the *Journal* is marked by self-distress and a sometimes morbid introspection.

1471. *To Charlotte Symonds Green*

Am Hof, Davos Platz, Switzerland. June 9 1885

My dearest Charlotte

I wonder how you got on upon your travels yesterday & if you did not enjoy arriving at Basel so much as I have done the pure cool air, the good sleep, the exquisite sense of rest & freshness in my home.

Davos is really radiant in the beauty of flowing grass & flowers upon the meadows, light sun-penetrated airs breaking over the whole surface of wavy green.

They had heavy snowfalls in May—once there was one of above a foot in depth. This together with the warmth & thunderstorms of the present month gives promise of a fine hay crop.

The drive up in the diligence was rather trying yesterday. Dust & heat intolerable. I really fear I cannot go again into the lower Switzerland while the weather remains so hot. [Dr.] Ruedi is to examine me tomorrow morning. I shall then know what I can do in the case of urgency. But I am sure that a few more days of such traveling as we had from Botzen & such heat as at Ragatz would knock me up.

How I wish Auntie [Mary Ann Sykes] could be here without getting here. I am certain she would like it. And yet I am afraid that the splendid summer may fail before she arrives.

We had the Spenglers[1] with us all the way, & spoke politely to them. At Klosters I left the girls, & took up Dr Ruedi. He said that he could see no reason why Janet should not come at once.

The house is quite fit for her. Only two W. C.s wet with paint—all the other work done & those ugly cracks in the plaster & papers quite obliterated. We have only 3 servants however. The kitchen maid is staying at home to nurse her sick mother. Elspeth [the maid] is here, doctors both at Davos & Chur assuring her that the air is better for her than that of her own home at Trins. She went home, & felt the heat. She must not do hard work.

But I am not afraid of being under servanted. I am sure we could get help if it were required.

Everything in fact seems to me peaceful & fairly satisfactory. And the sense of beauty wholesomeness & rest is to me delicious.

I will telegraph, as promised, tomorrow after seeing Ruedi. The enclosed letter from Auntie makes me hope that she will be *plastic* as to plans. Finding you at Basel will be almost an unexpected help to her if there is any difficulty.

Please tell her not to think about being useful to the girls. They will be at home soon—indeed they will leave Klosters, I think, now before Auntie could get there; & at home of course they are all right. She must only think of what would be pleasant to herself.

Tell her how very much I should enjoy her coming here if she thought that would suit her. There will be plenty of room in the house for her & her maid, & her man too if he comes. Or should I find our servants a difficulty, I will engage rooms for her at Buol's.

I only wish you could come also to Davos! But I know how many things call you back to England & must not even ask for this.

The time we have had together was to me very delightful in a thousand ways, & I hope I did not make myself to you more than moderately disagreeable by my habit of profuse & undisciplined speech. Of your help to me I cannot say as much as I feel. But without you I should not have been able to venture on Venice & that journey; & with you I never felt any real anxiety.

Ever dearest sister, most lovingly yours

J A Symonds

Love to Sophie [Girard]. I hope you find her better than seemed probable.

---

1. Dr. Alexander Spengler (1827–1901) and his family. He pioneered in exploring Davos as a place benefitting consumptives. (See W. G. Lockett, *Robert Louis Stevenson at Davos* [1934], pp. 43–45).

1472. *To Horatio Forbes Brown*

Davos, June 10, 1885.

[Dear Horatio]

I feel sure you will sympathise with me when you hear that Ruedi says the mischief in my lung (present actively last March) has considerably advanced during my visit to Venice. I was aware that I was not doing well, from the great languor and lassitude I felt, which I could only throw off by working myself into gaiety, and which I persistently ignored while sitting up late. Now, I suppose, I must pay again for all that. The truth is, I am in that dangerous state for an invalid of my temperament, that being ill so long has at least wearied my patience. My will, the volition to maintain feeble health at its maximum, has broken down. I am thoroughly bored, and boredom has betrayed me into petulance. Bad habits have been formed, and the whole man runs a risk unless he can pull himself vigorously together. Whence to draw the impetus for such an effort is my problem. I understand self-abandonment to a pleasureless deterioration. But I must remember how I have condemned that, and be still a man.

I am quite alone here. Davos is most radiant in the beauty of fresh young summer. Janet and Madge must stay awhile at Klosters still.

[Incomplete]

1473. *To the Rev. Augustus Jessopp*[1]

Am Hof, Davos Platz, Switzerland. June 10 1885

Dear Sir

A letter from my wife, enclosing one from you dated June 1, reaches me this evening.

I am very glad to hear that my sister in law Miss [Marianne] North means to purchase Roger North's[2] Mss & to give them to the British Museum.

I need not say that this resolution of hers puts an end to any scheme wh I may have entertained, & about wh I wrote from Venice to my wife a letter wh I think she sent on to you.

I was only anxious to prevent the Autograph of Roger's Autobiography getting into indifferent hands; & I never contemplated *the purchase of a copy of that Ms.*

Indeed of the existence of copies I hear only tonight, not having received from my wife the Catalogue of Crossley's Collection.[3]

I am in every way unqualified to edit Roger North's life. My own studies have not lain in that period of English History; & my enforced absence from London would make a work of research of that kind almost impossible.

When I spoke about wishing to reserve the right to edit, in case I subscribed so large (for me) a sum as £100 to the purchase, it was in order that I might retain a hold on the editing & see that it was properly carried out.

Now that point, to my relief, is also settled: for the original will, I hope, repose in the Br Mus: & for the copies I have no concern.

The object of my letter to you now is to thank you for the interest which you were willing to take in a matter concerning my wife's family. Independently of the fact that she, & through her my children, are descended from Roger, I have always been an enthusiastic admirer of the "Lives of the Norths."[4] Long before I knew her, I studied them on the recommendation of my (then) tutor, Professor Jowett, who used to say: "Next to Boswell, it is the best book of the kind in English!"

I have some personal right to be interested in Norfolk; for my paternal blood descends,[5] or claims to be descended from the Fitzsymons of Threxton & Suffield, an offshoot from whom settled at Croft in Lancashire in the 14th century, & gave off several branches of wh Symons of Pyrton Oxfordshire, Symonds of Great Yeldham Essex, flourished for awhile, while I represent that of Salop, transferred to Shrewsbury & Athepstone in Warwickshire. I dont much believe in these very complicated pedigrees of families wh have originated. But the evidence of seeing antique armory gives them some support. My forbears of Newport, for example, have "azure 3 trefoils slipped or" wh is very close to the coat of Symonds of Cley by the Sea, & for the branch of Essex this coat was differenced by a chevron engrailed.

You whose knowledge of the Medieval period is so extensive, might perhaps be able to inform me whether the descent of Symonds of Cley Suffield & Great Ormesby from FitzSymons of Threxton Suffield etc. is founded.

Through the Addingtons again I am connected with Norfolk, counting a Beymes of Overstrond in their pedigree.

But enough of such trifles! It is a pleasure from this land of exile to gossip even on paper to a man for whose services to English literature & history & life, & for whose style as a writer, I have long entertained admiration.

Believe me very faithfully yours
John Addington Symonds

Rev Augustus Jessop, D.D.

---

1. Augustus Jessopp (1823–1914), clergyman and author. After a period as curate and headmaster, in 1879 he became rector of Scarning, Dereham, Norfolk, where he remained until 1911. From 1902 to 1910 he was chaplain in ordinary to King Edward VII. His works include an edition, with a life, of Donne's *Essays in Divinity* (1855), *One Generation of a Norfolk House* (1878), *History of the Diocese of Norwich* (1879), and *Arcady for Better for Worse* (1881). He supplied some of the biographies of famous Elizabethans for the *Dictionary of National Biography*.

2. Roger North (1653–1734), lawyer, author of *The Life of the Right Honourable Francis North, Baron of Guilford* (1742; 2nd ed., 1808) and *The Life of the Honourable Sir Dudley North . . . and of Dr. John North . . .* (1744). As members of the noble family of Guilford, Roger North and Mrs. John Addington (Catherine North) Symonds were directly related.

3. Probably the catalogue, published by Christie's, listing the collection of the Rev. Thomas Crossley, H. M. Chaplain at Hampton Court.

4. Possibly as ed. by Henry Roscoe (3 vols., 1826), later reprinted with Roger North's autobiography, ed. by A. Jessopp (3 vols., 1890).

5. Much of the Symonds' genealogical detail appears in Symonds' *On the English Family of Symonds*, privately printed by his cousin Horatio Percy Symonds (the son of Dr. Frederick Symonds) at Oxford (1894).

1474. *To Mary Robinson*

Davos June 14 1885

Dear Miss Robinson

Your letter of June 7 was welcome, since it gave me good news of your journey, & showed you strong enough to see much & retain much in memory of those well-filled days at Paris.

I am glad that I had not to attend at Victor Hugo's funeral.[1] To be on the top of a cab was good—for I suppose you could always get inside & drive away. Fancy what it would have been to be a Member of the Institute!

V. H. was a man certainly of very distinguished talent, & in the art of words he was what deserves the name of genius.

It is very kind of you to remember your visit to us at Venice with any sense of pleasure. I felt, when you first came, how cold & repellent you must find us after Florence, where so much had drawn you out with genial warmth. I learned to respect you & admire you for taking your environment so sweetly. And then I was very harsh & quarrelsome.— It is my misfortune to miss what only health gives, the harmony of self. And as my implacable foe advances, I find the internal discord & discomfort objectifies itself more & more to the injury of the ideal of decent social intercourse.—It seems that I had better be shut up alone, taking my chance in intervals of speaking to others through written words.—

My doctor here says that at Venice I must have established a new bad process in the lung. He condemns me to a life of blisters, hammock in the woods, & mental inactivity.

I read M: Bourget's book of Psychologie[2] there today among the pine trees. It is good criticism, from a deep & imaginative mind. I could wish however, that he did not yield to what I am sure is a literary illusion, the illusion of a clique, that human nature in our age is decadent & that therefore the disease of Baudelaire and the unhealthy strain in Flaubert are normal.

At Ragatz[3] I read Amiel.[4] What a pity it is that those imperfect shoots of a sickly soul should have been preserved & published. They remind me of Kirke White![5] Of course, when they have been made the subject of études by Scherer[6] & perhaps Mat Arnold,[7] robuster people who expend their unction on them, they will be eventually absorbed into oblivion. But they did not print such things upon the banks of the Ilissus.[8] Nor on Mount

Zion. Ought we not, if we *are* decadent, to live Ilissus-ward & Zion-ward? Janet & Madge joined me here yesterday. Write to me. Ever yr

JAS.

To Night

The Mother of Sleep & Death.
Oh Mother, holiest Mother, Mother Night!
Thou on thy marble throne of ebon hue
Hast still the everlasting stars in view,
The slumbering earth & dusk heavens infinite.
Turn thou those veiléd eyes, where never light
Smote rudely yet, but dim cerulean blue
Broods in the dawn of moonbeams, on these two
Dread angels folded on thy bosom white!
Sleep & his twin-born Death; entwined, embraced;
Mingling soft breath, deep dreams, dark poppied
Lips pressed to lips, & hands in hands enlaced;
Thy children, & our comforters; the pair
From whom poor men, by earth enslaved, debased
Find freedom, & surmount their life's despairs

This sonnet I add to my dreary letter, to show you that I am still sometimes visited by the Muse—by such a Muse, at least, as deigns to visit me.

Literature, in snatches, is a great consolation to me. I have just read—or rather my wife read aloud to me all day when I was in bed—the very interesting & most judicious life of George Eliot wh Miss Mathilde Blind[9] kindly sent me. Your Emily Bronte[10] & this George Eliot are both of them above the average of Morley's[11] series—not above one or two of the best in that series—but quite above the mediocrities. The subjects are of course good in both—& if it comes to Mrs Barbauld[12] we may find a touch of unavoidable meritorious mediocrity. But I feel inclined to lay heavily on the women for doing the women on the whole better than the men have done the men. You women have a great storytelling faculty; & when a fairly good biographical tale is set you, you make more of the narrative motives than all but a few men are able or willing to do.

---

1. Hugo died on May 22, 1885, and was buried in the Panthéon. The funeral fête (June 1) was stately, one of the grandest ever seen in Paris. Crowds were held in check

by careful plans drawn up by the authorities. There had been disturbances after the death, particularly over the secularization of the Pantheon in honor of Hugo, a renowned freethinker.

2. Paul Bourget (see L 1465), *Nouveaux essais de psychologie contemporaine* (1883). See *OOP*, p, 246, for Margaret Symonds' account of a dinner party she attended with Bourget.

3. See L 1470.

4. See L 1470.

5. Henry Kirke White (1785–1806), poet. His *Poetical Works and Remains* (3 vols., 1807–22) were edited by Robert Southey. He wrote *Clifton Grove, A Sketch in Verse, with other Poems* (1803).

6. Edmond Henri Adolphe Scherer (1815–89), French journalist, protestant clergyman (1843), and professor at Geneva (1845–49); ed. *Les Temps* (from 1860) and wrote articles for it later published as *Études sur la littérature contemporaine* (10 vols., 1885–95).

7. Some of Matthew Arnold's early essays dealt with French and German writers, the Guérins and Heine among them.

8. The Ilissus (or Elisson), a river in Greece, flowing from Mt. Hymettus, skirting Athens on the southwest. It is usually dry because of the destruction of the forests at its watershed. It was "much sung among ancient poets." Symonds' point, however, may be contained in this account: "Under Solon, Peisistratus, and Pericles the festival of Demeter at Eleusis was adopted by Athens, and raised to higher elaboration and pomp. In the Lesser Mysteries, held near Athens in the spring, candidates for initiation underwent a preliminary purification by self-immersion in the waters of the Ilissus." Also, some of the dialogue of the *Phaedrus* occurs on the banks of Ilissus, while Socrates and his pupil cool their feet in the stream.—Will Durant, *The Life of Greece* (1939), pp. 188 and 514.

9. Mathilde Blind (1841–96) published her life of George Eliot in 1883.

10. Mary Robinson, *Emily Brontë* (1883).

11. The "English Men of Letters" series, ed. by John Morley.

12. Symonds' friend Janet Ross published a sketch of Anna Letitia Barbauld (1743–1825), the poet and essayist, in *Three Generations of Englishwomen* (2 vols., 1888).

1475. *To Horatio Forbes Brown*

Davos, June 18, 1885

[Dear Horatio]

My Davos life and climate are working their usual effects of stringing me up and pulling me together, making a nervous man of me, but curing the old lung trouble for the moment.

What a helter-skelter human life is—a hurrying to reach the tomb—a retardation by refinements of the process—an inevitable decadence in all of us when we have touched the thirty years—a choice of means to save the maximum and pare the minimum of what we know that life has put within our reach. It is all a matter of saving and spending—as the fearful allegory of the "Peau de Chagrin"[1] puts it; and the irony of the whole business is that when we think we save we often spend; and spending sometimes find that unexpectedly we have made a gain. We cannot calculate. We want too many things, self-contradictory and diverse, to make a balance.

[Incomplete]

---

1. Blazac's *La Peau de chagrin* (1831) presents one of his favorite themes, the dissipation of one's energies through the pursuit of desires.

1476. *To Horatio Forbes Brown*

Davos, June 21, 1885

[Dear Horatio]

It is snowing hard here this evening—the whole valley white—and the grey twilight of the longest day in the year gradually fading through grey brooding clouds.

I don't think I have more than this to say to-night. It seems funny, when I think of you in your casino at La Favorita, with your brick floor and the little acacia bushes round you. Probably it is not hot there, but damp and chilly.

I have nearly finished my studies in [Giordano] Bruno. Difficult to seize. But I think he is the only great Italian of the sixteenth century, and perhaps the greatest mind in Europe—I am really afraid to say what I am inclined to think—well, I will out with it, the greatest pure intelligence since Aristotle.

As he was but a little past thirty when his light went out in the dungeons of the Inquisition, Aristotle with his long life had a long pull over him. But might have beens can't count. So I can't go on to say that he probably would have beaten Aristotle if he had lasted another quarter of a century.

I have come very slowly to form this opinion of Bruno; and I do not see my way to expounding it.

[Incomplete]

1477. *To Horatio Forbes Brown*

Davos Platz, June 26 [1885]

[Dear Horatio]

Thanks for your letter of the 22nd, and for the proof of my article on the Renaissance. It was rather selfish of me to ask you to read the latter; but I thought you might suggest some omissions I had made or some superfluities I had inserted, before it was too late. As you once said, each man sees history so differently as to make his insight an originality—and I wanted to test my view of the matter in question by yours.

You are quite right that this is not on the type of an Encyclopædia Article. It is an Essay. But it is the first article (I believe) under the heading "Renaissance" with the Encyclopædia Brit.[1] has yet printed. The period of history has only been defined during the last twenty-five years, and its importance recognized. Hegel, for example, skips it almost dryshod in his "Philosophy of History"—passing with no transition from the Middle Ages to the German Reformation, ignoring the part played by Italy in modern culture. I therefore felt bound to discourse after the fashion of a treatise.

I understand your longing for rest. It will not come, however, till the house is finished. But meanwhile I hold it good you should be relieved of visitors. [A. O. Rutson][2] was, you say, as inexacting as a guest could be, and I believe that. Yet the mere presence of a guest is something. I shall be very curious to hear from time to time what N——[3] is doing. I confess he did not strike me either as an interesting personality or as a powerful man. It is, however, a great point for his social chances that he delights in society and that women take to him. These qualities often advance a man—provided he has ambition and power of work—more than will or than creative force. Mrs. G—— sent me a curious report about him from Z——, which shows that he did not impress Z. with more than his acquisitive ability. But that opinion does not count for much. A tutor rarely has insight into the obliquely successful points in a man's character.

I have greater ups and downs than usual in my attempt to recover health. But I have set my work again on the anvil, and am hammering away at the Jesuits. I have a vast canvas to fill.

[Incomplete]

---

1. The 9th ed. (1885).
2. See L III.

3. Since these letters were so frequently mutilated in print, we have preferred not to make guesses regarding the persons involved. The initials may stand for either first or last names. No other letters elucidate our problem.

1478. *To T. S. Perry*

Am Hof, Davos Platz, Switzerland, June 29 1885

Dear Mr Perry

It is a very long time since we exchanged letters. And I fully believe that in debit credit account of correspondence, I am the debtor. I will tell you why. My health, which, I think you know, is always feeble, has been so depressed during the last ten months that something of the nervous force on which I live has suffered change, & I have had to accept the new nuisance of writer's cramp. I have the forlorn satisfaction of studying in myself the mind's resistance to physical collapse, & of observing the stages whereby the consummation of our complex human organism is gradually effected. There has been what seems to me now, as I look back on it, a considerable tract of time in which I was unable to pen a letter. What I could write, though that was little, I reserved for literary work. But I have never forgotten you & Mrs Perry. You have both (if you will pardon this frankness) been often near me in thought at times when I could not compell the means of communication with you from my hand. There is nothing exceptional or strange in my condition. I only allude to it by way of apology for silence:—because I should regret that any lacks of my own deprived me of the privileges of your friendship.

When I can work, I work at the continuation of my "Renaissance in Italy." I have to do the part of Italian History wh is controlled by the Catholic Revival.

If you, whose universal oversight of all departments of knowledge is exceptional, could put me on the track of studying the Jesuit method in *education* (humanistic, scientific, & other), I should feel deeply obliged.—I only say this because, when I write to you, I am accustomed to ask for something.

I want most of all to shake your hand again in correspondence. Life is somewhat hard here, alone, without like-minded people & with failing force.

A copy of the French translation of your book on English Literature[1] reached me. I congratulate you upon it. It seems well done. Tell me what you are about, & believe me most.

Sincerely yours
John Addington Symonds

---

1. *English Literature in the Eighteenth Century* (1883), trans. into French by L. Lemarquis (1885).

1479. *To Horatio Forbes Brown*

Davos Platz, July 6 [1885]

[Dear Horatio]

I have not responded to your letters for three reasons. First, the continued weakness of my right hand. Secondly, that I have been at work on my Italian History. Thirdly, that a good deal of my time and thought has been occupied by some business here.

You will be glad to get into the mountains. The heat must be very trying. If your weather at all resembles ours, however, you are pretty cool and damp just now. All you write about the "Favorita"[1] sounds very charming. What do you rent it by the month for? Do you think it would do for us in May one year?

The tale I wrote in the "Waring"[2] and in the train to Udine appeared in a Bazaar magazine,[3] together with a tale by Dan Cave,[4] a tale by my cousin Miss Abdy Williams,[5] and a lyric by St. Loe[6]—plenty for one family.

Is not this a nice coat? Quarterly: 1 and 4 "Azure, 3 eagles displayed, or," FitzSimon; 2 & 3 "ermine, on a bend gules, 3 eagles displayed, or," Baghault. I found it on a 16th-century brass in the Church of Great Yeldham, Essex, quartered with one variant of my paternal coat, viz. "Azure, a chevron engrailed, between three trefoils, or." This brass was to Richard FitzSymonds.

The British Museum has bought *all* the North MSS.,[7] I am pleased to say. Catherine writes me to say they form a large mass of very miscellaneous material, besides the "autobiography." There was a MS. copy of Roger North's autobiography which Miss North purchased from the Brit. Mus. agent, and which I hope will be to-day within my hands; for I expect my wife and little Katharine from London, and she has promised to bring the document. Miss North will, I hope, have it collated with the autograph and published. She thinks of entrusting this to Dr. Jessop, the Norfolk antiquarian and Arcadian parson.

Here you have a rambling epistle enough! Ruedi gave an improved account of me. He said three days ago that he thought me in a very serious state when I first returned from the journey (to Venice), but that he wished more of his patients had my power of reacting against grave organic disorder. It was the resumption of literary work—writing the chapter on the Jesuits—I am convinced, which gave me a turn to better health.

[Incomplete]

---

1. H. F. Brown's note: "A house on the Lido, built by a Duke of Brunswick."

2. "An Ancona-built sailing-boat"—Brown's note to L 1468.

3. The tale, "The Heroism of Giustina," in the *Artillery Bazaar Magazine* (1885), according to Symonds' note on his cutting, was written at the request of Charles Cave. Babington (p. 189) was unable to locate the magazine. We have no clue to the other contributions.

4. Daniel Charles Addington Cave (born 1860), Symonds' nephew, son of Sir Charles Daniel Cave.

5. Ellen M. Abdy-Williams (Mrs. Bernhard Whishaw), daughter of Mary Abdy and the Rev. James Williams of Matherne; first cousin of Symonds' mother, Harriet Sykes; editor of *Time,* a magazine in which several of Symonds' poems appeared; wrote novels: *Two Ifs* (1884), *For His Friend* (1885), *Forewarned!* (1885), and *The World Below* (1887), and dramas.

6. St. Loe Strachey, his nephew. See L 1061.

7. See L 1473.

1480. *To Horatio Forbes Brown*

Davos Platz, July 24 [1885]

[Dear Horatio]

This is I suppose the last letter I shall address to Venice before you leave for the mountains. It is stupendously beautiful, this summer weather. I have always been most sensitive to the beauty of the world in illness. Though the range of enjoyment is so narrow, the entrance into communion with nature is somehow more intimate. There is something in long restless nights and watchings from the window for the gradual approaches of the dawn, which fixes on the soul the sacredness of spiritual life in outer objects.

I have just decided to spend a certain sum of money in having all sorts of MSS. printed.[1] I told you about this project at Venice. Since then the Edinburgh printers have offered better terms. Gradually I should like to make a clearance of my yet remaining stores of prose and verse. They are going to print for me in slips, six copies. I may thus obtain the material for a book of miscellanies, more *intime* than anything I have as yet published. I look forward to the arrangement and revision of this stuff as a relief from the solemn, solid production of Chapters on Italian History. Thank you for the title of Manso's book on Tasso.[2] It is not so good a book as Fra Fulgenzio's "Sarpi."[3] But it has some of the *naïf* qualities so remarkable in that life.

August 1. I have long intermitted this letter. But my body has been imposing upon my spirit indignities which can be borne only with difficulty, and during the incumbency of which it is well for a self-respecting soul to hold its peace.

August 4. I do not know where to send this better than to Venice. It is not worth sending, except in so far as the dates show that I have not ceased thinking of you. Until I have something livelier to say, I will henceforth hold my tongue.

[Incomplete]

---

1. The *Miscellanies*. See L 1482 and Babington, pp. 55 ff.
2. Giovanni Battista Manso, Marquis di Villa, *Vita di Torquato Tasso* (Venetia, 1621, and later eds.).
3. Fra Fulgenzio Micanzi, *Vita del Padre Paolo dell' Ordine de' Servi* [Pietro Sarpi] (1646, and later eds.).

1481. *To T. S. Perry*

Am Hof, Davos Platz, Switzerland. August 1 1885

How glad I am to think
you may come here!
Do come.
Did I tell you I was
invited to lecture at
the Johns Hopkins Univ? I have had
4 or 5 invitations recently
from America for literary work of all sorts.

Dear Mr Perry

Your two very kind and valuable letters of July 13 & 15 have found me here. I am basking in the most perfect summer I ever remember to have enjoyed in the high Alps. Days & nights are equally delightful. There is no drawback but that persistent one of physical weakness. I cannot do the things I want, & am perforce engaged with books & studies more than I care to be. Accident, not inclination, made me a sort of bookworm years ago. I have never become a successful creature of the sort, & do not understand Mark Pattison. By the way, I suppose you had read his volume of autobiography?[1] If so, did you also chance to see a paper of recollections of him by Lionel Tollemache?[2] It is remarkably good.

As usual, your letters convey a mass of information. I have already got & used Dejob's "De l'Influence"[3] etc, & another work of the same order, Philippson's "Contre-Revolution Réligieuse."[4] Both I found to be of much assistance. The latter has a really excellent abstract of the history of the Council of Trent, bringing out some points neglected by Ranke.[5]

My book is getting on. I have written chapters on 1) the Spanish Hegemony 2) the Papacy & Council of Trent 3) Inquisition 4) Company of Jesus 5) Social Morality 6) Life of Tasso 7) Giordano Bruno 8) Palestrina & Modern Music. Now I am reading through Tasso's poetry & prose again with a view to a chapter upon that. I mean also to make Sarpi the subject of one chapter, & the Bolognese painters of another, if I have strength to go on.

I wish I could talk to you about some of the more general aspects of my work. My period is 1530–1600. For Bruno I conceived the highest admiration after studying his original works. Have you come across Brunnhofer's book[6] on him? It is the best thing written about his philosophy.

I should also like to discuss your view of Tasso's madness. *Was* Tasso "out of his time?" The problem of Tasso's psychology is extremely obscure. I have found my best guide to a solution of it in the 5 vols of his letters edited by Guasti.[7] In some most important respects Tasso seems to me to have been too much *in his time*—i.e. too much inclined to observe its ordinances. That it was not a *good* time for a great poet I readily admit.

Can you send me a copy of your Welt Lit: Article?[8] I will send you one of mine on Renaissance in Encycl Brit when it appears. I should be glad if you would criticize it. Your grasp upon lity & social revolution is so much stronger than mine that I fear you will find the essay an antiquated production. By the way, my articles on Petrarch, Poggio Politian & Pontano in Enc Br are not worth looking at. All one can do is to make a précis of facts in such short pieces.

Tolstoi's "Guerre et Paix" I read with profound interest some years ago. What you say about its being a "loaf of life" is quite true. There is no realism like the realism of this new diffuse Russian style of novel. Men & women appear in it as they do in actual life, & leave the same impression as living people. A very wonderful book of the kind is [Dostoyevsky's] *Raskolnikow* [*Crime and Punishment*] wh in its German translation was introduced to me by Prince Emil Carolath[9] last winter. I strongly recommend it to any one who appreciates Tolstoi. Carolath showed me a great many recent Russian novels. But this was by far the most powerful. It is horrible also.

Falke's book[10] I shall now certainly get, & I must also try to have Paulssen.[11] I am obliged to buy books recklessly. My house is getting full of them.

Do send me more sonnets of Mrs Perry's. Of poetry I have myself written little lately, though I am ruminating a conclusion of Animi Figura, to express the faith (after the doubt) that is in me as adapted to the shadowy second-self of my fiction.

I must follow your advice & get quills. You see my handwriting is very bad—in spite of daily rubbing of the wrist & muscles, wh does a little good. I tried a typewriter[12] last winter, & mastered it fairly well. I could *copy* with it, but not compose. The more I write, the less do I manage to get "style" straight out. The Greek Poets were hardly blotted on their Ms. What I am now writing on Itn History is a mass of erasures & alterations.

I am sending to press (to be privately printed in slips) a great quantity of miscellaneous things in prose & verse written by me in past years, & am surprised with what ease they seem to have proceeded from my brain. Some of these things are too fluent. Others appear to have a sort of wilding grace wh I could not now recapture. The object is to see whether out of the whole mass I shall be able to extract enough ore to make a book of rather more *intime* utterances than I have yet published.

Apropos, what do you think of Amiel?[13] In spite of his marvellous style, the book makes me feel quite ill.

Please remember me to Mrs Perry & believe me ever sincerely as well as gratefully yours

J A Symonds.

I hope I did not write all this in my last letter.

---

1. Mark Pattison (1813–84), *Memoirs* (1885).

2. Lionel Tollemache (see L 125) wrote his "Recollections of Pattison" for the *Journal of Education*, VII, n.s. (June 1, 1885).

3. *De l'Influence du Concile de Trente* (Paris, 1884) by Charles Dejob (1847–1916).

4. *Contre-Revolution réligieuse au XVIme siècle* (Brussels, 1884) by Martin Philippson (1846–?), German historian and professor at the University of Brussels.

5. Leopold von Ranke (1795–1886), *Die Römischen Päpste* (3 vols., 1834–39).

6. Hermann Brunnhofer (1841–1916), *Giordano Bruno's Weltanschauung und Verhängnis* (Leipzig, 1882).

7. *Le Lettere di Torquato Tasso,* ed. by Gaetano Guasti (1835–1910), (5 vols., 1852–55).

8. Symonds had possibly misunderstood that Perry had published a book, *From Opitz to Lessing* (Boston, 1885), and not an article; or, he may have wanted a copy of Perry's "Recent German Fiction," *Atlantic Monthly,* XLV (1880), 566–68. Virginia Harlow, *Thomas Sergeant Perry: A Biography* (Durham, 1950), p. 104, is vague about the matter.

9. See L 1457.

10. Jacob von Falke (1825–1897), prolific German writer on historical and aesthetic subjects. Symonds may refer to one of the following: *Aesthetik des Kunstgewerbes* (Stuttgart, 1883); *Die Kunst im Hause* (Vienna, 1873, trans., Boston, 1879); *Hellas und Rom* (1878–80), or *Greece and Rome: Their Life and Art* (trans. by W. H. Browne, New York, 1882).

11. Probably Antonius J. Paulssen, *Anthologia Graeca* (1813, and various later eds.).

12. There had been many attempts, beginning at least as early as 1714, to invent successful writing-machines; Remington and Sons of Ilion, N.Y., in 1873 produced the Remington standard typewriter.

13. Symonds asked Sidgwick the same question in L 1470. See also L 1474.

1482. *To Horatio Forbes Brown*

Davos, Aug. 14 [1885]

[Dear Horatio]

I am exceedingly glad to know that you are off to the hills at last, and that you are out of anxiety about your household.[1] Your last letter made me really anxious. Nothing, as I too well know, is more trying than the persistence of that noisome complaint. It seems to me more demoralizing than any debauchery, and taints the imagination through the enfeebled nerves.

I did go up the Schwartzhorn with pain, and suffered much in consequence. Ruedi said I was mad, and took occasion to observe that all consumptive people are a little mad. Indeed I believe he is right about me, but not in the way he suspects. I am better though. Ruedi assures me that I must only have patience, that it is better to leave such things alone.

[T. Herbert] Warren is here; and there have also been three Balliol men on the Lake. We had a great symposium with the natives here last night—such a row, but very jolly. The house is full of women. I am very tired. It is altogether an odd life up here. Nothing seems capable of taking the edge off. My work goes on. The book [*The Catholic Reaction*] is approaching its completion. At least I see my way now to the end, and know pretty well what more I have to do—a chapter on the Bolognese painters, a chapter on miscellaneous literature, and perhaps a final one on the whole matter. Meanwhile I have begun printing "Paraleipomena"[2] (the MS.); 42 pages are already in proof. But 36 of these are a long essay on Goethe's Proemium to "Gott und Welt," which I wrote in 1864. My prose then had a lyrical cry which has for ever passed beyond my reach. I suppose it will chiefly be a matter of expense how much I print, for I find considerable stores that seem to me worthy of this kind of semi-preservation.

A copy of Mutinelli's "Storia Arcana"[3] reached me lately: cost a good deal, £1 16s. 6d. It is worth the money, a very valuable book.

[Incomplete]

---

1. Brown's note: "They all got gastritis on the Lido."

2. The *Miscellanies*. The "Commentary on Goethe's Proemium" occupied the first 36 leaves of the first part of the work. See Babington, pp. 55 ff, and L 1480.

3. Fabio Mutinelli, *Storia arcana ed aneddotica d'Italia, raccontata dai Veneti ambasciatori* (Venezia, 1855–58).

1483. *To Horatio Forbes Brown*

Davos, Aug. 21 [1885]

[Dear Horatio]

I cannot help laughing at the robbery of your wardrobe, and rejoicing at the prospect of a fresh start in clothes! But the misfortune is that last spring you were noticeably better dressed than used to be the case. So the thieves have got more than if they had come two years sooner. Have they stolen the lovely brown velveteen coat?

I can at last report a real improvement in my health. My right hand too is much stronger. Ruedi is not sanguine about the hand being ever quite well again. Already, however, I can use the pen and the alpenstock better than I did. So I have not much to complain of now. Only I have not enjoyed the summer altogether. There has been lots of work done. I am tired of the perpetual phraseology of criticism. I wish it were possible to invent a new form of sentence.

I will certainly send you my Fragments when I have a good show. I wish, indeed, that I dared call them "Aurea Opuscula"![1] But I believe they will contain some fairly decent pieces. Warren, who is still here, picked up "Fragilia Labilia"[2] yesterday and was pleased to be taken with them.

Tell me, would you really like me to send you Valtelline wine this autumn? I mean, do you care for it enough to pay the duty and carriage? for I find that it will be safest not to prepay the case. Properly speaking, Valtelline wine ought to pay no duty on entering Italy. But I suppose it will be impossible to have that advantage.

I am intensely stupid this morning after a riotous night. Also (wonder at me!) I read the whole of the "Adone" of Marini,[3] 45,000 verses, in two days—yesterday and the day before. It is a very extraordinary poem, and I shall have a good deal to say about it.

[Incomplete]

---

1. Golden trifles. He refers to the *Miscellanies,* privately printed. See Ls 1480 and 1482.
2. T. Herbert Warren had received 1 of the 25 copies Symonds had had printed for his own use. T. B. Mosher printed an edition in 1902.
3. Giambattista Marini (1569–1625), *Adone* (Venice, 1623), a long poem in octaves, treats of the love of Venus and Adonis and includes long mannered digressions, written in a florid and highly elaborate style.

1484. *To Herbert Harlakenden Gilchrist*[1]

Am Hof, Davos Platz, Switzerland. August 25 1885

Dear Sir

I must have missed the first announcement of your proposed collection of a testimonial fund to Walt Whitman.

From the Academy of last week[2] I see that he is willing to accept such a gift of gratitude and reverence.

If it is not too late, I should like to add my mite & my name to the list, by forwarding a cheque for £5.

This I will do on hearing from you, if you will kindly send me a p: c:, whether you are still able to receive it & to what address I should send it.

I am among those English people who feel deeply that the modern world owes a mental & moral debt to the Good Grey Poet.

Believe me to be truly yours
John Addington Symonds

Herbert Gilchrist Esq.

---

1. Herbert Harlakenden Gilchrist (1857–?), son of Mrs. Anne Gilchrist, friend of Whitman.

2. Symonds must have received an early copy. Whitman's letter, addressed to Gilchrist, appeared in *The Academy,* XXVIII (Aug. 29, 1885), 134. The announcement of the fund-collection appeared in XXVIII (July 11, 1885), 26. William Michael Rossetti was the fund's treasurer and Gilchrist the honorary secretary.

1485. *To Mary Robinson*

Davos Aug: 28 1885

My dear Miss Robinson

Thank you so much for your kind letter of the 23rd. I ought to have written to you before. But I have got out of the way of letter writing owing to my hand being still weak. The result is that I also get few letters.

I have had a good deal of health trouble this summer. I came back with my chest out of order, & had to live for that at first; & then there came quite a different bother wh for eight weeks has prevented me from taking enough exercise & has been very annoying in several ways.

That is getting gradually better I hope now. My hand too is not so weak as it was, owing to daily rubbing. But I have had a somewhat depressing summer altogether, & feel twenty per cent lower in physical energy than I like to be. The fact however is (as my friends tell me) that with any amount of physical energy I should always be discontented by craving for more & making myself a burden to others by my fractiousness.

I have done a good deal of literary work. Since I returned from Venice I have written a chapter on the Jesuits, one on Tasso's life, & one on his Gerusalemme, & am now pretty well on with a fourth chapter about Marino & such people—all these of course for the sequel to my Renaissance.[1] The labour has been against the grain because I am not truly in sympathy with the Jesuits or Tasso or Marino. I *am* in sympathy with my subject, wh is the contact of Reformation, Catholic Revival & Renaissance. But the manifestations of that collision of diverse forces are dreary, difficult to enliven, demanding more of nerve-force than they communicate.

It was so different when one used to write about Greeks! They gave everything. One had only to express in inadequate words one's sense of the blessing.

The doctors are right about you. You are overworked. You know I have been always telling you so; & in my savage semi-tyrannous semi-paternal & all-pedantically-pettish way I tried to treat you in Venice as one overworked. You are not exactly over-worked by actual study or production. But the advantageous conditions of your life have placed you in a highly stimulating milieu, wh is always making more demands upon your vital force than are quite healthy for the organism.

I should be very glad, with regard to you, if I could hear that you were going, for some long time together, to live in sweet air with only a few friends & with some definite piece of work to do.

Your new novel[2] for example. The subject of that appeals to me. I think it might be made a fine psychological study. Only, with so slight a fabric of pure plot, the character would have to be intensely apprehended & then projected in marble; & to do this would tax the strongest physique in existence.

Thank you for the sketch you sent me of a very interesting motif. It is a character-portrait wh appeals to me in a thousand ways.

What I should apprehend as perilous in the elaboration of it is i) that it would be difficult to make the world feel the *force* of this aspiring artist soul, ii) that the depression of the catastrophe would weigh too heavily upon the writer's sympathy. Under this double difficulty of projecting the man in vigour, & withdrawing him into the shades of defeated ambition, I seem to see before me a possible—one indeed of the most frequent cases of —failure in novelistic art: namely, *surroundings* realized out of proportion to the impressiveness of the *main motive.*

The odd thing about Russian literature is that it accumulates surroundings only with the result of making the chief characters emergent. How the Russians contrive to do this, I am unable to say. But in comparison with contemporary English writers, their success strikes me as remarkable.

I thought your sister's novel[3] (wh Catherine read aloud to me) a most promising book. If I should say frankly what it left upon my mind, it amounts to this—that though she interested us in all three of the chief actors she failed to make us love the girl, she led us to despise Bellingham more than she probably intended, & she used the young Irish hero too much as a cheval de bataille.[4] Here again the *surroundings* (as I call them) were all good—the early Irish life of the girl *eintreffend* [fitting], the French Abbey exquisite & subtle, the London life well seized in its relations to the characters. But after all, the three agonists were not so masterfully made out as to arouse a potent sense of human destiny in the midst of their complexities of interaction. They went too much into the background. The background, in other words, struck me as better made out than the central persons.

In the art wh we all aspire to, & wh so few in any generation achieve, the central human beings dwell in memory above the background, & though they are controlled by circumstance seem to colour & affect the circumstances wh they obey.

Forgive me, if I write now too much as I am wont to speak. I want the answering voice, the development of argument, the yielding to counter argument.

The upshot, however, is that I look forward with great interest to your sister's next novel. I think she has it in her to be a considerable writer in this way.

Is it worth suggesting the consideration how a man like the Abbé Prevost made Manon Lescaut[5] emerge from slightly sketched surroundings wh took from HER for us their value?

In addition to the Italian History, I am now at work upon another matter. This is the private printing[6] of a mass of papers. I am not sure it is worth doing. I am trying to put on record what I think to be the most distinctive parts of inedited literary MSS produced during the last 20 years.

It is rather trying business, getting those utterances of the past in order —not rhythmic—but in any kind of order. It makes me live back too much (for my own comfort) into former states of feeling. But it has occurred to me to do it. And so I go on.

How much you must have enjoyed your time with Vernon [Lee] in England! Merely to think of your mutual pleasure & profit gives me satisfaction.

It is good of you to think of me in all this—of me who was not very good to you at Venice, except only in the effort I made to get up a gondoliers' singing party for your amusement. For that tiny exhibition of will I take credit to myself, when I remember the noise there was etc.

You may be amused to hear that thieves broke into [H. F.] Brown's apartment at the Pal.[azzo] Balbi,[7] & stole all his good clothes! He has now, he writes, to provide himself with a completely new wardrobe. This will not be otherwise than a gain to the society wh he adorns.

Since we were at Venice, I have bought a second farm,[8] also on the Lake here. It is very large—has one house on the lake, one on the mountain, with meadows, streams, large tracts of woods alp, & pasturage upon the high fells for many cows. This is one of the prettiest things in the world. Madge & Lotta with my niece Miss Cave[9] & the governess are keeping house together now in the wooden chalet on the high pastures— 6000 feet above the sea—wh belongs to the new purchaser. I went to see them there this morning. They are having a good time except for the world-old beds mattressed with naught but sweet hay from the meadows round them. You do not know how funny & how kind this primitive life here is! In spite of solitude & exile & failing health we carve some wild good out of natural things.

But the doctors say that Madge is in a very critical state of the lungs; & Janet makes nothing wh can be called progress.

Enough. You will not read all this I reckon. But I have spent a couple of hours in talking to you. So goodbye. Yours ever

J A Symonds

---

1. *The Renaissance in Italy: The Catholic Reaction,* Chaps. IV, VII, VIII, and XI. In XI he treats Guarini, Chiabrera, Tassoni, and Testi in addition.
   2. Apparently never published. *Arden. A Novel* had appeared in 1883.
   3. See L 1462.
   4. A pet subject; literally, a charger.
   5. Abbé Prévost (1697–1763), *Histoire du chevalier Des Grieux et de Manon Lescaut* (1731).
   6. See Ls 1480 and 1482.
   7. On the Grand Canal in Venice; a favorite locale for artists in Symonds' day.
   8. For details about his farm see Ls 1452 and 1464.
   9. Edith Frances Cave (d. unmarried Nov. 17, 1949).

1486. *To William Sharp*[1]

[Davos, ca. Sept. 1885]

[Dear Mr. Sharp]

. . . The Preface[2] is more humanly and humanely true about Shakespeare's attitude in the Sonnets than anything which has yet been written about them. . . . You are one of those who live (as Goethe has for ever put it) in *the whole*. It is a great thing for modern criticism to get itself out of holes and corners, mere personal proclivities and scholarly niceties, into the large air of nature and of man.

[Incomplete]

---

1. See L 1324.
2. To Sharp's *The Songs and Sonnets of Shakespeare* (1885).

1487. *To Henry Sidgwick*

Davos, Sept. 3, 1885.

[Dear Henry]

Your diary, acceptable as ever, came this morning.

It fills me as usual with a kind of melancholy envy. Your life is so well filled, and your mind ripens in so much genial society. I cannot help contrasting one of your months with one of mine. I squander existence. My literary labour is the only backbone left to support the tottering frame of intellectual life. So I will talk about it.

I set to work just a year ago, after seeing "Vagabunduli Libellus" and "Wine, Women, and Song" through the press, at two volumes on the Catholic Revival in Italy. This book is part of my "Renaissance in Italy"; and if Smith will let me, I shall bring it out in sequence. Nine chapters are now written. Three more are on the stocks. Revision and rewriting will probably occupy me onward through the winter. I cannot say that I am not interested in the subject. There is something sublime in the spectacle of national ruin. The heroism of Bruno, the *maladie de l'âme* of Tasso, the impenetrable stoicism of Sarpi, the malign fervour of Loyola, the infernal machinery of the Index Libr. Prohib., the delirium of society asphyxiated by Spanish etiquette, the galvanisation of Latin Christianity into paralytic movement by the Tridentine Council, are all in their way striking.[1] Yet the word joy cannot be uttered. I sit down daily to my desk as an anatomist to the dissecting table—and each subject in turn is pathological. I have to deal with only two really healthy souls upon the road of progress—Bruno and Palestrina.[2] Palestrina, as you know, started music on the modern track. Bruno, before he was forty, had divined in a sort of incoherent way the whole of modern thought, and was burned for this audacity of vision. The extent to which Spinoza, Leibnitz, and the German idealists have lived

74

upon his ideas without, until Schelling, avowing their obligation, is quite amusing. There is a good new German book about him by a man called Brunnhofer.[3] It ought to be translated into English for such folk as are curious about the διαδοχή [development] of philosophical thought. Had it not been for the Catholic Revival, I believe that the Italian Renaissance, mainly through the work of thinkers in Magna Græcia,[4] Telesio,[5] Campanella,[6] Bruno, Vico,[7] men born on the old soil of Parmenides[8] and Pythagoras,[9] would have saved transalpine searchers after systems a good deal of trouble.

[Incomplete]

---

1. For Symonds' treatment of these topics, see *The Renaissance in Italy: The Catholic Reaction:* for Bruno, Chap. IX; for Tasso, Chap. VII; for Sarpi, Chap. X; for Ignatius Loyola, Chap. IV; for the Index, Chap. III; for Spanish society, Chap. I; and for the Tridentine Council, Chap. II.

2. *Ibid.,* Chap. XII.

3. *Giordano Bruno's Weltanschauung und Verhängniss* (Leipzig, 1882). See L 1481.

4. Name applied in ancient geography to that part of southern Italy colonized by the Greeks.

5. Bernardino Telesio (1509–88), Italian philosopher, leader in the attack on scholasticism, deemphasized theories of metaphysics and urged the value of scientific knowledge; Symonds in *The Renaissance in Italy: Italian Literature,* Chap. XVI, regards him as a forerunner of Francis Bacon.

6. Tommaso Campanella (1568–1639), philosopher and poet, anticipated the scientific attitude of empiricism. Symonds translated his sonnets (1878). He was born at Stilo, Calabria. See L 1059.

7. Giovanni Battista Vico (1668–1744), born at Naples, Italian philosopher and historian, regarded by many as the first modern historian, theorized that history is the account of the birth and development of human institutions and societies, not of biographies of great men or of God's will. In recent years his work was stressed by Benedetto Croce.

8. Born ca. 514 B.C., leading philosopher of the Eleatic School, lived at Elea, Lucania, southern Italy.

9. Ca. 582-ca. 507 B.C., founder of the Pythagorean school of philosophy, migrated from his native Samos, the island off western Asia Minor, to Crotona, in the toe of Italy.

1488. *To Horatio Forbes Brown*

[Davos] Sept. 3 [1885]

[Dear Horatio]

Davos is certainly an odd place as to climate. We never seem to get appreciably *bad* weather. While you have had that drip of rain at San

Martino, we have never had anything worse than a heavy shower or a day half-clouded.

I have sent Pinkie[1] a copy of "South Sea Idylls."[2] Make him lend it you and read "Chumming with a Savage." You won't like the man. Yet the picture he draws of savage kindness is very fascinating. I am squandering my time now abominably. It seems very hard to keep eurhythmic in Davos. I despise X. for submitting to the tyranny of a depressing climate, and here am I shredding myself to tatters by indulging in the tension of this stimulative air. My nerves are like the wires of a new spring bed—all aquiver about nothing. Addio.

[Incomplete]

---

1. Percy E. Pinkerton (?–?), author of *Galeazzo: A Venetian Episode* (1886), and translator of German, French and Russian works. See L 1407.

2. A series of travel sketches and stories (1873) by Charles Warren Stoddard (1843–1909), an American traveler and author chiefly of poems and sketches of travel. See L 2070.

1489. *To Albert O. Rutson*

Davos Sept: 9. 1885

My dear Rutson

I have been reading tonight with deep interest your speeches at Leith,[1] & I congratulate on the clearness & concision with which you expressed your programme, & not less the urbanity of your tone. Your answers to questions struck me as peculiarly happy.

It must be delightful thus to come in contact with the actualities of life, & to feel the power of dealing frankly with them.

Pray let us have information of all you do. We read with avidity what you send; & I can give your tones of voice to the printed word.

I am interested to see that my old school fellow Ch[arles] Darymple[2] (Puss Dalrymple we used to call him) is canvassing Midlothian. I once spent some weeks with him at his place Newhailes[3] near Musselburgh.

Ever yours. Macte virtute est! [Proceed in virtue!]

J A S.

---

1. Rutson had hoped to represent the Leith Burghs in Parliament. The *Leith Burghs Pilot* for September 5, 12, and 19, 1885, contains triple-column reports of Rutson's

appearances at Newhaven, Leith, Portobello, and Museelburgh. Despite his candor and humor, and his endorsement by such notables as Lord Aberdare, Rutson was bypassed by the Leith Burghs Liberals who endorsed William Jacks, a Glasgow merchant. Jacks defeated W. D. Thorburn, the Conservative candidate.

2. See L 41.

3. See Ls 77 and 78.

1490. *To Herbert Harlakenden Gilchrist*[1]

Am Hof, Davos Platz, Switzerland. Sept 14 1885

Dear Sir

I now enclose a cheque for £5 to the Whitman Testimonial.
It might be worth sending circulars to these people:

> H. G. Dakyns Esq.
> Clifton College, Bristol

> F. W. H. Meyers Esq.
> Leckhampton House Cambridge

> H. F. Brown
> Casa Torresella
> Zattere Venezia

> Prof: Sidgwick
> Cambridge

> R. Louis Stevenson
> Bournemouth

> Ernest Myers
> Albion Street W.

These men have been, all of them, more or less sealed of the tribe of W. W. But I cannot answer for their present fidelity.

My bad health, wh forces me to go on living for years in this out of the way place, has prevented my forming acquaintance recently with people who would be likely to care about Whitman.

Believe me to be very faithfully yours

John Addington Symonds

H. H. Gilchrist Esq.

P.S. I see you bear for second name Harlakenden,[2] with which I am familiar, a collateral ancestor of mine (b: at Gt. Yeldham Essex in 1595) having married Dorothy dr of Th: Harlakenden of Earl's Colne. This Samuel Symonds emigrated to America in 1637 & was Deputy Governor of New England. He had 16 children, one of whom was christened Harlakenden. Does the family of Harlakenden still flourish in Essex?

---

1. See L 1484.

2. See Meredith B. Colker, Jr., "The Harlakenden Claim of Royal Descent," *The American Genealogist*, XIV (1937–38), 209–14. Colker concludes that Thomas Harlakenden married Mary Londenoyes of Bread, Sussex, around 1532 (p. 213, note 1, p. 214). Roger Harlakenden (an American colonist) was the grandson of Thomas Harlakenden. His cousin Dorothy married Samuel Symonds who, after his wife's death, came to America and became deputy-governor of Massachusetts (he is frequently mentioned in *New England Historical and Genealogical Register*). He lived at Ipswich in the Massachusetts Bay Colony. For Harlakenden, Savage's *Genealogical Dictionary* gives Roger Harlakenden (1611–38), and Deborah (Dorothy) as the probable sister of Roger.

1491. *To Horatio Forbes Brown*

Davos Sept. 14 [1885]

[Dear Horatio]

I wish I could be with you in Venice this autumn. But, though I have smoked some pipes over the possibility, so as not to abandon the idea unconsidered, I must give it up.

Change I want. But I dare not take the change in Venice. To tell the truth, I always pay pretty heavily in physique for my visits to Venice; and this autumn I am really forced to economize resources. I shall probably take a little journey with Madge across the hills to Landeck, on to Munich, and back by the Boden See. If we make this excursion, I mean to take Sarpi's "Letters" and the three Lives[1] I possess of him as my travelling companions. I find that after all I shall have to give a chapter of my book to him.

What you call "Aurea Opuscula"[2] (I wish the title were deserved) shall reach you in due course. At present the printers have a mass of MS. still in their hands. This literary hay must be estimated to some extent by bulk and diffusion of interest. I do not care to send you 80 pp. when in a short while I may have 180 to send. As before, so now, I expressly deprecate the notion of being thought to want you or any one to read through all that. But I should like you to have a sufficient quantity of the stuff to browse on.

I am glad that what I said about your work gave you a lift. When you settle down into "Ca Torresella," you must go at it in earnest. Possibly you are upon the point of differentiating, determining your species as a student. You may find that your sphere is the unearthing and elucidating of documents, the doing of such bits of work as this inquiry into Venetian printing. But I advise you to give the other and wider sort of literature, history or biography in the liberal sense, a fair chance. In either department Venice will supply you with sufficient matter, and your love for Venice will lend you the energy of enthusiasm.

We are having heavenly weather just now. I am very content to enjoy it. In Italy it would be more entrancing. But I should not sleep so well there. *Spartam nactus sum; hanc ornabo.*[3]

[Incomplete]

---

1. See L 1218. The letters may have been any of these: *The Letters of the Renowned Father Paul . . .* , trans. by Edward Brown (1693); *Scelte Lettere Inedite . . .* (Capolago, 1847; Venice, 1848; Capolago, 1883); *Lettere raccolte e annotate da Fil. Luigi Polidari* (Florence, 2 vols., 1863). Two of the lives referred to are Fra Fulgenzio Micanzi's (see L 1480) and Aurelio Angelo Bianchi Giovini (1799–1862), *Biografia di Paolo Sarpi* (2 vols., 1836), both mentioned in the *The Renaissance in Italy: The Catholic Reaction,* "Works Commonly Referred to." See L 1480. The 3rd was Arabella Georgina Campbell, *The Life of Fra Paolo Sarpi* (1869). See L 1492.

2. His *Miscellanies.* See L 1483.

3. "I have reached Sparta; I shall enhance her": A variation on Cicero's "Spartam nactus es: hanc (ex)orna": "Sparta is your inheritance: make the best of her."

1492. *To Horatio Forbes Brown*

Davos Platz, Sept. 25 [1885]

[Dear Horatio]

Madge and I started for our journey on the 16th and returned yesterday, having had good weather all the time. We drove over Fluela, stopped at Pontresina, then over Bernina, rested at Tirano among the vines of the Valtelline, crossed the Stelvio and rested again among the orchards of Schluderns (whence we cast longing glances down the Etsch), returned by Münsterthal and Ofener Berg.

I am truly sorry to have abandoned Venice. But it could not be helped. Ruedi gave a bad report of me the day before I left, and would not hear of my going even to Munich.

Have you seen Ouida[1] upon the Gondoliers and Venice in general?

I read Sarpi's "Letters" and Miss Campbell's "Life"[2] of him on the journey. The letters are a most valuable source of history. Did you not once tell me that Miss C.'s life contained documents bearing on the point of Sarpi's being possibly surrendered to Rome? I can find none such. The English (which is the original of this life) is miserably written and quite ungrammatical. Does the Italian version give the originals of the documents she translates? If so I must get it. Pray tell me where it was printed. I get to like Sarpi more, and to admire his marvellous political penetration. Some passages in the letters are incomparable for insight. But I cannot seize his attitude towards religion. My belief is that he would willingly have accepted the Reformation if he could have done so without leaving Venice. There is a suspicion in my mind that the letters to Duplessis Mornay[3] may have been tampered with to make them appear more Protestant. If they are quite genuine, then I see not how Sarpi can be defended from duplicity. "Il travaillait sourdement à discréditer la Messe qu'il disait tous les jours,"[4] said Bossuet;[5] and certainly his language about Catholic dogmas to Duplessis M. is incompatible with sincere Catholicism. Have you formed any judgment about these letters? I shall write a chapter about Sarpi,[6] leaving, however, his *Venetian* services almost untouched. He comes into my subject rather for his attitude towards the Catholic Revival.

What you wrote from Asolo about experience is only sadly too true. I agree with R. L. Stevenson in holding that the right human life is to take our fill of all the activities and pleasures proper to each age. In that way man need have no regrets. But so many of us warped human beings invert the order of life, are never young, and so are never wholesomely middle-aged or old.

[Incomplete]

---

1. Louise de la Ramée (1839–1908), prolific novelist (pseud. Ouida) of French and English parentage who liked to write about the high life she did not know. Among her best novels are *Under Two Flags* (1862) and *Moths* (1880). Some of her stories for children are classics: *A Dog of Flanders, Two Little Wooden Shoes,* and *Bimbi.* Among her various enemies was Janet Ross. The specific reference is unknown to us.

2. See Ls 1218 and 1491.

3. The Huguenot statesman, Philippe du Plessis-Mornay (1549–1623), frequently called "the Huguenot Pope."

4. He worked blindly to discredit the mass which he recited every day.

5. Jacques Bénigne Bossuet (1627–1704), French Roman Catholic prelate; tutor to the dauphin (1670–81); bishop of Meaux (1681); famous pulpit orator.

6. See L 1487.

1493. *To* The Academy

Am Hof, Davos Platz, Switzerland. Sept. 27, 1885.

[Dear Sir]

There is an outcry in some quarters against Captain Burton's[1] translation of the *Arabian Nights*.[2] Only one volume of that work has reached me, and I have not as yet read the whole of it. Of the translator's notes I will not speak, the present sample being clearly insufficient to judge by; but I wish to record a protest against the hypocrisy which condemns his text. When we invite our youth to read an unexpurgated Bible (in Hebrew and Greek, or in the authorised version), an unexpurgated Aristophanes, an unexpurgated Juvenal, an unexpurgated Boccaccio, an unexpurgated Rabelais, an unexpurgated collection of Elizabethan dramatists, including Shakspere, and an unexpurgated Plato (in Greek or in Prof. Jowett's English version), it is surely inconsistent to exclude the unexpurgated *Arabian Nights,* whether in the original or in any English version, from the studies of a nation who rule India and administer Egypt.

The qualities of Capt. Burton's translation are similar to those of his previous literary works,[3] and the defects of those qualities are also similar. Commanding a vast and miscellaneous vocabulary, he takes such pleasure in the use of it that sometimes he transgresses the unwritten laws of artistic harmony. From the point of view of language, I hold that he is too eager to seize the *mot propre* of his author, and to render that by any equivalent which comes to hand from field or fallow, waste or warren, hill or hedgerow, in our vernacular. Therefore, as I think, we find some coarse passages of the *Arabian Nights* rendered with unnecessary crudity, and some poetic passages marred by archaisms or provincialisms. But I am at a loss to perceive how Burton's method of translation should be less applicable to the *Arabian Nights* than to the *Lusiad.* So far as I can judge, it is better suited to the *naïveté* combined with stylistic subtlety of the former than to the smooth humanistic elegances of the latter.

This, however, is a minor point. The real question is whether a word-for-word version of the *Arabian Nights,* executed with peculiar literary vigour, exact scholarship, and rare insight into Oriental modes of thought and feeling, can under any shadow of pretence be classed with "the garbage of the brothels." In the lack of lucidity, which is supposed to distinguish English folk, our middle-class *censores morum* strain at the gnat of a privately circulated translation of an Arabic classic, while they daily swallow the camel of higher education based upon minute study of Greek and Latin literature. When English versions of Theocritus and Ovid, of Plato's *Phaedrus* and the *Ecclesiazusae,* now within the reach of every schoolboy, have been suppressed, then and not till then can a "plain and literal" rendering of the *Arabian Nights* be denied with any colour of consistency to adult readers. I am far from saying that there are not valid reasons for thus dealing with Hellenic and Graeco-Roman and Oriental literature in its totality. But let folk reckon what Anglo-Saxon Puritanism logically involves. If they desire an Anglo-Saxon Index Librorum Prohibitorum, let them equitably and consistently apply their principles of inquisitorial scrutiny to every branch of human culture.

John Addington Symonds.

1. Richard Francis Burton (1821–90), explorer and orientalist; joined Indian army (1842); made pilgrimage to Mecca (1853); with John Hanning Speke (1827–64) explored Somaliland (1854), and the Lake Tanganyika region (1858); British consul at Fernando Po (1861–65), Damascus (1869–71), and Trieste (1872); accompanied Verney Lovett Cameron (1844–94) to the Gold Coast (1881–82); married (1861) Isabel Arundell (1831–96), who traveled with him, wrote travel narratives and a biography of him, and destroyed or mutilated a number of his works.

2. *The Thousand Nights and a Night,* a plain and literal translation of the *Arabian Nights' Entertainments* (16 vols., 1885–88). The outcries were against the first 2 vols. (1885): "Sigma" in "Pantegruelism or Pornography?" in the *Pall Mall Gazette,* XL (Sept. 14, 1885), 2–3, castigated the London *Standard* for favoring Burton's translation despite its frequent attacks on the *Gazette* for "pandering to pruriency"; he maintained that the argument that the work is for students is a hoax, that its reason for being is grossness (its character being that of filthy literature), that it is readily available in bookstores, and that it is unfit for the young. On Sept. 15, p. 2, "Anglo-Egyptian" answered: Burton's translation is one students will buy as the only literal one and in its coarseness is no worse than the classics given to school-boys. "Sigma" answered rather feebly on Sept. 17, p. 3. The editors themselves on Sept. 24, p. 3, asserted that to publish a page of Burton's translation would incur seizure of the *Gazette* by the police, but that it is a libel to compare even the worst passages of *Pericles* and *Titus Andronicus* with the *Arabian Nights;* and in the same issue, p. 6, "A Public School Master" called "Sigma" a representative of Mrs. Grundy, asserted that if the *Arabian Nights* must go, so must large parts of Shakespeare, Butler (*Hudibras*), Swift, Chaucer, Marlowe, Herrick, Byron, Juvenal, Martial, Horace, Catullus, and the *Old Testament,* and commented that "the dangers of evil books are among the least of the perils of a boy's life. . . ." On Sept. 25,

p. 6, the editors pointed out, clearly in disapproval, that Burton's book, issued privately by subscription to people supposed to be students, is available from almost every bookseller, an opinion supported by a correspondent quoted the next day, p. 3. "Sigma" answered in "The Ethics of the Dirt" (Sept. 29), 2, that the *Arabian Nights* corrupts not only boys, but also men who buy pornography, this practice being hypocritically defended at present in the name of "catholicity of culture"; as for boys, they should be protected from the obscene even in English literature, the classics, and the *Old Testament*.

For an account of the reception of this work, see Fawn Brodie, *The Devil Drives* (New York, 1967), pp. 309 ff.

3. *Scinde, or the Unhappy Valley* (2 vols., 1851) about India; *Personal Narrative* (3 vols., 1885), about Mecca; *First Footsteps in East Africa* (1856); *Abeokuta and the Cameroons Mountains* (2 vols., 1863); *Camoens: his Life and his Lusiads* (2 vols., 1881); and others before 1885.

1494. *To Mary Robinson*

Davos Sept: 29 1885

Dear Miss Robinson

I do not think I told you how much I liked the song you sent me upon our Venetian scuttle through the narrow Calli & emergence into the space behind the Pal: Dario & the flanks of the Salute[1]—or how much I should like to see more of these songs.

You would do me a great kindness if you could at some time without much trouble to yourself discover in the Br: Mus: what are the best sources for a study of the Bolognese painters—the Caracci,[2] Guido,[3] & Dominichius,[4] & Guercino.[5] I have to write a chapter on them; in the picture-gallery of my brain I can see a great many of their pictures almost as vividly as though I stood before them; but I want to work up their lives & the history of their eclectic revival.

It has been snowing here through the last four days, & the whole world is very white. Just the day before this bad weather set in, Madge & I returned from a nine days' journey in an open carriage over a series of high mountain passes—Fluela, upper Engadine, Bernina, Buffalora. We enjoyed it greatly; for we had delightful intervals of rest among the vines of Valtellina & the orchards of Vintschgow. And the high mountains were splendid in their majesty of glaciers under the serene September sky.

I go on working at my book on the Catholic Revival in Italy. It is a trying subject; little to sympathize with & very much to study & assimilate before a clear conception of anything can be gained.

Did I tell you that I am printing (for my own use) a lot of old MSS?[6] I think I shall send them to you when they are out of the printer's hand.

Life here rolls on very quietly with only its internal disturbances. So many of my old school & college friends are taking their part in the political struggle that I watch the English newspapers with more than common interest & feel myself more than usually out of the swim of life.

It is odd to be always filling notebooks & writing chapters upon things which do not very greatly signify to any human soul. When this long book is finished I really think I will try to do something toward the New Decameron. I have been reading the 1st vol of [Richard] Burton's Arabian Nights, & this has revealed to me for the first time in my life fully the strength and fascination of Oriental story telling. It is a pity that he should have wantonly

[three quarters page cut off]

truly glad to hear that you are giving yourself a fallow time. You know it is my idée fixe that you live at too high pressure.

[Incomplete]

---

1. The narrow streets leading to the Palazzo Dario—Amgarani, the American consulate, near the dome-covered church S. Maria della Salute.
2. Agostino; his brother Annibale; Antonio, son of Agostino; and their cousin Lodovico—Bolognese painters active in the last quarter of the 16th and the early 17th centuries. See L 1465.
3. Guido Reni, 1574–1642.
4. Domenichino (Domenico Zampieri), 1581–1641.
5. Il Guercino (Giovani Barbieri), 1590–1666.
6. See Ls 1480, 1482, and 1485.

1495. *To Albert O. Rutson*

Davos Oct: 3. 1885

My dear Rutson

Thank you much for sending me your Address.[1] It does not seem to me at all too advanced. Great sacrifices ought surely now to be made in England by all the wealthy classes, landowners & capitalists, for the bettering of the people & averting what seems to be the serious peril of crude socialistic revolutionary movements. If we could only find the means of descending by some gradual scale to conditions a society analogous to those of Switzerland! The even distribution of wealth in this land, the equal participation in government, the fact that everybody has some property in the land, & the political education afforded to each man by his voice in the affairs of the Commune, all together render the Swiss people contented soberly happy & good to be with. But what hope is there that England with its huge cities, ill-distributed population, & long past of slowly metamorphosed corrupted feudalism, should ever attain to such conditions?

I drove back from a village wedding just now with two men, a farmer & a glazier, who interested me greatly by their intelligent remarks upon the choice of the next parson for the parish. The present minister is old; & when he retires, each burgher of Davos will have a vote in the election of his successor. So they are beginning to discuss the matter among themselves —considering possible candidates from political as well as moral & religious points of view, especially considering the influence wh one or another is likely to exercise over the village school (where the parson has an indirect power) & over women.

Oct: 9.

This letter has been interrupted. Janet on Sunday (the 4th) had a hemorrhage from the lung which caused us much anxiety & has depressed us all. She is now out of danger, & will perhaps get up for a couple of hours today. But I cannot help fearing this is a downward step in her illness.

Last night came your letter of the 5th from Leeds. We watch all the steps you are taking with great interest; & the moment is becoming critical. I cannot say what I hope for. Surely, as events have hitherto gone, it will be best for you should Jack[2] retire. Thirsk[3] & Malton,[4] I now understand, is quite a forlorn hope—only, as you know, I have a strong leaning toward your working into & among your own folk:

I am glad Madge wrote to you about our driving tour. We both enjoyed it thoroughly, & we were very lucky; for the very day of our return the weather changed, & the whole world was soon white with those heavy snow-storms which have caused such serious innundations in the valleys of the Rhine & Adda.

I will give Madge your message. Since you left Davos, I have written three rather fatiguing chapters for my book on the Catholic Revival in Italy. One on the Gerusalemme of Tasso;[5] One on the Adone of Marini[6] & some other characteristic poems of the age; the third upon Sarpi[7] & his opposition to ultra-papal doctrines. Sarpi is a most interesting man; but his real opinions in religious matters are difficult to penetrate. He was more

like an English Whig than any Italian I have studied; & this is probably why
Macaulay liked him so. I wish I could lay my hands on what Macaulay
somewhere[8] wrote about him. Ever yrs

J A Symonds

---

1. Rutson was making political speeches. Which one he sent to Symonds is
unknown.
2. Rutson's brother, John (1829–1906), was Justice of the Peace for the North
Riding, Yorkshire. The third brother, Henry (1831–?), succeeded him in his office.
3. A small county-town of about 6,500 people at the close of the century, junction
of a branch railroad to Harrogate and Leeds. Rutson had apparently been thinking of
standing for Thirsk and Malton.
4. In 1894, a town of 4,900 persons, noted for its racing-stables and old priory-
church, between Whitby and Pickering.
5. Torquato Tasso (1544–95) published the first version of his masterpiece *Gerusalemme liberata* in 1573. It was completed 2 years later.
6. See L 1483.
7. See L 1218.
8. Macaulay's journal, quoted in George Otto Trevelyan (1838–1928), *Life and
Letters of Lord Macaulay* (2 vols., 1876), contains a paragraph on Sarpi, Macaulay's
"favourite modern Italian historian." See the 2-vol., 1931 ed: II, 542. See also I, 363, for
a passage from a letter to Thomas Flower Ellis.

1496. *To Horatio Forbes Brown*

Davos Platz, Oct. 8 [1885]

[Dear Horatio]

I should have written to you earlier but that since September 26,
whenever I took up a pen, it was to make notes or to work at a chapter on
Sarpi.[1] He is an impermeable, incommensurable man—ultimately, I think,
possessed with two great ideas, duty to God and duty to Venice. His last
words were for Venice, the penultimate consigned his soul to God.

To a mind like his the materials of dispute between Catholic and
Protestant must have seemed like Tweedledum and Tweedledee. He stayed
where he was, in a convent of the Servites, where he had taken root in
youth, because he could serve God there quite as well or better than in any
Protestant Conventicle. If Venice had inclined towards final rupture with
Rome, if indeed Venice had had the power to make that rupture, Sarpi
would have hailed the event gladly as introducing liberty of conscience and
purer piety and the depression of Papal supremacy in Italy. But the State of
Venice had chosen to abide in the old ways, and Sarpi knew that Venice

could not cope with Spain and Rome and Jesuitry. Therefore he possessed his soul in patience, and adored the God in whom he trusted, through those symbols to which he had from youth been educated, trusting the while that sooner or later in his Providence God would break those mighty wings of Papal domination. So I seem to read Sarpi. But after all construction of his character upon the lines of letters and signed writings, the man evades my vision. It was not for nothing that Sarpi made himself a friar at fourteen years of age.

In my History I am always grasping at shapes and souls of men; Bruno, Marino, Chiabrera, Tassoni, Sarpi, not to speak of the greater and the lesser Tasso,[2] with a host of others, have been flitting across the *camera obscura* of my brain for months. I am dizzied by the dance of personalities so diverse. I want rest and reaction, but where to find it, face to face with these inexorable hills, or in the company of peasants who inflame the brain with wine and noise? Fain would I fly away. But nowhere from my own soul and its responsibilities can I fly. I thought to devour thought in a diligence upon the road to Chur to-morrow. But Janet's state to-night forbids the journey. And should I have made it, I should only have carried my restlessness to a dull point from which I should then have carried it back again to a point of dismal industry.

There are dry stony substantial promontories in middle-life, shooting out into a surge of waters, upon which the self is impelled, unwilling yet incapable of resistance, and from which there is no exit except death's desirable determination.

[Incomplete]

---

1. See *The Renaissance in Italy: The Catholic Reaction*, Chap. X.
2. All in *ibid.*: Giordano Bruno: Chap. IX; Gabriello Chiabrera, Giovanni Battista Marino, and Alessandro Tassoni: Chap. XI; Fra Paolo Sarpi: Chap. X; Bernardo and Torquato Tasso: Chap. VII.

1497. *To Horatio Forbes Brown*

[Davos] Oct. 11 [1885]

[Dear Horatio]

Your letter of the 8th came last night. What you report about the Master of the Rolls[1] is most satisfactory. If you get that appointment you will be singularly happy: to have a public position connected with the studies and the place you love best, to be living in Venice with health to enjoy all these things and the society of so many interesting people as are always visiting Venice—all this constitutes a very fair share of human felicity.

When I reckon up my own goods and bads, I place an incurable discord in the soul first, next, chronic bad health, thirdly, the want of congenial society and external stimulus, and, lastly, want of success in literature. I think a man who has followed an art through a lifetime without making it pay and without securing some public distinction must be said to have failed.

I was reading Macaulay's "Life"[2] last night. It seems to me a little beyond the mark for a member of the Indian Council, living with the best Anglo-Indian Society, in perfect health, employing his time in framing the code for a great Empire, to complain of the "pangs of banishment."

By the way, both Macaulay and Hallam[3] take for granted that Sarpi was a Protestant. I find it difficult to state my opinion about Sarpi; but that he felt more sympathy with any of the then existing Protestant Churches than for Catholicism (apart from Papal tyranny and ecclesiastical abuses) I cannot admit.

[Incomplete]

---

1. Brown received the appointment. As master he edited and published *Calendar of State Papers, Venetian* (1891–1905).

2. George Otto Trevelyan, *Life and Letters of Lord Macaulay* (2 vols., 1876). Macaulay was appointed to the Board of Control of Indian Affairs in 1832, and in 1834, in financial need, he reluctantly left England for India as a member of the Supreme Council, returning to England in 1838. See L 1495.

3. See L 1495 and Henry Hallam (1777–1859), *Constitutional History of England* (3 vols., 1880), II, Chap. VII.

1498. *To T. S. Perry*

Am Hof, Davos Platz, Switzerland. Oct: 18 1885

Dear Mr Perry

Thank you very much for your line of the 2nd & the account of your ancestral hero in Harper's Weekly.[1] That interested me much, though I cannot say that I admire the statue.

Anything to do with American genealogy is of interest to me, as it ought to be to every Englishman. But I have made a hobby of heraldry &

pedigrees for many years. I take much interest in those members of my own family who had an early part in the foundation of America—Samuel Symonds[2] Depy Gov of New England & brother in law of Winthrop—the Harlakenden of Essex who went out in the Mayflower—and the Williams (for so we have some reason to believe) who settled Rhode Island.

I am glad to see that a Herald's College[3] is being established in the U.S.

Let me congratulate you on seeing the end of Aristotle![4] I wonder what you will have made of the Gk philosophers. They always seem to me most valuable as forgers of language capable of holding thought for centuries—glass phials, to use a metaphor, in wh thought has undergone slow chemic changes. But that any metaphysic, even this last metaphysic of evolution, introduces us to a solution of the world's secret, or helps to explain what everybody wants to know, namely the right relation of individuality & mind to the universe, I will not hold. The earliest & the latest appear to me equally feeble when the vital questions are touched.

I see before me now the results of a year's pretty hard work (for me who have small working power) in 12 chapters or 2 volumes on the Catholic Revival in Italy, rough-hewn. The next thing to do, is to sit down, re-write & polish the whole mass. But I am too tired to begin this yet.

I had a fine driving tour in an open carriage with one of my daughters this month. We crossed four of the highest passes in the Alps—one of them being the Stelvio—saw the vineyards of Valtelline & the orchards of Tyrol. Now I am settling down for the long winter—rather jaded & dispirited. My eldest daughter has just had a severe lung illness.

With kind regards to Mrs Perry believe me most sincerely yrs

J A Symonds

---

1. W. E. Griffis, "Perry and the Battle of Lake Erie," *Harper's Weekly*, XXIX (September 12, 1885), 605–06, on Oliver Hazzard Perry. The statue, by William G. Turner of Newport, Rhode Island, was erected by the citizens of Newport opposite Perry's childhood home. Griffis concludes his article: ". . . the sculptor has portrayed the moment of earnest action, when, with right arm aloft, he orders the flag hoisted and the vessel's course changed to renew the action."

2. See L 1490.

3. Eugene Zieber, *Heraldry in America* (Philadelphia, 1909), pp. 228–49, lists colonial societies and American heraldic orders, but mentions no national Herald's College. The English Herald's College was founded by Edward IV in 1464 and chartered by Richard III in 1483.

4. Symonds refers to Perry's work which resulted in *A History of Greek Poetry* (1890). Virginia Harlow, *Thomas Sergeant Perry* (1950), p. 139, confirms this opinion. The chapter on Aristotle is the 3rd in Book VI.

1499. *To Richard Burton*[1]

Am Hof, Davos Platz, Switzerland. Oct: 24 1885

Dear Sir

I do not know whether a letter which I wrote to the Academy[2] about your Arabian Nights has come under your notice. If so, I beg you to excuse the chary words I used in commendation of a work which now, from the literary point of view, I regard as one of great & original excellence.

I wrote in measured terms to the Academy, because I felt bound to make confession of my faith in opposition to what I esteem a pestilent heresy; & I did not wish to yield antagonists a point by seeming enthusiastic for the matter in dispute.

It is probably that you & I would differ upon some details of importance, involving artistic no less than ethical principles. I am not prepared to go as far as you do in the use of English vocably culled from all ages & sources of the language; & I doubt whether the information supplied in some of your notes might not have been conveyed with greater reticence. But I recognize that what you aim at, both in literature & in the illustration of manners, is not classical reserve so much as effective manifestation of the subject matter.

This seeking after truth at any price seems to me a very valuable quality. In science it is indispensable; & science rules our present modes of thought. In art it always brings its own reward. The reward wh it has brought to your translation is that when a reader has once familiarized himself with your method, he feels that method to be the right one for presenting to Englishmen the marvellous arras-work of fancy, wisdom, pathos, humour, passion, poetry, realism, sentiment, & plain prose, wh we term the Arabian Nights.

Not having read recent versions, I cannot compare yours with them in any way. I can only state that, my work having led me to the study of the Arabian Nights, I have read this book for the first time, with proper comprehension, in your translation.

It has effaced the pale image of the gallicizing *rifacimenti* [remaking] wh I read in youth. It has made me understand what the Mussulman races are; for whom it was composed, & from whom it emanated.

Can any book perform more useful service for an Englishman? I think not.

Therefore I disagree with those middle-class Censors of Morals who are now seeking to discredit it.

But I oppose them also on other grounds. It has been my business lately to study the means employed by Papal Rome in the 17th century to stamp out free political & religious thought through the Inquisition & the Index Librorum Prohibitorum. My heart has warmed at our own Milton's defence of the Freedom of the Press in his "Areopagitica." But I have also shrunk with loathing & dread from the approach of another tyranny, which seems now to menace England. Are Puritans, appealing to the passions of an uninstructed democracy, to substitute what they call obscenity for what the Roman Church called heresy? Are Jesuits drawn from the English bourgeoisie to follow in their train? Is literature to suffer an obscuration no less deplorable than that wh. it suffered in the days of Bruno, Sarpi & Galileo?

I do not regard the peril I have alluded to as an imaginary one. Pardon me therefore if I have spoken over-warmly, & believe me with thanks for your great services to literature to be yours faithfully

John Addington Symonds

---

1. See L 1493.
2. See L 1493.

1500. *To Horatio Forbes Brown*

Davos, Oct. 25 [1885]

[Dear Horatio]

I hope to get the corrected copies of what I call "Fragmenta Litteraria" or "Paraleipomena," in a few days.[1] Then I shall send you a copy. There are 142 pages printed—46 lines (I think) to the page, when uninterrupted —but for the most part, the pages are broken. I cut off the supply of copy for two reasons; one that it costs a good deal to print these things; the other that I have now a sufficient sample. Whether I go on with the affair will depend upon what I feel upon reflection about the utility of it. There seems to be an almost inexhaustible fountain of such stuff, in MS., as these 142 pp. represent.

If you take the sheets up for perusal I advise you to skip the first 36 pages. These contain a theological essay[2] written in 1864, to the main points of which I still adhere, but which can hardly be regarded as literature—in spite of its tumultuous incoherent quality of passion.

An autobiographical fragment, pp. 57–59, is perhaps worth looking at. Verses, pp. 66–74, are a jumble of several periods.

The chief point on which I seek your opinion is this: whether it is worth printing "Silhouettes"—pp. 74–103 and pp. 127–139. Of these I could commit to type almost any quantity; for it has been my habit to throw off such adumbrations and suggestions upon loose leaves of paper or copybooks—often retaining notes of conversations and sometimes passages from letters, as you may peradventure recognize.

Look at the poem "Music" on p. 103. It is a fragment eviscerated from a lengthy romance. Also look at the poem, "Two Dreams in One," on p. 106.

The jottings upon Clifton and Sutton Court landscape, pp. 108–125,[3] will probably be only interesting to myself.

[Incomplete]

---

1. Later published as *Miscellanies*. See Babington, pp. 55–62. See Ls 1480 and 1482.
2. "Commentary on Goethe's Proemium to 'Gott und Welt.'"
3. Published in *In the Key of Blue and other Essays* (1893) as "Clifton and a Lad's Love" and "Notes of a Somersetshire Home."

1501. *To Horatio Forbes Brown*

Davos, Nov. 11, 1885

[Dear Horatio]

I took Lotta and Madge to-day up to Fluela Hospiz, starting at 7.45 A.M. We tobogganed down the Fluela to Süs at a most furious speed—lunched there—took horses again at 1.45—arrived in a divine sunset of crimsons, oranges, and blues and beryls at the top again about 4.45—tobogganed back to Dörfli in the dark over snowy, soundless paths, through wood and meadow; reached our home at 6.45. It was a long day, and we covered I cannot reckon how many miles in the toboggan saddle—some passages extremely dangerous, owing to unprecedented pace of running.

[Incomplete]

1502. *To Charles Edward Sayle*[1]

Am Hof, Davos Platz, Switzerland. Nov: 19. 1885

My dear Sir

I am deeply & sympathetically touched by the gift you have made me of your book of poems "Bertha."

Such gifts have a special value for one who like myself suffers seclusion from the world, ill health, want of congenial society, & inadequate means of study in an Alpine valley full of sick people.

They remind me that my voice, even as that of him who is dead to the world, yet speaketh through the utterances of the press.

But the copy of "Bertha" wh reached me last night, is more than the friendly attention of a fellow worker in literature, more than the kindly recognition of an older by a younger artist.

Your inscription, & the Sonnet you have added,[2] make an appeal to me which constrains more than merely complimentary reply.

I cannot say that I have found those wells of life "wholly pure." I have found them bitter with disappointments & disasters, turbid with passions, poisoned with incurable maladies. And yet I drink of them, in the narrow sphere allotted to me now, with the confidence of one, to use your words, of "Nature's children."

God is in the world, & what we now call Nature, can be called God—will probably ere long be worshipped as God immanent in us & all, the only God, because the everything & all, of wh we form a living part.

Therefore, as to a Stoic, to me there comes nothing amiss, whether it be the slow process of wasting disease, or the tyranny of sin, or the exquisite visitings of fancy, or the physical enjoyment of the open road, or the students' labours.

You ask (in your Sonnet) "how I would answer one who taught me thus." Do you not mean, how I would reply to one who had expressed such thoughts as I have put into inadequate verse in "Animi Figura"? So at least I interpret your line.

Well: I have it in my mind to write an "Anima Raffigurata"[3] as the sequel & conclusion of "Animi Figura." And till I can fulfil my scheme, shadowy as yet, I must ask those few who find some value in my work to go on trust.

Death is always very near to me. And there are many other causes wh may intercept the execution of my task. But, if I live, & if I can discharge other now impeding literary obligations, I want to show forth (again in Sonnet form) that end to wh in my life's philosophy "Animi Figura" leads. I hope to make this a "word of peace."—But there is no peace in this world. For the wicked none. And Christ said he brought a sword.

You will see that I have first, as in duty bound, responded to your sonnet, & have followed its suggestions.

I now approach, with much diffidence, your own poems.

I will tell you at once that the two pieces which give me a sense of absolutest sincerity, most virile consciousness, & most accomplished expression, are the "Sea Song" and "Etude en Réaliste." Why this should be, what there is in your life experience to make it so for me, I cannot of course even to my own imagination say.

But this I am sure of. All the work in your volume shows much promise. To have written "The Last Echo," with its artfully conducted & yet facile strain of *Cantilena*,[4] is sufficient index of the lyrical power awaiting in you for accomplishment.

And so, throughout, as I turn the pages of "Bertha," I may say: this man, gifted with a natural command of melody, with a keen sensitiveness to external & internal conditions of emotion, with the lyrist's faculty of spontaneous self-revealing utterance, can go, & if he chooses, will go far upon the path of poetry.

Only, take to yourself strong food of real emotion & lasting furniture of solid thought. Learn to possess the essence of divinely human life in that which is actually felt & perenially enduring, so completely, that your gift of song shall command it & pour it forth transfigured into music. Do this and you take rank among the poets of an age.

To some writers of verse this would sound hard doctrine. But for a man who quotes Walt Whitman it will appear only as familiar truth.

If these words reach you, pray write to me, & let me hear from your lips what you think fit to tell me of yourself.

Meanwhile believe me to be in a true sense yours

John Addington Symonds.

If you have not got a book of mine called "Vagabunduli Libellus" shall I send it in exchange for "Bertha"?

---

1. Charles Edward Sayle (1864–1924), librarian at the Cambridge University Library (1893–1924) and co-editor of the Wyclif Society publications; educated at Rugby

and New College, Oxford. *Bertha: A Story of Love* (1885), a set of tame lyrics and sonnets addressed to the poet's mistress, owes a good deal more for its themes and diction to Dante Gabriel Rossetti than it does to Symonds. *Bertha* is dedicated to "Nostro Amori."

2. Sayle's sonnet "To J. A. Symonds" was not included in *Bertha*. It follows:

Master! For thou art master who best tried
   the wells of life and found them wholly pure
    though somehow Sin, whom we know not, can lure
Us from that water on the mountain-side:—
Master! Have patience e'en with one who cried:
   "There is no Sin, nor any need of cure
   For we are Nature's children,—and she, sure
It is, is wholly pure and sanctified."
Master, where now thou dwellest near the soil
   of Italy and lost among the hills—
    Hast thou no word of peace to send to us?
Speak, for we listen, thou whose daily toil
   Hath wrought us bread among our daily ills,
    How wouldst thou answer one who taught thee thus?

3. The soul recognized. Symonds means that in his sequel volume he will represent his own soul more frankly and clearly than he did in *Animi Figura*.

4. An oft-repeated song, a catch; Symonds compliments—or seems to compliment —Sayle on his command of conventional but facile lyric forms. As Symonds' next paragraph shows, Sayle lacks genuine feeling and experience.

1503. *To Charles Edward Sayle*

Am Hof, Davos Platz, Switzerland. Nov: 29 1885

Dear Mr Sayle

I received your letter of the 25th here this morning, & I thank you much for your candid & full reply to my question.

I thought you were a Rugbeian[1] from your writing, wh reminds me startingly of that of my old friend Arthur Sidgwick.

What you tell me about the reason for your going down from Oxford is serious. I am very sorry to hear it, for the greatest unhappiness I have seen in life is that of people who have got out of sympathy with the prevailing social feeling of their age.

You know also that I regard "L'Amour de l'Impossible"[2] with terror, & of all forms of this Impossible I fear you have set your heart upon the most impossible.

It is not easy to write on this subject—not that I find it at all painful, but that to touch it in any way with a stranger is embarrassing.

Therefore I will not pursue it further. If you have read my miscellaneous poems you will understand that you can count upon my discretion & intelligence.

Possibly we may meet, & then I shall beg for more of your confidence & offer you more of my counsel.

You may perhaps come to Switzerland next summer!

I shall tell Kegan Paul & Co to send you a copy of "Vagabunduli Libellus." Part of it, a series called "Stella Maris," forms an integral portion of "Animi Figura," as you will see if you read the Preface. What I there say about the episode not being autobiographical is strictly true.[3]

I shall be delighted to hear anything about yourself you choose to tell me. And if you will send me a photograph I shall esteem it. To the understanding of poetry a portrait is very valuable.

Believe me very truly yours

John Addington Symonds

My hand is so cold that I can hardly hold a pen. Looking over this letter later in the day, it seems to me cold & meagre. I am not well & have some cares upon me. Take this apology please. If you write again, tell me whether Bertha[4] was a real person.

---

1. Sayle attended Rugby School. See L 1502.

2. A reference to homosexual love. See Symonds' 14-sonnet cycle under this title in *Animi Figura*, pp. 36–49.

3. As the unpublished autobiography shows, Symonds addressed the sonnets to a series of male friends, especially to Angelo Fusato.

4. See L 1502.

1504. *To Arthur Symons*[1]

Am Hof, Davos Platz, Switzerland. Dec. 2. 1885.

My dear Sir,

I have only just received your gift of *Titus Andronicus,* the inscription of which to myself in your handwriting has given me two very real emotions. The first is one of delight that a scholar like yourself should have found anything in *Shakespeare's Predecessors*[2] of help or pleasure, I may say "surprised" delight; for this volume of mine has been so ill-accepted by the reading public that Messrs. Smith & Elder sternly refuse to hear of a continuation of the work. I therefore have come to think of it as merely a lamentable failure, which presumption led me to encounter. I have always loved our old dramatic literature. But I know that I am inadequately furnished with its scholarship; and I live so far out of the world here, among horrid Alps, as to be unable to make good my deficiences by recourse to great collections. That you should address me as you have done is therefore a source of deep-felt gratification. Later on, I hope, when I have studied your Introduction, to write to you again upon this subject.

My second emotion was caused by your date—Nuneaton[3]—in connection with your name, so like my own. My ancestors lived for a few generations in the neighbourhood of Nuneaton, at Tamworth and Atherstone whither they came from Newport in Shropshire, and whence my own immediate progenitor removed to Shrewsbury at the beginning of the last century upon marriage with a co-heiress of the family of Millington. I wonder where there is any connection, however distant, between us. Family history interests me deeply; and I like the heraldic side of this study. However, I will not annoy you with such antiquarian hobby-riding. Only from the winter snowscape of Davos my thoughts often turn to England, and sometimes they rest upon that angle of England where you dwell. A remote cousin of my forefathers Thomas Symonds, d: 1747 was the last owner of Merevale Abbey before it passed into the hands of the Dugdales (originally Geast) who obtained it by marriage with a Stratford of Merevale in 1767.

Believe me to be very truly yours

John Addington Symonds.

P.S. I fully mean to write again about your book. This letter is only a return of thanks by post.

---

1. This letter is apparently the first between Arthur Symons (1865–1945), translator, poet, and literary critic, and Symonds. In his unpublished "A Study of John Addington Symonds," in typescript in Princeton University library, Symons wrote: "It may be a matter of some interest to mention the fact that I had read some of the prose of Symonds before I came on the rare first edition of Pater's *Studies in the History of the Renaissance*. . . . I was then about seventeen. My first excitement in regard to tragic and dramatic events was derived from such books as these, before I had begun to build up about me the house of life I was to live in" (p. 15). Symons had sent copies of his facsimile edition of *Titus Andronicus* to Swinburne and Symonds. Swinburne, so Symons reports (*ibid.*, p. 15), seemed unmoved by the work and praised the type; Symonds was emotionally stirred. Symons edited the short-lived *Savoy* (1896) and was a prolific critic

of literature and art. Among his books are: *Browning* (1886), *Studies in Two Literatures* (1897), *Symbolist Movement in Literature* (1899), *Collected Poems* (1901), *Studies in Seven Arts* (1906), *Romantic Movement in English Poetry* (1909).

2. Symonds' *Shakspere's Predecessors in the English Drama* (1884). The typescript must be wrong. Symonds always wrote "Shakspere."

3. Nuneaton, Warwickshire, 22 miles northeast of Birmingham.

1505. *To Horatio Forbes Brown*

Davos Platz, Dec. 6 [1885]

[Dear Horatio]

I sent off last night the Fragments.[1] They had come at last. But they present so superb a margin that I somewhat doubt the letter post receiving them. You had better get them put into a limp cloth cover. This will take off the effect of proofs.

I have just been called away from this writing to look at an ermine which has taken to haunt our woodhouse. It is a lovely little beast; pure white, with large black eyes, a black tip to its tail, and a shade of yellow on the rump and hind legs. I did not know they were a common European beast. This is exactly like the creature on my crest.

[Incomplete]

---

1. See L 1500.

1506. *To Havelock Ellis*

Am Hof, Davos Platz, Switzerland. Dec. 7, 1885.

Dear Mr Ellis

Thank you very much for your essay on English Critics.[1] But for your kind thought of sending it, I should probably in this benighted place have missed it altogether.

To do that would have been a misfortune; for I regard this as a very sincere and penetrative piece of work.

What you say about myself gratifies me. It is the first word spoken clearly, which shows that anybody has taken my drift in criticism, and understood what I have been always aiming at.[2] You could hardly have stated my intention better, or have more kindly pointed out the impedimenta in the way of manner and descriptive tendency which I long used to carry about me.

I think you are very just to all of us now elderly critics: to our Dean, Mat Arnold; to Pater, Swinburne, Myers,[3] and myself, who are contemporaries past forty, hardly fifty.

I wish you had found a niche for Courthope,[4] who is in many ways, I think, worth notice as a critic. And Noel[5] deserves a word. Perhaps you will go on with your criticism of the critics.

It so happened that just before your essay reached me, I had been writing a digression on the essence of criticism in a book at which I am now working—the sequel to my Renaissance in Italy. I have there to deal with the curious vicissitudes of taste regarding the Italian painters of the 17th century.

If what I have written should meet your eye, you will see how well my profession of a critic's faith tallies with your account of me.

What you say about my not possessing the gift of a keen intuition is quite true. Perhaps I owe to this *défaut* the *qualité* of seeking to set at all events, I will not say succeeding in setting the things I have to deal with in relations to the whole.

That has been my steady purpose, and all life through I have resolutely pared away my own personal proclivities when I had to formulate or pass a judgment—indulging them, as you rightly observe, quite enough in places where I thought I might describe.

With many thanks to you for a most suggestive piece of work, believe me to be very faithfully yours

John Addington Symonds.

---

1. "The Present Position of English Criticism," *Time*, II, n.s. (December, 1885); reprinted in *Views and Reviews: First and Second Series* (1932), pp. 19–37.

2. Ellis says of Symonds: "Mr. J. A. Symonds, among English critics, promises, I think unquestionably, the most marked catholicity. . . . This allows him at once a large scope, both for analytic description and for mere description." Symonds is not always sparing of description, and is "sometimes almost oppressive." In *The Renaissance in Italy* he unites the two methods at their best. His chief characteristic is a "keen and restless intellectual energy."

3. F. W. H. Myers (see L 151) had published *Wordsworth* (1881), *Shelley* (1880), and *Essays Classical and Modern* (1883).

4. William J. Courthope (see L 566) was at work completing Elwin and Whitwell's edition of Pope (1871–89).

5. Roden Noel (see L 162) had the slimmest claim to recognition; but he was invited by Ellis to edit *Otway* for the "Mermaid" series. In 1886 he published *Essays on Poetry and Poets.*

1507. *To Mrs. Eleanor Boyle*[1]

Am Hof, Davos Platz, Switzerland. December 7, 1885

Dear Mrs Boyle

In the intervals of severer literary work I have found time to write an article on "The Pathos of the Rose in Poetry," wh I have based on your *Ros Rosarum,* so as to make it in part a review.

I have offered it to the Fortnightly. But I am not sure the Editor will care to have it. In which case I must try elsewhere.[2]

My purpose has been to trace two Latin sources (in Catullus and Ausonius) through modern rose poetry—Lorenzo de' Medici, Politian, Ariosto, Tasso, Guarini, Spenser, & afterwards Herrick & Waller & Ronsard too. This has enabled me to use your book, & also to supplement it with some fine passages.[3]

Looking over *Ros Rosarum* the other day I was struck with the coincidence between Ronsard's "Prendes cette rose amiable comme toi" and a thirteenth-century Latin song which Ronsard could not have seen since it was only discovered about 40 years ago.

I will copy out for you the version I have made of it in my unluckily misnamed book, *Wine, Women and Song.*[4]

Catherine, my wife, thinks & speaks so often of you & of your anxiously busy life in the fairy garden at Huntercombe.[5] Both she and I are very anxious now about our eldest daughter's health. It is terribly sad to see her gradually declining in strength.[6] The autumn here has been wretched and we have no prospect of other than a bad winter I fear.

Believe me to be most truly yours,

John Addington Symonds

1. See L 1424.
2. Printed in *Time,* III (1886), 397–411; reprinted in *E S & S* (2 vols., 1890). See L 1528.

3. The reprinted version of the article *ES&S* opens with a reference to the Hon. Mrs. Richard Cavendish Boyle's *Ros Rosarum ex Horto Poetarum:*

> Some five years ago there appeared a little volume . . . bearing upon its title-page the well-known initials of E. V. B., under which the . . . several works of combined literary and artistic merit [have been given] to the world. . . . Studying its pages with close attention, I observed that Mrs. Boyle had omitted two important passages in Latin poetry which may be regarded as the twin fountain-heads of a large amount of verses written upon roses in the modern world.

Among the works Symonds mentions in his essay are Catullus' 2nd epithalamium, "an idyll on the rose" by Ausonius, Lorenzo de' Medici's "Corinto," Politian's "Giosta" and "Orfeo," Ariosto's *Orlando Furioso,* Tasso's *Jerusalem Delivered,* Guarini's *Pastor Fido,* Spenser's *The Faerie Queene,* Herrick's "Gather Ye Rosebuds While Ye May," Waller's "Go, Lovely Rose," and Ronsard's "Comme on voit sur la branche" and "Mignonne, allez voir si la rose." He also cites Homer, Bion, Virgil, Ovid, Rufinus, Shakespeare, Milton, Samuel Daniel, and William Alexander. See L 1528.

4. Probably "Anni novi . . . ," "The Serenade to Flower-O'-the Thorn," (no. 16 in *Wine, Women, and Song, 1884*) which mentions the lover's wound and addresses the lady as "flower of flowers."

5. Huntercombe Manor, Mrs. Boyle's home at Maidenhead, Berkshire.

6. Janet, born 1865, died in 1887 after a long illness.

1508. *To Arthur Symons*

[Davos] Dec: 8th 1885.

Dear Sir,

Since I last wrote to you, I have read with attention and much interest your introduction to *Titus Andronicus.*[1] I think it is a good piece of critical work; and personally I believe you are on the right track in assigning the play, upon the faith of somewhat recent tradition, to an unknown amateur, who had the benefit of Shakespeare's[2] revision. This was my own view when I wrote on Shakespeare's Predecessors. It did not concern me to follow the point out in detail. And now I am delighted to see how ably you have conducted the argument.

Halfway down p.xiii you say: "Unless Shakespeare wrote *Titus Andronicus"*— But have you considered the very strong reasons which there are in favour of Shakespeare's having had at least a hand in *Arden of Feversham?* Swinburne has strongly contended for his authorship of *Arden;*[3] and I can never read that play without feeling the force of his pleading. But here we have a tragedy which is neither "lyrically pathetic" nor "piteously terrible". I do not think there are any positive proofs that Shakespeare had more [of] a hand in *Arden* than in *Titus Andronicus.*

The inscrutability of his author's personality before he began to shine like the sun, is one of the strangest facts of literary history. We seem to be always stumbling, in the midst of crude or stupid work, upon something which pulls us up and makes us exclaim "Shakespeare!"

I hope you will send me some of your poems.[4] I should much like to see them. Prepare yourself, if you go in for poetry, to meet with every rebuff, every neglect, and (what is more poignant) to pay for rebuff and neglect out of your own pocket by the act of publication. *Experto crede!*[5] And yet it is good to strive for the poet's wreath; and it were enough guerdon to be remembered by posterity in one song, one sonnet. A lyric lasts and lives vitally longer than whole tomes of history.

Perhaps we are cousins after all. My blood is derived through Symondses of Newport (Salop) and Croft (Lancashire) from FitzSimon of Norfolk. FitzSimon of Norfolk were cousins (descended from one ancestor) of FitzSimon of Herts, who by marriage with an heiress of Tregarthyn settled in Cornwall in the 14th Cent. Symons of Hatt represent these FitzSimons; and Symons of Chaddlewood claim a similar descent. Tell me what part of Cornwall[6] you come from. Lieutenant-Colonel Vivian[7] is printing a pedigree of Symons of Hatt and Tremayne in his Visitations of Cornwall, which, when it appears, may be of interest to you. What arms do you bear? I think I sealed my last letter with the coat of Symonds of Newport, which is the same as that of Symonds of Cley by the Sea—"azure 3 trefoils or".

Believe me to be very truly yours

John Addington Symonds.

---

1. See L 1504.

2. The typescript must be wrong throughout, for Symonds always wrote "Shakspere."

3. See Swinburne on *Arden* in *A Study of Shakespeare* (1880), pp. 129–44.

4. Symons' first volume of verse was *Days and Nights* (1889).

5. Trust one who has proved it.—Virgil, *Aeneid*, xi. 283.

6. Symons was born at Milford Haven, Pembrokeshire.

7. *The Visitation of the County of Cornwall in the year 1620*, ed. by John L. Vivian, Publications of the Harleian Society, IX (1869) and *The Visitations of Cornwall, comprising the Herald's Visitations of 1530, 1573, and 1620*, ed. by John L. Vivian (1879).

1509. *To Horatio Forbes Brown*

Davos Platz, Dec. 12 [1885]

[Dear Horatio]

(Therm: 4 ° Fahr. below zero outside, 10 a.m. 46 ° on writing table.)
Above details will explain why brain is numb and fingers stiff.

How very kind of you to look yourself into the Cases I asked about at
the Frari![1] I don't think I can go to the expense of having the whole copied,
or that I could spare the time. I should like such abstracts made as will
show the heads of accusation, the drift of the trials, and the causes for their
protraction after so many years.

Some light may be thrown on the men in question, especially the
Anabaptists, which will make an important modification of view with
regard to the Inquisition in general at Venice. Books like the "Histoires des
Martyrs" are quite unscrupulous in claiming as victims of Rome crazy or
antisocial creatures whom no State would tolerate.

I wish I had sent you my "Fragmenta"[2] in boards. The binder has
done a copy for me rather nicely. There are six copies in existence, of which
you have one and I have five.

[Incomplete]

---

1. Brown's note: "Papers of the Sant' Ufficio in the Archives at the Frari": the S.
Maria dei Frari. The monastery, adjacent to the church, contained the Archives of
Venice, "comprising ca. 14 million documents, the earliest of which dates from 883.
They are deposited in 298 different apartments."—Baedeker's *Northern Italy* (1886), p.
278.
2. The *Miscellanies*. See L 1500.

1510. *To Havelock Ellis*

Am Hof, Davos Platz, Switzerland. Dec. 16, 1885.

Dear Mr Ellis

Before I got tonight your kind note of the 13th, I was meaning to
respond to that of the 3rd.

I had only after all to say that I do not exactly plead guilty to feeling
"discouraged by the reception of my work."[1] I have indeed spoken after this
fashion to [Roden] Noel, partly because he is himself hurt by the world's

neglect, and partly because I am aware of not having made that mark which I ought to have made.

This I do not attribute to any want of sympathy in the public, but to certain moral and physical defects in myself. Ill health has separated me from the stream of life; and though it has not extinguished mental activity, it has, I think, so far taken the edge off my nature as to make me (as a writer) rather contemplative and curious than forcibly operative.

I needed contact with my fellow-workers; and one accident, a serious lung-illness at the age of 24, from which I have never more than partially recovered, threw my undeveloped character into seclusion slightly embittered by a sense of failure.

I set so high a value upon candour that I should not like you (who had shown true sympathy with the working of my mind) to be left with the notion that I blame any one but myself or anything but the circumstance of a maimed life for my short-comings as an effective writer.

I blush to talk so much about myself. Let me, however, add but this: that words like yours, the sense that a man like you finds something in me, will be of steady service in the future—if life is given me to work yet with purpose.

I also quite agree with you in thinking that publishers make a mistake when they send out books like mine (obviously of the vulgarisateur's production) at so high a price. Yet authors are in their hands. I am neither rich enough nor (I honestly believe) self-confident enough to take affairs of publication into my own hands at my own risk. So I have let Smith & Elder print and advertize—and give me £1 for what has cost me (in mere money) £20.

Thank you much. And pray do not take these hasty jottings for more than a wish to have you in true touch with one who esteems you. [W. J.] Courthope has hidden his best work in the Quarterly for which he-has been writing now some 19 years.

Very truly yours,

J. A. Symonds.

---

1. Probably a reference to a statement in a letter by Ellis, this remark nevertheless reflects Symonds' discouragement caused by reviews, especially of his poetry. See L 1447.

1511. *To Henry Graham Dakyns*

Am Hof, Davos Platz, Switzerland. Dec: 18. 1885

My dear Graham

Maggie's[1] letter to Catherine holds out hope of your coming to us. How very charming of you to think of this! You are real friends! I do hope that nothing will interfere to prevent you.

Yesterday & the day before I had been thinking of you much. Mozley has sent me his poem,[2] & I was reading it. It brought back memories of Clifton fifteen years ago.—By the way, there are many fine things in Dennell. The whole of Peraune is good, & the lyric on p: 189 is sublime— nobody but J.R.M. could have written that. The form, however, seems to me wrong.

I have just finished the last two volumes of the Renaissance in Italy. They are on the Catholic Reaction & the Spanish Hegemony. It is a dismal subject—the tragedy of a nation, the disappointment of a great European hope. I am very glad to have finished it.

I was going to ask whether you would care to have a copy of some Opuscula I had been printing privately for my own use: prose & verse of very miscellaneous quality. I have only had six copies printed; one I have sent H. F. Brown, & I design another for [T. H.] Warren. However, you need not answer this question; for if you come here, you will be able to see for yourself whether you will have the little pamphlet.

The sun has not risen yet, & my brain (as well as fingers) is stiff with cold.

Arivederci! God be praised, the sun has just escaped the Jacobshorn!

Yours ever

JASymonds

---

1. Dakyns' wife.
2. John Rickards Mozley (1840–1931), *The Romance of Dennell* (1885). Mozley was educated at Eton College and Cambridge University; B.A., 1862; M.A., 1865; fellow, 1861–69; assistant master at Clifton College, 1864–65; inspector of schools; wrote *Clifton Memories* (1921).

1512. *To Edmund Gosse*

Am Hof, Davos Platz, Switzerland. Dec. 23 1885

PRIVATE

My dear Gosse

I am very glad to hear that the letter I wrote you & to which you respond in yours of the 20th just received, had the right touch. When I wrote it, I felt sure that you must be suffering some pain from criticisms which I recognized to be malevolent:—I had indeed read that poisonous but not feeble shaft aimed at you in the P.M.G.[1] But I could not be certain that you would like ever so light a hand laid upon the smart.

What you tell me about your relations to the PMG is of course fully explanatory—but it is very saddening. It causes me real suffering to think of this ungenerous malignity. And the hypocrisy of a journal which professes to be fighting for the light, & acts thus, is sickening. I will not tell you what I think about Stead's[2] action: beyond this, that I regard his present sentence as too easy, & that I should like to see his instigatrix Mrs J. E. Butler[3] in prison too. A bourgeois Anglo-Saxon pack of Jesuits! Violating law: doing evil that good may come! Without even the solemnity, inscrutability, and perfect art of the real Jesuits!

Non ragion am di lor![4] But, as Sarpi said, when he fell stabbed by three daggers in the Ponte di Santa Fosca,[5] so may you say about that review in the PMG—Agnosco stilum Curiae Romanae![6]

However: What I wrote in my last letter, I firmly believe & now repeat. Attacks of this sort, not of course always so venomous as the one we have been talking of, are sure to be made upon a man just at the point in his career wh you have reached. They are signs of his taking an assured position; the efforts of some to drag him from his seat, the questionings of others who cannot quite submit to recognize him.

Experto crede.[7] I have suffered too. Indeed I am still in the zone of that meteoric shower of semi-unkindly semi-puzzled criticism. Just to get through it calmly & without losing heart or sweetness of temper, seems to me the right way. Christian preachers tell sufferers on earth to remember Christ. It is surely not presumptuous for a man of letters to remember Shelley then!

At all events, I trust that you will not withold from publication what you regard as good work, because of these ululations and latrations. Woolner told me that Tennyson[8] once took to his bed because of a spiteful review, & had the humiliation of finding that it was written by a prig of 16 years. And we know how much Rossetti's sensitiveness to Buchanan's brutality[9] is supposed to have cost the world. It were surely better to imitate the gentle persistency of Shelley than the irritability of Rossetti.

You ask me what I am at work on. Two volumes to conclude my "Renaissance in Italy." They discuss the Catholic Reaction, with its persecution of free thought; Inquisition, Indix Libr: Prohib:, Jesuits; Tasso and his works, Marini & such folk, the birth of modern music, the hideous Bolognese painters, Bruno, Sarpi, in a word all the ending of the Italian Renaissance in that strange jumble which Italians call the Seicento.

Believe me with best wishes to Mrs Gosse yourself & yours, very sincerely yours

J A Symonds—

---

1. The *Pall Mall Gazette,* XLII (October 26, 1885), 4–5, featured an article called "Why We Are Liberals." It sarcastically pointed out that "Mr. Browning leads the way, for it is now the fashion of poets to confess their political faiths." The reference to Gosse was this: "Take young Mr. Gosse, for instance, who says the place for the poet is the study, not the Senate. 'I am a liberal because I have been to America,' one might have expected him to say. Not a bit of it. It is the two bundles of hay over again—'How happy could I be with either. Canvassers of both parties may call.' Far different from the undecided twitter of the young rising poet. . . ."

2. William Thomas Stead (1849–1912), ed., *The Pall Mall Gazette* (1883–89). In 1890 he founded the *Review of Reviews.* He was a crusading editor, opponent of social ills and advocate of international peace. Partly because of his pressure the Gladstone Government sent General Gordon to Khartoum. His *The Maiden Tribute of Modern Babylon* (1885) exposed the outrages legally permissible upon children and women and earned him a 3 months' term in Holloway Gaol; this work was the action Symonds complains of. The final result was, however, an important Criminal Law Amendment Bill. Like Symonds' friend, F. W. H. Myers, Stead was an active member of the British Society for Psychical Research and conducted a journal, called *The Borderland* (1893–97), reporting spiritualistic experiences. He was one of the victims of the sinking of the *Titanic.*

3. Symonds' friend Mrs. George (Josephine Elizabeth) Butler, an advocate of higher education for women and a social reformer who helped to achieve the repeal of the Contagious Diseases Act and the reform of the law affecting white slave traffic. See L 210.

4. Let's not talk about them.

5. See *The Renaissance in Italy: The Catholic Reaction,* Chap. X.

6. I don't know the style of the Roman Curia.

7. Trust one who has proved it.—Virgil, *Aeneid,* xi, 283.

8. Thomas Woolner (1825–92) (see Ls 419 and 451) had sculpted Tennyson in 1857 and in 1873. The exact occurrence referred to here is difficult to pinpoint, although the reference may be to the *Poems* of 1832: their reception, and especially that of the *Quarterly Review,* was generally hostile. For Tennyson's sensitivity to criticism see

Thomas R. Lounsbury, *The Life and Times of Tennyson* [from 1809 to 1850] (1962; 1st ed., 1915), pp. 334–36 and 341–42.

9. Robert Buchanan (1841–1901), "The Fleshly School of Poetry," *The Contemporary Review*, XVIII (1871), 334–50.

1513. *To Mary Robinson*

Am Hof, Davos Platz, Switzerland. Dec 24, 1885

Dear Miss Robinson

This Christmas Eve has brought me much from you—a very charming card from Fra Angelico (wh will take a permanent place on my pine panelling) & a still more charming letter from you.

I too had been thinking that many days had passed since I had written to you. This means, please observe, that I have been thinking of you.

Davos is a Sleepy Hollow. Days slip by. I have worked on an average 6 hours per diem at the Catholic Reaction since June 25 last. This amount of "grind" exhausts me. I can write few letters.

There is the story in a few words.

Pray send me the proofs of your songs: If I can see some shrewd point, you shall have it submitted to you. But to read proofs of your songs at Davos is not quite the same as reading the Ms of them in a gondola! I shall be less daring of suggestion, more awed by contemplation of the printed lines.

The one Venetian waif of song you sent me (about our chiaroscuro ramble through the Calli of San Giorgio,[1] I thought very successful—that is, reproductive to me of the moments; whether to one who did not experience the moment, I know not. Artists always risk much by allusive treatment. And the odd thing is that they gain as much as they lose. Their least truthful work in that style seems to have a power of suggestiveness to readers—while the very marrow of observation goes lost!

I never met with any country people who talked of Daisies of Parnassus. You, who have lived in Arcady,[2] have the advantage of me; for I should dearly like to converse with such folk. I know a pearled white flower, dead-white delicately slashed with transparent grey, seeded with tiny kernels of the faintest amethyst, which botanists call Grass of Parnassus. If you have veritably plucked such Grass of Parnassus in song, you will have evaded the curse produced by Sappho on her who would not seek Aurian

Roses.[3] No roses are equal in shy dawn-&-dew loving charms of Oread[4] inspiration to these Grasses of Parnassus.

Any one who really loves flowers will recognize your intention, if you call your songs "Parnassia." But the critics are mostly Cockney, & know nothing about flowers. And they would jeer at you for claiming to bring "Roba di Parnaso" into Paternoster Row. So don't. How Gosse is catching it from the critics![5] He has succeeded at least in making himself well hated.

By the way, you are not right in saying that the Parnassia has no scent. Like the snow-drop it has scent as exquisite as its hue.

What a tirade,—you remember that I deal in tirades. The suggestion of a loved flower, particularly if there is a slight touch of inaccuracy in it, sets me off. But I may be wrong in my track. Of the "Daisy of Parnassus" send me a dried specimen. Enough then of this fooling.

I am just getting M. Bourget's new vol of Psychology.[6] Let me confess that I cannot abide Amiel.[7] I shall like what he says about the Goncourts, I doubt not. But I think Amiel ought to have been buried under the sentences which Goethe wrote[8] to that Self-mass of nerves & incompleteness — Plessing,[9] was the man's name? I cannot look it up. You probably know.

Goodbye. Thank you tenderly for your thought of me & mine. Thank you! As the bells of the Catholic Church here are ringing for the midnight mass, I close this letter with good wishes for you & yours at this season. God bless you. Grow stronger in frame. Spiritual wishes your friend need not send you. Believe him always yours

J A Symonds.—

Life is pretty "steep" here, as Stevenson would say. The usual solitude. Janet ill: hemorrhage in September: rheumatism: languid invalidism. Daily labour accepted by me, as anodyne for evils. The rest fairly well.

---

1. The streets of the Venetian island of S. Giorgio Maggiore.

2. A reference to Mary Robinson's volume of poems in a naturalistic vein, *The New Arcadia* (1884).

3. Mrs. E. V. Boyle (Ls 1424 and 1507) translates Philostratus: "Sappho loves the Rose, and crowns it ever with some praise, comparing the beautiful amongst the virgins with it" (*Ros Rosarum,* p. 5).

4. The oreads were mountain nymphs.

5. Gosse wrote to W. D. Howells, December 28, 1885: "I am in a mournful frame of mind, for I have come in for a veritable vendetta of criticism—the storm has long been brooding—and my new books this winter have caught it from the crawling things of criticism." According to Gosse's biographer, Evan Charteris, the criticisms began in the

November *The Academy,* XXVIII (1885), 350–51, over his *From Shakespeare to Pope,* the lectures he had presented in America during the winter of 1884–85 and repeated in Cambridge. These criticisms were mild, however, compared with the onslaught later unleashed by John Churton Collins in "English Literature at the Universities," *The Quarterly Review,* CLXIII (1886), 289–329.

6. Paul Bourget (1852–1935), *Nouveaux essais de psychologie contemporaine.*

7. Henri Amiel (1821–81), *Journal intime* (1883). See L 1470.

8. From Weimar on July 26, 1782:

I can assure you that in the midst of good fortune I prefer a persistent renunciation, and every day through trouble and work I see that there exists a will not mine, but that of a higher power whose purposes are not my purposes. . . . Tr. from *Goethe-Briefe,* ed. by Philipp Stein (8 vols., Berlin, 1902–05), II, 416.

9. Friedrich Victor Leberecht Plessing (1749?–1806), a hypochondriac and eccentric who wrote Goethe for advice about his emotional life; philosopher and professor; wrote *Osiris und Socrates* (1783) and *Versuche fur Aufklärung der Philosophie des ältesten Alterthums* (2 vols., 1788–90). See Chap. I of K. R. Eissler's *Goethe: A Psychoanalytic Study* (2 vols., 1963).

1514. *To Charlotte Symonds Green*

Am Hof, Davos Platz, Switzerland. Dec: 26. 1885

My dearest Charlotte

I want to send you my hearty best wishes for the coming year. I wonder how you spent Christmas Day at the Hospital. The girls had a very merry one here & enjoyed themselves. It is pleasant to see how happy they are in their own society. We have a nice Swiss governess too now. Indeed there are 11 females in the house; & I, the one man, living a bachelor life among them all. It is rather more of the so-called fair sex than I like.

I remember at Venice talking of the disadvantages under wh literature suffers in England, if it is neither distinctly popular (like novels) nor subsidized by the Universities in the shape of fellowship professorship & the like. You thought me unreasonable I remember. But you shall judge for yourself by my case. I have just made out with Smith & Elder the accounts of my "Renaissance in Italy." The last 2 vols are now ready to go to press. When they have been published, I shall have worked during 15 years at the whole book: or, deducting those periods in which I either could not work or sought a change of occupation, I shall have given 11 years of my life to it.

The total sum I shall have received will be £1100, or £100 per annum; but from this I must deduct £50 per annum for books & travel indespensable to the production. I have thus been paid at the rate of £50 a year, during the eleven best years of my life, for my work; wages equal to those of a clerk of the 3rd class or of a butler of the 2nd class (the latter being found too in food & lodging).

Of course I do not mean to say that my subject is an attractive one, or that I have the first sort of literary gifts. But the subject is not uninteresting or unimportant; & for myself, I think I may say without conceit that to treat it from so many points of view as I have done, indicates a somewhat unusual complex of intelligence & information. Also, the book has been accepted as a standard book in England, & as such reprinted in America.

Therefore I think what I observed at Venice was just. You cannot expect many men to give eleven years of their lives to a laborious & very complicated study of national culture for £550, or wages of £50 per annum. But those who are still connected with the Universities will in England employ respectable abilities upon such work, knowing that it gives them claims on academical income. And only a few venture to do *that;* for of course they run a great risk of not being rewarded at all—the academic prizes being few.

All this is not very interesting, except to those who care for what may be called polite literature—such work as Roscoe[1], Ticknor[2] & Hallam[3] in his History of Eur: Lit: produced. That branch of writing must perish I think in England; owing mainly to the action of the Circulating Libraries, wh have limited the demand for copies of such books by coming between the author & publisher on the one hand & the reading public on the other. The reading public will have novels, primers, personal talk in journalism, amply provided.

I am not to be pitied, because I can afford to work without wage; & yet it is rather hard to feel oneself practically so far behind an equally industrious & competent pork butcher. But what is to be regretted is the palpable impossibility of achievement under wh men without my means, but with my specific turn for a certain kind of production, must labour— precluded from applying themselves to the work for which they are qualified & from giving to society useful compendiums of knowledge, by sheer indigence.

It is rather incongruous to send these reflections from me in Davos to you in a London Hospital. But I have it in my head. And now at the close of a year, upon the completion of a life-task carried out under conditions of considerable difficulty, it is natural for me to review the subject & not unnatural to discuss it with my sister—especially after what I let fall at Venice. My position then was what I still maintain, that in England only

III

the Universities subsidize such unremunerative labour, & that they for the most part only subsidize their own members who have been engaged in education. Believe me ever with much love yours

J.A.Symonds.

---

1. William Roscoe (1753–1831), English attorney and historian, author of a popular *Life of Lorenzo de' Medici, Called the Magnificent* (1796) and of a *Life and Pontificate of Leo X* (1805).

2. Probably the American historian George Ticknor (1791–1871), best known for his *History of Spanish Literature* (1849). The work reached 4 eds.

3. Henry Hallam (1777–1859), *Introduction to the Literature of Europe in the Fifteenth, Sixteenth, and Seventeenth Centuries* (4 vols., 1837–39).

1515. *To Horatio Forbes Brown*

Davos, Dec. 26, 1885.

[Dear Horatio]

I have just heard from Smith & Elder about the publication of my two volumes on the Catholic Revival. They offer me 150*l*. In respect to "Renaissance in Italy," I have already received 950*l*. When, then, I have brought out these two volumes, I shall have had in all 1,100*l*. for this long bit of work. Allowing for periods in which I was unfit to work, periods in which I sought a change of work, I find that I have spent eleven years upon this task—and pretty hard years of daily labour. The education which enabled me to attempt it was a very costly one, and the abilities which qualified me for it, though not first-rate, were at least unusual in their combination of many-sided intelligence with acquired knowledge and literary style. I have, then, been paid at the rate of 100*l*. per annum; but I must deduct at least 50*l*. per annum from my gains for books and travel, quite indispensable to the production. This I reckon as really far below the just allowance. Say, then, I have received 50*l*. a year, during the eleven best years of life, for the execution of a laborious work, which implied an expensive education and unusual cast of intellect. The pay is about equal to the wages of a third-class merchant's clerk, or a second-class butler, the latter being also found in food and lodging.

These considerations are worth attending to. Few young men who projected such a book—(I say such a book, because there are many books to be written on more obviously attractive subjects; these will pay better)—as mine, could venture to anticipate for it a much more substantial success. Mine has been accepted in England, reprinted in America. It has given me a certain reputation. A young man, then, undertaking such a task, would, unless he were conscious of the commanding powers of a Macaulay, have to anticipate some such reward for some such labour as I have had. How many young men could afford to give eleven years of their lives between 33 and 45 for the net sum of 550*l.*?

The circulating libraries, intervening between the author and publisher on the one hand, and the reading public on the other, have limited the demand for copies of such books. The public has become a bad patron and paymaster.

Only one set of institutions in England subsidise such literature. These are the universities, who make it worth a man's while to compete for professorships by literary production of the sort I am discussing. But they dispense these rewards very uncertainly, and nearly always to members of their own body, and for the most part to such members as have been engaged in education.

The Crown does something small in the way of pensions from the civil list; but these are meagrely doled out to cases of proved destitution, or, as in the case of the 300*l.* a year voted to M. Arnold, are acquired by powerful interest with ministers.

The best advice to give to a young man contemplating unremunerative literature is, then, stick to a university, be prepared to do its educational work, and when you write, take care to hit the academical keynote; else you may acquire a modest reputation, but you will hardly gain enough to pay the rent of two rooms in an unfashionable street.

At the end of this year, upon the termination of my long task, I have taken stock of the whole position, and have poured my reflections out into your not uninterested ears.

[Incomplete]

1516. *To Arthur Symons*

[Davos] Jan. 4 1886.

Dear Mr Symons,

What you tell me about your age and the respective dates of the poems you sent me, is extremely satisfactory. Nothing of course can be more hopeful than the steady advance in style and firmness of touch which these dates indicate. I felt pretty sure that the "Idyl of Purgatory" was earlier work than "Forgotten Death" which was the piece in my opinion, most characteristic of all you sent me. I find the same style, yours individually, in the Sonnet on "Religious Toleration." There is a breadth, a simplicity of phrasing, what musicians call a Largo, here.

With regard to publishing a volume of poems. Of course I only gave you the advice which seemed to me most prudent. I think men do themselves an injury by coming with too early work before the world. And now that I know the dates of your pieces, this opinion is confirmed. It seems to me that you have a very good prospect of forming a style marked as your own; and that if you went on writing for yourself a year or two,[1] you might appear with a book which should be impressive from its unity of tone.

You speak of books of inferior verse appearing almost weekly, and getting their fair share of fame. I really hardly know which books you mean. It so happens that young poets very often kindly send me their ventures in poetry. During the last three months I have received seven. Not one of these is despicable. Two have points of remarkable excellence ("The Romance of Dennell"[2] in particular.) One of them called "Bertha"[3] shows lyrical promise of no common quality. Yet I doubt whether any one of these books will receive more than a hasty sneering notice in some article on "Current Poetry." I do not want to throw cold water on your plan of publishing. If you can afford to do so, there is of course no reason why you should not try. And certainly the fact that we have reached the public ear, has a healthy tonic upon our work. It makes us write with more consciousness of art and aim.

I am glad you like Eugene Lee Hamilton's poetry.[4] He sends me everything he publishes and I think much of it is decidedly good. He has been, poor fellow, for years unable to walk, unable to exercise his brain except in short swallow-flights.[5] He lies at Florence stretched out upon a sort of bed which can be shifted on to a kind of wheel chair. A robust man, as to build, in the prime of manhood, ambitious and energetic, till he was felled by some malady analogous to paralysis.

But to return to your work. Let me see some of your Blank Verse. Please put dates to the pieces. Thank you much for the Xmas Card and the too kindly flattering verses which make it very precious. I shall send you back a little pamphlet (unpublished) of verses[6] written mostly when I was about your age. You will see the influence of Swinburne in some of rather a later date. Of Tennyson in others.

Thank you, too, for your cousin's note about your family. I think he is wrong as to the coat of arms. No FitzSimon, Symons, or Symonds ever bore a shield with a chevron—except Symonds of Great Yeldham who differenced the hereditary coat "azure 3 trefoils or" by a "chevron engrailed or". If you could let me see it, I should sometime like to look at your Tree.

Very sincerely yours,

J. A. Symonds

P.S. You will think I ought not to have so much time to scribble letters. The fact is that the work of the last one and a half years (2 volumes of Italian History) stands piled in MS facing me, nearly ready for press. And so I can indulge hours of idleness for a while.

---

1. Symons apparently took this advice; his *Days and Nights* was published in 1889.
2. J. R. Mozley, *The Romance of Dennell* (1885). See L 1511.
3. Charles Sayle, *Bertha: A Story of Love* (1885). See L 1502.
4. See Ls 1182 and 1448.
5. Tennyson, *In Memoriam:* canto XLVIII, ll. 15-16:
   Short swallow-flights of song, that dip
   Their wings in tears, and skim away.
6. This was the pamphlet *Fragilia Labilia,* privately printed (1884) in 25 copies. His presentation copy, now in the Huntington Library, is inscribed: "Arthur Symons from John Addington Symonds (a sample of his earliest work in verse)."

1517. *To Mary Ann Sykes*

Am Hof, Davos Platz, Switzerland. Jan: 5 1886

My dearest Auntie

I am ashamed to see how far I have let both Christmas & New Year's Day slip by without writing you the letter I have been holding in my head.

Yours to Catherine from Beaumont Street[1] gave us all great delight. In spite of bronchitis, you are still the youngest & the cheerfullest of any company where you may be.

And that you may yet enjoy many years, to be a blessing to all who come within your influence, is the heartfelt wish not only of your nephews & nieces but of everyone who has felt the beneficial influence of your sunny age.

I know, dear Auntie, where you draw the sunbeams, & know *that* to be a source which cannot fail, although for too many it is partially obscured by the "earth-born mists" of Keble's Evening Hymn[2]—the vapours of their own perversities & evil habits.

Annie [Symonds][3] wrote to me while you were with them. I could see from her letter how much all the Beaumont Street people were valuing your company.

Things are tolerably bright with us just now. Janet seems really to have made a step in the right direction during the last few weeks. I do not count upon it yet. But a good report from Dr Ruedi shed a very pleasant ray upon our Christmas.

Little Katharine is going to have 7 teeth taken out under chloroform tomorrow. She is half frightened, & half proud, as children are. Ruedi will superintend the operation, which we believe to be necessary—for she suffers from tooth ache, & gets too little nourishment in consequence.

I have rather a bad cold. But I ought not to complain; for I have been able to do a great deal of writing in the last six months. The chief obstacle I suffer from in that, is the weakness of my right hand, wh has not left me. I use the cork pens you first suggested, & find them good. And I often have the wrist & hand rubbed by a "masseur" or professional rubber.

It is a great thing to be grateful for that all the girls are bright & happy, thoroughly enjoying the simple pleasures of our home life. And Lotta & Madge both take great interest in their work. I read Italian with them. We have a very nice Swiss governess, a real lady & yet quite a Swiss. Ever yours most affecte. nephew

J.A.Symonds.

---

1. In Oxford, the address of the family of Dr. Frederick Symonds (d. 1881).

2. The second introductory poem to *The Christian Year* (1827) by John Keble (1792–1866), clergyman and poet; professor of poetry at Oxford (1831–41); initiator in 1833 of the Oxford Movement.

3. Symonds' cousin, daughter of Dr. Frederick and sister of Dr. Horatio Symonds.

1518. *To Henry Graham Dakyns*

Am Hof, Davos Platz, Switzerland. Jan: 8 1886

My dear Graham

I am at last down with Laryngitis, or acute inflammation of the Larynx. It is tiresome, because I cough perpetually & cannot articulate a word.

But I am in nerves intellect & morals twenty per cent firmer & better than when you were with me.

The fiasco I made on Sylvester Abend[1] was caused I believe by the rebellion against this attack which I sub-consciously made.

In other words, I ought to have stayed at home & attended to myself. I would go out, & conceived that I might, by an effort of will & by alcohol, shake off the coming nuisance.

Such revolt against physical ailments wh threaten, but to which my will will not succumb, has always been frequent in my life. I do not remember one which brought me to quite the same disastrous issue. Indeed I am sorry to have flecked the otherwise fair surface of our intercourse with any note so base.

I hope you have performed your journey to your satisfaction, & have gathered Christmas Roses & have drunk no typhoid on the slack Ligurian sea, & have now returned to babes refreshed & fields of daily toil in delvesman's spirit dug.

Since you left, stimulated by the delivering Laryngitis, I have wound my two perplexing volumes on the Catholic Revival ⎫ My fields of
up for press, & have written the first chapter of my ⎪ daily toil, in
little book upon Ben Jonson in Lang's English ⎰ delvesman's spirit
Worthies ⎭ dug.

Nothing has happened. Only we are all down with colds of various sorts. And little Katharine had 7 teeth taken out under chloroform yesterday. She seems all right this morning.

Love to Maggie. Believe me very sincerely yours

John Addington Symonds.—

---

1. Symonds enjoyed Sylvester Abend (New Year's Eve) festivities in Davos; see "Winter Nights at Davos," *OLSH* (1892), pp. 334–60, and *Italian Byways* (1883), pp. 332–50.

1519. *To Albert O. Ruston*

Am Hof, Davos Platz, Switzerland, Feb 3/86

My dear Rutson

I must send you one word of friend-ship & good wishes long delayed, & of thanks for The Scotsman,[1] from this remote angle of the earth—where I work harder than I ought at my no-worth work of literature perplexed & eaten up by a burning sense of the confusion into wh. England is sinking. Perhaps out here it seems more glaring—as it does in some of the colonies. If I trod Pall Mall it might be less apparent.—I have a deep & daily deeper growing mistrust of the able but vain old man,[2] who has got the reins of Phaëthon's chariot again into his senile clutch.—But I need not bore you with this. I only wanted to shake hands. The report from our shanty in the snows is fairly good; The girls a great support to Catherine & myself; I somewhat enfeeble[d] for literary turning [illegible] upon the road no whither.

J.A.S.

---

1. A newspaper.
2. Early in 1886, Gladstone returned to the premiership, defeating Salisbury's Government over the Irish problem. But Gladstone's favoring home rule led to so serious a split in his party that at a new election in the summer of 1886 he was defeated.

1520. *To Mr. and Mrs. Robert Louis Stevenson*

Am Hof, Davos Platz, Switzerland. Feb. 4 1886

My dear Friends

It is long since I tried to touch your hands. A new year has opened for us all, and we are already in the second month.

I hope eternity will not drag on in this way. If so, there is a punishment in store for people of the XIXth Cent: wh Dante was too vigorous to have imagined.

Mr Dew Smith[1] sent me a copy of Louis's portrait—he calls it the "portrait of a smile"—wh I have pinned upon the panelling in front of me. It gives me a faint adumbration of the Sprite. But the luminous liquid play of his personality is not there. Unless we deal with men and women, it seems that we must be content with caricatures and phantoms.

I have read Prince Otto twice. It is very cleverly written; but I don't like so many pages of continuous Blank Verse.

The new book "Dr. Jekyll and Mr. Hyde"[2] I am just going to get. I expect that it will give me, to some infinitesimal extent, the shudders. It seems wrought upon a theme that is only too close to all of us.

I go on at my own business: husks that the swine did eat: saw-dust to stuff the bowels of a spiritual doll: what I like to call it; or any body is at liberty to say about it. Most of the work anybody produces now is sewerage and sediment.

I am in no good humour, and should be in much better if I could climb a little hill from my house to one which you once occupied—and laugh with you, and shed a flood of tears.

Ever yours

J A Symonds

Forgive. Discern the heart beneath the false-teeth cackle.

---

1. Albert George Dew-Smith (1848–1903), noted amateur photographer, collector of books and jewels; educated at Trinity College, Cambridge; connected with the Cambridge Scientific Instrument Company and the Cambridge Engraving Company.

2. Stevenson's romantic tale *Prince Otto* (1885) and *Strange Case of Dr. Jekyll and Mr. Hyde* (1886).

1521. *To Mary Robinson*

Am Hof, Davos Platz, Switzerland. Feb: 27 1886

My dear Miss Robinson

I do not like to hear of some of the things you tell me in your letter just received. That you have been indoors for weeks & weeks & weeks, & yet always working at state papers,[1] seems to me bad; & I wish that the next I hear may be that you are off for Tuscany.

I have never talked to you about the plan of your work on Queen Eliz & the Valois. And I have a very dim notion of what it is to be. And do you mean that some preparatory essay on the subject is getting ready for Creighton's review?[2] I should much like to know.

I have nearly lost my bad throat & cold on the bronchial tubes; but it has lasted now nearly two months & given me much trouble. I got better by change of air—from Davos to a bleaker drearier place 1000 feet higher.

In Ms before me on the table stand 3 volumes ready for press, the work of the last eighteen months. Two are the sequel to the Renaissance, "Italy & the Catholic Revival"; one is "Ben Jonson" for the English Worthies.

I suppose my time will be spent now much in proof-reading. Somehow, I suspect that the whole of this work is bad. I can't judge it. But I have not felt fresh enough while writing. Life here is gradually deadening what little wit I had.

Janet, according to the doctor's report, has neither progressed nor gone back since last June. She has a weary lot, but bears it patiently & bravely. Madge is in splendid spirits, the life of our household. She went to a fancy ball the other night in amber satin & black lace with red trimmings & looked very handsome I thought.

By the way, Angelo [Fusato] (the Venetian gondolier) is with me now. He came about a fortnight ago. Some weeks ago his wife & little girl died, & he wrote me a letter passionately begging to be sent for to Davos. One of my friends here, who photographs,[3] has made some magnificent studies of his face. If you care I will send you one. He is going tomorrow. We have some vague plans of going in the spring.

Now I must stop. I look forward to "In an Italian Garden."[4] Certainly I did not do justice to your poems in the proofs. I was very much out of sorts then.

Ever yours

J A Symonds

Many happy returns of tomorrow! & when you are as old as I am, may you be less tired!

---

1. She was at work on her *Margaret of Angoulême, Queen of Navarre* (1886), which contained genealogical matter.
2. *English Historical Review,* which Mandell Creighton founded and edited 1886–91. Mary Robinson's "Queen Elizabeth and the Valois Princes" is in II (January, 1887), 40–77.
3. Percival Broadbent (1852–86), the photographer whose studio was behind the Buol Hotel in Davos. See *H & P,* p. 204. He was a pioneer in early photography during the 1880's. His photographs of Symonds and his family appear in *OOP,* facing pp. 194 and 292.
4. *An Italian Garden: A Book of Songs* (1886).

1522. *To Robert Louis Stevenson*

Am Hof, Davos Platz, Switzerland. March 3 1886

My dear Louis

At last I have read Dr Jekyll. It makes me wonder whether a man has the right so to scrutinize "the abysmal deeps of personality." It is indeed a dreadful book, most dreadful because of a certain moral callousness, a want of sympathy, a shutting out of hope. The art is burning and intense. The Peau de Chagrin[1] disappears; Poe is as water. As a piece of literary work, this seems to me the finest you have done—in all that regards style, invention, psychological analysis, exquisite fitting of parts, and admirable employment of motives to realize the abnormal. But it has left such a deeply painful impression on my heart that I do not know how I am ever to turn to it again.

The fact is that, viewed as an allegory, it touches one too closely. Most of us at some epoch of our lives have been upon the verge of developing a Mr Hyde.

Physical and biological Science on a hundred lines is reducing individual freedom to zero, and weakening the sense of responsibility. I doubt whether the artist should lend his genius to this grim argument. Your Dr Jekyll seems to me capable of loosening the last threads of self-control in one who should read it while wavering between his better and worse self. It is like the Cave of Despair in the Faery Queen.[2]

I had the great biologist Lauder Brunton[3] with me a fortnight back. He was talking about Dr Jekyll and a book by W. O. Holmes,[4] in wh atavism is played with. I could see that, though a Christian, he held very feebly to the theory of human liberty; and these two works of fiction interested him, as Dr Jekyll does me, upon that point at issue.

I understand now thoroughly how much a sprite you are. Really there is something not quite human in your genius!

The denouement would have been finer, I think, if Dr Jekyll by a last supreme effort of his lucid self had given Mr Hyde up to justice—wh might have been arranged after the scene in Lanyon's study. Did you ever read Raskolnikow?[5] How fine is that ending! Had you made your hero act thus, you would at least have saved the sense of human dignity. The doors of Broadmoor[6] would have closed on Mr Hyde.

Goodbye. I seem quite to have lost you. But if I come to England I shall try to see you.

Love to your wife.

Everyrs

J A Symonds

---

1. Balzac, *Peau de chagrin* (1831).
2. Spenser, *Faerie Queene*, I. ix.33 ff.
3. Sir Thomas Lauder Brunton (1844–1916), a Scottish physician who did research on circulation and the physiological action of drugs; in 1867 discovered effect of amyl nitrate in treatments of angina pectoris.

4. Oliver Wendell Holmes' first novel, *Elsie Venner* (1861).
5. Dostoyevsky, *Crime and Punishment* (1866).
6. An asylum for the insane in Berkshire.

1523. *To Henry Sidgwick*

Davos, March 10, 1886.

[Dear Henry]

Your diary for February 7 has just come. Though brief, it has things which interest me deeply. Watching, "as from a ruined tower" out here, "how goes the day of England's power,"[1] I get more and more impressed with a sense of impending disaster, of some dark and dreadful place into which we are insensibly drifting. I keep telling myself that it is wrong to yield to alarmism, natural to take gloomier and more conservative views with growing years, and only too painfully reasonable for a man so separated as I am from his peers to become bizarre in opinion.

You echo back my apprehensions from the centre of English life. How sad it is that all our study of history, all our reflection upon principles in politics, never helps us at a pinch. We cannot apply what we feel we have learned, and the green tree of life laughs at our grey theories. Nay, worse, the unexpected evolutions of the organism force us to doubt what we confidently thought we had learned.

Surely England has reached a crisis at which, if ever, principles ought to suggest the way to right solution. And yet none are applicable. Sternly, blindly, patiently, perhaps sufferingly, we shall have to live it out—just like the meanest mollusc.

I should much like to get some lucrative literary work. I really feel anxious to that extent about the social and political prospects of England that I want to make literature, so far as in me lies, remunerative.

Pray keep this in mind, in case you should hear of an opening however humble, provided paying, for the talents you know me to possess—such as they are.

As it is, I have lately neglected the money side of my art.

[Incomplete]

---

1. A variation on Tennyson's "Two Voices," ll. 76–78:

Were this not well, to bide mine hour,
Tho' watching from a ruin'd tower
How grows the day of human power?

1524. *To Mrs. Eleanor Boyle*

Am Hof, Davos Platz, Switzerland. March 12, 1886

Dear Mrs. Boyle

My article on "The Pathos of the Rose in Poetry" is to come out next month in *Time*.[1] I have asked the editor to send you a copy. The *Fortnightly* found it too long and too technical. It consists, indeed, as you will see, chiefly of poems & translations. I call your attention especially to the Idyl of Ausonius & the passage from Guarini.

We are having a terribly cold spring—often from 42° to 47° Fahr of frost at night. Yet the sunshine is most glorious in the day. One sits basking and dreaming in it. Davos in winter is like some enchanted crystal palace on the top of a mountain—the place where the magician Atlante shut up young Ruggiero.[2] Soon we hope to escape from its long monotony of light & snowdrifts into the paler skies & softer hues of the Italian spring.

Your drawing of the olive wood has been a great pleasure to me. It reminds me of the low land at Mentone on the way to Cap St. Martin [3] before that was spoiled. I am very truly yours,

J A Symonds

1. *Time*, III, N.S. (1886), 397–411; included in *E S & S* (2 vols., 1890), II. For Mrs. Boyle see L 1424.
2. *Orlando Furioso*, Canto XX; Ruggiero is imprisoned in *l'incantate castel del vecchio Atlante*.
3. On the French Riviera.

1525. *To Mary Robinson*

Written in the middle of March, I suppose, and not sent because I knew it was to feeble in expression.

Am Hof, Davos Platz, Switzerland. March [15], 1886

Dear Miss Robinson

Is it true that in Mag of Art they have published an illustration to a Venetian Nocturne by you:—& if so, is it the Nocturne (dear to me as a momento of an hour wh comes back presently like photographic vision on my senses)—p: 16 of your Book?[1]

Please answer me this. I should so much like to have the illustration to *that* Nocturne, if it be that.

Only tell me if it is not *that,* & then I do not so much care. But if it is *that,* I want to see how the artist has matched by fancy a moment I well remember.

Fancy! I am writing this note, dead-tired past midnight, because a young English versifier writes to me (among other things) to say that, though he never was in Venice, your Nocturne inspired a something dreadful wh he sent. [And I don't like not to reply to these people.][2]

Only there came the thought:—Palazzo Balbi Valier, Le Zattere, round by Corte Vecchio San Vio, into Campiello Barbaro, and so on to the [S. Maria della] Salute: & just there, as Mary & I pattered by, the hoarse voice of Angelo [Fusato] from the Cà Forati crying "Comandi Signore?" and so on to the Salute.

And of this is there then an artist's vision in the "Mag of Art"? If so send it or tell me how to get it.

Yours ever

J A Symonds

---

1. *An Italian Garden: A Book of Songs* (1886), p. 16, "Venetian Nocturne." The poem is part of a design by Clara Montalba, *Magazine of Art,* IX (1886), facing 257.
2. Symonds' brackets.

1526. *To Henry Graham Dakyns*

Am Hof, Davos Platz, Switzerland. March 22 1886

My dear Graham

I have behaved like a brute to you, in not responding to two delightful & precious letters which you wrote me. My thanks at any rate for the trouble you took about L. M.[1] were long since due. The discovery of the word *levidense* in another dedication by Jonson makes the conjecture of *levidense munusculum* tolerably certain. I hit upon it while turning up *levis* in the dictionary; but it is odd that he should have indicated so rare a phrase by two capital letters only.

Soon after your departure I began to work hard again. I first did the book on *Ben Jonson*,[2] & then revised the whole of *Italy & the Council of Trent*.[3] These three volumes are now in the printers' hands. Then I wrote the Introduction to a book of selections from B. Jonson[4] I have undertaken, & next I had to produce an article on Tasso[5] for the Encycl Brit. These things, together with some reviews, which were promised, kept me so incessantly scribbling that I had little energy for correspondence.

Here then are my excuses! Also I got a bad cold & went over to the Engadine for change of air. I spent a week at Maloja,[6] which I cannot say I much liked *qua hotel*. I was always either too hot or too cold because of the freaks of the huge Calorifère.[7] Also the contrast between that big Belgian palace and the severe sublimity of nature all round it oppressed me. What one craves for in this winter landscape is Gemüthlichkeit.[8]

[H. F.] Brown & my Venetian gondolier Angelo came up to see me there. We crossed the passes & spent some days together at Davos. Brown was in good health & spirits. He works hard & thoroughly at the Venetian Archives: is on his way, I think, to be a first class student of historical Records. This development from his aesthetical & inaccurate boyhood is somewhat singular. Men of his kind make me often wonder what is wrong in public school education. Perhaps it is the nature of some people to find their real selves very slowly. But education ought to be maieutic of the real self, which in a case like Brown's it certainly was not.

My amateur photographer friend Mr Broadbent[9] has made a splendid study of my head—large, haggard, angular, wrinkled, & with a curious look of anxiety in the eyes; but very truthful I think. When I get some copies I will send you one, unmounted, to stick into the fragments. He also made some noble studies of Angelo, who is a very handsome fellow of the black-haired blue-eyed bronze Venetian type. One of these, nude to the waist, is worthy of a place beside the finest chalk drawings of a realistic master.

We have had a very cold spring. All through March the thermometer has marked from 15° to 5° below zero Fahr. But the sun has been splendid. This frost broke suddenly on Saturday. The temperature rose to 36° & now we are everywhere in a state of doleful deliquescence. The change is trying. I am sorry to say that Lotta has been really ill for a week past at Wiesen— sore throat at first, & then continued fever with no apparent cause. Her mother is there, nursing her. Janet too has been going down hill. It will be well when all of us can get away for our spring-change. [Dr.] Ruedi wishes us to go to Badenweiler in the Schwartz Wald [Black Forest]. And that will probably be our destination. I always feel the long residence at Davos (in this case hardly broken since early in last June) to be very trying. The stimulation of one's nerves & the comparative isolation of one's intellectual being put a severe strain on my morale. It is difficult to rest here when one is not sleeping.

I hope that things have been going pretty comfortably with you this term, & that you have taken up the position of Plato's philosopher under the wall. The last letter you wrote described an assault in force upon the οἰκεῖα κακά [domestic flaws] of your domicile. I trust they have been subdued. It is certainly pleasant to have a snug house such as I do possess here, even though there is too much wine to too few books in it—a half-pennyworth of bread of life to this intolerable deal of sack!

Our toboggin races went off well. One Swiss friend of mine Peter Minsch[10] netted prizes to the amount of 350 francs here & at S. Moritz. Since his expenses were paid, he made a fine business. So I go running on to you about my trifles, when the great House of England seems gradually crumbling into dust. The 'αμηγανία [ineptitudes] of politics is a dismal subject for reflection. How difficult it is to be wise in the present or to learn anything from the past. Each crisis in human affairs seems to present a new quantity or set of quantities wh render the solution of the problem impossible by prudence. We are reduced to the same evolutionary laws as molluscs, in spite of our power of looking before & after. Love to Maggie.

Ever yr

JA Symonds

I am writing to Nutt[11] to send you a copy of a book of verses by a friend of mine. Skip the story. Read the lyrics.

---

1. *Levidensis munusculum:* slight, poor; *levis:* light in weight.
2. In the "English Worthies" series (1886; 2nd ed. with corrected errata, 1888).
3. Part of *The Renaissance in Italy: The Catholic Reaction,* Chap. II.
4. *The Dramatic Works and Lyrics of Ben Jonson,* with an Essay, Biographical and Critical, by John Addington Symonds, "Canterbury Poets" series (1886).
5. In the 9th ed. (1888), XXIII, 75–79.
6. In the Grisons, Switzerland, on the route to the Engadine Valley and Italy.
7. A warm, dry wind, common in the Swiss Alps, occurring in any season.
8. Meaning, generally, warm friendliness.

9. See L 1521.

10. See L 1452.

11. Alfred Trübner Nutt (1856–1910), head (1878) of the publishing house Trübner & Co., in which his father was a partner; English folklorist and Celtic scholar: published W. E. Henley's works; founded the journal *Folklore* (1890); wrote *Studies on the Legend of the Holy Grail* (1888). The book Symonds sent is unknown, though it could have been by Edmund Gosse, Roden Noel, or Mary Robinson, works by all of whom Nutt had published. Also, Nutt may have distributed Pinkerton's *Galeazzo,* published in Venice (1886), which Symonds describes in similar terms in L 1533.

1527. *To Horatio Forbes Brown*

Davos, March 25, 1886.

[Dear Horatio]

Mrs. Symonds, Madge, and I walked up the Dörfli Berg to-day in pretty deep snow—an hour or so up to our waists. We nearly lost Ciò [a black Spitz dog] in a torrent. We got over it splashily but safely. He was getting sucked in under a roof of ice by the water, when I beheld him going, and Madge, in answer to my shouts, pulled him from the frozen cavern by the scruff of his neck. We descended the mountain gloriously, if perilously. On steep, but also well-selected slopes, we set avalanches going, and rode them downwards till they heaped themselves in masses six feet deep. Of course I knew what we were about, and took care there should be no extraordinary danger. We only devoted ourselves to a total wetting and a partial smothering. It was very exhilarating. The Dörfli Berg is furrowed with long triangular fan-shaped avalanches, indicating the points we severally selected for our start, and the wild animals we rode in the descent. The snow helps this method of progression just now, for the ground is frozen into ice, and upon that icy bottom lies a foot of melted snow, which slides off with a human being's weight upon it, accumulating volume and spreading as it goes. It was enjoyable, and we all of us have a thrill of quickened life in us to-night. I never experienced this sort of glissading in the summer on glaciers. The state in which we walked back from Dörfli to our house leaves itself to be imagined. There was not a dry thread on the three of us, and our hands were bleeding. Life here is funny; that one can turn so easily out of our home into a four hours' madness of the sort.'

[Incomplete]

1528. *To Arthur Symons*

[Davos] March 29. 1886.

Dear Mr Symons,

I have been so neglectful of you that I really cannot remember whether I answered your letter of Jan 11 (which lies before me), or whether I told you what I thought about the specimens of blank verse you sent me. It is true that I was not well in the winter. I got discouraged about things in general. And I had to work hard. The revision of two volumes of my *Renaissance in Italy*[1] for press cost me more labour than I had reckoned on. They are now, I am glad to say, in the printers' hands. When published, *that* long book will have been finished. I had also to write a short book (for Lang's English Worthies) on Ben Jonson.[2] This I finished at the end of last month. There were besides some smaller jobs to do. In short I have been scribbling so much since the New Year that correspondence went to the wall. Now pray tell me whether I did or did not write to you; and in case I did not, whether you would still like me to send you observations on your blank verse?[3] I will gladly do so; and indeed would proceed to do so now, if I felt sure that I should not be serving you a dish of critical *crambe repetita* [twice-cooked cabbage]. I liked the Ballad of Kings[4] you sent me. By the way, we have both contributed to the April number of *Time*.[5] Did I not think you would have a copy, I would send you one; for I should like you to see my article on Roses. If you do not already know the Idyll of Ausonius,[6] I am sure it will interest you. There is something singularly "modern" in its tone; and its influence over some of the best poets of the modern age[7] is striking.

Again I have to thank you for your generous gift of the Quarto Henry V.[8] A good piece of work. Shakespeare's attitude toward his own dramas seems to me one of the most inexplicable problems. That he should take such pains in recasting and remodelling them, always to the augmentation of their beauty and the enriching of their brain-stuff, and that he should not have thought it worth while in his retirement at Stratford to prepare a correct edition of them, indicates an unintelligible mixture of artistic conscientiousness and literary indifference. But I agree with you in taking the Quarto Henry V. for one of those short-hand piracies which seem to have been common. I suppose Marlowe's *Massacre at Paris*[9] is of the same species.

Your remarks on my *Vagabunduli Libellus*[10] interested me greatly. I shall keep them by me with a view to future consideration, if such an unhoped for piece of good fortune should come to me as the call for a second edition. I will revert to one or two of the points you raise.

LV. l. 7. You doubt the scansion. It is, I grant, peculiar. I wanted to have it read thus:

'Dríven my soul's bliss" fórth across the sea.

XXIV. l. 13.14. Your ear here is probably correct. I had written first:

'Communion with thee—even in the clasp of sin.'
From *even* onwards is a sort of after-thought, or
sudden swerve of thought in the man's mind.

XII. l. 1 & 2. You are quite right. *Gone* ought to be repeated.
XIV. l. 5. "twined" is rather an obsolete word for "separated from." You get it in one of the Yarrow ballads.[11] "I lie twined o' my mar-row." I fancy it is Scotch rather than English; and I suppose I am familiar with it through the ballad.

These notes I make because I am sure I did not write them to you before.

Very sincerely yours,

J. A. Symonds.

I think you over praise the quality of Swinburne's prose in general. Sometimes it is splendid, certainly, but how often it is Johnsonese of the very most cumbrous and cloying kind. The odd thing is that it is *catching*. Nobody can read it without finding himself writing to its tune. You have done so in your review.[12] I did so in some parts of Shakespeare's Predecessors.[13]

---

1. The final volumes of *The Renaissance in Italy: The Catholic Reaction,* appeared in October, 1886, published by Smith, Elder & Co.

2. *Ben Jonson* (1886). Andrew Lang edited the series.

3. Symonds had published his ideas on blank verse in an appendix to *Sketches and Studies in Italy* (1879). A separate edition of the essay was published by Nimmo in 1895.

4. Symons' poem appeared in *Time,* III, N. S. (March, 1886). His "Religious Tolerance," a poem, appeared in January, 1886, and "The Shelley Society," an essay, in February, 1886.

5. There is nothing by Symons in the April issue, but Symonds' "The Pathos of the Rose in Poetry" is on pp. 392–411 (III, N. S., 1886). It was reprinted in *E S & S* (2 vols., 1892), II, 197–224.

6. Symonds printed the Idyll by Ausonius, 4th century A.D., classical poet, translated it, and analyzed it in his essay on the "Pathos of the Rose in Poetry." He regarded this poem and Catullus' "Epithalamium" as "twin fountain-heads of a large amount of verses written upon roses in the modern world." His friend, Mrs. Eleanor (Richard Cavendish) Boyle, in her *Ros Rosarum* (see L 1507), had omitted these two Latin poems. Symonds detected in the Idyll coming at "the latest close of antique culture, something of the spirit which appears in mediaeval, and which pervades modern literature, the spirit of sympathy with nature, and the sense of pathos in ephemeral things." Ausonius, Symonds believed, was the first of the ancient poets to draw pathos from the rose and apply it to man. "Hitherto . . . the rose had been a symbol of love and gladness, celebrated as the ornament of Aphrodite, the pledge of passion, and the chief decoration of life's banquet. . . . It remained for Ausonius, in the crepuscular interspace between the sunset of the antique and the night which came before the sunrise of the modern age, to develop thus elaborately the motive of fragility in rose life and in human loveliness."—*E S & S*, II, 199, *passim*.

7. When Symonds compared passages from Catullus and Ausonius with stanzas by Poliziano, Ariosto, Tasso, Guarini, Spenser, Herrick, Waller, and Ronsard he "was so much struck with the examples of literary derivation they afforded" that he composed his article (*E S & S*, II, 198).

8. Symons published editions of both the First and Third Quartos of the play in 1886.

9. Marlowe's last play deals with the religious wars in France between Catholic and Huguenot, 1572–89.

10. The passages are all from the sequence of sonnets "Stella Maris." The published version of XXIV. ll. 13. 14 is: "Communion with thee, even in the clasp of pain. . . ." The passage from XII. ll. 1–2 follows: "Hushed is the music, all those crowds are gone./ Flown are the passing strangers, whose dark eyes. . . ." Finally, XIV. l. 5 reads: "Yea, those who love, twined from the loved one. . . ."

11. Ballads issuing from Yarrow, a parish and a stream in Selkirkshire, Scotland. The ballad to which Symonds refers is "Rare Willie Drowned in Yarrow," Child's example A, stanza 2, line 1: "I lie twin'd of my marrow." See the reprint of the 1st ed. (1882–98) of Francis James Child, ed., *The English and Scottish Popular Ballads* (5 vols., 1965), IV, 179.

12. Symonds means Symons' "remarks" on *Vagabunduli Libellus* and not a published review of Swinburne, which in any case we have not been able to find. In the unpublished "A Study of John Addington Symonds" Symons followed this letter with some sample passages demonstrating the contagion caught from Meredith and Swinburne.

13. The typescript is probably wrong because Symonds almost always used the spelling "Shakspere."

1529. *To Arthur Symons*

[Davos] April 5. 1886.[1]

Dear Mr Symons,

I have been reading over your blank verse pieces again to-night—having heard that I did not tell you what I thought of them. And now I am going to say something which will seem to contradict my previous advice. It is this: all your work in verse seems to me so far mature, and my own judgment about it is so very doubtful to myself, that I can see for you no other test than *publication of the pieces which you think best,* in one volume. Only I do not recommend you to publish if you have to pay. To tell the truth, I am frankly puzzled by you. That you are far too fluent seems to be apparent. But that you have already great metrical facility, command of diction, and dramatic force to some extent, is equally obvious. The Interruption in Court (very painful) is certainly powerful. You make me see the scene. I don't care for Master Stephan and the Fauns² so much. The former somehow remind me of Browning and the latter of Landor. But nobody in the world, except Posterity the public Vox Dei can really say what the value of your work is.

My general advice to young men is: Wait, and cook your talent like a peach upon the wall until it be ripe. This I gave you.³ But you seem to be so early ripe, that really I think you may attempt a harvest:—only do not pay some publisher to accept your peaches. That is ignominious—and worse ignominy is paying critics to praise them after they have been paid for by the author to the publisher.

I am so tired and stupid that I doubt whether I have made my meaning clear. It really amounts to this:

(1) That I am too diffident of my own faculty, to judge your verse, especially in MS.

(2) That I am sure you write too much and on too slight suggestion.

(3) That in these circumstances I believe it might not be bad for you to risk a volume, provided you can launch it without actual payment to the publisher.

When you are as old as I am, and when you know your limitations as well as I know mine, you will yawn over these affairs of literature (so far less poignant than life)—unless you have to gain your bread by them. Pray, at any rate, do not take them too seriously. Good work will find its own level. Do good work, and don't bother yourself further. Get it published, if you can. Serve your apprenticeship, as you can. Remember how many years a carpenter or doctor or attorney serves before he makes fame or money in his craft. Remember how cheap the mastery over decent metre and a fair vocabulary is. Then with these somewhat depressing thoughts in your head, march boldly forward.

I think it probable that if you attempt a volume of poems now, you will come a cropper. But that will do you good. In truth, I have changed my mind and think that you require the test of publication. I believe you are strong enough to stand a failure; and I see that you have qualities which are likely to be over-exercised in the present state of expectation.

You tell me you wrote a poem on a "Venetian Nocturne"[4] (Miss Robinson's title). And you have not been in Venice?—Her Nocturne[5] describes a walk alone with me last May in moonlight through labyrinths of narrow alleys out into the airy spaces of the lagoon by S. Maria della Salute. She has made a good sketch from nature.

You ask me about Browning and Greek and Italian. I think his touch on Greek is always extremely bad, and his touch on Italian good. As to Italian I distinguish. It is *good* in occasional pieces. *The Bishop Orders his Tomb in St Praxed*—*Up at a Villa*—*Holy Cross Day*—*Toccata of Geluppi* and *Fra Lippo Lippi*—*Andrea del Sarto*—*Englishman in Italy*). In such work as *The Ring and the Book* it is as good (i.e. as true to Italy) as Webster's *Duchess of Malfi* or his *White Devil of Italy*. Views expressed by me in my article (Italian Byways)[6] on Vittoria Accoramboni and Webster. The work is not Italian, but a splendid moral study of Italy from the Northern point of view of conscience.

Read De Stendhal[7] for the *real* Italian, or Cellini.

Yours ever

J. A. Symonds.

Excuse, if I have spoken naked truth. I am horribly tired to-night.

---

1. The letter was sent as an enclosure to L 1543.

2. These poems were published in *Days and Nights* (1889). "An Interruption in Court" is a short dramatic poem in which an old father pleads with the court to free Jenny, his daughter, who is finally declared guilty of some unspecified crime. "An Altar-Piece of Master Stephan" is a Browningesque monologue by a devout admirer of Master Stephan, spoken on his deathbed; "Fauns at Noon" is a dialogue between an old faun and a young one ranging over death, the transitoriness of beauty, and the nature of Pan.

3. See L 1516, January 4, 1886.

4. "Venetian Night" in *Images of Good and Evil* (1900).

5. Mary Robinson. See L 1137. Her "Venetian Nocturne" in *An Italian Garden: A Book of Songs* (1886). The volume contained a section, "Tuscan Cypress," of 16 rispetti, one of Symonds' favorite folk-forms.

6. The 8th essay of *Italian Byways* (1883).

7. Symonds was thinking of Stendhal's *Rome, Naples, et Florence* (1817) and *Chroniques et Nouvelles* (Paris, 1855). The latter he consulted for details on the Cenci and Vittoria Accoramboni. See also L 1548.

1530. *To Mary Robinson*

Am Hof, Davos Platz, Switzerland. April 13 1886

Dear Miss Robinson

My post-bag brings me strange bed-fellows: I mean the letters that have slumbered in it, are curiously matched. Tonight's for example turns out yours from Florence, & a very passionate cry from Venice, into my lap. I have long had by me on the table a written but unsent letter to you—wh I think I shall now send.

= = = = =

It is the cry from Venice, from the Corte San Vio, wh makes me send it, blending with your reproach that I have not a long time written.

= = = = = =

I remember ill. I thought I had written last & sent you what now seems to me a bad photograph of Angelo. In fact I did write & did send this photo & I believe, speaking like a money changer, this put me in your debt.

Mind you: I never treat correspondence upon such terms. But I rebut your accusation that I have not written.

And now I really want to know about the Venetian Nocturne.[1] The post bag is answerable, wh brings your letter & a Venetian letter (not from Angelo, but from the Corte San Vio) into singularly plaintive accord.

I am so glad you are in Florence & with your friend [Vernon Lee]. No such luck for me this Spring.

I am to go to Badenweiler,[2] wh is in the Scholarly World. Perhaps to London later.

The book about Jesuits etc is just lumbering into print; I have written another about Ben Jonson; & I am getting up steam for one upon Sir Philip Sidney.

Miss Violet Paget's [Vernon Lee's] Baldwin[3] is upon my list to get as soon as it appears. I expect it to madden me. Tell her that this is a compliment. For "the world-wearied flesh" of this romance is only excited by very pungent passages.

We are all here in fairly good sort. I think I am the least viable of the lot at present.

It is nice for your Sister Mabel[4] to be present at the great game of her friends the Irish. I sympathize with her. But fancy the attitude of people who lionize the Irish heart when really the fate of England hangs in the balance, & good patriots should be pandering & praying in their chambers!

Addio. Pray remember me to Miss Paget & to Mr Lee Hamilton.

Yours ever J A Symonds

Tell Miss Poynter, if you see her, that I thoroughly enjoyed "Mme de Presnel."[5] It has throughout the aura of good company. This is extraordinary merit in that these days.

---

1. Mary Robinson, in *An Italian Garden: A Book of Songs* (1886). See L 1525.
2. In Würtemberg, Germany, half way between Freiburg and Basle, Switzerland.
3. *Baldwin: Being Dialogues on Views and Aspirations* (1886).
4. See L 1485 for comments on *Mr. Butler's Ward* (1885). She also wrote *Disenchantment: an Every-Day Story* (1886), and *The Plan for Campaign: A Story of the Fortune of War* (1887). Her *An Irish History for English Readers* (1886) was written under the pseudonym "William Stephenson Gregg."
5. Eleanor Poynter's novel, 1885.

1531. *To Unknown*

[Postcard]

April 19 1886

Dear Sir

Pray excuse this p:c:, but I am very hurried today & have no time to write a letter.—This is in answer to yours of 15th.—I am very fond of lecturing, & should gladly accept your flattering invitation if my health allowed.—For eight years I have had to live in this place 5,000 feet above the sea, on account of lung disease. You will comprehend that lecturing is out of the question for me. Many thanks for your words about my work.

[Printed] J. A. Symonds
Am Hof
Davos Platz, Suisse

1532. *To Horatio Forbes Brown*

Badenweiler, May 7 [1886]

[Dear Horatio]

Your letter from Asolo by its sympathy induces me to write more openly than in the incoherent lines[1] I sent you last night.

The case with Janet is very sad. She has been a fortnight in bed, growing daily weaker. I apprehend no immediate calamity. But she has never been so ill before. We are at sixes and sevens. We do the best to keep each other in exercise and spirits. But what a life!

This place is certainly beautiful. Thick woods of silver pine, mingled with oak and beech upon the lower levels, sometimes opening into meadows of the richest grass, sometimes so tangled that the sun scarcely pierces their roof of branches. There is an undergrowth of ferns, with "frail wood-sorrel and bilberry bell" in rippling sheets among the mosses. Abundant water flows through the grass, which is everywhere enamelled with marsh-marigold and white narcissus and orchises and lilac cuckoo-flower. Far away stretches the Rhine-valley, bordered on the west by that exquisitely pencilled outline of the Vosges—a poetic country, a modern Arcady, with simple folk inhabiting its comfortable old farm-houses.

I write a good deal in the open air; upon the wall of the Castle, or in the open spaces of the Park, or further away in wooded glades by streams where green lizards whisk about half-tame around me. I have rough-hewn "Sidney,"[2] all but the last two chapters (two out of eight). It is all stippled with small touches, except the critical essays on his writings.

One afternoon I climbed the Blauen, the highest point here, and one of the highest in the Schwartzwald. The prospect was dreamily fine, illimitable: fancy the Rhinethal, from Basel to Strasburg, and the Bernese Oberland, Eiger, Mönch, etc. It is all sweetly sad: made for poetic melancholy and tender meditation. But I am not tuned for it: too much on the fret, dispirited, discouraged.

The inn is good. Excellent wine of many sorts at rather less than three marks the bottle. But what does that signify?

[Incomplete]

---

1. Not available.
2. *Sir Philip Sidney* (1886) in "English Men of Letters" series.

1533. *To Havelock Ellis*

Badenweiler, Baden, Germany. May 10 1886.

Dear Mr Havelock Ellis

I have just got your letter of the 5th. The plan you propose is one which has often occurred to my mind. I think nothing could be better than a series of *select* Elizabethan plays;[1] and I should much like to take part in its execution.

Ben Jonson I really feel to have written enough about. I have just finished him for the *English Worthies* and for the *Canterbury Poets.*

I would willingly undertake *Webster* and *Cyril Tourneur* in one volume; and I should like to do *Heywood. Massinger* might, I think, be allowed a volume by himself.

With regard to collaborators, I would suggest Mr A. H. Bullen[2] (editor of Old Plays, Marlowe, Middleton, etc). Of course you have thought of Gosse. I should like to recommend my friend and nephew Mr John St.Loe Strachey, who is an excellent literary critic and a good writer (he writes much both for the Saturday and Spectator and has written for the Quarterly), and who has the El. Dr. at his finger-ends. I dedicated my "Shakspere's Predecessors" to him. Also I might mention Mr Percy E. Pinkerton,[3] editor of Marlowe in the Cant. Poets, and author of an exquisite little book of Venetian Lyrics (called *Galeazzo,*[4] Sonnenschein & Co) which I warmly recommend to your attention. (The *lyrics* are good; the story Galeazzo not so good).

When your plans are more fully settled, I will if you like give you the addresses etc. of these men. Strachey would do B and F well, I am certain. Bullen would be excellent for some of the less known authors.—Middleton for instance, or a collection of single plays by obscure hands, some of which, as you know, are the best.

I should myself enjoy doing *Domestic Tragedies*—Arden of F[eversham], Two Ty in one,[5] Yorkshire Trag[edy], and the one about Sanders.[6]

But it is early to talk yet of these things.

My writing table is loaded with the proofs of the last 2 vols of Renaissance in Italy. They are going slowly but surely through the press.

With regard to payment; 10 or 12 guineas would suffice for such playwrights as have a fairly good modernized text. But were it necessary (as in the case of Heywood and Domestic Tragedies) to print from recent reproductions of the old texts, I do not know how anyone could undertake the labour of modernization at that price! In fact you will have to consider this question about text very thoroughly.

I am here for a change from Davos, and expect to stay about a fortnight longer. One of my daughters is very ill—has been 15 days in bed with haemoptysis, poor girl. My life is made up of literature and sickness.

Most truly yours

J.A.Symonds.

1. Ellis' "The Mermaid" series. Symonds wrote the general introduction on drama during the reigns of Elizabeth and James I, which accompanied Ellis' edition of Marlowe (1887). He also introduced A. Wilson Verity's *Heywood* (1888) and introduced and edited *Webster and Tourneur* (1888). Roden Noel edited *Otway* (1888); Arthur Symons, *Massinger* (2 vols., 1887–89); Ernest Rhys, *Dekker* (1888); and Edmund Gosse, *Shirley* (1888).

2. See L 1546.

3. See L 1407. Pinkerton edited none of the volumes.

4. See Symonds' review of *Galeazzo, A Venetian Episode, and Other Poems* in *The Academy*, XXIX (April 10, 1886), 249–50.

5. *Two Tragedies in One* (1601), attributed to a Robert Yarrington.

6. Anon., *A Warning for Fair Women* (1599), about the murder by his wife and her lover of George Sanders, a London merchant.

1534. *To Charlotte Symonds Green*

Badenweiler Baden Germany May 11 1886

Dearest Charlotte

It is some time since I received your last letter, & I ought to have written to you sooner. Up till now there was nothing very pleasant to say. Janet had an attack of blood-spitting the first night of our arrival (Saty Apr 24), & she has been in bed ever since. Today I am able to report some marked improvement. But she is more pulled down, thinner, weaker, & shakier than I have ever seen her.

We were very anxious. It seemed for some time as though the bleeding could not be stopped; never very much, but always there. Her mother has had a hard bout of nursing. Yet things will now, I hope, be going better.

We shall be delighted if you come out this summer to Davos. You can choose your own time entirely & stay as long as you like. You know the place so well that I need not recommend one month more than another.

Of course there is some uncertainty when we shall be able to return, on account of Janet. But I think some of us are sure to be back (all going otherwise well) in the middle of June.

This is an exceedingly pretty place overlooking the Rhine valley from the edge of the Black Forest. I had no notion that the scenery was so lovely.

It is quite ideal for strolling leisurely in woods of fir & beech, over meadows, & by little streams. Only, we have not had the joy of it, in this perpetual uneasiness about Janet. To think of her being dragged from Davos only to go to bed & suffer in a hotel here!

I am working rather harder than usual, having a great deal of literature on hand. I want to begin making money again, if possible, by writing. The future of people without a bread-earning profession in England seems to me dark, & already I notice considerable shrinkage in some sources of my income.

Therefore, I am undertaking small jobs, wh pay. We had had Sophie [Girard] here a week. It was very nice. She went back to Basel yesterday.

Believe me always with much love your most aff brother

J A Symonds.

P.S. I am going to send this to c/o Auntie [Mary Ann Sykes], because Catherine wrote to you to Edgware Road 2 weeks ago, & we think the letter must have missed.

1535. *To Horatio Forbes Brown*

Badenweiler, May 11 [1886]

[Dear Horatio]

I can give you a better account of our affairs here this evening. Janet has to-day shown decided improvement. The doctor now hopes she will advance to recovery.

I might have been in London to-night, dining at Miss North's with the Holman Hunts, the Frank Galtons, Scherer, the French critic, Haggard, the author of "Solomon's Mines," Miss Gordon Cumming, Lord and Lady North, Newton of the British Museum, and a few others.[1] I had thought of going to England. But this plan is now abandoned. It is not absolutely necessary, for business, that I should be there. And every year I find the inclination to keep away more overwhelming. There must be some evil in this growth averse to English life. I suppose the base of it, however, in my nature is the weakness which I feel when I try to undergo the conditions of English society.

I got a letter from Pinkie to-day in which he says you were returning upon the 9th. He speaks of the cholera as serious. Frankly I doubt whether your book of poems will be as reviewable as Pinkie's.[2] That lent itself to the quoter. I believe we are all asses (I first and foremost in offending) when we publish our poems. Yet the doing so eases our souls—for some quite inscrutable reason; and if we can afford the consolation, and expect nothing from the public in return for our gifts, I suppose there is no reason to be urged against it.

Discouragement weighs like a cloud here. Life appears certainly not in smiling colours. There is a heavy soft rain falling. Writing at "Sidney" has become a weariness now that the work is all finished.

[Incomplete]

---

1. Marianne North's home: William Holman Hunt (1827–1910), the Pre-Raphaelite painter; Frank Galton (see L 915); Edmond Scherer (see L 1474); Henry Rider Haggard (1856–1925), the novelist; Constance Frederica Gordon Cumming (1837–1924), missionary to Ceylon and China and author; William Henry John, 11th Baron North (1836–1932), his wife Frederica Cockerell North (d. 1915); and "Halicarnassus" Newton (see Ls 915 and 928).
2. See Ls 1407 and 1533.

1536. *To Edmund Gosse*

Hotel Sommer Badenweiler Baden May 16, 1886

My dear Gosse

Your postcard of the 10th has reached me round by Davos. I am sorry that I cannot find you any exact information about Bertini[1] here. I remember his name but cannot attach any definite recollections to his work, and therefore am inclined to think he was not much.

When I get home (wh will be at the end of this month I hope) I shall probably be able to send you more information.

I shall ask you a return question. Have you formed an opinion as to the authorship of "The Doleful Lay of Clorinda" ascribed to the Countess of Pembroke[2] but printed at the end of Spenser's "Astrophel"? I am not versed in recent Spenserian criticism, I have no right edition of his works with me here. But the style of this elegy seems to me suspiciously like that of Spenser.

I should be sorry to find that good judges had him for the author.

When is your Raleigh[3] coming out? Longmans sent me the first 2 vols of the English Writers ["English Worthies" series], so I suppose they mean to send the series. I have not therefore ordered Raleigh from my bookseller, and it may be already out.

Here I am at a German Bath with a sick daughter, up to my eyes in proofs of the last two vols of Renaissance in Italy [*The Catholic Reaction*].

Please thank Mrs Gosse very warmly from me for the kind letter she wrote me. I cannot excuse myself for having left it unanswered.

The brutality of the PMG to Saintsbury[4] (and its ignorance) must have gratified you if it is true what the poet says [undecipherable].

Believe me most truly yours

J. A. Symonds

---

1. Pietro Bertini is elusive. In 1583 he published in Florence *Delle Rime di M. Pietro Bertini . . . Parte prime.*

2. Mary Herbert, Countess of Pembroke (1561–1621), Sidney's sister. Her poem was attributed to Spenser.

3. *Raleigh* (1886).

4. In a review of George Saintsbury's *Marlborough* ("English Worthies" series) in the *Pall Mall Gazette,* XLII (December 10, 1885), 11: It criticizes Andrew Lang, editor of the series, for his fault in not recognizing that

> Mr. Saintsbury's treatise . . . is scarcely the sort of thing to inspire popularity. There is, indeed, a curious perversity in the whole-souledness with which Mr. Saintsbury handicaps himself out of the possibility of his book finding favour with the general reader. He is wholly in error in holding that it is only to the purely military historian—and consequently to the purely military reader—that the soldier Marlborough dwarfs Marlborough the politician, the diplomatist, the honest man or, in Macaulay's phrase, the "prodigy of turpitude." To the great mass of the people of today, the career and the character of Marlborough have interest solely as the career and character of a military conqueror. . . . Mr. Saintsbury has shirked this portion of his task because of a consciousness of his inability to do justice to it. . . . Most people will be glad to turn with relief from Mr. Saintsbury's involved sophistries and wearisome, abortive hair-splitting, to Macaulay's clear and direct utterance, with its fine ring of sarcasm, that "there was no guilt and no disgrace which Marlborough was not ready to incur in order to escape the necessity of parting either with his places or his religion."

1537. *To Arthur Symons*

Badenweiler May 23 1886

Dear Mr Symons

I have a long letter in my portfolio addressed to you.[1] I wrote it some weeks ago at Davos, & did not send it. This is a frequent occurrence with me, if I think the scrawl was ill-considered. But it always blocks correspondence.

I get yours of 19th here today. I will tell you distinctly what the case is, so far as I am concerned, with regard to Mr H. E.'s[2] Eln Dr.

He asked me to take 2 vols, proposing Webster & Tourneur as one. I agreed to W & T, & said I should like Heywood, if I did a second. I refused Jonson. I forget how Massinger came in. To tell you the truth, I do not feel as though I could do Massinger justice. I have notes enough on Heywood to make the matter as concerns him easy; & he has always been a special favourite of mine.

If therefore you will take Massinger, the arrangement would be simple. But I should not like to stand in your way. Rather than that, I will, if you like, propose to retire in your favour from Heywood: but at the same time I should decline Massinger. Mr Ellis might not object to this arrangement, seeing that one vol has been already assigned to me. His scheme too might succeed better if he extended his list of editors.

I expect to return soon to Davos. *That* then is still my address.

If you like to send this letter on to Mr Ellis, it may save time & facilitate his arrangements. I have his letter of the 20th & I will answer it when I have more leisure. At present I am very busy & very feeble in health.

Believe me most truly yours

JASymonds

---

1. The letter of April 5, 1886, L 1529.
2. See L 1533.

1538. *To Horatio Forbes Brown*

Badenweiler, May 24, [1886]

[Dear Horatio]

It is very long since I wrote to you.[1] You asked why I suggested anonymous publication. It was really because of my own discouragement as a poet. I do not think that any verses I have published have brought me reputation. I could just as well have watched their effect, if they had gone out without my name; and then, in your case, you are going to embark upon so very different lines of work, that I believe the sort of name one gets

nowadays for poetry may be injurious to you. This is the brief statement of
the matter as it strikes me. But I dare say that I am jaded and taste with a
distempered appetite. I believe I am right in saying that Louis Stevenson
sold the *copyright* of "An Inland Voyage" for £20. And the *copyright* of
"Virginibus Puerisque" for £50. Smith treated me always better. He paid
£60 for the right to publish 1000 copies of each volume of the Greek Poets,
and the same sort of sum for "Italian Sketches," leaving the copyright in
my hands, and paying again for a second edition of 1000 copies.

Catherine and I have taken a short driving tour. We were out three
days, seeing all the valleys of this end of the Schwartzwald, and getting up
to the top of the biggest hill—Feldberg, 5000 feet above the sea. It is a
wonderful country for woods: endless trees of all sorts, and some of them
superb; beautiful old farmhouses nestling among the forests; river scenery
of the finest, when one has descended upon the Rhine at places, Säckingen
and Laufenburg. I am glad to have made acquaintance with the country. It
is like a very perfect England in detail—with breadth and space of
mountain and plain to make up for the absence of ocean. The heat has been
terrific. I have corrected 120 pages of my book in the last twenty-four hours,
and I cannot write a good letter.

[Incomplete]

---

1. On May 11, L 1535, which is incomplete and may have contained the suggestion
of anonymous publication.

1539. *To Mary Ann Skyes*

Am Hof, Davos Platz, Switzerland. June 12 1886

Dearest Auntie

I must write you a line upon your settlement with Charlotte at Oxford,
to tell you how very much the plan has interested me & occupied my
thoughts, & how deeply I hope it may turn out of good for you.

I have no hesitation in saying that I think you are doing right, & that it
is a great satisfaction to me to know that you now have chosen a permanent
home with one of your own children.

I do not forget what you are giving up, of friends in London especially.
But I remember that, if you are blessed with a fair measure of health, you

can move about in England from Oxford quite as freely as from London. Meanwhile, if you are unable to pay visits, it is surely better to be at home with Charlotte than alone in a London house.

Both you & she have lived so long in your own ways that I cannot but perceive you will at first have need for mutual tolerance & forbearance. You have such a fund of humour & good spirits, & are so sustained by the eternal sources of cheerfulness & fortitude, that I expect you to be able to accommodate yourself to these new circumstances. I will not enlarge more upon the matter. I think I have said enough to show how truly I enter into the circumstances of you both, & how eagerly I shall look forward to hearing details of your life in common.

The whole thing is so natural, so right, so consonant with the wishes of all who love you, & you are both so truly good, that I am sanguine about the plan being successful.

Dearest Auntie, it has grieved me to hear how much you have been suffering from bronchitis. You must take great care of your diet, & learn even now, at the eleventh hour, to masticate your food well so as to get the maximum of nutrition. Mr Gladstone says that he chews each piece of meat 36 times before he consigns it to his stomach. And see what he is! Able to break up the Liberal Party, & shake the very pillars of the English Empire. Not wisely, I think. But how mightily, with what a young man's thews & sinews, burning brain & resonant voice! I verily believe he owes his force to mastication.

We had a sad time with Janet, when we went away, & a most trying journey home ward. She is rather better now. But it is a slow decline. Each illness leaves her weaker, thinner, more short of breath, more transparent.

Everything combines to keep me here. Catherine is very much occupied with her. The other girls are full of life, thank God! I am able to walk with them. And just at present we seem to hang together in a way that would make a change of the situation bad for some one or another.

But, though I am not now indulging the notion of going to England, knowing that if I go for mere pleasure I may risk fresh troubles in the family by some break-down of my own health, yet I have nothing to prevent my setting off to see you at a word from you. Please remember this. I can be in London after rather less than a day & a night from Davos.

Ever with true love yours

J A Symonds.—

1540. *To Charlotte Symonds Green*

Am Hof, Davos Platz, Switzerland. June 12 1886

My dearest Charlotte

It was a great pleasure to get your letter of the 8th yesterday. I think I must have unintentionally seemed to blame you more than I meant, by the general reflections I made in my last letter. I was really feeling, when I wrote, a sort of isolation (common to Catherine & my family), & speculating upon my own faults in creating it.

I am averse to calling any life, which is lived out to the full, either selfish or useless. It is tantamount to blaming God, in my opinion, to be critical of human activity in its various forms.

But I often recognize in myself, & sometimes in people round me, the error of making what we call our work, wh is usually our easiest form of occupation, an excuse for laziness in discharging the kindly offices of kinship society & friendship. The fact, of course, is that any sphere of activity wh absorbs a man or woman demands the whole being's forces.

The spirit in which people do the work they have chosen, is undoubtedly much. But I seem to divine a noblest type of character, which constantly makes sacrifices even of the chosen work to what I will only describe as geniality, kindliness, sympathetic pressure, the diffusion of affection over all surrounding it. These were the things I had in my mind when I last wrote to you; & I was taking stock among the Mss & proofs of six half-completed volumes, of my own poverty in regard to wealth so far more valuable than mere achievements in my chosen business.

I am glad & proud to be able to exchange thoughts with you so freely upon these topics. I talk to you on paper, or mouth to mouth, as I talk to my own heart. It is good of you to accept the conditions frankly, & distance will not harm our love, so long as this is so.

There is no doubt that you are engaged at present in a very difficult & delicate relation to Auntie [Mary Ann Sykes]. There is a Greek proverb which says that "all fine things are difficult." This is worth remembering, for it is very true. The vulgar things, the things too which come by instinct out of our own nature or our talents, are comparatively easy. But, in making a common life with Auntie, you have to discharge a duty which involves daily contradiction of your own instinct for another kind of business, & daily contact, with a character you cannot wholly sympathize with. Therefore the right discharge of the task will be difficult. To attempt to discharge it is a duty. To succeed in it, will be a fine, a morally distinguished & beautiful thing.

I cannot tell you plainly enough how much I sympathize with you both in this beginning of your joint household. I feel certain that it will be a trial to both of you. And the deadweight of any jars, the irritation of any disagreement, must inevitably be felt most by the younger.

I hope you will keep me informed about the progress of your life together. The least details will interest me. Though I shall not be able to give you practical advice, you can rely upon my sympathy, & I will promise a quick response without fail. Indeed I am co-interested with you in this matter; for if circumstances had not placed me where I cannot offer A[untie] a home fit for her, I should have been the one to whom she would naturally have looked first.

Janet has slowly emerged again into half-life, but on a decidedly lower level than she held two months ago. Her mother & I have nothing exceptional in this trial. How many parents have watched the gradual decline of their first-born in the bloom of life!

Ever yours with true love

J A Symonds.

1541. *To Horatio Forbes Brown*

Davos Platz, June 13 [1886]

[Dear Horatio]

I think of you much and often in your stricken city. If it rains there as it has been doing here, the melancholy will be deepened. Here we are blessing the heavens for the continual downpour, which is saving the hay-harvest, it is hoped. I never saw the valley more parched with drought than when I came back ten days ago.

I wonder whether it would trouble you to discover whether the Marciana[1] contains the second edition of the "Rime di Nic: Franco contra P. Aretino," 1546.[2] A scholar, unknown to me, has written to enquire about it. He is privately printing an edition of the 3rd edit., 1548. The same man, Robert S. Turner,[3] asks about Francisco Delicado (in Spanish, Delgado),[4] who worked a great deal (he says) at Venice and published there, and was imitated by Aretino, who lived in familiarity with him. I have told Mr Turner that I meant to refer these questions to you. I will ask you also, on my own account, whether Rawdon Brown[5] has anything about Philip

Sidney's visit to Venice. Sidney was there from the autumn of 1573 to the summer of 1574. He had his portrait painted by Paolo Veronese.

I have written, since I came to Davos, an introduction to a book of selections from Sir Thomas Browne,[6] which is going to form a volume of the Camelot Classics. I read Pater's essay.[7] I did not think it quite up to his mark. The best passage was a curious discourse upon Browne's "Letter on the Death of a Friend."

Literary work, fortunately, does not fail me, and I am always having invitations to do more. Fancy being asked to produce a new translation of "Cellini's Autobiography" for an illustrated edition *de luxe!*[8] If I can make good enough terms I feel inclined to undertake it. Only it ought to be paid well, and time allowed to do the work artistically. Goethe translated it, and Comte put it into the Positivist Library.

I have promised to do selections and introductions to Webster, Tourneur, and Heywood for a series started by Havelock Ellis.[9] He also wants me to write a short general introduction on the Elizabethan Drama. Sometimes my hand gets very tired with writing, and English words seem to fail me.

I wish indeed I could get hold of the "Carmen de Moribus Stud."[10] *Beanus,* by the way, is a Freshman! The mediæval students treated him atrociously.

[Incomplete]

---

1. The library of St. Mark at Venice, founded according to legend in 1362 with Petrarch's donation of manuscripts. The library is in the Palazzo della Zecca. Its collection contains ca. 400,000 printed volumes.

2. Niccolò Franco (1515–70), *Rime contra l'Aretino* a scurrilous work widely circulated in its time.

3. Probably the collector, R. Samuel Turner, who in 1888 published *Bibliotheca Turneriana, Catalogue of the first portion of the library of . . . R. S. Turner. . . .*

4. Early 16th century Spanish novelist and publisher who lived in Rome and Venice. His *Amadis* (1533) and *Primaleón* (1534) were published in Venice.

5. Rawdon Lubbock Brown (1803–83) resided in Venice 1833–83, making careful investigations of the Venetian archives. His *Calendar of State Papers . . . Relating to English Affairs . . . in the Archives of Venice* (1864–84) is still important. He wrote other works on English and Italian history.

6. Published, 1886.

7. "Sir Thomas Browne," *Macmillan's Magazine*, LIV (1886), 5–18, was included in *Appreciations* (1889).

8. 1887; still frequently published.

9. See L 1533.

10. A poem on the habits of students.

1542. *To Charles Edward Sayle*[1]

Am Hof, Davos Platz, Switzerland. June 13 1886

My dear Mr Sayle

My long silence must have seemed to you quite unpardonable. It can only be explained, hardly excused, by the enormous mass of literary work I have had on my hands—2 new vols of R. in Italy [*The Catholic Reaction*] to correct & print, a book on Ben Jonson, a book on Philip Sidney, & two minor introductory essays to write—since January. This has tired & occupied me, & I suffer also from a stiffness of the right hand wh makes the constant use of the pen painful.

I have also had much anxiety about the illness of a daughter, with whom I went in May to Badenweiler. It was with difficulty that we brought her home alive.

Your last letter of May 26, has been going from Davos to Badenweiler & back again, so that has prevented my sending an earlier answer.

I hope to be here till the beginning of September, & I should be delighted if you were to pay me a visit on your journey. I am sorry that I cannot offer you a bedroom in my own house. But the invalidism of the daughter I mentioned, makes her mother wish to receive as few guests as possible this summer.

There is an excellent hotel within 5 minutes of my house: Hotel Buol. If you put up there, you will see as much of me as you like.

Your letter, & your portrait, far from "displeasing" me (as you suggest) were extremely interesting to me.

I advise you not to go to Venice just now. A friend of mine there [Horatio F. Brown], also is devoting himself to the poor people, writes a sad account of the city. Three people died in the house next his, & his own gondolier was only saved by prompt measures taken with heroic severity in time.

Believe me to be very truly yours

John Addington Symonds

If you are a pedestrian, a good way to come from Chur is to drive up to Langwies & walk over the Strela Pass.

---

1. See L 1502.

1543. *To Arthur Symons*

[Davos] June 14 1886.

Dear Mr Symons,

In the last I wrote you from Badenweiler[1] I think I told you I had a letter by me addressed to you, which I had refrained from sending. I was just going to tear this up to-night among a lot of lumber which is always eddying round me, when I gave it a glance, and thought I might forward it. It will at least show you that more than two months ago, I tried once to pay my debt of correspondence and to say things which seemed to me applicable. The long delay you must attribute to great diffidence in giving such advice as I have ventured on in the letter, and to the sense that I had said things crudely. I do not think I can better them by saying to say them more maturely; and the hesitation I have confessed to will convince you that what I now enclose (dated April 5)[2] must be taken by you with allowances. I should not send it, except that I must purge myself of an apparent neglect of *officia* toward you who have always been generous and kind to me, that in the main I hold by what I then wrote, and lastly that I think my explanations will enable you to discount "crudity."

Yours very sincerely

J. A. Symonds.

---

1. See L 1537.
2. The letter appears in its chronological place, L 1529.

1544. *To Charlotte Symonds Green*

Am Hof, Davos Platz, Switzerland. June 16 1886

My dearest Charlotte

I think you & Auntie [Mary Ann Sykes] may like to hear what Dr Ruedi has reported about Janet. It was only this morning that he examined her, since her last illness:—he had been in England.

His opinion is most serious. Up to the beginning of last April her right lung had been in a fairly good state, the left becoming gradually worse. He now finds extensive & active mischief extending from the top to the bottom of the right lung. This he explains by the hypothesis that the hemorrhage at Badenweiler was from the apex of the right lung, not as we thought from the left lung; & that much of the blood was re-inspired; & lodging in the tissues of the lung, set up the inflammatory processes at present at work.

He thinks Janet's state one of immediate danger, & holds out no hope for the future. But we all know of course how useless it is to predict anything in cases of consumption. I have myself been feeling quite certain ever since the first week at Badenweiler that Janet had entered upon a new phase of disease, & when we were dragging her home the other day from Chur, & she was suffering so terribly from pain & weakness, it struck me as obvious that she must be in the last stage.

Still I have always hoped that Ruedi might give a better account than what we dreaded. Now, so far as his diagnosis is worth anything the worst fears are confirmed. I cannot doubt the accuracy of his comparison between her present state & that of April last.

He wants us, as long as possible, to postpone getting a permanent house for her. He does not want us to proclaim the fact to her that we are making up our minds for the worst. She, however, is aware of her condition, I feel sure.

One thing surprises him: that she has now no fever. He says the disease is of a nature to make him expect a daily rise to 104° F. This fever she had at Badenweiler & on the journey. But now her temperature is not much above normal.

Goodbye & believe me most affecty yours

JA Symonds.

My hand is particularly stiff today.

1545. *To Arthur Symons*

[Postcard]

to: Arthur Symons
114 Abbey St.
Nuneaton, Warwickshire, Eng.

[Davos] June 17 1886

I had despatched my old belated letter[1] to you before I got yours of the 11th.

My R: in It: has got to p:112 of Vol 2; & the proofs of Ben Jonson have begun. I too am doing a Vol for the Camelot Classics, Sir Th: Browne. Miss Abdy Williams[2] broke down in health, had to give up time, & is gone to Italy with her husband. She is now Mrs Wickham. Mr [R. L.] Stevenson is & has long been a great invalid. He can do so much, however, & his constitution seems to hold out so well, that I hope he may over come in the end. I found yr Henry V[3] here, & thank you greatly for it. My eldest dr [Janet] was very ill at Badenweiler, myself quite as well as usual. I even thought of coming to England, & might have done so if I could have left her. I had no time for a letter, but wanted to answer yours.

JAS.

----

1. The letter of April 5th (L 1529), which he did not send until June 14. See L 1543.
2. Miss E. M. Abdy Williams, Symonds' distant cousin, edited *Time,* which published Symonds' "The Pathos of the Rose in Poetry" and some of his poems. See Ls 1479 and 1528.
3. Symons had published facsimile editions of the First and Third Quartos. See L 1528.

1546. *To Havelock Ellis*

Am Hof, Davos Platz, Switzerland. June 17 1886.

Dear Mr Ellis

My answer to your letter has been unavoidably postponed by the anxiety caused by my eldest daughter's serious illness. It was only by great care that we were able to bring her from Badenweiler to Davos.

Here I found yours of May 26 and also one from Mr Bullen.

It seems I made a mistake, when I suggested his collaboration. He writes very kindly about you. But he says that Messrs Nimmo regard this scheme as injurious to their own edition of the Dramatists.[1]

I never regarded the matter in this light. The Dr have been so often republished, and by so many firms, that they seem to me common property. I should also have thought that whatever popularizes an interest in such literature is likely to do good to scholarly and critical editions. But publishers never take this view.

Before I give a definite answer to your proposal regarding a general Introduction (which is flattering to me, and attractive) I must ask some questions.

1) How long would it have to be?

2) Into which volume would you put it?

3) What do Messrs Vizetelly offer in payment?—In your first letter, May 5, you mentioned ten or twelve guineas for a dramatist; in your second, May 20, you spoke of four guineas for a minor dramatist. In the last you speak of 12 guineas for the General Introduction.

I should like, in fine, to know whether for *Webster and Tourneur* (for example) they offer say 15 guineas; for *Heywood* 12 guineas. It happens to be of importance to me, in view of other work, to have precise terms fixed.

4) Do you rely on Messrs Vizetelly's solvency? I have heard that the firm has been more than once bankrupt. The general introduction would go well with some pre-Marlowe pieces: e.g. an interlude by J. Heywood, a play of Lyly, and one of Greene or Peele, or both. Who, by the way, is going to do Marlowe?

When these preliminaries are settled, I will take up *Webster and Tourneur*. The plays will be probably: Duchess of Malfi; Vitt. C.; Cure for a Cuckold (indicating by brackets the non-Websterian parts); and Revenger's Tragedy. Will this be a large enough volume? If not, could Appius and Virginia be added; or a selection of scenes?[2]

Believe me to be very truly yours

J.A. Symonds.

P.S. The Webster and the Tourneur have not reached me yet. But of course, as this letter indicates, I am in no hurry. I have my hands too pretty full of work.

---

1. Nimmo was a London publisher known for his artful products. His copyrights were bought up by Swan Sonnenschein in 1902. See Frank Mumby, *Publishing and Bookselling* (1954), pp. 298 and 312. We find no record of Nimmo's series; Routledge, however, had one which paralleled "The Mermaid" series.

2. *Webster and Tourneur* (1888) included "The White Devil," "The Duchess of Malfy," "The Atheist's Tragedy," and "The Revenger's Tragedy."

1547. To Edmund Gosse

[Postcard]

Am Hof. Davos Platz. June 26 1886

I cannot find much about Pietro Bertini.[1] He published 4 vols of *Rime* (Sonnets & Odes) between 1583 and 1588. These were addressed to princes of the Medici & Urbino. He also wrote a Sonnet of Introduction to the Sacrificio of Beccari[2] & a Lecture addressed to the Svegliati [Academy] of Pisa.[3] I have not got anything of his in any of my collections here. This makes me pretty certain that the Italians have not accepted him in their catena of good authors. There is a list of his publications in Mazzuchelli.[4] Tiraboschi[5] just mentions his name in a long list of inferior versifiers.

Yrs

J A Symonds

---

1. See L 1536, where one of Bertini's volumes is mentioned. A second of the four Symonds mentions is *Sonnetti parimenti e madrigali* [1586].
2. Agostino Beccari, *Il Sacrificio*, a pastoral (1555).
3. *Lezzione del s. cavalier Pietro Bertini, . . . necitato da lui nella fioritissma Accademia de gli Svegliati di Pisa* (Florence, 1588).
4. Giovanni Maria Mazzuchelli (1707–65), Italian literary encyclopaedist. His principal work is the *Scrittori d'Italia* (6 vols., Brescia, 1753–63).
5. Girolamo Tiraboschi (1731–94), *Storia della letteratura italiana* (14 vols., 1772–81).

1548. To Arthur Symons

[Davos] June 26, 1886.

Dear Mr Symons

Your letter of the 21st shows that my instinct not to send you what I wrote about your poems[1] was right. It is almost impossible to avoid hurting people in these matters, and I see that you are a little hurt by what I said. I wanted to tell you that I felt very doubtful myself about the quality of your work in verse; that it seems to me mature enough to justify appeal to the public; and that failure, by which I mean the kind of non-recognition you are almost certain to get, will do you good—not by taking down your conceit (for I have no reason to suppose you conceited) but by compelling you afterwards to work on quietly by yourself. As to finding a publisher who will publish a book of poems without money paid or guaranteed by the author, I must say I am not sanguine. If you find one, I shall at once congratulate you. It will be a sign that he expects unusual things from the book.

When Kegan Paul published my *Vagabunduli Libellus*[2] without payment from me, they wrote to say that they were departing from their usual method because I had a certain position in literature. But their terms were such that I shall never get a penny from that book. As for subjects to write on: I recommend you to read the Italian Novellieri, especially Bandello[3] and Masuccio,[4] in the original. I think you will find many hints and suggestions. I agree with you that it is important, if you want to make poetry the work of your life, not to get a reputation as a prose-writer first.

Now I must say with much regret that I cannot undertake to review your book[5] in the Academy. I write very few reviews, and can ill afford the time. I am by no means a competent critic of Browning, and should feel awkward about it. My own belief too is that it is best in literature for a man to cast his bread upon the waters, and not to trouble his head about how his books will be treated in this or that newspaper. I am not in the least offended by your asking me. It is natural that you should be anxious about a first attempt. And you were justified in turning your thoughts to me. It gives me cause for regret that I cannot accede to your request. About de Stendhal I see you ask a question. His *Nouvelles et Chroniques* and *Rome, Naples et Florence*[6] are worth looking at for picturesque Italian subjects.

Pray do not be offended by anything I have written. You will always find me frank in saying what I think.

Believe me most truly yours

J. A. Symonds.

P.S. I have published, as you know, a great many books. I can say with absolute sincerity that after each was out, I began at once to think about another, and let the fledged bantling take its chance. This has been the source of much peace of mind to me; and I do not believe that, if I had bothered my head about reviewers, the result would have been different.

---

1. L 1529, which Symonds did not send until June 14.
2. In 1884. The work sold slowly.

3. Matteo Bandello (1480?–1562), Italian prelate and novelist. His *Novelle* (4 vols., 1554–73) served as sources for Shakespeare and Massinger.

4. Masuccio da Salerno (ca. 1420–ca. 1476). Fifty of his novels written in Neapolitan dialect were published (1476) as *Il Novellino*.

5. *An Introduction to the Study of Browning* (1886). Symonds had reviewed Browning's *Aristophanes' Apology, The Inn Album,* and *Jocoseria* in *The Academy*, VII (April 17, 1875), 389–90; VIII (November 27, 1875), 543–44; and XXIII (March 31, 1883), 213–14.

6. See L 1529. Symonds was thinking of Stendhal's *Les Promenades dans Rome* (1829) and his *Rome, Naples et Florence* (1817).

1549. *To Havelock Ellis*

Am Hof, Davos Platz, Switzerland. June 27 1886.

Dear Mr Ellis

In reply to yours of June 19. I am quite satisfied with your arrangements and the terms offered. It seems to me that one play of Tourneur ought to go with Webster; and you know this (The Revenger's Tragedy) is sufficiently modernized in Hazlitt's Dodsley.[1] I will send some corrections of the text there. I have just carefully read Tourneur. But if you prefer to have a vol of Webster alone, I will do that.—Now that I understand your views about the Introduction, I will undertake it; and I hope you will put it into the Marlowe vol, *by yourself.* That would (to my mind) be the most agreeable and natural arrangement. You, as editor in chief, ought to start the series; and if you like me to write the Introduction, it would please me to be associated with you.

As to Messrs Vizetelly's solvency,[2] I do not know anything more than what Mr [A. H.] Bullen wrote me about their having been bankrupt. Please do not mention his name; and I think it would not be very wise to show my letter to the firm. What I said to you, was only on hearsay. But I wished to communicate it to you, thinking you might be able to make enquiries. Bullen's words are "From enquiries I have made I learn that Messrs V. are not very reliable and have been bankrupt several times of late years".

Believe me very sincerely yours

J. A. Symonds.

I have left the question of Arder of F.[eversham] & other Domestic Tragedies open. If you wish me to do it, I will. But it will have to be modernized, and I cannot engage to do that.

1. The play was included by Robert Dodsley (1703–64) in his *A Select Collection of Old English Plays* (12 vols., 1744), IV; in the 4th ed. (15 vols., 1874–76), by W. Carew Hazlitt, it is in X, the works having been chronologically arranged.

2. See L 1546, where Symonds raised the question.

1550. *To Arthur Symons*

[Davos, July, 1886]

[Dear Mr Symons]

. . . You are quite right to regard art, literature, as the noblest function of your life. What I gently said, and somewhat cynically perhaps, to the contrary, is very much the result of a long experience in renunciation and patience, the like of which you have not yet had to undergo. I think it best for men to arm themselves with stoicism as regards success (in the external or in proportion to their own ideals) and to maintain as a guiding principle what is the ultimate fact—namely, that art and literature are and never can be more than functions of human life. Life therefore first.

[Incomplete]

1551. *To Douglas William Freshfield*[1]

Am Hof, Davos Platz, Switzerland. July 3. 1886

Dear Mr Freshfield

I must not delay longer to answer your letter though I am sorry to say that I cannot be of much use with regard to this district of Graubünden. I am laid up with inflamed eyes & find it almost impossible to read my own proofs. Those you sent me I return, having looked them through sufficiently to see that they need no important alteration. There is one mistake about the inns in Davos Platz. Hotels Belvedere & Buol are not under the same management. The district has not changed materially since the last edition of your guidebook,[2] except that the Landwasser has been corrected which has improved the sanitary condition of the valley.

If you are doing anything for the guide to Tyrol, I should like to call your attention to a new hotel the Schweizerhof which has been opened in the village of Schluderns that is at the opening of the Buffalora Pass & is about a quarter of an hour's distance from Spondinig—at present the halting place between Stelvio, Finsturmünz, Etsch Thal & Buffalora. Spondinig is a very disagreeable place. Schluderns on the contrary is charming & the new inn kept by Swiss people is comfortable though unpretending. I wrote an article about Schluderns in the Pall Mall Gazette of April 10th of this year.[3]

I am sorry to send you such a stupid letter; but I am a very bad hand at dictating, & the failure of my eyes is only the sign of an overworked brain.

Believe me to be very sincerely yours,

J.A.Symonds.

---

1. Douglas William Freshfield (1845–1934) published several works on mountaineering in Switzerland and worked on Murray's *Switzerland, Alps of Savoy and Piedmont, Italian Lakes and Part of Dauphiné*, 2 parts, in the Foreign Handbook series. Freshfield edited *The Alpine Journal*, 1880–89.

2. Presumably *Across Country from Thonon to Trent. Rambles and Scrambles in Switzerland and the Tyrol* (1865).

3. "Among the Orchards of Tyrol," *Pall Mall Gazette*, XLI (April 10, 1886), 4–5. Babington does not list this item.

1552. *To Thomas Duff Gordon-Duff*[1]

Am Hof, Davos Platz, Switzerland. July 14 1886

Dear Mr Gordon Duff

I am so glad (as are we all) to hear from yours of Sunday that Mrs Duff enjoyed the journey to Pontresina & that she is not permanently the worse for it.

This proves, I hope, considerable strength of constitution & power of reacting against fatigue.

It is always disagreeable settling in a new place, especially when one has the cares of a polyglot family instead of the "ease of my inn."

By this time, however, the newness will have worn off, & you will be tasting the sweets of your own fireside

We thought much of you all during the doleful wet days wh followed your installment, & were only glad that you had not to face the bad weather on the road.

I get oil from
>Marchese della Stufa
>>Castagnolo

Lastra a Signa
Toscana
Italia

He sells it at his price to everybody, & will send it anywhere. You can write to him (in English) for details. Mr & Mrs Ross (née Janet Duff Gordon) go shares with him in the working of his estate. It so happens that my wife wrote today to order 24 bottles of the oil for us. As for the cigars, I will send you the man's price-list. He quotes per 1000, but tells in another column whether he supplies boxes of 100 or of 50. The price *per cigar* is equal for 1000 or 100, if he supplies 100; & so with 50. He will send samples at so much per cigar according to the rate quoted for the 1000. I should advise you to have samples (five or more) sent of any brands you fancy. You can write in English. If you like to mention my name, you will be well served, for I am a pretty good customer. Tell him whether you like dark, light, or medium.

What you say about our conversations here is very gratifying to me. I assure you I enjoyed them all, & I have only felt that I ran on to unwarrantable lengths in my monologue. I hope we may live to have many more. It seems to me that not only sermons (wh are good things, very) but also the frank speech of friends in colloquy may be of infinite service. Only you must come down upon me, if I prose & wander. This you can always do, though you cannot check a pulpit orator.

My eyes are still giving me much trouble. I write rather wildly from not being well by candlelight.

Yesterday I guided my wife & Lotta & Madge alone from Glarus over Monstein & Jennisberg—all along the precipices of the Züge, where there is no proper path—to Wiesen. I was very thankful when I got to Jennisberg. We lost our way in a wood for ¾ of an hour & I felt then what a fool I had been to bring them into such a place. However, all ended well; & after 5 hours we were lunching with [unclear] at [Christian] Palmy's.[2]

With our kindest regards to Mrs Duff, believe me ever most sincerely yours

J A Symonds

If I come to Pontresina, I shall certainly pay my respects, & shall be delighted to try Edgardo Ferrario's[3] art. I should put up at the Krone, wh I take it is not far from you.

---

1. Thomas Duff Gordon-Duff (1848–1923) of Drummuir, Castle Keith, Banffshire;

educated at Harrow and Trinity College, Oxford; married (1875) Pauline Emma (died of consumption, 1888), eldest daughter of Sir Charles Tennant (1823–1906) and therefore sister of Margot Tennant (1864–1945). See Ls 1571 and 1619.

2. Christian Buol's cousin who succeeded Buol as Symonds' favorite.

3. Probably the chef at Gordon-Duff's hotel.

1553. *To Charles Edward Sayle*

Am Hof, Davos Platz, Switzerland. July 20 1886

My dear Mr Sayle

I am very glad to get your letter from Bellagio. Often have I wondered how you had made the journey.

You need no excuses for your manner of leave-taking here. I think that I rather should excuse myself for lecturing & monologizing to the extent I did.

In either case, life is not long enough to make much of such matters.

It is good that you are well settled & in Italian quarters, at Bellagio. I am afraid that I can send you no literature upon the Lake [Como]. It was not Roden Noel who wrote the poem I spoke about. A tolerably learned essay by myself on Giangiacomo Medici, il Medeghino[1] would not interest you much, I take it.

I suppose you reached Como from Tirano through the night. This was as it ought to be.

You mention a pretty good list of Italian books. But you have left out one, wh I must recommend: viz Benvenuto Cellini's Autobiography That teaches more about Italians in the past, & the present too, than any book I know.

I am just now beginning to make a new English translation of the same, & find the work agreeable.

I followed Mr Broadbent[2] to the grave this morning. He died on Friday night.—R.I.P.—Life here is not all laughter & hob-nobbing with peasants; though of that side of it you saw quite enough. Indeed it is so tragic that the escape into common pastimes justifies itself to me.

Broadbent has left me all his fine negatives of portraits. We were to have made many experiments in the art, as an adjunct to sculpture & painting, this summer. But now he lies in the grave smothered with exotic white roses, waiting for the snows of—how many wild Decembers?

I shall like to hear how things go with you, & how you get along with

Sapine & Italian. I hope he will prove a good fellow & a good linguist. You engaged him rather rashly. I know how jealous those men are if their padrone changes for another boatman.

Thanks very many for the Fame[3] wh you will send me. I shall appreciate it fully. Thanks too for the Sonnet. I like the terzets much, except for the one word *madly*. If you could get a word with the value of *negligently,* I should like it better. I will mention one or two other little things. Line 1. I should prefer *sprang* for *spring—heart* for *thought.* Line 5. I don't like *chime* for 2 reasons—rhyme exactly repeated, & rather a vague word. I should prefer

caves
prisoner in the chains of Time.
bonds

This carries out the vaguely indicated Platonic thread of thought.

Line 9. *Sprang* again.

Line 12. For *madly,* query *coldly.*

these suggestions, if you don't like them. Take them as proof that I have studied the sonnet.

I am just going off to live for a few days in one of my farm houses on the Lake here. I go alone, to live with the peasants after peasant fashion.

Send me further news of you, & believe me yours truly

J. A. Symonds.

Labor Improbus [work of inferior quality] goes on here. The proofs of 3 vols accumulating, with a 4th vol in sight.

---

1. "Como and Il Medeghino," in *Sketches and Studies in Italy* (1879), pp. 323–38. Symonds links the corsair Medeghino (1498–1555), one of the blonder of the Medicis, with the Cathedral of Como because, he says, "We are compelled to blend our admiration for the loveliest and purest works of art amid the choicest scene of nature with memories of execrable crimes and lawless characters."

2. Percival Broadbent, the photographer, died on July 16, age 34.

3. A photograph of "Fame," a painting by Annibale Caracci (1560–1609), the Bolognese painter. Sayle included this sonnet, "The Genius of Fame," inspired by the painting, in his *Erotidia* (Rugby, ed. ltd. to 220 copies, 1889), p. 54. The only suggestion of Symonds he followed was to change *spring* to *sprang.* See also L 1554.

1554. *To Charles Edward Sayle*

Davos July 25 1886

Dear Mr Sayle

Thank you very much for the photo of [Annibale] Caracci's Fame,[1] wh duly arrived three days ago.

It is certainly a very charming composition, though the execution in parts (espy the cherubs) betrays Bolognese coarseness & superficiality.

The genius holds a golden crown in his hand. That looks as though he meant to confer honours on somebody, & not as though he were soaring after the Ideal.

I cannot write much today. My eyes have given way, & I have also got my lung wrong.

Beside that the Master of Balliol [Benjamin Jowett] & Lyulph Stanley[2] are staying with us. They came from Bellagio. I wonder whether you saw them there.

Very truly yours

J A Symonds

---

1. See L 1553.
2. Edward Lyulph Stanley (1839–1925), 4th Baron Sheffield of Roscommon and 4th Baron Stanley of Alderley; lawyer and educationist; Symonds' friend from Balliol College days. (See L 125.)

1555. *To Edmund Gosse*

Am Hof, Davos Platz, Switzerland. July 31 1886

My dear Gosse

I duly received from Longmans your "Raleigh" a few days ago, together with two other volumes of the ["English Worthies"] series. I have read yours first, & with deep & sustained interest. It seems to me in all points an excellent piece of work; exhaustive of the material, judicious in spirit, & animated by flashes of literary originality. I could not write too strongly about the chapters "Cadiz," "In the Tower" and "The End." They have made a deep and, I hope, a lasting impression on my mind.

I feel that, working within the narrow limits of a book of this kind, under the obligation of being complete & historically conscientious, you have had (owing to the copiousness of matter & the variety of events in your hero's biography) to charge your pages with multitudes of names facts & dates which must have made the artistic presentation of the main personage very difficult. But I think you have succeeded; & it is no drawback to your "Raleigh" that it demands a careful or an impassioned student to apprehend its true merits.

It is an extraordinarily interesting history: most interesting perhaps because of the mystery which still envelops the secret of Raleigh's fall. You have indicated the kernel of the problem in the pages you write upon his sudden & unaccountable unpopularity. Do not you feel that the historian's greatest difficulty lies in estimating the effect of personality (physical & moral)—a quantity at once so undefinable & so potent—upon the otherwise appreciable factors in a man's career? It is just *this* wh always eludes our analysis, when we have to deal with a man like Raleigh. I have recently been puzzled and baffled by this elusive factor while attempting to explain the fate of Torquato Tasso.[1]

But I will not write an essay on the subject. I only feel, after reading your "Raleigh," that there is an irreducible element in his misfortunes which, if we had personally known him or had conversed with both his friends & enemies, we should have better comprehended as inseparable from his incommunicable *self*.

I hope you will receive from Longmans my "Ben Jonson," wh I have just finished—a very slight performance in comparison with your book. By the way, I see that you refer [to] young Raleigh's escapade with Jonson to London, whereas (on the authority of Drummond)[2] I took it certainly to have taken place in Paris.

I shall soon have a life of Sir Philip Sidney in the press. As a contributor to the English Men of Letters, you will probably receive it. If you do not, please let me have a p[ost]:c[ard]: so that I may give myself the pleasure of sending you a copy. I found it difficult to make Sidney interesting to myself, & so I fear that I shall have failed to present him in a interesting light to the public. But you will see & judge. Having written what I had to write, I need not inflict on you here my difficulties & reluctance with regard to him.

Pray remember me most kindly to Mrs Gosse, &, with sincere thanks to you again for this masterly contribution to English biography, believe me to be most truly yours

John Addington Symonds.

1. See *The Renaissance in Italy: The Catholic Reaction,* Chaps. VII and VIII.

2. William Drummond (1585–1649) preserved the record of his visit to Ben Jonson in *Notes of Ben Jonson's Conversation with William Drummond* (Shakespeare Society, 1842).

1556. *To Charles Edward Sayle*

Am Hof, Davos Platz, Switzerland, August 25 1886

Dear Mr Sayle

You must excuse my writing both ill & little: for I am suffering greatly from weak eyes & can only just see out of one of them.

Thank you for your account of your Itn tour. You tell me, however, so often "not to mind" what you found & saw in the places you came to that I have no clear notion of what you did see & find.

I should like indeed to hear more of what interested you in Venice.

I fear I know of no better photographer at Naples than Saumer. Marion in Soho Square used to be a great depot for European photos of all sorts.

We have had such a dismal summer here, raining incessantly. I have been ill too in the most cheerless of ways, & am now, as I said, more than half blind.

Goodbye & believe me very truly yours

J A Symonds—

1557. *To Havelock Ellis*

Am Hof, Davos Platz, Switzerland. August 30 1886

Dear Mr Ellis,

I must not delay longer to write to you, though I have but bad news to send.

My eyesight has failed, and I can neither read nor write now. I am going on Wednesday to consult an oculist at Zürich, whose directions I shall follow—with I hope good results.

Until I know the nature of my trouble better and the way to meet it, I am unable to foresee what sort or amount of work I shall be allowed to do.

I will promise to pay the best and first attention to the "general introduction";[1] and as I have the matter pretty well in my head, I trust that I may be able to discharge my debt to you without serious delay.

Indeed, if need were, I think I could dictate the small number of pages in a few days to one of my daughters, even though I should be unable to see. But I do not like dictation. It interferes with proportion and spoils style. I should prefer to wait until I can do something with my own eyes.

At present I am writing with one eye, the other being bound up; and I am warned that to do this for more than five minutes at a time may seriously compromise my use of it.

I am sorry; but no one suffers so much as I do from this mishap. Habitually ill and weak, I have overtaxed my strength, it seems.

Roden Noel, who has been staying here three weeks, will tell you how serious the affliction is.

Very sincerely yours

J. A. Symonds.

---

1. See L 1549.

1558. *To Horatio Forbes Brown*

Soglio, Val Bregaglia, Sept. 16, 1886.

[Dear Horatio]

I cannot tell you how much I am enjoying this escape from the "narrowing nunnery walls"[1] of Davos. It is the first time, for I know not how long, that I have got away without preoccupations, without work to be done, without the demands that friendship with humble folk of different breeding from oneself entails.

After we parted at Samaden, Catherine, Madge, and I spent some hours at St. Moritz, and then walked by a beautiful lake-path from Sils Maria to Maloja. There we met no less than seventeen English acquaintances of all sorts and descriptions. But on Monday we broke away from these for a seven hours' walk up the sublime Muretto-thal and on the Forno Glacier—a really stupendous piece of high Italian, not Swiss, scenery. The valley, though it starts upward from Maloja, drains into Bregaglia; and the Muretto pass leads easily, past Disgrazia, to Sondrio in Valtellina. This, I suppose, accounts for the wild exuberance of vegetation and the romance of cloven rocks in the ravine. Such cedar-like *cembras*[2] I have nowhere seen.

Next day we explored the immediate neighbourhood of the Maloja, which, too, is far richer in detailed beauty than the winter led me to expect. A walk of about two hours' winding along the precipices above the pass, in spite of its hideous name, "Promenade des Artistes," is certainly one of the finest things in the Alpine region.

Paul[3] had come up to see me; so I took him on Tuesday to Soglio; and here we have been since. I don't know how long we shall stay. It is quite one of the most remarkable places I have ever been in. Just 1,000 feet above Promontogno on a precipitous grassy bracket between chestnuts and pines, it commands the whole Bregaglia—to N.E. the mountains of Maloja, to S.W. the mountains heading Lago di Como. In front expand the marvellous jagged outlines of the Albigna and Bondasca glaciers and their peaks, of which one sees a part at Promontogno.

The inn is a corner of an old Salis palace, with its panelling, stoves, pictures, armour, beaten iron-work and furniture intact; very well kept in a somewhat negligent Italian way—picturesque and characteristic and un-tourist-like to heart's content.

I walked this morning through one huge forest of chestnuts, over those turfy swards you know, and among the purple granite boulders, to Castasegna. It was a long dreamy idyll, of the most musical poetry, in fact.

Yesterday I spent wholly basking on the rocks that dominate Bondo—plunging my eyes downward those sheer thousand feet, and lifting them to the airy pinnacles of ice and crag men call Bondasca.

I wish in many ways that it had suited your plans to come with us here. I am certain it would have fascinated you—the thoroughly Italian feeling, the grand old palace to live in, and the wild intolerable beauty of nature. I specially affect chestnut forests, and have seen and loved many; but I never saw one equal to this between Soglio and Castasegna.

[Incomplete]

---

1. Tennyson, "Guenevere," ll. 340 and 671.
2. A species of pine: the Swiss stone pine.
3. We have not been able to trace Paul.

1559. *To T. S. Perry*

Dear Mr Perry

I am really surprised at your goodness in going on writing to me such bright & interesting letters, when I have been so long dumb. It is very kind of you, for I always intensely enjoy what you send me, & only wish often that you could be talking to me instead.

I have some excuse. It is this. My eyes, which were always a weak point, have given way, & I have, all the same, had to do a great deal of trying work. The result is that I have been unable to read any thing for some months, & have been obliged to economize correspondence. I am just on my way (circuitiously) to consult a great oculist at Zürich.

I will tell you what I have been doing since Jany 1. First of all, I finished & prepared for press the two last vols of my "Renaissance in Italy." They deal with the Catholic Reaction. Then I began to print them; & while the proofs were being corrected, I set about writing two books—one on Ben Jonson (for Lang's series of English Worthies)— the other on Sir Philip Sidney (for Morley's English Men of Letters). These were finished in May; & then they had to be seen through the press. Meanwhile I had undertaken several minor things; & engaged in a work of considerable length—a new translation into English of Cellini's Memoirs, if you please! I enjoy doing this much, now that I have got into the style. But after finishing 150 out of the 495 pp of Le Monnier's edn,[1] my eyes grew so alarmingly bad that I had to stop.

We have had multitudes of visitors at Davos this summer, the names of most of whom you would not know. But among them were B. Jowett, Henry Sidgwick, Lylulph Stanley, Roden Noel, Oscar Browning,[2] Mary Robinson (the poetess), & H. Forbes Brown (of Venetian repute). I have derived much good from their society. What I most suffer from at Davos, is the lack of congenial friends & stimulating conversation.

We are (my wife & one of my daughters) reading in the Italian sunlight of this wonderfully coloured place with the wild granite crags of Bregaglia tossed around it—the roaring streams, the russet pines, & the velvety depth of chestnut woods. I muse & meditate, vaguely dimly seeing into things I want to handle. My ladies spend their hours in drawing. Both can paint in water colours well. There has been a great shooting-festival here; the little town is full of Italian soldiers—carbonieri Delle Alpi—& fiery-eyed dusky contadini. Two military bands perambulate the streets. A camel & three monkeys are performing in the piazza, beneath the ruined castle of Gian Giacomo de' Medici—Il Medeghino.[3]

My wife & I take monthly delight in Lemuel Barker.[4] It is through & through good; & we are so glad to hear that you call it truer Boston than [Henry] James's work.

Please remember me to Mr [W. D.] Howell[s]. I am so pleased to have the fine portrait of him you sent me, also his article on the Russian D.[5]

Now forgive my stopping! My eyes forbid my doing more. Please give my best regards to Mrs Perry & believe me most sincerely yours

J A Symonds—

1. *La Vita di Benvenuto Cellini, scritta da lui medisimo, restituita esattamente alla lezione originale . . . per cura di B. Bianchi* (Florence, F. Le Monnier, 1852). Symonds' translation was published by John C. Nimmo (1887).

2. Benjamin Jowett, Symonds' Balliol master (see L 36). Henry Sidgwick (see L 316). Lylulph Stanley (see L 125). Roden Noel (see L 162). Oscar Browning (1837–1923), author, master at Eton, 1860–75, lecturer in history and political science from 1875, wrote lives of George Eliot (1890), Dante (1891), and Peter the Great (1898), several studies in 19th century history, a *History of Educational Theories* (1881), and 2 autobiographical works: *Memories of Sixty Years at Eton, Cambridge, and Elsewhere* (1910) and *Memories of Later Years* (1923). Katharine Symonds Furse (*H & P*, p. 134) reports that Browning, during his stay at Am Hof, made Margaret Symonds "very angry by asking her where, in Davos, he could get his corns cut."

3. For Symonds on Gian Giacomo de' Medici (Il Medeghino) see *The Cornhill Magazine*, XXXVIII (1878), 342–51, and *Sketches and Studies in Italy* (1879).

4. William Dean Howells, *The Minister's Charge, or, Lemuel Barker*, appeared serially in *The Century*, XXXI, XXXII, XXXIII (February–December, 1886).

5. William Dean Howells on Dostoyevsky, *Literary World*, XVII (October 30, 1886), 364; an unsigned essay.

1560. *To Havelock Ellis*

Hôtel z. weissen Kreuz Chur, Sept. 23, 1886.

Dear Mr Ellis,

I am travelling about for the sake of my eyes, and having a few minutes here to spare, write to tell you I received your last note at Reichenau. I am glad to hear the General Introduction seems right to you. I have lately written three extra paragraphs to insert on the proof: 1) on the

London theatre 2) on the specific note of the Eln Drama as a whole 3) on its main periods, with short characterizations of all the prominent playwrights.

I have also during the last days jotted down my introduction to Webster and Tourneur; so that when you can send me Dyce's edn[1] of the former and Dodsley's "Revenger's Tragedy"[2] by the latter, I can almost immediately place that book in your hands.

I have made up my mind that there is no proof, and no great probability, of Webster's having had a hand in "A Cure for a Cuckold." But if your publishers could get permission from Mr Spring Rice[3] to reprint his "Love's Graduate," I think I would put it in the volume. The plays would be:

Vitt. Cor.

Duchess of M.   Webster

Appius and Virginia

Love's Graduate   ?

Revenger's Tragedy   Tourneur

I must say I should prefer to omit "Love's Graduate" and include Tourneur's "Atheist's Tragedy." But then you would have to get that modernized from Collins' edn.[4] What do you say to this?

Thank you for your enquiries about my eyes. I find that rest, and driving about our mountains have done them good already. But I am now on my way to consult Prof Horner at Zürich.[5]

Yours very truly

J. A. Symonds.

---

1. The Rev. Alexander Dyce, *The Works of John Webster* (4 vols., 1830).

2. See L 1549.

3. Stephen E. Spring-Rice had edited *Love's Graduate,* a comedy by John Webster (1885); Edmund Gosse supplied a prefatory essay.

4. Symonds included only *The Atheist's Tragedy* and *The Revenger's Tragedy* in his edition. John Churton Collins had edited *The Plays and Poems of Cyril Tourneur* (1878).

5. Friedrich Horner (1831–86), Zurich physician, professor of ophthalmology and director of the Ophthalmological Clinic of the University of Zurich.

1561. *To Mary Robinson*

Am Hof, Davos Platz, Switzerland. Sept: 28. 1886

My dear Miss Robinson

I am writing to you with blind eyes which must not follow the letters. So excuse, as I think you will, mere symbols.

I got your card from Rue Alger, & was glad to think that you had fallen into so nice an old-world French appreciative colony. I can see you in the midst of them.

You came here, & vanished, like a dream. We have a heavy tread up here, like the oxen & the peasants we consort with.

I am afraid you found us only such. And yet, your good dear thrill of emotion at parting with my wife & myself in the upper chambers abides with me as token that you will not forget us.

Do not forget us, even though we are purblind & more than uncommonly stupid through failings in the corporeal environment that means eyes & nerves.

I think you care for us. And I feel grateful for this. I should like to retain it as a precious possession for ever.

I am one who can say more from the heart on paper than I can in words or in personal contact. I do not choose that the feelings I have should overcome me. And so I now remember an hour when you were here, in this same room, half-fainting, & I wrote at the present table, half-laughing at you.

Forgive me, if I seemed brutal. Let me always have the thought of you, as of one who will not lightly let my hand-touch go.

We had a fortnight's journey in the mountains, part Italy, part Switzerland. This did me good. But at the end of it came an oculist, who said I had abused my eyes & must give them rest. So I wrote to you out of the dark now into your clarity of vision.

A riverderci!

J A Symonds.

I hope your Mother was not the worse from being here—that your Father was not too much bored—& that your friend Mr Mc Coll[1] is in good cue as he ought to be.

---

1. Dugald S. MacColl (1859–?), champion of the French Impressionists; educated at

Oxford and the Westminster and Slade Schools of Art; art critic (1890 and after) for the *Spectator, Saturday Review,* and *Week-end Review;* editor of *Architectural Review;* keeper of Tate Gallery (1906–11) and of the Wallace Collection (1911–24). John Rothenstein, *Men and Memories* (1931), p. 171, calls MacColl "the Ruskin of the Impressionists." His "independence and his high intellectual gifts gained him a foremost place among the critical writers of the 'nineties, and he became a power in the land." His most influential book was *Nineteenth Century Art* (1902).

1562. *To Janet Ross*

Stalla-Bivio Oct: 6 1886

Dear Mrs Ross

I am detained at a little wayside inn upon the Julier by bad weather, and find in my pocket what I thought I had lost—the pieces you wanted me to translate. So I have turned them into English, badly I fear; for these Stornelli[1] never get anything like their wayward careless prose in another language.

Catherine & I have been making a long walk in these mountains, long for such elderly people as we are; & were wanting to cross a high pass into one of the most tempting valleys of the Alps—a long secluded gorge, where the folk talk a language of their own—some very primitive Romansch—& where they had no communication with the outer world from the first snow-fall in the autumn until April. The weather was glorious yesterday: but today it looks suddenly ugly, & the old landlord of the inn (like the old man in "Excelsior")[2] warns us that if we are overtaken by snow in Avers, we may have to stay there in the minister's house—for there is no hostelry in the whole long valley of thirty miles—till spring melts the snows again. The prospect is not pleasant, for the inhabitants have no wine or fresh meat or wheaten bread. Therefore, much to our disgust we must for this year abandon our enterprise of penetrating into what is surely one of the oddest old-world places left in Switzerland.[3] There is some thing to my mind attractive in the mere thought of such a dale in this land of roads, railways & Cook's tourists.

Well. I will come to the Stornelli.

> Flower of July!   (Fierdistate)
> Like a loadstone you draw me, & there must I lie,
> Wherever you lure me & force me to fly.

Flower of the peach!   (Fioria di pesca)
You've cast me a spell enclosed in a peach;
In my pocket I put it, nor knew where 'twould reach.

O flower of gold!   (O fior d'oro)
Love's prisoner am I, when your face I behold;
Your beauty & grace by no tongue can be told.

Flower of the apple!   (Fiorin di vola)
Your sweet pretty face is a picture, I swear:
You're made all of manna & sugarcane rare!

Of floweret of flowers!   (Fiorin fiorello)
Of all the fair flowerets that ever shall flower
The flower of my love will be first at all hours

Fair blossom of Love!   (Fiorin d'amore)
Let it talk that sharp impudent tongue of all ill,
Love him who loves you, let him prate who prate will.

These versions are not worth sending you. Take them only as a sign that I gladly try to do what you ask.

    With kind regards to Mr Ross & to the Marchese[4] believe me very sincerely yours

                         J. A. Symonds.

P.S. I have done the songs into anapaestic rhythm. I think the iambic in English would be too heavy. But as I cannot hear you singing them, I fear my measures may not suit the tunes. If that is so, I will try to do them again, if you will send me some indication of the musical accent.

---

    1. Plural for stornello, a short popular lyric, especially Tuscan, sometimes improvised.

    2. Longfellow's "Excelsior," ll. 16–17, a warning to the banner-carrying youth:

        "Try not the Pass!" the old man said;
        "Dark lowers the tempest overhead."

    3. Brown, Biography, p. 412:
The return to Davos was made over the Splügen, and, as Symonds writes to Roden Noel, the party had "three jolly days at Reichenau, exploring the demesne of the old castle of Rhäzüns," a place which fascinated Symonds by its grim situation above the valley of the Hinter Rhein. The autumn ended with an attempt to penetrate the Averserthal.
The letter to Noel is lost.

    4. The Marchese della Stufa, whose productive estate the Rosses shared. See L 1552.

Davos, October 8, 1886.

[Dear Horatio]

I have been wandering again, partly for my eyes' sake. Walked one day up to Fluela. Had a superb night ascent of the Schwartzhorn, with an indescribably splendid morning star, and a long autumnal dawning round the Alpine circle. Walked with Catherine over the Kuhalpthal and Tuorsthal to Bergün—seven hours—the finest piece of scenery in this neighbourhood, and I have only accidentally stumbled on it. Drove to Stalla on the Julier in order to penetrate into the mysterious valley of Avers—a valley about thirty miles in length, blocked by the Septimer at the head and by terrific gorges (so they say) at the exit into Splügen. There the weather broke, and the good old host told us we might be snowed up in Avers for at least a fortnight, perhaps six months, and must certainly then live on rye and milk and cheese and dry flesh without wine. Like the old man in "Excelsior,"[1] he warned us off. We rushed back with extra post, and here we are again.

October 15.—I have just made a discovery of this and another unfinished letter, the second to the Editor of the "Fortnightly,"[2] both of which I thought I had completed and sent to their addresses. This, I fear, is only too characteristic of me, and of the state in which I keep my papers, to demand more than the ordinary apologies.

Well, what I thought I had already written to you was an apology for my hasty remark to A——, that you had from me so and so much money for him.[3] He shall hear from me how it is, and that I have plenty of things to do with my money besides sending him lump sums of two or three hundred francs four or five times a year. Only, I cannot jabber this out in Italian as fluent as that which I heard you producing last night in a dream I had of you and some Venetian workmen. You overwhelmed the fellows with voluble argument, expostulation, and abuse—mingled *à la* Cellini.[4]

Of course the humour of my brain came out of this Cellini translation, which I have been pushing vigorously forward till, last night, I completed half of the whole. I find it a stiff exhausting job. It makes demands upon every department in the faculty of language.

Could you do me this service? Ask your locksmith, the man who made your staircase railings, what the exact meaning of *"bandelle,"*[5] when used in relation to a prison door, may be. I want to hit the precise significance of this feature in a door, in order to explain some hazy points about Cellini's escape from St. Angelo.

And now, since I have asked one service, I will ask another. It is this. Do you know of any book which treats of the old modes of reckoning time in Italy? They reckoned differently in different places, and at different seasons of the year. Half the picturesque value of a narration, in which the exact hour of day or night means something, is lost if one cannot present the moment in time to an English reader.

You ask me a question which I will at this late season answer. It was whether I know of anybody who has treated the ethics of tyrannicide in Italy outside my book. I can point to no source. I collected all I could find, scattered in the histories I read, upon the subject; but, except the few pages in Machiavelli, to which I must have given reference, I have never come across a treatment of the subject on principles. The Jesuits at a somewhat late date, Mariana,[6] for example, did so in the polemical works of ethical philosophy they prepared against Protestant princes. But the far more interesting question of tyrannicide in Renaissance Italy was discussed partly upon the records of Plutarch, &c., and partly upon the authority of Thomas Aquinas.

[Incomplete]

---

1. See L 1562.
2. See L 1591.
3. Probably Antonio Salin, Brown's gondolier.
4. Cellini was known for his volatility.
5. Literally "running straps."
6. Juan Mariana (1536–1624), Spanish Jesuit theologian; his chief works were *De rebus Hispaniae* (20 vols., 1592; 30 vols., 1605) and *Historia General de España* (2 vols., 1601).

1564. *To Horatio Forbes Brown*

Davos, Oct. 27 [1886]

[Dear Horatio]

I have been drowned in a morass of Cellini,[1] working eight hours a day, and sleeping afterwards like a pig. I have got through four-fifths of the translation. But it is a very heavy bit of work, taxing all the resources of the English language in two very different ways—first, to match his immense vocabulary of popular speech and technical terminology; next, to cope with the wearisomeness of his perpetual repetitions in the connective tissues of a narration. Just now I am well-nigh worn out again; though, thanks to good regime and the Zürich doctor, my eyes are perceptibly stronger. I wish Venice were not so far off! In these golden lingering autumn days I think too often with a pang of Italy. The snow delays long this year; yet it must come at last. Meanwhile, it seems at times a sin to waste the last glad hours in work, which could be done as well in winter when the magic of the world is over.

Do you know the Trichinopolies[2] you gave me have proved a great success. I have sent for another box and am smoking one now while I write. I have also ordered more of several sorts. I believe they are good to lay down here. They lose less in flavour than Havannas, and are very wholesome.

À propos of assassination and the feeling about tyrannicide and homicide in general, I will send you, if you like it, references to Jesuitical Casuists whom you will doubtless find in the Marciana.[3] I believe the earlier Italian sentiment was founded upon mere *Faust-recht* [club-law], bolstered up by some words in S. Thomas Aquinas and the great examples of Plutarch.

It is curious that we remain so vague about Italian reckoning of time. In some places they certainly reckoned from sunrise and sunset. But in Rome they reckoned, I think, only from sunset, for the latest hours of *afternoon* are in summer 22 and 23. After the latter begins *una ora di notte* [first hour of night] and so onwards. I imagine it is impossible to fix the exact hour now with precision, in dealing with a document like "Cellini's Memoirs," where the season of the year is generally undefined. But I shall be truly grateful if your own researches indicate an authority upon this topic. How many of these once familiar things seem to escape the human mind after the lapse of a few years!

[Incomplete]

---

1. The translation of Cellini's *Autobiography* (1887).
2. Cigars made from tobacco grown near Trichinopoly, 250 miles southwest of Madras, India.
3. The famous Venetian library.

1565. *To Edmund Gosse*

Am Hof, Davos Platz, Switzerland. Oct 28 1886

PRIVATE

My dear Gosse

I must not delay longer to thank you for the special copy of your reply to the Quarterly,[1] or to postpone telling you how deeply I feel for yourself & Mrs Gosse in this most cruel time of trial.

I have not read the Quarterly article. Therefore I cannot express an opinion on the merits of the case.

But whatever those merits may be, the personal animus displayed by Mr Collins,[2] the PMG,[3] & Punch,[4] seems to me as unmistakeable as it is unwarrantable.

This gives me a deep sense of pain, as though I had been hurt myself; & I feel that the whole republic of letters suffers.

Criticism, both severe & thoughtlessly wounding, we must expect if we write books. We ought to be glad to have our blunders pointed out, & to be patient if our style is ridiculed. I at least am well used to these things.

But I hardly see how literature is to be carried forward, if this tyranny of journalism continues. It will be necessary to keep our thoughts locked up in our own hearts & studies. When I think what we earn in wages by the thankless Muse, & what we are exposed to of annoyance, time can be better employed in breaking stones than in giving the best we have of our own mind & heart to an ungrateful public.

I find it more difficult to write to you now than I did when the PMG first opened its guns upon you. Living quite outside the sphere of English literary society, I am forced to deal in generalities. But you can see how very painfully I feel, & how distressed I am not only for yourself but also for the whole commonwealth of letters.

I hope & feel sure that you will be sustained by the sympathy of friends. I know that your work can endure even this fiery ordeal, & that your reputation will survive it. But it is terribly hard to bear.

Believe me with kindest regards to your wife to be

Very sincerely yours

J ASymonds—

---

1. Gosse's reply, "The 'Quarterly Review' and Mr. Gosse," was a letter to the editor

of *The Athenaeum*, No. 3078 (Oct. 23, 1886), 534–35. Gosse later printed this letter privately (1886).

2. John Churton Collins' review of Gosse's *From Shakespeare to Pope. An Inquiry into the Causes and Phenomena of the Rise of Classical Poetry in England*, "English Literature at the Universities," *Quarterly Review*, CLXIII (1886), 289–329, is a thorough and devastating attack on Gosse. The book, the reviewer observes, reveals many "gross . . . blunders" of fact and chronology, and pretentiousness and poor style. It may be useful, since by its illustration of the way English literature "should not be taught," it "may direct attention to the manner in which it should be taught" (p. 312). See also L 1513.

3. The *Pall Mall Gazette*, XLIV (Oct. 10, 1886), 6:

The *New York Tribune* says that Mr. Edmund Gosse's servants have given notice . . . because of the insults to which they have been subjected by their fellow menials on account of the *Quarterly Review's* attack upon their master! We take this paragraph from the New York *Critic* . . . "[T]he story—so we are informed—was told by Mr. Gosse of his cook, who, he says, gave notice to leave because 'master's name had been so much in the papers.'" We are glad, however, to be able to state that this admirable woman has subsequently changed her mind: a friend . . . having assured her that "you needn't mind them newspapers; they do say such things."

4. Though we have not found the actual reference to the remarks in *Punch*, some stanzas, "Poet Gosse and the 'Quarterly,'" in the tone of the quarrel, appeared in XCI (Oct. 30, 1886), 209.

1566. *To Charlotte Symonds Green*

[Davos Platz Nov. 3, 1886]
[Notes following T. H. Green's death copied from Symonds' journal Nov. 3, 1886.]

[Dear Charlotte]

I find these notes of talks with Tom, wh may interest you.

J.A.S.

Norfolk Square, London[1]
"God is to the world as a man is to his life: his work: his life-work." This was probably condensed by me from much Green said to explain how he thought God lived the world out, & yet the world was separate from God—to us work.

A definition of current poetry: "The ordinary articulation of much that might as well remain inarticulate."

I can guarantee the essential accuracy of these remarks.

After reading over what the most intimate & eminent friends of Green wrote about him, & comparing their recollections with my own conception of his character, I am powerfully struck with the *unity of impression* stamped by him on men & minds so different. The divergent lines of reminiscence are more attributable to the divergences of temperament in his friends than to any divergence of effect produced by him—one man seizing what suited his own nature most, but all exhibiting the same personality as vigorously energetic. Through the differences of statement shines forth the single man. This is to me very noticeable; for this is exactly what a strong self-centered individuality ought on a priori grounds to effectuate.

Green's practical grasp on political conditions & his sympathy with the vast masses of a nation, the producers & bread-makers, the taxpayers & inadequately represented, strike all alike. Personally I may say that he inducted me into the philosophy of democracy & socialism—not in any sentimental or visionary or reactionary way—but on the grounds on wh both democracy & socialism are active factors in modern politics. I should say that in this respect he showed a singular statesmanlike faculty—the faculty of feeling by a kind of penetrative instinct that modern society had ripened to a point at wh the principles of democracy & socialism had to be accepted as actualities.

His broad view of human nature & his thoroughly English character saved him from taking up these principles with the feverish & revolutionary passions of the French & even of the extreme German School. He grasped them rather with the spirit of a philosophical Puritan & a Christian who loved his fellow-men—with the justice of one who felt that decaying feudalism was inequitable, & who had drawn a truly English teaching from the lesson of the French Revolution.

Carlyle & Bright undoubtedly helped him to these conclusions; & I believe that Wordsworth also helped him. The great American War, by its splendid display of heroism for principle, fortified the growth of his political opinions.

But the root of the matter was in himself—in the beneficent working of congruent influences upon a character which was politically shrewd, a character gifted with what the French would call the *fraire* of actuality in politics.

It is no doubt that the social questions wh he thought paramount; viz: the well-being of the masses & their physical & spiritual hygiene, their proper educational development & their opportunities for unimpeded energy; are the vital questions in European politics. If they could be solved in his spirit —a spirit wh I may observe he largely though not wholly shared with Bright—there would be fair hope for the future.

Unfortunately, there are few democratic leaders who are so well-balanced, & so gifted with human toleration, respect for the past, understanding of class-weaknesses, determination to deal with abstract subjects upon a practical platform, as he was.

It was just this power of instinctively apprehending the actual as separate from the doctrinaire of the dazzling aspects of political questions, wh made him remarkable.

It always seemed to me that had this man been born the member of a powerful oligarchy, he would have stamped himself beneficially on the whole being of his nation. But whether if he had been so born, he would have developed the independent & clear-sighted intuition wh he gained as an onlooker, may of course be doubted.

As it was, it was his distinction to have early recognized that Democracy (implying political & social advantages on equal terms) & Socialism (implying an equitable distribution of wealth) are the cardinal questions of the modern world; & while recognizing this, to have been led astray by no glittering theory or enthusiasm for impossible Utopia, but to have steadily considered how & at what points the needful evolution might be constitutionally (i.e. without rupture or reaction) & beneficially (i.e. with regard for those ground-elements of human nature wh are religion, domesticity, reverence, discipline, etc) effected.

---

1. After Thomas Hill Green's death, Symonds wrote two sets of notes. The longer was sent on Oct. 7, 1882 (see L 1298), the shorter one on Nov. 3, 1886.

1567. *To Horatio Forbes Brown*

Davos Platz, Nov. 6 [1886]

[Dear Horatio]

Please forgive me if I seem somewhat neglectful. I am working this Cellini against time, and have now only about seven days more of the translation. But revision, annotation, introduction, will occupy much of the short space at my disposal; and till I see the *opera venuta* [the finished work] (in Cellini's language) I am anxious about my power *"sfinirla"* [running out] (also his).

Thank you for the note about *bandelle* [metal straps] and the drawing.

I find I had got the right idea of the sort of hinge which other commentators and translators appear to have missed. I wish I could spend some hours in a brass-foundry, first at Venice and then in England, so as to catch the technical terms used by my author when describing the casting of his Perseus. Perhaps I may bore you with a few questions to the address of Ponte Pinelli before I have done with my translation.

I look eagerly to hear some more about the way of reckoning time. Cellini reckoned *usually* on the Venetian system—from sundown onward up to 24.[1] But I believe there were other methods of computation present at the same moment often to his mind.

I will write again soon on more general topics.

[Incomplete]

---

1. See L 1564.

1568. *To Horatio Forbes Brown*

Davos, Nov. 10, 1886

[Dear Horatio]

I have just finished the translation of Cellini, just before midnight. And I remember that on this 10th of November, in the year 1864, I married my wife at Hastings.

Strange and curious reminiscence—for me at least. How little did I then think what the twenty-two years now elapsed would bring me; how much of physical weakness through long early times of waiting, how much of struggle and of pleasure; how much in the last fourteen years of this long period (since I first began to print books) of perpetual literary labour.

God be praised for it all. Looking back over that long space of time, I see how I have been inevitably moulded into the sort of artist which I am. The work which I have done, when compared with my then expectations, is enormous; but, compared with what it ought to have been, if my life had not by ill-health been continuously warped, and by will continuously directed to the most convenient channels, appears in my eyes very poor. I see its defects far more than its qualities; for the defects remain inherent in the production, while no one but myself can estimate the cost of that production.

So will it probably be with any one who takes a candid reckoning of all his doings after such a lapse of time.

Pardon me if I write thus much about myself. I have been living into a personality which was nothing if not self-expressive. Also, I want someone to speak to, here alone, when the moon is sailing out there through turbid clouds above the chary snow. Alone to-night, however, I was not, while I brought my work to its conclusion. My wife sat by me—for she is interested in Cellini—having often held the pen while I dictated.

The whirligig of time astounds me at whiles. I do not know how it is, we do not seem to heed it for weeks, and months, and years; and then, on some occasion, its inevitable, slow, sly, swift, progressive, many-featured movement makes itself appallingly felt. At such moments I know not verily whether I am one man or a hundred men, dead, living, and to be, compacted in a something I call I, which is not I, but rather an expression of unapprehended forces.

[Incomplete]

1569. *To Edmund Gosse*

Am Hof, Davos Platz, Switzerland. Nov: 17 1886

PRIVATE

My dear Gosse

Thank you very much for your article on Sidney,[1] wh I have read with great interest & pleasure. If you look at my little book when it appears—& I really cannot imagine why it has not already come out—you will see how far we agree in our estimate. I think I rate his poetry, at least the Astrophel & Stella series, higher than you do, & am not quite inclined to limit his political capacity so strictly to diplomacy. By the way, it is rather too strong, do you not think, to say as you do on p: 640, "It does not seem that he took any interest in politics." On page 641 you remark "In Sept: 1580 she becomes Penelope Rich."[2] I should be very much obliged if you could indicate the authority for this date. To my shame I have been writing Sidney's life without knowing that the date of her marriage had been so accurately determined. There is one little slip by the way upon which Mr Churton Collins[3] would have come down heavily. You have printed the Duke of Parma's name Palma in three places.

Your account of the idealization of Sidney on p: 637 is most felicitous.

I cannot scan the second line in your note on p: 644. If we read *to* instead of *unto,* it would be a lame iambic. I see that the line has got wrong in Collier's[4] edn of Spenser, from wh perhaps Church[5] extracted it. I have not Church's Spenser by me.

By this time I sincerely trust that the great Quarterly row with all its unutterable baseness & blackguardism will have subsided. I had a long letter from Arthur Sidgwick about the matter, quite taking your side. He asks me whether I do not think it is absurd to lay so much stress upon a few slips here & there & none at all upon a man's power to stimulate the interest of his audience. With this I heartily concur. He says he hears on good authority that Ch. Collins is himself a very inadequate & inaccurate Greek teacher at some crammer's.[6]

I believe you might have made a far better answer to the Quarterly than you did, & have stopped the matter sooner. I should have enumerated all the slips & mistakes wh I acknowledged, very briefly in the first place; & have then proceeded to deal with the unfairness & misrepresentation & animus of the article more in detail. It is quite preposterous to suppose that a man should be impeccable in every trifling detail.

You asked me about M[ontagu] Butler.[7] He is a very old friend of mine, & I hope to go out for a walk with him this afternoon. He is staying here with a sick daughter, but returns to Cambridge next Monday.

Believe me as always most sincerely yrs.

J ASymonds—

Pray inform me about the date of Penelope Devereux' Marriage to Lord Rich. I feel anxious about it, feeling pretty sure that some discovery since 1873 (the date of Grosart's edition of Sidney's poems) has upset all Mr. Julius Lloyd's elaborate argument about Lord Huntingdon's letter in March 1580.

Apropos of nothing; did you observe in my Ben Jonson, p:40, that Ben himself refers the wheelbarrow incident[8] to his French journey with young Raleigh? Have we other authority for the story? I should like to know.

---

1. *The Contemporary Review,* L (1886), 632 ff.

2. Penelope Devereux (1562?–1607), the inspiration for Sidney's *Astrophel and Stella,* was intended by her father to marry Philip Sidney. After her father's death, her relative and guardian, Henry Hastings, Earl of Huntingdon, arranged her marriage in March 1581 with Robert Rich, 3rd Baron Rich.

3. See L 1565 for the Gosse-Collins controversy. See also L 1573.

4. John Payne Collier (1789–1883) published his edition of Spenser in 1862.

5. R. W. Church published *Spenser* as part of the "English Men of Letters" series (1879).

6. Schools that "cram" students to enable them to pass tests. Symonds felt that this was a shoddy practice. Collins taught Greek and English literature at such a school run by a W. P. Scoones.

7. Henry Montagu Butler (1833–1918), headmaster of Harrow until 1885, then dean of Gloucester; in 1901, a governor of Harrow; master of Trinity College (1886–1918); vice-chancellor of Trinity (1889–90). See Ls 40 and 1597.

8. In 1613 Jonson went to France as governor to Sir Walter Raleigh's eldest son. He reported the wheelbarrow incident to Drummond, quoted by Symonds with comment, *Ben Jonson*, pp. 48–49:

This youth (young Raleigh) being knavishly inclined, among other pastimes, caused him to be drunken and dead drunk, so that he knew not where he was; thereafter laid him on a car, which he made to be drawn by pioneers through the streets, at every corner showing his governor stretched out, and telling them, that was a more lively image of the Crucifix than any they had: at which sport young Raleigh's mother delighted much. . . . Pardon must, peradventure, be craved for introducing this unseemly picture of Ben Jonson and his pupil, the lad Raleigh, in the streets of Paris. Yet it gives so vivid a notion of Englishmen as they then were, and of Englishmen as they now are . . . in foreign parts, that I cannot deny myself the satisfaction of the quotation. I feel that it will not hurt Jonson; for the next two chapters shall display him in the very blaze of glory as a dramatist whom no contemporary touched in his own line of art.

1570. *To Mary Robinson*

Am Hof, Davos Platz, Switzerland. Nov 17 1886

My dear Miss Robinson

I have not yet thanked you for your Margaret.[1] My wife read it aloud to me, & we both enjoyed it very much. I think it is charmingly written, with great mastery over the history of those complicated times & grasp of their characters. Both Athenaeum & Academy[2] seemed to me very unjust to the book. By the way, the review in the former, admitted by your friend Mr McColl,[3] would be a lesson to Roden Noel! I shall tell him about it. He would have taken it as a personal affront. I agree with your critics in thinking that you have got too much of Michelet[4] in your description of Diane de Poitiers,[5] & that you draw too fast a line between the Francois i & Henri ii periods of the French Renaissance.

By the way, there is one little mistake which Mr Churton Collins, if you fall into his claws, will make the most of.[6] You talk of Charles V retiring to the Escorial, which was built by his son Philip after the battle of St Quentin. You meant to write Yuste.[7]

I should like to have been in London while this war was waged among the critics. I wonder what you think of it all. It seems to me clear that Gosse has been pitifully & unfairly dealt with; but he made a most ridiculously feeble reply to the Quarterly. He ought very briefly to have enumerated all the mistakes wh had really been detected & then to have explained his point about those which were wantonly misrepresented. Gosse is certainly an inaccurate writer. I notice, in an article he sent me on Sir Ph: Sidney, the Duke of Parma spelt invariably Palma—& without his title. He also gives the precise date of Penelope Devereux's marriage to Lord Rich, which, unless it has been discovered in the last year or two, must be some confusion. However, until I have heard from him about that, I may be myself to blame for not knowing so important a detail of my own work.

I have been going ahead with much industry of late, & have just finished the translation of Cellini. It was a heavy piece of work, but very interesting. Much is left to do still: polishing & writing notes. At present I feel tired & out of sorts.

Will you give my kindest thanks to your father for the letter he wrote me about anthracite coal? I shall talk the subject over with the Davos people on the first occasion when our smoke-nuisance is raised, & shall then be able, through his kindness, to give them some details about cost. From what they have already told me on the topic, I fancy they will think it too expensive. I am not inclined to try the experiment upon my own account; for it is not a little house like mine which spoils the air, but the large hotels bakeries etc. & the whole question will soon have to be considered in a very serious spirit.

I hope that you are well again now, & are able to work at your great subject—also that Mrs Robinson feels some benefit from her draught of mountain air. Please give her & your sister my kindest regards & believe me ever most sincerely yours

J A Symonds.

---

1. *Margaret of Angoulême, Queen of Navarre* (1886).

2. W. H. Allen, "Eminent Women—Margaret of Angoulême, Queen of Navarre. By A. Mary F. Robinson," *The Academy,* XXX (1886), 303–04. Though Allen is more favorable than Symonds suggests, he belabors Miss Robinson's use of the word "dense" for her subject because he thinks it indicates a misconception of Margaret's character.

3. In *The Athenaeum,* No. 3080 (November 6, 1886), 596, by Dugald S. MacColl, the art critic. See L 1561. MacColl says that the book "would have been much better if the author had taken less pains." This is the "lesson" Roden Noel required.

4. The French historian, Jules Michelet (1798–1874). His masterpiece was the *Histoire de France* (16 vols., 1833–67).

5. Duchesse de Valentinois (1499–1566), mistress of Henry II of France (1536 ff.) and an influence throughout his reign (1547–59).

6. A reference to the treatment Gosse had supposedly suffered from Collins. See Ls 1565 and 1573.

7. The Hieronymite convent of Yuste, 24 miles east of Plasencia, prov. of Cáceres, Spain.

1571. *To Horatio Forbes Brown*

Davos Platz, Nov. 24, [1886]

[Dear Horatio]

I have been hard at work writing an Introduction to "Cellini." It is always difficult, I find, to deal with matter into which I have been living. Close familiarity makes me lose the right touch on the public. Anyhow, this portion of my work is finished, and I have now the notes and revision in front of me.

I sent the volume of your Venetian Almanac (a very interesting book) back registered. I fear it was a couple of days delayed, since I would not have it committed to the post except by one of my own family.

I am stupid—having spent three days in tobogganing up and down vale in various directions with Margot Tennant,[1] introducing her also into *Wirthschaften* [inns] where the peasants smoke and drink—and where she drank and smoked. She is a mad girl, with a pocketful of familiar letters from Gladstone, Tennyson, and Mat. Arnold.

[Incomplete]

---

1. For an estimate of Margot Tennant's (1864–1945) list of acquaintances, see her *Margot Asquith: An Autobiography* (4 vols., 1920–22). Her father was Sir Charles Tennant (1823–1906); see L 1619. Her sister Laura was a favorite of Tennyson, who was their father's friend. Another sister was Pauline Emma (Mrs. Thomas Duff Gordon-Duff); see L 1552. Margot was the second wife of Herbert Henry Asquith (1852–1928), 1st Earl of Oxford and Asquith, and was noted in London society for her wit. The publication of her autobiography caused a minor sensation. Oscar Wilde's "The Star-Child," *A House of Pomegranates* (1891) and Symonds' *E S &S* (2 vols., 1890) were dedicated to her. She wrote a novel and works of personal reminiscences: *Persons and Places* (1925), *More Memories* (1933), *Off the Record* (1944).

1572. *To Mary Robinson*

Am Hof, Davos Platz, Switzerland. Nov: 25 1886

My dear Mary

I answer your postcard at once. Bernardino Corio[1] was born 1459. He was Chamberlain to Gian Galeazzo Sforza[2] & held other offices, wh gave him access to archives. His history is generally accepted as trustworthy about many Milanese facts wh cannot elsewhere be ascertained.

Isabella of France[3] was married in 1360, & died at Paris (in the childbirth of her third son) Sept 3. 1373.

Her eldest son Azzone d: Oct 4. 1387.

Her second Giangaleazzo d: in infancy.

Her third Carlo b: 1373 d: 1374.

I think that is all you wanted. Litta[4] does not give dates for the birth of Azzone & Giangaleazzo, but says that the former died early. He grew up enough to take some part in affairs, however, & survived his mother, as you see, eight years. Probably he lived to be nearly 20.

I hope you will find time to tell me something about the Gosse Collins affair.[5] I got a very nice letter from Gosse about it, wh shows more manly strength of disposition than I had given him credit for. Apropos of the Fortnightly you say "I must tell you all about that extraordinary young man." Do you mean Frank Harris? I want very much to hear about him. He is always sending me letters & telegrams. I never saw him; but I shall be very glad to work regularly for him, wh he seems to want, when I have done Cellini. I have been slaving hard at that nearly always since you left Davos. The translation is finished, & so is the introductory essay. But both will have to be carefully revised, & there are lots of notes to write.

Macmillan has not sent me a copy of my Sir Philip Sidney. I wonder whether it is out. I will send you one. The publishers forget me here, & what is bad, a good many of them forget to pay me. This is literally true; & I shall soon be roused into making a public row about their ways.

Janet continues to be fairly well. She cannot do much, however. I gave her a new piano, a very nice one, wh is a pleasure to her. I am keeping well enough, but am a good deal troubled by my eyes. I feel the intense cold & glare of sun upon the snow painfully. It very much detracts from my enjoyment of our Alpine winter. We have not snow enough yet.

Ever yrs

J A Symonds

1. Bernardino Corio (1459–1512) completed his history of Milan (*Patria Historia*) in 1499; it was published in a magnificent edition in 1503.

2. (1469–94), Duke of Milan (1476–81) under regency; expelled by Ludovico Sforza (1451–1508).

3. Isabella of France (born 1348), daughter of John II (1319–64), King of France. She was married at age 12 to the 13-year-old Viscount Jean-Galeas of Milan, the marriage being arranged by John II who needed money—he had been captured by the English at Poitiers and his ransom was fixed at 3,000,000 crowns—and appreciated the dowry. It was understood that she would eventually be Duchess of Milan; this never occurred.

4. Count Pompeo Litta (1781–1852) began to publish his *Famiglie celebri italiane* in 1819; it was continued by others until 1899.

5. See L 1565; also L 1576.

1573. *To Edmund Gosse*

Am Hof, Davos Platz, Switzerland. Nov: 26 1886

My dear Gosse

I must send you hearty thanks for your last letter, & tell you how highly I value it as the expression of a fine & manly nature taking the right lesson from shrewd accidents of fortune.[1]

Please do not be angry with me if I seem to be impertinent. I must say frankly that I think your attitude with regard to the whole of this miserable affair gives me a far finer conception of the point to wh you will attain (you now hardly in your prime) than I had before.

Forgive me if I hint that it had occurred to me fair weather might have spoiled your voyage. Now that I know with what good temper & the Knight's true virtue of Humilitas—not the humility of nonconformist ministers, but of Folgore da San Gemignano[2]—the Umiltà of the princely Borromeo family[3]—you affront the evil that has happened to you so unjustly, I expect the very highest things of you. Ecco chi crescerà la nostra gioia.[4] But, to abate this elevated note, I am really extremely pleased to see that you take the fiery trial you have had to undergo, in the right spirit—the spirit of the man devoted to his mission, who will make the uses of adversity sweet by turning them to profit for his own intellectual advancement & the greater benefit of us who listen to him.

Thank you much for what you say about the date of Stella's marriage in your Sidney article.[5] I have so long learned this lesson of Humilitas, that I always quake when I give anything to the public—feeling that I may have erred through negligence, supineness, want of materials at my command, &

so forth. I invariably expect to be caught out somewhere; & God knows it is easy enough to catch a fellow out, if a Collins is waiting at the corner!

I did not, in my last letter, tell you how much I felt your allusion to my forth-coming book on Sidney in your article. It made me almost uncomfortable; for I do not believe I have advanced the Sidney criticism in any point whatever, except perhaps in the discussion of his "Astrophel & Stella."

You are wrong when you say that I am a sound scholar. I take indeed great trouble about any bit of work I do; & I have burrowed myself into familiarity with one small section of the world's history in Italy. But otherwise, I am not & cannot here make myself a scholar in the supreme sense of that word.

I wonder also whether I have the fire that burns in you for literature! I love it, but I love life more.

Goodnight. It is very late. The Pleiads soaring to the Zenith persuade to sleep. Believe me always yours

J ASymonds.—

---

1. See L 1565.

2. Folgore da San Gemignano, 13th cent. Italian poet. Some of Folgore's sonnets were translated by D. G. Rossetti and by Symonds. *The Renaissance in Italy: Italian Literature,* Appendix II, contains translations of 10 sonnets. The first chapter of Symonds' *Sketches and Studies in Italy and Greece,* with prefatory note by H. F. Brown (3 vols., 1898), is devoted to Folgore.

3. A noble family including pious ecclesiastics like Saint Carlo (1538–84), who was created cardinal and archbishop of Milan (1560) and founded the order of Oblates of St. Ambrose (1578); and Conte Federigo (1564–1631), also cardinal and archbishop of Milan, and founder of the Ambrosian Library at Milan (1609).

4. That shall increase your joy well. See Dante, *Paradiso:* Canto V, l. 105.

5. In *The Contemporary Review,* L (1886), 632 ff. Stella was Penelope Devereux Rich. See L 1569.

1574. *To Charlotte Symonds Green*

Am Hof, Davos Platz, Switzerland. Dec: 6. 1886

My dearest Charlotte

Thank you very much for your last letter, which gave a fairly good account of your housekeeping with Auntie,[1] a matter in which I take the greatest interest.

Probably Lotta is even now staying with you. She has enjoyed herself all through in England, I think.

There was some trouble with Edith about her not going to Sidbury. I could not see why she should not go. But Catherine had made her mind up against it (on the strength of what happened last year at Oxford); & I think, as Lotta's mother, she has the right to settle such things for her more than I.

I have been toiling along at a translation of Cellini's Autobiography, wh is a long business, longer than I thought it would be. It has to be done against time. In consequence of wh I have been occupied more than I like or is good for my eyes.

We are all pretty much in status quo. Janet seems not worse, though [Dr.] Ruedi is anxious about a continual decrease in her weight. Madge works with spirit & profit at her drawing. Katharine is quite well.

Catherine feels the cold more than she used to. We have had some smart pinches lately.

I have just told my bookseller to send Auntie a copy of my Sir Philip Sidney. I think she may like to look at it.

Please give her my best best love. I shall write to her about Xmas.

We are expecting St Loe Harry[2] & B Mallet[3] on the 12th.

Ever most affectionately yours

J A Symonds

---

1. Mary Ann Sykes had moved to Oxford to live with Charlotte. See L 1539.
2. St. Loe and Harry Strachey, Symonds' nephews.
3. Possibly Edward Baldwin Malet (1837–1908), English diplomat who from 1879–83 had been agent and consul general in Egypt and from 1884–95 was English Ambassador to Berlin.

1575. *To Henry Graham Dakyns*

Am Hof, Davos Platz, Switzerland. Dec 6 1886

My dear Graham

One line in answer to your letter about plans.

Catherine, I think, wrote to say that your kind thoughts of helping us with regard to either Lotta or Madge need not influence them at all. But I hope that, if you find a visit to us in any way combinable with your desire to go further South, you will manage it. We can afford not to write to one another if we sometimes meet.

The longer you stay with us, the better pleased shall we be. If you like to bring work to do, I will see that you have a room to do it in. You can have one of my two studies to yourself.

However, all you write about Corfu or Sorrento or Sicily makes me prepare my mind with patience & philosophy in case the strong attraction of those Southern shores & seas draws you far away from our too too familiar monotony of winter.

I have been grinding on of late at a translation of Cellini's Autobiography. It is getting nearly finished. I have worked hard this year at this & at my two books on Jonson & Sidney—& shall have earned just 400.* Of course there has been a lot of tedious work in printing the two volumes of the Renaissance also. I really don't think literature worth doing, espy when one gets such reviews of one's best efforts as one wh appears in the Athenaeum for Dec 4 upon my "Catholic Revival."[1] It is not disrespectful. But the man who wrote it, does not seem to have chosen to understand what I was driving at.

Over & over again I say to myself I will lay my pen down for ever. Over & over again I take it up again for διαγωγη's [amusement's] sake.

Love to Maggie. Ever yrs.
JASymonds.

*N.B. I never earned so much before in one year by literature!

---

1. No. 3084, pp. 737–38.

1576. *To Edmund Gosse*

Am Hof, Davos Platz, Switzerland. Dec: 16 1886

My dear Gosse

I am rather amused at the vehemence of your letter of the 13th just received. I admit that I was put out by the Sat[y] P.M.G. article on you & me.[1] Nor did I like that beast Churton Collins' article[2] on my Ben Jonson also in P.M.G.—I suppose it was by him. But I do not see why a newspaper is bound to issue respectful reviews of books by people who send them signed communications! Entirely as I disapprove of the PMG's line on many subjects, particularly upon this last literary dispute, I think it a very useful channel for communicating one's opinions to the public.

What has embittered Mr Collins against me, I cannot imagine; & it is indeed too bad to insinuate that you & I have been log-rolling! I was fearful lest he should come down upon us in this very way when I read your kind words in the Contemporary about my forthcoming "Sidney."

Literature is becoming a most ungrateful task, & I think I shall give it up. After really trying to do my best in my vocation for fifteen years, I find myself getting more kicks than halfpence.

There is, however, after all, only one line to take about spiteful reviews. That is, to forget them. They spoil any interest or pleasure one may have in one's past work. But they cannot trouble the pure fountain of the pleasure we derive from literature & art.

I am glad you like my "Sidney." You are quite right in saying it is not as "fresh" as the other little book on "Jonson." The fact is that I wrote it under conditions of great depression. My oldest daughter is a confirmed invalid, & we had taken her to a German bath for change of air. On arriving there she had a dangerous hemmorhage & lay in a very critical state for four weeks in bed. I used often to write my "Sidney" all through a night while watching anxiously for any alteration in her health. This, together with a very sincere attempt to repress my natural tendency toward rhetoric, and a no less earnest effort to be scrupulously accurate, combined with the want of any strong enthusiasm for Sidney's character, made my work perfunctory in execution.

Do you observe how a creature like Churton Collins omits in his reviews all real discussion of the material in books, confining himself to the one object of carping sneering & personal insult? He must be a most unhappy man—poor little wretch! But of him & of his sort let us always say:

Non ragioniam di lor, ma guarda e passa [Let us not speak of them; look and pass on]. One more word anent him, however. You perhaps noticed that he quotes Fulke Greville's words about America as though they were Sidney's.[3]

Well, well! Instead of writing to you on such sad humiliating trifles as the spite of a Chaffers[4] or a Churton Collins, I wish we could meet & have ambrosial hours of talk about the great dead & the ingenious living!

Addio. With best wishes for Christmas & many happy years to yourself & Mrs Gosse believe me most sincerely

Yours

J A Symonds.[5]—

---

1. A review, "Two Biographies of Sir Philip Sidney," about Gosse's and Symonds', appeared in the *Pall Mall Gazette,* XLIV (December 11), 5. The reviewer was Oscar Wilde. The opening paragraph follows:

In an article on Sir Philip Sidney in the *Contemporary Review* of last month Mr. Gosse told us of the pleasure with which he looked forward to a monograph on the same subject from the "genial and learned pen of Mr. J. A. Symonds." This monograph has now appeared in Mr. Morley's "English Men of Letters Series," and "learned" Mr. Symonds certainly shows himself to be, though "genial" seems to us hardly a felicitous term by which to describe his style. Still Mr. Gosse was more than justified in making use of this expression as it had been previously applied to himself by no less a person than Mr. Symonds, and in matters of this kind reciprocity is everything. It now only remains for Mr. Symonds to speak of the "learned" Mr. Gosse and the balance sheet will be fully made up.

2. The reviewer was not Collins but Oscar Wilde. In his review, XLIV (September 20), Wilde was, in general, complimentary to Symonds, reserving a slap on the wrist for a precious style:

Eloquence is a beautiful thing, but rhetoric ruins many a critic; and Mr. Symonds is essentially rhetorical. When, for instance, he tells us that "Jonson made masks, while Dekker and Heywood created souls," we feel that he is asking us to accept a crude judgment for the sake of a smart antithesis. It is of course true that we do not find in Jonson the same growth of character that we find in Shakespeare, and we may admit that most of the characters in Jonson's plays are, so to speak, ready-made. But a ready-made character is not necessarily either mechanical or wooden, two epithets Mr. Symonds uses constantly in his criticism.

Symonds probably thought that by making the review seem more injurious than it was, Gosse would feel better.

3. Wilde proceeds:

Mr. Symonds however has this advantage over Mr. Gosse that he knows a good deal about the subject on which he is writing. . . . He knows that Sidney was fully conscious of the necessity of England maintaining her supremacy by means of her navy, and worked stoutly for that end; that from his seat in the House of Commons he rendered valuable assistance to Raleigh on the subject of the Virginia plantation; and that, in words which as we read them now seem almost instinct with the spirit of prophecy, he may be said to have traced the future of America, appealing to England to make of it, "not an asylum for fugitives, a *bellum piraticum* for banditti, or any such base *ramas* of people, but an emporium for the confluence of all nations that love or profess any kind of virtue or commerce." Mr. Gosse, however, calmly informs us that "*it does not seem that he took any interest in politics,*" which is really the most astounding statement ever made about Sidney by any writer.

4. Possibly Thomas Chaffers of Brasenose, who gave up the curatorship of the Bodelian Library in 1860 (see *London Times,* January 20, 1860, p. 12).

5. Symonds did not abandon Sidney after his book was printed. He wrote the

following lengthy note on three pages (title page and the two pages on either side) of his own copy of *Sidney,* now owned by his granddaughter Dame Janet Vaughan:

Sidney was a man of beautiful person & gentle nature, gifted with more head than heart. He never, upon any important occasion of life, allowed his feelings to master him; he never lost his head. Yet there was that sweetness of temper, that sympathy with divers kinds of human excellence & that real charity in him, which blent together made him use & diffuse his heart to good purpose in kind offices. By not yielding to passion except in poetry, by engrossing himself in no one tyranny or vulgar pursuit of the heart's desire, by keeping his head cool to serve his will & rule his conduct, by distributing his affections in just measure & proportion over a wide variety of worthy objects, by "plying compliment with compliment" (as his sagacious father phrased it) in a genial & at no time ignoble or ignorant spirit, he spread his character abroad over an immensely wide surface to the admiration of less well-balanced if often far more intense natures. Then too he became the model of aristocratic culture. Few men, as my friend H F Brown remarks, continued to be so accomplished without being professional.

Is it possible, I have sometimes speculated, that Sidney caught from the Italian Renaissance the ideal of a perfect patron, & that he adopted this with exquisite tact to his own modest position in life, to his own high principles as a Protestant gentleman?

Did he, in fact, realize the humanistic noble of the Italian type (so far as in him lay) after the same fashion as Milton realized the humanistic man of bits & learning—both of them upon the soil of Protestant England?

Xmas eve 1886

2. *The four Symonds daughters, ca. 1886; Davos in the background.*

3. *Margaret, Lotta, and Katharine Symonds, 1893.*

4. *Mr. and Mrs. J. A. Symonds with their daughter Katharine and the dog Ciò, taken at Davos, ca. 1886.*

5. *Poggio Gherardo, home of Janet Ross near Florence.*

6. *The Countess Almorò Pisani.*

7. *The pulpit given by Symonds in memory of his daughter Janet to the English Church of St. Luke, Davos. Photo by the Rev. George Dolman.*

8. Painting by Marianne North of the Native Vanilla Orchid hanging from an orange tree in the Seychelles Islands. From the North Gallery, Kew Gardens.

9. Drawing from the library archives, University of California, Riverside, by Marianne North.

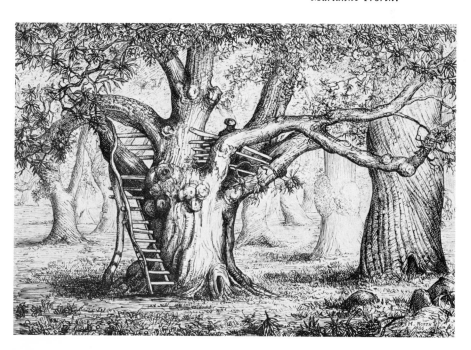

10. *"Evangeline Discovering Her Affianced in the Hospital,"* by Samuel
Richards. Courtesy the Detroit Institute of Arts.

11. *"Whitman,"* by H. H. Gilchrist. Frontispiece to Richard M. Bucke, Walt Whitman (*1883*).

12. Symonds and two un-
identified friends.

13. Symonds' study at Am Hof.

14. *Symonds in his study.*

15. *Tea time at Am Hof.*

16. *"Boy with Spear" by G. Plüschow, from R. W. Schufeldt,* Studies of the Human Form for Artists . . . *(1908). See L 1945.*

17. Portrait of Edward Carpenter by Roger Fry. National Portrait Gallery, London.

18. Charlotte Symonds Green, age 84; a drawing by F. A. de Biden Footner, 1925, in Melvin Richter, The Politics of Conscience *(1964).*

19. Henry Graham Dakyns at Inchnadamff, Loch Assynt, 1903.

SEXUAL INVERSION

BY

HAVELOCK ELLIS

AND

JOHN ADDINGTON SYMONDS

LONDON

WILSON AND MACMILLAN,
16, JOHN STREET, BEDFORD ROW, W.C.

1897

20. Title page of Sexual Inversion, *second and final publication on sex by Ellis and (posthumously) by Symonds; bought up for destruction by Horatio F. Brown.*

21, 22. Two hitherto unpublished ink drawings by Margaret Symonds illustrating two of Symonds' favorite poems. A large sketchbook containing these and other drawings is part of the Symonds Collection, Bristol University Library.

II

Prose Translations and
Janet Symonds' Death

1887–1888

1577. *To Horatio Forbes Brown*

Davos, Jan. 1. [1887]

[Dear Horatio]

. . . He is mentally very fit just now;[1] but oddly anxious about health. He fell on his back, tobogganing, and got a bad headache; thought he had concussion of the brain; ate a huge dinner; and slept well; organized charades; sent for [Dr.] Ruedi, and sickened; then, on Ruedi's saying he was as sound as a fish, suddenly jumped up again into Jack-in-the-box activity—I think he will go far in life; and these sanitary panics signify little, if they can be set at rest by paying a doctor ten francs at Davos or one guinea in London.

I have made £475 by my pen in 1886. This is the most I ever made in one year, and I don't mean to work as hard again to get such miserable pittance.

I wonder whether you will come here. I mean to go, health permitting, into Vintschgau, in order to bring pecuniary succour to a friend at Schluderns. He wants about £20. But I cannot discover exactly why. I think it would be amusing to carry the cash, and, as I know there is no hotel there, to cut into the winter life of a Tyrolese village.

It is 11.30 p.m. and Graham is sitting by me, reading Dowden's "Shelley."[2] I have still got the bells of last night in my ears, on the brink of a vast black, frozen chasm.[3] So good night.

Jan. 4. I have been knocked down by a bad and sudden cold. This letter was forgotten for three days. As I see there is no actual insanity in it, I send it for a token.

[Incomplete]

---

1. Symonds is probably talking about himself.
2. Edward Dowden, *The Life of Percy Bysshe Shelley* (2 vols., 1886).
3. For a description of the ritual Sylvester Abend (New Year's) bells see *OLSH*, pp. 346–51.

1578. *To T. S. Perry*

Am Hof, Davos Platz, Switzerland. Jan 4 1886 [1887][1]

Dear Mr Perry

While you have been loading me with benefits—letters, books, articles, & every mark of kindness—I have kept a glum & seeming-surly silence. Truly those epithets do not adequately describe my gesinnung [disposition] toward you all this while. I have not written only because it was next to impossible for me to do so. You know that I have been overworking myself for about a year past, & that my eyes began to give way in the early summer. I believe I did write so much of my news. But then I had to translate the whole of Cellini's Autobiography[2] & to write an introduction with illustrative notes. In order to meet the publisher's wishes I raced this through before Xmas, & got my Ms ready at the promised time—when the wretched creature casually informed me that he found it would be more convenient not to publish before August—he had miscalculated his press arrangements etc—was hopeful that I should be glad of the postponement.

However, of these grievances, no more. It is enough to show that with weak eyes & incessant toil at Cellini (a constant average of 6 hrs hard writing per diem) I really *could not* write letters.

Meanwhile I read with great interest & amusement your book on Snobs.[3] It is a charming application of the evolutionary criticism; & I think the view expressed, though at first sight startling, is quite correct. We are now so familiar with Snobs, especially in Anglo Saxon society, that it makes us rub our eyes to discover that they did not exist before the beginning of this century. The style of the essay was charming. Its free & easy swing, regardless of repeated words, always pithy & vivid, is so delightfully brightened up by unexpected coruscations of epigrams. "The poor noble man hiding his nakedness with leaves from his family tree."—"The aristocracy cultivating wood for its own guillotine"—remain in my memory, with many more besides, as in the highest sense aphoristic.

I found the same qualities of style in your survey of world-literature. But I could not help somewhat regretting the expenditure of so much learning thought & pains upon an impossible task. I wished, over & over again, that you could have dispensed with quotations & occupied the space thus gained with dissertation. That, however, was of course not in the scheme of the whole work.

I wanted to write first some of the things wh have been waiting in my mind to say, before I thanked you for your letter of Nov 19 & Dec 23, wh reached me this morning, together with the book of poems. The poems I have as yet only glanced at, & recognized their authorship of course. But pray tell me whether a portion of them are not *yours?* I shall study the whole collection with care, & if Mrs Perry would like to hear details of my opinion, I will write about it to her. Probably I shall discover, on closer inspection, that there is not a double authorship, but a double strain of feeling.

You are the possessor of a great literary treasure, if you have the autograph of L. Barker.[4] It ought to be bound in crimson morocco with blue watered silk linings—as some unknown person bound a set of Shelley's First editions wh I once obtained, & sold again (alas!) for 50 guineas.[5] I sold them in order to justify to my own mind the purchase of Litta's great collection of Italian pedigrees.[6]

What you say about my vols vi & vii [*The Catholic Reaction*] gives me the most unqualified delight. Living as I do away from learned society, away from libraries, recasting the old familiar sources without the advantage of a voluminous new literature upon my subject, I always feel that what I write may be quite arriéré [backward]. You can therefore comprehend how such remarks as yours, made by a man who keeps upon the highest crest of the huge tidal wave of learning, encourage me. I did indeed feel, while I was writing those vols, that I grasped my subject more firmly than I had done in the earlier parts. It is sad that the composition of a sustained work like "R. in It." involves of necessity the end being better written than the beginning. However clear a conception we may have of our method at the commencement we only learn how to command & apply it by practise. Yet I do not know that I ought to regret this. If anyone takes the trouble to read the whole work through, he will feel, I think, that the whole subject has a kind of unity—that what seems scattery in the earlier parts gathers & condenses, acquires momentum & unity, as the final issue becomes manifest. Of course too the Catholic Reaction introduces a dramatic element wh the Renaissance itself had not.

I am just now trying to remodel my own little book on Shelley[7] by the light of Dowden's[8] great biography. I find very little to alter in the general view, much of detail to correct. And I am inclined to be severely polemical against the main new point introduced into the "Parting from Harriet" episode. Dowden, I think, has been guilty of a real, if not an intentional *suggestio falsi,* when he tries to make out that Shelley believed in Harriet's adultery *before* the separation took place.

I shall probably publish a note upon this point in the Fortnightly[9]—a periodical wh is opening its arms wide to receive my writings.

Believe me to be, with sincere wishes for this year to yourself & your wife, not without a prayer that its months may bring us personally acquainted, ever most truly & gratefully yours

John Addington Symonds

---

1. The year of this letter is clearly 1887. In January, 1886, Symonds had not yet begun his translation of Cellini's life, which is first mentioned in L 1559.

2. His translation was published by John C. Nimmo in 1887.

3. *The Evolution of the Snob* (1886).

4. William Dean Howells, *The Minister's Charge or the Apprenticeship of Lemuel Barker* (Edinburgh, 1886; Boston, 1887).

5. Symonds sold the works to a Mr. Warren. Gosse was the agent. See Ls 1036 and 1048.

6. See L 1572.

7. *Shelley* (1878; new ed., 1887).

8. Edward Dowden, *The Life of Percy Bysshe Shelley* (2 vols., 1886).

9. See L 1591.

1579. *To Mary Robinson*

Am Hof, Davos Platz, Switzerland. Jan: 9 1887

My dear Mary

How can I thank you for your generous New Year's gift to me? It is very precious, & "The Roman Actor"[1] happens to be a great favourite of mine. I have always liked it the best of Massinger's plays.

I am delighted with what you say about my "Sidney."[2] I do not think, however, that there is much art in my treatment of the historic background. Or rather, the art consists in resolutely not knowing too much about the general European environment. I have always held that writers of biographies (espy short ones) should be careful not to engage in too profound a study of the period. They must only endeavour not to be wrong or ignorant.

I thought you managed the historic background in your "Marguerite"[3] very well indeed. Only I had a feeling that she did not detach herself against it as a character quite as sharply as I should have liked. I would have had you deliberately blur the background in order to bring her out. But then she, unlike Sidney, was a real & potent actor in the world-drama.

I am vexed about a little literary matter. Macmillan is going to reprint the "English Men of Letters" in a cheap form, & has advertized my "Shelley" for April. Now some passages are rendered quite ridiculous (e.g.

pp: 81 & 83) by the recent publication of the Shelley archives.[4] I therefore proposed to remodel my book (without asking to be paid for the trouble) in such a way as to make it a correct sketch of Shelley as we now know him. Macmillan writes refusing leave. He will only allow such minor alterations as may be made without injuring the old plates. I cannot submit to changing a date or name or figure here & there, while I leave important opinions unaltered. So I have just written to say that, if he will not reconsider his decision, the book must be reissued as it stands, & that when it appears in the cheap form, I shall review it, explaining how the matter stands. If I cannot get my review published in some periodical, I shall have to print it as a pamphlet.

This is very annoying; & I think it is extremely mean of Macmillan to go on disseminating a book wh he knows to be inadequate to present knowledge of the subject.

I wonder what you think of Dowden's Life.[5] I am greatly interested in it—a little surprised & disappointed, however, at no more light being thrown on the separation from Harriet—& considerably indignant at what looks to me almost like a disingenuous attempt to prejudice the public against Harriet by the very ill-supported suggestion that Shelley believed in her unfaithfulness during the summer of 1814.

However, we certainly know much more about Shelley than we did before, & all, I suppose, that we are ever likely to know.

Believe me always most sincerely yours

J A Symonds

I have had a bad cold lately, wh has made me more than usually lazy.

---

1. Philip Massinger, *The Roman Actor: A Tragedie* (1629). Arthur Symons included the play in Vol. II of the edition of Massinger (1887–89) in Ellis' "Mermaid" series.

2. *Sir Philip Sidney* (1886).

3. *Margaret of Angoulême, Queen of Navarre* (1886).

4. See n. 5 and L 1591.

5. He refers specifically to the new material in Edward Dowden's *The Life of Percy Bysshe Shelley* (2 vols., 1886). See Ls 1577 and 1578. H. Buxton Forman had published a *Bibliography* in 1886. Symonds' new ed. appeared in 1887.

1580. *To Horatio Forbes Brown*

Davos, Jan. 19 [1887]

[Dear Horatio]

I am writing in bed, to which I have finally betaken myself after dragging out a miserable existence since the beginning of the month. I cannot imagine how or when I am to throw off this cold. Probably I shall have to go away for change of air. I only wish the prescription would be Venice and the "Mandragora."[1] But that is not to be thought of. I fear that, until I see how things are going with me, my plans must be of necessity vague. And this has some bearing on the date of your visit. You mention the 25th. That would in ordinary circumstances suit very well. On the 26th we have fixed our International Toboggan race, and I ought to attend. But it may be desirable for my health that I should avoid it. In which case, if I am at all fit to move, I may go and stay a while at Chur. There we could meet and come up together. But I am so prostrate now that I can foresee nothing. It does seem as though I could not be well, unless I had some hard piece of grind on.

I am interested about Sarpi's Monument.[2] I agree with you that Venice is not meant for statues. Manin's[3] is an abomination, and we can't hope for another Colleoni![4] Yet Sarpi ought to have his memorial. I hope it will be put in some great church—S. Zanipolo perhaps. But the Clerics will not allow that, I suppose. I will subscribe, and, if you like, will help to make the matter known in England. One ought to write to several newspapers; perhaps to get affiliated Committees up in Oxford and Cambridge.

I have been having several literary annoyances lately—one was a really unjust review in very spiteful tone of my "Sidney."[5] This could have been answered, as I think, by a complete refutation. But I think on the whole it is better not to get into newspaper controversies about anything.

[Incomplete]

---

1. Probably Machiavelli's play (1524).

2. A committee had first been formed in 1876 to collect money for a statue, but the project fell through and was revived in January 1888 when a new international committee was formed. The plan was to erect a large bronze statue in the Campo di Santa Fosca, through which Sarpi had passed daily from his monastery to the Doge's palace. Designs from Venetian artists were solicited in July and again in December 1888, the latter models being exhibited in May 1889 in Robert Browning's palace. Emilio Marsili was commissioned to do the work. After hostile pressures from the Vatican, the work was unveiled on September 20, 1892.

3. Statue of Daniele Manin (1804–57) the Italian patriot.

4. The equestrian statue, by Andrea del Verrocchio (1435–88), of Bartolommeo Colleoni (1400–75), the Italian general, located in Venice.

5. See L 1576 to Gosse.

1581. *To Charles Edward Sayle*

Am Hof, Davos Platz, Switzerland. Feb: 12 1887

My dear Mr Sayle

I have been ill in bed with a very bad cold for some weeks & am only just beginning to get about again. This must be my excuse for not answering your letter of the 30th Jany earlier, & also for the stupidity wh will reign supreme over my present attempt at writing.

I was very glad to see your handwriting again & to have news of you. For I often thought about you during the autumn & early winter, wondering how things were going with you after your return to Oxford.

You have asked me to do something for which I am eminently unfit & it is supremely disagreeable to me: that is to write one of those inept things called testimonials.[1] I enclose a few lines, however, not wishing to decline the officium. In order to be effective, I ought of course to know you far more intimately than as yet I have the pleasure of doing. —Please excuse the poverty of my performance. No one had ever cause to congratulate himself upon a testimonial written by me; for I do not possess the gift.

You do not tell me much about Oxford, except that you are in for Greats. I wish you well out of them. And all success to your Drama![2] You were certainly quite right to accept the offer of half risks & half profits.

I will write again when I feel fit for a literary letter, & have more time. Just now I must work off arrears of correspondence wh my illness has caused to accumulate.

Everyours

J A Symonds.

Do you know a Mr Arthur Galton[3] of New College.

1. The testimonial, i.e., a reference, a recommendation, was evidently for a position Sayle hoped to attain at the British Museum. See L 1637.

2. *Wiclif: an Historical Drama* (Oxford, 1887).

3. The Rev. Arthur Howard Galton (1852–1921) attended Cambridge and then became a Roman Catholic priest before he entered New College, Oxford, in 1886, age 33; he was to write regularly for the *Century Guild Hobby Horse,* reviewing some of Symonds' work on the Renaissance and writing excellent pieces on Matthew Arnold; *Our Attitude Towards English Roman Catholics, and The Papal Court* (1902); *Church and State in France, 1300–1907* (1907).

1582. *To Horatio Forbes Brown*

Locarno, Feb. 18 [1887]

[Dear Horatio]

I write to you from this unexpected place. Soon after you left us, I felt I could stand my nightmare cold no longer. Upon [Dr.] Ruedi's advice I came hither. He said I should find the Grand[1]—got up for a winter season —English Chaplain and all the rest of it. I found the Grand' Albergo closed, no winter season thought of by the Locarnesi, and one fair hotel of the airy summer Italian-Lake sort ready to house me.

We left Thusis yesterday and slept at S. Bernardino. I have never seen an Alpine pass in winter so grimly glorious—such vast masses of fallen snow—and such a terrible wind sweeping it up from every crag and cranny and whirling it down across the plains of Italy in drift. Through that drift we crossed the mountain. And that I do not speak at random I may quote the *padrone* here. I asked him if it had snowed in the last few days. He replied that it had not exactly snowed, but that the north wind had been deluging them with drift from the high Alps. I could not have conceived anything more extraordinary than our journey from Bernardino this morning, enveloped in whirling snow, plunging down pure trackless drifts into a great boiling chasm of vapour, which, when we got inside it, was a seething mass of frost spicules. This is a strange attempt at a cure for a cold. I suppose we shall scuttle back over the Gothard. But I cast a hungry eye at Venice—not so very far away—and your *mezzanino* which you speak of as open to my use. No; I feel it would be risking more than I ought, to come to Venice.

I had to-night a letter from that Belgian Professor Philippson[2] about the Chapter in the Jesuit Constitutions. I wrote to him and he has answered very kindly and fully—sticking staunchly to his guns and mine upon the interpretation of the passage.

Meanwhile I sent a letter to Father Parkinson,[3] omitting my offer to cancel the allusion in my book, and demanding an explanation of the grammar of the chapter. To this I have received no answer. I feel now better prepared to fight the question out, if need be, which I would do by printing the original Latin and appealing to scholars of all sorts upon its obvious meaning.

[Incomplete]

---

1. The Grand Hotel had an English chapel. The Albergo Svizzero was another Locarno hotel.

2. Martin Philippson, the German historian, professor at the University of Brussels (1878–90). See L 1589. His *La Contre-Révolution Religieuse au XVIme. Siècle* (1884) was a source for *The Renaissance in Italy: The Catholic Reaction,* Chap. IV, dealing with the Jesuits. Brown notes (*L&P,* p. 198) that the controversy was over the meaning of *obligatio ad peccatum.* Symonds sent "an apologetic note" to the *Fortnightly Review* in June, 1887, which note, said Brown, "was hardly an apology." Symonds' letter was apparently not published, though "A Jesuit Doctrine of Obedience" published posthumously in *The Fortnightly Review,* LIII (May, 1893), 745–52, may be an expansion of it.

3. The Rt. Rev. Mons. Henry Parkinson (1852–1924), author of *A Primer of Social Science* (1913); born in Cheadle, Staffordshire; educated at Sedgley Park, Douai, Olton, and the English College, Rome; held various positions in Roman Catholic seminaries and cathedrals; assistant-general for England and Wales of the Apostolic Union of Secular Priests.

1583. *To Charlotte Mary and Margaret Symonds*

Locarno Feb 19 1887

My dear children, Lotta & Madge,

Here am I sitting on the shores of the Lago Maggiore, whitened all over with snow, with your mother, & thinking about you both.[1]

Your mother left Madge at Davos before she joined me at Thusis to cross the Bernardino.

From Lotta we have already letters full of Madge's expected arrival in London.

Our hearts therefore are full of thoughts about your meeting together and of the fine things we hope will come of it. I anticipate a good time for both of you now, & a good time for me also, if I am able to come to England & bring you back to Davos.

Your mother & I often said, as we were crossing the Bernardino, that we were glad to have sent Madge to England instead of bringing her here.

What was there upon the pass except snow in its grandest develop-ments, snow heaped thirty feet above the roads, snow whirled by the N.E. winds from every peak over into Italy?

And what is there here but snow, frozen roads, misty silvery lakes, & great mountains covered to their summits with a mail of snow?

I like to sit here by the open wood fire (itself a grateful novelty) & to think of you two together in London. You will have pictures, people, and theatres & music perhaps. If you want money, you will get it from me.

Tell me, both or either of you, if you want anything to make the life you are now living more agreeable.

We are expecting on Monday Madge's first letter from London. This, we are sure, will be one of excitement & pleasure. It is good that you are both together now in England. But how we shall miss you both, when we return to Davos, I dare not say.

I believe that your mother faced the snows of the pass & the frost, in order to put between her past & future a little bit of travelling wh should make the desolation of our home less sensible.

Enjoy yourselves both, & learn: that is my wish. There is an immense amount for both of you to learn where you now are, which you could not learn at Davos. I believe you will learn most by enjoying simply & healthily.

Goodbye to both now. I will not mix this letter up with casual details. They might amuse you. But my own thoughts are too much with you in London together, for trifles to have any articulate value.

God bless you both

JA Symonds.

---

1. See L 1582. In L 1585 he says: "Our two girls, Lotta and Madge, are in London with Miss [Marianne] North, learning and enjoying greatly."

1584. *To Herbert P. Horne*[1]

[Davos, March, 1887]

[Dear Sir]

. . . discourse, "Credo in unam Artem"[2] etc certain for me a truth to wh I have always sought, although with poor success, to tune my own labours.

That my book on the Renaissance should receive so respectful, so conscientious, & so excellently written a notice as that by Mr Galton,[3] in a publication of so ingeniously high a spirit, gives me true pleasure—not, I hope, merely the pleasure of finding work appreciated, but that of discovering it recognized as valuable to fellow-workers. Pray convey to him from me a message of thanks. I know him already at a distance as the author of "Urbana Scripta",[4] a book which I studied last year with great interest, & the sound critical stuff of which I fully appreciated.

I have no adequate gifts to return for yours. "Silver & gold have I none." But I send you, as a token, two sonnets on the Daffodil.[5] It always struck me as curious that this flower should be dedicated to two creations of the Aryan

[Incomplete]

---

1. See L 1452.

2. I believe in a single art.

3. Arthur Galton's review, "The Italian Renaissance," in *The Century Guild Hobby Horse*, II (January, 1887), 20–28. For a note on Galton see L 1581. Though Galton on the whole liked Symonds' work, he was critical of it:

Mr. Symonds' style is far removed from the conciseness, the simplicity, the severe restraint which even an English prose classic should possess. And, as an historian, he is still farther removed from the minute accuracy, the calm impartiality of a Stubbs or a Gardiner; and from the due, and admirable, subordination of multitudinous details which is the characteristic excellence of a Gibbon. Mr. Symonds' book is rather a storehouse of materials and authorities for some historian of the future, than a history which may be considered as classical or final; but the future historian of the Renaissance will owe Mr. Symonds an immense, an incalculable debt.

4. Galton, *Urbana Script: Studies of Five Living Poets; and Other Essays* (1885).

5. The sonnets, "Narcissus' Flower" and "Balder's Flower," appeared in *The Century Guild Hobby Horse*, II (October, 1887), 121–22.

1585. *To Henry Sidgwick*

Davos, March 5, 1887.

[Dear Henry]

If I have not written to you earlier respecting your Diary for January 7, it is not through lack of interest and sympathy. When I come to speak about myself, I will tell you the hindrances I have had to contend against, and the difficulties in which I still find myself placed.

You will of course know that I am alluding to the passage of your

Diary, in which you announce your expectation of having to abandon in this life the hope of obtaining proof of the individual soul's existence as a consciousness beyond death. What this implies for yourself, in its bearings I mean, upon Moral Philosophy, and its bearings upon the sustained quest of twenty years, I am able to appreciate.

And I may add that it was for myself also a solemn moment, when I read that paragraph in the Diary, through the measured sentences of which a certain subdued glow of passion seemed to burn. I do not pretend that I had ever fixed my views of human conduct clearly or hopefully upon the proof of immortality to our ordinary experience. I do not deny that I never had any confidence in the method you were taking to obtain the proof. I will further confess that, had you gained the proof, this result would have enormously aggravated the troubles of my life, by cutting off the possibility of resumption into the personal-unconscious which our present incertitude leaves open to my sanguine hope.

Ethics, I feel, can take care of themselves—that is to say, human beings in social relations will always be able to form codes of conduct, profitable to the organism and coercive of the individual to the service of its uses. In humanity, as in nature, "est Deus, quis Deus incertum."[1]

I have no apprehension for civil law and social and domestic institutions, even though the permanence of personal consciousness after this life remain undemonstrated. Those things are necessary for our race, of whose position in the universe we are at present mainly ignorant; and a sanction of some sort, appealing to imagination, emotion, unformulated onward impulses, will always be forthcoming. Man has only had about 6,000 years of memory upon this planet; and the most grudging physicists accord him between ten and twenty millions to come. Dislocations of ethical systems, attended by much human misery, possibly also by retrograde epochs of civilisation, are likely to ensue. History, if it teaches anything in its little span of past time, prepares us to expect such phases in the incalculably longer future. But our faith lies in this: that God, in the world, and in humanity as a portion of the world, effectuates Himself, and cannot fail to do so. I do not see, therefore, why we should be downcast if we cannot base morality upon a conscious immortality of the individual.

But I do see that, until that immortality of the individual is irrefragably demonstrated, the sweet, the immeasurably precious hope of ending with this life the ache and languor of existence, remains open to burdened human personalities.

A sublime system of ethics seems to me capable of being based, in its turn, upon that hope of extinction. Demonstration, *ex argumento ipso* [by the argument itself], will not here be attained. But I am of opinion that the persuasion, if it comes to be reasonably entertained, of man's surcease from consciousness when this life closes, will afford quite as good a basis for submission to duty as any expectation of continuance in its double aspect of hope and fear has lately been.

This long monologue is only the expression of that interest and sympathy whereof I spoke at the beginning of my letter, and of the deep feelings which your Diary aroused in me.

Our points of view with regard to the problems in question are so different, you being the critic and constructor of philosophy, I the creature of intense personal instincts, and the student more as poet than historian of the past, that I can well believe I shall have bored you with flimsy reveries.

Now I will come back to the affairs of this *Naturwesen* [physical being]. Ever since you left us in the summer, I have been suffering from a chronic inflammation of the eyes. This made my literary work painful. And I was under obligations to do a heavy bit before the end of the year. I translated Cellini's "Memoirs" into English. Under this pressure I broke down, and I have been seriously ill for more than two months with a very exhausting fever. It is of the nature of ague, I think, and has implicated the lungs. The result is that now I spend wretched days of helpless prostration without brain, suffering in every joint, alternately icy cold and burning hot, sleepless at night or pursued by tedious dreams, incapable of moving beyond my house and its wooden shed outside, the mere shadow and vision of a man.

I really do not know why any one who has to suffer in this life should wish to go on living. I know that I am hardly the man to say this; for I have had exceptional good things here compared with myriads of my fellow-creatures. But in so far as I have suffered, it has always been borne in upon me that not to have to live again would be the boon for which I would bless God, and for the certitude of which I would more contentedly agree to do my duty.

Our two girls, Lotta and Madge, are in London with Miss North, learning and enjoying greatly. Here it goes on as usual with the small remnant of us. *Addio.*

[Incomplete]

---

1. There is a God; what God is is uncertain.

1586. *To Mary Robinson*

Am Hof, Davos Platz, Switzerland. March 9 1887

My dear Mary

I read your first article on Valentine Visconti[1] last night, & was charmed with it. The work is so conscientious, & the presentation is so fresh & coloured.

I do not feel convinced that you have got the matter of the French claim to Milan right on pp 412 413.

The deed of Clement vii[2] & Gian Galeazzo's will could not have much value in what concerned succession to an Imperial Fief. Everything indeed rests upon the three Imperial Investitutes to Galeazzo. Will you show me how *"their claim (V's sans) is tacitly recognized?"* I looked up the Investitute of 1396 in Muratori[3] xvi p:828 and I cannot see how the words you quote (*descendentes tui enumque descendentes masculi*) can be referred to the male descendants of a daughter. The whole tenor of the document seems to indicate a careful limitation to heirs males *filii legitimi et naturales* born in wedlock, on the failure of whom the succession is extended to *descendentes tui J. G. V. legitimati* etc, wh I take to mean legitimated natural sons. Further down I find that the succession is limited to the heirs of such legitimated male offspring *per lincam masculiniam in infinitum* etc.

Now I should be greatly obliged to you if you would let me know whether you were following any good authority in your interpretation of the Privilegium 1396,[4] or whether you have a text different from Muratori's.

It quite puzzles me to understand why the word *filia,* or even the name of Valentine, was not used in this Privilegium, if the intention was to give her male heirs[5] a reversionary succession. The total absence of a single feminine noun adjective or pronoun (what you quote is *tui*) in this part of the *Privilegium* is most significant.

Pray excuse my insistence on the point. You know I became interested in it through you partly & partly as bearing on my own work. Also I should like you to make your point out fully. You have adduced a row of authorities upon the side-question regarding Clement's deeds & Gian G's will. But this vital question of the *Privilegia* is treated vaguely, & (so far as I can read Priv: 1396) your quotation in brackets does not bear out your assertion.

The conscientious thoroughness of your research is so conspicuous & so charmingly combined with graces & piquencies of style that when the study comes to be reprinted, it must be impregnable upon the kernel of the whole point.

Can you tell me what the French equivalent for *Tesoriere dei Risparmi* at the Court of Francis i was? I find the phrase in Cellini; & having to translate it, must give the proper official title. Was there a *Trésorier des Épargnes?* He seems to have administered the Privy Purse.

I am so glad you have been seeing something of my girls, though I am sorry that on the occasion when your sister so very kindly proposed to take them to the House, their Aunt [Marianne North] put a veto upon it. She feels strongly about some things, & her father was for 30 years an M. P. In the case in question I think she was right. These two girls have no opinion one way or the other about the Irish question. But they have relations, Members of the House of Commons, & perhaps they were rightly prevented from making their début there on a stormy day of battle in the company of the Irish Party. I am always in favour of keeping very much on the safe side in the case of young girls; & so I do not call Miss North's judgment in question. But I wish that she had written to Miss Mabel Robinson herself, explaining simply her reasons instead of leaving the task to Lotta. I can see that Lotta is a little afraid lest she should have seemed rude & careless of your sister's kindness. This was not the case. She felt the disappointment greatly.

I am still very unwell. Nine weeks of my life have been made useless for any purpose & utterly miserable by a lingering exhausting cold. The doctor was with me today, & spoke seriously about it. He speaks about sending me to *Bournemouth* or *St. Leonards* for two months! Fancy that! To go & live in a lodging by oneself on the South Coast, & to be as far away from friends & society as I am here. I really do not think I can endure it. Everyours

JASymonds.

I wonder whether you have read any part of my last vols of the R. in It. I am dispirited about them now, though I think there is good stuff in Vol 7.

---

1. A. Mary F. Robinson, "Valentine Visconti," *Fortnightly Review,* XLVII (1887), 407–20 and 573–86. In 1395, Milan was created a Duchy for Gian Galeazzo (1378–1402), descendant of the ancient House of Visconti who had become the masters of Milan and of a vast surrounding territory. Galeazzo's armed conquests included Verona, Pisa, Siena, Perugia, Assisi, Bologna, and Spoleto. He had visions of himself as

King of Italy and, in fact, demanded the title from the Pope. By his wife Isabella of France he had an only daughter, Valentine (1366–1408), whom he betrothed to Louis, Duke of Orleans, brother of Charles VI of France. From this marriage arose the claim of the House of Orleans to Milan, which led to many wars for both France and Italy. By a second marriage, to Caterina Visconti, Galeazzo had two sons, Giovanni Maria, who succeeded him in 1402, and Filipo Maria, the last of the Visconti, who succeeded his brother in 1412.

2. Robert of Geneva (d. 1394), anti-pope, was declared Pope Clement VII by the French cardinals in 1378; supported by the king of France and the Angevin queen of Naples; ruled from Avignon during part of the so-called "Babylonish Captivity," the Great Schism.

3. Lodovico Antonio Muratori (1672–1750), between 1723 and 1751, published 25 volumes of his *Rerum Italicarum Scriptores,* containing the chronicles of Italy, 5th–16th centuries, illustrated with commentaries and critical notes.

4. For details see L 1589 and Symonds' *The Renaissance in Italy: The Age of the Despots,* Chap. III.

5. Valentine's son was Charles, Duke of Orleans (1391–1465). His son was Louis XII (1462–1515) of France.

1587. *To Horatio Forbes Brown*

Davos, March 10, 1887

[Dear Horatio]

I wrote you a scrap[1] three days ago. I have been and still am very ill—on the verge, says [Dr.] Ruedi, of a serious collapse. He recommends me to go off for two or three months' change, and suggests St. Leonards or Bournemouth! Can you fancy me in a lodging alone there, within reach of London and not able to enjoy my friends? No: I can't do that. My thoughts, on the other hand, turn toward Venice. Your letter of the 6th, which came to-day, says that your *mezzanino* is still vacant, though you speak as if Henry James might take it. I should be very sorry to stand in the way of a more useful tenant. But if you do not find one, I should like nothing at Venice equally. But I am in doubt as to how I should find myself with regard to housekeeping. I do not want to engage a cook, and I should not like to have to risk dining out in all weathers. I must add that Ruedi is against the idea of my going to Venice at all, and I have just had an invitation to join my old friend Lord Aberdare[2] in the south of Italy, which might climatically be thought better for me.

[Incomplete]

---

1. Unavailable.
2. See L 1458.

1588. *To Horatio Forbes Brown*

Davos, March 15 [1887]

[Dear Horatio]

I am very much obliged to you for the telegram I got on Sunday anent the *mezzanino*.[1] There is little doubt, I think, that when I am fit to travel, I shall come to Venice. I cannot say exactly when this may be. For I have been getting weaker since I last wrote to you, and the weather has suddenly turned off to winter.

Jowett writes *more suo* that I have reached "eminence"; but that now is the time to win a permanent place among the first writers of my generation, for which I have the "natural gifts," but which I am still considerably far away from. His well-meaning exhortations reached me when I was half frantic with pain in the joints, wholly to bits in nerves, and terribly depressed by the sense of the difficulties under which I have to labour as an author at Davos. So I exploded a fantastic fire-work of words on this *tema:* "Damn success! *À bas la gloire! Vive la vie* under the ribs of Death, and in the prospect of fifteen millions of fame-annihilating years of human existence." I don't know how he will have liked it. But I am an old panting cab-horse; and can't bear to be flogged up the last hill with the prospect of most dubious bays to crown my carcass at the top.

[Incomplete]

---

1. See L 1587 to Brown.

1589. *To Mary Robinson*

Am Hof, Davos Platz, Switzerland. March 26 1887

My dear Mary

In an official document published by Plon,[1] I find that the title of the French functionary I want is "Trésorier de nostre épargne."[2] But I am not sure whether épargne corresponds to our *Prinz Purse*. I shall be grateful to you, if you can inform me.

The bulky Ms of my "Cellini," about 870 close pp, is now in the printer's hands. I wrote the whole between July 7 & Nov 10. This it is wh broke my health down.

211

With regard to the French claim to Milan, I think it may be worth your while to read Sismondi³ Vol vi Ch: 6 at the beginning. He seems to me to have a sensible view of the hollowness of all claims founded upon Imperial Investitutes in Lombardy.

But of course there still remains the obligation of ascertaining whether the French had even such a claim.

Now I think we may at once eliminate Gian Galeazzo's will.⁴ He could not leave the Duchy by will, when it passed into the hands of Filippo Maria who was acknowledged as 3rd Duke any more than my father's will regarding our family estate would have any effect after I became possessed of it. If F. M. V. died intestate (that is if his will in favour of Alfonso of Aragon & Naples was a figment) & if he did not declare Francesco Sforza his successor (wh I do not believe he did in any effectual way), then the Duchy either lapsed or went by the line of inheritance laid down in the Imperial Privilegia. F.M.V.'s tenancy of the Duchy rendered Gian Galeazzo's will in any case ineffective.

Now as to the Investitures, where the real tug of war is.

I hear in all of Six

1) 3 to *Gian Galeazzo:* 1395, 1396, 1397. That of 1396 pointedly excludes females. That of 1397 is not known to me; but unless females are clearly indicated in it, I should be of opinion that *descendentes sui* would have to be interpreted by that of 1396. What authority is there for this *Privilegium?* It was not known to Sismondi.

ii) 1 to Filippo Maria in 1425-6. This I have not seen. But if it exists, it ought to be carefully studied. For F. M. V. was Duke *de jure* through the Investitures granted to his father; and any fresh Imperial Settlement of the Duchy during his tenure must have affected Valentine's claim (supposing she had any) under that of 1397.

iii 1 to Lodovico Sforza in 1493. Dubious, _____ _____ but I think probable, because of the clauses inserted in the next to be mentioned.

iv) i to Louis xii in 1501. (Renewed 1508 1509?) Louis was then *de facto* Lord of Milan. Yet Maximilian especially reserved the rights of Lodovico Sforza's children, which, as you are doubtless aware, was the Spanish pretext for restoring the Sforzas & eventually obtaining the Duchy by the will of the last Duke Fr: M. S.

Have you seen the Privilegium of 1501 to Louis xii? It would be interesting to see whether Valentine's claim is recited in it.
‡ ‡ = = = = = = = =

Well: I do not think this will be very helpful to you anyhow. My firm

belief is that Milan was intended to be a male fief. Yet all depends 1) on the genuine nature of the Privilegium of 1397 2) on the interpretation of the words used in it regarding the succession. I argue that as females were pointedly excluded in 1396, they ought to have been pointedly included in 1397, if the Imperial policy with regard to Milan had changed.
= = = = =

You are quite right that I pitched too fiercely & unfairly into the Jesuits.[5] I am sorry for it now. But I cannot stomach their manipulation of the conscience while they affected to be the special servants of Jesus; & the end they had in view, the establishment of a religious despotism, is one that is to me odious above measure. Those views of determinism may be held by philosophers. They can not be squared with the teaching of the law or the gospel.

I wish I had not been so petulant, however. It has deformed my book. How I wish I could have got some friend to read the Ms! I am so lonely here, & write too much to myself. The next volume is, I think, much better than the 5th. I hope you will like it.

I had a nice letter from Miss [Violet] Paget [Vernon Lee] today. She seems rather to regret your historical research. I do not, because I see how well you do it. But I fear it will fatigue you too much. You look very tired in Hollyer's[6] photograph, which, however, seems to us by far the best was ever taken of you.

I am still ill: both lungs irritated, says the doctor. In a few days I hope to go to Ragatz for change, & thence if I am well enough to Venice. Everyrs

J A Symonds

---

1. Eugène Plon, *Cellini, orfèvre, médailleur, etc.* (Paris, 1883).

2. See L 1586. Symonds wanted to be accurate in translating Bk. 2, Chap. XXIII, of Cellini's autobiography.

3. Jean Charles Sismondi (1773–1842), Swiss historian, noted for his *Histoire des Républiques Italiennes du Moyen-Age* (1807–18) and *Histoire de la Renaissance de la Liberté en Italie* (1832).

4. See L 1586. Filippo Maria Visconti was Galeazzo's son.

5. See *The Renaissance in Italy: The Catholic Reaction,* Chap. IV. See also L 1582.

6. Hollyer, the photographer. See L 617.

1590. *To Margaret Symonds*

Am Hof, Davos Platz, Switzerland. March 26 1887

My dearest Madge

I received your letter this morning. I cannot tell you what pleasure we all take in your & Lotta's letters. They are eagerly seized upon & read by the small remnant of your family, & then your mother copies the most interesting parts into a Ms book. She likes doing it, & I think the plan is good.

I decidedly recommend you to buy the Metastasio.[1] He was the last great Italian poet of the 18th century, & wrote dramas for all the great Composers of his age. Hasse, Jom[m]elli, Cimarosa, Zingarelli, Paisiello, Mozart,[2] turned them into operas. The great ladies & gentlemen of the age of bagwigs & ruffles wept over their romance & sentiment. And really, allowing for the conventionality of their form, there is great lyrical beauty in them. You shall read Miss [Violet] Paget's *18th Cent in Italy,*[3] wh is all about Metastasio & the Opera—a most wonderful book for a girl of 22 to have written.

I want you to send 4/ by post order with the enclosed note to the address you will find at the bottom.

I believe that, if all is well, I shall go to Venice soon. You mother thinks of taking Katharine as far as Ragatz; where I propose to stay with them about a week, & if I feel well enough to go on by Arlberg & Bremer.

Dr. Ruedi has the measles. So I cannot consult him. But Florian Buol[4] examined me the other day, & said that he found mischief going on in both my lungs. He did not much like me to undertake a journey in this state. Yet I cannot progress here. At least I do so very slowly, if at all, & life has become dreary. So I think trying what change to Ragatz does for me will be a good experiment to begin with.

The huge Ms of Cellini, about 870 pp, & *you* know how much there is in *some* of the pages, has arrived safely in London; & I may soon expect proofs. Otherwise I have no literary work on hand, & mean to give myself a holiday.

I shall try to come to England later on. If so, I shall certainly hope to get to Alderley.[5] It is possible that we might travel back together. But these plans are still vague.

I am again in negotiation for buying Bätschi's farm at Meierhof.[6] If I can get it for about £ 700 or £ 800, I think it is worth while. Did I tell you that I have arranged with old Frau Friedin at Meierhof to have the

Stube looking on the Lake reserved in future for my own use? I think it would be nice to make tea there & write sometimes perhaps. Your remarks on the Nat[ional] G[allery] are very interesting. Have you seen the Pheidian [Elgin] marbles at the Br Mus? You ought to go there. Best love to Lotta.

Ever yr most loving father   JAS

It has been snowing hard these 3 days. But it melts as soon as falls. What a pity we had it not in Jany. This is a truly [A.O.] Rutsonian letter. All scraps & additions.

---

1. Pietro Antonio Domenico Bonaventura Metastasio (1698–1782), famous poet and opera librettist. His opera texts number about 35; some were set to music 60 or more times. Symonds' list of composers employing Metastasio's texts should also include Handel and Gluck. See Handel's *Siroe, Re di Persia* (1728), *Poro, Re dell' Indie* (1731), and *Ezio* (1732); Gluck's *Artaserse* (1741), *Demofoonte* (1742), and *Demetrio* (1742).

2. Johann Adolph Hasse, German dramatic composer (1699–1783): *Artaserse* (1731), *Cleofide* (1731), *Tito Vespasiano* (1735), *Didone Abbandonata* (1742), *Antigone* (1743); Niccolò Jommelli (1714–74), opera composer of the Neapolitan school: *Ezio* (1741), *Demofoonte* (1743), *La Didone Abbandonata* (1747), *Artaserse* (1749); Domenico Cimarosa (1749–1801), Italian composer, whose forte was comic opera: *L'Olimpiade* (1784); Niccola Antonio Zingarelli (1752–1837): *Artaserse* (1794); Giovanni Paisiello (1740–1816), Italian dramatic composer: *Demofoonte* (1773) and *Alcide al Bivio* (1779); Wolfgang Amadeus Mozart (1756–91): *La Clemenza di Tito*.

3. Vernon Lee, *Studies of the Eighteenth Century in Italy* (1880).

4. A doctor, brother of Christian Buol.

5. Marianne North lived at Alderley.

6. Symonds had bought another farm earlier. See L 1464. See also L 1452.

1591. *To* The Fortnightly Review

Davos, March 27, 1887.

Sir,

Professor Dowden's *Life of Percy Bysshe Shelley*[1] is based upon a considerable mass of letters, journals, and other manuscripts in possession of the poet's family, which were hitherto inaccessible; from it we learn all that has been ascertained about Shelley's domestic affairs, nor is it probable that much more concerning him remains to be discovered. To speak too highly of the skill with which this long biography has been composed would be difficult. It is a masterly portrait, executed with the most perfect fidelity and impartiality in the minutest details. Professor Dowden helps us to know Shelley far more intimately than we knew him before; and many of the legends which perplexed the student of his life are now finally disposed of.

The most important episode in Shelley's history was his separation from his first wife, Harriet Westbrook, in the summer of 1814. Lady Shelley in her *Shelley Memorials*,[2] and Dr. Garnett in his *Relics of Shelley*[3] had warned the public to suspend their judgment upon this point. They told us that documents existed which, without casting a slur on Harriet, would completely vindicate her husband's conduct. Mr. Dowden has had access to these documents, and we look therefore to his account of the circumstances with keen interest. It may be said at once that he has cleared away the last suspicions of Shelley's heartlessness and inhumanity. Shelley did not abruptly desert his wife without providing for her material needs. After a considerable period of gradual estrangement and mutual misunderstanding, he felt that their union must terminate. She agreed, not willingly indeed, but after personal explanations with her husband, to a separation which she possibly imagined would be only temporary. So far the matter has now been made plain. But very little that will alter our opinion of Shelley's morality has been added. It is true that Mr. Dowden is able to show that Harriet treated her husband with coldness in the spring of 1814, and he prints for the first time some tender and pathetic stanzas addressed to her by the poet in the month of May.[a] These prove convincingly that Shelley then was pleading for a reconciliation; but they do not disprove the fact that his final rupture with Harriet was caused by the sudden passion he conceived for Mary Godwin in the following June.

Mr. Dowden makes one assertion which very materially influences our judgment, and which demands close investigation. He says, "From an assurance that she (Harriet) had ceased to love him, Shelley had passed to a conviction that she had given her heart to another, and had linked her life to his."[b] This statement he repeats without qualification: "He had left her, believing she was unfaithful to him."[c] The documents which Mr. Dowden quotes to establish Shelley's belief in Harriet's unfaithfulness before the separation are three in number.[d] First, a letter from Shelley to his second wife, dated January 11, 1817. Secondly, a letter from Godwin to Mr. W. T. Baxter, dated May 12, 1817. Thirdly, a note appended by Miss Clairmont to transcripts from her mother's letters, made some time after 1832. I have enumerated these in chronological order, because their greater or less remoteness from the year 1814 considerably affects their value as evidence regarding Shelley's belief at that period.

It must be borne in mind that Harriet committed suicide in November, 1816, and very soon after this event the Westbrook family began a suit in Chancery with the object of depriving Shelley of the custody of his two children by her. On the 11th of January, 1817, then, Shelley wrote to Mary: "I learn just now from Godwin that he has evidence that Harriet was unfaithful to me *four months* before I left England with you. If we can succeed in establishing this, our connection will receive an additional sanction, and plea be overborne."[e] As a matter of fact, when the pleadings began, he did not establish this, nor did he allude to the matter in the memorandum he drew up of his case.[f] Godwin writes upon the 12th of May: "The late Mrs. Shelley has turned out to be a woman of great levity. I know from unquestionable authority, wholly unconnected with Shelley (though I cannot with propriety be quoted for this), that she had proved herself unfaithful to her husband before their separation." On the strength of these two passages, the pith and kernel of which is that Godwin, some months after Harriet's death, credited a tale told him by an unknown person, which he repeated to Shelley, we are asked to suppose that Shelley in July, 1814, two and a half years earlier, was convinced of Harriet's infidelity. But Miss Clairmont has still to be heard. She, writing at some uncertain date subsequently to 1832, and therefore at least eighteen years after the separation, recorded that: "He (Shelley) succeeded in persuading her (Mary) by declaring that Harriet did not really care for him; that she was in love with a Major Ryan; and the child she would have was certainly not his. This Mary told me herself, adding that this justified his having another attachment." When we come to examine Miss Clairmont's reminiscences, we find them untrustworthy in so many instances that her evidence carries no weight.[g] In the second place it is unquestioned and unquestionable that Shelley firmly believed the second child he had by Harriet to be his own. He announced the boy's birth to his friends, had him named Charles Bysshe, used him in his efforts to raise money, and passionately claimed him when Harriet's relatives refused to give him up. Yet we are invited to accept the memorandum of an inaccurate woman, penned at least eighteen years after the event, and including one palpable and serious misstatement, as proof that Shelley judged his first wife unfaithful before he eloped with Mary.

No one contends that Harriet actually broke her marriage vow before the separation. What Professor Dowden asks us to believe is that *Shelley thought* she was untrue to him at that period. Miss Clairmont's evidence I reject as valueless. At the most she only reports something which Shelley is supposed to have said to Mary with the object of persuading her to elope with him, and which his subsequent conduct with regard to his son Charles Bysshe contradicted. The true inference to be drawn from Shelley's and Godwin's far more important letters in 1817 is that it was not until the latter date that the suspicion of Harriet's guilt before the separation arose. This suspicion did not, however, harden into certainty, nor was it found capable of verification; else why did not Shelley use the fact, as he proposed, in order to strengthen his case against the Westbrooks? I admit that his letter to Southey in 1820 supports the view that, having once begun to entertain the suspicion, he never afterwards abandoned it.[h]

If now we turn to contemporary records between the dates, June, 1814, and May, 1815 (at which time Harriet disappears from our ken), we find no intimation either in Mary's or Miss Clairmont's diary, or in Shelley's words and writings, or in the conduct of the Shelley-Godwin set, that Harriet was believed to have broken faith so early with her husband. When Shelley in the summer of 1814 sought to lower her in the eyes of Mary Godwin, he did so by hinting that she only cared for his money and his prospects.[i] Mary talks about her "insulting selfishness," calls her "nasty woman," and exhibits a good deal of resentment at Shelley's welcome to his son and heir by her (December 6, 1815).[j] The pained reiteration of the words *wife* in her diary on this occasion proves how bitterly she felt her own position as *mistress*. Shelley invited Harriet to establish herself in the neighbourhood of Mary and himself. She was visited in London by the whole party. But while they continued upon awkward terms of half familiarity and mutual irritation, nothing by word or act implied a knowledge of her previous infidelity. What is further to the point is that Mrs. Shelley, in her novel of *Lodore,* which Professor Dowden rightly judges to be a history of Shelley's relation to Harriet, painted a wife's gradual alienation from her husband without hinting at misconduct.[k]

In conclusion, I am bound to express my opinion that nothing now produced from the Shelley archives very materially alters the view of the case at which sane and cautious critics arrived before these were placed in the hands of his last biographer. We ought, moreover, to remember that Shelley, of all men, would have most resented anything like an appeal to popular opinions regarding the marriage tie. His firm conviction was that when affection ceased between a married couple, or when new loves had irrevocably superseded old ones, the connection ought to be broken. In his own case he felt that Harriet's emotion towards him had changed, while an irresistible passion for another woman had suddenly sprung up in his heart.

Upon these grounds, after undergoing a terrible contention of the soul, he forced on the separation to which his first wife unwillingly submitted.

John Addington Symonds.

---

a. Vol. i., p. 413.

b. Vol. i., p. 429.

c. Vol. ii., p. 65.

d. These three documents will be found in Vol. ii., p. 98; Vol. i., pp. 424, 425.

e. Mr. Dowden omits the second sentence in his quotation. Vol. i., p. 426.

f. Vol. ii., p. 88.

g. See Mr. Dowden's own critique of this witness in Appendix B. to Vol. ii. Compare Vol. i., p. 440.

h. Vol. i., p. 428.

i. Vol. i., p. 415.

j. Vol. i., p. 465.

k. Vol. i., pp. 436–438.

---

1. Edward Dowden, *The Life of Percy Bysshe Shelley* (2 vols., 1886).

2. Jane (Gibson) Shelley, *Shelley Memorials. Edited by Lady Shelley. To which is added an Essay on Christianity, by Percy Bysshe Shelley* (1859).

3. Richard Garnett (1835–1906), *Relics of Shelley* (1862) included unpublished poems and letters.

1592. *To Roden Noel*

[Davos, April, 1887]

[Dear Roden]

I should call my own attitude a spiritualised stoicism rather than Calvinism; the latter assumed *inequality* in the divine dealings with man. All my notions about law and the homogeneity of the universe lead me to expect absolute equality. I am therefore in the peculiar position of an optimist, who is prepared to accept extinction. This enables me to feel a really passionate interest in the spectacle of the universe, and a firm conviction that its apparent injustice and inequalities must have a meaning, imply *a good in process*. At the back of my thought lie two perceptions—

(1) our incapacity to formulate the future and what we want in it; (2) our right to assume that manly acquiescence, combined with continued effort to get the utmost out of our lives by work in our own way, is the best preparation for any grace that may be granted to us.

[Incomplete]

1593. *To the Rev. Arthur Galton*[1]

Ragatz April 5 1887

I have told my publishers to send you Itn Byways merely in return for your many more valuable gifts to me.

Dear Mr Galton

I received your letter of the 30th March in this place, & your lecture on the relation of Literature to Life.[2]

I read the lecture with great interest, & agreed with its main drift. But I should like to talk over principles with you. It seems to me that you rest too easily contented with the doctrine (or Gospel shall I say?) of Mat Arnold. That leaves out a whole & very vital element of human life; the ignoring of which makes his Gospel jejune for disciples, though it has been aptly uttered by himself.

However, I cannot write an essay, & tell you what Mat Arnold does not allow for in life.

I had started on a journey to recover my health, was going in fact to Venice.

News reaches me that my eldest daughter (a confirmed invalid) is at the last stage of her life through a sudden development of disease. So I am off again to Davos, there to stay & abide the decrees of fate.—Has it ever been born in upon you that religion culture philosophy art etc are mere bubbles in comparison with life? JAS

---

1. See L 1581.
2. See Galton's essay, "Matthew Arnold; His Practice, Teaching and Example: An Essay on Criticism," *The Century Guild Hobby Horse*, III (1889), 83–108.

1594. *To Henry Sidgwick*

[Davos, April 6, 1887]

[Dear Henry]

I have just come home and found your March Diary, which is intensely interesting on several grounds. What interests me most is your meditation called forth by a letter I wrote about the relation of morality to our belief in immortality. I wrote that in the hope that you might answer. I cannot see why we should attempt to demonstrate such felt things as Morality, Beauty, God, or why we should cumber ourselves with searchings after a life "im seligen Jenseits" [in the blessed beyond]. It is, no doubt, quite idiosyncratic on my part to prefer the prospect of extinction. But I am no more sure of getting this than you are of getting a prolongation of conscious being. So, as far as morality goes, we are just at the same point; and if I behave worse than you, which I assuredly do, it is not due to my not having a firm expectation of immortality.

Why should not morality rest upon legality, as it does always in the first place, and on the social need of approval—self-respect?

So far as I am moral at all, it is not from a sense of Duty. I think a great deal of humbug has been talked about this word, which in the course of some centuries will be analysed away into the real principles of action it has masked.

The only sure thing is that we have to live and have to die—why either we do not now know; if we come to know, well; and there is no harm in seeking to discover the why and the whereto; but meanwhile we ought to be able to get on without it. Least of all ought we to rely upon an unproved bribe and unproved deterrent for right action. The problem about this bribe and this deterrent being insoluble, as you observe, by all methods, were it not well to accept the fact boldly, and leave ourselves resolutely in the hands of that power which put us here? This is not Comtism. The miserable spectre of humanity is quite *de trop*. He calls this the *Grand Être*,[1] doesn't he?

I am so indebted to you for writing what you think about these matters, that you must excuse the crude tone I take in order to elicit more of the same sort.

Indeed I do not think of the problem without great tenderness and deep searchings of heart now.

I have been ill since Christmas, and a long sojourn away from Davos was recommended. I left last Thursday, but was too weak to travel fast. I meant to go to Venice after spending a week at Ragatz. At this latter place I heard alarming news about Janet on Sunday. I came here to-day.

How am I to help her if she asks for help? I have my own answer: which is unlimited submission to the Supreme will, resolute abstention from all imaginative efforts to forecast the future, sustained belief that come what may the world is not diabolically ordered. This is only what Socrates in Plato told his judges.[2] But is this not enough to live and be a man and act and die by?

The impulse of curiosity I am not such a fool as to ignore, and I honour every effort which may render mankind clearer upon the great issue. But I cannot divest myself of the *Ahnung* [presentiment] that such solution of the problem as our very limited reason may arrive at will not greatly affect either our conduct or our happiness. And at present, at all events, we have to live and die without the gratification of our curiosity.

There is something grim in all this. But everything has a grim side. The hopeful point is that the total sum of things has so many sides which are not grim. This hypothesis of immortality seems to me also to be a phase in morality out of which we are passing.

[Incomplete]

---

1. The term used by Auguste Comte (1798–1857) for humanity, a supreme reality to which all others are subordinate. Cf. L. Lévy-Bruhl, *The Philosophy of Auguste Comte,* authorized translation with an introduction by Frederic Harrison (1903), p. 333; and Auguste Comte, *Système de Politique Positive* (4 vols., 1851–54), II, 57 ff. and 255 ff., for example.

2. See *The Apology.*

1595. *To Mary Robinson*

Am Hof, Davos Platz, Switzerland. April 7, 1887

Dear Mary

I must tell you that our dear Janet died this morning at 5.15. The last crisis was very rapid. She seemed much like herself, only a little weaker in the heart, up to last Friday. A serious change then set in, & the doctor warned us that the beginning of the end had come. She suffered a great deal from those alarming stoppages of the heart & partial suffocation. But she kept her brave calm spirit clear to the last. She had not the slightest fear of death, & died at last almost imperceptibly just after her mother had got her out of bed on to a chair to help her breathing. A gentler purer more reasonable & more unselfish soul was never "added to heaven's happiness."

Yrs ever

J A Symonds

1596. *To Charlotte Mary and Margaret Symonds*

Am Hof, Davos Platz, Switzerland. April 7 1887

My dearest girls

Your mother has just written you a long letter, telling you all about our loved Janet's last hours. No one could have wished that her life should be prolonged; for though she did not suffer pain exactly, she had a continual battle for breath.

The end was unexpectedly sudden. [Dr.] Ruedi thought she might hold out until the middle of May. Janet would have liked to have you here, & we should have sent for you. But this rapid failure of her heart forestalled all plans.

Ruedi telegraphed to me at Ragatz on Tuesday *not to come home;* for there was no immediate danger, & he wanted me to get rid of my cold. But I could not stay there longer. I am thankful I came yesterday. It seemed to give Janet pleasure, & she talked with me quite like herself last night. We even discussed plans about her going to a lower level where her breathing would be easier.

It is very very sad for you to get this news at such a distance. My heart yearns for you; & I am thinking every moment that I should like to have you sharing our deep sorrow & talking over our darling.

The whole house seems now calling out for Janet & reminding me of her. She lived in it more than any of us; & there are certain parts of it, especially the shed[Wandelbahn:[1] KF], which will never cease to recall her.

We must not regret what has happened. She could not get better. So far as it went, she enjoyed much in her life; and now we have the absolute certainty that her guileless, beautiful, brave, unselfish, reasonable spirit is with God, close to God; there was nothing in her nature to separate her from God, no passion, no carnal grossness, no evil thoughts or feelings. Her long trial purified & refined her, so that she at last was spiritually fit to pass at once into the choir of Angels. Oh, how we ought to long & strive to make ourselves like her! When I compare my weak wilful imperfect erring nature with hers, I feel how far less fit I am to die.

The whole thing has been very sudden. My last observation about her just before we left for Ragatz last Thursday, was that she was playing a duet for piano & violin with remarkable vigour. Heim[2] came in the morning then. It was, however, unfortunate that Ruedi (owing to his own illness) had not examined her for 4 weeks. She did not want to send for another doctor; & though she was more breathless, she ascribed this to the Spring & began to take tonics.

The next day, Friday, she collapsed; & there has not been a shadow of hope since then.

It is difficult this morning to do more than just dwell upon the fact, without thinking of anything beside it.

Ever my dear girls your most loving father

J A Symonds.

Since I wrote this your mother & I have been thinking much of what you will be wishing to do under these circumstances. We mean, if possible, to come together to England, & very likely with little Katharine also. But we should not come yet. I know it would be unsafe for me. Probably we should spend a couple of weeks here & another two at Badenweiler. If you feel that you can live in England, as at present arranged, chiefly with Aunt Pop [Marianne North] until we arrive, this would do very well. But you must take time to think over it. There is plenty of time for consideration, as you have no fashionable engagements; & the places you are going to are all quiet. You might however wish to cut off your Cambridge visit.—You must tell us what your mind is.

---

1. The covered porch built so that Symonds and his family could take the air on inclement days.
2. Probably a local physician.

1597. *To Edmund Gosse*

Davos April 7 1887

My dear Gosse

I am certain as I can be that my daughters did not receive Mrs Gosse's invitation, & that when they hear of what they lost they will be very sorry.

I can only conjecture that the letters were addressed simply to 3

Victoria St S.W. This most unlucky street has several No 3's in it—a state of things which has subsisted there since my father-in-law Mr North first took a flat in those regions more than 20 years ago. If therefore the name of "Miss North" was not included in the address, the letters are deposited probably in some other No 3 than hers. England alone is capable of such extravagances.

My daughters only left London about a week ago for Hastings where they are staying with another member of the North family.

Poor girls, they have a sad day today. For their elder sister, my dear first born, died this morning early. She had suffered much for five years of gradually progressive illness. But when the crisis came, it came so suddenly advanced to the end so rapidly that we feel now as if it had been some awful accident.

She is at rest. That comforts her mother & myself. And she passed from life in full consciousness, without a sign of apprehension.

I have been ill myself ever since the New Year, & quite incapable of doing anything. I overworked myself last year, & collapsed.

Else I should have written to thank you for the very cheering letter you wrote, chiding me for my pusillanimity, & promising me success if I would hold on. Indeed I have often & often thanked you for those words. I do not think I deserve what you generously say. But I shall keep the memory to stimulate me to more sincere & painstaking effort in the future.

Jam satis jocati sumus [enough frivolity]—that is the motto of Modern literature! The "channering worm"[1] of criticism & the Churton Collins[2] of the "vociferous PMG" have their uses, if they goad us into deeper earnestness.

Butler[3] is here again, & he has been very kind to me in my sorrow today. I find from other quarters that what you hinted about his want of tact (shall I call it?) at Trinity last term has been pretty widely noticed. He might with advantage meet a candid friend. But this should be one who can see through the whole situation. He has great private anxieties at present. Yet he ought to make a point of knowing all his college. His function is to be a centre.

I am proud to hear that you & Mrs Gosse like my two daughters. They wrote to us with enthusiasm of the visit they paid to your house. And when the mistake (whatever it is) about your last invitation is cleared up, I expect to find that they regret one of the most pleasant opportunities they could have had in London. Believe me with kindest regards to Mrs Gosse to be yours ever   J A Symonds.—

1. Muttering:

> The cock doth craw, the day doth daw,
> The channerin worm doth chide. . . .
> —"The Wife of Usher's Well"

2. See L 1565.
3. See L 1569.

1598. *To Charlotte Mary and Margaret Symonds*

Am Hof, Davos Platz, Switzerland. April 10 1887

My dearest girls

Your mother & I were very much pleased to get both sets of your letters this morning—those written on the 6th & those on the 7th for they show that although you would like to have come straight here, you were prepared to do what we thought best.

The end came so quickly that you could not have arrived in time to see Janet alive. Yet I feel deeply for you in not having been with us during the last three days. We have found great peace & consolation in seeing Janet, who looked even more beautiful in death than in life. She was just like one of those marble statues of the sleeping dead carved by a Tuscan sculptor, & was covered with flowers.

Everybody has been extremely kind; not only English people, but also the Davosers. Marie Godmer[1] brought a little wreath of myrtle wh finished off her hair & just defined her forehead. Tobias Branger[2] sent a splendid wreath of white flowers. All the snow-flakes, narcissus, camellias, white stocks, late Christmas Roses, hyacinths, cyclamens, that you can think of covered her bed. Colonel Pearson[3] sent a wreath, with a card and "Adieu Janet" written on it.

She was taken away last night without any fuss, & she is to be buried at 12 tomorrow. I fear this will be a very trying time for all of us. So many of the Davos people mean to come I believe.

I think you will like to see the enclosed letter which Herr Heim[4] sent with a wreath of flowers. Please keep it for me. I think his words "ihre edle Sanftmuth und Güte" [her noble gentleness and kindness] are just right.

I did not know how much I loved her, & I am always regretting that I did not do more for her while there was yet time. I know she felt for me a deep & peculiar affection; & I might have given up some of my eternal scribbling, wh engrossed me always & made me irritable & nervous, in order

226

to read to her or to talk about things she liked. Instead too of sitting with the door ajar in my room smoking, & thinking "how nicely Janet is playing!" I might have pleased her by going in & listening. (She was pleased, I could see, that last evening by what Madge wrote about her music.) And also I think it would have been kind if I had more often alluded to her symptoms of illness. She liked talking about such things. But I deliberately avoided doing so, for I judged her life would retain more of naturalness if its painful elements were not constantly touched upon.

It is of little use to make these reflections now. Death is a great teacher. We only learn through him too late how we might have acted better.

One of you said in your letter that Janet was Christlike. And this is perfectly true. Like Christ also she suffered for others. Being our first-born, we did not understand how to treat her health; & our experience has been of advantage to you & little K. And now that she is the first to die, she will I hope make me less neglectful of small matters if any of you come to suffer in like ways.

Your mother embroidered a golden daffodil upon a little Satin cushion for her head in the coffin; & I made her add beneath it these Greek words οὐκ ἔθανες πρώτη. These are the beginning of a beautiful Greek epitaph: "Thou art not dead my Proté."[5] Proté means "the first." She looked wonderful in her coffin—like a bride—only as Greeks would say "the bride of death," or better as the early Christians would say "the Spouse of Christ."

To pass thus away at the very threshold of live, without any of the joys of womanhood, is very sad. But again I must remember an old Greek saying: "Whom the gods love, dies young."

Little Katharine has been very sweet & sensible. She seemed to grow accustomed to seeing Janet in death, & was often in the room.

I find myself always saying to myself "Ah, I will tell Janet that!" & then catching myself up with "I can't." I used to refer many things to her, & told her a great deal about my work.

We want to go soon to Badenweiler for a little, & then to Alderley.

I must, however, wait to see what [Dr.] Ruedi says about me. You can fancy that, being weak before, I am not very strong now. My long cold had pulled me down, & at the last examination (about a month ago) I was told that both of my lungs were in a bad way. It was most fortunate in this respect that I had those six days at Ragatz. I revived greatly there & got enough healthy exercise.

Ever with much love yours

J A Symonds.

1. A Davoser.
2. A Davos saddler and upholsterer.
3. See L 1405.
4. Possibly a local doctor. See L 1596.
5. The first line of a poem from the Greek Anthology: "Thou art not dead, my Proté; thou art flown into a land much fairer than our own." For a translation by Dr. Symonds, see *Miscellanies by John Addington Symonds, M.D.* (1871), p. 412.

1599. *To Charlotte Mary and Margaret Symonds*

Am Hof, Davos Platz, Switzerland. April 10 [11] 1887[1]

My dearest girls

We have just come back from the funeral, & I must tell you something about it.

It was a lovely morning, very warm & sunny with crocuses sprouting all over the meadow. Wreaths & flowers kept coming in every quarter of an hour until the very last minute. Burgers[2] said he had sat up all last night to make them. And very many came from the other man. They were of all sorts. Fedele sent one of bay & magnolia leaves decorated with bunches of blue violets & yellow daisies. Old Frau Büsch sent yellow & black immortelles, grim & old-Davoser-like. Mrs Willing[3] gave a box of delicate white & pale yellow flowers, ixias, lilies of the valley & double ranunculuses with one white carnation wh I took out & wore. Your mother gave it me. Besides all the flowers I wrote of yesterday, there were roses & bigonias & lilies & the allium Neapolitanum in profusion. About equal quantities came from English & Swiss people. Mrs Freeman[4] plaited a wreath of moss & wild anemones from the Alps here, wh I thought the prettiest of all.

Your flowers from Hastings addressed to Janet arrived yesterday. These your mother made into a bouquet & threw herself into the grave. Also a large box of white violets wh Isabella[5] sent came in time. Katharine showered these, together with Mrs Willing's flowers & a quantity of crocuses she had picked this morning.

I thought of Webster's Dirge:

> Are the flowers of the spring
> Meet to perfume our burying;
> For these have but their growing prime,
> And man doth flourish but a time.[6]

228

Service began at 12 in the English Church. The hearse was brought in covered from top to bottom with those multitudes of pale blossoms. I cannot tell you all the people who attended. There were quite as many men & women from Davos as English people. It struck me that we had realized what I always wanted—to gain the common Sympathy of both strangers & natives.

Mr Battersby[7] read the Service with great feeling. Then we drove to the Cemetery: your mother, Katharine, Fr: Schmid[8] & I in one carriage; the Rose & the 2 big Margarets & Elspeth in another. Our friends followed on foot; & all along the street Davos men & women fell into the procession. It was warm & sunny at the grave, & it seemed to me that a large part of the ground was taken up with people all of whose faces I knew. But one cannot afford at that last moment, when the first wish is to concentrate thought upon her, & the second to behave without stupidity—one cannot see & note everything one would wish to do. It goes too quickly, & is too solemn. I only had the happy sustaining feeling of large human kindness round us.

Your mother bids me tell you what a great part bay-leaves played in the floral decoration. They are emblems of immortality. And they were abundant in Janet's grave. She says that this will give you a deeper feeling about the bay trees in the Croft with the Sea-wind swaying them to & fro.

I think Janet would have been astonished, after her long quiet patience on this Wandelbahn [covered porch] where I am writing to you now, after her shyness & seclusion & gentle acquiescence in the coming doom, if she had been able to see the grave & elevated but yet joyous spectacle of all that Sympathy expressed in action round her tomb. I could not quite remember at some moments whether it was a burial or a marriage—though I knew that the marriage was with no mortal bridegroom. All those white crowns of flowers seemed to me more fit for her union with immortal things, with God, a kind of mystic marriage-rite, than for some mere committal to the earth.

And remember, this funeral took place on Easter Monday; & the Lesson read over her coffin is the Lesson appointed by our Church for this very day, a reminder of the Supreme doctrine of the Resurrection. Those wonderful periods of S. Paul's XVth chapter in his first Epistle to the Corinthians[9] are being read today to all Christians of our Communion in all quarters of the globe. And they were read in the little English Church here at Davos with special reference to the hope we have of Janet.

She trusted, I know, as I too trust, on religious truths which are even more firmly based than St Paul's expectation of a life with Christ in God.

She had made a deep & perfect sacrifice of her self to God who made her, & was willing to abide his ordinance regarding her Soul as she submitted to the same regarding her body.

This more perfect holocaust of self, this more entire resignation, & more conscious acceptance of laws we do not wholly comprehend, does not, for me at least, exclude reverence for the faith in which so many generations of our fathers lived & died. And I am sure, where she is now, whatever she is, she will have felt the pathos & the beauty of that religious sympathy extended to her by men & women who loved her & who must also die.

Janet was scientific in the right sense. She accepted the order of Nature; & she also felt God in Nature. She knew that all religions are the attempts of the human Spirit in its upward struggle to express the sense of our dependence upon God in Nature. She knew that they also enshrine the aspirations & the hopes of man, feeling blindly after something solid in the void around us. But she was never anxious, never in a fuss about her particular self. She has often told me here in this place that she could calmly leave her future in the hands of Him who brought her into being.

"I know not whence I came, & I know not whither I go. But I know that I came well, & I know that I shall go well."

Also she agreed with me in this prayer:

"Lead thou me, Lord Father God, & thou, the World's Law, whithersoever I am appointed by you to go. For I will follow unreluctant; & even if my will fails, through cowardice upgrown in me, none the less shall I follow."

To that confession of faith & prayer we may add the flowers of Christian expectation. They harmonize together. There is nothing insincere in cherishing a hope we can demonstrate.

After all these higher contemplations I should like to tell you how curiously Ciò [the dog] has sympathized with us today. He seemed, I think, to feel that somebody was going on a journey. He asked with all his eyes & ears what the wreaths meant, & the black clothes, & the coming & going. When we came back from the funeral, he seemed to be contented that your mother & little Katharine had not disappeared.

Ever, dearest children, your loving father

J A Symonds.

---

1. Clearly this date is in error, Easter Monday, the day of Janet's funeral, was April 11.

230

2. Burgers, "the other man," Fedele, and Frau Büsch were local Davosers.

3. Possibly wife of Barton Willing of Oxford, who often stayed at the hotel Buol; or Mrs. T. J. G. Willing, wife of a German author, in Davos at the time.

4. Mrs. Edith Freeman, wife of Dr. Harold Freeman who helped organize winter sports at Davos.

5. Possibly Isabella Gamble, Symonds' cousin. In 1888 she married Symonds' friend and executor Robert Otter. See L 345.

6. John Webster, *Vanitas Vanitatum*, first 4 lines. In the fourth line *a* should be *his*.

7. The clergyman for the English Church at Davos.

8. Frau Christina Schmidt, the German governess: See *OOP*, p. 192. Rose, the two Margarets, and Elspeth were servants.

9. Paul preached about the resurrection of Christ and of the dead. See Symonds' critical response to this text in L 1600.

1600. *To Henry Sidgwick*

Davos, April 14, 1887

[Dear Henry]

The pain of losing Janet was very great, and the *desiderium* [yearning] will remain permanent. There seems to be something pitiful in this extinction of a nature formed for really noble life. It is extraordinary from how many unexpected quarters the echo of her personality, the impression she made on those who knew a little of her, comes to us.

You tell me that you have "no consolation to offer." But really I do not want any. I know that I cannot get any. The loss is there, and may not be made up to me. I have long since bent and schooled myself to expect no consolation of the ordinary sort. And I do not think I feel less brightly and less resignedly than those who are basing their hopes upon unimaginable re-uniting with their loved ones, in heaven only knows what planet. You go on to say that "despair in our ignorance is the prompting of blind passion, not of reason." I have no comprehension what "despair" is. I have ceased to wish for immortality, and therefore ceased to hope for it. If I am to have it, I have it at the hand of the same Power which gave me mortal life. If I am not to have it, is a matter of contentment to me; for I have found that all life is a struggle, and neither for myself nor my fellow-creatures do I desire the prolongation of the struggle. Being what we are, it is obvious that the continuation of consciousness in us must entail a toilsome *Entwickelung* [evolution].

So I am content to leave these things until the very end, until the very new beginning if that comes, upon the knees of It, of Him, who is for me responsible.

231

Such a word as "despair," the counterpart of hope in personal immortality, does not exist in my vocabulary. This fact I have tested while sitting by my daughter's corpse, while consigning it to the earth. And I want to utter this now, because, as you observe, "the perplexities of theory have strangely entwined themselves with the inexorabilities of life in our correspondence."

The net result of my present experience is to corroborate my previous opinions. It has roused in me no new longings, no new regrets, laid its finger on no lurking hope and no concealed despair. Only it has confirmed my conviction that the main point in the whole position is that of Euripides, τοὺς ζῶντας εὖ δρᾶν [those who are alive are well off]. Upon this point I have only the purest satisfaction with regard to Janet. She attained to spiritual perfection in her life. What troubles me about myself is the sense of shortcomings, rendering the part I play in life less worthy of man's station in the world.

I have proved in my own person that St. Paul was wrong when he exclaimed, "If Christ be not risen, then are we of men most wretched."[1] We may be happy and calm and submissive to the supreme order, to Zeus and ἡ πεπρωμένη [destiny], without a resurrection. I perceive that his *argumenta ad hominem* in 1 Cor. xv., "Else what shall they do that are baptised for the dead," &c., "If after the manner of men I have fought with beasts at Ephesus," &c.,[2] are blots upon the splendid inspiration of his rhetoric, appeals to human love of profit. Love and good, and the desire of righteousness, do not need the bribe of immortality, and have to be reasoned now upon quite different principles.

I would not willingly bore you with these observations, but it is incumbent upon me to tell you how the last week of severance from my first-born has acted like a test upon the convictions I began to express some weeks ago.

[Incomplete]

---

1. A combination of I Corinthians 15:14 and 19.
2. *Ibid.,* 29 and 32, respectively.

1601. *To Edmund Gosse*

Am Hof, Davos Platz, Switzerland. April 15 1887

My dear Gosse

I received yours dated 11th? this morning, & only write this scrap to tell you that I wrote you a long letter on the night of the 7th wh you ought to have received by this time. I hope it did not go astray; for besides suggesting what I thought had been the cause of the mistake about my two daughters, I also told you of my eldest girl's death,[1] & touched on many things I had to say. This has been a severe blow to us; for though our dear child had been ill several years, & we had little hope of her eventual recovery, there was no warning of immediate danger. I had even started on a journey, for the sake of my own health, to Venice. But fortunately I had not got far, & could be recalled in 7 hours. So I was able to see the last of Janet. Indeed I enjoyed three hours of quiet talk with her before she tried to go to sleep. The end came quite suddenly.

She was in the truest sense a *schöne Seele* [beautiful soul], & no one was more fitted to pass without a pang of apprehension into the unseen.

With gratitude for your sympathy believe me most

truly yours

J ASymonds.

---

1. For poignant accounts of Janet, and of her death, see Katharine Symonds Furse, *H&P*, pp. 27 ff., and Margaret Symonds' *OOP*, pp. 282–83 and 309–10. See Ls 1597–1603.

1602. *To Unknown*

Am Hof, Davos Platz, Switzerland. April 18, 1887

My dear Friend

Thank you heartily for your letter of sympathy. Like many others which I have received at this time, it has greatly helped to soften the blow we have sustained in our dear daughter's loss.

Nothing is to be regretted concerning her. She died without a pang, either physical or mental. Only the end came distressingly abrupt to the survivors.

My wife & I, who had gone to Ragatz, leaving her apparently in her usual condition, though rather weaker than I liked, were both able to return in time to see how quietly & unconsciously of any evil she was preparing for the last sleep.

I am not one of those who cling, passionately to hopes of immortality. Nor was she. We felt alike upon this subject, though she always felt more wisely & gently than I can do. She, veritably face to face with the mystery of death, told me that she could cheerfully & contentedly give back her life to Him who bestowed it on her, without repining even though it should be renewed upon the same inadequate terms of happiness as she enjoyed in this world.

That seems to me the perfectly *religious* spirit; & it is the spirit in which I try to take her loss. To expect all things from God, to hope for nothing wh might gratify our human achings & longings of this moment— not to challenge the universe with St. Paul's "If Christ be *not* risen, then are *we* of men most wretched"—to forgo these egotisms in the spirit of pure obedience—that appears to me the highest faith, & Janet has greatly confirmed me in it.

We start tomorrow for Badenweiler (Black Forest) & then on to England.

Everyrs   J. A. Symonds

1603. *To Margaret Symonds*

Am Hof, Davos Platz, Switzerland.[1] Badenweiler April 29 1887

My dearest Madge

I think it is the turn to write to Lotta. But I must break my rule, because I want to send you your cheque for £5 (wh I stupidly forgot to do before), & also to tell you that I only yesterday got from the Post the letter you wrote me on the 19th. They sent on most of the Poste Restante things at once; but kept back two or three letters in a pigeon hole I suppose.

This letter had a great deal which interests me about your feeling for English landscape. I agree with what you say. Though I was bred in very beautiful English country, I seemed always to be wanting something which the mountains, when I came to know Switzerland and Italy, supplied. There is a sense of limitation, of being cloyed with fatness & pent in with hedges, even in the best English Scenery. We do not get enough of wildness, enough of solitude with nature & with God. But, on the other hand, no country is so perfect in its details; none realizes so completely Tennyson's phrase "a home of ancient peace." And its real outlet into "the infinities," a very melancholy one sometimes, & always very dreamy, is the vast hazy luminosity of sky & brooding clouds. At Davos I sometimes yearn for what I always had at Clifton—the Sun rising alone above a mighty city, flooding wood & pasture, & Sea-going river, & all the many works of men—the Sun setting in glory beyond that strip of sea & low Welsh hills, with the wonderful tenderness of pure yellow spaces & tremulous stars. In a Sonnet I printed about the pines at Davos[2] I condoled with them for never in all their lives of 300 years having seen a sunrise or a sunset. I don't suppose anybody understands what I meant.

You will get to love English landscape I am sure. But you will find it very difficult to paint. I should like, too, to take you & Lotta to see some really grand Sea-coast. There, perhaps, is the true *sublimity* of Nature in England. But, after all, I quite feel with you that I want the friendship, stern & wild, yet closer & tranquillizing, of mountains. Of course they really coop one up more than hedges & copses. But they do not coop the spirit up. There is no fatness about them.

You ask me what I think about those whom we loved in life being present with us after death. In a spiritual sense I feel Janet nearer to me now than when she lived. I do not mean that she comes & speaks to me, or that I imagine her soul is in the air unseen. But her thought, her ideal self, what she truly was for me, seems to be more inside my own spirit now than when she was there—an objective human being with her own personality in contrast to mine. This Christ promised to his disciples; & this explains how the memory of Christ developed into a religion.

I believe it to be my own duty not to be anxious about the question of survival after death. I feel that we are unable to know. And the purest religion seems to me to consist in leaving this absolutely to God. But there is no reason in the world why one should not exercise both faith & hope upon this topic. The immortality of the Soul, even after the Christian Revelation, is a matter of faith not sight.

Of one thing I think we may be quite certain; that Janet is not disturbed by any thing wh happens in our lives. If she watches what we are doing & thinking, she is aware of it much more as God is aware of it than as we are. And my faith in God makes me believe that what appears to us Sin & pain & struggle bears in His Sight some different aspect. I am sure He makes allowances for us, wh we have no right to make for ourselves. I am sure that in some way Sin & pain & disease & unrest are education; & that a liberated Soul, like hers, if it is still aware of them, cannot be distressed by them because it knows what they are intended for.

Did I ever read you Landor's poem about the meeting of Agamemnon with his daughter Iphigeneia in Elysium?[3] You know that he had killed her with his own knife in obedience to an oracle. But the Greeks thought that the Soul on entering Elysium drank of the river of Lethe, which erased all memory of what had been painful in life. Therefore, Iphigeneia had forgotten this last dreadful act; & only remembered her father's love & their happiness together. She therefore ran to meet him with joy: but he, who had not yet drunk of Lethe, stood apart, remembering her cruel death & his own murder by the hands of her mother. She cannot understand his misery. But just at that moment, the Spirits of the Hours descend, bringing the waters of Lethe to Agamemnon's lips. The poet leaves us with the blissful prospect that when he has partaken of that draught, nothing of earthly sorrow will remain between him & his daughter.

This is a most sublime & touching allegory. And it seems to me fairly to represent what may still be hoped about the relation of the liberated Soul to people & things on earth.

I have spent 3 days in writing a very difficult article for the Fortnightly[4] on the remoulding of religious thought by Science. The editor asked me to do it; but I wonder whether he will print what is very much like a sermon! At any rate, deeply stirred as I have been by our great loss, I took great pleasure in my task.

This letter is quite as much for Lotta as for you. I write it to you because I think you may have felt that I was neglecting the very direct things you said in yours of the 19th.

The proofs of Cellini are coming in.

We are exactly in the 3 ground floor rooms Janet your mother & I had last year. It is pleasant & restful. We expect Albert [O. Rutson] soon.

I feel better. This air suits me. I hope I shall get to England.

Everyour most loving father

JASymonds.

---

1. Symonds is using printed stationery. In *OOP*, p. 282, Margaret Symonds wrote: My sister and I were in England at the time of Janet's death. My parents wrote constantly to us—they did not wish us to return, but came to join us in England. My Mother's beautiful letters cannot here be printed. But she told me how when Janet died two birds—two mountain thrushes whom we loved—came on the sill

outside her window and sang their song in the early morning stillness; and how Janet sat up to listen to them, and then my Mother laid her back: "my gentle, sinless child."

2. Sonnet III of his 4-sonnet sequence, "Winter Nights in the High Alps," in *Vagabunduli Libellus* (1884).

3. *The Complete Works of Walter Savage Landor,* ed. T. Earle Welby and Stephen Wheeler (16 vols., 1927–36), II, 211–17.

4. "The Progress of Thought in Our Time," *The Fortnightly Review,* XLVII (1887), 885–98; reprinted in *E S & S* (2 vols., 1890) as "The Philosophy of Evolution."

1604. *To Herbert P. Horne*[1]

Badenweiler April 30 1887

Dear Sir

Your letter followed me to this place, where I am halting for a few days on my way to England.

It would give me pleasure to contribute a prose article, such as you suggest, to the Hobbyhorse; & I wish that I had known of your proposal before I left Davos. All my literary accumulations & notes for studies are there; & I have nothing with me but what is necessary for work in progress. —I do not feel as though I could conscientiously promise anything by June 1, though it is not improbable that something may present itself to my mind capable of treatment.

I happen to have with me here a complete essay on the "Heir of Linne"[2] (the old English ballad). But I fear this is too much of a "folklore" study to suit you; & besides I find it has nearly 5000 words.

When I come to England my time will be much taken up with society. So I fear I have little prospect of setting quickly to work at something worthy of your notice. Nor do I like to make a half-promise; for I am sure you will want to arrange at once for your next number.

I was much interested in the last.

I will not omit to send you something when I have what will harmonize with the tone of the Hobbyhorse.

Believe me very truly your

John Addington Symonds.

---

1. See L 1452.
2. The essay was never published.

1605. *To Unknown [Edmond Scherer?]*[1]

Badenweiler April 30 1887

My dear Sir

I received your kind letter of the 28th today, & have written to my booksellers in London to send you the two volumes (*Animi Figura* & *Vagabunduli Libellus*) to your address.

I am sorry to hear that you are suffering from over-work—only a too common complaint with the industrious in literature—& hope that the rest you mean to take will quite restore your health.

If you do me the honour to read these books, may I request that you should notice the connection between them? An integral part of *Animi Figura* was omitted from that work, & first published in *Vagabunduli Libellus*. It is called "Stella Maris" & ought immediately to follow the section entitled "Intellectual Isolation."

I spoiled my own scheme by this misplacement. But when I put forth *Animi Figura* it seemed to me that the large space given to passion in "Stella Maris" would be out of proportion in the analysis I had attempted. Reflection made me afterwards convinced that this large element of passion is true to life & therefore admissible in art.

If then I should ever have the opportunity of remodelling my work, I mean to divide *Anima Figura* into three sections, whereof the central will be "Stella Maris."

I really do not presume to think these verses are worthy of your study. I wanted to correspond to the kindness of your gift. But having chosen this way of doing so, I am bound to say as much as I have now done about the relation of the books to one another.

I am delighted to hear that you are at work upon some of the elder English poets. The younger ones, like Miss [Mary] Robinson, Miss Blind,[2] [Roden] Noel, etc, have no immediate claim upon the attention of the French public. You are engaged in a task of great difficulty, considering how little the English poetry of this century is known in France. It will be enough to act as the interpreter of what after all has still to be experienced regarding those writers whom we have admitted almost to the rank of English classics.

Thank you for accepting in so kind a spirit the letter I ventured to address you on your book of Studies.[3] I have a great deal more to say than I there expressed. Cela va sans dire [That goes without saying]. But I will not trespass on your time with further correspondence. Allow me only to

238

add that I have made in you the acquaintance of a critic, whose work I shall always study with respect, in the certainty of desiring from it not only pleasure but instruction also.

Bad health compels me to live, remote from the world, in a little Alpine village, more than 5000 feet above the sea. I have left it now with the view of spending a few weeks in England. But I must doubtless soon return to my mountain home. The address which I will add at the bottom of this page is my permanent abode.

Believe me to be very
truly yours
John Addington Symonds
Am Hof
Davos Platz
Switzerland

---

1. We have been unable to identify the addressee of this letter. He was, it appears, an established French critic, possibly Edmond Scherer (1815–89). See L 1474.

2. Mathilde Blind (1841–96), *Poems by Claude Lake* (1867), *The Prophecy of Saint Oran* (1881) and *The Heather on Fire* (1886), *The Ascent of Man* (1888). She translated Strauss' *The Old Faith and the New* (1873–74), and published biographies of George Eliot (1883) and Madame Roland (1886).

3. See L 1474 for a reference to Edmond Scherer's *Études,* which Symonds read and which may support our conjecture in note 1 above.

1606. *To Ernest Rhys*[1]

Badenweiler May 4 1887

Dear Mr Rhys

I have your letter of the 29th April with enclosure from Walt Whitman.

As yet, I have not been in any way concerned with the proposed author's vol of Whitmaniana. Though, if such a book is contemplated, I should be glad to take part in it.

It would interest me much to look at Mr W. Sloane Kennedy's[2] work. I am not sure that I can do more, however, than advise.

Will you send it to me at Athenaeum Club, Pall Mall? I am on my way to England now.

I did not know that you would so soon have room for my projected

selections from Milton's prose works. But I have the scheme in my head; &
when I return to Davos I will take it in hand.

A sad thought is now added to our home at Davos. We lost our eldest
daughter there early in April.

Believe me to be sincerely yours

J A Symonds.

---

1. Ernest Rhys (1859–1946), author, editor, and critic. During 1887 and 1888 he
lectured in the United States, where he met Walt Whitman. As editor of the "Camelot
Series" of popular reprints and translations (65 vols., 1886–91), he invited Symonds to
edit Milton's prose works. He was the first editor of the "Everyman's Library." His
Letters from Limbo (1936) contains some of Symonds' letters.

2. William Sloane Kennedy (1850–1929), American writer and translator from the
French and Italian, published works on Longfellow (1882), Whittier (1882), O. W.
Holmes (1883); and *Reminiscences of Walt Whitman* (1896) and Whitman's *Diary in
Canada* (1904); it was the *Reminiscences* which Symonds was asked to examine. See
L 1626.

1607. *To Robert Louis Stevenson*

Badenweiler May 4 1887

My dear Stevenson

Behold an example of the malignity of fortune! I am on my way to
England, and was meaning to come to see you at Bournemouth. Now I get
your letter proposing I should meet you at Aix les Bains.

It is really too bad. I cannot change my plans; for I have some special
reasons for going to England.

Our eldest daughter Janet died at Davos on the 7th of last month,
while two of the younger girls were away in England. They want their
mother and me much. It has been a sad blow to my wife, and I have felt it
most deeply, for Janet had grown to be the best and closest friend I had up
there. She was spared much misery, poor child, by what was at last an
unexpectedly sudden close of her long illness. So it would be selfish to
regret what has happened. It only leaves a blank in our lives, and some
thing missing wh shall not be replaced.

I am very sorry to think that our paths cross just now—perhaps you
are already starting for Savoy! I cannot write letters wh are worth anything,
unless I write nearly every day, and you know that this sort of correspond-

ence becomes an impossibility. Therefore I wanted truly to have speech with you again.

Davos goes on, so far as I am concerned, much as usual. I grind at the literary mill a good deal. I have got so thoroughly accustomed to it, and it is so indispensable to me in those circumstances, that I suppose I shall not stop so long as I can drive a quill.

You do not say anything about yourself or Mrs Stevenson. I hope then that both of you are holding on as bravely as before. You certainly do not grow less in the fair creations wh issue from your hands and brain.

Poor naughty spiteful Wogg [the dog]! R. I. P.

With truest friendship, I beg you both to believe me always and ever yours

J A Symonds
(address Athenaeum Club S.W.)

1608. *To T. S. Perry*

Badenweiler May 10 1887

My dear Mr Perry

I have just received your letter of the 25th here; & I doubt whether this will reach you before your departure from New York. I will however take the chance, in order to express my best wishes for your journey.

I am on my way to England with my wife & youngest daughter. Since I last wrote to you, we have had a severe trial in the death of our eldest daughter. She had been an invalid some years—indeed her illness began before she was sixteen, poor girl; & so she may be said to have had no youthful pleasure of life since childhood. I cannot say that her death was unexpected, though it came so suddenly at last that I had just been sent off to Italy by my doctor for change of air. Fortunately, I was able to retrace my steps in time to enjoy some quiet hours of conversation with her before the end came.

This will add painful memories to our home at Davos, wh I built as much for her sake as for my own need.

You do not, I hope, know what it is to lead a life controlled in all its outer circumstances by considerations of ill-health.

There is no prospect held out in your letter of your coming to

Switzerland this summer. I hope this part of Europe will be patronized by you in 1888!

I suppose I shall be back at Davos before you are settled into life in France. I mean if possible to leave London again in the middle or end of June. My address in London is

Athenaeum Club

Pall Mall.

I am laid up with a sprained ankle, stupid accordingly, & writing on my knee. Pray accept this as excuse for a letter wh I would not have thought fit to send, except to convey to you my best wishes & to inform you of my movements.

With kindest regards to Mrs Perry

believe me very sincerely yours

J A Symonds—

1609. *To Ernest Rhys*

74 Eaton Square [London] Sunday May 22 [1887]

Dear Mr Rhys

I found the Ms about Whitman[1] at the Athenaeum, and have it safely here. I have not had time to look at it yet.

Will you dine with me here at 8 tomorrow? I expect Roden Noel (whom I think you know) and Courthope.

I am staying with an old friend Mr A. O. Rutson. But he will not be at home tomorrow night. So we shall be by ourselves.

Please send a telegram as enclosed, to say whether you will come or not. I should be very glad to make your acquaintance.

Believe me very truly yours

J A Symonds.

---

1. By W. S. Kennedy. See L 1606.

1610. *To T. S. Perry*

(Ry Station Charfield on the Midland)

Mount House Alderley Wotton Under Edge Gloucestershire June 7 1887

My dear Mr Perry

I have just received your letter of May 25, & write this line of welcome to our English waters! May you have had a prosperous journey, & may your wife (to whom my best regards & wishes) be none the worse for her experience of "the pond."

I wish I could fly off to you, or that I had a house in England to invite you to. I am unfortunately for the present myself a sojourner only here, & have no London abode open. So I cannot put any, as I should have liked, at your disposal.

When you do come to Davos, you must let me know in time, & take up your quarters with us.

Pray keep me informed of your plans. On my return journey to Switzerland this summer, if not before in England, I may be able to make out a meeting.

I am staying with wife & daughters at my sister in law, Miss [Marianne] North's country house in a most lovely rural district, sixteen miles from Bristol, close to Berkeley Castle, on the spurs of the Cotswolds. I wish you could see us. It is so absolutely the best English country here.

Good luck to all your enterprises! Ever yours

J A Symonds

Are your children with you?

1611. *To Robert Louis Stevenson*

[Wotton Under Edge, Gloucestershire] June 21 1887

My dear Stevenson

You will think I am always coming and never going to come—when I tell you that I must postpone yet one day, and *fix my arrival for Thursday.* I hope this will not trouble you. After your kind telegram duly received at Sutton Court I shall come straight to Skerryvore,[1] probably by the fast train wh leaves Waterloo (I think) about 2.

I have just seen the shew[2] (not in the Abbey) but in Whitehall and here. It has gone off splendidly.

Ever yours

J A Symonds.

1. Stevenson's house at Bournemouth, which he sold in July 1887. He sailed on August 17 for New York.

2. Victoria's Jubilee, commemorating the 50th anniversary of her accession to the throne. In state, Victoria attended a solemn service in Westminster Abbey that day.

1612. *To T. S. Perry*

Alderley Wotton Under Edge June 25 1887

Dear Mr Perry

I have just returned from a round of visits (the last to Louis Stevenson at Bournemouth) & found your card of the 23d.

It is stupid that I should have missed you. I thought, however, from what you wrote me, that it was no use trying to hit you in London at the Jubilee time. I left it myself on Thursday. But I hope to be there again soon —that is early in July. Please tell me of your movements.

This is scribbled to catch the post wh goes early from our village.

Very sincerely yours always

J ASymonds.

I have found here a card from Ld Ronald Gower[1] asking me to meet "some American friends of yours & mine"[2] this morning at Stopford house. I wonder if they are you?

---

1. Lord Ronald Gower (1845–1916), sculptor, author, and friend of H. F. Brown and Symonds. His *My Reminiscences* (2 vols., 1883) contains references to Symonds, as does *Old Diaries 1881–1891* (1902). Gower's chief sculpture, an indifferent work, was the Shakespeare Memorial set up by him near the Stratford-on-Avon Shakespeare Theater.

2. Unidentified.

1613. *To Mrs. R. L. Stevenson*

Mount House Alderley Wotton under Edge June 25 1887

My dear Mrs Stevenson

My thoughts have been so constantly with you and Louis all this day that I must, before I go to bed, sit down for a few minutes' *causerie* with you.

Seeing you again has given me the truest deepest pleasure. I am a man of little faith, and always think that something may have come over my friends to change them.

I don't think you are either of you changed, except that you seem to me to have grown better. Louis is one of the very few people I have known who have the unmistakeable mark of genius. But what strikes me more than his mental distinction, is his goodness. And this goodness, a something rarely beautiful in his nature, appears far more eminent in him now than ever it used to be.

You are very happy in each other, although there are so many things to make life difficult. I cannot tell you just what I personally feel about you two, and what it is I envy in your lot.

Yesterday in the afternoon I fear that I distressed you by my talking and my queries. Forgive me if you can, and as I trust you have forgiven me.

I am in a very different scene from Bournemouth. In the midst of a garden full of wonderful flowers, brought together by my sister-in-law from all parts of the world. There is no Sea near. The hills above. Masses of cedars and old Scotch firs enclosing the near ground—and a prospect over vale and Severn to Welsh mountains—with such a wonderful still afterglow from sunset and the thinnest sickle of a crescent moon.

These English landscapes touch me with [a] deep penetrating sense of beauty, a sort of pathos and peace mingled, after the long years of monotonous Davos and naked Italy.

I have nothing to say, you see. Or rather, I have too much, and so say nothing. The soul rarely speaks in any man, and I do not know why mine should try to be articulate.

It will be the best of news if I ever hear from over seas that Louis has found a place where he can preserve the strength that still is vital in him. I am sure that if he can be saved from spending too much of his energy, and can get into the right conditions, he will be for you and for the world the beneficent paver of his destiny. But I cannot look at him wihout being aware at what a cost such a rare creature lives.

You see I cannot talk about him, and will not talk about myself.

The hours I spent with you remain an everlasting possession in my memory. They form a very sacred spot in this many-coloured experience of England revisited. Thank you for the gift.

It is good to have a clear conception of your party—you and Louis and Lloyd [Osbourne] and your two faithful friends the servants—who will cross the seas [for Colorado] so soon. Do not forget me, who shall be again in my narrow valley, possibly, before you go.

Ever yours
J A Symonds.

I found a letter here from my wife, not forwarded to Bournemouth, in which she very specially begs to be remembered to you and Louis.

1614. *To Herbert P. Horne*[1]

Alderley Wotton under Edge June 27 1887

Dear Sir

Thank you for your kind note of the 24th.

I am not sure yet when I shall come to town—probably upon the 7th. It is true that I shall not be many days in England, & that I am pretty well taken up with engagements.

It would be a great pleasure to me to come to you, & to meet your friends.

When I can see my way more clearly, may I write again? Of course I must take my chance of finding you disengaged.

With many thanks believe me very truly yours

John Addington Symonds.

---

1. See L 1452.

1615. *To T. S. Perry*

Alderley July 1 1887

My dear Mr Perry

I was sorry that you could not come yesterday, but I quite understand why.

I wondered whether the memory of the great scene in Marlowe's Edward ii would have drawn you to Berkeley Castle![1]

My Oxford address will be 9 Banbury Road.[2] I hope to get there by a train wh leaves Bristol at 10 a.m. on Tuesday. Please let me hear what your

Oxford address is—whether ancient Mitre, or Clarendon, or modern Randolph.

The Master of Balliol [Benjamin Jowett] is away at Malvern until Thursday, 7th else I should have been with him, & should have much liked to introduce you to one of the most important figures in literature & society.

Very sincerely yours

J ASymonds

---

1. In Act V, scene v, of *Edward II*, Edward is murdered in Berkeley Castle, near Bristol.
2. His sister Charlotte Symonds Green's address.

1616. *To A. O. Rutson*

Alderley July 2 1887

My dear Rutson

Catherine & the girls returned last night after a very lazy journey, in spite of the heat. They enjoyed their visit in the twilight to Gloucester Cathedral.

They are all of them full of delights of Nunnington[1] & its beautiful country. The sketches they have brought, gives me an idea of how lovely it must be. And your brother has been infinitely kind & thoughtful for them.

Catherine Lotta & little K are going on to Sutton Court[2] today.

With reference to your letter of the 30th & your plans for us in London, I will now tell you, having arranged our own affairs, that I shall come to you alone upon the 7th & stay if you can really have me till the 14th or 15th. If you can really also take in Madge a few days later than the 7th she will much like to join me having spent some more time than I can spare at Oxford.

Catherine means to bring Lotta & the little K[atharine] up to town only the day before we leave for Switzerland; & Miss [Marianne] North has put the flat in Victoria Street at their disposal. On the 13th (yr dinner party) Madge can go to them; & I have always too many people whom I ought to see; so do not think of me for that day.

It is extremely kind of you to take so much care for us. But we could not trespass on your hospitality to such an extent as all to fall upon your arms at once!

The arrangement we have made, as above, is definite & need not be reconsidered.

Do tell me to 9 Banbury Road Oxford[3] how your affairs have gone *tomorrow*.

Ever your affte.

J A Symonds

I shall think of you much for the next 48 hours! Thank you again for your kindness too.

---

1. A. O. Rutson's home, Nunnington, Yorkshire; Oswald Kirk was the post-town.
2. Home of Sir Edward Strachey, his brother-in-law.
3. His sister Charlotte Symonds Green's home.

1617. *To Horatio Forbes Brown*

Wotton-under-Edge, July 4, [1887]

[Dear Horatio]

You must have thought me very irresponsive to your letters; and I am truly ashamed of my remissness in writing. But it is as much as I can do to bear up against the great heat there is in England now. I have also to write at least ten letters a day about plans, engagements, and business. Everybody I know or don't know wants me to come to them, and I have to keep saying "No!" or fitting things in. *E.g.* a note yesterday from Lord Ronald Gower,[1] whom I never saw, and only this: "Do come at 11 to-morrow morning." Then the printers have been rushing "Cellini"[2] through the press. Each sheet of 16 pages costs me four hours to correct; for I find it needful to work through my translation with the Italian carefully again. So you will I hope understand why I have drawn a large draft upon my friends' indulgence. So far as health goes I have got on pretty well. But I am so thin and sleepless from heat that I feel it risky to stay much longer.

I am sorry to hear that you cannot go to Newhall[3] this summer. Everybody seems to be getting poorer. I have been trying to sell my three Clifton houses, and cannot get a decent price: and every bond I renew is reduced in interest. So grumbling is my portion also. But I have always so arranged expenditure that I do not feel reduction of income as much as those who live up to theirs.

I spent a day at Bournemouth with the Stevensons. He has gone downhill terribly. They are all off to Colorado next month. I expect his father's death will have made his circumstances easier. But he is still nervous about money. "Dr. Jekyll" has been worth £350 to him, he says. I should have thought he would have got more for it.

[Incomplete]

---

1. See L 1612. We have been unable to locate any letters between Gower and Symonds.

2. *The Life of Benvenuto Cellini*, translated by Symonds (2 vols., 1887). Standard reference works (*The Encyclopaedia Britannica, The Cambridge Bibliography of English Literature*, et al.) and Babington, pp. 65–68, give 1888 as the publication date. Brown (*L & P*, p. 278) correctly gives 1887. It appears that the publisher Nimmo's sales-expectations were exceeded by far, the issue being quickly sold out. The 2nd ed. appeared in 1888 with a prefatory note by Symonds dated Feb., 1888. In our Chronology in Vols. II and III we have corrected the date of this work accordingly.

3. Brown's family home outside Edinburgh.

1618. *To A. O. Rutson*

Clifton Tuesday [July 5] 1887

[My dear Rutson]

I have been so very busy since I came here, & so confused with the blending of new & old impressions, that I could not write to you till now.

I wanted to tell you what a peaceful happy time I spent with you in London, & how very often you are in my thoughts.

It is indeed a matter of deep concern to me to know how you are getting on with your many most fatiguing occupations. The house [Nunnington], I am sure, will of course arrange itself in time. It is an excellent house, & I am sure you will do nothing to spoil its capabilities of being made also beautiful.

I need not say that the other things on which you touched the last night we spent together, preoccupy me more. And just here nobody can help you, except by the assurance of the truest Sympathy & the most earnest prayers (I think all really heartfelt wishes are prayers).

I was so happy with you. I never felt so much at home in London. You are the best of hosts, & you have friendly servants. Do you know, I have been regretting 74 Eaton Square ever since I left it? Now this is a great gift

249

you have; to make an empty house a home at once! God bless you for this, & for the kindness you showed me at every moment.

I wonder whether you went to Alderley. I take it, not yet. I had a letter from

[Incomplete]

1619. *To Margaret Symonds*

Please keep this letter.

[The Athenaeum] July 8, 1887

My dearest Madge

I shall make you the depository of my experiences last night at 35 Grosvenor Square.—When I drove up in a Hansom at about 20 minutes to 9, I found a little crowd assembled outside to see the illustrious guests—of whom I proved to be the last. The gorgeous house was ablaze with lights and alive with flunkeys; the drawing rooms full of people. The Tennants[1] all welcomed me most kindly, and Margot[2] informed me I was to take down Lady Ribblesdale[3] and sit next Gladstone.[4] The great old man had been making a long passionate speech in the House, and was sitting quite exhausted on a chair. Mr. Gladstone sent the word round that no one was to talk to him. Soon we all marched down to dinner. The dining room groaned with silver plate and heaps of roses; nothing but masses of dazzling embossed vases and candelabra all smothered in red and white flowers intensely odorous.

Gladstone at once began to ask me where he had last seen me. He had spent many hours in the company of my mind (books), but could not remember if he had ever seen my face. I reminded him of a dinner party at Woolner's where he first met Tennyson, and where my father and I were.[5] That was very very long ago he said. Then I had to tell him all about Davos, and to give minute particulars about our house, and how it was built, and how old the trees were we used for wood-work in it; and what sort of books I had collected. His voice was husky and weak at first. In fact it never recovered its tone through the evening. He drank brandy and water, and ate a very good dinner, selecting the most wholesome articles out of the sumptuous menu. His face is full in flesh, with a healthy rosy complexion, and his eyes are very bright. He looks like a vigorous old man; but is clearly aged. Speaking of his age, he told me that he felt it most in incipient deafness. And deaf he certainly is. I found it difficult with my weak voice to make him hear. But I noticed age in him more in a certain curious inconsecutiveness of his talk. He took up one subject after another, just as though his brain were acting of itself and working independent of his will.

Apropos of very old wood, he now began to talk of Norway, and told me many interesting things about the old wooden churches he had seen there. What had struck him most was that the pine timbers of their outside grew dark brown, not grey, with centuries—just as our chalets do. Then he described the fiords, and their peculiarity of being several thousands of feet in depth while the sea at their mouths only measures by hundreds. Then he went on to the people: such a fine race: "Nature's own democracy": the conditions of the country, divided by fiords and mountain ridges, sparsely populated by small landowning freemen, had developed a real natural democracy, which no revolutionary process could produce. The fine manners of the peasants. Their pride of descent from Vikings. One old man with a long pedigree he knew, who had entertained the king of Sweden at his own table in the homestead, sitting with him as an equal at the board, but sending the king's suite to feed with his farm servants. Next he swerved aside to talk about their Church in Norway. It is purely Lutheran in doctrine, "the bare Confession of Augsburg." But in ritual it is strictly Catholic. "They use the wafer instead of bread in the Sacrament; the Communion Service is like the Mass, performed before the people almost in dumb show; the vestments are unchanged from Catholic tradition; I saw one officiating priest with a cope on, which had a Crucifix, yes a Crucifix, and highly embossed too, patent in the Cross upon the back." This mixture of Lutheran doctrine and Catholic ritual seemed to delight Mr Gladstone; and he explained it by the intention of the men who adopted Reformed principles, to maintain for the eyes of the people what they were accustomed to and what had secured their reverence in the forms of the earlier Church.

Norway lasted us a long time. Then he spoke about Lord Acton,[6] and his way of collecting about 2000 vols wherever he happened to be stopping. Also about his place on the Tegern See, where Gladstone was last summer.

All of a sudden the subject changed; and now I heard a lecture on the suicidal policy of the English publishers, who had encouraged circulating libraries like Mudie's,[7] thereby limiting their own profit, starving authors, and preventing the public from being able to buy good books cheap. You may imagine that I entered into this part of the conversation with enthusiasm. Gladstone seemed much interested with what I reported from Mr [T.S.] Perry about the vast extent of the book trade in America, where it flourishes under very different conditions from ours.

Here there was a pause. He turned to Lady Tennant, and I to Lady Ribblesdale. But he soon began again to me about Italy. He does not think we ought to have an embassy at the Vatican. "The Pope has ceased to be a temporal sovereign. Diplomatic establishments are kept up to manage secular affairs. How can we compell the English taxpayer to maintain an embassy at the Vatican, where policy is all for spiritual interests? Besides, I am by no means sure that the Papal Court does not intend still to trouble the peace of Europe, if it sees the chance, for the recovery of its former position." This was all he said on politics during the whole time. But he soon left the Vatican, and told me about some little villages of the Abruzzi and Sorrentine promontory, where the clergy are still elected by the people, as in the oldest times of the Christian Church. "It would be right good if we could trust the people with the election of their clergy. But they would be sure to make it a matter of politics; and heaven forbid that we should have the scenes of hustings and so forth in connection with the choice of priests! Nor indeed do I see why folk should grumble at the aristocratic element having come into the constitution of the Church at an early date."

Somehow or other he now got on to the subject of the Mortmain Act,[8] and how people evade it in England. I told him in outline what had happened to me with regard to Mr Sisson's property; and this appeared to interest him, as a very modern instance of the *fidei commissum* [bequeathed in trust] with entire trust in a man's personal honour.

Gladstone did not talk to the Company: only to Lady Tennant and myself. There were a great many people—about 30 I think at dinner; and it seemed to me that the buzz of voices confused him, with his incipient deafness. I rather think the Tennants had intended that he and I should hold forth for the benefit of the rest of the company; or rather that I should be the means of stirring him up to a Monologue. But he was not in the physical force requisite for that. He struck me as fatigued. There was certainly no sign of the excitability and irritability people often say they notice in him. I think his long speech in the hot afternoon had lowered his whole tone.

He often quoted Greek; and was amused (on asking me whether I had not plenty of time at Davos for literature) when I reminded him of something Prometheus chained on Caucasus says in a play of Aeschylus.

It is this: Io comes and tells him a long tedious story all about herself. Prometheus says: don't mind boring *me;* I have only too much time on my hands here— λίαν σχολή [great leisure]. "Ah," says Gladstone, "what a strange history that word σχολή, school, has had!"

Well: I think I have told you the principal things we said to each other. I can't tell you who all the grand people were, lords, ladies, and so forth. One very ugly woman (Lady Margaret Beaumont[9] I think) absolutely blazed with diamonds, which seemed to be piled together like a corselet on her withered throat and breasts. She had a strong crimson dress on. Lady Ribblesdale was lovely, in a kind of Maria Stuart dress of pale yellow brocade embroidered with red and lilac peonies. Margot was in screaming crimson, but very jolly and like a comrade.

I got away at midnight. When I reached Eaton Square I found A[rthur Rutson] waiting for me, and had the whole Nunnington[10] affair discussed. I see that there are two sides to the story; and, as I half suspected, [mutilated] him by [mutilated] manner. [Mutilated] does not know when [mutilated] does this. His great anxiety is about a dinner party on the 13th. He cannot have the whole family then.

Now I have settled for you to come here on Monday and stay till Wednesday at Eaton Sq. On Wednesday we will go to Dover and meet your mother and the two girls there. If you come by an early train on Monday, I will meet you, and then we can see some pictures. The *affaire de coeur* is advancing prosperously. Every most affly yours

J A Symonds

Love to Auntie [Mary Ann Sykes] and Aunt Char[lotte]

---

1. Sir Charles Tennant (1823–1906), 1st Bart. of The Glen, Innerleithen, county Peebles and of St. Rollox in Glasgow; businessman; M.P. for Glasgow, 1879–80, and for Peebles and Selkirk, 1880–86; a trustee of the National Gallery; created baronet in 1885; in 1849 married Emma Winsloe, who died in 1895; his sixth daughter, Emma Alice Margaret ("Margot"), in 1894 married Herbert Henry Asquith, 1st Earl of Oxford and Asquith, and Liberal Prime Minister. She wrote of him: he "was a man whose vitality, irritability, energy and impressionability amounted to genius," *Margot Asquith: An Autobiography* (4 vols., 1920–22), I, 20. See L 1571.
2. Margot Tennant, a favorite of Symonds (see L 1571) had visited Davos in the winter of 1885 to help nurse her sister, Mrs. Pauline Emma (Thomas Duff) Gordon-Duff, who had gone to Davos in the last stages of consumption. See L 1552.
3. Charlotte Monkton, daughter of Sir Charles Tennant, in 1877 married Lord Ribblesdale.
4. Gladstone would be 78 years old in December.
5. See L 451.
6. John Emerich Edward Dalbert Acton, 1st Baron (1834–1902), the historian and

Catholic layman. Since Cambridge at the time refused degrees to Roman Catholics, Lord Acton was educated at the University of Munich. Tegernsee is a lake in Upper Bavaria, about 32 miles south of Munich.

7. Charles Edward Mudie (1818–90) began his famous lending library in 1842.

8. The act restricts the amount of his estate a dying person with issue may leave to charities. Symonds had acted as executor of William Sisson's estate, which was meant, after the death of Sisson's insane sister, to devolve to Bristol charities. The will is mentioned in L 574.

9. Lady Margaret Anne de Burgh (d. 1888), daughter of the 1st Marquess of Clanricarde, in 1856 m. Wentworth Blackett Beaumont (1829–1907), of Bretton Park, Wakefield, M.P. for South Northumberland.

10. The reference is to an unidentified unpleasant occurrence at A. O. Rutson's home, Nunnington, York.

1620. *To A. O. Rutson*

Am Hof, Davos Platz, Switzerland. July 17 1887

My dear Albert

I write to you the forlorn hope that you may have found some MS pages of my "Cellini" in your study. They came on Monday the 11th & I laid them down on the mantelpiece. I am afraid they must have looked very dirty & untidy, & it is possible that you or the housemaid may have destroyed them. Anyhow I could not find them when I was putting my things together before leaving your house. I thought I might have already packed them up: but upon unpacking here, I do not discover them.

I should not make enquiries about Mss which have been to press, unless the circumstances were exceptional. But the fact is I was very anxious to keep the whole of my "Cellini" MS intact, since it is the joint work of myself Catherine Janet Lotta & Madge.

Ever yours,

J A Symonds

1621. *To Horatio Forbes Brown*

Davos, July 31, 1887

[Dear Horatio]

If I had known beforehand what a trouble this translation of Cellini would have been, I do not think I should have undertaken it. I have now been working pretty hard for four months at the proofs, and have still one-third of the whole to do. I suppose I must reckon on the whole of August being devoted to it. I do not believe that such a translation is worth all this labour, especially as I hear that the edition is to be restricted to five hundred copies. My chief satisfaction is that I am at least more accurate than Roscoe.[1] To count his bad blunders would be impossible.

I think I told you that I have begun some Essays on the Principles of Art and Criticism.[2] These I can push forward when there are no proofs. I have already got four pretty well finished, viz. Realism and Idealism; The Model; Beauty, Composition, Expression, Characterisation; On the Application of Evolutionary Ideas to the Study of Art and Literature. Then there is another on The Validity of Nature-Myth and Allegory, and another on Arnold's paradox, "Poetry is a Criticism of Life," ready. I am thinking of a short study on Landscape, and another on Democratic Art, in which I shall try to say my say about the lines for future art-work opened out by Whitman. I am also vaguely planning one on Hybrids, which might, I think, be curious.

We had a very violent thunderstorm on Friday evening, the finest I have ever known here. The rain fell in volumes; and suddenly, in the middle of the uproar, a great noise made itself felt—like a dozen express trains tearing through a deep cutting. We could hear some obviously human shrieks also. What they call a *Rüfe* or sudden swelling of the torrent from the Jacobshorn, which comes down above Huldi, the carpenter's workshop, had taken place. Usually this is a thin thread of water. But now it was bringing down thousands of tons of rock per minute. I went to examine the scene this morning, and saw some really incredibly huge blocks of granite which the miserable little rivulet had brought from above. It only lasted fifteen minutes. But in that time many acres of grassland were ruined, and several homesteads inundated.

I have just been to hear a sermon in the Davos Church. They have a new clergyman,[3] to go to listen to whom is now the fashion among the young men. He preached on the kingdom of God; implied that Christ was a man; said that you could not be sure of Christ's own words from the contradictory statements of the Gospels; denounced the theory of the Church; poured contempt upon Bibliolatry. I never heard such a bombshell of Rationalism—very eloquently expressed too. Curiously enough, the Davos peasants are keen on the new theology. I heard of this clergyman by accident at a *Wirthschaft,* [an inn] where the whole conversation turned upon his definition of the Deity. I used to imagine that the young men at least cared about none of these things. It appears now that they did not care about the humdrum orthodoxy of their previous teachers.

[Incomplete]

---

1. Thomas Roscoe (1791–1871), translated Cellini's *Autobiography* (2 vols., 1822). He was a writer of topographical works (*The Tourist in Switzerland and Italy,* 1830; *Wanderings in North Wales,* 1836, 1852; *Windsor Castle and its Environs,* 1838; *The Book of the Grand Junction Railway,* 1839; *Belgium in a Picturesque Tour,* 1841), fiction and drama (*Gonzalo, the Traitor,* a tragedy in verse, 1820; *The King of the Peak,* 3 vols., 1823), miscellaneous books (*Legends of Venice,* 1841), poems (*The Last of the Abencerages, and Other Poems,* 1850), and translations.

2. Became *E S & S* (2 vols., 1890).

3. The Rev. Harford Battersby, clergyman, English Church of St. Luke, Davos; later the Rev. Dundas Harford of Seaford.

1622. *To Horatio Forbes Brown*

Davos, July 31 [1887]

[Dear Horatio]

I wish you had sent me Creighton's letter of which you speak in yours of the 26th. I should like to see *how* he is disappointed about the reception of his book.[1] From no motive of vulgar curiosity, I think, but partly from sympathy and fellow feeling, partly from a wish to understand the attitude which a solitary worker, conscious of having done his best, must assume against the blank indifference of the world. I have suffered from the sense of irresponsiveness, and have done my utmost to steel myself against it from the first, having had a pretty clear prevision of how it must be. But no sensitive personality can ever attain the point to which he aims of self-preservative cynicism. We are destined to feel that our wings are beaten and broken against iron bars. We all go through it, who do disinterested work. Creighton is, professionally speaking, well paid with a good professorship,[2] and what I should like to observe in him is whether *that* seems nothing, whether he does not crave for the response of spirit to his spirit; never to be got. Let us be like Jenny Lind, who told me she sang not to the people but to God.

[Incomplete]

1. Vols. III and IV of Mandell Creighton's *History of the Papacy during the Period of the Reformation* (5 vols., 1882–94).

2. Creighton was the first Dixie professor of ecclesiastical history at Cambridge (from 1884).

1623. *To the Editor of* The Fortnightly Review[1]

[Davos, August 11, 1887]

Sir,—It is told of Louis Napoleon, Napoleon le Petit, that after reading M. Victor Hugo's voluble abuse of him, he laid the book down with this one word—Ignoble! Walt Whitman might surely do the same, if his eyes should light upon the pages of Mr. Swinburne's "Whitmania,"[2] in the August number of your Review.

The argument of this essay is indeed directed less against the author of *Leaves of Grass,* than against those foolish people who have Whitman on the brain. Mr. Swinburne, moreover, is careful to show that he retains some sense of what is good and great in the writer, to whom he formerly addressed not the least inspiring lyric in his own *Songs before Sunrise.** Nor will his statement of the fact that Whitman is not a poet in the technical sense of that term provoke contradiction.

What calls for protest and correction is the following passage from Whitman's conception of womanhood:—

"But Mr. Whitman's Eve is a drunken apple-woman, indecently sprawling in the slush and garbage of the gutter amid the rotten refuse of her overturned fruit-stall: but Mr. Whitman's Venus is a Hottentot wench under the influence of cantharides and adulterated rum. Cotytto[3] herself would repudiate the ministration of such priestesses as these."

I do not pretend to have any means of judging what sort of priestesses Cotytto would repudiate or welcome; but I am sure that neither Whitman's Eve nor Whitman's Venus ever sought admission to that sisterhood. I am not about to defend Whitman's method of treating sexual matters, which is far too physiological for my taste. I only wish to point out that Mr. Swinburne's account of the type of woman held up by Whitman for admiration and respect—the mate and mother of stalwart men—is palpably unfair. Whatever Whitman's Eve is, whether she bores us or attracts us, whether we like her company or shun it—"athletic American matron,"

257

white-capped Quakeress, Indian squaw, or what not—she is the exact opposite of Mr. Swinburne's caricature. The "drunken apple-woman," "the slush and garbage of the gutter," "the cantharides and adulterated rum," exist solely in Mr. Swinburne's own brain, and are conspicuously absent from the homely and coarse, but clean and healthy, ideal of Whitman. Passages indeed may be cited from *Leaves of Grass,* in which, applying his doctrine of democratic religion, Whitman extends the hand of sympathy to outcast women, and avows a comradely feeling for Bohemians and bullies. Yet he remains rigidly consistent in his exaltation of robust and wholesome womanhood, to tally, as he would phrase it, rigorous and self-respecting manhood.

We may not care for Whitman's gospel of the sexes. We may think, as I for one do, that it is bawled with superfluous vehemence into our ears. Yet we ought not to forget that Whitman's familiarity with the American proletariate convinced him that this message, delivered through a speaking trumpet, was needed, in order to bring men back to sound ways of thinking and feeling upon matters fundamentally important to society. Against the dram-drinker, the slave of secret vice, the victim of habitual excesses, the adulterous couple, the obscene dreamer, the nympholept of unnatural erethism, he deemed it his duty to protest. He felt that the core of material life in the great American cities ran a risk of being corrupted by such folk. Accordingly he promulgated his own conception of the primal attraction of normal womanhood for normal manhood, he glorified an ideal of average and natural reciprocity between the sexes. Even those who heartily admire the great qualities of this singular and puzzling writer, will admit that there is something repulsive in the presentation of the ideal, something grotesque in the deliberate and detailed inculcation of his doctrine, something incurably devoid of the restraining sense of humour in his *Children of Adam,* something ungraceful, indelicate, and dull in the picture of his muscular and well-conditioned Venus. This does not, however, alter the fact that the sentences I have quoted from Mr. Swinburne's essay contain a serious misrepresentation. They impute the vice, uncleanliness, and corruption against which every page of Whitman's didactic writing is directed. For this, I feel sure that a man so generous and sincere as Mr. Swinburne, a poet who himself endured so much unsympathetic criticism after the appearance of his *Poems and Ballads,* will, "on better judgment making," be sorry.

JOHN ADDINGTON SYMONDS

* "To Walt Whitman in America." One poem begins: "Send but a song over sea for us." It is worth noticing that *then,* in 1871 or thereabouts, Mr. Swinburne regarded Whitman as a *singer.*

---

1. "A Note on Whitmania," *The Fortnightly Review,* XLVIII (Sept., 1887), 459–60.
2. "Whitmania," *The Fortnightly Review,* XLVIII (Aug. 1887), 171–76; reprinted in *Studies in Prose and Poetry* (1894).
3. In Greek mythology, an orgiastic goddess, often identified with the moon goddess Semele, worshipped by the Cottians whose ancestor was Cottus, one of the hundred-handed giants among the first semi-human children of Mother Earth; her worship spread from Thrace throughout northwestern Europe.

1624. *To Herbert P. Horne*[1]

[Davos] August 12 1887

My dear Sir

I was unable to call on you when I was last in London (early in July); for the heat of the summer forced me to leave England sooner than I wished—I could not stand it.

Please use the sonnets on the Daffodil[2] as you think fit, & I wish they were more worth your attention.

I was very sorry indeed not to have the much desired pleasure of meeting some of the members of the Hobbyhorse (as you so kindly promised) at your house. But my poor health renders me always liable to such disappointments.

I do not forget that you asked me to send something in prose. I am at work now upon some essays in criticism—chiefly on principles;[3] & if it seems to me that any part of this production is worth sending, I will do so.

Very truly yours
John Addington Symonds

---

1. See L 1452.
2. "Two Sonnets—The Daffodil—I. Narcissus' Flower. II. Balder's Flower," *The Century Guild Hobby Horse,* II (October, 1887), 121–22.
3. *E S & S* (2 vols., 1890). See L 1629.

1625. *To Charlotte Mary and Margaret Symonds*

In the 3d floor of the Gasthaus zum Rössle
Bühler Cn. Appenzell
August 13. 1887. 9.30 p.m.

My dear girls

Before I go to bed I shall relate a little of the amusing but very fatiguing experiences of today. You saw me start—about a century ago it seems—why does time seem so very long when one has only travelled from Davos to Bühler? I think it is because I have been always with some of the nicest men I know anywhere, but who are never still or silent, & whose language I imperfectly comprehend. Hold, Tobias [Branger], Jost & Louis[1] were all of them good company; & we kept up a continual flow of innocent cheery talk, enlivened by jokes, occasional singing, & some horseplay, till we reached Landquart. Those young men (not Louis) are just like boys—like good English boys, not overburdened with wits & education, but more experienced in life because they have learned to labour. But oh! their innocence, their limpid Unschuldigkeit [innocence]! and oh! the physical disturbance occasioned by their outbursts of animal spirits! all of them colossal-"stramme Kerle" [vigorous fellows], as a gymnast called them in conversation with me just now.—At Landquart we all went different ways. Louis stopped there. Jost went to Glarus—though he heard on the way that his father-in-law had died this morning:—we met his wife near Grüsch all in tears, poor thing, but anxious that her Jost should go & win a Crown at Glarus! Hold went to somewhere in Lichtenstein, also to win if possible a Crown. Tobias & I came hither. They all of them have ulterior business objects, wh they combine with their amusements.—It is a very fine drive up from Altstätten to Gais & on to Bühler—finer than I remembered it at the distance of fifteen years. The widening plain of the Rhine, breaking on toward BodenSee [Lake Constance] & Baiern [Bavaria], lies beneath you: a mass of Graubünden hills in the far distance: & the jagged noble ridge of Säntis, broken like a forefighter of the mountains conquered in some Titanic combat, singing above the wonderfully rich green meadow lands of Appenzell.—Tobias was delighted to find Bühler decidedly Fest-stimmig [in holiday-mood]— i.e. bands braying, flags flying, & incomparably funny Bürschen in all sorts of grotesquely festival costume stumping around.—He established me in a little room of this inn, where all the Fest-stimmigkeit goes forwards—bands, beer, Bürschen, with a prospect of dancing & drinking when the "event" is over. Then he found his own quarters: & reappeared in full blossom. You should be able to see him! A huge straw-hat with patterns in red upon it (conveyed hither in a bandbox), wreathed round with what he calls an "englische Schleier" [English veil], i.e. puggsle, & the puggsle trimmed in graceful festoons with a silver filigree imitation of the edelweiss made for him & presented to him by some adoring Schatz [sweetheart]. Under this wonderful erection his good honest face looks very handsome: really handsome: the only fault is that he does look so like an Italian Opera [Rossini's] (Guillamme Tell) version of the Swiss peasant. Splendidly worked flannel shirt; broad red sash; breeches; red bows at the knees; open-worked white stockings; & a flaming ribbon across the breast. He is superb, & is awfully good & kind & unaffectedly serviceable to me. I too wear one of those "Sektion Davos" ribbons. It belongs to Luzi Kinschi. But I have a right to wear it; & the Turners ask me if I am "Kunst" or "National."[2] No more cards.

good night. JAS

---

1. All local Davosers. Branger was a saddler and upholsterer.
2. Whether his ribbon indicates that he is a professional or of a national representative or enthusiast.

1626. *To William Sloane Kennedy*[1]

Am Hof, Davos Platz, Switzerland. August 21 1887

My dear Sir

I have perused your collections[2] for a book upon Walt Whitman with very great interest. They show an extraordinary depth of study in his works & an intelligent sympathy with his mind. You ask me, in your favour of June 6, whether I can propose "any radical amendments." To speak quite frankly, I should like to see the whole of Chapter 1 (Enfans d'Adam)[3] altered. I agree with the substance of what you say regarding Whitman's treatment of sexual things, & I think it is important to utter it. But I can see no use in mixing up controversy with exposition & descending to railings against Messrs Harlan & Allen.[4] Whitman does not need that sort of defence, which has, besides, been fully exhausted by O'Connor.[5] His cause even in the past has suffered, I think, from the abuse & invective poured out upon his persecutors. The time has come for his friends to take their stand upon simple exposition & analysis.

I find something also to criticize in Chapter 2. It seems to me that the time has gone by in which any good can be done to Whitman's cause by repeating the testimonials given him by men of more or less eminence. There is quite enough of this sort of thing in Bucke.[6] What seems to me the valuable part of chapter 3 [2] is the attempt to *analyse* the constituents of Whitman's greatness.

Chapter 3 I think in all ways valuable as a resolute attempt to solve the problem of poetic form—although I do not wholly agree with your conclusions.

I will not inflict further remarks upon you, except to say in general that I think you quote too many people. Instead of hearing what *you* have to say, we are constantly hearing citations from a miscellaneous mob of writers. Now what we want, is to hear you—insofar as you can explain Whitman to us, & make his place in literature & philosophy more evident by lucid criticism. It is enormously difficult to write on Whitman. No one has quite succeeded up to this time. This I am able to affirm from experience; for some years ago I formed large collections for a work on Whitman, & I have masses of MS by me on the subject, which I found to be so formless, so obscure, so inadequate to the man, & yet so blatant & exaggerated, that I put my work aside & acknowledged to myself its failure.

I sent to the "Fortnightly" about 10 days ago a temperate reprimand to Swinburne for his ignoble attack on Whitman.[7] I should not be surprised, however, if the editor declines to print it.

As yet I have heard nothing about a memorial volume by authors writing with special reference to Whitman. I should think your collections are too voluminous to form *a part* of that. They constitute a book.

Believe me dear Sir to be very truly yours

John Addington Symonds.

If you see Whitman assure him of my constant sympathy & hearty love.
Wm. Sloane Kennedy Esq.

---

1. See L 1606.
2. Kennedy had solicited Symonds' help. Kennedy reports in the "Preface" to *Reminiscences of Walt Whitman* (1896), that "a pretty full concordance to *Leaves of Grass* . . . together with portrait and autograph manuscript of Walt Whitman's, and the first cast of much of the present volume, was stolen from me in Europe, after receiving the benefit of suggestions from John Addington Symonds and other English friends." Kennedy goes on to criticize Symonds who "was singularly unfortunate in his published

utterances on the man he loved most passionately of any on earth. We here in America were astounded that it seemed to him necessary in his work . . . to relieve the Calamus poems of the vilest of all possible interpretations. It was a sad revelation to us of the state of European morals. . . . But Symonds had the best of motives." To prove this he provides extracts from two of Symonds' letters to him, the present one and L 1632.

3. The section of *Leaves of Grass*, 3rd ed., containing most of the poems on sexual themes.

4. Kennedy did not take Symonds' advice, but pointed to the "disgrace" of the Boston preachers, the Rev. James Harlan "who turned Whitman out of office in Washington, in 1865, for being the author of *Leaves of Grass*, and . . . Reverend Baylies Allen . . . who suppressed it in Boston in 1882."—*Reminiscences of Walt Whitman*, p. 118. Kennedy was wrong about James Harlan (1820–99), who was not a Boston preacher but a politician from *Iowa*: senator (1855–65, 1867–73), and secretary of the interior (1865–66); in 1865 he dismissed Whitman after a few months' clerkship in the department of the interior. The Rev. Baylies Allen (?–?) was assistant pastor of Trinity Church, Boston, and secretary of the Society for the Suppression of Vice; he was instrumental in the banning in Boston of a proposed issue of Whitman's work by the publisher Osgood, but who was directly responsible for the banning is still a matter of question.

5. W. D. O'Connor (1832–89), American journalist, *The Good, Gray Poet: A Vindication* (New York, 1866).

6. Richard Maurice Bucke (1837–1902), Canadian alienist and psychologist, published *Walt Whitman* (1883), the authorized life.

7. See L 1623.

1627. *To Ernest Rhys*

Am Hof, Davos Platz, Switzerland. August 21 1887

PRIVATE

Dear Mr Rhys[1]

Mr W. S. Kennedy's collections on Walt Whitman[2] seem to me to illustrate the impossibility of writing coherently upon the topic. Nobody has succeeded as yet in presenting at the same time a sympathetic & an orderly view of the man & the poet. And I am bound to state my opinion that Mr Kennedy stands forth among the most chaotically minded of his interpreters.

This being the case, I find it useless to suggest alterations in detail & omissions.

What the book most suffers from is the habit of perpetual quotation & allusion. You never hear Mr Kennedy's opinion without a mass of citations, wh are often irrelevant.

In the next place there is a vast amount of mere assertion & vociferous declamation in places where the proof of an opinion or the analysis of an argument would be to the purpose.

The whole of Chapter 1, on Enfans d'Adam, seems to me written in a wrong tone. At this time of day nothing can be gained by declaiming against Messrs. Harlan & Allen.[3]

Chapter 2 I like better. But mere lists of people who have admired Whitman prove but little; & up to the present time panegyrical Whitman literature has dealt mainly in such testimonials. The part of this chapter which goes into details upon topics such as *Handling* etc, seems to me valuable in criticism.

Chapter 3 I like better than the two others. It is a resolute attempt to grapple with the aesthetic problem of *form* in poetry.

Chapter 4 has some very interesting matter. The treatment of Whitman's fundamental conceptions upon p: 188 seems to me both true & also helpful to a beginner in the study of his works.

Chapter 5 interests me much. I like the account of Calamus on p: 207. Chapter 6 has the same sort of merit. But I do not find that Mr Kennedy penetrates very deeply into the differentia of Whitman's religious ideas.

Chapter 7, for quite special reasons, seems to me a very valuable & interesting chapter. It contains a great amount of personal anecdote which is quite new to me.

The Bibliography is of course valuable; but I have not gone into it minutely enough to judge whether it supersedes Bucke in this matter. The phrase Concordance, if complete, would be of great assistance to Whitman students.

Now it is clear that Mr Kennedy has before him material for a considerable volume; & I do not see any course open to him but to publish the whole as an independent book. But if he does so, I should strongly recommend him to omit Chapter 1, or to recast the matter of it in an uncontroversial form. Injury is done to Whitman by railing. It is quite sufficient for his interpreters to take their stand upon positive ground—exposition of his intention with regard to sexual things, not interwoven with polemical abuse. O'Connor has done the latter once & for all.

Should a part of Mr Kennedy's book come to be used in a memorial volume I almost think that Chapter 3 would detach itself best from the whole mass. Will you kindly inform me what I am to do with the Ms? Shall I return it to you?

I have received a letter from Mr Kennedy himself, which I will answer.

Believe me very sincerely yours

J A Symonds.

---

1. See L 1606.
2. See L 1626.
3. See L 1626.

1628. *To Havelock Ellis*

Am Hof, Davos Platz, Switzerland. August 22 1887

Dear Mr Ellis

On looking into Heywood today, I find that it will cost me very little trouble to get the Introduction ready.[1] If you could procure me copies of the Academy for *July 18* & *July 25* 1874, or have my articles on Heywood in those numbers transcribed by typewriter, I will immediately set to work & get these into shape by ommissions & additions for our present purpose.

I enclose a list of plays. Counting *Edward iv* & *Fair Maid of the West* as 4, I have suggested 12 plays. Should that number be too large, it seems to me that *Edward iv* could best be sacrificed. I should be sorry to omit *Love's Mistress* for many reasons—& mainly because it displays a curious form of the chorus (Midas & Apuleius) & illustrates the habit of supplying a drama with a running criticism. The Rape of Lucrece has also special claims, for its analogy with Shakespeare's poem.

But please tell me what you think. If you incline to keeping *Edward iv* which would you reject? I confess that I am very loth to lose the Tanner of Tamworth & Mistress Shore, wh we shall sacrifice if *Edw iv* goes out. But how can we do without the *Fair Maid* also—I mean her of the West?

In the Introduction I shall of course allude to [A. H.] Bullen's discovery of *The Captives*.[2] But I hardly think this play is wanted in the series. If you can meet my wishes by sending the Academy articles I have requested, you may rely upon an early delivery of the copy.

Yrs very truly

J ASymonds

1. Symonds was preparing an edition of Heywood for the "Mermaid" series being planned by Ellis.

2. A. H. Bullen (1857–1920) discovered *The Captives: or, The Lost Recovered,* now generally ascribed to Thomas Heywood, in a British Museum manuscript in 1885, and printed it in *A Collection of Old English Plays;* limited to 150 copies and privately circulated (4 vols., 1882–85), IV.

1629. *To Herbert P. Horne*

Am Hof, Davos Platz, Switzerland. August 26 1887

Dear Mr Horne

I return the proof of my two sonnets.[1] I wish I could make them better. But they seem to me incurably imperfect.

With regard to essays on the principles of art & criticism, I will not fail to communicate with you, & to give you the opportunity of using some part of what I am at present producing. I should only wish to reserve to myself the right of reproducing them in a volume; for anything you may care to print in the Hobbyhorse,[2] will form a portion of a corrected scheme of studies.

I have thought among other things, of commenting on some passages in Eckermann's Goethe;[3] & it occurs to me that this section of the work would suit the conditions of your journal.

I will, however, write again on the subject.

I am much interested in what you say about [E.] H. Le Sueur.[4] At present I do not know of anything to add to your sources. But I will see whether I can get upon the trace of Gian Bologna[5]—a man whose work & life deserve to be studied in detail.

I am at Zürich today upon an anxious mission regarding the health of one of my family. But when I get back to my books, I *may* have something to report.

Very sincerely yrs

J A Symonds—.

---

1. The sonnets on the daffodil. See L 1624.

2. The only one of the essays later in *E S & S* (1890) to appear in *The Century Guild Hobby Horse* was "Is Music the Type or Measure of all Art?" III, (April, 1888), 42–51.

3. The projected essay, if written, did not appear in *E S & S*.

4. Probably the French painter, Eustache Le Sueur (1616–55), one of the founders of the French Academy.

5. Symonds refers to Jean Bologne (Italian name, Giovanni da Bologna, 1524–1608), Flemish sculptor. He settled in Florence, where his best works are located.

1630. *To Horatio Forbes Brown*

Davos, Sept. 9 [1887]

[Dear Horatio]

From your mother's and your own letters I see that I can safely address you now in Venice. I hope the Piave[1] has not carried you away from Mr. Malcolm's. If it has been raining on the watershed of that river as it is now raining on that of the Rhine, you must have been in peril of flood. There is the usual wintry weather of early September here, which will, I suppose, be succeeded by a tranquil brilliant autumn—the weeks in which the high Alps are at their best in all respects, and especially in colouring.

I have almost entirely abandoned the hope of seeing Venice this year. I feel, as you do, that it is preternaturally long—longer than mere lapse of days implies, since we were together. It is not the same whether we meet there or here; and, for the twining of life in common, I wanted a turn at Venice. I do not believe that this sense of distance and lapse of time means any sort of refrigeration. But I do think it means a settling down to different ways of thinking and living: an amount of daily labour and of hourly experience, which, as individuals become less plastic through development, has heavier effect upon them.

I thoroughly sympathized with your feelings at finding that extract in the *P.M.G.* from Stevenson's poems.[2] Odd man, if he never sent you such a pretty symbol! A copy reached me here, of his book. He meant to send me one, I know—for I saw him at Bournemouth in June. But I wonder whether it was not meant for you—through me. I have lost the wrapper, which, as so many books reach me by the post, I stripped off at once. If you have got a copy you must consider it his gift anyhow, for I am sure he meant to send you the book. But he was very ill before he left England for America. Mrs. Stevenson wrote to me on their last day in London with really heavy accents of discouragement about their journeys, and my heart has often throbbed in imitation of the screw which was propelling them

267

across the Atlantic. Now, I suppose, for better or for worse, they have arrived and are gone up country towards Colorado.

I work on at my Essays upon art and criticism.[3] Gradually they are accumulating. I do not think they will make "a book." But they are going to have a lot of my life-thoughts in them. The odd thing is that one has so little to say upon subjects which have occupied a lifetime. I often find that what I wrote between twenty and twenty-five is no shallower than what I can arrive at now.

The night has fallen gloomily over this valley, and I am not the cheerfullest of souls in its narrow compass.

[Incomplete]

---

1. A river several miles above Venice. Mr. Malcolm is unidentified.
2. "Mr. Stevenson's Poems," *Pall Mall Gazette*, XLVI (Aug. 20, 1887), 5. *Underwoods* (1887) was the book.
3. *E S & S.*

1631. *To Horatio Forbes Brown*

Davos, Sept. 14, 1887

[Dear Horatio]

On Monday I gave myself a holiday by taking a new walk. It was the ascent of a mountain called "Pischa," 9,300 feet, which rises from the Fluela Thal, S.E., and commands a finer view, in my opinion, than the Schwartzhorn, since by its position the whole Landwasser valley, as far as the Julier and Schyn, is surveyed, together with Prättigau; and the huge pyramidal peaks of the Silvretta group are seen immediately in front. From this peak we scrambled down very rocky places to the head of the Vereina Thal, where a Club-hut has just been built in a most romantic place—the meeting of four vales, with roaring cataracts pouring down into a tangle of dwarf pine. Then to Klosters—about three and a half hours' descent, rapid walking. The whole expedition had more of the picturesque and romantic than is common in these hills; and, though long, it was not difficult. I was out twelve hours; nine hours pretty hard walking, the rest divided between a rest on the peak and a rest in the Club-hut.

It does me good morally to take a walk of this sort—I mean it keeps my sense of living up; and I do not think it hurts me physically, though I got a slight chill from being wetted by a storm of rain.

I have made friends with a guide at Klosters called Guler,[1] whom I like.

[Incomplete]

---

1. Leonhard Guler, carpenter by trade, who made much of the panelling for Symonds' home, Am Hof; a favorite Swiss guide; listed in *The Davos Courier* among guides holding certificates from the Davos section of the Swiss Alpine Club. See the *Courier*, Aug. 17, 1889, p. 384.

1632. *To William Sloane Kennedy*

Sept. 17 [1887]

[Dear Mr Kennedy]

. . . . I should like to add a few sentences expressing as plainly as I can what it is that I for one most admire in him after 22 years of intimate acquaintance with his work.[1]

I am afraid that his friends may have thought my rebuke to Swinburne (in the *Fortnightly* of this month) lukewarm.[2] It was printed, or rather misprinted, without my being able to modify my utterance upon the proof. I meant to keep my tone very low, and to say far less than I feel; for I am sure that this is the right way to win a wide recognition of Whitman's merits. Yet when I saw my note in print, I felt very sorry that I had not been allowed the opportunity of striking out a phrase here and there. It does not represent my thought. It is almost impossible to say exactly anything about so astounding and incommensurable a thinker and writer as Whitman is. . . . I am, very sincerely and with comradely greetings, yours. . . . From a peak 9500 feet above sea, I saluted you and W.W. three days ago! . . .

[Incomplete]

---

1. Kennedy explains in his *Reminiscences of Walt Whitman* (1896), p. viii, that Symonds was writing about Kennedy's plan to publish European eulogiums of Whitman.
2. They did, see Grosskurth, pp. 233–34. For the rebuke see L 1623.

1633. *To Horatio Forbes Brown*

Davos, Sep. 22, 1887

[Dear Horatio]

I told you in my last letter that I was thinking of an excursion into the Averserthal. This is what I have done now; and it has quite repaid me. Without going into details of description I will say that I have never seen anything in the way of high river scenery to equal this. The Averser Rhein beats the Sesia and the Mastalone hollow, and has long odds against the streams of the Dolomites, which I have always thought enchanting. It has a tremendous volume of the purest azure water, which sometimes hides itself in cembra-tufted gorges, sometimes swims through grassy meadows with wide swirling curves that hollow out the turfy margin to their liking, sometimes carves a narrow monumental way through solid marble pure as Parian or Pentelican, sometimes falls thundering in cataracts encircled with a dozen changeful rainbows, sometimes glides deep and solemn in dark pools, which make one dream of death and long to dive in them and find the mystery.

It is a long valley—forty kilometres. I had not thought that this Canton held anything so highly poetical. And tourists have not touched it. I slept with my guide in a room which held the Archives of the valley in one chest, and had the Eucharistic vessels of ancient pewter on a window-sill. There was nothing to eat but eggs and bread. This, however, signified little.

Well, I will not tell you more of Avers. It is enough to have mentioned the stream, and to that deity I sacrifice.

[Incomplete]

1634. *To the Rev. George Bainton*[1]

Am Hof, Davos Platz, Switzerland. Sept: 30 1887

My Dear Sir

I received your letter of the 26th, in which you speak so far too highly of my literary work, this morning. To the best of my ability I will answer your question regarding the formation of my style.

I never gave myself any special or conscious training in this respect. I was always fond of reading and of learning poetry by heart; and my father, a man of very cultivated mind, used to read select passages from the best authors aloud to us. In this way I heard, while yet a boy, much of Milton's,

Jeremy Taylor's, Sir Thomas Browne's, Lamb's, Landor's, and Bacon's prose.

I was educated at Harrow. But here did not distinguish myself at all in English Composition. I failed signally to win either English Essay or English poem. Yet I think I must have been forming a style unconsciously; for I came the other day upon a diatribe in Ms of that period, and it seemed to me not without merit of a rhetorical dreamy kind. It was written for my own amusement on the conceptions made severally by Homer Virgil and Dante regarding the state of souls in the next world. The influence of De Quincey (of whom I was a diligent student then) is apparent.

During my time at Oxford I practised writing assiduously, and began to feel that I had some power. Hardly a day passed without my composing something in verse or prose for my own pleasure—while I also spent great pains upon a weekly Essay for my tutor Professor [Benjamin] Jowett. His observations and the criticisms, my father occasionally gave me were extremely helpful. They checked my tendency to a vague and sentimental rhetoric.

Great facility of expression has always been my bane, combined with a natural partiality for sensuous imagery. I attribute any degree of strength and purity of style to wh I may have subsequently attained in no small measure 1) to the composition of Essays on dry metaphysical topics for so good a critic as Jowett 2) to the habit of translation from Greek.

I was fortunate in enjoying the intimate friendship of Professor [John] Conington, who also helped me by sound advice. His own style was clear & vigorous, without affectation. He laughed me out of many of my conceits & prettinesses.

All this while I kept on composing English verses: the style modelled (by sympathy rather than calculation) upon Tennyson & Keats. But Conington was convinced that I could not be a poet; & his discouraging influence prevented me from studying poetry with system. The only wrong direction I am aware of having received from anyone, was from him; when he once said "Your forte lies in poetical prose." I took the hint too literally; & when I felt inclined to write verse, used often to *compell* myself to prose-expression. The result of which was that I got into a hybrid habit of writing, wh has given offence to many of my critics.

I ought to add that from the age of 18 to 24 I kept a diary, chiefly for the description of impressions made on me by landscape & works of art. This, I am quite sure, helped to form my own style more than all else. The emotional passages of the diary are in verse, the descriptive & critical passages in prose.

If you happen to know my books of Italian sketches, you may be interested to know that they are mainly extracts from this journal.

On leaving Oxford I began two kinds of study, wh had a powerful effect upon my style. One was writing for the Saturday Review. I was just 21[2] when I first became a regular contributor to that periodical. The other was a systematic reading of the Elizabethan Dramatists. In the course of three years I read them from beginning to end, & wrote a complete series of studies on them—which I refrained from publishing, feeling the work too immature.

I reached the age of 31 before I published a book under my own name. Severe illness spoiled for me the years between 23 and 30. I could not use my eyes, & broke down in the lungs. But I am of opinion that the enforced inaction of that period was not an entire evil. It made me reflect more, & checked my natural fluency; although it prevented me from acquiring exact knowledge & prosecuting *études fortes* at the time when the intellect is best fitted for such work.

To sum up. My training in style has consisted in:

1) early habits of reading with love, for pleasure, in a desultory way, without the sense of obligation.

2) Sustained practice in several kinds of writing—partly under the eyes of strict criticism—partly as journalism—partly with a view to arriving at self-expression, & to recording impressions with fidelity while they were fresh and present to the mind, in diaries:

But it has never been a systematic or deliberate training. My belief is that Composition is not a thing to be acquired by rules. I never read a book upon the subject, though I believe that both Prof Bain and my friend Prof Nichol[3] have written good handbooks.

Cicero's motto *Nulla dies sine linea*[4] is the first precept for a would-be author. In the second place he should learn to respect the criticism of his elders, even though it goes against his own tastes. Although it may not be possible to teach style, it is certainly possible to direct the young by sound advice from mannerisms & affectations.

I fear that I have been rather long-winded & egotistical in these remarks. But the warmth of your letter tempted me to put forth my foliage! And now that I look back on what I have set down, I see that I have been able to communicate very little which is useful.

> Believe me, dear Sir, to
> be very sincerely yours
> John Addington Symonds

The Rv. George Bainton

1. The Rev. George Bainton, *The Art of Authorship . . . Advice to Young Beginners, personally contributed by leading authors of the day . . . Edited by G. Bainton* (1890). Bainton supplied a complimentary sentence and then published Symonds' letter (Chap. III, pp. 170–75).

2. Actually, he was 22, if Babington is correct: "A Painter's Camp in the Highlands" appeared in *The Saturday Review,* XIV (Dec. 27, 1862), 777–79. It is an unsigned review of a travel-book by Philip Gilbert Hamerton (1834–94), artist and essayist, and founder and editor (1869–94) of the art periodical *The Portfolio.* Symonds noted the influence of Ruskin on the writer.

3. Alexander Bain (1818–1908) wrote several once-popular texts on grammar and rhetoric (1863, 1866, 1872, and 1874). John Nichol (1833–94) wrote *English Composition* (1879).

4. No day without a line; no day without something done.—Apelles, the Greek painter, labored to improve himself, especially in drawing, and practiced daily; hence, the proverb.

1635. *To Horatio Forbes Brown*

Davos, Oct. 26, [1887]

[Dear Horatio]

Madge and I arrived here on Monday evening. We had a fairly pleasant journey, sleeping well in those cubicles over the Gothard, and getting to Landquart on Sunday. We found the road from Klosters to Davos on half its length tobogganable. Some snow has fallen and will last I think. The cold last night was severe: 5° Fahr.—27 degrees of frost.

I am very glad to learn from your letter that you enjoyed our visit to you—I will not say as much as we did, for that would be rating your enjoyment as high as ours was.

I have just sent off a telegram to you. "Sì. Letter." I could not do so before. It took some time to turn the question of the *mezzanino*[1] over in all its aspects. We all of us have a hankering after it. But we all feel that it commits us to a certain line of action—removes us to some extent from England—ties our hands in some degree from making exploratory journeys into other parts of Italy. For myself the latter consideration is not of much importance; I am old enough and have seen enough to know that I like going to Venice and slipping into accustomed ways there. But I feel that for Madge's education it may be somewhat limiting. Then there is the question of Lotta to be considered. We can decide on nothing without thought for Lotta. However, the upshot of the whole debate is that we should like to take the *mezzanino,* provided you will alter the arrangement of the kitchen by putting it on the basement. I have little doubt that, provided we agree upon the detail, and provided I do not become a poor man, we shall all be delighted to know we have a home in Venice.

I am going to send you Roger North's "Life."[2] We are disgusted with the binding—a coronet out of place—and the father's coat wrongly displayed; for Roger's mother was an heiress of Montagu, and if her arms were to be used, they ought to have appeared in a scutcheon of pretence. Otherwise the book is good. I have slipped into it a pedigree of North (leaving out the Earls of Guilford).

To Sir Henry Layard[3] I am about to send my "Cellini." The book pleases me; and I regard my part in it with modest satisfaction. It has been already well reviewed in the *Scotsman* and *Spectator*.

[Incomplete]

---

1. Symonds was thinking of renting Brown's Venice *mezzanino*. See L. 1587.
2. The autobiography of Roger North (1653–1734), the lawyer and biographer. He is best known for his *Lives of the Norths,* published in 1744 after his death. Symonds refers to a complete edition, with North's autobiography and some letters, to be published with Symonds' sanction and edited by Augustus Jessopp (1890). See L 1473.
3. See L 1327.

1636. *To Sir Henry Layard*[1]

Davos Platz, Switzerland Oct:27.1887

Dear Sir Henry

I am sending you my translation of Cellini[2] in two packets, with the anxious hope that you may not find it too poor to look at.

I am not responsible for the illustrations, all of wh, except the French etchings, are middle-class below contempt.

I hope you and Lady Layard[3] forgave my daughter and me for flitting like shadows from Venice. We were not fit to present ourselves before you, having been wafted down by bad weather to Venice with only the rough clothes needful for a driving tour in the mountains of Lago d'Iseo and Lago di Garda.

We have some expectation of getting a *pied à terre* in Venice, if Brown and I agree upon the lease of his mezzanino. We shall not then be quite such salvage creatures.

Believe me to be with true respect yours
John Addington Symonds—

1. See L 1327.
2. See L 1635.
3. Lady Layard was Enid (d. 1912), daughter of Sir John Guest and Lady Charlotte Guest, Layard's cousin and translator (1838–49) of the *Mabinogion*.

1637. *To Charles Edward Sayle*

Am Hof, Davos Platz, Switzerland. Nov: 13. 1887

My dear Sayle

You say my silences are "not inexplicable." I wonder at this, because they are almost inexplicable to myself. I get into the bad way of letting correspondence drift altogether. It is partly because I have such lots of letters I am forced to answer, & partly because I set apart no fixed time, & partly from a great dislike to writing either mere banalities or confidential communications of feeling & thought to friends.

You know I did get your 'Wiclif,'[1] & you must know I did read it. But just then my eldest daughter died; & this grievous pain was followed by an exodus to the Black Forest, where my wife was ill, & then by England, where I was pretty well engulfed by people—besides having to work 4 hrs per diem at the correction of the text of my Cellini. I left England, overdone by the heat & society.

I thought "Wiclif" very unequal, I must confess; & I do not like the attempt to present in dramatic shape a view of an epoch & a great historic character. I think the world is no longer naive enough for this to be successful. But I delighted in the lyric passages, & I felt the power, the intellectual spring, of the whole performance. As I have been frankly critical, I will go on in my frankness, & tell you that, when you talked to me of "Wiclif" here, I did not anticipate anything so good. I was pleased to see that Mr A Galton[2] took interest in your play. He is a critic for whom I have respect, & whom I should much like to know personally. He ought to make much of literature, having not only mental qualifications, but moral tone of the right sort for serious enduring work.

I don't know whether to congratulate or condole with you about the Br: Mus:[3] Pray alter the words you propose in my wretched testimonial.

I was passing over the Lago di Como last October, & thought, at Bellagio, of you. What curious slim, sleepy-faced fellows, with almost Japanese eyes, some of the boatmen in those places are. I went on to Venice, where I have taken the lease of an apartment in a friend's big house.[4]

I wish we could meet there in the spring, or somewhere else where there is room & time to talk. I should like to have some more long wandering conversations with you.

I am working at a collection of essays on—what shall I call it?—well: perhaps, the principles of Criticism.[5] But then Criticism has no principles; & my book ought to be like the hackneyed chapter on the snakes in Ireland.[6] By the way, I wish there are no snakes anywhere, & espy in the Zool: Gardens. My friend [J.W.] Courthope took me twice to see them last June; & I have been obliged to dream of them ever since, amalgamating their shapes in "the anarchy of dreaming sleep" into most abhorred monsters.

You will perceive that, if I am bad at writing, I am not bad at remembering my friends. So: give me the pleasure of sometimes hearing from you. I will do my best to respond; & anyhow, I shall be a sympathetic listener.

Believe me, dear Sir, as Dr Johnson says, to be your affectionate faithful & humble servant

John Addington Symonds

---

1. *Wiclif: An Historical Drama* (Oxford, 1887). The best part of this tiresome play is the dedicatory lyric written to commemorate Sayle's friend, Thomas Bagot Oldham, who died in India, age 23. It is by far the best poem Sayle published.

2. See L 1581.

3. Sayle hoped for an appointment to the staff of the British Museum. He had asked Symonds for a reference, a task Symonds disliked. See L 1581.

4. Horatio Brown's house.

5. This became *E S & S* (2 vols., 1890).

6. A reference to St. Patrick's legendary dismissal of the snakes from Ireland; to write a book on principles of criticism would be like writing a book on snakes in Ireland —neither exists.

1638. *To Horatio Forbes Brown*

Davos, Nov. 15 [1887]

[Dear Horatio]

I was pleased to read what Creighton[1] said about my "Cellini," and thank you for sending me those words. This book has been uniformly well reviewed, and Nimmo tells me that all the copies will have been sold by the end of this month. He only allowed me two copies; else I would have sent you one. But I was obliged to buy three for necessary presentation and I really cannot afford 36s. over and over again. Besides, you don't need an English translation of Cellini.

Nimmo proposes that I should translate Gozzi's "Life."[2] Do you know anything of Gozzi? I fancy it would be a pleasant book to do. I do not think it very much matters not having very many reviews of your book. There was a spiteful little notice in the *Athenaeum*.[3] You will probably have seen it. But as it may miss you, I send it. What is said about Carmagnola at Arbedo may be worth your notice. Publishers say that reviews make little difference to books. I dare say that is true in the case of a book like "Cellini." But I agree with you in thinking that a book like your "Essays" must be affected by the number and frequency of reviews.

[Incomplete]

---

1. Mandell Creighton (see L 1521). Anonymous reviews appeared in *The Saturday Review*, LXIV (1887), 703; *The Spectator*, LX (1887), 1425–26; and later in *The Athenaeum*, no. 3140 (Dec. 31, 1887), 887–88.

2. Count Carlo Gozzi (1720–1806), the dramatist whose best-known work is *Turandot*, published his *Memorie inutili* in 1797. Symonds published his translation of the work in 1889 (a new ed., 1963). Symonds found translating Gozzi far less congenial than translating Cellini. For a lengthy complaint over the task see L 1646.

3. *The Athenaeum*, No. 3134 (November 19, 1887), 673: this anonymous notice found Brown's *Venetian Studies* "pleasant" but condemns his underrating of Francesco Carmagnola (ca. 1390–1432), Italian condottiere, and his admiration of the *relazione* of Giovanni Sagredo (1617–82), Venetian ambassador to England.

1639. *To Horatio Forbes Brown*

Davos Nov. 15, [1887]

[Dear Horatio]

I have been lecturing to-day[1] to 200 people in the Konversations-Saal of the Kurhaus. This is a new experience for me at Davos. It went off well enough. I talked to the people about Davos in the Middle Ages, using the old Landbuch, or Digest of Common-Law, date 1598, which illustrates the manners of the place. The Trustees of the English Library[2] asked me to give the lecture for the benefit of the Institution, and I suppose I have put about £10 in their pockets.

I do nothing else but write now. The weather is too dreadful. Next to

London in November, I suppose Davos is the worst place on earth, in November, I have ever lived in.

Nov. 17.

The weather changed after I had written the beginning of this letter, and we have had two fine days. Yesterday I spent in exploring my wood upon the Seehorn with the forester. We marked thirty big pines to fell this winter, which ought to give me firewood for two years. It was a very pleasant excursion. Wading in snow above our knees, among the broken rocks and fir-roots and alpen-rose plants, from the Lake-basin to the top of the Seehorn,—tapping the trees and settling which were fit to keep and which were ripe for felling. I suppose we crawled over about a twentieth part of the wood, but got enough for my purpose. I spend about £100 a year on firing now. If I can get these trees economically cut, sawn, carried and split, I shall save something next year.

To-day has been spent in tobogganing. They have made a fine new road from Clavadel to the Landwasser, about a mile in length, on the shady side of the valley. There is plenty of snow there in good condition. It makes a fine run.

[Incomplete]

---

1. "Davos in the Olden Days," *OLSH*, pp. 28–58.
2. The English Library, still at Davos, is used only infrequently.

1640. *To Margot Tennant*

I am so glad that you like my Cellini. The book has been a success; and I am pleased, though I am not interested in its sale. The publisher paid me £ 210 for my work, which I thought very good wages.

[Davos, ca. Nov. 17, 1887][1]

My Dear Margot,

I wrote to you in a great hurry yesterday, and with some bothering thoughts in the background of my head.[2]

So I did not tell you how much I appreciated your critical insight into the points of my Introduction to Cellini. I do not rate that piece of writing quite as highly as you do. But you "spotted" the best thing in it—the syllogism describing Cellini's state of mind as to Bourbon's death.

It is true, I think, what you say: that I have been getting more and more nervous and less elaborate in style of late years. This is very natural. One starts in life with sensuous susceptibilities to beauty, with a strong feeling for colour and for melodious cadence, and also with an impulsive enthusiastic way of expressing oneself. This causes young work to seem decorated and laboured, whereas it very often is really spontaneous and hasty, more instructive and straightforward than the work of middle life. I write now with much more trouble and more slowly than I used to do. This gives me more command over the vehicle, language, than I used to have. I write what pleases myself less, but what probably strikes other people more.

This is a long discourse; but not so much about myself as appears. I was struck with your insight, and I wanted to tell you how I analyse the change of style which you point out, and which results, I think, from colder, more laborious, duller effort as one grows in years.

The artist ought never to be commanded by his subject, or his vehicle of expression. But until he ceases to love both with a blind passion, he will probably be so commanded. And then his style will appear decorative, florid, mixed, unequal, laboured. It is the sobriety of a satiated or blunted enthusiasm which makes the literary artist. He ought to remember his dithyrambic moods, but not to be subject to them any longer, nor to yearn after them.

[Incomplete][2]

---

1. In the printed version by Margot Tennant Asquith, *An Autobiography* (II, 65, 68), this letter was attached without date to our L 1776, at the beginning of 1890. The reference to Cellini clearly places the present letter in 1887.
2. The letter is not available.

1641. *To Mrs. Thomas Duff Gordon-Duff*[1]

Davos Nov: 25 1887

Dear Mrs Gordon Duff

It is pretty late; but before I go to bed, I must tell you that Margot [Tennant] arrived here about 6 this evening in high spirits—quite herself,

& full of the amusements which her long & tedious journey had afforded. How admirable is the soundness of nature in her, which makes her great physical & mental energy delightful to herself & to others! I think the quality is very rare of such large force & universal adaptability so simply & unaffectedly employed. Many people have the same energies. But they generally combine some egotism, some palpable self-seeking, with their use. Margot's complete freedom from such things, her disengagement, & her essential goodness of nature, render her brilliant personality not only dazzling but loveable.

Please do not mind my saying this. It strikes me always when I see her. And I am impelled to express (being nothing if not analytical) what I feel about her.

I can tell you that we are all highly flattered by her coming so far to see us—when there is worse than nothing to find here. Flattered is not the word. We are warmed & made better by her kindness.

Thank you very much for the two photographs of yourself & Gordon Duff, both of which will soon be placed (in the best little frame I can find at Davos) in the corner of my study, where a few portraits of my friends are.

Alas! they will only serve to remind me that you are both absent. When I think of you, I feel—as one so often does in life—how little use I made of either of you for my own happiness, & how much I miss you. I am always missing the friend who used to come & talk to me, when I was tired at night, & bore with endless dissertations upon things in general, & always left me the better by what he suggested or by what he advanced in discussion.

How strange it is that you should think kindly of Davos. There is so little to love here. And yet I suppose that one really loves most what has the least to offer. We like what we are forced to make something out of. And so you retain a feeling for this valley. I do not think you need regret being elsewhere at present. It is a dreary gloomy autumn, slowly dwindling into the death of the year, with grey skies, & abominable snow-slush on every path which feet can tread.

It is not so bad for us, who have home-occupations, as for the wretched strangers sent up to get rid of their maladies in miserable hotel rooms.

I do not spend time in lamenting the weather. I have always a lot of things to plan & write about—only too much work on hand. But the ugliness outside depresses me.

Yes: we are breaking out into Lectures & Literary Societies. It is very comic. I find that I can lecture comfortably in that public room, the Conversations Saal, at the Kurhaus. And I like lecturing. Your husband will say that I do so pretty stiffly in my own room by the stove-side! I read a paper, not with the same comfort, in the dining-room of the Hotel Angleterre, upon Elizabethan Lyrics, yesterday.

You ask me a question about Cellini's nimbus.[2] I noticed the phenomenon quite independently of his narrative. But when I came to read his Memoirs, before translating them, I saw that he had happened to observe the same phenomenon. It is a very common one. Only one needs the level light of early morning & dew upon the grass to see it. All sportsmen must have had it within their observation. Other people do not generally go abroad early enough. Here in the Alps, for many reasons, it is particularly easy of detection—partly because the sun's level light is often concentric by mountain-gaps, & because the dews are heavy upon *grassy* slopes at a convenient angle.

I am going, probably, to complete another amusing Italian life, that of the Venetian Carlo Gozzi.[3] "Cellini" is already sold out, the publisher writes me; & he wants something to take his place.

Pray give my love to your husband, & tell him that I think of him daily. I do not need his welcome picture to remind me. I shall write to him soon, when I have something worth his hearing. But what I most want is to talk to him. Ever yours most truly

J A Symonds

---

1. See L 1552.
2. As Cellini approached Rome and reached rising ground, he looked towards Florence and exclaimed: "Oh God of heaven! what is that great thing one sees there over Florence?" It was "a huge beam of fire, which sparkled and gave out extraordinary lustre" (*Autobiography,* translated by Symonds, Chap. LXXXIX).
3. Symonds published his translation of Gozzi's memoirs in 1890 [1889]. See L 1638.

1642. *To Thomas Duff Gordon-Duff*[1]

Am Hof, Davos, Dec. 6, 1887.

My dear Duff

We are thrilling with heightened pulses & improved intelligence by Margot's [Margot Tennant's] wonderful life-giving goodness. I put goodness in the place of honour on purpose; because it seems to me that I have discovered for myself *this* as her ruling quality. And I think I ought to say so to you, in equity & honour; since I have in former days spoken with less certainty of conviction. Other people, who have had the advantage of knowing her in the way that we do now, would say that there is no good reason to say what is so obvious. But I am bound to mark the discovery, if only in correction of my earlier judgment when I felt Margot's fascination & enjoyed her brilliancy, but when her character was still somewhat of a puzzle to me. She has made herself beloved & quite unselfishly adored by my wife & daughters. They almost forget me in their love of her   how clever & bright she is. What a gift this is! And I am bound to say, being nothing if not critical, that I think she uses this gift in a right & wholesome way. It is somewhat startling to find anyone with her gift; more startling to find that the gift is used so excellently. She makes people to be in love with her. But she is able to make them go further, to love her. You know what I mean by those balanced sentences. And really I maintain that the power to do that, to convert "being in love" into "loving" is one of the rarest & most beautiful qualities. And now she is going away

> "O saw ye bonnie Leslie,
> As she gae'd o'er the border?
> She's gone, like Alexander,
> To spread her conquests further."[2]

God go with her. I think she carries God & his angels with her & I cannot believe that she will go or come except rightly.

[Incomplete]

---

1. See L 1552.
2. By Robert Burns.

1643. *To Horatio Forbes Brown*

Davos, Dec. 21 [1887]

[Dear Horatio]

The "Introduction to Boccaccio,"[1] which prevented me last time from writing you a proper letter, and which you say you had not heard of, is now over. It was an Essay on Boccaccio as man and author (like my Prefatory Essay on Cellini), intended to go before a new translation of the "Decameron" which Vitzetelly is bringing out. He proposed to pay me £35, which is nearly a year's rent of your *mezzanino* by the way, and I agreed to do it. But I had to get it out of hand in time to begin Gozzi. Thank you very much for the information you have already sent me about Gozzi. I will not trouble you to copy Cicognara;[2] when I come to Venice you will show me what he says. The great difficulty is to get a copy of the "Memorie Inutili."[3] I feel rather indignant with myself for going in for lucrative literature, as I am doing. I should not have thought of Cellini except for the £210, or of Boccaccio except for the £35, or of Gozzi except for the £210 to come. But my choice has been deliberate; and I do my work as well as I can. By the way, a second edition of Cellini[4] is called for; and I am going to make alterations in the Introduction at two points to which you called my attention.

Miss [Margot] Tennant spent a fortnight here; very pleasant it was. She is a wonderful companion. I have never seen a woman like her. And she corresponds with all sorts of people. Letters are always coming from Gladstone, Jowett, the Prince of Wales, Arthur Balfour, Lords Rosebery, Granville, and Pembroke, the Lytteltons, and innumerable ladies of society, all of which have things of interest in them. She keeps her friends up to her mark.

[Incomplete]

---

1. Published posthumously by Nimmo (1895) as *Giovanni Boccaccio as Man and Author*.

2. Count Leopoldo Cicognara (1767–1834), Italian archaeologist and author. His chief work was the *Storia della scultura dal suo risorgimento in Italia al secolo di Napoleone* (1813–18).

3. See L 1638.

4. 1888.

1644. *To Herbert P. Horne*[1]

Am Hof, Davos Platz, Switzerland. Dec: 23. 1887

Private

Dear Mr Horne

Your letter of the 20th reached me this morning, & I will immediately reply to it. In my last I told you that I was gradually preparing a volume of essays upon critical & artistic subjects, & that I thought some parts of these might suit you. I have already finished several. Two of them, on *Idealism & Realism* & the *Model,* have appeared in the Fortnightly (Sept & Dec). And two, in continuation of the argument, are booked for the same periodical.

I have by me at present the following numbers. 1) *On Principles of Criticism.* 2) *On the Application of Evolutionary Ideas to Literature & Art.* 3) *On Democratic Art,* with special reference to Whitman. 4) *On Landscape,* with special reference to modern ideas regarding Nature. 5) *On Nature Myths & Moral Allegories,* somewhat mystical. 6) *On Some Relations of Art to Science & Ethics.* 7) *On a theory of Pater's that Music is the Standard Art,* a plea for the prevalent belief that art requires an intellectual & moral content against critics who would fain find in it only a handling of agreeable forms etc.

Numbers 1. 2. 3. 4 are, I think, larger than you would care for. Number 5 is not too long; but I doubt whether, detached from its context in my book, it might not seem too fanciful; it attempts to prove that the elder mythologies have still their value for us. Number 6 is partly an attempt to define the relations between Beauty Truth & Goodness, partly an enquiry into the moral paradox presented by Renaissance art. Number 7,[2] again, seems to me perhaps somewhat difficult to separate from its context.

After this frank explanation of my position, you must tell me, if you think fit, whether any of these numbers seem to you at all likely to suit. Written as they all have been in close connection with each other, I am rather diffident about their effectiveness in isolation.

I have another essay by me upon two volumes recently published by Mr A. H. Bullen "Lyrics from Elizabethan Song Books" & "More Lyrics from do."[3] This is distinctly popular, & deals largely in citations of songs which have appeared for the first time in these remarkable anthologies. I want to publish it, for the sake of diffusing an interest in what seems to me a most surprising new treasure of English lyric verse. This I could give you, if you feel it likely to be more suitable than any one of the others. But I must beg you in that case to let me hear at once. I have promised the publisher of Bullen's books to get my essay somewhere placed ere long.

You will notice that I have marked this letter *private.* I did so only because I would rather not have the contents of my projected volume of essays freely discussed as yet. I wish to take time over its preparation; & I have not decided what form I shall ultimately give it, or what other subjects I shall discuss.

Thank you for your kind enquiries about my health. It is fairly good now, except that I am rather over-worked. But the solitude, long leisure &

bracing climate of these Alps enable me to do more than I could in England.

With best wishes for Christmas & New Year believe me very truly yours

John Addington Symonds—

Thank you much for your proposed gift of the Jany number. I will write to you about it.

---

1. See L 1452.

2. The essay on Pater, "Is Music the Type or Measure of all Art?" appeared in *The Century Guild Hobby Horse,* III (April, 1888), 42–51.

3. *Lyrics from the Song-Books of the Elizabethan Age* (1887) and *More Lyrics from the Song-Books of the Elizabethan Age* (1888) are the full titles and dates. Symonds' essay on them, "Elizabethan Song-Books," was published in *In the Key of Blue* (1893), pp. 265–302, as the concluding essay.

1645. *To Henry Graham Dakyns*

Am Hof, Davos Platz, Switzerland. Jan: 15. 1888

My dear Graham

I am redirecting a letter & a p:c: for you to Clifton. I feel that I must send a tender with the train.

It is lonely here by the square green stove without you & Arthur [Sidgwick]. The wooden walls of my little den seem to be ringing & whispering with friendly voices in debate or droning in familiar colloquy.

These walls will echo mainly, for some time to come, the voices of men like Franz the postillion or Fridolin the porter. I enjoy both spheres of comradeship; but I should like to have a little more of the sort which you two friends of my youth & manhood gave me. I should like to blend the two. I imagine an impossible pleasure.

But while I imagine this, & know I cannot get it, I am very grateful to those enlarged facilities of intercourse wh have given me three weeks of Arthur & Graham in the midst of months of Franz & Fridolin.

We had a good time on the whole I think, & one which is ideally profitable by continuing the far past into the transitory present—making me at least feel younger & more defiant of the injuries of Time.

I wish you could have been longer with us. And I wish that the strain upon my small stock of nervous strength had not made me incapable of conducting you upon your journey.

I ought to remember that if I were as elastic as I desire, I should not have been living here, & you & Arthur & I would not have been together in Davos & at Wiesen.

Thank you both heartily, dear friends, you & Maggie, for the pledge of your love you have given us in coming all that way to see us here. I do not say this for myself alone, but for all my family, Catherine & the girls feel it quite as much as I can do.

I will not write more. These lines should be only the continuation of tones of voices wh are still thrilling in my ears—yours & Maggie's & ours, now divided by swift-hurrying steam-engines, but wh twelve hours ago were vibrating together in this little house.

Ever yours
J A Symonds.

1646. *To Horatio Forbes Brown*

Davos, Jan. 21, 1888

[Dear Horatio]

Something has happened to me lately, whether temporary or permanent remains to be seen, which has reduced my vitality and induced a sort of somnolence by no means natural. However, without somnambulising upon paper, the upshot is that I am uneasy on reflecting, in a wakeful interval, how much time has elapsed since I wrote you a letter, and how you may have interpreted my inattention.

I am doing no good in my literary work. I believe this is the secret, or a secret, of my state. Gozzi will not do.[1] And yet I do not see my way to getting out of Gozzi. Excellent to read through rapidly for a student of *roba italiana* [Italian trifles], his Memoirs are hardly worth translating, and their interest depends upon such trivialities—the decadence of Venetian society in a putrid mass of political corruption, Brummagem[2] French philosophy aped by Italians with no revolutionary force inside them, prostitution, theatrical cabals, vain efforts to rehabilitate Dante in the city of Casanova,[3] Baffo,[4] and the Doge Renier,[5] bad style, bad morals, effeminacy, hypocrisy, sloth, *dappocaggine* [ineptitude] of every sort—with an odd unsympathetic bastard between Don Quixote and a pettifogging attorney, a man of cramped genius and of respectable sentiments turned sour, to serve as central figure—all this is so irrelevant to the main current of world-history, so *bizarre,* so involved in masses of petty details which have lost the accent of humanity, that I despair of making anything out of my work. And yet I am engaged.

Basta! I enjoyed the visits of A.[rthur] Sidgwick and Dakyns three weeks. But it was a tiring time, from the vast amount of talk. And there is all the tobogganing business afloat now: squabbles, petty arrangements, &c., &c. Every scrap of the small affair comes eventually to this house. Since I began this letter I have had a solemn deputation to attend to from the natives of Clavadel, where we shall run the International Race, intimating that, unless their particular demands are met, they mean to shut the road up; and the race is next Thursday.

[Incomplete]

---

1. See L 1638.

2. Cheap and gaudy: after *Birmingham,* formerly *Bromwycham,* England, where cheap jewelry and gift toys were made.

3. The implication, based on the characteristic works of the two writers, is sufficiently clear. Casanova (1725–98) was born in Venice.

4. Giorgio Baffo (1697–1768), Venetian patriot and writer of licentious verse. His *Raccolta universale* (1789) reflects the corruption of the culture of his day.

5. Paolo Renièr (1710–89) was elected Doge of Venice in 1779.

1647. *To Horatio Forbes Brown*

Davos, Jan. 28, 1888

[Dear Horatio]

Our luck in tobogganing has been indeed great. We arranged to hold the International Race at Clavadel, providing a mile course, and running two heats. This was fixed for 10 A.M. on the 26th, and thirty-two competitors of all sorts and nations entered. The usual public luncheon for one hundred and twenty people was ordered in the Rathhaus. I saw on the morning of the race by my barometer, and a strange look in the sky, that the weather would change. However, we had it fine up to 1.30, when the race was at last over—fancy how long! And I was standing all that while upon the snow, helping to record the time, identify the racers, and keep the course clear.

Then a furious wind swept down the valley, tearing the snow from the forests and house-roofs, and tossing a tempest of finely powdered snow-sand up into the clear blue sky against the blazing noonday sun—a striking and splendid sight, as the swirl of snow shifted, and took various effects of light.

The race was a very good one. An American, called Child,[1] who rides head-foremost on a flat toboggan, came in first, beating two old racers, Freeman[2] and [Charles] Austin[3] equal, by three seconds, while Minsch,[4] who came on purpose from Montreux, where I have placed him to learn French, ran in fourth at another interval of five seconds. I am always happy when this race and all that belongs to it is well over. On Thursday I did not get home till seven, having started in the morning at nine, and never stopped talking all the time; and then I had to entertain here until midnight. Such a day.

As President of the Club, known alike to English and Swiss, everything falls eventually on my shoulders,[5] and I am held responsible for anything which may go wrong. I have resigned the post, and trust that my resignation will be accepted.

But about our luck; if the weather had changed two hours earlier, the whole thing would have come to grief. And the valley is in such a state now, that no running will be possible for days, weeks perhaps. The higher passes are blocked, Fluela impassable, and those dreadful creatures, "dust-avalanches," *Staub-lavinen,* playing at will upon the mountains.

The University of Oxford has chosen me as one of its three delegates to Bologna, for the festival which begins on June 13, to celebrate the eleventh centenary of that University. I doubt whether I shall accept. It is risky to think of anything so late in the summer.

[Incomplete]

---

1. See Margaret Symonds, *OOP,* p. 62, for a notice of Mr. Child and his toboggan. He had arrived in Davos the preceding year.

2. Harold Freeman, who served at various times as Treasurer of the Buol Toboggan Run Competition, resided with his family and servants at the Hotel Buol. See L 1452.

3. See L 1452.

4. Peter Minsch of Klosters, who figured in all toboggan races from 1883–93, won the Symonds cup twice, in 1884 and 1887. Through Symonds' influence he became a station master in the postal service.

5. Symonds' contributions to the cause of winter-sports were the Symonds Cup and the Symonds Shield. See L 1684.

1648. *To Herbert P. Horne*

Am Hof, Davos Platz, Switzerland. Jan: 28 1888

Dear Mr Horne

In reply to your letter of the 24th I think that the article which I should prefer to send you will contain about 4800 words—rather fewer than more. But when I have copied out some passages wh form a part of it, I shall be able to give a nearer estimate.

This article has for title "Is Music the type or measure for all Art?" It consists of an enquiry into the theory (expressed by Mr Pater in a very interesting Fortnightly essay called "The School of Giorgione"[1]) that art is always striving to free itself from the mere intelligence.

It is not controversial in any hostile spirit. But I find that the discussion of the Pater's essay enables me to say what I think about the wrongness of a too sensuous theory of art; just as some time ago Mr M. Arnold's[2] phrase of "poetry being in the main a criticism of life" enabled me to say what I think about the wrongness of a too intellectual & didactic theory of art.

Please let me hear whether you would like to have this article, & whether the length will suit you.

Two others I selected to consider: on "Some Principles of Criticism" and on "The application of Evolutionary Ideas to art & literature" appear to me too long. So is a third on "Democratic Art" coupled with the name of W. Whitman.

Believe me very truly yours

J A Symonds—

---

1. *The Fortnightly Review,* XXVIII (1877), 526–38.

2. The review, "Matthew Arnold's Selections from Wordsworth," reprinted later in *E S & S* (1890) as "Is Poetry at Bottom a Criticism of Life," appeared in *The Fortnightly Review* XXXI (1879), 686–701. Symonds included in *E S & S* all of the essays he mentions in this letter.

1649. *To Herbert P. Horne*

Am Hof, Davos Platz, Switzerland. Feb: 3 1888

Dear Mr Horne

I find that I overestimated the length of my article on Music as the Type & Measure of all Art.[1] Now that the whole is written out, it amounts to about 4000 words.

When I hear from you, I shall be able to send it off at once.

I do not think I told you how much I admire the new type of the Hobbyhorse & the increased beauty of the ornamental work. The last number was a very choice specimen of typography.

Believe me very truly yours

J A Symonds

---

1. See L 1644 and 1648.

1650. *To Horatio Forbes Brown*

Davos, Feb. 9, 1888

[Dear Horatio]

It began to snow last Saturday at 2.30 P.M., and it has been snowing almost incessantly since then.[1] Our only safe communication with the rest of the world is by the Prättigau. Avalanches are streaming down both sides of the valley below Frauenkirch. One man[2] was killed on the road near Glaris yesterday; another,[3] whom I know, was blown by the blast of an avalanche from the road near Tschuggen on the Fluela, right across the stream to the other side of the valley, and then buried in the torrent of snow which followed him. It is very difficult to get out of our house, though I have three men always working, cutting us out. And I begin to feel uneasy about the masses of snow upon the Schiahorn right above our heads. If the snow does not stop, I think seriously of migrating to Hotel Buol to-morrow; that house is in a safer place than ours. This state of things does not agree with mental activity. I am stupefied merely by gazing at the perpetual whirl of snow-flakes, the gradual ascent of snow-walls round me, and the recurrent noise of snow descending with a heavy thud from the house-roof.

I always wanted to see a "great snow" here; and now I have my wish, so I ought not to grumble. There has been nothing like it since I came in 1877.

I wonder what part Lord Salisbury is playing in the European crisis.[4] The suspense is terrible, something like the expectation of a "Staub-Lavine" [dust-avalanche] from the Schiahorn.

[Incomplete]

1. The *Annual Register* (1888) reported the effects of this Swiss storm; its resulting avalanches: "Between Hallstadt and Aussee [in Austria] a pine forest covering the mountain side was wholly swept away. On the Vorarlberg Railway the Langen station was completely overwhelmed, and one end of the tunnel stopped, enclosing a mail train." All passes over and through the Alps were blocked ("Chronicle," pp. 8, 9).

2. Anton Broher. See L 1653.

3. Caspar Valär. See L 1653.

4. The crisis involved Germany and Russia. The German Parliament required only 10 minutes, without discussion, to vote £14,000,000 for war and add 700,000 men to the army. Robert Arthur Gascoyne-Cecil, 3rd Marquis of Salisbury (1830–1903), the prime minister and foreign secretary, claimed that Russia's character was "pacific" and that Prince Bismark had declared that Germany had no interest in Eastern Europe.

1651. *To T. S. Perry*

Am Hof, Davos Platz, Switzerland. Feb: 9 1888

My dear Perry

I am very glad to hear from your letter of the 1st that you are all comfortably established in Paris, & I hope that Mrs Perry is enjoying her art-work in the Louvre.

It was very good of you to send me Howells' notice of my last 2 vols (R: in It:).[1] I see no American reviews of my work at any time, & do not exactly want to do so—finding the English criticisms by no means unkindly or non-eulogistic, but unhelpful & unintelligent. Howells' I prize, since it takes my point & shows that he felt what I was driving after. You & he are the only two men who perceived the argument of those concluding volumes. No doubt it is my fault that I didn't make it clearer, & your merit that you discovered what I was feeling after.

You speak about going to "the Darmesteters."[2] Do you mean the Professor of Oriental Languages in the Rue de Vaugirard 192? He is a bachelor, is he not, & somewhat deformed in physique? I have special reasons for being much interested in him personally at present, which I am not at liberty to mention. I have never seen him. But if this is your friend, please tell me some impressions he has made on you. My interest in him, I must say, is quite disinterested—nothing to do with myself or with my work.

Among other things he has recently published a French version of selections from Miss Mary Robinson's poems[3]—done with charming sympathy.

Do you go to Renan's[4] Lectures? People say they are always touched with humour. I should like to have heard him monologize at the Vaudeville.

It is just now 10 p.m. on Thursday evening; & it has been snowing ever since 2.30 p.m. last Saty. Life is getting dangerous here. The avalanches are thundering into the valley at all points. They have blocked the post-roads, destroyed three men at several places in the immediate neighborhood, confined seven men for a night & two days in a tunnel, buried five more who were dug out alive, & finally reduced the village to darkness by choking the water-supply wh gives electric light. We are being smothered in snow. I keep three men all day working round my house, & work with them at the shovel.

But it is like a labour of the Danaides.[5] We cut channels of approach out, the walls of which are far above our hats; huge bastions of snow block all the ground floor windows. Meanwhile on the mountain side above us to the height of 3000 feet above the floor of the valley, the vast masses of snow are piling themselves up on perilous ledges & precipitous slopes, ready to descend & bury the house. Our safety depends upon a thin wood of old pines & larches. Sometimes when the wind wails at night, prowling about those frightful wildernesses of snow, & threatening to dislodge & hurl them down into the vale, I tremble in my bed. This house happens to be in a critical position. But it is better to abide like a passenger in a ship upon a stormy sea. When a snow-fall reaches these dimensions in a mountain valley, every point in it offers insecurity. The odd thing is to think how many hundreds of invalids etc are cooped up here. They do not know their risks as well as an old-stager like myself. But in ten years here I have seen nothing like this.

If I find means of communication, I will send this off tomorrow. But I was told today that the post would cease in all directions. Till tonight we had one route, the easiest, open for vehicles with one horse.

Goodbye. Ever yrs J A Symonds

---

1. In "The Editor's Study," *Harper's New Monthly Magazine,* LXXV (1887), 963–65.

2. James Darmesteter (1849–94), French Orientalist; succeeded Ernest Renan (see n. 4 below) as secretary of Société Asiatique de Paris; editor of *La Revue de Paris;* married Mary Robinson in 1888. See L 1137. Her correspondence with Symonds apparently ceased after her marriage.

3. The *Poésies* (1888).

4. Ernest Renan (1823–92), the famous French religious historian and philosopher. His renowned *Vie de Jésus* appeared in 1863.

5. All 50 daughters of Danaüs, except 1, were condemned to pour water eternally into sieves as punishment for the murder of their husbands on their wedding nights.

1652. *To Miss Desvoeux*[1]

Am Hof, Davos Platz, Switzerland. Feb: 16/88

Dear Miss Desvoeux

My little daughter Katharine tells me you would like a bit of my writing. I find these sonnets tonight in an old Ms book, & think they may serve as well as anything else. At least they are a bit of original work with the corrections of the moment.

Very truly yours

JASymonds

The Daffodil[2]

i

Narcissus' Flower

"Ah me for youth! Ah me for dolorous eld!
    This comes apace while that fleets fast away!"
    So sang Theognis in the birth of May,
        When grace & love o'er Hellas empire held.
He sat beside the brook, & watched the belled
    Beauty of daffodils that laughed a day,
    Then sank into decrepitude's decay—
    Thin shrivelled husks where through the
                north-wind knelled.
He sat & watched the blossoms: from their bloom
    Upgrew before his dreaming poet's eyes
    A youth of mystic loveliness, inclined
Face-forward o'er the hurrying streamlet's gloom,
    Bending dark brows of yearning, dim surmise,
    To search time's turbid flood with prescient mind.

ii

Balder's Flower

Whene'er one looks upon the daffodil,
    Let him remember golden Balder's death:
    In Asgard's hall He yielded up his breath,
    Whom all the gods were impotent to kill,

Save Loki with sly mistletoe: then chill
    Winter descended, & the world had Scathe;
    And Odin wandered, a pale wailing wraith,
    What time his darling dwelt with Hela still.
Yet Balder had not wholly died, for spring
    Returning brought pure summer airs again;
    And jocund harbingers of that sweet birth
Were new-fledged daffodils on bare grey earth,
    Balder's own flowers, bright cups of golden grain,
    Girt with frail sunbeams in a silvery ring.

                         John Addington Symonds.

---

1. Probably Frances Emma, the daughter of Sir Henry Dalrymple Des Voeux, 5th Bart. (died 1894), who married Lady Alice Egerton Grey, youngest daughter of the 2nd Earl of Wilton. There were 3 daughters. Frances Emma died in 1892, age 27. Mrs. Des Voeux and a daughter appear on the guest list of the Hotel Buol for 1889 and 1892.

2. These poems had been published in *The Century Guild Hobby Horse*, II (Oct. 1887), 121–22.

1653. *To* The Pall Mall Gazette

[Davos, Feb. 28, 1888]

[Dear Sir]

It may interest English people to receive a succinct account of the somewhat exceptional snowfall which has happened in the health resort of Davos Platz this winter. I have resided in the valley since 1877–8. But I have witnessed nothing to be compared with this snowfall in magnitude. With a view to clearness I will make extracts from my diary of the last fortnight, adding such explanatory notes as seem to me useful:—

Feb. 4.—It began to snow at 2.30 P.M. The barometer has been rising slowly during the last three days, and now it stands pretty high. The only intimation of bad weather I have noticed was a well-defined and brightly-coloured solar halo between eleven and twelve yesterday morning. At 9.20 P.M. this evening a brilliant flash of lightning was noticed, while the snow was falling heavily.

Feb. 5.—About two feet had fallen before 8 A.M. It snowed all day.

Feb. 6.—We reckoned another foot of snow this morning. The Fluela

Pass, which connects us with the Lower Engadine, was closed to traffic. Just before noon a man called Anton Broher, known among his comrades as "the Knave of Spades," because he had a bushy black beard, was swept away by an avalanche below Tschuggen, on the Fluela road, about three miles from Davos Platz. Eye-witnesses saw him carried by the blast of the avalanche, together with his horse and sledge, three hundred yards in the air across the mountain stream. The snow which followed buried him. He was subsequently dug out dead, with his horse dead, and the sledge beside him. The harness had been blown to ribbons in the air; for nothing could be found of it, except the head-piece on the horse's neck.

This violence of the wind which precedes an avalanche is well authenticated. A carter, whom I know, once told me that he was driving his sledge with two horses on the Albula Pass, when an avalanche fell upon the opposite side of the gorge. It did not catch him. But the blast carried him and his horses and the sledge at one swoop over into deep snow, whence they emerged with difficulty. Another man, who is well known to me, showed me a spot in the Schaufigg valley (between Chur and the Strela Pass) where one of his female relatives had been caught by the wind of an avalanche. She was walking to church when this happened. The blast lifted her into the air, swept her from the road, and landed her at the top of a lofty pine, to which she clung with all the energy of desperation. The snow rushed under her, and left the pine standing. It must have been a trifling avalanche. Her friends, returning from church, saw her clutching for bare life upon the tree, and rescued her. Many such cases could be mentioned. A road-maker named Schorta this winter was blown in like manner into the air below Zernetz, and saved himself by grappling to a fir tree. I have been shown a place near Ems, in the Rhine Valley, not far from Chur, where a miller's house was carried some distance through the air by an avalanche blast. Its inhabitants were all killed, except an old man above sixty and a child of two years. Again, I may mention that the tower of the monastery at Dissentis was on one occasion blown down by the same cause. In order to understand the force of the "Lavinen-Dunst," as this blast is called here, we must remember that hundreds of thousands of tons of snow are suddenly set in motion in narrow chasms. The air displaced before them acts upon objects in their way like breath blown into a pea-shooter.

Feb. 7.—It is still snowing. We reckon that there is an average depth of five feet in the valley. In the woods, and where it has drifted, the snow is of course much deeper. Four large avalanches fell to-day between Frauenkirch and Schmelzboden. One of them, in the Rutsch-tobel, below Monstein, caught some men working on the road. The man in advance, Caspar Valär, was blown across the stream and buried. The others managed to extricate themselves.

I have since then seen this avalanche. It covers about five acres in the valley, and has a depth in the deepest place of at least sixty feet. The trees on a hill above it have been mown down by the violence of the wind it carried.

Feb. 9.—It is still snowing. The road between Davos and Wiesen is said to be impassable. The electric light is extinct in Davos Platz to-night, owing to an immense avalanche, which fell in the Dischma Thal and choked the water supply.

Feb. 10—The weather seems inclined to mend. I took a sledge and drove to Klosters. All the usual road tracks are obliterated and we passed through enormous masses of snow on either hand.

Feb. 11.—A fine day; clear and sunny. The thermometer stands at −2 deg. Fahr. at night. This renders the snow safe. When not snowing, the cold is very considerable this winter.

I must observe that when there is a considerable frost the snow does not get easily into motion, and so there is less risk of avalanches. The greatest danger is when a thaw, with blustering warm winds, sets in while the snow is still falling. There are, roughly speaking, three sorts of avalanches. One is called "Staub Lavine," and descends when the snow is loose and recently fallen. It is attended with a whirlwind, which lifts the snow of a whole mountain side into the air and drives it onward. It advances in a straight line, overwhelming every obstacle, and is by far the most formidable of the three sorts. The second is called "Grund Lavine." It falls generally in the spring time when the firm winter snow has been loosened by warm thawing breezes. The snow is not whirled into the air, but slips along the ground in enormous masses, gathering volume and momentum as it goes, and finding a way forward by its own weight. The third is called "Schnee-Rutsch," or snow-slip. It consists of a portion of snow detached upon a mountain slope, down which it slides gently, heaping itself gradually higher till it comes to rest on a level space. Small as the slip may be, it is very dangerous. The snow in motion catches the legs of a man, carries him off his feet, creeps up to his chest, and binds his arms to his side, being compressed by motion into a firm substance like hardening plaster of Paris. I once saw a coal cart with two horses and a man swept away by a very trifling slip of this sort. The man and one horse managed to keep their heads above it and were rescued. The other horse was stifled before he could be dug out.

Feb. 12.—Drove over the avalanches to Wiesen. At Glarus saw fifty-two men digging for the body of Caspar Valär. They have been digging since the 7th, but in vain. His corpse will not be found until the spring. Meanwhile his widow is lying in a house which overlooks the place where her husband was overwhelmed. Avalanches have descended on both sides of the hill on which this homestead stands. The gorge that separates Davos from Wiesen, called the "Züge," or the "Paths of Avalanches," is a mere wilderness of snow shot down from either side. Horse and sledge have enough to do to climb up one heap and descend upon the other side before another is reached. I was glad to come safely out of it.

Feb. 13.—The warm wind, or Föhn, sets in. Drive to Chur. It snows heavily on the Lenzer Heide. A furious snowstorm at Parpan, which is buried in drifts, sometimes six feet above the sledge.

Feb. 14.—Drive to Thusis, and visit the Via Mala. There is compara-tively little snow here, and the gigantic icicles which drape these precipices are magnificent.

Feb. 15.—At Thusis it has been snowing all night, and there is a foot of fresh snow on the road. Not safe to regain Davos by Wiesen and the Züge. Consequently I drive to Chur, and take the post from Landgrost to Davos—thirteen hours journey in continuous snowfall. A strange and weariful experience of wintry desolation. Pines knee-deep in snow, draped from top to bottom in winding-sheets of snow; monstrous folds, and furls, and ledges of snow, blurring all landmarks; huge lolling lips of snow upon the cliffs above our heads; vast billowy breasts of snow, swelling round smothered cottages; writhed spires and pinnacles and heav-ing waves of snow where the raw wind has worked and fretted; silent, drowned depths of snow, without a track or wrinkle for successive miles, through which we noiselessly plod onward. The jolts, lurches, and stagger-ings of the sledge are tremendous. But the horses contrive to find their path.

Feb. 16.—At Davos again. It is still snowing. The posts on all the mountain passes—Fluela, Albuela, Julier, Splügen, Bernardino—stop run-ning. Telegraph communication is interrupted.

Feb. 17, 18, 19.—Fair weather. But continual avalanches on the moun-tains. Cold nights; hot sun by day.

Feb. 20.—A strong storm-wind gets up; intense sun-heat; clouds of snow are whirled from all the mountain tops high up into the air. The woods in the valley are shaken, and explode with sudden bursts of snow. Snow is scurfed from the meadows, and whirled about around our houses. Avalanches are to be expected. One fell in the afternoon above Glarus, in the Bärenthal. It caught two men engaged in gathering wood, one of them saved himself, the other, Christian Ettinger, was swallowed up. His wife saw the snow close over him from the windows of their home. While the villagers were trying to dig him out, a second avalanche descended in the same place. At Davos Platz the average depth of snow is now at least 6 ft. On the shady side of the valley it has been measured, and reached 8 ft.

These facts will show how wild the winter may be in this mountain health resort. I have carefully eliminated rumours, hair-breadth escapes, and mere inconveniences (such as men being shut up in tunnels for twelve hours), from my narrative. I have also refrained from recording what has happened in our neighbour valleys, the Engadine, the Vorder Rheinthal, and so forth. Else the list of casualties and the havoc wrought by avalanches would have been vastly increased. The loss of life through avalanches within a radius of four miles from Davos Platz amounts as yet to only three men. Some have suffered severely from frost-bite, and have lost their toes or fingers. But accidents of this sort are not reckoned. No such snow has been known here since the winter of 1874–5. Much has still to be expected from avalanches, for very little of the snow has left the mountain heights as yet. There are parts of our village which cannot be considered safe from these fearful scourges of nature. Living here now may be compared to living on the slopes of Vesuvius in eruption.

[No signature]

1654. *To Horatio Forbes Brown*

Davos, Feb 29, 1888

[Dear Horatio]

. . . I see that you and I fully agree about Creighton.[1] The book has been one of absorbing interest to me, not only in these last two volumes, but also in the first couple. I think it a really great book, which does honour to the school of English historians. The grasp of the whole field shown in his treatment, his power of turning from a Pope in Rome to the same Pope in Europe, is very remarkable. And I think that we may in part ascribe his rehabilitation of men like Sixtus IV. and Alexander VI. to his feeling that their personal conduct ought to be reduced to scale with their cosmopolitan importance. Here, however, I should make two observations. One is, that their personal behaviour was decisive in the germination and development of Reforming Teutonic antagonism, and that therefore the main problem of his book becomes more difficult to solve in proportion as he whitewashes the protagonists, the Popes. The second is, that he has hitherto overlooked a large sphere of Pontifical activity: *e.g.* Sixtus IV.'s part in the Spanish treatment of Jews and Moors, and Alexander's part in the formation of what became the Index Expurgatorius, and with it the suppression of free thought in Catholic kingdoms. He alludes to these points, but so faintly that the anomaly of the Papacy, that anomaly which justified the insurgence of Reform and liberal science, and brought about the Catholic Reaction in its historical form, is unexplained.

I look forward with much interest to the next portion of his work, when we shall see how he solves the problem of the Reformation after having weakened the old lines of explanation. I doubt not but that he will be able to state the phenomenon by using forces extant in Germany which were independent of Papal scandals.

I am very dull, brain-tired, engaged in correspondence of all sorts. An English D.D. writes to consult me about the ways of reconciling Providence and Natural Law. Is not that odd? This is only one among many instances of correspondence which has fallen on me through my article in the July "Fortnightly."[2]

[Incomplete]

---

1. Mandell Creighton, *A History of the Papacy during the Period of the Reformation* (5 vols., 1882–94). See L 1622.
2. "Progress of Thought in our Time," XLVII (1887), 885–98. The issue was published in June, not July.

1655. *To Sir Henry Layard*

Am Hof, Davos Platz, Switzerland. March 11 1888

My dear Sir Henry

I am quite ashamed of having so long postponed writing to thank you for the copy of your "Early Adventures"[1] wh duly reached me.

I wanted to read it before I wrote, in order that I might tell you how much I enjoyed it. I was sure beforehand that I should do so, but I was not prepared for so much of vivid interest and for such a romance of real life.

It is indeed singular that you should have been able to keep a book of this kind so long in your portfolio—that Murray,[2] if he knew of it, should not long ago have forced your hand.

But it has lost nothing of its interest by keeping.

What a varied full adventurous life you have enjoyed!

Thank you very much for this gift, which I value greatly for its own sake and for yours.

I hear from Brown this morning that you have returned to Venice. But he also tells me that your niece[3] is ill of typhoid. I am very sorry to hear this. It must be a great anxiety to Lady Layard.

I hope that we may soon meet. I have taken Brown's mezzanino, and propose to come to Venice with two of my daughters in a few weeks. It has been a rather trying winter here. The amount of snow, which fell in February, made our mountains unsafe. We have been living in the midst of avalanches.

Believe me very sincerely yours
John Addington Symonds.

---

1. Sir Henry Layard, *Early Adventures in Persia, Susiana, and Babylonia* (2 vols., 1887). On Layard see L 1327.
2. John Murray (1808–92), the publisher.
3. Lady Mary Enid Layard (née Guest) had 5 brothers and 6 sisters; it is difficult to say whose daughter Symonds meant.

1656. *To Horatio Forbes Brown*

Davos, March 17 [1888]

[Dear Horatio]

You must think I have not received your letter or that I am very unmindful of your kindness. Neither is the case. Your last letter came when I was upon another "snow-tour," and I found it on my arrival here.

I had the experience of driving in an open sledge from Landquart while it was snowing incessantly—thick wet snow.[1] All my outer garments were soaking. But as soon as we reached Laret, all the wet things began to freeze, and, when I got to Dörfli, I was as it were enclosed in a panoply of ice.

I am rather sorry that you missed this winter at Davos. I wish you could be here now. I have never seen anything in the Alps which impressed me so strongly with the force—the cruel, blind force of nature. Of course the impression deepens into tragedy in the Züge. That gorge is really sublime in its ruin, its awful danger, its abandonment to the havoc of desolating accidents. Millions of tons of snow, forest, rocks, which have swept on both sides from 3000 ft. above, are lying huddled up together there. A horse can just get across the frozen deluge, climbing and descending, climbing and descending on a narrow track delved by the road makers. Here there is a tunnel 30 ft. below the upper surface of an avalanche; there the marble walls, where excavation has been made, rise fifteen feet above our heads; and always rocks rolling down with a sullen roar.

[Incomplete]

---

1. Brown (*Biography,* p. 431) notes:
The extraordinary snowfall of the winter of 1887–1888 fascinated Symonds's imagination. He refers again and again in his letters, and he eventually worked the subject out in an Essay on Avalanches . . . in "Our Life in the Swiss Highlands." . . . The spring outing to Venice led . . . over several of the passes, and allowed Symonds to see much that had taken place during this memorable winter.
See also Ls 1653 and 1662.

1657. *To T. S. Perry*

Davos March 27 1888

My dear Perry

I do not know what you will think of me for suddenly interrupting our correspondence, just at the point when you were taking so much interest for me in the essay I sent you on Greek Morals, & when you were clearly expecting further communications.

What happened was this. I have been working this winter off & on at a subject suggested to me by the publisher of my Cellini. He asked me to undertake a translation of Carlo Gozzi's *Memorie,* with a study of Venice in the decadence of Italian Comedy. At first I took to the scheme. But we found great difficulty in getting hold of a complete copy of Gozzi's

Memorie. I had 2 vols of it in December. At last, early in March, a complete copy (including vol 3) reached me. I read it through, & judged that the execution of my task would be more difficult & less worth than I had imagined. I wrote to Nimmo[1] on the subject, & at the same time promised to send him a specimen of the Memorie translated. When I sat down to this, I immersed myself in it, & finished off 100 pages of the original at a blow. This occupied some days, & put all other matters out of my head. It came just when I ought to have been writing to you.

I do not think I have any questions to ask about the subject of my Essay.[2] It is clear that I must get hold of Meyer's article on Paederastie,[3] and study it thoroughly, before I take any step of any kind.

If it is as complete as you report (and of this I can have no doubt), the necessary work has been already done. Information is accessible to scholars. And I think I shall be wise to keep my own essay in obscurity. I shall not, however, let it lie by, particularly after what you have said upon the subject. On the contrary, I will go through the whole matter again, whenever I can get at Meyer's article—at Zürich perhaps—& at some other books wh bear upon the topic of wh I have just got. I can then [form] a judgment whether my essay possesses any independent value.

I hope that the chance you hold out of coming to Venice may be realized. We expect to leave this for there next Monday; & I suppose we shall stay through June. My address will be

   Cà Torresella [Mezzanino][4]
    Zattere
     Venezia

Please tell me whether it is likely that you will come. I wish I could offer you quarters; but our apartments—the entresol in a friend's house, wh I have taken for five years—will only hold ourselves.

It seems that you are resolved to miss Switzerland out of all your plans. Surely between Greece & France & Germany, you might take a line through Davos. If we do not meet at Venice, you ought to be able to pay Davos at least a flying visit in the summer.

Write to me at Venice, & believe me always to be your most sincere & obliged

           J A Symonds

I hope that you are getting on with your magnum opus. I doubt whether it will not be novel to men of Science; & I feel pretty sure that it ought to mark an epoch in criticism. I am putting in type a short essay on evolution applied to literature, a proof of which, when I get it, I will send you. I find this method of "seeing my work" convenient though costly.—Please send me anything you have written. I shall devour it. Your Ms gives me no trouble. But register it to Venice.

1. See L 1638.

2. Eventually called *A Problem in Modern Ethics* (1891). See Babington, pp. 75–76.

3. M. H. F. Meier, "Paederastie" (Ersch und Gruber's *Allgemeine Encyclopädie der Wissenschaften und Künste*, 1837).

4. Symonds' brackets.

1658. *To Horatio Forbes Brown*

Chíavenna, April 7, 1888

[Dear Horatio]

Madge and I settled finally to leave Davos alone. We had a tremendous journey[1] over Julier and Maloja, but arrived here safely yesterday. I telegraphed to you, but was so stupid that I did not also write. I hope, however, that this will arrive before we do.

I wish I could tell you something of our journey. It was in many respects very impressive. The descent from the top of the Julier to Silva-plana in perfect darkness and a blinding snowstorm, with whirling drift and the road buried, was particularly so. The postillion at one point said: "We must now trust to the horse, and if he does not find the road, *es ist mit uns um*—it is over with us." The horse did find the way, pausing, feeling each step with his hoof, putting his nose down to smell, sometimes hardly stirring from the spot, and sometimes breaking into a trot for a few minutes. His bells were taken off for fear of avalanches. The snow is so deep up there that you can touch the telegraph wires with your fingers. They made the most hideous shrieks in the wind close to our ears, like the voices of Banshees and wailing women, with a curse in them.

We are resting here to-day. This place, which I always admire, looks very beautiful in the stormy April sunlight.

[Incomplete]

1. Because of the heavy snows. See Ls 1653 and 1656.

1659. *To Henry Graham Dakyns*

Cà Torresella Zattere Venezia April 9 1888

My dear Graham

I arrived here last night & found the enclosed,[1] sent by Henry [Sidgwick] to Davos, & forwarded to Venice.

I have signed it, being quite of Mr Pirie's opinion, & taking the same course about consols in my own trust fund.

There is no time to write you a letter because you want the assent returned as soon as possible. Madge & I are come to establish ourselves in the part of Brown's house wh I have taken on lease.

We are very busy today.

Goodbye with much love.

Everyr

J A Symonds.

I am going to send you (in print) some lucubrations & speculations upon the universe soon, in wh you will recognize a reminiscence of our 3 cornered talks[2] at Am Hof.

Love to Maggie.

---

1. Through the lawyer Mr. Pirie, Dakyns' father-in-law, Dakyns was arranging for Symonds to act as his executor.

2. Talks between Arthur Sidgwick, Dakyns, and himself during the winter of 1887. See L 1646.

1660. *To T. S. Perry*

Cà Torresella Zattere Venezia April 14 1888

Dear Perry

Your letter of the 11th with its very welcome news has just come in. I only send this to tell you that we *are* here: that is to say, my daughter & myself, in the midst of furnishing our little apartment. By the time you arrive, I hope it will be in moderate order.

Till then, I must content myself with wishing a good journey & "bien divertimento" to Mrs Perry & yourself, in wh my dr begs to join.

Ever yrs

JASymonds

1661. *To T. S. Perry*

[Venice, ca. April 28, 1888]

My dear Perry

I write to propose that you should come with me in my gondola to the Lido this afternoon and so get our talk then instead of in the evening.

The reason is this: I am working at the Italian Comedy of Masks,[1] & tonight they give a play of Goldone's Con le maschere.[2] I really cannot resist the temptation of going to it.

I am sending now to take a box. Will you & Mrs Perry help me to fill it tonight? Otherwise I shall bloom alone in it: for my dr must not go.

I will call for you soon after 2 p.m. to go to the Lido, if I hear that you will change your plans in my favour. I am afraid I can not entreat Mrs Perry to accompany us thither as I have only one oar.

Very sincerely yr

JASymonds

Yr Ms has arrived. Many thanks for it & Mrs Perry's note I read all her epigrams last night.

---

1. The essay was one of the supplementary pieces published in the 2nd volume of Symonds' translation of *The Memoirs of Count Carlo Gozzi* (2 vols., 1890).
2. Carlo Goldoni (1707–93), Italian writer of comedy. His *La Mascherata* was produced in 1751.

1662. *To Henry Sidgwick*

Venice, 560 Zattere, May 11, 1888.

[Dear Henry]

I do not want to speak about my own psychological circumstances, more than, in a parenthesis, to observe that life at Davos has become for me a permanent sort of tunnel. When friends come there, as A.[rthur Sidgwick] and G[raham Dakyns] did last Christmas, I do not think they notice this, because they polarise and externalise me by their own being. But when friends are not there, I live in the worst sort of tunnel I know, which is the burrowed gallery in the middle of a marble-hard avalanche, fifty feet beneath the frozen air of Alpine winter in a stony ravine.

Well, I return from this parenthesis to your letter of April 8. What you proceed to say there is very deeply interesting, and I have been thinking about it all along. I am sure that I can contribute nothing to the solution, feeling confident that you have exhausted every *pro* and *con* of the problem as it appears to you. But, frankly, it does not appear to my mind as a problem. The object is to arrive at truth, if that can be arrived at; at any rate to search after it. A negative result may be discouraging and disappointing, though I for one do not find it so. I am so sure that sooner or later morality must be based upon analysis of the growth to-us-ward of human opinions and institutions, must enter the sphere of evolutionary philosophy and discover principles *a posteriori,* that it seems to me a pity for a thinker of authority not to accept and proclaim this.

But here, probably, we come to a radical difference of opinion, as I think we did about a year ago, when I contended that the immortality of the soul was not a necessary postulate for moral science, even though in course of time we should obtain the certainty of this, and ethics gain the force which comes from the conception. "Magna est veritas, et prævalebit" [Great is truth, and it will prevail]. Surely the truth at present is, that while the moral law is a fact persistent under all its human variations, we cannot account for the fact any more than we can account for our existence. If we do not know why we are, how can we expect to know why we differentiate our behaviour as right and wrong? All we ought to expect is that we should learn how we exist and how we differentiate.

I have been staying during the last five weeks with Madge at Venice, in an apartment of my friend H. F. Brown's house, which I have taken for some years. It is a pleasant change from the terribly severe winter in Graubünden, when we were literally drowned in snow. I hope to be able ere long to give an extended account of this great snow,[1] and of the play of the avalanches, which exceeds anything I had imagined. I kept well through the winter, and took many driving journeys, in order to see those dreary wildernesses and ruins caused by nature in her wildest, cruellest moods. Now, though I enjoy the colour and the vault of heaven above these waters, I am not good for much in health.

[Incomplete]

---

1. "Snow, Frost, Storm, and Avalanche. Studies of Winter in the Grisons," *The Cornhill Magazine,* XII, N.S. (1889), 246–69; also in *OLSH,* 59–104.

1663. *To James Payn*[1]

Am Hof, Davos Platz, Switzerland. June 9 1888

My dear Mr Payn

Thank you for your kind letter about my article on Avalanches,[2] in consequence of wh I send it registered. I hope you will be able to print it. But if you do not, may I beg the favour of having it returned? I have no copyright here, & I should be sorry to lose this essay, which has (for me at least) some of the best writing in it I have done in the line of description.

I do not care in the least about my name being appended. When I said that I should like it, I was thinking of the personal nature of a good deal of the article. The word I is often used, because the whole matter has been collected from first hand reports made to me or from my own observations & experience. But if you think so egotistical a piece of work can go without the egotist's signature, I do not want to advertize myself.

Very sincerely yours

John Addington Symonds

---

1. James Payn (1830–98), English novelist, journalist, poet; editor of *Chambers's Journal* (1859–74) and of the *Cornhill Magazine* (1883–96); published ca. 100 novels, including *Lost Sir Massingberd* (1864) and *By Proxy* (1878).
2. See L 1662.

1664. *To Horatio Forbes Brown*

Davos, June 13, 1888

[Dear Horatio]

I have been doing the most incongruous of things since I arrived here last Friday. After settling my affairs, which you know takes some time after a nine weeks' absence, I have been writing the history of last winter's avalanches.

I can tell you that this is precious difficult to do. You have to paint with a palette on which there are no colours—pure *grisaille*—absolute monotony. And yet I think I have succeeded; and therefore I suppose I shall not get my essay printed.

It is funny, coming back from that variegated life in Venice into the fresh beauty of the Alps—and they are quite coquettishly attired this early summer; it is funny that a man should sit down and sweat his brains out over a description of the grim ascetic winter, which is past. I think this shows—and perhaps you will agree with me—that, in the long run, we really love the sternest things in life best. They seem to cling to us, and wrap us round, and haunt us. The rest we take and leave, as recreation prompts. Facile ephemeral pleasures—deep penetrating sadnesses.

I am not reconciled yet to Veltliner Wein. I fear that the various facile vintages, Verona, Valpolicella, Venosa—these many V's are good—have seduced me. Yet there is a V in the Valtellina, and a V in Venice, which is innocent of vintages. So perhaps I shall become reconciled to my Veltliner after all.

But I have played on the letter V enough, and I ask you to notice that I am now using the Fabbriano paper (Campo S. Luca) which you recommended. I like it greatly, and shall see to getting a supply here. Eighty of these pages have gone into the article upon the avalanches. Good gracious, what a subject! Yet I flatter myself that I am about the first to polish that rough diamond.

[Incomplete]

1665. *To Horatio Forbes Brown*

[Davos, June, 1888]

[Dear Horatio]

I do not know whether it can be good to be mentally and morally starved. But I do know that, if people who are worth anything have been starved so, their sudden invitation to a full, refined, passionate and sympathetic banquet of the most varied delights, exercises a very peculiar influence.

We are neither of us apt to take things elegiacally, or to ignore the substantial advantages of any situation in which we find ourselves. The extraordinary cleanliness and comfort of our little house, the splendid air and water, the resuscitated energy communicated by the climate—weigh with us, and are appreciated; but we know that we want something else, something which we had at Venice.

[Incomplete]

1666. *To Horatio Forbes Brown*

Davos, July 17 [1888]

[Dear Horatio]

I finished the translation of Gozzi[1] yesterday. I am rather surprised at the fact; for I find that the whole memoirs will be about 150 pp. less than Cellini's. That is a bulky book. And, except for the lazy time at Venice, I have only been working five weeks. I am afraid there is no chance of my coming to Schluderns[2] before you leave. Do not overwork yourself. Your hours look formidable to me. But mine might look worse to you. When I am hard at it, I do work as follows:

9 a.m.	. . . .	12.30
1.30 p.m.	. . . .	3.0
8 p.m.	. . . .	1 a.m.

I go to bed very tired. But I hope not to continue these bad habits. It is the vice of ageing people to throw their labour on the night.

When I began this I meant to write you a letter. But I have not done so. My brains have become mechanic things.

[Incomplete]

---

1. The translation of Carlo Gozzi's *Memoirs*. See Ls 1638 and 1646.
2. Near the Ortler, in eastern Switzerland.

1667. *To Horatio Forbes Brown*

Davos, Aug. 25 [1888]

[Dear Horatio]

I am looking forward greatly to your visit, and am happy to think that we shall neither of us be overburdened with our work. Gozzi is practically finished. Jowett and Prof. Sellar[1] and Miss Poynter[2] are staying with us, and we are hoping for a visit from Sir Robert Morier.[3] I don't know him, but he is a great friend of Jowett's, who always brings friends about him. Jowett is much better than he was last year, and is still grinding away at Plato. We are doing the "Symposium" together. I take the Greek and he reads out the English. I find a good many mistakes or misses of *nuance,* which is rather absurd. But the whole effect of the English is very good—peculiar to Jowett—governed by a delicate sense of the fitting, *il decoro,* in language.

All my girls have taken to riding. I rode with Madge to Klosters yesterday, and found it not as tedious as I expected, going down and up that long hill; one certainly enjoys scenery on horseback. I have a good mind to ride to Brescia in the autumn *en route* for Venice. One could do it in five days, I think, from here.

[Incomplete]

---

1. William Young Sellar (1825–90), Scotch classical scholar, from 1863 professor of Latin in the University of Edinburgh; published *Roman Poets of the Republic* (3rd ed., 1889).

2. Eleanor Frances Poynter. See L 1024.

3. Sir Robert Burnett David Morier (1826–93), educated at Balliol College. English diplomat, Minister at Lisbon (1876) and at Madrid (1881–84), and Ambassador to St. Petersburg (1884–91).

1668. *To Henry Sidgwick*

Davos, Sept. 3 [1888]

[Dear Henry]

I do not know of any treatise on the relation of Art to Morality which treats the topic lucidly and fully. There are good things in one of Ruskin's Oxford Lectures,[1] and of course all Ruskin's works are penetrated with his peculiar views about it. I should much like to see your remarks on this subject, since I have had the audacity to write an Essay on "The Relations of Art to Science and Morality"[2] for my forthcoming book. Naturally, while engaged on this, I looked about for accessible dissertations on the theme, and read a good deal "about it and about." But I found little that was helpful. I confined myself to defining the limits of the inquiry, and putting as clearly as I could what seemed to me the common-sense view of the matter.

Things have been going pretty well with me—"speaking κατ' ἄνθ."[3] I have finished my long work on Carlo Gozzi, which is ready for the press as soon as the publisher likes to send it there. And now I am going back to the Essays *de omnibus rebus,*[4] fifteen of which were written six months ago.

We are all well, and all together here, enjoying occasional visits from touring friends. Jowett stayed ten days, and I worked about three hours each evening with him at the translation of the "Symposium."

[Incomplete]

---

1. Ruskin's "The Relation of Art to Morality," delivered on February 23, 1870, the third of the first series of lectures given during his first professorship (1870–78).

2. In *E S & S* (2 vols., 1890), I.

3. According to the capacity of man: as human affairs go.

4. Concerning all things: a book which rambles.

1669. *To Horatio Forbes Brown*

Davos, Sept 25, 1888

[Dear Horatio]

I hoped to spend this morning on the Schwartzhorn. It has turned out one of the worst days of all this dismal summer. So I am here at Am Hof, and have been making acquaintance with a young Russian, instead of sweeping the horizons of the Alps.

I finished my Essay on Elizabethan and Victorian Poetry.[1] What it will be like, under the conditions of its composition, Heaven only knows.

One brain is more than one man ought to have to put up with. But a couple of brains, pulling in different directions, such as I possess at present, is distracting.

[Incomplete]

---

1. "A Comparison of Elizabethan with Victorian Poetry," *The Fortnightly Review*, LI (1889), 55–79, and in *E S & S* (2 vols., 1890), II.

1670. *To Horatio Forbes Brown*

Davos, Oct. 2, 1888

[Dear Horatio]

I am afraid I must have disgusted you with the flippancy of my last letters. The fact is, I was falling ill. The usual thing happened. 1. Too much writing for a long space of time—Cellini, the Essays, Gozzi, the Essay on Victorian Poetry. 2. Too much sitting up and talking with Jowett and you; I cannot fill my friends' Leyden jars, if I do so, as you say, without a great expenditure. 3. A superexcitability of emotions, a physical restlessness, attaching itself to this or that object, as a first result of failing energy.

I have been unfortunate this summer. The weather prevented me from getting proper air and exercise. If I could have taken those mountain walks with Guler[1] I had planned, to explore the Silvretta glacier and the valleys of the upper Vorarlberg, I should have kept my health.

The weather is terribly against me. It storms and rains perpetually, so that I cannot get out enough, and always run a risk when I do so.

I have chosen the strongest hour of my day to write this, and here is the result. Go some times on credit with me. I must emerge. But it is difficult. I cannot put myself just now into the C major key of this life, in which you are living. It is serious, this physical, mental, spiritual struggle of the nervously strong man at odds with malady. People think—I dare say you think—that I yield too easily to passing illness, and flit away hypochondriacally from Venice or from London. No, no, no.

[Incomplete]

---

1. Leonhard Guler. See L 1631.

1671. *To The Rev. Harford Battersby*

Zattere 560 Venice Oct: 22 1888

Dear Mr Battersby[1]

I am very much obliged to you for your letter & the notes of your sermon, which seems to me thoroughly appropriate, & with which (in spite of differences of view between us, more essential perhaps in your opinion than they seem to me to be) I can cordially agree.

It is a great satisfaction to hear that people on the whole are satisfied with the pulpit.[2] I am sure that it is a thorough, honest, durable piece of work; while in point of design it has the merit of great originality & appropriateness to an English Church in a Graubünden Valley.

If the position chosen for the pulpit prove to be unsatisfactory, it will of course rest with the authorities of the church to change it. So far as Mr Read[3] & I are concerned, the matter was carried out according to the decision we arrived at with you last spring. But these things must be experimental, when we have not the controlling mind of the architect who designed the church to aid us.

I am very glad that Mr Read's part in the work received the hearty acknowledgment. Nobody except his wife & myself will ever know what labour of the brain & what constant watchful care he bestowed upon this pulpit. He has spent himself freely & often to the injury of his health, in order to carry out a conception of true originality; and, as you are aware, he has generously given all this—so that his gift to the English Church is far greater than my contribituon of money.

I hope that this is fully understood by the English Colony.

It would have been very pleasant to me to have been with you last Thursday. But [Dr.] Ruedi wished me to lose no time in going away. We certainly got at once into good weather, wh we have enjoyed ever since. I am not however as yet the better for the change. Venice is always a difficult place to manage health in, & I have got too many friends of various sorts here.

Believe me with kind regards from my wife & daughters to be most truly yours

John Addington Symonds.

You do not ask me to return the notes of your sermon. I shall therefore keep them in order that you may have them again if you desire.

---

1. The Rev. Harford Battersby. See L 1621 and *H&P*, pp. 52 and 67.

2. The pulpit, dedicated on Oct. 18, was given by Symonds to commemorate his daughter Janet.

3. The designer of the pulpit: Henry Read (1862–?), English painter, with wife and son resident of Hotel Schweizerhaus, Davos; painted a well-known picture of Davos (see announcement of its completion in *The Davos Courier*, Jan. 11, 1890, p. 176); organizer of Davos and St. Moritz Photographic Society; designer of the chalet housing the Davos English Library; had a studio behind the Hotel Buol, which was occupied for a time by Samuel Richards. Eventually he moved to Denver, Colorado. In *OOP*, pp. 200–01, Margaret Symonds says:

> Some years later my Father gave the church a pulpit. He and an English artist together made the design for the pulpit, taking as their model some of the beautiful old woodwork of the country. I fancy that the pulpit was not entirely to the taste of the British community, but this we ourselves were not likely to hear of. The question arose: Where should the pulpit stand? Some cried to the right, others to the left of the chancel. I was in the church at the time, and I beheld my Father with an enthusiastic and friendly clergyman and one or two Swiss carpenters racing all

round the church to pitch the pulpit in an orthodox position, till at last, in the general flurry, it swayed to the side and almost toppled down on top of them. When this point had at length been determined another one arose—a reading-desk was required, and a pleasing idea came into my Father's head to copy, in wood, one of those entrancing bronze beasts of Donatello in the choir at Padua, and to fix this on to the wooden pulpit. As the church at Davos was dedicated to St. Luke, the ox was naturally chosen as the proper symbol, and my Father proceeded to have this copied. But news of his choice got abroad in the community; it was screamed at; it was descried as 'popish' and even 'pagan.' Fresh struggles and fresh submission; and an eagle was substituted for the ox, just as hassocks had been substituted for priedieux; though why an ox should be more popish than an eagle, and why a bench more pagan than a hassock, who shall say?

1672. *To Sarina Browning*[1]

[Venice] November 1 [1888]

Dear Miss Browning

I am delighted to accept your kind invitation to lunch tomorrow at 1.
Very truly yours
John Addington Symonds

---

1. Robert Browning's sister. The following diary account of an evening with Browning appears in *L & P*, pp. 210–12:

Venice, Oct. 30.

Dinner at the [Daniel] Curtises', Palazzo Barbaro. Robert Browning and his sister. Browning, who is a Unionist, talked about the Parnell letters. He was dining at the same table with [George] Buckle [1854–1935], editor of the *Times* [1884–1912], and Buckle was explaining his own views about them. Browning wanted to listen; but a man kept talking to him on the subject, why there is such a dearth of young poets. "You must ask God, who made them; I don't know," said Browning.

Browning told a good story about himself and a Chinese ambassador in London, who had been an Executioner (High Sheriff?) and was one of the best poets of the Empire. Speaking through an interpreter, Browning asked him what sort of poems he had chiefly written. He answered: "My poems are mostly enigmatical." "Then," said Browning, "we are brothers." By "enigmatical" the Chinaman meant allegorical or symbolical.

Browning talked about metres. He thinks there are four controlling beats in all verses; illustrated this by hexameters, Shaksperian blank-verse, Æschylæan iambics. The metrical stave, independent of its scansion and also of its rhetorical effect, is gathered up, for him, into four groups marked by four beats. I don't know whether this will really work. Monumental verse, like Milton's, he seemed to exclude. He noticed rhymes, double rhymes, as tolerably frequent in the "Iliad." Said he read the

"Iliad" once a year, and could point to more than twenty of these instances. Were they intended or signs of neglect?

Browning read "A Grammarian's Funeral," "Andrea del Sarto," and "Donald" gladly. Liked reading. Emphasized the dramatic values, but always in a low key, bringing out the prose-aspect—or rather the fact-aspect—of each piece. It was a lesson as to his intention, a rebuke to declamatory reading of his poems, an illumination of the asides and parentheses and reserved indications in his style— these to be indicated by brief, pregnant modulations of voice, with something of a rasp in it.

Said he had burned the greater part of the letters he wrote to his family, a great mass of letters covering all his past life, which had fallen into his hands. Did not know what to do with his wife's letters; could not destroy them, would not let anybody have them. Once permitted [Richard Hengist] Horne [1803–84] to publish some [2 vols. 1877 (1876)], because these were written to Horne before he (Browning) knew his wife, because Horne wanted to sell them for money, and because he (Browning) would not take a money equivalent. Mrs. Browning carried on her conversation with men of parts by correspondence mostly. Said he conceived the "Grammarian's Funeral" at Ancona. Graphically described the bells bursting out as he sat on the top of the hill there.

1673. To Mrs. Arthur Bronson[1]

Zattere 560, [Venice, Nov. 3, 1888]

Dear Mrs Bronson

I shall have great pleasure in dining with you on Saturday at 7 in "the little garden at Ognissanti,"[2] which I doubt not I shall duly find.

Yours very truly

John Addington Symonds.

---

1. Katherine de Kay (Mrs. Arthur Bronson), a leader of the Anglo-American coterie in Venice, a frequent host to Robert Browning, and author of "Browning in Venice," *Century Magazine,* LXIII (1902), 572–84. An American, she lived in Venice for more than 20 years. Her home was the Casa Alvisi on the Grand Canal opposite Santa Maria della Salute. She also kept a suite of rooms in the adjoining Giustiani Palace so that she might better dispense hospitality. Henry James wrote of her: "She sat for twenty years at the wide mouth, as it were, of the Grand Canal, holding out her hand with endless good-nature, patience, charity, to all decently accredited petitioners, the incessant troop of those either bewilderedly making or fondly renewing acquaintance with the dazzling city."—Leon Edel, *Henry James: 1870–1881. The Conquest of London* (1962), pp. 440–41.

2. A spot in or near the Church of Ognissanti, a few streets north of the Fondamenta delle Zattere where Symonds was living.

1674. *To William Barclay Squire*[1]

560 Zattere Venice Nov: 11 1888

My dear Squire

I take the liberty of dropping the Mr & beg you to do the same if you favour me with a letter.

Since you went away on that sad afternoon at Monselice, sad for you because you were leaving Italy, & sad for us because we were losing you, I have thought often & much about you.

More than once I have had it in my mind to write, & there was always enough to say.

Only all things which one wants to say are not convenient.

It is a far cry from Venice to the British Museum, & from a soul thrilling with sight & sound & sense to a soul thrilling with memories.

I am not well, & have been cooped up for two days. Brown lent me "Camping with Cannibals."[2] I have read it.

The battered personalities of modern men need to drink of impossible fountains—wells of eternal & fadeless Beauty & heroic Strength [undecipherable] Divine Health—before they can even make themselves transported into a sphere of nature wh allures their ever quick & ever impotent desires so.

Sympathy & imagination carry their curse with them, as "Lust at her girdle carries her own whip."

I am scribbling cobwebs, which spin in my brain as I cannot but hope they have spun also in yours—else you may think me an impertinent madman.

Fact is after all a good thing, even though it sometimes wears the mask of [undecipherable], and to fact I return: the fact that I hold it very good to have come to know you, & the corollary that I wish to know you better.

Do not forget me, or the days we spent together this autumn.

Believe me very truly & affectionately yours

John Addington Symonds.

---

1. William Barclay Squire (1855–1927), English musicologist, curator of printed music at the British Museum (1885–1917) and chief of the Royal Music library (1917 and after).
2. Alfred St. Johnston (ca. 1858–91), *Camping among the Cannibals* (1883).

1675. *To Alfred W. Goodman*[1]

Am Hof, Davos Platz, Switzerland. Dec: 2. 1888

Dear Mr Goodman

I ought to have acknowledged your kind letter earlier. It found me at Venice, where one is always soothed into the languor of inertia; and when I returned to this brisker air ten days ago, I was too ill to write even a letter.

I had already read and enjoyed the style and humour of your account of the Spa Tournament of Beauty in the P.M.G.[2] When you sent me the paper, it gave me pleasure to be able to connect a bit of writing I so much liked with the recollection of a man whose company I so much enjoyed that afternoon between Chur and Lenz.

Do you remember how it rained, and how I tumbled out of your carriage into the cottage of my Romansch friends? I spent a very agreeable evening there, and the tall young man who greeted me that afternoon in Lenz drove me up next day in an open carriage through the snow to Davos. I thought of you crossing the Albula[3] alone in that bad weather.

If you come back to these regions, you must not forget your promise to pay me a visit.

Living out here in the wilds, and occupying myself with literature rather remote from the things of the day and England, I do not see as many books—especially books of fiction and so forth—as I should otherwise do. This must be my excuse for not having made acquaintance with you as a writer. Will you do me the favour of telling me what you think I should like to read of yours?—and Nutt shall send it in his next parcel.

Hours like those we spent together that gloomy 1st of Sept bring people quickly acquainted in a kind of way. And I have often thought of you, and have wished to know you better.

I am flattered to hear that you liked my little Italian sketch-book.[4]

Believe me very truly yours

John Addington Symonds

---

1. Of Heath House, Belvedere, Kent.
2. "The 'Beauty' Show at Spa," *Pall Mall Gazette,* XLVIII (Sept. 24, 1888), 5; an ironic rather heavy-handed account of a "beauty" competition Goodman had seen at Spa on his return to England from Switzerland.
3. A pass and valley in the Swiss Engadine.
4. *Sketches and Studies in Italy* (1879).

1676. *To Sidney Colvin*[1]

Am Hof, Davos Platz, Switzerland. Dec: 10. 1888

Dear Colvin

It is rather difficult to answer the main question of your letter—as to whether S. Moritz is good for such nervous over-strain as you describe.

The climate of this valley & the Engadine operates very differently on different people. It makes some people sleep, & drives others mad with sleeplessness. To me it has been most beneficial in this respect. Since I lived here, I have rarely had recourse to potions.

I think it all worth trying. But you must be prepared to watch yourself, & after three weeks or so, if you find that the uneasy symptoms increase, quit the high regions.

It is impossible to know beforehand what will happen. But you have already had experience regarding the Alps in winter, wh ought to be of service.

I advise you to go to the Hotel Kulm.[2] It is a large place, with a mixed society; generally some pleasant people, & none very ill. They go in for social amusements a good deal: also skating, tobogganing, & sledging.

The Fluela[3] is at present open. I was up there today.

Suppose you were to come to us on your way. We should be delighted to see you; & you could make the journey from Davos onward according to the circumstances of the roads.

I hope to have a visit this winter from your colleague in the Museum Squire.[4]

Thank you for the news of Louis [Stevenson]. I envy him among those lovely islanders. It has always been my dream to learn to know something of them. But eccomi qua! [Here I am!] Very truly yrs

JASymonds

---

1. Sidney Colvin (1845–1927), the critic and friend of R. L. Stevenson; published *Letters of Robert Louis Stevenson* (1911) and assisted in the editing of the Edinburgh edition of Stevenson's works (27 vols., 1894–98) and of the *Vailima Letters* (1895). He was to have written the authoritative biography but relinquished the work to Graham Balfour. He was (1884–1912) keeper of prints and drawings at the British Museum.

2. In St. Moritz, the highest village in the Engadine.

3. A mountain pass near Davos-Platz.

4. See L 1674.

1677. *To William Barclay Squire*[1]

Am Hof, Davos Platz, Switzerland. Dec: 12. 1888

My dear Squire

It was a very great pleasure to all of us here to get the first letter you wrote me, & to think that we may look forward to a possible visit from you this winter. I hope you still meditate the journey.

Now I have received your second letter of the 5th which stirs me up to write again.

I have been really ill since I left Venice—that is to say for the last three weeks—so ill that I have not been able to work & have had no enjoyment of my life—Only many anxieties added to the depression of physical weakness.

I will not bore you about all this. In some respects I hope the evil time is passing.

It was very kind of you to send me the notes on Gozzi's bibliography in the Br: Mus: Very little seems as yet to have reached English ears about him.

Will you kindly tell me whether Galuppi,[2] Il Buranello, wrote an opera on La Caduta dei Giganti & when? I have a notion that he did, & that Gluck afterwards rehandled the libretto. But I find nothing in Grove's dictionary[3] on the subject of Galuppi's operas.

I have just, with pain & grief, finished a chapter, for my Gozzi book, on Longhi.[4] I wondered whether those hideous frescos we saw in the Palazzo Sagredo[5] were inspired (!) by music of Galuppi. An opera on the Titans might have suggested the theme to Longhi's patrons.

Did I tell you how much I enjoyed "Camping with Cannibals"?[6] When I am ill, I am always sighing for the South Sea Islands. They are lost to me, however, so far as this life goes—those lovely places—

> Where the sands are smooth & golden,
>   And the flowers bloom, one by one,
> Unbeloved & unbeholden
>   Save by the all-seeing sun.
>
>   =
>
> I shall ne'er with friend or lover
>   Wander on from glade to glade
> Through those forests, or discover
>   Silvery fountains in the shade.
>
>   =

319

But another's foot shall linger
  Mid the bowers whereof I dream,
And perchance a careless finger
  Strew the roses on the stream.

=

Happier men shall pluck the laurel
  For the tresses that they love,
And the passionate pale coral
  Wreathe round brows I know not of.

=

This is silly & sentimental. There is snow enough in Davos, & the cold moon shines by night.

When I am well enough to overhaul my manuscripts, I will get at the facts about those verses out of a Ch:[rist] Ch:[urch] Ms: wh I think may possibly be [John] Ford's—the question I sketched out to you at Vescovana.

How far away the Euganeans seem now—Noverolo, Agria, Monselice! Do you remember talking about Monte Amiata?[7]

Ah me! No more for us
Spreads the clear world—old Tuscan land divine;
Fold over billowy fold
Of fertile vale & tower-set mountain old,
Innumerous
As crowds of crested waves that shine
In sun & shadow on the spaceless ocean brine.

=

Soul-full we said farewell—
What time those tears from flying storms were cast
O'er Thrasymene & thee
Loveliest of hills whatever hills may be
Loved for the spell
Of names that in the memory last,
And with strange sweetness link our present to the past!

=

Mont' Amiata, thou
Shalt take the envoy of this sorrow-song!
For thou still gazest dawn
On Chiusi, & Siena's marble crown,
The bare hill-brown

Where gleams Cortona, & the strong
Light of the lands I love, the lands for which I long.
=

I am in such a mood tonight as not to be able to write sensibly or straight forward, but must needs wander off into waifs & strays of weak rhymes wh expressed my earlier & ever abiding cravings for a lovelier life.

I ought not to complain, except that I am restless ill unable to think or do at present.

You have fogs & the hard dull grind of wh you write to me.

Caraggio, amico! [Courage, my friend!]
Are the souls so too,
When they depart hence, lame & old & loveless?
Ah no! 'tis ever youth there!
So addio!

Yours

J A Symonds

---

1. See L 1674.
2. Baldassare Galuppi (1706–85), composer, born on the island of Burano near Venice, called the father of Italian comic opera. There is no record that Galuppi wrote *La Caduta dei Giganti*. Gluck did, however, in 1746, with a libretto by F. Vanneschi.
3. George Grove, *Dictionary of Music and Musicians* (4 vols., 1878–89).
4. Pietro Longhi (1702–85), Italian painter of domestic and social Venetian life. Symonds' essay appeared in *The Century Guild Hobby Horse*, IV (April, 1889), 42–55, and became a chapter in his translation of the *Memoirs of Carlo Gozzi* (2 vols., 1890), II.
5. A palace along the Grand Canal, Venice.
6. See L 1674.
7. In Umbria.

1678. *To Herbert P. Horne*

Am Hof, Davos Platz, Switzerland. Dec: 13. 1888

Dear Mr Horne

You have once or twice said that you should like some article from me, & once you suggested I might send something on an Italian Painter.

I have recently written a chapter on Pietro Longhi[1] (little known in England, but a really interesting painter of Venetian manners in the last century). This chapter will form part of my forthcoming book on Carlo Gozzi—on wh I have been at work during the last year.

Gozzi will appear in the spring. But I do not think the publisher, John C. Nimmo, would object to the chapter on Longhi appearing in yr spring number—if you liked to have it under these conditions.

My book is to be illustrated with drawings by Longhi.

I was at Venice when your letter of the 10th Oct. reached me. I was very busy there, & have been ill since I came up here again. This is why I am so late in answering. I may say that the last number of the Hobbyhorse (old style!) wh I received was April 1888. This is only because you told me you had kindly ordered it to be sent.

The change of title I approve of. I think *The Sibyl* a decided improvement on *The Hobbyhorse*.[2] And the only thing I should have demurred to, had I been assisting at the debate, is the didactic intention of the words "in attempt to rouse a finer interest in the Arts." The object you have in view is clearly defined in the quality of your performance. And it always seems to me impolitic to press such intentions on the notice of a possible unsympathetic public. It gives reason to the energy to sneer.

Excuse this freedom of remark. Believe me very sincerely yours

J. A. Symonds

What I have written here about Longhi is only to express my wish to serve you. I daresay it will not meet your views. In which case I will not forget to send anytg wh seems likely to be of more use.

---

1. See L 1677.
2. The title of the journal was not changed immediately, but in 1893 it was shortened for 3 numbers to *The Hobbyhorse*.

1679. *To* Pall Mall Gazette

[Davos, Dec. 14, 1888]

[Dear Sir]

Abler pens[1] than my own have already taken up the defense of Marlowe in your columns. I would only point out that the accusations against Marlowe of atheism and blasphemy exist only in the manuscript signed by an informer, Richard Bame, upon which no action was taken by the English government. Similar accusations were delivered to the Venetian Inquisition by an informer and traitor against Giordano Bruno at very nearly the same date. The minutes of Bruno's trail showed how he repelled and repudiated them. Marlowe was dead, and had no voice wherewith to utter his defence. It was too common in the sixteenth century to blacken the fame of a political, a literary, a religious, or a social enemy by such charges. Witness the whole invective correspondence of the Italian Humanists. This seems a feeble reason for denying a monument to one of England's noblest poets in the nineteenth century.

[Incomplete]

---

1. The letter appears among a number of selections from other letters on the topic of a monument for Christopher Marlowe in Westminster Abbey.

1680. *To Charlotte Symonds Green*

Am Hof, Davos Platz, Switzerland. Dec: 20. 1888

My dearest Charlotte

I must write to you one line tonight to send you my wishes for Christmas. Something this year makes me think of the old years in our childhood when we used to go with Sophie [Girard] into Leigh Woods[1] & bring back loads of ivy for wreaths. It is so different here. My little Katharine collects frozen moss in small quantities from the roots of trees where the snow is not too deep—to make a Church decoration.

Catharine's being at Alderley with her sister [Marianne North], & writing to me from that moist land wh sees the Bristol Channel, has perhaps put these old thoughts in my head.

At any rate, I am thinking of you now. And I want to thank you for the book of Tom's Life,[2] which found me in Venice. I read the biography with very great interest; & it left upon my mind the sense of having been extremely well done—as well as pains, & love, & sympathy with his high aims & noble character, could do it. Yet the man is not there. He cannot be there. Nothing which we can write about anybody is worth much. It is certainly worth no more than a copperplate engraving from the live man's face we knew—& that is better than a staring photograph. [That is not true. One of the things I love best here is Tom's face in the large photograph you gave us. I often go to this face in my troubles.][3] The older

I get, & the more I learn to know folk, the more I feel it is not what a man thinks about the universe & politics & art & social questions & all the rest of such matters, which signifies—but what *we are*, personally *are;* that is the great fact. And that is always incommunicable. That is how we touch the people whom we mould in life unto our likeness. And that, the real essential man, lives onward in a way which no species of photogravure or copper-plate-engraving in words will manifest.

What was Christ, as an individuality, I wonder? We know well what has been made of his reported words, & of the loving portraits drawn by his disciples.

I have been very ill since I came back from Venice at the end of November. If you had been here, I should have liked to talk to you about my state of health. It is a case of over-wrought nerves & painful disturbance of the ordinary thought functions, which makes me sometimes uneasy about my reason: I do not think it can be written about with any profit. And I do not expect much from doctoring: more from self-discipline & an attempt to curb my tyrannous volition.

Goodnight dearest sister! Ever yours

J A Symonds.

In this letter I want to add a word of Christmas greetings to my dear Auntie [Mary Ann Sykes]. I am thinking tonight of our old Clifton home. I see & feel & even smell the winter there—& am so far away from England. Give her my best love, & tell her that the thought of England & the past is always for me connected with a thousand memories of her. I hope for her many years of happy life!

---

1. A favorite spot near Clifton.
2. Thomas Hill Green's *Works,* ed. by R. L. Nettleship (3 vols., 1885; 2nd ed., 3 vols., 1889–90). Vol. III, *Miscellanies and Memoir,* is probably what Charlotte had sent to Symonds.
3. The brackets are Symonds'.

1681. *To Herbert P. Horne*

Am Hof, Davos Platz, Switzerland. Dec: 23, 1888

Herbert P. Horne Esq.
  26 Southampton Street
    Strand London W.C.
Dear Mr Horne

I am sending you my Ms on Longhi.[1] If you find it too long or do not want it, I beg you to return it kindly at once.

If you wish to use it for your April Number, please let me have *two* proofs as soon as possible. I told you already that this essay will go into a book on Carlo Gozzi wh I am preparing. It is therefore of importance for me, to have either the MS back or a proof, in case I should have to send the thing to press.—I had much trouble with our Post here last summer; & now I hope that I shall not lose any packets addressed to me. Very sincerely yrs

J A Symonds.

---

1. "A Venetian Painter of the Last Century, Pietro Longhi." See Ls 1677 and 1678.

1682. *To William Barclay Squire*

Am Hof, Davos Platz, Switzerland. Dec: 24. 1888

My dear Squire

We are delighted to hear that you still think of coming to Davos. I will tell you the best way of travelling.

Starting as you propose, you will arrive next morning early at Basle, and will find that the express reaches a station (short of Chur)[1] called *Landquart* at 12.46. The diligence leaves Landquart at 2.20 P.M. wh allows you time to get your luncheon there. Take your place and book your luggage to Davos Dörfli, wh you will reach at 9 P.M. I will send to meet you at the post at Dörfli.

It would be well, if you have time, to telegraph from Basle to the
  Lit: Post Direktion
    Landquart
for a place in the Coupé.[2]

I am sorry to say that this year we have very little snow as yet. So that our mountains do not look their best. I hope before you arrive that they may have put on some more snow.

Be sure to bring plenty of warm clothing, espy for the feet and legs. I find gaiters here quite indispensable in winter.

I am so glad you liked those verses about M. Amiata.[3] I felt them when I wrote them, which is the great thing.

My wife is in England with her only sister Miss [Marianne] North[4] who is hopelessly ill. I expect her back soon however, and it is not impossible that you might be fellow travellers.

In haste believe me affy yours

J A Symonds

What a piggish mess I have made!—I hope that your Xmas will not be very dismal. Ours cannot be very cheerful in the absence of my wife on so sad an errand.

---

1. Chur is the capital of the Canton of the Grisons. Landquart is approximately 27 miles from Davos-Dörfli.
2. The diligence ran between these points twice daily. The trip required about 7 hours and cost 12 francs or 65 cents. The *coupé* was the enclosed, more private, more expensive, portion of the vehicle.
3. See L 1677.
4. Miss North died August 30, 1890.

1683. *To* Pall Mall Gazette

[Davos, Dec. 28, 1888]

[Dear Sir]

I see in the "Art Notes" of your issue of the [Dec.] 27th [1888] that the reported robbery of Raphael's "Entombment" from S. Pietro at Perugia has turned out to be a hoax. The report ran the round of Europe. But well-informed persons like your correspondent "M.H.S." were satisfied that no such picture ever existed in the Church of S. Pietro. I believe that I can explain the origin of this report, which is not altogether a hoax, but which is the revival of something that took place under my own eyes exactly fifteen years ago. I must begin by saying that the celebrated so-called "Borghese Entombment," which Raphael painted for Atalanta Baglioni in 1507, remained at Perugia, in the Baglioni Chapel at S. Francisco, until 1787, when it was taken to Paris, and replaced by a copy executed by Arpino. (See Crowe and Cavacaselle's "Life of Raphael, Vol. I, p. 319, note.) A very careful copy of the same Entombment, made by Sassoferrato, also adorned the Church of S. Pietro at Perugia until the winter of 1873. In December, 1873, I happened to be at Perugia with a servant called Jean Tairraz, of Aosta. At that time I was writing an article on "Perugia and the Baglioni," and I wished to see the celebrated copy of the Entombment, which had been originally painted by Raphael for the mother of the murdered Grifonetto Baglioni. I went, accompanied by my servant, to the Church of S. Pietro, and walked up to the spot where I expected to find Sassoferrato's copy. The picture was covered by a thick dark curtain, which we could not draw aside. So far as I remember, the cords which control these curtains in Italian churches were either removed or tied in a knot beyond our reach. I sent my servant for the *custode,* who arrived, and showed the most positive disinclination to uncover the picture. I insisted, and said that I knew very well what the picture was, and that I had particular reasons for wanting to see it. At last he sullenly consented. But when the curtain was drawn, lo and behold! nothing but an empty frame and a rough plastered wall was to be seen behind it! The *custode* thereupon displayed all the signs of frantic grief, whirling around in his long soutane upon the pavement like a teetotum, and tearing what the tonsure had saved of his scanty hair. The picture had been stolen, and I had accidentally been the means of bringing the theft to light. In the evening I was visited by the Procuratore del Re, who took the depositions of myself and Jean Tairraz regarding what we knew about the theft. He warned us that we might be required to give evidence in court, and therefore took down our addresses; but at the same time he comforted our minds by adding significantly that the thief was pretty well known already, and that he would probably be sent to the galleys on his own confession. I was leaving Perugia the next day, and I cannot now say with confidence who the thief was, or whether Sassoferrato's copy of the "Borghese Entombment" was restored to Perugia. But when, some weeks ago, I read in the Coire [Chur] newspaper, *Der Freie Rhätier,* that an "Entombment by Raphael" had been stolen out of S. Pietro, I rubbed my eyes, and asked whether history ever repeated itself so accurately.

[Unsigned]

III

*Literary Essays and Winter
Sports at Davos*

1889–1890

1684. *To William Barclay Squire*

Davos Jany 12 1889

My dear friend

Since I rose to see you off this morning, I have been continually thinking of you—& now it is about the hour, 10.30, at which we used to be drawn into the Maelstrom of long intimate confidences. I shall not go to bed without greeting you with one written word or two, in lieu of the millions of words you would have had to suffer from me if you had been here;—kindly & patient & sympathetically humorous as you are, front to front with my incorrigible garrulousness.

It has been a long day. The dawn was such an age arriving, & I kept considering how far you were upon your way to Chur. It mortified me, after rectifying my computations, to discover that you would not have Franz[1] to drive you from Wiesen to Lenz. His comrade is an inferior person to Franz.

Then when the sun got up, I went to sit in the shed & there received deputations (who uninvited come, like the abominable Até[2]) from all sorts of people about the "Bob-Sleigh."[3] Poor dear amiable "beastly" Benn came among them & poured forth the woes & indignities he had received from gobbling Freeman & swollen Austin,[4] since yesterday's event at Klosters. (How long ago that Klosters scene appears to me, since you are so far off; & I think you will have erased it already, in its squalor, from your memory).

Truly I foresee not what the tragi-comedy of the "Bob-Sleigh" is likely to end in. The combat thickens; & I shall have to preside over a most tempestuous meeting on Monday. Sunday, the day of divine rest, is going to be spent in the brewing of venom and sharpening of tongues & careful calculation of insults on both sides.

This sort of thing was continued until late into the afternoon. Such waste of time! I wish you had stayed here to control the parties of Davos ("A plague on both your houses!") while I were cataloguing Music Hall & Salvation Army ditties in your place fog-asphyxiated at the Brit. Mus: !—[5]

I hoped for a quiet evening. But instead of talk with you about poetry & people & comradeship & the impossible, I have had too several men on visit with plans of houses they are going to build here—wanting my advice: —& latterly the eccentric Mr Gordon,[6] of whom you dimly heard, attacking me about the misunderstood ideality of Bouguereau.[7] If you do not happen to know what Bouguereau paints the point of that epigram will be lost. But the argument lasted more than an hour: & then all my womankind returned in a high state of excitement from a spectacle of Schatten-Bilder[8] at Hotel Buol[.] One remarked for champagne & I found Heidsiech[9] for them. Now they are gone to bed. As I finish these stray notes of a day wh began with you and has kept your memory all through, I forget to say that we have just drank the Heidsiech to your health at Delle,[10] or a little further on, the hour being now past eleven. Goodnight. Do not forget me. JAS. Past midnight. to bedwards. addio   a rivederci

---

1. Symonds' friend, Franz Willy (see *Biography*, p. 447).
2. In Greek mythology, the daughter of Zeus and Eris (strife).
3. A full announcement of the Davos International Toboggan Race, dated Dec. 27, 1888, appeared in the *Davos Courier* of Jan. 3 in both German and English. The English announcement follows:

Davos International Toboggan Race 1888–89.

The Committee of the Davos International Toboggan Race invites competitors of various nationalities in the sections stated below, to take part in the annual race.

Sections	Competitors
English and American Visitors to Davos	8
Visitors to St. Moritz	5
German visitors to Davos	3
Visitors to Maloja	2
Turnverein of Davos	2
Swiss from Klosters	4
" " Davos-Platz	2
" " Davos-Dörfli	2
" " Unterschnitt	2
" " Wiesen	2
" " Upper Engadine	2
Other Nationalities	5

The race will be run in one heat on the Klosters Course on Thursday, 17th January 1889. The first start will take place at 9.30 A.M. precisely.

The prizes will not, as formerly, be given in money, but in objects of value, as follows: First Prize, A Silver Cup of the value of 200 fcs.

The winner of this prize will also hold *the Symonds Cup* for one year under the conditions stated below.

The other prizes will be of the following values:

2nd Prize 70 fcs., 3rd Prize 50 fcs., 4th Prize 40 fcs., 5th Prize 30 fcs., 6th Prize 20 fcs.

The Symonds Cup, hitherto named *The Challenge Cup,* is now offered to competitors under the following altered conditions. The Cup will in future be held by the winner of the International Race for one year only, and will not under any circumstances become the private property of a winner. But the names of the winners of the International Race since the institution of the Cup in 1885 will be inscribed on a stand attached to the Cup, and presented by Mr. J. A. Symonds for this purpose. The Cup must not be removed from the Canton of Graubünden, and the holder for the time being must make such arrangements for its safe custody and return to the Committee as the President may approve.

Each of the Sections above named is invited to choose its representatives, and to intimate their names in writing to the Secretary, Major-General M. R. Haig, Hotel d'Angleterre, Davos-Platz, not later than Monday, 14th January, after which date no nominations will be accepted on any account whatever.

Committee

J. Addington Symonds, President
A. Blackwood, Vice-President
H. Freeman, Hotel Buol
Col. Munro, Hotel Belvedere
Capt. Bulpett, St. Moritz
A. Herbert, Treasurer
C. Austin, Hotel Belvedere
S. Whitney, Hotel Victoria
Major-general M. R. Haig, Hotel d'Angleterre, Secretary

The same issue of the *Courier,* printed the following rules:

Rules
for the
Davos International Toboggan Race
for the season 1889–9.

1. The Committee will decide the order of running by drawing for places.
2. Competitors shall be started at such intervals as the Committee shall appoint.
3. Competitors shall start at the time, and in the order stated in the official list.
4. Competitors must start in riding-position on their toboggans which must be kept motionless till started by order.
5. A starting-line shall be drawn across the course, which line must not be overlapped by any part of a toboggan about to be started.
6. No competitor may deviate from the prescribed course.
7. A competitor must not get off his toboggan, or carry or lift it, except for the purpose of avoiding an obstacle, or in the case of being upset; in either of which cases he must resume his position on his toboggan as soon as possible.
8. A competitor who is overtaken by another must keep well to the left to allow the overtaking competitor to pass clear on the right.
9. If any competitor start before the signal is given he shall be reported by the starter to the Committee, who are empowered either to disqualify him, or to deal with the case otherwise as they may think fit.
10. In case of a tie for the First Prize the competitors concerned shall either run it off, or shall decide the matter by declaration to the Committee of the withdrawal of a competitor, or competitors; and in the case of a tie for other prizes the Committee shall adjudge the prize by lot in the presence of the competitors.
11. In the event of ties, or heats, the competitors shall not be allowed to change their toboggans, or in any way alter the racing conditions of the same.

12. There shall be no restriction as to the pattern of toboggan or weighting of the same.
13. All disputes must be referred to the Committee immediately after the race, and their decision shall be final.
Davos, 15th December 1888.

J. Addington Symonds, President.
Davos I. T. R. Committee.

Symonds eventually resigned as President of the Davos Toboggan Club (see Ls 1687 and 1688). He had organized the first regular races anywhere in the Engadine. See Katharine Symonds' account of the growth of winter sports at Davos, *H & P*, pp. 59–67, and Margaret Symonds' *OOP*, pp. 201 ff.
4. Harold Freeman, Charles Austin, and H. Benn were bobsledders. The Freemans, a family of seven, including servants, were guests of the Hotel Buol; Austin, of Wickham Market, Suffolk, and Benn, of London, were at the Hotel Belvedere.
5. Squire was curator of printed music (1885–1927) at the British Museum. See L 1674.
6. Probably Thomas Duff Gordon-Duff. See L 1552.
7. Adolphe William Bouguereau (1825–1905), popular classicist painter, to more serious artists a symbol of insincerity and vapidity.
8. Silhouettes.
9. A favorite wine.
10. French frontier station west of Basle.

1685. *To T. S. Perry*

Davos Platz. Jan: 14. 1889

My dear Perry

For my long silence I have nothing to plead. No letter has gone wrong, like the one which has not returned from Spain; because I have written none.

I only received yours in the summer, which told me that you were going to Germany, but that you could give me no address.

The mere refrigeration [?] of not knowing where you were prevented me at first from writing.

Then the fact that I had not written, began to freeze me up; & I crystallized into a glacial state of inertia. And all this while, there has been throbbing in me, sharp within the ice which gathered round, a painful sense of having been disagreeable to you & Mrs Perry when we last met,[1] a dreadful recollection of the night we spent together at Goldoni's Comedy after I had expressed myself to a lady in words wh were only suitable for a comrade of the pen. But the words expressed the truth as I see it.

Well: here is my confession: & now you know that my silence has been for me haunted in my solitude by far more thoughts, & tender thoughts, for you, than you can possibly have had for me.

Other things during the last two months have weighed upon me. They are so personal that perhaps I ought not to speak of them. The sudden development . . .[2]

How is this to reach you? Am I to send it to you in your unknown German cave through the hands of a French Banker[3] I never heard of?

What was his name? Poirot, I think. It seems so stupid to communicate with friends in a German city or a German forest by means of Poirot or Poisson or Peyron in Paris!

This I must do; if I can find the last letter you wrote me; where the banker's name, I think, was given! I will put my pen down, & investigate the precipice of letters.

Imagine a delirious search, & a triumphant evocation of the right document! Such really took place; my heart beating with the dread that I might have destroyed the letter & lost the address.

Eureka! I have got the address. I laid my hands upon your letter swiftly, dated July 3, & telling me that, wherever you are, *Perier Frerès* will find you. So here goes for *Perier!* How stupid I am!—If I had considered a banker's name, I should by memoria technica have connected it with *Perry!*

Forgive me. I am not fooling. These things are very serious to me. I only hope that Perier will find out Perry for his friend

J. A. Symonds.

If you vouchsafe me a life, please tell me how Mrs Perry has been since you wrote. In yours of July 3 you say that she had been "enjoying" wretched health. I hope she has enjoyed something better since.

---

1. See L 1661.

2. This intermediate section of the letter has been lost.

3. Perry was apparently using the French banking firm of Périer as his continental address.

1686. *To Stephen Whitney*

Am Hof Davos-Platz January 16th 1889.
[Published *Davos Courier,* Jan. 26, 1889]

Dear Mr. Whitney,[1]

The Davos International Race Committee having been forced to decide whether Bob Sleds are admissible under the published Rule No. 12, by the receipt of three protests against that type of toboggan, came, after long and anxious deliberation, to the conclusion that they are not admissible.

The members of the Committee now wish to express to you their extreme regret that, through an insufficiently considered and informal expression of opinion at a late Committee Meeting, they led you to believe that you were authorized to run a Bob Sled.

They further desire to record their sense of your perfectly straight-forward and honourable conduct under specially trying circumstances; and this letter will, with your permission, be printed in two of the leading newspapers of the district.

Believe me to remain

Very faithfully yours

John Addington Symonds
President

for the Committee of the Davos Int. Tob. Race.

---

1. Stephen Whitney, an American (New York City) guest at the Hotel Victoria, hoped to race with a bobsled which differed from the old type popular with the Swiss at Davos. Whitney was entered in the race and placed first. He was not placated by Symonds' letter and on behalf of himself and his team-mate, Mr. H. Benn, of London (Hotel Belvedere, Davos) asked the editors F. de Beauchamp Strickland and Leonard W. Paitson to print the following letter, which they did, immediately following Symonds':

Hotel Victoria Davos Platz 21st January 1889

Dear Mr. Symonds,

In reply to your letter of 16th inst. I regret that I cannot consider the letter of the Committee satisfactory. I take exception to the use of the words "insufficiently" and "informal"; opinions may differ as to the first, but on the second I do not think there can be any doubt, I considered "the expression of opinion" as formal as anything discussed at the meeting, and I understood that the Committee as such authorized the running of bobsleds in the International Race. I am sorry that it should have been thought necessary to absolve me from blame in the matter. I had thought that an apology was due to Mr. Benn and myself from the Committee for its change of mind at the last moment, and that no further explanation was required. I am surprised that the letter of the Committee should have been sent for publication before it was submitted to me, and I can only say I very much regret that it should have appeared in print; since it has been published I will supply Mr. Strickland and Mr. Paitson with copies of this letter, and request them to insert the correspondence in full this week,

Yours sincerely
Stephen Whitney

Katharine Symonds Furse (*H & P*, pp. 62–63) describes the difficulties her father and his committee met in trying to keep the Symonds Cup Competition fair:

In 1887 an upheaval took place, and it was as though a dog-fight had been let loose in the tobogganing world. . . . An American, Mr. Child, came to Davos and had built for himself, by a local carpenter, a new-shaped toboggan which he called "America"; she was long and low, built of solid wood with spring steel runners attached fore and aft. Mr. Child, who rode head first, entered "America" for the International race which led to the upheaval, because no other toboggan had a chance against her. It was finally decided that the Symonds Cup should be kept for the old type of toboggan and the Symonds Shield was instituted to cover all sorts. . . . From 1888 onwards the sport developed fast and furiously, each new invention from "America" to bob sleigh and skeleton producing the usual outcry from the more conservative people. Quarrels grew hot in places like Davos and St. Moritz.

See also Margaret Symonds, *OOP*, pp. 201–02:

The tobogganing element was perhaps even more tempestuous, though certainly more exhilarating, than that of the English church in the life of Davos, and my Father threw himself into it heart and soul. . . . First as the promoter of this race [the international toboggan race], and then as its President, it may well be imagined that a very heavy part of the business connected with it fell on my Father, and a considerable amount of exercise in the old capacity of judge and mediator. To live 5,000 feet above the level of the sea may be very good for the health, but it excites the nerves of anyone accustomed to the lowlands; the gentlest spirits take sudden fire into themselves, and the more naturally irritable develop quite turbulent tempers in such a setting. Hot and fierce, therefore, were the battles which sometimes occurred between members of the tobogganing committee who, as a rule, happened themselves to be competitors, and on the night before the . . . race, the bookshelves in my Father's wooden study . . . sometimes seemed to rock; and the old Italian chronicles . . . must have felt fresh blood come back to them during these tempestuous saturnalia.

1687. *To Alexander Blackwood*[1]

[Davos] Jany 20. 1889

Dear Mr Blackwood

I shall be obliged to you if you will kindly communicate this letter to the Committee of the Davos Int: Tob: Race.

Last winter, as you will remember, I wished to retire from the post of President; & you also know that I accepted my reelection with some reluctance.

I now resign definitely; & at the same time I sever myself altogether from the Association I helped to form in 1882–83.

Society in Davos Platz has greatly changed since I first attempted, with other gentlemen, to promote the sport of tobogganning here.

I can no longer devote the time & energy & trouble which under these altered conditions are required from an active Member of the Committee.

While taking leave of my colleagues, I thank them cordially for the support they have always given me, & for the forbearance they have shown me.

I am sorry that I shall not officially cooperate in future with gentlemen & friends whose company has given me much pleasure in the past.

It is neither their fault nor my own that I feel compelled to leave them.

I will settle with the Treasurer about the money remaining in my hands for the association, & will send the minute book to you.

Believe me very sincerely yours

John Addington Symonds.

P.S. Enclosed is a copy of a letter[2] which I am sending for publication to the Davoser Blätter, Davos Courier, & St. Moritz Post.

I wish to make it known through your columns that I have retired from the Davos International Race Committee.

While taking this step, I thank the members of the Committee for their invariable courtesy & kindness toward myself, & express my sense that they have served the public faithfully.

Your obt servant

John Addington Symonds.

---

1. Alexander Blackwood, of Scotland, a guest of the Hotel Belvedere, Davos; during Symonds' presidency of the Davos International Toboggan Race served as vice-president; president of the Committee for the Davos English Library during its first two years (1886–1888); was succeeded in Nov. 1888 by Major General M. R. Haig (see L 1753); apparently left Davos after the winter of 1889—he is not on the hotel lists after this time.
   2. See L 1688.

1688. *Leonard W. Paitson*[1]

[Davos] January 20th 1889.

Sir,

I wish to make it know [sic] through your columns that I have retired from the Davos International Race Committee. While taking this step, I thank the members of the committee for their invariable courtesy and kindness toward myself, and express my sense that they have served the public faithfully.

Your obedient servant

John Addington Symonds

---

1. The Paitsons, from Cumberland, were guests of the Villa Collina. He was an editor of the *Davos Courier*. The issue of the paper (Jan. 26, 1889, p. 141) that printed the resignation also carried the following item:

The Committee of the Davos International Toboggan Race, in accepting Mr. Symonds' resignation of the office of President and of his seat on the Committee, desires to place on record some expression of the extreme regret which they feel that for reasons, the force of which they fully appreciate, he finds himself under the necessity of severing his connection with a body over which he has so ably presided since its formation six years ago.

As one of the originators and a liberal supporter of the International Race and the donor of the Cup, which is its chief prize, Mr. Symonds has laid under obligation to him the large section of the Davos Community which takes an interest in the sport of tobogganing. To him is largely due the idea of bringing together the members of different nationalities in friendly rivalry for supremacy in this popular sport and to his knowledge of the native population, as well as to his tact and judgment, it is owing that the annual contest has now happily become a recognized bond of intercourse. For his services in Committee throughout the long period of his Presidentship the members—more especially the old members—of this body feel that their warmest thanks are due to Mr. Symonds. They gladly bear witness to his constant aim to settle differences, to reconcile conflicting opinions and to make their meetings not less agreeable as social gatherings, than useful in promoting the interests of the International Race.

In parting with him the Committee indulges the hope that Mr. Symonds may long continue to take an interest in the race, which he has been the chief agent in raising, to its present pitch of popularity; and they trust that, though his official connection with them now ceases, they will still, should occasion arise, be able to count on his friendly and valuable counsel.

1689. *To Alexander Blackwood*

Am Hof, Davos Platz, Switzerland, Jany 24 1889

Dear Mr Blackwood

I am very grateful to you for the kind of letter wh you wrote me regarding my retirement from the Committee & wh duly reached me at Wiesen.

The official letter signed by you. wh Mr Herbert[1] brought me this morning, is highly gratifying to me; & I beg through you to thank the Committee heartily for the cordial & handsome words in which they speak of me.

I am sorry that the note I sent to the newspapers seems to you liable to misconstruction. I wished it to be short. But it is difficult to attain brevity without curtness.

The publication of the official letter would, as I told Mr Herbert, be only regarded by me as an honour; & I hope that you will carry out your idea of printing it or the substance of it.[2]

You know already that I retired almost solely because I cannot afford so much time & worry as the affairs of the Int: Race now involve, & because my health has lately caused my family & myself considerable anxiety. I am particularly unfit for work involving such friction as we have unfortunately had during this & the last winter.

It is very unwillingly that I break such an old tie: and my interest in the Race will be undiminished, as also my encouragement of my Swiss friends to take their part in it. Believe me very sincerely yours

J A Symonds

---

1. Arthur Herbert, English resident of the Hotel Belvedere, secretary of the Davos International Toboggan Race Committee, secretary of the Davos and St. Moritz Photographic Society; auditor of the accounts of various Davos societies (library, literary, etc.).

2. See L 1688. In the *Courier* on January 17 appeared a letter by Norwood Young, a guest at the Hotel Victoria, protesting Harold Freeman's part in the toboggan trials. Hector Munro replied to this letter in the January 26 *Courier* and Young asked for a correction. In the February 2 issue, another letter from Young was printed, followed by a note from Leonard W. Paitson, the editor, hoping that the discussion was now dead. But in the February 9 issue, Munro had the last vexatious word.

1690. *To Horatio Forbes Brown*

Davos, Jan. 26. [1889]

[Dear Horatio]

Another long fit of silence. I have ever since the beginning of the month been taken up with bothers and rows about the International Toboggan race.[1] It has been really dreadful this year, the state of trivial squabbles our mixed society has got into. At last I retired from the Committee of Management of which I was President, having, however, got the race itself run successfully. The first prize was won by a young American, on a peculiar sledge which rendered competition impossible. Minsch[2] and an Englishman tied for the second prize, and Freeman came fourth. If I were not too sick of the whole thing to write you the details of our quarrels I think they would amuse you.

I don't know whether you will have seen my review of Roden's poem in the *Academy*.[3] He seems wild with delight about it. I was quite sincere when I wrote it, and yet I feel a great bewilderment as to his actual merits. This poem of his exactly hit the mood I was in and echoed my own despondency.

A book by Richard Garnett, "The Twilight of the Gods,"[4] would interest you. Stephen[5] brought it me. I also think you might find Whitman's "November Days"[6] worth reading. I cannot work much at my Essays. But I have recently rewritten one on "Democratic Art,"[7] which is about Whitman to a large extent.

Visitors and local quarrels and the pleasant society of many Swiss comrades distract me from literature. However, they also distract me from my own attendant ever-watchful spectres of the mind.

We have one pageant of splendid skies by day and night. Since October 11 there have been only four or five clouded days. My tenant, old Hans Ammann, tells me he cannot remember a winter with so little snow.

Jowett wrote me a most interesting letter from Faringford, where he was staying with the dying Tennyson.[8]

[Incomplete]

---

1. See Ls 1684 and 1686–89.

2. See L 1452.

3. "A Modern Faust, and Other Poems. By the Hon. Roden Noel," *The Academy*, XXXV (January 19, 1889), 33–34. The review was reprinted in *Collected Poems of Roden Noel* (1902).

4. 1888.

5. Leslie Stephen (1832–1904), editor of the *Cornhill* and the *Dictionary of National Biography;* was an inveterate traveller to the Alps; between 1855 and 1894 he made some 25 excursions there. The Stephen's children, Thoby, Vanessa (Bell), Virginia (Woolf), and Adrian were of the generation of Symonds' daughters. On several occasions Symonds' daughters stayed with the Stephens in London and in St. Ives. See L 1911.

6. Whitman's *November Boughs* (1888); see L 1692.

7. Printed in *E S & S* (2 vols., 1890), 11.

8. Tennyson died October 6, 1892. Farringford is near Freshwater, Isle of Wight.

1691. *To William Barclay Squire*

Am Hof, Davos Platz, Switzerland. Jany 27 1889

My dear Squire

Thank you very much for your letter, & for having so faithfully & kindly remembered the [mutilated] I troubled you about.

With regard to Longhi,[1] I do not yet know what Nimmo wants to do. It is possible, when he has considered the sketches as revealed in those dim blurred photographs, that he will decide to abandon them altogether. But if they are still to form the basis of the illustrations to Gozzi, I will certainly propose to him the course you suggested.

I wonder what had [mutilated].

If I were to tell you all that followed from the intrusion of the Bob Sled into our peaceful valley, the Iliad of woes would perhaps amuse you.[2] But I am so sick of the whole thing that I cannot do this. I want Madge to write you a mock-heroic account. The upshot of the matter, so far as I am concerned, is that I had retired from my post of President—not in wrath, but in good humour, & I believe regretted by all. I could not allow my time to be wasted & my nerves worried another year by the internecine quarrels of contending champions, printed calumnies, formal apologies, threatened actions against newspapers for libels, long wrangling debates in delirious Committees, & so forth ad infinitum—& all about a child's toy.

We have the Leslie Stephens[3] staying here now. Their society is a pleasant relief after the fuss & mess of the last fortnight. What you saw beginning at Klosters on the 11th came to a final explosion of poisoned fireworks in the "Davos Courier" yesterday. I don't know to what extent the mischief will spread. But I hope that I may now be a spectator only.

I am going to ask you to do another little commission for me. It is to see whether you can find a little silver owl to hang on a watch chain. It is for Madge. She has a menagerie of bears, dogs, cats, monkeys, trolls, etc already; & yearns for an owl—with yellow eyes, if possible. It ought to be

about this size or *a little larger*. I cannot find one here, or I
would not   trouble you.

Just now, the Schlitten Fahrt [sleighride] of young men & maidens, lovers, from Klosters is parading before the windows. There are about forty sledges, each holding its happy couple. Every colour in the paint-box has been used to make the procession gay; & queer it looks under a softly falling snow.

How long ago it seems since you were here! I have so much to say to you, wh I cannot write. I like, however, to think that you know how I live here, & that you remember some of my peasant friends.

Keep out of mischief, & do not get quite stifled by the dust of the Br Mus. I am longing to come to London & to stay with you.

Don Antonio[4] sent me a book the other day, & an odd letter in which he says that he feels for me "stima e se non le spiace amicizia" [esteem and friendship, if you like]. I am proud.

Addio caro! Stia bene.

JAS

---

1. Symonds' essay on Pietro Longhi, the painter of Venetian society during the period of Gozzi and Goldoni, in his translation of Carlo Gozzi's *Memoirs* (2 vols., 1890), II. See L 1677. The book did not include illustrations of Longhi's work. There were, however, a portrait and 6 original etchings by Adolphe Lalauze and 11 illustrations of Italian comedy by Maurice Sand, engraved on copper by A. Manceau.

2. See Ls 1684 and 1686–1689.

3. See L 1690. Stephen's second wife was Julia Prinsep Duckworth, a widow, whom he married in 1878.

4. Probably the colorful priest who served the estate of the Countess Pisani (see L 1717): "a tall, fat form, cased in a marvellously cut priest's garb of the wearer's own design, a pair of immense flat feet with gaiters, and a small head with the most inscrutable expression."—Margaret Symonds, *Days Spent on a Doge's Farm* (1893), p. 49. Symonds had met the Countess in 1888.

1692. *To Walt Whitman*

Am Hof, Davos Platz, Switzerland. January 29 1889

Dear Mr Whitman

I have to thank you for many mementoes in the shape of newspapers. One which lately reached me, of Dec 27 1888, contains the welcome news that you are recovering from your last severe and tedious attack of illness.

Your "November Boughs" has been my companion during the last week. I have read it with the deepest interest, finding the autobiographical passages regarding your early life and the development of your great scheme particularly valuable. Rejoicing also in the delightful vigour of your critical notes.

Now I am eager to get the 900 page volume of your complete works, and do not know where it is published. I shall try to obtain it through my London bookseller.

I have long wished to write about your views regarding the literature of the future. Each time I have attempted to do so, I have quailed before my own inadequacy to grapple with the theme. But I have in preparation a collection of essays on speculative and critical problems, one of which will be called "Democratic Art"[1] and will be based upon your "Democratic Vistas" and "Leaves of Grass." This I have been working at during the last month; and however imperfect it may be, I have contrived to state in it a portion of what I think the world owes to you both for your suggestions and for the illustrations you have given in your poems—not only by asserting the necessity of a new literature adequate to the people and pregnant with the modern scientific spirit, but also by projecting and to a large extent realizing that literature in your own work.

Meanwhile I am able to echo the words of your friend Dr Bucke[2] in his "impromptu criticism," and to congratulate you now in the autumn of your life upon the achievement of a monument "more enduring than brass or marble."

Believe me, dear Master, to be, though a silent and uncommunicative friend, your true respectful and loving disciple

John Addington Symonds.

---

1. Published in *E S & S* (2 vols., 1890), II.
2. See L 1626.

1693. *To James Sutherland Cotton*[1]

Am Hof, Davos Platz: Jan. 30, 1889

Sir:

Dr Moore,[2] in his letter about Dante's references to Alexander the Great, mentions a story which Boccaccio could not find in "William of England," nor Benvenuto da Imola in *"Gallicus ille qui describit Alexandreidem Metrice"*. Dr Moore asks also who these two authors, William of England & the French poet of the Alexandreis, are. The latter is certainly Walter of Lille or Gualtherus de Insula,[3] famous for his Latin epic on

Alexander & also for his Goliardic poems. He has frequently been confounded with our English Walter Map,[4] whose contemporary he was, since he visited England in 1166, & held a diplomatic post at the Court of Henry ii. I venture to suggest that Boccaccio, when alluding to William of England—if indeed he did not write Walther instead of William, the constructions of Gualtherus & Guglideus being similar—was pointing to the same authority, Walther of the Island. Notices of Walter of Lille will be found in Giesebrecht's *"Vaganten (Allg: Monatscrift für W. und K. 1853)*, & Hubatsch's *"Lateinischen Vagantenlieder."* (Görlitz 1870.)

Yours faithfully

John Addington Symonds.

---

1. James Sutherland Cotton, editor of *The Academy*. See L 1448. Symonds' letter appeared in *The Academy*, XXXV (February 9, 1889), 96. Babington does not mention it. Symonds had published a discussion of some of these matters in *Wine, Women, and Song* (1884), pp. 21–22.

2. Edward Moore (1835–1916), principal of St. Edmund Hall, Oxford, wrote 4 series of *Studies in Dante* (1896, 1899, 1903, 1917) and in 1890 published *Dante and His Early Biographers*. He also edited Dante's works. His letter appeared in *The Academy*, XXXV (January 26, 1889), 58–59.

3. Also called Walter of Chatillon, or Walter of the Island, or Gualterus (Philippus) de Castellione (fl. 1170–80), French poet: *Gesta alexandri magni* (a poem in 10 books) [Rouen, 1487?].

4. Or Mapes (ca. 1140–1209), medieval Welsh ecclesiastic; canon of St. Paul's Cathedral, Lincoln; archdeacon of Oxford (from 1197); author of *De Nugis Curialium* ("Courtiers' Triflings"), reputed author of goliardic verses, and supposed author of lost prose romances linking the Arthur legend to the cycle of the Holy Grail.

1694. *To Benjamin Jowett*

Am Hof, Davos Platz, Switzerland. Feb: 1, 1889[1]

My dear Master,—I am glad to hear from the last letter you wrote me that you have abandoned the idea of an essay on Greek love. Little good could come of such a treatise in your book.

It surprises me to find you, with your knowledge of Greek history, speaking of this in Plato as "mainly a figure of speech."—It surprises me as much as I seem to surprise you when I repeat that the study of Plato is injurious to a certain number of predisposed young men.—

Many forms of passion between males are matters of fact in English schools, colleges, cities, rural districts. Such passion is innate in some persons no less than the ordinary sexual appetite is innate in the majority. With the nobler of such predetermined temperaments the passion seeks a spiritual or ideal transfiguration. When, therefore, individuals of the indicated species come into contact with the reveries of Plato, (clothed in graceful diction, immersed in the peculiar emotion, presented with considerable dramatic force, gilt with a mystical philosophy, throbbing with the realism of actual Greek life), the effect upon them has the force of a revelation. They discover that what they had been blindly groping after was once an admitted possibility—not in a mean hole or corner—but that the race whose literature forms the basis of their higher culture, lived in that way, aspired in that way. For such students of Plato there is no question of "figures of speech," but of concrete facts, facts in the social experience of Athens, from which men derived courage, drew intellectual illumination, took their first step in the path which led to great achievements and the arduous pursuit of truth.

Greek history confirms, by a multitude of legends and of actual episodes, what Plato puts forth as a splendid vision, and subordinates to the higher philosophic life.

It is futile by any evasion of the central difficulty, by any dexterity in the use of words, to escape from the stubborn fact that natures so exceptionally predisposed find in Plato the encouragement of their furtively cherished dreams. The Lysis, the Charmides, the Phaedrus, the Symposium—how many varied and unimaginative pictures these dialogues contain of what is only a sweet poison to such minds!

Meanwhile the temptations of the actual world surround them: friends of like temper, boys who respond to kindness, reckless creatures abroad upon the common ways of life. Eros Pandemos [carnal, or earthly love] is everywhere. Plato lends the light, the gleam, that never was on sea or shore.

Thus Plato delays the damnation of these souls by ensnaring the noblest part of them—their intellectual imagination. And strong as custom may be, strong as piety, strong as the sense of duty, these restraints have always been found frail against the impulse of powerful inborn natural passion and the allurements of inspired art.

The contest in the Soul is terrible, and victory, if gained, is only won at the cost of a struggle which thwarts and embitters.

We do not know how many English youths have been injured in this way. More, I firmly believe, than is suspected. Educators, when they diagnose the disease, denounce it. That is easy enough, because low and social taste are with them, and because the person incriminated feels too terribly the weight of law and custom. He has nothing to urge in self-defence—except his inborn instinct, and the fact that those very men who condemn him, have placed the most electrical literature of the world in his hands, pregnant with the stuff that damns him. Convention rules us so strangely that the educators do all this only because it always has been done —in a blind dull confidence—fancying that the lads in question are as impervious as they themselves are to the magnetism of the books they bid them study and digest.

Put yourself in the place of someone to whom the aspect of Greek life which you ignore is personally and intensely interesting, who reads his Plato as you would wish him to read his Bible—i.e. with a vivid conviction that what he reads is the life-record of a masterful creative man—determining race, and the monument of a world-important epoch.

Can you pretend that a sympathetically constituted nature of the sort in question will desire nothing from the panegyric of paederastic love in the Phaedrus, from the personal grace of Charmides, from the mingled realism and rapture of the Symposium? What you call a figure of speech, is heaven in hell to him—maddening, because it is stimulating to the imagination; wholly out of accord with the world he has to live in; too deeply in accord with his own impossible desires.

Greek love was for Plato no "figure of speech," but a present poignant reality. Greek love is for modern students of Plato no "figure of speech" and no anachronism, but a present poignant reality. The facts of Greek history and the facts of contemporary life demonstrate these propositions only too conclusively.

I will not trouble you again upon this topic. I could not, however, allow the following passage in your letter—"I do not understand how, what is in the main a figure of speech should have so great power over them"—to go unnoticed without throwing what light I can upon what you do not understand.

I feel strongly on the subject, and where there is strong feeling, there is usually the risk of over-statement. But I hope I have not spoken rudely. It is indeed impossible to exaggerate the anomaly of making Plato a text-book for students, and a household-book for readers, in a nation which repudiates Greek love, while the baser forms of Greek love have grown to serious proportions in the seminaries of youth and in great centres of social life belonging to that nation.

Ever most sincerely yours

J. A. Symonds

1. This letter, from the unpublished autobiography, appears through the kindness of
Mr. Stanley Gilliam, the librarian, London Library. According to Symonds in L 1709
Jowett intended to publish an essay on Greek male love as part of his edition of Plato's
dialogues.

1695. *To Henry Graham Dakyns*

Am Hof, Davos Platz, Switzerland. Feb: 1. 1889

Dearest Graham

More than a year, and not a word exchanged between us. I take the blame, because I know that I deserve to bear it. We keep some people in our hearts so that their deaths even would not seem to be matters of any great consequence. I don't know whether this is a compliment to them or a condemnation of us—an index to our confidence in the eternities or a confession of our preoccupations with the passing moment.

Henry [Sidgwick] sent me a letter upon your trust, wh I return formally answered upon my part. I suppose he has done the like, through you, by Mr Pirie[1] for I cannot forward his form of acceptance, it would look so unbusinesslike and contains some personal matter.

Among other things Henry told me that you had lost Mss in a portmanteau,[2] the labour of many years. If I had heard that you had lost a leg, I should have been sorry, but not *so* sorry. Without jesting, I am alarmed, and stirred with keen sympathy, and want excessively to know that the lost sheep have returned. Write & ease my mind. My prophetic soul warns me that Xenophon is involved.

It is more than a year since you were in this room with Arthur [Sidgwick]. What a year for me! If you were here again, I would talk about it. I cannot do that. And writing is just an impossibility—the stupidest method of communication: made for comfortable people.

I am not comfortable. Ergo, I cannot write. I can write nothing now, nothing any more, though I can make a ghastly book—wh I am doing to my utter humiliation—a book of Essays.

Life is such an acute thing. As we grow older, its gets shriller—at least I find it so. And as it deepens in its madness, & its sin, its degeneracy, & its gasping escapements into empyreans where the facts of experience are shrivelled into nothingness, the old ambitions dwindle, the old occupations lose their hold upon one, the old diurnal ways of working disappear & mingle with the mountain mist.

What is there, after all is done, & more than all is said, but the soul face to face with its greater self, God, the eternal mirror?

How ugly the soul looks in that looking-glass! And yet how beautiful!

I am Narcissus-like enamoured of my own shadow, scathed by the vision of my own deformity, haunted with the aching sense that my own portraiture is part of the inevitable.

What am I saying to you? Pouring out the distilled quintessence of the past twelve months. Since we cannot speak, & write once in the 70th part of a human life, we must needs communicate by the intensest quivers of exasperated finger-tips.

If anybody can understand this, you will; & you perhaps above of all human beings, will perceive that there is a deep truth hidden in my rhetoric.

Goodnight!

JAS

Feby 12. Dear Graham, I am very sorry to find this on my desk tonight unsent—& the business letter together with it. A young diplomatist from Munich came to stay with me—a Henry Cadogan[3] by name—& he absorbed my energies so completely for ten days that I forgot my correspondence. Now that he is gone I return to it.

In this interval I have received a letter from you, which explains the loss of the Mss, but adds the information that you have lost £1100. I hope that the former loss may still be made good by the capture of the errant portmanteau. But I have heard *nothing* hitherto about the loss of money, which seems to be irreparable. Will you tell me about both losses now?

My dear Graham, I am sore at heart for you about both losses. In my present mood I reckon it better to lose Mss than £S.D. But the choice between the two kinds would still be agonizing, & if I lost my Mss I almost think I should be cross with Providence for not having made my loss my gold.

I wonder what [T. H.] Warren with his "adipose wit" has been doing to you. You say that you will have to castigate him.

You did not mention Henry—your own Henry.[4] How is he going on? His physical health? O my beloved Graham, I cannot write one little word! I will send you the proofs of my lucubrations—? triple talk.

JAS

1. See L 1659 for the first reference to Dakyns' trust fund. Pirie, Dakyns' father-in-law, and Symonds were co-trustees (see L 1733).

2. Possibly a section of his prolonged edition of Xenophon.

3. Henry George Gerald Cadogan (1859–93), secretary at the British legation, Teheran.

4. Dakyns' son Henry entered Clifton College in Sept., 1888.

1696. *To Henry Graham Dakyns*

Davos Feb: 14, 1889

My dear Graham

I am sending you the proofs of my essays[1] etc, the first of wh contains a good deal of the matter we discussed with Arthur [Sidgwick] here last winter.

While doing so, I should like to tell you a little about a book which I am gradually forming. It will be a collection of Essays on all sorts of things. I send you a list of the articles, so far as I have as yet made them out. All are written except that on the "Art of Style."

Do you think that "Suggestive Essays" would be a good title, & not too ambitious, for such a publication? This expresses my intention, which is to stimulate thought & to arouse speculation rather than to treat the subjects I handle *excathedra* or in an exhaustive way.

My chief difficulty about the book is that the essays have been written at different times & in very different moods. Myself has changed rapidly, &, of late, immensely, since I began to think of this collection.

Many of the essays have already appeared in the "Fortnightly", "Time", "Century Guild Hobbyhorse", & elsewhere.

I may add that the Appendices I mention as *Group vi* on the list I enclose, would contain some of the short pieces in the proofs I send you—as "Darwin's Thoughts about God," "The Limits of Knowledge," "The Criterion of Art," "Note on Realism & Idealism," "Note on the Model," "Colour-Sense & Language," "Priority of Thought to Language," "Notes on Theism."[2]

I don't know why I should bore you with all this. I wish I could talk with some competent friend. At times I feel inclined to chuck the whole scheme up, & to keep silence from these words for ever.

It would not serve any useful purpose if I were to go into things about myself. But I have been living through very trying times this autumn &

winter; & while I cannot say that I have come out in any sense of the term, I shall never be the same man I was before. I am more & more doubtful about my own capacity to say anything which could be of the least use to any body. I think I have been nearly mad, & am not sane now.

I hope to come to England next spring. Paget[3] went from London to see Miss [Marianne] North a few days since. He pronounced her disease (in the liver) incurable; but gives hope of her life being prolonged.

Everyr aff

J A Symonds

If you care to note anything on the margin of the proofs, you will do me a service. And if you care to have a clean copy to keep, I will send one.

---

1. *E S & S* (2 vols., 1890).

2. All of these pieces appeared in the appendix to the second volume.

3. Sir James Paget (1814–99), surgeon to Queen Victoria and the Prince of Wales, president of the Royal College of Surgeons.

1697. *To Horatio Forbes Brown*

Davos, Feb. 16, 1889

[Dear Horatio]

I must write, lest you should think I am more actually dead than I really am. Time has become for me a category of no value whatsoever. I gain in this life a relative conception of life in the eternities. I don't want to discourse. So I will bind myself down to facts.

We had a long visit from Cadogan,[1] which was in all ways pleasant. He is a good fellow, enjoyed every minute of his time here, made us feel that he did so, which is a great thing in guests, and let me learn him very intimately.

I have been writing, with immense toil and grief, four essays upon Style.[2] I don't know what devil has got possession of my own style and dried its wells up.

Just now I am negotiating the transfer of a gymnasium,[3] which I have helped to build here, into the hands of the Commune. I have offered the sum of 10,000 francs, as a free gift, in order to effect the consolidation of the debts and other financial interests involved. This keeps me up to the chin in small transactions, and I discover how difficult it is to spend money generously and yet effectively. That I knew before. But I did not anticipate quite the same rebuffs as I am experiencing now. Yet I hope to bring affairs to a right conclusion. Only I never got rid of 400*l.* with more diplomacy and more management than I am doing now. I doubt whether anybody ever flung so much money away, so virtuously, and so irksomely. All this makes me appreciate the grit and pride of my beloved Graubündeners. I love this people for the obstacles they put before me; and I hope they will appreciate what I am doing, when they fully comprehend my scope. These are the main facts of the moment.

There are other things beside what I have written of—longings, experiences, sympathies with my growing children, anxieties about Miss North,[4] readings in books, correspondences with the four quarters of the globe. But the whole is got mixed up for me and blurred with Maya.[5] I have not recovered, and perhaps shall never recover, from four months ago. —Yours ever, *so wie so.*

[Incomplete]

---

1. See L 1695.
2. "Notes on Style: Part I.—History and Usage of the Word. Part II.—National Style. Part III.—Personal Style. Part IV.—The Art of Style," *E S & S* (2 vols., 1890). II.
3. See also Ls 1702, 1707, and 1712.
4. See L 1696. Marianne North died the following year, after a long illness.
5. To Symonds, Destiny or Fate.

1698. *To Alexander Blackwood*[1]

Am Hof, Davos Platz, Switzerland. Feb: 23. 1889

Dear Mr Blackwood

Before the tobogganning season comes to an end, I wish to record the fact that my Cup for the International Race will in future be run for by toboggans of the old Swiss type only.

This is consistent with one of the resolutions passed at the last Meeting of the Committee over wh I presided as Chairman, pursuant to wh the Int: Tob: Race was fixed in future for Swiss toboggans.

It is also according to my original intention when I gave the Cup, & to my present wishes with regard to it.

I think it best to place this statement in your hands, in order that no further difficulties may arise next year. Should the Committee wish me to meet them at any time about the Cup, after this announcement, I shall be happy to do so.

Believe me very sincerely yours

John Addington Symonds

Alexander Blackwood Esq
Chairman of the Davos
   Int: Tob: Race Committee

---

1. See L 1687.

1699. *To Charles Edward Sayle*[1]

Am Hof, Davos Platz, Switzerland. Feb: 24. 1889

My dear Sayle

I have behaved very badly to you, but not worse than I have been doing for a long time to all my friends. Writing letters has become almost impossible for me.

Several people have told me about Berenson.[2] [T. S.] Perry wrote & talked quite enthusiastically. I wish I could make his acquaintance. The only people at Florence I think he would care to know, whom I know, are Miss Paget (Vernon Lee) & the Villaris.[3] Please tell me if it is worth while sending him introductions to them—& where his address is.

I look forward to *Erotidia*[4] with curiosity. I will try to conquer my besetting sin, & write to you about the poems. For the rest, though I am so bad a correspondent, I never forget friends nor alter in my regard for them.

I go on working very continuously. Am just seeing a book on Carlo Gozzi—essays on Itn Impromptu Comedy, & a translation of a very curious autobiography[5]—through the press. This occupied me from April till August.

I have also a collection of 20 essays[6] on all sorts of literary artistic &

speculative topics nearly ready. A few of them have already appeared in the Fortnightly.

I am sorry you found Noel's Otway[7] infelicitous. It made me think a great deal about whether our Elizn mania is just, & sent me again to Otway whom I now admire & understand better. I thought "the Elizabethan unsoundness" a good phrase.

Tell me what you are doing, & heap coals of fire on my head by writing about yourself. Why did not you send Berenson with a card to my door? He may find me at Venice (Cà Torresella Zattere 560) if he comes there in May. That is my Venetian "pied à terre."

Believe me always yours

J A Symonds.

What do you think of Lord H. Somerset's poems?[8] Why is he cross with me? He sent me the book.

Pray do not "Mr" me, if you write again. And write. Write without affectation or reserve. I want to know about you, for I have forgotten nothing which concerns you.

---

1. See L 1502.
2. Bernard Berenson (1865–1959), the American art critic.
3. Vernon Lee: see L 1182; Villari: see L 1297.
4. *Erotidia* (Rugby, privately published, 1889).
5. *The Memoirs of Carlo Gozzi,* tr. into English by John Addington Symonds . . . (2 vols., 1890 [1889]).
6. *E S & S* (2 vols., 1890).
7. Noel's edition of Thomas Otway's plays in the "Mermaid" series (1888).
8. *Songs of Adieu* by Lord Henry Richard Charles Somerset (1849–1932), prolific song-writer; second son of Henry Charles Fitzroy Somerset, 8th Duke of Beaufort (1824–99). See also L 1868, note 4.

1700. *To Mary Ann Sykes*

Am Hof, Davos Platz, Switzerland. Feb: 24 1889

My dearest Auntie

I see from Charlotte's last letter to Catherine that you are interested in the pulpit I have given to the church here. So I send you a photo of it. The pulpit does not stand in the middle of the choir now. It was photographed there before being put into its proper place. I am going to have a brass plate made, recording that it is erected to Janet's memory. It is made entirely out of wood from in this canton: pine of two sorts, larch, walnut, sycamore, & oak; & is in the style of the old Grisons furniture.—We are very glad to hear that you are keeping pretty well. I am thankful to say that, up to this time, we have been all in good health. I am better than I was when Catherine was in England. But I still suffer from my head at times. I go on working at my books. This exercise has become a necessity to me.

Ever yr most aff nephew

JASymonds

I shall soon send photos of myself & study.

1701. *To George Rea*[1]

[Davos] Feby 26. 1889

My dear George

Rather reluctantly I send you three volumes of my verses—: since you asked, & I promised.

I could not choose one volume, & send that, because I have not one which I think better than the rest.

As books, I think that they are all failures; & the world has also decided in this way. But even modesty & candour allow me to believe that, here & there, in the rubble of imperfect poetry, a grain of gold-dust—of the actual poetic metal—may be found.

I do not like you to hunt for these few grains among so many pages.

If you would care for this, I would write you out a little book of tiny pieces in Ms,[2] where I think my work is best—or, at the least, creditable. And this I would give you, instead of the loan of these three volumes—& there are two volumes more—as a momento of the kindness I feel for you, & of the days we have passed together here & at Venice.

So take this offer, & return the printed books. Or read in them, & see if there is anything which suits your mood.

Yours very sincerely

John Addington Symonds.

1. A passage from an unpublished letter of Samuel Richards (see L 1708) to his wife has enabled us to identify George Rea (?–?). Richards wrote (December 30, 1890):

Miss [Mary] Robinson and George Rea left Monday, she for Paris, he to Hanover, they meet in Bremen Nov 9 for home, he is going to go in for Civil Engineering with his cousin who is President of some R R in Pittsburgh. (Gallini collection)

The cousin was probably Samuel Rea (1855–1929), civil engineer, assistant to the vice-president of the Pennsylvania Railroad, 1883–89, and president of the railroad, 1913–25. George Rea resided at the Hotel Buol with his aunt Mary Robinson of Pittsburgh (not the poet, who married James Darmasteter in 1888. See L 1651). He was named as grandson in the will of William C. Robinson (d. 1872), whose youngest daughter married a James Rea. Mary Robinson (1836–1916) was Rea's aunt and left him the bulk of her estate, which made payments to him in Lausanne, Switzerland, until 1924. His death date is unknown to us. In 1928 payments from Mary Robinson's estate were made to Dixie Rea, his widow.

2. Apparently a group of poems in manuscript, now in the Huntington Library, San Marino, California.

1702. *To Horatio Forbes Brown*

Davos, March 3, 1889

[Dear Horatio]

Madge and I had a good time in the Vorder Rheinthal We drove about incessantly in sledges for seven days. Both came back to Davos, and had severe colds on our arrival. I am still sunk below the surface of vitality in a deep sea of cold.

But, such is the oddness of man's nature, I have chosen this particular moment to begin a new literary work of the utmost importance—my "Autobiography"—and at the same time I am overwhelmed with Gozzi proofs, which keep pouring in by every post, so that I have to spend at least four hours a day upon them, and look forward to a speedy completion of the printing. I shall be glad when it is done. My heart was never in that subject. And yet I think it is a workmanly performance. The book will be about eight hundred pages, of which two hundred pages are original essays, the rest translation of Gozzi's "Memoirs."

God bless you, dear friend. Looking to times less dark and less confused than these, which overwhelm me with innumerable cares and miseries of health, I am your ever loving.

P.S.—I have not yet persuaded the *Gemeinde* [common folk] to accept my 10,000 francs.[1]

[Incomplete]

1. The Davosers were balking over accepting his gift of a gymnasium. See Ls 1697, 1707, and 1712.

1703. *To Arthur Herbert*

Am Hof. March 9. 1889[1]

Dear Mr Herbert

I returned from a six days' driving tour last night; & now I am able to answer your letter of the 2nd.

The resolution of the Davos Int: Tob: Race Committee[2] which you forward, is in the deepest sense gratifying to me. I feel the kindness of it toward myself most truly, & wish to express my cordial thanks to the Committee for the honour implied in calling the proposed shield by my name.

In the circumstances, I am of opinion that this project of establishing a second Race & founding a second Challenge Prize is the best possible. I believe too that it will greatly conduce to the development of the sport, & will add further interest to our annual event.

Personally, I shall be ready to do all I can to further the end in view; & if I am able to be of service to the Committee as a resident in Davos, they may count on my assistance.

You will see that I have returned a full affirmative to your communication. I must only express again my sense of the unexpected honour you have done me by proposing to connect my name with the Shield.

Believe me to remain very truly yours

John Addington Symonds

To Arthur Herbert Esqe
& the Committee of the Davos Int: Tob: Race.

Dear Mr Herbert

I wrote on the previous page just what I feel—in hearty acknowledgment of the Committee's handsome intentions with regard to me.

I could not find it in me to refuse what is so kindly meant & so very honourable to myself.

Yet I think it might be worth considering whether the Shield ought not to receive some other name. I should like to talk about this with

357

Members of the Committee, & shall take an opportunity when it occurs of doing so.

Whatever may be finally decided, I shall always retain a lively recollection of the resolution passed unanimously, & shall treasure up your letter announcing the same to me.

Very sincerely yours

John Addington Symonds

---

1. Symonds seems to have gone on 2 successive driving tours, one ending March 3, the other ending March 8.
2. See L 1689. Readers especially interested should see the "Special Race Supplement" of the *Davos Courier,* Feb 25, 1893.

1704. *To Henry Sidgwick*

Davos, March 10 [1889]

[Dear Henry]

On the receipt of your note, gently chiding me for silence, I sat down and wrote you a very elaborate letter about myself. I think it, however, almost wiser not to send this, for it would cause you anxiety, and you cannot help me by being informed of my mental troubles.

Briefly, I have been seriously amiss in my brain during the last four months, and am beginning to perceive that the constant literary work, with which I am accustomed to keep my mental maladies at bay, has its evil side as overtaxing the cerebral energy and increasing the nervous susceptibility. My distress has been very great, and my uneasiness about the future is sometimes almost more than I can bear. This is enough to explain, in part at least, why I hold myself aloof from correspondence. I never could write formal letters.

Did you see a review I wrote of Roden's book?[1] It is rather high-pitched. But I was resolved to say out once what I thought about him. I admire his "Modern Faust," with all its faults of form, immensely. The intense sympathy for, and intuition into mental and moral anguish, which it displays, vibrates through every chord of my own tormented being. Perhaps this adaptation to my special circumstances rendered me a little too enthusiastic. Still, it is a merit in a poem of that sort to have fitted on to a

358

sufferer's mood. I do not feel the same about Thomson's or even Leopardi's[2] pessimism—and am superbly scornful over the weak modern German pessimism which seems to me begotten of *Byronismus und Bier.*

Have you read an Essay called "Accent and Rhythm"[3] Pt. 1 (no author's name), published by Blackwood? You are one of the very few people it would interest. I do not see how the man's laws are to be applied to classical metres. But they suggest a clue which I have always been fumbling after with regard to English blank verse.

I sent you two photos of my study here. I had to sit four minutes for the one in which I appear. The result is not very luminous. I wish I could talk to you instead of writing. I have, however, had some pleasant visits from friends lately, and expect another on Wednesday next.

[Incomplete]

---

1. See L 1690.

2. Two of Symonds' earlier favorites: James Thomson, author of "The City of Dreadful Night," and Giacomo Leopardi. See Ls 1369 and 1277.

3. *Accent and Rhythm: explained by the law of monopressures* (1888), possibly by James Largie Blake.

1705. *To Charles Edward Sayle*

Am Hof, Davos Platz, Switzerland. March 21 1889

My dear Sayle

I duly received "Erotidia."[1] I thank you for the book heartily. I have read it through from cover to cover with real pleasure & deep interest.

Whether you ought to *publish* it I cannot say. Looking into my own heart, I am inclined to think that you will publish it when three lustres more have passed over you.

But whether this is the moment, I doubt. The book stands high among books of poems issued from the press now, & is far above anything a man like me could invite the public to read.

But there are so many books. I get so many that are confused & wonder whether any poetry is "viable" in our generation.

You see that I am depressing & depressed. As time goes on I think less of literature & more of life.

I do not quite understand the difficulties of Cambridge.[2] Yet I hate universities, despise the academic mood of mind, & prefer peasants ten thousand times to professors.

So I suppose you are already suffering from my own malady of disgust for "culture." If you are, I congratulate you.

Write to me again. I like hearing from you. Ever yrs

JAS.

---

1. Sayle's book of poems. See L 1699.
2. Sayle was sub-librarian at Cambridge University library, a position he held for over 30 years.

1706. *To Arthur Symons*

[Davos] March 21, 1889.

Dear Mr Symons,

I have been very bad toward you, shut up here in this mountain valley of oblivion, and you have been very good toward me in many mindful ways. Last of all, you have sent me your volume of poems,[1] some of which, you know, I already possess in your handwriting. I have been reading them slowly through during the last days and now I should like to say some thing to you about them. But the older an old critic grows, worn with the continuous flowing over him of floods of literature, the less can he rightly say to a young eager poet. It is best, I think, for such a man as I am, not to utter opinions upon this or that of your poems, but to tell you that the net result left upon my mind after sympathetic and critical reading of your book is—that you *are* a poet.

If I were to pass from this generality to particular, I should tell you that I rate highest in the scale—looking at the poems of *Days and Nights*—the transcripts from life; realistic and penetrated with strong human emotion; next the sonnets (the form of which in many cases seems to me of admirable quality); afterwards the translations from the French. I have no hesitation in urging you to go forward in the path of poetry. It seems to me that you might take a great stride on that path, if you were to concentrate your powers of sympathetic intuition, analysis, dramatic presentation, and poetical treatment, upon some central theme—viewed by you as

360

artist more objectively than you have as yet viewed anything. This is tantamount to saying that I believe you have the gifts to produce a substantial work of art, if you will gird your loins up to what is the supreme adventure. I speak in all humility, knowing that what I indicate is the touch-stone of attainment in our art of writing, and confessing that such an adventure would have always been beyond the scope of my own faculty. But I think you have the stuff in you to make it worth your while trying to gather all your forces together for some comprehensive deeply-meditated poem.

I do not believe that much can be done with the drama in this age. Yet there are forms which serve as substitutes for the drama. And I submit as a mere opinion that you would find yourself braced up to the best by attempting some work planned upon a big scale—a large canvas.

Do not think ill of me because of my long silence. Distance only. Diurnal drudgery deadens. Besides, we have not yet touched hands[2] or exchanged the magnetism of spoken words.

Believe me very sincerely and unforgettably yours

J. A. Symonds.

---

1. *Days and Nights* (1889), dedicated to Walter Pater.
2. Symonds did not meet Symons until Nov., 1889. See L 1750.

1707. *To Horatio Forbes Brown*

Davos, Mar 24, 1889

[Dear Horatio]

Gozzi has been literally pouring. Torrents of proofs come daily. I worked literally ten hours at them yesterday, and have just had another bout of three hours this morning. The result is that the book is nearly all in print. There only remain some pages of my continuation of the life and an essay on Longhi[1] to complete it. The whole will be longer, I think, than Cellini.

I have also had a good deal of business about my donation to the Commune.[2] At last I believe that I shall force my 400*l.* down their throat, and put them thereby into the position of buying an excellent gymnasium, which cost over 1,000*l.* to build, for the comparatively small outlay of 160*l.*

I cannot quite understand, and am rather mortified by, their reluctance to accept my offer. My object was to secure the gymnasium for the public, and at the same time to retain for the *Turnverein*[3] their right of using it, while I relieved the latter of a serious debt. Their debt amounts to 14,000 francs. I offer 10,000, on condition the *Gemeinde* [common folk] discharges the balance of 4,000, by which means the building becomes the property of the *Gemeinde,* with rights of use reserved for the *Verein.*

There was a three hours' meeting at the Rathhaus yesterday about it; and now a plan, arranged between the members of the Council of the Commune, the managers of the *Verein,* and myself, will be submitted to the *Landsgemeinde,* or general assembly of the burghers of Davos.

In the interval of other things, I have written a good deal of Autobiography.[4] I should like to talk to you about my plan, and I will certainly bring the work to Venice if I come.

[Incomplete]

---

1. See L 1681.
2. The local council which was proving difficult over his transfer of the gymnasium. See Ls 1697, 1702, and 1712.
3. The local gymnasts club.
4. The still largely unpublished work, in manuscript at the London Library; under the terms of Brown's will it remains withheld from publication.

1708. *To Samuel Richards*[1]

Am Hof, Davos Platz, Switzerland. [March 25, 1889]

Dear Sir

It will give me great pleasure to make your acquaintance. Instead of calling this afternoon, will you come to lunch here at 12.30?

Very truly yours

J A Symonds

---

1. Samuel Richards (1853–93), the American painter, born in Spencer, Indiana, studied art in Munich, suffered from tuberculosis, sought relief in Switzerland, returned to the United States to direct an art museum at Denver where he died shortly after his arrival. His best-known picture is "Evangeline," now in the Detroit Institute of Arts. (See

plates.) Symonds acknowledged his help with "technical and critical observations upon several intricate details of Michelangelo's work" (see *Michelangelo* [2 vols., 1893], I, Preface). Glimpses into Richards' life at Davos appear in *The Davos Courier,* in Nov. 30, 1889. On Jan. 17, 1891, the *Courier* referred to Richards' pen and ink drawing of Symonds which is the frontispiece to Vol. I of this collection of letters. Of the drawing Richards himself wrote to his wife Bettie, Oct. 8, 1890:

> I got a fine pen & ink head of Symonds with hulap hut [hat] on, the best thing I ever did. He is perfectly delighted with it as is everybody else & its the talk of the place: it is strong, got some stuff & art in it, and I think he would have bought it but for a silly criticism of Mrs. Symonds. He sent for me to send it to the house for a day or two. Mrs. S. came over, said it was grand and art work of the very highest character, only it was so very *strong and bold,* it "killed every thing else in the house" (a lot of photos. & washed out water colors) that the likeness was a speaking one, simply perfect in every respect. She had one objection, the hat—(which is a most happy hit) She would like to have it, but they *had no room* big enough to hang it in. So thats the way, you can make a masterpiece in the most difficult material in the world, and a portrait of greatest truthfullness, but if you dont satisfy every silly childish idiotic *whim* of some one else its no good. When they can find no *real* fault, they fall back on some cursed fancy, until it is enough to drive a serious artist insane to do portraits at all, the highest art is nothing against an imbecile fad. I told Symonds I was going to send it to a London Ex. where it would be seen & appreciated. I know there is not another man could do it with a pen, and if it don't sell, I can leave it to you & the baby & they will be glad to give 25 £ for it some day. (Gallini Collection)

On December 23, 1893, the *Courier,* noted Richards' death in Denver, Colorado, and published a warm account of him, apparently a reprint from a Denver paper.

1709. *To Henry Graham Dakyns*

I hope I have not scribbled all
this to you before. My memory is
bad about [what] I may have written
in letters.

Am Hof, Davos Platz, Switzerland. March 27 1889

My dear Graham

The long & delightful letter wh you wrote me on the 10th bridged over the hiatus in our correspondence, & left me deep in your debt.

I am very sorry indeed to hear how serious the loss of your manuscript[1] was. It seems to me that I could not gird up my mental loins to rewrite a considerable portion of a book wh had got lost in this way. Yet I suppose I should do so, & probably the second edition would be better than the first. I hope it will prove so in your case.

I have much reason to be contented at the present moment, having just finished the printing of my book on Gozzi 2 vols of about 320 pp apiece. Until all the Ms of a work has got into type I never feel easy.

This book which has cost me a great deal of trouble since last March is not altogether worthy of the time & labour bestowed upon it.[2] Having begun it, I stuck to it out of pure cussedness. Yet it has the merit of originality. Nobody in England except "Vernon Lee"[3] knows anything about Gozzi, & she did not know his Autobiography. This contains a vivid picture of Venetian life in the last century. I have added about 200 pp of essays on the development of Italian impromptu comedy & kindred subjects, including a criticism of the almost unknown painter Longhi.[4] The whole work will therefore be a contribution to the Italian Cultur Geschichte which has occupied me so many years.

My occupation with Cellini & Gozzi has infected me with their Lives Autobiographica; & I have begun scribbling my own reminiscences.[5] This is a foolish thing to do, because I do not think they will ever be fit to publish. I have nothing to relate except the evolution of a character somewhat strangely constituted in its moral & aesthetic qualities. The study of this evolution, written with the candour & the precision I feel capable of using, would I am sure be interesting to psychologists & not without its utility. There does not exist anything like it in print; & I am certain that 999 men out of 1000 do not believe in the existence of a personality like mine. Still it would be hardly fair to my posterity if I were to yield up my vile soul to the psychopathical investigators.

I do not know therefore what will come of this undertaking. Very likely, I shall lay it aside, though the fragment is already considerable in bulk & curious in matter—& I feel it a pity, after acquiring the art of the autobiographer through translation of two masterpieces, not to employ my skill upon such a rich mine of psychological curiosities as I am conscious of possessing.

This may appear rather conceited. But it is not so. I speak as an artist, who sees "a subject" of which he is confident. *Infin del corti* [to make a long story short] I believe I shall go forward, & leave my executors to deal with what will assuredly be the most considerable product of my pen.

You see I have "never spoken out." And it is a great temptation to speak out, when I have been living for two whole years in lonely intimacy with men who spoke out so magnificently as Cellini and Gozzi did.

I ramble on like this, because I want to talk to you.

What you say about the printed essays & fragments I sent you is very satisfying to my mind. I am encouraged to proceed with that book. The whole collection is *there,* on a shelf beside me. But three or four of the essays have to be rehandled, & I am too slack with the severe work of printing Gozzi to attack that kind of business. In my literary life I find sudden transition from extremely concrete work (like biography) to abstract thinking difficult. That is why the groove of memoir-writing carries me along with it at present.

By the way, I will certainly send you a clean copy of the printed essays.[6] You can show them to whom you like. But as they are going to be published, people must be asked to be discreet about them. And of course so private a document as the notes of Tennyson's & Gladstone's talk[7] must not be divulged to the public in this age of interviewing & random publication.

I have been receiving letters from Mrs Wilson[8] (School House) about a book wh once belonged to me & is full of Ms notes—how many of such indiscretions had got into circulation I am afraid to think. The Wilsons bought it of George the bookseller [in Bristol].[9] They tell me that not only Vaughan[10] is leaving Clifton, but also that Grenfell[11] means to retire I rather like the tone of Mrs Wilson—abundant παρρησία [freedom of speech] any rate.

I have also had a correspondence with Jowett on the paradoxical topic of Greek Love.[12] He wanted to write an essay about it for his new edition of Plato. But I have fortunately checked this project. He is so thoroughly off the spot that no good could come of it. He says, for example, that παιδεραστία [paederasty] in the Phaedrus, the Symposium, the Charmides, the Lysis, is a "matter of metaphor." What he means I cannot imagine. But an excursus written to demonstrate this point of view could not fail, I think, to be infelicitous, & might lead to scoffing criticism upon his sophistic habit of mind. The fact is that he feels a little uneasy about the propriety of diffusing this literature in English, & wants to persuade himself that there can be no harm in it to the imagination of youth. We went through the whole Symposium last summer word by word; & I must say I thought it very funny to be lending my assistance to a man of his opinions in the effort to catch the subtlest nuances of that "Anachronistic" dialogue.

I must stop, or else I shall flow on for ever.

I am sending a little silver toboggan to Frances.[13] It will serve as a model if you want to have one made on the right pattern. The great point is to get the runners quite straight, & to have them shod with perfectly polished iron of exactly the same width as the wood. Beech & ash are the best material.

Every very affecly yours

JAS

Callander House[14] will not let. It is a great pity. I am willing to take less than £150 a year for it now, but get no offers.

---

1. See L 1695.

2. See Symonds' earlier references to his lack of real conviction about the Gozzi *Memoirs*, particularly L 1646.

3. See L 1182.

4. See L 1677.

5. The unpublished autobiography; see L 1707.

6. *E S & S* (2 vols., 1890).

7. See L 451.

8. Mrs. J. M. Wilson, wife of the headmaster of Clifton College.

9. George's, Bristol bookshop, is still in business.

10. Charles Edwyn Vaughan (1856–1926) was appointed a master at Clifton in 1878; he left in December, 1888, to become professor of English at Durham College of Science and then at Leeds University. See his introductions to *English Literary Criticism* (1896) and *Types of Tragic Drama* (1908), and his *The Romantic Revolt* (New York, 1907).

11. John Granville Grenfell (died 1897) served at Clifton 1871–89; educated at Rugby and Pembroke College, Oxford, he had worked with Sir Charles Newton (1816–94), the discoverer of the site of Halicarnassus, in the Greek and Roman Dept. of the British Museum (1861–68).

12. See L 1694.

13. Dakyns' daughter. See L 261.

14. The house adjacent to Clifton Hill House; both places are now owned by Bristol University and are joined.

1710. *To Samuel Richards*

[Postcard]

Am Hof, Davos Platz, Switzerland. Tuesday [April, 1889]

Dear Mr Richards[1]

Will you kindly let the enclosed paper circulate at the Belvedere table d'hote today?

Very truly yrs

J A Symonds

---

1. Because of the formal salutation (Symonds' later salutation was simply "Dear Richards"), this card was written early in the friendship. See L 1708.

1711. *To Horatio Forbes Brown*

[Davos, April 3, 1889]

[Dear Horatio]

I am writing away at my Autobiography, and have reached the age of thirteen. It is interesting work, but I see that it tends *ad infinitum,* and that it will be hardly fit to publish.

[Incomplete]

1712. *To Charlotte Symonds Green*

Am Hof, Davos Platz, Switzerland. April 9 1889

My dearest Charlotte

Will you kindly pay these two bills for me? They are just too small to be worth writing cheques on Coutts.[1]

I have been waiting for proofs of my study photos. At last they have come but not very good prints. Such as they are I send you a couple, & should be much obliged if you would take some opportunity of letting Edith [Symonds Cave] have the other two.

The girls & Miss Hall[2] left for Venice last Saty. They got safely over Fluela[3] I am thankful to say. At this season avalanches are really dangerous.

Catherine & I think of going tomorrow.[4] Our plan is, if it is fine, to drive to Chiavenna, then through the Valtellin & Aprica Pass to Iseo & Brescia, then up into the mountains above Lago di Garda to Trento & from Trento (not as you & I did by Val Sugana but) to Schio & then to Bassano. The drive ought to last a fortnight. If we get good weather & are well, it ought to be an excellent thing for me. I am very tired & have been again suffering from trying symptoms in my head & my lung has got fidgety. Nothing is healthier & more resting than a long driving tour. Catherine & I both feel as if [we] were returning to long past days when we wandered about Italy together.

My book on Gozzi, a very troublesome piece of work, has come to an end so far as I am concerned, & only awaits the publishers' will to finish off.

I have already begun another book—two in fact. Here at Davos I cannot escape from this incessant brain-work. But you can understand that it is trying to my strength.

I have just succeeded in accomplishing a scheme I have long meditated.

I am a member of the Turnverein or Gymnastic Club[5] here. We built a Gymnasium on wh there is a heavy debt—say 15,000 frs. I wanted the Commune to take over the Gymnasium, paying the debt, keeping the property, & allowing the Club the free use of it. I knew they would not do this straight away. So I offered to pay 10,000 frs of the debt. After considerable haggling & long negotiations an agreement satisfactory to both parties has been drawn up & I believe that I have secured something of permanent value for the boys & young men of Davos. An excellent gymnasium is secured for them in perpetuity.[6]

I am sorry you could not take up Somerville Hall.[7] You would, as the St. J. G. said, have been an "ideal Superintendent." But I understand why you were unable. I am afraid Auntie must be very trying & depressing at intervals.

With best love to Auntie, I am ever your loving brother

J A Symonds

---

1. His English banker.
2. The governess who appears frequently in these letters.
3. The leading mountain pass out of Davos.
4. According to Symonds' diary quoted in *Biography,* pp. 441–43, the Symondses left for Venice on the 12th. They were delayed for 2 days by the threat of avalanches in the passes:

April 12, 1889.—After some days of indecision, Catherine and I left Davos this morning for Süs by the Fluela. It was misty, yet I thought with the promise of a fine day in it. A large post and four passengers, and six luggage sledges, with only four drivers to all the ten horses. We were in the conductor's sledge. Up to the Hospiz things went well, and the heat was absolutely awful. It burned more than I ever felt it burn, except upon the *névé* of a glacier in midsummer. A splendid liquid sky, full of the spring, seeming to portend storm. The road to Süs combines all the dangers of an Alpine road—avalanches, upsettings, falling stones; and they were all imminent to-day. When the first four sledges plunged into the great gallery I felt comparatively safe, but the rest did not arrive. After about ten minutes a fifth horse came plunging down the dark passage over the ice, with a pack-sledge and no driver. When he reached our train, he kept whinnying, neighing, and looking back as though to tell us that something had happened. We waited another five minutes, and still the rest did not arrive. The conductor had sent the chief postillion back. He could not leave the five horses alone in the tunnel—yet he was now anxious. Accordingly, I proposed to run back and see what had happened. The tunnel was pitch dark and as slippery as glass. . . . When I emerged into the blaze of sunlight and snow, I saw nothing at first; then met Herr Lendi of Davos Dörfli walking to me. One of the sledges (with a driver) had been upset. The two passengers, a man and woman, and the postillion, had all been flung over a wall on to snow and rocks, and had fallen and rolled about fifty feet down the steep place. The woman was

368

badly cut about the head; the young man, a Swiss, had sprained his hand; the postillion was all right.

'Fortunately,' added Lendi, 'the horses and sledges remained above the wall, else they would all have been smashed together.' I saw the girl, dazed and faint, and the place where she had fallen; then ran back to tell the conductor. But it was bad going in that tunnel with my gutta-percha shoes, and soon I heard the rest of the sledges come thundering into the pitch dark passage. I tried to keep close to a wall, and in moving shufflingly onward as fast as I could go, fell once heavily upon the rock and ice, bruising my right arm and loins. I did not think much of it at the time, being eager to get to my own sledge before the rest of the train arrived.

I ought to mention the curious optical phenomenon in this black gallery—black because fallen avalanches had stuffed up all its apertures with snow. On entering it, with eyes dazzled by the brilliance of the outer day, any object which caught a reflex of light from behind looked as green as emerald or sun-illuminated lake-water. In the middle there was no colour, nothing but night. Toward the end, when light again caught icicles and snow-heaps from the furthermost opening, these points shone bright crimson, as though a score of red Bengal lights had been lighted far ahead.

We reached Süs without further accidents. There . . . I found that I had lost a ring from my watch-chain, to which was hung these objects—1, funeral gold ring of John Symonds, my great-grandfather; 2, alliance ring of my great-grandfather and great-grandmother Sykes, two clasped hands opening, one heart inside; 3, a ring belonging to Admiral Sykes, with the name of his friend Captain Gathorne; 4, my father's guard-ring; 5, my seal ring of bloodstone engraved with the crests of Symonds and Sykes; 6, my gondolier's ring engraved with the arms of Symonds; 7, a Napoleon 'Rép. Fr.' 1848; 8, a cow-bell given me by Patt.

Drove up Engadine in diligence to Samaden. Reached it at 7.

April 13.—Up at 4. On at 4.50 in diligence to Silvaplana. There changed to sledges, in which we drove over Maloja to the wood beyond Casaccia. Then changed to diligence again, and reached Chiavenna at noon. A glorious spring day, very cold at first, so that beards and faces, &c., were frosted over. But the sun was glorious, and the mountains shone like crystals. Piz Badile especially beautiful. Picked flowers with Catherine.

5. See Symonds' chapter, "Swiss Athletic Sports," *OLSH*, pp. 222–39.

6. See Ls 1697, 1702, and 1707. The gymnasium was recently demolished to make room for a new one.

7. *St. James's Gazette*, March 14, 1889 (p. 6), reports:
The *Oxford Magazine* announces the retirement after midsummer of Miss Shaw-Lefevre, the Lady Principal of Somerville Hall. . . . Speculation is already busy concerning her successor. . . . [W]e believe that overtures are being made to Mrs. Green (the widow of the late Professor T. H. Green), who would make an ideal Head.

1713. *To Horatio Forbes Brown*

Davos, April 10, 1889

[Dear Horatio]

On the eve of departing from Davos, if spring storms permit, across the dreary and now dilapidated Fluela snow-road, my thoughts turn to you.

All this winter my health has been very queer. It is one of the reasons why I have corresponded with you infrequently and reticently. And just now I feel upon the brink of an absolute collapse. A diurnal drive of from eight to twelve hours in fine scenery ought to do me good.

The Autobiography has been going on. I have written a decent octavo volume, and got down to my nineteenth year, rather beyond it. According to my conception of such a work, the years of growth are the most important, and need the most elaborate analysis. But if I do not fling the whole thing aside, I see my opportunity for "panning out" considerably *de omnibus rebus* [concerning everything] in the future. It is a fascinating canvas, this of a *Lebensschilderung* [life-painting], for a man who has been hitherto so reticent in writing, and who is so naturally egotistical and personal as I am. Heaven knows what will come of it, and what will be done with it.

[Incomplete]

1714. *To Edmund Gosse*

Brescia April 19 1889

My dear Gosse

I have got so far on a long driving journey from Davos to Venice, having traversed the Engadine and the Valtellina, and the Val Camonica and the Lago d'Iseo, in seven days of snow and sunshine and rain.

Your book on "Eighteenth Century Literature"[1] has been my companion. I always take a book or two to feed upon slowly during these journeys; and I find that I never enter so thoroughly into the spirit of an author as when I do so. The matter of the book detaches itself in quite a peculiar way against the background of avalanches, wayside hostelries, and postillions, with whom one drinks litres of red wine in smoky chimney-corners. This being the case, I reserve for my wallet a couple of books which I desire to study.

I must write to you my gratitude for the good company during these laborious and eminently picturesque days which you have unconsciously given me. I like your book greatly, and have learned from it very much indeed. It seems to me most admirable in its analytical power—the precision and the justice and the novelty of critical observation applied to the problem of unravelling what looks, to less accurate and learned students of the epoch than you are, like a confused skein. In your preface you apologise for the abundance of dates. I bless you for your copious use of them. Dates, in so intricate a matter of inquiry, are like the kilometre stones upon the long and perplexed roads I have been travelling. They are the final measures for sites and fountain-heads, for paths of origin and paths of divergence. With some of your unorthodox points of view I warmly sympathise, especially in your bold thrusting of Addison[2] back into the second rank, and your no less audacious but quite genial recognition of Goldsmith[3] as a reversion to previous ideals.

I wish I had enjoyed the privilege of reading this book before I wrote an article upon Elizabethan and Victorian Poetry for the "Fortnightly."[4] It would have enabled me, under your auspices, and with reference to your work, to have brought out less crudely the point of neo-Elizabethanism in our century. By the way, when you spoke of Pepys, I think you might have said a word about Roger North.[5] I regard his "Lives of the Norths" and his own Autobiography as remarkable essays in the composition of memoirs. Jowett used to tell me, twenty years ago, that, next to Boswell, Roger North was the best biographer in English. Exaggerated, certainly, but the man has some right to "a niche." Thank you again. I am so sleepy and so shaken with posting that I must say good-night.

J A Symonds

---

1. *A History of Eighteenth Century Literature* (1889).

2. Gosse sees Addison as an aesthete in prose whose influence in his day "was out of proportion with the mere outcome of his literary genius."—*Eighteenth Century Literature*, pp. 193–94.

3. Gosse denies Goldsmith's "verse . . . any great importance in the procession of English literature" . . . but declares his prose among the "most delicate" in English.—*Eighteenth Century Literature*, pp. 322 and 345.

4. In LI (January, 1889), 55–79; the essay was included in *E S & S*, I, 225–77.

5. Roger North (1653–1734). See L 1473.

1715. *To Horatio Forbes Brown*

Salò, April 20 [1889]

[Dear Horatio]

Many thanks for your letter, which gives such a bright account of the girls. I wish I had not missed Margot [Tennant]. But cannot help it. She is,

371

as I told you, a very remarkable young woman. I dare say she rather raised the hair of some people. But she is really good. I can fancy the meeting of the three girls in the Campiello[1] which you describe so graphically.

We have had a good journey so far on the whole—travelling entirely with horses, except for the trifling bits between Chiavenna and Sondrio, Iseo and Brescia. We had snow on the Aprica, rain in Val Camonica, for the rest, good weather.

I had a very heavy fall in the icy tunnel on the Fluela, by which I lost that bunch of gold rings I carried on my watch-chain, and did some injury to my back.[2] This has made the constant driving less enjoyable than it would have been, and less of a rest to my nerves; for I have been always in pain of a dull and disagreeable sort.

I found in a deserted church at Sondrio, high up above the town, a most extraordinary series of *graffiti*. I never saw anything like them: very literary, and written in an odd stiff way as though a dead language were being used. One was pretty:

"Chi ama molto, riamato,
    Gli verrà molto perdonato."[3]

This Salò[4] is a fascinating place. But it has the trail of the slug over it, in the shape of sundry German invalids. A very good inn, and lovely views. We hope to reach Venice about the 27th, *viâ* Rovereto, Schio, Bassano, and, perhaps, Asolo.

[Incomplete]

---

1. Campiello Querini-Stampalia, a palace housing an art-gallery, Pinacoteca Querini-Stampalia.
2. See L 1712.
3. He who loves much [will be] loved in return; much will be forgiven him.
4. On the southwest shore of Lake Garda.

1716. *To Margaret Symonds*

[Vicenza] April 23 1889

My dearest Madge

A load is off my mind now that I hear of the arrival of my "boule" [travelling case]. It has got all my company clothes & white shirts in it.

Since we cannot have the Gritti rooms[1] till the 27th & rest is good for my sore back & it is raining a little today, we have decided to stop here over tonight. I doubt whether I ought to take the drive from Rovereto to Schio at all yet.[2] Shaking in a carriage hurts me considerably, & I don't know what is amiss. Probably Miss Hall,[3] if she were here, would fix me up.

Your mother & I went to call on the Contessa Martinengo Cesaresco,[4] a literary lady who admires my books on Italy. We found her & a funny little Conte, her rather aged but well preserved husband, in one of those vast Palazzi wh look like villages—stretching its long frontage for quite a kilometer between lake & mountain—once a very fine old place; but it has been three or four times occupied by soldiery, sacked, bombarded etc, with the result of now being a huge dilapidated shell.

The poor young lady is affligée with the most hideously projecting discolored & tusk-like front teeth; but gentle, intelligent, sympathetic & well bred. Her husband is short fat round flabby, with a flat face out of wh greenish eyes goggle affably but inscrutably like the eyes of an automaton —reddish yellow hair grizzled in his eyebrows moustache & trimmed beard —a black skull-cap on his presumably bald head, from beneath wh a few long & straggling wisps of dull red hair straggled down his shoulders, as much as to say "There is still some left." He too was excessively polite kind & ingenious, showing us & telling us everything, but remaining shut up in a sort of sphinx-like polish. How these two curious people came to marry kept puzzling me. She was a Miss Carrington—that is a noble English name—& her parents live in Essex. Perhaps the omniscient Miss Hall will know all about her.

Your mother was delighted to get Miss Hall's letter last night. You are having "larks" I see.

Now goodbye with all love. Writing makes my back ache.

Tell Mr Brown that I was in the villa where the Duke of Bracciano[5] died, & whence poor Vittoria Accoramboni escaped to her death-scene in Padua. It will interest him.

Everyrs

J A Symonds.

If Margot [Tennant] is still there give her my love, & tell her I would have written—but that she gave no address, & I thought her already gone to Florence.

---

1. The Cassa Gritti, a palace-become-hotel on the Grand Canal in Venice.
2. A popular excursion ran from Vicenza to Schio and on to the Tyrol at Loveredo.

3. See L 1712.

4. Both Countess Evelyn Lillian Hazeldine (Carrington 1853– ?) and Count Eugenio Martinengo-Cesarasco (? – ?) earned modest reputations as writers; he published works on riding and horses; she published stories and sketches of Italian history and setting. Her books include *Essays in the Study of Folk Songs* (1886); *Italian Characters in the Epoch of Unification* (1890); *The Liberation of Italy, 1815–1870* (1895); *Cavour* (1898); and *Lombard Studies* (1902).

5. The husband of Vittoria Accoramboni. See "Vittoria Accoramboni," *Italian Byways* (1883).

1717. *To Herbert P. Horne*

Venice April 29 1889

Dear Mr Horne

I duly received at Davos one copy of the Hobbyhorse containing my article on Longhi;[1] & let me congratulate you on your beautiful design for a "grande bella Cacciatrice Diana" [great sweetheart huntress Diana] as my friends here might say.

Last time I sent you something, you were so kind as to allow me more than one copy. And I hope you will do so in this case. There are three people here who would like my article, & to whom the Hobbyhorse might be profitably introduced.

They are: La Contessa Almorò Pisani[2]
Stranghella
Provincia di Padova

Mrs Curtis[3]
Palazzo Barbaro
S. Stefano Venice

H. F. Brown
Cà Torresella
Zattere
Venice

Will you kindly send a copy to each of these? And if you can spare one for La Contessa Martinengo Cesaresco[4]

Salò

Riva di Garda

You will oblige yours most faithfully

J A Symonds

---

1. See L 1677. The essay in *The Century Guild Hobby Horse* IV (1889), 42–55, was accompanied by a drawing of two butterflies on intertwined grain-stalks.

2. Countess Evelina Millingen Pisani (ca. 1832–?), daughter of Dr. Julius Michael Millingen, who attended Byron at his death and married a French woman. See L 1852. She married Count Almorò Pisani of an old Italian family. It is her farm which is described in Margaret Symonds' *Days Spent on a Doge's Farm* (1893; 2nd ed., 1908). According to Leon Edel,

> The late Count Pisani, "a descendant of all the Doges," had married her for her beauty thirty-five years before [ca. 1852]. Now [1887], at fifty-five or sixty, "widowed, palaced, villaed, pictured, jewelled, and modified by Venetian society," she impressed Henry James as the sort of woman one might have found in the early years of the century "receiving on a balcony at two o'clock on a June morning."— *Henry James: The Middle Years* (1962), p. 228.

Symonds had known Mme. Pisani, as he always called her, since 1888, a year for which few of his letters are available. Though the present mention of her is the first in these letters, Margaret Symonds writes:

> On a night in May, 1888, . . . I visited Vescovana for the first time. My father and I, Mr. H. F. Brown, and his mother, and our two Venetian gondoliers, left Venice in the afternoon, and in the dusk, some five hours later, drove up to the doors of the great villa on the mainland to which we had been bidden by its owner.

Mme. Pisani wrote a novel, *Only an End* (3 vols., 1869).

3. Ariana Randolph Wormeley Curtis (1833–1922), wife of Daniel Sargent Curtis (1825–1908) of Boston, daughter of an English admiral, Ralph Randolph Wormeley, by birth a Virginian but an admiral of the British navy who returned to America. Her sisters, Elizabeth Wormeley Latimer (1822–1904) and Katharine Prescott Wormeley (1830–1908) were both authors. With her husband Mrs. Curtis wrote *The Spirit of '76, or, The Coming Woman* (1868), a parlor play given in all parts of Europe and America. The Curtises purchased the Palazzo Barbaro on the Grand Canal in 1885. Henry James was their guest for as many as 5 weeks. Here he wrote *A London Life in Venice* (1888) and drew upon the Palazzo Barbaro for *The Wings of the Dove* (1902).

4. See L 1716.

1718. *To Henry Sidgwick*

Venice, May 12 [1889]

[Dear Henry]

Owing to frequent changes of place during a prolonged journey from Davos to Venice (driving most of the way), some of my correspondence has been delayed. I have been four weeks away from Davos now, and I find the variety of life here, as contrasted with its monotony there, very soothing to my nerves. When I last wrote to you I was in a very morbid state. Things are not, I believe, much improved with me essentially. But it is a relief to find distraction. The people of Venice—Italians, English residents and visitors and some Americans—amuse me greatly. The mixed society of the place goes far to realize the ideal of an urbane and unprejudiced *Kleinstädterei*.[1] Royal princesses and Bourbons, descendants of Doges and occupants of those vast palaces which line the Grand Canal, mingle freely with artists, advocates, journalists. If there were less gossip and rather more intellectual interest, the social atmosphere would be charming.

It is difficult to *know* Italians. I doubt, indeed, whether we really know or understand any people of a foreign race. But they admit one with charming readiness into the outer court of their familiarity; and I am at home now in several houses, both here and in the country, where I can study the last relics of Venetian aristocracy. Their apparent simplicity and real ignorance are quite delightful. There is one young gentleman who combines in his single person the blood of the Pesaros, Gradenigos, Donàs and Zons—houses which were illustrious in the times of Frederick Barbarossa[2] and whose splendid architectural monuments stud the plains of Lombardy from the Friulian Alps to the Po—who has not the faintest tincture of historical knowledge, and who cannot recognize the arms he quarters when he sees them on the façade of the Ducal Palace, the gates of tributary cities, the palaces of Sansovino and the canvases of Titian. I have spent the last year in studying Venetian decadence (1720–1815) and translating a very rare autobiography by a Venetian nobleman [Carlo Gozzi] whose life covered that period. So you can understand that it interests me to meet with the survivals from that age, who continue to some extent the habits of their ancestors under the altered conditions of *Italia unita*.

The way these people muddle away their fortunes—sometimes very considerable fortunes—without magnificent expenditure, without conspicuous vices, without ruinous tastes, is beyond belief or comprehension. A certain Marquis who owned a villa with a spacious park in the neighbourhood of a rising town on the mainland, recently sold it, at the rate of 25 francs the square metre, to a building company. His eldest son, not without his father's connivance, is employing a fortune he inherited from an uncle in repurchasing the land from the same company at the absurd rate of 200 francs the square metre. Such *naïvetés* seem impossible, but they verify what we read about Venetian folly in the memoirs of the 18th century.

A gentleman told me that his great-grandfather was the last High Admiral of the Republic of San Marco. He had his table laid every day for forty guests, whether he expected company or not. He was particular about the decoration of the board, and very capricious in his taste. At the same time he would not give his majordomo any direct instructions. The custom of the house was to prepare the dining-room some hours before dinner. The Admiral walked in, and if he observed anything which displeased his eye, he twitched the cloth with all its plate, glass and china off the table and left everything in a smash on the floor. This man was in no way notable for eccentricity.

These things will not interest you, however, and if I let my pen flow on, I should fill volumes with maundering ancedotes.

[Incomplete]

---

1. A system of small towns.
2. During the 12th century.

1719. *To Frank Thomas Marzials*[1]

560 Zattere Venezia May 27 1889

Dear Mr Marzials

I am sorry to say that I have done nothing to Boccaccio.[2] I looked over the Ms before I left Davos, & saw that I should have to remodel it throughout. I had not time then, & have been continuously occupied with the printing of a book in two vols on Carlo Gozzi. That is now about half finished; & when I get back to the mountains next June (I hope to be there about the 10th) I will try to take up Boccaccio.

If I once sit down to it, the work will go quickly. But there will be more of criticism than of biography in it—by the necessity of the case. We know very little wh is not more or less conjectural & hazy about the facts of his life.

I will try to give a background to this little by dwelling on the social aspects of Italy in the 14th century. You know that to do this artistically, not drily, in a sufficiently scholarly way & yet so as to interest that nondescript "the general reader," is not easy.

377

Since I have been here, that is during the last six weeks, I have seen something of your brother Theo.[3] He appears & disappears like a sprite, always eloquent & always bizarre.

Very truly yours

J A Symonds

---

1. Frank Thomas Marzials (1840–1912), editor and translator; later Accountant-General of the Army (1898–1904); created knight, 1904; poet (*Death's Disguises and other Sonnets,* 1889) and biographer (of Victor Hugo, 1888; Leon Gambetta, 1890; Thackeray, 1891; and Molière, 1904).

2. This became the posthumous *Giovanni Boccaccio as Man and Author* (1895).

3. Theophilus Henry Marzials (1850–1920), English poet, composer and song-writer.

1720. *To Horatio Forbes Brown*

Sunday Davos, [June 14] 1889[1]

[Dear Horatio]

I went off last Monday for an escapade to Ems, in order to be present at the wedding of my friend, Franz Willy. It lasted from 8.30 A.M. until 2.30 A.M. Tuesday and Wednesday mornings. I at least went to bed at 2.30. The other guests did not go to bed at all. The whole affair, though exceedingly fatiguing, was interesting and amusing. It will help to form a "page of my life."

On Thursday I was driven to Thusis, where I met a friend, called Anton Juon, who took me to his home in Reuschen, on the hills above Andeer. There I stayed, in one of the most perfect peasant houses I have seen, until this morning, when he and his handsome brother came up with me to Davos. They are staying here now; and I am to give a banquet to the Turnverein [athletic club] to-morrow evening in one of the Wirthschafts [inns] here. So you see I have been going it.

It was very cold on this journey, and I am rather the worse for wear in my breathing apparatus. But I shall try to hold out until to-morrow night is over.

The Via Mala at 5 A.M. to-day was ghostly-glorious. The undefined light of approaching dawn dilated all its heights and depths; and a waning moon hung far away to westward in a melancholy space of sky between the crags. I have been living for these five days with Romansch-speaking folk, which has added to the usual nervous tension of conversing with natives. But it has been a good time on the whole—yet a cold time—so cold that I could not wash except at the pump. Every fluid in my bedroom froze— down to a mixture of quinine and sulphuric acid.

If you are still ill, this will read to you like madness; and it was somewhat mad of me to take a frolic which made such constant demands upon my nervous force.

[Incomplete]

---

1. This letter can be exactly dated from information in L 1721.

1721. *To Horatio Forbes Brown*

Davos, June 15, 1889

[Dear Horatio]

We reached Davos last Friday after four pretty hard days from Schio. I had business here all Saturday. On Sunday, Chr. Buol drove me down to Thusis, in company with twenty-five of the Davos gymnasts, who went with music and banners in two five-horse brakes. It was a merry party.

The *Turnfest* at Thusis on Monday was exceedingly pretty—on a long level upraised grassy terrace, with that fine theatre of valley and wood and precipice. There were some 130 competitors, many of them extremely fine men.[1]

. . . . . .

It is time to close this letter, for the night is far advanced, and I am very tired. That *Turnfest* on the top of a long journey was pretty steep upon my strength. I stood about upon the ground yesterday from 7 A.M. till 8 P.M., and then sat in company till 1 A.M., and these excellent Swiss lads are noisy.

[Incomplete]

---

1. Symonds wrote an essay on this Turnfest; "The Athletic Sports for Canton Graubünden: At Thusis 1889," *Davos-Courier*, June 15, 1889, pp. 340–41.

1722. *To Lord Ronald Gower*[1]

[Davos, June 16, 1889]

[Dear Ronald]

If Michael Angelo could have learned anything about muscles and postures, he might have picked up a crumb at this feast.[2]

[Incomplete]

---

1. See L 1612.
2. A reference to the *Turnfest* at Thusis. See Ls 1720 and 1721.

1723. *To Horatio Forbes Brown*

Davos, June 20, 1889

[Dear Horatio]

In this day and yesterday, I have taken a fast grip upon my work—the remodelling of those "Essays, Speculative and Suggestive." But I do my task with reluctance. I hate the uncertainties of these critical determinations. They are good enough to talk out, with a pipe or a cigar, among acquaintances. But to write and print them?

"Grün ist der Baum des Lebens, grau ist alle Theorie."[1] That will be a motto for my next book. The uncertainties of even occasional contacts with human beings seem to me now so far more pregnant and more real than what we can achieve with thought. At my age, this is like standing on one's head; for I ought to have got to the point when ideas are paramount, and I have only just arrived at the point where things of life and sense appear at all significant. It has therefore been for me troublesome to finger again the old Gordian knot of what we mean by criticism, and whether there is any substratum for its exercise.

I know your woods and vales and meadows on the slope at Serravalle —a gracious landscape, a sweet place to breathe again in. I thought it, last spring, one of the most attractive spots I had ever visited—if the Bersaglieri [infantry] bugles had not rung so shrilly there at night.

[Incomplete]

---

1. The tree of life is green; all speculation is grey (Goethe).

1724. *To Horatio Forbes Brown*

Davos, June 23 [1889]

[Dear Horatio]

The "Soldiers Three"[1] has arrived. I mean to get more of this man's books—and perhaps to write to him. I cannot quite understand the Envoy. When first I read it I *felt* the lover in it; and then I got confused because it seemed to be the artist in a mysteriously religious mood. It is singularly touching—especially these lines,

> "Because I wrought them for Thy sake,
> And breathed in them mine agonies."

What does that mean with reference to so humorous and remarkably realistic a sketch of character?

Have you seen "Looking Back,"[2] an attempt to state, in semi-novel form, what American Society will be like after the institution of Socialism? It is worth getting.

I suppose you have heard little about the shameful way in which Germany is bullying Switzerland.[3] I am, of course, in the thick of the talk. In the last Diplomatic Note the Germans say that unless the Swiss alter their Constitution as they dictate, they will consider the advisability of *setting at naught her neutrality*—which can mean nothing else except going to war with a view to annexation. They have also actually proposed to set up a *German Police* inside Switzerland! The odd thing is that both Russia and Austria are morally backing Germany up on the point of asylum rights.

"Gozzi" is expected to come out first week of October.

An Italian from Bassano is working in my garden now. He has such a typical face. Really looks as if he had come out of one of those ugly pictures of the Da Ponte family.[4]

[Incomplete]

---

1. (1888), by Rudyard Kipling (1865–1936).

2. Edward Bellamy (1850–98), *Looking Backward; or, 2000–1887* (1888). Though not purposely so intended, the book became something of a gospel of socialism, and Bellamy clubs were formed.

3. In late April, 1889, a German policeman, Herr Wolgemüth, was arrested and deported when he tried to arrest a supposed spy on Swiss soil. Bismarck declared that if the Swiss did not withdraw their expulsion order and apologize, he would establish a

German police force in Switzerland. The Swiss demurred. The Germans finally backed down but only after further notes and threats.

4. A family of genre, landscape, portrait, and historical painters: the chief, Jacopo da Bassano (1510–92), took his name from the town in which he lived near Venice; studied with his father, Francesco da Ponti; was assisted by his 4 sons: Francesco (1543–91); Giambattista (1553–1613); Leandro (1558–1623); and Girolamo (1540–1622).

1725. *To Horatio Forbes Brown*

[Davos Platz June 28, 1889]

[Dear Horatio]

. . . Am rewriting Essays:[1] am now doing the one on Landscape. I think it has some good writing in it. But the book will be an odd collection. . . .

[Incomplete]

---

1. *E S & S* (2 vols., 1890).

1726. *To Horatio Forbes Brown*

Davos, July 4 [1889]

[Dear Horatio]

I suppose you are at Schluderns or will be there soon.

I am in bed here, where I have been since last Saturday, when I sprained my right foot very badly. What happens if a slave in the centre of Africa meets with such an accident and has to go forward—or a soldier in the retreating column of a defeated army? The actual injury is so slight, and so completely disabling. After twenty-four hours of march the man's leg must swell so that he cannot walk and has to fall—and then, in the plenitude of vigour, death stares him in the face. This must have happened over and over again. We do not need legend to make us feel the atonement of sin through suffering. In some way or other this is going on every day.

But the point to which these reflections carry me, I will not dwell on now. For I am not firm enough of brain to grasp conclusions. In moments of weakness we often seem to be on the point of a discovery—a complex of thoughts ready to be solved in some higher and luminous synthesis. It is like the illusion of dreams which makes things so clear; but which have no logic when we wake from them.

I have not much to write about. Only to keep touch. So good-bye.

[Incomplete]

1727. *To William Barclay Squire*

[Davos] August 1 1889

My dear Squire

No indeed. You have said or done nothing to offend me—how could you? But I have been unpardonably indolent, & through my extraordinary torpor of many months now have risked the losing of several cherished friends—yourself among the number.

I have, it is true, been both ill & worried. But this I do not count a valid excuse, except insofar that what had been annoying me was something of which it is better not to write.

I went putting off writing a letter week after week, until at last the effort seemed intolerable.

All the while of course I have been working, & this in itself explains a great deal. Since you were here, I finished my Gozzi book; & then came the printing of the two volumes. While this was going on I composed my own autobiography[1]—a very large part at least I got done—having been moved thereto by certain considerations connected with my ill health, & also by the autobiographical habit acquired in doing Cellini & Gozzi. But my toughest bit of work has been the revision & in large part rewriting of 20 essays upon all topics of criticism art & literature wh I hope to put forth soon.[2]

My hands you see have been full. But nothing excuses my neglect of friends whom I value.

With regard to the future. I shall have to come to England on business early in September. If you are in London about October, may I come to see you on my way back? I fear there is no chance of our meeting at Venice.

We spent eight pleasant weeks there last spring. The friendship with Mme Pisani strengthened.[3] She & my wife have taken to each other wonderfully. From Vescovana[4] Brown & I went to the enchanted Val San Zibio[5] where we passed two idyllic days with Antonio [Salin] & Angelo

[Fusato]. One of these we spent in ascending the highest peak of the Euganeans—Venda, where at the top is a ruined convent hanging upon precipitous cliffs; & here we spent three dreamy hours, tracing the silvery coast line from Venice to Rarigo, & the Alpine chain & the vast vapoury Lombardy outspread with cities & long lapse of rivers—Brenta, Adige & just a film of distant Po. A goatherd, more like a faun than a peasant, joined us & kept up a sort of obbligato accompaniment to our thoughts by singing those odd montonous vilote[6] wh seem to my unpractised ear to have no tune at all, and rise at the close into a wail. By this time, the child of nature is sweating under the Conscript's sack-cloth in some hot city, Padua or Verona.

Brown & I thought much of you on Venda. I am sure it would have suited you right well.

Brown is at Schluderns, working furiously at the magnum opus on the Venetian Press[7]—9 hours a day he tells me. At Venice he gets too little time for work, & when he goes away he gives himself these intellectual orgies. I wonder how he stands his life—for at Venice he is more & more in a whirlpool of small duties & irritations. But he seems to have toughened into a very strong man.

I never even told you how pleased Madge was with the owl.[8] Now I send you what I owe you. And I must let you know that the painter who was engaged to do up the tombstone died a few weeks after you left Davos. I cannot remember the young man's name (Mr Cust's friend). If you will send it, & tell me whereabouts the grave is, I will get it done by a man who is to paint the whole of my house soon.

We have been improving the neighbourhood of Am Hof—by enclosing a garden space within walls after a very old Graubünden fashion & by building out a kind of transept to the shed or "Wandelbahn." Here I am sitting now on a hot summer morning with plenty of green shrubs & flowers to temper the keen Alpine sunlight.

In my laziness, I rather shrink from England & country-house visits & business with lawyers & the probability of getting my lungs ill in autumn fogs. I should prefer to watch the seasons change here in the quiet round among my peasants.

We are all of us well, as things go, & get now plenty of visits from English friends upon their travels.

Everyone, hearing that I am writing to you, sends their greeting.

This sort of thing—"epistolary correspondence"—is a poor exchange for the delightful intercourse of conversation. One cannot write about the most real things; & so the second best seems hardly worth having. But that sounds like yet another feeble excuse for indolence.

Goodbye & believe me ever affectionately yours

J A Symonds

If you have not yet read E. Fitzgerald's Letters,[9] you should do so. There is something unique in them.

---

1. Now in the London Library.
2. *E S & S* (2 vols., 1890).
3. See L 1717.
4. Mme. (Countess) Pisani's home.
5. A villa in the Euganean Hills. It then belonged to Count Donà dalle Rose.
6. Name used in N. Italy for rispetti. See L 1336.
7. *The Venetian Printing Press* (1891).
8. See L 1691.
9. *Letters and Literary Remains,* ed. W. A. Wright (3 vols., 1889).

1728. *To Horace Traubel*[1]

Am Hof, Davos Platz, Switzerland. September 3, 1889

Dear Sir

Owing to circumstances connected with the fact that I inhabit one house at Venice in the spring & another here at Davos in the summer, your letter of May 24 has only just reached me—too late, I very much fear, to be of any use.

Nevertheless, I enclose what may be styled an expression of my creed with regard to that noble, (& here rightly named,) grand old man.

Whether it would in any way have suited the scheme of the pamphlet which you wrote me was to appear after the celebration of May 31, I do not know.

But it has at least the merit of sincerity & of careful consideration. I took thought before I set on paper what will perhaps to many persons who have read my books, appear an exaggerated expression of my intellectual & moral obligations to Walt Whitman.

Will you, if you are in personal relations with him, convey to him my hearty though belated congratulations? And pray believe me to be cordially & in all good comradeship yours

John Addington Symonds

P.S. I cannot read your signature distinctly. Therefore, in order to avoid miscarriage, I have cut it from the foot of your letter & pasted it upon the envelope of this.

[Enclosure][2]

I find it extremely difficult to write anything about Walt Whitman: not because I have little, but because I have far too much to say./—

"Leaves of Grass," which I first read at the age of twenty five, influenced me more perhaps than any other book has done, except the Bible; more than Plato, more than Goethe. It is impossible for me to speak critically of what has so deeply entered into the fibre & marrow of my being—

Walt Whitman helped me to understand the harmony between democracy, science, & that larger religion to which the modern world is being led by the conception of human brotherhood & by the spirituality inherent in any really scientific view of the universe. He gave body & concrete vitality to the religious creed which I had previously been forming upon the study of Goethe, the Greek & Roman stoics, Giordano Bruno, & the Founders of the Evolution hypothesis. He taught me to attempt to free myself from many conceits & pettinesses to which academical culture is subject. He opened my eyes to the beauty, goodness & greatness which may be found in all worthy human beings, the humblest & the highest. He made me try to strip myself of social prejudices. Through him I have fraternized in comradeship with men of all classes & several races, irrespective of their caste, creed, occupation & special training./—

Though my energy, as a writer, has been mainly devoted to those critical studies for which my education prepared me, my life, as a man, has been sweetened, brightened & intensified by the good Gray Poet's invigorating & ennobling influence. Before long I hope to publish a collection of speculative & philosophical essays, in which the debt I owe him & the benefits I have received from him will be apparent to all who, like myself, call themselves his disciples.

John Addington Symonds.

---

1. Horace Logo Traubel (1858–1919), author, friend and literary executor of Walt Whitman, founder and editor (1890–1919) of the *Conservator*. Among his works are

With Walt Whitman in Camden (3 vols., 1906–14) and *The Complete Writings of Walt Whitman* (10 vols., 1902).

2. This is published in Horace L. Traubel, ed., *Camden's Compliment to Walt Whitman* (1889), p. 73.

1729. *To Horatio Forbes Brown*

Sidmouth [Devonshire], Sept. 12 [1889]

[Dear Horatio]

We arrived here this afternoon. This is a very beautiful place; a large modern house set down in a cup of English hills, reminding me of the far narrower yet finer chalice of Val San Zibio.[1] It is all broad and smooth and sweeping here, in long, slow, undulating lines, broken at the extreme limit by the southern sea, and crested with tiny spaces of moor at the summit of the ridges. There are magnificent gardens such as only England can produce.

I read "Le Disciple"[2] with much labour on the journey. I cannot understand Bourget's reputation as a man of *esprit*. He is so conscientiously and painfully laboured. It is like eating very acrid saw-dust. Of course I recognize the power with which he has interpreted *le crime littéraire* and the *crime Chambige*. But he does not convince me of the reality of the situation, and leaves me with the feeling that the *jeune homme d'aujourd-hui* is a confounded simpleton more than anything else. The philosopher is of course sheer absurdity. I like and admire de Maupassant much more. The more I read of him, the more I feel the feebleness of James' criticism. Before I knew de Maupassant, I thought James' Essay[3] on him good. But like the Essay on Loti it is based on a real critical obtuseness of conception.

[Incomplete]

---

1. See L 1727.

2. Paul Bourget (1852–1935), *Le Disciple* (1889), deals with morbid psychopathology. The last two paragraphs of the introduction to the novel describe two young men of "today."

3. Henry James, "Guy de Maupassant," *The Fortnightly Review*, XLIX (March 1888), 364–86, reprinted in *Partial Portraits* (1888); "Pierre Loti," *ibid.*, XLIX (May, 1888), 647–64, reprinted in *Essays in London and Elsewhere* (1893).

1730. *To Henry Graham Dakyns*

Sidbury Manor, Sidmouth. Sept: 18 1889

My dear Graham

Thank you very much for your kind letter from Charing Cross. As you can take me, I propose to come next Monday, which will perhaps be more convenient than if I were to arrive upon the very first day after your beginning of the term.

I had not heard of your brother in law's death.[1] I can well understand that it must have been a great blow to Maggie & even more perhaps to her sisters.

I am looking forward greatly to seeing you. Till then yours

J A Symonds

---

1. Arthur Lindsay Pirie (1853–July 15, 1889).

1731. *To Horatio Forbes Brown*

Sidmouth, Sept. 20 [1889]

[Dear Horatio]

I am still lingering on here in this lovely country, getting myself accustomed to the luxuries of life, but not exactly loving them.

Did I tell you Nimmo talked to me about your book (The Venetian Press)?[1] He is going through with it, I can see. But he does not expect it to do more than just cover its expenses. I like the man. He has a real affection for the books which he has published.

I have bought a photographic machine called "Kodak." My nephew, Arthur Cave, gets excellent results from one he has; and I am inspired by his example. But I doubt whether I shall succeed as well as he does.

My wife writes that they have had 14° of frost already at Davos and her flowers are killed. It is madness to make gardens there. Here, though the autumn air is crisp, the flower-gardens are in gorgeous bloom, and the woods have yellowed—a herd of deer is slowly feeding across my line of vision on the hill-slope opposite, beyond a vast Persian carpet of zinnias, Japanese anemones, scarlet lobelias, etc.

[Incomplete]

---

1. *The Venetian Printing Press* (1891). See L 1727.

1732. *To Margaret Symonds*

I will write from Tortworth to Lotta, & a more cheerful letter I hope. There have been many things to oppress & annoy me here. Do not withdraw your confidence from me. You & Lotta can help me & educe the best I have in me by your sympathy & candour.

Clifton Sept: 29. 1889

My dearest Madge

I will begin by saying that I am going to "The Countess of Ducie[1] Tortworth Court Charfield Gloucestershire" on Tuesday, & to your Aunt Pop [Marianne North] on Thursday. Probably I shall go on to Oxford on Saty.

If you have anything urgent to communicate, you might telegraph to Tortworth. Anyhow, I hope to hear from one of you at Alderley.

Your letter & Lotta's give me a great deal to think about: espy yours; & I am very glad that you write to me like that. It makes me proud to have your confidence. You must always give it me.

This affection which has been aroused in you for England, English people, English ways, is a matter to be very thankful for. It is right, natural, most to be desired.

You write to me as if I did not know the land where I was born, & where I lived till 37. I have not so much to learn as you have in it. If I cannot be quite as enthusiastic as you are, it is only because I know so much more, & because I have no glamour or romance.

I do not think that it is only romance which makes you appreciate the infinite beauties of English scenery, life, personal character. No: that is only just & natural—what you ought to feel. But I can see that romance heightens & gives a glow to the natural enthusiasm. And on this point you will have to be a little careful. Do not forget that Arthur[2] is your first

389

cousin, & the lieutenant of a regiment on foreign service: two reasons against either of you becoming too much attached to the other.

All that you say about the real superiority of English life to the life we lead at Davos & Venice is very true—at least there is a very great amount of truth in it. I do not resent anything which you have written about that. It made me sad, because the problem of life is very difficult now. But I am deeply grateful to you when you treat me as a friend & brother.

Perhaps I have reached the point at which it would be better to quit the scene or be removed from it—if only one could "fade upon the midnight without pain."[3] I have long been aware, to my great uneasiness, that by not dying when I went to Davos in 1877, I put the whole of my family upon a false line. And I do not yet see my way to retrieve the blunder, wh was forced upon me by health, & wh has been maintained for health's sake as well (in my case) as for choice & inclination.

I would rather be talking to you than writing. It is difficult anyhow to touch these matters; & almost impossible to see a way out of the perplexities.

But one thing I want you to consider. It is the question of staying on with Mrs [Leslie] Stephen in London. Has she spoken to you about this!

My own opinion is that it would be excellent for you to have a fair trial of daily English life, under circumstances less exciting than those of Sidbury & even than those of visiting from house to house as you are doing.

I believe & hope that you will have your new love for your native land —"this dear dear England"—confirmed & solidified. But I should also like it to be sobered; & I should not be sorry for you to reach a point at which you would be able to value both its advantages & those of the different life which you have led in Switzerland from a point of comparative experience. Six months of regular life & of work at drawing in London would be, I think, of the very greatest benefit to you.

Both you & Lotta have remarkable gifts of mind & character (very different), which have hitherto been remarkably developed by what is an unfairly exceptional training. *You* particularly need to be rectified by a course of that normal experience wh people can only acquire in their own country. You have neither of you been spoiled or rendered unfit for England by your past bringing up. And I am thankful to perceive that you appreciate England, even to the extent of being perhaps for the moment a little unfair to the training which has enabled you (at the most sensitive period of expanding womanhood & maturing mental powers) to recognize its special beauty by the face of contrast. *Now* I should like you to live into

English life. It is my conviction that you will reach a point of view—a point of perspective vision—from which you will recognize that your education under these double influences has been for you a singular & rare advantage.

What there is in store for myself I do not know; & I am sometimes, nay always, sombred by the prospect of the future—to the extent of wishing, in moments of dissatisfaction with myself, that it had pleased God to lay me, instead of our dear Janet, in that bleak churchyard among the hills.

I have not time to write to Lotta. If you do not object, I should be not sorry if she were to read this letter of your loving father   JAS

---

1. Julia Langston (d. 1895) married (1849) Henry John, 3rd earl of Ducie (1827–1921).
2. Arthur Stephen Cave (b. 1865).
3. Keats, "Ode to a Nightingale": st. 6, l. 6.

1733. *To Henry Graham Dakyns*

9 Banbury Road Oxford Oct: 7. 1889.

My dear Graham

Does your Marriage Trust[1] hold £1595 North British Ordy Pref Stock?

I have just received a dividend warrant for the sum of £23.6.6. made out to "John A. Symonds Esq Bristol & ors." It was sent to Clifton Hill House.

I do not know, supposing it to be yours, exactly how to deal with it. And certainly these warrants ought not to be sent to my address at Clifton Hill House. They run the risk of being lost. The money ought to be paid periodically into the Trust Account.

My impression is that some of your Capital was reinvested in this stock during the Spring.

If Maggie or you will answer by return of post, I will sign the Warrant & send it to you, so that it may be paid to the trust account. Or what would really be more businesslike, if you will give me the address of my co-trustee Mr. Pirie.[2] I will send the Warrant to him, & at the same time call his attention to the necessity of getting the dividend in future paid by other means.

I came here on Saty after two very successful visits to the Ducies[3] & Miss [Marianne] North. The latter seems to me extraordinarily well & strong. She is looking more vigorous than when I last saw her three years ago.

I am getting very tired, throwing myself into sympathy with series of people & also doing some of my literary work.

I often think of you & Clifton & all your kindness, to return to which is my desire. But I am going into Cumberland & also to Cambridge first, & shall also be here again.

Best love to Maggie.

Yours ever J A Symonds

P. S. I shall leave this Wednesday morning; will keep the Warrant till I hear from you—unsigned.

---

1. For Symonds' role in the trust see Ls 1659 and 1695.
2. Dakyns' father-in-law. See L 1695.
3. See L 1732.

1734. *To Henry Graham Dakyns*

9 Banbury Road Oxford Oct: 9. 1889

My dear Graham

The simplest thing is to sign & send you the Warrant, wh I will do. You will see that in future the money is properly paid straight into the Trust Account.[1]

With regard to my English Address: instead of Clifton Hill House, I have adopted

c/o Mess. Miles Cave & Co
Old Bank
Bristol.

All business letters thus go through my brother's & nephew's[2] hands.

I ought properly to have told you this before.

I am waiting to hear whether I ought to go to Penrith tomorrow. My Co-executor[3] seems to be sleeping & on a journey.

What a wonderful sign in the heavens you describe. I have seen nothing but a great moon entangled among the pinnacles of Magdalen [College].

Love to Maggie

Ever yr

J A Symonds

---

1. See L 1733.
2. Sir Charles Cave, his brother-in-law, and possibly Sir Charles' son Charles Henry. See L 1.
3. Dakyns' father-in-law. See L 1695.

1735. *To Benjamin Jowett*

35, Beaumont Street[1] Oxford Wednesday Oct:16 [1889]

My dear Master

I am very sorry to say that we must leave Oxford again on Saturday, & that therefore we cannot accept your kind invitation for either day.

I shall try to see you somehow before I go.

England has hitherto agreed with me very well in physical health, & has been extremely good for me in other ways. I have seen many places & people, & shall carry much back with me, I hope, to my barbarian haunts.[2]

Everyours

J A Symonds.

---

1. The address of the family home of Dr. Frederick Symonds, who died in 1881.
2. Davos-Platz, Switzerland.

1736. *To the Rev. Arthur Galton*[1]

35, Beaumont Street, Oxford Oct: 18. 1889

Dear Mr Galton

I am sorry to think I shall not see you again before I leave Oxford. I enjoyed talking with you very much & have now a different feeling about you from that former shadowy impression conveyed by letters.

There are some hard things in my life; & the hardest is the necessity of living, in that magic castle of the snows, so far away from people. I feel that deprivation far more than the withdrawal from libraries, pictures, music. There I have only Lycidas & Colin Clout, instead of Lysis & Charmides,[2] to converse with.

Thank you for introducing me to Mr Johnson.[3] If we come to know each other better, I think we shall discover a good many tastes in common. Please tell me his proper names, in case I should have occasion to write to him.

I wonder whether it would be possible for me to get that symbolic design by S.S.[4] of his besetting sin?

It may be nothing worth. But also it may have a psychological value. One of the most remarkable things I ever saw was a similar picture painted by a young Neapolitan artist in his madhouse.

Please also let me have Mr Horne's[5] address. I hope to be in London next week, & may be able to call on him.

By the way, my book on Carlo Gozzi[6] reached me yesterday. I think it is better-looking than Cellini, though far from perfect in taste. The etchings by Lalauze are certainly nice in their way.

Now believe me very sincerely yours, & do not forget to write to yours

John Addington Symonds.
(next address) c/o Prof: H. Sidgwick
Hillside
Chesterton Road
Cambridge

---

1. See L 1581.

2. Lycidas: the dead youth of Milton's elegy; Colin Clout: nom de plume employed by Spenser in his pastoral poem "Colin Clout's Come Home Again"—also a shepherd in Gay's pastoral, *The Shepherd's Week;* Lysis and Charmides: figures in Plato's dialogues. Symonds contrasts Davos with its life of books, dreams, and peasants with the Socratic climate at Oxford of youth, love, and ideas.

3. Lionel Pigot Johnson (1867–1902), the poet and reviewer interested in the Irish literary revival, though not himself Irish; became Roman Catholic in 1891; ardent champion of Irish nationalism. See L 1839.

4. A reference to Simeon Solomon's homosexuality. The work is "Sintram," a work now lost. Julia Ellsworth Ford, *Simeon Solomon: An Appreciation* (1909), p. 76, includes the work in her "Partial List: Photographs after Solomon."

5. Herbert Horne, editor of *The Century Guild Hobby Horse.* See L 1452 and later references.

6. See L 1691.

1737. *To Charlotte Symonds Green*

14, Albert Place. Kensington [London]. Oct: 25. 1889

Dearest Charlotte

I am going to stay with the [A. O.] Rutsons[1] (74 Eaton Square) next Wednesday, Oct: 30. Will you kindly send registered, or insured, both the portmanteau & plate box to that address? A. O. Rutson Esq etc I shall be in dire need of clean shirts. It is impossible, living as I do, to get things washed. I go tomorrow to Roden Noel at Burgess Hill, on Monday to the others if they can have me.

I have got a rather bad cold in my throat & bronchial tubes. The irritating fog of London does me no good. So I hope to leave England again perhaps on Nov 2.

It was impossible for me to go to see Auntie yesterday, & I fear I cannot go today. Except absolutely necessary things, I avoid fatigue & exposure from a fear of being laid up in a friend's house.

Chapman & Hall seem very eager to publish my Essays—in 2 volumes.[2] I saw them yesterday. What offers they will make I do not know. But I shall not try to bargain. I can't.

I was very much touched by the line you sent me to Cambridge. I did not know that I had left an impression of "brilliance" behind me at Oxford. But I am not sorry I did. I always feel the duty of trying to be as agreeable & entertaining as I can to people who are kind & hospitable toward me. For yourself, what you say about my feeling, that is one of the really deep things which I think grow firmer & stronger in me as I grow. . . .

[Omission]

Conferences which will leave me at least with the sense of having taken a line & acted for the best according to my lights.

On my way to you I hope to visit Alderley, & may pay a visit to Lady Ducie[3] if she is at Tortworth. I wrote to her in consequence of a very kind invitation she sent to Davos. But as yet I have not had an answer.

It is possible that I may not go to the North at all. Yet I think I should like to see the surviving co-executor of Mr Sisson's will,[4] who lives on Ullswater. It is only fair to consult him, although I am the sole person now responsible & exposed to risk if I act prematurely.

The equinoctial disturbance seems to have set in. We have high gales & driving rain. But Clifton is looking very beautiful all the same. My business took me yesterday to a house in Leigh Woods, the loveliness & rich

395

luxuriance of which struck me with wonder. It is so unlike anything in Switzerland or Italy.

The girls have been with their relatives the Enyses of Enys[5] in Cornwall, & are now, I hope, with the Leslie Stephens at St Ives.

Best love to Auntie, & tell her I am coming as quickly as I can but not as quickly as I would.

Ever yr most affectionate

JASymonds—

P.S. The above details about the Sisson affairs are private. It is part of the anomaly of my position that I cannot tell everybody how I am circumstanced.

I have had a box of small plate (with a key wh will come in a letter) sent to your address. Please keep them for me.

Also I told Coutts[6] & [sic] send my pass book to your address. If that comes tomorrow Saty or Sunday, will you post it on to me here?

---

1. See L 111.
2. Chapman and Hall published *E S & S* (2 vols., 1890).
3. See Ls 1732 and 1733.
4. See L 574.
5. Distant cousins by way of their mother. The head of the family was Francis Gilbert Enys (1836–1906), whose mother Catherine (d. 1893) was still living. Francis Enys had two brothers: John, who succeeded to the family property in 1906, and Charles (1840–91); and one living sister, Mary Ann. An older sister, Jane Mary, died in 1874, leaving 7 sons and 1 daughter.
6. His banker.

1738. *To William Barclay Squire*

[Harrow] Oct: 26. 1889

My dear Squire

After I had said goodbye to you, breakfasted, written four or five letters at your desk in that delightful room, packed my clothes up, & flown in a hansom to Harrow Road upon a visit, I at least reached this sordid "cave of care."

And here I am, waiting half an hour until it is time to go down to Burgess Hill.

You will understand me when I say that my thoughts are naturally turned to you.

The confidences of the night prolong themselves into the waking moments of the day, & keep their deep mysterious bourdon going through all our sordid-business & the discords unresolved of necessary traffic.

Not this alone, however. For I am living in thought with you far more under a sense of gratitude for your great kindness, & of vivid memory of the pleasure I had in your Society—yours and your friends'.

I left the Magazine Mr Fuller Maitland[1] lent me on your table somewhere. In returning it, please tell him from me how much & how often I shall think of our evening together on Thursday. When I come forth from the snows, I am a savage: but a savage who dearly likes to chumm with agreeable people.

And then, last night! The best memory I retain of that is the recollection of a few minutes talk to your friend Russell.[2] He will forget me, but I shall not forget him; & I shall think of you more happily in the knowledge that you have this friend.

You have done so much for me; & I can do little or nothing for you, except to keep you always in my heart. This I shall do, & shall always eagerly welcome any opportunity which brings you near to me.

Goodbye, dear friend.

Yours John Addington Symonds.

P.S. If a letter (wh I expected to find here) has come to me at your house, please send it at once to me

c/o Honble. Roden Noel

Livingstone House

Burgess Hill.

---

1. John Alexander Fuller-Maitland (1856–1936), musicologist and critic; in 1889, appointed music critic of the London *Times*.

2. Probably Walter Westley Russell (1867–1949), painter and teacher at the Slade, and Keeper of the Royal Academy; friend of the painters Henry Tonks and Wilson Steer; began his career with illustrations and etchings after the work of the illustrators of the 1860's; exhibited at the New English Art Club; during his twenties studied at the Westminster School of Art under Frederick Brown; first exhibited at the Royal Academy in 1898. Among his works are a series of Venetian scenes, and several of his pictures are at the Tate Gallery.

1739. *To Henry Graham Dakyns*

Greenwood, Chertsey, Oct: 28. 1889

My dear Graham

I received the enclosed from Henry [Sidgwick] yesterday, & return it signed to you.

I am afraid that I shall not be able to come back to Clifton. Business does not seem to make it necessary, & fatigue & fog warn me that I ought to be thinking of Davos again.

Since I left you, I have visited ten houses of friends, & worked myself into more or less of sympathy with ten different sets of people—together with the company they had invited to give me pleasure. This is rather laborious, though very delightful & improving. In fact I want to be alone & savage again.

I am going to meet the girls tomorrow at

74 Eaton Square,

& I think I shall take Lotta back with me to Davos on Saty. Madge will probably stay in London: that is, if I find her well enough—there come to me reports I do not quite like about colds on the chest; & I must see to this before consigning her to that City of Dreadful Night. It was precisely so, when I entered it yesterday from the south—a lurid yellow fog, sullenly shot with some celestial splendour of Sunset far away, & broken with the glare of electric lamps—infernal & fuliginous at 4.30 p.m.

I wish I could see you again! One of my happiest memories of this English visit will be that of your house.

Love to Maggie. Congratulations on Xenophon finished![1] Ever Yrs

J A Symonds

---

1. Dakyns' translation of the complete works of Xenophon, over which he labored for many years, was published by Macmillan between 1890 and 1897, but the *Cycropaedia* seems not to have been issued until Dent did so in 1914.

1740. *To William Barclay Squire*

74 Eaton Square [London] Nov: 1. [1889]

My dear Squire

After all I am staying over Sunday. If you will be really at home, I have a great mind to bring my two girls to tea with you about 5 on Sunday afternoon. They want to see you at home, having heard from me much about it.

You did quite right about [Simeon] Solomon's Sintram.[1] I should have been really glad to get it, & should have asked you perhaps to keep it for me. But I feel that his art is hardly what I want. In so far as it expresses anything, it is not quite good—is too much like what one has more than enough of upon one's own premises. And the actual artistic execution is now so shamelessly slovenly, that I am pained at the heart when I see ideas wh might have been wrought out so recklessly abused.

Send me one line to the above address to say whether we may come on Sunday.

I shall be at home & alone I think all Sunday evening. I wonder whether you & your friend[2] would come & see me. We can talk about this. The Rutsons are going out of town, & leave me & my daughters alone. Yrs ever JAS

---

1. See L 1736.
2. Walter Westley Russell. See L 1738.

1741. *To William Barclay Squire*

74. Eaton Square S.W.[London] [Nov. 2, 1889]

Dear Squire

If it is not bad for you to come out in the evening, will not you dine here at 8 tomorrow, Sunday?

Yrs ever

JAS.

1742. *To William Barclay Squire*

14, Albert Place, Kensington. Saty 4 p.m. [Nov. 2, 1889]

Dear Squire

I sent you two notes[1] today which you need not attend to; for I have just got your card.

I will come with my daughters about 4.30 tomorrow, & I should be so very glad to meet your sister & your other friends.

Will you & Mr Russell[2] dine with us at 8 in Eaton Square, 74? We shall be alone, i.e. my hosts are gone into the country; but I believe dinner will be there. This is better than coming in the evening.

Everyrs

J.A.S.

I may have to leave you rather early in the afternoon tomorrow because of an engagement at the Leckys.[3]

---

1. Only one, L 1741, is available.
2. See L 1738.
3. William Edward Hartpole Lecky (1838–1903) and his wife, Elizabeth van Dedem, maid of honor to Queen Sophia of the Netherlands. Lecky was a vigorous historian and essayist. In 1892 he declined the regius professorship of modern history at Oxford. A chair of history was founded in his name at Trinity College, Dublin.

1743. *To Albert O. Rutson*

[London] Nov: 3. 1889

My dear Albert

Sitting in your room tonight before going to bed, I must talk to you on paper, as I cannot say anything in words.

I spent a very delightful half hour alone with Mr & Mrs Lecky.[1] I came just after he had returned, & I really think they liked my visit. I am sure that I enjoyed it. And I am grateful to you for having suggested that I should go to call on them. When I am again in London, I feel sure that they will greet me as a friend.

I had two of my friends to dinner: Mr Squire[2] of the British Museum, who keeps the musical books there, & a young Mr Russell[3] whom I wanted to know. Both of them nice men.

They did not stay late. But at 10.15 I told Kemp[4] (as you suggested) that he might put the gas & lamps out. So that, having duly locked the housedoor, I have only to extinguish your lamp & retire myself.

When you return, Lotta & I will have departed, I suppose. Carrying vivid memories of your kindness & your wife's over the plains of France.

I wish there were a chance of your coming in the winter. This I must not build on. But you know how much I should like it.

Goodbye. Ever yours

JAS.

---

1. See L 1742.
2. See L 1674.
3. See L 1738.
4. A servant.

1744. *To Edmund Gosse*

[London] Nov: 3. 1889

My dear Gosse

I want to remind you of your promise to send me "Bouchard."[1] I will take great care of the book, & return it to you with every precaution for its safety.

I enjoyed that only too short a time we spent together at the Savile[2] yesterday.

The worst of such occasional meetings—with chasms of decades between them—is that the natural vivacity of men of the artistic temperament efferveses into something which leaves so much of the deeper things unsaid.

We make a beginning—a title-page—a sketch; & then we find that the threshold has hardly been crossed, the real serious good work of life & friendship scarcely touched upon.

Lonely as I am in the main part of my life, I feel this no doubt more than you do, who are broken in to occasional contact—Gelegenheits gedichte [occasional verses] of intimacy.

Mrs Myers,[3] who made some photographs of me at Cambridge, (wh I have not seen yet), has promised to send me her study of you. I shall value it greatly.

Please remember me to Mrs Gosse.

Sincerely & truly yours

[No Signature]

1. *Les Confessions de Jean Jacques Bouchard Parisien, suivies de son Voyage de Paris à Rome en 1630* (1883).

2. The Savile Club, founded by Auberon Herbert May, 1868, took its name from its second home, 15 Savile Row. See Edmund Gosse, "The Savile Club," *Silhouettes* (1935), pp. 375–80.

3. Eveleen Tennant, daughter of Charles Tennant of Cadoxton Lodge, Neath, Wales, married F. W. H. Myers in 1880.

1745. *To Margaret Symonds*

Am Hof, Davos Platz, Switzerland. Nov: 7, 1889

My dearest Madge,[1]

I am very glad indeed to hear that, as I always hoped, you found your purse when you got back to Eaton Square.

In the abominable bustle of that departure I did something very silly; left 15/10 of change on the counter where I registered our baggage. By the way, I hope you gave the footman that 10/-.

Lotta and I had a very uneventful journey, and brought all our things safely up to Davos. Your Mother and K. met us at Landquart—more bleak and 'Care of Carey' than ever. Both were looking in splendid health. K. of really Amazonian beauty. She is worthy to pose to some great sculptor for Artemis or a Nymph of the Woods, with her pure classical profile and her virginal nobility of form.

I think constantly of you, and begin already to miss you far more than anything I left behind in England. There is a comfort, however, in thinking how easily you can get here if you want. The journey offers no difficulties.

I told you that I should write you some directions. I have not much to say. The main thing is that I want you to begin this London life very quietly. Get first into regular ways of going to your studio, and do not think much about anything else until you have become accustomed to that. Remember to be at home at sunset. The two hours after sunset are the worst in London at this season, especially near the Parks. When you have quite settled down, I shall have no objection to your going out occasionally in the evening; very rarely, and only for some real object—good music or a dinner party. But if you do this, you must be very careful to note the effect on your health—(1) whether you sleep restlessly or are hot afterwards, or perspire at night; (2) whether you rise in the morning with a headache or a tendency to feel shivery, or with a husky throat.

If your throat gets at all congested, dry, lumps, sore, etc. you must go to a doctor. The one who comes to the Stephens is the one you had better consult in ordinary. Mrs Stephen will tell you how to pay him his fees.

Mme Pisani has settled to have Miss [Hall]. She will go there soon, I think. Goodbye, my dearest child. Be a good girl, better than your father ever was. God bless you.

Ever your loving,

J. A. Symonds

I shall miss our Ariosto! Remember me to both the Leslie Stephens.

---

1. Katharine Symonds Furse comments in *H & P*, p. 56:

Now that they were growing up plans were made for my sisters to see more of the world and Lotta was sent on a round of visits in England while Madge spent the winter of 1889–90 with the Leslie Stephens at 22 Hyde Park Gate, so that she might meet more people and also have drawing lessons. It must have been a very stimulating life for her and she became much attached to the beautiful Mrs. Leslie Stephen and also to her daughter Stella Duckworth. Two of Father's letters to Madge [see Ls 1747 and 1753] are interesting as showing a side of him which his readers may not know but which we, his children, appreciated greatly. Perhaps I value these letters especially because they show his awakening interest in his youngest daughter and also stress the Victorian rules of health.

Katharine Furse had often thought her father undervalued her.

1746. *To Horatio Forbes Brown*

[Davos Platz, November 8, 1889]

[Dear Horatio]

. . . . I find it not very easy to settle down again to literary work after all that intellectual and social racket in England.[1] . . . The longer I live, the more trouble proofs[2] give me.

[Incomplete]

---

1. His visit during September and October covered by Ls 1729 through 1744.
2. For *E S & S*.

1747. *To Margaret Symonds*

Am Hof, Davos Platz, Switzerland. Saty. Nov: 10. 1889

My dearest Madge

Your letter, the first you have written me from London, came last night, & was read (I need not tell you) with absorbing interest. I read it aloud to your mother in my little study.

It will not be a duty, but a pleasure to write to you; & I shall make it my business to write often & as much as I can. If you like letters from me, you must on your side also write. That will keep me "talking"—& the only correspondence human Souls have is in "talking," of which "writing" is a poor (but also a permanent) reflex.

You need not my telling you with what anxiety & sympathy we watch all these first steps of yours in a life away from us.—

I began to live this life of a personality making itself in the world—at 13, when I went to Harrow. And I know all the stages of it.—

It is my firm belief that parents can help their children best—& even older people, the younger whom they love—by providing them with wholesome surroundings, chosen at first & mainly for their *social* advantages. Life is larger, deeper, more difficult, more permanently interesting, more evocative of all our faculties, than literature or art or science.

And so, I shall not be disappointed even if you do not get just what we both of us desire for you in the way of art-teaching, this winter. These months are experimental. And I, for your sake, have sacrificed beforehand the best conditions of art-study to the best conditions of social life.

You have gained the standpoint for looking around you, & for comparing different courses of study. And I am disposed to think that, so far as art goes, you must be content at present with something less than the best.

Another winter—another summer, if you wish—you may do more what you crave for. And I tell you plainly I am glad to see that you crave for work—reject dilettantism. That is right. But we must begin cautiously. As regards health, as regards your larger mental life, as regards society, you have now to be in a good milieu. And I believe you have got this.

Later on, you may see your way—& I shall not oppose—to far more strenuous efforts.

Your way of dealing with the two schools offered you by Mrs Stephen, is practical. I like it; & I hope to hear that the second choice seems better to you than the first. A little further away does not signify. You will want a daily walk. The main thing is to get it in a quiet neighbourhood.

404

I shall not look closely into money. That you know already. But I must say that five guineas for the privilege of being taught water-colours by the red-nosed man up to Christmas, seems to me a big price for a little gain.

We are, thanks be to God at the present moment, in a situation where money is not a main consideration. So, if some should be spent unprofitably upon experiments, it will not distress me.

Art is very long; & life, they say, is short. But life, as I have found it, is long enough to acquire a considerable command over art.

The first steps are tedious & often disappointing. If you want to draw well, & to colour well, you must not expect to get far in one winter.

This I do not say to discourage, but to encourage you.

Look around now, learn what you really want, be thankful for the singularly felicitious home-life you have in London.

If you see that it would be better, for another season, to break up these conditions, & to go in for the severer student life, I shall approve. I trust you down to the ground. And, anyways, your character is being formed.

Your loving father

J A Symonds.

1748. *To Margaret Symonds*

Am Hof, Davos, Platz, Switzerland. Nov: 13. 1889

My dearest Madge

I have been writing like a horse the last two days. Mr Frank Harris kept telegraphing to me to send him "A page of my Life" for the Fortnightly.[1] My desk diary opened at the page of our journey to Nancy last March. I at last sat down; & with great difficulty wrote it out in large for Harris. It is very disagreeable having to throw one's most intimate existence into a form for the public.

This has tired & irritated my brain. Also, the night before last, I sat up until half past two, because I received notice that our house was likely to be attacked by burglars. Some suspicious men had been seen prowling round it in the daytime & again after dusk. The Police had it under the one eye of their constable. But it was judged better that the inhabitants should be on the alert. I sat up & went on writing. That is the sort of thing wh takes it out of one.

So I am now only sending you a line of welcome. To tell you too that I am glad you have settled your studio.

There are no news in particular here. We have had two glorious autumn days with frost clinging round the selvage of the woods in the shadow. And the nights are wonderful. I walked home from the Turnhalle last night under such flaming stars as are only seen here. [Peter] Minsch[2] is going off on the 1st of December as a Conductor of the Post. This is a great step for him, I hope, wh he owes partly to the opportunities I gave him of learning French & Italian. So I ought to be glad.

Johannes Ammann[3] in the Turnhalle last evening was radiant; more like a laughing Greek hero of the world's young prime than a Bündener peasant. He is not breaking his heart, it is obvious.

I get enthusiastic letters from Italy—Villari,[4] Memmo,[5] Sir Henry Layard,[6] Mrs Curtis,[7] Mme Pisani[8]—about my Gozzi. If it were not so expensive to send heavy letters by the post to & fro I would send them to you. But you have so much to think of that it would not make much difference to you.

Keep well. Ever yr most loving father

JAS.

---

1. Frank Harris was editor of *The Fortnightly Review*. The "page" was printed in *The Fortnightly Review*, LII (1889), 764–75. See L 1751; Ls 1758 and 1759 deal with this episode, distressing to Symonds.

2. Symonds' Klosters friend. For a detailed account of Peter Minsch at the time of his departure, see L 1756.

3. See L 1452. According to Katharine Furse (*H & P*, p. 58) Ammann "was probably one of the reasons why Madge went to London that winter."

4. See L 976.

5. Probably Ricardo Memmo (1863–1943), Venetian noble living in Rome, an electrical engineer.

6. See L 1327.

7. See L 1717.

8. See Ls 1717 and 1727.

1749. *To W. Kineton Parkes*[1]

Am Hof, Davos Platz, Switzerland. Nov: 15. 1889

Dear Sir

It will give me great pleasure to receive a copy of your book on the Preraphaelite Movement.[2]

Mr. Jobbins is a friend of whom I can sincerely say that his good fortune in India has been a piece of ill luck to those who often miss him here in Europe. At Venice in particular he is much desired & regretted.

If you correspond with him, please convey to him my sincerest regards & congratulations on his marriage.

Among Italian painters & artists who have written poetry I know:

Orcagna
Giotto   L. B. Alberti
Raffaello d'Urbino (bad verses)
B. Cellini (some of his pieces, in my translation
Salvator Rosa (exquisite songs & some fine satires
Bronzino (Sonnets & Indecent Capitoli[3]

So far as I know, none of these men's writings have been Englished, except those of Cellini by me.

I think I have by me two sonnets translated from Leo Battista Alberti wh I could fish out. And I once tried to lick Raphael's poor sonnets into English prose.

Almost all Italians who followed art, wrote verses.

This is all that occurs to me at the present moment to communicate. In a book called "Felsina Pittrice" (2 vols)[4] I think you will find sonnets by some of the Bolognese School—the Caracci.[5]

Believe me very truly yrs

J A Symonds—

---

1. W. Kineton Parkes (1865– ?), editor (1890–92) of *Igdrasil*, novelist (*Life's Desert Way*, 1907; *Hardware*, 1941), essayist (*Thomas Carlyle*, 1887; *Shelley's Faith*, 1888), and art-critic (*The Art of Carved Sculpture*, 1931).

2. *The Pre-Raphaelite Movement* (1889), an essay of 52 pp.

3. Andrea di Cione (called Orcagna) (1308?–68), Florentine painter, sculptor, and architect; Giotto di Bondone (1276?–1337), Florentine painter, architect, and sculptor; Leon Battista Alberti (1404–72), Italian architect, painter, organist, and writer; Raffaelo (1483–1520), Italian painter, architect, sculptor; Salvator Rosa (1615–73), Italian painter and poet: wrote satires in terza rima: *La Musica, La Poesia, La Guerra* and *L'Invidia;* Agnolo di Cosimo (Il Bronzino) (1502–72), Florentine painter. For their poetry see Symonds' *The Renaissance in Italy: Italian Literature* (2 vols., 1881), Chaps. I, III, IV. He does not discuss the poetry of Raffaelo and Salvatore Rosa. Cellini see Symonds' translation of the Life (1887).

4. Bologna, 1841.

5. Family of painters, founders of the Eclectic school and the Accademia degli Incamminati: Lodovico (1555–1619); Annibale (1560–1609), his cousin; Agostino (1557–1602), Annibale's brother; and Antonio Marziale (1583–1618), natural son of Agostino.

1750. *To Arthur Symons*

Am Hof, Davos Platz, Switzerland. Nov: 16. 1889

My dear Mr Symons

I have been back here ten days, & I suppose that you too have left London.

I often think of the morning we spent together, & of the very energetic way in which you besought me to be more autobiographical.

Oddly enough, Mr Frank Harris at the same time kept poking me up with letters & telegrams to the same effect. He wanted what he called "A Page of My Life" for the Fortnightly.

Accordingly I sat down & wrote out a page at random, happening to select from my desk diary March 2–6 of this year.

If Harris has the brass to print this, it may end in my being in future more autobiographical.

I wish I could see my way to publishing a great many poems I wrote between the age of 24 & 30. These would satisfy your theory of self-expression in literature. And on looking over some of them the other day, I was surprised to find in them more psychological force & poetical intensity—though of a rough loose kind—than I remembered.

If you ever come to see me here, we will talk about these things. Davos is a good place to talk in.

By the way do you remember my asking you in the hansom whether you read the classics much? I will tell you why I did so. It was because you twice spoke of Commŏdus. This made me wonder whether I had been wrong all my life in saying Commŏdus. I find here that the dictionaries give it Commŏdus. There is too much pedantry in academical scholarship. But a man of general culture, & a poet, ought to avoid false quantities. I will not mention the name of a living poet, well known & of excellent performance, who rasped our ears with a poem on a Greek theme wh had in it three Greek names all falsely scanned.

Pardon this excursion. It is very likely that you are right after all about Commŏdus. In wh case please inform me. I remember when I used to say Holiogabălus.

Everyours

J A Symonds

1751. *To Horatio Forbes Brown*

Davos, Nov. 18 [1889]

[Dear Horatio]

It is good that you have Allen[1] with you now. This will give you a great sense of security about your book. I have often wished, in similar circumstances, that I had some competent friend to look over my proof sheets.

I liked what I saw of Allen that day at Queen's very much indeed. Of course one cannot understand a man at one or two meetings. What struck me in him was an external air of scornfulness and boredom. But he became bright and friendly in conversation.

Frank Harris has bothered me into writing for the *Fortnightly* what he calls "A Page of My Life."[2] I doubt whether he will print it, now that I have done so. This making a man interview himself, produce a "celebrity at home" on his own account, is a new departure in journalism which I do not much like.

I find it not very easy to settle down again to literary work after all that intellectual and social racket in England. And yet I have a magnificent subject in Georg Jenatsch[3] already half studied.

We have splendid autumn weather. I drove up the Fluela yesterday and found winter there in all its crystal purity.

I was just going to close this letter without thanking you for Sir A. Lyall's poems,[4] and telling you how much I enjoy what I have read of them. I took the book up and did not lay it down till I had gone through half. They lift you along. And the sympathy—two-sided, with the natives and the English in India—is very remarkable. The man is a real poet. When I was at Cambridge, Mrs. F. Myers[5] (who is an admirable photographer) showed me a fine portrait she had made of him—a fine head.

Did I tell you of my making the acquaintance of Rudyard Kipling (the author of "Soldiers Three") in London? He turns out to be a nephew of Mrs. Burne-Jones[6]—a very extraordinary young man. I wish I could have got to know him well. It seems to me that he is going to make a name in England. The Savile Club was all on the *qui vive* about him, when I lunched there once with Gosse. Rider Haggard[7] appeared really aggrieved at a man with a double-barrelled name, odder than his own, coming up. Literally.

[Incomplete]

1. We have not been able to identify this person.

2. See L 1748.

3. Georg Jenatsch (1596–1639), Swiss soldier and leader during the Thirty Years' War. K. F. Meyers published an historical novel, *Georg Jenatsch* (Davos, 1876) and Ernst Haffter a biography (Davos, 1894).

4. Sir Alfred Comyn Lyall (1835–1911) is better known as the author of a life of Warren Hastings and a study of Tennyson than as a poet. The volume of poems is *Verses Written in India* (1889).

5. Mrs. F. W. H. Myers had also photographed Symonds and Gosse. See L 1744.

6. Rudyard Kipling (1856–1936) was the son of John Lockwood Kipling (1837–1911), who in 1860 married Georgiana Macdonald, sister of Alice Macdonald (1837–1910), who married Sir Edward Burne-Jones (1833–98), the painter.

7. 1836–1925, novelist who saw British government service in South Africa, the background of his romantic novels, *King Solomon's Mines* (1883), *She* (1887), and others.

1752. *To Horatio Forbes Brown*

Am Hof, Nov. 19 [1889]

[Dear Horatio]

I am greatly interested by what you tell me about the Harlequin photographer. His saying that "Brighella" must remain "Brighella," etc., accords exactly with what I made out about the masks, and tried to express in my introductory Essays to Gozzi. It seems that the old *Commedia dell'arte* is living on, as everything does live on, in Italian customs.[1] Probably some one in Pompeii before the eruption would have shown the same book of *generici*[2] and *doti*,[3] and described his art in the same way.

Parenthetically, I should much like to hear what the general effect produced on your mind by the reading of my "Gozzi" was. I don't want details; and I know you don't care about Venice at that period. I never did anything with less spontaneous sympathy, and with a greater sense of merely mechanical dexterity. The whole of the first edition has already been sold out. Nimmo is going to issue a second; and the price of the first is rising rapidly. This is the working of the "limited issue" system.

I cannot say that I agree with you about "The Master of Ballantrae."[4] It has all Stevenson's power of style—but the story is decrepit—does not go on four legs. There is no reason assigned for the domination of that shadowy and monstrous person, the Master, over his family. The best thing in the book is the old steward's character. I regard the book as an inartistic performance; feeble in what it has been praised for—psychological analysis;

silly in its episodes of pirates and Indians, which Stevenson does with a turn
of the wrist and a large daub of blood. There is nothing in it so human as
the disagreement between Alan Breck and David Balfour on the moor.

[Incomplete]

---

1. In "Introduction: Part II," *The Memoirs of Count Carlo Gozzi* (2 vols., 1890), I,
35, 47, Symonds treats similarities betwen Harlequin and *Commedia dell' Arte* figures.
Brighella was the brighter and more knavish of two country brothers, figures in the
Commedia dell' Arte.

2. Brown's note: "Commonplaces, fixed in form, which could be applied *ad
libitum*."

3. Brown's note: "Passages not left to improvisation. See J. A. Symonds's 'Carlo
Gozzi,' i. 62."

4. 1889.

1753. *To Margaret Symonds*

Am Hof, Davos Platz, Switzerland. November 23, 1889.

My dearest Madge,

Katharine, who is more like the Russian Giantess[1] now on view at the
Aquarium than anybody else, and also grows hourly, began her 15th year
today, i.e. she calls herself now 14. She has had a very happy event and
heaps of presents. Yours was specially admired and proclaimed 'so thoroughly English' until I mildly pointed out that the whole thing came from
Bavaria. 'Then', said Miss Hall [the governess], 'it was made for the English market.' Your Mother and I gave K. a new watch. . . .

Johannes[2] [Ammann] was here again last night. He *is* rather disconso-
late. It is a pity that he cannot always go about like a Masai Chief, with
nothing on but a waistband. He is quite splendid, plastically a superb
model. But the bauer homespun is like a London fog, veiling the radiance
of the deity of light.

I have been working pretty hard at proofs (Intr. to St. of Dante going
on), at Graubünden history in the pre-historic period, and at autobiographical studies. I get less time for correspondence than I did in country houses.

Tell me exactly what you are doing at the school.

We have a real treasure in Col. Napier,[3] a man of culture, acumen and
breeding. Your Mother and I take to him, and he to us. There was a dinner

here the other night to celebrate him—the Haigs[4] & Pearson[5] assisting. As always in this house, the guests enjoyed themselves exceedingly. I think this is due to our fair cookery, excellent wine, & refined Bohemianism—a home & ways of its own, with a remarkable woman at its head, & a very clever man for companion; not to speak of "beautiful" but alas! hardly dashing Lotta. We miss you as much as any one can desire to be missed; & I think I am right in saying that a wish to be missed is the finest form of human egotism—it is such a compliment to one's personality. Next evening came the two Hagens,[6] alone. It was a grim occasion. Neither Lotta nor Miss Hall would do anything to make Frau Hagen go. I suppose I frightened her. With Hagen alone, smoking, I got on. He is an odd man, what Germans call a "Sonderling" [odd character]; & I fancy I could get to be fond of him as I am of my peasants. He is handsome, has a soft voice, & open-air tastes: all this combined with a sort of effeminacy.

I have sent a poem to Mr Strickland for the New Year's Number of his newspaper.[7] It is a rather good copy of verses which I wrote in 1864. When it comes out, you shall have a copy.

I wonder what you think of "Ionica."[8] I used to dote upon that book when I was a lad at Oxford. But the best things in it (those written about Eton) are morbidly sentimental. The art of the verse is fine.

Kipling wrote me another jolly letter with a very funny pen & ink sketch in it, of Mr Gosse discoursing with a soldier. I will put this into your autograph box.[9]

Now I think I have run on long enough. Like the river in Virgil, I can "flow & flow for ever."[10] But it is good to know when to stop.

I cannot tell you how often I miss you. It is no use talking about this.

Goodbye my dear girl. Ever yours

J A Symonds.

Remember me to your kind & eminent hosts.

---

1. The Russian giantess, Elizabeth Lyska, 12 years old and 6′ 8″ tall, was being shown with other curiosities at the Royal Aquarium in London.
   2. See Ls 1452 and 1748.
   3. "Colonel Napier was the man who brought the first pair of skis to Davos, so the date of this letter of November 1889 marks the beginning of an epoch in the history of Winter Sports."—*H & P*, p. 58. Colonel Alexander Napier, M.D. (1851–1928), Scotch doctor, commanded the 4th Scottish General Hospital, Glasgow. The sentence describing Col. Napier, and the first word of the following sentence, do not appear in Symonds' handwriting on the original letter. Katharine Furse says that it "is evidently Madge's copy of part of J. A. S.'s letter on a former sheet of paper."

4. Major-General and Mrs. M. R. Haig and family lived for several seasons at Davos in Villa Rossweide. Haig was active in all English affairs at Davos, serving as president of the library and as an official of the literary society. He was known as a student of Indian affairs, the subject of lectures he gave.

5. Lieutenant Colonel Alfred Pearson; see L 1405.

6. Since there are no Hagens on the guest lists of the various Davos hotels of the time, we assume that these were Davosers.

7. F. de Beauchamp Strickland, owner of *The Davos Courier* and editor of the *St. Moritz Post*. The poem was possibly "Past, Present, and Future," published in the Christmas number, 1889, of the *St. Moritz Post*. See Babington, p. 201. It had appeared earlier in Symonds' *Miscellanies* [1885]. See Babington, p. 57.

8. A volume of poems originally published anonymously in 1858, written by William Johnson Cory (1823–92). Five hundred copies were printed; by 1872 only 311 had been sold (Faith Compton Mackenzie, *William Cory: a Biography* [1950], p. 189). *Ionica II*, also published anonymously and at the author's expense, appeared in 1877. A collected edition, *Ionica*, appeared in 1891.

9. This tantalizing sketch has not turned up.

10. The river Oceanus.

1754. *To Horatio Forbes Brown*

Am Hof, Nov. 26 [1889]

[Dear Horatio]

I quite agree with you about the boredom of Gozzi.[1] Think how bored I must have been, boiling him down and trimming him up! "Not worth it" is the word. And I felt it all the while I was doing it. I am not in good trim; suffering again from trouble in my head.

[Incomplete]

---

1. Symonds' translation, *The Memoirs of Carlo Gozzi* (2 vols., 1890).

1755. *To Margaret Symonds*

Davos, [November 28, 1889][1]

. . . what I think. I shall not tell you; for some things ought not to be written down in black and white. I am sorry you have to vacate that curious room, and to abdicate from the bookshelves.

I will send you some more money, *mine,* for your expenses. I suppose you find no difficulty in cashing my cheques. If you don't, I will send you a cheque on Coutts[2] for £ 10 after I hear from you.

And your two cousins: Arthur,[3] Dudley![4] They are different enough. But they belong to families which have many points in common. Especially stiffness, family pride and holding together. The Caves, I think, are far more conventional, but then they are also more rigid and persistent than the Norths.—[You see now why I chaffed you for thinking you could be only a friend to a young man].[5] Walter![6] How have you come to dislike him so much! I share your opinion of his character. Conceit with very little bottom to support it is his main characteristic. He is also a snob, a bourgeois.

When I read your letter about Barnum,[7] how I did envy you! The acrobats, the charioteers, the lightly clad girls and well-set-up tall men, in Nero! I should like to give Thoby[8] a guinea for saying, after it was over, that he wanted to be naked. That was a fine word. It expresses much which goes to the very root of our passions. We desire the savage, *l'homme primitif,* as Loti[9] says, when we are deeply stirred.

This is not the Gospel of Wordsworth or Mat Arnold; but perhaps of Whitman, certainly of me. And Thoby, with the mouth of a babe and suckling, (a swearing babe and an obstreperous suckling), has put the philosophy in the form of an incomparable epigram.

We get along here much as usual. Mourn though we do with "decent sorrow decent tears" for Miss Hall, K[atharine] seems stimulated by her absence and by the learning from Herr Meier in companionship with Vera.[10] I hope that this will last. Lotta remains the same. I do not quite seem ever to comprehend her nature. But she too is more of herself now, and is looking forward to Vescovana.

For myself, I regret Miss Hall in many ways. She was a practical person, and though she did not keep things together, as nobody can except the master and mistress of a house, she was always to be relied on for a pinch.

I think it best to write you off £10 tonight on the Caves. So goodnight.

Yrs ever

JAS

---

1. This interesting fragment to Margaret Symonds seems to be the letter which Symonds on November 29 said that he had written the night before. Margaret was

staying with the Leslie Stephen family at 22 Hyde Park Gate, London, during the winter of 1889. See *OOP*, p. 267. There is a note by Margaret Symonds at the top of the original letter: "I had been describing in my letter some of the many conventional, good-looking male cousins in the family."

2. Symonds' English banker.

3. Arthur Stephen Cave (b. 1865), son of Edith Harriet Symonds and Sir Charles Daniel Cave, Bart. of Cleve Hill, Gloucester. See L 1.

4. Dudley North (1840–1917), Col. North Lancashire Regt., served in Ashanti and Zhob Valley; 1st cousin to Mrs. Symonds; died unmarried.

5. The brackets are Symonds'.

6. Walter Frederick Cave, son of Sir Charles Cave, born 1863. See L 1.

7. Phineas Taylor Barnum (1810–91), the American showman; in 1881 formed Barnum and Bailey Circus.

8. An 8 or 9 year old, Julius Thoby (1880–1906), son of Leslie Stephen, brother of Virginia Woolf.

9. Symonds admired the French novelist Pierre Loti's *Mon frère Yves,* a fictional treatment of homosexual psychic undercurrents.

10. Miss Hall, the governess, had gone to Vescovana. Her tutorial chores had been taken over by a Herr Meier and a Vera (unknown).

1756. *To Margaret Symonds*

Klosters Nov: 29 1889

My dearest Madge

I did not say all the things in my letter last night wh I meant to do. For I saw you were in need of money, & would not miss a post without sending you a cheque. I hope you have now got £6 on Coutts of your own money, & £10 on Miles & Cave[1] of mine.

I have been sleighing today for the first time. The snow came suddenly, just on the day after Miss Hall [the governess] left us, & we were snowed in after the good old tradition of Davos. At Davos there is but little as yet. But on this side of Wolfgang there is much, & the forests have put on their strange pure sleepy burdened aspect. As I drove down, it snowed softly incessantly & was very cold. There is a chastity, the chastity of a wild animal or of a strong shy young man, in all this winter world which has not ceased to take my fancy. If we find no excitement, we have no noise, no dirt, no darkness caused by human habits.

I wish it were possible to combine what is good in this life with what is good in England. For myself, I will never voluntarily go to live in London. I should not live. I might not die. It would be death-in-life, against which, if I were strong enough to react at all, I should react by outbursts of excitement dangerous to my health. But I have always thought that your mother & you girls might do something to make an English home for yourselves. I do not see why your young life should be condemned to the limitations which suit my old life, & out of which I draw some satisfaction.

It is a difficult problem. The first condition for solving it is to understand its fixed terms. And one of these is the impossibility of my settling for a permanence in London. Three months of winter there would bring my health, by one way or another, into peril; & then there would arrive a violent disturbance of the family.

When you come home, you must think something out with your mother, who, I know, would like, if she could see her way, to sit more lightly on Davos.

I, for my part, do not grow in liking for Davos. The place interests me less & less. The Kurgasts[2] annoy me, & I have given up the tobogganing affairs. But I thrive in the climate, work well, & enjoy my Swiss friends. For these things I am willing to put up with much that is tiresome.

All this comes out of something in your letter. As to adding to the Davos house, I do not think you need be afraid. Even were I, wh is not certain, to decide on laying out £ 700 in bricks & mortar, it would not ruin the estate. And now there is no good investment for superfluous cash. Perhaps I could not find a better than in the improvement of a house, which wants very little to make it the best private residence in Davos.

I came down to see my friend Peter[Minsch], who is too busy to come up to see me. On Sunday he enters on a new career, as Conductor of the Post; & we shall have few opportunities of meeting (except by chance upon the mountain roads) during the rest of our lives. Conductors, as you know, never sleep two nights together in the same place. I have just lunched with him, expect him again for a few minutes, & then must drive back.

He is very sad & anxious. The life before him, now that he has got what he has been desiring, seems difficult & full of dangers & discomforts. His mother makes it worse to face, for she cries over him, & says she will not have an easy hour all the winter for thinking of where he may be. Of course she feels like the mother of a sailor.

It is curious to see those great hulking fellows saddened & made tender. Their simplicity has a great attraction for me. I wish, if I were to go to live in England, that I could make friends with such people. But that is quite impossible.

I am not writing you a cheery letter. My head, tired with painful work for many days, is full today of problems & anxieties.

Goodbye, my dear. I am your ever loving father

JAS.

Three days ago Casanna was freer of snow than when we climbed it in August. I used often to look up at those cliffs in evening red or yellow light. It is now scrawled against the sky in white & black. One likes a hill wh one has trodden.

How wise is this line about life in Tennyson:[3]

Pain rises up, old pleasures fall.

Then he says:

There is one remedy for all.

Death.

---

1. All banks.
2. Guests at a spa-resort.
3. "Two Voices," lines 166–67.

1757. *To Horatio Forbes Brown*

Davos, Dec. 5 [1889]

[Dear Horatio]

I am relieved to find that the *P.M.G.* selects "A Page of My Life" as the most interesting article in the best magazine of the month.[1] I really wondered whether people would stand it. But if they like such "pages," I can supply them with dozens at the rate of from £12 to £15 apiece. I almost think that I am getting considerable enough in literature, if God grants me a few more years and the consecration of old age, to say out a great many things which have been pent in me, and which I should like to tell my brothers before the breath is out of my body. Well, well. This is neither here nor there.

Old Walt Whitman sends me, with autograph and inscription in his shaky hand, the final and complete edition of his works—one book, a sort of Bible. It is a grand present to the spirit, and (for the future) of incalculable pecuniary value. I wish I could write about him.[2] But I am so saturated with the man's positive electricity, so paralyzed by the negative, that I can come to no formula—sink and swim alternately in turn as in an

417

ocean or an ether. The critic is nowhere, face to face with him. But, as you know, "Naufragar in questo mare,"[3] etc. Now I must shut up.

[Incomplete]

---

1. "A Page of My Life" appeared in *The Fortnightly Review*, LII (1889), 764–75, and was printed later in *OLSH* (1892), pp. 281–306.

2. Symonds' *Walt Whitman* (1893) included a short life plus 10 sections of criticism.

3. Brown supplies (*L & P.*, p. 230) the line from Leopardi's "L'Infinito": "E il naufragar m'è dolce in questo mare [and in this sea, shipwreck is pleasant for me]."

1758. *To Margaret Symonds*

Am Hof, Davos Platz, Switzerland. Dec: 6. 1889

My dearest Madge

To answer your question about Xmas presents. I think you had better give parlour maid, housemaid, cook, each 10/; and if there be a scrub, a boy who comes in, or a poor old charwoman, that individual will be gratified if you can bestow a half-crown on it.

These tips you will of course pay out of my money in your hands. If you want to give a really nice present of a book to anybody, I can recommend Mr A. A. Bullen's "Songs from the Dramatists" (Nimmo & Co). Supposing it is too late now to buy a copy, through their all being bought up, which is extremely possible, go yourself to—

J. C. Nimmo

14 King William Street

Strand W. C.—

& present yourself to Mr Nimmo as J A Symonds's daughter. If there is a copy of the book to be had, he will find it for you. And you will anyhow experience something rich & rare (à la Dickens) by half an hour's talk with the funny Scotch publisher.

That is a long parenthesis. Sir A Lyal's[1] poems is a nice little book to give as a memento. Kegan Paul is publisher—same size as Dobson & Lang[2] etc. You shall have my copy when you come back. It is a gift from H. F. Brown, who rarely gives any thing but infinite kindness.

I have just completed the painful book I told you I was writing.

Though not a large one, it is a book—not an Essay. If I were to publish it now, it would create a great sensation. Society would ring with it. But the time is not ripe for the launching of "A Problem in Modern Ethics" on the world. The Ms lies on my table for retouches, & then will go to slumber in a box of precious writings, my best work, my least presentable, until its Day of Doom.

I am glad to have got through the fierce tension of this piece of production, even though I am left with a gnawing pain in my stomach—stomach or heart, I know not which:—but the pain of the hard brain-work is stabbing like a stiletto in my vitals, at the middle of my body.

This often happens at the end of an exhausting literary labour. I have bored holes in my lungs in old days by the process, & bored so many that I was at last sent to strand here.

I want you to know your father; & so I scribble thus, pretty recklessly, yet not without intention. I would rather write than speak about my life.

A propos of this, the "Page of My Life,"[3] wh I told you about, has appeared already in the Fortnightly of this month. I cannot look on it without aversion, because it is defiled on every page with twenty to thirty printer's errors. I spent 3 hours in correcting the proof. But Harris, the editor, in his eagerness to publish the article, ran it through the press without attending to my corrections. I cursed him by all my gods in a letter last night—a letter not fit for ears & eyes polite. But *das nutzt nichts.*[4] The thing is published, with me at 13 in *Hanover* instead of at *Harrow,* & so forth—*glories* instead of *glaciers*—*history* where *industry* should be,—& every blessed name of place or person misspelled—& every shade of punctuation altered in its values. All the same, I am glad to see that the Pall Mall Gazette says this is the most interesting article in the best magazine of the month December 1889.

Voilà! I write to you as one artist writes to another. I wish you to know your father's ways.

Gran Dio! This pain in the entrails is too much. I can hardly sit up in my chair before the cyclamen root in flower, & write to you.

I am glad that you have discovered that your family is liberal in Soul beyond most people. I think that we are. Your mother & I form a rare combination. There is nothing middle-class or *bourgeois* here. Many & many a time have you heard the prate about the gospel of the Spirit. Not words, serious facts, are these. A large part of human life, the largest part, is involved in not being bourgeois. I do not know whether one gets felicity there. I rather think that doubtful. But I am sure the Spirit lives—suffering perhaps, enjoying greatly, sinning deeply, risking the passage from this world into another in a state of nudity & keen vitality. When we ever find God, if we ever do find Him face to face, it will be well for us, I fancy, to have been as true, as naked, as incisive, as active, as vital, as devoid of prejudices & conventions, as we can be. Only, we must ever bear in mind that we shall face God, & be held responsible for our deeds & feelings & desires. In some way or other, here in this life, or elsewhere in the everlasting life, God will ask about the Soul committed to us—the spark of his divine existence, which we help to constitute. And that conviction abides with me ever, controlling me.

Ein guter Mensch, in seinem dunklen Drange,
Ist sich des rechter Weges wohl bewusst.[5]

Alas! How difficult it is to walk in the right way! Wherefore, my daughter, & my brethren all, let each of us in fear & trembling work out his own salvation.

So the sermon ends. Out of your manifold London life you send us animated pictures. I return meditations from my mountain eyrie, plunged in star-fire & smoke of Tophet.

"Ma Religion" writes Tolstoi on the title page of his book, "*Ma religion*"; *ma fille; à toi!*

Now to go back to business. About your coming home. I think you ought to settle this for yourself. I am very well contented with the way you are living now. Your mother would keenly like to have you again soon; & if she wants you to come & says so, you have a plain duty. For my part, you know well enough that you are always a great joy to me. But I will never allow my own happiness to interfere with the good of another creature.—

He who binds to himself a joy,
Doth the wingéd life destroy;
But he who kisses the joy as it flies,
Lives in Eternity's sunrise.[6]

Descending quite to practical details. I think that if you do not come about the New Year, you had better live on in London till we return from Venice. You can choose between doing this, or coming here in January, going to Venice with us in April, & settling at Davos in June. You prefer the London life (& your mother does not decide matters by calling for you at once), then you shall come home in the summer.

Miss Hall is very happy at Vescovana. We get on here as usual, well, but I wish I had not this ache in my belly.

Goodbye. Do not think me mad. Learn to know me.

Everyrs

JAS.

1. Sir Alfred Comyn Lyall (1835–1911), British administrator in India and writer: *Verses Written in India* (1889).

2. He refers to pocket-sized works by Austin Dobson (1840–1923) and Andrew Lang (1844–1912); Longmans, Green and Co. published Lang's volumes, and Kegan Paul, Dobson's.

3. See L 1748.

4. It will make no difference.

5. In his moments of dark distress the good man is conscious of the right way.— Goethe, *Faust, Pt. I*, "Prolog im Himmel," ll. 328–29.

6. William Blake, "Eternity."

1759. *To Edmund Gosse*

Am Hof, Davos Platz, Switzerland. Dec: 8. 1889

My dear Gosse

I am glad to hear that you got Bouchard's Confessions[1] safely. The book proved very interesting to me, as a piece of pathological psychology— the purest type wh has come under my notice of an originally bad & vulgar nature ruined, by self-abuse, yet not quite destroyed for the intellectual life & observation. Some of his details of fact I thought worth transcribing. The sexual inversion which breaks out at one period of his experience, has nothing to do with the real nature of the man, who was clearly devoured with curiosity about the female.

I am afraid that it will be impossible for me just at present to respond to your flattering suggestion that I should write for the periodicals you have in charge.[2]

I have a too large amount of work on hand, as it is. A republication of my "Introduction to the Study of Dante" to superintend & see through the press. Two vols of "Essays, Speculative & Suggestive" in course of printing. Then besides, a book on Georg Jenatsch[3] to be studied & composed. And while so much is claiming, the old waywardness of us literary artists has driven me on my own private account, into the writing of an elaborate essay[4] which I daresay will never be published, but to which I now dedicate all my spare hours.

Frank Harris badgered me into writing a bit of autobiographical *causerie*.[5] It came out in this No. of the Fortnightly—without my corrections of the press—much to my disgust; as I am sent to Hanover instead of Harrow at 13, & so forth through innumerable blunders.

I wonder whether you have seen this article, & whether you think anything is to be done in that line. I wish I could have your opinion; & if I could meet you face to face, should ask you.

The form of causerie, gossip, is extremely convenient for many purposes. My life here is by its nature so curiously mixed of different elements that I have unlimited opportunities of producing pot-pourri both of Switzerland & Italy.

I wonder what it is that you find fetching in Kipling. I do not think I could define my own feeling about him. But I believe it is the keen appreciation wh the man has of raw native humanity. I am sorry to be brought gradually to the conviction that, for literary purposes, he cooks this raw humanity & makes clever salines out of it. But the underlying sentiment is strong.

Goodbye, with real friendship, yours

J A Symonds

---

1. See L 1744.
2. Gosse had written for the *Century,* the *Athenaeum,* the *Spectator,* and the *Academy.*
3. The 2nd ed. of his *An Introduction to the Study of Dante* and the *E S & S* appeared the following year. So far as we know, he did not complete the book on Georg Jenatsch, the Swiss soldier-leader. See L 1751.
4. The autobiography, still largely unpublished, now in the London Library.
5. See Ls 1748 and 1758.

1760. *To Arthur Symons*

Am Hof, Davos Platz, Switzerland. Dec 9 1889

Dear Mr Symons

I am glad to hear, by your letter of the 5th, that those introductions have been of use to you.

I do not think you will get much money out of the Academy. I have never drawn a penny from its *caisse* though I wrote from the commencement. But it is good to be able to sign your name, to come before the world —I suppose you will extort something from them if you try.

With Wemyss Reid[1] the case will be different. I advise you to stick to this ticket. There is money there, & a very sound business to be done—the extent of which will be gauged by your own ability & willingness to work.

I am annoyed by the appearance of that "Page of my Life"[2]—full of misprints. Harris said he wanted it for Jany: sent me a proof, on wh I spent three hours, & wh I returned by the next post. And after all, the thing comes out with all the errors, of wh I think only Virtue & Co. City Road are capable, sered deep upon its forehead.

You know that I am averse to this personal delivery of oneself in current literature. I have a modesty about the matter, wh I broke at Harris's insistence. I should therefore have liked what I did write in the demanded way, to be verbally & typographically faultless. And now I find myself sent to *Hanover* instead of *Harrow* at 13; *glaies* instead of *glaciers; history* instead of *industry;* & every blessed name of place or person I have mentioned mangled by the brutalest compositors a sixth-rate firm of printers ever got together.

I am annoyed. But I possess my soul in patience. Literature, after all, as I say, is a pastime. One wants the game played fairly. If one can't get it, one can withdraw.

I wonder whether you are right about Kipling. You do not seem to think that an "unusual insight into the average soldier's nature" is a very extraordinary gift. I regard it as almost priceless. Only I fear that Kipling has dressed his soldiers up with more of literary buckram than they ought to have. He knows the barrack-room. He has not given it *Cru* [crudeness].

Yours always   J A Symonds

---

1. Wemyss Reid (1842–1905), editor of the *Speaker* (1890–99) and manager of Cassell and Company (1887–1905).
2. See Ls 1748, 1758, and 1759.

1761. *To Walt Whitman*

Am Hof, Davos Platz, Switzerland. Dec: 9. 1889

To Walt Whitman
   Camden New Jersey
      U.S.A.

Dear and honoured Friend and Master

I thank you from my heart for the gift of your great book—that beautiful complete book of your poems and your prose,[1] which I call "Whitman's Bible."

But my heart has not the power to make my brain and hands tell you how much I thank you.

None of your eleves, your disciples, will be able to tell the world what they have gained from you, what they owe to you, what you are for them.

I cannot even attempt to tell yourself (upon this page of paper with this pen in my hand), what it is that makes me ask you now to bless me.

If my health, riven to the bottom like a tree in me, twelve years ago,—and the cares of a family, complicated with this affair of health—had not prevented, I should long ago have come to see you in the flesh, to ask counsel of you, and to assure you of my inviolable fidelity.

We are both growing old, and nearly half a hemisphere divides us. Yet nothing can divide souls, or separate that which is inseparable in the divine nature of the world.

Perhaps we shall yet meet: and then, beyond the death of this life, I shall ask you about things which have perplexed me here—to which I think you alone could have given me an acceptable answer. All such matters will probably sink into their proper place in the infinite perspective; and when we meet, a comrade's hand-touch and a kiss will satisfy me, and a look into your eyes.

But, if we come to be judged, I shall go to the judgment-seat and say: "Call out Walt Whitman. Let him pronounce upon the doings of this man, this me; and let me be confronted with him; before you judges pass your sentence."

I cannot find words better fitted to express the penetrative force with which you have entered into me, my reliance on you, and my hope that you will not disapprove of my conduct in the last resort.

As I cannot talk to you, I feel the need to say this; because you have exercised a controlling influence over me for half a century. It is not often, I take it, that one man can say so much as I am saying to a man whom he has never seen.

Those lines which I wrote in September of this year,[2] and which I am glad to see now circulated, were calculated for the public mind. They do not tell the half; but, as an old Greek proverb puts it, "the half is better than the whole"—in print at any rate.

When I read your Bible, I miss—and I have missed for many years in new editions—the poem which first thrilled me like a trumpet-call to you. It was called: "Long I thought that knowledge alone would suffice me" [Calamus 8. ed: 1860–61].[3] Why have you so consistently omitted this in the canon of your works?

Upon me, your disciple, it made a decisive impact. "I put down the book, filled with the bitterest envy." And I rose up, to follow you. I miss the words now.—

I am old now, and you are older in years, though everlastingly young, in ways not given to all men to be so. So perhaps I ought not ask why you omitted that poem from "Calamus," and what you meant by it. It means for me so infinitely much. I cannot say how much.

Well: the disciple weighs his Master's words, too scrupulously—and thinks perhaps too much of his omissions or dark sayings. He must not ask for answers to his questions, but express the total of the teaching in his works and ways.

That I shall do ever, so far as I am your man—marked with your seal and superscription; and what my addiction to you will later bring forth, is a matter for the literary historians of England to decide—if only I have life and time for future working.

More and more of you will be found in me, the longer I live and the firmer I become in manhood.

Goodnight, dear man!

Yours

John Addington Symonds

---

1. The *Complete Poems and Prose of Walt Whitman, 1855–1888* (1888) in 600 copies. See L 1757, where he speaks of the future "incalculable pecuniary value" of the autographed books.
2. See L 1728.
3. Symonds' brackets. The poem follows since it is not easily come by:

Calamus.

8

LONG I thought that knowledge alone would suffice me—O if I could but obtain knowledge!

Then my lands engrossed me—Lands of the prairies, Ohio's land, the southern savannas, engrossed me—For them I would live—I would be their orator;
Then I met the examples of old and new heroes—I heard of warriors, sailors, and all dauntless persons—And it seemed to me that I too had it in me to be as dauntless as any—and would be so;
And then, to enclose all, it came to me to strike up the songs of the New World—And then I believed my life must be spent in singing;
But now take notice, land of the prairies, land of the south savannas, Ohio's land,
Take notice, you Kanuck woods—and you Lake Huron—and all that with you roll toward Niagara—and you Niagara also,
And you, Californian mountains—That you each and all find somebody else to be your singer of songs,
For I can be your singer of songs no longer—One who loves me is jealous of me, and withdraws me from all but love,
With the rest I dispense—I sever from what I thought would suffice me, for it does not—it is now empty and tasteless to me,
I heed knowledge, and the grandeur of The States, and the example of heroes, no more,
I am indifferent to my own songs—I will go with him I love,
It is to be enough for us that we are together—We never separate again.

1762. *To Margaret Symonds*

[Davos, ca. Dec. 15, 1889]

[Dear Madge]

Well, poor old Browning—glorious old Browning, as happy in his felicitous death[1] as in his vigorous and manly life—lies dead in the Palazzo Rezzonico[2] . . . I fear that by his last book of poems, now consecrated by the aureole of a poet's death, he will have turned a flood of tourists into Asolo.[3] The inn is to be 'improved' in order that the middle class may go round 'Asolando.'

[Incomplete]

---

1. Robert Browning died Dec. 12.
2. Browning's home in Venice, bought for his son in 1887.
3. Browning had been living at Asolo, about 30 miles from Venice. The title of the book, *Asolando: Fancies and Facts* (1889), which appeared on Dec. 12, the day of Browning's death, comes from Asolo and from *asolare,* meaning "to disport in the open air." See Browning's dedication to Mrs. Arthur Bronson.

1763. *To Charles Sayle*[1]

Am Hof, Davos Platz, Switzerland. Dec: 16. 1889.

My dear Sayle

I am proud that you should turn to me for advice or for sympathy in your present situation.

It was inevitable that you should come to some such a choice of ways, about this time of your life; & those who have been interested in your career, cannot but have expected it.

I think that I comprehend how you are standing in the material relations of the matter. Work at John's undertaken,[2] to last another year. No immediate anxiety about money. Family duties.

The question then is: What are you, at the age of 25, to begin for yourself: it being understood that you have elected literature as your line.

I think you are right to discard poetry as the main-work of your life. I do not say this on the strength of my opinion of what you have already published; but because your own instinct leads you to this decision. To put it very frankly, I do not think your poems of that quality to make a friend say: "poetry is your vocation—anything else would be a mistake." But nothing is more liable to mislead a critic than the early work of men in poetry. Vide Shelley, Byron. Therefore, if you told me that poetry was your line, the line you must pursue, I should say: Macte virtute esto [Be strong]! & wait the issue. But, as you do not tell me this, rather the contrary, I am justified in perceiving that the obscure impulse of a developing consciousness in you does not lead imperatively in that direction. That being so, I think you are wise to abstain from it, except as a $\pi\alpha\rho\epsilon\rho\gamma o\nu$ [useless addition], the channel of occasional expression.

Upon this point I feel a deep sympathy with you. At your age, or a little earlier, I made the renouncement of poetry as my work. And I must tell you, to be fair, that I have often doubted since whether I was right. What I have done in literature, has been done on the strength of this renouncement; & what I have published in verse or translation of verse has been, as I said above, a $\pi\alpha\rho\epsilon\rho\gamma o\nu$.

No man can venture to counsel another upon this most important decision. He can only say, as I have already said, that if the poetical impulse is not overwhelming (as it was in the cases of Shelley & Byron), then it is safe to renounce; & the consequences will have to be accepted.

Now I attack the immediate problem facing you: what to begin upon. I agree with O.B.[3]—*something big*. But I am not sure that a man can find out what the big thing he ought to do is, so very easily. I am inclined to believe that he has to feel about some while before he finds it.

To go back again to my own experience. Between 25 & 30, I wrote essays on Greek Poets, Dante, all sorts of things, always trying to take up an adequate subject, & to put my whole strength (such as it then was) into what I did. I also wrote pictorial pieces about Italy, sketches & so forth, preluding to the work I eventually chose.

That was, as you know, the R. in Italy. But I did not attack this till I was past 30; & I think I ought to have waited longer.

One thing I feel I am right in recommending to you. That is, to collaborate with *nobody* in literature at the beginning. For instance, I warn you off such a gigantic undertaking as a final edition of the text of Dante, with OB for collaborater. The reasons are manifold why you should not engage in that. Literature ought to be the final expression of a man's personality. And he cannot divide it with another. Then the long years absorbed in such a labour would leave you only as the co-editor of Dante—unprepared for other work, inefficient in the use of literary expression as the vehicle of a decisive impact on the mind of your contemporaries.

I am writing so rapidly that I doubt whether I shall make my meaning quite plain. But you are quick of intelligence, & will seize what I want to say.

What you need to find, is such a method of working as will in the next fifteen years make you a clear somebody, a voice, the voice of a man speaking through books. And then, when you have won your position as such, you may pour your personality out upon the willing ears of the world in any or every way.

But you must win your spurs (to mix metaphors emphatically) off your own bat.

My friends, when I was of your age, gave me the same advice as they give you—to do something Big. Following it, I began a history of the Elizabethan Drama, & finished it, & put it away dissatisfied upon a shelf. A fragment survives in the volume called "Shakspere's Predecessors," wh was a *refacimente* of the first part of that old history. I also undertook a translation of Zeller's "Geschichte der Griechischen Philosophie,"[4] two bulky volumes of wh I consigned to the flames.

I found that I could not follow their advice by "taking up some big subject," as they bade me. My task was to *find* a subject for myself. And very hard it was. But through the many efforts I made, I think that I discovered *myself* & my capacities.

And I really, *in fin de conti,* cannot recommend to you another way than this of exploration for yourself. Go to the discovery of your real impulse, your leading capacities & passions in literature; & pursue this quest by earnest studies & copious composition.

You have one leading indication for the choice of your work—as you told me recently,—an aroused interest in Catholicism.

Would it not be well to follow that lead? It is one which offers you an ample field. Write *études* here & there, & make them not only thorough but attractive, upon Catholic personalities, curious questions relating to the growth of Catholic belief, remarkable episodes in the history of Catholic opinion.

Pardon me if I seem to be telling you to bathe in Jordan.

Bathe in any streams you like. The great thing is to bathe. Not to stand wondering what *big* task to choose.

Work with your young brain—& with what I never had, your young health—but work, so far as in you lies, upon some certain line; & regard all you do for a few years to come, as essays in the art of style, & expression, & exact study.

I do really believe this is the best advice I can give you, in answer to the question of your letter.

But it looks so naively simple, so much as though I said "learn from me," that I am quite ashamed of giving it.

Do you know? Very many young men come to me, & ask: "What shall I begin? I want to do literature!!." I always say to them: "Do you *see a subject?*" If they answer: "No: I do not see a subject yet; but I feel my power of handling one; & I want you to advise me what to take."; then I reply invariably: "Find a subject for yourself; good literature is the utterance of a man's self; what another man puts into his mouth to say, or dictates to him on paper as a theme, will never express the man. He must discover it, be it, present it as a portion of himself. In this way only he will become somebody in literature."

Now all this is unsatisfactory to you, I doubt not. But you will see, from my lengthy scrawl, in what way I think you ought to approach the problem you put before me as to your immediate work; & how much I wish to serve you—wishing infinitely that I could be of better service.

Yours affectionately

J.A. Symonds

I am glad you keep a memory of our meeting at Cambridge. I keep a very pleasant one. All, up here, is so different, and, as you remark, so "unexpected."

Write to me again, & say whether I have been in any way ignorantly disagreeable to your sense or sensibility.

---

1. See L 1502.
2. The reference is unclear.
3. Oscar Browning. See L 1559.
4. See index for references to this work in Vol. I of these letters.

1764. *To Edmund Gosse*

Am Hof, Davos Platz, Switzerland. Dec: 19 1889

My dear Gosse

I was both surprised & delighted by the charming volume, your gift,[1] which reached me here a few days ago, & to wh I have been constantly turning in moments of leisure since.

I should before this have ventured to send you verses of my own; but that I was under the impression that my work in this way seemed to you mistaken. I feel so uncertain as to its quality myself, that I am far from resenting any such opinion.

At any rate I thoroughly enjoy your poetry, & thank you greatly for "Firdausi." I love the poet's books which have been given me by the poet's self.

"Firdausi in Exile" seemed to me successful in what I know to be a difficult style—narrative in verse deliberately sustained at a level above the pedestrian, so as to admit of occasional "soaring" without the danger of imperilling simplicity. My Italian Studies in ottava rima *novelle*[2] make me know how very difficult it is to preserve the exactly right pitch.

But I believe I shall always turn, when I take up your book, to Liber Cordis & the Sonnets.[3] Some of the latter have the mark of immortality upon them. I cannot believe that "I stand before you as a beggar stands" will fade from the memory of Englishmen. It so happens that the lines next to this Sonnet "Illusion" have taken my fancy. So too "Apologia" touches me.

I am glad to see that even a critic who grudges you praise[4] has felt the charm of "A Ballad of the Upper Thames."

Among many (to me) new faces of poems, I hail one or two old friends: "Gilead," "Palingenesis," "Theocritus."[5]

I notice that in the last sentence but one I have let slip a word about criticism of your poems. I trust you will not think it impertinent if I remind you that every man who is tending to a confirmed position in literature or art, after he has put forth considerable samples of his work, reaches a point at which he is subjected to scrutinizing & what often looks like unkindly criticism. I have always observed the curious operation of this φθόνος [envy]. We must each in turn be prepared for it & just endure it, passing through those vapours like the angel who came down to gain for Virgil & Dante entrance into the city of Dis.[6] But considering how meagerly the singer's & the writer's labour is rewarded, it does seem hard that he should also get harsh words, sneers, taunts, & odious comparisons hurled at him by the brotherhood of his own craft. Pray excuse me if I have transgressed the limits of reserve. But I live so out of the way here that I take liberties I might not venture on in London. Believe me always very sincerely yours

John Addington Symonds.

---

1. Gosse, *Firdausi in Exile* (1885).

2. He refers to unpublished verse sketches.

3. "Liber Cordis" and "Sonnets and Quatorzains" were two groups of poems in the *Firdausi* vol., pp. 171–200 and 201–18, respectively.

4. Gosse is praised in *The Athenaeum*, I (1886), 130–31. *The Academy*, XXVIII (1885), 386–87, calls "Firdausi" and "The Island of the Blest" poor, but praises "A Ballad of the Upper Thames" and some sonnets.

5. Reprinted in *The Collected Poems of Edmund Gosse* (1911): "Gilead," p. 175, "Palingenesis," pp. 211 ff., and "Theocritus," pp. 181 ff.

6. *Inferno,* Canto IX, ll. 64–106.

1765. *To Margaret Symonds*

Am Hof, Davos Platz, Switzerland. Dec: 20 1889

My dearest Madge

Your last letter to me brought great joy to the family. And I am thankful that your doubts and hesitations about returning are at an end. I

431

quite understand what it must be to be going on so long in a strange household, & so peculiar a family.

I want you, when you get near a Japanese shop (there is a very good one at Oxford in the Corn market) to buy me half a dozen knickknacks—especially metal match boxes in the shape of fishes ugly faces etc. I gave my friend Anton Juon[1] one wh I had brought from England, a shiny silvery fish it was, wh caused so much satisfaction that I feel I should like to have an assortment on hand.

I also want you to get me at Liberty's[2] another of those golden-looking Indian bowls. I gave one to K[atharine], & the other I gave away to a man here. I never can keep anything of this sort.

If you tell me what these things cost, I will send the money.

I hope you got my cheque for £2.2.0. enclosed in the last letter I wrote you. I fancy it had not come when you wrote.

Please give my love to Robert & Isabella [Otter] & Bobby,[3] with all good wishes for the season. The same to you from yr most aff

[No signature]

---

1. A favorite Davos athlete. In L 1864 Symonds writes to Janet Ross soliciting her aid in locating a position for Juon in Florence.

2. "Liberty & Co., of Regent Street are perhaps the most popular firm of London of To-Day, at all events with ladies. Their windows are fitted up with consummate taste, and comprise one of the attractions of the main thoroughfare. It is difficult to say what Liberty & Co. do not sell."—Charles Eyre Pascoe, *London of To-Day: An Illustrated Handbook for 1891* (1891), p. 406.

3. Robert John Charles Otter (1881–1915), son of Isabella Gamble, Symonds' cousin, and Robert Henry Otter (1836– ?), one of his literary executors.

1766. *To Arthur Symons*

[Davos] Dec. 21, 1889.

Dear Mr Symons,

I have your letter of the 16th and your poems.[1] You ask me a very difficult question about these, which I feel it almost impossible to answer. A reviewer of Gosse's last book said a very true thing; that nothing but a whole nation's verdict can confer the title of poet on a versifier. I am utterly incompetent, and I believe any single critic is incompetent, to help you to assurance in this matter. I hold, however, that the strong thirst to be a poet is a sign of the vocation. And I can say this much with confidence—that you already possess the power of versifying with skill and also of constructing energetic single lines. I should like to know how old you were when you wrote the pieces you have sent me. You told me that you are still quite young. This makes me think less than I should otherwise do, of the Swinburnian reminiscences in your work—felt certainly in the blank verse. The Sonnet to Aeschylus is decidedly good. I find a wrong note in

shamed

The craven Greeks.

Some Greeks were craven in that crisis. But with the morn-song of the Hellenes ringing in our ears from Aeschylus' Persae, this touch seems to me wrong. The version of Du Bellay's lyric is very right, I think that shows real command of language and real poetic feeling. There is force of imagination in "By an Empty Grate" and a sweet human note upon the close. You use the word *shudder* too often in it. And for the grimness of the subject I think the first 6 stanzas are a little too prolix.

To tell you the truth of my impression: the poem on Casella strikes me as inadequate in its working out to what is highly original in the idea. I should much like to know exactly how old you are[2] There is so much promise as well as already acquired mastery of rhythm and language in these pieces that, if you are really very young, I should wish to beg you wait and work some years in solitude before you try the issue of publication.

I should indeed be glad if I could utter more uncertain notes than this. But art of all kinds has to be pursued alone; and none but the divine spirit in the man sustains him on that arduous path. It is as dangerous to stimulate as to repress the impulse, if one outside by words of encouragement or coldness can do either. If you are perfectly free to choose your vocation and if you feel that ardent desire for poetry, then you have shown me enough to make me say with decision: Labour hard at the poet's task, but do not be precipitate in publishing. Learn the craft. Fortify your mind by select reading and assiduous study of nature. Gain mastery by translation from the best models. Write from your heart only at your highest moments. I shall be glad to hear from you again about this ambition which is so noble and has taken so strong a hold on you. Remember how very diffident in judging I must be who know so absolutely nothing about your past and present and yourself. Send me, if you will, a photograph.

Very sincerely yours

J. A. Symonds.[3]

1. Symons seems to have sent Symonds poems in manuscript which were intended for *Silhouettes* (1892). Symonds had received *Days and Nights* (1889) earlier. See L. 1706.

2. He should have been able to guess since they had met in November. See L 1750.

3. In the typescript Symons added that in an unspecified letter Symonds said: "You are quite right to regard art, literature, as the noblest function of your life. What I gently said, and somewhat cynically perhaps, to the contrary, is very much the result of a long experience in renunciation and patience."

1767. *To Samuel Richards*[1]

Am Hof Dec: 24. 1889

Dear Mr Richards

Very many thanks for the photographs, some of which are excellent & suited to my purpose.

I hope, as you say, that we shall be able to look through them together later on in the week.

And let me add, I hope that you will soon be through with the influenza. I cannot help fearing you caught it in my draughty shed.

I shall keep several of these studies.[2] But if another lot comes, it will interest me to see more of the male figure. For the particular object I have in view the male nude, in photography, is more instructive owing to the greater salience of the muscular & bony structure.

Wishing you, Mrs Richards, & your lovely little girl, a very Merry Christmas (as if that were possible at Hotel Belvedere) & many many happy years,

I am very sincerely yours

John Addington Symonds

---

1. See L 1708.

2. Photographs of nude males assisted Symonds in forming principles for his "The Model" and "Realism and Idealism," 2 essays in *E S & S* (2 vols., 1890).

1768. *To Samuel Richards*

Am Hof, Davos Platz, Switzerland. Dec: 26. 1889

Dear Mr Richards

I have now enough (& more than enough) proofs of those essays to make it worth while your looking at them—if you still feel any inclination **to do so.**

The two I most wanted to ask your opinion on are called "Realism & Idealism" & "The Model." (Slips 44–56).[1]

I should much like some day to compare with you the studies of the nude & the photographs of Raphael's drawing & Flandrin's picture wh I talk about in "The Model."

You will also see why I am at present interested in getting reproductions both of the nude in life & of artists' transcripts from the nude in drawings.

I hope sincerely that you are quite well again & remain very truly yours

J A Symonds

---

1. See L 1767.

1769. To Alfred W. Goodman[1]

Am Hof, Davos Platz, Switzerland. Dec: 27. 1889

Dear Mr Goodman

I write this line to thank you for your Christmas Card, & heartily to reciprocate the good wishes contained in it.

I often think of the only time we passed together. If you have read "A Page of my Life" in the Fortnightly,[2] you must have been reminded of that afternoon from Chur to Lenz we spent in a retour-wagen.[3]

Should it come to other pages . . .[4] episode into one, & you will then see how I passed the evening at Lenz, while you were rolling on to Bergün & supping there alone.

Your kind recollection of me makes me bold to ask whether you will not some times send me what you write. I am out of the way here for following up the traces of friends in literature, as you will well imagine— living as I do in my own house, shut off even from such Magazine Societies as there may be in the hotels.

A happy year & many of them to you from yours. . . .[4]

[Incomplete]

---

1. See L 1675.
2. *The Fortnightly Review*, LII (1889), 764–75. See also L 1748.
3. A round-trip carriage.
4. A section has been cut from the letter.

1770. *To Edmund Gosse*

Am Hof, Davos Platz, Switzerland. Dec: 28 1889

My dear Gosse

I have been waiting all this while, since I wrote on Christmas Eve, for the book (Pria-etc).[1] It has not come; & I fear there must have been some mischance.

If it has been lost in the post, I need hardly say that I shall be prepared to take the pecuniary loss upon myself. But I should like to know how it was sent, & whether it can be traced & recovered.

Meanwhile I will no longer delay this letter & the little essay[2] I spoke to you about in my last.

The Sandow[3] photographs arrived. They are very interesting, & the full length studies quite confirm my anticipations with regard to his wrists ankles hands & feet. The profile & half-trunk is a splendid study. I am very much obliged to you for getting them for me.

My wife, I believe, wrote to Mrs Gosse, urging you to come here, on the strength of something you had said to my daughter Madge. I cannot say how glad I should be to welcome you both here, & to have some of those long talks which are so easy & delightful in this solitary place.

If you are not afraid of influenza, I do hope you will come. But I am in duty bound to inform you that it is raging here. We have at present three cases in the house; & all the hotels are full of it. Up to the present time I have escaped. But I see from the state my friends are in after they have had it, that it is no slight matter for delicate people.

I hope that "A Problem in Greek Ethics"[4] will fare better than the book you sent me. Keep it as a gift from me, & again I say—please be discreet with it.

For the New Year all good wishes:
from your friend

J A Symonds

---

1. Since the letter referred to seems to have disappeared, the book mentioned is not known.

2. In L 1764 of Dec. 19, 1889, there is no mention of the essay.

3. Eugene Sandow (1867–1925), German strong man and physical culturalist; exhibited at Chicago's World Fair (1893).

4. Symonds' study of Greek male love published in only 10 copies (1883).

1771. *To Arthur Symons*

[Davos, Dec. 28, 1889]

[Dear Symons]

. . . . They come from my part of England where my paternal home is. Miss Cooper's study of the Faun is quite admirable. That seems to me the highest point to which Michael Field[1] has reached.

I congratulate you on the good time you have had at Paris. It is the duty of the human soul to give itself good times, and to get the most it can out of them. This philosophy of life is the reverse of the Calvinistic. But I believe that it is just, and squares with the nature of me. But we must have enough of the theologian left in us, to know that we have to use our opportunities for our own benefit. I hope to see the result of your experiences in Paris in literature very shortly.

Meanwhile, I wish you would come to see me here—or in Venice, where I hope to be again next autumn. If we cannot meet, I pray you not to lose touch with me.[2]

[Incomplete]

---

1. Joint pseudonym of Katherine Harris Bradley and her niece, Edith Emma Cooper. See L 1216. The relationship began when Miss Bradley was 19 and Miss Cooper 3, and continued until their deaths, 9 months apart. They wrote 8 volumes of poetry, 27 poetic tragedies, a masque, a journal, and letters.

2. Symons followed this section with this comment:

As this letter contains some of the writer's own confessions, it is inevitable that I also should make confession: that whenever I read this letter in the original I cannot imagine why I did not accept so kind and so unexpected an invitation to stay with him at Davos or to see him in Venice: it seems more inconceivable than ever; for if I had seen him in Venice or stayed with him in Davos I should certainly have wandered with him, and it is probable that he might have read aloud some chapter or other out of his Autobiography. . . .

1772. *To W. Kineton Parkes*[1]

Davos Jan 1 1890

That first wise man of yore who Love portrayed—
    A naked child, with wings that woo the air,
    And hands that are so marvellously fair,
    And round his beauteous eyes yon bandage laid—

He truly Love only too well displayed;
  Seeing how lovers are constrained to bare
  Their fervid thought, that master well was ware,
  And knew how reason's light they ne'er obeyed.
He gave Love arrows, torch in hand, a bow
  Wherewith from far & near those wounds to deal;
  Sweet wounds; but to the heart eternal sorrow.
Who flies, Love faces: feeds who with him go,
  On hopes uncertain: useth men to feel
  Infinite fear, derision night & morrow.

My dear Sir

Above is one of my translations from Alberti,[2] wh has not yet been printed. The other you will find (& it is by far the better & more characteristic sonnet of the two) in my *Vagabunduli Libellus* (Smith & Elder, 1884) at page 178, where too (on page 179) is a version of Da Vinci's Sonnet.

I am so confused with influenza that I am not fit to write more, or to thank you as yet intelligently for your Preraph: Movement.[3]

Very truly yrs

J A Symonds

1. See L 1749.
2. See L 1749.
3. See L 1749.

1773. *To Mary Ann Sykes*

Davos Platz. January 9, 1890.

My dearest Auntie,

You will think I have been forgetting you all this time. But I have been ill with the influenza, and have had it pretty badly. . . . And I have been always more or less delirious for the last fortnight. That is the worst of having educated one's brain from childhood up to now in old age, out of all proportion with the rest of one's body.

That is a kind of crime, which revenges itself upon the culprit sooner or later.

In the case of great poets and prophets and artists—Shakespeare,

Isaiah, Michael Angelo—it is right perhaps to over-educate the brain. The world gets something by the hypertrophy of this organ—as we get something (in the shape of *pâté de foie gras*) from the hypertrophy of liver in geese.

But it does not really do for little people like me to cultivate their brains so much. We cannot give a great tragedy, a great prophecy, a great statue, to the world—and are not even so happy as the Strasburg geese are, in being able to give a good *pâté de foie gras*—in exchange for our comfort and our life.

Since this illness fell upon me, I have felt the truth of all that. It has made me the sport of my own brain—the fever going into it, and rendering life intolerable as well as humiliatingly inefficient.

There is a great deal too much of education in this age. We force and force—and what do we get by all the forcing? Miserable people like me and . . .

. . . The real thing is that I love you very dearly and wish you a good year, and many good years, and tell you that, as I grow older, I want always to be humbler, simpler, nearer to the truth of human nature, closer to God in the world—to cast away the trifles of culture, to grasp the facts of life, and in a steadfast frame of mind to prepare myself for the closing of our earthly accounts.

How small the life of men is; and yet how much we have to learn in it. I began so wrongly, that I shall go out of life with much less real knowledge than the simple folk have, whom you have always loved and from whom I am every year coming to learn more than books can teach me. . . .

Your grateful and ever loving,

J. A. S.

1774. *To W. Kineton Parkes*

[Postcard]

Am Hof, Davos Platz, Switzerland. Jany 18. 1890

My dear Sir

I shall gladly see the Sonnet of Alberti in "Igdrasil."[1] Please send me a copy of the magazine when it appears—& let me have a proof of the Sonnet for correction.

By the way, the number you say you sent me has not arrived.

Very truly yours

J A Symonds

Kineton Parkes

P.S. I open this to make a suggestion. It is—whether you would like to have some original & hitherto unpublished piece of poetry lyric for "Igdrasil"?

---

1. See L 1772.

1775. *To Horatio Forbes Brown*

Davos, Jan. 19. [1890]

[Dear Horatio]

This influenza is a very singular thing. It has left me all to bits. What I resent most is that my head is gone. I cannot write—literature I mean—and hardly a decent letter. And I cannot follow a difficult book. I tried Pater's "Appreciations" to-day, and found myself wandering about among the precious sentences, just as though I had lost myself in a sugar-cane plantation—the worse for being sweet.

I have not seen T. E. B.'s[1] poems. I think I don't want to read any more poems. "Demeter"[2] and "Asolando"[3] both bored me beyond words. The fuss people make about art and books begins to annoy me in a way which is really stupid. I have no doubt it is my own fault. And I am chief of sinners, having written so much about books and art. But I know when I have had enough and have lost my joy in such things. The time seems to have come; and I am not going to be a hypocrite, and pretend that I care for what I regard as froth and bladders.

[Incomplete]

---

1. The Manx poet, T. E. Brown, whose collected poems were edited by W. E. Henley, Graham Dakyns, and Horatio Brown in 1900. See L 501.
2. 1889, by Tennyson.
3. 1889, by Browning.

1776. *To Margot Tennant*

[Davos, Jan. 19, 1890]

[Dear Margot]¹

Do you know that I have only just now found the time, during my long days and nights in bed with influenza and bronchitis, to read Marie Bashkirtseff?² (Did ever name so puzzling grow upon the Ygdrasil³ of even Russian life?)

By this time you must be quite tired of hearing from your friends how much Marie Bashkirtseff reminds them of you.

I cannot help it. I must say it once again. I am such a fossil that I permit myself the most antediluvian remarks—if I think they have a grain of truth in them. Of course, the dissimilarities are quite as striking as the likenesses. No two leaves on one linden are really the same. But you and she, detached from the forest of life, seem to me like leaves plucked from the same sort of tree.

It is a very wonderful book. If only *messieurs les romanciers* could photograph experience in their fiction as she has done in some of her pages! The episode of Pachay,⁴ short as that is, is masterly—above the reach of Balzac; how far above the laborious, beetle-flight of Henry James! Above even George Meredith. It is what James would give his right hand to do once. The episode of Antonelli⁵ is very good, too, but not so exquisite as the other.

There is something pathetic about both "Asolando" and "Demeter,"⁶ those shrivelled blossoms from the stout old laurels touched with frost of winter and old age. But I find little to dwell upon in either of them. Browning has more sap of life—Tennyson more ripe and mellow mastery. Each is here in the main reproducing his mannerism.

I am writing to you, you see, just as if I had not been silent for so long. I take you at your word, and expect Margot to be always the same to a comrade.

If you were only here! Keats said that "heard melodies are sweet, but those unheard are sweeter." How false!

> Yes, thus it is: somewhere by me
>> Unheard, by me unfelt, unknown,
> The laughing, rippling notes of thee
>> Are sounding still; while I alone
> Am left to sit and sigh and say—
>> Music unheard is sweet as they.

This is no momentary mood, and no light bubble-breath of improvisatory verse. It expresses what I often feel when, after a long night's work, I light my candle and take a look before I go to bed at your portrait in the corner of my stove.

I have been labouring intensely at my autobiography. It is blocked out, and certain parts of it are written for good. But a thing of this sort ought to be a master's final piece of work—and it is very exhausting to produce.

[No signature]

---

1. See L 1640, n. 2.

2. In Russian, Marya Konstantinova Bashkirtseva (1860–84), painter and diarist of a wealthy noble family; lived most of her life in Paris; exhibited in Paris Salon (1880); author of *Journal*, which caused much discussion (pub. Paris, 1887; Engl. tr. by Mathilde Blind, 1890), and *Letters* (correspondence with Guy de Maupassant) (1891).

3. In Scandinavian mythology, the great tree whose branches and roots extend through the universe.

4. The original of this letter is not available and Margot Tennant may have transcribed "Pacha" as "Pachay." "Pacha" was a Paul, Bashkirtseff's first cousin, with whom she fell in love: Bashkirtseff, *Journal,* Aug. 23 (Aug. 11), 1876 ff.

5. *Ibid.,* Jan. 10, Jan. 22, 1876 and ff. She fell in love with Pietro Antonelli, nephew of Cardinal Giacomo Antonelli (1806–76), prelate and statesman serving under Pope Pius IX (1792–1878), who proclaimed the dogma of the Immaculate Conception (1854) and through the Vatican Council of 1869–70 promulgated the doctrine of papal infallibility.

6. Browning's *Asolando* and Tennyson's *Demeter* both appeared in 1889.

1777. *To Horatio Forbes Brown*

Davos, Jan. 21, 1890

[Dear Horatio]

I have got your letter of the 19th with its continued bad news—of fog and lingering bronchitis. We are better off in many respects; for our sunshine has been all but uninterrupted for six weeks, and the frost by no means as hard as usual. I am also able to report a considerable advance towards health. My head, which suffered so severely from the influenza, is recovering a normal tone. Unfortunately, to balance these benefits, I sprained my ankle again the other day. I have cut thirty-four noble pine trees in my wood upon the Seehorn; and I went to see which I would keep for planks, and which I would saw up for fire-wood. Scrambling about upon the huge smooth stems coated with smooth snow and ice, I slipped—

and have been three days lame with arnica bandages on to keep swelling down.

The beauty of the scene in the wood, the purity of the air, the perfect stillness, the flooding sunlight, the solemn giants all around, and the men at work athletically hauling those unmanageable boles down chasms and ravines—all this was worth a sprain!

We have had our Toboggan Races at Klosters. Two days of two sorts of competition. The prizes on both days were divided between an American, S. Whitney, first in each event, and Swiss people. No English and no natives of any other nation touched them. Minsch was away. My friend Ammann came third in one race and second in the other, which pleased me. The Committee disqualified him because he was 1½ minutes late at the starting point. I do not think they were wrong.

I have had no proofs of either of my books[1] since Dec. 17. When I look at the proofs of the "Essays" already here, I am almost glad that no more come. This is in many ways the most important book I have written for publication. You will agree that my trials on the path of publication (regarding a book I set very great store on) are enough to provoke a saint: I go back to the fourteenth century in Graubünden[2] when I am vexed. They are printing it infamously with a typographical carelessness which makes one sick.

I am immersing myself in the mediæval history of Graubünden. It is a thorny subject. The chronicles are very defective; and the literary histories are written in absolutely sixth-rate style. The two eyes of mediæval history are pedigrees and geography. Both fail me. Of the baronial families who strove and expired here, I have only scattered names. What would I give for a Litta![3] Of their castles again I have only names. No maps exhibit them. It is dreary plodding. But I disentangle a great deal. And the work is not quite so feverish as a psychological autobiography.[4] By the way, the house of Matsch was one of the four or five most eminent feudal families of Rhaetia. Not very old or brilliant nobility, but (like the house of Hapsburg) intensely acquisitive and tenacious. It rose into eminence as a chief vassal of the See of Chur, held bailiwicks for the Bishop in all the Vintschgau, Engadine, Münsterthal, Bormio, Puschlav. One of my brothers is dealing with German feudal terms. The modern dictionaries do not help. And I doubt whether there are exact analogues, for all the several sorts of tenures, in English mediæval nomenclature.

You will observe that I have recovered tone after the last letter I wrote to you. I am reconciled to literature and study as *palliatives*. I do not believe in them as substantial factors in life. Only when I am in fairly good spirits do they amuse me and help me to pass the time.

[Incomplete]

---

1. "An Introduction to the Study of Dante," new edition, and *E S & S*. The former was published by A. & C. Black, Edinburgh (1890), the latter by Chapman and Hall (2 vols., 1890).

2. The Swiss canton, site of Davos.

3. A reference to Count Pompeo Litta's *Famiglie celebri d' Italia* (1819–38).

4. Parts of this study appeared in his "Davos in the Olden Days," *OLSH* (1892), pp. 28–58.

1778. *To A. & C. Black Co.*

[Postcard]

[Davos] Jan 27. /90

Dante[1]

Last sheets received tonight. Will correct & return them immediately.

But *Preface* is wanting. Send me that please. I have no copy. I will alter it in the paragraphs wh require adjustment, & add a *dedication page*.

J A Symonds
Davos Platz

---

1. See L 1777.

1779. *To Samuel Richards*[1]

Am Hof, Davos Platz, Switzerland. Jany 27. 1890

Dear Mr Richards

Thank you heartily for your very kind & far too flattering note of yesterday.

I too have been more or less ill all this month, at first with the influenza, afterwards with bronchitis. I cannot shake the latter off, & am suffering a good deal in general health by the want of my usual amount of air & exercise.

It is exactly 5 weeks since the proofs of my essays stopped coming. I cannot imagine for what reason; & must make enquiries. Nothing of moment has been added to those you saw. But when they begin again, I will communicate them to you.

I was not sorry, while in bed, & very miserable with a confused stupid brain, to be free of them. But now I am beginning to be anxious.

My wife & I are going down to meet my daughter [Margaret] tomorrow. She is coming from England. I too have some business which I must transact at Chur. I hope to be back again on Thursday.

After that, we must look forward to some more meetings & pleasant talks. Perhaps you will be well enough to come to me—even to carry out our project of your staying a few days in this house.

I can assure you that I enjoy & profit by your society quite as much as you can possibly find any good in mine.

Very sincerely yrs
John Addington Symonds.

---

1. See L 1708.

1780. *To W. Kineton Parkes*

Am Hof, Davos Platz, Switzerland. Feb: 14. 1890

Dear Mr Parkes

I have returned tonight from a short absence, & find the proof of Alberti's Sonnet,[1] wh I return at once corrected.

If you should print anything else of mine at a future time, I shall esteem it a favour to have the copy with the proof. It saves much time in correcting.

I will send you a poem for your approval. It is not quite in the manner of "Lyrics of Life & Art," which you say you like. But it is one I should be glad to print somewhere, & which has I think good work in it.

All the same, I shall not be surprised if you feel it unsuitable to Ygdrasil, & even if you tell me that it arouses a certain amount of repugnance in your mind.

It is called: "With Caligula in Rome."[2]

Should you not care for this I have an abundant store of personal lyrics, some of which I would gladly place at your disposal.

Believe me very truly yrs

J A Symonds—

Kineton Parkes Esq

---

1. See L 1772.

2. It appeared in *Igdrasil,* I (1890), 245–48. It had been printed privately in *Pamphlet V* (see Babington, p. 25).

1781. *To W. Kineton Parkes*

Am Hof, Davos Platz, Switzerland. Feb: 15. 1890.

Dear Mr Parkes

In order to fulfil my promise, I am sending you that poem about "Caligula."[1]

I do not think it will be of any use to you; for when I read it over after the lapse of many years, I see how painful it is.

The vision was a very real one, epitomizing, as dreams do, all that I had read & thought about that imperial madman.

The surcharged imagery came as a natural relief from the underlying inhumanity of the motive.

It went into print, as masses of my private work do, to save me the trouble of dealing with Ms. But it has never been published, & perhaps only three or four people have seen it during the fifteen years since it was written.

You will notice that *terza rima* is treated here upon the systems of blank verse. At one time I had a notion that the rhyming structure of the former, & the periodic structure of the latter, could be usefully combined! I think now that this was a mistake. But the experiment perhaps was worth making.

Anyhow I send the thing to you; & if you do not use it, I beg you to return it.

Believe me very truly yours

John Addington Symonds.

March 12. This letter I did not send, thinking Caligula impossible as well as too long. However, since you remind me of it in yours of March 9, I will forward the poem.

I feel proud to hear that Mr Skipsey[2] whose own work I greatly admire found anything to like in my verses.

You have a complete list of my published poems, unless you cared to include the translations of medieval Latin student songs called "Wine Women & Song," wh include in my opinion some of my best productions in the way of rhythm.

---

1. See L 1780.
2. Joseph Skipsey (1832–1903), self-taught; from age 7, a pitman in coalpits of Northumberland; edited the "Canterbury Poets" series (1884–85); custodian of Shakespeare's birthplace, Stratford upon Avon (1899–91); author of *Book of Miscellaneous Lyrics* (1878) and *Carols from the Coalfields* (1886).

1782. *To Samuel Richards*

Am Hof, Davos Platz, Switzerland. Feb: 20 1890

Dear Mr Richards

I have been desperately bad with my cold & have quite lost my voice. Else I should have asked you to come & lunch & chat with me again ere now.

I don't like to let the days pass without informing you of the reason of my silence.

Very sincerely yrs

J. A. Symonds.

1783. *To Edmund Gosse*

Am Hof, Davos Platz, Switzerland. Feb: 28. 1890

My dear Gosse

The Sonnets I alluded to in my last letter are in "Animi Figura,"[1] a copy of wh I have told Nutt[2] to send you. The whole centre of that volume (pp. 32–70) might be indicated.

Thank you for your letter of the 24th. When I last wrote, my soul was troubled & perplexed not so much with any sorrows of my own—for I can truly say with S. Augustine & yourself "jam tempore lenitum est verbum meum"[3]—but I had been musing on the insolubility of the whole problem & the terrible amount of pain & misunderstanding in the world of men around us—once more wondering whether nothing can be done to put things straighter & saner.

You will not doubt, I am sure, that what you call "the central Gospel" of that essay on the Greeks,[4] has been the light & leading of my own life. But I had to arrive at this through so much confusion of mind & such a long struggle between varied forms of inclinations & abstentions, that a large portion of my nervous force and mental activity was engaged in the contention during the years when I most needed them for tranquil study & patient labour at art. It was also the main reason of the break-down in my health.

It seems to me not only sad & tragic, but preposterous & ludicrous, that this waste should have to be incurred by one man after another, when the right ethic of the subject lies in a nutshell.

"To refine and cultivate": Yes, that is the point. To see the making of Chivalry where the vulgar only perceive vice. To recognize the physiological & psychological differences in individuals, wh render this process of elevation necessary, & the process of extirpation impossible, that is the duty wh society neglects.

Ever yours

JAS.

---

1. *Animi Figura* was published in 1882. Symonds was dissatisfied with the motivation he had provided for his persona.
2. Albert Trübner Nutt (1856–1910), head of his father's publishing business. See L 1093. Smith, Elder and Co. had published the book.
3. Already my word has been softened by time.
4. The *Problem in Greek Ethics* (privately printed, 1883).

1784. *To Margot Tennant*

[Davos, ca. March 1, 1890]

[Dear Margot]

I am at work upon a volume of essays in art and criticism, puzzling to my brain and not easy to write. I think I shall ask you to read them.

I want an intelligent audience before I publish them. I want to "try them on" somebody's mind—like a dress—to see how they fit. Only you must promise to write observations and, most killing remark of all, to say when the tedium of reading them begins to overweigh the profit of my philosophy.

I think you could help me.

[Incomplete]

1785. *To A. & C. Black Co.*[1]

[Postcard]

Davos Platz March 3/90

I send today proofs of Preface & titlepage *Intro to Study of Dante* corrected.

Please let Mr J. S. Black see the revise in case he should wish for any alteration.

I have sent the dedication to Countess Pisani,[2] & must await her answer as to the form of her name.

J A Symonds

---

1. Edinburgh publishers of the 2nd (1890) and 3rd (1893) eds. of *An Introduction to the Study of Dante*. Smith, Elder & Co. were the original publishers in 1883. A. & C. Black also published *OLSH* (1892) and the 3rd ed. of *Studies of the Greek Poets* (1893).
2. See L 1717.

1786. *To Edmund Gosse*

[Davos] March 25 1890

My dear friend

You will readily believe that I have been reading "The Taming of Chimaera"[1] with absorbing interest. Nearly all the poems which belong to this series had been favourites of mine before, & I had felt in some of them a peculiar afflautus, an *aura* of their own—espy with regard to those on pp:

182. 185. 187. 127 (a most lovely poem). 214. 215. 194. 196. 197. I had felt, I say, that these pieces breathed of friendship, rather than of what is commonly called love.

But now that I see them in their right succession, & seize their proper values—with the final accent, necessary to the leading motif, given by the three Ms Sonnets—I must even sit down upon the ground & complain to heaven that Mrs Grundy's tyranny deprives us of the natural enjoyment of such works of art as these.

You have mutilated the offspring of your heart & Muse, no less than I have, & have cast the *disjecta membra*[2] of the beautiful winged being out upon a world that cannot be expected to recognize its organic deity.

I am indeed grateful to you for having given me the Ariadne clue in this heart's mystery. Poems, which were always beautiful as verse, have become now (what is far more weighty for me than mere art, however lovely) a life-history expressed in moments of authentic inspiration, fact & feeling translated into high poetic utterance.

It is very sad, however, to reflect that the real autobiographical value, the ethical import, of such a poem as your "Taming of Chimaera," should be remorselessly and irrevocably sacrified to the prejudice of society.

Who can appreciate the organic relation to each other & to the rest of the series; in the lyrics upon pp: 194, 196, 197, without the key wh you have given me? Who can understand their ethical significance without a sense of the whole situation?

Coventry Patmore,[3] who has his hand upon the very heart-pulse of emotion, could not mistake the true deep inspiration of "Love feeds upon the fiery trial." But he would surely have rated it higher (not perhaps in poetry, but in the history of souls), if he had understood the strife of feelings, out of which that supreme Sublime Atonement was won by the poet & the man.

Imagine for a moment that the whole sequence of "The Taming of Chimaera" were put together, & its motive properly avowed; how exquisitely would then the Ms. Sonnets A.B.C. harmonize in their high lights of emotion with the cool tones of "Thou hast gone back to Arcady" & with the celestial music of "Love feeds upon the fiery trial"! And all the intermediate Sonnets would fall into their right place. Whereas, now, the world has nothing but a mangled mutilated god, the ethical & real artistic power of whom is practically undiscernible.

I feel very bitter about this. Quoque tandem Domine?[4] How long are souls to groan beneath the altar, & poets to eviscerate their offspring, for the sake of what?—What shall I call it?—an unnatural disnaturing respect for middleclass propriety.—I find no phrase for my abhorrence.

So I return to thanking you for showing me what your real force as poet & as man has been. Without the key you placed in my hand, I must have always groped & wondered.

I do not mean that the disjecta membra of your poem are not lovely & useful in their published state. But how absurd it is that they should not appear together in their proper connection, when they teach a consistent life-lesson & lead men on the path of righteousness.

For I firmly think that the 3 MS Sonnets, read together with the rest, & in particular relation to the climax expressed in the poems on pp: 194,196,197, of "Firdausi in Exile," form a piece of the highest ethical importance.

You are so much a greater artist in verse than I am, & your conclusions are so much more morally right, that I do not regret the mangling & mutilation of my own child of the Muse as I regret the fate of yours. Will you not restore the broken statue of your god? You invite me to do this for mine. I am not unwilling. But I should be happier if you undertook the work of reconstruction too.

Yours very affectionately J.A.S.

P.S. In your notes of indication you repeat the lyric on p:185 "The circle of the wind-swept ground" as Nos. 8 and 12 of the Series. Did you mean this, or was there a mistake?

---

1. Since we have been unable to locate Gosse's poem (or set of poems) "The Taming of Chimaera," we can only speculate that they were a "key," unpublished, to the meaning and the sequence of poems in *Firdausi in Exile* (1885) and were on homosexual themes. On February 24, 1890, Gosse had written to Symonds of his homosexual tendencies, and they had exchanged other letters skirting the subject.

2. A reference to Symonds' own series of sonnets on the "Chimaera" theme, "L'Amour de l'impossible," in *Animi Figura* (1882), pp. 36–49. Sonnet II, "The Furies," begins: "Chimaera, the winged wish that carries men/Forth to the bourne of things impossible." Sonnet III is entitled "Chimaera" and VI, "The Tyranny of Chimaera."

3. Gosse had probably shown the work to Coventry Patmore (1823–96), poet and assistant librarian at the British Museum (1846–65) who contributed to the Pre-Raphaelite organ *The Germ* and published a poetic celebration of married love, *The Angel in the House* (1854–62). His *Unknown Eros* (1877) may have been the inspiration for the series. The direct reference is to Patmore's "Renunciation." Patmore did not give homosexual love as high a rating as heterosexual love because, as Symonds explains, he did not understand "the strife of feelings, out of which that supreme Sublime Atonement was won by the poet & the man."

4. How long, O Lord. Revelations 6:10.

1787. *To A. & C. Black Co.*

[Postcard]

[Davos, March 29, 1890]

I write this line to say that I am going tomorrow to Italy. My address will be:

560 Zattere
Venezia
Italy

I should like to have the opportunity of seeing what cover you mean to use for the *"Introduction to Study of Dante." When do you propose to publish* the book?[1]

J. A. Symonds.

---

1. See L 1785.

1788. *To Samuel Richards*

Chiavenna March 31 1890

Dear Mr Richards

I am going to avail myself of your kind offer of help already. It is by asking whether you would go to my house & find the black leather cover of a Kodak wh I left behind. The thing is on the floor in the corner by the stove in my larger study. I should like the servant to send it, together with whatever may be found in it, on to my address at Venice

Zattere No 560
Venezia
Italia.

I stupidly left the case behind, when I sent the Kodak to be refilled the other day.

We arrived here safely yesterday morning at 11, having had a prosperous but rather eventful journey in the most superb weather.

On the further side of the Fluela from Davos, we had to run the gauntlet of three very large avalanches[1] which came down just in front of the post & blocked the road for about 500 feet. It was of course impossible to drive over them, & it was very dangerous to stay in their neighbourhood. I made my party therefore get out & walk. We scrambled over the avalanches & walked on for another 1½ hours sending all the men we met upon the road (the Wegers [road men] as they are called there) back to dig out a road for the post sledges horses etc. Avalanches were falling more or less the whole way, but none of such serious dimensions as to further impede the post; & at last we reached Süss very late, in time still to get up late to Samaden.

This sudden & unexpected shower of avalanches was due to the intense heat of Saty.

Chiavenna is one of the loveliest spots in Italy; & it is just now radiantly beautiful—such a feast of colour to the snow-starved sense of sight! The masses of broken granite cliffs here take those extraordinary hues of brown & purple wh are peculiar (in my experience) to the sub-alpine region of N. Italy. Spring flowers & rivulets hurrying through steep green lawns fill the landscape with life & promise. Indeed the air is summer.

Believe me with kind regards to Mrs Richards

to be very sincerely yours,

J A Symonds

I am going to Milan tomorrow, & shall pay a visit near Padua afterwards. So I do not expect to reach Venice before Saty.

Enclosed is a fair copy of my Proposal to the Julian School of Art.[2]

Condition

of a Prize Competition for

Six Drawings from the Nude

proposed by

John Addington Symonds

to the

Students of the Julian

School of Art

Paris

1) A prize of 600 francs, in 3 equal portions of 200 francs, is offered for six nude drawings to be made by 3 men, under the following conditions:

(a) The model is to be man between the ages of 25 & 35 years, of *strong muscular* development, not stout, showing a well-defined anatomical structure.

(b) The model is to be posed in full light standing; & students are to take their places in the usual manner by lot.

453

(c) At the end of one week the drawings shall be placed on view in the School Studio, & a jury consisting of the 3 Professors of the School shall decide upon the three best drawings made from this model.

(d) The draughtsmen of these three selected drawings shall now proceed to make three other drawings from the same model, posed in the same position, light, etc; on the following week; it being provided for by balloting that no one of the three students occupies the same place as on the previous occasion.

(e) The second set of three Drawings being thus obtained, they must first receive the approval of the Jury, one week being allotted as in the case of the former set; & then shall be given, together with the other three to the Secretary, who will immediately pay the prize money in equal sums of 200 francs to each of the selected students.

2) The drawings must not be over 18 inches high or under 17 inches, & must be on white paper. The material to be either charcoal or black crayon.

No restrictions whatever are placed upon the manner or the method of work, or the management of materials; each student being left at liberty to render the truth of the model as he best can.

3) If these prize drawings are found available for the illustration of a book, due credit will be given to the artists; & for this reason it is requested that each student sign his name plainly to his drawing.

(signed) John Addington Symonds

---

1. See the passage from the Diary, March 29, in *L & P,* pp. 237–38. Catherine, Margaret, Katharine, and Rosa, a maid, were travelling with Symonds.

2. Unfortunately, nearly all the records of the Académie Julian were destroyed by the Germans during the Occupation, World War II. We are grateful to Professor Albert Farmer of the Sorbonne for his efforts to determine whether or not the competition was in fact ever instituted. The Académie itself closed its doors in 1968.

1789. *To Samuel Richards*

560 Zattere Venezia April 8 1890

Remember me to [Henry] Read[1]

Dear Richards

When I wrote to you this morning, in a somewhat exuberant mood of rapid utterance, I forgot to send the last batch of proofs of my Essays.[2]

These complete what you already have, & finish the body of the book.

I want to call your attention to two numbers of the Appendix: namely "Note on Realism & Idealism," & "Note on The Model." The former ought, I think, to be inserted into the pamphlet you have in contemplation: since it is an extension of the main principle to other matters beyond the sphere of art.

I am not so sure about the "Note upon the Model." That consists of mere jottings, suggestions thrown out to indicate my artistic sympathies regarding the Nude.

I wish I could talk with you about the Model—Ask you whether you feel the same as I do about the inferiority of the female form in *unveiled* attitudes of movement.

In the Scala Theatre at Milan, where I saw many scores of *clothed* women dancing, I felt inclined to query my own opinion. But I resolved my doubt, to my satisfaction at least, by saying that the short skirts of the Ballerina are admirably invented to conceal what is defective in the female frame—the pelvis, & the spread of the thighs from that part of the body outward.

I will post these remaining proofs to you; & if you feel inclined to make any observation on what I have jotted down in my Appendix about "The Model," you will do me a great service. Were it desirable, & did I feel that my own instincts there expressed were just, I could form those notes into a separate section.

I am glad, for your sake, that you were not in Venice today. It has rained pitilessly; & nothing is sadder than this City of the Waters, when the Heavens are weeping over it.

Always yours

J A Symonds

---

1. See L 1671.
2. *E S & S* (2 vols., 1890).

1790. *To Samuel Richards*

[In pencil across top:] I duly received the proofs.[1] But I am very troublesome still; for the sheets I wanted were earlier ones, at the end of vol i, which form also a part of the essay on Style. Could you do me the kindness of sending them? It is not worth while to register.

560 Zattere Venice April 24 1890

My dear Richards

Your letter of the 20th with its enclosed photographs reached me yesterday, & has since been studied with the greatest attention, interest, & profit.

Last night I compared the nudes with Flandrin's étude,[2] which my friend Brown (in part of whose house I live) has here. We both agreed that Flandrin, as regards delicacy of outline & truth to nature, was "smashed up." The curve of the back, mass of the head, narrowness of the waist, bulk of the thigh, in Flandrin, seem impossible after making even large allowances for peculiarities in his model.

Of course the horizon, as you convincingly demonstrate, is wrong. I always thought, as you do, that his picture was an "académie" provided with a simple landscape background in order to give it more suggestiveness to the imagination than belongs to a plain study of the nude. Viewed from that point, & without the accurate perceptions of a trained draughtsman, I had hitherto not been disagreeably impressed by the false relation of the horizon to the pose of the figure. But now I shall never forget the discord this involves.

I am very much obliged to you, my friend, for what you have done to please & instruct me. With you I shall learn much, if you allow me to do so. Also I admire the accuracy with which you have posed the model. If we cannot in the summer get another subject which you think better or as good, photographed upon a somewhat larger scale, I should like to have plate 1 reproduced by Obernetter[3] with a copy of the Flandrin done to the same scale, as an illustration to our proposed pamphlet. So I am glad to hear that the negative has been preserved.

Walsh[4] is certainly built on a fine scheme; & I am sorry for the man who had his right arm propelled by that trapezoid pounding on his face!

I always fear that you exaggerate the importance of what I have written about these matters. Are not my ideas mere commonplaces, put out in naiveté and ignorance, which a subtler or more scientific thinker would not take the trouble to express?

All the same, it is intensely satisfactory to me to hear that an accomplished master of the art, like yourself, & one who is conversant with what is said & thought in the circles of the practical workers, thinks the utterance of such views useful.

I received a letter from Read[5] by the same post as yours. Strictly private. But what he tells me explains his situation, & throws light on many things I did not understand before. I am extremely sorry for him, chiefly because I fear there is a radical want of business faculty in some of the main points of life. I do not like to write upon the topic, lest I should break his confidence. But I will talk to you about it when we meet. I do not see how it is possible to help him effectively now. But the information he gives me makes me believe that he will not have difficulty in getting to Colorado. At this distance, I do not understand all the circumstances however. I wish his troubles had occurred before I left Davos.

I am living (for me) a rather dissipated life still, & keeping very late hours. We spent last evening with the Princess of Montenegro,[6] & did not get to bed till past 2. Those are the hours Venetians keep. The night before, I went to hear Boito's "Mefistofile," an interesting opera, wh only came to an end at 1. And so on & so on.

I shall have to put the drag on. However, I am out on the water a large part of the day, & do not do much work—except that I have been drawing up a memorial to one of our English law-peers on the subject of a modification of an antiquated statute. This sort of thing has got to be done with the greatest care.

I often wish for the air, the water, & even the wine of Davos! & think you happier in my shed than I am in this Venetian room with carved beams of the 16th century some fifteen feet above my head.

Ever gratefully & affectionately yrs

J A Symonds.

---

1. Of *E S & S.*
2. See illustrations, Vol. II.
3. The photographer, Johann Baptist Obernetter (1840–87), who invented a way of burning photographs into porcelain, enamel, and glass. At first (1867) he manufactured celluloid paper; then (1869) he turned to photogravure and gave it the form it had under the name of "Albertogravure." Later he improved dry plates and printing by colored lights.
4. A model.
5. See L 1671.
6. Princess Olga Alexandra Eugenie Marie (1859–96), daughter of Prince Danilo I [II] (1826–60) and Princess Darinka Krekvíceva of Montenegro, and cousin of Prince Nicholas (1841–1921), who succeeded her father after the assassination of her father in 1860. See Ls 1958 and 1959.

1791. *To Havelock Ellis*

560 Zattere Venice May 6 1890

Dear Mr Ellis

I want to thank you for your book [*The New Spirit*], which you so kindly sent me—and to congratulate you on it.

I thoroughly sympathise with the point of view from which it is written, and admire its criticism.

How far we agree, and why I welcome "The New Spirit", will appear to you if you look over my forthcoming "Essays Speculative and Suggestive", of which I have ordered a copy to be sent to you to the care of Messrs Bell.

I must say that I did not expect another man to group so frankly Whitman, Millet and Tolstoi together! You will see in my essay on "Democratic Art" that I have done so implicitly—not with the same directness perhaps as yourself. But the mere fact is enough to indicate a deep critical sympathy between us.

You seem to me to have succeeded as well as it is possible to succeed in the hopeless task of setting forth Whitman. I have tried over and over again (at any time during the last quarter of a century) to say what I think and feel about him, to express what I owe to him. It has never come to anything with me.

I wish you had said more about "Calamus": or, if you have formed an opinion, that you would tell me what you think. In many ways Whitman clearly regards his doctrine of Comradeship as what he might call "spinal". Yet he nowhere makes it clear whether he means to advocate anything approaching its Greek form,* or whether he regards that as simply monstrous. I have tried but have not succeeded in drawing an explicit utterance upon the subject from him. But I felt that until my mind is made up on this important aspect of his prophecy, I am unable to judge him in relation to the gravest ethical and social problems.

I have ventured to touch on this point to you because I see, from the note to p. 108, that you have already considered it—and, as it seems to me, have both arrived at the conclusion that Whitman *is* hinting at Greek feeling, and also that his encouragement of "manly love" would necessarily and scientifically imply a corresponding degradation of women.

I am inclined to think that Whitman in comradeship includes any passionate form of emotion, leaving its mode of expression to the persons concerned. It is also obvious that he does not anticipate a consequent loss of respect for women. And are we justified in taking for granted that if modern society could elevate manly love into a new chivalry, this would prejudice what the world has gained by the chivalrous ideal of woman?

His own deepest utterances on the subject are, I think, in "Primeval my love for the woman I love" and "O earth my likeness."

I should much like to hear your views upon the matter; because, as I said before, I cannot estimate Whitman in his most important relations without being more sure than I am of the ground he takes up in Calamus: nor can I so forecast the future as to feel certain what would happen to the world if those instincts of manly love which are certainly prevalent in human nature, and which once at least were idealized in Greece, came to be moralized and raised to a chivalrous intensity.

In one word, does Whitman imagine that there is lurking in manly love the stuff of a new spiritual energy, the liberation of which would prove of benefit to society? And if so, is he willing to accept, condone or ignore the physical aspects of the passion?

If you see Arthur Symons please remember me to him. Are you going together to Paris?

Very sincerely yours

J. A. Symonds.

* "When I peruse" comes nearest to this.

1792. *To Edmund Gosse*

560 Zattere Venice May 12 1890

My dear Gosse

My last letter (with I hope Pinkerton's verses[1] & some Sicilian photographs) must have crossed yours of the 8th wh I received yesterday.

You will see that I do not forget you, even though my life here is full of "exciting interests & pleasures"—& there are very many, only too many perhaps, of them.

I cannot describe the curious mosaic of this Venetian existence. I write the "pages of my life" in a diary; but I do not suppose they will see the light. It is a jumble of palaces & pothouses, princesses & countesses, gondoliers & facchini [porters], hours & hours by day upon the lagoons, hours & hours by night in strange places of the most varied description.

Work does not enter into the scheme. And "das was uns alle bändigt, das Gemeine,"[2] is almost wholly excluded.

I will send you, when I get them, the portraits of three Venetian friends, with whom I pass a good deal of time, & whom I took to the best photographer here, Vianelli, the other day. They will be more eloquent than my words.

It is good for me, meanwhile, to be able to string all these things upon the thread of my dear old friend H. F. Brown, who is both sympathetic & wise, & upon the sense of duty to my wife & three daughters who are with me.

If you care for all or any of those Sicilian Studies, please keep them. Otherwise send them back. But if you keep them, pray let me have the numbers—wh I forgot to note down. I should like to get duplicates. The pair of men crowned with fruit & leaves, with a wall background, struck me as fine.

I am touched by what you wrote about yourself. But I do not know whether I do not envy you. I have never had the sobering influence of routine. I have never really worked at anything; & though people often say they wonder at my productiveness, they have no idea how very little part literature has played in my life except as a pastime—how very unproductive I have been relatively to what I ought to have produced. The last twelve years of Swiss-Italian life, most necessary to my physical health, have detached me from ambition, society, everything that is not a mode of my self-effectuation subordinate to the prime duties & engagements of life.

Believe me yours always with affection

JAS

---

1. The last was L 1786 (March 25), but the one here referred to must be unavailable. Symonds reviewed Percy Pinkerton, *Galeazzo, A Venetian Episode, and Other Poems* in *The Academy*, XXIX (April 10, 1886), 249–50.

2. That which binds us all, the commonplace.

1793. *To the Rev. Arthur Galton*

560 Zattere Venice May 13 1890

My dear Mr Galton

I have been thinking not unfrequently of you, & of my glimpse of you at Oxford. I thought too of writing to you about your interesting (if, in my eyes, rather paradoxical) essay on the so-called Renaissance in the Hobby-Horse.[1]

But I did not write; & now comes your letter of May 8 & the little book of poems.[2]

I have read the poems through for the first time, skimming them rapidly. I will take them out again when I go to the Lido in my Sandolo,[3] & will read them on the dunes.

It is the sort of book which interests me very much, & makes me want to know the people.

Binyon[4] is very remarkable indeed, & so (in a different way) is Phillips.[5]

I somehow do not feel the note of veracity in Ghose[6]—but "Raymond & Id"[7] is a piece of rare work.

For Cripps[8] at present I feel that I care but little. You need not tell him so; for "on better judgment making," I may very likely come to more flattering conclusions.

I wonder whether those four poets would like me to write something about their book in the Academy?[9] That is almost the only place open to me—unless the HobbyHorse would do. Let me know.

"Psyche"[10] is an interesting poem. I do not seem to catch the note of a woman in it though. It has the tone of having been written about a friend or an abstraction.

You say nothing about your own academical life. Have you taken your degree—or are you, like Johnson,[11] going into the Schools in July?

Please remember me to him, & wish him good luck. You both of you forgot to come & see me at Davos, this winter. Will you come in the summer—or to Venice in the autumn? I shall be here probably alone in October, & could give two bedrooms to my friends if they would share the simple fare & service provided by the noble animal my gondolier & his little wife.

It is exceedingly pleasant at Venice now. I am as idle as the lilies, but, I fear, not so simple in my life as they are. I go to bed at all hours of the morning, never of the night. This is a Venetian habit. And I see the greatest possible variety of people—from princesses to facchini [porters]. Nowhere except in Venice can the social gamut be so nonchalantly played on.

Do you know my book on Dante wh has just been republished?[12] If you don't, would you care to have a copy?

A two-volumned set of "Essays Speculative & Suggestive"—such is the grim title—was worked by me through the press with *ribrezzo* [disgust] this winter. It is like S. Johnston's[18] mutton "badly bred, badly fed, badly cooked, & badly served," I fear—certainly abominably printed, owing to my careless abandonment of details to Chapman & Hall.

I do not know why the thing has not appeared yet. Ch & H never reply to any letter I write them.

I see little chance of coming to England. I want the mountains in the summer, & Venice calls for me in the autumn. I fear only business would draw me to England.

Very sincerely yrs.

J ASymonds

---

1. "Some Thoughts about that 'Movement,' which it is the Present Fashion to Describe too Absolutely as 'The Renaissance,' and to Admire Inordinately," *The Century Guild Hobby Horse,* V (1890), 15–27. Galton said that "the great figures of the Middle Age are . . . more complete and more valuable human beings than any of the [Renaissance] Humanists"; that the "antagonism" set up between the Renaissance and the Middle Ages is false; and that "humanists" have been too much admired. Early in the essay there are flattering references to Symonds and to Pater. There was also a second essay by Galton in this issue: "Some Letters of Matthew Arnold," pp. 47–55, containing letters from Arnold to Galton.

2. *Primavera: Poems by Four Authors* (1890), a slim pamphlet in brown cover, now scarce. We have examined a copy in the Huntington Library, one presented by Laurence Binyon to Lionel Johnson, and containing on the front and back end papers Binyon's hand written copies of Lionel Johnson's "Now is there any love at all/ In England left, for simple song?" and Dowson's "The Nuns of the Perpetual Adoration," "Cynara," "My Lady April," "The Dead Child," and "Amor Unbeatido." The theme which seems to unify the book more than any other is the death of the Muse. Stephen Phillip's "invocation," untitled, has as its opening line: "No Muse will I invoke; for she is fled!" With the exception of Binyon's brief but sprightly "O summer sun, O moving trees!" and Arthur S. Cripps' "The Seasons' Comfort," the poems are melancholy and elegiac. Thomas B. Mosher, in 1900, printed a handsome edition of four copies "ON REAL VELLUM" and included as the "Preface" Symonds' brief review of the work. See note 9 below.

3. The *sandolo* is a boat similar to the gondola, but is smaller, lighter, without benches, and without the high prow of the gondola.

4. Laurence Binyon (1869–1943), poet and Orientalist, assistant in the British Museum's department of printed books (1893–95) and later chief of Oriental works in the department of prints and drawings.

5. Stephen Phillips (1866–1915), the poet and dramatist, contributed his first published poem to *Primavera* (1890).

6. Manomohan Ghose (1869–1924) became a professor at Presidency College, Calcutta. He published *Love-Songs and Elegies* (1898) and *Songs of Love and Death,* edited and introduced by Laurence Binyon (1926).

7. Ghose's poem in *Primavera.*

462

8. Arthur Shearly Cripps (1869–1952); B. A., Trinity College, Oxford, 1891; ordained Anglican priest, 1893; missionary in Rhodesia, 1901–52; wrote *Titania* (1900). *Lyra Evangelistica* (1909), *African Verses* (1939).

9. He did: "Primavera: Poems. By Four Authors," *The Academy,* XXXVII (Aug. 9, 1890), 104.

10. Binyon's poem in *Primavera.*

11. Lionel Pigot Johnson. See Ls 1736 and 1839.

12. By A. & C. Black Co., Edinburgh.

13. See L 1674.

1794. *To* The Pall Mall Gazette

560, Zattere, Venice, May 21 [1890]

SIR,—There is one point in the flattering notice of myself which appeared in the *P.M.G.* lately that I should like to have corrected. It is said that I went at the age of thirteen to Hanover. I have never been in Hanover; and the error is copied from a villainously ill-edited essay of mine which was published in the *Fortnightly Review,*[1] where, among countless misprints, Hanover was substituted for Harrow.—Yours faithfully,

J. A. Symonds.

---

1. "A Page of My Life," LII (Dec., 1889), 764–75. See L 1795.

1795. *To* The Pall Mall Gazette.[1]

Davos Platz, June 9 [1890]

SIR,—I must ask to be allowed to say one word in answer to Mr. Frank Harris, although the point at issue has no interest for the public. My complaint was not that I have been injured in my reputation by the substitution of *Hanover* for *Harrow.* I did and do complain of this: namely, that I wrote at Mr. Harris's request an article of a personal character, which was printed without my corrections. The proofs were sent me, and I returned them by the next post, fully revised. But the editor rushed the article through without waiting for, or regarding, my corrections; and when it appeared it contained a very large amount of blunders some of which spoiled it from a literary point of view, while one at least gave the sanction of my signature to an incorrect statement about my life.—Faithfully yours.

John Addington Symonds.

---

1. The reason for this letter was this:

MR J. A. SYMONDS AND THE "FORTNIGHTLY."

To the EDITOR *of the* PALL MALL GAZETTE.

SIR,—My attention has been called to a letter of Mr. J. A. Symonds in your issue of May 27th [see L 1794], in which Mr. Symonds speaks of a "villainously ill-edited essay" of his "which was published in the *Fortnightly Review,* where among countless misprints 'Hanover' was substituted for 'Harrow.'" On the appearance of the essay I received from Mr. Symonds a most intemperate letter, which, however, was promptly followed by a postcard apologizing for the language he had used. I wrote to Mr. Symonds explaining the mischance under which he had suffered. The fact is that while preparing the *Fortnightly* for press I fell ill, and was compelled to leave the editing of Mr. Symonds's paper to the gentleman who assists me, and who is not so well acquainted with the peculiarities of Mr. Symonds's handwriting as I happen to be. I must not be taken as objecting in any way to Mr. Symonds's language. He is of course the best judge whether or not such a mistake as the substitution of Hanover for Harrow is calculated seriously to injure his reputation. The one thing of interest to the public is the fact that Mr. Symonds's choice of expressions now entitles him to claim high rank in what Mr. Coventry Patmore calls "the tomahawk school."—Yours faithfully,

FRANK HARRIS,
11, *Henrietta-street, Covent-garden,*   Editor of the "Fortnightly Review."
June 3.

[The only "peculiarity" we have ever noticed in Mr. Symonds's handwriting is that it is peculiarly clear and scholarly.—ED. *P.M.G.*]

1796. *To W. Kineton Parkes*

Am Hof, Davos Platz, Switzerland. June 9. 1890

Dear Mr Parkes

I was pleased, & I must say surprised also, at your printing my "Caligula."[1] I wrote the poem long ago, & thought it (in a turgid sort of way) good of its kind. But I somehow felt it would repell people.

May I have six copies of the number it appears in? I should like to send the poem to some friends & judges I esteem.

I do not know whether my "Wine Women & Song" is out of print. Chatto & Windus published the book; & I have got £2. odd out of the sale of it. That is all I know about it up to date. If you cannot find a copy, I can lend you the only one I possess—wh I should be obliged to beg you to return.

And now I come to the last, but to me the most interesting point, of this letter. It is to thank you for the proposed dedication of your forthcoming work to me,[2] which I accept with a sense of the honour that you do me, & with true thanks for the kindness that prompted it.

I am writing a whole mass of letters tonight, having only just returned from Venice where I spent nine weeks of almost total (& yet blissful) idleness.

Believe me most truly yrs

John Addington Symonds.

P.S. I forgot to say that if you send me the 6 copies of Ygdrasil I asked for, I am ready to pay for them.

Some lyrical poems of a different sort, I would willingly send you from time to time, if you care to have them for yr magazine.

1. "With Caligula in Rome," *Igdrasil,* I (June, 1890), 245–48; privately printed in *Pamphlet V* (see Babington, p. 25).

2. *The Painter-Poets,* selected and ed. by W. Kineton Parkes, in the "Canterbury Poets" series [1890].

1797. *To Edmund Gosse*

Venice is so far away from you, & so near to me, that I shall not send you the photographs I spoke of: only I will send one of myself wh was done there.

Am Hof, Davos Platz, Switzerland. June 13 1890

My dear Gosse

I have been here rather more than a week. I came from Venice over the mountains, wh were enjoyable in the early summer; but I had left Venice behind, my wild life there, & beauty, & so much.

I have written you many letters since I came. And I have torn them up, one after the other. There is nothing left to say, now that I have stifled all I had to say.

I felt at Venice, & I feel here, very deeply the injustice of the world—that a man like myself, who has no merits to distinguish him from the rest, should be, through luck of birth and money merely, enabled to play upon the lyre of life so largely to his satisfaction—sea, city, islands, pictures, palaces, there—here, mountains, fine air, forests, homely houses, flowers—& in both situations, intellectual enjoyment, responsive human beings, energies of heart & head.

I wish that it could come into your plan for the summer to spend some time with Mrs Gosse here. It would give my wife & myself real pleasure. We expect to stay here till the end of August.

I am getting again to work, in rather a desultory way. I was wholly idle at Venice.

Should you care to have a copy of two vols of "Essays, Speculative & Suggestive" by me, wh are announced? Essays, I find, are mostly poor stuff: twice removed from talk in energy, & thrice from life in substance. But I should be glad to give you anything I do, wh you think worthy of acceptance: as I am also satisfied, if you say you do not care for this or that.

I am too poor, I spend too much on things which make no show, to buy a bronze of Thornycroft's.[1] The offer of "Teucer" or "the Mower" tempted me. But I must keep my money for people who want it in their lives.

Goodbye tonight. I only write now to make you feel that I have been this while in touch with you. I will write again, as I beg you to do to me.

There is an odd poem of mine in this month's "Ygdrasil."[2] How it finds itself in company with so much Ruskinism is a marvel. I will send you a copy, if I get some

yours ever

JAS.

---

1. William Hamo Thornycroft (1850–1925), leading Victorian sculptor. "Teucer" (1881), regarded as his masterpiece, is in the Tate Gallery. "The Mower" (1884) is in the Liverpool Gallery. For the former and "The Sower" (1886), see plates Vol. II.
2. See L 1796.

1798. *To the Rev. Arthur Galton*

Am Hof, Davos Platz, Switzerland. June 13 1890

My dear Mr Galton

As you see, I have returned to my Alpine home. The wrench from Venice to Davos is always very trying—irritating to my nerves. This time, for certain reasons, it was more so than usual. I left so much beauty behind.

In rather a fretful mood then I took up my book of the Greek Idyllists the other day, & soothed myself with the bounding hexameters & wild Phrygian melodies of Bion.[1]

So I fell at last upon translating the Lament for Adonis.

I send this to you, with the request that if you think it could be printed in the Hobby Horse, you would forward it to Mr Horne. I do not go straight to him; for I should like you first to form an opinion. Should you decide against it, please return the Ms to me.

Perhaps I ought not to trouble you with these literary matters while you are either in or on the verge of the Schools. But after all a version of Bion's Lament is Κοῦφόν τε καὶ πτηνόν [light as a bird]—no great burden on your mind!

Do you ever see a magazine called Ygdrasil? In the June number appeared a poem of mine (written years ago) called "With Caligula in Rome." I should like you to see it; & if I obtain copies, I will send you one. It is written in terza rima treated after the free fashion (as regards break & pause) of blank verse.

Please remember me to [Lionel] Johnson, & believe me very sincerely yours

John Addington Symonds.

---

1. Bion (latter part of 2nd century B.C.), Greek bucolic poet, imitator of Theocritus. His "Lament for Adonis," in 98 hexameters, provided a model for later elegies, including Shelley's "Adonais." Galton approved of the translation and passed it on to Horne, the editor. The "Hexameters and a Note upon the Lament for Adonis, out of Bion" appeared in the *Century Guild Hobby Horse,* V (October 1890), 121–26.

1799. *To Horatio Forbes Brown*

Davos Platz June 19, 1890 1.30 at night

[Dear Horatio]

. . . . I have to-night received a copy of my Essays [*E S & S*]. . . . I am glad it is out. It is a weight off my mind. And the book has so much stuff of myself in it that I am rather glad it goes forth to the world *in forma pauperis* [in its poverty]. . . . It is off my mind: and even though one has sent some twenty-nine volumes out, one is always glad when the last has flown. I think this feeling of impatience about the rupture of the umbilical cord of authorship grows more intense the more one publishes.

[Incomplete]

1800. *To Horatio Forbes Brown*

Munich July 5 [1890]

[Dear Horatio]

Madge and I had rather a weary journey to this place—a day and a half. And at the end of it we found that the object of our pilgrimage, Mr. Richards,[1] was laid up with ice bags on his chest; the result of excitement at escaping from Davos into his old artist-haunts rather than of any organic disturbance.

All the same I felt very blue. For my only reason for coming here, as I told you—and I always speak the truth about my reasons for going to places, though people don't believe me, because I generally find so much to do in them which I did not go for—my only reason for coming to Munich was to study the modern German school of painters at the Exhibition, under his guidance.

Speaking broadly I hate Munich, and have hated it ever since I first saw it in the summer of 1860, when I wrote a dismal emotional poem among the willows of the Englische Garten. I had not then, nor in many subsequent visits, learned to mitigate its blatant pedantry and priggishness, its air of a small slice of culture-butter spread very thin over a huge expanse of German *natur-schwarzbrod*,[2] the hollow, unsubstantial, imitative, mediocre art of the place in flagrant contrast with the dull Bavarian plain and the honest Bavarian bumpkindom. The Munich Bier-Kellers are colossal; and the whole *genial* life of the place throbs in them. More than 2000 people crammed together in the Löwenbräu, listening to the Würtemburg military band, is a sight to see, as much as can be seen of it through the tobacco smoke. We are in a small pension—the very temple of the bourgeois. We have seen and are going to see oceans of works of art, old and new. I must confess that the more I see of these things the less I care for them. The old Greek statues and the old pictures are always interesting, with a certain pallid Elysian glow about them dimly reminding me of the passion they once inspired. The modern work is far more refined, delicately perceptive,

468

true in method, sincere and modest, than it used to be. But it has no ideas, no centrality of inspiration, nothing but common-sense and good method. These people, sculptors and painters, try at least to get close to nature. But nature eludes, and is better to look at than their work. And they put no passion, no emotion, no religion, no ideality into what they do, to make up in some sort for their conspicuous inferiority to nature.

[Incomplete]

---

1. See L 1708. A few days before (June 27), Richards had written Dr. William R. Huggard, his physician, about Symonds:

. . . Mr. Symonds has been a great and powerful helping arm to me, he can be to us all, let us this winter live that intellectual life and help each other to stem the dwarfing, stupefying effects of a diseased, dying, mortality, which will otherwise corrode and poison us as sure as we cease to swim against the stream, for in Davos, it is above, below, around us, even in the air and dust we breathe. I'm lonesome here. . . . (Gallini Collection)

2. Natural black bread: hence, heavy, uninspired art.

1801. *To William Barclay Squire*

[Postcard]

Davos. July 9. /90.

[Dear Squire]

If you chance to see this month's Fortnightly,[1] look at p: 116, where you will see a reference to you,[2] proving that at Rovolone this May I was not forgetful of you. Hope to write you a letter soon.

JAS

---

1. "Among the Euganean Hills," LIV (July, 1890), 107–18.
2. *Ibid.*, p. 116: "[My friend] had to leave Lombardy next day for London and the British Museum."

1802. *To Samuel Richards*

Davos July 9 1890

My dear Richards

We reached home safely last evening at 6.30. I am greatly obliged to you for recommending the Krone at Lindau, wh is a charmingly characteristic old place, & where we were most hospitably entertained at very moderate charges. The town too interested me much.

I found at Munich that I could not book further than Lindau. But the 9.30 a.m. boat for Rorschach sets one going straight for Davos. N. B. no time to eat at Landquart.

The rail had been carried away by a landslip on the steep slopes between Küblis & Saas. About 50 metres of it just fell off into the fields, leaving a chasm over wh we scrambled, to join another train. This Prättigau line is a horridly dangerous affair. In the last days of June another piece was swept away at a point called Fuchs[en]winkel.[1] This is now patched up.

It will not be opened to Davos before the 20th[.] My daughter & I both carried away extremely pleasant memories of Munich. It is all very well for me to jeer at the sham Greek Italian Byzantine buildings[2] etc. I do not think I am wrong in disliking such a museum, as disagreeable to the cultivated sense, & as confusing (or what is worse vulgarizing) to the uninstructed eye. But I got to like the leafy spaces of the town, & dearly to like what I saw of the cheerful honest friendly burghers in their Beer-palaces. What Omar Khayyam says in his mystic way about the True Light or Eternal Wisdom, has wide applications:

One Glimpse of It within the Tavern caught,
Better than in the Temple lost outright.

And so the Hofbräuhaus is to me more profitable than the Ludwig Strasse.

The weather up here has been horrible they say; & I see how much damage is done to the only harvest our people have, the hay.

This morning, however, the sun shines, & the air is light with a genial caressing warmth wh I have not enjoyed since I left Davos last Wednesday.

I hope that you are getting along nicely, & that you will soon return. If you break the journey anywhere between Lindau & Davos, I advise you to do so at Klosters. The Hotel Vereina there is a good one & close to the station. There is some peril in taking your chance of post places at the end of a long railway trip, & climbing up into a cold air toward sunset. I *felt* this last evening.

I find here a terrific accumulation of letters & literary work. It will keep my pen going for some days. It appears from some of my letters, that the "Essays" has at last been sent out. Accordingly I hope that your copy is at the Belvedere.

Please give the love of both of us to Mrs Richards & baby. I feel as if I knew you all better now, after seeing you at Munich; & am grateful to Mrs

Richards for her kindness to my daughter in the midst of her anxiety about you.

Remember me also to Frau Weilhammer, & to Messrs Clark, Hughes, & Wilber.[3]

Believe me now, dear friend, with sincere hopes for your speedy recovery & reappearance here, to be yours very affectionately

John Addington Symonds

My wife left for England last Saty. The news about her sister Miss North[4] is very bad. We fear that she must be sinking; & so it is good that my wife did not delay.

---

1. Fuchsenwinkel on the Prättigau line, a rocky defile near Schiers about 10 miles from Landquart in the direction of Klosters.

2. See L 1800.

3. Frau Weilhammer, not on the guest lists published by the *Davos Courier,* was probably someone in Munich, where Richards apparently was staying; the 3 men were tourists; Hughes and Wilber were soon to be caught in a homosexual scandal.

4. Marianne North, who died August 30, 1890. See L 1831.

1803. *To Herbert P. Horne*

Am Hof, Davos Platz, Switzerland. July 9 1890

Dear Mr Horne

Your letter of the 21st June gave me real pleasure. I am very glad that you like my version of Bion's Adonis.[1] To tell truth, I felt that it was not a bad piece of work; & for that very reason I immediately thought of the Hobby Horse, aspiring to see my hexameters produced in so perfect a way. It would be soaring too high on the wings of hope to wish that Mr Selwyn Image[2] might combine anemonies & roses, or weave briars, in one, of his exquisite designs to symbolise the passion of the poem. How I do envy that power of suggestive design! If I possessed it, I would make for Bion weeping roses & windflowers interlaced, & cupids entangled in blackberry sprays.

If I do come to London this summer or autumn, I shall not fail to visit you—perhaps you & [Arthur] Galton & [Lionel] Johnson all together.

If Galton is with you now, pray give him my kindest regards & ask

Believe me to be very truly yours

John Addington Symonds.

---

1. Symonds' "Hexameters and a Note Upon the Lament for Adnois, out of Bion," *The Century Guild Hobby Horse,* V (October, 1890), 121–26.

2. Selwyn Image (1849–1930), the artist, created many of the designs published in the magazine. Symonds' poem, however, was immediately preceded by a reproduction of a drawing, "A Prophetess of the Resurrection," by Frederick Shields. Herbert Horne supplied the tail-piece, a depiction of a stag leaping past an oak tree.

1804. *To Oscar Wilde*

Davos Platz July 13 1890

My dear Mr Wilde

I am so sorry that a note, wh was really left by carelessness in one of my essays,[1] should have given you pain.

It was by no means intended to imply that you imagined yourself to be the originator of the William Hughes theory:[2] I give you greater credit for your scholarship, espy in a matter of such subtlety & interest as Shakespeare's Sonnets & their criticism. But I remember that when I was writing that essay, yours appeared; & many stupid people & some periodicals, so far as I can recall the facts, gave you the credit of having done so. It was not to *you* but to *them* that I addressed my note; using the word resuscitated, to indicate your use of an old & obsolete hypothesis. The note ought to have been deleted on the proofs of my book: for it is obviously a mere *obiter dictum,* wh has nothing to do with the argument.

Pray accept this apology, wh is very sincere. And tell me if you would like me to make some public recognition.

I wish, while we are upon this topic, that you would send me a copy of your essay.[3] The hypothesis is ingenious, & I should much like to examine it again at leisure. If you possess only one Copy, I will take care of it, & duly return it.

I once wrote a poem on the complications of sex arising out of the position of a boy-actor in the London theatres of that time—imagining an

Italian visitor to England, unacquainted with our customs, being seriously smitten on the evening of his arrival with the person who played Bellario in Fletcher's "Philaster." But this poem went the way of all things that border on the strange & dubious: i.e. tumbled into the "vindices flammae" [avenging flames] of my hearth eventually.

To think that I should have spoiled five minutes of a sunny afternoon for a true lover of beauty & the gladness of the world, grieves me. But I do not believe I did. It is only your way of putting what I can see annoyed you.

Believe me very truly yours

John Addington Symonds

We are badly off for sun here now. We have had deep snow over the whole of the valley for two days & nights, & a canopy of low cold cloud above our heads.

---

1. "William Hughes had been in literary existence a century before Mr. Oscar Wilde resuscitated this hypothetical youth in a magazine of 1889."—"On Some Principles of Criticism," *E S & S* (2 vols., 1890), I, 118 n.

2. The theory apparently began with Edmund Malone over a century before the appearance of Wilde's essays in *Blackwood's Magazine,* CXLVI (July 1889), 1–21. For a brief history of the theory that William Hughes is the "Mr. W. H." to whom most of Shakespeare's sonnets were addressed see Clifford Smyth's "Introduction" to Wilde's "The Portrait of Mr. W. H.," in *The Writings of Oscar Wilde* (1925), pp. 167–81.

3. "The Portrait of Mr. W. H."

1805. *To Horatio Forbes Brown*

Davos, July 15, 1890

[Dear Horatio]

I envy you that storm in the Piave valley. Those are the kind of things which do the soul good—in some obscure way; like most of the disturbances of nature, external or internal. It is also very pleasant to hear that you are reading my book [*E S & S*], and that you find it so far stimulating. I am interested in this book more than I have been in any other; not in its success, that must take care of itself, and really does not matter, but in what people think of it, for I put a great deal of myself into it, and what they think of it is what they think of me, the man here. So I hope you will some time tell me where you find me "flinging out" in a way you do not like. I thought I had only indulged in one fling—in a passage on the *bourgeois* in the essay on Democratic Art.[1] But it seems I must have already done so in the first four essays. This, for me, is a very important point, and I want much to be enlightened on the subject. For my aim at present in writing is not to "fling out," except when the occasion makes it necessary. And yet I know that, living so much alone, I am not always in proper *rapport* to my audience, and probably I take many things for accepted truths which may appear to others sallies of my own humour. So tell me, if you will do me this service, where you felt the personal kick-out or the "privy nip."[2] It is of the utmost value to me to know.

I hope you will not think I am boring you for mere opinions, which I shall afterwards discuss with you. That I promise not to do; it is not what I am after. But I do want to see with your eyes, and feel with your senses, what impression my way of obtruding myself has made. The mere indication of pages where the "flinging out" occurs, will suffice for my intelligence. The rest must be left to my judgment, the lesson to my capacity for profiting by it.

[Incomplete]

----

1. See the concluding paragraph of Part IV, *E S & S* (2 vols., 1890), II, 46–47. Among other things he says: "Snobbery and Pharisaism, in one form or another, taint the middle-class to its core. Self-righteousness, and personal egotism, and ostrich-fear corrode it."
2. See Ls 1821 and 1839.

1806. *To William Barclay Squire*

Am Hof, Davos Platz, Switzerland. July 16 1890

My dear Squire

You ask me what my plans are for the autumn. If I am not forced to go to England, I hope to be at Venice alone after the second week of September.

Why should not you come here & travel with me to Venice? [H. F.] Brown, I am sure, will have a spare-room vacant; & I could give you one in my little *mezzanino* part of the time. I am not able, however, to promise this at a certain date—having invited one or two guests to stay with me, upon whose movements I must wait.

Anyhow, if you would come to Venice, we should be together; & we might make the journey in some pleasant way. I want to go over the Aprica & Tonale passes (from Tirano in Valtellino to Trento). If you do not know these, we might perhaps

[Incomplete]

1807. *To Henry Graham Dakyns*

Am Hof, Davos Platz, Switzerland. July 19 1890

My dearest Graham

The post brought me tonight your letter. It is very dear to me, because I have been for a long time ignorant of where you are, mistrusting old addresses, wondering whether you had found your desired country home, & at least resorting to the villain expedient of sending my book of essays (as much your book as mine, since it is born out of our communion, ours & others, comrades of the New Life) to you through that "harmless drudge" the publisher.

Now I know again all about you, & see you fixed for a part of the earth's revolution round the sun.

I cannot communicate with a man, whom I cannot locate in space. This is a miserable limitation of my spiritual freedom.

But from this time forward I shall locate you for some months in a part of the world well known to me. I thought you might have escaped to other regions—Hampshire, Kent, Essex, what not.

I am glad you take to Loti.[1] He is a man after my heart—in a certain way—I do not know what under lies his art—if it is love for the sailor, I like it—but I sometimes dread that he uses the sailor as an artistic ingredient. What do you think? Anyhow, he touches me upon a most sensitive point of my nature—which you know, & the truth of wh I tried to communicate in my essay on "Democratic Art."

But how stupid all these efforts are to say the big things of our lives "by indirections." It is only the coarse rank cheek-by-jowl comradeship which pays for our immortal soul's destiny—one way or the other.

I feel that Loti, the novelist, or that an essayist evades the main point of the situation. What that main point is, the ultimate issues of life-contacts, remains insoluble for expression, the turning-point for our vitality & future.

Henry Sidgwick is here, & is dissecting my essays [*E S & S*] under my eyes. He is doing me the compliment of reading them & trying to get something useful out of them.

Good Lord! in what different orbits human souls can move.

He talks of sex, out of legal codes, & blue books.[2] I talk of it, from human documents, myself, the people I have known, the adulterers & prostitutes of both Sexes I have dealt with over bottles of wine & confidences.

Nothing comes of discussions between a born doctrinaire & a born Bohemian. We want you to moderate between us. And you are not enough. We want a cloud of witnesses.

Shall we ever be able to see human nature from a really central point of view? I doubt this now. Though we redouble our spectacles, put scores of our neighbours' glasses on our own, in order to obtain the typical impression, shall we reach the central standpoints?

Books are trifles in the current of life. What we write, is the smallest part of what we are. And what we are, is an insignificant globule in the vast sea of nature.

So we must be content to remain with pores & tentacles wh find no sympathetic response in our dearest brethren—nay in the wife of our bosom, the comrade who sleeps beside us & the children who grow up separately from ourselves; all of whom, soul & body, in their several ways we passionately love. /—

Good night. I touch you with this written word, which is hardly intelligible owing to a thorn in the flesh you wot of—eyesight incapable of functioning at night by artificial light.

Your own

J A S

---

1. Pierre Loti's *Mon frère Yves*. See L 1405.
2. That is, Sidgwick speaks of sex as codified in laws and discussed in authoritative manuals or reports (blue books).

1808. *To Percy William Bunting*[1]

Am Hof, Davos Platz, Switzerland. July 21 1890

Dear Sir

I write to ask whether you would care to consider an essay I have been writing on "The Platonic & the Dantesque Ideals of Love?"[2] It is in reference to the sexcentenary of Beatrice, going on at Florence now. The treatment I have adopted seemed to me not unsuited to the Contemporary; & for this reason I have ventured to offer it to you.

I do not send the ms. unless I hear from you.

Very faithfully yours

John Addington Symonds

---

1. Percy William Bunting (1836–1911), editor of *The Contemporary Review* (1882–1911). He was an astute politician, active in the National Liberal Federation, and, as a leading Methodist, edited *The Methodist Times* (1902–11).

2. The essay appeared in *The Contemporary Review*, LVIII (1890), 412–26, and was reprinted in *In the Key of Blue and Other Essays* (1893).

1809. *To Horatio Forbes Brown*

Davos, July 22 [1890]

[Dear Horatio]

Our railway was opened on Sunday—great festivities in horrid weather —and it works now, as if it had been going all the century.

We have the Henry Sidgwicks staying here and Miss Poynter.[1] Lord Langton[2] and a Cambridge friend[3] are coming on Thursday. So all the resources of the house are strained. The Sidgwicks are in excellent form, and I learn much from them.

Oscar Wilde sent me his novelette, "The Picture of Dorian Gray." It is an odd and very audacious production, unwholesome in tone, but artistically and psychologically interesting. If the British public will stand this, they can stand anything. However, I resent the unhealthy, scented, mystic, congested touch which a man of this sort has on moral problems. He and a good many other people have written applausively about my "Essays."[4] But I have seen no reviews yet.

[Incomplete]

---

1. Sister of the painter. See L 1024.

2. Probably William Stephen Gore-Langton, 4th Earl Temple of Stowe (1847–1902); B.A., Christ Church, Oxford; M. P. for Mid-Somerset (1878–85). Lord Langton had received the earlship on March 26, 1889.

3. Unidentified.

4. See L 1804.

1810. *To Edmund Gosse*

Am Hof, Davos Platz, Switzerland. July 22 1890

My dear Gosse

Very many thanks for yours of the 16th. I am so sorry to hear of your being troubled with that painful & wearing affliction, sciatica. This summer, following an unhealthy winter, is bad for all of us. I am out of sorts in my chest, & prevented from taking proper exercise by an injury to my foot.

I have taken your advice about the essay[1] on Dante & Plato, & have offered it to the Contempy without going into particulars.

I am not surprised that you do not sympathize with "Caligula."[2] It is turgid; & I now know that there is something radically wrong in the way I have handled terza rima on the lines of blank verse.

Oscar Wilde sent me his Dorian Gray, wh I read yesterday with interest. I do not like the morbid & perfumed manner of treating such psychological subjects. It seems calculated to confirm the prejudices of the vulgar. The touch I want, is Loti's.[3]

I will reflect upon your suggestion as to printing my "Problem"[4] essay at the Chiswick Press. It is a matter in which I must move very cautiously. Before taking any further step, please expect to hear from me again. Meanwhile I am sincerely obliged to you for your offer to sound Jacobi,[5] of which I would gratefully avail myself if I do not abandon the idea of privately printing altogether.

I am going to send you a packet of nudes, chosen rather at haphazard. I cannot remember what I sent before, but hope there are some new ones here. Please return them if possible in the same or similar boards. Photographs get so unmanageable when they are curled up.

It seems clear Chap: [Man] & H:[all] have neglected my order as to the Essays[6] for you (& some 2 or 3 other friends). I will send you a copy from Nutt.

Everyrs

JAS.

---

1. See L 1808.
2. "With Caligula in Rome," was published in *Igdrasil*, I (June, 1890), 245–48; printed earlier in *Pamphlet V* (see Babington, p. 25).

3. Pierre Loti, the French novelist. Symonds admired his *Mon frère Yves*.

4. *A Problem in Modern Ethics*. Symonds had printed a private edition of 50 copies. These are undated (Babington's guess is 1891). A surreptitious edition appeared in London in 1896.

5. Unidentified, but obviously a printer.

6. *E S & S.*

1811. *To the Rev. Arthur Galton*

Am Hof, Davos Platz, July 24.1890

Dear Mr Galton

Messrs Chapman & Hall have made a muddle about the copies of my "Essays" wh I wanted sent to friends.

I have had to rectify their errors in several cases; & I have just done so in yours, by telling Nutt to send you the book.

It is stupid of the publishers. But, between ourselves, they have been tiresome all through the printing of this work. And I particularly wanted a few people, yourself among the first, to have it from me at the earliest opportunity.

I wish I could see you all together at 20 Fitzroy St. I should like to be able to fly to you now, instead of penning a few lines in the minutes I can snatch from five very miscellaneous guests, who are staying in my house.

One of these, by the way, is Henry Sidgwick, a good judge of metre. He read my version of Bion,[1] & suggested some alterations in lines wh he thought too licentious. I may perhaps be able to get the *quantitative* effect of the verse better, when it comes to print.

Oscar Wilde sent me his story.[2] I have read it with interest. But I do not like this touch upon moral psychological problems, wh have for myself great actuality, & ought I think to be treated more directly. I am afraid that Wilde's work in this way will only solidify the prejudices of the vulgar—to wit, that aesthetics are inseparable from unhealthiness or inhumanity, & that interest in art implies some corruption in its votaries. My Essays are meant in a large measure to remove this error.

Pray remember me to [Herbert P.] Horne & [Lionel] Johnson, & believe me to be very sincerely yours.

J A Symonds.

I am subscribing to all Nutt's reprints.[3] As to Villani,[4] I think you ought to get a copy of the Magheri edn (Florence 1825), in about 14 vols, for something like £2.2.0. I will write again about editors. Why do not you join the Fortnightly: I think F.[rank] Harris would take to your work. There, or with the P[all] M[all] G[azette], or with any journal where I have influence, I will do what I can, if you would like it. But I hope you will go in for longer articles than dailies & weeklies have room for.

JAS.

---

1. "Hexameters and a Note upon the Lament for Adonis, out of Bion" in *The Century Guild Hobby Horse,* V (October, 1890), pp. 121–26.

2. *The Picture of Dorian Gray.* See L 1809.

3. Probably a reference to Alfred Trübner Nutt's reprints of folklore, fairy and ghost stories, and popular studies in mythology. See L 1526.

4. Giovanni Villani (ca. 1275–1348) wrote a history of Florence in the vernacular, *Chronicon Universale.* Villani carried the work to 1348; his brother Matteo continued it, in 11 books, to 1363; Matteo's son Filippo brought it to 1364. R. E. Selfe translated parts of the work into English (2nd ed., London, 1896). It is difficult to see exactly what edition Symonds had in mind. Magheri published Giovanni's chronicle (8 vols. in 4) in 1823, Matteo's (6 vols. in 3) in 1825–26, and Filippo's in 1825–26 as the last vol. of Matteo's.

1812. *To Horatio Forbes Brown*

Davos, July 29, 1890

[Dear Horatio]

You make me feel that the long discipline I gave myself in preparing that book—altering my nature, correcting my proclivities, working toward a conscious aim—has not been thrown away. For I have lived a strange life in many ways of late; and all the time I have striven to gain preciser views and methods of expression—I have wanted to be as sincere in sense, and in thought and sympathies, and in the training of the intellectual moral part of me, as I could hope to be. I thank you very gratefully for all you write. It makes me feel that I have rather grown than lost in the process of self-effectuation, which is the only business of an individuality.

Who can judge for himself? We must see ourselves in the mirror of others. Not in the mirror of the reviews. They have their place in forming the jury which condemns or acquits the inner man. But they do not enable one so narrowly to test the decline or the growth in himself, as what a friend who knows and loves him says.

Henry Sidgwick here has helped me in the same way, or a similar. These Essays [*E S & S*] have suggested for twelve days constantly recurring conversations, and have set speculation on the wing. They would not have done so with him, had they not had stuff. And do you know, I was beginning to fear I had no stuff left in me? So through my friends I feel that, if I am allowed some years of energy, I may go on to new things with freshly trained faculties. Thank you, and God bless you.

[Incomplete]

1813. *To Percy William Bunting*[1]

Am Hof, Davos Platz, Switzerland. July 31. 1890

My dear Sir

In reply to your kind note of the 24th, I beg to say that the article on "Platonic & Dantesque Ideals of Love" will be sent so soon as I can get it type-written. This takes more time here than it does in London.

Very truly yours

John Addington Symonds

Percy Wm. Bunting

---

1. See L 1808.

1814. *To Walt Whitman*

Am Hof, Davos Platz, Switzerland. August 3 1890

My dear Master

I received your card of July 20 in due course two days ago. It makes me feel how very remiss I have been in not acknowledging the volume of your Complete Works, which I am already in the habit of calling to myself "Whitman's Bible,"[1] and which remains the colossal monument of your arduous Life-Labours—monumentum aere perennius,[2] as Horace says.

Reading this great book, I found on p: 291 in "Collect" the passage I quoted from the essay known to me under its old title of "Poetry of the

Future." But it was then too late to alter the reference in my own essay on "Democratic Art" which had been printed a considerable time before it was published. I hope to have a second edition of my "Essays Speculative and Suggestive" (for only 750 copies were printed); and if I do so I shall remodel the whole drift of that article.[3]

Now I must thank you for the generous and to me most highly acceptable, by me most reverently guarded, gift of your portraits—a sheaf of portraits unique in their significance and interest. Many friends have shared with me the pleasure and profit of studying and comparing them. If you have no objection to the idea, I should like to have some of the *photographs* of middle and later life reproduced by a permanent process, which has recently been invented by a very able chemist at Munich: Obernetter.[4] I will send you a specimen of his skill, the reproduction of one of Rembrandt's etchings, which will bear the closest comparison with the original.

I want next to ask you a question about a very important portion of your teaching, which has puzzled a great many of your disciples and admirers. To tell the truth, I have always felt unable to deal, as I wish to do, comprehensively with your philosophy of life, because I do not even yet understand the whole drift of "Calamus." If you have read Mr Havelock Ellis' "New Spirit,"[5] which contains a study of your work in thought and speculation, you may have noticed on p: 108 that he expresses some perplexity about the doctrine of "manly love," and again on p: 121 he uses this phrase "the intimate and physical love of comrades and lovers."

This reference to Havelock Ellis helps me to explain what it is I want to ask you. In your conception of Comradeship, do you contemplate the possible intrusion of those semi-sexual emotions and actions which no doubt do occur between men? I do not ask, whether you approve of them, or regard them as a necessary part of the relation? But I should much like to know whether *you are prepared to leave them to the inclinations and the conscience of the individuals concerned?*[6]

For my own part, after mature deliberation, I hold that the present laws of France and Italy are right upon this topic of morality. They place the personal relations of adults of both sexes upon the same foundation: that is to say, they protect minors, punish violence, and guard against outrages of public decency. Within these limitations, they leave individuals to do what they think fit. But, as you know, these principles are in open contradiction with the principles of English (and I believe American) legislation.

It has not infrequently occurred to me among my English friends to hear your "Calamus" objected to, as praising and propagating a passionate affection between men, which (in the language of the objectors) has "a very dangerous side," and might "bring people into criminality."

Now: it is of the utmost importance to me as your disciple, and as one who wants sooner or later to diffuse a further knowledge of your life-philosophy by criticism; it is most important to me to know what you really think about all this.

I agree with the objectors I have mentioned that, human nature being what it is, and some men having a strong natural bias toward persons of their own sex, the enthusiasm of "Calamus" is calculated to encourage ardent and *physical* intimacies.

But I do not agree with them in thinking that such a result would be absolutely prejudicial to Social interests, while I am certain that you are right in expecting a new Chivalry (if I may so speak) from one of the main and hitherto imperfectly developed factors of the human emotional nature. This, I take it, is the spiritual outcome of your doctrine in Calamus.

And, as I have said, I prefer the line adopted by French and Italian legislature[s] to that of the English penal code.

Finally, what I earnestly desire to know is whether you are content to leave the ethical problems regarding the private behavior of comrades toward each other, to the persons' own sense of what is right and fit—or whether, on the other hand, you have never contemplated while uttering the Gospel of Comradeship, the possibility of any such delicate difficulties occurring.

Will you enlighten me on this? If I am not allowed to hear from yourself or from some one who will communicate your views, I fear I shall never be able to utter what I want to tell the world about your teaching, with the confidence and the thorough sense of not misinterpreting you in one way or the other which are inseparable from truly sympathetic and powerful exposition.

The precise drift of "Whoever you are"—what the one indispensable thing is—I cannot get at; and I am not sure what the drift of "Earth my likeness" is.—Ah, if I could only once have spoken to you, you would certainly have let me know—Lieber Mann, geehrter Meister, das fehlt mir doch!—[7]

It is perhaps strange that a man within 2 months of completing his 50th year should care at all about this ethical bearing of Calamus. Of course

I do not care much about it, except that ignorance on the subject prevents me from forming a complete view of your life-philosophy.

Believe me truly gratefully and affectionately yours

John Addington Symonds

---

1. *The Complete Poems and Prose of Walt Whitman, 1855–88* (1888), an edition of 600 numbered copies.

2. *Odes,* Book III: 30, line 1: I have constructed a monument more lasting than bronze.

3. See *E S & S* (2 vols., 1890), I, 38. In a lengthy note, in which he quotes from Whitman's "Poetry of the Future," Symonds was unaware that Whitman had republished the essay: "It may appear," Symonds closed his note, "in one of the many collections of his works in prose and verse with which I am unacquainted." In the 1893 1-vol. ed. the note remained unchanged (pp. 260–61).

Symonds had sent a copy of *Essays Speculative and Suggestive* to Walt Whitman who in a note, published here for the first time, acknowledged its receipt. The note was pasted by Symonds into his personal copy of *Leaves of Grass* (Philadelphia, 1884), now in the possession of Symonds' grand-daughter, Dame Janet Vaughan. It reads:

328 Mickle St—Camden New Jersey

U S America   July 29 1890

Yr fine "Essays Speculative & Suggestive" two vols: have just come—thank you —I shall write soon ab't them more at length—Have you rec'd my *Complete Works* in one big vol: 900 pp? Sent to you by mail—Also the L of G. latest ed'n (in pocket b'k binding?)—Also the portraits in large envelope?—Say in yr next if so or no. I keep up yet—paralyzed almost completely—get out in wheel chair—sleep & appetite fair—my Nat. Rev: piece is in "Spec:[imen] Days" call'd "Poetry to-day in America"—Y'r letter three months ago rec'd

Walt Whitman

4. See L 1790.

5. Havelock Ellis' *New Spirit* (1890). See L 1791.

6. Whitman's famous reply to this underscored question, in which he boasts of 6 illegitimate children, was written on Aug. 19, 1890. See L 2088 for Symonds' quotation from this letter; see also L 1822.

7. Dear man, honored master, I cannot do it.

1815. *To Ernest Rhys*[1]

Am Hof, Davos Platz, Switzerland. August 4 1890

Dear Mr Rhys

I want very much to have some information upon a topic which you may probably know more about than I do—since it concerns Walt Whitman, with whom I believe you had personal relations in America,[2] while mine with him have only been by way of correspondence—owing to "shadowy mountains & the sounding sea" between us, & my incapacity for taking long journeys.

Briefly, I want to know exactly what he means by "Calamus,"[3] & whether, in his propagation of the gospel of comradeship, he has duly taken into account the physical aspects of manly love.

I have interrogated him pretty plainly by letter on this subject,[4] but have received no direct answer. In fact, he seems to wish to leave the ethical questions involved in what he calls "manly love" untouched. But does his silence imply ignorance of the problem? I can hardly think that. Does it imply a belief that the solution of the problem has to be left to individuals?

He has uttered his opinions about the "veneralee" & the "onanist" so frankly, that his reticence (in the matter of sexual deflections from the normal standard) in regard to an emotion which he exalts to such an altitude of passion as "manly love," is peculiarly perplexing.

Critically, I could never grasp for my own mind, & I feel certain that I would never present to the world, a view of his philosophy of life, without having arrived at some coherent opinion upon Calamus. It is so important in his system, & the interpretation of this section of his work involves moral questions of such moment.

I ought to add that, after mature deliberation, I am inclined to think that the Penal Laws of France & Italy are right in placing the personal relations of adults of both sexes upon the same level—i.e. protecting minors, punishing violence & offences against public decency, but leaving individuals within these limitations to their own inclinations & the care of their own conscience.

Whether Whitman takes this view, which is at open contradiction with the principles of English & American legislation, is what I want to know. Till we are informed upon this point, it is impossible to deal with his Calamus; & yet we cannot treat of his whole teaching upon life, without being sure of what he is driving at—in that part of his doctrine—so subtly is it interwoven with the most potent of his utterances (not only in "Leaves of Grass," but also in "Drum Taps" & "Democratic Vistas").

If you can throw any light upon the problem I have suggested, I should be grateful to you. I do not like to bother him again. He is clearly unwilling to explain his own prophecy.

I hear indirectly that you wrote the article upon me in the P.M.G.:[5] and I want to tell you that I think your criticism of my literary activity is just, as I feel sure you meant it to be appreciative, & I own that it is more than liberal in its commendation. I think it is just, precisely in the indication of a versatility, a restlessness, a receptivity, a curiosity about ideas & mental images, which preclude the concentration of energy on monumental work. It is no bad compliment to be called a child of one's age! And, outside the sphere of pure science, I see nothing whatsoever that deserves the name of monumental, in our age. Art & literature seem destined now to tremble like the magnet in a period of electrical perturbation. Instead of taking the lead, they must be sensitive to influences. I only wish (apropos of yr article) that you had not mentioned an autobiography[6] of mine, wh is something very different from what you described. But that is not your fault—mine rather, who ought not to have mentioned to anyone that I was engaged on what will probably be consigned to the fire now.

Very sincerely yrs

J. A. Symonds

---

1. See L 1606.
2. Rhys on a lecture tour visited Whitman in the spring of 1888.
3. See L 1814.
4. See L 1761. In *Letters from Limbo* (1936), p. 4., Rhys prefaced this portion of this letter thus:

He [Symonds] had asked me what construction I put upon the poems in *Leaves of Grass* called 'Calamus,' and I told him I did not think Whitman ever thought people would read into those poems anything more than an ardent feeling for comradeship. But Symonds was not satisfied, and wrote to Whitman asking him if he had not in mind when he wrote 'Calamus' a relationship akin to the Greek conception of physical love between men.

5. "Men and Women Who Write. No. 1. Mr. John Addington Symonds," in the *Pall Mall Gazette*, L (May 17, 1890), 1–2, with a small picture of Symonds. The writer signed himself *θ*.
6. See L 1707.

1816. *To Henry Holt and Co., Publishers, New York*[1]

[Davos Platz, August 7, 1890][2]

[Gentlemen]

I wish to explain to you a scheme which has been suggested to me by a distinguished American painter (Mr. [Samuel] Richards) of the Munich school, well-known in Europe, and also in the United States. He thinks that the Essays in this book [*E S & S*] upon the principles of art are original, sensible, and convincing enough to deserve separate publication with illustrations.[3]

What I have attempted to demonstrate in these Essays is that the personality of the artist inevitably makes itself felt in any attempt to imitate nature, and that this fact renders a thorough realism in art impossible, while it forces idealism of one sort or another on the artist's work.

Now, to prove this, we propose to offer a prize[4] for the best studies from the same nude figure to be competed for in the famous Ecole Julien, at Paris. When the best studies have been selected by impartial judges, we propose to photograph the model in the several attitudes copied by the students, and then to reproduce both the photograph of the model and the studies of the successful draughtsmen by a mechanical process of first-rate excellence invented by Herr Obernetter,[5] of Munich.

[Incomplete]

---

1. Established by Henry Holt (1840–1926) in 1873. Holt was also lecturer and novelist and founder and editor of the *Unpopular Review*.

2. Brown, Preface to 3rd ed. of *E S & S* (1907), was not certain that this letter was actually sent. Symonds' plan was never realized.

3. Richards may have been making illustrations for Holt's issues of volumes of *The Renaissance in Italy*, though Holt did not re-publish Vol. III, *The Fine Arts*, and Vol. II, *The Revival of Learning*, until 1908. He had issued, presumably from the plates of Smith, Elder and Co., Vol. I, *The Age of Despots* (1881, 1888), Vols. VI and VII, *The Catholic Reaction* (1887), Vol. II, *The Revival of Learning* (1888), and Vols. IV and V, *Italian Literature* (1888).

4. See L 1788 for the prospectus for this prize.

5. See L 1790.

1817. *To Samuel Richards*

[Davos] Friday [August 8, 1890]

My dear Richards

I could not stand the inaction of all these days. So I am going over Fluela[1] with a carter whom I know in his wagon. It will be a long process, & I shall probably not return till tomorrow. I enclose the draft of a letter I have scribbled to Holt.[2] Will you kindly look it over? I have left the estimate for illustrations in blank. Of course this letter is open to any alteration. I tired you so much yesterday that anyhow you ought not to have had another sitting from me today.

Very affly yours

JAS.

---

1. The Alpine pass Symonds usually took from Davos. The date of this letter is conjectural, but the letter itself illustrates the impulsiveness with which Symonds took short trips to get away from the ennui of Davos.

2. See L 1816.

1818. *To Richard Burton*[1]

Am Hof, Davos Platz, Switzerland. August 15 1890.

Dear Sir Richard,

As I mentioned to you that I had written an essay on paiderastia among the Greeks,[2] I am going so far upon the path of impudence as to send you a copy of it. It was composed some while ago, before I had seen either Meier's article in the Leipzig Encyclopaedie,[3] or your own Terminal Essay.[4] If you look at it, you will see that I have treated the subject from a literary and historical point of view, without attending to the psychology and physiology of the phenomenon. Since I wrote this essay I have been able to add a great deal to it, which if I ever dared to publish it, would go to confirm my theory about the Dorians (p. 23), and to make the discussion more interesting. If you do not care to read, or to keep, the opuscle, please send it back, as I have not many copies.[5] Otherwise take it as a very little sign of my respect for you; and anyhow believe me sincerely yours

John Addington Symonds.

---

1. Richard Francis Burton (1821–90) had completed the publication of his *The Thousand Nights and a Night* in 1888. He was nominated for a KCMG in 1885, but was never knighted. See L 1493.

2. *A Problem in Greek Ethics*, privately printed in 10 copies, 1883.

488

3. Moritz H. F. Meier (1796–1855), German classical scholar and authority on Athenian law; coeditor of the *Allgemeine Encyclopädie der Wissenschaften und Künste* (1830–55). His papers posthumously published as *Opuscula* (1861–63). The article Symonds refers to is Meier's "Paederastie," in Ersch und Gruber's *Allgemeine Encyclopädie* (Leipzig, 1837). In *Problem in Modern Ethics* [1891], p. 76, Symonds refers to the earlier *Problem in Greek Ethics*, "composed by an Englishman in English. The anonymous author was not acquainted with Meier's article before he wrote, and only came across it long after he had printed his own essay. This work is extremely rare, ten copies only having been impressed for private use."

4. Symonds listed this essay from Vol. X (1885) of *The Thousand Nights and a Night* in the bibliography to *A Problem in Modern Ethics*.

5. Burton's copy eventually came into H. F. Brown's possession.

1819. *To Ernest Rhys*[1]

Am Hof, Davos Platz, Switzerland. August 27 1890

Dear Mr Rhys

Thank you very much for your letter of the 20th wh reached me here tonight. I see that you substantially take the same view as I do about Whitman's attitude toward what he calls Comradeship. I do not think he wants to raise the question of what people call unnatural relations; & I believe that, like Plato in the Phaedrus, he would regard the occurrence of them as a pity, but not as a matter of the extreme & peculiar moment wh the opinion & laws of Christian countries ascribe to them.

It is odd, however, when he speaks so decidedly about the consequences of excess & bad habits in other sexual affairs, & when he cannot be ignorant of what history & Society have plainly to tell about the nature of passion between people of the same sex, that he should have left this aspect of Calamus quite open—without an ethical suggestion of any kind.

I have again written to him very candidly upon the topic—& possibly may obtain some sort of answer. Since he is much interested in reading my two volumes of Essays wh have recently appeared. By the way, I got from him tonight a sort of reply (in print) to my Essay on him called "Democratic Art." It does not break fresh ground but is the reiteration & reinforcement of what he has before said about the necessity of great literature growing out of an age, a nation—if the age, the nation are really great. Also of his views regarding the totality of Art.

With regard to my autobiography, please do not think that I resent what you said in the PMG, or that this would make me suppress the work.

I meant only to remark that now—when the thing is almost done—I do not see how it could be published.

What I did demur to was the description of the autobiography. If you had read it, you would have seen that it is a close psychological study, & that there is very little anecdotal matter or gossip about people in it. I do not like to acquire the reputation of preserving for publication things about "the people I have met." On the other hand I feel that the intelligent & careful study of any person's development & psychical history, written from inside with sincerity, is what he may legitimately give to the world if he likes, & what is a valuable contribution to our documents of human experience.

Believe me very sincerely yours

John Addington Symonds

I do not know Mr E. Carpenter[2]—wish I did, for I admire & sympathize with his attitude toward life. If you think he would communicate to me any views he may have formed on "Calamus," I should be grateful to get them.

---

1. See L 1815, for the initial discussion of the matter of this letter.

2. Edward Carpenter (1844–1929), educated at Brighton College and at Trinity Hall, Cambridge; ordained 1869 but was gradually alienated from his orders, which he relinquished in 1874; joined the University Extension movement as lecturer on astronomy; visited America in 1877 where he met Holmes, Lowell, Bryant, and Whitman; moved to Sheffield (1879) where he lived with a working-class family and wrote his unrhymed Whitmanesque poem *Towards Democracy* (1883); in 1883 he moved to Millthorpe, near Chesterfield, Derbyshire, where he lived for nearly 40 years writing and market-gardening; travelled to America a second time (1884), saw Whitman again, embraced socialism (1885), and thereafter lectured and wrote widely for the movement; published *Civilization: Its Cause and Cure* (1889), *From Adam's Peak to Elephanta: Sketches in Ceylon and India* (1892), *Love's Coming of Age* (1896), and *Iolaus* (1902), which deal with friendship and relations between the sexes; from 1898–1928 he lived with a companion, George Merrill (d. 1928), first at Millthorpe, but from 1922 onward at the Mount, Guilford, where he died on June 28, 1929.

1820. *To Margot Tennant*

[Davos, ca. Sept., 1890]

[Dear Margot]

I am sorry that the Essays I dedicated to you have been a failure—as I think they have been—to judge by the opinions of the Press. I wanted, when I wrote them, only to say the simple truth of what I thought and felt in the very simplest language I could find.

What the critics say is that I have uttered truisms in the baldest, least attractive diction.

Here I find myself to be judged, and not unjustly. In the pursuit of truth, I said what I had to say bluntly—and it seems I had nothing but commonplaces to give forth. In the search for sincerity of style, I reduced every proposition to its barest form of language. And that abnegation of rhetoric has revealed the nudity of my commonplaces.

I know that I have no wand, that I cannot conjure, that I cannot draw the ears of men to listen to my words.

So, when I finally withdraw from further appeals to the public, as I mean to do, I cannot pose as a Prospero who breaks his staff. I am only a somewhat sturdy, highly nervous varlet in the sphere of art, who has sought to wear the robe of the magician—and being now disrobed, takes his place quietly where God appointed him, and means to hold his tongue in future, since his proper function has been shown to him.

Thus it is with me. And I should not, my dear friend, have inflicted so much of myself upon you, if I had not, unluckily, and in gross miscalculation of my powers, connected your name with the book which proves my incompetence.

Yes, the Master [Benjamin Jowett] is right: make as much of your life as you can: use it to the best and noblest purpose: do not, when you are old and broken like me, sit in the middle of the ruins of Carthage you have vainly conquered, as I am doing now.

Now good bye. Keep any of the letters which seem to you worth keeping. This will make me write better. I keep a great many of yours. You will never lose a warm corner in the centre of the heart of your friend.

J. A. Symonds

P.S. Live well. Live happy. Do not forget me. I like to think of you in plenitude of life and activity. I should not be sorry for you if you broke your neck in the hunting field. But, like the Master, I want you to make sure of the young, powerful life you have—before the inevitable, dolorous, long, dark night draws nigh.

1821. *To Horatio Forbes Brown*

Davos, Sept. [2] 1890

[Dear Horatio]

I have been in bed since Thursday with continuous fever. I only get an hour or two in the morning when I can use my head.

The review of my Essays in the *Athenæum*, last number,[1] please read if you can. This is the kind of review which makes one wish to publish nothing again, which blights any pleasure one may have had in one's work, and which puts truths about one's self, apparent as soon as expressed, in a way to dishearten.

It does not matter after all. The day's headache has begun, and I must stop. That is worse than the "privy nip."[2]

It was really kind of you to tell me what Sir James Hannen[3] said about my Essays. When I get better again, I shall be glad of any reassurance as to that book.

[Incomplete]

---

1. *The Athenaeum*, No. 3279 (August 30, 1890), 279–80: the essays (*E S & S*) are "pleasing, but somewhat scrappy" and lack "solidity." There are "hints" of the inspiration he finds in mountain solitudes, conveyed "in the prettiest manner" and "hints and compendia not above the level of the most superficial dabbler." "In easy, unforced eloquence . . . these volumes abound. It is not exactly the style of the sequestered philosopher or a learned student; it is something too voluble for weight, too reminiscent for originality. But its brightness and facility will be grateful to readers as facile in their way and by no means so bright."

The next appearance of *The Athenaeum* was on September 6; Symonds wrote his letter prior to the 6th; hence, our dating of it September 2.

2. A rhetorical figure *charientismus:* gracefulness of style; saying an unpleasant thing in an agreeable way. See Ls 1805 and 1839.

3. Sir James Hannen (1821–94), judge, president of probate, divorce, and admiralty division of high court, 1875–91. What he said is unknown.

1822. *To Walt Whitman*

Am Hof, Davos Platz, Switzerland. Sept: 5. 1890

My dear Master

I am sincerely obliged to you for your letter of August 19.[1] It is a great relief to me to know so clearly and precisely what you feel about the question I raised. Your phrases "gratuitous and quite at the time un-dreamed and unrecked possibility of morbid inferences—which are disa-vowed by me and seem damnable," set the matter as straight as can be, base the doctrine of Calamus upon a foundation of granite.

I am not surprised; for this indeed is what I understood to be your meaning, since I have studied Leaves of Grass in the right way—interpret-ing each part by reference to the whole and in the spirit of the whole. The result of this study was that the "adhesiveness" of comradeship had no interblending with the "amativeness" of sexual love.

Yet you must not think that the "morbid inferences," which to you "seem damnable," are quite "gratuitious" or outside the range of possibility. Frankly speaking, the emotional language of Calamus is such as hitherto has not been used in the modern world about the relation between friends. For a student of ancient literature it presents a singular analogue to the early Greek enthusiasm of comradeship in arms—as that appeared among the Dorian tribes, and made a chivalry for prehistoric Hellas. And you know what singular anomalies were connected with this lofty sentiment in the historic period of Greek development.

Again, you cannot be ignorant that a certain percentage (small but appreciable) of male beings are always born into the world, whose sexual instincts are what the Germans call "inverted." During the last 25 years much attention, in France, Germany, Austria and Italy, has been directed to the psychology and pathology of these abnormal persons. In 1889 the Penal Code of Italy was altered by the erasion of their eccentricities from the list of crimes.

Looking then to the lessons of the past in ancient Greece, where a heroic chivalry of comradeship grew intertwined with moral abominations (I speak as a modern man), and also to the Contemporary problem offered by the class of persons I have mentioned—who will certainly have somehow to be dealt with in the light of science, since the eyes of science have been drawn towards them: looking, I say, to both these things, it became of the utmost importance to know for certain what you thought about those "morbid inferences." For you have announced clearly that a great spiritual factor lies latent in Comradeship, ready to leap forth and to take a prominent part in the energy of the human race. It is, I repeat, essential that the interpreters of your prophecy should be able to speak authoritatively and decisively about their Master's *Stimmung* [disposition of mind], his radical instinct with regard to the emotional and moral quality of the comradeship he announces.

I am sorry to have annoyed you with this discussion. But you will see, I hope now, that it was not wholly unnecessary or unprofitable.

With the explanation you have placed in my hands, and which you give me liberty to use, I can speak with no uncertain voice, and with no dread lest the enemy should blaspheme.

The conclusion reached is, to my mind, in every way satisfactory. I am so profoundly convinced that you are right in all you say about the great good which is to be expected from Comradeship as you conceive it, and as alone it can be a salutary human bond, that the power of repudiating those "morbid inferences" authoritatively—should they ever be made seriously or uttered openly, either by your detractors or by the partizans of some vicious crankiness—sets me quite at ease as to my own course.

I will tell my bookseller in London to send you a copy of the "Contemporary" in which there is an essay by me on the "Dantesque and Platonic Ideals of Love."[2] You will see something there about the Dorian Chivalry of Comradeship to wh I have alluded in this letter. It seems to me, I confess, still doubtful whether (human nature being what it is) we can expect wholly to eliminate some sensual alloy from any emotions which are raised to a very high pitch of passionate intensity. But the moralizing of the emotions must be left to social feeling and opinion in general, and ultimately to the individual conscience.

I am greatly interested in your "Rejoinder" (wh by the way has been reprinted in the PMG).[3] Anything you say about the inception and performance of your great life-work has value.—I have been ill; six days in bed with high fever, a lung-inflammation serious to me; only just up again for a few hours. Ever yours with deep gratitude and true affection.

John Addington Symonds.

---

1. See L 2088 for Symonds' quotation from this letter; see also L 1814, note 6.

2. *The Contemporary Review*, LVIII (1890), 412–26, later reprinted in *In The Key of Blue* (1893).

3. *Pall Mall Gazette*, LI (August 26, 1890), 7, reprinted from the New York *Critic* (August 16, 1890): "'An Old Man's Rejoinder' Mr. Walt Whitman's Reply to His Critics." In this rejoinder Whitman refers to Symonds' essay on "Democratic Art" in *E S & S* and expresses gratitude to Symonds for his "invariable courtesy." "Democratic Art," Whitman says in a footnote, caused the "offhand lines" of the rejoinder.

Am Hof, Davos Platz, Switzerland. Sept: 5 1890

My dear Squire

I am very glad to hear from you. Almost immediately after Horatio left Davos, I was taken ill with an inflammation of the old healed wound in my lung—a serious affair, which kept me for eight days in bed with continuous fever.

I am rather better again now. But for a long while I shall not be fit for much exercise; and I shall have to keep very regular and early hours.

I tell this in order to make you see beforehand clearly what the manner of my life will have to be, if you pay us the visit which would give me very great pleasure. It seems a poor way for you to pass a part of your short holiday.

My sister in law Miss North died,[2] while I was still ill in bed; and though my wife needs me much in the transaction of necessary business, I am unable to go to England. Very probably I shall have to give up my visit to Venice: or at all events shall have to postpone it till quite late in the autumn.

This illness is the climax of a long unhappy period of malaise.

We have had the most horrid weather. Thunderstorms with snow on the mountains and deluges of rain—innundations everywhere.—and great damp cold. It does not promise well even now. But I should not be surprised if a golden halcyon season of calm skies and mild sunshine were yet in store.

Make your own mind up about coming here. The railway brings you up to Davos Platz, where the Hotel Buol omnibus will drive you to my door, if you come. And welcome you will be. But I shall understand if you find a better use for your precious weeks of freedom.

Please remember me to Blumenthal.[3] His villa near Chernex[4] is lovely as a dream. Ask him if he has forgotten the autumn we passed together at Glion (in 1868 I think)[5] with Brabazon Courthope and other friends. I wonder whether he remembers "Harriett," the colossal daughter of a Countess Tolstoi, for whom Courthope wrote burlesque rhymes, wh he (Blumenthal) passed off as a serious love-poem

[omission]

The sun shines, without great warmth, but always with enough for me to sit out in the open air, drinking coffee, and talking with friends; and in the evenings English visitors dine with us, or I drink wine with Swiss folk.

I am working as hard as is at all good for me, at a new Life of Michelangelo Buonarroti,[6] wh I have rather unwillingly undertaken. The subject is old and well-worn. I must absorb whole libraries of books. And after all, I do not feel sure that the English need a biography of that eminent artist. Mr Nimmo thinks they do. And his offers, both as to the form of the projected book, and as to the pecuniary value of it for myself, are so enticing that I have given way. It rains books and photographs and prints concerning Michelangelo in my house now.

My peasant friends, with their huge bodies, can hardly turn round in my room, when they come to greet me of an evening.

So I live. What an odd thing life is. Here, at least, it is not exactly as commonplace as it would be in S. Kensington (at home there) & the Athenaeum[7] (to go down to).

Goodnight. Yours ever

JAS.

Write to me sometimes. I love my friends, and always long to hear from them.

---

1. See L 1674.

2. Marianne North died August 30, 1890.

3. For notes on Blumenthal, Courthope, and Brabazon, and an account of the experience see L 566.

4. Chernex is south of Freiburg and Bulle in western Switzerland.

5. It was in 1867. See L 566.

6. *The Life of Michelangelo Buonarroti* (2 vols., 1893, though it appeared late in 1892). The work contained an etched portrait and 50 reproductions of Michelangelo's works.

7. The exclusive London club patronized by writers and civil servants. Symonds was elected to it in 1880.

1824. *To William Barclay Squire*

[Postcard]

Am Hof. Davos Platz. Sept: 6. [1890]

[Dear Squire]

Sent you a letter two days ago.[1] Yours of Friday to hand tonight. This only to repeat that we shall be delighted to receive you, under the circumstances which I mentioned. Am getting slowly better—but not yet out-of-doors.

JAS.

---

1. L 1823; the letter is dated Sept. 5, however.

1825. *To Margaret Symonds*

[Davos, Sept. 6, 1890]

[Dear Madge]

If ever you come to the real pains of authorship, and printing and publishing what you have written in your own chamber, I wish you more joy of it than I have got. It is a dreadful toil. Masses of proofs and MSS. Perpetual corrections of details, alterations of plan, attention to typographical insanities. The technical work wears down the free birth of your spirit to a dead dumb level; and yet you have always to keep spurring yourself to final effort of pure style and sharp delineation. And so it goes on for months until your 600 or 700 pages go forth to the public, and you call it then your 'vomit.'

[Incomplete]

1826. *To Horatio Forbes Brown*

[Davos Platz, September 7, 1890]

[Dear Horatio]

. . . I wrote in a night-marish mood to you about an article in the *Athenaeum* on my Essays.[1] I see now that there is a great deal of truth in what the reviewer said. He has spoiled that book for me for ever. But I admit that he had the right to spoil my conceit of it, because he has shown me that my conceit was ill-founded.

[Incomplete]

---

1. See L 1821.

1827. *To W. Kineton Parkes*

Am Hof, Davos Platz, Switzerland. Sept: 8. 1890.

Dear Mr Parkes

In one of the recent letters you wrote me, you said that you should like to have some personal lyric of mine for "Ygdrasil."

I happen this morning to have had to look over a whole bundle of such things in Ms & have copied out one wh I send.[1]

It is rather morbid in tone, & was written very many years ago. But I think the mood expressed was very genuine at the time I wrote it.

I am looking forward with great interest to your Anthology,[2] & to the dedication wh you told me you wished to prefix to it. Let me know if it has appeared.

Believe me very sincerely yours

John Addington Symonds.

---

1. "Waiting (Heart and Head Converse Together)," *Igdrasil,* II (November, 1890), 55–57.
2. *The Painter Poets.* See L 1834.

1828. *To Horatio Forbes Brown*

[Davos Platz, September 8, 1890]

[Dear Horatio]

. . . . You will see that I have taken the *Athenaeum*[1] in good part. . . . It is over now, however; and I am already the better for feeling humbled.

The days in this fever-prison go so sadly, and the nights so strangely, that I am losing count of time; [Dr.] Ruedi holds that the principal irritation is a recrudescence of the old wound in my lung.

[Incomplete]

---

1. See L 1821.

1829. *To William Barclay Squire*

Am Hof, Davos Platz, Switzerland. Sept: 16. 1890

I advise you to come to Davos Platz, the station which the omnibuses meet, & take the Buol omnibus to us. If indeed you come!

My dear Squire

Since I wrote to you, my state of health has not improved—rather the contrary. But if you do not mind coming from your pleasant life at Chernex to an invalid host, you will be welcome, & my daughters will do all in their power to make up for my deficiencies.[1]

I have had more than three weeks of almost incessant fever, without any adequate apparent cause. You will understand that this has tired me very severely. But I have the shreds & patches of a man left in me for a friend; & my three girls are robust. Yrs JAS.

---

1. Squire did make the trip. See L 1833.

1830. *To Herbert P. Horne*

Am Hof, Davos Platz, Switzerland. Sept 21 /90

/Herbert V. Horne Esq
20 Fitzroy Street
Bloomsbury, London. W.C. England/

Dear Mr Horne

I return the proof of my Bion's Lament corrected. May I have a revise?

You will see I have adopted most of your suggestions. I must, how-ever, preserve the form *Ah for Adonis!* It is necessary to mark the Greek αἰαὶ ὦ τόν' Ἀδωνιν [Wail, O, for Adonis].

Some alterations I have made in the text I originally sent you, always with the object of getting the rhythm of the English hexameter quantitatively more right.

I fear there is no hope of my getting to either England or Italy. I have been very ill for six weeks, & am even now only able to get up for a few hours in the day.

Very sincerely yours

J A Symonds

1831. *To Henry Graham Dakyns*

Am Hof, Davos Platz, Switzerland. Sept: 24 1890

My dear Graham

Your letter to Catherine arrived last night; & as she is expected here ere long, I shall keep it for her, sending this line of acknowledgment meanwhile.

It is terribly long since I wrote to you, & I am in your debt for a very kind letter about my Essays.[1]

I have been ill all the Summer: overworked nerves originally; ending at last in an attack of continued fever & pulmonary inflammation, wh has now lasted six weeks & seems inclined to keep up. Of course I am a complete invalid again; & one of my difficulties has been to conceal the fact from Catherine during her anxieties & business duties at Alderley.[2] I could not go there to be of any assistance.

But enough of this. You see it will prevent my coming to England or getting to Italy.

I was much interested to hear of your final arrangements, & settlement at No. 5 Downleaze Road.[3] It seems easy to transport myself into that region in this misty autumn season of changing foliage: the peculiar quality of "Clifton" landscape—atmosphere is found at its height just there.

I wish I could talk to you about the work I have been privately engaged upon, & wh has broken my nervous health down. It is too long a subject to discuss for the first time by letter. And yet it is so much the main thing about me that I have little else to say.

I envy you having been in Norway. I want to go there to see the people. One cannot be everywhere or see everybody. But I should like to meet some of the young Norwegian men & Swedes, of whom friends tell me pleasant things.

If it had not been for this lung trouble, & four large open blisters, I ought to have been now at Mme. Pisani's villa,[4] helping her to entertain the empress Frederick.[5] This is an opportunity I am sorry to have missed. Mme Pisani is herself so remarkable a woman & so genial in conversation that I am certain a week in her country house with that other interesting woman would have been worth having. Then I was going on to stay at Trieste with Sir Richard Burton,[6] who is composing a treatise on what he calls "the third sex"—& who had never heard (when I last saw him) of either Ulrichs or Krafft-Ebing.[7] I am sorry also to miss this; for though Burton is not exactly sympathetic, he is a perfect mine of curious knowledge about human nature, & one of the very few men who talk without reserve & with abundance of information upon its strangest problems.

It is quite true that the H.M. of Clifton was offered to G.H.W.[8] & very strongly pressed upon him (espy by J.P.).[9] I was consulted in the matter. On the whole I thought W. had better stay where he is. It was a difficult choice for that child of fortune; & I really did not know that he had utterly rejected the invitation. Do not quote me; for, though of course I played no official part, I should not like to be mentioned in the matter.

We are all fairly well here, except my own useless & sore afflicted self.[10] July, August, September, 1890, lost months, worse than lost, unless the discipline of pain & fever & utter prostration can be reckoned good for a character so rebellious against the laws of salutary life. And Catherine away from us all these months; & the daily correspondence & anxiety about Miss North; & then the break-up of Mount Alderley & all her collections; & here I have felt near to dying, & have had to think so often how if the Davos home wh has been made for me, should next come to be broken up—& wife & children left stranded in the world with the debris of so many homes around them, & no house to call their own, & only a coagulated cake of capital. The pity of all these things—the absurdity of our system of property —the clogging & congesting & shattering & saving of fragments & final floating upon a deep wide sea with salvage from a score of shipwrecks.

Ever yours—with love to Maggie, Henry etc—

J A S

---

1. *E S & S*. Critics and reviewers had not, on the whole, taken kindly to the work. Brown claimed that this reception "hurt" Symonds "more than he was ever hurt before or after. He looked upon the book as in some ways a new departure in his literary career, and he felt that in it he had given more of himself to the public than in any previous work except 'Animi Figura.' "—*Biography,* p. 453.

2. Marianne North's home (Gloustershire), where Mrs. Symonds was settling her sister's estate. Marianne North died August 30.

3. Downleaze Road, Snyed Park (near Clifton Downs).

4. He made the trip to Contessa Almorò Pisani's estate, Vescovana, in November. See L 1717.

5. 1840–1901, born Her Royal Highness Princess Victoria Adelaide Mary Louisa, Princess Royal of the United Kingdom; daughter of Queen Victoria and Prince Albert; wife of Emperor Frederick III (1831–88) and mother of Kaiser William II (1859–1941). She was known as Empress Frederick after her husband died shortly after ascending the throne.

6. See L 1818. Burton died shortly, on October 20.

7. Symonds drew for his *Problems* books upon several of Karl Heinrich Ulrichs'

works: the most important, according to Symonds, was the essay by "Memnon," *Die Geschlechtsnatur des mannliebenden Urnings* (1868). In the bibliography prefacing *A Problem in Modern Ethics* (1891) Symonds lists 10 others of Ulrichs' works on the same subject, written between 1864 and 1870. Ulrichs published initially under the nom de plume Numa Numantius. Karl Heinrich Ulrichs (1825–95), attended the Universities of Göttingen and Berlin; his specialties were jurisprudence and theology; and he was also fully acquainted with science and philosophy. The *Jahrbuch für Sexuelle Zwischen-Stufen unter besonderer Berücksichtigung der Homosexualität,* I (1899), carries a short biography and 4 letters about homosexuality addressed to members of his family. For a poignant description of Symonds' visit to Ulrichs, see L 2084 to Edward Carpenter.

Richard, Baron von Krafft-Ebing (1840–1902), German neurologist. His *Psychopathia Sexualis* (12th ed., 1903) was a landmark in its field.

8. George Hyde Wollaston, who had been a master at the college since 1873, was apparently considered for the headmastership, left vacant on J. M. Wilson's retirement in December, 1890. Michael George Glazebrook was appointed, however.

9. John Percival, the first headmaster of the college, was headmaster of Rugby School and member of the Clifton Council at the time.

10. On September 25, 1890, Samuel Richards wrote to his wife Bettie:
Symonds has been ill all summer off and on and [I] have only had [him] sitting now & then for his pen & ink portrait, which is nearly finished. He & every body else say it is the finest thing they ever saw in way of a head & technical work. I've got his happiest expression took. . . . He is going to have Obernetter reproduce them size of my two, & send to his friends everywhere I think if I send it to some black & white Exhibition in London it will do me lots of good and may sell. Symonds asked me what I would want for it, and I said £25 ($125) and I wont take less. There is no one else who can make a life size pendrawing and I don't care to do many of them, what I do must pay. I think I may get some to do here this winter, and I am going to try to sell this to one of the London illustrated Magazines. It does me good to feel I can earn a little something, even if I am a poor Cripple; I mean to do my best & hope on. Symonds went on one of his tares over the Fluela in Aug. [See L 1819] & has had hectic fever ever since. Ruedi says there is a healed wound 5 inches long in his bad lung, which has become inflamed again from his foolish reckless way of doing & if he is not more careful he will get on his last legs again. (Gallini Collection)

1832. *To Horatio Forbes Brown*

Davos, Sept. 28, 1890

[Dear Horatio]

It is time, I think, to end the tedious scene. I am a failure in the one thing I have tried to do—literature. The way in which that book of Essays has been received shows this. Did you see the "P.M.G."?[1] It cannot be the mistake of so many people. It is my own fault; and I am old and stupid.
[Incomplete]

1. "Mr. Symonds on Things in General," *Pall Mall Gazette,* LI (September 25, 1890), 3. To the reviewer of the book (*E S & S*) is "unfinished," too long and unrefined, full of "scaffolding" and "ornamental details," and stylistically dull. "Some of Mr. Symonds's acutest and most valuable remarks occur in his 'Notes on Style.' Quite admirable is his discrimination of the merits and defects of Greek, Latin (classical and ecclesiastical), Italian, French, German, and English, as vehicles of literary expression. But when he proceeds to treat of English style in particular, he becomes perfunctory and unhelpful, lapsing now and then into the flattest truism. That is Mr. Symonds's besetting sin."

1833. *To William Barclay Squire*

Am Hof, Davos Platz, Switzerland. Tuesday Oct: 1 1890

My dear Squire

It seems to me so odd to be sitting here alone this evening while you are starting from Basle for London, that I must send you a word on paper.

Though I have nothing to say. You know how my days pass, and how dismally little there is in them.

I only hope you will not have sent the Shakespeare[1] back . . . [mutilations] friend of mine—Fehr . . . [mutilation] in your luggage, which she says the fellow did with a grin, comprehending some sort of mischief.

You did me a great deal of good by your visit. This may be some very slight compensation to you for the waste of so much of your precious holiday on so slow a place. Whether you wrought the change, or collided contemporaneously with the blisters, I do not know. But I have much less fever. And what is better I look back to many delightful talks of intimacy with you.

Alas, too few! And one never says the whole of what one wants, or the best of it, or indeed anything which the soul and heart desire to say.

Still it is very good to exchange thoughts in freedom. . . .

[mutilated passage]

This is no letter. I have nothing cheerful to communicate. It is a mere shake of the hands.

Remember me very kindly to Russell;[2] and love to Horatio if he is with you. When I hear of Johannes' [Ammann][3] address I will send it. At present he is "Lost in London" rather to my annoyance.

Yrs very affecate JAS.

1. So spelled in the letter.
2. See L 1738.
3. See L 1452.

1834. *To W. Kineton Parkes*

Am Hof, Davos Platz, Switzerland. Oct: 2. 1890

Dear Mr Parkes

I duly received the copy of your "Painter Poets,"[1] & I think that it was well worth while to collect those compositions into one anthology. It is singular with what towering preeminence Blake & Rossetti emerge. Scott,[2] however, is a good third.

I greatly appreciate your dedication. These signs of sympathy & kindness touch me deeply in my somewhat irksome life—especially when, as is now the case, I am battling with a bad attack of my old enemy. It has destroyed the last nine weeks for me.

I wrote that poem "Waiting" in 1870 at Clifton.[3] It was about a friend who did not care for me as much as I for him.

Believe me very sincerely yrs

J. A. Symonds.—

1. In the "Canterbury Poets" series (1890).
2. William Bell Scott (1811–90), known for his paintings of Northumbrian history; modelled his poetry on Blake and Shelley: *Poems* (1854); *Poems*, ill. by the author and L. Alma-Tadema (1875); *A Poet's Harvest* (1882).
3. In *Igdrasil*, II (November, 1890), 55–57. The friend was surely Norman Moor. See L 602.

1835. *To the Rev. Arthur Galton*[1]

Am Hof, Davos Platz, Switzerland. Oct: 9. 1890

My dear Mr Galton

I have been very ill during the last six weeks, trodden close to the ground which waits to receive all of us, by continual fever & by the gnawing malady in the lung of which that fever is the symptom. For a man who has just completed his 50th year this is an austere Memento Mori.[2]

If it had not been thus with me, & I had not had other sources of anxiety in the death of my sister-in-law Miss [Marianne] North, you would have probably heard from me sooner.

Now your Camelot volume of Tacitus arrives—with that admirable Introduction,[3] to taste which—slowly to *degustare* [to taste], as one tastes an opened flask of ripened Tuscan wine—has been my chief pleasure in this gray day of illness.

I think it a most remarkable piece of literary work, & one which carries with it to my mind the hope of a new revival of style, the outcome of a movement which proceeds (as all fine things must do) from Oxford & your particular School there.

The lightness with which your erudition is borne, the mental force with which views of history & character are insinuated, the general urbanity made tart at proper intervals by irony & subrisive humour, the felicity of quotation, the nice maintenance of modernity in thought & judgment under turns of phrases studied on the classics of the last century, the weight of criticism displayed in sallies like that on punctuation: all these qualities, with their fragrance of the living man of whom they are a spiritual outcome, give me extreme delight.

Emeritus, at the end of my career, I salute the advent of something unexpected from this end of the century. It seems to me too infinitely superior to the style of the decadents across the Channel.

I wonder how far you & your school will go: what latent forces you will evoke from our language, our national style.

In one way it is a pity that such a piece of art in writing should be thrown away upon the introduction to a Camelot volume. But then I remember that you have your manhood in hand to use; & I hope that you will not spend it upon any vulgar issues.

You see that I am deeply moved by the literary beauty of your work. And I should not feel this beauty so profoundly, were it not for the vital force of personality which throbs in it.

So I leave you, with no word more tonight. I cannot write much at a time now. And I do not want to repeat the Iliad of my own personal woes. I will only add that it gave me true pleasure to see a phrase or two of mine imprisoned in the amber of your prose. Do not imagine, however, that if this pleasure had been absent, I should have formed any different opinion of your work.

Commend me to my friends; & think of me as a man who is fighting a hard fight with fate. Pray for me.

Yours always

John Addington Symonds—

1. See L 1581.

2. A reminder of death; a genre of poetry common in the Middle Ages.

3. *The Reign of Tiberius, one of the First Six Annals of Tacitus; with his Account of Germany and Life of Agricola,* tr. by Thomas Gordon, and ed. by Arthur Galton, the "Camelot Classics" (1890).

1836. *To the Rev. Arthur Galton*

Am Hof, Davos Platz, Switzerland. Oct. 10. 1890

My dear Mr Galton

I have been re-reading your Introduction to Tacitus[1] with undiminished interest & pleasure. How effective is the passage on the death of the Emperor Frederick: p:xv: "Everyone must remember" etc[2]: so truly Tacitean in its style & accent.

I did not, however, begin this second epistle to congratulate you again upon the literary merits of your work.

I have been pondering the psychological problem offered by Tiberius; & I do not see why we should not accept the stories told about him during his retirement. No amount of sexual eccentricity is incompatible with the finest humanity, the strongest faculties of brain & will & judgment.

Tiberius seems to have been an eminent example of those exceptional people whom Krafft Ebing has studied in his "Psychopathia Sexualis."[3] In his case it is not improbable that inherited neuropathy determined the abnormal extravagances of wh he is accused, because the same phenomena appear in several of his collaterals. But I do not believe that it is necessary, as Krafft Ebing & his school do, to postulate hereditary nervous disorder in all persons thus abnormally constituted.

It is also a mistake to suppose that the brain breaks down under "unnatural" pleasures any more than under the "vulgar & trivial ways of coition." On this point the cases collected by Ebing & the testimony of Ulrichs[4] in his "Memnon" are conclusive.

506

This very curious branch of psychology is only just beginning to receive the attention it deserves, in Germany, Austria, Italy & Russia. What the medical & juristic authorities write about the Roman Emperors seems to me usually in contradiction with the conclusions drawn from their own observation of facts: the remnant of old historical idées fixes. Yet the theory that Tiberius, Nero, Caligula inherited a specific sexual morbidity, which Caligula
did not interfere with their mental & moral equilibrium in other respects, is a probable one. If you care for such enquiries you might consult Moreau: "Des Aberrations du Sens Génétique."[5] He maintains that the sexual sense is literally a sixth sense, which can be physically & psychically disordered without affecting the general sanity of the individual.

Were it to be established that this view of the phenomenon is correct, there would be no *contradiction* in the character of people like Tiberius— only a peculiar diathesis, due perhaps (as Ulrichs suggests) to an imperfect differentiation of sex in the embryonic stages of growth. How to treat such people is a difficult problem:—what society will have to do with them, when it awakes to the conviction that their congenital abnormality is not vice or crime, but imperfection, aberration from the standard.

In Italy (Il Nuova Codice Penale of 1889) they have totally abolished what are called unnatural offences. The law takes no notice of them, so long as they are not accompanied by violence, infringement of the rights of minors, or outrages to public decency. This new legislation is possibly due to the influence of Lombroso's School.[6]

But I must not go running on upon a topic wh you see has completely occupied my attention.

Believe me very sincerely yours

J ASymonds.

---

1. See L 1835.
2. In his "Introduction," pp. xv–xvi, to illustrate the ease by which we are apt to misinterpret ancient history, Galton draws upon the more recent example of the Emperor Frederick:

Everyone must remember the last hours of the Emperor Frederick: the avenues to his palace infested by armed men; the gloom and secrecy within; without, an impatient heir, and the footing to and fro of messengers. We must own, that the ceremonials of the Prussian Court detracted in a certain measure from the ordinary mild usage of humanity; but we attributed this to nothing more than the excitement of a youthful Emperor, or the irrepressible agitation of German officials. But if these events should find a place in history, or if the annals of the Kings of Prussia should

507

be judged worth reading by a distant Age, who could blame an historian for saying, that these precautions were not required for the peaceful and innocent devolution of a crown from a father to his son? Would not our historian be justified, if he referred to the tumults and intrigue of a Praetorian elector; if he compared these events to the darkest pages in Suetonius, or reminded his readers of the most criminal narratives in the authors of the "Augustan History"? From Sejanus and the Emperor William, I return once more to Tiberius; from the present *Kaiser,* to a genuine Caesar.

3. See L 1831.
4. See L 1831.
5. Paul Moreau (?-?), *Des Aberrations du sense génétique* (3rd ed., 1883).
6. Cesare Lombroso (1836–1909), Italian criminologist, held that there is a definite criminal type to be distinguished by easily determined anatomical features and psychological traits. His most influential book was *L'uomo delinquente* (1876).

1837. *To Ernest Rhys*

Am Hof, Davos Platz, Switzerland. Oct: 12 1890.

Dear Mr Rhys

The day after I wrote you the enclosed,[1] I fell very seriously ill and have been ill ever since: worn out with fever & unable to use my brain—I had not posted your letter before this came on me; & very soon after, I received a remarkable reply from Whitman,[2] part of wh I felt I ought to transmit to you—but I had not the energy to copy it. Here it is:

'As to the questions on Calamus etc: they quite daze me. L[eaves] of G[rass] is only to be rightly construed by & within its own atmosphere and essential character—all of its pages & pieces so coming strictly under. That the Calamus part has even allowed the possibility of such construction as mentioned is terrible. I am fain to hope the pp: themselves are not to be even mentioned for such gratuitous & quite at the time undreamed and unrecked possibility of morbid inferences, wh are disavowed by me & seem damnable.'

That is clear enough; & I am extremely glad to have this statement—though I confess to being surprised at the vehemence of the language.

Believe me very sincerely yours

J. A. Symonds.

---

1. Possibly L 1819.
2. Possibly the letter of Aug. 19. See L 1822.

1838. *To Henry Scott Tuke*[1]

Am Hof, Davos Platz, Switzerland, October 15, 1890.

My dear Sir,—My old friend, Horatio Brown, has just been here and has talked to me a great deal about your work and life at Falmouth, so much indeed and with so much enthusiasm that he made me almost feel I knew you. I say this to excuse myself for writing to you—I want to tell you how much I admire the photograph of your 'Perseus'.[2] I had already singled out that picture is one of those indifferent illustrated catalogues, and I was delighted to be able to study a better reproduction of it. The feeling for the nude in it seems to me as delicate as it is vigorous. I wish you would take pity on my isolation here, an isolation made this year still more strict by renewed ill health, and send me some photographs of your various pictures and studies.

I had a very kind visit here from your father,[3] who was a friend of my own father. He touched me by the warm affectionate way he spoke of my father. . . . Well, try to forgive me if you do not like my want of ceremony, and believe me very truly yours, John Addington Symonds.

---

1. Henry Scott Tuke (1858–1929), the Cornish painter noted for his studies of adolescent bathers and marine pictures.
2. Tuke's "Perseus and Andromeda" was exhibited at the Royal Academy in February, 1890, and in the Salon of 1891, where it received honorable mention. Maria Tuke Sainsbury, *Henry Scott Tuke: A Memoir* (1933), p. 89, says: "At the Academy . . . 'Perseus' was not considered a complete success, some of the critics warmly praising the figures, some making easy game of the monster, and all crying out for more bathers instead of classical subjects."
3. Daniel Hack Tuke (1827–95), London physician and alienist, specialist in mental disease, and visiting physician to the York retreat for the insane. See L 1846.

1839. *To the Rev. Arthur Galton*

Am Hof, Davos Platz, Switzerland. Oct: 16. 1890

Dear Mr Galton

I am glad that what I wrote about your Introduction to Tacitus gave you pleasure, am proud that you should value my opinion, & am particularly delighted by the sympathetic letter from you to myself of which my sincere & spontaneous words of congratulation have been the occasion.

I wrote indeed with all sincerity, & with something of that enthusiasm which is engendered in ageing men by their perception of the advent of a new force into the sphere of thought and work where they have moved. Without hinting at prophecy, I mean to shadow forth the stirring in me of what I believe to be a veracious instinct.

I had a good friend staying with me these last days, Horatio Forbes Brown, who has just brought out a book (by John Nimmo) of sterling merit & original research upon the history of the Venetian Press.[1] He came from England, where I had told him to try to form alliance with your circle. But this fell through, chiefly from the time of the year being unpropitious—his own leisure occupied in sumptuous country-houses of the West of England, & his ancestral place upon the Pentlands. The opportunity will therefore be deferred. But I made him read your Introduction; & was gratified: since I value his opinion greatly: to find that his judgment coincided with my own. My health obliges me to retire early; & I left my friend with his pipe to the perusal of your writing. In the morning, he was full of its classic elegance of phrase, its nervous pith, its hidden irony, its urbane delivery of (what Puttenham I think calls) the "privy nippe."[2]

I do not think that you will fail to make the mark which every artist seeks to make upon the world of readers. You have one great quality, in addition to your search after form & your sacrifice to concentration, humour.

Were I to venture to criticize your fellow-workers, the young men of this rising school, I should be inclined to suggest that they do not treat matters with a light touch. They are too much in earnest. This exposes them to the vulgar imputation of conceit & pedantry. Lionel Johnson,[3] for instance, always seems to me to write admirably. But he approaches his subject in a very serious spirit. The review on Sommer's Mort DArthure wh he lately printed struck me as excessive in this way.

I am also inclined to wonder whether, with your aims, literature of the periodical species—as this is now carried on—is properly the sphere you ought to work in.

Pater[4] made his great mark in letters by a volume of carefully finished essays, penetrated through & through with the unity of his peculiar personality. Ought you not to seek this channel of expression? Or, if you were not to do this alone, could you not produce in concert with your friends a book which should arrest attention by its worth & weight?

I cast these suggestions out, & please take them only as an expression of my sympathy, because I am really anxious that the vibrations of the spirit stirring in you all should not go to waste.

Meanwhile, please think of me as one who is deeply & affectionately interested in all you do, & who could have no greater pleasure than to improve his acquaintance with you by personal intercourse. I wish you could come to see me here!

My health is a great trial to me now. Matters are not improved by a heavy snow-storm wh has drowned all our woods & vales in white. It is not winter, but the first feeler put forth by the coming foe, who will I fear obstruct my passage to another land before the long cold season settles in.

Ever yours

JASymonds

---

1. Brown's book on the Venetian Press appeared in 1891. Symonds may be referring to a previously printed copy.

2. George Puttenham (?–ca. 1590), reputed author of *The Arte of English Poesie* . . . (1589). See L 1821.

3. See L 1736. By October 1890, Johnson had published "A Note Upon Certain Qualities in the Writings of Mr. Pater," *The Century Guild Hobby Horse*, V (January, 1890), 36–40; "A Brief Notice of 'Strafford,'" *The Century Guild Hobby Horse*, V (April, 1890), 74–77; "In the Character of Nero," with Hugh Orange, *Macmillan's Magazine*, LXII (June 1890), 135–39; and in *The Academy*, XXXVIII, "'The Tragic Mary.' By 'Michael Field'" (August 16, 1890), 123–241, and "La Morte Darthur by Sir Thomas Malory. . . . Edited by H. Oskar Sommer" (September 20, 1890), 237–39.

4. *Studies in the History of the Renaissance* (1873).

1840. *To Henry Sidgwick*

Davos, Oct. 18, 1890

[Dear Henry]

I have overlived my interest in those two volumes of Essays, and do not care what the Press says.[1] I think I made a mistake in supposing that I could do things of that sort well, and that I could acquire distinction by pruning off my personal proclivities toward certain kinds of rhetoric—perhaps the only point I had in literature. What do books matter in relation to the soul, when life is trembling in the balance, and the days and nights have no savour in them? Even so, I have love still, and am yours.

[Incomplete]

---

1. *E S & S*. The press was severe. See Ls 1821 and 1832.

1841. *To Samuel Richards*

Am Hof, Davos Platz, Switzerland. Saturday [Oct. 25, 1890]

My dear Richards

I am going away tomorrow.[1] It seems rather mad. But the step is going to be taken.

Business overwhelms me in these last hours of being here, & I cannot come over to see you.

If you like to drink a cup of tea with my wife & me about 4 p.m. we shall be delighted, & I shall shake your hand. Anyhow I will write to you from Italy. I feel your kindness to my daughter Madge more than I can tell you, & am always your hearty friend

J A Symonds.

[Date in pencil on envelope] Oct. 25.1890
[Note on back of envelope:] I wrote & sent this in the afternoon. But you were not at the Studio. So it must now come after my departure with the friendly greetings of yours most sincerely JAS.

Saturday Oct 25/90
8.30 p.m.

---

1. Symonds was going to Venice. On Nov. 1, 1890, Richards wrote to his wife Bettie: "Symonds & Mrs. S. put off yesterday in a snow storm for Venice & [Dr.] Ruedi is furious he curses Symonds in unmeasured terms. Symonds did not even tell him he was going: he is by no means well. . . ." (Gallini Collection). Since dates do not correspond, Richards must be mistaken in "yesterday."

1842. *To Margaret Symonds*

Venice, Oct. 30, 1890

[Dear Madge][1]

I am a different man from what I was in the spring. I wish that it were possible to make a just division between these contrary periods of over-excitability and physical exhaustion, to which the artistic temperament—and for that matter the pulmonary subject too—is peculiarly liable. The intense work I did all last winter at the volumes of my Essays [*E S & S*] . . .

made me so sensitive and excitable in the spring that I almost lost control over myself, and finally sank down into that state of semi-collapse which you watched over in the summer. It will be long before my constitution re- covers anything like tone and elasticity, and at 50 nature's forces are dimin- ishing. I write all this to you, not only because I am apt to analyse but also because you share what I call the artistic temperament and will probably have at some time to combat with its perils.

[omission]

Do not give up drawing under Richards's direction. It is a great opportunity for you of getting a good grip on method; and if you take seriously to writing, times may come when painting would be a relief to you. I have often regretted that I had no alternative to study and composi- tion, so that in the periods of illness and prostration I have just had to eat my heart and abide in irritable patience—to loaf around and suffer.

[Incomplete]

---

1. Margaret prefaced this letter with the following note: "I was beginning to write a little myself at that time, and my Father was very anxious that I should take seriously to writing, but he spoke and wrote to me constantly about the needful discipline and sup- pression of a nature just a little like his own." Margaret's essay on an expedition to the Silvretta Glacier appeared in the *Pall Mall Gazette,* LI (October 27, 1890). *The Davos Courier,* Nov. 8, pp. 53–54, printed the following notice of it:

In the *Pall Mall Gazette* of the 27th ult, Miss Margaret Symonds gives an interesting and thrilling description of an expedition to the Silvretta Glacier. Miss Symonds was accompanied by a friend, a guide and his son. The object of the ex- cursion was apparently to toboggan down the snow fields. To many of those who like tobogganing in a mild way, the idea of climbing 4,000 feet and taking a 5 hours walk for the sake of a "run" may be a little incomprehensible—the climbing to the top of the "long run" is almost too far—but those who have read Miss Symonds' description of the scene from the highest point they reached and of the wildly exciting descent on the toboggan will readily understand how the writer was repaid for the long climb. The friend did not fare so well, having her fingers somewhat frostbitten, and the run down could hardly have been enjoyable to her being towed by the guide at a pace "as moderate as the steepness of the descent allowed."

1843. *To Janet Ross*[1]

560 Zattere Venezia Nov: 6. 1890

Dear Mrs Ross

I found your very kind letter when I came here a week ago, & ought to have answered it sooner. But I was so uncertain about my movements after the journey which tired me, that I thought it best to wait & see how things went. On the whole I have been doing well, in spite of miserable weather. And now, if you are really ready to receive me, I should greatly like to pay you the proposed visit.

I think of leaving this on Sunday & sleeping at Bologna (Albergo d'Italia), so that at the last moment, if anything alters your plans, a word directed to me there would find.

It is most kind of you to say that I may bring my gondolier. He is an old servant, has been with me for ten years, & is a very good fellow. Just now I am really dependent on him while travelling.

With kind regards to Mr [Henry] Ross, believe me most truly yours

J. A. Symonds.

I will telegraph my train from Bologna, so as to secure your Cabby!

---

1. See L 976.

1844. *To Herbert P. Horne*

Venice Nov 9 1890

Dear Mr Horne

I have been expecting the [Century Guild] Hobby Horse for October for some time. Has it not appeared? Galton told me there was to be something of his in it, & a poem by L. Johnson. Also I thought it might perhaps contain my Adonis.[1]

I want now to tell you that I should like to *subscribe* to the Hobby Horse, & if you will inform the publishers, I will send them for the year 1891 my subscription for one copy. I do not know what it is, but they will tell me.

I hope, at the same time, that if I write anything in it, you will let me have the six copies you said you gave to writers.

In the case, for example, of Bion's Lament, I should like to send a copy to some scholar friends. I want particularly to let Prof Henry Sidgwick & Sir Charles Bowen[2] see it.

I have been at Venice ten days, in bad gloomy weather. But it is a great rest to the nerves & brain after that narrow Alpine valley I live so much in.

I am going on to Florence: & if you send the Hobby Horse, please do so to *Am Hof Davos Platz.*

Believe me very sincerely yours

John Addington Symonds.

---

1. The number did include Symonds' poem (see Ls 1803 and 1830) as well as Lionel Johnson's poem, "In Praise of Youth" and his reviews of Dowden's ed. of *The Lyrical Ballads of Wordsworth and Coleridge* and W. Kineton Parkes' ed. of *The Painter-Poets,* and also Galton's review of P. Hume Brown's biography (1890) of George Buchanan (1506–82), the humanist and reformer.

2. Sir Charles Synge Christopher Bowen (1835–94), Balliol College; B. A. and president of the Oxford Union Society, 1858; Hertford Prize, 1855; and Ireland Prize, 1857; a distinguished jurist; in 1890, one of the Lords Justices of Appeal.

1845. *To Edmund Gosse*

560 Zattere Venice Nov: 9. 1890

My dear Gosse

I left Davos this day fortnight, worn out with my long illness in that narrow valley (two months & three weeks just sponged out of active or enjoyable existence). I have been here since, alone in my own little house, with my gondolier friend Angelo [Fusato] & his wife to look after me, & a great many friends of different nations near. The change has been beneficial to nerves & brain; but I am not myself yet.

Tomorrow Angelo & I are going to stay with Mrs Ross at

Poggio Gherardo
Via Settignanese
Firenze.

I wish, if you have time, that you would write to me there. I should much enjoy a letter. But your own troubles of illness & overwork are enough to make the writing of letters irksome. So I expect nothing.

My essay called "A Problem in Modern Ethics" is being printed. I will send you a proof of the title, contents, & books used, from which you will see what line I am taking. I think the whole thing will be as long as the other "Problem" ["in Greek Ethics"] I gave you. But it is being printed differently: only on one side of the page & with a large margin.

Did I tell you of the very interesting & explicit answers I drew from Whitman about "Calamus"?[1]

Burton's[2] death was a sad blow. Had I been able to get to Venice as early as I wished, I might have seen him again, for I was going to Trieste to stay with him. I had a heart-rending letter from Lady Burton the other day. She says nothing about his books papers & immense collections of notes. Nor does his doctor, Baker,[3] who has also written, giving me a full account of his last hours. At Davos I feared such a catastrophe was inevitable. Baker told me he never left him for 10 minutes together; & as he spoke of gout, I suspected that the muscles of the heart must be affected.

I am really "up to the discussion of things of interest"; & just at present, being not fit yet for literary work, take a pleasure in writing letters & keeping a pretty full diary of impressions.

My window here, where I write, is so charming & the whole via of the Zattere & the canal of the Guidecca, in part, crowded with all kinds of craft, yellow & red sails, etc, leading on to the distant mainland & the Euganean Hills behind wh the sun sets. I am just above a bridge (it is an entresol [mezzanine floor] I live in) up & down wh go divine beings: sailors of the marine, soldiers, blue vested & trowsered fishermen, swaggering gondoliers. I can almost see their faces as they top the bridge. By rising from the chair a little I do so at once and get some smiles from passing strangers. A Princess Dolgorouky[4] has a house next ours (across a little canal or *rio*), wh stands behind an old walled garden; the trees of this garden, cypresses maritime pines olives etc, make an excellent side foreground to the expansive water view.

I am almost sorry to be leaving for Florence. But I want to see Janet Ross[5] again. She is a very old friend; & though most people do not like her, I do. A thorough *bon comarade*.

Please remember me to Mrs Gosse, & tell her how much I sympathize with her in her trouble. And do not forget yours affectionately

J ASymonds

[Across front of p. 1:] I wonder if the Oct: [*The Century Guild*] "Hobby Horse"[6] had a version by me of Bion's Adonis? Did you see it? I wanted to send you a copy. But Horne has not given me any. Did you notice Tuke's[7] pastel "Leander," & did you think it had the *aura?*

---

1. See Ls 1814, 1815, 1822, 1837.
2. Sir Richard Francis Burton had suffered from gout and was ill enough from 1887

onwards to require the personal attendance of a doctor. He died on October 20 in Trieste. Mrs. Burton, a devout Roman Catholic, had the last rites of the Church administered to him. As his literary executor, one of her first acts was as "a moral act" to burn his manuscript translation of the Arabic *The Scented Garden*. After completing his biography, she destroyed his private diaries. She allowed nothing of her husband's to be published without the stamp of approval of the secretary of the National Vigilance Society.

3. Dr. Frederick Grenfell Baker (?–1930), born in Lahore, India, travelled with Burton for 3½ years, 1887–90.

4. Princess Ekaterina Mikhailovna Dolgorukaya (1846–1922), second wife (1880) of Czar Alexander II (1818–81) and author of *Alexander II* (1882).

5. See L 976.

6. V (Oct. 1890), 121–26.

7. See L 1838.

1846. *To Edmund Gosse*

Poggio Gherardo[1] 23. Via Settignanese Firenze Nov: 15 1890

My dear Gosse

I shall certainly not be without your Beddoes.[2] It is upon a list I keep to send to Nutt: & if you had been able to send me a copy, it would have collided with the other—whose fate would then have been a place in the English Library at Davos,[3] to wh I send duplicates. Beddoes always had a powerful attraction for me; some of his lyrics being perfect except for (to my ear) a want of absolute cadence. I look forward to what you have said about his life.

Here I am in a very old castle of the Gherardi family, where Boccaccio is said to have come first when he fled from the plague. It surveys the whole Valdarno with of course Florence spread out beneath. But to my mountain-loving eye, the most charming points in the landscape are snowy Vallom-brosa & the tossed crests of the Casentino & the great white spires of the Carrara hills to westward.

I have been very ill again since I came here. Lost what I thought I had gained at Venice. I don't know how or why. Were I not with the kindest of friends I should have been miserable. The malady I suffer from has not received a name yet from the doctors. But as it includes incessant fever with headache sickness stomachache & shivering fits, you can imagine that it is inimical to any joy in life.

The only thing I have seen here is M.A.'s David in its new place at the Accademia.[4] I had not seen it there before: & till now I never knew how beautiful it was. Among other things plenum juvenis et testiculous mirabili arte ad veram effigiem modelli sui singulariter conformati perfecit sculptor.[5] The whole statue is full of the model.

You remark on my not including "Alcibiade" etc. I notice this book (a copy of wh I have) in a note.[6] But it does not throw any light on the psychological problem, & is in the strictest sense of the term too "paiderasti-cally-sodomitical" to be of much use to any enquirer. Tout ça c'est suffisam-ment cornu: e pur troppo![7]

Yes. I have seen reproductions of Tuke's[8] things, & I feel certain about their character. It would not be right to say more in writing than that they strike me in this way. He is a son, I believe, of a mad doctor[9] (horrid & opprobrious name), who was a great friend of my father's. Lives and works at Falmouth. His father paid me a visit at Davos this summer. I tried to draw him about "Sexual inversion," but found that he preferred to dis-course on "hypnotism."

I was always afraid that Kipling would go up like a rocket & come down like a stick. If you remember, I talked enthusiastically last autumn about him,[10] before he was widely known. But this was wholly on the strength of "Soldiers Three" and "Studies in Black & White." As he mul-tiplied, it seemed to me that what one felt to be the weak side of his work became more apparent, while the stuff dwindled for a want of aliment.

He is so young that he may well yet find the *via artis,* which is very different from the *vita vitae* strongly felt & lively seized.

Probably his milieu is not a metropolis. And then why, why did he go in for a boom. I fear he determined to force himself up; & no talent can do this with impunity. Es bildet ein Talent sich in der Stille.[11] Distinction he lacks.

They say Stevenson has gone back to Samoa after all.[12] Well: if we want to see him, we must go to Samoa. If I were not a "povero vecchio senza denti e senza cazzo"[13]— if I were a young man I would go there. But I am afraid it would be like deliberately dooming oneself to the fate of Tantalus.

What a silly letter this is. Italian brains are light, & I am always listening to their chatter in this house.

Do not write to me again here. If I do not get unexpectedly better, I shall travel back in 3 days to Davos, prepared like a Roman to wrap my cloak around me & endure my wretchedness in my own house.

Everyrs

JAS.

1. Janet Ross' home outside Florence, once owned by the Della Gherardesca, a noble Italian family first recorded as being in Tuscany; most famous member was Ugolino, count of Donoratico (died 1289), immortalized by Dante (*Inferno*, XXXII, 124 ff.); family dominated Pisa (1316–47) and in the 16th cent. part of it moved to Florence.

2. Thomas Lovell Beddoes (1803–49), poet and dramatist, born at Clifton, where his father, Thomas Beddoes (1760–1808), physician and author, had founded (1798) a "pneumatic institute." Gosse edited his *Poetical Works* (1890) and his *Letters* (1894).

3. Symonds helped to found the English Library at Davos. It is still in existence but rarely used.

4. In 1882 Michelangelo's statue was taken for safety from the site on the terrace of the palace of the Signory, a site it had held since May 1504, to a hall in the Academy of Fine Arts.

5. The sculptor has executed (a form) full of youth and virility, with remarkable skill corresponding amazingly with a true image of his model.

6. In *A Problem in Modern Ethics,* privately printed in an edition of 100 copies (1891); the note, p. 16, mentions "the remarkably outspoken [Italian] romance entitled 'Alcibiade fanciullo a scolla.' "

7. All that is sufficiently absurd: and unfortunately.

8. See L 1838.

9. See L 1838.

10. At the start of his career Kipling wrote laudatory letters to Symonds. One of these is at Bristol University.

11. Talent is formed in silence. Goethe, *Tasso,* I, ii.

12. Stevenson moved to Vailima in November 1890.

13. Poor old man, without teeth and without genitalia.

1847. *To Edmund Gosse*

Poggio Gherardo 23. Via Settignanese Firenze Nov: 23. 1890

My dear Gosse

I am still here, you see; but I am going off today to stay with the Contessa Almorò Pisani at Vescovana,[1] & then to Venice for a short while, before I return to Davos.

Your gift of Tolstoi's book "War etc"[2] reached me here; & I value it far more for your "appreciation" of the author than for the confused & sermonizing story wh that introduces. You have indeed been very successful in giving a broad survey & a general estimate of Tolstoi's puzzling career & of his relation to Russian literature.

I want to ask you something in the interest of my hostess here, Mrs [Janet] Ross. She has some translations from Heine's poems in the hand-writing of her mother Lady Duff Gordon,[3] wh Lady D. G. who was a friend of Heine's made at his special request. I was reading these the other evening, & I pointed out nine or ten (including a complete version of "Almansor"), wh I told Mrs Ross I thought quite the best things done from Heine into English. This is what I do think; for they reproduce Heine's rhythm & spontaneity of phrase, without conscious effort on the part of the translator. In fact, they retain what I feel to be the essential part of the original.

Well: Mrs Ross would like to publish these; & I have promised to ask you whether you thought they might do for the Century. Her idea was to preface them with an account of Lady Duff Gordon's personal relations to Heine, & then to print the 10 selected pieces. I suggested that, as these ten fall apart into 4 groups—Almansor, one set of pathetic, one of sarcastic, & one of purely fanciful lyrics—she might separate them & lead from one group to the other by a few remarks.

What then I come to ask is whether you would write Mrs Ross a line, saying whether or no you would look at the Ms for the Century,[4] & in the next place (if you give her any encouragement) how you think the versions ought to put forth.

I hope you will forgive me for giving you this trouble. I cannot help thinking you would take the same view I do of Lady D.G.'s translations; & in that case you might not be sorry to have them.

My proofs of the essay on "A Problem in Modern Ethics" come in rather slowly. I have got through about one half. It will run to 90 pages, I think. The style is arid & severe.

I will write to you again from Venice (560 Zattere is my address there).

Ever yours

J A Symonds.—

---

1. For a note on Evelina Van Millingen Pisani, Countess di Barbana, see L 1717.

2. Tolstoi's *War and Peace* (1866).

3. Lady Lucie or Lucy Duff-Gordon (1821–69), woman of letters; daughter of John Austin (1790–1859), the jurist; in 1840 married Sir Alexander Cornewall Duff-Gordon (1811–72); lived in Egypt from 1862 and died in Cairo; known for translations from the German and for *Letters from the Cape* (1862–63), *Letters from Egypt* (1863), and *Last Letters from Egypt* (1875). See L 976. See Janet Ross, *Three Generations of English Women* (2 vols., 1888).

4. The translation did not appear in the *Century* but in *Murray's Magazine*, IX (1891), 769–76, and in the *Eclectic Magazine*, CXVII (1891), 167–73.

Vescovana Stranghella, Wednesday Nov. 26 [1890][1]

My dear Janet

This is how I am going to call you, if you will allow me. We had a very quiet journey on Sunday & found at Bologna a letter from Mme Pisani begging me not to pass her by without a visit. So here I have been since 2 oclock on Monday, & now I am going on to Venice 560 Zattere.

Fortunately the weather is extremely beautiful, & so this vast plain intersected by the Canals of the Adige looks its very best—like a silvery dreamy Holland with richer soil & more luxuriant vegetation, & the Euganean Hills for great permanent blue clouds upon the nether horizon.

I drove with the Contessa [Pisani] over a large part of her estate yesterday, visiting I don't know how many farm-houses, inspecting (she said) nearly 300 head of huge white oxen, & blowing up—at least the Countess blew up—every unfortunate man woman & child that came in our way. It took nearly four hours, & gave me considerable respect for the Pisani property. They have one fascinating old house for villeggiatura [summer residence] right on the Adige, built deep below the level of the dykes, but rising to a high aerial story wh looks down into the swirling mass of water, & across it to the Apennines, & backwards to the Euganeans & the Alps. I should like to inhabit that "altana" [the top story] for awhile.

I have heard all about Osman Bey, Mme Pisani's wicked brother.[2] He has been living 4 months in the village at the gates, abusing her & when the Empress Frederick came on a visit last month, he used to harangue the contadini against them both. She seems half annoyed & half amused at the infliction, says he has been a misery to her for the last 40 years. It is altogether a very odd family history, hers.

I find in the back of an envelope this rhyme, done I think from one of your Tuscan lullabies.

What are	Carnival, Carnival, fly away home.
you to do	They've made a fool's cap to set on your crown:
with	tag's a black-pudding
fegatello?[3]	Each tag is a sausage that dangles down.
	Carnival, Carnival, fly away home.

Angelo & I talk a great deal, & I think more, about Poggio Gherardo, & all the pleasant time there. I wish I had been stronger or more capable of enjoyment. In some strange way "j'ai perdu ma force et ma vie."[4] I wonder whether they will ever come back again, even in part!

Please remember me with affection to Mr Ross, & believe me always most sincerely yours

J A Symonds

---

1. Katharine Furse dated this letter 1889, but it clearly was written in 1890.

2. See Ls 1717 and 1850. Osman Bey (Frederick Milligen, 1839?– ?), as a Russian assumed the name Alexis Andrejevitch. He wrote *Les Anglais en Orient, 1830–76* (1877) and *Les Femmes en Turquie* (1878).

3. Slice of pig's liver.

4. A tag from de Musset which Symonds frequently used, especially in the letters of Vol. II.

1849. *To Henry Sidgwick*

Venice, 560 Zattere, Nov. 27, 1890

[Dear Henry]

You see I am in Italy: and to-day the whole of Venice is under snow. It looks like a bad imitation of Davos in July bad weather, while the ships along the canal of the Giudecca, seen from my windows, present the appearance of blurred illustrations to a book of Arctic exploration.

I only came here yesterday. I have been staying in the Tuscan country, not far from Florence, with Mrs. Ross; and then at Vescovana, near the Euganean Hills, with the Contessa Almorò Pisani.

I can't say that these Italian "peregrinities" (as Carlyle calls such wanderings in "Sterling's Life"[1]) have done me much good. Three months of illness at Davos, continual fever, and a general disturbance of the whole system, including brain, lungs, and stomach, pulled me down terribly; and I find at fifty that the recuperative force, with which I was once singularly gifted, is upon the wane. Thank God I have been brought to mortification, and now am willing to accept the advent of old age. I do not even hanker feverishly after Koch's miraculous lymph.[2] If it be of any good, it comes for me too late, and I shall only regret it did not come when Janet first began to fade. But at present I suspend my judgment, and refuse to be sanguine for my fellow-sufferers.

Ah, me! what stuff Tolstoi has taken to write. "Work while ye have the light," says nothing toward instruction and edification. The "Kreutzer Sonata"[3] is of course full of true things; but you cannot eradicate sex from human nature.

Publishers want me to write all sorts of things. I found three letters here yesterday: one clamouring for a little book on Boccaccio; one offering me something like 500 guineas for a new grand "Life of Michael Angelo"; the third suggesting that a prose version of the "Æneid" from my pen would be a certain success. If I were more elastic, I would bite at Michael Angelo, rewrite the history of Tuscan art, and illustrate my æsthetic principles by reference to that colossal manifestation of wayward force. But I do not know; I want to sleep more than to think.

[Incomplete]

---

1. Thomas Carlyle, *The Life of John Sterling* (1851).

2. Robert Koch (1843–1910), German physician and pioneer bacteriologist; first to isolate anthrax bacillus (1876) and to publish (1883) a method of innoculation against this disease; isolated tubercle bacillus (1882); identified comma bacillus causing Asiatic cholera (1883); produced tuberculin (1890); awarded Nobel prize for physiology and medicine (1905).

In November 1890, Samuel Richards wrote to his wife:

The greatest excitement here exists from Dr Kochs cure of Consumption, and Ruedi is the most excited of all. He says it is the greatest discovery the world has ever seen, and will be the death of Davos in no time. He has been in Correspondence with one of Kochs assistants & knows much of the process but not all. . . . They are erecting hospitals all over Berlin & hundreds are flocking there begging to be treated. The German Emperor has taken it in hand and says the world shall have the benefit of it. . . . Ruedi told Coester in 12 months from now he would be glad to take for a whole floor what he charged for a room now, and old Halsboer said if it was all true, they might as well touch a match to Davos & pull up the rails on the R.R. I hope to the heavens it is true and I would like to be the happy man to touch the match to the hateful nest. Ruedi said he hoped in 3 or 4 weeks every Doctor would be in possession of the Discovery & wanted to know if I was willing to be treated & I said yes only an idiot would refuse. (Gallini Collection)

The news had been prematurely released by a student in November 1890. Amid the ensuing clamor, Koch remained silent about his methods of preparing the "lymph" (he called it paratoloid) and conservative about its efficacy. The news of Koch's discovery was a featured story in *The Davos Courier*, Nov. 15, 1890.

3. In *The Kreutzer Sonata* (1889) Tolstoi assumed that the effect of music on sexual morals is deleterious, his illustration being the effect of Beethoven's *Kreutzer Sonata* for violin and piano (Opus 47).

1850. *To Janet Ross*

My dear Janet

I did not come back to Venice with a cold caught at Florence. But I found Venice under snow & very disagreeable. I have hardly been outside my own apartments, which are extremely snug & comfortable, & have the most amusing windows to look out of, since I arrived.

Of course I do not mind the mention of my name in your "forewords" on Heine.[1] They introduce the translations very well.

I will tell you the story of Mme Pisani[2] Her father was Dr. Millingen,[3] the man who was with Byron when he died. He married a handsome French Levantine woman, connected fairly well in France I believe. They did not get on well; & she went, when Evelina (Mme P.) was 5 & Frederick (Osman Bey) was 4, to Rome. There they stayed with Mrs Millingen, the grandmother, & a "Signorina Millingen dei Conti di Millingen," also called "Contessa Millingen," a maiden aunt, who had been dame d'honneur to the Duchess of Lucca. Both of these ladies & also Mrs (Dr) M were R. Catholics. So Evelina was sent to the Sacré Coeur in Rome & Frederick to the Jesuits. After awhile Mrs (Dr) Millingen decamped, leaving her children at Rome; & Mme Pisani never saw her again. When she turned up, it was as the wife of Kibritzi Pasha at Constantinople. Her life in the Harem was written & published, & she attempted to purge herself of the crime of murdering a female slave. Well: to wind up her history, she got divorced from Kibritzi, went to Paris with her precious son, & committed suicide at last by throwing herself out of the windows of a hotel.

Now for Frederick. He remained with the Jesuits till he was 18. His father than determined to make him an English Protestant. So he went to London with a small allowance, wh he increased by sponging on friends & fraudulent transactions. Thinking his mother's position as a Pasha's wife to have its advantageous side, he made himself a Musselman & entered the Ottoman army. He used to boast that he was instrumental in the betrayal of Kars[4] to the Russians; & it is certain he had a pension from Levikoff[5] through that man's life. Also he became a Russian subject, & remains so to the present day—if he has any nationality at all after all this muddle. He left the Turkish army under some cloud.[6]

For the last 40 years he has been publishing books abusing his father and Mme Pisani, pretending to defend his mother, etc. One of these, wh was suppressed, was lent me by the Princess of Montenegro,[7] who told me he came to her for money (to her! she has not a pezzo) on the score of being a Servian! The book is full of the vilest scandals & dirtinesses: how far justified by the facts of Dr M's life of course I cannot say. Mme P lent me another of these libels, wh is still in circulation—in French, Russian, Italian, & German.

I must tell you that when Mme Pisani came out of the Sacré Coeur, she sided with her father,—lived some time in his house at Constantinople. It was at Venice, in the house of her school friend, the Princess Giovanelli,[8] that she met the Conte Almorò Pisani, who being informed that she was a young Turkish lady come to be baptized & made a Christian, begged to be presented. He was agreeably surprised to find her a good Catholic & a perfect Italian. So he proposed marriage to her.

Venetian society still calls her la Turca. The Princess of Montenegro, e.g., who does not like her, does so when she wants to be nasty.

And, as she says, it is almost impossible for her to disentangle herself from the complications of her family. People will not take the trouble to understand that she is practically an English orphan educated by an aunt at Rome.

Osman Bey is now the agent in Italy for a Socialist, or anarchist, society. He has been doing politics in the 2d Collegio di Padua, & at the same time trying to extort money from his sister. She has not yielded one inch to his threats & calumnies & persecutions. And there is the situation.

This is a long history. I hope it will not bore you. Probably Mr Ross will remember plenty about part of it. Kindest regards to him.

Yrs even affely

JASymonds

I think of leaving for Davos on Wednesday. Angelo [Fusato] begs me to send his respects to you & the Padrone. He wrote a letter to Fortunato[9] I believe.

---

1. Mrs. Ross was editing her mother's translations of Heine's poems. See L 1847.
2. L 1717.
3. Julius Michael Millingen (1800–78), physician and writer; studied at Rome and Edinburgh; went to Corfu, 1823; attended Byron in his last illness; surgeon in the Greek army, 1824; settled in Constantinople, 1827; court physician to 5 successive sultans; discovered ruins of Aczani; defended himself at length in his *Memoirs* (1831) against charges that he had caused Byron's death; married 3 times; died at Constantinople.
4. In the Russo-Turkish war of 1877–78, Kars, in N. E. Turkey, fell to the Russians on Nov. 18, 1877.

5. Probably a mistake for Melikoff: Count Mikhail Tarielovich Loris-Melikoff (1825?–88), Russian soldier and statesman who took Kars in 1878.
6. See L 1848.
7. See L 1790.
8. Probably Princess Maria, née Chigi-Albani, wife of Joseph, 2nd and last Prince Giovanelli (1824–86), upon whose death the title became extinct. The Princess' adopted son Alberto was made Prince Giovanelli by King Humbert in 1897.
9. One of Mrs. Ross' servants.

1851. *To Margaret Symonds*

[Venice, Dec. 2, 1890]

[Dear Margaret]

The sort of conversation I had at Florence with various literary men, and more or less literary ladies and pretty countesses and ugly Scotch dowagers, is of absolutely no use to any human soul except in the way of superficial pastime. You only touch the epidermis of these people, and the *obiter dicta* of somebodies are as unsatisfying to the spirit as the remarks of nobodies. Indeed, the table-talk of nobodies, if they are peasants and artisans, seems to me really more succulent than that of somebodies—unless you are living with the people of importance in close intimacy and sustained sympathy.

Now, of the very peculiar conditions of really profitable intercourse which I have described, I have always had plenty, and there has been an atmosphere of it around me. So that it is natural to feel the vacuity of anything else. How vacuous you would have thought Mme. R.'s tea-party at Florence, in spite of its numerous 'eminent authors,' or Lady Z.'s reception in her princely Villa, in spite of its grand names and solemn toilettes!

I had good talk with Mrs. Ross at Poggio Gherardo—she is full of spark and spirit—and good talk here with P., and last evening with Van Haanen.[1] But in these cases there was the intimité of truly interesting people moving in a circle of mental freedom.

No amount of intimité with the European scholar——or the famous ——or the learned——, would make these celebrities other than tiresome. You get the best of them in their books: and a man like Dakyns, who cannot write a book, is better company—a man like myself, who talk better than I write, is excellent company. I do not deny that, when one is quite young, there is interest in seeing what are called eminent people, and also that the mere accidents and varieties of society are amusing and educating.

526

But I remain sure that the right way to form both character and talent is to do this by means of study and the exercise of creative or critical faculties.

'Es bildet ein Talent sich in der Stille.'[2]

And this is what I have always been seeking to impress on you; putting it even in Clough's stoical way:

'Seek, seeker, in thyself, submit to find
Life in the stones and life in the blank mind.'[3]

J. A. S.

---

1. P. may be for Percy Pinkerton. Van Haanen is unidentified.
2. Talent is formed in silence—Goethe, *Tasso*, I, ii.
3. "Dipsychus," Part II, scene ii, ll, 102–03.

1852. *To Janet Ross*

Am Hof, Davos Platz, Switzerland. Dec: 11 1890

My dear Janet

You see I am here. I arrived on Saty evening, having had a very dull & gloomy three days' journey from Venice. But within five miles of Davos we emerged from thick fog into the glorious clear sunset of the upper Alps— white pyramids, tinted like red & amber coloured jewels by the sun's rays, shooting into cloudless serenity of blue. And so it has been ever since. All the while I was in Italy I did not get as much & as intense sun heat as I have had these four days. It is an odd climate; for of course the frost is severe: thermometer at night generally about zero Fahrenheit, more usually below than above that point.

I feel on the whole really the better for my Italian holiday, for the delightful days of gentle summer at Poggio Gherardo.[1] And I am going to rest as much as I can from work for some time. Grazzini[2] is quite right about that. By the way, when you see him, do give my kindest salutations to that charming man.

I hope Gozzi[3] & the Norths[4] reached you. I will write today to have my poems sent. But I do not expect you to care for them. They are a very mixed lot, & the best are sonnets in Vagabunduli Libellus: wh means, you know, the little books of a little wanderer or vagabond.

ἀμωσγέπος is Greek for higgledypiggledy, or something of that sort.

Catherine has been reading out to me passages of Pop's [Marianne North's] autobiography.[5] The chapter on her early life is excellent, & some part of the later, about Borneo, Australia, etc, seem to me very good. I think it will be a difficult Ms to deal with, just because of its average merit, wh will render the work of excision hard. I do not know who is likely to edit it. I hardly think that Catherine can, & Fred North[6] cannot. He is coming here in ten days, & there will be some talk about the matter then. I will not forget that Pop once put the Ms. into your hands.

Mr Gosse wrote me about Heine: "I will consult the editor of the Century, & let you know: I don't much expect it will suit him." I hear nothing more than this, which is not very hopeful, & wh shows that Gosse has only the power of suggestion.

Angelo [Fusato] is here. He enjoys the frost & hot sun, & is very well. Were he in the room I am sure he would insist on having all sorts of messages sent to everybody at Poggio Gherardo.

With my kindest regards to Mr Ross, believe me always

Yours

JASymonds.

---

1. Mrs. Ross' home.

2. Reginaldo Grazzini (1848–1906), composer, director of the Instituto musicale di Reggio Emilia and of the "liceo" Benedetto Marcello at Venice, and *insegnante di composizione al conservatorio di Firenze;* composed liturgical and sacred music.

3. His translation of Gozzi's *Memoirs* (2 vols., 1890).

4. *The Lives of the Norths.* See L 1473 for details of this work on Mrs. Symonds' ancestors.

5. Marianne North's *Recollections of a Happy Life* being edited by Mrs. Symonds.

6. Frederick Keppel North (1860–1948), Symonds' brother-in-law, a lawyer of distinction; chairman of Norfolk Quarter Sessions, chancellor of the dioceses of Norwich, 1908, and of St. Edmundsbury and Ipswich, 1914; Justice of the Peace for Norfolk, 1912.

1853. *To Horatio Forbes Brown*

Davos, Dec. 15 [1890]

[Dear Horatio]

It is nine days now that I have been here, and never a cloud. Very cold at night. Ruedi came to see me yesterday. He says there is still serious mischief in my lung, quite enough to account for the physical weakness and other things I complain of. From time to time at night I tear myself to pieces with fits of the most frightful coughing, which leave me almost helpless, and shaky all the following day.

I do not think I was cut out to be loved; admired, liked, befriended, run after—*si, pur troppo* [it's so, unfortunately] but love is something else. I often think it is that I do not know how to love. No animals or birds take fancies for me, "nor women neither." "Are the souls so too, when they depart hence—lame and old and loveless?"

I am intoxicated by your phrase about Pennance Cove.[1] What is there in the nerve-value of a phrase? I believe that phrases carry with them sometimes whole moods and spiritual effluences of the man who makes them. You will think me pretty mad. Yet I am writing on a cold morning, before the sun has climbed the Jacobshorn, in my cave of care—care-haunted study—after a strange night of fever. And out there—on the void infinite, the unexpected, unexplored, intangible—what is to become of a soul, so untameably young in its old ruined body, growing hourly more impassioned as life wanes! Well: the sun has reached the crest and is flooding my table with heat and light. It is 10.20 a.m. Good-bye.

[Incomplete]

---

1. A cove on Falmouth Bay in Cornwall, near Penzance. Brown had visited the painter Henry Scott Tuke at Falmouth in 1890. See Maria Tuke Sainsbury, *Henry Scott Tuke: A Memoir*, p. 90.

1854. *To Janet Ross*

Am Hof, Davos Platz, Switzerland. Dec: 16 1890

My dear Janet

I have come across my old translation of "Auf Flügeln des Gesanges",[1] & I send you a copy—though it is not worth much, except for the rhythm. In the impossibility of securing perfect double rhymes, I fell back you see on jingles.

Angelo [Fusato] is very anxious that the enclosed photographs of himself & me should be given to Fortunato.[2] I daresay you will kindly bestow them with our joint saluti; & I am certain that you will not be tempted to detain mine by the way.

I have read a good deal now of Pop's [Marianne North's] Memoirs.[3] It is a fatiguing book from its dead level & voluminousness of detail. But each paragraph by itself seems good.

We are so near to Christmas that I send you & the Padrone all the best wishes of the season. We have had ten days of quite unbroken sunshine ever since I came here: cold at night, but very enjoyable for walking or sledging in the day.

Ever yrs.

JAS

When my poetry books arrive you may take the enclosed list as a guide to what I think about the best in them.

---

1. "On the Wings of Song" (Heine).
2. Mrs. Ross' servant.
3. Marianne North's *Recollections of a Happy Life* being edited by Mrs. Symonds. See L 1852.

1855. *To Dr. John Johnston*[1]

Am Hof, Davos Platz, Switzerland, Dec 22nd, 1890.

My dear Sir,

I want to send you very hearty & very kindly greetings, with thanks for your "Notes of a visit to Walt Whitman". I appreciate the little book in the first place for its own sake: among the many attempts to delineate Whitman as he is none have brought him so freshly & livingly before me as this. The moderate compass, & the unaffected unegoistic simplicity, of the narrative give it a high place in the Gospel of the Good Grey Poet. It is like a bit of literature descending from a purer, less affected age than ours, & will play a very considerable part in the formation of that tradition wh Whitman is destined to hand down to the future.

Next, I am touched with the request that you should send it me, & by the fact in your first Coloquy with the man I venerate so deeply you should have handed him the reprint of my humble essay on Dante. For a broken & ageing man of letters up here among the Alpine snows, these particulars have an almost tender, pathetic, interest. They bring a film before the eyes,

530

through which swims so much of life, of the irrecoverable past, of the unequal battle with circumstances, of spiritual forces wh have sustained, & of the failures wh have saddened. I do not know whether you have seen a short piece of writing by me, in which I said that Whitman's work had influenced me more than any thing in literature except the Bible & Plato. This expresses the mere fact, so far as I can read my inner self, though perhaps my own industry in life, on the lines of author mainly may not seem to corroborate my statement.

I owe to him a great debt, & had I not been fettered by the chains of an unpardoning disease, Consumption, with which it has been my duty to fight, I would long ago have crossed the seas to visit him.

So you see that anything wh bring him near to me is dear to me. And you have done this so vitally that I am writing to you more than with the measured terms of ceremonious courtesy.

I wish I could see a copy of the photograph you took of him "& Warry"[2] even were it imperfect I am trained to see, an artist of any kind sees more than the uninitiated can.

Whitman himself sent me a sheet of very interesting portraits of himself, taken at various periods of his manhood. These, with his permission, I am trying to get reproduced by a Munich Artist[3] who has great skill in such matters. He is doubtful whether he can succeed. But should the result prove worthy in any degree I will give myself the pleasure of sending you copies.

Believe me, meanwhile, to be very sincerely, & in Whitmanly friendship.

yours,

John Addington Symonds.

---

1. Dr. John Johnston (d. 1927), honorary surgeon to the Bolton Infirmary, Lancashire; M. D., University of Edinburgh (1877); published his *Notes of a Visit to Walt Whitman and Some of his Friends in 1890* in 1898. See L 2014. The copy of this letter was probably made by Dr. Richard Maurice Bucke (1837–1902) of London, Ontario, who met Whitman for the first time in the autumn of 1878. Bucke, head of an insane asylum in London, was a notable alienist. His meeting with Whitman had mystic significance for him: Whitman "was either actually a god or in some sense clearly and entirely praeter-human." Bucke's *Walt Whitman,* a biography, was published in Philadelphia in 1883. Bucke and Johnston were friends.

2. Johnston's photograph of Whitman and Warren Fritzinger (Whitman's male nurse) on the Camden Wharf is p. 55 of Johnston's *Notes of a Visit.* . . . See L 1907.

3. The Munich chemist, Johann Obernetter. See L 1790.

IV

Michelangelo, Whitman, and the Homosexual Question

1891–1892

[Jan. 1891]

[Dear ——]

I find it difficult to express all the feeling which your little book of poems has aroused in me to-night.[1] I took it up, curious, expecting to find things rare in it; but I was not prepared for "infinite riches in a little room."[2] These, having rapidly read the book, I find there; and then I begin to meditate: why is it possible that I should not have discerned the book before, in all the nine years of its printed and published life? What is the function of the critical press, if it failed to force it on my vision and my sense of hearing? What spilth and waste of melody and genius must be going on, if these lyrics fail to arrest attention?

Such, indeed, is the first tide of emotions roused by reading your poetry.

I am not going to pretend that I regard your poetry as very wide in range, and so forth, or to seek in it a philosophy of life, &c. I do not think it aims at that, or has it. But it is the real note of a really poetical, gifted, sensitive, and exquisitely cadenced individuality.

It is like the poetry of some of our most beloved Elizabethans; with a smack of the decade (or two decades) which produced it, a touch of Swinburne, a grace from the French, fused in the alembic of the writer's self.

To-night I am bee-drunken with the harmless honey of your song. But if morning hours, and another reading, do not alter my opinion, I will send these unpremeditated words to you.

I should so much like to make an *étude* of your poems. But I am ignorant—I do not know whether they are not already far more widely known than I could make them known, and loved than I could teach men how to love them.

Tell me if you would like me to write what I think about their excellence—not dithyrambically, as here, but soberly as art requires. If you would, are you willing to tell me something about yourself, and how your lyrics came out of your heart and life, and whether you go on writing still?

How I envy you your gift of rhythm, and inevitable melodic phrase. No, envy is not the word; but if God had given me that gift I could have said what I wanted, and what I must never say through want of magic.

[Incomplete]

---

1. Since H. F. Brown does not name the recipient of this letter except by calling him one of the younger generation of poets, we have not been able to identify this work or the author.
2. Christopher Marlowe, *The Jew of Malta,* Act I.

1857. *To Henry Graham Dakyns*

Am Hof, Davos Platz, Switzerland. Sunday night, Jan: 4 1891

Heaven only knows whether the wild address on the envelope will find you. I can't find your last letter.

I have been very ill since July—: With frequent attacks of fever. I cannot work, & any enjoyment of life is a secondrate imitation—shoddy.

My dear Graham

I know not what there is in the night—a lonely night & sad enough for me, heavy with cares & weariful through sadness—wh makes it imperative that I should write to you.

The injunction has come once, twice, thrice, unbidden & resisted. I have nothing particular to say; & what I should say, if you were with me, must not be written. Yet I have to write. It is a case for the Psychical Research Society.[1] I am not anxious about you. I know you cannot help me in my troubles. And I have no heart head or will to write about indifferent matters.

Yet I have to indite to you an epistle, as they say.

I received the newspaper you sent to me or Catherine with the final fireworks of Wilson's[2] exit in it.

I wonder what Glazebrook[3] will do at Clifton. I knew him here, two years ago—did not think him a strong man—as a Master perhaps—but certainly not as an intelligence.

536

How much intelligence is wanted to make an efficient figure-head for a Public School!

I hope they are going to give up the study of Greek. They teach it so infernally that it had better be done away with. And the Greek voice sings in accord with few souls now.

Will the Greek classics survive in translations? I doubt. That, as you know, is Jowett's hope! But they do not form a Bible—have no relation to religion & the bourgeoisie, & finally unless "set to the tune of Amanda"[4] are indecorous.

Tell me on a p:c: whether you would like to have a little book I have just been printing privately: called "A Problem in Modern Ethics." It is about unisexual love, what the Germans call "die Conträre Sexual Empfindung."[5] If I do not hear, I will not send it. Else, when I get my copies of the treatise, I reserve you one.

Goodnight. I wish I could talk to you. The years do not freeze my feelings or my soul; but they are playing the deuce with me in other ways. Always yours

JAS

1. The society to which Symonds' friends F. W. H. Myers and Henry Sidgwick and others belonged.

2. J. M. Wilson resigned as headmaster of Clifton College in December, 1890.

3. Michael George Glazebrook (1853?–1926), assistant master, Harrow, for 9 years (1879–88); headmaster January 1891 to July 1905; canon residentiary, Ely, 1906–26. Of minor importance, but interesting nevertheless, is the fact that Glazebrook was the first Englishman to jump 6 feet (1874).

4. Symonds is using a device used for hymn words which can be sung to a variety of selected tunes. What he means is that unless the classics are "set" in conventional ways (forms) and are also re-chorded so as to be conventionally and morally acceptable, they are indecorous in English (as they are not in their original languages). Amanda may be Amanda Smith (1837–?), the American Negro gospel-singer who attended the Broadlands conference of 1870. See L 712.

5. Literally, the contrary sexual sense, meaning homosexuality.

1858. *To Janet Ross*

Am Hof, Davos Platz, Switzerland. Jan: 5 1891

My dear Janet

I only read last night the news of Kinglake's[1] death. I thought at once of you, & what you must feel at the snapping of so old & long a chain. I hope that the end came without much previous suffering. It is a privilege of old age that even such terrible disease as he developed, has less power to pain.

I have been here four weeks & two days now; & have only seen three days with any cloud in them. The rest of the time we have basked in unbroken sunlight, which has enabled me to sit out of doors for many hours a day, to drive, & to take other forms of exercise, among wh tobogganning comes first. The only thing I do not do is to work my head: although I am slowly renewing acquaintance with the various sources of Michelangelo biography. I really think of taking that book up.

The fourth vol of the Journal des Goncourt[2] came to me some days ago. It is not as interesting as the first three. But it gives a very vivid account of the daily hourly sensations of a very observant subjectivity during the siege of Paris & the Commune.

There is nothing much to write about. We are all of us fairly well, & I really hope that I am making solid progress toward better health.

Angelo [Fusato] only left me yesterday for his home in Venice. I was sorry to say goodbye to him. But he had nothing to do here, & was waxing fat—not [illegible].

We have also had Fred North[3] of Rougham staying here: a bright-minded old-young man, whom I was glad to learn to know. And H F Brown from Venice comes to pay a visit of some weeks soon. For the rest, the place is full of people, & we rarely lunch or dine alone. Some of the visitors are really nice, & some are old friends. It is a very odd place, Davos.

With all best wishes for the New Year to yourself & the Padrone I am very sincerely yours

JASymonds.

---

1. Alexander William Kinglake (1809–91), *The Invasion of the Crimea* (8 vols., 1863–87) and *Eothen* (1844). For an account of Janet Ross' friendship with Kinglake see her *The Fourth Generation: Reminiscences* (1912).

2. Edmond de Goncourt (1822–96) and Jules de Goncourt (1830–70), *Journal des Goncourt,* ed. by Edmond de Goncourt (9 vols., 1887–96), the 4th being published in 1890.

3. Mrs. Symonds' brother. See L 1852.

Davos, Jan. 7. [1891]

[Dear Horatio]

I went last night—what is rare with me—to a concert at the Kurhaus [Sanitorium]; and what is rarer still, I went in a mood sensitive to music. I heard a young American, called Lockwood,[1] play one of Beethoven's pianoforte Concertos. I am going now to set down the thoughts which came into my mind.

The pianoforte, in contrast with a full orchestra, brings up before our picture-making brain a crowd of images. Here are some which came to me. I seemed to see and feel a rill of cold pellucid water flowing unharmed and unresolved into steam-particles, athwart hot masses of ebullient lava; or moonlight glancing over a great pyrotechnical display above the sea at Naples; or the bluish beams of *Aurora Borealis* palpitating upwards through red oceans of the trembling Arctic lights; or sprays of alamanda flowers detached upon a background of burning taxonia stars and bunches of flushed Bougainvillæa bloom smothered in veils of woven verdure. But Beethoven had the power to make the pianoforte capable of symphonious effects. He brought the cold, pure water-rill, the moon's frigidity, the pale auroral pulse, the amber bloom, into vital art-relation with volcanic forces in his sympathetic orchestra, with the gloom and glory of intercepting, sustaining tones from wood and brass and string, with tumultuary colours tossed from clustering volumes of contrasted, intertwined, and interpenetrating instruments of throbbing sound. Beethoven, first of modern masters in the poetry of tone (unless peradventure Weber broke the path as a pioneer before him), gave its right place to the clavier among the organs man has fashioned to translate his soul's emotion into music. He brought the pianoforte's specific quality into relation toward those elder and more potent instruments of metal, wood, and string. He made us feel it as a liquid, candid, self-eliminating, self-detaching spirit—a spirit fit to raise its voice of clear transparent utterance among the host of congregated soul-compelling, sense-subduing, force-evoking *daimons* of the orchestra. Not indeed as a seraph to command, but as an angel to be loved and tended by them, to evoke their sympathy and their collaboration—standing the while somewhat aloof, though still with kindred feeling, as the pure soul of woman or of saintly man stands in the turmoil of the world, and adds a clarity of accent to the concert of contending cries and hymns and groans and passions.

This is a dithyramb. But it is good, in our old age, to have the dithyrambic stuff still left in us. And, as is usual with me now, everything poses itself before me as a problem. Last night the problem was: how can that poor instrument, the clavier, be made to play its part against and with the violin, the hautbois, and the rest of them? In a sort of emotional or Bacchic way I seemed to find the solution. At all events I felt the Concerto, though Mr. Lockwood is not Anton Rubinstein[2] and the Davos band is not the Philharmonic orchestra. Last time I heard it, I had Rubinstein at a Philharmonic meeting. But I do not think I got the same thoughts. Moral: to be grateful for the least; and to bless God for undiminished sensibilities in the *Götterdämmerung* of old age.

Jan. 8.

I did not finish this yesterday—and I doubt whether it is worth the postage stamp. Am I going to form a third manner, as you predicted? The prospect of Michel Angelo[3] makes me wonder as to how I shall do the style part.

[Incomplete]

---

1. Albert Lewis Lockwood (1871–1933), American pianist, became head of the piano department, University of Michigan School of Music; wrote *Notes on the Literature of the Piano* (1940). The concert at which Lockwood appeared was a benefit for the Poor Invalid's Society of Davos. *The Davos Courier,* Dec. 20, 1890, p. 134, has the following notice:

> Some of our readers will have already heard the piano-forte playing of Mr. Albert Lockwood. It is seldom that we have so gifted a performer amongst us in Davos. Mr Lockwood is a favourite pupil of Herr Reinecke at the Leipzig Conservatorium; and at a recent "Abend-Unterhaltung," in which he was taking part in a Concerto of Beethoven, he earned the hearty plaudits of a master not often given to much expression of approval.

2. Anton Rubenstein (1830–94), Russian pianist and composer, gave frequent London recitals during the seventies and eighties.
3. *The Life of Michelangelo Buonarroti* (1893).

1860. *To Janet Ross*

Am Hof, Davos Platz, Switzerland. Jan: 9. 1891.

My dear Janet

I am going to ask you to do me a favour. This is to go to Alinari,[1] the photographer in the Via Tornabuoni, & to tell him that I am beginning a new Life of Michel Angelo in English, for the preparation of which I shall want a large quantity of photographic matter. Then to ask him whether he will send me at once a price list of all the photographs he can supply of all extant work by Michel Angelo—statues, frescoes, pictures, architecture, models, & original drawings. They must, the photographs, be executed from originals only; & I shall prefer to have them unmounted. Only he must say what the price mounted is; for some of them I may need in one way & some in another.

When I have made my selection, my London publisher will give him the order.

I am doing the same with the Autotype Co for [H. F.] Brown's reproductions, & hope between them & Alinari to get a tolerably complete working apparatus.

This is asking a great favour of you. But I think it better to open negotiations with Alinari through the mediation of one who is so well known at Florence as you are. He may probably never have heard of me. You can tell him that a part of one of my books (vol 3 of R. in Italy) has been published by Le Monnier in an Italian translation made by Mme Fortini Santarelli.[2] Also refer him to Villari.[3] The great thing is that he should understand that this is business.

I hope you will excuse me giving you this trouble. I would have written direct to Alinari but that I thought he might not execute my order with *the fullness I greatly desire,* unless he knew that he was being asked to cooperate in an important undertaking.

Believe me ever yours

JASymonds

---

1. The Florentine publishing house specializing in art-books and reproductions of paintings.
2. *Il Rinascimento in Italia. Le belle Arti,* traduzione di Fortini-Santarelli (1879),
3. Pasquale Villari, the Italian historian. See Ls 976 and 1297.

1861. *To William Barclay Squire*[1]

Am Hof, Davos Platz, Switzerland. Jan: 12. 1891

My dear Squire

I come to bother you with a question.

An old friend of my daughters', a Miss MacMorland,[2] has been studying music at Milan, & has written an amusing article on the working up of raw male & female material into second rate theatrical or operatic stars there.

She of course comes to me, & asks whether I cannot introduce her lucubrations to the press. I read the Ms & see merit in it, both of fact & of humour. But I do not think it the sort of thing to send to one of the general monthlies.

My question, wishing to help her, is whether there is any musical, stage, or operatic journal, wh would take a moderately long article (it is too long for a daily, & I think also for a weekly) of the sort as above described.

I only want to use your special knowledge in these matters, in order to obtain information inaccessible to myself here—viz: whether there exists a magazine of the particular musical, operatic, sort; & if so, what it is called, & where it hangs out.

The rest of the business Miss MacMorland must transact for herself, with such poor assistance as a letter of introduction from me may give her.

I should like to hear a little about yourself, but do not demand this, since I know what your life is, & what alas! it must be now during the bondage of this tyranny of arctic weather.

You are always affectionately remembered by all of this household & by me particularly, your

affectionate friend

J A Symonds

My essay not yet come. When it comes here, it shall go to you.

---

1. In charge of printed music at the British Museum. See L 1674.

2. Bessie, the daughter of the Rev. and Mrs. John [Elizabeth] MacMorland, among the first English settlers at Davos. See L 1065.

1862. *To Dr. John Johnston*[1]

Am Hof, Davos Platz, Switzerland. Jany.12.1891

My Dear Sir,

I thank you most sincerely for your friendly letter of the first of this month, and also for the inestimable gift of photographs you sent me.

We keep a sort of Whitman archive here, where his letters and portraits are treasured, together with some of the rare editions of his works (among these the first 4to edn of Leaves of Grass in its original green binding), also photographs supplied in a great measure by himself. And now you have added to this collection a series of the greatest interest, not only as showing the (*really*) grand old man as he is in 1890, but also as illustrating his material surroundings, of street & sleeping room, daily wheel chair ride & bright-eyed young attendant.

It is, indeed, extremely good of you to do so much for a stranger. I take it as a sign that our Master Walt has the power of bringing folk together by a common kinship of kind feeling.—I suppose this is the meaning of "Calamus", the essence of the doctrine of Comradeship. He has not only preached the gospel of mutual goodwill, but has been a magnetic force ("telepathetically" potent, as the Psychical Research people might say) to create the emotion.—

I wonder what more than this "Calamus" contains, whether the luminous ideal of a new chivalry based on brotherhood and manly affection will ever be realized.

Such are the problems suggested to me in my decrepitude by Whitman's impassioned vital prophecy.

Very truly yours

J.A.Symonds—

---

1. See L 1855. In L 1761 Symonds had written to Whitman about "Calamus."

1863. *To Henry Graham Dakyns*

Am Hof, Davos Platz, Switzerland Jany 16 1891.

My dear Graham

I was very glad indeed to get your letter last night. It gave me great delight & made me long for you. Now that you are your own master,[1] why will you not come out & see us? You cannot plead professional duties any longer: and if the winter goes on behaving as it has hitherto done, this is no bad place to be in. I came back from Italy on Dec: 6. Since then there have been only four cloudy days—the rest clear sunlight, with a sharp frost. Very cold it is. The thermometer stood at *minus 21° Fahr* [53 degrees of frost] outside my window when I rose at 8 this morning. But, as you know, we do not feel the cold here enough to suffer from it.

One reason for writing to you so soon again is that I have had a copy of my essay "A Problem in Modern Ethics" addressed to you at Rockleage Stoke Bishop Bristol.[2] I am not sure from your letter whether you have given that house up already. If so, please write at once to Messrs Ballantyne & Hanson, Paul's Work,[3] Edinburgh, & make them send the essay to your present address. I think there will be time, in this way, to avert some confusion, & the straying around of an essay not intended for all eyes.

I have had a great deal of experience, both personal & through the communications of friends, relating to the subject of that essay lately. It is a strange chapter in human psychology, and the issues are not, I think, as yet to be forecast or apprehended. I feel that, as Whitman says, there is "something exalté previously unknown" ready to leap forth in the due time of the Spirit—which spirit will possibly have to work with man for yet 5 millions of years (more not impossibly) upon the planet.

I wish I could tell you some of the strange things—sweet & dear & terrible & grim—which I have learned in the course of my experiments & explorations.

I do not believe that Greek is destined to perish. So far, I am optimistic with you. But I agree with Jowett & Henry [Sidgwick] that the study of Greek is bound to enter upon a new phase, & we cannot forsee how the struggle for existence, in things intellectual, & in practical life, will affect that. Therefore, I am of opinion that all engaged upon the work of translation from the Greek are doing good service to culture. One of the best pieces of verse, by the way, which I have written, is a translation of Bion's Lament for Adonis into English Hexameters. It was printed in last Oct: number of the "Century Guild Hobby-Horse"—what Gosse calls "a cryptic publication", but typographically perfect. If I had more than one copy, I would send you the poem.

I wish rather you would order a copy from your newsagent. I want this more remarkable magazine to get currency. It is a thing of beauty, & the organ of a very curious band of artist-men-of-letters—Selwyn Image, Horne, Lionel Johnson, Arthur Galton, & the poets of "Primavera."[4] I do not believe the School is as potent as those Preraphaelites who sustained "The Germ."[5] But they have force, character, assured aims, & a high ideal of art—like "le cenacle" in Balzac's "Illusions Perdues."[6]

By the way, have you read "Les Journal des Goncourt",[7] "Sous Offs,"[8] "Le Crime de Sylvestre Bonnard"![9] Three French works of very different quality, but of first-rate style & absorbing interest. In French books, I would also mention Maupassant's "Cher Ami"[10] & [Paul] Bourget's "Physiologie de l'Amour Moderne"[11]—for different reasons.

I read fewer & fewer books. But I keep my self going in French. Did I tell you that my old essay on Dante has been translated into lovely French![12] I think I may have. It has not yet been published, but I revised the Ms with pleasure, & with pride.

The task at present before me is a new life in English of Michelangelo Buonarroti, to be splendidly illustrated, & issued with typographic pomp by Nimmo. I doubt myself whether a new life is really wanted. But I love the subject—especially as a relief from sexual inversion and its cruel problems.

I am writing on my knees—I mean on a desk upon my knees—after lunch, under the blaze of our unmitigated sunlight. So I can hardly see my words.

With much love & true, yours ever

JAS

---

1. On his retirement from Clifton College in 1889, Dakyns moved to Higher Coombe, Halsmere, Surrey, where he pursued his translation and life of Xenophon.

2. Stoke Bishop, a village near Bristol.

3. An Edinburgh printing firm with the address Paul's Work, 212 & 224 Causewayside.

4. For Selwyn Image see L 1803; for Lionel Johnson, L 1736; for Arthur Galton, L 1581; for Herbert P. Horne, L 1452; and for the *Primavera* poets, L 1793.

5. The Pre-Raphaelite journal of which only 4 numbers appeared (1850).

6. A novel (1837). A reference to Mme. de Bargeton's salon. Her presentation of the poet Lucien at one of the evening gatherings was a disaster.

7. The diary of Edmond and Jules Goncourt began to appear in 1887. See L 1858.

8. Lucien Descaves (1861–1949), *Sous-Offs,* a military novel, 1889.

9. Anatole France (1844–1924), *Le Crime de Sylvestre Bonnard* (1881).

10. Guy de Maupassant (1850–93), *Bel-Ami* (1885).

11. Paul Bourget (1852–1935), *Physiologie de l'amour moderne. Fragments Posthumes d'un ouvrage de Claude Lancher, recueillis et publiée par Paul Bourget, son exécuteur testamentaire* (1891).

12. *Dante. Son temps, son oeuvre, son génie.* Traduit par C. Auguis (1891). The preface, in English, is by Symonds. In the Balliol College library is a presentation copy inscribed thus in ink on the flyleaf:

> A Monsieur J. A. Symonds,
> Témoignage d'admiration
> et de Sinceré gratitude;
> et Souvenir d'un travail en commun
> qui restera un des honneurs et
> uni des joies de notre vie.
> Caroline Auguis
> Adrien Auguis
> Bordeaux, Octobre 1891

1864. *To Janet Ross*

Am Hof, Davos Platz, Switzerland. Jany 18. 1891.

My dear Janet

Thanks to your energetic action, for which I am sincerely grateful, I received a whole mass of photographs from Alinari.[1] I only wish now—this is my fault—that I had asked to have them mounted. They would have taken more room indeed, but would not have curled up like so many hundreds of Aaron's rods[2] turned into serpents on my tables & my floor as these superb shadow-pictures of great art-work are doing now. I can hardly grapple with them. But, as I hope to buy a very large number, I can have them mounted for me here: & the residue Alinari will have to deal with.

The fact is that we live just now in climactic conditions hostile to unmounted photographs. The thermometer register last night was 27° Fahr below zero, or 59 degrees of frost. The house is well heated, & the sunheat in the day is high. And there is not a scrap of moisture anywhere, except in human bodies. Consequently things like wood, paper, leather, woollen garments, acquire an extraordinary dryness.

Tell the Padrone of our temperature. It will remind him of Erzeroum[3] —except that here we have little wind. I do not know whether there, in Erzeroum, he profited by as much sun as we have, wh enables me to sit out in my wooden loggia, when the thermometer behind the planks registers 15° below zero at noonday.

I am going to plague you with another request. I have a friend here, called Anton Juon, (aged 23)[4] who wants to find a place in Florence. His object is to learn Italian. He can correspond excellently in German, well in French, & understands book-keeping by double entry etc. He comes of one of the most honourable families in the Canton, & is a thorough gentleman. We have him often at our table, as also a brother of his, who lives upon the ancestral homestead. Like all the Swiss, he is willing to work for very little pay, if he can secure his object—which, in his case, is the acquisition of Italian. A house of business could not find a more trustworthy servant. Lodging & board & something for pocket-money in the way of wages would satisfy his wishes. I do not ask you to take any trouble for this man. But it is just possible that you & Mr Ross may know of some post which would do for him. In that case, I should be grateful to you if you would introduce him; & I fully guarantee the man in moral & other respects. I will enclose his photograph. He is here represented in the costume of a member of the Davos Turnverein, & the picture shows him to be, what he is, a powerful, well-built fellow of six foot or upwards. This is the only portrait of him wh I have.

Now you will exclaim: "A plague on the Historian! He comes, in each letter, to make some claim upon our friendship!" True, dear lady; true, Padrona Cara, Donna Signora di Poggio Gherardo! But your poor historian does not really make demands. He only asks whether, in the multiplicity of your connections with Florence, you can think of some place in which to stow away Anton Juon for a season. If you do not know of anything to suit, then the historian will ask no more. But he will have taken the best step to help his friend Anton.

Catherine is reading aloud to me your book "Three Generations." I had only done what people call "seeing it" before. It interests me deeply now. But what did Sarah Austin translate of Henri Beyle's work, to call forth that letter from him?[5] There are lots of little questions of this sort I want to ask.—Love to you all, including Moschino & Fortunato!—

Yrs ever JASymonds

---

1. See L 1860.
2. See Exodus 7:8–13.
3. A city in Turkish Armenia known for its frigid winters.
4. See L 1765.
5. Janet Ross, *Three Generations of English Women* (2 vols., 1888), II, 76–77, is not very helpful on this matter. She prefaces Stendhal's letter to Sarah Taylor Austin (1793–1867), her grandmother: "A very different letter is the following from that *spirituel* writer, M. de Beyle (Stendhal), which is full of what Miss Aikin calls 'airy French grace'." The translated letter opens "Mister Translator. . . ." Mrs. Austin was known as a translator of French and German works, but there is no evidence that she translated Stendhal's.

1865. *To Henry Graham Dakyns*

Davos Jany 23. 1891

My dearest Graham

The sap of so many summers rises in my old veins when I touch you, or your letters touch me. We are getting to be gnarled & weathered seniors of the forest; beaten by many storms & frosted by inclement winters. Yet the heart beats, & the blood responds—I think it does this even more purely, more decisively, through the stress & pressure of the previous years, than it used to do before their purgation. Only air & fire remain of the life-long man-engaging affection. —Is this a promise of immortality? or is it the final perfect flicker of the soul, in its gradual process of emancipation into nothing by the cremation of the body through oxygen?

I am glad to hear you have got my Essay.[1] If you would do me a kindness, please scribble over its blank pages etc, something of your thoughts, & send the printed thing back to me. If you like, I will return it to you. But, as you know, it is only sent forth to stimulate discussion. I thought that the best way to do this would be to give it the form of a Ms in print, wh I have done.

Enough of that. Though I must say that I am eager about the subject from its social & juristic aspects.

You know how vitally it has in the past interested me as a man, & how I am therefore in duty bound to work for an elucidation of the legal problem.

I am in daily correspondence with Ulrichs.[2] He lives at Aquila, & edits a newspaper in Latin there—styled "Alaudae." He does not seem to care for Urnings[3] anymore. How odd! The last letter I got from him (tonight) was a request to interpret Tennyson's "Crossing the Bar." He wanted me to translate two difficult passages into any language except Latin. I did them into Italian. It seems that he had got (through an American newspaper) a copy of one of the many Latin versions wh H. M. Butler[4] has made of this poem: he could make the Latin out, but *not* the English. "The bar" stumped him up: *u:s:w:* [and so forth].

Butler sent me his little book of translations, as I no doubt he did to you. They are very clever. But I think Ulrichs is right in saying that the Latin does not correspond to the violent (violently coloured & symbolic) language of the magnificent original poem.

It is not funny for me & Ulrichs, me only interested in him because he championed the slave-cause of the Urnings, & him mainly interested in me because I can expound Tennyson's odd English—is it not funny, I say, for us to be brought together upon this extraordinarily trivial trifle—the Master of Trinity's Latin translation of the Poet Laureate's "Vale" to the public—when our original *rapport* was in the *hearts* & *viscera* & *potent needs* of thousands of our fellow-creatures.

So goes the world. And—well I will not say what I was going to say: only I fear that a free legal course, with social sympathy attending, will not be given to my brethren—the Urnings.

JAS

---

1. *A Problem in Modern Ethics* (1891).
2. See L 1831.
3. In *A Problem in Modern Ethics*, p. 53, Symonds follows Ulrichs in calling

Urnings men who have a feminine soul in a male body. On p. 54, in a note, Symonds says that a Dr. Kaserer of Vienna is said to have invented the term.

4. Henry Montagu Butler (1833–1918). See L 40. He published some volumes of sermons, of verse, and of translations into Greek and Latin of English verse. "The bar" probably means Tennyson's "Crossing of the Bar."

1865a. *To Janet Ross*

Am Hof, Davos Platz, Switzerland. Feb: 12 1891

My dear Janet

I have been knocked down again by worry, on the top of wh I caught cold, & the cold degenerated into bronchitis. Else I should have written before now to thank you for your efforts on behalf of my friend Juon.[1] I ought not to have troubled you at all about him, because I know by experience how almost impossible it is to get a place for a young man without his applying personally etc. Still one does ask one's friends these questions, in the forlorn hope that they may have what is "just the thing," by good luck in their pocket.

The worry wh has been annoying me is of a private nature, uninteresting to anybody but myself. It has, however, taken a great deal out of me.

There is a young man living here, who came with an introduction to me. His name is Rimington;[2] his mother was a Gordon, sister of the Captain Gordon[3] who owned Fyvie [Castle]; & here Mr Rimington says he spent the best days of his boyhood. He is a sort of cousin of yours, you see. And will you give him, he asks, a copy of your little book on the Castle?[4] You gave Catherine one, wh is somewhere in the house, but we cannot lay our hands upon it. There is no order in the books here (except a sort of order rooted in disorder among my own), because they have accumulated by thousands in a dwelling wh was never designed for them.

Do you think there is any reason to be afraid of Florence in April on account of typhoid? I want to bring Madge there. Please tell me What Pension you recommend. You said there was one better than any of the hotels. If I come to work at Michelangelo, I ought to live in Florence for some while at least. That would not prevent me from giving myself again a taste of the great pleasure I had last autumn at Poggio Gherardo, & which your warm hearted invitation to come again would, I feel, allow me to enjoy for a few days, provided you are free for guests. But I ought to concentrate attention on MA in a way which is impossible while living in society with friends: to take notes, receive impressions, & to work these into MA upon the spot.

I cannot tell you how thoroughly I enjoyed your "Three Generations":[5] every word from cover to cover. I only here & there regretted the absence of slight editorial notes. And I must say that I very eagerly expect the "fourth generation"[6] promised in your preface—your own notes of your early life. You told me nothing about that: but I hope you have not laid it aside. The "Dichtung und Wahrheit"[7] of your life would be a remarkable addition to this series, which has the notable value of presenting a similar strain of family genius under the conditions of social evolution—the type altering with the alteration of environment.

Do you know? I find that book on Boccaccio[8] is really a book. It wants very little doing to it. Yet I am too indolent or impotent to work. Business & bronchitis have stopped even MA wh is now on engagement.

With kindest regards to the Padrone I am always affecally yrs

J A Symonds

---

1. He was trying to find a place in Florence for the young Davoser Anton Juon. See L 1864.

2. E. Rimington resided at the Victoria Hotel, Davos.

3. Captain Alexander Henry Gordon (1813–83) of Fyvie Castle, who in 1842 married Catherine Douglas. He was grandson to Alexander, Lord Rockville, and after his death the castle went to Sir Maurice Duff-Gordon (1849–96), brother to Janet Ross and father of Lina Duff-Gordon (Waterfield). See the latter's *Castle in Italy* [1961], pp. 15–20.

4. *Fyvie Castle and Its Lairds* (1885).

5. *Three Generations of English Women* (2 vols., 1888).

6. *The Fourth Generation: Reminiscences* (1912).

7. Literally, poetry and truth: the title of Goethe's autobiography (4 vols., 1811–33).

8. Symonds' *Giovanni Boccaccio as Man and Author,* though written in 1887, was not published until 1895 by Nimmo. See Babington, p. 93.

1866. *To Edmund Gosse*

Am Hof, Davos Platz, Switzerland. Feb: 19. 1891

My dear Gosse,

Since you last heard from me, I have been down with bronchitis & bother—the latter being the cause of the former. I have often thought of you and your bothers with Archer about Ibsen;[1] & annoying as these must have been, I have rather envied you. My troubles touched & touch me more personally; & being almost tied here by my health, I cannot deal with them except through correspondence.

I do not, however, allude to these matters, which have no interest to any one but myself—except as explaining why I have not written to you.

I do not want you to write anything about my "Problem" unless you feel impelled to do so. Only I should like sometime to know whether you found anything in my treatment, my moral attitude, or my views on legislation, which seemed to you wrong.

This, as you see, does not press for immediate attention. It is, however, of some moment to me—pioneering as I am in the matter—to hear what you think.

My wife is tomorrow going to begin to read aloud to me the life of your father.[2] We always spend nearly 2 hours in reading aloud, she to me, per diem; & we have read through our provision of books to this biography. We look forward to it: for the delights in natural science, & I feel sure that I shall have a literary treat.

Affectionately yours

JAS

---

1. Gosse translated *Hedda Gabler* (1891) and, with William Archer, *The Master Builder* (1893); both are in *The Collected Works of Henrik Ibsen,* revised and edited by William Archer (13 vols., 1906–13) to which Gosse contributed a life of Ibsen (vol. XIII).

2. *The Life of Philip Henry Gosse* (1890). Philip Henry Gosse (1810–88) was a naturalist who visited Canada and Jamaica: *The Canadian Naturalist* (1840), *Birds of Jamaica* (1847), and *A Naturalist's Sojourn in Jamaica* (1851).

1867. *To Horace Traubel*[1]

Am Hof, Davos Platz, Switzerland Feb: 21 1891

Dear Mr Traubel

Your letter of the 7th & the beautiful verses, original in thought & graceful in expression, which you sent with it, bring back to my memory a letter which I once wrote you on the occasion of the paragraph I sent for Walt's anniversary.

I wrote the letter, & tore it up, because I thought that the friendly feeling expressed in it from me to a stranger whom it was not likely I should ever see, might appear to you sentimental or unreal.

I feel I was mistaken; for yours which lies before me now, is full of that confidence & straightforward comradeship which inspires a like return, & would have justified the warmth of my spontaneous utterance.

We English people, especially those of us who have "aristocratic" connections, & who have been bred at a public school like Eton or Harrow, & at Oxford or Cambridge, we, I say, find it hard to break the conventional husk, & be as simple as God made us.

These national peculiarities have great drawbacks, & offer obstacles to the free currents of manly sympathy. Yet they have stood the Anglo Saxon in good stead during his long brutal warfare with new lands & savage populations. So I ought not to complain. Only I feel it rather ridiculous to have written you a long letter of sincere feeling, & to have torn it up, because I thought it "too forthcoming"—now that I am sure you would have liked it.

I hope that the spirit of our Master, if it wakes and leavens the whole mass, will eventually do much to lift what is free & noble in men above the petty pens of their castes & creeds & prejudices. It has already done this in those of us, who carry written on our hearts (if hearts can be tattooed by life-long thought-preoccupations), the letters W. W. Queen Mary said that "Calais" would be found tattooed upon her heart, poor woman!²

Still we must be careful, walking in the footsteps of the Master, not to break the limits of a masculine reserve. It is very difficult, I think—at least, it requires a wonderful equipoise of forces in the man—to be as fluid & responsive, as elastic in sympathy & as full of buoyant impulse, as Walt Whitman is, without tumbling over into what the English call "gush."

This sort of preachment is drawn forth from me by the very keen interest I take in all that you have said to me about your life with Walt. I want to tell you, candidly & sincerely, how grateful all disciples of our Master must be to those who tend & brighten with their service & affection his declining years: & how much I personally thank you for the good thought which inspired you to write to me as you have done. I am easily drawn to love those who have a clear transpicuous nature, such as I find here among my dear friends of these Swiss mountains—people whose only faults are hereditary love of hard blows, love of the wine-cup, & love of mastering their neighbours in business; but who, for the rest, give their hands & hearts to a comrade. I am sure I owe it to Walt that I am able to appreciate this grand stuff of humanity, in spite of my culture & my criticism & the burden of book-learning I carry about with me, & like a pedlar display to the public in my literary products.

And I owe it to him that my heart warms to you, who are helping him, & who are so generous in friendly feeling toward myself. What a man he is! who can make the world kin by common touch & central throb of his own vital self!

Write to me again, & send me, if you will, a photograph by which I may know you as in a glass darkly. I seek & feel after the bodily presentment of a man who occupies my thought. And it is only too probable that we shall never meet; for life is growing for me yearly more & more difficult. I find it every year more troublesome to live, more irksome to do my daily tale of work.

I exchanged some words by letter with Walt lately about his "Calamus."[3] I do not think he quite understood what I was driving at. But that does not signify. I wish you would tell me what you & your friends feel to be the central point in this most vital doctrine of comradeship. Out here in Europe I see signs of an awakening of enthusiastic relations between men, which tend to assume a passionate character. I am not alarmed by this, but I think it ought to be studied. In true friendship yours

John Addington Symonds

---

1. See L 1728.
2. Mary I (1516–58) declared war against France on June 7, 1557. Opposed by the Pope, who took France's part against Spain, and forsaken by the Scotch who declared war on her, Mary suffered her greatest and final calamity on January 5, 1558, when Calais fell to France, a disaster for her.
3. See L 1814 to Whitman.

1868. *To Edmund Gosse*

Am Hof, Davos Platz, Switzerland. Feb: 23. 1891.

My dear Gosse

I was very down in the mouth when I last wrote to you, & felt a sort of seeking after sympathy. But I am not so impatient or so vain as to want quick responses to things I send my friends, as poems, essays, or the like.

What I should dearly desire, apropos of "the Problem," is just what you express, namely that we might come together, & have a good talk about it—*inter alia* of course, for we should have a thousand topics to discuss.

Do entertain the possibility of paying us a visit in the summer. I feel sure that both Mrs. Gosse & yourself would find our mountains worth seeing, quite apart from the otia dia [too much leisure] & vast streams of conversation to which the life conduces. I have never talked so much, so openly, so brilliantly, & so sympathetically, with so many remarkable & eminent men, in any place, as I have done here.

That sentence was badly worded. I did not mean to put "I never talked" etc. Yet "I never enjoyed talk" etc "with so many" etc.

As you observe, the great thing, with regard to "The Problem," is to reach the opinion of sensible people who have no sympathy with the peculiar bias. I have sent the essay to two such men: T. S. Perry of Boston, quite one of the most learned & clearest-headed men in the USA; & to my old friend John Beddoe,[1] MD FRS., eminent as an ethnologist. Both reply emphatically that they agree with my conclusions & suggestions on the legal point, but that they do not think it possible for the vulgar to accept them. I had an interesting conversation with Lord Hannen,[2] a [dis]cussion on the subject in Venice last May. He also agreed with me in the main, & told me some very remarkable things about the way in which a judge evades the law, while charging Grand Juries. I talked the other night here about it with a young German nobleman of the highest rank & very large estates, who most decidedly took the same view, & communicated curious facts about the manners of the peasants on his property. Henry Sidgwick again, in his own cautious hedging way, after reading my essay, told me he thought that I had removed all the utilitarian objections to an erasure of those statutes from our Code. One of the P & O officers[3] at Venice, during a state dinner to which I was invited, began upon the subject of Cleveland Street,[4] & volunteered the opinion that it was absurd to disqualify by law passions which seemed so harmless & so instinctive, although he added that his own (I suspect very free) self-indulgences were in the opposite direction. The way of thinking among the proletariate, honest artizans, peasants, etc, in Italy & Switzerland—where alone I have fraternized with the people —is all in favour of free trade.

Gradually, then, I collect from various sources the impression that if our penal code could be freed from those laws *without discussion,* the majority of unprejudiced people would accept the change with perfect equanimity. It is also curious how much the persons I have interrogated knew about it, & how much they accept it as a fact of human nature. What everybody dreads is a public raking up of the question; & as the vast numerical majority has no personal interest in it, things remain as they are.

554

Hannen said he should like the English laws altered, but added "there is no one who cares to take the matter up."

I am very ill, & have lost my power of living like an invalid. The constant effort of a life-time to control my health & create the best conditions for repelling disease, has worn my faculties of endurance out. So I do things now, which are not prudent. I drove yesterday to a village two hours away from here, attended a peasant theatre, (wh was tremendous fun), dined with three topers & good companions, Swiss, & drove home at midnight in an open sledge under the most glorious moon & icy wind from the glaciers. This is not a cure for bronchitis. And again today, I started with my girls & our toboggans, & ran a course of four miles, crashing at lightning speed over the snow & ice. We did the journey in about 11 minutes, & I came in breathless, dead-beat, almost fainting. Then home in the railway with open windows & a mad crew of young men & maidens excited by this thrilling exercise. It was solemn & beautiful upon the rim. The sun had set, but all the heavens were rosy with its afterglow, & the peaks & snow-fields which surrounded us shone in every tone of crimson & saffron. Then, from behind the last black bulk of a mountain mass, the rising full moon swam rapidly upon our sight, a huge transpicuous dew-pearl of intensest green, bathed in the warm colours of the burning skies. People who summer in the Arctic Circle, describe these luminous effects. Our rapid motion through the celestial wonders & over the myriad tinted snow-path added an intoxicating glory to the vision—until, as we descended from the upper heights, the splendours & the path we sped upon were swallowed up in vast chasms of primeval pine-forests, from which we emerged again into the flooding silver of the moon, which at a lower level strove victoriously with the sunset incandescence we had left behind. But this again was no cure for bronchitis. I have just supped at 11 p.m. & am writing to you with pipe in mouth before I turn into bed.

Goodnight. And believe me yours

as ever JAS

Have you read any of Rosegger's village stories?[5] They are first-rate, & might do for Heinemann.[6] My friend Prince Emil Carolath zu Schönaich[7] brings them to me. He rightly says that they beat Auerbach[8] & all that crew into nothing. I read them at night, when I cannot sleep for coughing. (Carolath is not the German alluded to above)

I am glad to see that Thornycroft[9] is elected to the Athaeneum by the Committee, an honour wh was conferred upon me some years ago. Tell him, if you see him, that I am delighted with this recognition of his eminence in sculpture. Do you, by the way, know Donoghue,[10] the sculptor of a "Sophocles"? He sent me a photograph of the statue, wh is good in its way. I never saw the man. But I seem to feel the *aura in* him.

---

1. See L 753.
2. See L 1821.
3. The P & O Orient (Pacific & Orient) British steamship line.
4. Timothy d'Arch Smith has supplied the following information about the Cleveland Street affair:

In the *North London Press* of November 16, 1889, a piece appeared mentioning that the premises of No. 19 Cleveland Street (a small road near Tottenham Court Road) were being used as a homosexual brothel. Various high-ranking people were mentioned. The editor (Parke) was had up for criminal libel, lost his case and went to jail (see *The Times,* Reg. v. Parke, January 16–17, 1890). However, enough evidence had been uncovered by the paper to alarm several people, who left the country. Lord Arthur Somerset, an officer in the Prince of Wales' household, was one of the victims. Frank Harris' autobiography (1923) and E. F. Benson's *As We Were* (1932), mention the case. Lord Henry Somerset published a book of verse entitled *Songs of Adieu,* (1889) [see L 1699], all of which echo a great regret at leaving someone in England, which may tie in with the case. An interesting backfiring occurred at the publication of *The Picture of Dorian Gray.* An anonymous article (now known to be by Charles Whibley) appeared in *The Scots Observer* (July 5, 1890) saying Wilde had brains and art and style "but if he can write for none but outlawed noblemen and perverted telegraph-boys, the sooner he takes to tailoring . . . the better." The article is to be found in [Christopher Millard], *Art and Morality,* new revised edition (1912), pp. 76–77. The Earl of Euston, son of the Duke of Grafton, also had to skip. I imagine the customers at No. 19 were entertained by telegraph boys for which there seems to have been a kind of vogue in the nineties. Lord Alfred Douglas had a penchant for them, and we note that Robert Kemp in Corvo's *Nicholas Crabbe* [1958] is a telegraph boy.

5. Peter Rosegger (1843–1918), prolific Austrian fiction writer, poet, and dramatist. A popular edition of his tales was published in 3 series and 40 volumes.
6. William Heinemann (1863–1920), London publisher (from 1890) of Stevenson, Kipling, and others; of translations he commissioned (of Dostoevski, Turgeniev, Tolstoi, Ibsen, and others); and of translations in the Loeb Classical Library.
7. Prince Émile-Rodolphe Osman zu Schönaich-Carolath. See L 1467.
8. Berthold Auerbach (1812–82), German novelist and story writer, known especially for his descriptions of life in the Black Forest (*Edelweiss,* 1861; *Auf der Höhe,* 1865). He also wrote about Spinoza (1837) and translated his works (5 vols., 1841).
9. William Hamo Thornycroft (1850–1925), the sculptor, was elected to the Athaeneum Club of London.
10. John Donoghue (1853–1903), American sculptor, exhibited his "The Young Sophokles Leading the Chorus of Victory after the Battle of Salamis" at the Royal Academy in 1890.

1869. *To Janet Ross*

Am Hof, Davos Platz, Switzerland. Feb: 25. 1891.

My dear Janet

I am greatly obliged to you & Biagi.[1] I will certainly write an application. Of course I knew about the will etc (in his Life of MA) makes an awful fuss about it. I doubted whether I should be allowed to have even a peep at the archives. And I am most grateful to Biagi! In some way or other I will try to make it up to him if he stands over me! Dreadful thought! If he is there, he must help me to work; & so the time will not be so ghastly for both of us. What you send from the good physician is reassuring. I hope, if I can get free of my bronchitis, to leave this direct for Florence in about 4 weeks. It may perhaps (supposing the bronchitis to be stubborn) turn out that we go to the Genoese coast first.

I hope you will do something for Gosse's translations[2] (Heinemann[3] is the publisher). I was thinking of calling your attention to some German village stories by Rosegger,[4] wh seem to me thoroughly excellent. My friend Prince Emil Carolath[5] first introduced me to them. He is a very good judge, & he says that they are extremely "tasted" in Austria & S. Germany. The last volume I have read is the 10th of his collected works: P. K. Rosegger. "Wald heimat," 2ter Band, "Lehrjahre." Harleben, Wien.

I wrote to Gosse last night recommending him to take up Roseger for his Heinemann series; & you ought to do the version, if you think the things good enough.

I can't send you any of Roseger's books. Carolath lends them to me from time to time, & I send them back. We exchange literature thus.

Do you know his (Carolath's) poems, & a prose-tale called "Thauwasser"? This latter is really charmingly written; but wd not do to translate.

I am in an awful hurry. Yours ever

J A S.

---

1. Dr. Guido Biagi (1855–1925), librarian of the Laurentian Library, Florence, and friend of Symonds' friend Janet Ross (see L 976). Symonds dedicated his life of Michelangelo to "The Cavaliere Guido Biagi . . . in Respect for his Scholarship and Learning/Admiration of his Tuscan Style/And Grateful Acknowledgement of his Generous Assistance." Biagi himself published a monograph, "Un' Etéra Romana, Tullia d'Aragona," *Nuova Antologia*, IV (August 1886) (which Symonds referred to in *Michelangelo*, II, 169), and *Aneddoti Letterari* (1887). See L 1873.
2. Gosse was translating Ibsen. See L 1866.

3. See L 1868.
4. See L 1868.
5. See L 1868.

1870. *To Horatio Forbes Brown*

Davos, March 6, 1891

[Dear Horatio]

I have been working hard at "Michael Angelo," and have got through a great deal of preliminary business. The analysis of his correspondence taught me much about him.

You tell me I ought to come to Venice, and not to wring something out of my life here. But I do not think I should be better there. I like Davos quite as much as I do Venice, and far more, inasmuch as it has so far more enjoyable a climate. Still I shall not be sorry to get away into Italy—Tuscany, most likely—at the end of this month. This, because I have been a good deal bothered, as you know, here; and every place in which one does not live seems a rest.

The problem of life and self is not, however, to be solved by change of place. One place is as good as another for the soul, though some are far better for the body, and I find that the people in all places are equally attractive and almost equally annoying. On the whole, I am better satisfied with Graubünden than with any other region I have dwelt in. And that is good.

As I once wrote in a Sonnet,

It is the centre of the soul that ails.[1]

Like you, if you are speaking truth, I do not know what *ennui* is. I know what a lot of other disagreeable states of the spirit are. But I never suffer from vacancy. Unsatisfied hungers of the heart are not *ennui*.

I have invested 2,400 £. out of income in various ways since January 1. This business takes up some time and thought. But my old age and failing strength are what really fatigue me. Literature is but a side matter. I don't do it as easily as I used to do—in some ways more carefully and conscientiously—but not with the same pleasure. I get numbers of letters now from strangers about my work. It seems that one must live to be old and rather indifferent to such things, before they come to one.

[Incomplete]

---

1. The first line of the fifth sonnet of the series "Intellectual Isolation" in *New and Old* (1880), p. 119.

1871. *To Janet Ross*

Am Hof, Davos Platz, Switzerland. March 6 1891

My dear Janet

My bronchitis has made me very ill again, & I have also been hard at work at Michelangelo—nine hours writing yesterday.

For this reason, I have delayed writing to Biagi.[1] I am not quite sure of his address; to send you the letter I have written, & pray you to forward it.

I hope to get this precious permission; & if I cannot work enough in the spring, I shall come again (D: V: [God willing]) in the autumn.

I am sitting out in my open loggia, & have been writing here since 10.30 until now 3.30 *pm*. Luncheon comes & finds me here.

This is a great point about our climate. When I am really ill, as I am now, I can still spend a large part of the day in the open air under the tonic sunlight.

So many greetings to the Padrone [Henry Ross], & much love to yourself, from your friend

JAS.

Anton Juon makes,[2] I find, no difficulty now about staying several years in Italy. He has decided not to come there till the autumn. If I could find him a place I should be glad. Perhaps in April!

---

1. See L 1869.
2. See Ls 1765 and 1864.

1872. *To Horatio Forbes Brown*

Davos, March 6 [1891]

[Dear Horatio]

I wrote you a rather snappish letter to-day. But to-night I am softer-hearted. Sad too: life is failing me.

Harry Strachey[1] has painted a picture of "Football" on a Somerset meadow, full of the *aura*. Do you know what I mean by the *aura*? His picture I am going to buy. It is in the key of Tuke's[2] work but not artistically so strong. A very refined sense of beauty in it, all the same. Of course I have only seen the photograph.

Talking of football, my M. A. studies led me to read through the poems of "Il Lasca"[3] again. I find there a *Capitolo*[4] on football with this passage in it on a scrimmage—

> "Ma il bello è quand e vengono alle prese
> Che van sossopra, onde si veggon spesso
> Otto o dieci persone in terra stese," etc.[5]

Grazzini was a delightful writer of pure Tuscan; and this passage seems to me deliciously *naïf*.

[Incomplete]

---

1. Henry Strachey (1863–1940), Symonds' nephew and brother of St. Loe Strachey, was a painter and art critic of *The Spectator* (1896–1922).

2. See L 1838.

3. Antonio Francesco Grazzini, called "Il Lasca" (the roach), (1503–84), Italian poet and dramatist. The poem is probably in his *Canti Carnascialeschi*—full title: *Tutti i Trionfi, carri, Mascherate a Canti Carnascialeschi, andati per Firenze, dal tempo del magnifico Lorenzo de'Medici, fino all' anno 1559.*

4. A *capitolo* is a division of a poem, like a canto; literally, chapter.

5. But the beautiful part is when they come to encounters so that they go topsy-turvy, whence often eight or ten people are seen stretched out on the ground.

1873. *To Guido Biagi*[1]

Am Hof, Davos Platz, Switzerland. March 6. 1891.

Dear Signor Biagi

Mrs Ross told me of your very kind & generous offer to procure for me the permission to study in the "Archivio Buonarroti"[2] & to make copies of the Mss.

You know that I am engaged upon an English Life of Michelangelo. It is to be brought out with great typographical beauty & with the best illustrations, in 2 large volumes.

It would be of the greatest value to me to gain access to the Archivio, & I pray you earnestly to forward my humble request to the Italian Government.

I enclose a list of books which I have published in England upon Italian matters. It will be seen from this that a large part of my life has been devoted to Italian Studies. Perhaps this may give me some claim to be regarded as a student worthy of the great favour I request.

I should have written earlier, but I have been ill again with bronchitis. I hope to come to Italy early in April.

Your "Aneddoti Letterari" was my travelling companion from Venice to Davos last December. I read it through with very great enjoyment on the journey, & found a hundred things to interest me. What a charming sketch is that of the "Abate Verista"!—& Mario Pieri, how comical a figure!—& Verri, how genial—& Longo, how thoroughly Venetian![3]

Thank you, dear Biagi, for all those delicate portraits you have drawn with so much sympathy & humour.

We share a common partiality for autobiographies. This "touch of nature" makes us "kin."

Bouchard[4] always interested me. But it is impossible to deal with his "psychologie maladie" frankly & openly. If a monkey wrote its memoirs, they would be like Bouchard's.

Again thank you for the valuable essay on the "Rassettatura del Decamerone."[5] There were many facts & considerations there, quite new to me.

I want to make you a "contraccambio" [return] with one of my books. Tell Mrs Ross which you would like to have. If you do not tell her, I shall send you a short study I wrote upon the "Carmina Burana."[6] But pray choose, & please your very grateful & obliged friend

John Addington Symonds.

---

1. See L 1869.

2. In 1858, Michelangelo's descendant the Commendatore Cosimo Buonarroti bequeathed the family papers, including the artist's manuscripts and letters, to the city of Florence, placing them under the trusteeship of the Syndic, the director of the galleries, and the prefect of the Laurentian Library. The Commendatore willed that access to these archives be denied even to the learned, except in rare instances. Symonds' biography appeared in late 1892 under the imprint of John C. Nimmo, with an etched portrait and 50 reproductions of Michelangelo's works. A 2nd ed. appeared the same year. Sir Edward Poynter supervised the illustrations.

3. In *Aneddoti Letterari* (1887): "Un abate verista," pp. 63–76, Mario Pieri a Bologna," pp. 35–48, "Alessandro Verri a Londra," pp. 95–109, and "Una gita a San Lazzaro (Ricordi di Venezia)," pp. 142–58.

4. Biagi, "E un quarentena nel 1630," *Aneddoti Letterari*, pp. 115–21, criticizes *Les confessions de Jean-Jacques Bouchard Parisien, suivies de son Voyage de Paris à Rome en 1630, publiées pour la première fois sur le Manuscrit de l'Auteur* (1883).

5. In *Aneddoti Letterari*, pp. 282–326.

6. *Wine, Women, and Song* (1884).

1874. *To Dr. J. W. Wallace*[1]

Am Hof, Davos Platz, Switzerland. March 7 1891

My dear Sir

There was no need of excuse for writing to me. On the contrary, I am grateful to you for doing so, & thank you heartily for all the warm appreciative words you use about me.

It is pleasant too to feel we are linked together by the common tie of Whitman. I have now many unknown friends in America & England, who are only connected with me through him, & yet with whom I feel myself to have a real & not a fictitious comradeship of heart & mind & will.

The disciples of our poet B. Jonson, used to say that they were "sealed of the tribe of Ben." We can say that we are "sealed of the tribe of Walt."

You must not think that I am alone & miserable here. I have a wife & three bright handsome daughters, the youngest (aged 15) a girl after Walt's heart—tall, strong, fond of horses, clever at all sports & capable of bearing great fatigue. (While I write, she comes down from the upper snow fields, crossing my window, on her Norwegian Skij).

Also I have very good friends among the Swiss inhabitants, true fellows & sturdy, simple, shrewd & sweet-natured, whom it does one good to live with.

But all the same, the shades of evening are closing round me, & I suffer much from the exhaustion of a constitution tried to its last resources by phthisical disease sustained & combated through 26 years.

My comparative ease & power to enjoy life, as also to have battled with outward conditions, I owe simply & solely to the circumstance of having been comparatively well-off, & having married early a woman of noble nature, who has stood by me & helped me always.

I cannot tell you with what deep feelings of sympathy & pity I am stirred when I come across men who are failing or have failed in life through the want of material well-being & loyal companionship. Then I feel indeed what my blessings have been & are.

Yet, in the twilight of life, I would gladly be among my own people, in my own England. And this exile makes me anxious for the future of my family. It seems to me sometimes as though they were being sacrificed to the necessities imposed upon us by my health. But I think I ought to repell these doubts as morbid. The children have been brought up in the midst of a wild & splendid nature, & they have not lacked society & opportunities of gentle culture.

562

Many of the first men in Europe come to stay with us under this roof; & they (the girls) go often to England.

You wrote so very kindly to me that I wanted to tell you how it is really with me; & if there is a note of pathos in my speech occasionally, to let you know what that means. I do not wish to pose as an exceptionally ill-used son of step-mother Nature. For I think, on the whole, I ought to regard myself as exceptionally fortunate.

And, anyhow, it seems to me man's duty to accept with thanksgiving what God & the World have appointed for him as his lot in life.

Enough of all this. Take what I have written in Whitman's spirit.

Does Dr Johnston keep a forger to copiy [sic] his correspondence, or does he do this by photography? Some of the leaflets from Whitman are exact facsimiles of his Ms, & doubly precious thereby. I am glad to have them, & very glad to hear from Warry's[2] & Traubel's letters[3] that the present crisis seems to have passed over. But of course, as Traubel says, the future cannot long be reckoned on; & what is beautiful in this sunset of a great strong soul, is the man's own cheerful & calm acceptance of the situation. "It will be all right either way." *Ab eo disce vivere ac mori!* [From this learn both to live and to die!]

Kind regards to Dr Johnston. And believe me, with true gratitude & friendliness, to be your most faithful

John Addington Symonds

J. W. Wallace Esq.

P.S. You say that you liked to see an old worker in the field of scholarship & criticism, come out in his own person & speak out of his own heart. It may then interest you to hear that I have lately written an autobiography,[4] which perhaps may yet be published: if its candour permits publication.

---

1. Dr. J. W. Wallace of Anderton, Lancashire, and Dr. Johnston (see L 1855) were Whitmanians and together formed the "Bolton College" of Whitman enthusiasts. Wallace visited Whitman in 1890 and wrote *Diary Notes of a Visit to Walt Whitman and Some of his Friends* (1898). Gay Wilson Allen, *The Solitary Singer* (New York, 1955), p. 537, describes Johnston's and Wallace's interest in Whitman:

> For some years a group of men in Bolton, England, had been meeting to read and discuss *Leaves of Grass*. It included a physician and several ordinary men without much education, and they had humorously named themselves "Bolton College." In 1890 they had decided to send one of their group to see the great poet and bring back a report. Accordingly on July 15 Dr. John Johnston arrived in Camden, and then he made a visit to Brooklyn, where he talked with a ferry pilot who had known Whitman. Afterward he visited the poet's birthplace and talked with some of the older residents of West Hills and Huntington. He completed his tour with a visit

to John Burroughs. The following year another member of "Bolton College," J. W. Wallace, came over, had a talk with the poet (which he duly wrote down), collected more information about the great man's life, and returned to make his report to the group. Later the two reports were published in one of the most interesting of the early books on Whitman's life.

2. See L 1855.

3. Horace Traubel, Whitman's friend and literary executor. See L 1728.

4. In the London Library archives, still largely unpublished.

1875. *To Horatio Forbes Brown*

Davos, March 8. [1891]

[Dear Horatio]

Carolath[1] brought me a wild poem written by him on "The Death of Don Juan." It is extraordinarily in the key of Roden's [Noel's] work. There is one magnificent image in it. Ahasuerus, the Wandering Jew, meets Venus by the roadside. She brings to birth twins, Don Juan and Faust. That is to say: the eternal restlessness of the human spirit, forcing eternal beauty to work its momentary assuagement, begets the lust of the flesh and the lust of knowledge. Do not you think this, in its naked bareness, a fine conception? It seems to me awfully true.

[Incomplete]

---

1. Prince Schönaich-Carolath. See L 1467.

1876. *To the Rev. Arthur Galton*[1]

Am Hof, Davos Platz, Switzerland. March 8 1891

My dear Mr Galton

It was a great pleasure to hear from you again. I hardly know what has made me a bad correspondent lately. One of the drawbacks of living so much out of the world as I do, is that I lose touch with friends & from not knowing exactly where they are, omit to write to them.

I am interested in what you tell me about your change of plans, & your settlement in that fair country. For my part I prefer the outskirts of the Lake district (especially on the side which you have chosen) to its central spots. The outlines of the hills from the crests of Moorland between Windermere & Kendal are lovely.

We have had such a wonderful winter here. I came back from Florence on the 6th of Dec, & it is a mere truth that we have not had fourteen days of clouded weather since that date. The sunshine indeed becomes fatiguing; & except for the pleasure it affords me of walking in the open air all day, I could even wish for a respite from its radiance.

In spite of this fine weather I have not been well. My powers of literary work decrease. Michel Angelo, on whom I am engaged, is of course an extremely attractive subject. But I feel that Grimm,[2] Gotti[3] & Heath Wilson[4] leave but little room for a new biography. I undertook this book at the suggestion of Mr John Nimmo [the publisher] & under strong pressure from him. Now I feel that, if I do it at all, I must aim at doing it completely.

But, like Petrarch,

> Io son sì stanco sotto 'l fascio antico
> de le mie colpe e de l' usanza ria
> ch' i' temo forte di mancar tra via
> e di cader in man del mio nemico.[5]

Moreover, taking this task in hand has suspended another, upon wh I was engaged—the History of Graubünden.[6] I hope I may have length of life enough to write this, when Michaelangelo is finished. From the point of view of constitutional development the History of the Grey Leagues[7] is extremely interesting; & many of its episodes remind one of Medieval Scotch story.

I will send your message to H F Brown about his book[8] & the HobbyHorse.[9] For a book of that kind, it has already had success; & I think myself that it is very well done. He has recently been appointed editor of the Venetian Archives for the English Government, carrying on the State Calendar begun by Rawdon Brown[10]—with whom, by the way, he is not connected.

I am very glad to hear that you will put forth a volume of Essays.[11] By the way, you once said you would like an introduction to the Pall Mall Gazette. Are you still of this mind? Unless you want to earn the few pounds of the reviewer, I do not see much use in writing for a newspaper. I threw away much time & many thoughts on work of this kind; wh I began while I was still an undergraduate at Oxford. I think it did me harm as a writer.

I wish you would come & pay us a visit in the summer. At the end of this month, I hope to go to Florence & Venice. But I shall probably be here again about the middle of June.

Believe me very sincerely yours

John Addington Symonds

---

1. See L 1581.

2. Hermann F. Grimm (1828–1901), *Das Leben Michaelangelos* (2 vols., 1860–63). Symonds used the 5th (1879) ed.

3. Aurelio Gotti (1834–1904), *Vita di Michelangelo Buonarroti, Narrato con l'aiuoto de nuovi Documenti da Aurelio Gotti* (2 vols., 1875).

4. C. Heath Wilson (1809–82), *Life and Works of Michelangelo Buonarroti* (1876).

5. Sonnet LXXXI, in Symonds' translation:

> I am so tired beneath the ancient load
> Of my misdeeds and custom's tyranny,
> That much I fear to fail upon the road
> And yield my soul unto mine enemy.
> —*Sketches and Studies in Italy and Greece*
> (3 vols., 1898), II, 367.

6. One version was published in *The Engadine, A Guide to the District,* ed. by F. de Beauchamp Strickland (London and Samaden, 1890); also see Symonds' "Davos in the Olden Days," *OLSH,* pp. 28–58.

7. For Symonds' sketch of this scrap of 15th and 16th century Swiss history see *OLSH,* pp. 34–39.

8. *Venetian Studies* (1887).

9. Galton reviewed frequently for *The Century Guild Hobby Horse.*

10. Rawdon Lubbock Brown (1803–83). See L 1541.

11. Galton had published his *Urbana Scripta: Studies of five living poets and other essays* (1885). His *Two Essays upon Matthew Arnold, with some of his letters to the author* was reprinted from *The Century Guild Hobby Horse* (1897). *The British Museum Catalogue* mentions no other collection of his essays.

1877. *To Horatio Forbes Brown*

Davos, March 10. [1891]

[Dear Horatio]

I have written almost the whole of the first chapter of my Michel Angelo, and an important passage on his poems. In fact, if I were to stay here, I should probably steam ahead till I was worn out. It seems very difficult to make a new Life of this man *fresh*. But I am doing my best; and I think I shall clarify the whole liquid of his biography. A laborious analysis of his correspondence brings many things to light; and I find, as usual, how very casual are Italian scholars. Cesare Guasti,[1] the editor of the

566

Rime, did fairly good work. And Aurelio Gotti,[2] the biographer, is conscientious. But for Milanesi[3] I do not think I can find eulogistic words: yet he
is the man who edited the Letters, and whose edition of Vasari is our *codex
receptus.*

We shall not be leaving this yet. Davos is horrid just now. I have to
shut myself up and work—about nine hours a day. I am willing to put this
strain upon my nerves, feeling that a good bit of work done on M. A., and
the style of my book settled, will justify me in taking a holiday and looking
round for impressions in the region of my subject. The older I get the more
I am a machinery of nerves and vehement sensations. Where will it all end?
Do not mind these reflections and questions. The little Etna is in momentary eruption.

Get hold of Rosegger and read his "Wald Heimath."[4] This is one of
the real books written in the last half-century. You may not be attuned for
it. But if you want the sincere poetry of peasant-life and a pure soul, you
find it there. It cools me every night.

I close this letter because I am going into the theatre at the Kurhaus.
Amateurs give three plays, in German, French, and English. The last is
Mrs. Curtis's "The Coming Woman,"[5] and I want to see this. If I enjoy it I
shall write to her.

Strange, wild, feminine letters from [Karl Heinrich] Ulrichs;[6] torrents
of letters from the friends around W. W., expecting his death; letters
asking for money—they snow upon me. Why in old age do we get so much
together?

[Incomplete]

---

1. Cesare Guasti (1822–89), bibliographer, art-critic, and art-historian, edited Michelangelo's *Rime* (1863).

2. *Life of Michelangelo* (1875). See L 1876.

3. Gaetano Milanesi (1813–95), curator of the Florentine State Archives, *Le Lettere
di Michelangelo Buonarroti* (1875); he also published 1 volume of Vasari's edition of
Michelangelo's letters in 1890.

4. Rosegger's *Waldheimat* (1873). See L 1868.

5. *The Spirit of '76, or, The Coming Woman* by Ariana and Daniel Curtis. See L
1717. Margaret Symonds acted in the Kurhaus productions. The reviewer for the *Davos
Courier,* Feb. 28, 1891, p. 80, wrote of Margaret's performance as the Marquise de St.
Maur in T. W. Robertson's *Caste:* "The cold, selfish, and haughty aristocrat was
excellently done by Miss M. Symonds, who retrieved the old lady's character in the final
scene so far as to show that even she had a heart."

6. See L 1831.

1878. *To Dr. Daniel Hack Tuke*[1]

Am Hof, Davos Platz, Switzerland. March 19 1891

Dear Dr Tuke

You will see, from the letter I have marked No 2, that I wrote to you in January, & was about to send you an essay I have printed.

I suppose I should have sent neither letter nor essay, but for your kind communication of the 10th, which makes me feel that I am not wrong in thinking I may trespass upon your sympathy so far as to call your attention to my venture in psychological analysis.

With regard to what you ask about my father, I will very gladly write you a letter on the subject of his psychological studies,[2] & I feel proud to be requested by you to do so—though you cannot fail to be aware that I am no expert. It pleases me to think that you are disposed to recall to the inhabitants of Bristol the memory of his name & work.

I forget whether you told me that you had seen a volume of his Miscellanies which was published o [deleted] immediately after his death? This contains those papers which seemed to me most valuable for general circulation. It also has some excellent aesthetical philosophy.

I am deep in the study of a great character, being engaged upon a new life of Michelangelo Buonarroti. It is to be brought out with magnificent illustrations; & I want to make it as complete a presentation as I can of an unique artistic personality.

This work is very exacting; for, as you know, the subject has been handled over & over again. My task is to clarify the turbid liquid of innumerable documents, biographies, & criticisms of greater or less value.

I am just starting for Florence, with one of my daughters, to look up monuments & archives.

Koch's lymph[3] I will have nothing to do with. I am too old to hope, anyhow, for much more from life; & I see no reason why I should confuse my remaining years, few or many, with such experiments.

I very much wish I knew your son Harry.[4] I admire what I know of his work greatly.

Very sincerely yours
John Addington Symonds

---

1. See Ls 1838 and 1846.
2. Symonds' father had written "Apparitions" (1832), "The Relations Between Mind and Muscle" (1834), "Sleep and Dreams" (1851), "Habit" (1853), and "Criminal

Responsibility in Relation to Insanity" (1869). These all appear in Symonds' edition of his father's *Miscellanies* (1871).

3. See L 1849.

4. Henry Scott Tuke. See L 1838.

1879. *To Janet Ross*

Am Hof, Davos Platz, Switzerland. March 30 1891

My dear Janet

Madge & I are going to start tomorrow. She has to be at Vescovana on the 3rd having promised to make one of a party to celebrate Mme Pisani's birthday. When she is there I shall probably be at Mantua, where I want to grub about & endeavour to rediscover a lost statue by Michelangelo.

I suppose we should come on to Florence on Monday the 6th. And if we may come straight to you for a few days at least, we can consider our further plans. It is very tempting, the idea of going down to Leucaspide[1] with you! I do not think I ought to do so; for my business is really Michelangelo.

Will you kindly tell me the name of the Pension in Florence wh you spoke about. I shall have to be in the town itself when I am at work in earnest.

I have been tiring myself pretty considerably of late & shall not be sorry to get a change of scene. This last day is busy. So pray excuse a miserable scrawl & believe me, all impatient to see you again, to be yours most sincerely

J A Symonds

Many saluti to the Padrone.

I forgot to say that I shall be at Albergo Rebecchino until Saturday morning. Also that I shall bring Angelo [Fusato] with me to Florence; but that I think I will leave him in the town. I do not want to inflict a tribal settlement on hospitable Poggio Gherardo.

----

1. To visit Sir James Philip Lacaita (1813–95), Italian scholar (especially of Dante) and politician; adviser to British legation at Naples; the center of political storms; lived in the British Isles from 1852; professor of Italian, Queen's College, London, 1853–56; naturalized British citizen, 1855; during the last 15 years of his life wintered at Leucaspide, near Taranto.

1880. *To Guido Biagi*

(Milano) April 3. 1891.

Dear Signor Biagi

I am greatly obliged to you for your kind letter, which I should have answered sooner (before I left Davos) had my plans not been very uncertain.

I could not say when I should be able to come home, & I was fully occupied with business.

I hope now to come next week to Florence, & shall probably stay a few days at Poggio Gherardo,[1] before settling down.

It will be to me of the utmost service if you will give me some help with the Buonarroti Archivio—as you kindly promised.

I should most like to examine his own letters & those of his correspondents: especially, to find out if any exist written to Michelangelo by Messer Tommaso Cavalieri of Rome, Gherardo Perini, & a certain Febo.[2]

Milanesi's edition of MA's own letters[3] seems to me upon the whole very well done, in spite of Grimm's attempt to disparage it.[4] I do not suppose there is much more to be gleaned. But it will be interesting to see the documents.

Believe me your most obliged & faithful

John Addington Symonds

---

1. Janet Ross' home in Florence.

2. Symonds published letters from these 3 persons to Michelangelo in his *Michelangelo*, II, 400–406. Cavalieri nursed Michelangelo during his last illness and afterwards carried on his work in the Capitol; Perini, one of the artist's best friends, received gifts of drawings (*ibid.*, II, 131); and Febo di Poggio, a shadowy youth, a favorite of Michelangelo's, figured in the artist's life during the 1530's. See L 1891.

3. See L 1877, "a monument of respectable scholarship and industry."—*Michelangelo*, I, ix.

4. See L 1876. We have been unable to trace Grimm's disparagement of Milanesi's edition of the letters. Fanny Bunnètt, in her 1884 ed. of Grimm's *Life of Michelangelo*, printed a prefatory letter in which Grimm complains of the inaccessability of the Buonarroti archives, but there is nothing specifically about Milanesi.

1881. *To Guido Biagi*

[Florence. ca. April 17, 1891]

Caro Cavaliere, Per non occupare troppo del suo tanto prezioso tempo scrivo questa riga: domandando Lei si sarebbe possible di darmi domani

Buonarroti Cod VI—insino Cod X. Non so se si trovano qui alla Laurenziana.

Divmo serv

J.A.S.[1]

---

1. Translated:
Dear Sir

    In order not to take up too much of your most valuable time I write this line asking
if it would be possible for you to send me tomorrow Buonarroti Cod VI up to Cod X. I
do not know if they are to be found here at the Laurentian [Library].

Your most devoted

J.A.S.

1882. *To Horatio Forbes Brown*

Firenze, April 27 [1891]

[Dear Horatio]

It is difficult to imagine worse spring weather than we have had. Cold
winds, dust, damp, rain, *scirocco,* by turns; and sometimes apparently all
together. I caught a bad cold and went to Poggio Gherardo to recruit [*sic*].
I came back yesterday rather better.

I have not yet got access to the Archives. It seems far more difficult
than I was led to expect. Probably, if I do get permission, I shall not be able
to use it till the autumn. Meanwhile I am translating a good many of
M. A.'s letters in Milanesi's edition,[1] but not working hard.

On Wednesday I hope to take Madge and Lina Duff-Gordon[2] to
Lucca, Pisa, and Siena. We shall be out about a week; and soon after our
return to Florence I hope to set off for Venice.

Tuke's[3] letter I return; it is very nice, and the impression of the
Winged Genius[4] jolly. When that drum from Ephesus[5] first was found,
how the figure thrilled me! Just for the reason Tuke gives. It is so flesh and
blood.

I cannot yet get Verlaine's "Poems."[6] He, I think, must be rather of the
sickly school. The last line of his sonnet to Parsifal, fine as it is, looks like
it:

"Et oh! ces enfants chantants dans le chœur"!

[Incomplete]

---

1. See L 1877.

2. Lina Duff-Gordon (1874–?), niece of Mrs. Janet Ross and close friend of

Symonds' daughter Margaret. She arrived in Italy shortly after the death of her mother in the spring of 1891. In 1902 she married Aubrey William Waterfield, of Poggio Gherardo, Florence, youngest son of Ottiwell Charles Waterfield, of Nackington House, Canterbury. See her *Castle in Italy* (1961) for an account of Symonds' friendship with Janet Ross. She collaborated with Margaret on *The Story of Perugia,* illustrated by M. Helen James (1898).

3. The painter, Henry Scott Tuke. See L 1838.

4. Presumably the winged Victory of Samothrace in the Louvre (4th century B.C.).

5. The drum from Ephesus was undoubtedly one of those from the Temple of Diana at Ephesus, unearthed by J. T. Wood in the early 1870's and now in the British Museum. The figure probably represents an attractive nude Hermes leading Alcestis back to the world of light. Hermes stands with head thrown back and lips parted. He has a chlamys wrapped about his left arm and bears a caduceus in his right hand.

6. Paul Verlaine (1844–96), French poet; leader of the Symbolists. The line is from "Parsifal—à Jules Tellier" in *Amour* (1888). Symonds (or Brown) misquotes the last line, which should read:

Et, ô ces voix d'enfants chantant dans la coupole!

1883. *To Guido Biagi*

2 Via Vigna Nuova [Florence] 3° p: [April 30, 1891]

Caro Signor Biagi

Lo ringrazio tanto dello suo biglietto, e sono contentissimo di avere la permissione. Infinite grazie a Lei!

Domani ho promesso a mia figlia e alla Signorina Lina di andare con loro a Lucca Pisa e Siena.

Subito tornato, dopo forse otto giorni, verrò la mattina a trovarlei alla Laurenziana.

Intanto mi recomando, suo

servitore

J A Symonds[1]

---

1. Translated:

Dear Signor Biagi

I thank you so much for your note, and I am very pleased to receive your permission. A thousand thanks!

I have promised my daughter and Miss Lina [Duff-Gordon] to go with them tomorrow to Lucca Pisa and Siena.

As soon as I have returned—after about eight days—I shall come on a morning to look for you at the Laurentian [Library].

Meanwhile I remain

Your humble servant

J A Symonds

1884. *To Horatio Forbes Brown*

Firenze, May 1 [1891]

[Dear Horatio]

I am getting along very much to my own discontent and with considerable danger to my health. I have an awful cold which I cannot shake off; and yet I do not like to leave Florence without having had a go at the Buonarroti Letters. The permission has come: "Valuable for two months." Still I fear I shall have to go away before I do anything. We went last Saturday to Siena. I thought the finer air would do me good. I think it did. But I proceeded on Monday to Montalcino (a quite divine upland city, crowning slopes covered with venerable olive trees and orchards and vineyards, and commanding that vast Tuscan plain with all the hill-cresting towns and Monte Amiata to supply the final accent: excellent country inn, good food cooked by the landlady, and a wine of first rate quality, both red and white: no objects of art interest except one Luca della Robbia[1] in the whole place)—well, I went there on Monday in great heat, came back yesterday in a deluge of rain followed by cold wind, and went to the theatre at night. I was ill enough this morning.

[Incomplete]

---

1. In Montalcino the church of San Francesco has della Robbia terra-cottas and the Palazzo Comunale has a Madonna and saints by the della Robbia school.

1885. *To Horace Traubel*

[Florence, ca., May 1, 1891]

[No salutation]

Speaking about Walt Whitman has always seemed to me much the same as talking about the universe. You know what Whitman himself said of *that:*

I heard what was said of the universe,

Heard it & heard it of several thousand years;

It is middling well as far as it goes,—But is that all?[1]

When I read panegyrics or criticism of Walt Whitman, these words always recur to my memory. "It is middling well as far as it goes,—But is that all?" My own helplessness brings the truth of these words home to me with overpowering effect, whenever I attempt to express what I feel about him.—

In order to estimate, to interpret, to account for a hero, it is necessary to be the hero's peer, or at least his comrade. Only a Plato penetrates the sphere of Plato: only a Dante dives into the depths of Dante's soul.—

In the case of the illustrious dead, this task of comprehending the hero's aim, & of interpreting his prophecy, is not so difficult as in the case of the illustrious living. By the mere fact of having survived successive centuries, of having been absorbed into the best thoughts of the best intellects through many generations, a Plato, a Dante, a Shakespeare [sic], becomes in some sort measureable, & acquires a certain ponderable quantity.—

We classify the fixed stars according to their magnitude. But when "a new planet swims into our ken," when an effulgent comet streams across the firmament, uncatalogued by previous astronomers, then it behooves us to observe, suspend our judgment, study the law of the celestial wonder.—

This is no less true, when we meet a moral & mental influence like Whitman's. Incommensureable, all-embracing, all-pervasive; exhilarating, elusive; alluring, baffling; defying analysis, refusing to be classified; Whitman's genius cannot be gauged, cannot be grasped, cannot be adequately presented to the world by any literary process during his own life-time. His contemporaries must be satisfied with responding to his magic, assimilating his doctrine, thrilling beneath his magnetism. They dare not attempt to evaluate or elucidate him. Only, by saturating their minds with him, they will prepare the soil for future growths of criticism.—

Let us live & think & act in Whitman's spirit—to the best of our ability —according to the measure which is granted us of understanding him—by the light which each one has derived from him. Doing so, we shall help to form just & sane views about our Master as man, as poet, & as prophet. Imperceptibly his influence will be felt through what we say & do. But let us not pretend to measure & interpret him. The bow of Ulysses proved too strong for all the suitors of Penelope: not a man of them could bend it. Even so, the critique of Whitman lies beyond the scope of any living student. His panegyric—even when poured forth by an Ingersoll[2]—is "middling good as far as it goes,—But is that all?"

John Addington Symonds.

Dear Mr Traubel, Here a few sentences about Walt, if you can or care to use them.[3] They are dictated in simple truth by an earnest sense of the impossibility of saying aught to the point yet on Walt's work.

Yours   JAS.

---

1. "Song of Myself," 41, ll. 3–5.
2. Robert G. Ingersoll (1833–99), American lawyer and agnostic; noted lecturer

attacking popular Christian beliefs; author of *The Gods, and Other Lectures* (1876), *Some Mistakes of Moses* (1879), *Why I Am an Agnostic* (1896), and *Superstition* (1898).

3. This letter was read at a dinner given by Whitman's friends on his 72nd birthday, May 31, 1891. See Horace L. Traubel, "Walt Whitman's Birthday," *Lippincott's Magazine*, XLVIII (Aug. 1891), 230–31.

1886. *To Guido Biagi*

Poggio Gherardo [Florence] May 11 1891

Dear Signor Biagi

I have been ill with a cold for some time. But now I hope to get out again soon. I write to ask whether it would suit you for me to come on Wednesday morning next, May 13, to the Casa Buonarroti, & at what time I had better meet you? I shall drive down from here, & can call for you wherever you choose to name.

Believe me very sincerely yours

John Addington Symonds

P.S. I have told my London bookseller to send you three little books of mine.

1887. *To Charles Kains-Jackson*[1]

Poggio Gherardo Firenze May 14 1891

Dear Sir

I do not know whether I owe two numbers of the Artist, one of which reached me at Davos & the other here, to your kindness. At any rate I think I may venture to tell you how much I have been interested in the paper, & how much I liked some of the Verses, espy the lines to Lysis.

I should like to send you some stanzas from time to time if you would care to print them.

I have been here a fortnight looking up various matters about Michelangelo, of whom I have undertaken to write a new biography. After a stormy spring, summer leapt upon us at one bound two days ago. And I am soon going back to the Alps: Am Hof, Davos Platz, Switzerland is my address.

Very truly yours
John Addington Symonds

---

1. Charles Philip Castle Kains-Jackson (1860–1935), journalist, son of Henry Kains-Jackson, editor of *The Farmer* and agricultural correspondent of *The Times;* studied law; friend of Alfred Douglas, Oscar Wilde, Robert Ross, Gleeson White, and other figures of the nineties; edited *The Artist,* to which Symonds contributed several poems, and *The Chameleon;* like his father, was an expert on agricultural matters, contributing features and statistics to *The Times* and other papers and journals.

1888. *To Margaret Symonds*

Venice May 15/91

Dearest Madge

I have just arrived here, & am taking a cup of tea in the solito [usual] room. The place looks fresh & clean & feels very pleasant. A hearty welcome from Maria[1] who looks fatter than usual.

I opened a letter to you from Mr Halle,[2] & sent it on this morning: i.e. left it at Poggio to go.

He writes from Bournemouth that he has got yr Ms, thinks it will read very well, must alter the beginning a little to get it in with the rest, & will try to find illustrations. But the most important thing is he says you have left the S. Moritz people out in the cold: espy Bulpett.[3] This is true I think. I suggested you ought to write to Halle, & propose to remodel the part about S. Moritz *on the proof.* Otherwise he will be doing it himself.

These lines, in case my letter should have missed by some accident.

Best love to the Countess [Pisani]. Let me hear soon about yr plans. I have your sun shade here.

Ever yr.
JAS.

---

1. Wife of Angelo Fusato, the gondolier.

2. We have been unable to identify either Margaret's essay or Mr. Halle. The context suggests that the essay appeared in the *St. Moritz Post.*

3. The *Davos Courier* calls him Captain Bulpett. He was a tobogganer from St. Moritz.

1889. *To William Barclay Squire*

[Venice, May 18, 1891]

[Dear Squire]

I should so much like to come with you. But I have all that big book[1] upon my shoulders, and am losing so much time through being ill now, and besides feel so very uncertain as to a complete recovery, in time to take a hot journey across Germany—that all things put together I ought to go up to Davos before very long and stop at work there.

It is stupid, at my age, to go on undertaking things like a Life of Michelangelo, when I neither want nor make any money to signify, instead of doing just what I like from day to day. But engagements are engagements and I must stick to this one.

Please let me hear about A.R.[2] When the thing is settled, I assure him of my profound sympathy and continued good wishes.

Ever yrs affecty

JAS

---

1. His life of Michelangelo. See L 1823.
2. The reference is unclear.

1890. *To Guido Biagi*

560 Zattere Venezia May 19 1891

Dear Signor Biagi

I have written to Prof: Sidney Colvin,[1] telling him about your intentions with regard to the Botticelli drawings, & preparing him to receive a letter from yourself.

If I can ever be of any service in this or other matters to you, I shall esteem it a small way of showing how much I value the courtesy & kindness wh you showed me at Florence.

I find that it would be useful to me to have copies of the letters addressed to Michelangelo by

Angiolini Bartolommeo.[2]

They must be in the first volume of the Lettere de diversi.[3] Those I need most are three of the year 1533, dates August 2, Oct 11, Oct 18. But I should be glad to have the whole of Angiolini's letters copied, if there are more.

I hope that you will not find any great difficulty in getting the letters I have asked for copied.

With best wishes to Mme Biagi & your infant son, believe me to be your very sincere & obliged friend

John Addington Symonds.

---

1. Colvin (see L 1676) was in charge of drawings and prints at the British Museum.

2. Bartolommeo Angelini (whose name Symonds in his letters spells Angiolini) corresponded frequently with Michelangelo. The letters cease in October 1533. See Symonds' *Michelangelo*, I, 466; II, 142–47, 386–99. (This last section contains 19 of Angelini's letters.)

3. The collection of letters from various persons in Michelangelo's papers.

1891. *To Henry Graham Dakyns*

560 Zattere Venice May 20/91

My dear Graham

I was very glad to get your letter yesterday. Horatio showed me one to him in wh you said you meant to write. And now I have your new address; & hear about your house—what certainly seems promising.

I have been at Florence (a place I detest) the last five weeks, getting up steam about Michelangelo, whose life I have stupidly promised to write. The Italian Government gave me permission to examine the Buonarroti Archives, a privilege wh has hitherto been granted only to one other foreigner, a German who could not read the Mss when he got there. My studies in this place brought out into clearness some curious points about M.A.'s character. The relation he had with Vittoria Colonna, for example, has been made to take much too large a place in his life; whereas some other affections & friendships, wh caused him pain & joy, have been very unintelligently slurred over.

There is something inexpressibly pathetic in turning over the passionate letters & verses, indited by aged genius & youthful beauty, after the lapse of four Centuries and a half.

Persons quite unknown to fame—a certain Febo di Poggio[1] especially, who could not spell or write grammar, & principally cajoled & caressed for money—acquired for me in that Library a sort of vivid personal reality by the answers he drew out from him who was carving the Night & the Day, & the two Twilights.

I have received a great abundance of interesting & valuable communications in consequence of sending out a few copies of that "Problem in Modern Ethics." People have handed it about. I am quite surprised to see how frankly ardently & sympathetically a large number of highly respectable persons feel toward a subject which in society they would only mention as unmentionable.

The result of this correspondence is that I sorely need to revise, enlarge, & make a new edition of my essay; & I am almost minded to print it in a PUBLISHED vol: together with my older essay on Greek Morals & some supplementary papers.

The oddest information sent me has come from 1)America,[2] in the shape of sharply-defined acute partisanship for Urningthum, 2)London, in the shape of about twelve Ms confessions of English Urnings, & two extraordinary narratives made by professed Hypnotists of "cures(?)" effected in cases of inveterate sexual inversion.

This sort of thing, at my time of life, is much more amusing—interesting I ought to have said—& more valuable—than recooking the jaded cabbage of a Florentine Sculptor.

Soon hope to get back to Davos—work, wine, etc. There is no wine, no work, & too much etc. here.

Goodbye. I suppose no human being really *changes*. But I am now 50, & am as unlike what I was at 30 as it is possible for 2 men to be.

yrs.

JAS

T.O. I *do* like English hexameters: very very much. But I do *not* like the version of *Theocr: Id:*.[3] What I do *like* is my version of Bion's Lament for Adonis,[4] written when I was sobbing myself upon the mountains for Augusto's [Zanon's] wound. I think those English hexameters have go & flow & music—though they are my own.

---

1. Michelangelo's friend, Febo di Poggio, about whom little is known. See Michelangelo's letters to him printed in Symonds' *Michelangelo*, I, 466–67; II, 119, 155–157, 384, 403–04. See L 1880.
2. From Benjamin Osgood Pierce (1854–1914), mathematician and physicist; graduated from Harvard, 1876, with highest honors in physics; Parker fellow in

Germany, 1877–80; studied at Berlin with Helmholtz; taught at the Boston Latin School for 1 year, then began teaching mathematics at Harvard; wrote *Elements of the Theory of the Newtonian Potential Function* (1886); edited the *Physical Review*. See L 1897.

3. Idyll II deals with Simaetha's efforts to win back the youth Delphis' love. Delphis, Simaetha suspects, is in love with a man.

4. "Hexameters and A Note upon the Lament for Adonis, out of Bion," in *The Century Guild Hobby Horse*, V (October 1890), 121–26.

1892. *To Janet Ross*

560 Zattere Venezia May 21 1891

My dear Janet

This beginning of your sketch of John Austin[1] seems to me very good, leaving nothing to be desired. I envy you the direct & unaffected style of narrative wh you possess, & wh gives an unpretentious air to these family records. What you want, it seems to me, is only a little more fullness of detail, & slowness in writing.

I am sorry to say that my bookseller says: "We are unable to supply a copy of Mr Symonds' *Sketches & Studies* in *Italy,* wh is at present out of print." The editors Smith & Elder had never vouchsafed me any information on the subject. I ordered one copy for you, & one for Biagi.[2] Please tell Biagi, when you see him, that only two of the books I promised will arrive, & why.

Madge is still at Vescovana. But I expect her here next week. She will doubtless have kept Lina[3] informed of her plans. It would be very nice if you came too to Venice. I do not think we shall stay long into June; for I am quite idle in this place & want to get to work. It is very likely that the Princess of Montenegro & her daughter Olga[4] will come to pay us a visit at Davos. So Lina will have society. She will like Olga, who is a great friend of Madge's. The old Princess is not quite as nice, & has a very sharp tongue.

Your friend Hallam Murray[5] is expected at Vescovana. Madge says he is going to help her with some sketches to illustrate a history she is writing of the place & the Countess,[6] to present to the Empress Frederick.[7] Madge is a very odd girl.

The weather is cold again here, & today it rains.

Best regards to the Padrone & to Lina. Ever yours

JAS.

Would you like one dama gianna [wine jug] sent back empty? I have put the wine into fiaschi [flasks], but have not opened the other yet. The wine is excellent; far better than what my friends give me at their parties. The Veronese and other wines in vogue here have been wretched for 3 or 4 years.

---

1. Janet Ross' grandfather, John Austin (1790–1859), jurist and professor of jurisprudence, University College, London (1828–32). His daughter Lucy (or Lucie) (1821–69) in 1840 married Sir Alexander Cornewall Duff Gordon (1811–72).
2. See L 1869.
3. Lina Duff-Gordon. See L 1882.
4. See Ls 1790 and 1958.
5. Probably Alexander Henry Hallam Murray (1854–1934), son of John Murray (1808–92), the London publisher, and himself for 25 years a partner in the firm.
6. *Days Spent on a Doge's Farm* (1893).
7. See L 1831.

1893. *To Janet Ross*

560 Zattere Venezia Monday. May 25 1891

My dear Janet

Thanks for yours of the 22nd.

I will send back the empty dama gianna [wine jug]. But I should be much obliged if you would keep the third (faltoria wine)[1] until I write for it.

I hope you did find after all the 1550 edition of Vasari.[2] That is the first. The second, of 1564, is of no use at all to me. I wrote to Miss Turton[3] warning her to be careful about the date.

I have got a really sharp attack of rheumatism & neuralgia. The pain has been incessant since Saty morning at about 4 when it first came on, & I have not had three hours of sleep since.

It makes it difficult to write even like this; & I cannot read even a French novel without increasing the ache.

So I sit, lie, walk about the room, quite vacant.

Do you know, this sort of thing, & what you have twice seen of me at Florence has been my normal state since I was 22. It has only been varied by really dangerous illnesses & by occasional bursts of too intense mental or emotional energy.

C'est bien etrange d'etre un homme de cette espêce, et je ne pas pouvoir vieillir dans l'âme et dans le coeur.[4]

Madge still at Vescovana. Comes here Wednesday. She is very eager to hear about Lina [Duff-Gordon]. I shall be able to arrange for them in one way or another. But I fear, in the present state of things that it would be useless to hope for a good time all together if you came also. If I have to stop here ill, I could hardly make you comfortable in our little house. The girls would have a quarter of it to themselves.

Yrs JAS.

The doctor says, if I do not catch cold or fatigue myself, the trouble can be *localized*. It seems to be everywhere.

----

1. Wine made on a farm.
2. The well-known *Vite de' più eccellenti architetti, pittori e scultori italiani* (rev. 2nd ed., 1568).
3. Unidentified; possibly a librarian.
4. It is very odd to be a man of this type [homosexual], and I am not able to age in soul & heart: i.e., his cravings, as he grows older, remain undiminished.

1894. *To Herbert P. Horne*

Am Hof, Davos Platz, Switzerland. June 6 1891

My dear Mr Horne

I returned from Venice two days ago. I found the Hobby Horse awaiting me, for which many thanks. I have read it with great interest, & do not quite understand what there is in this number which can have given the offence you indicated.

As a matter of detail I do not care for Mr. Shannon's drawing;[1] what is intended for a mystical *volupté* seems to me slovenly; & I think the choice style & real good sense of Mr L.[ionel] Johnson's essay[2] are spoiled by the affectation of archaism in his diction.

But beyond this, I have no objections to make. Legendre's letters[3] are quite delightful, & I congratulate you on your article on M. Aurelius.[4]

You asked me to give my opinion, & I have done so frankly.

You also asked if I could send you some prose. I have a short piece wh is at your service, if you care to use it. I saw a Tiepolo[5] for the first time at Venice, under very favourable conditions for inspecting it, since it was placed on an easel in good light. Upon this I have written a kind of descant.[6] Tiepolo is a painter who interests me greatly.

I am come back to work at a Life of MA Buonarroti. But I am ill & out of spirits.

Very sincerely yours.

J A Symonds.

Please say by P:C: if you wd like to see my paper.

---

1. Charles Hazelwood Shannon (1865–1937), English painter, etcher, and lithographer. A drawing on stone, "Umbilicus Tuus Crater Tornatilis, Numquam Indigens Poculis. Venter Tuus Sicut Acervus Tritici, Vallatus Liliis," is a study of a nude sleeping woman, vigorously rendered. Lily motifs are sketched into the background. See *The Century Guild Hobby Horse*, VI (April, 1891), facing p. 41.

2. Johnson's review, "The Painter-Poets: Selected and edited . . . by Kineton Parkes," is more self-consciously archaic than his briefer review of Dowden's edition of the *Lyrical Ballads*.

3. "The Letters and Papers of Adam Legendre: now First Published from a Manuscript, in the Possession of the Editor," pp. 91–106, edited by Lyall Aubryson. Legendre's dates are missing. Aubryson conjectures that his "considerable" estate was located in Devonshire. The letters range from 1629–36.

4. Horne's "The Thoughts of the Emperor Marcus Aurelius Antoninus," *The Century Guild Hobby Horse*, VI (April, 1891), 68–80.

5. Giovanni Battista Tiepolo (1692–1769), Venetian painter.

6. "On an Altar Piece by Tiepolo," *The Century Guild Hobby Horse*, VI (October, 1891), 121–26, and in *In the Key of Blue* (1893), pp. 43–53.

1895. *To Herbert P. Horne*

Am Hof, Davos Platz, Switzerland. June 13 1891

Dear Mr Horne

I will make my man pack up the notes upon a picture by Tiepolo[1] tomorrow, & send them to you. They are not worth the name of an article, though I have tried to define what (for myself) is the real point about this extraordinary painter. If you have not seen his pieces in the Pal: Labia at Venice,[2] & two or three of his easel pictures, you can have no conception of the wonderful glamour he is capable of throwing over art-work for even winds so jaded by criticism & so worn by life as mine is. A good Tiepolo is, in a high & noble sense of the bar-phrase, a "corpse-reviver."

There is one of his pictures at Udine,[3] a great study of warm blues & blacks, wh, if life permits, I must revisit Udine to see.

I very much wish that, before my work on Michelangelo is finished, I may have the privilege of studying your essay, & using it with due acknowledgments, your letter interested me very greatly. I can tell you that it is very rare to find any competent judge of architecture, who is sympathetic (as you are) to his style. I do not believe much in any criticism wh is not sympathetic; & for myself, I know my own incompetence to deal properly with architecture—except as historical document.

I spent a long time in the Library of S. Lorenzo[4] last May, & my house is full of photographs of it & other buildings by MA. I am fairly puzzled & at sea. So much of his work in this way seems mere decorative quibbling; & yet the total effect is so pictorially impressive. It seems so wrong in its principles & still so genial in its results.

And then, did he really determine that curve of the Cupola of S. Peter's?[5] If he did, if it was not a Da Porta,[6] we must concede to him the discovery of a quite stupendously delightful ovoid.

I am dreadfully maimed by neurologic rheumatism, caught in those damned Italian churches.[7] Write nonsense in spasms of pain.

Yours very sincerely

J A Symonds

---

1. See L 1894.

2. See L 1894. In 1745 Tiepolo decorated the grand hall of the Palazzi Labia with themes from Cleopatra's life and illusive architectural decorations.

3. Either a fresco in the Oratorio della Purità or a painting in the Archiepiscopal Palace, Udine.

4. Michelangelo worked from 1523–27 on the Medici Chapel, the sacristy of San Lorenzo. The architecture was conceived as framing for Michelangelo's sculpture.

5. In 1547 Michelangelo was appointed chief architect of St. Peter's. The cupola alone was carried out according to his plans.

6. Giacomo della Porta (1542–1604), Italian architect, pupil of Giacomo da Vignola (1507–73); completed works left unfinished by Michelangelo, especially the cupola of St. Peter's.

7. Symonds' fellow sufferer, Samuel Richards, wrote thus to his wife on June 14, 1891:

. . . [Dr.] Huggard says I must keep quiet, sit in my Studio balcony & lay on the Sofa when tired, and not commence work for 6 or 10 days till I get used to the altitude again. I can hardly breathe here, and I loathe the place worse than ever. Have seen no one yet but Symonds who got back only two days ago. Am invited there to lunch tomorrow & to Huggard Tuesday. Symonds came back much worse for his stay & has been in bed since, he has an accute attack of rheumatism, & Madge says he makes the air blue with execrations . . . You may say what you like about America, but Hell is preferable to me rather than an existence here—and this is my candid & considered opinion. (Gallini Collection)

1896. *To Janet Ross*

Am Hof, Davos Platz, Switzerland. June 16 1891

Dear Janet

I happened to see, in a Second Hand Book Catalogue, a copy of my "Sketches & Studies in Italy."

I bought it, & now am sending it on to you. It was obviously purchased by its previous possessor for the sake of the essay on Antinous.

I advise you to read the Appendix on English Blank Verse. Lina [Duff-Gordon] seems to thrive here, & the four girls, with some friends from outside, make up a very very merry party.

I am still tormented with the nerve trouble in my arm. It does not leave me night or day. And I really cannot write to you a decent letter.

Work goes on at a slow rate, & the pages I now produce about M.A.B. will always be redolent for me of pain.

JAS

1897. *To Edmund Gosse*

Am Hof, Davos Platz, Switzerland. June 22 1891

My dear Gosse

Your welcome gift of Couperus' book,[1] for wh I thank you greatly, reminds me how many weeks have passed since we exchanged letters.

I have been away in Florence & Venice, making the best I could of a very bad spring & much physical discomfort. I was eventually disabled by acute neuralgic rheumatism, & got back here in a suffering condition wh continues.

There is only one remedy, I think, for maladies; & that is mental work. I consequently have never been very idle, & am making considerable progress with my book on Michelangelo. But I was unable to study con *amore* in the libraries & museums, which I frequented agueishly shuddering; & I could not drink in the pleasure of Italian nature. So I fear my labours will be dry enough in their results.

I spent a few days at Siena & the jewel-hill-town of Montalcino. Here I composed an appendix to my "Problem,"[2] combining several new considerations brought home to me by the correspondence wh that sparely circulated essay has educed. I found a fierce & Quixotic ally, who goes far beyond my expectations in hopes of regenerating opinion on these topics, in a Prof: Pierce (?)[3] of Cambridge Mass. He ought to be in Europe now—or "here" as the Americans so oddly call the whole region bounded by Atlantic, Arctic Ocean, Ural Mountains, Egean Sea, & northern Mediterranean coast-line. If he crosses your path in London, look after him, & mention me. I hear he professes Mathematics.

If the appendix gets into print, I will send you a copy.

It is my present desire to remain here, writing about 5 hrs on the average a day, through the summer; & then I suppose I must go again, about Michelangelo, to Florence & Rome.

Some points, wh I think I communicated to you, about MA's emotions, were fully confirmed by the Ms correspondence I studied at Florence. It is a difficult matter to tackle, for I think there has been a conspiracy on the part of his Italian editors & biographers to throw dust in the eyes of the public about things which even the public would not judge blame-worthy. My book will, to some extent, be revolutionary. But I am afraid of the task before me: truth-telling, without seeming to dot i's wilfully. I need not say that I have discovered no scandal about MA. I did, by the way, about Cellini. He was actually imprisoned a long time for a very flagrant case. Milanesi,[4] who pretends to have published all accessible documents about him, withheld those bearing on the point. And so, biographies are always "a rifare" [remaking].

What a number of Urnings are being portrayed in novels now! "Dorian Gray," "Un Raté," "Monsieur Venus," this "Footsteps of Fate."[5] I stumble on them casually, & find the same note.

Tell me about yourself, if you have time. I mean to buy the novels of your series as they appear.[6] It seems to me a most excellent scheme. What a woman Mrs Bell[7] is. Is she polyglot exceedingly? Sister of Poynter?
Yours ever affectionately & of closer intercourse desirously

JAS

What do you, & people, think of the "humanity of genius"?

---

1. Louis Couperus (1863–1923), Dutch writer of fiction; *Footsteps of Fate,* tr. from the Dutch by Clara Bell, with an introduction, "The Dutch Sensitivists," by Gosse (1891).
2. The pirated edition (1896) contains a section, following the Epilogue, called "Suggestions on the Subject of Sexual Inversion in Relation to Law and Education."

3. See L 1891.

4. See L 1877.

5. Oscar Wilde, *The Picture of Dorian Gray* (1891); "Gyp" (pseudonym of Sibylle Gabrielle, Countess de Martel de Janville, 1849–1932), *Un Raté* (2nd ed., 1891); "Rachilde" (pseudonym of the French novelist Marguerite Eymery Vallette, 1860–?), *Monsieur Vénus* (1889), a sensational treatment of homosexuality; and see note 1.

6. Gosse edited Heineman's International Library.

7. Clara Bell (1834–1927), sister of the painter Sir Edward Poynter, daughter of Ambrose Poynter, an English architect; married Robert Courtenay Bell; was a prolific translator.

1898. *To Havelock Ellis*

[Davos] July /91

[Dear Mr Ellis]

. . . . the problem on me. It reappeared in my researches into Italian social conditions of the Renaissance period. And I have privately printed two essays, which deal with the psychological problem in ancient Greece and modern Europe. The latter I sent to Tuke,[1] who is an old friend of my father's. But he shrinks from entertaining the question in any practical way. The real point now is legislative. France and Italy stand in glaring contrast to England and Germany. And the medical and forensic authorities who are taking it up, seem quite ignorant both of history and fact. Their pathological hypothesis will certainly not stand the test of accumulated experience. What the whole thing tends to, seems very doubtful; I do not believe that you and I would disagree at bottom about the ethical views. But we cannot discuss this on paper without knowing more about our principles and sympathies. After all, the phenomenon is there, and for England is a very serious one. It ought to be scientifically, historically, impartially investigated, instead of being left to Labby's[2] inexpansible legislation.

The only book of Verlaine's[3] I have not yet seen (I think) in verse, is Bonheur. I must get that.

I will send you a photograph of myself, not so nice as Hollyer's of you. —Try to let me have the number of the *Arch. di Psych.*[4]

Very sincerely yours

John Addington Symonds.

---

1. Dr. Daniel Hack Tuke. See L 1838.

2. Henry du Pré Labouchère (1831–1912), in the House of Commons from 1880–1906, supported Gladstone, founded *Truth,* a magazine devoted to the exposure of

social fraud (1877). See Hesketh Pearson's *Labby* (1937). In 1885, he sponsored a clause in the Criminal Law Amendment Act making the punishment for homosexuality two years at hard labor. Oscar Wilde was sentenced under the terms of this clause.

3. Ellis had called Verlaine's *Bonheur* (1891) and *Parallèlement* (1889) to Symonds' notice.

4. *Archivio di psichiatria* . . . , XI (1890). It contained an essay by Cesare Lombroso (1836–1909), Italian physician and criminologist; Ellis brought it to Symonds' attention. See L 1984.

1899. *To Horatio Forbes Brown*

Davos, July 2, 1891

[Dear Horatio]

There are some things in your last letter (June 30) which make me want to respond at once; and I hope this will follow you to England, and that you will think over a friend's word there. It is about the relation of passion to intellectual energy. You know how little I seek after fame, and how little I value the fame of famous men. You also know how much I value self-effectuation: how I deeply feel it to be the duty of a man to make the best of himself, to use his talents, to make his very defects serve as talents, and to be something for God's sake who made him. In other words, to play his own note in the universal symphony. We have not to ask whether other people will be affected by our written views of this or that. Though, for my part, I find now, with every day I live, that my written views have had a wide and penetrating influence where often least expected. That is no affair of mine, any more than of a sunflower to be yellow, or a butterfly to flutter. The point for us is to bring all parts of ourselves into vital correlation, so that we shall think nothing, write nothing, love nothing, but in relation to the central personality—the bringing of which into prominence is what is our destiny and duty in this short life. And my conclusion is that, in this one life, given to him on earth, it is the man's duty, as recompense to God who placed him here, or Nature, Mother of us all—and the man's highest pleasure, as a potent individuality—to bring all factors of his being into correspondence for the presentation of himself in something. Whether the world regards that final self-presentation of the man or not, seems to me just no matter. As Jenny Lind once said to me, "I sing to God," so, I say, let us sing to God. And for this end let us not allow ourselves to be submerged in passion, or our love to lapse in grubbery; but let us be human beings, horribly imperfect certainly, living for the best effectuation of themselves which they find possible. If all men and women lived like this, the symphony of humanity would be a splendid thing to listen to.

I have been writing out of the heart's depth. And as Achilles says in Shakespeare—

> My soul is troubled like a fountain stirred,
> And I myself see not the bottom of it.[1]

But, after all, dear friend, do not do what you seem inclined to do; do not let your intelligence imagine that any work you can produce is useless; do not delude your conscience with the seductive dream of becoming corrupt. Corruption is too terrible a Siren. Some part in us loves her so. You must keep your intelligence alive to its humble function, as a necessary energy for your own diurnal happiness. And you must make your conscience feel that, living for unselfish and no ignoble ends, you do not sink into corruption.

At the end of the whole matter I say this:

Brain work, whatever its value may be, is the best balance to passion; and passion, however despised it may be, is wholesome when it helps the man to will and labour with his mind.

[Incomplete]

---

1. *Troilus and Cressida*, III, iii, ll. 314–15, where "soul" is replaced by "mind." See L 1995.

1900. *To Guido Biagi*

Am Hof, Davos Platz, Switzerland. July 15 1891

Dear Professor Biagi

I received the copies of the letter you sent me on the 13th this morning, & am exceedingly grateful to you.

It only really pains me to think that you should have spent your own valuable time & given yourself trouble for this.[1]

Is there no way of employing some one to do what ought really not to be put upon your shoulders?

It makes me very diffident about asking for other letters, though in the course of my work I find that some more would be desirable: unless you will allow me to make some arrangement with you, by which this work would not be unremunerative. My publishers are very liberal toward me with money, & I can rely on getting a good grant from them for information & material so precious as original documents supply. The letters you have already sent me are worth a great deal to me, & are most carefully copied. They enable me to establish with certainty a point which, though small, is of much importance.

I wanted Angiolini's letters[2] because he was Michelangelo's Roman correspondent during some years which offer a good deal of difficulty to the biographer as regards Buonarroti's own movements, his occupations & his friendships. It seemed to me possible that I might be able to fix through them the date of his coming to be acquainted with Vittoria Colonna,[3] if, as Milanesi[4] suggests, that was before 1534.

There is one question I will ask you if you go to the Archivio. That is; Guasti has printed a series of 14 Stanze beginning
"Io crederei se tu fussi di sano"
& ending
"Ti troverei grand' io fussi ben cieco":
does it seem to you from the state of the Ms that they were all addressed to *one* person, & have the words undergone important alterations by Michelangelo's own hand? Guasti prints it (Rime, p: 329) from the *Autografo*.[5] MA the younger's[6] *rifacimenti* [revisions] contains more than the usual alterations, & as far as I can see omits entirely the *first* stanza.

As a direct expression of strong & simple emotion some of the stanzas are more than usually good from the literary point of view, & I should much like to know all I can about them.

If I come to Florence, as I hope, again this autumn, shall I be able to go to the Museo Buonarroti & read without getting another permission? My work goes on apace, & I have written eight of the chapters of my book—which will have I think about 14 in all.

I hope you will consider this question about the honorarium I proposed, & let me know. I shall feel very awkward & uncomfortable if you do not.

Believe me meanwhile with sincere gratitude & the kindest feeling, to be yours

John Addington Symonds.

P.S. I can leave it to you not to copy out absolutely uninteresting letters from Angiolini.
=============================
If you will agree about the honorarium, I should like to ask you to look

through the letters of *Pietro Urbano*.[7] But I cannot ask further favours until we come to an understanding. It will always & in any case be a great obligation to me that you should have undertaken the drudgery of copying.

---

1. See L 1869. Biagi himself made copies of various letters in the Buonarroti archives for Symonds.

2. Symonds translated these for the text of his *Michelangelo*, but put their Italian versions in an appendix.

3. Symonds settled on 1538 as the possible date of the first acquaintanceship: *Michelangelo*, II, 93. See L 1890.

4. See L 1877.

5. *Le Rime di Michelangelo Buonarroti . . . cavate dagt; autografia e pubblicate da Cesare Guasti* (1863). See L 1877.

6. Michelangelo Buonarroti (the younger) (1568–1646), *Rime di Michelagnolo Buonarroti. Raccolte da Michelagnolo sua nipote* (1623).

7. Pietro Urbano, one of Michelangelo's workmen, was charged with completing the statue "Christ Triumphant" in Rome, bungled so badly that Michelangelo was forced to dismiss him and thus terminate a friendship. See *Michelangelo*, I, 360–62.

1901. *To Janet Ross*

Am Hof, Davos Platz, Switzerland. July 31. 1891.

My dear Janet

I should have written before. But I mislaid the letter in wh you told me what I owed you. I have now found it, & enclose a cheque. I do not know what the carriage of the oil from Chiasso[1] was, so I cannot deduct it.

As regards Carlo Orsi[2] & Venice. Angelo does sleep in my house; but there are four bedrooms. If Carlo likes to go there as my guest, he will be very welcome to a bedroom & whatever accommodation the little place has. It is *560 Zattere*. He would have Mrs Angelo [Fusato] to do the rooms for him & cook, if he wanted. He ought to pay her something a day, perhaps one franc. I think she is expecting to be confined. But Angelo will find a Donna.

Should he care to accept this proposal, I will write to Angelo & tell him to expect Signor Orsi. Please therefore let me know at once.

Here I am quite alone: Lotta at Danzig; Madge & Katharine at Gawthorpe Hall;[3] my wife, I don't know where (for she went off on Monday & has not written since). I think she is at Thun.

I grind away at Michelangelo, & am very tired. I hope you will enjoy [Richard?] Wagner. Ever yr affec

JAS.

---

1. A Swiss town on the Italian border.
2. (?–1898), a sculptor and artist, friend of Mrs. Ross. Orsi illustrated her *Italian Sketches* (1887). "Everyone loved gentle, kindly Carlo, the talented artist and charming singer; to us he was like a son."—Janet Ross, *The Fourth Generation* (1912), p. 366.
3. Burnley, Lancashire. They were visiting the Kay-Shuttleworths. See L 148.

1902. *To Margaret Symonds*

[Davos] Aug: 5 Wednesday [1891]

My dearest Madge

I wrote you one letter to Gawthorpe.[1] But in the confusion of your plans I did not think it worth while to send more.

It is a pity your mother made you go to England after Rougham[2] broke down. I agreed with her at the time. But I had forgotten for a moment the smallness and selfishness—the miserably mean scale of life and conception—of the upper English bourgeoisie: people who ask you to the ends of Lancashire for 3 days and the rest of it: not because they are bad, but because they are so infernally stupid and hedged in (like their own petty fields and petty parks) with palings of conventionalities, and stuffed with the artificial manures of comfort like their own fat flowerless meadows.

I am not exactly sorry that you should be reminded of the remarkable freedom of our life. If there is one set of human beings I detest, it is the English upper middle class. Buxtons etc.

It has rained incessantly ever since you went away, except last Sunday. I have been alone and working hard at Michelangelo. I am very tired and feel odd in my head. But I can't stop.

Your mother came back last evening, bringing Herr and Frau Caveng[3] whom she had found pacifically waiting on the platform at Landquart.

[T. H.] Warren and his wife are here and the only son of the great Lord Acton.[4] They all seem happy, which is well. [H. F.] Brown is settled alone at Wiesen, for 2 months, he says! His letters have been increasingly delirious since he went to England; and the last from London exploded like a sky-rocket. Wiesen will sober and sadden him.

Rucock[5] has succeeded admirably I think with Mme Pisani.[6] The odd thing is that his reproduction is so much clearer than the original.

Obernetter[7] has done equally well with Aunt Pop [Marianne North]: and so quickly that little viper Richards[8] has been up to some mischief between Obernetter and me, I am certain. I must find out. For this job for your mother has been executed with businesslike despatch and in a thoroughly workmanlike way.

Give my love to Auntie [Mary Ann Sykes] and Aunt Ch.[arlotte] and also to K.[atharine].

You can always come back when you are sick of your life.

Yrs ever

JAS

Margot [Tennant] is at S. Moritz. Her Sisterinlaw Helen (Gordon Duff)[9] is dying of galloping consumption there, she writes me!

---

1. Where she was visiting the Kay-Shuttleworths. See L 1901.
2. The North family home was Rougham.
3. Her mother's Swiss friends.
4. Richard Maximilian Acton (1870–1924), son of John Emerich Edward Dalbert, 1st Baron Acton (1834–1902); Baron Acton was writer and historian; head of the Liberal Roman Catholic movement in England and vigorous opponent of papal infallibility; regius professor of modern history, Cambridge (1895–1902); planned the *Cambridge Modern History*. Richard Maximilian became lord in waiting to Edward VII (1905–10) and George V (1910–15).
5. A photographer.
6. See L 1717.
7. See L 1790.
8. See L 1708.
9. Helen Elizabeth Gordon Duff of Drummuir, Banffshire (b. 1866), in Oct. 1889, married Harold John Tennant (1865–1935) and died May 9, 1892.

1903. *To Margaret Symonds*

Am Hof, Davos Platz, Switzerland. August: 10. 1891. Monday

My dearest Madge

I have been working awfully at M.A.B.[1] Last Saturday I wrote in the morning from 9 a.m. till 12.30 p:m. Then again in the evening from 8 p:m: till 2. a.m. & when I got up yesterday, I wrote from 9.30 until 12.30 in the forenoon.

That makes quite 12 hours of sustained work of the most strained quality in the space of 27 hours.

I often reckon my own brain-work out for myself in such calculations. And I do not mind speaking to you about them, because the bond of sympathy between us is very subtle & vibrant, & I should like you to comprehend the sort of excessive life I often lead.

Well: I felt the pace was killing, & went off with Edwin,[2] who can only laugh, & be as clear & pure as lake-water—nothing more—but how much that is in an active healthy person—to Wiesen; where we dined & talked with Brown, slept, & came back.

In the interval, your letter (for which I thank you warmly) came to Am Hof, & your mother naturally read it. Between her & me & my children there cannot be secrets.

I am glad to find that she is now quite happy about you. I left her yesterday on the point of packing up her portmanteau & going to England. But now she only says that you are getting on well enough; & that I have corrupted your mind with my talk about the English upper middle class.

Well: if that's all, then "all's well that ends well." And I only hope for my part that you are now a little more settled, & feel a little more of warm kindliness, less of plans & compressed schemes, around you.

There are as splendid men & women in the English bourgeoisie as any nation ever produced. The individuals, when you discover them, are magnificent, superb. It is only the way of living that I rail against—what I call the hedge-row scheme of existence.

A most noble Marchioness, who took me up when I was a lad,[3] once said to me: "Dear boy, take care never to over-stay a three days' visit."

I made a mental memorandum to avoid people with whom such precepts passed as oracles. Life, I thought, was not worth living on that scale of philosophy.

With time, I found out that the three days' visit has its uses & its charm, & also that the people brought together in this social scheme can often diverge into beautiful relationships.

Still, I do not appreciate the hard rind of selfishness, calculation & established comfort, which forms the stuff of the Marchioness's maxim. It is the want of pliability in the nature of my home-bred country men I most resent; & the way they have of hiding their real selves under shells of convention, which have to be cracked, & lie always open cracked for the initiated.

I am so very glad to hear that you miss me. It means so much. It means

594

that, in our case, the relation of father & child brings something real of vitality to both. For myself, I never doubted this. Without you, I am a man who has lost a finger. I often go into your empty room, & touch the things upon your table, & look at the flowers outside the window.

So: though I want you to drink of the well of life at large, to learn, to take the bitter, & to love the sweet, it cheers me to hear from you a frank acknowledgement of a bond between us. I do not believe that such bonds are other than imperishable: that is, if one person has found, or can find, that another is a bit of himself—felt in presence, lacked in absence.

The post boy (actually) brought your Straf Karte [card of reprimand] (worth to my pocket 10 centimes, & to the post boy, for my pleasure in getting it, 50) of the 9th just now, while I am writing after lunch.

I am so glad to hear you are today (Monday) on your way to Sutton Court.[4] God bless you. You cannot imagine how much I think of you, & how angry I am if things do not go as I should like with you. And what a joy it is to hear that you are started right at last on what I think is good for you!

God be blessed!

So I close, begging you only to give my love to Sir Edward [Strachey], my kindest regards to Constance,[5] & to say to Harry[6] that I love his picture & am going to write to him.

A hug of love to K.[atharine].

Your loving father JAS.

Tell K that her Nelken [carnations: KF] are a cataract of lovely blossoms & that I took Tike [foxterrier:KF] with me to Wiesen. The little dog was good & "Folgsam" [obedient].

---

1. *The Life of Michelangelo Buonarroti* (1893).
2. A Davos friend, Edwin Brugger. See Ls 1975 and 1988.
3. Possibly Emily Jane Elphinstone de Flahault (d. 1895), who in 1843 married Henry Thomas Petty-Fitzmaurice, 4th Marquess of Lansdowne (1816–66), of Bowood, Colne, Wiltshire, a close friend of Symonds' father.
4. Home of the Sir Edward Stracheys.
5. Constance Strachey, wife of Symonds' nephew, Edward Strachey, junior. She was the daughter of Charles Braham and the niece of Frances, Countess Waldegrave. The marriage occurred January 17, 1880. On the Stracheys, see L 122.
6. Henry Strachey, painter, Symonds' nephew and son of Sir Edward Strachey. See L 1872.

1904. *To Margaret Symonds*

[Davos] Aug 15 1891 Saty.

My dearest Madge

I have bad news. The Cardinal [bird:KF] died this morning at 11. Up to Thursday evening he was as vigorous & joyous as ever. But yesterday it became clear that he must have poisoned himself while flying about the room. He was so very ill today at breakfast time that your mother sent for Dr Huggard.[1] The Orâtor was kind, & prescribed; but all to no purpose. And poor Cardy died at last in the hands of his sorrowing mistress.

I am very sorry for your Mother, & wish I had never chaffed her about her pet. She will miss him greatly, as shall I—for it was a pleasure to have a creature in the house enjoying life so hugely & so innocently.

I sent you through your mother £20 yesterday. Do not be anxious about expenses. Of course I know that going about England three persons will cost money. And I trust you to be as economical as is consistent with comfort.

I think, as you have your own servant with you, that 15/ spent in the house you stay at is enough: 5/ to housemaid, 5/ to butler or footman, 5/ to the coachman if he has done much for you. It is not usual to tip coachmen however, unless as at Bexley [Kent][2] they have served you a great deal.

Our weather has changed suddenly (rather too much so) from abominable to perfect. Yesterday your mother & I climbed the alp meadows above Buol's chalet over [Davos] Dörfli. It was glorious, & some flowers still in fine bloom.

I go on working at Michelangelo, & am getting rather tired. I feel as if the works of the clock were running down. I ought to get away for a holiday.

Give my dearest love to Auntie & Aunt Char. I hope the latter is well again. It is too late to congratulate her on her birthday!

Yours ever JAS.

I was so interested to hear about C. H. House.[3] Is it not beautiful, that garden & that view! I wish I cd get a photo of the new front.

---

1. Dr. W. R. Huggard, leading British doctor and Consul at Davos; according to Katharine Symonds Furse, "A great character, with a stammer of which he made full use, who was always good company." He helped her organize the British trained nurses at Davos.—*H & P*, p. 175. He wrote an article, "The Standard of Sanity," in the *British*

Medical Journal (November 28, 1885), pp. 1013–14, in which he discusses the definition of insanity and the confinement of the insane. See Symonds, *A Problem in Modern Ethics* (1891), pp. 34–35.

2. The manuscript has "Bexley," but we have not been able to discover whom Margaret visited there. This spelling may be a mistake for Burnley, Lancashire, where she visited the Kay-Shuttleworths at Gawthorpe Hall.

3. Clifton Hill House, Symonds' former Clifton home.

1905. *To Janet Ross*

[Davos] Aug 21 1891

My dear Janet

I am very sorry to hear of your bronchitis & non-enjoyment. The journey is so long that you ought to have got a great deal out of it.

Carlo[1] wrote me a nice little note soon after getting to Venice. He seemed to feel at home. Angelo [Fusato] too writes that he will do everything he can to make him comfortable.

I hope he has found out a charming ostereia close by (called the Speranza), kept by a very good friend of mine Cenzi.[2] It is a pretty pergola place, as though in the country.

Tell Poldo[2] how very much I am obliged to him. I will go & thank the young priest when I come to Florence.

I think of leaving this for Italy about the end of September; & if you could take me for a few days, it would be such a pleasure to me.[3]

I shall have to go on to Rome. I cannot properly remember the MA[4] architecture there.

Since I came up here, I have now spent 10 weeks on my work, writing about 8 hrs a day. It is a tremendous strain. But I have finished (or at least laid down on paper) 11 chapters out of the 14 I planned. My book[5] is already a substantial thing before me.

Thanks for the Daily News (Andrew Lang).[6] Walt [Whitman] is very funny. He sent me the whole account of his supper, with much more in it about me.

We have hideous weather here, rain, snow, thunder, snow, rain.

Everyr

J.A.S.

I never told you how very grieved I was to hear about yr money losses.[7] You must tell me all about it when I come.

If you write to Carlo tell him from me that Val San Zibio (near

Battaglia) in the Euganeans is one of the most picturesque & romantically beautiful places in Europe. It is worth going to see, perhaps to paint its grand old gardens.

---

1. Carlo Orsi. See L 1901.

2. These were probably officials of the Laurentian Library who assisted Symonds in consulting the archives. Mrs. Ross had, through Dr. Guido Biagi, taken the initial steps.

3. The visit was made in October. See L 1920.

4. Michelangelo, who succeeded Antonio da Sangallo, in 1547, as chief architect of St. Peter's, Rome, designed the main architectural features of the church, including the famous dome. He also supervised the remodeling of the baths of Diocletian into the Church of Santa Maria degli Angeli and designed the façades and court of the palace group on the Capitoline Hill.

5. *The Life of Michelangelo Buonarroti* (1893).

6. Roger Lancelyn Green has been able to resolve Symonds' reference for us: it refers to an article called "A New Jersey Celebration" which appeared in the London *Daily News* on August 15, 1891, and which described a dinner honoring Walt Whitman. Symonds had sent a message: " 'Whitman's genius cannot be gauged,' says Mr. Symonds, on which the good Walt observes 'I like Symonds.' " Lang based his account on the report in *Lippincott's Magazine*, XLVIII (Aug., 1891), 230–31. See L 1885.

7. See L 1922.

1906. *To Horatio Forbes Brown*

Davos, Aug. 23.[1891]

[Dear Horatio]

I suppose you are not coming to-day. So I hope "fervet opus" [the work goes on briskly]. I did a good day's work yesterday. Then came a night of uproar. The Landammann [Swiss cantonial president] invited me with others to play hosts to the officers. It went off well on the whole. But I thought the Landammann's wine bad. And the Swiss officers are, I think, less well bred than the Swiss peasants or artizans. But they had all marched over the Strela yesterday, and you know what sort of a day it was. They had the right to take their ease in their inn.

The Sidgwicks are coming on the 30th, Margot [Tennant] on September 5th, R. G.[1] a little later. You must come up and see some of these folk. I think you would like the Sidgwicks best.

My article on the Turnfest at Geneva came in proof last night.[2] I expect the thing will only puzzle the general reader. I read a phrase of Thoreau's the other day, to this effect: "Do not look for inspiration unless the body be inspired too."[3] That is what I feel about the effect of the passions upon the intellect. It puts sanely before you, what I wanted to say. But I doubt whether I am right in thinking that this inspiration of the body is a source of mental excitement in the way of work for all men.

[Incomplete]

---

1. Ronald Gower, i.e., Lord Ronald Charles Sutherland-Gower (1845–1916). See L 1612. His *Old Diaries 1881–1891* (1902) contains several references to his visits with Symonds.

2. "Swiss Athletic Sports," *The Fortnightly Review*, LVI (1891), 408–15; see also *OLSH*, pp. 222–39. A brief article in the 100th anniversary issue of the *Davoser Zeitung*, February 6–7, 1965, commented on Davos as a health resort and sports center in which the English played an important part.

3. "A man is never inspired unless his body is also."—*Summer: from the Journal of Henry D. Thoreau*, ed. by H. G. O. Blake (1884), 197–98.

1907. *To Horace Traubel*

Davos Platz, Switzerland. August 24. 1891.

My dear friend & comrade

I am a brute beast before you. I have been thrilling to all your messages sent over sea and shadowy hills to me. I participated in your marriage,[1] thanks to your kindness. And I sat at the feast with Whitman, when he spoke so like his grand old self about his friends—so simply falling like pure light upon their personalities, & giving them relief of sun and shadow.

All this I have had from you, & your portrait too, showing me what my friend Traubel is. It came to me in a high upper room at Florence, where I was ensconced, poor old man that I am, with my Italian "Warry."[2]

Give Warry a good grip of the hand from me. Tell him that a fine young man must work his own life-drama through, but that he will not regret the time spent in assisting a hero so triumphant as our Walt, or even a poor fellow so inferior as one who does his best & comes to little. Love is fellow-service; & as Paul said, of these three Love lasts longest.

I have been so tired with the unremitting calls upon my force to write a Life of Michelangelo, when I am physically unequal to the task, that I have lived only in sympathy with my dear friends—absorbing too much of their affection, giving out too little, accumulating the whole produce in my own miserable egotism.

599

Forgive me, friends. Take it not amiss. It is only the old worn workman's instinct to conserve his energy for what his present task is.

What you tell me about Walt's daily life now, is infinitely precious. He teaches us, in his latest years, as in his youngest, how to deal with life. In the long run, this will be his real mission.

Tell him from me that his sick-bed, his death-bed,[3] is the Seal of the magnetic inspiration he has sent to quicken spiritual life in others. I am sure of this. He ascends sublimer, as the mere material force of life declines. And I believe that in this he clinches the whole of the philosophy he gave us. We need not look beyond the grave. But Whitman teaches us to live & die.

The Universe is responsible for those who live & die. The Universe sends men, from time to time, to show us how to live & die.

Whitman is the last of these Avatars.

I am writing just as though I were talking; tired out with my day's work. But I mean every word of what I have said above. And when Whitman joins "the majority," he leaves a rule of sane & social conduct for the disciples lingering round his grave—not with tears; that spirit needs no sign of Sorrow; rather with acceptation of the destiny, which he taught us to face bravely & hopefully.

Dear friend, from the remote Alps to you, I am writing these words, very late & tired.

Please take them in good Comradeship. And do not be vexed with me, if they seem to you stupid or simple. The heart speaks sometimes; & then it asks too little from the head. The heart wants eyes.

You tell me you would like to have something from my pen about Whitman, to put into a volume of essays.

What I should like to put there is a poem in Terza Rima I once wrote, about his prophecy of Comradeship.[4] He got it, & responded to it in a letter, wh I have religiously preserved.

Elsewhere I have not published it. But I stand by the opinions & feeling I expressed in verse there.

Could you make use of this poem, I am able to send you a (privately) printed copy of it. And I do not think I could add anything to your volume more characteristic of what I feel about our Master's influence.

Give him my dear dear love, & show him this letter.

I am yours in fellowship

J ASymonds

Symphony on Love & Death

Written to Whitman about the year 1871. The whole was suggested by his teaching of Comradeship as the binding emotion of the nations; & in particular by some poems out of Calamus. [Scented Herbage. I dream'd a dream. Primeval my Love]

First Movement. The address to Whitman as the Poet-prophet of a new Chivalry, & to the God in man's heart revealed by him, are blent together like two motifs.

Second Movement. Example from the history of two comrades, who in the early age of Athenian liberty, voluntarily devoted their lives to save the city from a plague.

Third Movement. Vision of the Future, when Whitman's teaching on Comradeship & Democracy shall have imbued the nations with a new religion & a new audacity.

Though the 20 years which have passed since I wrote this ode have damped youthful ardour, I still believe Whitman's doctrine to have the essence of a great possibility for human expansion in it.

Aug 25. I think I may, on the whole, send you straight off this poem.

If you use it please let it appear that it was written in 1871 & has not been published.

I add inside this, a few notes to explain my meaning to you as you read.

JAS.

---

1. Horace Traubel married Anne Montgomerie of Philadelphia, May 28, 1891.

2. Warren Fritzinger, Whitman's young male attendant. See L 1855. Symonds saw a parallel between his own relationship with Angelo Fusato, the gondolier, and Whitman's with Fritzinger.

3. Whitman died March 26, 1892.

4. *In Re Walt Whitman* (1893), ed. by Horace L. Traubel, Richard M. Bucke, and Thomas B. Harned, opens with Symonds' "Love and Death: A Symphony." There are also extracts (p. 412) from L 1761 (Dec. 9, 1889) to Whitman, in which Symonds thanks him for his edition of poems and prose. "Love and Death" had been printed in *Pamphlet V* (possibly, 1880), where it was subtitled "To the Prophet Poet/ of Democracy Religion Love/ this Verse/ A feeble Echo of his Song/ is Dedicated"; parts of it were published in *Many Moods* (1878). See Babington, pp. 24–25.

1908. *To Margaret Symonds*

Am Hof, Davos Platz, Switzerland. Wednesday August 26 [91:KF]

My dear Madge

I hope you are now upon that fairy terrace, among "the sleepy woods embowered in Summer Seas,"[1] of Glenthorne.[2] It is a place I used to admire

601

very much twenty years ago, & to be ill in, for the climate hurt my lungs; & where also Mr Halliday taught me to appreciate the qualities of wines for their own sake—he had such a cellar!

I got your excellent letter from Oxford last night. What you say about the Japanese things fills me with joyous expectation. I like to have a lot of those knick-knacks.

We go on as usual. The weather seems turning well. Your Mother has a big Italian tinkering at her garden.

I write, like a demon, at Michelangelo. The work is drawing to its conclusion: so far as the ground-plan & first composition are concerned. It will want a lot of "chasing," as bronze-founders say of a statue they have cast.

The main part of my life is contained in this strenuous effort to produce a piece of literary art. For relaxation I have walks with the dogs, talks with [T. H.] Warren & his young men,[3] wine with Swiss comrades.

Il solito giro, n'est pas? Well: ça marche.[4] But the big thing is the Michelangelo. The rest fades off into soothing & diluting shadows.

I am often very weary, with a vexed brain & irritable nerves. This career of art is not indeed what the French poets call it, "un Calvaire"; but it is a very exhausting business, which brings the whole man into play & drains him out. Also, ennobles him.

There will [be] a mixture of other elements soon. [H. F.] Brown & the H. Sidgwicks here next Saturday & Sunday. Then Margot [Tennant] & Ld Ronald Gower. After that two Americans,[5] personally unknown to me.

I will write to Auntie about the tureen. Till I get to Bristol, I cannot have it got out from the Bank. But I will let her do what she will with it. She ought to be humoured in her old age. She will probably steal it from me, & give it to a Cave.[6] But we can do without it: as we have done many years.

Tell Katharine, with dear love from me, that Tike [terrier:KF] is very well & happy. He has taken to me, but not so much that she will not find him her own dog again. Only she must indulge him more. He wants this & deserves it: he is so good & obedient & affectionate.

Everyr JAS.

Remember me most warmly to Mr. Halliday.

---

1. A misquotation of Keats' "And float along like birds o'er summer seas."—"Epistle: To Charles Cowden Clarke," l. 57.

2. She was with William Halliday (1828–98) and several of his daughters. His wife had died in Dec., 1889. See L 943.

3. Probably Magdalen College undergraduates.

4. It [his life] keeps going around, doesn't it? Well, that's the pace [march, tread].

5. The Americans were Jeremiah Lynch and S. Pary (whom we have not been able to identify). See L 1910.

6. His sister, Edith's, family.

1909. *To Henry Graham Dakyns*

Davos Sept: 4. 1891

My dear Graham

I am grateful to my dithyramb about the Swiss athletes,[1] because it has brought me such a charming letter from you: fresh & sweet & unexpected, full of yourself.

You think me more through with my work than I really am. The jaunt to Geneva was only a pause in a very long labour. I go toiling on at Michelangelo daily & nightly—the rate being about 8 hours out of the 24.

And I am still far from being near the end.

Enough for these conditions of the journeyman's existence.

Only they leave his heart & head barren. He cannot use the pen with purpose for his friend. The nibs are so worn down with reams of sentences.

I escape, as usual, out of literature into crude life. I drink in taverns with Robert or with Edwin (both true Swiss), & sleep sometimes with young Achilles.[2]

There is my life expressed. Ardent literature, & moving fact: each reacting on the other, & driving the soul of the man to what God only knows his destiny will be.

By way of episode, the Henry Sidgwicks are staying here now. Henry is himself; but perhaps physically less than he used to be: not morally or mentally. I feel a little anxious about his health.

I cannot talk to you in this way, with the pen. I get more & more impatient, using the instrument of my industry. If you cannot come to see me here, then we must be content to fast. I cannot come to you. Michelangelo demands me in Rome & Florence this autumn; & again at Davos, in the winter, for the consummation of my work about him.

How stupid it all is! Operose nihil agunt![3] Books on Politics, books on Michelangelo, books on God, books on Gladstone!

Books, books, books! Goodnight. "The tree of Life is green, & grey is every Theory:"[4]

How long will the tree be green? And when the tree is withered, how awfully discoloured will all theory seem?

Yours

JAS

---

1. "Swiss Athletic Sports," *The Fortnightly Review*, LVI (1891), 408–15.

2. He refers elsewhere to Christian Buol as "young Achilles."

3. Seneca: they are busy about nothing.—"De Brevitate Vitae": I, 13.

4. Goethe, *Faust*, Part I: scene iv: Mephistopheles (disguised as Faust) to the student, ll. 2038–39:

> Grau, teurer Freund, ist alle Theorie,
> Und grün des Lebens goldener Baum.

1910. *To Margaret Symonds*

Davos Sept: 8 1891

My dearest Madge

Many thanks for your letter which shows how much you have been enjoying yourself at Glenthorne.[1] Spite of rain, it must have been a splendid time, & I am very glad you have made these warm friends.

We are rather busy with people here. Margot [Tennant] came on Sunday & has been pouring on like a mill wheel ever since. We are expecting Mr Cobham[2] & Horatio [Brown] to stay today, Mr Lynch[3] & S. Pary [?][4] to lunch, Lord & Lady Lingen[5] in the evening (they would not come to dinner). He is a dear old gentleman, who in his life time organized the modern system of English education.

I was delighted with what Dr Kinglake[6] said to you about me, & my father. He is a very remarkable man, & the surviving brother of one of the greatest writers of this century. It is pleasant to me to hear about the appreciation people give my books.

The writing of them out here seems to get so mechanical, to be so much like shoe making, that I forget often how they go forth & are read by thousands of intelligent persons, who agree or disagree with the opinions, learn or criticize.

I am pausing in my work on MAB. The purely biographical part is nearly done.

The rheumatism has come back very badly during the last week. This time it is in the back, & bends me quite double. I have a feeling that it keeps me from getting ill in the lungs or brain. The weather is most variable.

You have certainly been most unfortunate in some of your visits. I think Edith [Symonds Cave] at Sidbury might have had you in spite of Frances [Cave].[7] Gussie [Noel:KF][8] is of course lying—at least your mother thinks so—in order to avoid having Emily[9] at Rougham. English people seem to me selfish in such things; yet the same people would be very kind & hospitable, if you were under their roof.

It would be nice to take the Halliday's farm on Exmoor & hire some ponies. Of course one would be quite out of the way. But the country is nice.

Love to K & to both Aunts.

Yrs ever JAS.

---

1. With the Hallidays. See L 1908.

2. See Ls 247 and 1004. We might add that Cobham was Commissioner of Larnaca, Cyprus, 1879–1907, that he translated the *Turkish Laws of Evqaf* and the *Story of Umm al Haram* and the Italian *Bishop Graziani's Sieges of Nicosia and Famagusta.*

3. Probably Jeremiah Lynch (1849–1917), American capitalist; travelled widely in the Klondike, Europe, and other places; member of the Royal Geographical Society; member of the California Senate (1882–86); published *Egyptian Sketches* (1891); *Three Years in the Klondike* (1904); and *The Lady Iris in Bohemia* (privately printed, 1914), on the occasion of the bequest of a mummy to the San Francisco Bohemian Society. These facts fit well with the Lynch of Symonds' letter—the affinity between the Alaskan Klondike and Davos-Platz is obvious, as is Lynch's membership in the Royal Geographical Society.

4. See L 1908.

5. Ralph Robert Wheeler Lingen, Baron Lingen (1819–1905), friend of Benjamin Jowett; fellow of Balliol; secretary to the Education Office, 1849–69; permanent secretary of the Treasury 1869–85; married, 1852, Emma Hutton, who died in 1908.

6. Dr. John Hamilton Kinglake, executor of the estate of Alexander William Kinglake (1809–91), the historian of the Crimean War. See L 1858.

7. Symonds' niece and Margaret's cousin. See L 1.

8. Probably Roden Noel's daughter Frances Gertrude (b. 1864).

9. Emily Symonds (d. 1936) Symonds' cousin, wrote plays and novels under the pseudonym of George Paston. Rougham was the home of the Norths.

1911. *To Edmund Gosse*

Davos. Sept: 18 1891

My dear Gosse

It was very good of you to think of me & write from Dunster,[1] lovely place! My daughters are in England, have been at Glenthorne with the Hallidays,[2] are now at S. Ives with the Leslie Stephens.[3] Their raptures about the beauty of the English Sea & land make me sigh to be there. I am tired of mountains, tired of Italy—& yet I must go soon to Florence & Rome. I want, do so want English beauty. Dunster thrills me, the very name.

I am greatly excited by the news about your prose romance[4] & the subject. I wish I could see it at once. Can you not send it?

Will you never come here? Won't you try it about the New Year time?

I have had heaps of guests lately. Some of them stimulative to the mind. Three of them horribly irritating to the nerves. Do you know Ld Ronald Gower?[5] He is a dreadful man to live near, though very interesting. The same may be said about Claude Cobham.[6] They saturate one's spirit in Urningthum of the rankest most diabolical kind.

In spite of these visits I have written 11 chapters of my Life of M.A.B. since June 14. There are 13 chapters done now—all the purely biographical part of the book. Two more remain to be composed, more critical than biographical. You can imagine that I have very often worked through the 24 hours with only brief intervals for sleep & food. I get 1½ hrs sleep in the afternoon before dinner; & then write again from 8.30 p.m. till about 2 a.m.

The pace is killing. And I can hardly say *why* I have steered along so. Nor do I know in the least what the literary result is; for I have read over nothing, being able to carry every detail of the work done in my head so as to avoid involuntary repetitions & omissions without turning backward.

I want you to read my account of the Geneva Turnfest in the Sept Fortnightly.[7] It is very bold in its plain proclamation of a passionate interest in masculine beauty.

I have been making a great many lyrics & sonnets in odd moments (you will ask when I found them?) & have found a divinely charming friend. I wish you could see him. In body, soul, mind, emotion, he is absolutely transparent—like pure blue shallow water of a lake shot with limpid morning light.

Next week, i.e., on the 28th (probably), I hope to start for Italy, & shall probably take a devious path over very unfrequented passes. I want to visit my Italian soldier friend, an Alpino or Chasseur des Alpes, in his lonely garrison at the head of Val Camonica.

Then that delectable place Florence takes me. Rome I go to merely to grub at Michelangelo's ugly architecture.

With the man's spirit I am intoxicated, & I have wrestled with his "psyche" so that I seem absorbed in him. But I cannot say that this close study makes me sympathetic to his artistic ideal. I think it has even dispelled some illusions I had formed.

One thing is certain, that if he had any sexual energy at all (wh is doubtful) he was a U.[rning].

Now addio! I wish I could fly to England & cool my fever* there.

JAS

Fever of the over excited nerves. I think I am pretty well in other ways. But I shall see when the bow unbends. Do you know MAB's red chalk drawing of the Archers at Windsor?[8] It is about the finest of his things. Brown has made a splendid red autotype of it. Get it, & tell me what you think about the allegory.

---

1. Dunster, less than 2 miles from the Bristol Channel.
2. See L 1908.
3. See L 1690.
4. *The Secret of Narcisse: a Romance* (1892).
5. See Ls 1612 and 1906, and *Biography*, pp. 468–69.
6. See Ls 247, 1004, and 1910.
7. "Swiss Athletic Sports," *The Fortnightly Review*, LVI (1891), 408–15.
8. Symonds reproduced the drawing in his *Michelangelo*, I, 298. See L 1924.

1912. *To Margaret Symonds*

Am Hof, Davos Platz, Switzerland. Sept: 27 1891

My dearest Madge

It seems as though I had been very neglectful of you for a long while. I have really of course thought much about your doings, of which your letters have been giving us such ample & lively information. But I have felt little inclined to write letters. My work on MAB has gradually dwindled down to the very end of what I can do here; & has left me extremely jaded. It is always so at the very close of a great effort of the brain.

I have 13 out of my 15 chapters written, & of these 11 have been worked off since June 14. I never did so much in the same space of time. The two chapters I still need to write will be upon the Genius of MAB as shown in the Sistine Chapel & the Sacristy of S. Lorenzo. I want to get rested before I attempt these: & I may get new lights if I go, as I hope, to Rome.

We have been quiet since [Clyde D.] Cobham left upon the 14th. The weather has been glorious, & I have got a certain amount of mild walking most days.

[Samuel] Richards wrote me a very animated letter from Liverpool on the eve of sailing. His release from Davos seems to have restored him to mental activity. London he enormously admired, dwelt much upon its beauty. I also have had a very good letter from [Dr.] Ruedi,[1] who is happily settled at Denver.

It is delightful to think what a good time you have had at Glenthorne & S. Ives.[2] I can see however that you are still tired & apt to be overexcited by what you enjoy, fretted by what annoys you. I am glad there is a quite tranquil time coming now, & I advise you to keep as free as possible from little fussy distractions this winter.

I wish I could see you taking to a line of occupation: not, as I seem sometimes to have preached, because it is your duty to cultivate your gifts, wh are certainly above the average: but because I feel it would steady you & introduce an element of sobriety into your life.

Did you ever fancy you could take up translation? You might do worse than try yr hand on Wald Heimaten.[3]

Ever your most loving father

JAS

I hope to set off about Thursday & go pretty straight to Poggio Gherardo.[4] But I have a cold & the same sort of stomach trouble I had last year.

---

1. We do not have this letter, but the *Davos Courier* for Oct. 24, 1891, reports:
    Private letters from Denver bring good news of Dr. Ruedi and his family. They arrived there towards the end of July, and Dr. Ruedi was very well received by the local members of the Medical Profession. He was invited by the organisers of the Medical Congress, held in Washington on September 1st and the three following days, to read a paper before the Congress upon the "Koch treatment."
Dr. Ruedi, disappointed at Denver, was to return to Switzerland to practice medicine at Arosa. See the *Courier* also for Feb. 21 and April 25, 1891.
    2. With the Hallidays at Glenthorne and the Leslie Stephens at St. Ives, Cornwall.
    3. *Waldheimat*, by Peter Roseger. See L 1877, where Symonds praises his work for its "sincere poetry of peasant life."
    4. Janet Ross' home near Florence.

1913. *To Margot Tennant*

Am Hof, Davos Platz, Switzerland, Sept. 27th, 1891.
My Dear Margot,

I am sending you back your two typewritten records. They are both very interesting, the one as autobiographical and a study of your family, the other as a vivid and, I think, justly critical picture of Gladstone.[1] It will have a great literary value sometime. I do not quite feel with Jowett, who told you, did he not? that you had made him *understand* Gladstone. But I feel that you have offered an extremely powerful and brilliant conception, which is impressive and convincing because of your obvious sincerity and breadth of view. The purely biographical and literary value of this bit of work seems to me very great, and makes me keenly wish that you would record all your interesting experiences, and your first-hand studies of exceptional personalities in the same way.

Gradually, by doing this, you would accumulate material of real importance; much better than novels or stories, and more valuable than the passionate utterances of personal emotion.

Did I ever show you the record I privately printed of an evening passed by me at Woolner, the sculptor's, when Gladstone met Tennyson for the first time?[2] If I had been able to enjoy more of such incidents, I should also have made documents. But my opportunities have been limited. For future historians, the illuminative value of such writing will be incomparable.

I suppose I must send the two pieces back to Glen.[3] Which I will do, together with this letter. Let me see what you write. I think you have a very penetrative glimpse into character, which comes from perfect disengagement and sympathy controlled by a critical sense. The absence of egotism is a great point.

[no signature]

---

1. Probably included in her *Autobiography* (4 vols., 1920–22), respectively, I, Chap. I, and I, 105–06 and 219–35.
2. See L 451; privately printed in *Miscellanies* [1885]. See Babington, p. 60.
3. The family home of the Tennants.

Am Hof, Davos Platz, Switzerland. Sept: 28. 1891.

My dear Janet

I am wretched to think (from what you say in your last letter) that [Guido] Biagi probably did not get the last I wrote him from up here. I thanked him for the photograph of a sonnet & the copy of a document; & told him that he was laying me under the greatest obligation by doing these things himself, & by refusing the offer wh I made him, on the part of my publishers, that, if he gave his valuable time away, he should at least accept from him an honorarium. Well: Since then, I have heard nothing from him, & received no further documents.

Of course I was unable to ply him for more copies, when I knew he was making them himself, & when he would not accept any remuneration. So I just had to be silent.

From your saying he does not know *where* to send to me, I fear he did not get my letter.

I have written now to explain, & to ask him to keep these things till I come to Florence.

I hope to be able to start upon Oct 1. I have some business to do upon the way at Thusis & at Milan. But from Milan I hope to come straight. Will you be able to take me in? I shall of course write again when I know more exactly.

I am sorry to hear you have your German cold still. A German cold is sure to be nasty—like one caught from someone one dislikes. I am rather out of sorts with a cold etc. But it is more being overworked and worried.

The girls are still away. Please give my kindest messages to the Padrone. I am glad to think I may soon see him.

Evr yrs.

JAS

1915. *To Guido Biagi*

Am Hof, Davos Platz, Switzerland. Sept: 28. 1891

My dear Cavalieri

Something in a letter from Mrs Ross makes me fear that the last letter I wrote you[1] did not reach you. It was immediately after I received your photograph of the Sonnet & the Copy of a letter by Luigi del Riccio.[2]

I should be very sorry if you have not received this, for I wanted you to know at once how very deeply indebted I felt to you for the great services you have been willing to render me. I told you that you were laying me under too great an obligation by not accepting a certain proposal I made you.

It is not impossible that this letter may have gone astray. I remember some years ago writing from here to Villari[3] in Florence. The letter only reached him after about four months & a long journey in India!

I had been rather hoping you might have sent me some more copies. But I know that you are going away into the country at some time, & I could not expect much from one so busily engaged with more important matters.

So I have been proceeding steadily with my own work here, & soon I shall, if all goes well, reappear at Poggio Gherardo.

What made me think you never got my last letter, is that Mrs Ross says you *have* more copies of Mss ready for me, but do not know where to send them.

Altogether I am annoyed at the thought of your missing the expression of my true gratitude to you for all your generosity. I must have seemed to you a barbarian.

Well: Now I hope that we shall soon meet. Till then believe me to be your most obliged & sincere friend

                                                                J A Symonds.

---

1. On July 15. See L 1900.
2. A Florentine merchant, friend of Michelangelo. Symonds reproduces the letter in his *Michelangelo*, II, 404–05.
3. Pasquale Villari. See Ls 976 and 1297.

1916. *To Margaret Symonds*

                                                        Davos Sept 30 1891

My dearest Madge

What a good time you seem to be having at Rougham.[1] I hope you won't break your neck over fences. After all, the plan of your mother &

myself has been successful for you. It would be difficult to have seen more varied & nicer English homes than you are now doing. I advise you not to be in a great hurry to come back. Wait till the snow is down.

I am going to start for Italy tomorrow. Rather the Solito gino, n'est ce pas?[2] But if I get to Rome, it will be a diversion. There is, as usual, a horrid scrimmage before getting off. I feel to be standing on my head although it is only eleven o'clock.

If you like to write to me, please do so to Poggio Gherardo.[3] I may take a week getting there—or more—for if it is very fine, I shall perhaps drive across the Apennines from Modena to Pistoja.

Do not forget to try to go to the Noels if you are at Hastings. I told you the address:

St. Aubyns'
W. Brighton.

Did I ever tell you that I liked the Japanese things very much, & the silk? Those red handkerchiefs are lovely. I shall want more. My set is getting filthy. I have already given away 2 match boxes & a red kerchief to three several "Bündner Bumpkins."[4]

Oh, I am so tired.—I am reading Lombroso's[5] great book, in wh he proves that genius is a form of neuropathical disturbance. Among other things he detects as a very morbid sign the extraordinary faculty of producing immense masses of work at a go, which weak & nervous men of talent have. Eccomi! [Behold!] Few strong & healthy men turnips, could have born what I have borne this summer. But now I am as empty as a bladder, & fit to be filled with the gusts of all passions & iniquities.

Your most loving father

JAS.

Remember me most warmly to Charley,[6] also to Gussy [Noel][7] in a less degree.

---

1. See L 1910.
2. Circling around, isn't it?
3. Janet Ross' home.
4. His favorite peasants.
5. See L 1836, and, for Symonds' final estimate of Lombroso, L 1984.
6. Charles North (1828–1906), Mrs. Symonds' brother.
7. See L 1910.

1917. *To Margaret Symonds*

Poggio Gherardo, 23. Via Settignanese, Firenze Oct: 11. 1891.

My dearest Madge

I found your letter of the 2nd here, when I arrived on Thursday.

I quite understand what you write about the Rougham[1] people, & the troubles you have had in arranging your plans. I hope your last visits will be pleasant, & that you will settle down ere long again into a quiet life at home.

You must never imagine that I forget you or that in absence I do not feel even more strongly for you than I do when you are near me.

But it is really very difficult for me to write letters, when I am working so hard as I have been & still am. A great book on a great subject is an immensely absorbing task, which takes the energy out of one. I want relief & distraction when I am not at it. The pen too becomes irksome.

This October weather here is most glorious, so far more radiant & glowing than the spring. The vintage is over, & has been good. Poggio Gherardo is just as it was. The Padroni & I are alone in it. Cockey[2] I have not seen. He lives in the garden.

I have been always in Florence from 9 A.M. till 5 P.M. working hard on the Buonarroti documents. I have done more in the last three days (Thurs: Fri: Sat:) than I did in all those weeks of April & May. The Mss are brought for me to the Laurentian Library. In fact all the restrictions seem suddenly removed.

What I have now acquired will curtail some important modifications of my work. But I do not mind that. The great thing is get it well done.

When I have done here, I hope to go on to Rome, & study there. It will be better to postpone the journey awhile, for it is still very hot.

I suppose I shall be right in sending this to Aunt Bella's. Give her my love. Best & truest love to dear big Katharine.

Everyr loving father   JAS.

Aunt Ch[arlotte] writes me that Jowett[3] is very ill: quite broken down.

---

1. The home of the North family.
2. Probably one of Janet Ross' dogs.
3. Benjamin Jowett, died Oct. 1, 1893. Charlotte Symonds Green nursed him in his last illness.

1918. *To Guido Biagi*

Poggio Gherardo 23. Via Settignanese Firenze Oct: 13. 1891.

My dear Biagi

I could not come to the Library today; for my eyes are very tired with reading those old letters.

I hope to come tomorrow & to finish Cod: xi. Might I have either Cod: vi or vii or x to go on with?

From what I have as yet seen, it would be very desirable to edit in full the Letters of Giovan: Francesco Fattucci[1] and those of Lionardo Sellajo.[2]

Though Gotti[3] has made good use of both series, he has not exhausted them I think.

I wonder whether, if you can carry your plan out of publishing *fascicoli*[4] it would not be good to begin with some one important set of letters, like the Fattucci series? This would certainly attract the attention of students to the scheme.

Believe me very sincerely yours

J A Symonds.

Please give my servant, who brings this, Viesseux's[5] copy of Gotti.

---

1. Giovanni Francesco Fattucci (?–?) Michelangelo's Roman agent. See Symonds' *Michelangelo*, I, 372; II, 376–79.
2. Symonds (*Michelangelo*, I, xv) lists Lionardo Sellajo's (?–?) letters among those he found especially useful for valuable side-lights on his subject.
3. Aurelio Gotti *Vita di Michelangelo Buonarroti* (1875). See L 1876.
4. Special dossiers, or collections, of letters and papers peripheral to the main subject.
5. Probably Giampietro Viesseux (?–?), compiler of obituary notes at Florence.

1919. *To Horatio Forbes Brown*

Firenze, Oct. 13 [1891]

[Dear Horatio]

I have been working pretty hard at the Buonarroti Archives, which come to me at the Laurenziana. About four hours a day. But I have to stop to-day as my eyes gave way. I hope to read through the whole of the inedited correspondence of diverse persons addressed to him. It consists of six big folios. Three I have already pretty nearly done. There is a German called Frey[1] working on the text of the Rime. He hates me, and tries to keep all the MSS. to himself. It is really very annoying. We have to use the same index to the Codices, which causes a perpetual rub. It is odd how suddenly and totally the restrictions on the Archives have been broken down.

[Incomplete]

---

1. Karl Frey (1857–1921), *Die Dichtungen des Michelagniolo Buonarroti. Herausgegeben und mit Kritischem Apparate versehen von Dr. Carl Frey, etc.* (1897).

1920. *To Benjamin Jowett*

Poggio Gherardo 23 Via Settignanese Firenze Oct: 15 1891

My dear Master

Ever since I heard some three weeks ago that you were ill,[1] I have been thinking of you; & lately we have been very anxious. But news today seemed somewhat better. So I feel that I dare write to you, & tell you what a source of thanksgiving it would be if you were still spared for some time: to teach us, as you have always taught, how to live.

I heard this morning from Mrs Warren[2] that my Sister Charlotte [Green] is with you. This is good, for she has a great power of communicating some of her own strength to others.

I hardly like to write to you about Common things. But I may tell you that I have come to Florence in order to read the Mss collected by the Buonarroti family. I have been working very hard at a Life of Michael Angelo all the summer, & hope to get it finished in the course of the winter.

I left my wife at Davos busily engaged in seeing the Autobiography of her sister Miss [Marianne] North through the press.

Now that you are very ill & suffering from sleeplessness & weakness, hardly less difficult to bear than acute pain, it must be some Comfort to feel how many hearts far & wide are beating in sympathy with you, not one of which does not owe to you some of its best things in life. God bless & preserve you to us. Your very affectionate friend

John Addington Symonds.

---

1. See L 1917.
2. Mary Isabel Brodie Warren, wife of T. Herbert Warren, president of Magdalen College (1885–1928) and Symonds' friend.

1921. *To Janet Ross*

Bibbiena Saturday, Oct. 25, 1891.

My dear Janet,

We reached this place all right on Wednesday, and found the Albergo Amorosi all that could be desired in the way of good beds, wine and service. It poured next morning, and I thought we were in for a wet day at least. At about one however it began to clear, with splendid rolling clouds and broken sunlight all along the mountains of the Casentino. So I took a vehicle and drove to Poppi. That is indeed a very interesting place. The old Castle of the Conti Guidi is quite splendid, and the view from its battlements over the field of Campaldino, back to Bibbiena with La Vernia rising above it, and then up to Camaldoli is one of the finest I have seen in Italy. The Hotel Michelangelo seemed to me good, and I should say that the place would do well for villeggiatura [country holiday] for people of quiet tastes.

Yesterday I got a little carriage and two good horses, and left at 7 for La Vernia. It is a tremendously steep ascent. The drive is just under 3 hrs. We rested the horses, and then rode them to Chiusi (a bleak old ruined castle just on the watershed between the Arno and Tiber valleys) and on to Caprese. The roads execrable. We were 5½ hours in the saddle going and coming. Caprese is a lovely country—I cannot call it town or village—for it is a sort of scattered district made up of hamlets buried in vast woods of chestnut and oak. The old castle, where M.[ichel]A.[ngelo] was born, stands by itself on the top of a wooded rock, and would make I think a good sketch. You look down the Tiber valley toward Citta di Castello, and then far away via the Apennines beyond and round Perugia—Monte Aquito etc. We returned in time to visit the convent and Bosco of La Vernia before the sun set at last in glory behind the hills toward Florence.

I cannot bestow unmixed praises on the Inn at La Vernia. Bad wine. No meat, butter or milk. Beds fairly good. The whole house filthy.

We have just returned, and are going at 3.30 to Arezzo, meaning to take the express for Orvieto in the evening.

If this weather lasts, I propose to reach Rome by Terni, Aquila and Sulmona, which will take four or five days. But I shall be greatly obliged if you will send my letters to the Hotel du Quirinal, Rome, after the receipt of this. I wrote there, begging them to keep my correspondence till I come.

I hope that you and the Padrone are both well: as also Moschino.[1] Remember me most kindly to the Padrone, and believe me to be always

Affectionately yours

J.A.S.

If there is anything urgent wh I ought to hear, please telegraph to P.R. Terni. But I do not want letters sent there.

---

1. This letter is only available in typescript by KF; thus this name may be misspelled; we have not been able to identify the person.

1922. *To Janet Ross*

Hotel du Quirinal, Rome. Oct: 29. 1891.

My dear Janet

I have just arrived here, & found your letter & those you so kindly forwarded.

I must tell you how deeply grieved I am to hear of your troubles in money affairs. It makes me feel what I [a?] nuisance I must have been, & makes me very reluctant to seek your hospitality again at such a troubled time.

I am not exaggerating when I say this. For I know by experience how much better people who have a bother to endure are able to bear it, when there is no small talk of intrusive friends to disturb them.

These things, brave as one may be, are real trials so long as they last, which tell upon the nerves of the strongest & most courageous.

In spite of mixed weather, I have enjoyed my journey since I wrote to you from Bibbiena. Orvieto, as usual, left upon my mind a sinister impression of ancient guilt, & Signorelli,[1] as formerly, dominated my imagination almost painfully.

We passed through Terni without stopping, & came to Aquila by an interesting mountain railway. The upland where Rieti is, struck me as excellent in air. But the Appennines are so stony & ugly, destitute of charm or sublime beauty. Aquila is worth a long journey.[2] (Albergo sole good, wine poor). Its position in the very centre of the highest Apennines is highly characteristic, & there are some interesting relics of art—not much, since a great earthquake in 1703 destroyed nearly the whole of the old city.

Sulmona is hardly worth going to. It has an Angevine acqueduct of some picturesqueness, & a fine façade of a build[ing] wh is now a hospital. The city is filthy, & the hotel (del Toscaro) ditto. Nothing more to my eyes at least: except the stony Apennines, & the people also are as ugly and rude as the abominable twangle wrangle jangle music of the Superficial South.

I could not get de Nino's book on Ovidio[3] in the arty bookshop of the town!

The railway to Rome is on the whole uninteresting. Endless barren hills—stones, stones, stones, & a few black olive trees, three or four large oaks. One passes Tagliacazzo—the great battlefield of the Hohenstauffen tragedy[4]—& then Tivoli, Tivoli seen from a railway & on a dreary day! Then down into the grand dramatic Roman Compagna, all indigo and Venetian red under a brooding heaven of cloud.

I do not want to stay here longer than is necessary for my work on MAB. I hate a hotel like this.

Will you kindly send me what comes for me during the next four days? I will write again.

Probably I shall go to Seravezza & Carrara (on MAB business), & then —I do not know. Be good & write to me frankly if you would not rather not see me again, at Poggio Gherardo just now! I should esteem this a sign of true friendship: & it would help me to decide on future plans.

My sister Mrs Green writes me much about Jowett. I see that she has no hope of his return to any real health.

My best regards to the Padrone. Angelo's service & thanks for your saluti.

Ever yrs

JAS.

---

1. Luca Signorelli (1441–1523) created his greatest paintings, frescoes, for the cathedral in Orvieto; the subjects include "Fall of Antichrist," "Punishment of the Wicked," and "Last Days of Earth."

2. Karl H. Ulrichs, the psychologist, lived at Aquila. See L 1831.

3. Antonio de Nino (?–?), *Ovidio nella tradizione populare di Sulmona* (1886).

4. At Tagliacazzo in the province of Aquila, 56 miles northeast of Rome. Here, at the close of 1268, a battle occurred between Conradin of Hohenstaufen and Charles of Anjou. Conradin was defeated.

1923. *To Horatio Forbes Brown*

Rome, Oct 29, 1891

[Dear Horatio]

Angelo [Fusato] and I arrived here to-day, after making a very good journey in spite of mixed weather, something trying by reason of scirocco.

We saw a good part of the Casentino: Poppi, a thoroughly grand old Tuscan eyrie (of the Conti Guidi), and Bibbiena, a milder hill-set city, where the inn is kept by the Fratelli Amorosi, and the wine is "Tuscan Burgundy." We drove over the most breakneck roads to La Vernia, and then rode to Chiusi and Caprese (Michael Angelo's birthplace) on the watershed of Arno and Tiber, a ride of five and a half hard hours over stones and through cataracts. Of course we visited the *sacri luoghi* of S. Francis, and spent the night in a filthy charming inn, crooning over the open kitchen fire with *contadini* working their way to a distant market.

After this Orvieto, and its sense of ancient wickedness. I wonder why that place has such a strong moral pungency, for me at least. And why Signorelli[1] dominates my imagination so cruelly.

Next, by Orte and Terni, into the very heart of hearts of Apennines, to Aquila below the Gran Sasso d'Italia. They are ugly mountains, with no grace but that of rarely manifested atmospheric charm. Still Aquila is worth a long journey. It has great character, and some unexpected beauties of art. The main thing there was Ulrichs. I spent a whole afternoon and evening in his company. Ulrichs is *Chrysostomos*[2] to the last degree, sweet, noble, a true gentleman and man of genius. He must have been at one time a man of singular personal distinction, so finely cut are his features, and so grand the lines of his skull.

I left Aquila yesterday for Sulmona (Ovid's birthplace), a dirty place, hardly worth a visit, except for its position among those heartless and prosaic Apennines. Repellent, stupid mountains at the best; at the worst, abominably mediocre and vulgar. I have travelled just now through so many hundred miles of them that I may abuse them with knowledge. Below Umbria, I do not see any good in them at all; and the people are ugly—loud—like the twangle, wrangle, jangle music of the shallow South.

To-day we came in seven hours from Sulmona to Rome, passing through Tagliacozzo[3] (memorable historic name, but nothing else), and Tivoli, into the sullen Roman Campagna, all indigo and Venetian red, under a heavy cold sky of imminent rain. I found your letters here.

I expect to stay in Rome long enough to see the principal things of M. A. B. again with care, and if possible to examine the codex of his poems in the Vatican Library. This big Americano-Germanico cosmopolitan *caravanserai*,[4] with an English Bible in each bedroom, does not please me. In fact, it is just what I loathe, and brings out the worst side of my temper. I had a bitter passage of wordy arms with a patronising polyglot head-waiter just now, while eating a fifteen francs dinner *à la carte*. It was about a bottle of wine, which I had not ordered, and he thought fit to bring instead of the one I chose. *"Satis et super satis"* [Enough, and more than enough]. But you know how nasty I can be in my mood, and how I regret it afterwards.

Probably I shall go to Carrara from here, and then again to Florence, Poggio Gherardo. Tell Ronald Gower[5] where I am, and write to me here once again, if you feel the impulse—if not, to Poggio Gherardo, to wait for me. After that I hope to come to Venice.

You know, perhaps, that Jowett is very ill? My sister, Mrs. Green, is nursing him in Balliol. She writes me (a letter I found here) that the prospects are almost hopeless.

Once at Aquila, again at Sulmona, I had the deepest strangest dreams of him, in which he came to me, and was quite glorified, and spoke to me so sweetly and kindly—as though he understood some ancient wrong he had not fathomed in me before, and blessed me and made me feel that this and all else would be right.

I cannot say that I have been much occupied with the thought of him, though I knew him to be ill. M. A. B., and the places I saw for the first time, absorbed my energies and sympathies. Still, these two dreams have haunted me with a sense of atonement and softness. I am deeply touched to find by my sister's letter how near to death he was when she wrote.

[Incomplete]

---

1. See L 1922.
2. The reference is to Karl Ulrichs. See Ls 1831 and 1922. Symonds compares him with John, Saint Chrysostom (ca. 345–407), noted for his gentleness, warrmth, and brilliant preaching on behalf of his ideals. A sect of followers, the Johannists, sprang up after his death. Ulrichs was a prolific writer and polemicist, as was Chrysostom. An English translation of the latter's works appeared in the 1st series of the "Nicene and Post-Nicene Fathers" (1889–90). Symonds undoubtedly knew the work.
3. See L 1922.
4. The Hotel du Quirinal. See L 1921.
5. See L 1612.

1924. *To Horatio Forbes Brown*

Roma, Oct. 30 [1891]

[Dear Horatio]

I am getting accustomed to this *Caravanserei* and falling back into the old bad habits of my youth, and accepting the fate of infinite waiters in black swallowtails.

I have had a long day at M. A. B. The Capitol,[1] S. Pietro in Vincoli,[2] Palazzo Farnese,[3] Cristo Risorto at the Minerva,[4] Pietà,[5] and general structure of the church at S. Pietro,[6] S. Maria degli Angeli.[7] As an architect, the man is incredibly unequal, a veritable amateur in this branch, as he always said he was.

The weather is very trying. After enervating *scirocco,* we now are suffering a strong frigid *tramontana.* Rome was brilliant enough to-day, but cruel in its coldness. The city has altered immensely since I was last here—about six years ago. The old quarters are in ruins, being rebuilt after a Haussmann fashion.[8] A great deal of its charm has disappeared: that ancient suavity which brought its various aspects (Republic, Imperial, Mediæval, Renaissance, Baroceo) into harmony: that is gone for ever.

The Rome I loved in 1863 is lost. But I cannot deplore change when change means prosperity. Does it so here? The Ludovisi Villa has become a nest of bourgeois habitations. The Palazzo Borghese was shut when I went there to-day to visit the "Bersaglio"[9] [or the "Arcieri," the archers] of M. A. B., because of the Prince's bankruptcy.[10] Rising nations pull through. I hope this is the case with New Italy. But I see little of real wealth about. The faces of the shops in the vast new quarters are poor, like stores set up by squatters in some Californian mining station. They have opened a new museum in the Baths of Diocletian. I could not get in to-day.

[Incomplete]

---

1. Michelangelo designed 3 buildings on Capitoline Hill: the Palazzo di Conservatori, the Capitoline Museum of Sculpture, and the Palazzo del Sanatore.

2. Symonds visited the celebrated "Statue of Moses" in the Church of San Pietro in Vincoli.

3. The Palazzo Farnese, begun by Antonio da Sangallo the younger (1483?-1546), was revised, continued, and completed by Michelangelo.

4. Michelangelo's statue of Christ, to the left of the principal altar of the Santa Maria sopra Minerva.

5. Michelangelo's last work in marble, in the Duomo, Florence.

6. Symonds devoted much of Vol. II of *Michelangelo* to Michelangelo's role as architect of St. Peter's.

7. This church was constructed from designs by Michelangelo.

8. Georges Eugène, Baron Haussmann (1809-91), French city planner, who under Napoleon III, made bold alterations in the layout of Paris, widening old streets and creating new ones and adapting space to accommodate monuments and vistas.

9. A fresco in the Borghese Palace based on an engraving by Niccolò Beatrizet (1515-65), a designer and engraver, who followed the design of Michelangelo's "Bersaglio," no. 424 in the Windsor Castle Collection. See Symonds' *Michelangelo,* I,

296–98, and for the question of attribution, A. E. Popham and Johannes Wilde, *The Italian Drawings of the XV and XVI Centuries in the Collection of His Majesty The King at Windsor Castle* (1949), pp. 248–49. See L 1911.

10. Don Paolo, 2nd Prince Borghese (1845–1920), like the Italian government, was in financial straits. On Dec. 1, 1891, the Borghese family sold its library to a bookseller for 55,000 lire.

1925. *To Janet Ross*

Hotel du Quirinal Rome Oct: 31. 1891.

My dear Janet

I cannot resist the impulse to write to you, because I have just done something which is entirely out of your line, I think.

Rome is whipping its enthusiasm up about Mascagni & Amico Fritz.[1] Tonight is the first representation. At the Table d'hote (to wh I go for penance & discharge of duty) I sat next a friend of his. A pleasant young man, who talked very agreeably & listened to my bad Italian, being somewhat Anglo-maniac. Well: he offered to take me to Mascagni's private box, introduce me to the Maestro & let me share the tremors of the situation. I refused. With abundance of thanks & pleading previous engagements, which exist only in my own imagination.

I don't suppose you would have done this. And I am not sure that I am right to have neglected such an opportunity.

Alas! I can only do two or three things at one time. Not four or five. The Sistina has exhausted me today: & a visit to a German artist of great skill in painting nudes.

I am going to make him pose models in the impossible positions discovered by MAB.[2]

MAB is my Vampire at present. If only the work would come out worth the pains I take about it.

He beats every artist quite clean out of the field. Raffaello is insipid. The Stanze after the Sistina are like milk or gruel after wine. Only the antique bears the comparison. And I must confess that the bronzes, recently discovered, & placed in a new Museo at the Baths of Diocletian, beat Michelangelo.[3] There is a young man there in bronz[e] called Meleager, who is stupendous.

Addio. I am sorry Carlo Orsi[4] found Assisi so little to his liking. The wind (if it was there such as it is here) was enough to drive him away.

Everyrs

JAS

---

1. Pietro Mascagni (1863–1945). His *L'Amico Fritz* was premiered in 1891 and *Cavalleria Rusticana* the year following.

2. And rendered on the ceiling of the Sistine Chapel as garland bearers.

3. Apparently Symonds was mistaken. Prof. Olga Pinto, the director, Biblioteca Dell'Instituto Nazionale d'Archeologia e Storia Dell'Arte, Rome, writes us that an English guide to Rome by Russell Forbes, *Ancient Sculptures, the Masterpieces of Greek Art in the Museums of Rome* (1891), pp. 34–35, guesses that the work was a Meleager by Lysippus.

4. See L 1901.

1926. *To Janet Ross*

Rome Nov 5 1891

My dear Janet

I think of leaving Rome tomorrow, & of stopping at Perugia. If I may come to you on Saturday for a day or two, I shall enjoy it greatly.

Ronald Gower[1] has arrived here, & we go about together. He has a quite extraordinary sense of what is distinguished in art & nature.

I hope to go with him tonight to L'Amico Fritz.[2] They say it is being done not badly. The only person who has seen it whom I have met, Rennell Rodd,[3] seems to have been disappointed by the quality of the music.

I have made a pretty thorough study of the Vatican Ms of MAB's poems. It is interesting, for the Ms is nearly all autograph; & one can trace the immense pains which he took with his compositions, in spite of their ruggedness.

Goodbye, with love to the Padrone.   Yours

JAS.

A long letter from my sister gives a rather better account of Jowett.[4]

---

1. See L 1612.
2. See L 1925.

3. Sir Rennell Rodd (Lord Rennell) (1858–1941), councillor at the British Embassy, Berlin, and British representative at other foreign posts; author of several vols. of verse and of *Social and Diplomatic Memoirs, 1884–1893* (1922; 2nd series, *1894–1901*, 1923; 3rd series, *1902–1919*, 1925); *Frederick, Crown Prince and Emperor,* with an introduction by H. M., the Empress Frederick (1888).

4. Benjamin Jowett was ill and Charlotte Symonds was nursing him.

1927. *To Arthur Symons*

[Zürich] November 13, 1891

. . . the last crop of sonnets which have to be put into *Vagabunduli Libellus.*[1] I do not suppose I have ever expressed my deepest self so nakedly before as I have here. The question is whether they are too naked. They seem to me, read together, to be inebriating. The world is a dream, but who is dreaming it? No one ever expressed this mood. But it is the deepest, truest mood of man's existence which has made me an impassioned sceptic —so hard! I even write these words with that weird and supernatural feeling of my unreality.

[Incomplete]

---

1. The sonnets constitute the "Stella Maris" group. In dating the excerpt Symons may be wrong, since the volume was published in 1884. See L 1355 to Dakyns, in which Symons says largely what he says here about the group. It is possible that Symons miscopied and the "have" of the first line should be "had"—Symonds, in other words, was at this later date explaining to Symons undercurrents in the *Stella Maris* poems.

1928. *To Janet Ross*

Hotel Baur Zürich. Friday Nov 13 1891

My dear Janet,

Since I left the hospitable feudal keep of Poggio Gherardo yesterday, I have got along well enough, except for coughing, & find myself alone with my foot upon my Swiss heath. I left Angelo at Milan. He was desolated not to be taken along with me to Davos. But lately he has rather assumed at times the airs of a spoilt & indispensable old servant. So I judged it wise to bring him round to his bearings; & I felt that the assertion of my padroneship is worth more than the luxury of having my Hand-Gepäck attended to. There was a really impressive scene in the Milan station, when Angelo took leave of me in tears—real tears—not feigned—nor wholly mercenary:—for he does enjoy his life on the loose with me much more than his life with wife & babies & bills in Venice. Well. The Gothard [Pass] was never more drenched, dripping, grand in a vast style of Alpine squalor, than I saw it today. We got into thick snow & icicles at Aivolo. Then, emerging from the tunnel, spring or Lady Summer reappeared. On the Swiss side, all was a respectable late autumn evening, tuned to preciseness. The lakes of Luzern & Zug brooded, steely-grey, with their crags & woods, under an innocent dove-coloured heaven. A great change from the deluge-devils of the Italian "versant."[1]—I found none of my family here, & no news of them. So I hope to get up to Davos tomorrow, & to go ahead in earnest again on MAB.—I think of you both so much & your continual kindness that I spend this atom of time in talking to you. It makes up for not being able to sit dreaming, gossipping, sauntering across a thousand fields with irresponsible feet of meditation, ventilating paradoxes, dissecting neighbours, over the wood-fire in your dear drawingroom; while the presence of the Arno valley & the hills is always felt inside the house, adding a dignity & charm, not airs, to what we say.—For this poor wanderer on this world your room in the evenings, with you & Mr. Ross, both so tolerant of nonsense, & so delicately kind to weakness, will retain an abiding & ineffaceable impression of genial & active life. May you both live long & prosper, amid all your projects for the good of selves and others, & may you have no more hard times.

This is the heart-felt wish of your obliged & humble well-wisher—as the old letter-writers often put it.

J.A.S.

Bourget's[2] book is, on the whole, good. I have given it full justice, read it all "à petites gorgés" [in small mouthfuls]. It is made up "a stento" [stuntedly]. Not an effusive spontaneous from the heart & fashion of the man. On a small scale. But a good book, a good boy, naively anxious to secure sensations, & still sufficiently devoid of cynicism to cook them for his appetite out of cabbages & the bushes by the wayside. It seems to me wholly original, so far as it goes. A very striking contrast to his novels. Which is the real man? the man of the novels, or the man of the pretty diary? The latter is the real man I think. The modern French novel is a sort of a machine.

---

1. The Italian side, slope.
2. Paul Bourget (1852–1935), who wrote more than 60 novels, published a travel book in 1891, *Sensations d'Italie*.

1929. *To Janet Ross*

Davos Nov 14 1891

My dear Janet

I am arrived. This morning, at Zürich, when I was selecting my carriage, I heard the voices of my two daughters Madge & Katharine calling loudly to me from the train. They had travelled from London with a large party—their cousin Col: Dudley North,[1] Sir Charles & Lady Tennant,[2] Margot Tennant,[3] & Lady Farrer.[4] North had returned to England. The rest of the party gone to Brindisi for Cairo. So I took up my girls just at the point when they were journeying alone. In spite of the horrid weather, we had a very sociable time together, after our separation of three months. Much to tell on both sides.

And finally; as so often happens, out of the unutterable fog & filth of Lombardy, the drenched squalor of the Gothard, the repellent dullness of Lower Switzerland; we emerged before sunset into the aerial splendour of our snowy mountains, with their pure clear air & graceful summits clearing upward to the stars. It is like getting back into an enchanted crystal palace, after the humdrum of a mediocre world.

The luxury too of finding a house with perfectly dry air in it & an equal temperature.

Many as are the drawbacks of spending one's life at Davos, it has aesthetically & sensually the greatest pleasures wh an epicure can hope for.

All the Apennines, from Consuma to La Verna, through Rieti, Aquila, Sulmona, Tivoli, have not a single line of poetry in them equal to what lies about us everywhere in this region. The beauty here, of line & profile, is so overwhelmingly rich that artists cannot deal with it. I understand their seeking after poorer districts, where "bits" make a distinct picture effect, & where atmospheric influences & varieties of vegetation suggest subjects. But here we have the greatest beauty, that which defies art. The only supreme beauty in nature which art can grapple with is the human nude.

There. I have written an Aesthetik in small paradoxes. So goodnight. My chest is raw. But what of that?

Love to the Padrone, from my wife as also from me.

Ever yours   JAS.

---

1. See L 934.
2. See L 1619.
3. See L 1571.
4. Possibly Anna Maria Shaw-Lefevre (d. 1892), wife (1856) of Sir William James Farrer (1822–1911).

1930. *To Charles Kains-Jackson*[1]

Am Hof, Davos Platz, Switzerland. Nov: 16. 1891

Dear Mr Jackson

I returned on Saturday from Rome, where I have been studying Mss of Michelangelo, and found two numbers of the Artist. Some things in Oct: interested me much. I want to know what "Sonnets by E. C. L."[2] are, and who is Harmodius.[3] I agree with his views, and have expressed something in harmony with him in my "Swiss Athletic Sports" (Fortnightly Sept).

Do let me have the means of procuring these "Sonnets by E. C. L." Do not neglect this please.

You ought to be ashamed of printing the French lines to Antinous with so many villainous mistakes. What in the world is *Ausdir?*

[Incomplete]

---

1. Charles Kains-Jackson, editor of *The Artist.* See L 1887.
2. Edward Cracroft Lefroy (1855–91). Symonds wrote an essay on him in *The New Review,* VI (1892), 341–52, reprinted in *In The Key of Blue* (1893). For a brief biographical sketch of Lefroy and a checklist of his works see Timothy d'Arch Smith, "Some Uncollected Authors XXX: Edward Cracroft Lefroy 1855–1891," *The Book Collector* (Winter, 1961), pp. 442–45; also see W. A. Gill, *Edward Cracroft Lefroy: His Life and Poems* (1897). For Gill see L 1933a.
3. So far as we know, Symonds did not receive an answer to his question.

1931. *To Horatio Forbes Brown*

Davos, Nov. 20 [1891]

7.30 p.m.

[Dear Horatio]

You are having the same change of weather as we are here. It is very
mild. At the same time it is well that I am here. Davos is safer than Venice,
and I have had a sharp warning. I have not been out of doors since I
arrived here last Saturday.

The time is spent oddly enough. I begin work at 9.30 and go on till
12.30. After lunch, at 2.30 I go to bed and sleep two hours; have tea in bed
and talk to my wife. Dine at 6.30. Begin work again at 8 p.m. and go on
with it till 1 or 2 a.m. Then to bed and sleep again.

I have written a difficult chapter here upon the Sistine and M. A. B.'s
design-conception of form in general. Of course I had brooded over this
during my Italian journey. Now I am tackling his architectural work at
S. Lorenzo and the Medicean Sacristy.

Madge acts as my secretary all the forenoon. She copies out the
quotations and translations from M. A. B.'s letters. (Ronald[1] always calls him
"Mab," and Angelo [Fusato] calls him *"il suo vecio"* [his ancient man].)
She is getting through all the chapters under my dictation, and I think she
likes the work. There will really be very little of importance when this last
aesthetic chapter and the copying are finished. The routine suits my health.
I feel already to be better, with more power of breathing in the lungs.

Nimmo showers gorgeous editions as gifts upon me. I found a select
cabinet-library awaiting me. Among them a very interesting thing by
Pollard,[2] on "The Title Page," full of facsimiles. Should you care to have a
copy of the last "Hobbyhorse"? It has an essay by Pollard[3] on the ugliness
of Greek type, I think—(I forget), and an "appreciation" by me of
Tiepolo's "Last Sacrament of S. Lucy." I will send you one if you like.

12.30 a.m.

Since I wrote to you at 7.30 I have been pounding on at "MAB"—the
difficult chapter (xii.). It will be the novelty of my book, and certainly in
Florence a rebuke unacceptable to Florentine scholars. I am going to
dedicate the book to Biagi.[4] But, I suppose, as it is not in Italian, they won't
care. They are to blame for nidificating mares' nests with eyes open to the
truth. The stupidest thing a fellow can do.

To-night I enjoyed rather a grand piece of translation—the peroration

628

of Varchi's discourse on M. A. B.'s philosophy of Love and Poetry,[5] winds up with a sonnet, very learned and difficult in style, but so much less trying than the effort to grapple with one's own sincere feelings about things like the Laurentian staircase.

Angelo was so nervous and giddy in the dome and on the top of S. Peter's that I trembled for him. I thought he would faint or throw himself down. And yet he is so strong and impervious to things which thrill me. I could stand tip-toe on the very summit of the Cross upon St. Peter's if it were wanted.

[Incomplete]

---

1. Ronald Sutherland Gower. See L 1612.

2. Alfred William Pollard (1859–1944), keeper of printed books, British Museum; *Last Words on the History of The Title Page* (1891).

3. "Some Remarks on the History of Greek Types, and Upon the Reasons of Their General Lack of Beauty," *The Century Guild Hobby Horse,* VI (1891), 127–35.

4. The dedication reads: To The Cavaliere Guido Biagi Doctor in Letters Prefect of the Mediceo-Laurentian Library, etc., etc. I dedicate This Work on Michelagnolo In Respect for his Scholarship and Learning Admiration of his Tuscan Style And Grateful Acknowledgement of his Generous Assistance.

5. Benedetto Varchi (1503–65), Italian scholar: *Due lezzioni . . . nella prima delle quali, si dichiara um Sonnetto di Michelagnolo Buonarroti . . . con una lettera d'esso Michelagnolo . . .* (1549). He also wrote *Storia Fiorentina* (pub. 1721), a history of Florence for the period 1527–38, commissioned by Cosimo de' Medici.

1932. *To Guido Biagi*

Am Hof, Davos Platz, Switzerland. Nov: 21. 1891.

My dear Biagi

I was so very sorry not to be able to see you in Florence, when I came there from Rome. But I caught a bad cold in the chest on my way from Rome, & after a few days in the house at Poggio Gherardo felt that I must go straight home.

My health has always stood in this way of my doing what I wanted.

I am here trying to cure myself with blisters on the chest & bed. I go on working however.

I want now to ask you whether Signor Gherardi[1] has sent the copy of M A. Buonarroti Simoni's Decime?[2] I should much like to have it. In [unclear] Cod 13 No 13

And can you clear up a small point for me? Guasti says that Bugiardini wrote a letter to MAB in Rome, from Florence, Aug 5 1532.[3] It has the Sonnet "S'un casta amor" etc on the back. The *date* does not agree with Sebastiano del Piombo's[4] letters & those of Angelini wh you copied for me. These point to MAB having been in Florence in Aug: 1532. In my notes taken from the Epistolario I do not find anything about this letter. The matter is of some slight chronological importance.

I had a long talk with Villari[5] in Rome, & made, I think, an impression on his mind. I pointed out that, while Milanesi was publishing unauthorized copies of the letters, & the Arch: Buon: was theoretically shut to students, all the work wh men like Gotti,[6] myself, or Frey[7] do there, has no value for the learned world—*because* it cannot be verified.

Villari begged me to draw up a Memorial, wh I shall do shortly.

I carefully examined the Codex of the *Rime* in the Vaticana. The larger part is in MAB's autograph, & all these poems seem to me to be subsequent to the date (circa) 1540. Some forty compositions are copied in another hand at the beginning of the Ms. It was clearly a copy-book into wh MAB began to have his poems copied, & after a time used for his own pen. To this old book have been added fragments of letters & separate sheets; the whole bound up in one vol by Fulvio Orsini.[8]

Now the odd thing is (if you look to Guasti's Rime) that he gives a wrong description of the Codex, on the faith of Prince Piombino.[9] BUT he gives a right description of it when he comes to describe MAB the Younger's copy of the Codex. In fact this grand nephew left a precise record of the Orsini Ms. And why Guasti calls the Ms an *autograph* without noting the *changes of handwritings* seems to me inexplicable.

If you care to have my notes on the Codex, I will send them. I made them without having Guasti's book, or remembering what he said about it. But my conclusions, I find now, exactly agree with those of MAB the Younger when he made his copy,[10] now in the Arch: Buon:

Believe me most sincerely yours

John Addington Symonds.

Pray send me the copy from the *Decime,* & tell me the date of Bugiardini's letter [given by Guasti as *Aug. 5. 1532.*][11]

Also, let me have the title of yr essay on Tullia,[12] & the No of the

Antologia. I want to refer to it—on the point of Varchi's *rifacimento* of her verses.

---

1. Probably Alessandro Gherardi (?–?), who published materials from the Florentine Archives, particularly *Le Carte Strozziane del R. Archivio di Stato in Firenze* (1884, etc.), begun by C. Guasti.

2. The archives of the Decima at Florence. See Symonds' *Michelangelo*, I, 468.

3. Giuliano Bugiardini (1475–1554), one of several Florentine painters summoned from Florence to assist Michelangelo with his fresco painting in the Sistine Chapel. See Symonds, *Michelangelo*, I, 201. Symonds makes 2 references to this letter, agreeing finally with Cesare Guasti's dating (*Michelangelo*, II, 137, 143) and placing the sonnet "Se un casto amor" in the Cavalieri series. Guasti published the sonnet in *Le Rime di Michelangelo Buonarroti* (1863), p. 190.

4. Sebastiano del Piombo or Piombino (1485?–1547), Italian painter, wrote his gossipy, racy letters mainly between 1520 and 1533. Symonds examines the friendship between the two painters, *Michelangelo*, I, 345–63; 449–69 *passim*.

5. See Ls 976 and 1297.

6. See L 1918.

7. Karl Frey, *Denunzia dei Beni della Famiglia di' Buonarroti* (1885). See L 1919 for Symonds' personal reactions to Frey.

8. For Symonds' account of the Codex Vaticanus see his *Michelangelo*, II, 407–08. He was apparently unable to resolve the question of Orsini; this person is not mentioned in his account.

9. Symonds treats Guasti's falsifications in *Michelangelo*, II, 128, 131, 173. Prince Piombino: see n. 4 above.

10. Symonds, *Michelangelo*, I, x:
Up to the date 1863, his [*Michelangelo's*] sonnets, madrigals, and longer lyric compositions were only known to the world in the falsified and garbled form which Michelangelo the younger chose to give them when he published the first edition of the "Rime" in 1623. The history of what may be called this pious fraud by a grand-nephew, over-anxious for his illustrious ancestor's literary and personal reputation, will be found in the twelfth chapter of my book.

11. The brackets are Symonds'.

12. "Un' Etéra Romana, Tullia d'Aragona," *Nuova Antologia*, IV (August, 1886). Symonds, *The Renaissance in Italy: Italian Literature*, Chap. XIII, characterizes the poetess thus: "Tullia di Aragona, the mistress of Girolamo Muzio, who ruled society in Rome, and lived in infamy at Venice. . . ." Biagi had examined the extent to which Benedetto Varchi, the historian of Florence, revised Tullia's verses. Also see Symonds' *Michelangelo*, II, 169.

1933. *To Janet Ross*

Davos. Sunday. Nov: 22/91

Pray look up the word *gorna*[1] in the Della Crusca Vocabolario[2] & tell me what examples they give of its having being used for the jacket of a man, or for any male raiment.

You will do a great service to your poor Historian.
It is snowing hard today. My chest is still raw.

JAS.

---

1. A kind of skirt.
2. The Accademia della Crusca was a Florentine academy established in 1592 for the purpose of cultivating Italian language and literature. In 1612 it published the *Vocabolario degli Accademici della Crusca, con tre indici della voci, locuzioni, e proverbi Latini, e Greci,* etc. There was a 5 vol. ed., Venice, 1741: *Vocabolario degli Accademici della Crusca Compendiato secondo la quarta ed ultima impressione di Firenze Corretta et accresciuta,* etc.

1933a. *To Wilfred Austin Gill*[1]

[Davos] Dec. 2, 1891

[Dear Gill]

   . . . for the little book[2] has only been in my hands a couple of hours. . . . I feel sure already that here is the work of a poet born with a gift of wide compass in the line he chose to follow, and how sincere, direct, spontaneous, rich in fancy! It is so difficult to feel clear and sure about most books of the kind; and so sad to think that the singer has already been taken from us. . . .

   . . . I should like to understand his views upon the relation of Hellenism to Christianity. For myself, it is difficult enough to adjust Hellenism to modern ideas. Nothing which Lefroy said, even were it severe stricture of my own writings (in the "Studies of the Greek Poets," &c.), would break the impression which he has made on me. I am not a dogmatist, but a perplexed seeker, whom length of life has made diffident. . . .

[Incomplete]

---

1. Wilfred Austin Gill (1856–99), educated Magdalen College, Cambridge; B.A., 1879; M.A., 1882; fellow King's College, London, 1885–99; Edward Cracroft Lefroy's executor, of Magdalen College, Cambridge. Gill published *Edward Cracroft Lefroy: His Life and Poems including a Reprint of Echoes from Theocritus . . . With a Critical Estimate . . . by the late John Addington Symonds. . . .* (1897). See L 1930.
2. Edward Cracroft Lefroy, *Echoes from Theocritus and other Sonnets* (1885).

1934. *To Janet Ross*

Davos Dec: 10. 1891.

My Dear Janet

You will have some right to be cross with me for this prolonged silence. I never thanked you for your notes upon the use of the word "gorna",[1] nor have I told you how very much I was flattered by your verses to me.[2] They are indeed a delightful compliment. I only wish I deserved it.

I have been dreadfully hard at work, finishing up MAB. The whole book is now complete, & I shall send it to London in a few days. It will make 2 vols I reckon of about 350 pp apiece.

We have had no snow to speak of yet. The lake is frozen & affords splendid skating.

Madge & I are going to produce a book in common. Did I tell you about it? It is to be all about Graubünden & our life here. I cannot find a good title. What do you think of

High Alps

"Our Life in the Alpine Highlands"? I wish you would invent a good one. I have no talent for this. Your "Land of Manfred"[3] shows that you have.

I shall be very glad to get the photo of the Stufa MAB.[4] I see the picture is mentioned in Fortnum's essays on the "Portraits of MAB."[5] He doubts its attribution to Bugiardini.[6] My impression is that it may be by Jacopo del Conte.[7]

Colvin[8] sent me eight photographs of Or: Dr:[9] in the Br Mus wh have been of use to me lately. But I am in great difficulties about the illustrations.

Remember me to the Padrone & believe me affectionately yr

J. A. Symonds.

We expect Lotta home today. Madge had a very nice letter from Lina [Duff-Gordon] a few years ago.

---

1. See his request in L 1933.
2. See Janet Ross, *The Fourth Generation*, pp. 312–13:

> Faithful and truthful, generous, modest, kind,
> Many the virtues which in thee I find.
> So wise art thou that flattery is vain
> To fill with vanity thy steady brain.
> Made to discern the characters of men

And calmly trace their real meaning, when
They would dissemble. Large and just thy view
Of all humanity, and clear and true
Thy judgment, which nor fear nor favour rules,
But justice metes to sages and to fools.

3. Her series of sketches on the "Manfred region" of Italy in *The Land of Manfred, Prince of Tarentum and King of Sicily* (1889).

4. Symonds supplies the following note, *Michelangelo*, II, 274:

There is a puzzling easel-picture, formerly in the possession of the Marchese Lottaringo della Stufa, which deserves mention here. The face is nearly full, turned to the spectator over the right shoulder; very pallid, with rugged features and a fatigued expression; wrinkles strongly marked. The right eye is out of drawing with the left. The lower lip is dragged a little toward the right side, showing more beneath moustache and beard than elsewhere. The head is covered with a black felt hat. . . . A doubtful piece of work, yet interesting as divergent from the types named above.

5. Symonds acknowledges, in *Michelangelo*, II, 261–62, Fortnum's kindness in supplying data on Michelangelo's portraits. C. Drury E. Fortnum's essays were: "On the Original Portrait of Michelangelo, by Leo Leone," and "On the Bronze Portrait Busts of Michelangelo," in the *Archeological Journal*, XXXII (1875), 1–6, and XXXIII (1876), 168–82.

6. See L 1932. Symonds had attributed a portrait of Michelangelo to Bugiardini (*Michelangelo*, II, 274).

7. Jacopo del Conte (1515–?1598), according to Vasari, painted a portrait of Michelangelo. The picture has disappeared.

8. Keeper of prints and drawings at the British Museum. See Ls 1191 and 1676.

9. Original Drawings. In the preface to *Michelangelo* (p. xxi) Symonds acknowledges Colvin's help in allowing him to photograph 8 original drawings in the British Museum.

1935. *To Horatio Forbes Brown*

Davos, Dec. 10, 1891

[Dear Horatio]

The abrupt finish of my M. A. B. work is rather trying to my nerves. How can a writer escape from being neurotic? He has such tremendous changes of mental climate and revulsions of emotion. He is always vehemently growing or being violently amputated, and he is not a vine, to suffer these alternatives in the due course of natural seasons. If genius is connected with insanity, this must be due in many cases, not merely to a congenital diathesis, but also to the abnormal vibrations set up in the nervous system of an author by the conditions of his labour. A pendulum has rhythmic action, so long as the motive force lasts, but here the creative rhythm is suddenly suspended, just when the nervous energy is over-stimulated to its utmost. I feel the fact acutely at the present moment, and am tingling, jumping.

The only way out is to begin some new work. But how exhausting all that is to vital resources.

. . . The Blacks of Edinburgh, meanwhile, are going to publish Madge's and my book on our life here,[1] and Nutt is going to publish a volume of Poems and Translations[2] by me. In spite of spiritual bankruptcy, it seems, then, that the first people I offer a book to, take it without questioning. It is likely, then, that if I live during the next six months, I shall be engaged in printing three books—M. A. B., Life in the Swiss Highlands, Verses. . . .

So I sit groaning on this awful night's glacier, thirty degrees below zero.

Life of the Universe, God, everlasting Law, from which no soul can flinch, soon must I go back to you, bruised, maimed, afflicted in my sense of dwarfdom. My hope is that you made me thus, and that I play a part in the unknown drama. Blind and stupid, like a cockchafer, I have buzzed in crepuscule. Brain and heart, with all their light and heat in me, are inefficient. Yet I have striven in my own gross way. And, after all, a man may be tested by strife, even though he feels at life's ending that strife is only one line, and not the finest line of action.

[Incomplete]

---

1. *OLSH* (1892), published by A. & C. Black.
2. Apparently the transactions with Nutt fell through. On Nutt see L 1526.

1935a. *To Wilfred Austin Gill*[1]

[Davos], Dec. 11, 1891

[Dear Gill]

. . . I fully understand what he Lefroy felt about Pater and me. In fact it (the paper) recalls vividly an attack which a Mr. Tyrwhitt[2] made upon my morals at a time when he thought I might be elected to the Chair of Poetry at Oxford. . . . I am undoubtedly open to criticism. And it is just for this reason that I welcome Lefroy so much, because at heart he was at one with me, but in him "the elements were kindlier mixed," the spirit purer. . . .

The sonnets cannot die. They have the stuff of immortality, and will stir every generous soul to sympathy, if only they are not whelmed beneath the mass of late Victorian literature. . . .

[Incomplete]

---

1. See L 1933a.
2. See L 1040.

1936. *To the* Pall Mall Gazette[1]

Am Hof, Davos Platz, Switzerland, Dec. 11. [1891]

SIR,—I do not much sympathize with the makers of cyclopaedias for poets recently committed to their mother earth; nor do I admire poets who deal with word-puzzles and perplex the senses they should sing to by their eccentricities of language and of learning. Our literature ought not to lapse into Lycophron and Byzantine Scholiasts yet awhile. Still, after reading what you published about Dr. Berdoe's forthcoming book,[2] I feel inclined to call attention to one little point of criticism.

Browning is reported to have put into the mouth of Caponsacchi: "Yes; I wrote these [letters] when St. John wrote the tract De Tribus." Dr. Berdoe seems to have adopted the theory that the tract alluded to is a verse in one of St. John's Epistles, probably spurious upon the Three Witnesses. But, allowing for Browning's habitual carelessness and liking for conundrums, would he have styled a verse in an Epistle "tract," or have credited Caponsacchi in the seventeenth century with foreknowledge of a German textual criticism belonging to the nineteenth? Is it not more rational to suppose that our poetic sphinx was alluding to that treatise, "De Tribus Impostoribus" (one of the impostors being Christ), which haunted the imagination of the later Middle Ages, although it is doubtful whether it existed except in a late version made to order? Caponsacchi's answer, I submit, is to this effect: "I did not write these letters any more than St. John wrote a tract accusing Christ of imposture." It does not matter greatly one

636

way or another. But one ought to be just even to Browning in his game of hide-and-seek with the public.—Yours faithfully,

John Addington Symonds.

1. Printed under the title "A Browning Puzzle" in the *Pall Mall Gazette,* LIII (Dec. 16, 1891), p. 2.

2. Edward Berdoe (1836–1916), *The Browning Cyclopaedia* (1892); earlier he had published *Browning's Message to His Time: His Religion, Philosophy, and Science* (1890).

1937. *To Guido Biagi*

Am Hof, Davos Platz, Switzerland. Dec: 13. 1891.

My dear Biagi

I have long waited to answer your kind letter of Nov: 25, & to thank you for the transcript of Palla's letter.[1]

My publishers in England have been urging me to finish the book, or as much of it as would enable them to start printing. On this account I have worked incessantly & had no time for other things.

I now send you the copy of the notes I made upon the Codex Vaticanus of the poems. They are by no means exact in detail, but give a fair notion of the composition of the Ms. What Guasti has printed from the copy made by Michelangelo the Younger agrees with my observations of the original.[2]

I cannot understand the account he gives of the Cod: Vat: itself.

Do you think it would be possible to find the date of [the death of] *Lodovico* di Leonardo Buonarroti *Simoni?* (MA's father). It must have happened either in 1533 or 1534.[3] I incline to the end of 1534. But no one has published the exact date. I should be very glad to get it if I could. It has an indirect bearing upon Michelangelo's departure from Florence for the last time.

Believe me most sincerely yours

J A Symonds.

1. Giovanni Battista Palla (? –?) in 1530 purchased Michelangelo's now lost statue of Hercules and sent it to France as a present to the king. Palla was Francis I's agent for

Italian art and bric-à-brac. He was eventually imprisoned and poisoned. For one of his letters to Michelangelo see Symonds' *Michelangelo*, II, 380.

2. See L 1932 for the details of this matter.

3. In his "Pedigree of the Buonarroti Simoni Family," *Michelangelo,* II, Table B, Symonds sets the date as 1534.

1938. *To Guido Biagi*

Davos Platz. Dec: 16. 1891

My dear Biagi

I am anxious to determine with certainty the date of Michelangelo's final departure from Florence for Rome.[1]

Arch. di Stato

In a letter to Vasari (date May 1557, Milanesi[2] No. CLDxxxii) he says himself that he arrived at Rome 2 days before the death of Clement vii, i.e. Sept 23. 1534. But Milanesi assumes that he returned to Florence afterwards. There is no proof of this; & the thing seems improbable, for he was very much afraid of the Duke Alessandro.[3] Condivi says he owed his life to the fact that he was not in Florence when Clement died.

A good deal depends upon the examination of letters. And I am going to ask you to look at the originals of two at least, in order to see whether Milanesi has authority for the dates he gives.

Arch. Buonarroti

No. CDXX to Febo di Poggio[4] is important, because MAB says in it that *he is going to leave Florence next day, & never to return.* Milanesi assigns this to Dec: 1533. Is there any sign upon the autograph which proves this date?

Febo's answer is dated Florence Jan: 14. 1534 (Arch: B: Cod: viii. 303). Now if Febo used the Florentine style,[5] this would be Jan: *1535.* In that case MAB's letter was written in Dec: 1534, & we should have distinct proof that MAB returned to Florence after Clement's death.

No. Cxxix, to Giov: Simoni Buonarroti, is dated by Milanesi under the year 1533. Is there any evidence upon the autograph? It refers very distinctly to Lodovico's[6] death as a past event.

If I could get the exact date of Lodovico di Lionardo Simoni's death, it would be an important aid toward settling the date of MAB's final retirement to Rome.

I should be grateful to you if you would tell me whether you think it probable that a young Florentine like Febo would use the *Roman* style (anativitate) instead of the *Florentine* (abincarn) in writing a letter. The question really turns greatly upon this.

Pray pardon me for giving you all this trouble, & believe me most sincerely yours

J A Symonds.

P. S. Some light might be thrown upon this question of dates from Fattucci's Correspondence.[7] Are there any letters written by him to Michelangelo in Florence or in Rome, between Dec: 1. 1533 and Jan: 1. 1535?

Fattuci's Correspondence ought to be published. It is very important for one period of MAB's life; but not so amusing as Sebastiano del Piombo's.[8]

---

1. For Symonds' formal discussion of the complicated matters that follow see his *Michelangelo*, I, 465–69.
2. See L 1877.
3. Alessandro di Medici (1510–37), natural son of Lorenzo, duke of Urbino (1492–1519) and last of the direct male line of the elder branch of the Medici family; 1st duke of Florence; murdered for his tyrannical rule. For the story of the Duke Alessandro's undisguised animosity towards Michelangelo, Symonds relies on Ascanio Condivi (1520–?), *Vita di Michelangelo Buonarroti* (1823), still regarded as "the original font" of all biographies of Michelangelo, the 1st. ed. appearing in 1553, possibly under the artist's own supervision, and rewritten in Vasari's 2nd ed. of his *Lives*, 1568. See Sidney Alexander, *Michelangelo the Florentine* (1957), p. 462.
4. The elusive young Florentine, favorite of Michelangelo, See Ls 1880 and 1891.
5. The same calendar styles are mentioned by Michelangelo's father as quoted in Symonds' *Michelangelo*, I, 5. The former is Gregorian, the latter Julian.
6. Michelangelo's father. See Symonds' *Michelangelo*, I, 468–69; also L 1937.
7. Michelangelo's friend and Roman agent. See L 1918.
8. See L 1932.

1939. *To Agnes Strong*[1]

Am Hof, Davos Platz, Switzerland. Dec: 19. 1891.

My dear Agnes

In reply to yours of the 16th. I think the simplest way will be to pay Jane Bates[2] £2 per month beginning with the 1st of Jany. And for this purpose I will now enclose a cheque for £ 12, so that you will have six months' in hand. It is very kind of you to see to this. There will be no difficulty in continuing the payments if you give them up. Supposing her able to walk or to send a duly accredited person to the Bank, I am sure Prescotts[3] will undertake it for me.

You did not tell me where Dawsonne[4] is settled or going to be settled. I look forward much to seeing him again.

We are all very well here. It has snowed heavily, but now we have glorious sunlight & sharp frosts. It was 20° below Zero Fahr (52 degrees of frost) last night. And yet I am sitting now with open windows: & had my bedroom window open in the night. The climate is singular.

I am glad to hear that your father[5] has a successor[6] at All Saints whom you both like. Please give Uncle Clement our best love, from all, with all good wishes for Christmas & the New Year.

Lotta has returned from Danzig, looking extremely well & beautiful. She seems to me also to have developed in mind & character.

Your affectionate Cousin

John Addington Symonds

---

1. Symonds' cousin. See L 891.

2. A check of the Bristol archives has failed to produce any information about Jane Bates.

3. Bankers, affiliated with Symonds' brother-in-law, Sir Charles Cave.

4. Symonds' cousin. See L 28.

5. The Rev. Clement D. Strong. See L 176.

6. The Rev. Harry Wilson Boustead succeeded the Rev. Mr. Strong as vicar of All Saints', Corn Street, Bristol. He served from 1891–1905, moving to Basingstoke (Hampshire) as vicar; he was educated at Magdalen College.

1940. *To Mary Ann Sykes*

[Davos] Dec: 21. 1891.

My dearest Auntie

I must write you one line to send you my best wishes for Christmas & New Year. I hope you will have many more of these seasons, although I daresay that you agree with me in feeling the sad side predominate over the exhilarating as years advance.

I find it difficult to believe often that I am 51. I feel so young in many ways, having I suppose inherited this together with a very nervous temper from your blood.

We are all together now here. Lotta has greatly improved in health & developed in character by her visit to Germany. Madge is preparing a book with me, wh we are going to publish under the title of "Our Life in the Swiss Highlands." Katharine is careering about on little sleighs & snow shoes.

Give my best love to Charlotte. We were all very proud of her while Jowett was ill. I heard from so many of his old friends.

Believe me most affecly yours

J A Symonds

1941. *To Dr. J. W. Wallace*[1]

Davos Dec 24. 1891

My dear Mr Wallace

How can I thank you for your immense kindness, in sending me these three telegraphic messages about our dear great friend & Master![2]

It is too late evidently now to hope that his life may be continued, & we must look forward to a restful ending. Traubel wrote me already six weeks ago that he did not think Whitman could live through the winter.

My thoughts are continually with him, & I find them taking shape in verse as I wander across these snowfields.

How I wish it were possible to express anything adequate to the man's real greatness! But that I have always held is not to be done in this age.

In many respects the feeling provoked by this news throws a sadness over the fall of Christmas tide. But I feel serious rather than sad for has not Whitman taught us to be unterrified by Death, to regard him as the deliverer?

Again, thanking you I am most sincerely yours

John Addington Symonds

---

1. See L 1874.

2. The content of the messages is not known, but they must have been related to Whitman's declining health. In January 1873, Whitman had suffered a stroke and was forced to leave Washington for Camden and his brother's home. After 1885, his strength further declined, and in 1888, after a series of heart attacks, he became incapacitated. He died on March 26, 1892.

1942. *To A. & C. Black, Ltd.*[1]

Am Hof, Davos Platz, Switzerland. Dec: 25. 1891.

To Messrs A & C Black.

Dear Sirs

I duly received from you a statement of accounts regarding the "Study of Dante," together with a cheque for £7.15.3 for wh I thank you.

I also received a letter about the terms of publication of the book "Our Life in the Swiss Highlands." I am prepared to accept your present offer, which is that you should print an edition of 1500 copies, paying the £50 on publication & a further sum of £20 when the sale reaches 1500, the copyright remaining in authors' possession.

I should like the book to be titled "Our Life in the Swiss Highlands" By John Addington Symonds and his daughter Margaret. I will shortly send you some photographs which seem to me suitable for illustrations.

Believe me very truly yours

John Addington Symonds

---

1. Publishers of the 2nd ed. of Symonds' *An Introduction to the Study of Dante* (1890) and of *OLSH* (1892).

1943. *To Horatio Forbes Brown*

Davos Dec. 29, 91

[Dear Horatio]

. . . it [the autobiography] was so passionately, unconventionally set on paper. Yet I think it a very singular book—perhaps unique, in the disclosure of a type of man who has not yet been classified. I am anxious therefore that this document should not perish. It is doubtful when or whether anyone who has shown so much to the world in ordinary ways as I have done, will be found to speak so frankly about his inner self. I want to save it from destruction after my death, and yet to reserve its publication for a period when it will not be injurious to my family. I do not just now know how to meet the difficulty. And when you come here, I should like to discuss it. You will inherit my MSS if you survive me. But you take them freely, to deal with them as you like, under my will. I have sketched my wish out that this autobiography should not be destroyed. Still, I see the necessity for caution in its publication. Give the matter a thought. If I could do so, I should like to except it as a thing apart, together with other documents from my general literary bequest; so as to make no friend, or person, responsible for the matter, to which I attach a particular value apart from life's relations.

We have Fred and Dora North[1] from Rougham here [very English], and [T. H.] Warren's brother[2] [the architect] expected tomorrow. There were a lot of people to dinner tonight, including a Mr Coke [W Leicester][3] whom perhaps you saw here last year—a very odd man—also a nephew of John Morley[4]—also a young doctor from British Guiana.[5] Such an odd lot. They talked about insanity and genius, hereditary proclivities, and sexual inversion until I got quite nervous. Not to much purpose the talk. The difficulty was how not to cut into the pomegranate and reveal the truth. Fortunately I refrained from taking that extreme step.—Soon you will be back with A.S. and G.F.[6] God bless you.

J.A.S.

Thanks for your words of heartening and comfort. I [omission].

---

1. Mrs. Symonds' nephew Frederick North (1860–1948) and niece (d. 1923). The brackets in this sentence are Symonds'.
2. Edward Prioleau Warren (1856–1937), architect of many collegiate, domestic, and religious buildings, especially at Oxford and Cambridge and in London; writer of many architectural articles.
3. Thomas William Coke Leicester, 2nd Earl of Leicester (1822–1909), Keeper of the Privy Seal to the Prince of Wales from 1870; distinguished lawyer.
4. Probably Guy Morley, mentioned in F. W. Hirst, *Early Life and Letters of John Morley* (2 vols., 1927), I, xi, as having been the recipient at his full discretion of John Morley's papers, John Morley's father had three sons: the oldest, Edward, succeeded to his father's practice as a doctor in Blackburn; the second was John; the third was William, who died in India and left three children. One of them was Guy, whom John Morley adopted (*Early Life and Letters,* I, 7–8; also II, 55–57).
5. Unidentified.
6. The first person is probably Antonio Salin, Brown's gondolier; the second eludes us.

1944. *To A. & C. Black, Ltd.*

Am Hof, Davos Platz, Switzerland. Jan: 2. 1892

Dear Sirs

In reply to yours of Dec 30, I may say that I am willing to frame our agreement in this way "Mr J. A. S. sells to Messrs A & C. B the right to publish an edition of Our Life in the Swiss Highlands of from 1500 to 2000 copies, but not exceeding 2000, on condition that Messrs A & C. B pay £50 on publication & a further sum of £20 when 1500 copies have been sold."

If this is satisfactory to you I hope you will soon put the book into the printers' hands.

I send you up some photographs numbered at the back, & indicate here what parts of the book I think they might serve for.

Believe me very faithfully yours

John Addington Symonds

Messers A & C. Black

P. S. Please let me have the photos back which you do not want.[1]

1) Am Hof. Davos Platz. Our House. For frontispiece
2) Davos village
3) Davos church   for *Winter at Davos* etc
4) View of valley from Hillside
5) View of postroad in snow
6) Interior of Hall in the Rathaus
                   (for *Davos in the Olden Days*

7) Lake in early winter
8) Corner of Mr Symonds' study
9) Mr S. at his writing table
10) Corner of Mrs Symonds' sitting room
11) Details of Alpine
12) garden at Am Hof
13) Gallery in Avalanche
14) Cutting an Avalanche   for chap on Snow Storm etc
15) Men digging for the body of a comrade
      in Avalanche
16) Post Houses (Sledge Drive)
17) Icefall on Silvretta Glacier
             (for Tobaggoning on a Glacier

18
19 } Tobaggoning Incidents
20

21 } Two Members of the Gymnasium
22   (for Swiss Athletic Sports
23) In the Prättigau. For chapter on Conters[2]

24) The head of a young peasant you already have, I should like if possible used for Melchior Ragetti the Swiss Porter.

---

1. The book actually contained the 5 following plates: Symonds at his writing table (frontispiece); By the Lake Shore: Early Winter; The Old Church of St. Johann, Davos Platz; Men of Glarus-Davos Digging in an Avalanche for the Body of Caspar Valär; Margaret Symonds on a sled.
2. A small village in the Prättigau.

1945. *To Charles Kains-Jackson*[1]

Am Hof, Davos Platz, Switzerland. Jan: 2. 1892.

Dear Mr Jackson

I received back the Plüschow Studies,[2] for which many thanks. Your observations on them are just. I wish I had sent you more to look at. But Plüschow if you choose to write to him will be glad to furnish you with a selection. The model you seem to have liked best is a Roman lad called *Luigi*. You might ask for Studies of *Luigi, Filippo, Cazzitello, Edoardo*. These are some of his best models.

You do not mention "Midnight at Baiae"[3] in your letter, a copy of which I sent you. Perhaps it did not reach. Or you may not have had it at home. If the poem is not to hand, please let me hear.

Thank you for the Xmas Sonnet, wh I like greatly. I am a believer enough to have written a Christmas Lullaby (published with illustration in the American number of English Illustrated Mag 1891)[4] & three Latin Hymns published in Loftie's "Latin Year."[5]

Always yours

J.A.S.

---

1. See L 1887.
2. Guglielmo Plüschow (?–?), of Rome, specialized in studies of nude youths. Examples of his work were published in *The Photogram* (London), IV, Nos. 41, 42 (May and June, 1897), and discussed briefly by Robert H. Hobart Cust (1861–1940), translator of Cellini's autobiography and student of Italian painting, in an essay, "Photographic Studies," pp. 130–33 and 158–61. Cust also featured samples of photographs by Count Wilhelm von Gloeden (?–?), of Taormina. Von Gloeden's work had been exhibited "at the Photographic Salon and at the Exhibition of the Royal Photographic Society, some three years since"; Plüschow's work, however, was hardly known in

England at the time. Some of the plates from *The Photogram* were reproduced in R. W. Schufeldt, *Studies of the Human Form for Artists* (1918), Chap. XIII, "The Form in Youth," pp. 186–217. See plates.

3. A verse-transcript of a dream appeared in *Pamphlet I,* and in *The Artist,* XIV (March 1893), 69–70, and as a separate pamphlet in 1893. See Babington, p. 88.

4. "Sleep, baby, sleep! the Mother sings," IX (Dec., 1891), 209.

5. William John Loftie (1839–1911), *The Latin Year* (1873) contained Symonds' "Dominica Tertia Post Epiphaniam" (pp. 294–96), Ecce Chorus Angelorum" (p. 255), and "Sol Cordis, Jesu Care" (p. 226).

1946. *To Janet Ross*

Am Hof, Davos Platz, Switzerland. Jan. 3 1892

My dear Janet

I have been terribly overworked—& lately ill also. This must be my excuse for long silence.

The wine came, & was superlatively good. I say was, alas, because I drank the last of it yesterday. Shall I send the little cask back?

It bore the journey so well & kept so well here that I should like to buy of you a cask of about 300 litres, if you can send me the same sort. But please do not send it off till the weather gets warm. We have fierce cold here—14° fahr last night! [46 degrees of frost.

I send you a note on that passage in Boccaccio.[1] I imagine Poggio Gherardo[2] is the Palace.

I am probably going to produce a new translation of the Decameron[3] for an illustrated "edition de luxe." The publishers treat me as Eurystheus treated Herakles.[4] They won't let me alone.

Every copy of MAB was sold about 6 weeks ago; & the price of the book rose up to double towards the end. Nimmo says it would not be fair to bring out a new & cheaper edn before next autumn.

Your new edn of the three generations[5] came. Many thanks. Catherine has been reading out to me the new parts. It is a very charming book.

As for that novel on Florence[6] I should like to have it; but can't you set it for less than 36 frs?

Remember me to Lina[7] & the Padrone.

Please give my Saluti & those of Angelo [Fusato] (who is here) to Fortunato.[8] How does Alfredo[9] get on at Barbaro?

Yr Aff

JAS.

Mezza terza is an hour of the morning, exactly half way between Sunrise & the *terza* or Canonical hour at wh for the 3d time in the day services were performed. Anglicà *terce.*

So what Boccaccio says is "Considerably before the time which comes between sunrise & the terce."[10]

I should translate it

"at a quite early hour of the morning."

---

1. See the postscript to this letter. The preceding single bracket is Symonds'.

2. Janet Ross' home. The palace is described in the introduction to the *Decameron.*

3. Symonds died before he could undertake this work.

4. Hera, wife of Zeus, was always hostile to her husband's children by mortal mothers. After she failed to destory the infant Heracles, son of Zeus and Alcmene, by sending serpents to his cradle, she rendered him subject to Eurystheus and compelled him to perform all commands. The 12 labors were arranged by Eurystheus.

5. Janet Ross, *Three Generations of Englishwomen* (1892) (1st ed., 2 vols., 1888).

6. Possibly Margaret Vere Farrington (1863–?), *Fra Lippo Lippi* (1890).

7. Lina Duff-Gordon, Janet Ross' niece, later Mrs. Aubrey William Waterfield. See L 1882.

8. One of Mrs. Ross' servants.

9. Formerly a servant with Mrs. Ross, but then of the Palazzo Barbaro, Venice, where the Curtises (see L 1717) and Mme. Pisani (see L 1717) lived. See Clare Benedict, ed., *Constance Fenimore Woolson* [1930], p. 382.

10. In the introduction of the *Decameron.*

1947. *To Janet Ross*

Am Hof, Davos Platz, Switzerland. Jan: 6. 1892.

My dear Janet

I am so sorry about that photograph of the MAB portrait. Of course it cannot be reproduced. The old one may be of some good. I will see that you get it again. What shall I do about Mr Spence?[1]

I am not at all well. Catarrh of the lungs, wh will not go away. Also I feel the loss of my long work, & cannot take to any other occupation.

Will you ask Sir James[2] if he thinks it would be possible for me to get permission to have a drawing by MAB, wh is at Chatsworth,[3] photographed? It is in black chalk, said to be a realistic likeness of Leo X; & if so, *the only extant portrait sketch* by the master in existence.

Colvin[4] has had a number of the Br Mus drawings done for me. But I don't get along with the plan for illustrating my book. I ought to be in London.

Your letter to C[atherine] makes me melancholy. It is so full of life. We lack not light here. But all this snow is deathly; & a fine young man I know[5] was swept away two days ago in an avalanche. His beautiful strong body will lie frozen until May or June brings it to light, with forty or fifty feet of snow above it.

I should like to see the people in the olive fields & the dancers in the evening.

Please remember me most kindly to Sir James & thank him warmly for his message. But, but—

Es ist in Leben hässlich eingerichtet [Life is badly arranged]. How very saddening the Diary of Walter Scott[6] is, wh I have just read!

Give too please my kind regards to Miss Zimmern;[7] & ask her to photograph some Faunlike young men if she can for me. I want to know what the type of those folk is.

I hope you are going to prosper this year. Yrs affectionately ever

JAS.

---

1. We cannot identify Mr. Spence, who probably had something to do with Symonds' attempts to secure a photograph of the oil portrait of Michelangelo, in the possession of the 9th Earl of Wemyss (1818–1914), which eventually appeared as the frontispiece of Symonds' *Michelangelo*.

2. Sir James Lacaita. See L 1879.

3. Symonds suspected that the attribution of the drawing of Leo X at Chatsworth to Michelangelo was wrong; see his note in *Michelangelo*, II, 125.

4. Sidney Colvin. See Ls 1191 and 1676.

5. There is a reference to this youth in the "Epilogue," in *OLSH*, p. 362; a more detailed account of an earlier loss of a similar man, Caspar Valär, pp. 72–74; and a photograph of men digging for the body, facing p. 73.

6. Symonds probably refers to *The Journal of Sir Walter Scott, from the Original Manuscript at Abbotsford* [with illustrations, and a preface signed, D. D., i.e., David Douglas] (2 vols., 1890). This journal was also published in part in J. G. Lockhart's (1784–1854), *Memoirs of the Life of Sir Walter Scott, Bart* (1st ed., 1837); here it was called the "Diary."

7. See L 1409.

1948. *To Horatio Forbes Brown*

Davos Platz, Jan. 12 [1892].

[Dear Horatio]

Your last letter was interesting, except for the bad news about the health of people. I have rather a bad account of my own to give. Ever since M. A. B. was off my shoulders, I have been drooping; and it is now serious. I cannot encourage you to make plans for coming here yet awhile. I am fit for little, and, when [E. P.] Warren[1] goes, I feel as though I may have to go to bed and stay there some time. The matter is extensive bronchial trouble. My own fault. When I feel well I will not live as befits a damaged man of fifty-one. And so I have to pay heavy bills from time to time. Now good night.

[Incomplete]

---

1. See L 1943.

1949. *To Horatio Forbes Brown*

Davos Platz, Jan. 15 [1892]

[Dear Horatio]

I am still what I must call ill. I don't know what I have written to you lately. The days and nights go by as in a sort of dead dream. A letter of the 22nd comes to me from you to-night, and I am glad to see you are working at the "Calendar."[1] I feel sorry for my Venetian friends, who seem to be doing badly now, with influenza and the winter season. But I hope that most of them will pull through. They have at least health and manhood. It strikes me that nobody ought to complain who has these things: in my present lack of them, all else seems worthless.

I sent you the little book by Lefroy[2] you write of. I thought I had told you about it in a letter. It struck me that his views about friendship would suit you, as they have done. The dead man speaks to me in his verse and in his prose. I want to diffuse his influence, it is so good and true. I mean to write about him, when I am less a wreck.

Walt Whitman, from his death-bed, sends me the final edition of "Leaves of Grass."[3] It is a beautiful book. I will procure you a copy. At last his life-work reaches a form, in which it will snuggle to a man's breast and lie there—what he always wanted. Poor Whitman! He is dying hard. They cablegram to me from Camden almost daily. All of him, but his *heart*, is dead. He lives and lives and longs for death.

[Incomplete]

---

1. Brown was editing the *Calendar of State Papers, Venetian, 1891–1905*.

2. Brown's note: "E. C. Lefroy, *Counsels for the Common Life*." It has the added title: *Six Addresses to Senior Boys in a Public School* (1885). For Edward Cracroft Lefroy see L 1930.

3. Published by David McKay, 1891–92. See Carolyn Wells and Alfred F. Goldsmith, *A Concise Bibliography of the Works of Walt Whitman* (1922), p. 35; "Whitman was very ill at the time, and, wanting to see the edition, Horace Traubel had a few copies hurriedly bound in wrappers for him, and Whitman had them sent to intimate friends. This issue is extremely rare and did not exceed fifty copies."

1950. *To Henry Graham Dakyns*

Am Hof, Davos Platz, Switzerland. Jan: 15 1892

My dear Graham

I return the business letters & thank you very much for your own, though I wish it gave a better account of health. I am a poor creature just now, & am obliged to keep my bed. My long book on M. A. Buonarroti was a very tough job; & when I finished it just before Christmas, I collapsed. This is always the way. One's strength holds out while the strain is on, & then just when one looks forward to holiday & rest, flop one goes. And the lungs always feel the decline of nervous energy.

It has been most interesting doing this book. I have found out a lot of new things about MAB & a lot of lies connected with his memory. Fortunately nothing scandalous.

It took me a good deal to Florence & Rome. In the latter place I lived with that odd fellow Ld Ronald Gower.[1] He is a most interesting but very fatiguing companion. When off worked [sic] we romped around like [sic] 2 o clock in the mornings. He knows everybody, from the cabbies corporals & carabinieri up to the painters princes & plenipotentiary envoys.

I also went to Aquila, on a visit to old Ulrichs.[2] He is a beautiful & dignified old man, living in great poverty. We talked much about "inverted Sexuality." I wish I could see more of him. Fancy, he supports himself entirely by the sale of a little Latin newspaper wh he writes himself. If you think him worth helping, write to

Sign: Carlo Enrico Ulrichs

Aquila Italy

& ask to be abonne [a subscriber] to *Alaudae*.

It is so disagreeable writing in bed that stop I must. I hope to come & see you next summer.

Ever yr affecate

JAS

1. See L 1612.

2. Karl Heinrich Ulrichs. See L 1831 and Symonds' *A Problem in Modern Ethics* (1891).

1951. *To Albert Trübner Nutt*[1]

Davos Jan 21 1892

Dear Mr. Nutt

I have been confined to bed with a sharp attack of bronchitis which left me very weak. Else I would have replied to your kind letter earlier, & have told you how very pleased I am to hear that you will take up my suggestion regarding a volume of Poems & Translations.[2]

I dare say we shall be able to find a better title than this: for I do not want to include any translations which have not been for me poems—spontaneous transfusions of myself into a previous mould.

I will busy myself with making a selection. This cannot be done very quickly, & it requires a good deal of tact.

Should you object if I make this book one that appeals to the artist temperament rather than the public? I have a good many things which both as to form & matter would be caviar to the general, & some that might even offend a scrupulous stickler for conventions. But I think that the poems I allude to are neither immoral nor enfeebling. And they are as good in workmanship as I can do.

It seems difficult to get back numbers of the Century Guild Hobby Horse. I want Oct: 1890. It has a translation by me of Bion's Lament for

Adonis[3] wh I should like to include in this volume. Will you kindly try to get a copy?

Believe me very truly yours

John Addington Symonds.

---

1. See L 1526.
2. Symonds did not live to complete this book.
3. V (Oct., 1890), 121–26.

1952. *To Edmund Gosse*

Davos Platz Jan: 21. 1892

My dear Gosse

I should have responded earlier to your letter of the 9th & have reciprocated your kind wishes, had not the year begun badly for me, with a very serious attack in the lungs.

I am getting up strength again. But I fear that there is little prospect of anything in store for me which I enjoy here—the sleighing & journeying through snow scenes.

How delighted I am to hear of your experience at Dunster,[1] whatever it was. I divine of what nature, & congratulate you. "Many a green isle needs must be."[2] Only these islands have been so sparsely pitifully scattered over the deep wide sea—like plums in a workhouse pudding.

I hope we shall meet next year—I mean this. I must go to my brothers-in-law—Sir E Strachey[3] at Sutton Court & Charles Cave[4] at Sidbury, probably also to the Hallidays[5] at Glenthorne & to the Stephens[6] at St Ives. It would be odd if I did not make out a day at Dunster.

I am getting ready a vol of verses, wh will be pretty risky.

I long for your story.

I am so weak that I cannot write much. So glad the Ms of MAB is in London!

Yrs JAS.

Kindest regards to Mrs Gosse.

---

1. Dunster, Somerset. The experience remains a mystery.
2. The opening line of Shelley's "Lines Written Among the Euganean Hills."
3. Sir Edward Strachey married Symonds' sister Mary Isabella (Maribella), who died in 1883.

4. Sir Charles Daniel Cave married Symonds' sister Edith in 1859. One of the family seats was at Sidmouth, Devonshire.

5. See Ls 943 and 1908.

6. The Leslie Stephen family.

1953. *To Edward Carpenter*[1]

Davos Jan. 23/92

Dear Edward Carpenter,

I think I know you somewhat, & had long felt toward you, as one who has been able to simplify his life. Am I right? It is what, if I had health, I would wish to do. But I am tied down & clogged physically. Nothing survives energetic in me but the unconquerable mind: often a torment to itself, in these distracted times.

I will post [Horace] Traubel's[2] letter to Dr. [John] Johnston.[3]

Great Whitman, we must not call him poor, or commiserate him. But would that he could be released. It is very painful this hard-dying and the irony of nature, or her equity; in return for his firm grip (as you observe) upon the material world.

We are all of us the better for having come to know him. I did not think you lived so far north.

Goodnight. This is a poor scrap of paper. But I am too tired & weak to reach out for better writing gear.

Thank you for your kind words. I respond with the greetings of a sincere comrade and herzlich grüssend [greetings from the heart], as we say here.

John Addington Symonds

---

1. See L 1819.

2. See L 1728. Presumably a letter Traubel wrote for passing around among Whitman's friends in England.

3. See L 1855.

1954. *To Janet Ross*

Am Hof, Davos Platz, Switzerland. Jan: 27. 1892.

My dear Janet

I go on ailing: chest bad, & a racking cough. It is the sudden stoppage of MAB wh hurts me.

If you see Biagi,[1] will you ask him whether he got a long letter I wrote him about the end of last year. It was mainly about some dates in MAB's letters.

Tell him that I wrote a full report to Villari[2] (at his particular request) in support of the Ente Buonarroti's[3] application to be allowed to publish the archives.

We are all so sorry to hear of your various troubles: espy Lina's[4] fragility. Poor Fortunato[5] too! I wonder whether you could try packing the whole of his trunk in water compresses. It relieved me greatly at the time when this bronchial affection was most distressing.

I quite understand about Ovidio;[6] & if de Nino got half the oof [money], you were more than just—generous. Forgive my pedantry.

The proofs of Madge's & my book are beginning to come. We have decided to call it "Our Life in the Swiss Highlands." Kindest regards to the Padrone. Yr affecate

JAS.

1. See L 1869. The letter Symonds refers to is probably L 1938.
2. Pasquale Villari, the historian. See L 1297.
3. The *Ente* or "Society" Buonarroti consisted of scholars and other persons anxious to publish Michelangelo's letters and papers given to the city of Florence in 1858 by the Commendatore Cosimo Buonarroti with strict stipulations that no one was to divulge their contents. In the preface to his *Michelangelo,* Symonds explains the details of his own efforts, finally successful, to examine the collection. The *Ente* was also successful: it received permission to publish an official edition of the correspondence.
4. Lina Duff-Gordon, Mrs. Ross' niece. See L 1882.
5. One of Janet Ross' servants.
6. Antonio de Nino, (?–?), *Ovidio nella tradizione populare di Sulmona* (1886).

1955. *To Guido Biagi*

Am Hof, Davos Platz, Switzerland. Feb: 12. 1892.

My dear Sign Biagi

I cannot thank you enough for your long letter of the 5th & all its valuable information.

There seems no doubt now that Lodovico died in 1534,[1] & that Michelangelo must have been at Florence in December of that year. This is what I was inclined to believe. I had noticed the point about the Decmia of 1534.

It is curious how inaccurate some of Passerini's[2] statements are. I will give you an instance, wh is puzzling me at present.

In the Buonarroti pedigree he makes this entry: (*Gotti*[3] *vol 2: p: 5*)

(*a*) 1472 16 gennaio [January] m[arried]
   Francesca di Neri etc
   Morta il di 9 juglio *1497*

(*b*) *1485*. Lucrezia di A. Ubaldini.

That is to say, he makes the second marriage take place 12 years before the death of the first wife. I sent him a long report upon the subject, which he acknowledged a few weeks ago, intimating that my arguments had weighed with him. I am delighted to think that we shall have an authoritative text.— Milanesi's vol of Seb: del Piombo's letters[4] is defective in several documents wh were published previously by Gaye[5] & others. I hope that you will publish the whole Mss irrespective of whether they have been previously edited.[6]

The way in which you propose to divide the correspondence seems to me admirable. It might be possible to add an index to the work when it is finished, arranging the dated letters in their chronological order, & giving a list of the undated with probable dates. To [so] many of the undated are clearly written from correspondents who were living in the same town with Michelangelo, that we can often assign an approximate date. This is the case with one of Angiolini's, one of Cavalieri's, one of Pierantonio's, etc.[7]

I made for myself a chronological Index to all the Letters in Milanesi's edition,[8] wh I have found useful while working.

Whenever this project begins to take shape, I will do my best to make it known in England. And I suppose that I may be permitted to call attention to it in the introduction which I mean to write upon the Sources of Michelangelo's Biography.

By the way, have you ever seen a critical article wh Villari told me he wrote upon Guasti's edition of the *Rime*?[9] I forgot to ask him where to find it & he is so dreadfully busy. I should like to see it; for Villari said he found it needful to be severe in his remarks.

Believe me to be most sincerely yours

John Addington Symonds.

P. S. Do not forget to help me about the dates of Lodovico's marriages.

Do you know Gotti? He might be able to say whether 1497 is a misprint for 1477 in the pedigree.

I wonder whether he could be induced to explain his "Spaccato del

Modello in Legno della Cupola di S. Pietro" (Vol: 2 p:136–7? It shows *three* separate sheaths or *volte* to the Cupola. Now the Modello in Legno has only *two volte*.[10] This drawing misled (I believe) both Heath Wilson[11] & Garnier in "L'Oeuvre et la Vie de Michelange."[12]

Do you think it would be possible to find out the real date of the second marriage?[13]

The question is whether Giovan Simoni Buonarroti (b: 1479) and Sigismondo (b. 1481) were whole brothers or only half brothers of Michelangelo.

Springer,[14] the best German authority on MA's life, adopts 1485 as the date of the second marriage. But oddly enough, in the pedigree he publishes, Giovan Simone & Sigismondo (in spite of their births having been in *1479* & *1481*) are called sons of the second wife. I will copy his pedigree.

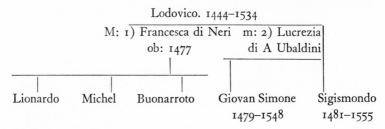

Lodovico. 1444–1534

M: 1) Francesca di Neri   m: 2) Lucrezia
ob: 1477   di A Ubaldini

Lionardo	Michel	Buonarroto	Giovan Simone	Sigismondo
			1479–1548	1481–1555

On page 7 of his book, he says "Lodovico gave a Step-mother (Lucrezia) to his son Michelangelo in 1485.

You will see from what I have written that there is a hopeless confusion in the dates of three marriages & births. What do you think is likely to be the truth? I much want to clear the point up.

My book is being printed. I have the proofs here of the first 152 pages.

I hope that I may be able to come to Florence, if the work goes on as quickly as it has begun. But I ought to finish the correction of the press here, where all my books are.

I should greatly like to talk over your plan for publishing the Carteggio.[15] I am greatly pleased to hear that Villari is favourable.

1. See L 1938.
2. Luigi Passerini (1816–77), genealogist, historian, and bibliographer, *La bibliografia di Michel-Angelo Buonarroti, e gli incisori delle sue Opere* (1875).
3. Aurelio Gotti, *Vita di Michelangelo Buonarroti.* See L 1876.

4. Sebastiano Luciani, called Sebastiano del Piombo [*Letters to Michael Angelo*], Italian text ed. by Gaetano Milanesi, translated into French by A. Le Pileur (1890). In the published pedigree (Symonds' *Michelangelo*, II) Symonds dropped Francesca di Neri's (i.e., di Miniato del Sera's) death date. She was the daughter of Neri di Miniato del Sera.

5. Giovanni Gaye (1804–40), ed., *Carteggio inedito d'artisti* (3 vols., 1839–40).

6. Biagi apparently never completed an edition of Sebastiano de Piombo's letters.

7. Bartolommeo Angelini (see L 1890); Tommaso Cavalieri (see L 1880). We have not been able to identify Pierantonio. See Symonds' *Michelangelo*, II, 138–39.

8. Milanesi's edition of Michelangelo's letters (1875).

9. *Catalogo Generale della Libreria Italiana* (*1847–1899*) (3 vols., Milan, 1922), III, 592, indicates that Pasquale Villari and Guasti exchanged published letters on various questions, although it does not record one dealing with *Rime*. See L 1877.

10. On the cupola of St. Peter's, Rome, see Symonds' *Michelangelo*, II, 236–44.

11. See L 1876.

12. By Charles Garnier (1876).

13. Symonds resolved the problem by dropping Francesca's death date, presumably Springer's error.

14. Anton Springer (1825–1891), German art critic, historian, and professor, *Raffael und Michelangelo* (1st ed., 1877; 2nd ed., 2 vols., 1883).

15. See n. 6 above. The reference to Villari (see L 1297) is obscure.

1956. *To William Barclay Squire*[1]

Davos Platz. Feb: 14. 1892

My dear Squire

I was glad to hear again from you, though sorry to know that you have had bronchitis. London must have been most trying this year.

Here we lie in danger of avalanches. There is more than 7 feet of snow on the valley—in places where the wind does not make drifts. You can imagine what it is, where the snow has been heaped together.

The railway has ceased to work. And we have only one road open, that to Klosters. It is like the Middle Ages.

I am going to ask if you could employ anyone at the Br: Mus: to examine for me some of the Herald's Visitation in the Harleian Mss.[2]

It is for two points in my own pedigree. I will enclose a draft wh shows what I want, with references to the Mss.

The marriages with Congreve & Grosvenor in the 15th century are only recorded in our "tree" without dates. Yet they are important, as both families were distinguished, & I am immediately descended from them.

It is possible that the Harleian Society has published these Visitations of Staffordshire & Cheshire. But I doubt whether the descents, so distant from the period of the visitations, will appear.

657

My book on MAB is being printed. I have proofs of five chapters out of fifteen. Owing to the letter you wrote me, I got some original drawings in the Br Mus photographed; & I am much obliged for the hint.

Madge & I are printing a book together wh will be called "Our Life in the Swiss Highlands", & my wife has just published her sister Miss North's Autobiography in two volumes. Am Hof is a workshop of literature.

Thank you so much for your invitation for the summer. I shall not forget it, & hope to be able to avail myself of your hospitality.

Ever affectionately yrs

JA Symonds

John Symonds of Croft, Lancashire	= in year 1372 m:
	Alice dr & heir of
	Hugh Leighton of
	Forton, Staffordshire.
William Symonds of Croft	= a daughter of Sir Wm Lording, bt.
Robert Symonds	= dr & heir of Richard^x Congreve
	of Stretton Staffordshire
John Symonds of Stratton or Stretton	= a dr of _____^{x} Grosvenor
	of Belloport, Cheshire

^{xx}. I want to know if the pedigrees of Congreve & Grosvenor record these marriages.

Congreve of Stretton. Harl: Ms ~~1100. fo. 21b 1173. fo 113—1570. ff. 57. 71b b 128 ff. 55.64~~ *Grosvenor of Bellaport.* ~~1535. fo. 146 b.~~

---

1. See L 1674.

2. There is no record among Symonds' papers of Squire's reply. The search that Symonds requested was formidable; there are over a hundred volumes of Visitations published by the Harleian Society. The Visitations were investigations made by the king's heraldic officers into pedigrees and claims to bear arms. They ceased ca. 1686.

1957. *To Horatio Forbes Brown*

Davos, Feb. 14 [1892]

[Dear Horatio]

I wrote you a letter some nights ago,[1] which I kept back, thinking no news better than what I had to give then. But I will send it, since it thanks you for your offer to come here, which touched me. I hope you will come before the winter is over. Things are going more happily with me at last. In the first place my health is certainly improved.

The whole thing is trying enough. And yet I do not think I should have wished God to make me other than I am. He justifies His ways to men by leaving them contented with a puzzled page. He helps them, too, by nature's gradual process of killing, stifling, numbing.

Of my book,[2] I have five chapters out of fifteen in proof. I cannot judge the work. I only see that it combines more of the "grubber's" industry with more of recklessness in language than anything I have published.

Nature is very interesting here this winter. We are shut off from the whole world, except by one-horse traffic with Klosters. Avalanches descend. Eggs have ceased to be purchasable. I sent notes about the snow to the *P.M.G.*[3] which perhaps will be printed and you will see. I walk two or three hours a day, visiting various points of interest.

The snow has reached such a point of width and depth now that no figures are of any value. We simply wallow in it. I employ two men daily (for the last ten days) to keep the access open to the house, and prevent the burying of the whole up to the second storey. In the basement they burn lamps by day.

This is a rest; as storms at sea have been a rest before to me. Nature annihilates the petty grievances which conscience weaves. Is this the reason why sailors are so humane? Good night. Late as usual.

[Incomplete]

---

1. Not available.

2. *The Life of Michelangelo Buonarroti.*

3. We have not located this piece; nor does Babington mention it. *The Davos Courier*, Feb. 13, 1892, devoted considerable space to the storm (including most of the first page):

The absorbing topic of conversation during the first half of this week was the abnormally heavy snowfall. It may interest our readers to know that since the beginning of the winter snow has fallen to the depth of 13 feet, of which nearly five feet was contributed by this last fall between Friday and Tuesday. The total fall of this year is said to be much heavier than that of any previous year since 1817, though there has been no single fall this winter so heavy as in the winter of 1874–75.

For the first time since the opening of the Prättigau Railway, the train service has been interrupted. This is partly owing to the mass of snow along the line, and partly to one or two heavy avalanches, which have fallen across the track. There have been 200 men working on the line, chiefly between Davos and Klosters, though a good deal of work had also to be done just below Klosters: indeed it was feared that if much more snow had fallen, the trains would have been unable to push their way further than Küblis. Considerable interest was excited on Wednesday by the two engines slowly forcing their way between Platz and Dörfli station. The front engine armed with a snow-plough, having got up steam, charged into the barrier in front of it, and sometimes, when it was lucky, would succeed in making way for two on three hundred yards. The second engine then came to the rescue of its mate, and after retiring some distance, a fresh charge was made, and so Dörfli was reached after a hard and wearisome battle.

Our connection with the outside world, however, has been wonderfully well preserved. As soon as it was found that the trains were unable to work, the Post arranged for sleighs to go to Klosters, the chief inconvenience to passengers being a slightly earlier start than usual, and the only difference in the delivery of mails being that instead of getting the English papers on the evening of the day following publication, they have been delivered early the next morning.

Several avalanches have fallen in the neighbourhood, the nearest being near the Brewery at Dörfli. This occurred about 11 o'clock on Monday morning and came from almost the top of the mountain, bringing with it a hay chalet, which it had overtaken in its descent and sweeping away 3 cow-sheds about 300 or 400 feet above the road. In one of these cow-sheds a man was feeding the cattle, and he appears to have had a narrow escape, having been found pinned down by a heavy beam across his throat. This, however, was quickly sawn through and he was released in a semiunconscious state, but has since completely recovered. Three cows were buried in the avalanche, which travelled as far as the Villa Wieseli, one side of which is completely blocked up with snow and debris. Some English residents in a house close by were advised to move as it was thought possible that another avalanche might come down and sweep them away. They therefore wisely took up their quarters at the Fluela Hotel. On the falling of this avalanche alarm was given by the ringing of the Church bell, which quickly brought a willing band of helpers to the spot.

A considerable avalanche has fallen in the Dischma Thal, by which nine cows were killed and a shed swept away. Also an avalanche at Frauenkirch in which one man is reported to have lost his life. Reports also come of avalanches in the Sertig, the Fluela, the Züge (five having fallen since Monday) and at Laret at a point where an avalanche has never before been known to fall. The Fluela and Züge have therefore of course been entirely blocked for traffic. The telegraph arrangements have also been sadly interfered with and for a short time no telegraphic communication could be held beyond the valley; but that, of course was very soon rectified.

It is often the case that when we have a heavy fall of snow here, in the neighbouring valley—The Engadine—there is very little, and *vice versa*. It is so in the present instance for only about 11 or 12 inches have fallen at St. Moritz during the last week, and unless any further alteration is made, the Grand National Toboggan Races will be held on the 25th.

1958. *To Janet Ross*

Am Hof, Davos Platz, Switzerland. Feb: 16 1892

My dear Janet

I never told you how deeply I felt for you in the loss of Mrs Higford Burr.[1] I know well what the sorrow must have been, coming also so closely after Kinglake's[2] death. The memories of a lifetime interrupted.

I have heard tonight of the sudden death at Venice—from influenza, after only two days' illness apparently—of a friend I esteemed greatly: the Dowager Princess of Montenegro.[3] She was one of the very few foreign women whom I ever seemed to know intimately.

Perhaps this made me revert to you for deeper source of grief, & remember that I had not spoken of it.

The parcel of books duly arrived, & I thank you sincerely. It was too good of you to send your own Osservatore.[4] I do not like to keep it. I do not know what you want me to do. Please to tell me. You ought to keep it at Poggio. But if you like me to buy it, I will gladly do so, & see that it somehow comes back in time to its former owner. So you must let me hear. (This is stupidly said. I mean that if I am to buy it, I shall regard you as joint-owner.)

I have been really ill—after bronchitis, nervous disturbances of a distressing kind. Catherine became anxious, & we have had rather a disagreeable time lately. It is all the fault of grinding at MAB too much, & then being at a loose end when he was finished. Things are going better now, & I can take my 2 to 3 hours walk—but oh! in such snow! through drifts, over avalanches, along roads like ploughed fields!

Measured by the snow-gauge, 13 feet of snow have fallen since Dec 1. You can fancy what the drifts are. And, quite contrary to our usual winter weather, we rarely see the sun. It is not very cold. But en revanche there is a perpetual dread of being swallowed up in an avalanche. Were I not obliged to stop here for the printing of MAB, & Madge's book with me, I believe we should have migrated to Capri or Rapallo.

Five Chaps out of 15 of MAB are in proof. Should you like to read the proof? I think I could send you a copy, if you would return them. You said in your last that you wanted to see the book. So I make this proposal. But if it bores you, say so.

I do not think the publishers would like any press-notices of it to appear before it is published. So, you will kindly remember this, if you read the proofs. But you may care to get the book up, & write some reviews of it, & have the start of others.

I often wish I were living at Poggio, correcting proofs, within reach of [Guido] Biagi, & the Libraries. But I am not fit—even if other things permitted. I have already got one useful note out of the Osservatore.

We are so glad to hear how well Lina [Duff-Gordon] is getting. Give her my love. Also remember me to the Padrone.

Yours ever JAS

Tell Fortunato[5] how pleased I am to hear that he is better.—How kind of Lacaita[6] to send me that letter from Lady G. Croft![7] I already got a photo from that odd fellow R Gower[8] of the drawing I wanted. It seems he had it done once by Brown.

---

1. Mrs. Higford Burr, née A. Margaretta Scobell (?–1892), water-colorist; during her many travels copied old frescoes, some of which were published by the Arundel Society. Janet Ross in *The Fourth Generation*, p. 313, says that Mrs. Burr "had been like a second mother" to her.

2. Alexander Kinglake, author of a history of the Crimean War and *Eothen*. See L 1858.

3. Princess Darinka Krekvíceva of Montenegro. See Ls 1790 and 1959.

4. *Osservatore Romano*, the Vatican City newspaper.

5. Janet Ross' servant.

6. Sir James Lacaita. See L 1879.

7. Possibly Lady Georgiana Croft (d. 1925), wife of Sir Herbert George Denman Croft (1838–1902), of Croft Castle, Herefordshire; inspector of constabulary for the north of England.

8. Ronald Gower. See L 1612.

1959. *To Horatio Forbes Brown*

Davos, Feb. 23 [1892]

[Dear Horatio]

I thought I would just stipple to-night a few things casually to restore the tone which has been strained.

I was greatly interested by your jottings about the Princess of Montenegro's funeral at Venice.[1] It was as if I saw it all. Glad too that this emphatic recognition of her worth and rank was given. She had a great deal to bear, I fancy, in her subdued and impecunious life at Venice. Olga[2] will appreciate the honours paid her mother, though she may wish that a little more of the world's sunshine had cheered her while yet living. She was a fine and brave and I believe a large-hearted woman.

We are living, after our enormous snowfall, in a state of continual thaw. You can imagine that the snow begins to look unbeautiful and draggled. It has shrunken, and lost its colossal plastic outlines.

I get a daily letter from New Jersey, U.S.A., about W. Whitman. He lies, dying hard and gradually. His devoted friend there, Horace Traubel, writes. Seems to hope against hope for a recovery, which could be only temporary. I wonder what the meaning of this clinging on to life is, in persons who surround a death-bed? Is it callousness in myself which makes me rather, in these circumstances, pray for a speedy despatch, a *euthanasia,* when the whole sad scene would not have to be overacted again?

Most remarkable fragments from Lefroy's correspondence are being sent me by his friend and literary executor, Mr. Gill of Magdalene College, Cambridge.[3] Lefroy disliked my attitude, and published a discourse[4] against it, which Gill has also sent. I feel that if we could all be made like Lefroy, we should get just what I desire. I have printed an Essay on Lefroy's sonnets for the *New Review,* which may appear next month.[5] If you are not here in March I will see to sending you a copy. I think he is a real discovery.

Robinson Ellis[6] has translated into Latin elegiacs four sonnets of my "Stella Maris." He is going to send them, and says I may pass them on to Ulrichs to print in "Alaudae."[7] How oddly the whirligig of the world moves! Ellis says he thinks "Stella Maris" *"very* fine," but cannot follow the drift of the emotion. But suffers and submits to it. And so he, I, and Ulrichs meet in a Latin Version of my verses.

I heard a young German violinist, Krasselt,[8] to-night play Bach's supreme Chaconne[9] extremely well. It was a real κάθαρσις τῶν παθημάτων.[10] If we could hear Bach and Händel, and a dessert of Gluck, every day!

M. A. B. goes on, and costs me about five hours a day labour on proofs. I change my views about it. I do not think I was made to do what I have tried to do—to be what Nimmo calls exhaustive. Now it seems to me that I am demonstrating what is a truism—viz.: "L'art d'ennuyer est de vouloir tout dire,"[11] also that πλέον ἥμισυ παντός.[12]

Well: we shall see. In doubts about one's life, one's work, one's method, one's principles, one's practice, there is always *living.* It is a sign of not being dead, to doubt and be discomfortable.

Now, I have stippled enough. I could go on all night. But I only wanted to give a *"Stimmung"* [mood]. "Screw thy divine theorbo two notes lower," not higher, or shriller.

[Incomplete]

---

1. Princess Darinka Krekvíceva, widow of Prince Danilo I [II]. She was interred at Cettinje, beside her husband. See Ls 1790 and 1958.
2. Princess Olga Alexandra Eugenie Marie of Montenegro. See Ls 1790 and 1958.
3. See L 1933a.

4. In *Undergraduate Oxford* (1878).

5. "Edward Cracroft Lefroy," in *The New Review*, VI (1892), 341–52; reprinted in *In the Key of Blue* (1893).

6. Robinson Ellis (1834–1913), editor and translator of Latin literature, translated some of Symonds' poems into Latin. For the reactions of Symonds' children to Ellis, see *OOP*, p. 224. See also L 153.

7. A news-sheet published in Latin at Aquila by Karl H. Ulrichs. See L 1831.

8. Alfred Krasselt (1872–1908) studied violin in Leipzig; concertmaster in various orchestras, especially in Weimar.

9. *The D minor Chaconne for violin alone*, frequently transcribed for piano (Busoni) and for orchestra.

10. Purging of emotions.

11. The art of being boresome is wishing to say all.

12. Better than half of all (everything).

1960. *To Edmund Gosse*

Am Hof, Davos Platz, Switzerland. Feb:25.1892.

My dear Gosse

Your very acceptable letter of the 16th reached me duly. I would have written again earlier but for the usual impediments—proofs, bronchial colds, & such things. We are having a very trying winter; immense masses of snow (13 feet have fallen since Dec), followed by warm sultry weather. It is difficult to get exercise, almost impossible to drive out, & very risky about catching or repeating colds. Then the proofs of two books come pouring in. First, my MAB, wh gives me a lot to do still. Then a volume of descriptive articles by my daughter & myself "Our Life in the Swiss Highlands." I fancy I must have talked to you about this.

Have I written to you about E. C. Lefroy's Sonnets? They interested me deeply, & I sent an article upon them to the New Review.[1] I am in correspondence with his oldest friend & literary executor (Lefroy died last summer), who has sent me extracts, from his letters, extremely curious about the love of Comrades & the admiration for male beauty. Lefroy was an earnest Christian, a Clergyman, & of irreproachable morals. All this makes his Hellenic aspect interesting.

I don't know what to do about my own poems. I find it difficult to satisfy my sense of what is good in workmanship & strong in feeling with what is safe & decent from the public's point of view.

Your gossip concerning the Kiplings[2] gave me great amusement. I wish I had known him as well as I knew Louis Stevenson. They are two of the most typical eccentricities of genius—so idiosyncratic, & yet so impossible to conceive of except in the second half of the 19th century. Stevenson has long been lost to me. I cannot keep in touch with a man in the South Seas who does not live like a native & with the natives.

I put this aside on being interrupted the other day. Among announcements of periodicals for the month, I see my essay on Lefroy. Do look at the sonnets to Bill, Football Player, Palaestral Study.[3]

I have been ill again the last few days, & am getting tired of this long variable winter. But I cannot go away till MAB is printed, & as usual, the pen seems to have come to an inexplicable stop when not quite half-way through. I feel a little anxious what effect my essay on Lefroy's love affairs with young men and the smash up of the mythic part of his [Michelangelo's] friendship with Vittoria Colonna will have.

The catena of evidence supported by previously inedited documents is fortunately as strong as a ship's anchor chain. But some people do not like to hear unpalatable truth.

I think I shall try to spend a good part of the Summer in England. Somehow or other, we must meet: if possible, out of London, in a quiet country.

My wife is having a success with her sister Miss North's autobiography.[4] An edition of 1250[5] copies seems to have been sold out in ten days. It is very much due to the careful & judicious way in wh Mrs Symonds dealt with the MS.

It seems as though I could not write a letter. My brain does not work. I will write something more worthy of the name soon.

[Portion cut off]

---

1. See L 1959.
2. See Gosse's "Two Pastels:—I. Mr. Robert Louis Stevenson as a Poet [1887] II. Mr. Rudyard Kipling's Short Stories [—1891]," in *Questions at Issue* (1893), pp. 237–54, 255–93. Gosse says, p. 261: "The private life of Mr. Rudyard Kipling is not a matter of public interest, and I should be very unwilling to exploit it, even if I had the means of doing so." These articles were first published, respectively, in *Longman's Magazine*, X (1887), 623 ff., and *Century*, XX (1891), 901 ff.
3. Reprinted in Symonds' essay on Lefroy and in *In The Key of Blue* (1893), pp. 97, 99, and 100–101.
4. Marianne North's *Recollections of a Happy Life* (2 vols., 1892). The work is chiefly an account of Miss North's travels in Canada, the United States, Jamaica, Brazil, Japan, India, Borneo, Australia, South Africa, and Chili. Obernetter (see L 1790) and Mrs. Julia Margaret Cameron supplied pictures, as did Mrs. Bryan Hodges, a neighbor of Miss North's at Mount House, Alderley. This work was followed by *Some Further*

Recollections of a Happy Life, which are selections from her journals, chiefly from
1859–69, also edited by Mrs. Symonds (1893).

    5. L 1965 says 1350 copies.

1961. *To Horace Traubel*

Davos. Feb: 27.1892

My dear Traubel

    Hearty thanks for your letters to myself.

    Johnston, Wallace, & Carpenter[1] have sent on to me, by wire your
cablegrams, & under cover your letters to them—which latter have been by
me duly returned to their owners.

    So, out here, in these Alpine Snows, where we have been blocked by
avalanches for some time, with only an express post bringing mails in &
out, I have been daily & punctually informed of what is going on by our
dear great Master's sick-bed in Camden.

    I have got to know you more closely through the perusal of this
painfully interesting correspondence, & to sympathise most deeply in all
your hours.

    And then I have your photograph upon my working table. Altogether
then you see that I have been living in near relation to your spirit.

    It is a good & great thing this which the love & service of Whitman has
wrought for us all. It is what his spirit, if it soon arrives at a fuller
knowledge of the whole, will appreciate as the best outcome of his teaching
—this creation of Comradeship, sensitive pulsations of emotion noble in its
quality, between men so far apart.

    Are we to hope, in Whitman's case, for a prolongation of life after all
he has been going through?

    I do not venture to answer the question.

    But the attitude which he preserves upon his couch of mortal weakness
is worthy of his previous life, the seal set upon his teaching.

    Please tell Wary [Warren Fritzinger] that I think of him, & am
grateful to him. He may never have heard of me.

Believe me your true friend & comrade

John Addington Symonds

---

    1. On Dr. John Johnston see L 1855; on Dr. J. W. Wallace, see L 1874; on
Edward Carpenter see L 1819.

Davos. Feb: 27. or 28. in the deep night. 1892.

My dear Traubel

I scribbled to you a very hasty note this evening—a mere handshake—to catch the night's post.

I am overwhelmed with proofs: two books going on together: one a big new Life of Michelangelo, which costs me hours of labour in its final revision through the press: the other a volume of descriptive essays by my daughter Margaret & myself (she is the little girl on my back in an old photograph I once sent to Whitman, & some one told me he still keeps) about our experiences here. It is to be called "Our Life in the Swiss Highlands"; & when it comes out, I will send you a copy, as it has much personal about myself & life here in it.

Well, I wanted only to say that I wrote a few lines under great pressure of work, for which my strength is not quite adequate at present. And then there came to me a good peasant friend of mine here, with a trouble of his own to communicate. Our interchange of counsel & sympathy lasted a couple of hours; & I am refreshed again by this wholesome contact with true loving confiding human life.

And, to wind my story up, I return now in the dead hours of the night —to you & Whitman; he[1] may die this year or that, & a great light will be extinguished; but he lives for ever in the words which he has left behind him, in the spirit he has created beneath the very ribs of intellectual & academical death in such poor men as I am.

You do not know, & I can never tell any one, what Whitman has been to me. Brought up in the purple of aristocratic school and university, provided with more money than is good for a young man, early married to a woman of noble name & illustrious connections, I might have been a mere English gentleman, had not I read Leaves of Grass in time.

I am not sure whether I have not abused the privilege of reading in that book. It revolutionized my previous conceptions, & made me another man. Revolution is always a bad thing. And so, bred as I have described myself, it is possible that I have not attained to that real & pure nobility of nature in dealing with my fellowmen which Whitman teaches & exemplifies.

I only know that he made me a free man: he helped me to work at my chosen trade, literature, for better or for worse, as I was made to do it: but he also made me love my brethren, & seek them out with more perhaps of passion than he would himself approve.

667

Working upon a nature so prepared, as mine was, the strong agent of Whitman's spirit could hardly fail to produce a fermentation.

He says himself: I shall do harm as well as good.

To clinch all, he has only done for me good; & the harm which may have come to me, from intemperate use of his precepts, is the fault of my previous environment or of my own feeble self.

I pour all this out upon you now, because, while Whitman is lying on his deathbed, you must hear what one of his disciples—a man sworn to him unto the grave—has to say about the effect of his prophecy.

If I have seemed to be cold, here & there, about Whitman, it is not because I am not penetrated with his doctrine; but because I know by experience how powerfully that doctrine works, & how it may be misused & misunderstood.

Yours

JAS.

If Whitman is able to hear a word from an old friend, whisper in his ear that so long as I live I shall endeavour to help on his work, & to the best of my poor ability shall try to do this in his spirit.

J.A.S.

---

1. Beginning at this point, portions of this letter were printed in *Goodbye and Hail Walt Whitman: At the Graveside of Walt Whitman* (March 30, 1892), p. 25. They were prefaced by the paragraph beginning "It is a good and great thing" from L 1961.

1963. *To Edmund Gosse*

Am Hof, Davos Platz, Switzerland. March 2. 1892

My dear Gosse

I did not think, when I wrote in a dull mood yesterday, that I should "seize the pen" so soon again, to address you.

It so happens that I want an opinion about a book-plate, the photograph of wh I enclose. And I know from your delightful "Gossip"[1] that you are an amateur of Ex Libris.

The book-plate belonged to my lineal ancestor Joshua Symonds (nat: 1656, ob: 1735).[2] It is taken from the French translation of Lionardo da

Vinci's Treatise on Design,[3] showing that my ancestors even then delighted in polite studies.

Joshua was a rather remarkable man. He married Elizabeth, the sister & heiress of James Millington of Shrewsbury, in whom one line of that family expired. Joshua & his brother-in-law were both of Puritan, Commonwealth, blood & opinions; & one of the regicides, Gilbert Millington, was closely related to them. James Millington wanted to make Joshua Symonds' eldest son his heir; but he added this condition—that the boy should be christened Gilbert, & should take the surname of Millington, in order to perpetuate the memory of the regicide. Joshua refused the bargain, on the ground that he disapproved of the execution of Charles. So James Millington left his fortune to found the beautiful old Hospital at Shrewsbury, wh is called after him—the Millington Hospital. I narrowly escaped being called Millington, owing to this transaction: &, in any extended achievement, I still display the Millington quartering "argent a double-headed eagle displayed sable, beaked & clawed azure."

The arms in the bookplate are my own: viz: 1 & 4, Symonds "party per fere sable & or, a pale & three trefoils counterchanged," 2 & 3, Mainwaring, "bony of twelve pieces argent & gules" (see Guillim[4]). But the metals tinctures etc have not been heraldically attended to by the engraver of the bookplate. What I should like to know, from some one familiar with such matters, is to what probable date one may assign the plate. Joshua's life, as I have noted above, falls between 1656 and 1735.

I do not know when the fashion of Ex Libris was first introduced into English Society, & what the earliest examples are.

We possess some pretty specimens of my wife's, the Norths', family, who seem to have adopted bookplates in the reign of James ii or Charles ii. There is one, not in my own possession, wh was used by the Honble Roger North,[5] author of "Lives of the Norths."

You see that the topic of this letter is of no pressing importance. But the writing of it indicates my wish to correspond on points beyond such miserable jottings as I yesterday produced.

Ever yrs. J.A.S.

Humi tutus refers to the "grass of the field," the trefoil. It is not our family motto. Indicates perhaps old Joshua's sense of personal security, through insignificance, in troublous times.

---

1. *Gossip in a Library* (1891).
2. See L 58.

3. Probably the edition *Traité de la peinture* by Roland Fréard, sieur de Chambray (1651).

4. John Guillim (1565–1621), English authority on heraldry.

5. See L 1473.

1964. *To Charles Kains-Jackson*

Am Hof, Davos Platz, Switzerland. March 4 1892

My dear Mr Jackson

I see that you continue to be very indulgent to the claims of "lovely Knights" upon public attention. A Chant Royal, of Hylas, Hyacinth, Narcissus, Agathon & Charmides, followed by a Sonnet on Hyacinth & Zephyrus,[1] is not bad.

I like both poems, wh I take to be yours. When will you collect your Doric lays into a volume?

Do you think it would create a scandal if four or five people who have written lyrics in this vein should publish an anthology of chosen pieces? I often thought that artistically the result would be both novel & effective.

You ought to look to the proofs of "The Artist" more. That list of Wagner's legends on p: 72 is excruciating.[2] My time is spent now in correcting the proofs of MAB & "Our Life in the Swiss Highlands." Misprints give me a kind of mental neuralgia.

I am flattered by the par: upon my MAB,[3] p: 82. But I do not think the book will expound "the principles" of Renaissance Art so much as explain the psychology of a very peculiar artist-nature. Out of fifteen chapters only three are devoted to distinct criticism of art: one dealing with MAB's ideal of form & successive manners; another with his architecture; the third with his poetry & its underlying emotions.

Have you come across any one who has seen the proofs? Nearly half the book is now in type, & I fancy Nimmo may have shown it in progress to critical friends. Prof: Middleton[4] at Cambridge is kindly helping me with the proofs.

Very truly yours

John Addington Symonds

An Essay by me on Lefroy's Sonnets is announced for this month's no. of the New Review. Look at it, if you can. His Lit: ex: Mr. Gill of Magd:

Coll: Cam:[5] has sent me some very interesting extracts from private letters, illustrating his sense of beauty.

---

1. Anonymous, "Chant Royal: Of the Princes of Old Time," and Anonymous, "Sonnet. On An Old Legend," from Ross, *Mystagogus Poeticus* (1672), p. 179, in *The Artist*, XIII (March 1, 1892), 69 and 83.

2. Anonymous, "The Legends Adapted by Wagner," *The Artist*, XIII (March 1, 1892), 70–72. The "excruciating" aspect of the list on p. 72 of versions of the legends used by Wagner is a series of atrocious misspellings. But Jackson seems to have paid no attention. The December 1 issue, p. 379, has a similar list even more defective.

3. *The Artist*, XIII (March 1, 1892), 82: "The book will be the most exhaustive and authoritative exposition of the principles of Renaissance Art yet published."

4. John Henry Middleton (1846–96), archeologist and architect; Slade Professor of Fine Art, Cambridge, 1886; director, Fitzwilliam Museum, Cambridge, 1889–92; published *Engraved Gems of Classical Times* (1891), *Illuminated Manuscripts in Classical and Medieval Times* (1892), and other works.

5. See L 1930 and L 1959.

1965. *To Henry Sidgwick*

Davos Platz, March 4[1892]

[Dear Henry]

I am fascinated by Myers' treatise on the Subliminal Consciousness.[1] I doubt whether he himself suspects how far the hypothesis involved in his argument carries. Rightly, he confines himself to proof or plausible inference from more or less accredited phenomena.

I could talk more than it seems convenient to write, upon the deductions and corollaries which must ensue from this doctrine, if it is established. It will prove a great prop to Pantheism, the religion of the Cosmic mind.

Life wears away here, much as usual.[2] A great deal of book-producing. Catherine has edited two volumes of Miss [Marianne] North's "Autobiography," with great success, since the new year: an edition of *1350* copiess sold already, and another of 1000 in course of printing. A French translation of my book on Dante,[3] revised and partially re-written in the French speech by myself, has burst on Paris during the same space of time. My daughter Madge and I have brought forth a volume called "Our Life in the Swiss Highlands." And lastly, there are the two heavy volumes of my "Life of Michel Angelo," under which burden the press still groans—and I groan; praying daily for deliverance.

If it is at all virtuous to make books, then Am Hof, Davos Platz, may smirk! A cottage, 5000 ft. above the sea, hemmed in by avalanches, drowned in snow-drifts, has not often furnished a record of six volumes between January and April. My M. A. B. still lags a little. But the MS. is right enough and in the printer's hands.

The man is ill and tired, after all is said and done, and cares little about what he does or does not do in life. The parable of Ixion[4] was not a bad one: except that it was devised for Hell: whereas it suits phenomenal existence here more nicely: perhaps this *is* Hell. We go round and round, turning our phrases, polishing our rhymes, committing our aimless follies, doing our senseless acts of charity and benevolence, buying, investing, squandering, swilling, a dismal merry-go-round upon wooden hobby-horses in the artificial light of a Fair which does not deserve the name of Vanity, rather of Commonplace. *Everybody does the same. There is no difference of values in lives.*

[Incomplete]

---

1. Possibly the manuscript of "On Indications of Continued Knowledge on the Part of Phantasms of the Dead," published later in the *Review of Reviews*, VI (Sept., 1892), 191–4; or, parts of *Science and a Future Life: With Other Essays* (1893).

2. Symonds did, however, enjoy diversion during this period. The toboggan races, postponed because of the severe winter, were eventually held with Symonds playing a prominent part in the proceedings, as reported in the *Davos Courier* for March 12, 1892.

On March 15, he presented an address, "Culture, its Meaning and its Uses," to an audience in the dining room of the Hotel Buol. See the *Davos Courier*, March 19, 1892, p. 301.

3. *Dante. Son temps, son oeuvre, son genie*, trans. by Mlle. C. Auguis (1891). The preface, in English, is by Symonds.

4. For boasting of his supposed enjoyment of Hera's favors, Ixion was punished in Hades by being fastened to an ever-revolving wheel.

1965a. *To Wilfred Austin Gill*[1]

[Davos] March, 1892

Dear Gill

. . . I am deeply possessed with the desire to extend the influence which Lefroy's poems and ways of feeling ought to exert; and I think I am right in saying that there exists a medium in our modern life which would be receptive to them, and for which they cannot fail to be beneficial if once received. What I should like to do is to strengthen and expand the exposition I made in this first attempt, so as to present a more perfect view of Lefroy's mind from the side of his artistic and sympathetic qualities, and in particular, to discriminate the specific quality of his neo-Hellenism and to prevent anyone from imagining that his athletic poems implied the least sympathy with licence. If one could only put quite rightly what he was in these matters, I am certain we should do something to draw some young souls of men and boys out of a Cretan labyrinth where lurks a minotaur. . . .

[I intend] to make some excerpts from his address on Muscular Christianity,[2] showing in what way he defined himself against the line taken in 1877 by myself and Pater. . . .[3]

[Incomplete]

---

1. See L 1933a.
2. A paper read before the Keble Essay Club at Oxford (1877) and afterwards reprinted in *Undergraduate Oxford* (1878).
3. By Symonds in the conclusion to *Studies in the Greek Poets,* Second Series (1876), and by Pater, *Studies in the History of the Renaissance,* 2nd ed. (1876).

1966. *To Charles Kains-Jackson*

Am Hof, Davos Platz, Switzerland. March 14 1892

Dear Mr Jackson

I promised to send you some verse which should be proper to print before the eyes of the vulgar.

It came to me today to translate a very ardent piece of poetry by Michelangelo.[1] Like all his work in this sort, one hardly knows what he meant by it.

But it is so passionate in its complexity & tumultuosity of emotion that I think it has some psychological value.

So I send it to you, as a waif & stray from the strenuous studies which engage me now upon the great perplexing Master.

The incompleteness of the Sonnet gives it (in my eyes) a special interest. It seems to have been a fragment cast forth from the very entrails of the man's being.

Yrs J A Symonds

---

1. "On Love and Beauty in the Artist's Heart," *The Artist,* XIII (April 1, 1892), 99.

1967. *To Janet Ross*

Am Hof, Davos Platz, Switzerland. March 19. 1892

My dear Janet

I am so sorry to hear of your bad illness. Laryngitis is one of the most irritating of all that family of disorders.

I have been pretty well, except for a persistent cold in the head & bronchial tubes wh has gone on since the beginning of Jany. I don't expect to get rid of it till I change the climate.

And I can't go away yet. The printers go on so slowly with Michelangelo. Nothing is more tiresome than to be expecting proofs daily; wh come irregularly. It prevents one from settling down to other work, & also from going away.

We have been having glorious weather during the last week. A perpetual blaze of sunshine. Only too hot.

By the way I will send you another batch of proofs today. I do not want the first lot back yet. I shall be glad of them some time however. The marks in pencil are made by an old friend of mine, a Col Pearson,[1] whose taste in style I value.

I am so deathly stupid with my cold & other things that it is no use trying to write a letter. Let me hear that you are improved in health. I envy you getting down to Leucaspide.[2] Please remember me to the Commendatore. You will see my hyacinth anemone narcissus, I suppose, all over the bare earth.

Everyrs

JAS.

---

1. Colonel Alfred Pearson. See L 1405. Symonds acknowledged his assistance in the preface to *Michelangelo*.
2. The home of their friend, Sir James Lacaita, the Commendatore. See L 1879.

1968. *To Edward Carpenter*

Am Hof, Davos Platz, Switzerland. March 20 1892

My dear Carpenter

I duly received the gift of your book "Towards Democracy" in its third edition,[1] & have been reading it with sustained interest ever since it came into my hands. It is certainly the most important contribution which has as yet been made to the diffusion of Whitman's philosophy of life, & what I think we may now call the new religion.

You must not mind my saying that I somewhat regret the doubtless inevitable circumstance of the form of your work suggesting an echo or imitation of Whitman. It has so much that is original, individual to yourself in it, that this seems to me a pity and as likely to make careless or hostile readers lay it aside as a mere sub-species of "Leaves of Grass."

And yet I do not know in what better way an extended commentary or exposition of the principles involved in that "incommensurable" production could have been given to the English public. Mere criticism I feel to be helpless face to face with Whitman. As I have said in print,[2] I feel that talking about him is much the same as talking about the Universe.

What you have done has been to give a thoroughly personal, a specifically English, & if I may so put it, a feminine (as implying other strains of sensitiveness, humours, ways of regarding particular modes of social life), interpretation upon the leading ideas.

Insofar, then, as "Towards Democracy" is read & appreciated, it will do more than any amount of analysis or criticism to diffuse the teaching wh inspires you.

You know how deeply I sympathize with all that is involved in the new religion. The circumstances of my own existence & having been early married, & then reduced to a state of comparative physical inefficiency, have rendered it not only a necessity, but a duty also, & what is more, the best practical form left for me of service—to carry on my own work as a scholar, a writer, a student of history, an analyst. I have been unable to do what I should have preferred, had I been vigorous & unentangled, namely to join the people in their lives. Still I have endeavoured more & more to approach them, & have learned more & more from them. A large portion of my happiness in later years has come to me from frank companionship, wholesome comradeship, & mutual fellow-service with these Swiss mountaineers among whom my lot has been cast.

There is much in your way of regarding the world & human life, wh I do not feel able to grasp. I cannot be so optimistic, cannot feel so sure that all things are really right for all, cannot find in nature so clear an exit from human pains & troubles, finally cannot divest myself of self so utterly:—or indeed understand exactly what that means.

I intensely accept what you say on pp. 20–27, 50–62. I wish people would take these passages to heart. And I recognize how the healing is to come from the spirit expressed in pp 42–47.[3] I too have felt, and feel continually in my daily life, the deliverance which you have sung so ably in the poem "In the Drawing Rooms" 139–144.[4] The postilion on Alpine passes with his hard life & simple ways & strong unselfish service is a perpetual aid to my soul toward a higher spiritual frame: an escapement from the stifling air of the "better vulgar" & so much the "higher vulgar" than those who are called the vulgar.

So far as all this goes, I am one with you to ground down. But the "joy" you utter so frequently,—that note, I take it, is more a matter of individual temperament than of aught else, & is hardly to be gained by any shifting of our mental or emotional attitude.

I will send you a little book just about to appear, written by one of my daughters with myself,[5]

[Incomplete]

---

1. First ed. 1883; 2nd ed. 1885; 3rd, 1892. See L 1819.
2. See Ls 1728 and 1885.
3. These passages are a sustained complaint against England's "false shows and pride," which the poet threatens to tear off: "you shall be utterly naked before me, in your beauty and in your shame." The British have lost "a passionate attachment" to nature. Healing is to come from "naturalness." All comes from the rejuvenated self, and self speaks to self.
4. The poet is freshened after a session in the drawing-room: "A grinning gibbering organisation of negations—a polite trap, and circle of endlessly complaisant faces bowing you back from all reality!" by meeting the eyes of a grimy railway stoker:
Close at my elbow on the foot-plate of his engine he was standing, devouring bread and cheese,
And the firelight fell on him brightly as for a moment his eyes rested on mine.
That was all. But it was enough. . . .
For in a moment I felt the sting and torrent of Reality.
5. *OLSH*.

1969. *To: Charles Edward Sayle*[1]

Am Hof, Davos Platz, Switzerland. April 8 1892

Dear Mr Sayle

I am glad to hear from you again, & amused by your Wildeian paradox of there being salvation in music. I congratulate [you] on having so little that wants saving, if music can do it for you.

I am just at the end of a long piece of work, the Life of Michelangelo, & am looking forward to some restful days at Venice, 560 Zattere.

Though Rome has lost a great deal of its charm (I was staying there last December) it is still the most attractive place on the whole.

Did you ever go into the Cupola of S. Peter's when Mass was being sung just below? It is a very singular & thrilling musical sensation:

Et ôh ces voix d'enfants
chantant dans la cupole!²

If you care for extremely artistic studies from the nude, done mostly in the open air, go & see my friend G. Plüschow³ 34 Via Sardegra. He has made an immense collection wh he will be delighted to show you.

Very truly yours

J A Symonds.

---

1. See L 1502.
2. From Verlaine. See L 1882.
3. See L 1945.

1970. *To Dr. John Johnston*

Davos, April 11 1892.

Dear Dr Johnston

When I returned all the letters from Traubel the other day in a registered packet, I was too much overwhelmed with work on my Michelangelo book, for which my physical condition is not really adequate, to write to you.

It cannot be regretted that the life of our Master and friend Whitman has ended.[1] The last weeks were painful and must have been inexpressibly so to the friends who gathered round his sick bed, especially to the excellent and highly emotional Traubel.

I am going to Venice soon, where my permanent address is

ZATTERE 560

The hard work of Michelangelo has been got through, and there only remains to see it through revised proofs.

If possible I shall write something extended upon Whitman in prose while sailing and floating on the lagoons.[2] And for this purpose I mean to take books with me. But I feel the task to be one of gigantic difficulty. One must let Watts in the Athenaeum[3] & the New York Independent[4] snarl & bark. They are not worth attending to. When the Angel came from heaven to open the gates of the Castle of Dis for Dante & Virgil, he brushed the fiends away who rose from the waves of Styx with his left hand, as though they were frogs.[5]

Very sincerely yrs

J.A.Symonds.

---

1. Whitman died on March 26th.
2. *Walt Whitman: A Study* (1893).
3. Theodore Watts-Dunton (see L 1416a), a long article in *The Athenaeum*, No. 3362 (April 2, 1892), 436–37, explaining his views on Whitman and his reason for christening him the "Jack Bunsby of Parnassus."
4. The first paragraph of the New York *Independent* (March 31, 1892), p. 11, reads:

> The designation of Walt Whitman as "the good, gray poet" fails of the complete and supreme infelicity of the famous definition of the crab, in that time had made him at least gray. He wrote the noisiest, noisomest stuff ever called poetry, in lines beginning with a capital letter, and whose elusive dactyllic suggestion had a habit of dribbling out into utter prose.

5. Dante, *Purgatorio*, IX: 74 ff.

1971. *To Janet Ross*

[Davos] April 12. 1892

Dear Janet

I have received all my slips of MAB back up to 100. I now send you the rest of the book with the exception of a chapter upon architecture, wh has gone to an architect friend in London. Those slips shall follow.

I had already (on my own copy) attended to della la sana.[1] Gualfonda was, I think, that part of Florence where the new quarter between the Ry Station & the Arno now is. (The Cupid is so described in the S. Kensington Catalogue.[2]

I sent off my first correction of the whole book yesterday, & am going to start tomorrow for Italy by the Gothard. My fixed address will be

Zattere 560

Venezia.

I hope, however, if weather permits, to dawdle about the Lago Iseo & Lago de Garda on the way to Venice.

Catherine Madge & Katharine are going to Sta Margherita, (on the Gulf of Spezzia), Pisa & Rome then possibly to Florence. I am left thus alone, for Lotta is on her way to London. I must, however, be in one place because the revised proofs of MAB will soon begin.

I am exceedingly tired & sad. And now having just got through one big task Providence prepares another for me. One postman laid on my table a new & important History of Graubünden[3] at the moment when he took up the last proofs of MAB to register for London.

Now I had not expected this History to appear for 6 months, & then I meant to begin my own English work on the subject.

But eccomi [behold]! Supplied with the needful for labour just when I meant to take a holiday.

I wish I could come to you this spring. It is not outside the range of possibilities.

Please remember me to Sir James [Lacaita]—also to the Padrone & Lina [Duff-Gordon].

Yours affectionately

JA. Symonds

---

1. Probably a misprint in the proofs of the book.

2. The *Cupid* in the South Kensington Museum was discovered ca. 1852 in the cellars of the Gualfonda (Rucellai) Gardens at Florence, by Professor Miliarini (?-?) and the Florentine sculptor Emilio Santarelli (1801–86) (Symonds' *Michelangelo*, I, 62). Symonds reproduced two photographs of the cupid.

3. Peter Conradin von Planta (1815–?), *Geschichte von Graubünden* (1892). See also L 1995.

1972. *To Janet Ross*

560 Zattere Venezia April 21 1892

My dear Janet

I am sending you the last of my proofs: the part omitted from the batch I sent off before leaving Davos.

I shall be much interested to hear what you think about Chapter Xii,[1]

679

which is really the most novel portion of the book. I fear it will not be acceptable to the general reader. Yet the time has come when the truth about Michelangelo must be told. The true reason of the odd will of the last Buonarroti providing that nobody should study in his family archives is explained by the evidence they contain of Michelangelo's peculiar temperament.

I came into Italy just a week ago with Catherine Madge & K[atharine]. We parted at Milan, they for the Riviera di Levante, & I for Venice. Here I am alone, enjoying myself much, & not working. It is delightful to be free after the hard work of the winter.

Believe me affectionately yours

J A Symonds

I will send you a copy of Madge's & my book "Our Life in the Swiss Highlands," to Poggio.[2]

---

1. The chapter is entitled "Vittoria Colonna and Tommaso Cavalieri—Michelangelo as Poet and Man of Feeling." Symonds explores the relationships between Cavalieri, Febo di Poggio, Luigi del Riccio, and Cecchino dei Bracci and Michelangelo, and Michelangelo's alleged homosexuality. See also L 1977.

2. Poggio Gherardo, Mrs. Ross' home.

1973. *To Katharine Symonds*

Venice April 22 1892

My dear Katharine,

We have glorious weather here now, and I hope you have the same. I spent the whole day at Malamocco yesterday. The line of the Alps was quite clear from Vicenza all the way into distant Friuli. Antebao, above Cortina, as usual, being most eminent in form. All so white with snow and blue with air, forming a noble background to the city and lagoon and many islands in their dress of green.

This morning I conducted the Toynbee Hall[1] People over San Rocco and the Scuola di San Giovanni. A function of more than two hours, during which I talked. There were about 40 very intelligent men and women, full of questions, but oddly like a flock of sheep. It was an experience which amused me. I said everything which I think true about the pictures in a loud voice, regardless of any considerations except my own mature impressions of these things which I know so well. And I told them stories; anecdotes; odd sayings; a mixture of feelings profane and sacred, casual and permanent. I should not like to make a trade out of this showman's business. But, once in a way, it was funny to take a taste of it.

It is nice being here, I enjoy life immensely, when I am not ill or overworked.

Cultivate all ways of enjoying life innocently and in sympathy with various sorts of people—if possible mainly with the simple or the serious. The middle sort of minds, who are neither simple nor serious, but are sophisticated by a quantity of adulterated sentiments and secondhand knowledge, do not help the human soul much any way.

Mr. Barnett and his wife,[2] who have done so much for the poor of Whitechapel, were at S. Rocco with the Toynbees. I was glad to meet them . . . They told me the English people in our train over the Gothard were Toynbees going to Rome.

April 23. Mr. [W. B.] Squire and Lionel Cust[3] arrived here yesterday. They dined with me, as H. F. B. was going out. Edward Clifford writes that he and Mary[4] will come in the middle of May.

I am glad to hear from Madge's letter how much you all enjoy Sta. Margherita. I cannot make out whether you both scrambled from Portofino to the top of Monte Venere. It must be a lovely region.

[Incomplete]

---

1. Toynbee Hall in London, opened in 1884, was the first social settlement. See n. 2 below.

2. Samuel Augustus Barnett (1844–1913), clergyman and social worker; B.A., Wadham College, Oxford; pioneer in social settlement movement; vicar of St. Jude's in slums of London; persuaded university men to live in neighborhood to work for social betterment; helped found Toynbee Hall; active in university extension movement; Canon of Bristol (1894–1906) and of Westminster (1906–13). His wife Henriette Octavia Barnett (1851–1936) worked with him and collaborated in some of his books, especially *Practical Socialism* (1888); wrote his biography (1918).

3. Sir Lionel Henry Cust (1859–1929), art critic; an assistant in the dept. of prints and drawings in the British Museum (1884); director, National Portrait Gallery (1895–1909); author of studies of Dürer (1894), Eton College (1910), Van Dyck [1911], and the royal collections.

4. See L 712.

1974. *To Edward Clifford*[1]

Zattere 560 Venice April 23/92

My dear Clifford

I do not think that May is at all too hot for Venice & Florence, or that it matters which you take first.

For flowers I can safely recommend the Monte Generoso. It was probably in an article[2] about it that you read my account of the lilies there —there are literally "lilies in lieu of snow"—white S. Bernardino lilies, lilies of the valley, tiger lilies. And then the peonies, auriculas [kind of prim-rose], narcissus etc.

You can go up the mountain from Lugano in a railway, & there is an excellent inn on the top.

I am down here having a holiday after the very hard work of writing a new long Life of Michelangelo. I did a great deal of original research in the Archives[3] for this book.

Yours ever affectionately

J A Symonds

---

1. See L 712.

2. "Monte Generoso," *Cornhill*, XXI (1870), 605–10, especially pp. 606 and 609.

3. The Buonarroti Archives, which had been closed to all but Florentine scholars, but which the Italian government allowed Symonds to consult. See L 1954.

1975. *To Charles Kains-Jackson*

Zattere No. 560 Venice April 24, 1892

My dear Mr Jackson

I am glad to get another letter from you. It always does me good to hear from you. I am down here in my own little abode, living en garçon, with my dear friend Angelo, my gondolier. There are two Sonnets about him somewhere in my books—I think in "Vagabunduli Libellus." One begins "Rebellious Angel" another "Wide lucid eyes."[1]

It is quite a mistake to suppose that no Swiss are handsome. I will send you a few photographs when I go back to prove the contrary. And better, I

682

will send you *Edwin*[2] in person when he goes to London as he means to do. Edwin has a most remarkable beauty & delicacy—transparency. A friend of mine,[3] an attaché at Petersburg, says what is true: "You do not feel the beauty of a nation till you have slept with one of them."

The young fellow mentioned in my "Swiss Athletic Sports" at p: 233,[4] is divinely beautiful. I have compared him often, posed nude, with Michelangelo's David, whom he resembles in type, but far exceeds in heroic loveliness. I will scribble for you from memory some verses I once wrote about him. A friend who admires them, gravely suggests that I might render them publishable by altering *young Achilles* into *Amaryllis*.[5]

Do you care to read inedited "damned poems"—damed as doomed to silence & suppression? If so, I will send you some from time to time. I get them printed privately or type-written. It is very pleasant to hear that you like some of my writings. The "Greek Poets" would be republished at once if Smith & Elder had not some spite against the book & me. They *Keep* the remainder of Edn 2 of Series 2. And I can do nothing. There is a good American edition.

Yrs

JAS.

For insomnia did you ever try drinking red wine? A bottle of good claret or burgundy taken about an hour before your usual bedtime might help. I have found this excellent. I used to suffer awfully from sleeplessness and drugs.

---

1. See "Angelo Ribello" and "A Portrait" in *Vagabunduli Libellus*, pp. 119, 120.

2. Edwin Brugger was in London in June: see L 1903 and L 1988 to Jackson.

3. Possibly either Russell James Kerr (1832–1910), who married (1860) Rose Mary Ann Griffiths of Castle Hill, Englefield Green (formerly owned by Admiral John Sykes; see L 61), or his son, Russell James Kerr (1863–?). The *Almanack de Gotha* for 1891 and 1892 mentions an R. Kerr as an attaché at Petersburg.

4. In *OLSH*, Symonds reports that he asked his young Achilles how he and his fellow athletes came to be so brotherly: Achilles replied: ". . . that is because we come into physical contact with one another. You only learn to love men whose bodies you have touched and handled."

5. The manuscript of this poem, owned by Goodspeed, Inc., is reproduced below:

> At a Jura Feast in Thusis
> On the meadow young Achilles
> Laughed & raced beneath the sun:
> 'Neath his feet the bending lilies
> Tossed their gold-dust one by one:
> Mother-naked he was racing,

From the Rhine's cold fierce embracing,
   Where the Alpine torrents run.

On the pillow young Achilles
   Laid his head beside my own;
And the curls like clasping lilies
   Down his low smooth brow were blown:
Mother-naked he was lying,
Sinking into sleep, replying
   Faintly to my undertone.

I with him the young Achilles
   [Passed] that blissful night all through,
Intertwined as twine the lilies,
   Drinking draughts of heavenly dew:
Mother-naked friend & brother,
Lying, twisting each the other,
   While the hours so swiftly flew.

1976. *To the Rev. Matthew Russell*[1]

Venice, April 27, 1892

[Dear Mr Russell]

   . . . I have received your note here to-day, and reply that I shall be glad to see my three Sonnets[2] on the Sonnet reprinted in your book. Only, I must make one condition, that I should see the proofs. A good many poems by me have got into the hymn-books and anthologies, and have suffered greatly from careless editing.

[Incomplete]

---

   1. Matthew Russell, S.J. (1834–1912), founded the *Irish Monthly Magazine* in 1873; published *Sonnets on the Sonnet* (1898), *Life of Mother Mary Baptist Russell, Sister of Mercy,* by her brother (1901), and *The Three Sisters of Lord Russell of Killowen and their Convent Life* (1912).
   2. The sonnets printed in Russell's compilation, *Sonnets on the Sonnet,* are: "The sonnet is a fruit which long hath slept," "There is no mood, no heart-throb fugitive," and "The sonnet is a world where feelings caught," all three from a section titled "The Sonnet" in *Vagabunduli Libellus* (1884).

1977. *To Janet Ross*

Zattere 560 Venezia May 2 1892

My dear Janet

I am glad to hear you got home safely.[1]

Thank you for what you say about Chap. xii.[2] I know the matter is one which requires delicate handling. I should be greatly obliged to you if you would mark on the proof exactly the sentences wh you think might be omitted or altered.

The critique of people like Parlegreco,[3] Lombroso,[4] Von Scheffel,[5] is quite necessary because this view of MAB is only just beginning to be adopted, because it is in the main true, & because a thorough definition of his real temperament ought to be made once & for all.

I want to do this. But I should be sorry to render the book unreadable by anybody.

I believe you have proofs of Chap. xii. If not, I will send a duplicate.

I dined with the Layards[6] last night: Sir Henry pretty well: his friend Sir Henry Thompson[7] there, very anxious about himself.

Catherine & the 2 girls are at Albergo d' Italia in Rome.

I got a long letter today from Edward Poynter,[8] who is, I am glad to say, managing the illustrations of MAB for Nimmo.

Ever yrs aff

JAS.

---

1. From Leucaspide. She had been visiting Sir James Lacaita, to whom she dedicated *The Land of Manfred* (1889). See L 1879.

2. Chap. XII of *Michelangelo*. See L 1972.

3. Symonds regarded Carlo Parlagreco's (?–?) *Michelangelo Buonarroti (Il Vecchio)* (1888), as "the most important and serious essay" on Michelangelo as "the subject of neurotic disorder" to appear. Parlagreco "strongly insisted upon Michelangelo's indifference to women and his partiality for male friends as the sign of radical psychical unsoundness."—Symonds' *Michelangelo*, II, 361, 382.

4. The exact reference is unclear; possibly to *The Name of Genius* (1891). On Lombroso, see L 1836.

5. Symonds meant Ludwig von Scheffler (?–?), *Michelangelo: eine Renaissance-studie* (1892). He also edited *Jahrbuch für sexuelle Zwischenstufen, unter besonderer Berücksichtigung der Homosexualität* (Leipzig, 1899), I, *Bibliography*.

6. The explorer Sir Austen Henry Layard. See L 1327.

7. Sir Henry Thompson (1820–1904), English surgeon and amateur painter, educated at University College, London; created a knight (1867) by Leopold I of

Belgium, owing to the success of an operation; in 1874 founded the Cremation Society of London.

8. Sir Edward John Poynter, Royal Academician (1836–1919). A reviewer in *The Artist*, XIII (1892), 338 and 360 commented:

The sixty illustrations to the two sumptuous volumes are a triumph of care, and all artists will be grateful not to Mr. Symonds alone, but also to Mr. Poynter, R. A., whose supervision and counsel were most kindly accorded during the passage of the plates through the press.

We believe that Mr. Poynter, R. A., made it a labour of love to see these illustrations through the press, and when we add that Mr. Emery Walker practically supervised the technical handling of the process work, we have said enough to show that pictorially the book is all the most fastidious taste could demand.

1978. *To Janet Ross*

560 Zattere Venezia May 7 1892

My dear Janet

I find that I cannot send a fresh copy of the proofs of Chap. xii.[1] If you will use those you have, please write on the margin in red chalk, irrespective of what is already written there; or else write on the back of the slip opposite to the one you wish to remark upon. I.E. on back of 142 for slip 143.

I am anxious to get these observations; & I can assure you I shall give them due weight, &, wherever possible, alter what I have written in their sense.

My own belief about Michelangelo is that he was a man who had the highest degree of sensibility for male beauty, little or none for the female. If this be so, the particular quality of his passion in any special case, whether more or less platonic, does not signify. The fact must be insisted on, simply because it is the truth about his temperament & the explanation of his art & poetry. There is, however, no reason why one should needlessly shock people who dislike any allusion to sexual eccentricities.

Edward Poynter[2] RA is helping with the illustrations. I had a long & interesting letter from him about them.

I daresay it is odd to turn from Mrs Barbauld & her friends[3] to MAB & Febo di Poggio[4] & me. They are both of them very attractive sets of people.

The weather here is awful. We had half a fine day yesterday. Then came a superb storm on the lagoons—lightning in four parts of the horizon at the same time—in wh my gondola was nearly drowned. At night one of the crashingest thunder storms I ever lived through. And this morning the Canal of the Guidecca is like the English Channel in a gale.

Everyr aff

JAS.

---

1. The chapter in *Michelangelo* dealing with his homosexuality.
2. See L 1977.
3. Janet Ross had just published a new ed. (1892) of her *Three Generations of Englishwomen* (2 vols., 1888), which includes sketches of Mrs. Anna Letitia Barbauld (1743–1825), the writer-friend of Sara Taylor Austin, Mrs. Ross' grandmother. See L 1946.
4. Symonds explores the question of Michelangelo's friendship with the mysterious Febo di Poggio. See Ls 1880 and 1891 and *Michelangelo*, II, 154–59.

1979. *To Guido Biagi*

Venice May 31. 1892.

My dear Signor Biagi

I feel a brute for not having ever thanked you for the most valuable information contained in your last letter which I have used.

The only point I could not feel quite clear about was the date of Lodovico Buonarroti's death.[1] It does not appear to me certain that he died in 1533. If you could make me see your reasoning more clearly, I should be greatly obliged. There is still time to deal with the proofs.

My publisher John C. Nimmo, 14 King William Street, Strand, London W.C., would feel very grateful to you if you could let him have the negative you took of the autograph of the Sonnet to Giov: da Pistoja[2] on the Sistine. He could get a much better reproduction from the glass than from the proof. [Of course he would return the negative safely.

I will ask him about the wax models.[3] Could permission be got at once? The illustrations are being done, & time is a consideration.

A Prof: Wiel[4] here, who married an English lady, Alethea Lawley, sister of Lord Wenlock, wants to translate my Life of Michelangelo into Italian. He is a fairly good Italian writer. But I have not promised him permission. I thought I would consult you first. You may know of someone who would like to do it. The book would be easy to translate: for nearly half of it consists of letters, passages from Vasari & Condivi, Cellini, etc, with poems, all of wh would only have to be entered in Italian from printed books.

If you know of anyone you think better fit than Prof: & Mme Wiel to do the translation pray let me hear.

I am most sincerely yours

J A Symonds
I leave Venice   Am Hof
on Thursday.   Davos Platz
                                                        Svizzera

---

1. The problem of the dating begins in L 1937. In his published table (*Michelangelo*, II, Appendix) Symonds established the date of Lodovico's (Michelangelo's father's) death as 1534.

2. Symonds printed a facsimile of the sonnet in *Michelangelo*, II, facing 160, and his translation of it in I, 234–35. It is one of the most trenchant Michelangelo wrote; the subject is the discomfort he endured while painting the Sistine ceiling. Symonds' translation follows:

> I've grown a goitre by dwelling in this den—
>   As cats from stagnant streams in Lombardy,
>   Or in what other land they hap to be—
> Which drives the belly close beneath the chin:
> My beard turns up to heaven; my nape falls in,
>   Fixed on my spine: my breast-bone visibly
>   Grows like a harp: a rich embroidery
> Bedews my face from brush-drops thick and thin.
> My loins into my paunch like levers grind:
>   My buttock like a crupper bears my weight;
>   My feet unguided wander to and fro;
> In front my skin grows loose and long; behind,
>   By bending it becomes more taut and strait;
>   Crosswise I strain me like a Syrian bow:
>   Whence false and quaint, I know,
> Must be the fruit of squinting brain and eye;
> For ill can aim the gun that bends awry.
>   Come then, Giovanni, try
> To succour my dead pictures and my fame,
> Since foul I fare and painting is my shame.

Giovanni da Pistoja is identified by Elizabeth G. Holt, *Literary Sources of Art History* (1947), p. 201, n., as someone "known for his jocose and bizarre tone in verses addressed to Michelangelo."

3. Symonds used photographs of various wax models in his book. The preceding bracket is Symonds'.

4. Cavaliere Professore Taddeo Wiel (?–1920), principal of the Marciano Library, Venice. Alethea Lawley was second daughter of Beilby Richard Lawley-Thompson, 2nd Baron Wenlock (1818–80), a soldier and politician. We are unable to locate an Italian translation of *Michelangelo*.

1980. *To Janet Ross*

Venice 560 Zattere May 31 1892

My dear Janet

Thanks for the proofs.[1] I am delighted to hear how much you like the book now that you have read it all. The printing still goes on very slowly, & I shall have to work at it when I return to Davos.

We are going in a day or two i.e. Catherine, Katharine & I, leaving Madge with Contessa Pisani at Vescovana. Venice is getting hot, Scirocco heat.

I do not know whether Carlo Orsi[2] would care to come here again, as he did last Summer. If he does, he is very welcome. But I fancy that Venice did not suit him. I had given this mezzanino up, since having rented it 5 years (at £36 the year) I found that altogether in that time I had occupied it about 8 months. But after all I am going on. I cannot tear myself away from the people here.

I cannot give Biagi[3] advice about his lecture tour except that it is certain, if he goes to America, he will need a Barnum.[4] I should doubt that kind of lecture being very attractive in England. It always seems to me the English care next to nothing about Italian subjects. In connection with "Venice at Olympia,"[5] a lecture on Venetian life might have been successful. That show has sold off Brown's "Life on the Lagoons."

I wish I had seen Biagi on Shelley.[6] There is a considerable public of specialists who are sure to buy a new book on Shelley. So I should think it would be worth doing.

I sent you a copy of "The Author."[7] If you want a fair opinion about Chapman,[8] the agents of our society[9] are the people to go to.

There is a great thunderstorm blowing up—9 a.m.—& I am head-heavy with it.

Everyrs

JAS.

---

1. Proofs of Symonds' *Life of Michelangelo*.
2. See L 1901.
3. Dr. Guido Biagi, Prefect, Mediceo-Laurentian Library. See L 1869.
4. P. T. Barnum (1810–91), the great American showman; in other words, he would require someone to beat the drum on his behalf.
5. The title of Biagi's lecture.

6. Guido Biagi, *Gli Ultimi giorni di P. B. Shelley, con nuovi documenti,* etc. (1892; English trans., 1898).

7. The English quarterly, *The Author,* founded in 1890, edited by Sir Walter Besant (1836–1901), novelist, critic, and social reformer, and founder of the Society of Authors.

8. Possibly Dr. John Chapman (1822–94), the physician, author, and publisher and editor of the *Westminster Review.* But the reference is unclear.

9. See n. 7 above.

1981. *To [Margaret Symonds]*

Venice, June 1, 1892

[Dear Madge]

The business I began for X.[1] has been completed, and I am sanguine about it. It is my hope that I shall have saved a life from misery, and have given a man the sort of work which he is fitted for and which will yield him a good subsistence. I have taken infinite trouble, more than I ever take about things which concern myself. If I have done harm, it will not be for want of a good unselfish will.

I am tired with the strain of the transaction. Still it is honest hard work; not niggling about one's feelings or repining upon thoughts. It is contact with all sorts of men and minds.

[Incomplete]

---

1. Specific person unknown.

1982. *To Arthur Symons*

[Davos] June 13, 1892

[Dear Symons]

. . . . I am unfeignedly glad to hear that you wrote that review in the St James' Gazette.[1] It went straight to my heart, and made me do what I have only once before done: sit down and talk to the anonymous reviewer of a book of mine. After yielding to such an impulse, one always feels shy, as though one might have made a mistake. But to discover that one has only been approaching a man with whom one is already thoroughly in touch—that is charming.

. . . I am greatly interested in what you say about your Degas poems.[2] At Venice last month I tried my hand at nine studies (Verse) "In the Key of Blue," with a prose setting. Something in the line of impressionism. I have a friend there, who is a facchino [porter][3] of 20, and dresses in a costume of three modulated blues. He poses in my studies, in combination with other colours. Of things like this, I have always been doing plenty, and then putting them away in a box. The public thinks them immoral. You ought not to be attached to a young man in a blouse, and see how beautiful he is combined with blacks and reds and golds, etc. People criticize me severely for "A Page of my Life" and "Swiss Athletic Sports" in the book you reviewed.

I shall get hold of your article on Verlaine.[4] His work interests me, and his history. How charming "Pierrot" is. And such a line as "Et oh, les voix d'enfants chantant dans la coupole"[5] is a treasure for ever.

Apropos Verlaine, will you ask Havelock Ellis[6] if he would take a book from me on "Sexual inversion" for his Science Series? I have written and privately printed two essays on the phenomenon in ancient Greece and modern (contemporary) Europe. These could very well be fused; and the historical study of Greece is absolutely essential to the psychological treatment of the subject now. It is being fearfully mishandled by pathologists and psychiatrical professors, who know nothing whatsoever about its real nature. Sir Richard Burton in the year before his death was very urgent on me to publish these treatises. But I cannot see my way at present to doing so.

I envy you your life in the coulisses of the music halls. My own experience for some years in these mountains and on the Venetian lagoons, has been a comparatively free and happy one. The parlour has not a place in my existence. The study—sì. The tavern—sì. The wide world—sì. The parlour-nossignore! [no, sir!] . . .

I am coming to London in July.[7] Will you take me to see some acrobats? I hope I shall see you when I am in England. You are so good to me, and so understanding of the real man who has "never spoken out" yet, that I should like to tell you some things about myself wh cannot well be written.

[Incomplete]

---

1. The unsigned review, "Essays from The Alps," of OLSH appeared in *St. James' Gazette*, May 17, 1892. Symons copied it in its entirety on pp. 43–46 of his manuscript, "A Study of J. A. Symonds" (in Princeton University Library).

2. See "Décor de Théâtre," A. Symons, *London Nights* (1892).

3. Augusto Zanon.

4. "Paul Verlaine," in *The National Review*, XIX (1892) 501–15. Symons said of the poetry: "It is an art of impressionism—sometimes as delicate, as pastoral, as Watteau, sometimes as sensitively modern as Whistler, sometimes as brutally modern as Degas." One of the best chapters of Symons' *The Symbolist Movement in Literature* (1899) is on Verlaine.

5. See L 1882.

6. Symons and Ellis first met in 1886. Ellis was drawn to Symons after he had read Symons' essay Frédéric Mistral," *The National Review*, VI (1886), 659–70; on the strength of this review Ellis invited him to edit the Massinger volume for the "Mermaid" series. See Roger Lhombreaud, *Arthur Symons* (1964), pp. 34–36.

7. For an account of Symonds' meeting with Symons see the latter's "A Study of John Addington Symonds," *The Fortnightly Review*, CXXI (1924), 228–39.

1983. *To Margaret Symonds*

Davos June 16 [1892:KF]

My dearest Madge

We drove all the way yesterday from Münster to Davos, over the Ofener Berg & through long galleries of snow—thirty feet high but not roofed in—partly with the diligence & partly with galloping extra post horses. I am glad we got in last night, for this morning it is snowing heavily.

I am rather out of it here, for I have lost all my keys. Whether I left them behind me somewhere at Venice, or never took them away from here, or where they are, I know not. But I can get at no papers & no nothing.

Also I find my books etc in even worse confusion than when the oracle[1] was here. It is so bad that I shall not try to put it to rights except by degrees.

We had a delightful evening & morning at Verona. I enjoyed that greatly, & I must say that my dear Bündners[2] look very homely after all the beautiful people I have lately been seeing. I console myself by remembering that it is not particularly good for me to be always stirred up & impressed by living beauty.

On the whole the journey has been achieved without any very great discomfort. Your mother has been exceedingly difficult to live with, & her behaviour to me is something extraordinary: such an odd mixture of dead indifference with peevish disapproval. She has hardly spoken about anything except flowers. I always liked flowers, but it annoys me to see them placed far above all human interests. I am glad your mother has the resource, but it seems to become a monomania, & I really think it deadens her sympathies toward people.

Katharine is all right, & I think she enjoyed being with me, as I certainly did with her.

She had a good orgy of soldiers at Verona: dragoons, hussars, lancers, gunners, bersaglieri, & infantry without end. It was the anniversary of Garibaldi's death,[3] & the military must have been let loose in more than usual numbers & allowed to stay out later than usual.

I am beginning to think of that awful Lecture at Oxford.[4] Have not yet decided on the subject.

Remember me to the Contessa [Pisani]. Yr most aff father

JAS.

---

1. Probably the governess, Miss Hall.
2. His peasants.
3. Giuseppi Garibaldi, the Italian patroit, died June 2, 1882 (b. July 4, 1807).
4. "A Ceremonial Lecture on the Renaissance," delivered on July 29. See L 1984 to Havelock Ellis.

1984. *To Havelock Ellis*[1]

Am Hof, Davos Platz, Switzerland. June 20. 1892

Dear Mr. Ellis

I am glad to hear that Arthur Symons told you what I wrote to him about a book on "Sexual Inversion," and that you are disposed to consider it.

This, I feel, is one of the psychological and physiological questions which demand an open treatment at last. The legal and social persecution of abnormal natures requires revision. And enquiry may lead to some light being thrown upon that *terra incognita,* the causes of sexual differentiation.

I have written and privately printed two treatises on this subject. One deals with the phenomenon as recognised and utilized in Ancient Greece; the other with the same phenomenon, under adverse conditions, in the modern world.

It is absolutely necessary to connect those two investigations in any philosophical handling of the problem. The so-called scientific "psychiatrists" are ludicrously in error, by diagnosing as necessarily morbid what was

693

the leading emotion of the best and noblest men in Hellas. The ignorance of men like Casper-Liman, Tardieu, Carlier, Taxil, Moreau, Tarnowsky, Kraft-Ebing, Richard Burton[2] is incalculable, and is only equalled to their presumption. They not only do not know Ancient Greece, but they do not know their own cousins and club-mates. The theory of morbidity is more humane, but it is not less false, than that of sin or vice.

If it were possible for us to collaborate in the production of an impartial and really scientific survey of the matter, I should be glad. I believe it might come from two men better than from one, in the present state of public opinion. I would contribute the historical analysis (ancient Greece), which I am sure must form a basis for the study. You are more competent than I am to criticize the crudest modern medical and forensico-medical theories. But I might be of use here by placing at your disposition what I have already done in "getting up" the material, and in collecting data of fresh cases. We should have to agree together about the *legal* aspects of the subject. I should not like to promulgate any book, which did not show the absurdity and injustice of the English law. The French and Italian Penal Codes are practically right, though their application is some-times unfair. (Do not imagine that I want to be aggressive or polemical.)

I am almost certain that this matter will very soon attract a great deal of attention; and that it is a field in which pioneers may not only do excellent service to humanity, but also win the laurels of investigators and truth-seekers.

If you do not feel able to collaborate with me, I shall probably proceed to some form of solitary publication, and I should certainly give my name to anything I produced.

I agree with you that we had better meet and talk the matter over. I hope to be in England after July 15. I have to deliver a solemn Address upon the Renaissance at Oxford on the 29th.

I will send you the No. of *"Arch: di Psich:"*[3] which you lent me, if I can find it. But I understood you to say that it was a duplicate you did not want. Lombroso's article is worthless, and so I have chucked the No. aside. He only abstracted a little opuscule by *Parlagreco,*[4] which, if you like, I will send. Lombroso is entirely untrustworthy from the historico-critical point of view. What his own powers of observation are, I cannot judge. But he stuffs into his books at second hand whatever suits his purpose.

Very sincerely yours,

J.A.Symonds

Allow me to congratulate you on your marriage,[5] of which I had not heard. I hope it may prove as true a source of happiness as mine upon the whole has been to me.

J.A.S.

---

1. There are two versions, both typescripts by Katharine Furse, of this letter at Bristol University. The shorter was apparently a draft; the second, according to her, contains corrections in Havelock Ellis' writing and was obviously the one that Symonds sent and that we print. Since the substance of the letters is identical (the longer one is more expansive and stylistically smoother) we see no reason to publish both.

2. Except for Taxil, the works which follow Symonds included in "Books Consulted" in *A Problem in Modern Ethics*:

J. L. Casper and Carl Liman, *Handbuch der Gerichtlichen Medicin* (Berlin, 1889)

F. Carlier, *Les deux prostitutions* (Paris, 1889)

A. Tardieu, *Attentats aux moeurs* (Paris, 1878)

Leo Taxil, *La prostitution contemporaine* (Paris, 1884)

Paul Moreau, *Des aberrations du sens génétique* (Paris, 1887)

B. Tarnowsky, *Die krankhaften Erscheinungen des Geschlechtssinnes* (1887)

Richard von Krafft-Ebing, *Psychopathia sexualis* (1889)

Richard Burton, "Terminal Essay," *The Arabian Nights*, Vol. X (1885)

3. Vol. XI (1890) of the *Archivio di Psichiatria;* it contained Lombroso's essay on Michelangelo. Ellis had written to Symonds about the essay on July 10, 1891. See L 1898. Symonds paraphrased the argument of the work in *A Problem in Modern Ethics*. He used the German edition, he said, because of the translator's fine preface and notes.

4. See L 1977.

5. In 1891 Ellis married Edith Mary Oldham Lees (1861–1916), a long-time intimate of his and, after their marriage, an author: *Three Modern Seers* [1910] [James Hinton, Nietzsche, Edward Carpenter].

1985. *To Margaret Symonds*

Hofkellerei Chur June 26 1892

My dearest Madge

I wrote to you in a hurry before I left Davos on Friday.[1] I have written to Florian Buol, who is at Rheinfelden, asking him, as it seems he can do nothing, to get my previous correspondence with Birkenstädt back.[2] I shall probably put the whole into the hands of a lawyer.

This is that tall old tower, through the gate of wh one goes up from the town of Chur to the Cathedral & the Bishop's Court. I am living at the very top of it. My view extends over the whole town, the Vorder Rheinthal up to Tödi, the cliffs of Calanda, the lower Rheinthal down to Landquart, a bit of Scesaplana—& then on the back, the hills & dales toward Langnau & Churwalden. The Bp's garden, adapted into niches of the old grey walls—orchards, flowers, vegetables, elder trees in heavy-scented blossom—work in & out all round the place at our feet. We have two most magnificent Gothic halls to eat & lounge in, are vaulted, the other cieled with wood panelling, both mullioned in the windows with great twisted columns of stone. The tower forms an integral part of the old Bridle. Bishop's palace, & these State rooms, seem to have been arranged in it at a time when the Bishop made peace at last with the Burghers of Chur. In feudal days, it was the outpost of the ecclesiastical fathers against the city.

Yesterday (Saty) I made my brain wake me at 3.30 am, got up alone, & journeyed by the first train 4.20 a.m. to Zürich. I had business with the Italian Consul. He was away, & I could not see him till 2. After transacting my business it was too late for any but the last train. So I rolled slowly into Chur again at 10/30 p.m. Such a day! Stewy, soaking dull. If I had not had Zola's last great novel with me—La Débacle[3]—I don't think I could have got through.

Yr most affate JAS.

I told you my fixed date is to be at S. Moritz on the 10th & 11th. I may leave for London on the 15th. If well enough I must read an Address at Oxford on the 29th.

---

1. Letter not available.
2. The legal matter here involved is unknown to us. See L 1992.
3. Emile Zola's (1840–1902) *La Débacle* (1892), the second last of 20 vols. of a series called "Physiological History of a Family under the Second Empire."

1986. *To Henry Sidgwick*

(Chur), June 26 [1892]

[Dear Henry]

It was very rude of me not to answer your kind letters about coming to meet Arthur Balfour[1] at Cambridge. I should of all things like to know him. As a matter of fact there was no chance of my being in England so early.

But this did not excuse my neglect. It can only be explained by the extreme weariness which my book on Michel Angelo, dragging on through the final stages of printing, produced in me.

I hope to get to London about the 17th of July, and then to go down to Oxford, where I have promised to deliver an inaugural address on the hackneyed subject of the Renaissance. I have just succeeded in screwing the lecture out of my reluctant mind. I cannot say anything which I have not said before.

If I get to England, I shall try to stay there till well into autumn. I do not want to begin another book of any great importance, though the time will probably arrive when I shall begin the History of Graubünden. Meanwhile I am going to put a volume of Essays together, perhaps too another volume of verse! I have been touched and gratified by the decided sympathy shown for my more personal and autobiographical work on the "Swiss Highlands."

Lotta is in England, Madge with Countess Almorò Pisani[2] on the Paduan plain, living a semi-princely life on a huge estate, and enjoying herself. I am at the top of a mediæval tower in the Bishop's Palace at Chur, 150 ft. above the town, with all the Rhinethal at my feet. I am going back to Davos to-morrow.

[Incomplete]

---

1. Arthur James Balfour (1848–1930), 1st Earl of Balfour, philosopher and statesman, educated at Eton and at Trinity College, Cambridge; wrote *A Defence of Philosophical Doubt* (1879), *Foundations of Belief* (1895); M.P. for East Manchester, 1885–1906; entered the Cabinet, 1886. His sister, Mary, married Henry Sidgwick. See L 989.
2. See L 1717.

1987. *To Horatio Forbes Brown*

Davos, June 28 [1892]

[Dear Horatio]

I paid my bill (a mere flea-bite, 23 frs. 10 cts.,) and got off all right, with the knave carrying my portmanteau on his back. I had a pleasant journey, and fraternized with an Italian from Verona (elderly, handsome man, look of probity and prudence), who sells lemons about this land. I would not have mentioned him, however, except that he tells me he has set up a little shanty for the sale of fruit and liquors at Landquart, and that the wine comes to him direct (he says) from Valpolicella. It struck me you might like to taste Veronese in a strange land. You must ask for Francesco Campagnari: or "der Italianer mit der Weinschenke in dem Wald" [the Italian with the wine-tavern in the forest].

My portmanteau appears to have lost itself at Klosters. You will sympathize. It has my *Lecture* (on Culture)[1] in it; of which there is no copy; and all my keys. I am sanguine, however, that it will turn up.

The two $\left.{C \atop K}\right\}$atherines are gone up into the glaciers. So I find myself alone here, and am smoking an Indian cheroot from the Missionshaus Basel. It is not equal in flavour to Cotton's. But the 100 cost 8 frs. I intend to make a considerable purchase. As I promised, I will send you a sample or two down, of the best I discover, with prices. At present I have only lighted the first. A list of nine sorts ranges from frs. 4.50 to 8.50 *per* 100. *Est-ce possible?*

I enjoyed myself at Chur and am all the better for my two walks with you. Here it is too lonely for a healthy life, I get sunk in sloth—with *tempeste.*

I am enamoured of the Tower.[2] "You damned luxurious mountain goat," you, living there at 4.50 frs. *per diem,* when it costs another 15 frs. at least to carry on existence in a Zürich inn.

I wrote the fifth sonnet of my series coming up to-day. Shall I send you them? I think not. My verses must be very bad, because none of my friends like them. And I think the reason of this is, that they do not like my quality of feeling. I enjoy your verses,[3] and Pinkie's,[4] etc., although of course I know that they are only mediocre as art. In the region of writing we are thinking of now, all turns on personal flavour. *N'importe.* I will go on writing, because I am sure that I love, in my way, and love finds a voice of some sort. I have no pretension "to dine late." Has proud, poor Landor ever really dined at all?[5] Ghosts do not dine. He hardly in fame even.

I will send you some new photos of myself, unbearded. One is decidedly good. It has the merit of psychological veracity, this photograph.

The world is worth living in. How pure the air is to-day, how light, how keen the sun, how tender, wonderfully green the meadows and the little boughs! Passionately beautiful our world, and all that moves in it; and blessed be every man and child. Only we must go—just when we have learned to love the whole dear thing, and to take its disagreeables calmly.

[Incomplete]

1. Published in *The New Review*, VII (1892), 105–15, and in *In the Key of Blue* (1893).

2. See L 1986: "I am at the top of a medieval tower in the Bishop's Palace at Chur. . . ."

3. Brown's volume of poems, *Drift*, was not published until 1900.

4. Percy Pinkerton. See L 1407. These may have been manuscript poems or *Galeazzo: A Venetian Episode with Other Poems* (1886)

5. Walter Savage Landor (1775–1864), poet and prose writer of intractable temper who was removed from Rugby, rusticated from Oxford (1794), and alienated from his family; friend of Robert Southey, Robert Browning, and Swinburne; lived in various places on the Continent; wrote a long poem (*Gebir*, 1798) a tragedy (*Don Julian*, 1812), and short poems; best known today for his *Imaginary Conversations* (5 vols., 1824, 1828, 1829).

1988. *To Charles Kains-Jackson*

Am Hof, Davos Platz, Switzerland. June 29. 1892.

Dear Mr Jackson

I have taken the liberty of telling M: Edwin Brugger,[1] a young Swiss, whom I like & who is I think a good specimen of Swiss looks, to call upon you on a Wednesday in Chancery Lane. He talks French.

Here is a photograph of myself, just made, & also one of the "Young Achilles"[2] lifting a bolb stone.

I cannot send you any of "In the Key of Blue"[3] because it is going to form part of a vol of essays to be published by Elkin Matthews,[4] who wants it to appear there fresh.

Will Tuke[5] be in England this summer? Our friend H F Brown, with whom I have been living in a feudal tower above the town of Chur lately, says that since Tuke took to living in the little hut— σπιτι μικρος, or something of that sort—with his Alexandros, he has heard nothing of him.

Every yrs J. A. Symonds

I hope to be in London about the 17th July, at 18 Cowley Street Westminster.

1. Symonds first mentioned Brugger to Jackson in L 1975. See also L 1903.

2. Probably Edwin Brugger.

3. Symonds refers to the title essay itself, a series of sketches describing Augusto Zanon in varying shades of natural and artificial light.

4. See L 1989.

5. Henry Scott Tuke, the painter (see L 1838), returned to England from his Italian visit in late July. Tuke was Horatio Brown's guest in Venice during part of March and April, and then went on to Corfu, Rome, and Naples.

1989. *To Elkin Mathews*[1]

Am Hof, Davos Platz, Switzerland. June 30. 1892.

Dear Sir

Mr Percy E Pinkerton[2] writes me that you would like to publish a vol: of my essays. I have corresponded with him on the subject. He says that he has communicated with you.

I should like to hear from you personally, & to know whether you approve of the list of articles which I suggested.

The copy for the book is ready to be sent; & I shall have no objection, if you think the list too long, to drop one or two of the numbers.

I should like to call the book: "In the Key of Blue, with Other Pieces."[3]

The essay wh gives the title, comes in the body of the book. But it is quite new, & tunes the whole.

As for terms, I read what Mr Pinkerton wrote me on this subject. I should like, however, to hear your own views.

I hope to be in London after the middle of next month.

Believe me very faithfully yours

John Addington Symonds
Elkin Mathews esq

Prospectus for *Essays in a Key of Blue*

1) *In the Key of Blue.* (Unpublished)
   A study in prose & verse of the effects of blue in the dress of a Venetian Facchino.
2) *Among the Euganean Hills.* (Fortnightly)
   Descriptive Article.
3) *An Altar Piece by Tiepolo.* (Hobbyhorse)
   Criticism & Description of a Venetian Picture

4) *Platonic & Dantesque Ideals of Love*. (Contemporary).
   A psychological study in prose.
5) *Edward Cracroft Lefroy*. (New Review)
   Account of his life & poems.
6) *La Bête Humanine* (Fortnightly)
   Critique of Zola's Idealism.
7) *Old Norman Songs*. Translations of popular poems, with a prose setting.
8) *Clifton and a Lad's Love*. Prose & Verse written about 30 years ago, & put together recently. Autobiographical & Inedited.
9) *A Somersetshire Homestead*. Description of Sutton Court, my brother-in-law Sir Edward Strachey's place. Inedited.

10) *Culture. Its Meaning & its Uses* (New Review).
11) *Notes on Fletcher's Valentinian* (Fortnightly).
12) *On the Lyrism of the Elizn Drama* (Fortnightly).
13) *On Lyrics from Elizn Songbooks* (Inedited)

   I should be glad to have your careful opinion about Nos. 1 and 8. I am not sure whether certain things in No 1 may be inappropriate for publication, & whether the whole of No. 8 is not too immature.

If any of the essays are discarded I should recommend the omission of the last four. *10. 11. 12. 13.*

J A Symonds

---

1. Elkin Mathews (1851–1921), bookseller and publisher, Vigo Street, London; published editions of various English poets of the 1890's; with John Lane (see L 2061) formed Bodley Head publishing house, the partnership lasting from 1892–94; publisher of the Garland and Vigo Cabinet Series of poets—W. B. Yeats, Laurence Binyon, Robert Bridges, John Masefield, J. M. Synge, W. H. Davies, James Joyce, and Ezra Pound. A collection of Mathews' papers, including some 500 letters, manuscripts, and books, is owned by the University of Reading library.

2. See L 1407.
3. See L 1982.

1990. *To Margaret Symonds*

Am Hof, Davos Platz, Switzerland. July 1892. Evening.

[Dear Madge]

Since I wrote to you this morning, your letter to your mother has come in, with the account of your Sunrise experience on Venda. I think that finely written and in a solid and yet glowing style, free entirely from vularity. It will be well worth preserving and publishing.

When you come back here, which I hope you will do immediately, you should settle down to adjust all these memories and put together the impressions you have already given in letters.

I think you ought to be able to produce a book with some title like "Harvest Weeks on a Venetian Farm."[1]

You would begin, as the Contessa wishes, with an account of Vescovana and the Pisani. Then you can proceed to all your personal experiences in the form of what I call "vignettes." Larger and smaller sketches from your life during the last months.

It requires a certain delicacy of touch to finish these things off well, and to begin the next. But I want you to try the genre, out of the abundance of your materials. Many subjects (gleaning e.g.) will occur to you for separate treatment, when you are alone here.

I expect you to produce a book. Not a pretentious one. But a pleasant and vivacious one.

I enclose a note from an old gentleman who seems to have liked your work in The Swiss Highlands.[2]

[Incomplete]

---

1. The work became *Days Spent on a Doge's Farm* (1893).
2. *OLSH.*

1991. *To Guido Biagi*

Am Hof, Davos Platz, Switzerland. July 2. 1892

Dear Signor Biagi

I talked to Mr Fisher Unwin[1] at Venice about those illustrations to Dante,[2] & told him I would write a short preface. I do not like much having to fix my own Remuneration. The sort of sum, however, wh people give me for this kind of work is about £10. I should like to have copies of the prints, & also your own Introduction. The latter is quite indispensable to me, as I should be sorry to repeat anything wh you have said.

I have been waiting to get a decided answer from my publisher about an Italian translation of my Michelangelo.[3] At first he was rather adverse to the project. However, he now writes: "There is no harm whatever in its being translated by the Contessa Rasponi,[4] if she is willing to leave the arrangements for its publication with me." Will you communicate this to her? Should she really care to do the work, I should be glad to hear.

I am informed by Mrs Ross that you are appointed Capo di Gabinetto[5] by Martini.[6] I congratulate you, & I am glad to think that your influence will be felt in the Ministry of Instruction. I hope it does not mean, however, that you will leave Florence for good.

I am still in difficulties about Michelangelo's Model for the Cupola of St Peter's.[7] *All* the eyewitnesses say there are only 2 vaults; but Gotti's plans show 3 vaults, so do also those of a German architect Durm.[8]

Would it be possible for you to get from Gotti the *photographs* he says he had? Very sincerely yrs

J A Symonds.

---

1. Fisher Unwin (1848–1935), the London publisher.

2. *Dante: Illustrations to the Divine Comedy of Dante . . . by the Flemish Artist Jo. Stradanus,* 1587. . . , introduced by Doctor Guido Biagi and with a preface by Symonds (1892). See L 2051.

3. See L 1979.

4. Possibly Countess Rasponi-Bonanzo, who as Princess Donna Luisa, daughter of Don Marco, the 5th Duke of Fiano, in 1882 married Count Carlo Rasponi-Bonanzo and lived in Rome.

5. Head of the department.

6. Ferdinando Martini (1841–1928), secretary-general of the Ministry of Public Education (1884–92).

7. For Symonds on the problem of the cupola see his *Michelangelo,* II, 238–44, and 2nd ed., 1893, I-xxi-ii. He concludes that "Michelangelo himself abandoned the third or semi-spherical vault, and that the cupola, as it exists, ought to be ascribed entirely to his conception. It is, in fact, the only portion of the basilica which remains as he designed it." See also Ls 1994 and 1995.

8. See Aurelio Gotti, *Vita di Michelangelo Buonarroti* (2 vols., 1875), II, 136 and Joseph Durm, *Die Domkuppel in Florenz und die Kuppel der Petruskirche in Rom* (1887). On Gotti, see L 1876. Joseph Durm (1837–1919), German architect and archaeologist. His *Die Baukunst der Renaissance in Italien* was part of his massive *Handbuch der Architektur.*

1992. *To Margaret Symonds*

Am Hof, Davos Platz, Switzerland. July 2. 1892

My dearest Madge

Birkenstädt[1] has become so very troublesome that I went to see him today, & had a long conversation. Of course he is quite mad, & his madness consists in thinking that I have had him under my malign influence during the last four years. He describes it as "Mystificiren, Mystification." But he cannot give any clear account of what the matter is. Only, in some way or another, you are mixed up with it. I told him if he went on annoying us, I should put his correspondence into the hands of my lawyer. He replied he would like nothing better; for then he could explain his case & defend himself before the public. But, he added, it would be better to settle the matter in a friendly way if possible, & that one thing would satisfy him: that is to get from you a couple of lines to say you are quite ignorant. I wish you then to copy out what I will enclose. Use the Vescovana paper with the Como Ducale, & get the Contessa [Pisani] to witness your signature adding her rank etc. This cannot compromise you, & it may end the persecution. I fear it will not, but it may. Let the Contessa read this.

Everyrs

J A Symonds.

---

1. See L 1985.

1993. *To Henry Graham Dakyns*

Have you read a volume of Sonnets called "Love in Earnest"? It is written by a Schoolmaster in love with a boy called Ernest.[1]

Am Hof, Davos Platz, Switzerland. July 2. 1892

My dear Graham

This is only to tell you that I am coming to England in the middle of July. I have to give an Address at Oxford on the 29th.

I should be glad to know when it would suit you for me to come to see you. Naturally I have to sketch out plans, since I must be in Cumberland & the South of Scotland on the one hand, in Cornwall Devonshire & Somersetshire on the other, & in many places besides. I hope to be in England about 2 months. Short time enough considering all I ought to do—desire to do, in it.

My Venetian, Angelo [Fusato], will be with me.

Let me know your plans, so that, if I cannot find you at Haslemere, as I should like, I may light upon you somewhere else.

With me life burns ever more intense, as my real strength wanes, & my days decrease. It seems to me sometimes awful: the pace at which I live in feeling—inversely to the pace at which my self is ebbing to annihilation.

I shall have a great deal to say to you, if only it can be said. I never seem to have lived until quite lately; & just when the times are out of joint for self-externalizing life, I seem drawn into it.

It is true I go on writing books, & even poems. But literature has long since lost for me reality of interest.

One reads certainly. Copious reading fills the vacuum which remains when feeling & sensation are abeyant.

Yours with true affection

JAS

---

1. John Gambril Francis Nicholson (1866–1931), *Love in Earnest and Ballads, Sonnets and Lyrics* (1892). Nicholson, who taught at Rydal Mount School, Colwyn Bay, was a school-friend of Charles Kains-Jackson, and had an uneasy friendship with Frederick William Rolfe, Baron Corvo. Nicholson later published *A Garland of Ladslove* (1911), a duodecimo volume of verse, and a novel, *The Romance of a Choir-Boy* (privately printed, 1916).

1994. *To Horatio Forbes Brown*

Am Hof, Davos, July 3 [1892]

[Dear Horatio]

I do not want to send you any more of my verses. I can always tell you what I think. But verse is form. I hope this will not prevent you from sending me what you write. About twenty years ago I used to show my verse productions to Henry Sidgwick and F. [W. H.] Myers. I discovered that they were curious about them on account of what I said, but did not like the form. So I stopped doing so, and there has been no interruption of the freest closest exchange of thought and feeling. Henry is only a little plaintive when "Vagabunduli Libellus" appears, and I do not send it him, and will not discuss it with him. But he has made the situation. It is easy enough to do without a man's sympathy, but difficult to go on seeking it and not getting it.

Like many better men than myself, I suppose that I have fallen between two stools in art. My own dearest, nearest mode of self-expression is verse, and the indulgence of that has interfered to some extent with the development of my power as a prose-writer. But it is clear, I think now, that nature did not endow me with the poet's gifts. At least not with the gift of making my song acceptable even to my comrades. When that is said, the case is desperate! And if I must sing, I will sing to myself and God, not to you and Henry and F. M. It does not matter a bit. We are all going to die soon, and we can all love each other apart from words. I notice that even the omnivorous Ronald [Gower] does not catch on at my verse. What a funny thing it is to be so eager for sympathy in what apparently one cannot get the trick of, and yet, after all, to feel sincerely that the matter is one of real indifference! Life, life, is the thing. I believe the most vital forms of character are in perpetual antagonisms.

July 4.

A long letter came last night from Dr. Durm[1] about the Cupola (of St. Peter's). It convinces me that he is right, and that the third inner shell *is* in the model. I have this morning rewritten the chapter. The whole thing is still very strange. For Stillman[2] keeps sending me excellent testimonies to the contrary. It shows how difficult it is to see accurately, unless you measure by millimetres. My life is pretty full of incidents in this small way. It is such a relief to have no huge piece of literary work on hand. And yet I liked to get back to M. A. B. this morning.

I go on writing to you. I wonder whether I shall send the whole budget, or put it in a drawer! There was also a *Turnfest* [gymnastic competition] in my *Verein* [club] yesterday at the Waldhaus, part of which I saw. Fairly good.

July 5.

I am glad you had such a good time at Lenz. Zola's book[3] is grand but fatiguing. I agree with you about the passage on friendship. The ending is exceedingly dramatic.

[Incomplete]

---

1. See L 1991.
2. William J. Stillman (1828–1901), American painter, journalist, and art critic,

who for his style of painting (influenced at first-hand by Rossetti and Millais, and by Ruskin and Turner) was known as "the American Pre-Raphaelite"; during the American Civil War, United States consul at Rome; founder and co-editor of *Crayon: A Journal Devoted to the Graphic Arts, and the Literature Related to Them* (1855–56); correspondent of the *London Times* in Rome (1886–98), when Symonds was at work on Michelangelo. In *Michelangelo* (2nd ed., 1893), I, xxi, Symonds acknowledged Stillman's aid. See W. J. Stillman, *The Autobiography of a Journalist* (2 vols., 1901) *passim.* and David H. Dickason, *The Daring Young Men: The Story of the American Pre-Raphaelites* (1953), Chaps. IV and V.

3. *La Débacle* (1892).

1995. *To Margaret Symonds*

Davos July 7. 1892 Thursday.

My dearest Madge

I am alone here, & have been so since Monday. Your mother & K are at the Au.[1] They may come back today, & possibly Aunt Char too. I hope she will, for I am bound to go to the Turnfest at S. Moritz on Saturday. Lord Ronald Gower is coming all the way from Viareggio, near Pisa, on purpose to be present. Well, I have finished my Inaugural Address for Oxford.[2] It is very carefully composed. The question of the Cupola of S. Peter's is at last settled—against me & all the eyewitnesses who have inspected the model— by a certain German architect called Dr Durm.[3] He published a book on the subject, & he has written me a letter wh convinces me against my own eyesight. The odd thing is that a Sign: Volpini,[4] who was Keeper of the Models in the Vatican for 30 years, supports the view wh I originally took, that there are only 2 vaults (not 3 as Durm maintains) in MAB's model. The printing of the book is not yet finished. Meanwhile I have put together another short vol of essays, wh will be called "In the Key of Blue, & Other Pieces."[5]

I am rather melancholy & not at all well. I have quite lost my power to eat. Something is very wrong with my inside. Enclosed is one of my new photographs, not the best I think, but I have got none of the others.

I retouched what you wrote about Fishing, made K copy it, & sent it to the PMG.[6] They are so taken up in England with the Election[7] now that I hardly think they will attend to it. I liked it on the whole, though it is slight & incoherent. It has, what you always give, a great sense of enjoyment.

I find the chief fault in what you write, especially in your letters, to be

707

a certain self-important bustle. This strikes one as vulgar, at least as wanting in distinction. Pure egotism is different. No artists can keep themselves out of their work. Yet there is a way of being extremely egotistical—as in Shakspere's Sonnets, Heine's Lieder, De Musset's Les Nuits—wh has not this disagreeable quality of self-importance. I believe what I am now taking you to task for, comes in great measure from your not being simple enough in style. Castiglione in "Il Cortigiano,"[8] a book worth yr reading if the Contessa [Pisani] has it, says with absolute truth that no one can be a perfect gentleman if he has the least affectation. The affectation with you is not in thought or feeling, but in expression. If you remember what you wrote lately to K[atharine] about her letters, you will know the sort of style I call self-important, bustling, affected, ill-bred.

I wonder whether you really mean what you wrote your mother, that you would like to settle down in England. It seems to me that you have so formed yourself to enjoy what is exceptional that the humdrum life either of English Country or English town would make you restless. I do not know;—but I am willing to further any schemes for the good of the family. I suppose they will be discussed with Aunt Char. Little good can come of that, however; for after all, we have to suit ourselves, & no outsider can do anything to help us.

Your mother had some notion of shutting up Am Hof, & taking a really good apartment in Rome, setting up a carriage there, & going with you into Society, this next winter. To that I should have no objection. Only I doubt whether she will like going to balls!

When I am in London I hope to stop with E. P. Warren.[9] I shall be able to see, I think, whether there is anything on his side about Lotta. I wish some thing could come of that, for I am sure he is a good fellow & hope he is going to be prosperous.

It is not likely now that we shall meet before I go to England. I did not want to hurry you away from what you so keenly enjoy, merely to say a few words of affection. I am depressed, however, & filled with apprehension —due to being out of health partly. But as Achilles says in Troilus & Cressida:

> My mind is troubled like a fountain stirred,
> And I myself see not the bottom of it.[10]

My love to the Contessa & Don Antonio [the priest].

Everyr

JAS.

I am going to try to get Birkenstädt[11] removed. Florian Buol says the Landammann [Swiss cantonial president] will do nothing. I must employ a lawyer—A. Planta V: Reichenau.[12]

---

1. Near Zürich.
2. Delivered on July 29.
3. See Ls 1991 and 1994.
4. Information regarding Salvatore Volpini is extremely scarce. According to Dr. D. Redig de Campos, of the Vatican Museums and Galleries, Salvatore Volpini was a nephew of Mgr. Volpini, custodian of the Vatican Museums under Pope Leo XIII: "C'était un de ces dilettanti très fréquents à celte époque." Mgr. Volpini carried the title "capo custode dell'Apportamento Borgia." He apparently wrote a description of these rooms (2nd ed., 1897) and translated Catullus into Italian.
5. Published in 1893.
6. See L 2003.
7. The Liberals, under Gladstone, defeated Lord Salisbury's Conservatives, largely over the issue of Home Rule for Ireland.
8. Baldassare Castiglione (1478–1529), Italian author and statesman, known for his *Libro del cortegiano* (1518), the book of the courtier, setting forth the whole duty of the gentleman. English trans., 1561.
9. See L 1943.
10. III, iii, ll. 314–15. See L. 1899.
11. See Ls 1985 and 1992.
12. Alfred von Planta (1857–1922), a member of an old Grisons family originating in the Engadine (Zuoz) and acting as leaders in Swiss government and administration; author of *Beitrag zur Kenntniss der deutsch-schweizerischen Hypothekarrechte* . . . (1883). See also L 1971. Reichenau is 10 miles south-east of Chur.

1996. *To Havelock Ellis*

Am Hof, Davos Platz, Switzerland. July 7 1892

My dear Mr Ellis,

I was very glad to receive your letter of the 1st and to learn from it that you think we might do something together about Sexual Inversion.[1] Had I know that you were seriously contemplating a special study of Sex phenomena, I should not have written to you in the way I did. I should have felt that to propose anything like collaboration would be an impertinence. However, now that you have met me so kindly, I look forward to discussing the subject with you and seeing whether anything can be done. I feel that, in a matter of this sort, two names, and two men of different sorts would be stronger as attracting public opinion than any one alone of any sort, and also would be more likely to get a wide and serious attention.

With regard to "abnormal" and "morbid." I think sex-inverts can only be called "abnormal" in so far as they are in a minority, i.e. form exceptions to the large rule of sex. I doubt, from what I have observed in the matter, that sexual inversion is ever and by itself morbid. It may often of course co-exist with morbidity and I concede that it is liable to result from vicious habits which injure the nervous organism—like masturbation after the age of puberty—but not nearly as much as people imagine. One great difficulty is to estimate how much it is a matter of habit: that is to say, to what extent the sexual instinct is indifferent, and liable to be swayed one side or another by custom and surrounding. What I know about the Greeks and Persians (I know little about Eskimos) and what I observe in Italy, leads me to attach very great influence to custom and example: but the more one ascribes to such causes, the less can one talk on morbidity.

I am angry with the English Medical Psychologists, who will not discuss the subject. Especially with Tuke,[2] whom I know as an intimate old friend of my father, I have talked to him about this matter, and found him unscientifically prejudiced to the last degree.

I think it may be worth while to send you what I wrote some years ago about Greek Love. I have prepared it for republication with additions, alterations and translations of the Greek quotations. But it is more convenient not to send these extra MSS. The copy I do send belonged (as you will observe) to Sir Frederick[3] Burton, and was returned to me by Lady Burton after his death. Please let me have it again some time.

In my view, no survey of Sexual Inversion is worth anything without an impartial consideration of its place in Greek Life.

I think I will also send you what I have printed about the Modern Problem. I have not seen Moll's[4] book, you mention, but will instantly order it.

The legal state of things in England is very simple. Any act of "gross indecency" between males, in private or in public, is a Misdemeanour punishable with two years imprisonment and hard labour. Connection per anum, with or without consent, is a penal servitude for life.

Very truly yours

JAS

---

1. See L 1984.
2. Daniel Hack Tuke. See L 1838.
3. The typescript is in error. He means Richard. See L 1493.

4. Albert Moll, *Die conträre Sexualempfindung mit Benutzung amtlichen Materials* . . . with a foreword by Dr. R. von Krafft-Ebing (1891). Moll (1862–?), German psychiatrist, wrote *Der Hypnotismus* (1889) and various works on occultism.

1997. *To Margaret Symonds*

[Davos] [July 8, 1892: KF]

[Dear Madge]

I am impatient to see the photograph of beautiful Carbotte.[1] When I was your age, & for a long time after, I contented myself (as you say you do) with seeing & admiring people, entering my imagination into sympathy with their lives. I now want to love them also. I do not much believe in knowing anybody, even oneself. But I am sure one can love immensely. And I love beauty with a passion that burns the more I grow old. I love beauty above virtue, & think that nowhere is beauty more eminent than in young men. This love is what people call aesthetic with me. It has to do with my perceptions through the senses; & does not affect my regard for duty, principle, right conduct. I know well enough that there are more important things in the universe than beauty. But there is nothing I was born to love more. (With my soul & heart I love you more than the world. With my aesthetic perceptions I love physical perfection.)

I hope to go to S. Moritz tomorrow. Your mother & I came back last night. Aunt Char[lotte] comes today.

My soul is wrapped up in some cloud of inexplicable gloom & dread. I dream at night of ruined houses on the verge of black precipices, along the broken roofs & parapets of which I wander. I cannot eat.

JAS.

What vexes me is the thought that not only am I growing old, but that I have some unconquerable malady to face—death in fact is near. My soul keeps whispering this to my spiritual ear.

And before I go hence & see the lovely earth no longer, I want to do so much still. I want to write my History of Graubünden, to publish my work on Sexual Aberrations, & to get my Autobiography finished.

I do not think I should have written so candidly to you as I have done under this cover, were I not starting soon for a journey to England with this Fear upon me. I regard you, & always have regarded you, more as a comrade than a daughter. And I say now to you, as we shall not meet before you leave Italy, & I leave Switzerland, what I say to no one else.

Think well of me, when all is over. I have been a very unhappy man, as you will find out if you read the history of my life. But I have tried to be a brave one, & to work.

---

1. Unidentified.

1998. *To Janet Ross*

Am Hof, Davos Platz, Switzerland. July 8. 1892.

My dear Janet

I ought to have written. But I am dissolute & idle, & have been chumming with an acrobat—a glorious creature, who lives in a van, & risks his life every night on a trapeze 100 feet nearer to the stars than we are.

You will do my little mezzanino much honour, if you & Lina [Duff-Gordon] go there. I am sorry to say you will not find Angelo. I take him to England on the 16th or 17th. But his wife Maria will do for you, & procure a good gondolier if you want to set one up.

Her address is: Maria Fusato Dietro gli Incurabili

Dorsoduro 548

Venezia.

I am going to S. Moritz tomorrow for a Turnfest [gymnastic competition], & when I come back, shall get up steam for England. I have to give an Inaugural Address at Oxford on "The Renaissance"![1]

Everyrs.

JAS.

I will put a cheque into the envelope if I do not forget—for oil & book.

---

1. The address was delivered on July 29.

1999. *To Henry Graham Dakyns*

Am Hof, Davos Platz, Switzerland. July 14, 1892

My dear Graham

Thanks for your letter. It is very kind of you to leave matters like that about my visit. Till I get to England, I really do not know how I shall arrange my time after I leave Oxford. There seem to be so many things to do. I am first engaged to go north with Lord Ronald Gower[1] & to stay at Naworth [Castle],[2] Glen,[3] & Carlisle. But I think I shall be back in London about the middle of August, & that would be the best time to come to you.

Katharine got Tennyson's pastoral.[4] She has been severely rated by me for not writing to you. I read the play, & thought the lyrics very sweet. This is the 10th letter of the morning, & there are 20 more. So I must end.

Ever yrs

JAS

---

1. See L 1612.
2. At Brampton, Cumberland; the second county seat of the Earl of Carlisle, the first being Castle Howard.
3. Seat of Sir Charles Tennant.
4. *The Foresters, Robin Hood and Maid Marian* (written in 1881 but first published and produced in New York, 1892).

2000. *To Margaret Symonds*

Am Hof, Davos Platz, Switzerland. July 16. 1892.

My dearest Madge.

We had a very good time at St Moritz. I got there with 15 of the Davos Turners last Saty (this day week), & found Ronald Gower just arrived. On Sunday was the Fest, when Johannes [Ammann][1] shone forth in glory & threw the strongest men about the field like sacks of flour. Monday Ronald & I spent in walking. On Tuesday we came together to Wiesen, & on Wednesday morning here. He has gone this morning. I like him very much indeed. He grows on acquaintance into something really good & nice. He made an excellent impression on yr mother & Aunt Char. They both really liked him.

I am going off, if Dr [Florian] Buol lets me, on Tuesday, & shall travel straight to London. My best address there is

Athenaeum Club
Pall Mall S.W.

Your last long letter reached me in due course. I am sorry I depressed & saddened you so much, & that you hate my photograph. It is easy enough, if

I choose, to let my mangy grizzled beard grow again. Only I think I am better without it. What you do not like is the look of spiritual fatigue, of being haunted internally, wh my face in a photograph carries. I cannot help that. I was born with a temperament wh has given me immense worry & distress all through my life. It is, luckily, mixed up with great capacity for enjoyment & being merry.

I do not feel easy about my health. But no doctors can help much. Who can minister to a mind diseased? Neither divine nor physician. And the mind corrodes its organ, the nervous system, with me. Of rest there is no possible question left. I am glad to be having Angelo with me on the journey. There is no strain in his society, & he takes off the strain of solitude. Otherwise he will be of no great use to me, & some trouble.

I am not at all sorry that you made a formal statement before an Italian lawyer.[2] Unfortunately, I shall not have time to place the document & other papers in Planta's[3] hands, before I go to England. The Landammann [Swiss cantonial president] here will not return B's letters or some correspondence he had with B's family. The latter, it seems, are not ill-disposed to have the man removed, if it can be done without expense & trouble to themselves. It is on *them* I think that we must act.

As yr Aunt Char says, the bother might happen anywhere. She told your mother of the far worse annoyance to wh Miss Lefevre is subjected at Oxford by a crazy & vindictive woman.[4]

You will get on right in literature, if you keep your eye upon being sober & at the same time keenly sensitive to impressions. I like your style better in its subdued moods.

The affection you express for me is very dear & sweet to my heart. I really do not think it would have been worth bringing you back for a few last hours with me before I leave. We must hope to meet again, well & in good spirits. I will write to you from England. To hang about there & see crowds of people is for me inevitable.

Everyr most loving father

JAS.

---

1. L 1748.
2. Over the Birkenstädt affair, see L 1985.
3. See L 1995.
4. Madeleine Shaw Lefevre (1835–1915), daughter of Sir John George Shaw-Lefevre (1797–1879); first principal of Somerville College, Oxford, 1879–89. Her sister

Rachael Emily, in 1865, had married one of Symonds' friends, Arthur Gordon. See L 2003.

2001. *To Margaret Symonds*

Am Hof, Davos Platz, Switzerland. July 18 1892

My dearest Madge

Your mother & I both think you had better come home soon, as soon as possible in fact.

The reasons are many. Katharine would be better with you. She spends her time almost wholly with those Sickly Days. The part here will be very small when I am gone. And lastly, the cholera is coming. It would be a pity for you to be caught by quarantines.

I start tomorrow. I do not know why I am glad to go, because I do not see why I should be better off there than here. But I have been so wretched lately that any change seems promising. I cannot eat, & have perpetual diarrhoea, & sleep only 3 hrs at night. I don't know what the matter is. It seems to be a chronic irritation of the muccous membrane, wh keeps me in continuous discomfort.

I hope to travel with Aunt Char & Angelo from Basle. Perhaps also Lord Ronald & his servant Alfonso. What a party, if we all meet on the Basle platform!

I mean to go first to E. P. Warren's. If I find out anything about his feelings, I will inform you. I don't believe there is anything, except esteem.

Did my silver cow reach Vescovana? I should not be surprised if I were tempted to buy some old silver things in London. I like them so much.

I have taken to writing in the top spare-room, East. It is very pleasant, & I feel my head rested by not being in the rooms where I have worked & felt & suffered so much.

The last proofs of MAB were sent off yesterday; & I am going to pack up the Ms (wh has been bound in 3 big volumes) to present to Mr Nimmo [the publisher]. He seems glad to have it.

English address   Athenaeum Club
                  Pall Mall S.W.

for yours ever

JAS.

V

*Final Visits to England
and Rome
1892–1893*

2002. *To Horatio Forbes Brown*

[London, July, 1892]

[Dear Horatio]

I hope to be in England about two months. Short time enough, considering all I ought to do—desire to do—in it. With me life burns ever more intense, as my real strength wanes and my days decrease. It seems to me sometimes awful—the pace at which I live in feeling—inversely to the pace at which myself is ebbing to annihilation.

I shall have a great deal to say to you if only it can be said. I never seem to have lived until quite lately; and just when the times are out of joint for self-externalising life, I seem drawn into it. It is true I go on writing books, and even poems. But literature has long since lost for me reality of interest. One reads certainly, and copious reading fills the vacuum which remains when feeling and sensation are abeyant.

[Incomplete]

2003. *To Margaret Symonds*

[London] Sunday July 24 1892

Dearest Madge

I think it probable you may have left Vescovana. But I risk a letter.

I left Davos alone on Tuesday, saw Brown at Landquart, met Ronald Gower at Wiesen, and lastly Aunt Char at Basel. Angelo did not turn up, & there was no news of him. So I let the others (ill-assorted couple) go on their way to London, & slept rather forlornly in the Schweizerhof. Angelo arrived next morning, & endeavoured to explain how it was he had to sleep at Luzern, although he left Milano by the Express wh reaches Basel at 7.10. I don't understand it, but I do believe he was very anxious to join me, if only because he is so lost in foreign lands.

719

We arrived in London duly at 5 p.m. on Thursday, & the first thing I bought at the Victoria Station was PMG, & the first thing in it wh caught my eye was your article on Fishing.[1]

I think I told you that I regard your letter about Venda[2] as one of the best things you have written, quite the best I think.

Life goes very fast here, & it is nonsense to tell me not to get tired. I live en rapport with far too many sorts of people, & keep up far too diverse threads of sentiment & thinking, to be ever tranquil.

A long morning of business with Nimmo [the publisher]: a luncheon with Lord Lorne,[3] R[onald] G[ower] & Arthur Gordon[4]: the Academy & New Galleries: a dinner party given by Warren: "The Mountebanks" in company with Angelo & a Life Guardsman: "Venice" with Angelo & Warren: these have been my most prominent doings during Friday & Saty. Not including visits, correspondence, shopping.

Angelo [Fusato] in London is very nice. The place amazes & subdues him. [E. P.] Warren's servant, who is the retired Life Guardsman, takes a real affectionate interest in him, though they cannot exchange thoughts.

I hope you will go on with your book steadily when you get home. I believe you will make something good. One piece more or another might go into the PMG. That journal clearly appreciates your work. But do not write with your eye on the PMG—only on the subject. When you get a piece done, of the right length to print there, you might send it to me; & I will forward to editor as I have done before.

Everyrs   JAS.

---

1. See L 1995. Probably the unsigned "Fishing on the Lombardy Plain," *Pall Mall Gazette,* LV (July 21, 1892), 3.

2. See L 1990.

3. John Douglas Sutherland Campbell (1845–1914), Marquess of Lorne, educated at Eton and Trinity College, Cambridge, president of the Royal Geographical Society, 1884–85; constable of Windsor Castle, 1892; succeeded his father as Duke of Argyll, 1900.

4. Arthur Charles Hamilton Gordon (1829–1912), fourth son of George Hamilton Gordon (1784–1860), 4th Earl of Aberdeen; knighted 1st Earl of Stanmore 1893; educated at Cambridge and Oxford; secretary to his father, as Prime Minister, 1852–55; private secretary to Gladstone, 1858; governor of New Brunswick, Trinidad, Mauritius, Fiji Islands, New Zealand, Ceylon; 1865, married Rachael Emily Lefevre, daughter of Sir John George Shaw-Lefevre. See L 2000.

2004. *To Charles Kains-Jackson*

18, Cowley Street, Westminster.S.W. [London] July 24. 1892

My dear Jackson

I arrived here later than I expected, i.e. on Thursday evening, & have naturally not had a moment to spare.—I must go away on Wednesday again; & the only evening which is even possibly free, is Monday. I cannot be sure till I hear whether a half-engagement with some people I want to talk to, is made or not made. May I telegraph to you tomorrow? And if we go to the Vale,[1] shall we dine together somewhere first? Of course this is not my only visit to London. When I have finished with Oxford, I may return at once, & then I think I will stay at the Metropole.

Everyrs.

JAS.

I have promised to take Edwin [Brugger] & Angelo to a Music Hall, after a dinner at the Italian Restaurant in Great Compton St, on Tuesday. Which is the best show now?

Have not had time to think about the "Key of Blue." The illustrations to MAB are being badly done I fear.

---

1. A cul-de-sac in Chelsea. It contained a house inhabited at one time by Whistler and in 1892 by Charles Ricketts (see L 2050) and Charles Shannon (see L 1894).

2005. *To William Barclay Squire*

United Service Club, Pall Mall, S.W. July 27. 1892.

Dear Willy

When I wrote to you just now,[1] I forgot to remind you that you had not given me your friend's address at Oxford. I should like to meet him. So let me know. My address is

c/o The President of Magdalen College.[2]

Yrs ever   JAS

---

1. Letter not available.
2. T. H. Warren. See L 788.

2006. *To Arthur Symons*

United Service Club Pall Mall, S.W. Monday [July 27, 1892]

Dear Mr Symons

I will certainly come, if it is possible, to you tomorrow afternoon. As you say, it is by no means the conventional tea-party you invite me to.

Yours ever

J.A.S.

The Athenaeum is lying down like a lamb with the lions of the U.S.

2007. *To Elkin Mathews*

United Service Club Pall Mall, S.W. Monday [July 27, 1892]

Dear Mr Mathews

It occurs to me that, if we stick to the title "In the Key of Blue", we could obviate the book being taken for poems, by adding "and other prose pieces" or "essays."

Very truly yours

J A Symonds
(Athenaeum)

2008. *To Thomas Duff Gordon-Duff*[1]

United Service Club, Pall Mall, S. W. July 27. 1892

My dear Gordon Duff

I find your letter here (i.e. Athenaeum[2]) this morning. I was at 40 Grosvenor Square yesterday & saw yr brother & son,[3] & thought much of you. Your brother I had last met at S. Moritz in March, when your poor sister's fate[4] was already sealed. Two weeks ago I was again at the Kulm.[5] It is painful to have so many sad associations connected with those mountains.

I am enjoying myself in London hugely. But as I wind myself up at 10 a.m. I don't run down again till about 2 a.m. next morning, the pace is killing.

I have such a very miscellaneous set of friends, including all classes of society from a hairdresser to a Duke. This complicates social relations & taxes the range of sympathy.

I hope to be at Glen soon. I am going to Castle Howard & to Carlisle with Ronald Gower, & then it seems too near not to slip over the Border.

Today I go down to Oxford to deliver a solemn Address upon that old humbug "The Renaissance."[6]

Everyrs
J A Symonds

---

1. See L 1552.
2. Symonds was elected a member of the Athenaeum Club in 1880.
3. The brother was Archibald Hay Gordon-Duff (1863–1938); the son was Lachlan (1880–1914), whose mother, Pauline Emma Tennant Gordon-Duff, died in 1888.
4. Helen Elizabeth Gordon-Duff Tennant. See L 1902.
5. The Hotel Engadiner Kulm in St. Moritz-Dorf.
6. Possibly published as "The Renaissance in its Broader Aspects," *The New Review*, VII (Sept., 1892), 293–305.

2009. *To Dr. John Johnston*

The Hill, Stratford on Avon. August 4th 1892.

Dear Dr Johnston

Can you give me Edward Carpenter's[1] address? I have forgotten it, and want to write to him.

If you can do so please let me hear

c/o the Earl of Carlisle
Castle Howard,
Malton.

Is Carpenter at home now, do you know?

Very sincerely yours

John Addington Symonds—

---

1. See L 1819.

2010. *To Margaret Symonds*

Castle Howard, York August 5 1892

My dearest Madge

Your first letter from Am Hof was very welcome to me. I see that you are in good health & spirits. So am I—far better than before I left Davos—because I am living in the mid-stream of the world. And pretty hard.

I left Oxford with Ronald G[ower] & Hamilton Aide[1] (the Ranee[2] did not come) on Wednesday, & went to Stratford on Avon. We were hospitably entertained by the local magnate, a Brewer of course, as he was not a Banker, and a proper gentleman to boot, in his country house.[3] There were twelve large dogs in it, host & hostess, four handsome blonde haired sons, & five daughters. The whole family painted or sang, & the elders had given the Memorial Theatre & Museum to Stratford. A magnificent donation, enriched in the garden which runs along the lovely sleepy Avon, by Gower's really fine monument to Shakspere,[4] fine life-sized bronze statues, with bronze masks & decorations, on a great stone pedestal.

We spent the whole afternoon on our legs visiting Shakespere houses & relics. An authoress, Mrs Leith Adams[5] came down upon us, temptesuously assailed us, wanted to waft us away into her house. Finally wound up by rushing home, producing a volume of poems, & presenting it with an inscription to my Kleinigheit [trifle].

It was like one of your days. Shakespeare[6] is "Il Santo" of Stratford on Avon.

Yesterday, Ronald & Angelo & I came on to Castle Howard. We dined & saw York Minster on the way. Arrived at the station about 8.30, & drove in a dogcart through the vast Park, about 3 miles. The House itself is an immense Palace by Vanbrugh,[7] the architect of Blenheim, about as large as Stra,[8] but with far finer wood, & gardens—an immense park all round it. At the head of the grand entrance stood a maid with a candlestick, & after her came Lord Carlisle[9] with his white hair & bent back. Two solitary small figures relieved against the enormous mass of the façade with its crowning cupola. There are no manservants in the whole place, & there is no wine. It is stuffed with marbles, works of art, grand Italian & Dutch paintings, portraits of all the Dukes & Duchesses, Counts & Countesses of England, during the last 300 years, all relatives of Howards & of Gowers. Such a jumble of concentrated undiluted engrained aristocracy with a new diffused well-meaning but colourless democracy. I don't agree with your mother that people of this sort are hardly human. They seem to me very near to myself as human beings. But it cannot be otherwise than that they should become a little remote when they talk to each other in soft voices about masses of relations, not one of whom is less than ducal. The whole situation strikes me as singular, & Castle Howard is making a curious impression on my imagination.

Angelo, as I expected, gets on very well in all the various places we have been in. He does not lose his head, his spirits, or his manners, & takes everything with pleased amusement. Of course, he is very well looked after by Ronald & me. But it will be the same everywhere.

One thing I forgot to mention last night. The whole huge place is only lighted by gas, & as Carlisle[10] & his son Morpeth[11] are alone here, they have not had the gas made. Accordingly we had to grope about the immense corridor mysteriously with bedroom candles. Heaven save the man who loses himself in the labyrinth.

I hope your mother is well. I have not heard directly from her during the last eight days. But she has directed several of my letters to the Athenaeum Club.

I shall go from here to Carlisle (County Station Hotel), where I hope to be on Tuesday next. But perhaps it is safest always to address "Athenaeum." On the 13th or 15th I mean to go to [The Tennant's] "The Glen, Innerleithen NB."

There is a cricket match going on today. Among one eleven I found my old Clifton friend Gray Tylecote[12] looking very aged.

Love to all. Yr most affate JAS.

---

1. Charles Hamilton Aïdé (1830–1906), English poet, novelist, and amateur artist. Published several volumes of poetry and set some of his verses to music.

2. Probably Margaret de Windt (1849–1936), wife of Sir Charles Johnson Brooke (1829–1917), the 2nd Rajah of Sarawak. Brooke succeeded his uncle, Sir James Brooke (1803–68), who was made Rajah of Sarawak by courtesy for his services in Borneo. Oscar Wilde dedicated "The Young King" in *A House of Pomegranates* (1891) to the Ranee.

3. Probably Edgar Flower (1833–1904), of the Hill, Stratford-on-Avon, from which place Symonds wrote L 2009. The sons were Archibald, Richard, Oswald, and Spencer. See Burke, *Landed Gentry* (1937) and Ronald Gower, *Old Diaries* (1902), p. 174. His brother, Charles Edward Flower (1830–92), in 1864 founded the Shakespeare Memorial Association, under whose auspices the Shakespeare Memorial Theatre was opened in 1879. Symonds' "the elders" were probably Edgar and Charles Edward Flower.

4. Ronald Gower's monument, begun in 1876, completed in 1888. A seated Shakespeare, executed in bronze, is accompanied by figures of Hamlet (philosophy), Prince Hal (history), Lady Macbeth (tragedy), and Falstaff (comedy).

5. Mrs. Bertha Jane Leith Adams (d. 1912), daughter of Frederick Grundy, solicitor

from Cheshire; married Surgeon-General Leith Adams and after his death the Rev. Robert Stuart de Courcy Laffan; on the staff of *All the Year Round,* wrote voluminous popular novels and verse. *Bonnie Kate: a Story from a Woman's Point of View* (3 vols., 1891) and *A Garrison Romance* (1892; by 1893 5 eds. appeared) were among her successes.

6. The spelling is thus in the letter.

7. John Vanbrugh (1664–1726), dramatist and architect, was chosen by the Duke of Marlborough to build Blenheim Palace, near Woodstock. Vanbrugh was a close friend of the then Lord Carlisle, who had served as godparent to Carlisle's only surviving son Charles. Lord Carlisle's commission in 1701 to build Castle Howard was the first of Vanbrugh's projects of note. The castle, despite its inharmonious additions, is considered one of the best examples of the Corinthian Renaissance in England. The main building was not completed until 1714. It is at Malton, about 25 miles northeast of York.

8. The Pisani villa on the Brenta near Padua. See L 2011.

9. Probably Frederick John Howard (1814–97), the oldest member of the family, M.P. for Younghal (1837–41), private secretary to George William Frederick Howard, private secretary to the 7th Earl of Carlisle (1802–64).

10. Symonds' friend George James Howard (1843–1911), the 9th Earl, succeeded to the title on the death of the 8th Earl, William George Howard, in 1889; amateur artist; trustee for 30 years of the National Gallery to which he gave Jan Mabuse (1478?–?1533), "Adoration of the Kings"; lifelong temperance advocate.

11. Morpeth is the name applied to all eldest sons of earls of Carlisle. Charles James Howard (1867–1912), later (1911) became 10th Earl.

12. Henry Grey Tylecote (1853–1935), attended Clifton College and New College, Oxford, became master at the Golden Parsonage Preparatory School, Hemel Hempstead, Hertfordshire.

2011. *To Horatio Forbes Brown*[1]

York, Aug. 5 [1892]

[Dear Horatio]

When I arrived here late last evening, about 9.30, the first person whom I saw after Lord Carlisle's greeting, was Gray Tylecote. There is a cricket match on to-day.

At Oxford the junction with Ronald [Gower] and Hamilton Aidé was effected. The Ranee could not come. We went to Stratford-on-Avon, and stopped in the house of the local magnate, outside the town—Mr. Flower, with four handsome sons—"Angeli non Angli."[2] A terrible hard day of sight-seeing it was. Indefatigable Ronald poked us into everything and presented us to everybody. He is a sort of local Genius, and his monument on the brink of the Avon is really a fine thing.

There we slept, and yesterday came on here, lunching at Birmingham, seeing the Minster and dining at York. The drive in a dog-cart through three miles of park was very impressive. At the end of it, the lake under a low large moon, and the vast pile of this Vanbrugh Palace, enormous with its flanking wings produced to form a court, and the high central cupola. At the top of the flight of stairs in front of the grand entrance stood a servant girl in black and white, and behind her Lord Carlisle, very white and aged and round-shouldered. They had one bedroom candlestick between them. The house, lighted usually by gas, is now obscure, except by day; and any one who loses his way in it by night is lost. George Howard told us a story of John Bright[3] at Chatsworth, talking to Lord Northbrook on their way to bed, and abusing all the Governors and Viceroys of India. L. N. got cross, and said "good night" suddenly, and left Bright alone in the labyrinth without a clue. He slept—or did not sleep—at last upon a sofa in the billiard-room. Castle Howard is full of very interesting things: immense masses of family portraits, and some fine pictures, a few good pieces of sculpture. It has a lovely chapel.

There is no wine, and there are no men-servants. Nothing more concentrated and real in the shape of its aristocracy can be imagined—more diffuse and ideal, I should say, than the democracy of its present owners.

Vanbrugh designed Castle Howard. It is rather larger than Stra,[4] lighter in style than Blenheim. Its position on a vast park of very broken ground, surrounded by grass terraces with statues and balustrated staircases into the gardens, is splendid.

[Incomplete]

---

1. Since this letter contains the same materials as L 2010, see the notes to that letter on persons and places.

2. Angels, not Angles; attributed to St. Gregory.

3. John Bright (1811–89), English statesman, advocate of free trade, M. P. and leader of the Liberal party.

4. The Pisani villa on the Brenta near Padua.

2012. *To Mrs. John Addington Symonds*

Castle Howard York August 6. 1892

My dear Catherine

It is quite ten days since I heard from you. I know that somehow or another I should have had news if you had been in any difficulty. And there is little to say if things are going in their ordinary groove at Davos.

This is a delightful place to stay in. Lord Carlisle & his sons are so kind & friendly, & there are plenty of young people, lads & girls, about. The park is wonderfully spacious & filled with the noblest old trees in mile-long avenues, & ferney clumps, & sombre copses. Ronald [Gower] has taken me all over it in a series of walks. The beeches are the finest of the trees, next the oaks, then the Spanish Chesnuts, then the ashes, & lastly the ancient limes. Deer roam about it from end to end.

At the end of my long life I reap the benefit of having worked so hard at writing. People are very kind to me in consequence & this is pleasant for a naturally shy man.

The gardens here are vast, but not very well kept up. The best part is a huge kitchen garden, divided into sections, filled with fruit-trees, all the walks & alleys being planted with herbaceous plants of various sorts in flower.

Everything is on a gigantic scale.

I am going to sleep at York on Monday, & to go to Carlisle (County Station Hotel) on Tuesday. I may run down from Carlisle to Penrith, but I shall return there again before going to Glen [the Tennant's] upon the 13th or 15th.

I will finish this tomorrow. I must go to dinner now, 8.30.

August 7. Today is Sunday. I began it with family prayers in the chapel of the house, a beautifully decorated building with painted glass, frescoes, alabaster paintings, etc all done by Remp,[1] & a sweet organ such as would delight the soul of Miss [Edith] Fuller.[2] The German governess played, the Italian nurse sang with a powerful dramatic soprano—Signa. Raffaelli from Pesaro, who might make her fortune on a stage in Italy at all events. George Howard[3] read the prayers & parts of the Bible. Only members of the family & the maidservants attended. I do not know when I have been impressed with a thoroughly noble & good life, in the same way that I am here. The master is so beneficent, so gentle to all sorts & conditions of men, so exquisite in artistic taste, so modest & yet so widely cultured. The mistress,[4] with all her flightiness, has evidently a large & excellent nature. She is out of health at Naworth [Castle][5]. The sons & daughters seem to be so well brought up. Exceedingly natural. It is just this naturalness which, in the middle of such splendour, makes the reality of their simplicity difficult to seize. I think at root they remain intensely proud of their blood. And I cannot imagine how the daughters who are married get along in their restricted lives. Charlotte [Green] says that Lady Cecilia Roberts,[6] whose husband is a tutor at Oxford, living on his work, inhabits one of those small semi-detached houses, & is unpopular because of her brusque manners. That is because she has hitherto been "natural" in palaces.

Well: I will not run on upon a theme, wh you know is likely to interest me personally very much. These people are trying one of the most curious & difficult experiments.

Everyrs

J.A.S.

No letter today except from England. I mistrust the Athenaeum.

---

1. Probably Franz Carl Remp (1675–1718), German artist and decorator.
2. Organist of the Davos English Church.
3. See L 2010.
4. Rosalind Frances Stanley (d. 1921), daughter of 2nd Baron Stanley of Alderley, married George Howard in 1864.
5. See L 1999.
6. Lady Cecilia Maude Howard (d. 1947), daughter of the 9th Earl of Carlisle, in 1891 married Charles Henry Roberts (1865–?), Exeter College, and Boothby, Brampton, Cumberland.

2013. *To Charles Kains-Jackson*

Castle Howard. York. August 7. 1892.

Dear Jackson

Since I left Oxford (where the 1300 auditors of my Lecture were mostly an assortment of motley-aged women) I have been at Stratford on Avon with Ronald Gower & Hamilton Aidé,[1] & am now at my old friend Lord Carlisle's[2] with Ronald. It is very pleasant here. A huge Vanbrugh palace in a noble English northcountry Chase. The house is full of splendid works of art,[3] pictures mostly, also sculpture. The lives of the Howards in it are of an exquisite simplicity. [erased passage] Erased, because I ought not to write about my hosts.

J. A. S.

I received your letter this morning most gladly. That beautiful Ballade I know, of course, for it appeared in the Artist.[4] But I am glad to have it in autograph. The Superscription to myself delighted me & amused Ronald.

I am going to York tomorrow, & then to Carlisle, & then to Sir Charles

Tennant's[5] at The Glen, Innerleithen, N.[orth] B.[ritain]. When I shall come back to "the village" & its wigwams I don't know. It is probably that, if I am still well, I shall run from Edinburgh straight down to Bristol, see friends in Somersetshire, & then go on to Cornwall.

Let me hear something about your movements. Up to the 12th my best address, while moving about, will be

County Station Hotel
Carlisle.

After that date,

The Glen
Innerleithen N. B.

Send me some more verses which I have not seen.

Yours   J. A. S.

Angelo [Fusato] is in high spirits, & English life in palaces or in hotels or colleges by Isis shore delights him equally. Michelangelo drags rather, & is sick of the disease of "illustrations."

---

1. See L 2010.
2. George James Howard. See L 2010.
3. For Symonds' list of the artists see L 2019.
4. "Chant Royal: Of the Princes of Old Time," *The Artist,* XIII (March 1, 1892), 69. See L 1964.
5. See L 1619.

2014. *To Dr. J. W. Wallace*

Castle Howard, York. August 8 1892

Dear Sir

In reply to yours of the 5th wh reached me today, I must tell you that I left Venice for Switzerland on the 7th of June. I have not received the parcel you sent me on July 19.[1] But it is possible that this may have come to Davos since the date on wh I left my house there: viz the 19th. My family may not have thought it the sort of thing to send after me. I will write for information & will let you know.

I hope indeed that no accident has happened to records so valuable.

If the parcel is not at Davos, I will make enquiries at the Venetian

Post. They had my Paris address there. But the Post is badly managed. At anyrate, it, the parcel, will not have been done away with.

Believe me very sincerely yrs

John Addington Symonds

J.W. Wallace esq

---

1. Wallace had sent notes of his visits with Walt Whitman to Symonds, who used them in preparing his *Walt Whitman* (1893). They were returned by Horatio F. Brown after Symonds' death:

Am Hof, Davos Platz, Switzerland. June 28. 93.

Dear Sir,

I find among the papers of the late Mr Symonds a packet of diaries & extracts from letters which I imagine belong to you.

But the only signature is "Wallace." I therefore write this line first to make sure.

Please address to me
c/o John Torry Esq
13 Herid Row
Edinburgh
I am yours faithfully

Horatio F Brown

The notes were published in J. Johnston and J. W. Wallace, *Visits to Walt Whitman in 1890–1891 by Two Lancashire Friends* (1917). Johnston's *Visit to Walt Whitman* was originally published separately in 1898. See L 1874.

2015. *To Horatio Forbes Brown*

Carlisle, Aug. 12 [1892]

[Dear Horatio]

I got your first letter from Wiesen. It was pathetically interesting to me in this alien life. It gave me *heimweh* [homesickness] for the hills and Alps.

I read a book, type-written, by R.[onald] G.[ower] at Castle Howard, on Joan of Arc, quite ungrammatical. It is fine in chivalrous spirit and glow of feeling, the outcome of snorting aristocratic-democracy, that funny modern *mélange*.

Howards and Gowers, Cavendishes and Grosvenors, Campbells, Egertons,[1] coagulated in one slab mixture, stick together in a castle of more than Lucifer's pride.[2] Somehow or another, here and there, they show their

731

cloven feet. It is "we" against the world; too great, too luminous, to care about distinctions, secure in "our" impregnable and unapproachable superiority.

[Incomplete]

---

1. George James Howard, Earl of Carlisle (Symonds' host at Carlisle); Ronald Sutherland Gower, the sculptor son of the 2nd Duke of Sutherland; Spencer Compton Cavendish, the Duke of Devonshire; Hugh Lupus Grosvenor, the Duke of Westminster, married first, Lady Constance Sutherland-Leveson-Gower, daughter of the 2nd Duke of Sutherland, and second, Catherine Caroline Cavendish, daughter of 2nd Baron Chesham; George Douglas Campbell, the Duke of Argyll, married Lady Elizabeth Sutherland-Leveson-Gower (d. 1878), daughter of 2nd Duke of Sutherland; the Duke of Devonshire's sister, Lady Louisa Caroline, married Francis Egerton, son of the 1st Earl of Ellesmere.
2. Cf. *Paradise Lost*, Book X, ll. 422–26:

> the rest were all
> Far to the inland retired, about the walls
> Of Pandemonium, city and proud seat
> Of Lucifer, so by allusion called,
> Of that bright star to Satan paragoned.

2016. *To Elkin Mathews*[1]

Naworth Castle[2] Aug: 13. 1892

My dear Sir

I found your letter of the 12th in Carlisle today.

The specimen page you sent me for "In the Key of Blue & other Prose Essays" is very successful, I think; & I particularly like the italic type for the verses.

I suppose, since you say nothing on the subject, that you are satisfied with all the copy I placed in your hands, & find no objection, literary or other, to the pieces I requested you to consider.

If that is the case, we may consider the book formed.

Only, as I told you, I should be glad of your opinion as to the suitability for publication of some of the essays. You know the public taste better than I do.

In answer to one of your questions, I may say that all my recent books have been published (so far as I remember) in editions of 1000 copies or upwards. My new Life of Michelangelo is, I believe, going to be issued by Mr Nimmo with 1500 copies for England & 1500 for America. One little vol: on Latin Student Songs was published by Messrs Chatto & Windus in an edition of 750 copies, I think, under the title of "Wine Women & Song".

You propose a royalty of 10d. Do you mean in all copies sold?—I may say that I have no objection at all to an edition of 750 copies. It seems to me that you can judge better than myself upon the number to be issued.—But before deciding, I should like to know what sum of money down you could offer, & whether the royalty proposed would be on the whole edition of 750.

I am staying here with my old friend [George Howard] Lord Carlisle. On Monday I go to Sir Charles Tennant Bt

The Glen

    Innerleithen N. B.

for six or seven days. Please write to me there. Very truly yours

John Addington Symonds

To Elkin Mathews Esq.

---

1. See L 1989.
2. Symonds was visiting George James Howard (1843–1911), 9th Earl of Carlisle. He had moved from Castle Howard to Naworth Castle. See L 1999.

2017. *To Dr. J. W. Wallace*

Naworth Castle August 15 1892

Dear Mr Wallace

News reaches me from Switzerland that your packet [of notes on Whitman] is at Davos.[1]

It will be safe there, as safe as things can be, till I return.

If you want it please send to me. Address

        Athenaeum Club

        London S.W.

Very sincerely yrs

J A Symonds

---

1. See L 2014.

2018. *To Margaret Symonds*[1]

The Glen, Innerleithen, N.B. Aug. 16, 1892

[Dear Madge]

. . . The change from George Howard's house[2] to this house, which is light, airy, Frenchified too, a house too flowing with wine beer food & flunkeys—is too funny. Sir Charles is a kind old man, but not of excellent manners & awfully rich. He gave £600 the other day for a pair of ponies for Margot.[3]

Lady Tennant[4] loves flowers & has more fruit & plants under glass than Sidbury,[5] but all the houses arranged in nooky places of the garden, which breaks off into heathery moor & wild brisk woods from the ancient Ettrick forest.

I like Margot in her home. She is the life of it. The girl at heart is deeply religious & conservative in her feeling about life. She has a very singular naiveté & innocence underlying her fast ways.

She over-lives life, & is very pale, & much thinner.

Politics & correspondence with people in the swim of the great world are still her main interest. I don't think, however, that she enlarges her circle very much. The clique is not a wide one, but it touches society at several points. I see that Margot suffers, as most people do, from want of fixed work.

I went all over the garden with Lady Tennant today. She would appreciate your Aunt's Book,[6] & if your mother sent it to her, it would be graceful. Please let me hear if your mother cares to do this; for if she does not, I will send a copy of the book to Glen. I sent our "Swiss Highlands" to Naworth [Castle]. With Ld Carlisle I have made a very delightful friendship out of what was an old & rather timid acquaintance.

MAB still gives me a great deal to do. The Index is bothering now.

Love to K[atharine]. I hope your mother will settle her well at Lausanne. It would be very nice if you carry out the plan of staying on a little there.

Yr most aff father

JAS.

[Incomplete]

---

1. The first few words are in Katharine Furse's hand. She apparently copied from a preceding page, now lost.

2. Lord Carlisle's house, Naworth Castle. See L 2016.
3. Margot Tennant, later Lady Asquith. See L 1571.
4. Margot's mother, Emma Winsloe. See L 1619.
5. One of the homes of the Cave family.
6. Marianne North, *Recollections of a Happy Life,* edited by Mrs. J. A. Symonds (2 vols., 1892).

2019. *To Horatio Forbes Brown*

The Glen, Innerleithen, N.B., Aug. 17 [1892]

[Dear Horatio]

I wrote you last, I think, from Carlisle,[1] where I was doing business. It gave me a great deal of trouble. But now I feel I have moved a considerable way forward in my plans.

On Saturday we moved to Naworth,[2] which is, as you know, one of the finest inhabited feudal Castles of England. It is just on the English side of the border, and from its battlements one looks across the Roman Wall to the rolling hills and Cheviot range. The castle is built on the edge of a deep glen. This ravine is filled up with splendid trees, in the way of Nightingale Valley, but more so. I thought your glen must be like it. The weather was very stormy. All night "the wind was roaring in turret and tree."[3] Melancholy and sombre. Sleep fled. There is a great courtyard like a college quad. Indeed if Castle Howard is as large as Blenheim, Naworth is at least as large as Merton.[4] And such a hall, emblazoned with such arms. Fitzalan, Warren, Plantagenet, Dacre, Greystoke, Cavendish, De Valence, and I cannot go on.[5] As at Castle Howard, we lived poorly in the midst of it all. Carlisle said he had put me into a little room next Morpeth's[6] to save the servants, as there was only one chamber-maid. It was a little slip room, and all its cupboards were filled with clothes, china, books, papers. Angelo [Fusato] put my things out on the floor. Of course there are between forty and fifty state bedrooms, gorgeously furnished and adorned with rare engravings and water-colours or old portraits. But it is not the habit of the Howards to live into their splendours. The house, in addition, overflows with curious books and lovely pictures. The Giorgione *is* a Giorgione, no doubt, and a gem. It is a grave bare-headed knight, bearded and ruddy, clad in the rich shining mail Giorgione loved, having his corslet braced up by a lovely page with deep green sleeves, downcast eyelids, and just the faintest film of a moustache upon his upper lip. There is a very good

735

Signorelli, and the best Mabuse in existence. Plenty of Holbeins, Mores, Knellers, Lelys, Sir Joshuas [Reynolds]. Carlisle collects books and engravings. He must spend a great deal of money on them. Their parish church is part of the ruins of Lanercost Priory,[7] and a fine spacious early English building, which the Howards got from the Dacres.[8]

I came on here on Monday. This house is flowing with wine and food and flunkeys. Margot is, as usual, nice and clever. The house has lots of good modern pictures. A lovely unfinished oil picture by Walker, with a boy in it who dangles naked legs over the steep side of a running stream.[9]

The glen is like a Scotch Val San Zibio,[10] if you can fancy that. A hollow, *perdu* in the hills, filled in with cultivated lawns and gardens—and the pretty Frenchy modern house, which has its own coquetry.[11]

[Incomplete]

---

1. See L 2016.
2. See L 1999.
3. See Tennyson, "The Sisters," l. 15: "The wind is roaring in turret and tree."
4. Lord Walsingham's seat, Merton Hall, Thetford, Norfolk, built by Robert de Grey (1530–1601) about 1598, or by Sir William de Grey (1583–1632), his son.
5. Consult Burke's *Peerage* for details on these families.
6. Courtesy-title of the eldest son of the Earl of Carlisle, who was Charles James Howard (1867–1912).
7. In Carlisle; the monastery of the Scottish border. Edward I stayed there during the winter of 1306–1307. It was ruined by the followers of Robert Bruce after the Battle of Bannockburn (1314).
8. Lord William Howard, 3rd son of Thomas, 4th Duke of Norfolk (1536–72), was restored in blood by act of Parliament in 1603. He married Elizabeth, sister and co-heir of George, Lord Dacre, and became proprietor of Naworth Castle, the ancient seat of the Dacre family. In the same way Hinderskelfe, the site of Castle Howard, came to Charles Howard (1629–1684/5) who was created first Earl of Carlisle in 1661.
9. The painter was Frederick Walker (1840–1875). Sir Christopher Tennant writes us:

> The picture by Walker . . . is still in my possession and is called *The Sunny Thames*. Although said to be unfinished it does not really give this impression and is a large canvas, measuring about 60″ by 40″. It was I know a good deal admired in late Victorian and early Edwardian times.

10. Val San Zibio is in the Albergo alla Pergola, a few miles from Battaglia, Italy, in the Euganean Hills. When Symonds was there it was owned by the Conte Dorià dalle Rosa.—Symonds, "Among the Euganean Hills," *In the Key of Blue* (1893), pp. 26 ff.
11. For a photograph of *The Glen*, see Margot Asquith, *Autobiography* (4 vols., 1920–22), I, facing p. 46.

2020. *To Elkin Mathews*[1]

The Glen. Innerleithen. N.B. August 18 1892

Dear Mr Mathews

My "Studies in Greek Poets" was published (in partly piratical way) by Mess Harper.[2] A book of my poems by Osgood.[3] The "Renaissance in Italy" is published in two editions (dearer & cheaper) by Henry Holt of New York,[4] who also did a book of my Italian Sketches.[5]

I cannot remember any other publishers. Nimmo arranges for simultaneous publication in America. But I know nothing about that.

I feel that the royalty of 10d you offer would not produce as much as I am accustomed to on a book of this sort. £60 is what Smith & Elder have given me for vols of collected essays. Before final settlement of our agreement, could you not make an advance upon the royalty! I am not unreasonable, but I ought to consider the matter in question.[6]

Very truly yours

John Addington Symonds
c/o Professor Henry Sidgwick
Hill Side
Chesterton Road
Cambridge

P.S. My friend the Honble Roden Noel writes me that he wants to part with the remainder of editions of his poems at present published by Kegan Paul & Co.[7] Would you care to consider this? I ask because I noticed you were reissuing other of K. Paul verse publications. I shall be seeing Noel I hope after Cambridge.

J.A.S.

---

1. See L 1989.
2. In 1879. Harper also published *Sketches and Studies in Southern Europe* (a title presumably not devised by Symonds) in New York in 1880, his *Shelley* in 1879 and 1887, and his *Sidney* in 1887.
3. *New and Old,* Boston, 1880.
4. In various parts, 1881, 1887, 1888.
5. *Italian Byways,* 1883.
6. See L 2016.
7. Probably *A Modern Faust and Other Poems* (1888).

The Glen. Innerleithen. N.B. August 18. 1892

My dearest Catherine

You cannot think what pain such letters as your last give me, because they make me so exceedingly sorry for you.

You must feel, I am sure, that when I am seeming to hold or gird at you, it is that I am vehemently hoping you may be mistaken, hoping things may be more easily set to rights than you lead me to imagine.

A letter like Charlotte's (wh I sent you) & another I had from her before, render me from time to time sanguine. And then there comes one from yourself, with all the reality of suffering & dread in it.

One thing is certain. You must get away from Davos as quickly as you can. I do not think you ought to return to it for some time. But you are not in a condition of health which makes it right for other people to choose for you. I think you must choose for yourself, with the knowledge that I shall carry out your wishes.

For a great many reasons I do not want to make an abrupt separation from Davos. Indeed I could not well manage it, & I think it would be very unwise (in view of my own past health) to abandon what has been so beneficial. But we need not think of details yet. Fortunately we have money enough to afford experiments. I have made no investments yet this year, & I will keep my spare capital still floating so that cash may be at our disposal.

One thing distresses me greatly. It is the humble & abased way in wh you write about yourself, & your impression that we do not sympathize with you or believe in what you say. This is a false idea. It is natural, however, that we should endeavour to explain your troubles by all sorts of things rather than suppose that you are seriously wrong in your nervous system.

I do not however blink the fact that the state of your mother's & Pop's [Marianne North's] health makes anxiety about yours at this time of life reasonable. Also I have always believed that your nervous force was very inadequate under certain strains & in certain circumstances wh do not try an ordinary normal nature.

I therefore feel that, just as the family turned upon my illness when I came to Davos in 1877, so it ought now to be guided solely with a view to your benefit. You remember how very far gone I felt myself to be, & how instinct made me choose Davos, & how I chose it. I am certain nobody else could have settled my life for me. It is likewise for you to find, it may be, what suits you.

I am going on Sunday to the Sidgwicks Hillside Chesterton Road Cambridge. On Wednesday probably to Roden Noel's. I may pay visits to Gr: Dakyns & C.[ecile] W. Boyle before I go West. I could make a visit to Cornwall agree with your coming, if you will let me know when you go to Enys [Cornwall]. I would suggest your resting alone there somewhile; & if you liked to go anywhere with me, it might be done. Go to Enys as soon as you can conveniently. Corragio amica mia!

Yrs

JAS.

No need to send any of those books & parcels.

2022. *To William Barclay Squire*

Hill Side, Chesterton Road, Cambridge. August 21 1892

My dear Willie

I have been dallying about at Castle Howard, and Naworth, and other Cumberland places, and also at the Glen upon the Tweed. Came here[1] from Scotland this morning.

I ought to let you know what my plans are. Time is pushing me so much that I fear I cannot get to the Gloucester Festival.[2] Lady Ducie[3] wants me to be at Tortworth for it. I shall try. But visits of more absolute importance to me have to be made in Somersetsh, Devon, & Cornwall; & you cannot always arrange things right.

I am going to stay with Roden Noel (address the Honble R.N.
St Aubyns
W. Brighton

on Tuesday for a day or two.

If you should have anything to tell me about your movements, let me hear there. Angelo [Fusato] has been getting on well in these stately castles and great houses of the North.

Ever your affecate

JASymonds

---

1. He was visiting Henry Sidgwick.

2. This Gloucester festival, the 169th event, took place early in September. The joint choirs of Gloucester, Worcester, and Hereford performed Hubert Perry's oratorio

Job and lesser works by Miss R. F. Ellicott, Lewis Morris, and Charles Lee Williams, the conductor of the affair.

3. Lady Julia (Langston) Ducie, Symonds' life-long friend, lived at Tortworth Court, Falfield, Gloucester. She died in 1895. See Ls 319 and 1732.

2023. *To Elkin Mathews*

Hill Side,[1] Chesterton Road, Cambridge. August 22 1892

Dear Mr Mathews

I am in receipt of your letter of the 20th, & write to say that I am quite satisfied with your proposal of a royalty of one shilling per copy sold, & also as regards an American edition.[2]

So as far as I am concerned then, the agreement may be made at once,[3] & I shall be ready to read proof whenever you choose to begin printing.

I quite understand what you feel about [Roden] Noel's poems. I did not indeed think them entirely in your line, & expected that their *bulk* would prove a difficulty.

I suppose you could not give him any practical advise as the best way of dealing with these works wh seem to be now thrown upon his hands! He is not very capable of managing these things & does not know whom to apply to.

I am going to stay with him tomorrow at

St. Aubyns'

W. Brighton

If you write to me during the next 3 days please address the letter there—adding c/o The Honble Roden Noel. When I am next in London, I shall not fail to call on you.

Very truly yours

John Addington Symonds

---

1. Symonds was visiting Henry Sidgwick.
2. The American publisher of *In the Key of Blue* was Macmillan.
3. Accompanying this letter are notes written by Mathews about the letter Symonds is answering. They are unsigned:

copy of letter to Mr Symonds
written August 20, 1892
In the Key of Blue

Taking into consideration what you tell me, I think we ought to give you one shilling royalty instead of 10d. Wd you deem this satisfactory.

As already stated, we shall print 1000 copies and be prepared on Jany 1.1893 to pay you in a lump sum royalty on 500 copies—or more, if sold by that date. If an American edition can be arranged we agree to a further allowance of 10% on the net amount received (i.e. on such American edition)

If we go in for a Designed title page it will mean extra expense for production, etc.

We will see about an Agreement as soon as possible if you approve of the increased royalty now offered

Here followed thanks for kindness in offering to speak to Mr Roden Noel and explaining why we declined

2024. *To Henry Graham Dakyns*

Hill Side, Chesterton Road, Cambridge August 22 1892

My dear Graham

I have been up in the North staying at Castle Howard, Naworth, the Glen & doing lots of business at Carlisle & Penrith.

I came down on Saty & was here yesterday. Find the Sidgwicks very busy.

I am going to Brighton tomorrow, & am thinking that if you are able to receive me I should much like to come to you upon the 27th, wh is Friday

[Incomplete]

2025. *To Henry Graham Dakyns*

9 St. Aubyns W. Brighton Aug 25 [1892]

My dear Graham

I only heard last night from Lotta, after a silence of ten days. She was then at Sidbury Manor[1] in Devonshire on the eve of her departure for Switzerland.

I take it that she has already joined a friend in Hampstead for the journey.

As far as I can tell, it will do for me to leave this at 10.15. Whereby I can reach Haslemere[2] at 1:13 on Saty.

If there is room in your house for Angelo [Fusato] I shall bring him.

741

He does not talk English, & I like if possible to keep him near me. I daresay, if you have not room, something in the neighborhood might be found for him.

Ever yours

JAS

---

1. Lotta (Charlotte Mary), Symonds' daughter, was visiting her aunt and uncle, the Sir Charles Caves.

2. Haslemere, Surrey, 42 miles from London, where Dakyns lived.

2026. *To Janet Ross*

Brighton August 25, 1892

My dear Janet

I have just received yours of the 20th here, where I am staying with the Roden Noels.

I think that my Michelangelo will be out probably in October. The illustrations are nearly finished, & I am correcting the last proofs of the Index. The whole business has been wearifully slow.

That being the case I do not see why you should not offer the article, especially if you do so (as I think you said) to the Edinburgh.[1]

I have been working hard at society since I came to England. After London & Oxford I went to Stratford on Avon, then to Castle Howard, York, Carlisle, Penrith, Naworth Castle. My old friend George Howard (now Lord Carlisle) was partly my object in haunting those parts, & partly I have to spend £20,000 in good works in the Penrith-Carlisle district.[2] You may guess what trouble that costs me.

Then I went to Peebleshire—Sir Charles Tennant—at the Glen, a lovely quiet spot. Thence to Cambridge (Henry Sidgwick) & then here. Now I am off for Haslemere & then Falmouth![3]

It is very hot here also. I am grieved to hear of the Padrone's being ill. Pray remember me to him & also to Lina [Duff-Gordon].

Everyrs.

JAS.

I have read a good deal of Nitti's book[4] on my travels & like it. Of Biagi's

Shelley[5] I saw nothing, & of his Dante illustrations I hear vaguely from F. Unwin.[6]

1. The *Edinburgh Review* did not, however, accept the review of *Michelangelo;* the editor, writes Janet Ross in the *Fourth Generation* (1912), p. 317, "did not care for reviews written by an intimate friend." The review appeared in the *Nineteenth Century,* XXXII (1892), 818–30.

2. He was under the obligations set by William Sisson's will. See L 574.

3. At Haslemere he visited Dakyns; at Falmouth, the painter Henry Tuke.

4. Possibly Francesco Nitti (?–?), *Leone X e sua politico secondo documenti e carteggi inediti* (1892).

5. *Gli Ultimi giorni di P. B. Shelley, con nuovi documenti, etc.* (1892).

6. See Ls 1991 and 2051.

2027. *To Margaret Symonds*

Higher Combe, Haslemere,[1] August 29, 1892.

[Dear Madge]

. . . Graham and Angelo [Fusato] and I walked over to Aldworth to see the Tennysons yesterday. It is an hour's walk through the changeful scenery I have been describing. I do not care for the view from Aldworth as much as this one. The house is built above terraces, very narrow and rather overcrowded with conifers, which seem suspended on a steep descending slope. There is the broad prospect of the Weald in front, and nothing else.

We left Angelo in the shrubbery and went up to see Hallam Tennyson and his wife, a sister of Lieut. Cecil Boyle.[2] . . . After some talk, Hallam said he would see if his father would be able to receive us. Then Graham and I went down to see the old man's study, a large room longer than its breadth. He was sitting near a window at one end of a large lounge couch, shawls over his knees, and a velvet skull cap defining the massive bones of his forehead. He welcomed me very kindly as an old friend, and began at once to talk about old times. I reminded him how he asked me at Farringford what Shakespeare's "long purples" were. "Aye, aye, I think they are jack-in-the-box (his name for the arum); but I have used the words in my poetry to signify a hedgerow vetch with trailing flowers." He began to talk about grammar. "I don't understand English grammar. Take *sea-change.* Is *sea* a substantive used adjectively, or what? What is the logic of a phrase like *Catholic Disabilities Annulling Bill?* Does *Invalid Chair* Maker mean that the Chair-maker is a sickly fellow?" Then we got on to English rhy-

743

thms. I said that no one had reduced them to the rules of prosody. "Yes, and just as I don't understand English Grammar, so I don't understand English verse." "For one man who can read poetry, there are a hundred also can whistle a tune. I heard one the other day read a line of mine '*Lit bỳ a loẁ large mòon.*'"[3] We agreed that blank verse had five beats. I said you could often find but one iamb in a line, and quoted his own line *Ruining along the illimitable inane.*[4] The last two syllables are an iamb. "True," he said, "but you will find five beats." I replied there often seemed to be three beats, and instanced from Milton "Lancelot or Pelleas or Pellinore."[5] He admitted there were only three strong beats there, and cited one of his own from the Idylls constructed on that system. Then he began to talk of Milton and Virgil, and recited passages from both to show how the English poet had modelled his blank verse on the Latin hexameter. "Strange," he added, "considering the difference between the two languages and metres." He told me he was going to write a poem on Bruno,[6] and asked me what I thought about his attitude toward Christianity. I tried to express my views, and Hallam got up and showed me that they were reading up the chapter of my "Renaissance in Italy" on Bruno. Tennyson observed that the great thing in Bruno was his perception of an Infinite Universe, filled with solar systems like our own, and all penetrated with the Soul of God. "That conception must react destructively on Christianity—I mean its creed and dogma—its morality will always remain." Somebody had told him that astronomers could count 550 million solar systems. He observed that there was no reason why each should not have planets peopled with living and intelligent beings. "Then," he added, "see what becomes of the second person of the Deity, and the sacrifice of a God for fallen man upon this little earth!" (You notice how the thoughts which animate me are formed in all imaginative and reflective minds.)

At this point Capt. Brown[7] joined us. He was dressed in a very neat suit of lavender-coloured cloth. "How d'ye do," said Tennyson. "You look like the grey dawn, so fresh and clean." We all laughed, and he went on: "Well, so you do, look at these fellows (Graham and me), how dingy they are." The conversation turned on Ireland and Gladstone. Tennyson hates Home Rule[8] and thinks Gladstone mischievous. The Irish, in his view, are the people least capable of political freedom and self-management under the sun.

It was nearly time to go, when he accused me of having said he borrowed his Margery[9] from Dame Quickly. I forgot entirely what and who his Margery is—somebody in "Becket," I suppose—and vehemently protested I never said anything of the sort. "Oh, but you did, I have got the

article in print, with your name signed, pasted into that book yonder."
Then they wanted to see Angelo, whom I called up from the shrubbery. He
was in his gondolier costume, and looked very handsome as he bent over
the old man's hand and kissed it. I said in Italian: *"Questo Signore,
Angelo, e il più grande poetà di Inghilterra forsè del mondo!"* [This
gentleman, Angelo, is the greatest poet in England, perhaps in the world!]
"Eh! what's that you're saying to the fellow?". . . He then asked me about
Davos, and said he had once been in Chur, the only thing about which he
could remember was—well, too grotesque (to say the least) for me to
record here. Then suddenly, All the Tennysons have big calves. My brother
was bathing at Naples, and as he came up the hotel steps with a towel
round him, the maids exclaimed: *"Sanctissima Madonna, chè gambe!"*
[Most holy Madonna, what legs!]

We went to pay our respects to Lady Tennyson on her sofa, a pale
sweet S. Monica sort of face, looking just as when I saw her first more than
twenty years ago. After that, we walked home through the sunset and the
dewy woods.

[Incomplete]

---

1. He was visiting Dakyns.
2. Audrey Boyle Tennyson, died December 7, 1916, "a victim to the service in her
Military Hospital during the Great War." See a letter and piece on her by F. W.
Bourdillon in *Country Life*, Dec., 1916.
3. "The Palace of Art," l. 68: "Lit with a low large moon."
4. "Lucretius," l. 40.
5. *Paradise Regained*, Book II, l. 361.
6. Giordano Bruno (1548–1600), who figures frequently in Symonds' letters. See L
1460.
7. We have not been able to identify this person.
8. Gladstone and the Liberals had just won the general elections on this issue.
9. In Symonds' review of "The Holy Grail," *The Cliftonian*, I (February and April
1870), 239–42 and 269–73.

2028. *To Henry Graham Dakyns*

Sidbury Manor, Sidmouth[1] Sept. 1, 1892

My dear Graham

I came down here today, & am just going to bed after a rather heavy
evening of sporting gentlemen wearied with their first go at the pheasants.

Since I left Haslemere there was no time to say anything—a mess of

745

London medleys, including a Music Hall, two publishers, a lot of mixed friends (one being a hairdresser), & a dinner with Jack Bright[2] & his more than eccentric wife.

The time I spent with you was not singularly distinct in the present kaleidoscope of life. For yourself & Maggie, for the eminently beautiful environment—marvelously beautiful I think—& then for your children.

I felt a singular affection for Henry.[3] There is something extremely winning about him.

Things oppress me in my mood. I do not envy more fortunate mortals. But I seem to have mismanaged my own existence in company with the lively lives I see.

I thought yours a very pleasant lot to have fallen upon, at a time of life when the heart of man desires permanence & seeks repose.

To say more would be stupid. Thank you for the vision. I shall never forget it.

J A S

I have not said what I mean, I see, and I cannot.

Behüt dich Gott, es wär so schön gewesen.[4]

So beautiful for me if I could place myself where you are And yet I [unclear] you.

---

1. He was visiting the Sir Charles Caves.
2. Possibly John Albert Bright, son of the statesman John Bright (1811–1889), who succeeded his father as liberal unionist, M.P. central Birmingham 1889–95; or, the Clifton College student, John Henry Bright, who left the College in 1880.
3. Henry Graham Dakyns, Jr., b. Jan. 25, 1874.
4.   Behüt dich Gott! es war zu schön gewesen,
              Behüt dich Gott, es hat nicht sollen sein!
God guard you; it would have been too beautiful;/ God guard you; it was not to be. The refrain of the 12th of the "Lieder Jung Werners" in the 14th "Stück" of J. V. Scheffel (1826–86), *Der Trompeter von Säkkingen* (1853).

2029. *To Henry Scott Tuke*[1]

Sidbury Manor, Sidmouth. Sept 5 1892

My dear Mr Tuke

I am glad to hear from you today & hope to reach Falmouth on Wednesday. I suppose, when I come to see you, the thing is to get trans-

746

ported in a boat. Angelo [Fusato] & I will probably find out how to do that.

I will post the proofs of my new book to you.[2] The whole of the August article is there. You can give me the proofs back when I come.

Augusto [Zanon] is a charming personality, & I wish I could have praised him more worthily.

Please thank Kains Jackson for the letter I received this morning. I certainly did not try to "economize" the truth while talking to [John Gambril] Nicholson.[3] There is much in the man I like. But I think it would be better if he ceased to be a schoolmaster.

So long then! Very sincerely
yours

J.A. Symonds

---

1. See L 1838.
2. *In the Key of Blue* (1873); the title essay is based on color impressions of Augusto Zanon in various styles of dress and against various backgrounds.
3. See L 1993.

2030. *To Katharine Symonds*

Falmouth, England September 9, 1892

My dearest K.

I hope you will get along and be happy at this school.[1] You are old and formed enough to be superior to the petty annoyances of school life. But I daresay you will find it at first very cramped and petty. You must give the whole thing a fair chance, remembering that you wished to try it and feeling that it is perfectly easy to leave it alone if the experiment does not succeed.

I often think that the difficulties in our family, such as they are, come from everybody's having had too easy, various and idle a life, from your Mother downward. This breeds restlessness and discontent.

I hope to see your Mother at Enys[2] to-morrow. From her letter I gather that she got better before she left Davos—probably because her mind was occupied with visitors. I wonder how I shall find her now, and what sort of plans for the immediate and more distant future are in her head.

[Incomplete]

1. Mony Fleuri in Lausanne, Switzerland.
2. In Cornwall to visit relatives, the Enyses. See L 1737.

2031. *To Charles Kains-Jackson*

Royal Hotel College Green, Bristol, Sept 16. Thursday 1892

My dear Jackson

I have just come here, & found your startling letter. I cannot fully express the depth of my sympathy with you in this sudden & overwhelming sorrow.[1] I can only thank you for writing to me & letting me in some sense share it.—To think that when we were walking on Friday through those fields by Falmouth harbour, & you were telling me about your home-life & Cecil,[2] this tragedy should have been so near! —It is very terrible. My poor friend, I do grieve with you in your bereavement, & I ponder how you will manage to live on with your father, for whom this blow must be crushing.

I cannot say more. Silence is better than speech now.

Believe me to be affectionately & sincerely yours

John Addington Symonds

Should you have anything to write me, I shall be found

c/o the Earl of Ducie
Tortworth Court
Gloucestershire

till Saty morning. Then at

9 Banbury Road
Oxford

I hope to come to London again about next Tuesday.

1. Charles Kains-Jackson's mother had just died.
2. Cecil E. J. Castle (1870–1922), Kains-Jackson's cousin. Cecil was a companion of the young son of the Gleeson Whites (see L 2073), who lived in the area of Christchurch, Hampshire. Kains-Jackson met him ca. 1890 and was so fond of him that Cecil lived with him in London even after Cecil's marriage. They were sharing a house in Richmond at the time of Cecil's death, after which Cecil's widow continued to live with Kains-Jackson. She died in 1933.

Athenaeum Club, Pall Mall. September 21 1892

Dear Mr Ellis,

I found your note of the 19th here this morning. Thank you very much for your kind proposal to come to see me.

I fear I cannot ask you to do so, and I should not like to inconvenience you. Anyhow I have decided to cancel a good many engagements, and to leave England tomorrow. I have been here 9 weeks rushing all over the country, and am afraid of having some breakdown in health if I continue this sort of life.

I am very sorry to miss this opportunity of talking over the matter upon which we exchanged letters in July. But I suppose there is no hurry about it.

Writing on the subject would perhaps be difficult to you. I should, however, be glad to hear what you think in general of the two essays I sent you. And if you do not want it, I should be obliged if you would return to me the smaller one called "A Problem in Greek Ethics."

Please do not think that I wish to press you for any opinion you may have formed regarding my studies in the history and psychology of abnormal passion. Still, as I say, if you have anything to utter you would oblige me.

I am yours very sincerely

[No signature]

Am Hof,
Davos Platz,
Switzerland.

2033. *To Horatio Forbes Brown*

Basel, Sept. 23 [1892]

[Dear Horatio]

I came from London through the night, and am spending the day here. The relaxation of nerves which comes when one has had a very lively time, out of the common run, and returns to familiar scenes and things, is upon me. People, I expect, always feel limp, disillusioned, craving after some-

749

thing different from what they have just left, and from what they are going back to, at these moments. To-morrow I am bound for Lausanne, and then again for Davos.

My M.[*ichel*] A.[*ngelo*] B.[*uonarroti*] is just out. I hope the illustrations will not look as bad as I feared. In England I saw "In the Key of Blue" through the press. I suppose it will be out soon. I have got the "Studies in the Greek Poets" with me to prepare for a new edition.[1] If I come to Venice next month, I must try to do something at that book.

It is fearfully muggy and depressing at Basel, as if the dregs of a whole summer of thunderstorms and *scirocco* were in the air. I have slept like a pig and run down like a top all day. Reaction from the high strain of my life in England, I suppose.

I saw a good deal of Pinkie[2] and lunched with C——, who has one of those odd Scotch faces like a very whiskered cat. My old Harrow friend Sir Charles Dalrymple had one.[3]

[Incomplete]

---

1. The 3rd ed. published by A. and C. Black, 1893.
2. Percy Pinkerton. See L 1407.
3. See L 41.

2034. *To Katharine Symonds*

Chur, Switzerland Sept. 25, 1892[1]

[Dearest Katharine]

I got home all right last evening by the long hill and after you had opened my eyes to see them, I found plenty of glow-worms on the way. Some were actually crawling about in the mud, trailing their dimly phosphorescent stomachs there.

It was a splendid morning for that lovely journey, up from the lake and through such beautiful meadows and woods as I think there are not elsewhere to be found. It is a singularly fair land, that of Fribourg and the Berner low-countries. . . .

I might as well have gone on to Davos Platz and slept in my own bed to-night. As it is, being sick to death of railways, after all that tearing about in England and across France, I have elected to take the 6.30 a.m. post over the Lenzer Heide.

750

This is enough regarding myself and doings. I enjoyed that time with you yesterday very much, and I cannot tell you how much. Such little meetings bring a father and daughter closer together than months of living in the same house.

I am quite satisfied with all you told me and I saw concerning your present life. You seem to have taken up the question of learning something in quite a practical spirit. If you stick to it in the way you are beginning, you will be astonished at the amount you have acquired in two or three years. It has always been my belief that nobody learns anything until they really want to learn, and also, I think, they must have a certain sagacity as to the subjects they take up. I thought you spoke very sensibly about your work, which makes me feel that what you do with a firm will and a clear head is not going to be thrown away.

You may count upon me in any difficulty of any kind which may occur to you. I repose perfect confidence in you, and I shall understand anything you want to tell me or to ask. Though you are alone there, you are surrounded with loving thoughts and cares. All four of us, your mother, your sisters and I, are not very far away and all of us would come if called for.

Good-night, my dear Girl. I am almost as drowsy as one of the owls in the Bishop's garden up above here. I walked round the tower to-night. But no friends! Alone here!

. . . Tobias Branger[2] gained a gold medal at a Dutch exhibition of all sorts of Alpine winter gear—toboggans, etc. He has also been investing in real Norwegian skijs.

How do you like this way of doing up a letter? It is very old-fashioned. I rather like it, because I am fond of seals.

I am very busy and very tired. But I want to tell you how much we are looking forward to your arrival,[3] and also that I am mindful of what you wrote to me about wanting to take up History.

I think History a better preparation for life than Mathematics; and also I quite sympathise with what you said in your first letter. Still, it is a pity to give up a subject on which you have spent some time and in which you are making progress.

We must consider this in detail when you come. It is difficult to give more than general advice at a distance. I do not want you to be sacrificed to helping forward the studies of another girl. But if you think your mistress

751

is right in saying you make progress in Mathematics, then it seems to me that you may well continue that subject for a time.

Most depends upon your own mature convictions. And you must remember that the first steps in a subject are those which try our powers most surely and make us discouraged. It is, therefore, very possible that you are advancing without being sensible of it.

The difficulty, of course, is that you cannot take more things at the same time.

Thank you for your note to me. I see that you have settled down, and I hope that the various subjects you are studying will give you so much daily interest as to make life enjoyable. I think you have a cool and sensible head. You are able to take in a good many things at the same time. And I hope you are not possessed with that thirst for knowledge which in some folk (myself included) amounts to a disease providing fever and brain-irritation.

No: I trust that you will learn what Egypt had to do with Greece, and Greece, through Rome, with Italy, and Italy, by means of the Renaissance, with England, in a calm sagacious manner.

History, like every other subject, is a very big thing. The first step in learning it, is to discover how little we know—and how very many circumstances and nations, epochs, climates, of which we are wont to take no heed, contributed in an essential way to our own thought and feeling.

The second step in history is to keep our eyes and ears always open and slowly to accumulate facts. . . .

I drove over to the Pfarrer's [Johannes Hauri][4] last evening, and spent the night in his company (we went to bed at his house at 6 a.m.). It was a grand entertainment given to all the Post and Telegraph officials in Davos. Extremely jolly. But all through the night telegrams came pouring in, brought by rough fellows in greatcoats deep snowed over. The Post Master read them out to us: how one train had been snowed up at Sargans, another at Schiers: how 20 horses with their drivers were imprisoned by avalanches in a tunnel of the Fluela; how the letters would not arrive until this morning, and so forth.

It was a strange jumble of jollification inside and of a weltering sea of snow outside.

Good-bye, my dear. If you want anything, let your father know.

[No signature]

---

1. Katharine Furse received this letter (or these letters) in Switzerland, where she attended school (see L 2030); she published this letter (or these letters) as one in *H & P.*, pp. 113–15.

2. A Davos saddler and upholsterer. This section may have been written in October or November.

3. This section probably written in December.

4. Possibly the Davoser who, like Symonds, had written a section in the travel-book, *The Engadine* (1890), ed. by F. de Beauchamp Strickland.

2035. *To Arthur Symons*

Am Hof, Davos Platz, Switzerland. Sept: 27 1892

Dear Mr Symons

I came here again yesterday, & feel rather funny in these soberer hills after the full riot of my life in England.

I am glad I got that final glimpse of you. Your critique of [W.E.] Henley,[1] like all you do in that way, gave me real pleasure. I do not quite agree with you in admiring his impressions of the sea & moon. It is so comically alien to all modern thought & feeling about the universe for a little imp of the human species to fancy these great natural pairs as an obscene old troll & pickpocket.

I am sending the proof of a mixture of verse & prose wh will come out in a new collection of essays by me.[2] I wonder what you will think of it as a form for presenting one's impressions of nature?

When the book appears I will let you have a copy.

I have gone in for more of what you recommended, talking about myself. Would it not be easy to be only too garrulous on that interesting topic?

Very sincerely yours

J A Symonds—

---

1. "Mr. Henley's Poetry," *The Fortnightly Review*, LVIII (1892), 182–92.
2. *In the Key of Blue and Other Essays.*

2036. *To Havelock Ellis*

Davos. September 29, 1892.

Dear Mr Ellis,

Your letter of the 21st reached me in due course. I think that we may now consider that all important disagreement on the fundamental points is at an end. I most emphatically approve of the attitude you wish to take with regard to medical psychologists. Nor did I ever deny that sexual inverts are frequently neurotic. I only doubt whether neurosis can be regarded as the cause of sexual inversion.

"Sport" is not a word I should have chosen, unless you employed it as the alternative for neuropathic.

My feeling upon the point is that sexual inversion will eventually be regarded as a comparatively rare but quite natural and not morbid deflection from the common rule, due to mental imaginative aesthetical emotional peculiarities of the individual in whom it occurs. It would then be neither a morbidity nor a monstrosity—except in the same sense as colour blindness be termed either.

I do not think that legislation can affect the percentage of persons born inverts. It can only affect those who may have adopted inversion out of curiosity or for any voluntary reason. Consequently the inverts will be more apparent, as such, after Justinian's[1] age, because they are not confounded with the others.

I doubt very much whether the North Italians are more homosexual than the Germans for example. They regard the South Italians as essentially different in this respect from themselves. A male prostitute whom I once saw at Naples told me that he was a Venetian, but had come to Naples because at Venice he only found custom with Englishmen, Swedes and Russians whereas at Naples he could live in excellent Italian society and be abundantly supported.

I will send you some notes on the "[no words]".

I had a letter tonight from Edward Carpenter,[2] to whom I am glad to see that you have communicated our joint project. He ought to be able to give some useful information.

Believe me with all good wishes for the New Year very sincerely yours

[No signature]
P.S. I have a good deal to say about inversion in Switzerland, where I think it plays a prominant part.

---

1. Justinian the Great (483–565), whose *Digests* or *Pandects* (533) were a digest of all writings of Roman jurists and whose *Code* (534) was their revision; his *Novellae* (534–565) were new laws, in the preamble to number 77 of which he fulminated against "unnatural sinners." See Symonds' *A Problem in Modern Ethics* (1896), p. 7.

2. See L 1819.

Am Hof, Davos Platz, Switzerland. October 2, 1892.

My dear Mr Ellis,

I am very much oblighed to you for your letter, and quite agree with you in your criticism of my "Modern Problem" essay. I never regarded myself as really competent to deal with the psychology of this matter, and my sense of a great injustice having been done by law and social opinion has made me less judicial than the treatment requires. If it comes to collaboration, probably the best method would be for me to make myself responsible for the historical essay on Greek love. This, according to my own view of the topic, is an important part of the enquiry.

I have more than once called attention in my Essay to the difficulty of treating sexual abnormality of this sort from the point of view of simple disease, face to face with the facts of ancient Greek society.

I think that nothing could be better than what you propose: namely for you to sketch out the plan of the book as you conceive it, and to let me see it.

[Albert] Moll's book[1] I have not read, and should much like to do so. Will you on a p.[ost] c.[ard] let me have the title and publisher's address? I should be glad to add it to the works I already own upon the subject.

My big book on Michael Angelo has just reached me. I suppose it will be issued to the public in the course of the month.

Believe me very sincerely yours

J A S.

---

1. See L 1996.

2038. *To Janet Ross*

Am Hof, Davos Platz, Switzerland. Oct: 11. 1892

My dear Janet

I do not wonder at your thinking me very forgetful. But I really am wholly unable to keep up what is called a correspondence under certain circumstances. My life in England made it most particularly difficult. You will understand this when I tell you that I stopped in 19 big private houses & 7 hotels on the surface contained by Galashiels,[1] St Ives, Brighton & Cambridge; that I studied & settled how to spend £20,000[2] in good works; that I was always occupied with the proofs of MAB, & that I printed the whole of "In the Key of Blue"[3] (another 300 odd pages); finally that I settled my own affairs about the rent of houses shared;—you will understand that I had no time for letters.

My visit to England filled me with new interests & vigor. It is a great pleasure to me just now to have had a whole long afternoon with Tennyson at Aldworth on the 20th of August. No one could have imagined the end to have been near then.[4]

Since I came back to Davos, I have been busy & sleepy & not very well.

The first bound copy of MAB has reached me.[5] It looks very scrumptuous, & the illustrations are really not so bad. I have thanked you for the trouble you took about the proofs, in a passage of my preface. Both [Guido] Biagi & the Museo Buonarroti are to have copies. Alas, I cannot afford to send you one. That is literally true. The number allowed me free, are exceeded; & I make so little by books that I cannot afford to be generous or do what I wish.

A business friend up here, 2 weeks ago, struck the average of my literary gains during the last ten years. He saw the very detailed accounts I keep of all receipts. It comes to £215.5.6. per annum. And the years from 40 to 50 are the best of a man's life. I spent the whole of my literary income this spring, in Venice, on setting a young man up in business.

However, that does not matter. You know what MAB is; only I hope you will see the illustrations. They are dry, severe, grim. But fairly well executed.[6]

I will mention Dr Percival Wright's[7] wish about a large copy to Nimmo.[8]

Madge & I are so glad to hear that Lina's article[9] will be printed. My friend Miss M.[argot] Tennant with Mrs Horner[10] & a galaxy of rank & fashion (female) are going to start a new periodical.[11] I should not wonder if it were a success. At any rate it will have a list of contributors & supporters fit to make the mouths of bourgeois water. Should you like to be in it? as Italian correspondent, or in any other way?

I may come to Venice for a couple of weeks. But I fear I must not think of Florence. Since March I have only been in this place 6 weeks altogether; & I must soon begin to work at my "History of Graubünden." At present I grind here 6 hrs a day at a third edition of my "Studies of Greek

Poets."[12] It is good for a man to be a little tired. But I wish my literature were better paid. It would give me the sense of sacrificing whims & inclinations to a more serious end in life than I can now regard my scribble.

Remember me to the Padrone & believe me always unchangeably yr affate

J A Symonds

The book goes to the public on the 20th.

---

1. Galashiels, Selkirk, Scotland. There is no earlier reference to this place. Symonds is of course defining geographical boundaries and did visit Innerleithen and Carlisle nearby.

2. See Ls 574 and 2026.

3. His last volume of essays (1893).

4. Tennyson died on Oct. 6.

5. But it is dated 1893.

6. The artist, Edward Poynter, supervised the plates.

7. Dr. Edward Percival Wright (1834–1910), professor of botany, University of Dublin.

8. J. C. Nimmo, the publisher of *Michelangelo*.

9. Lina Duff-Gordon. The article is unknown and was probably to appear in *To-morrow*. See n. 11, below, and L 1882.

10. See L 1571. Frances Graham, who in 1883 married John Francis Fortescue Horner (1842–1927) of Mells, Frome.

11. Margot Tennant drew up elaborate plans for a magazine, to be called *To-morrow*. Her sister, Lucy Graham Smith, was to have been in charge of illustrations, and her contributors included A. J. Balfour, Lady Ribblesdale, Oscar Wilde, and Symonds, among others. See *Margot Asquith: An Autobiography* (4 vols., 1920–22), II. 81–88.

12. Published by A. & C. Black, 1893.

2039. *To Janet Ross*

560 Zattere Venezia Oct: 19 1892

My dear Janet

I am just very rudely sending you a telegram to ask you to send me some fiaschi of your wine—of wh you said you were going to send me a "compione" to Davos.

I came here last night, & found I had no good wine in the cellar. I should be extremely glad to get some of yours as soon as possible. I do not know in what quantities you pack fiaschi. But 10 pieces more or less is what I should at present like to have.

I caught a cold in my face before I left Davos, & have been in great pain coming across the mountains. I did the journey this time by two days' post to Chiavenna & then one huge day (5 a.m.-6.35 p:m:) in the train. I find now that an abcess has been forming under my right cheek-bone, wh sufficiently explains the pain of this purgatorial journey.

I have got a great man of affairs, as usual. Even if one only leaves one's home 3 days, a whole tide of business has collected for me to work through.

So I leave other matters for another time & remain yours affectionately

JAS.

2040. *To Margaret Symonds*

Venice Oct: 19 1892

My dearest Madge

I came here last night, & this morning arrived your letter & Lotta's, for both of wh I am very grateful. It is good to know that I bring you cheer & animation when I come home: for I have often felt that what in me gave pleasure to friends & strangers, was not in its right place in my family. But I see you mean what you say, & I will try to come back soon again in "good form."

I discovered yesterday what was the cause of those complicated pains in my face. An abcess was forming under the right cheek-bone. When it began to discharge, though this was repulsive & sickening, the pain grew blunter. I had, all the same, a sufficiently discomfortable journey from Chiavenna. I got up at 4, set off at 5, encountered the most violent thunderstorms or deluges of rain upon the Lake of Como & then wobbled slow & exhausted on to Venice wh I reached more dead than alive at 6.35.

The lightning was playing all round the sky. It is now zigzagging through a purple cloud above the Dolgoruki villa. But Maria [the maid] had heated all the stoves to furnace pitch. One could not be angry with this hospitality. But it gave me fever & a bad night. What an odd thing pain is —this sort of pain in the bone & fever in the brain for instance! One passes suddenly into the region of it, & in that region it is everything.

I remember that we once made that early morning start before the dawn from Chiavenna. So I will write out for you some verses I scribbled yesterday of impressions. They may remind you of that former occasion:

> In sombre thought I watch withdrawn
> The sad approaches of the dawn;
> While slowly crawls this tortoise train
> From Chiavenna toward the plain.
> Orion & the smouldering star
> Fade on the western mountain bar,
> Whose bristling peaks in serried row
> Are silvered with fresh autumn snow.
> Now feel the finger of the morn
> Through slaty cloud & clefts forlorn;
> And oh! with sudden splendour shines
> Venus entangled in the pines;
> Then swims a space of pallid blue
> Around her radiance into view.
> The stagnant pools the liquid lake,
> Which blocks of stunted poplar break,
> Like sheets of lead still slumber, blurred
> With shadows from huge crags, & stirred
> By curdling flows of wind, wh say
> "Awake, awake!" then faint away.
> How melancholy all this while
> Of waiting for the dawn to smile!
> Nathless she comes, & upward creeps:
> For now the swirling Adda sweeps
> All burnished neath a saffron sky,
> While horns immeasurably high
> With purest argent cleave the woof
> Of clouds, dove-hued, heavens dappled roof.—
> Thus day hath come, not over-bright,
> No harbinger of huge delight,
> But like a tired man well aware
> How far the stage that he must fare.

I thought you had a hankering to come with me to Italy. But I feel you ought to acquire the habit of making the best of a routine life. This has been forced upon none of you in the way it is forced on nearly everybody.

Nobody except some dry folk ever regarded their art except as a *pis aller*. "Life is more than literature." "Thoughts are but the pale spectres of emotions." But I wonder what it *is* your "hopes & wishes go out on far different ways" toward.

Meanwhile it is good right fitting & of great utility to acquire an art. (This sickening abcess makes me stupid & a noisome object to myself. I can't go on writing.) You are wrong when you imagine I did not much like what I saw of your Vescovana.[1] I found it terribly unequal & deficient in technical skill; but full of personality & a peculiar vigour, wh no amount of technicality will give. But I want to see some pieces type-written, as I told you. Look to this.

Love to Lotta. Ever yr

JAS.

Mrs Brown[2] had an accident in England. Fell headlong down a staircase of 13 steps. Is not much the worse, it seems. A letter telling me of this has miscarried I think. Please tell Miss [Edith] Fuller[3] that Mr Day[4] is not satisfied with my proposal about the Organ. This weighty matter must be settled up there, & I will follow. But I cannot do more than I have already done. So I send my own document back to Mr Day unsigned by me.

---

1. Margaret's book, *Days Spent on a Doge's Farm* (1893).
2. H. F. Brown's mother. See L 877.
3. Edith Fuller was for many years the organist for the English Church at Davos.
4. Possibly Lewis Foreman Day (1845–1910), F.S.A., decorative artist educated in France and Germany; designer of wall decorations, textiles, tiles, glass, and all manner of manufactures into which ornament enters; a family of Days were guests of the Hotel Victoria, Davos Platz.

2041. *To Janet Ross*

Venezia Oct: 20. 1892.

I am so glad you have got the book,[1] & think it "splendid." I did not like to promise it beforehand, but of course I wished that you should have it.

It would be charming if you could come here. After these disturbances of weather, I think we may expect a S. Martin's summer.

I am far from well, & had to see a doctor yesterday. Abcess under the cheek-bone (due to cold) with pain fever & noisomeness.

I shall be glad of your good wine,[2] wh I expect, to set me up.

"In the Key of Blue" is a volume of fugitive & flighty essays, chiefly inedited.

JAS.

---

1. *The Life of Michelangelo Buonarroti.*
2. Mrs. Ross was sending him a supply of wine.

2042. *To Mrs. John Addington Symonds*

560 Zattere Venice Oct: 23. 1892

My dearest Catherine

I have been very remiss in writing. But I have little to say & have also been far from well. It is a cold I caught before I left Davos, & wh has settled in my cheekbone & jaw, giving me a great deal of pain as well as making me stupid. The nip of winter seems to have come into the air prematurely.

You forgot to remind me about the servants' wages, but Fanny[1] did, & I paid her the day before I left—460 francs. I have set up a chequebook on the Bank für Graubünden, wh is convenient.

Edward Warren[2] talked to me about a young friend of his, who, [he] says, is particularly good at sculpture in bas relief. I told him to send you the man's name & address. You might see how you like his work. If you do this thing of Pop's,[3] it might be well to employ a young artist. Of course Gilbert[4] is *the* genius; but I expect he would be extremely expensive.

Things here in Venice are much as usual. I think the mezzanino is the warmest place in the town. This corner room where I am now sitting is charmingly cheerful & sunny. It is very luxurious being here alone & taken such good care of by Angelo & Maria [Fusato]. If you want a change after Jany I do not think you could do much better than to try this.

The Curtises[5] were expected home last evening. I may see them perhaps today. I have not seen very many people. The weather too has been bad.

I am much pleased with the success of my benevolence to that young man,[6] to whom I gave the boats last spring. He looks quite another creature —happy & strong—& has been able to save a good deal of money with wh he has bought more boats. Antonio[7] gives a most excellent account of him, & I can see that they have become fast friends.

The Century cabled me an offer of £50 for my "Recollections of Lord Tennyson."[8] This will be a short article of about 9 pages. The whole sum I have made by literature this year is £500 about. But then last year I made hardly anything.

I have invested £2200 during the year, & I find that since we left England in 1877 I have added about £22,000 to the Capital estate. The income of that sum considerably exceeds the shrinkage wh goes on in most stocks, although a good deal is [as] unremunerative, as land in Graubünden.

It is rather absurd to sit talking about these things from Venice to England! I will go out & look round the Accademia.

Your most affectionate

J A Symonds

---

1. Their cook.
2. See L 1943.
3. Catherine had in mind a memorial to her sister, Marianne North.
4. Sir John Gilbert, Royal Academician (1817–97).
5. See L 1717.
6. Unidentified.
7. Antonio Salin, H. F. Brown's gondolier.
8. "Recollections of Lord Tennyson. An Evening at Thomas Woolner's," *The Century Magazine*, XLVI (May 1893), 32–37. Symonds supplied the following note: "Evening at Woolner's in 1865 & Last Interview in August 1892." See Ls 451 and 2027.

2043. *To Margaret Symonds*

Venice Oct: 25 1892

My dearest Madge

I called at the Palazzo Barbaro yesterday afternoon, & saw the Curtises[1] who have just come back. Then I went to Mme Pisani. She arrived last Friday, but did not show herself till Sunday afternoon. She spent a day in decorating the whole appartment. It looked pretty & festive with quantities of such flowers as are still left. Her friend the Marchesa Guiccioli[2] was there: a sort of romp, a pleasant woman I thought. They seemed to be so young together. The Contessa [Pisani] rather overwhelmed me with praises of the whole family, espy you.

In the evening Horatio [F. Brown] & I repaired at 7.30 to Cà Capello.[3] There was a large assembly: the Spanish Ambassador Count Benomar[4] & his wife, Mmes Guiccioli & Pisani, Mrs Eden,[5] the Layards[6] of course & Ol[g]a[7] (with a very red nose). Then the Empress[8] arrived, with her suite: a pug-faced rosy curly daughter,[9] who is engaged to be married to a thin prim bloodless & utterly bored Princeling of Hesse;[10] Count Seckendorf[11] & Miss Cadogan[12] (sister of Henry) in waiting.

All the ladies bobbed in that awfully ungraceful way they have in front of royalty, & everybody stood stiff. The little plump woman, very quietly dressed in black, proceeded to waddle round the room stopping to speak to people here & there, & making the persons she did *not* speak to feel uncomfortable. When she came up to me, she began at once to ask about Michelangelo. I condensed as much information as I could in a convulsive 3 minutes talk, & wound up by asking to be permitted to send her a copy of my book. She accepted very graciously, adding "But you must write your name in it" & waddled away. At dinner I sat between Mme Pisani (whom I took in) & Mrs Eden, & was very happy. We were able to talk to the Guiccioli also, on one side, & to the Princess (Mary[13] I think) on the other. The Princess was instructed in the theory of Alpine gardens with a special description of Am Hof. Her *fiancé* sat by her, never spoke, looked dismal, & ate everything & lots of everything. I got quite apprehensive, for the dinner was atrocious. But it did not seem to harm him.

In the evening all Venice more or less arrived, & there was music—Fortini, Tirindelli,[14] Miss Stella Dyer & her violin. The Empress left before 11.

By the way, I am glad to hear that Fanny [a maid?] keeps right. See that she does not have a relapse. Jo Anna's cooking upstairs is fantastically villainous. I never saw such fearful messes. I lunch here off fish & roasted marrow.

Everyrs

J.A.S.

Carli [has] been here again. He can't stop this disagreeable discharge from my nose. But says it does not matter. Pain nearly gone.

---

1. See L 1717.
2. Wife of the Marchese Guiccioli, friend of Janet Ross and her circle. The Marchese became a prefect of Florence in 1893.

763

3. Sir Henry Layard's palace at the corner of the side-canal Rio di S. Polo and the Grand Canal.

4. The Ambassador was given his title by the King of Spain in 1878.

5. Sibyl Frances Grey (?–1945), wife of Sir William Eden (1849–1915), 7th Bart. of West Aukland and 5th Bart. of Maryland, whom she married July 20, 1886. She is the mother of Sir (Robert) Anthony Eden (1897–   ). See Janet Ross, *The Fourth Generation* (1912) for references to her.

6. See L 1327.

7. Princess Olga of Montenegro. See L 1790.

8. The Empress Frederick of Germany. See L 1831.

9. Princess Margarete Beatrice Feodora (1872–1954), youngest of Empress Frederick's and Emperor Frederick III's 6 children; married Prince Friedrich Charles Ludwig Constantin, Landgrave of Hesse, in 1893.

10. See n. 9, above.

11. Court Chamberlain to Empress Frederick.

12. Ethel Henrietta Cadogan (d. 1930), maid of honor to Queen Victoria; sister of Henry George Gerald Cadogan (1859–93). See L 1695.

13. Margarete, not Mary; see n. 9.

14. Pier Adolfo Tirindelli (1858–1937), Italian violinist and composer, appointed director of the Liceo Benedetto Marcello, Venice, in 1892. Fortini and Stella Dyer are unknown to us.

2044. *To Arthur Symons*

560 Zattere, Venice. Oct. 26. 1892.

Dear Mr Symons,

You will think I never received, or have forgotten all about your *Silhouettes*.[1] They reached me duly during a few days' visit which I spent to my Alpine home, on the way back from England. I did not care to acknowledge the gift at once, or when my impressions are still raw. So I took the book with me to this place. I can assure you that it has made deep and ineffaceable marks on my memory, not only for the singular felicity of phrase which distinguishes each separate poem, and also for the power of pictorial presentation—but far more for that indefinable something in the emotion and the style, which communicates the author's mood. Then too I find there has been such a sincere wish to pierce to the *vraie verité* of each situation as the poet felt it, and to reproduce that essence with the utmost economy of means. In all this I think you have been very successful, and have given us what is both delightful and original.

As perfect, each in its own way, I should mention "On the Beach", "In the Oratory", "April Midnight", "For a Picture of Watteau", "The Javanese Dancers". But then I like, in rather a different mood, "Emmy", "In the Haymarket", "Gipsy Love". I do not discover echoes and reminiscences —only the French influence to which you have committed your artistic self. It is stupid writing about these matters—so difficult to say just what one means.

I am going to send you a little volume which is being published for me by Elkin Matthews, *In the Key of Blue*. I don't know whether it has appeared yet. It is always a pleasure to hear from you and to read what you write. Will you sometimes remember this?

I am looking down the broad canal of the Giudecca, toward the hazy Paduan distance, the whole scene blurred with sad grey mists in which there are almost imperceptible touches of nacreous blue and green. And all the moving boats are very black. Such a sad Autumn aspect of a place which is so sheeny in the Spring! It is my own little house, and I like to be here alone in all seasons.

Ever yours

John Addington Symonds.

---

1. Published 1892.

2045. *To Elkin Mathews*[1]

560 Zattere Venice Oct: 27 1892

Dear Mr Mathews

It is some time since I finished the proofs of "In the Key of Blue." But I have not heard more of the book, nor have I seen the title page, or cover.

I should be glad if you could let me know when you mean to bring it out etc.

A young man, of whose promise in literature I think highly, Mr Percy Addleshaw,[2] has written a short book of sketches, prose & verse, about Cairo. Parts of it seem to me quite excellent in style & feeling. All the articles are not of equal merit, but none are bad.

If you write to me, will you let me know whether you think it worth while to look at a type-written copy of these things with a view to publication! I do not like to tell Mr Addleshaw to send them without

giving you at least the opportunity of saying that they are not of the sort
you care to see.

Believe me very truly yours

John Addington Symonds
My address, wh is that of my Venetian pied à terre, will find me for
another 10 days or so.

---

1. See L 1989.

2. William Percy Addleshaw (1866–1916) in 1897 edited Rodin Noel's *Selected Poems* and added a biographical and critical essay, but Elkin Mathews did not publish any of his works (e.g., *The Cathedral Church at Exeter,* 1898) until 1920, when he brought out Addleshaw's *Last Verses* (with a preface by Arundel Osborne).

2046. *To: Margaret Symonds*

Venice, Oct: 29, 1892

My dearest Madge

I am reading the "Doge's Farm." Put the whole of what remains of the copy into type-writing. The Ms gains by being read in this way.

I do not want to flatter you. But my artist's soul, which is not the parent's, forces me to tell you that this is something rare and wonderful in its blending of poetry and humour.

Unequal certainly, but so vivid. One little piece "In Early June" seems to me quite perfect. I am intoxicated by the extraordinary play of your imagination and emotion on your language.

Oct 30. I wrote the above yesterday before I had read the whole of your work. What I said is certainly not too strong for "In Early June," wh I regard as a remarkable piece of prose-writing. It is, however, too high pitched for most of the articles. You have spoiled "The Santo,"[1] by the way, by leaving out what was assuredly the best piece of your letter to your mother: I mean the description of the procession up the dusky church—the indistinct object like a great star at the entry, defining itself as the Saint's head in a blaze of diamonds & candles wreathed with lilies. This must be replaced.

I read "In Early June" aloud to Horatio. He was quite carried off his legs by it.

I almost wish you would send this to the PMG, & try whether the new editor[2] is going on with you.

As I say, get the whole of the rest (excluding the 2 in print) typed. They shall be arranged in their order and submitted to some publisher.

No more now. Yr most aff

J.A.S.

I crossed the Splügen this day 2 weeks ago. I don't think I shall stay here much longer. It is, however, pleasant enough to idle. Lovely afternoons of mellow golden light & sometimes a sad rich sunset.

What, by the way, *is* the undercurrent of melancholy in your work? Neuropathy?

---

1. "In Early June" became Chap. IV of *Days Spent on a Doge's Farm* (1893); the *Santo* is described in "The Festa of S. Antonio at Padua," Chap. XIII, and occurred on June 13, 1892.

2. We have been unable to find "In Early June" in the *Pall Mall Gazette*. The new editor was Clement Kinloch-Cooke (1854–1944), barrister, economist, and editor at various times of the *English Illustrated Magazine, The Observer, The New Review,* and in 1892–93 of the *Pall Mall Gazette;* educated at Cambridge in mathematics and law; knighted 1905.

2047. *To Charles Kains-Jackson*

Venice, 560, Zattere. October 30, 1892

My Dear Jackson,—It is one of those evenings charged with an inexplicable melancholy and what the French call "indicible tristesse." Outside upon the broad Canal of the Giudecca foghorns are calling from sea-going steamers, and now and then the weird sting of a siren—like a writhing sound-serpent or a Banshee's cry—shivers from nowhere, no whither, through the opaque mist.

I could never make up my mind whether it is from our own nerves, or from something altered and set wrong in natural things, that this sense of a profound gloom now and again settles down quite unexpectedly. So often too it happens on a Sunday. There is an excuse for that in England; none here in Italy. If I had energy enough to seek the Piazza I should find it ringing with a military band, while bright-eyed, sleek-necked sailors shot ceaseless invitations as they passed.

I always like my life here when I am alone. I have fair bedrooms, the sunniest of which I use as my own scribbling-place in early spring or autumn; a fairly large sitting-room with five small windows in a row, a dining-room next the kitchen, and Angelo [Fusato] for factotum with his wife for cook. It is a little Paradise for a bachelor. And then such a view! And all the shifting crowd, soldiers, sailors, *facchini* [& porters] in triple blues, girls with lovers, gnarled old men;—just under my nose; for I am in an *entresol* [a mezzanine].

My life is being spent too much among the great of this world. The Empress Frederick[1] is here with her daughter Margaret,[2] and the nice young Prince of Hesse—something, who is the girl's *fiance*. They make considerable demands on my society, and I am always plying in my gondola between this house and their palace on the Grand Canal. *N'importe.* It is good for a man to live in both worlds. The other World is Augusto [Zanon], and a little old-fashioned wine-shop in a garden of vines, where the gondoliers congregate.[3] There are many charming high-bred women in the circle of the Empress: my old friend the Contessa Almoro Pisani,[4] the Marchesa Guiccioli,[5] the Gräfin von Wolkenstein,[6] the Princess Hatzfeldt,[7] Lady Layard,[8] Mrs Eden,[9] Mrs [Daniel] Sargent Curtis.[10]

Then I have a third set: Pen Browning[11] in his vast Palazzo Rezzonico with Cullum,[12] and a corporal of the 2nd Life Guards in mufti, and old Sir James Lacaïta,[13] and Mrs Bronson,[14] and General De Horsey.[15]

One has to come and live in Venice to see how the various strata of society flow into each other naturally, and can be enjoyed by one and the same person daily, without any dislocation of conventions.

I need hardly say that it makes a great difference having such a friend and servant as Angelo. But then I doubt whether the same sort of person can ever be found outside the gondolier class. It also makes much for me that I am in the same house as my friend Horatio Brown, though separate as far as access goes. He forms by himself, with his associates, a fourth set.

November 5th.—I do not know what made me break off in this letter. The days go so nonchalantly that one realises that desire of Clough's "Were life but like the gondola!"[16] There have been a succession of sad sumptuous autumn days: the lagoons asleep, gently heaving, in long undulations, beneath the immense vault of varied greys, modulating from the warmest violet to the coldest slaty hues. Mournful pageants of sunset, hanging roses and flakes of crimson fire over the whole expanse of heaven's pavilion. And then, still misty nights with a touch of chill in them, when the concave of the sky, mingled in the concave of the water, made one sphere of mysterious blue, moving about in which was like being in the midst of some pale milky sapphire, all luminous with moonlight suffused into the vapour. Silhouettes of churches, masts of ships, blurred and *estampés* into shadows. Lead-covered domes and roofs, drenched with dew, glistening like dull silver. Only, at intervals, along the quays, lamps dilated into globes, with golden shadows sagging down along the imperceptible azure of the water floor. A divine Whistlerian Symphony, with infinite space and inimitable delicacy of superabundant detail added.

These things have been engulfed again in sea-fog, and I listen this night to the complaining fret of the boats moored close beneath my windows. I am alone for once, and sad, and disappointed of an expectation for the sake of which I contrived to elude a reception of the Empress. *Taci, taci, inquieto cuore* [Peace, peace, unquiet heart]. I do not think it is because I am defrauded of a longed-for opportunity that I am so weary. *Ich weiss nicht was soll es bedeuten dass ich so traurig bin.*[17] Moments come in the hyper-sensitive life of all artist-natures when, unlonged, unbidden, we are assailed by desolate perceptions of the inutility of life, the vanity of all things, the visionary fabric of the universe, the incomprehensibility of ourselves, the continuous and irreparable flight of time,—when all our joys and sorrows, our passion and our shame, our endeavours to achieve and our languor of inertia, seem but a mocking film, an iridescent scum, upon the changeful surface of a black and bottomless abyss of horrible inscrutability.

Alas for us, that we feel the realities of beauty and emotion so acutely, and have such power at times to render them by words or forms for others, should also feel with such poignant intensity the grim vacuity of the universe, the irrationality of life, the illusory and transitory nature of the ground on which we tread, the flesh that clothes us round, the passions that fret our brains, the duties we perform, the thoughts that keep our will upon the stretch through months of useless labour.

This is the mood which blurs my soul to-night in solitude, while the Princess Margaret and the Prince of Hesse are acting charades at Cà Capello,[18] and Sir Henry Layard is presenting a copy of my "Michelangelo" to the Empress Frederick.

I am sure I do not want to be there. And I do not think it is the absence of "the blue boy" [Augusto Zanon] for whom I renounced my part in those Court-triumphs, which has so dejected me. I feel it a relief even to be alone. For how could such a mood have been other than contaminating to the lamp of the soul—as the seamist blurs the moon?

Here I tired of writing about what cannot be described in the Soul's sickness—the *Maladie de l'âme*. I turned back to look at the beginning of my letter, and to my surprise I found that, a week ago, I had written to you in just such a melancholy mood. It is some instinct then that, when the mood is there, I turn in thought to you. Take this, if you will or can, for a compliment!

Now I will set down a sonnet I made lately.

L'Envoi à ces Passions

Hence, all ye vernal loves, light forms of joy,
　　Shapes of dim gods trampling the liquid air,
　　Ye lovely Knights & blonde squires debonair,
　　Blithe jocund youths descending on the boy!
Hence too, yet later loves, live men so fair,
　　Strong, sweet as wine of grapes that cannot cloy;
　　Your charm nor law nor custom may destroy:
　　Yet wisest Fate says No! Thou shalt forbear!
Hence then, ye floating dreams, of hope the blossom,
　　While young blood burgeoned into life's full spring:
Hence, potent puissances, clasped to my bosom,
　　When fruits of summer burdened passion's tree.
Autumn hath come, & doom, the stern sad king,
　　Beckons my tired Soul o'er death's frightful sea.

J.A.S.

---

1. See L 1831.
2. See L 2043.
3. See plate in Vol. II.
4. See L 1717.
5. See L 2043.
6. Probably Marie, Countess von Wolkenstein, who was a lady of the palace, daughter of Count Friedrich Schaaffgotsche and wife of Oswald, Count von Wolkenstein (1843–1913), whom she married in 1877.
7. Countess Natalie von Benckendorff of Trachenberg, who married Hermann, Prince of Hatzfeldt (1848–1933) in 1872, and was grand mistress of the court of Empress Frederick.
8. Mary Enid Evelyn Guest married Sir Austen Henry Layard, the discoverer of Ninevah (1817–1894) in 1869. See L 1327.
9. See L 2043.
10. See L 1717.
11. Robert Wiedemann Barrett Browning (1849–1912), son of the poet. In 1887 Robert Browning bought the Palazzo Rezzonico, a house "Pen" found a bit too

big.—Letter of Robert Browning to Mr. and Mrs. Charles Skirrow, Dec. 25, 1888, in C. D. DeVane and K. L. Knickerbocker, *New Letters of Robert Browning* (1950), p. 363.

12. Gerry Cullum (G. Milner-Gibson-Cullum, 1857–?), the only son of Thomas Milner-Gibson (1806–84), English statesman and M.P., described by Mabel Dodge Luhan, *Intimate Memories* (2 vols., 1935), II, 124, as "middle-aged and red and stout with a face quite like a mixture of a pig and a frog—rather repulsive." He had an attractive manner nevertheless—"a hearty, Irish laugh and a lovely North-Country accent —and there was a kind of magnetism about him."

13. See L 1879.

14. See L 1673.

15. Lieutenant-General William Henry de Horsey (1826–1915), entered the army, 1844; major general, 1878; retired, 1883; served in the Crimean war; owned Casa Semitecolo near the Palazzo Davio. Angelo Fusato was serving him when he entered Symonds' employ.

16. The refrain of Clough's "In a Gondola." The line properly reads "Were life but as the gondola."

17. I don't know what it means that I am so sad.—Heine, *Die Lorelei*, l. 1.

18. See L 2043.

2048. *To Janet Ross*

Zattere 560. Venice Oct: 30. 1892.

Dear Janet,

The wine arrived duly. I write return the two damigianne [demi-johns] & send you 30 lire to settle accounts.

If you can, please let me have another damigianna of the same size & same wine, & two bottles of oil.

We drink this wine like fishes with high approval.

I am asked tonight to dine at the Pal: Rezzanico[1] to meet Lacaita.[2] Cannot go, because of a self-made engagement. But hope to find him at home this afternoon. I do not think you can have come, else would have told me.

We are all of us bedevilled with Empress Frederick.[3] I have had to wait upon her three times—one of which, the last, being an evening of privacy in her own rooms, I found very pleasant.

Now & then Venice is her best this season. But the place is not so nice to autumn in as our hillside above Florence.

I am reading what Madge has written about Vescovana.[4] It is a book sure in fact. A most extraordinary piece of writing for its literary grace. I am carried off my feet by its purely technical existence here & there—in the management of language. Not much stuff of thought or incident. And excessively unequal.

What to do with it, after it is finished?

Everyrs

JAS

---

1. Pen Browning's palace on the Grand Canal. See L 2047.
2. Sir James Lacaita. See L 1879.
3. See L 1831.
4. It became *Days Spent on a Doge's Farm* (1893).

2049. *To Margaret Symonds*

Venice Nov: 4. 1892

My dearest Madge

Your & Lotta's letters make me restless, longing to be in your golden valley with the soft air & the sense of slumber coming. I think I must set off next week.

One of those sad moods, in which all life seems wasted, & the heart is full of hidden want, & one does not even know what one desires, but a sense of wistfulness is everywhere—one of these moods has been upon me several days.

It is very thankless. On all sides there come pouring in upon me proofs of my achieved renown—the success of my last big book—the sympathy of strangers. And yet I am not happy.

The world too has been very beautiful here at times. We went outside the Porto del Lido yesterday, & moved ourselves to one of the great pali. One tide was running out like a river, till it changed of a sudden, & new shivers in the reverse direction began to thrill the keel. The sky was a vast vault of infinitely varied greys—dove-breasted, slaty, violet, pure blue, rose-tinted, tawny—all drenched & drowned in the prevailing tone of sea-lavender: and the water, heaving, undulating, swirling, without a ripple on its glassy space, reflected those blent hues, making them here & there more flaky & distant in patches of azure or of crimson: out in the offing, waiting for a breeze to carry them toward Torcello, were half-a-dozen fishing boats with sails like butterflies atremble on a flower, red, orange, lemon, set by some ineffable fact of Nature just in the right place to heighten & accentuate her symphony of greys. And yet I was not happy.

And then the eclipsed full moon rose, & a cindery pall overspread the world, & we went home. And after the eclipse, as though that quarrel between sun & moon had washed heaven with tears of reconciliation & repentance, Luna sailed in a sky of brilliant blue. The colour was indescribable—so blue, so blue,—through the thin diffused mist wh lay low along the face of the lagoon, & through the pearly mackeral clouds lazily afloat above. The churches, S-Georgio, Redentore, Salute, loomed, dusky silhouettes, bathed in the blue, the clinging mist; & wherever the moistened lead upon their roofs & cupolas caught moonlight, it shone like silver. The only golden things were the lamps dilated into globes, with tremendous shuttle-shaped reflections sagging down along the water. I paced about—first from 7 till 8—then afterwards from 11 till 12—looking on all this. And yet I was not happy. On the contrary, so infinitely sad, restlessly longing for I know not what.

"Why do ye toil hither & thither upon paths laborious & peril-fraught? Seek what ye are seeking; but it is not there where ye are seeking it. Ye are seeking a life of beatitude in the realm of death. It is not there."

And indeed I know what I was wanting, & at the same time knew that even to want it was vanity, to possess it dust and ashes.

All these things appertain to the temperament which one calls neuropathic. But they belong also to the artist. In compensation for sensibilities to beauty & powers over language, sound, form, etc, far exceeding those of his neighbours, he is doomed to a life-long ache, a numbing paralyzing pain at the heart, a useless feeble craving, which renders him in some ways weaker, often far more wretched, than the most commonplace of men. The only way out, to avoid being mad or bad instead of only sad, is work.

J.A.S.

Something has happened, I think, about Mme Pisani.[1] She never answered by writing or speech my letter in wh I proposed going to Vescovana, & she has not acknowledged my Michelangelo. I don't think I shall try to go there.

---

1. Perhaps Mme. Pisani was displeased by Margaret Symonds' book about her farm, *Days Spent on a Doge's Farm.*

2050. *To Elkin Mathews*

Venice Zattere No 560 Nov: 6. 1892

Dear Mr Mathews

I am much obliged to you for your note about my book & the prospectuses. I shall be delighted to see Mr Rickett's[1] design copy as you tell me it is charming.

Will you let me have a copy of each edition for myself, & send in my name (from the Author) 14 copies (of the 8/6 edn) to the addresses enclosed.[2]

Of course you will charge against me those copies wh exceed the number you are in habit of allowing to the author.

The Cairo sketches wh I mentioned by Mr Addleshaw[3] cannot, I think, have yet come beneath your notice.[4] They are not his "Stories" (which by the way I have not seen. His work in verse seems to me usually too cold & self-restrained, deficient in force & energy of thought. But the Cairo book has much more of glow warmth & energy than anything I have yet seen of his. I think it might be worth your while to look at it.

I am delighted that you like my Michelangelo. As yet I have seen hardly any reviews of it, but Mr Nimmo says they have been "most favourable" & also that the edition is on the point of being exhausted.

Believe me very faithfully yours

J A Symonds

I have got no decent letter paper!

---

1. Charles Ricketts (1866–1931), painter, sculptor, art critic, and designer of stage sets; coeditor of *The Dial* (1889–97); founder and owner of the Vale Press (1896–1904): Babington (pp. 82–83) describes the design thus:

The front and back covers are filled with a design (Hyacinths and Laurel) by Charles Ricketts in gold, with the words *In the Key of Blue* in ornamental lettering (also by Ricketts) in the upper portion of the design. All edges uncut. A few copies were bound in *light blue* cloth, and the late Mr. Mathews informed me that the whole of the ordinary issue was to have been so bound, but that Mr. Ricketts came in and objected, making a jest about "Ricketts' Blue," and therefore the cream cloth was substituted. Copies in the *blue* cloth were few, and fetch considerably more than the others.

2. The addresses do not accompany the original letter.

3. See L 2045.

4. We find no evidence of the publication of these sketches.

2051. *To Janet Ross*

Zattere No. 560 Venice Nov: 11. 1892.

My dear Janet

I cannot take back the money & the wine. It is true that the wine has a cask taste. But I am drinking it, & except for this drawback, I think it most excellent stuff. Quite the best of your growth I should say.

If you like to square matters by sending me a few fiaschi [wine flasks] to Davos Platz, I shall be happy in drinking to your health there.

I ought to go home soon. But I find it difficult to stop loafing about in this divine St Martin's summer of soft air & superb sunsets.

I go out every afternoon beyond the Porto del Lido & get tied up to one of the pali in the open & stay there till the last red lights are fading in the West.

Sometimes I think with yearning of Fiesole at sundown, & sometimes of my own Davos, which Madge calls the golden valley in these days. It seems to be universally a splendid autumn. Catherine writes in excellent spirits from London—she thrives in the fog—does not mention that—but I gather from Ronald Gower's lamentation that it *is* foggy.

Miss Zimmern[1] writes a waspish little note because I told the truth about a vile English version she has made of a perfectly worthless preface which Biagi has drivelled out to introduce a set of utterly inept & indecent pictures of Dante's Inferno which a drunken Dutchman did in the days of Georgio Vasari & his Cupola which art-ignorant Fisher Unwin is bent on to make sense of *that*.[2] There is sense. I did not know that Miss Z was the translator. She seems to have the very devil of a temper. Poor I have had to write some critical words to introduce the whole lot of them—drunken Dutchman, conceited empty-pated Biagi, hornet-tongued Helen Z, & uncritical Unwin.

Everyrs

JAS

Margot [Tennant] writes she is so glad to get you. I hope you will see her. She is not only very clever, but really good & warm-hearted. In spite of her reputation for fastness, I know few purer-minded women—conservative in religion & moral principles.

---

1. Helen Zimmern. See L 1409.
2. The book Symonds refers to is *Dante: Illustrations to the Divine Comedy of*

Dante, executed by the Flemish Artist Jo. Stradanus, 1587, and reproduced in Phototype from the originals existing in the Laurentian Library of Florence, with an Introduction by Doct. Guido Biagi, and a Preface by John Addington Symonds (1892). It was published by Unwin and was priced at 126s. Symonds criticizes Biagi for unfairness to Signorelli's "chiaroscuro work," for completely neglecting Blake's and Flaxmann's designs for Dante, and for overpraising Stradanus: "to whom as it seems, only 24 designs for the *Inferno*, and perhaps four for the *Purgatorio* should be assigned with any certainty." Symonds supplies some further notes on Stradanus' life. There is no mention of Miss Zimmern as translator of Biagi's 11-page introductory essay. But see L 2059. For Biagi see L 1869.

2052. *To Margaret Symonds*

Venice Nov: 11. 1892

My dearest Madge

I began a letter the other day with more descriptions & emotions in it. But this I threw aside as morbid. Have you kept the one I wrote you about a sunset? I am going probably when I get back to attempt another little Venetian fantasia.

It is difficult to get unmoored from this divine place in this S. Martin's summer. Yet I will not delay more than till Wednesday next at the outside. I want to go out of Venice for a night next Monday. Then when I start, I propose to spend a day at Vescovana & come direct by Gothard. Do you recommend that route you tried by Goldau? Where did you stop the night? Please reply.

Horatio's History of Florence,[1] wh I am reading in proof, is a really solid & brilliant performance. He has done nothing equal to it before, & I do not think any extant history of the Republic is as good.

I am rather sorry to hear you sent your best bit of Vescovana work to "Tomorrow."[2] It is true that, if they put it into No 1, it will receive a great deal of notice. But I somehow feel the note struck in it is too high in quality, too poetical, for the periodical. I should not wonder if they felt this & returned it.

Here is a note from Margot [Tennant], wh really means: Do write a review of some book & let Madge sign it! I hardly think this would satisfy either of us.

Everyrs

JAS.

Interesting letter about Pfarrer [pastor] in the Dischma.[3]
I wonder I have not been asked for a cheque to pay the monthly bills.

---

1. He means Venice, published in March, 1893.
2. *To-morrow,* Margot Tennant's projected journal. See L 2038.
3. Dischma is a mountain valley near Davos. We have not identified the man referred to, but he may be Pastor Hauri (see L 2034). He may also be a Pfarrer Ziegler, who lectured in Davos on such diverse subjects as Martin Luther and Hannibal (see *Davos Courier,* March 29, 1889). Either clergyman may possibly be represented in Margaret Symonds' novel, *A Child of the Alps* (1920), by Pfarrer Caflisch, the main character. Caflisch is a Lutheran clergyman of "free and very unorthodox doctrines." Something of an actor, he is a powerful preacher who socializes with folk freely during the week: he "had the charm of a boundless and almost magnetic sympathy" and "loved life and love better than he loved renunciation and religious devotion."

2053. *To Horace Traubel*[1]

Venice. Zattere No. 560 Nov: 13. 1892

Permanent
Address
  Am Hof
Davos Platz
  Switzerland

My dear Traubel

I have been running about the world so much all this year—Venice, England, Switzerland, & again Venice, since the end of March—that I have neglected both serious work & correspondence.

Of a truth, I sorely needed a long holiday, rest from the tension of brain-labour, & collision with multitudes of men of all sorts & conditions.

This partly explains why I have not earlier responded to the call about Whitman's house. I now enclose a cheque for £5, which I wish I could make larger.

I think you would be surprised to hear what "a successful man of letters" makes in England. I struck the average of my literary gains for the last ten years (best years of life, between 40 & 50) & found that my income has been exactly £215.5.4 per annum. Journeys, purchase of books, all the expenses connected with the business, to be deducted from this magnificent total.

Don't publish this fact anywhere. I am going to publish a full balance sheet in some American monthly[2] soon.

A friend writes to me from London that a Circular is going around, being the prospectus of a collection of Letters addressed to Whitman,[3] which is in process of publication. He says there is a fragment of a "very private one" from myself, & begs me to take some measures to prevent its being printed. No such circular has reached me.

But I am certain that, if this is so, as my friend says, you must have something to do with the projected volume.

So I come to beg you not to publish any private letters of mine without my consent.

You know that, in England, & in Europe generally, doing so—i.e. publishing private letters without the writer's consent—is not only considered to be a very dishonourable action, but is also punishable by legal process.

I am aware that on one occasion I told Whitman things about my own past life (with the object of showing how he had helped me) which were not meant for the eyes of the public, & the diffusion of which would not only cause me great pain, but would also provoke me to a violent attack on Whitman's literary executors.

So I hope there is no truth in the report. I should attach little weight indeed to it, unless it had come to my friend through E. Carpenter.

Pray, my dear Traubel, set my mind at rest about this.

I may say incidentally that I have no objection to the publication of the POEM[4] which I see in the list of articles for the volume I subscribe to.

          Believe me most sincerely yours

               John Addington Symonds.

---

1. See L 1728.
2. Babington does not list any essay on this.
3. Traubel, Bucke, and Harned, *In Re Walt Whitman* (1893). See L 1907.
4. "Love and Death: A Symphony" appeared in *In Re Walt Whitman*, pp. 1–12, as did, on p. 412, extracts from L 1761. See L 1907.

2054. *To Margaret Symonds*

Venice Nov. 14 1892

My dearest Madge

This is the old-fashioned way of writing. I am going to adopt it, because I like the rough paper, I like sealing-wax, & I do not want to run the risk of a double letter. Be careful, my dear girl, how you cut or tear it open—cutting was the method used by Miss [Jane]Austen—or else you will lose a small portion of the precious contents wh may be written on the last of the 3 available pages.

I am all agog to come home. But the machine creaks & labours when it is being set in motion. So I may not come till the end of the week.

I shall bring Angelo [Fusato] with me. Let him have the red room, since the one on the ground-floor is useful for occasional events—luggage or a belated Bündner.

I send you an ineffably charming picture of myself in a periodical, as well as a general survey of my life. There is one splendid phrase in it, describing me as "the indomitable invalid."

There has appeared a very eulogistic review of MAB in the Daily News, by Lang[1] I think. He says "Mr. S's MAB is, so far, his masterpiece. He has found himself, as the French say, & his subject. He has given every proof of erudition, industry, & skill, directed by accomplished taste. It is a great work, & polished *ad inguem* (i.e. to the highest finish of detail)."

Nimmo, however, sends me no reviews.[2] So I do not know exactly how the book is being criticized.

I am going to telegraph to Mme Pisani & ask to come there on Wednesday. I should rather like to touch on the delicate question of your "First Impressions."[3] Perhaps she will let me read out parts. I don't think you could print it without her permission. I read a little to Mrs Brown [Horatio Brown's mother], who was amused immensely. I would not let her have the copy, feeling it might get about.

On Thursday I hope then to set off without further delay for Davos. Possibly I may leave Padua by the night train on Thursday & sleep at Zürich Friday night. The journey is difficult to decide, & from Vescovana to Davos without stopping rather makes me quail. One of the reasons which has kept me dawdling here is the memory of the very uncomfortable journey I had last month & the sense that in one way or another it must all be done over again.

Best love to Lotta. Your most affecate

JAS.

---

1. Mr Roger Lancelyn Green has been able to identify this unsigned review as Andrew Lang's: "Lang's style and outlook are so recognisable that he might just as well have signed most of his *Daily News* 'Lost Leaders.'" Lang's review appeared in the *Daily News*, No. 14,541 (November 9, 1892), 5: "For many years Mr. Symonds has been working at the Italian Renaissance, and now he may be said to have crowned his labours with his 'Life of Michel Angelo' (Nimmo). It is an admirable and most interesting book. Mr. Symonds's style, at one time rather floridly rhetorical, has run clear, like a flooded river. He has convinced himself that rhetorical effusions about works of art are not telling, and that plain and simple words do all that can be done. . . ." Mr. Green has also identified Lang's eulogy of Symonds (*Daily News*, No. 14,681 (April 21, 1893), p 5, a judicious complement to the review of *Michelangelo*. Lang wrote that Symonds' death "is a serious loss to English literature. He was not only a fine writer in the highest and noblest sense of the term, but a fine thinker. It would better express our meaning to say that he thought beautifully and wrote beautifully. . . . No writer who survives him can carry on his labour. Happily it is fairly complete as it stands. When he had finished the 'Renaissance' his work was really done."

2. Other reviews of Symonds' *Michelangelo* were these: Walter Armstrong, "A New Life of Michelangelo," *The Portfolio*, No. 37 (1893), 84–86; Anonymous, "*The Life of Michelangelo Buonarroti* . . . by John Addington Symonds . . . ," *The Athenaeum*, No. 3415 (April 8, 1893), 446–48; Maurice Hewlett, "*The Life of Michelangelo Buonarroti* . . . ," *The Academy*, XLII (July–December, 1892), 415–17; Herbert P. Horne, "Michelangelo," *The Fortnightly Review*, LIX (January–June, 1893), 64–79; and Anonymous, "Symonds' 'Michelangelo Buonarroti,'" *Spectator*, LXIX (July–December, 1892), 961–62.

3. A part of Margaret's *Days Spent on a Doge's Farm* (1893) which Mme. Pisani apparently disliked. See L 2049.

2055. *To Janet Ross*

Venice Nov. 15. 1892

Dear Janet

MAB seems to have been a real success. Not a word of blame or outraged sense of decency in any of the numerous reviews.[1] Edition all but sold already.

I am making arrangements for its translation into German & also into French. I have an offer for the Italian translation from M. & Mm: Wiel here (she née Honble Alethea Lawley),[2] wh I am quite willing to accept. Only there was a talk with Biagi about a Contessa[3] who wanted to do it—with his help.

Do you know anything about the Contessa? I have forgotten her name, & could you, if you do, discern whether she still wishes to do it.

Biagi is impossible. He has written an execrable preface to those foul pictures of Stradanus.[4] And he won't answer Fisher Unwin, Alinari,[5] Miss Zimmern or myself. So I suppose it is of no use thinking at him & his Contessa.

I don't want however to close with the Wiels before I make at least an effort to reach the Contessa.

I am off for Vescovana & then to Switzerland.

In haste yours

J.A.S.

So sorry to hear about your poor bracciante.[6] What a disturbo for you!

---

1. See L 2054.
2. See L 1979.
3. Contessa Rasponi. See L 1991.
4. See Ls 2051 and 2059.
5. The Florentine publisher of art books and reproductions of art founded in 1854 by Leopoldo Alinari.
6. Day-laborer. We have not been able to find out what happened.

2056. To Charles Kains-Jackson

[Davos, Nov. 19, 1892]

[Dear Kains-Jackson]

. . . you that at several times I have been thinking of . . . in moments moreover when I think it is a proof of real sympathy to remember a friend.

I have been up here in the Alps again since last Friday fortnight. Angelo [Fusato] has not quitted my side yet. The deep snow is piling itself up tonight, & there is not a sound, except the passage of a mountain spring which flows perpetually through the house.

One reason why I kept back the letter so long was that I wanted to use it for part of an article on "Venetian Melancholy."[1] That is now written.

How would you like to have that poem of mine "Midnight at Baiae"?[2]
I see no reason to withold it, now that I have not written anything for some
time in "the Artist."

Did you see how Sayle[3] has been praising Nicholson[4] in "The Hobby
Horse"?

[Incomplete]

---

1. A transcript of a diary, Oct. 30—Nov. 8, 1892, in *The Fortnightly Review*, LIX
(1893), 256–61.

2. The poem, subtitled "A Dream Fragment of Imperial Rome," was in the
privately printed *Lyra Viginti Chordarum, Pamphlet I* (see Babington, pp. 16–20), and
was written probably in the early seventies. It was published in *The Artist*, XIV (March,
1893), 69–70, and shortly afterwards as a separate pamphlet.

3. Charles Edward Sayle. See L 1502.

4. John Gambril Nicholson. See L 1993.

2057. *To Margot Tennant*

[Davos] Nov. 19 [1892]

Dearest Margot

I only came back last night from Venice—28 hours in the train—and
found your letter.

Here is a sonnet, if not too late to use. I am sorry about "Tomorrow."[1]
I doubt if any harm would have come of it. But it is better to be on the safe
side perhaps.

Keep an eye on Pinkerton.[2] He was to help of all sorts. Am sorry for
him that this has fallen through. Tell me what you think of him.

I have 12 letters of *pressing* importance to write. So goodbye. The 2
girls in rampant spirits, and the Alpine autumn lovely. But how lovely were
the Lagoons!!!

Yours

J.A.S.

On True & False Passion

No mortal thing enthralled these longing eyes
When perfect peace in thy fair face I found;

782

But far within, where all is holy ground,
    My soul felt Love, her comrade of the skies:
For she was born with God in Paradise;
    Nor all the shows of beauty shed around
    This fair false world her wings to earth have bound;
    Unto the Love of Loves aloft she flies.
Nay, things that suffer death, quench not the fire
    Of deathless spirits; nor eternity
    Serves sordid Time, that withers all things rare.
Not Love but lawless impulse is Desire:
    That slays the Soul: true Love makes still more fair
    Our friends on earth, fairer in death on high.
               John Addington Symonds—
               From the Italian of Michelangelo Buonarroti

---

1. Either Margot Tennant's plans for a journal had apparently fallen through; or, an earlier poem Symonds had sent to her for publication was too frank. See L 2038.
2. Percy Pinkerton. See L 1407.

2058. *To Guido Biagi*

Am Hof. Davos Platz. Switzerland. Nov: 19. 92.

Dear Signor Biagi:

I have been wandering about England & Italy all the summer & autumn & only returned here last night.

Meanwhile my Michelangelo has appeared, & every copy is already sold in London. Its reception has been very flattering.

I hope you received 2 copies I had sent to you in Florence, one for yourself, & one for the Mus: Buonarroti, & that you like the book.

It is going to be translated into German, & probably into French too.[1]

I write now to ask about the proposed Italian translation. I remember you spoke about a friend—a Contessa,[2] who wished to do this. But part of the idea was that you should help her with the book & citations. Now I am glad to see that your Ministry has received a new lease of robust (?) life from the Elections,[3] & this will no doubt prevent you in attending to mere literature.

I think it [indistinct] true that the notion of an Italian translation by the Contessa will have been abandoned. But I do not wish to accept any other offer without hearing what your own views are.

I must tell you that I have received a proposal from two persons in Venice, who are well qualified for the work. There are Prof: Taddeo Wiel, in the Marciana, & his wife who was the Honble Alethea Lawley.[4] Both write fairly well, & both together require a thorough knowledge of the 2 languages, also access to a large library.

I told them that I can not intrust the book to them without consulting you, & they expressed a strong desire not to interfere with your wishes.

Still it is desirable to get the Italian translation done soon. And if you do not feel disposed [to the] plan you projected in the spring, or have no other plan to propose, I should be inclined to close with the Wiels.

Pray let me have as speedy an answer as possible to this address. No matter how short. I know how valuable your time must be. And believe me to be always your most sincerely

John Addington Symonds

1. We have found no trace of translations into French, German, or Italian.
2. Contessa Rasponi. See L 1991.
3. The elections took place on November 6. Giovanni Giolitti (1842–1928) was premier of Italy in 1892 and the dominating figure in Italian politics later (1903–14). An able adminstrator, he skillfully handled these elections. For the complications in Italian politics at this time see the *Annual Register* for 1892, pp. 217–21.
4. See L 1979.

2059. *To Thomas Fisher Unwin*[1]

Am Hof, Davos Platz, Switzerland, Nov 19 1892

Private & Confidential

Dear Mr Unwin

I arrived here last evening. On Wednesday night in Venice about 2 a.m. I received this telegram: "New York. Write halluck. Century." Last night I received here a letter from the present Lord Tennyson,[2] wh has this passage about my Recollections.

"Your recollections of the dinner party chime in with a letter that I have just been getting Audry (Lady T)[3] to copy from my Father, saying that he had met you. I wonder whether you would like me to include the article in my memoir of him. I will gladly do so, if you would like it. This would give much interest to the bare facts that my Father mentions."

Here, you see, is the result of applying to him at all. He does not give consent to publication, but wants to have the document for his own book.

I shall tell him now, I think, that I want to print it *in extenso* in the Century[4] feeling sure it would be too long for a biography, & yet of sufficient interest to be published at length. He then may use what parts he chooses from it.

But all this is very delicate & disagreeable. I think the Century ought to double their fee if I transact the matter successfully! By the way I will wire at once to them when I have concluded one way or the other. Meanwhile please forward this sheet.

re *Biagi*.[5] Miss Zimmern wrote me an angry ill-bred letter, saying the faults of the preface are Biagi's & not hers. Alinari[6] sent me Biagi's Ms & a proof of Miss Z's *corrected* translation. The latter is still extremely ill-done —not English, & often mistaken as to the Italian sense. Biagi's original is slight, but quite intelligible. I have replied to Miss Zimmern in this sense. I could not help the matter without rewriting her work. I wish I had been asked to do the translation at once. It would have given me less trouble.

My proofs of Introduction came today. Shall go back to Alinari corrected tonight.

Thanks for yr congratulations on my book. It seems to be a success. Nimmo writes he has not a copy left on hand.

Thanks too for Leland.[7] It is a delightful looking book, wh I shall read with *gusto*. I only found it last night here.

May I send you some prose work of my daughter Margaret to look at? Some things, scenes of life in Lombardy (with the Contessa Pisani), & some short stories, have passages of singular force & beauty. I speak as a literary critic, not as a father.

Very sincerely yrs

J.A.Symonds

Please do not repeat the above to Miss Zimmern. It is right, however, that you should know what I think.

---

1. See L 1991.
2. Unclear. Probably misspelled for Hallam, 2nd Lord Tennyson (1852–1928);

author of *Alfred Lord Tennyson: A memoir* (1897). The editor of *The Century Magazine* was Richard Watson Gilder (1844–1909).

3. Cecil Boyle's (see L 400) sister whom Hallam Tennyson married in 1884. For the recollections, see L 451. See also L 2027.

4. *The Century Magazine,* XLVI (May 1893), 32–37; reprinted in *L & P,* pp. 1–10.

5. See L 2051.

6. See L 2055.

7. *Etruscan Roman Remains in Popular Tradition,* by Charles Godfrey Leland (1824–1903), American author and philologist, just published by Unwin.

2060. *To John Gambril Nicholson*[1]

Am Hof, Davos Platz, Switzerland. November 19, 1892

[Dear Nicholson]

After leaving England I went almost directly to Venice, where I spent the last month in a most delicious S. Martin's summer. The lagoons are almost too soft and glorious.

It is true that the sort of life I have been leading since [we] met at Brighton leaves little time for correspondence. In Venice I was mixed up with artists, Countesses, gondoliers, Facchini, an Empress, and all sorts of people. And then there is always work and business going on. . . . I am very tired, and have to write twelve letters of pressing importance before lunch. . . .

Michelangelo is a great success. All copies sold. German, Italian, French translations in view. Gives me quite a lot of fuss and trouble. But the book has consolidated my reputation for seriousness.

[Incomplete]

---

1. On Nicholson, see L 1993. We are grateful to Mr. Donald Weeks for locating this letter in *A Bibliographical Catalogue of the First Loan Exhibition of Books and Manuscripts held by the First Edition Club 1922. Privately printed for the First Edition Club 17 Pall Mall East London, S.W.1,* pp. 111–12.

2061. *To Elkin Mathews and John Lane*[1]

Davos Platz Nov 30 / 92

[Postcard]

Please send for me
"In the Key of Blue"
to Lawrence Binyon Esq[2]
19[1] Uhland Strasse
Dresden

J A Symonds

---

1. See L 1989. John Lane (1854–1925) continued the Bodley Head Publishing Co. after the co-ownership was dissolved in 1894, the year Lane founded the *Yellow Book*.
2. See L 1793.

2062. *To Havelock Ellis*

Am Hof, Davos Platz, Switzerland. Dec 1, 1892

Dear Mr Ellis,

Various pressing occupations have prevented me from replying earlier to your letter of the 14th Nov: which I found here upon my return from Venice.

With regard to your proposed plan, I will first consider it in general, and then in detail.

A). I like the principle you have sketched out for our collaboration and for our responsibility in the several parts. All this seems just as it should be. And I think your statement of our object as "primarily a study of a psychological anomaly" exactly right.

I only doubt whether we are completely agreed as to the part played in the phenomenon by morbidity. This is the most important question. And I apprehend that, while I have been growing to regard these anomalies as sports, that is to say, as an occasional mal-arrangement between the reproductive function and the imaginative basis of desire, *you* still adhere to the neuro- or psychopathical explanation.

I should be inclined to abolish the neuropathical hypothesis, and also suggestion, on the ground that impaired health in ancestors and suggestion are common conditions of all sexual development, normal and abnormal.

What I mean is this. Considering the wide and impartial distribution of "Erbliche Belastung" [hereditary taint], and the comparative infre-

787

quency of Sexual Anomaly, I regard neurosis in a Sexual Pervert as a *concomitant* not as a *cause*.

Considering that all boys are exposed to the same order of suggestions (sight of a man's naked organs, sleeping with a man, being handled by a man) and that only a few of them become sexually perverted, I think it reasonable to conclude that these few were previously constituted to receive the suggestion. In fact, suggestion seems to play exactly the same part in the normal and abnormal awakening of sex.

The only cases in which I should be inclined to accept the theory of psychopathy are those extreme ones in which there is a marked *Horror Feminae.* I do not believe that in perfectly natural and unprejudiced persons there is absolute Horror Feminae or Horror niasis[1] (?).[2] (Apropos of this, did you ever pay attention to the position of the "Concubinus"[3] in a young Roman noble's household? I could send you some notes I have made on it, if you think fit.) At the end of this letter I will return to the point, and will collect some information I have recently obtained upon the subject.

B). *Introduction.* As you suggest. N.B. In dealing with my "Problem" when you have to use it, you would always be at liberty to tace [sic:KF] expressions where it seemed too argumentative or heated.

Chapter i. History. Yes.

Chapter ii. History in Greece. This might well be my own Essay, as you say, with the last pages[4] omitted. (I never meant to publish those, they were intended to impress schoolmasters and Jowett.) I do not think anything important could be added about "Complete frigidity" or *horror feminae,* because the Greeks recognized the preference of male for male as a matter of course, and were not impressed by cases in which a male confined himself to males. Something may be gleaned from *Straton*[5] and from Glaucus in Plato's *Republic.*[6] (Also from Lucian's *Grôtes.*[7]) But the fact to dwell on about Greeks is that they were mostly sensitive to both sexes. They married and went on taking boys. Yes. What is said about Delphis in [omission] 18: ii. As to female Sexual Inversion we do not know very much. I think it would have to be alluded to: of course Sappho,[8] then Lucian's Brothel Dialogues.[9] I should notice the fact that while there are numerous paiderastic myths I do not know of one which sanctions female perversion.

Chapter iii. I feel serious difficulty about the history of the Transition to modern times. But it might be done by showing the effect of Justinian's Edicts[10] in making Perversion a *Crime.* Of course I know lots about it in Italy, and could largely increase the list of ancient people you mention. The problem would assume this shape: that in modern history there have been individuals with a specific perversion, frigid to women, or indifferent to them: but that there have also been (especially in the South) very numerous persons who for various reasons preferred the male, though they are potent for the female.

Part ii. 1,2,3,4. These you assign to H.[avelock] E.[llis] quite rightly. Any material you here would take from my "Problem", you would use as you thought best. By the way, I can supply you with duplicate copies of that essay, for scissor use, if you wanted.

Only I feel that it is just in these Chapters that our difficulty of collaboration will be felt. (We must come to some fundamental agreement about neurosis.)

Conclusion. This I would undertake, as you suggest, but should hope to have your assistance in correcting the outlines etc.

One great difficulty I foresee. It is that I do not think it will be possible to conceal the fact that sexual anomaly (as in Greece) is often a matter of preference rather than of fixed physiological or morbid diathesis. This may render the argument *ad legislatores* complicated.

If we succeed in producing this book together, I hope you will allow your name to stand first and mine second, because I feel my own want of scientific equipment. And I think it ought to be published by one of the medical publishers. But about this I am not sure, since one wants the subject to come under the notice of laymen.

Believe me very truly yours

[No signature]

---

1. For Symonds on the role of women in Greek society, see *A Problem in Greek Ethics* (1883), especially Chaps. XVI and XVII.

2. This letter is transcribed not from a manuscript but from KF's typed copy with her queries and omissions.

3. In the English (1897) ed. of Ellis and Symonds, *Sexual Inversion,* Symonds in Appendix E introduced "Notes on the Concubines." In the German edition (1896) it is an appendix to Chap. III. This work on sexual inversion, quite altered, eventually became Vol. III of Ellis' *Studies in the Psychology of Sex* (7 vols., 1897–1928).

4. Chap. III of the German edition, entitled *Das konträre Geschlechstgefühl* (1896), is Symonds' treatment of homosexuality in Greece.

5. Straton of Lampascus or Strato (fl. 288 B.C.), Greek peripatetic philosopher, succeeded Theophrastus as head of the Lyceum. He was called the "physicist" of the naturalistic school. He denied a transcendent deity, believing that the world was formed through natural forces. See *A Problem in Greek Ethics,* pp. 36–37.

6. Symonds refers to Glaucon, probably to Book V, in which are discussed the

merits, capacities, and duties of men and women, and more specifically the honor which the hero deserves from his fellows and lovers and the nature of the lover himself.

7. Greek satirist and wit of the 2nd century A.D., considered the most brilliant writer of the revived literature under the Roman Empire; wrote *Dialogues of the Gods*, *Dialogues of the Dead*, *Banquet of Philosophers*. See *A Problem in Greek Ethics*, pp. 39, 56–57, and 71, where Symonds discusses Lucian's *Amores* and the *Erores*, the latter a doubtful attribution.

8. Sappho, Greek lyric poet of the isle of Lesbos, flourished ca. 600 B.C.

9. Probably *Dialogues of Courtesans*.

10. See L 2036.

2063. *To Elkin Mathews*
[Postcard]

Davos Platz Dec: 6. 1892

Book-cover [of *In the Key of Blue*] received. Think it *admirable in design;* but in colour should have preferred a ground of greyish blue with the pattern in Silver or dull gold. Could some copies be sent out in that way?

J A Symonds

2064. *To Charles Kains-Jackson*

Am Hof, Davos Platz, Switzerland. Dec: 18. 1892

My dear Jackson

Many thanks for your charming letter, which, I am quite sure, was a generous gift in exchange for my Venetian Melancholy.[1] I am glad you liked those descriptions, & wonder whether you will like the article I am making out of them (with additions) for the Feby Fortnightly. Also I am glad the "blonde squires debonair"[2] pleased you. I would like to print that Sonnet. Mais comment le faire?

I have got the Ms of "Baiae" here, as returned by you.[3] The word you could not read is "creamed" essences. I will send you the Ms to be printed, if you are still of that mind. But pray stick to your resolve of letting me see a proof. What you say about March & April is so true.

I will send you my own photograph of Angelo [Fusato] "quel finissimo profilo" [that most exquisite profile], as Vianelli[4] called it, the same

790

you saw in the cab at Falmouth & which prevented you from noticing Mrs Drinkwater's[5] (is that her name)! Fairweather! signals. But I can only send it on the proviso that you return it, if I am unable to get another from Venice.

The strange thing about Angelo is that he has the shoulders, thorax, belly & thighs of a Bacchus, in spite of that delicate neurotic face. Nude, he is really very remarkable.

You can see from the tone of the blouse that he was "in the Key of Blue" when he was photographed.[6]

Pray tell me all you can about that affair at Bolton.[7] I am interested in watching the exact working of Labouchere's clause,[8] which is a disgrace to legislation by its vagueness of diction & the obvious incitement to false accusation.

I have a friend at Bolton, very W. Whitmanish.[9] I will write and ask him about it.

By the way, I spent 12 long days just now in composing "A Study of W. W."[10] It will have to come out as a separate little book I think.

Thank you so much for notice i of MAB.[11] I thought it well written, & of course I liked your kind sentiments with regard to book & writer.

Very sincerely yours

J.A.S.

---

1. *The Fortnightly Review,* LIX (1893), 256–61. See L 2056.
2. A line from the sonnet he had sent Kains-Jackson with L 2047. We find no record of the sonnet's publication.
3. One version of the manuscript is owned by Mr. Donald Weeks, Detroit. In the passage Symonds describes some ornate silver lamps:

> The lamps are silver: Satyrs love-elate
> Upraising cressets; phallic horns that hold
> Creamed essences, amber oil.

See L 2056.
4. The photographer.
5. Symonds' playfulness is of little help here.
6. Though the reference is to Angelo Fusato, it was descriptions of Augusto Zanon in various shades of blue which constituted the center of interest in the title essay of *In the Key of Blue.*
7. The reference is unclear. See L 2065.
8. Henry Labouchère (1831–1912), the English journalist and Liberal politician, sponsored a section, Sect. 11, to the Criminal Law Amendment Bill of 1885 punishing homosexuals, under which Oscar Wilde and Alfred Taylor were tried and sentenced.

9. The friend was Dr. J. W. Wallace. See L 1874. His friend and collaborator on the Whitman reminiscences, Dr. J. Johnston, was also attached to the Bolton Infirmary, Lancashire. See Ls 1855 and 2065.

10. *Walt Whitman: A Study* appeared on the day of Symonds' death.

11. The notice appeared in *The Artist*, XIII (Dec. 1, 1892), 354.

2065. *To Dr. J. W. Wallace*

Am Hof, Davos Platz. Switzerland. Dec: 19. 1892

Dear Mr Wallace

I returned a short while since from my long absence in England & Italy. Here I found the note-books of your American journey,[1] which are full of a deep & pathetic interest. I am reading them with care, & will return them duly registered.

I have nearly finished writing a "Study of Walt Whitman," the thinker & poet, not the man. It is an attempt to know the relations of Religion, Science, Personality, Sex, Comradeship, Democracy, Literature, in his writings. I think I shall have to publish it separately as a little book.

I am still perplexed about the real drift of "Calamus." Whitman once wrote me a very emphatic letter, repudiating the idea that under any circumstances the passionate attachment between friend and friend could pass into physical relations. Yet there are certainly a large number of men born with "homosexual" tendencies, who could not fail, while reading "Calamus," to think their own emotions justified by Whitman.

The subject is of considerable interest & importance for students of W. W. I have lately been obliged to study the most recent French, German, & Italian researches into the phenomenon, in course of writing my new Life of Michelangelo, who was certainly born with innate sexual inversion. I had not any idea what a large part this anomly plays in modern life.

By the way, I noticed in some newspaper that a prosecution was going on at Bolton under what is called "Labouchere's Clause."[2] Do you think that you or Dr [John] Johnston could give me any exact information regarding it? Whatever view the psychologist may take of homosexual passions, every citizen of a free country must feel that Labouchere's Clause is a disgrace to legislation, because of its vague terminology & plain incitement to false accusations.

This of course is not a matter of great moment. Still, if you can send me a report, you would oblige me.

Pray give my kindst regards to Dr Johnston, & believe me very sincerely yours

John Addington Symonds

If you have any advice to give me regarding the publication of my "Study of W. Whitman," or any suggestions to make about "Calamus," I shall be grateful to you for them.
P. S.
Since writing the enclosed, I spent the whole morning reading through your notes, & now I want to tell you what a profound & genial impression they have made on me. I seem to feel the whole of that Camden circle quite as old friends, & to have gained a vivid presentment of them to the inner eye. But what is even more, I am immersed in a definite atmosphere of friendliness, essential kindness, fine brotherly benevolence. Of course some of Whitman's own spoken words are very pregnant, & throw to a certain extent fresh light upon his works. I have been so free as to jot down a few phrases: & these, if you gave permission, might, I think, be used with profit to authorize the views I have taken in my "Study of W. W." on certain points. But I will most assuredly not do so without sanction from yourself.

It seems to me that you & other friends, to whom I feel linked in bonds of sympathy with W. W., must regard me as cold, irresponsive, apathetic. About him to some extent—& also about the kindness you have shown me.

But you must remember in what a huge mass of study & literature this matter of Whitman is for me of necessity embedded. Also I am alone, quite alone here, in all that concerns him. I have as yet nowhere found men of my own pursuits & condition who sympathized with me upon this point—I mean, found through personal society and contact.

So make excuses for me, & believe that my belief in Whitman is very permanent & real, if possibly less enthusiastic & exclusive than some of his younger disciples might desire.

---

1. See L 2014.
2. L 2064.

2066. *To Elkin Mathews*

Davos. Dec: 20. 1892

Dear Mr Mathews

I cannot tell you how charmed I am with *In the Key of Blue*. It satisfies my every sense of what is desirable in design, binding, typography, and paper. I only wish that my part of the book were more worthy of it all. . . . Will you tell Mr [Charles] Ricketts how greatly I admire the cover. The colour is quite right, the design lovely.

J. A. Symonds

2067. *To Horatio Forbes Brown*

Davos, Dec. 20 [1892]

[Dear Horatio]

We are having the most extraordinary weather I ever knew here. Day after day, night after night, the sky flames with sun or stars. It freezes, but so temperately that one wants no extra clothing and sleeps well under a light coverlid with open windows.

There is a thin but very hard snow-road, so that we toboggan with unparalleled rapidity. The last four days have been spent in that exercise, principally on the Klosters road. I ran to-day from Wolfgang straight into the village of Klosters in 18½ minutes.[1] The sunsets are extraordinarily fine. But, for all these things, the dryness and tension make me feel brittle.

I have just finished my study of W. W. It will have, I think, to be printed as a separate little volume. "In the Key of Blue" is said to be coming out on the 22nd. The cover is pretty—hyacinths and laurels by [Charles] Ricketts.[2] I wish "Venetian Melancholy"[3] had been in time for insertion. Of course that is a loaded colour-sketch, and over-loaded. I don't want to recall the lagoons precisely. I have used them as a theme for words —the background to a mood. But I think the gems are over-done. It amuses me now to try different ways of reaching the same result by language. Such experiments of necessity carry with them something of artificiality. But the artificial can always, if one chooses, be rubbed out. The true thing is that without art we do not gain effects, which at any rate will be permanent.

[Incomplete]

---

1. The distance down the mountain was nearly 6 miles.
2. See L 2050.
3. See L 2056.

2068. *To Charles Kains-Jackson*

Davos. Dec: 22. 1892

My dear Jackson

For a Christmas Card, I send you a Sonnet[1] which came to me this afternoon.

I had been reading the fragment of a Greek Lyrist (in Athenaeus),[2] who says that Hûpnos kept the eyes of Endymion wide open, in order that he might for ever contemplate & dote upon their beauty.

It is refreshing to learn that Artemis[3] had not her way alone with the divine youth. The masculine deity is more ethereal in his adoration.

I almost think that in line 11 one ought to read Hypnos or Hûpnos: & then perhaps in line 6 Artemis or Cynthia.[4]

Hot from the baking, I send you the little cake. But I do not think it will need much alteration.

In the first cast, I got for the final couplet:

> To ope those sleepy eyes, that each soft dream
> May be discerned on the dark spirit's stream.

But I do not want to close here with a rhyming couplet, which I think, in Sonnets, ought to be reserved for epigrammatic effect.

You can put this into the Artist if you like, & when the final form is settled.

Have you read the "Country Muse"?[5] It is excellent verse. A curious pendant to "Love in Earnest."[6] The two Loves have found spontaneous singers among the English youth. Gale and Nicholson are alike remarkable for their spontaneity & command of fluid form.—the latter *was* overdone by Sayle.[7]

795

Goodnight, my dear fellow. May the next year bring you no such heavy trouble as this did. Perhaps it cannot.

Best wishes at all events from your well-wisher & friend of the heart

J ASymonds.

I hope you will have got "In the Key of Blue." Matthews said it was to come out today. Read "Clifton & a Lad's Love." A wholly artless composition of my youth—1862.

---

1. Really, 2 sonnets, "The Lovers of Endymion" and "A Sequel," were published unsigned in *The Artist,* XIV (March 1, 1893), 75.

2. Athenaeus, a Greek writer, who fl. ca. 200 A.D.; best known for his *Deipnosophistae* (the banquet of the learned), in 15 books, a storehouse of miscellaneous information about cookery, music, songs, dances, games, courtesans, grammar, and literary criticism, and contains extracts from writings no longer extant. In *Deipnosophistae* (xiii. 546) he wrote: "Licymnius of Chios, after explaining that Sleep was in love with Endymion, says that Sleep does not cover the eyes of Endymion when he slumbers, but lays his beloved to rest with eyelids wide open, so that he may delight of gazing upon them continually." —*Athenaeus, the Deiphosophists,* trans. by Charles Burton Gulick (7 vols., 1951), VII, 49. Hypnos was the Greek god of sleep.

3. A reference to the legend where Artemis is identified with the moon-goddess who loved Endymion; the course of love ran unsmoothly.

4. In line 11, "A Sequel," Hûpnos was the form used; in line 6, "The Lovers of Endymion," *Diana* appears.

5. Norman Rowland Gale (1862–?), English poet; *A Country Muse* (1892), a collection of love and nature lyrics. A 2nd series was published in 1893 [1892], followed by selections from his poems (1894) and other volumes of prose and verse.

6. John Gambril Francis Nicholson, *Love in Earnest.* See L 1993.

7. Charles Edward Sayle, probably *Erotidia* (1889). See L 1502.

2069. *To Edmund Gosse*

Am Hof, Davos Platz, Switzerland. Dec: 23 1892

My dear Gosse

Since I wrote to you upon the 12th of September[1] from Leslie Stephen's house at St Ives, & told you why I was obliged to give up a visit I had projected to Glenthorne & Dunster & my friend [E. P.] Warren near Minehead, I have not heard from you. I fear something has gone wrong, or that you thought I ought to have made a greater effort to come to you. But my presence was urgently needed at Oxford. The disappointment was great on my part, as I had been looking forward to seeing you at last.

From Oxford I could not turn westward again. Business called me back to Davos, & from Davos I went to Venice, whence I returned only five weeks ago.

I do not like to let Christmas pass without writing to you, & begging, if you feel aggrieved with me, to tell me why.

I was exceedingly tired in the end with all my work on the Life of Michelangelo, & took a surfeit of writing which made letters odious to me. Nor have I yet recovered from the strain. At Venice I lived in absolute idleness & very mixed company—from the Empress Frederick[2] down to my facchino [porter] friend Augusto [Zanon]. It was a St Martin's summer of extraordinary warmth & colour. The lagoons were more sumptuous than I have ever known them.

Now send me a word, & accept my best wishes for yourself & Mrs Gosse & children. Yours

most sincerely

J A Symonds

---

1. Not available.
2. See L 1831.

2070. *To Edward Carpenter*

Am Hof Davos Platz Dec: 29. 1892

Private

My dear Carpenter

Thank you much for your letter & the promise of your book.

I will send you my last little book in return. It is called "In the Key of Blue." I fear you will not find much in it. /Look[1] at "Platonic Love," "Clifton," & the first Essay.

I am so glad that H. Ellis[2] has told you about our project. I never saw him. But I like his way of corresponding on this subject. And I need somebody of medical importance to collaborate with. Alone, I could make but little effect—the effect of an eccentric.

We are agreed enough upon fundamental points. The only difference is that he is too much inclined to stick to the neuropathical theory of explanation. But I am whittling that away to a minimum. And I don't think it politic to break off from the traditional line of analysis, which has been going rapidly forward in Europe for the last 20 years upon the psychiatric theory. Each new book reduces the conception of neurotic disease.

I mean to introduce a new feature into the discussion, by giving a complete account of homosexual love in ancient Greece.[3] I wrote this some time ago, & had 10 copies of it privately printed. If you like to see it, I will lend you one of my two remaining copies. I should indeed value a word from you about it.

All the foreign investigators from Moreau[4] & Casper[5] to Moll[6], are totally ignorant of Greek Customs. Yet it is here that the phenomenon has to be studied from a different point of view from that of psycho-pathology. Here we are forced to recognize that one of the foremost races in civilization not only tolerated passionate comradeship, but also utilized it for high social and military purpose.

/By the way, in the book I send you, you will find an essay[7] on the subject./

You raise a very interesting question with regard to physiological grounds for this passion. I have no doubt myself that the absorption of semen implies a real modification of the physique of the person who absorbs it, & that, in these homosexual relations, this constitutes an important basis for subsequent conditions—both spiritual & corporeal.

It is a pity that we cannot write freely on the topic. But when we meet, I will communicate to you facts which prove beyond all doubt to my mind that the most beneficent results, as regards health and nervous energy, accrue from the sexual relation between men: also, that when they are carried on with true affection, through a period of years, both comrades become united in a way which would be otherwise quite inexplicable.

The fact appears to me proved. The explanation of it I cannot give, & I do not expect it to be given yet. Sex has been unaccountably neglected. Its physiological & psychological relations even in the connection between man & woman are not understood. We have no theory which is worth anything upon the differentiation of the sexes, to begin with. In fact, a science of what is the central function of human beings remains to be sought.

This, I take it, is very much due to physiologists, assuming that sexual instincts follow the build of the sexual organs; & that when they do not, the phenomenon is criminal or morbid. In fact, it is due to science at this point being still clogged with religious & legal presuppositions.

Any good book upon homosexual passions advances the sound method of induction, out of wh may possibly be wrought in the future a sound theory of sex in general. The first thing is to force people to see that the passions in question have their justification in nature.

My hope has always been that eventually a new chivalry, i.e. a second elevated form of human love, will emerge & take its place for the service of mankind by the side of that other which was wrought out in the Middle Ages.

It will be complementary, by no means prejudicial to the elder & more commonly acceptable. It will engage a different type of individual in different spheres of energy—aims answering to those of monastic labour in common or of military self-devotion to duty taking here the place of domestic cares & procreative utility.

How far away the dream seems! And yet I see in human nature stuff neglected, ever-present—parish and outcast now—from which I am as certain as that I live, such a chivalry could arise.

Whitman, in Calamus, seemed to strike the key-note. And though he repudiated (in a very notable letter to myself) the deductions which have logically to be drawn from Calamus, his work will remain infinitely helpful.

South-Sea-Idyls. C. W. Stoddard. Boston. James R. Osgood. 1873. I got mine from Sampson Low, I think, through Nutt 270 Strand. If you cannot get a copy, let me hear, & I will send you mine. It was suppressed once in America.[8]

Now, dear friend, farewell. I put "Private" on this letter, qui habent sua fata epistolare[9]

Yours in affection

JAS

---

1. All brackets in this letter are apparently Symonds'.

2. For the details of this collaboration see L 1984 and subsequent letters to Ellis.

3. The *Problem in Greek Ethics* (1883).

4. See L 1836.

5. Leopold Casper (1859–?), German urologist who settled in New York. Symonds lists the following of his works in the bibliography to his *Problem in Modern Ethics:* (with Carl Liman) *Praktisches Handbuch der Gerichtlichen Medicin* (1856, 8th ed., 1889), and *Klinische Novellen zur Gerichtlichen Medizin* (1863).

6. See L 1996.

7. "The Dantesque and Platonic Ideals of Love," *In the Key of Blue* (1893), pp. 55–86.

8. On Charles Warren Stoddard, see L 1488. *South-Sea Idylls* was reprinted in 1892 by Scribner's, New York. If the book was "suppressed once in America," "Love-Life in

a Lanai," was probably the cause. In the 1892 reprint there is an introductory letter by W. D. Howells, dated August 11, 1892, addressed to Stoddard, in which Howells attributes the little success of the book in part to the "vulgar and repulsive" illustrations in the London (1874) edition and in part to the American panic of 1873. Howells himself had accepted the last story, "A Prodigal in Tahiti," for the *Atlantic Monthly*, XXX (1872), 610 ff.

9. Because letters have their own destinies: an allusion to *Pro captu lectoris habent sua fata libelli*—the fortune of a book depends upon the pleasure it affords the reader, a well-known tag from Terentius Maurus, *De Literis, Syllabis et Metris*, l. 1296.

2071. *To Guido Biagi*

Am Hof, Davos Platz, Switzerland. Dec: 31 1892

My dear Biagi

I am sorry not [to] have answered your letter of the 4th earlier. But I hoped to be able to communicate something definite with regard to the translation of Michelangelo.[1]

That has not been possible, since negotiations are proceeding with French & German translators & publishers at the same time, & Mr Nimmo wants to see his way all round. I will however not fail to send you an answer as soon as I can.

I may say that *the whole edition* of I believe 3000 copies was sold off some weeks ago.

With regard to the Conferenza.[2] I accept the proposal gladly, & consider that a very high honour has been paid me.

It must be understood that I shall compose my lecture in English, &, if I come in person to deliver it, I fear that I must also do so in English.

When will it be wanted? I could not produce it just at present, having an immense amount of work to do & not being at all well.

I wrote a short preface to Stradano.[3] The whole is now in print.

Thank you greatly for your book on Shelley,[4] which I only received & read with much interest. It is a really important contribution to the biography of the poet.

Now, with sincere good wishes for the coming year, believe me to be most truly yours

John Addington Symonds.

Should you like the copies of those letters from Angelini[5] which you made for me? I had kept your Ms. If the publication of MAB's correspondence takes place, these may be useful.

P. S. I think Signor Sansoni⁶ had better now correspond directly with Mr J. C. Nimmo.

Do you not believe that it would be better to publish the translation without adding the expensive illustrations?⁷

I may add that at present no French publisher has come forward for the book. Hachette who wished to do so, on account of his writing, did not care for the illustrations.

---

1. See Ls 1979 and 1991 and subsequent letters to Biagi concerning the translation. Symonds was apparently caught between Biagi's, his publisher's, and his own wishes.
2. A lecture Symonds was scheduled to give in April 1893. It was published in an Italian translation by Signora Ida Falorsi. Babington, pp. 89–90, records Mrs. Symonds' copy.
3. See L 1991.
4. *Gli ultimi giorni di P. B. Shelley, con nuovi documenti*, etc. (1892).
5. Bartolommeo Angelini, Michelangelo's friend. See L 1890.
6. Giulio Cesare Sansoni (?–?), the Florentine publisher and author of *Michelangiolo Buonarroti. Ricordo al pogialo Italiano* (1875). He was probably negotiating for an English translation of his work.
7. The translation of his *Michelangelo*.

2072. *To Henry Scott Tuke*

[Davos] Jan. 10, 1893

My dear Harry,—Yours of the 8th comes to-night and gives me what my Italian friends call 'una grandissima consolazione' [a superlative solace]. I treasure it because it is a very nice one. . . . Horatio [F. Brown] has been very hard at work. Few people give us literary fellows credit for the hatred we feel for our pen when we have driven it all day in labour. It will not obey our sentiments or fancy in familiar correspondence. Or, to put it more prosaically, our hand gets awfully tired, and we hate the sight of black words on white paper.

What you say about your pictures interests me greatly. I can *see* them, and so can follow your developments. If I were to give any advice, which I am really not competent to do, but the hint of a friend may be considered —I should say you ought to develop studies in the nude without pretending to make them 'subject pictures'. Unless you are inflamed with the mythus, the poetical motive, I do not think you will bring your mastery to bear upon the work in hand if it be mythological.

Your own inspiration is derived from nature's beauty. Classical or Romantic mythologies are not your starting point. Number your pictures Op. 1, 2, 3, etc. Do not find titles for them. Let them go forth as transcripts from the beauty of the world. It won't pay? No, I suppose it won't. But, damn it, nothing pays. Do you suppose I am not out of pocket by the ten years' work I put into my 'Renaissance in Italy'? I am going to publish an article on my 'Literary earnings,'[1] which will show the world that artists and men of letters have a small chance indeed of even feeding themselves on porridge by their best and most disinterested work. Goodbye, it is late, and to bed go I must. Yours ever, with love,

J. A. S.

---

1. We have not been able to trace this account, if it has been published.

2073. *To Gleeson White*[1]

Am Hof, Davos Platz, Switzerland. Jan. 10. 1893

Dear Mr White

Your request needs no apology. I am very glad to meet so reasonable and to me flattering wishes of a young man & fellow-writer. If I had known more about him I would have sent my autograph in the form of a bit of original writing. Is Royal Cortissoz[2] his real name or an anagram? And what line of work does he follow?

Please tell him that he ought to send me his portrait in return. I had a great collection of the pictures of the young here, who help me much by their bright and sometimes beautiful faces.

I wish my own work in "In the Key of Blue" were worthy of the charming cover and excellent typography. Please tell Mr Ricketts[3] how very much I admire his design. It is a pity, I think, that some copies have not been issued in blue.[4]

The pieces in the book I care for most are extracts from very early diaries, about Clifton & Sutton Court. It so happens that they are full of bluebells. So the cover strikes the right note in my judgment.

Very Truly Yours

John Addington Symonds

---

1. Gleeson White (1851–98), American editor of *Studio* and art adviser to a large publishing firm. His designs for book-bindings started a fashion for decorated cloth covers.

2. Royal Cortissoz (1869–1948), American connoisseur, art editor, and eventually art critic of the New York *Herald-Tribune* (1891–1948). He was "the last of the 'grand tradition' critics and master of the essay style of writing."—*Art Digest*, XXIII (November 1, 1948), 13. He wrote biographies of Saint-Gaudens (1907), John La Farge (1911), and others; books on art; and edited *Don Quixote* (1906) and wrote an introduction to Brentano's issue of Symonds' translation of *The Life of Benvenuto Cellini* (1906).

3. See L 2050.

4. See Ls 2050, 2063, and 2066.

2074. *To Edward Carpenter*

Am Hof, Davos Platz, Switzerland. Jan: 10, 1893

My dear Carpenter

I want to tell you how very much I have enjoyed your book about India.[1] My wife has just finished reading it aloud to me. We both of us are quite enthusiastic about its style & its feeling. Some passages are very beautiful—especially the last pages. We have a fine set of her sister Miss [Marianne] North's oil-sketches of Indian places & people here. Your book proved a running commentary to them, & they illustrated your words.

I am afraid that in my last letter[2] I wrote rather too emphatically. But I feel strongly upon the point, & just then I had received what seemed to me a remarkable verification of my views.

Believe me Very Sincerely Yours

John Addington Symonds

---

1. *From Adam's Peak to Elephanta: Sketches in Ceylon and India* (1892).

2. L 2070; Symonds wrote Carpenter his views of the benefits of homosexuality.

Am Hof, Davos Platz, Switzerland. Jan: 10 1893

My dear Gosse

You do not tell me in the letter I had from you recently, whether you got or did not get what I wrote you from St Ives in September.

It does not really matter much. But you leave me under the impression that you think I have been fabricating a mares nest.

That does not matter, however.—What is really more of moment is that I never find the time now to write properly to my friends. All the summer I was moving rapidly about,[1] & all the autumn I spent in very complicated society at Venice—from the Empress Frederick[2] down to My *facchino* [porter] friend Augusto [Zanon].

I daresay you would laugh at my literary work seeming to be a burden. It is, nevertheless, for me a serious weight. I am printing a third edition of my "Greek Poets,"[3] a second edition of "Michelangelo,"[4] am writing a monograph on "Walt Whitman"[5] & collaborating on a treatise[6] which will deal with morbid psychology (when this takes shape I hope to tell you about it), & finally had undertaken to produce a new version of the "Decameron."[7] All these things in addition to the fugitive fidgets of the literary life, take a great deal out of my time & nervous energy. And oh! I forgot to mention that, as a minor matter, I have thoroughly studied the new Greek poet Herondas[8] & made an English version of him.

I get so dreadfully tired sometimes, & yet I cannot stop. The little threads that entangle are so sly & subtle. Days & weeks go by in a dream of fusses wh mean nothing. And when a moment of rest comes, the tired brain writes a sonnet or a study of "Venetian Melancholy."[9]

Do not then imagine that I ever change. But, being an unmethodical creature & apt to obey the currents which sway temporary action, I seem to forget. The real thing is that I was not made to live in the Category of Time.

The tone of your letter, though it was very kind, seemed to have something forgiving in it—as though you thought I had erred—as though you pardoned me because you elected to imagine I was ill.

Well: I don't feel to have erred: & ill I have not been—yet. Carried away by currents, yes. So much so that I hardly am my own master.

All the same, always yours

J.A.S.

1. He was in England in the summer of 1892, gave a lecture at Oxford, and visited many friends.

2. See L 1831.

3. 1893.

4. 2 vols., 1893. He made a few changes in the illustrations and added (II, 408–14) an Appendix IX, "Replies to Criticism."

5. *Walt Whitman,* published by Nimmo, appeared on the day of Symonds' death.

6. *Sexual Inversion,* in collaboration with Havelock Ellis. It appeared first in Germany as *Das konträre Geschlechtsgefühl von Havelock Ellis und J. A. Symonds,* in 1896, as Vol. VII of a series "Bibliothek für Socialwissenschaft . . . herausgegeben von Dr. Hans Kurella." In the general preface to the English edition (1897) (Vol. I of *Studies in the Psychology of Sex*) Ellis explained that "unexpected difficulties and delays" occasioned a German edition rather than an English edition. For details on Symonds' contributions see Babington, pp. 124–25. He rightly says that this first English edition "is far the most important for the bibliographer of Symonds." Not only was the issue suppressed by Symonds' family, but when "a modified reissue" appeared the same year, Symonds' name was dropped from the title page. Even the appendix, "Ulrich's Views," which had borne Symonds' signature, was now authored by "Z." Ellis also deleted from the preface his account of Symonds' interest in the subject and the degree of his collaboration. The English edition was successfully prosecuted as an obscene work in England. Edward Carpenter thought the end of *A Problem in Greek Ethics* had weakened the case for tolerance which Symonds was making throughout the book. See L 2079.

7. Not completed, but published by Nimmo was *Giovanni Boccaccio, as Man and Author* (1895), written in 1887 to preface a new translation of Boccaccio to be issued by Vizetelly. See Babington, pp. 93 and 211.

8. Herodas or Herondas was new in the sense that his papyri had recently been discovered. Herodas' works portray the vulgar life of his era, 270–50 B.C. See Walter G. Headlam and A. D. Knox, *Herodas: The Mimes and Fragments* (1923), p. ix. The papyrus manuscript, in the possession of the British Museum, was printed by F. G. Kenyon in 1891.

9. See L 2056.

2076. *To Dr. John Johnston*[1]

Am Hof, Davos Platz. Switzerland. Jan: 15: 1893.

Dear Dr Johnston,

I have just finished writing a Study of Walt Whitman,[2] not as man so much as thinker & writer. This I hope to publish in small book form through Mr Nimmo. And I should like to illustrate it. Will you give me permission to reproduce some of those photographs you took in 1890 & wh you sent me? I think if Mr Nimmo is responsible for the reproduction it is sure to be well done.

The book cannot, I fear, be other than dear—relatively.

Very sincerely yrs

John Addington Symonds.

---

1. See L 1855.

2. *Walt Whitman* (1893) contained a portrait and four illustrations.

2077. *To Dr. J. W. Wallace*[1]

Am Hof, Davos Platz, Switzerland. Jan: 15 1893

Dear Mr Wallace

Many thanks for your last letter. I was glad to be reminded of that passage about Calamus.[2] Of course I knew it, but I had not sufficiently digested it.

I have just finished my essay on W. W. It is about his writings not himself. Yet I should like to put in certain illustrations. Portraits of course & views of places. Could you furnish me with any of those you took in America: on Long Island e.g.?

I am going to ask Dr Johnston whether he would allow me to have some of his reproduced.[3]

I doubt whether I shall induce my publisher (Mr Nimmo) to make a cheap edition at first. But if you & other admirers of W.W. think the essay worthy of wide diffusion, that can be managed later on.

Believe me to be very sincerely yours

John Addington Symonds

---

1. See L 1874.

2. For a summary of the details of the exchange between Symonds and Whitman over "Calamus" see Grosskurth, pp. 272 ff.

3. See Ls 2076 and 2080.

2078. *To Horatio Forbes Brown*

Davos, Jan. 17. [1893]

[Dear Horatio]

We go on having the same hard open weather with intense light. It is trying to the nerves. I have reason to be anxious about my brain just now. I have very curious sensations in it, which seem to show that there is something wrong. I do not work with vigour or contentment. I wish I could go to sleep like Endymion, and not wake up till my head and eyes were refreshed. But it is too late to hope for rest in this life.

Jan. 18.

This day has taken away from us Katharine; and my wife is gone with her as far as Zürich.

"Quomodo sedet sola civitas!"[1]

I wish I could write well to you again, as I used to do. It seems—I think because I am devoted to no work—it seems that I am devoid of ideas. I am full only of wants, which are shadows, till they get filled up with energy. Preludings to fresh upheavals of volcanic vigour?—Not impossibly. It sounds a little thing: but I am sorely exercised upon the question whether I ought to undertake a new literal English version of the "Decameron." John Payne[2] did it, not long ago, affectedly, euphuistically, in false archaistic diction. Of course I could do it in a smooth and vivid style of today. But is it right for me to translate these indecencies into my mother-speech? In my capacity of artist I don't mind. The indecencies do not disgust me. But is it wanted? So easy to begin to do it, and become engrossed in it, and bring another splendid book out on Boccaccio, and spread myself round again upon the field of Italian masterpieces! So easy. Yet is it right, is it what I ought to do for myself first, for the world next?

I would give the balance at my bankers' for six weeks of profound health-giving sleep. Worry, worry, no exit from worry. Not a good thought in me but what gets corroded by the devil of unrest.

[Incomplete]

---

1. How lonely rests my state (of mind).

2. John Payne (1842–1916), English poet and translator of Villon's *Poems* (1878), the *Arabian Nights* (9 vols., 1882–84), *The Decameron of Boccaccio* (1886), and other works. See also L 2075.

2079. *To Edward Carpenter*

Am Hof, Davos Platz, Switzerland. Jan: 21. 1893.

My dear Carpenter

Thank you for yours of the 17th. What you say about H. Ellis[1] in conversation is just what R.[oden] Noel[2] told me.

In correspondence I find him full, eager, open-minded, scientifically conscientious: the sort of man, I think, to lead our joint enquiry.

When you make notes on those matters for us, will you send them to me? Of course H.E. will see the bulk of them. But you might feel it more appropriate to let me have things wh you would not care to submit to him.[3] This is only a suggestion, arising from my desire to lose nothing you may have to say.

I will copy out for you Whitman's very singular letter to me about Calamus,[4] when I have time. I feel sure he would not have written it, when he first published Calamus. I think he was afraid of being used to lend his influence to "Sods" [sodomites]. Did not quite trust me perhaps. In his Symposium Speeches,[5] he called me "terribly suspicious," you may remember.

I will send my Greek Study[6] to Holmesfield.[7]

The blending of Social Strata in masculine love seems to me one of its most pronounced, & socially hopeful, features. Where it appears, it abolishes class distinctions, & opens by a single operation the cataract-blinded eye to their futilities. In removing the film of prejudice & education, it acts like the oculist & knife. If it could be acknowledged & extended, it would do very much to further the advent of the right sort of Socialism.[8]

I find a great deal of the emotion, in a wholly manly & admirable form, abroad among the people here. It does not interfere with marriage, when that is sought as a domestic institution, as it always is among men who want children for helpers in their work & women to keep their households.

We have a most awful snowstorm raging here, after 2 months of cold sunny weather. I think pensively with a troubled heart of many friends, carters, postillions, conductors of diligences abroad upon our passes—the highest in Europe, averaging (five of them) 7000 feet above the sea.

Goodnight. I respond to your greetings of affection, & return them with my heart.

J A Symonds

1. Later, Carpenter described Ellis as "a student, thoughtful, preoccupied, bookish, deliberate; yet unlike most students he has a sort of grand air of nature about him—a fine free head and figure as of some great god Pan, with distant relations among the Satyrs."—*My Days and Dreams* (1916), p. 225.

2. What Noel said is apparently not on record.

3. In the first English edition of the work Havelock Ellis reported that he had for "a year or more" considered "Symonds's proposal as to collaboration and distribution of the task" of writing *Sexual Inversion.*—See Babington, p. 124.

4. This is the famous letter of Aug. 19, 1890, in which Whitman declares that Symonds' suggestions about, "the Calamus part" of *Leaves of Grass* was "entirely undreamed of" and that he, Whitman, had 6 children. See also L 2088.

5. Whitman said Symonds was "terribly literary and suspicious" in Horace L. Traubel, "Walt Whitman's Birthday," *Lippincott's Magazine*, XLVIII (1891), 231.

6. The *Problem in Greek Ethics.*

7. Carpenter's address was Holmesfield, Millthorpe, Derbyshire.

8. Ellis believed that inverts are less prone than normal persons to regard caste and social position. This "innately democratic attitude" parallels Symonds' attentiveness to gondoliers and soldiers and Carpenter's to the British peasants of Derbyshire.

2080. *To Dr. John Johnston*

Am Hof, Davos Platz, Switzerland, Jan: 21. 1893.

Dear Dr Johnston,

I am greatly obliged to you for yours of the 19th, with its permission to use your photographs for my Whitman book.[1]

I should like to reproduce the Study Bedroom, the Street, the old man in his chair with Warry [Warren Fritzinger].

But I must consult the publisher about the choice.

I am loth to part with the proofs you gave me, even to yourself. But, as you request them, I will, look them up & send them off tomorrow.

I am sorry Wallace's did not come off.[2]

My meeting with E.Carpenter was pleasant, but too brief. I have enjoyed his Indian book immensely.[3] My wife read the whole of it aloud to me, and felt, as I do, that it reveals a singularly sweet and limpid nature.

People not inexcusably think Carpenter a little "faddy". But the man's personality is strong & distinguished enough to cover a few fads[4]

We have had a blaze of sun-&-star-light since Nov 16, when I returned to Davos from Venice. But last night an awful blizzard with piles of snow, came down upon us.

My heart is with my friends, the carters, postillions, diligence conductors, abroad upon those awful passes—five of them in this canton over 7000 feet—& I know so many of the noble fellows whose lives are in peril now like those of sailors upon the Atlantic in violent storms.

My health (thank you) is pretty good so far as lungs go. But my brain is overtaxed with deluge of literary work. Books & editions of former books keep up a continuous mill-race.

Believe me most sincerely
Yrs

John Addington Symonds

---

1. See L 2076.

2. Johnston had published a pamphlet, *Notes of a Visit to Walt Whitman* (July, 1890) for private circulation. But Wallace's (see L 2017) was delayed (*Diary Notes of a Visit to Walt Whitman* [1898]).

3. When Carpenter and Symonds met it is hard to say. In L 2070 (Dec. 29, 1892), Symonds writes "when we meet." Thus they must have met, presumably in Davos, in January, 1893, but before the 21st. Symonds refers to Carpenter's *From Adam's Peak to Elephanta: Sketches in Ceylon and India* (1892).

4. According to the *D.N.B.*, Edward Carpenter's life was a "reaction against Victorian convention and respectability"; he "abjured his social class as a protest against . . . the exploitation of the poor and weak by the well-to-do." He despised systems and rules and took as his ideal the simple life ordered "by no other code than that of charity and brotherly affection."

2081. *To Edward Carpenter*

Am Hof, Davos Platz, Switzerland. Jan: 29. 1893. (night)

Dear Carpenter

I sent you a copy of my "Problem in Greek Ethics", wh I found by accident in a drawer today. If you care for it, please keep it. I have another copy for reprinting when I need.

When you wrote to me upon the subject of assimilated semen,[1] were you thinking about a book called "Le Degenerazioni Psico-Sexuali" by Silvio Venturi?[2]

I got it, at H. Ellis's suggestion, with a view to our joint work. I have been reading it tonight, & find little for my purpose.

But it has this peculiarity, that it tackles the problem you raised.

The author has experimented upon patients by the injection into them of bestial & human semen, with results which (if one may trust his report)

810

show that semen received into the system is a powerful nervous agent. He draws the conclusion that the absorption of male semen through the mucous membrane of women may account for the thriving of girls who improve in physical condition immediately after marriage.

It is so strange to find this (otherwise tedious & stupid book) tonight under my hand, (but the only one in which I have seen the subject treated) —so strange that I think you must have been reading it or something similar.—Let me hear if this or any other literary work put you on the track.

Yrs

JAS.

---

1. Symonds and Carpenter were speculating on the possibility of transferring one man's virility into another through the absorption of semen. See L 2070.

2. Symonds refers to Le Degenerazioni psico-sessuali nella vita degli individui e nella storia delle società (1892) by Silvio Venturi (1850–1900).

2082. To Dr. John Johnston

Davos Feb: 3 1893

Dear Dr Johnston

I received your letter & the photographs last night. I am delighted to have the view of Whitman's birthplace, part view of house in Camden, & new view of W.W. in chair with Warry.[1] Also the portraits of Burroughs,[2] Bucke,[3] Wallace,[4] are very interesting. And I thank you heartily for your own, to which I respond by sending you one of myself. I am not sure whether you have not already got it, in which case pray excuse my forgetfulness.

It is very good of you to give me leave to reproduce the photographs. But are you quite sure you would not prefer to reserve them for your book and Wallace's![5] Of course I shall make full acknowledgment & shall allude to the importance of your Notes of Visit in my preface.[6]

It is true that copies of my Michelangelo have now run up to £4–£6. Of course I gain nothing by this. I sold my work straight out for 300 guineas, with 100 guineas upon each subsequent edition. There is a new edition being printed, wh will be sold at 21/—I believe the type will be the same, but not so expensively got up. There will be additional matter added by myself in the form of replies to criticisms.

On the whole, this will be the superior edition for students, not book-collectors, and your Librarian had better apply to J. C. Nimmo for an early copy.

We are wallowing here in an ocean of snow. There are some 7 ft (average) over the valley—in many places drifts of 30 ft & avalanches of 60 ft in depth.

Three men were blown by an avalanche 2 days ago over drifts 1500 ft in height. Their comrades saw them flying through the air. One has been found mere pulp. The others are either under snow or whirled into fragments by the fury of the blast. One of my carter friends spent 14 hours in a hole under a stone, blocked in my avalanches, with his two horses, no food or fuel, intense cold, & [omission]. They dug him out in time & he told me all about it with his cheery smile the other day.

I have been in bed 3 days with congestion at the base of the left lung. The machine is always getting out of gear. But I do not attend to it more than is absolutely necessary. I think that is the best way of bearing & of fighting chronic illness. The brain is what gives me most anxiety. I work that very hard.

Thanks for the Liverpool Daily Post. The writer of that leader twigged what I was after in my last little book. I liked his appreciation of my work.

Yours ever

J A Symonds

We have got Leslie Stephen & 2 members of his family, snowed up with us. Good company But I spend the days in bed alas!

---

1. Symonds' *Walt Whitman* included the following illustrations: autographed photograph of Whitman, dated 1880; Whitman's birth-place; Whitman's room, Camden; Whitman on the wharf, Camden, 1890, seated in a wheelchair backed by Warren Fritzinger, his male attendant; and facsimile of a postcard from Whitman, 1891.

2. John Burroughs (1837–1921), American naturalist; from 1863 a friend of Walt Whitman; first published book was *Notes on Walt Whitman at Poet and Person* (1867).

3. On Dr. Richard M. Bucke, see L 1626.

4. On J. W. Wallace, see Ls 1874 and 2077.

5. *Visits to Walt Whitman in 1890–1891, by Two Lancashire Friends* (1917).

6. The preface, however, contains no mention of Dr. Johnston. Symonds says instead that he is "indebted to the kindness of Mr. J. W. Wallace, of Anderton, Lancashire, for use of copious notes from conversations with the poet. . . ."

2083. *To Edward Carpenter*

Davos, Feb: 5 1893

My dear Carpenter

I did send you my Problem in Greek Ethics, & will now send you the Modern Problem—which please to keep if you care. Since the latter was written, Moll & Schrenck-Notzing[1] have done a great deal to whittle down the theory of "erbliche Belastung" [hereditary taint]. My elaborate polemic against Krafft-Ebing is hardly required now.[2]

Your notes are very interesting & valuable. Percy's[3] love-letter is quite charming, & the silhouette of the Sheffield show-boy delightful.

What the guardsman said to your friend accords with what I know about military prostitution. I made acquaintance last autumn in Venice with a Corporal of the 2d Life Guards who was travelling with a man I knew. He gave me a great deal of information. But it all pointed to the mercantile aspect of the matter. However, he said that some men 'listed on purpose to indulge their propensities. An Italian Colonel told me the same thing—i. e. that young men of the best families, after serving as volunteers, or in the natural course of conscription, would sometimes remain on in the ranks with a view to the opportunities afforded by barracks.

Referring to what you stated as to Case H, the only boy among 6 sisters, I have wondered whether cases of this sort do not support Ulrich's physiological hypothesis: as though the combination of the parents tended to female sexuality in the differentiation of the offspring, so that when a male came he was feminine in temperament.

I know a decided Invert, who grew up with 3 sisters. But his parents had produced before him 2 still-born males, & a third who died in infancy of acute inflammation of the brain. The sisters normal, & all married.

This will not prove much, however. I know two Ducal families in which there is Sexual Inversion. One is Somerset,[4] where males & females are pretty equally distributed. The name of the other I will not mention.[5] But here also males & females occur in balanced quantities. The eldest son, the Duke, was a man much given to women. The second married a cousin of mine, & died after the birth of their first child, a boy. The third is an invert of marked quality. He is a great friend of mine, & tells me that he thinks he inherited his temperament from a Ducal great uncle of a different race.

I wish the medical psychologists would study the phenomenon from this point of view. If only it had fallen into the hands of Fr. Galton![6]

Did you get a copy of South Sea Idylls?[7]

Apropos of yr friend the engine driver—I must tell you how much I admire that passage in "Toward Democracy" (pp 140–143).[8]

Yrs affectly

J.A.S.

---

1. Symonds has in mind Baron Albert Philibert Franz von Schrenk-Notzing (1862–19?), *Suggestions-therapie bei Krankhaften Erscheinungen des Geschlechtsinnes* (1892) or *Ein Beitrag zur therapeutischen Verwerthung des Hypnotismus* (1888). For Moll see L 1996.

2. See *A Problem in Modern Ethics,* pp. 43–61. Symonds quarreled particularly with Krafft-Ebing's theory that onanism was a prime cause of homosexuality. See also L 1831.

3. Unidentified, but probably one of the bases for Carpenter's *Homogenic Love* (privately printed, 1894).

4. See L 1699 for Lord Henry Somerset.

5. The reference is to the family of the 2nd Duke of Sutherland. The eldest son was George Granville William, 3rd Duke of Sutherland (1828–1892). The second was Frederick George Granville (1832–1854). The third, Albert (1843–1874) married Symonds' distant cousin Grace Emma Townshend (d. 1923), and the fourth was Ronald Charles Sutherland-Gower (1845–1916), the invert who figures largely in these letters. See L 1612. In numbering this family Symonds forgot the second son, who was already dead.

6. Francis Galton (1822–1911), the biologist.

7. By Charles Warren Stoddard. See L 1488. See also L 2070.

8. See Ls 1819 and 1968. The passage occurs in the poem "In the Drawing-Rooms."

2084. *To Edward Carpenter*

Am Hof, Davos Platz, Switzerland. Feb: 7. 1893

My dear Carpenter

I am sending off my "Problem of Modern Ethics" registered. It does not represent my views completely, since I have read & thought a great deal during the last two years. And on the Continent the subject has rapidly been gaining in completeness.

Did you ever come across any of Ulrich's works?[1] They are very curious. He must be regarded as the real originator of a scientific handling of the phenomenon. I went to visit him in Nov: 1891. He lives exiled & in great poverty at Aquila in the Abruzzi, under the snowy crests of "Il gran passo d'Italia". There is a singular charm about the old man, great sweetness, the remains of refined beauty. His squalor was appalling. I drove

814

to his house in a carriage, & then persuaded him to take a drive with me, which he did. He had no shirt & no stockings on. My magnificent Venetian gondolier & manservant was appalled at the sight of this poor beggar sitting next his padrone. However, I told Angelo [Fusato] that the old man was one of the men I prized & respected most in Europe. And Angelo got to like him in spite of his rags. (You saw Angelo on the top of the Brighton omnibus).

I do so much wish that we could meet & exchange thoughts in quiet somewhere, before this book on Sexual Inversion is begun. Could you not come out & stay with me in the early Summer here, or could you come to Venice & stay with me in May? I have a little house at Venice, wh is delightful for 2 people. If my wife & a daughter are in it, I would take apartments for us near. But as yet I know not what the family will do. In April I want to be in Rome.

Yours affectionately

J. A. S.

Do you know Plüschow's photographic[2] studies from the nude in open air?

---

1. See L 1831.
2. See L 1945 and plates.

2085. *To Henry Tuke*

[Davos] Feb. 11 [1893]

My dear Harry,—I was meaning to write you before your letter came. You seem to be getting along with your painting all right, it is good to hear you talk so hopefully. I wish I could be comfortably settled again to some stiff bit of work. At present I am fidgeting about at trifles—new editions of old works, review articles, and fresh matters. This sort of thing does not agree with me. We are living in serious danger of avalanches. There are about 7 feet of snow on the valley and the hills above, and it is still snowing to-day. The wind in the night was awful, raging about these cliffs and peaks, dislodging the huge snow masses in cloud and drift. But, thank God, no avalanche was brought down on the village. I can't tell what I shall be doing next summer. I hope to come to England. But how early I do not know. It depends too partly upon what the cholera does. I want to go to Italy for April, May and part of June. This is a stupid letter but I feel lifeless and depressed.

Ever affectionately yours,

J. A. S.

2086. *To Horatio Forbes Brown*

[Davos, Feb. 11, 1893]

[Dear Horatio]

I have been very ill . . . The way in which my nerves, as well as lungs, have been attacked looks like influenza; but, on the whole, I think it is a reaction from M.A.B. . . . Literature has pretty well come to an end with me. It loses its attractiveness, and I feel threadbare. Fate has made me much too young to grow old properly . . . I am writing in my study on a cold morning, before the sun has climbed the Jacobshorn. Out there—in the void infinite, the unexplored, intangible—what is to become of a soul so untamably young in its old ruined body, consuming its last drop of vital oil with the flame of beauty?

[Incomplete]

2087. *To Havelock Ellis*

Am Hof, Davos Platz, Feb. 12. 1893.

My dear Ellis,

(As collaborators, may we not drop the Mr?)

I wrote you a long and wordy letter last night. I have little time just now, and scribble when I ought to write propositions.

I hope to send you tomorrow or next day 16 selected autobiographical cases of English Inverts, for the genuineness of all of which I can vouch.

If you have only met with one recorded case in English sources, these may be interesting, and may be used with profit perhaps in your part of the work.

Only two of them, N and P, expressed a wish that their cases should not be printed. But with regard to some of the others I should like to exercise my right of veto, since the communications have been given me under a certain seal of confidence, and are quite different from those collected by physicians.

If I can possibly procure more, speedily, I will do so. I am rather afraid that the diffusion of books by Ulrichs,[1] Krafft-Ebing,[2] and others, may tend to the formation of a kind of "fixed style" in these confessions. It is important then to base conclusions upon obviously candid and uninspired records.

You will observe my method in eliciting these confessions. I framed a set of questions upon the points which seemed to me of most importance after a study of Ulrichs and Krafft-Ebing.

What struck me in the English notes, was the comparative frequency of *paedicatio*. The cases who object to it are few. Next, *onanism* seems to play a very feeble part in the business. There is a large preponderance of *Horror Faeminae*. *School-vices* do not seem to be taken into account at all.

Are you beginning to write your part of the book? I only ask this because I should like to go *pari passu* [side by side] with yourself. I have revised and prepared for the English public my Greek Essay[3]—adding translations in all cases of the Greek. This part of my work is finished, except that it will have to be worked into the scheme of the whole book by some introductory remarks, and a short notice of female Sex. In.[version] will be added.

The transition in history from the Greek, through the Roman and mediaeval periods, to present times, will have to be done very superficially. I do not see much good in making generalizations based on insufficient facts. —The point to insist upon is Justinian's Edict and theological legislation.[4] —Then the persistence of the phenomenon, in spite thereof.—Afterwards, perhaps, the selection of a few unchallengeable eminent Inverts in history down to the present time.—but anything like a learned or scientific discussion of special cases would occupy too much room.—In order to arrive at *tempus praesens* [present time] it should suffice to demonstrate that the phenomenon has always been vivid, in a more or less suppressed form.—

Shall I begin to write a section sketching out the transition from Greek customs, through the intervening centuries, until we arrive at the main issue of our work?

If you think this good, I will do so, and have it typewritten, so that you can place it among our documents?

I do not want to hurry you. I have such lots of work to do that I can postpone the Sexual Problem. And will do so gladly. Only I do not want to be behind-hand with my promised contribution. I prefer to be always to the fore.

Yours,

J.A.S.

---

1. See L 1831.
2. See L 1831.
3. *A Problem in Greek Ethics*, which, with *A Problem in Modern Ethics*, became part of Havelock Ellis and J. A. Symonds, *Das conträre Geschlechtsgefühl* (1896), and *Sexual Inversion* (1897) by the same authors, and *Sexual Inversion*, Vol. I of *Studies in the Psychology of Sex* (1897) by Havelock Ellis (American ed., 1901).
4. See L 2036 and *A Problem in Modern Ethics*, pp. 5–8.

2088. *To Edward Carpenter*

Davos. Feb: 13 1893

Dear Carpenter

I wrote in the Summer of 1890 to Whitman, asking him what his real feeling about masculine love was, & saying that I knew people in England who had a strong sexual bias in such passions, felt themselves supported & encouraged by Calamus. Unluckily I have not got a copy of my letter.

He replied (Aug: 19. '90)[1]

"About the questions on Calamus etc: they quite daze me. L[eaves] of G[rass] is only to be rightly construed by & within its own atmosphere & essential character—all of its pages & pieces so coming strictly under—: that the Calamus part has even allowed the possibility of such construction as mentioned is terrible—I am fain to hope the pp themselves are not to be even mentioned for such gratuitous & quite at the time undreamed & unrecked possibility of morbid inferences—wh are disavowed by me & seem damnable."

That is all that is to the point. He rambles on about his being less "restrained" by temperament & theory than I (J.A.S.) am—"I at certain moments let the spirit impulse (female) rage its utmost wildest damnedest (I feel I do so sometimes in L. of G. & I do so)."

That last passage seems meant to qualify the first. But if it does so, it implies that these inferences are not so gratuitous morbid & damnable as supposed.

At the end of the letter (wh is a long one) he resumes:

"My life, young manhood, mid-age times South, etc, have been jolly bodily & doubtless open to criticism. Though unmarried I have had six children—two are dead—one living Southern grandchild fine boy writes to me occasionally—circumstances (connected with their benefit & fortune) have separated me from intimate relations."

It struck me when I first read this p.s. that W.W. wanted to obviate "damnable inferences" about himself by asserting his paternity.

Section X of my Modern Problem[2] treats of Calamus you will find.

My "Study of W. W." is now in the hands of J. C. Nimmo. I am sure he will make a pretty book out of it, but I doubt a cheap one. I fear that the blind idolators of W.W. will not wholly like it.

Yours affcly

J.A.S.

"Civilization"[3] came last night. Have not had time to do more yet than look at p: 105[4]—which is firmly & delicately touched.

---

1. Part of the letter was printed in the 1896 edition of *A Problem in Modern Ethics,* pp. 118–19. The original of the letter, and Whitman's first draft, are in the Charles E. Feinberg collection in Detroit. See also Ls 1814 and 1822.

2. The section is entitled "Literature: Idealistic: Walt Whitman." Section X of the 1891 edition became VIII in the 1896 edition.

3. Carpenter's *Civilisation: Its Cause and Cure* (1st ed., 1889).

4. A reference on p. 105 is to Symonds' obsession, the "ideal passion" of the Greeks, comradeship, male love. Harmodius and Aristogiton are referred to as having this passion and as uniting in self-devotion to their country's good.

2089. *To Dr. J. W. Wallace*

Am Hof, Davos Platz, Switzerland. Feb: 17. 1893

Dear Mr Wallace

I was very sorry to hear of your trouble from Dr Johnston, but hope I may conclude from your letter to me that it is passing.

I am sincerely grateful for those copies of W. W.'s letters to Pete

Doyle.[1] As you say, they throw a distinct light on what he meant by comradeship, & do more than aught else could to explain Calamus.

Shall I not return to you all your notebooks soon?[2]

Dr Johnston told me he thought you would like to have my photograph. So I enclose the same I also sent to him. My wife & daughters do not like it, think it is too grim. But I often feel like that.

I am so delighted to possess the photograph of yourself & Dr Bucke. We have had some awful snow-storms this & last year. One avalanche brought down over £200 worth of trees on to a little farm I have here, & covered our railway to the height of 50 feet. But, as yet, there have been few accidents on the mountains.

Believe me very sincerely yrs

John Addington Symonds

---

1. Peter Doyle, a baggage master Whitman met in Washington around 1869, when Doyle was 18 years old. Whitman's letters to Doyle were published in *Calamus: A Series of Letters Written During the Years 1868–1880 by Walt Whitman to a Young Friend,* ed. by R. M. Bucke (1897). In *Walt Whitman* (pp. 78–79), Symonds says,

I have been privileged to read a series of letters addressed by Whitman to a young man, whom I will call P., and who was tenderly loved by him. They throw a flood of light upon *Calamus,* and are superior to any commentary. . . . The letters breathe a purity and simplicity of affection, a naiveté and reasonableness, which are very remarkable considering the unmistakable intensity of emotion. . . . There is something very wistful in the words addressed from a distance by the aging poet to this "son of responding kisses."

2. See Ls 214 and 2017.

2090. *To Havelock Ellis*

Am Hof, Davos Platz, Switzerland. Feb 22 1893.

My dear Ellis,

Yours of the 19th to hand. What you say about your work, and its affect upon our book suits me well. I am also burdened with other things, and not sorry to think that the main pressure of the book will come a few months later.

Also I thoroughly agree with your views about the tone to adopt. Let it be [omission] and analytical statement.

It is only in this way that we shall get a fair hearing from the English.

So anything that you think fit to use in "my problem" shall be worked over so as to erase it's bias and eliminate its literary quality. Since I last wrote I put together a short section on female sexual inversion in Greece,[1] and have composed the greater part of the transition from Greece to modern times. I have tried to deal with Imperial Rome, the Middle Ages, the Renaissance, and some special features of Italian and French life, with a glance directed to England at the time of James 1st.

What to do with eminent historical urnings[2] is very doubtful. It took me enormous trouble to work out the case of Michael Angelo and then I had pretty copious documents. But what can one do with people like Marlowe, Shakespeare, Henri III, Frederick the Great? Their contemporaries thought and called them sodomites. (Not even so much in Shakespeare's case.) But we possess no accessible records upon which to found any useful psychological observations in these cases. History yields a vague verdict on "imputed sodomy non proven" which can hardly be considered helpful to scientific determination of the phenomenon.

It might be worth while, however, to draw up a list of historical personages, in whom the aberration is fairly ascertained, without attempting to qualify its particular manifestation.

I am glad you liked my scheme of questions. I took some pains to draw it up. Please keep copies, if you like, of the whole lot of answers. I think I could get N[3] printed by permission. It is a curious one (if I remember the N rightly) because the man is of exceptional mental and moral vigour, has been able to marry and forget, and at the same time is so thoroughly an urning that, if circumstances had not thwarted his inclinations, he would undoubtedly have remained true to his specific homosexual bias.

I will send you [omission] by post tomorrow.

[No signature]

---

1. See *Problem in Greek Ethics,* Chap. XIX, pp. 70–72.
2. Homosexuals. For the origin of the term and Ulrich's uses of it see *A Problem in Modern Ethics* (1891), and L 1865.
3. Norman Moor? See L 602. It is possible that Symonds here tries to conceal "N's" identity, as he did in the autobiography, using "N" for Moor but saying the initial does not fit the true name. Moor died in 1895.

2091. *To Horatio Forbes Brown*

Davos, Feb. 22 [1893]

[Dear Horatio]

Last Sunday night I was lying awake, thinking of death, desiring death, testing the energy of my own will to seek it, when lost in this sombre mood, to me the bedroom was at a moment filled with music—the "Lontan, lontano" from Boito's "Mefistofile"[1] together with its harp accompaniment.

On Monday I went by train to Chur. Yesterday I drove in the post to Thusis, leaving Chur at 5.10 a.m. The dawn at Reichenau[2] was wonderful: crocuses, irises, and Corot: shy colours and luminous transparencies. I found Thomas[3] at Ems, brought him back to Chur, was elected an Honorary Member of the Gymnastic Clubs of the whole Canton, and had a tremendous drink with twenty-eight stalwarts from 8 p.m. to 2 a.m. Came up by train to-day, after seeing the Hofkellerei and the Cathedral bathed in tearful sun and wandering snowflakes.

"Lontan, lontano!" has not left my auditory sense yet—stays behind all other sensations—and seems to indicate a vague and infinite, yet very near . . .

[Incomplete]

---

1. Arrigo Boito (1842–1918), the opera *Mefistofile* (1868, rev. 1875). "Far, far away, o'er the waves of a far-spreading ocean," in the duet of Margaret and Faust, end of Act III. Symonds saw the opera in Venice, April 25, 1890. See *L & P*, p. 237.
2. These are all towns near Davos in the Canton of Grisons.
3. Unidentified.

2092. *To Robert Louis Stevenson*

Davos, Feb. 24 [1893]

My dear old Friend,

After all these years, since that last sight of you in Bournemouth,[1] I come to write to you. How strangely different our destinies have been! Here I am in the same straight valley, with the old escapements to Italy and England, with the regular round of work—I forget how many books I have written since we conversed; and I do not want to record their titles. You have been thrown into such very different scenes—and a sort of injustice has been done to our friendship, by the wistfulness I have for all that South-Sea life. Not that I am unhappy. I have found a great deal of happiness by living with the people here, though it is chequered with disappointments and pains.

I sometimes think I may still set sail, an old Ulysses, for those islands of magic charm. But I am past the age of doing more than dream of them.

A curious sense of being drawn to you is on me to-night. Partly because I read to-day news of Lloyd's[2] going to Trinity. Partly because I found time, first, to-night to read your book on the disturbances of Samoa[3] —that magnificent chapter on the Hurricane.

My inner life, in these nine or ten years of our separation, has been the most eventful that I have gone through. But of this I cannot write. To write well from Davos to Upolu[4] about burning points of experience is more than a sensitive soul can do. It is like screaming secrets to a vast void filled with listening unsympathetic ears.

I never pass your châlet without thinking of you and Mrs. Stevenson.[5] Give her my love. I think often of a dream she dreamed about me—and has probably forgotten.[6] As far as health, etc., goes, we are not otherwise than prosperous.

If this ever reaches you, think of me not unkindly. I will send you a little "Study of Walt Whitman," which I have just written, when it comes out.

"Lontan, lontano"—that duet in Boito's "Mefistofile"[7] with its dropping accompaniment of deep harpnotes, is in my ears—"Lontan, lontano" —Addio. A rivederci mai?

P.S.—I have just written your address. Will Samoa find you in the universe?[8]

[Incomplete]

---

1. Symonds had last seen Stevenson in June 1887, at Bournemouth, just before the Stevensons left for the United States.

2. Lloyd Osbourne (1868–1947), Stevenson's stepson and author; published *An Intimate Portrait of Robert Louis Stevenson* (1925).

3. *A Footnote to History: Eight Years of Trouble in Samoa* (1892).

4. The Samoan island on which Stevenson lived.

5. The Stevensons lived at Davos for 2 winters, 1881–82, near the Symondses.

6. This is probably the dream referred to in L 1307 (November 16, 1882). According to Brown's note the dream was a "warning [to Mrs. Stevenson] not to pursue the journey."

7. See L 2091.

8. Brown notes that this letter was never sent.

2093. *To Janet Ross*

Am Hof, Davos Platz, Switzerland. Feb: 26 1893

My dear Janet

I should much *like* to have my wine at once & in two casks, as you propose. The weather is mild enough. But I am rather frightened about Duty. The other day Brown sent me 7 bottles of ordinary Graspa from Venice; & I paid 15 frs for Monopole and Péages Suisses. This is ridiculous, for the Graspa costs 2 frs a bottle in Venice.—

Will you make enquiries what are export duties on wine in Italy, & whether Switzerland has raised import tariff with Italy in the same degree as she has with France? (No French wine can come into the country.) If the duty seems to be reasonable, then I will [be] glad [to] have the wine at once. If not, I must have it sent to Venice.

It is indeed ages since I wrote. I am a bad correspondent unless something makes me write almost every day. Lately too I have been far from well, over wrought in my nerves & worried by a disagreeable affair.[1]

Would you tell me when Sir James Lacaita[2] leaves Leucaspide? I doubt whether Madge & I will be able to go there. I must be in Florence for my Conferenza[3] on April 12. It is an absurd affair, but the honour so great I could not refuse. I am also honoured by Alinari[4] begging me to catalogue the drawings in the Museo Buonarroti wh he has received permission to photograph (together with its other relics) & publish in a handsome book.

Your letter came too late for me to drink your health on the 29th. But I did so heartily yesterday in Sanella of 1875, a rattling good wine & year.

I will write to Sir Charles Tennant about the Cassone,[5] & make Margot go to see it. He buys largely & gives good prices. He lives in Grosvenor Square.

When I come to you you must let me see your novel. And pray let me say this: if Madge & Angelo [Fusato] come with me, you must really allow us to pay something. I will not come unless you do, & this would be a real disappointment to all of us. In fact, I accepted the Conferenza because I knew it would make me come to you.

Goodbye from yr affectionate Historian

J.A.S.

I will write to Lord Carlisle[6] too about the Cassone. But I am afraid he is in Algiers now.

1. The letters supply no clue: he may have been worried over his projected translation of Boccaccio. See L 2078.

2. See L 1879.

3. See L 2071.

4. See L 2055.

5. Giacomo del Cassone, 16th century painter, served in the atelier of Antonello Gagini (1478–1536) of Sicily.

6. George Howard, Lord Carlisle. See L 2010.

2094. *To Dr. J. W. Wallace*

Am Hof, Davos Platz, Switzerland. March 2 1893

Dear Mr Wallace

I am so glad you like that photograph of myself which I sent you, & I thank you most warmly for the kind & affectionate terms in which you speak about me.

I have read Walt's letters to Pete[1] with the greatest interest. But what I most desire to see is—Pete's correspondence with Walt. I fully enter into Walt's feelings. Among my own dearest friends are a postillion, a stevedore, a gondolier, a farm servant, a porter in a hotel. I find the greatest possible relief & rest in conversing & corresponding with them. They do me so much good by their simplicity & manly affection. Their real life is such a contrast to that strange thought-world in which my studious hours are past—Italian Renaissance, Greek Poets, Art, philosophy, poetry—all the lumber of my culture. In fact the greatest thing I owe to Walt is his having thoroughly opened my eyes to comradeship & convinced me of the absolute equality of men.[2] My friends of this kind think me an exception to the rest of the world. But, having won their confidence, I see how enormously they appreciate the fraternal love of a man socially & by education superior to them. I verily believe that the social problems would find their solution if only the majority of rich & cultivated people felt as I do, & acted so.

The son of an English Duke,[3] a distant cousin of mine, was staying with me last year both here & at Venice. I made him acquainted with my working friends, & he tells me that it has been to him a revelation of the untold wealth of happiness lying close to people of his kind & undreamed of by them.

I never saw "The Carpenter."[4] Pray send me a copy. Yours most sincerely

John Addington Symonds

825

1. Peter Doyle, the baggage master. See L 2089. In his *Walt Whitman* (1893) Symonds says: "I regret we do not possess P.'s answers. Yet, probably, to most readers, they would not appear highly interesting; for it is clear he was only an artless and uncultured workman."

2. Symonds wrote: ". . . he taught me, as no enthusiasm of humanity could do, the value of fraternising with my fellows—for their own sakes, to love them, to learn from them, to teach them, to help and to be helped by them—not for any ulterior object upon either side. I felt, through him, what it really is to be a member of the universe I sought to worship."—*Biography*, p. 324.

3. Lord Ronald Gower. See L 1612.

4. A story eulogizing Whitman by William D. O'Connor (1832–89), American journalist and author of *The Good Gray Poet* (1866); in *Putnam's Magazine*, XI (1868), 55–90, reprinted in *Three Tales* (1892).

2095. *To Richard Le Gallienne*[1]

Am Hof, Davos Platz, Switzerland. March 15 1893

Dear Sir

I do not often write to people whom I have not the honour of knowing personally, about what they may have thought it right to say in criticism of my books.

But I cannot refrain from letting you know what true pleasure your treatment of my "In the Key of Blue" in the Academy has given me.[2] The sympathy sustained throughout & the delicate touch upon things are very grateful to me.

The Romans used to say that *laudari ab laudatis* [to be praised by those who receive praises] was the highest praise. To obtain the appreciation of me when I appreciate so highly as yourself in poetry & prose, is the truest gratification.

I hope that I shall sometime be able to meet & learn to know the author of "The Book-Bills of Narcissus" & "English Poems."

Possibly next summer in London?—

I am starting for Italy tomorrow, literally

> Tendens Venafrancos in agros
> Et (not aut) Lacedaemonium Tarentum.[3]
> [Making my way to the Venafrian fields
> And (not or) the Spartan Tarento.]

Believe me very sincerely yrs

John Addington Symonds.

Augusto [Zanon], for me, is a good deal more than a lay figure. He is a downright good fellow & good friend.

---

1. Richard Le Gallienne (1866–1947), American writer, born in Liverpool and educated at Liverpool College; after 1898 lived in the New York area; an accountant, he abandoned business for literature; literary critic for the London *Star;* wrote reviews for *The Century Guild Hobby Horse, The Academy,* and many other publications; by 1893 he had published *My Ladies' Sonnets* (1887), *The Book-Bills of Narcissus* (1891), and *English Poems* (1892); perhaps best known today as the father of Eva Le Gallienne (1899–), the actress.

2. XLIII (March 11, 1893), 213–14; reprinted in Le Gallienne's *Retrospective Reviews: A Literary Log* (2 vols., 1896), I, 233–43.

3. Horace *Odes* 3. 5. 56.

2096. *To Charles Edward Sayle*[1]

Davos March 15 1893

My dear Sayle

I think Gaston de Foix[2] is a very good subject, & I am glad you are going to take it up. I will tap for you the Venetian Archives—I mean, find what material there is there. Mme Darmesteter[3] would help you with the French Archives. You had better consult the Archivio Storico Italiano. I am not sure whether it has published documents. But there may be contemporary records relating to the Siege of Brescia.

For myself, I have only written a little vignette upon the marvellous portrait-statue of the dead youth in the Brera.[4] (Sketches & Studies in Italy. [1879] pp. 364–366). Also, I think, some touch of picturesqueness about the Stele at Ravenna (in Sketches in Italy & Greece).[5]

If you look up those passages, you will see that the Hero of the battle of Ravenna has been haunting my imagination.

I shall welcome a study of him. But pray refrain from precienté. He is worthy of a chivalrous straightforward treatment. And, before you write, go & see him in the Brera at Milan.

I start tomorrow for Milan, Venice, Taranto.

Yours always

JASymonds

---

1. See L 1502.

2. Probably Gaston de Foix (1489–1512), Duke of Nemours; brilliant French general in the Italian wars, especially in 1512; successfully laid siege to Ravenna, where he was killed. Sayle published nothing on this person. Symonds himself had written on him: see *Sketches and Studies in Italy and Greece* (3rd ed., 3 vols., 1898), I, 160–61.

3. Mary Robinson. See L 1137.

4. The Palace of Science Arts and Letters in Milan.

5. (1874), p. 262.

2097. *To Henry Graham Dakyns*

Clifton Hill House
Clifton, Bristol.

[Davos March 19, 1893][1]

My dear Graham

Once more I dedicate this book to you. When I first did so, I spoke of 16 years of [omission]. Those years have now grown to 30; and though during the last fifteen of these we have been divided by shadowy mountains & the sounding sea, I do not think that our common sympathies have failed or that our hearts have been far apart.

You know how the book grew up: at first from scattered essays written to amuse my leisure during winter wanderings in search of health, & afterwards from lectures addressed to the Sixth Form boys of Clifton College.

My friend R. L. Stevenson used to tell me how he read the Studies when they first appeared, & how lamentably, it seemed to him, the style sank here & there from literary charm & distinction to pedestrian commonplace.

I perceive, while passing this third edition through the press, that the inequalities he pointed out are there: in fact that the book is a young man's effort. Yet I do not think much would have been gained by rewriting the whole. It has a note of its own, a way of feeling & seeing things which seems to me fresh, & which maturer criticism sometimes lacks.

I have therefore contented myself with rearranging the Studies in their proper order & with making a few alterations & additions.

Such as it is, accept it as a token of the unchanging affection felt for you by your old friend

JAS.

1. This, possibly his last letter to Dakyns, is dated March 19, 1893, in the 3rd ed. (2 vols., 1893) of *Studies of the Greek Poets*. The 1st series (1873) was dedicated to Dakyns. Symonds apparently used old Clifton Hill House stationery—probably for sentimental reasons.

2098. *To Elkin Mathews*[1]

560 Zattere Venezia Italy March 20. 1893

My dear Mr Matthews

I am in receipt of your letter of the 15th, & am glad to hear such good news regarding "In the Key of Blue." Mr LeGallienne's review[2] gave me great pleasure. I thought it admirable in itself as well as favourable to the book, & wrote to tell him so.

The arrangement about royalties which you have suggested corresponds to our original notion, & I am not dissatisfied with the b[3] on American copies. Please therefore pay the 57. 10.0 to the credit of my account with Messrs Coutts & Co.[4] & do me the favour of writing to inform me when you have done so.

Since the type is moulded, there will be no question of making additions or alterations in a second edition; & the book can be printed without my seeing proofs. I suppose royalties will go on upon the same system.

I should be glad to undertake an edition of Whitman's poems. (Those just finished correcting the proofs of a "Study of W. Whitman"—about 200 pp—wh Nimmo will publish immediately.)

Let me hear what form you would like the edition to take, & whether you would care to have it annotated. The text ought to be based on the complete edition of 1888. I have most of the editions of "Leaves of Grass." But I should want the 2nd, that of 1872 (1856) & also the edn of "Drum Taps" (1865) if I were to undertake a complete & critical work.

Let me hear about these things. This address will find me, though I am just starting for a regular scamper over South Italy.

Believe me very truly yours

J. A. Symonds.

When you write to tell me that you have paid that money to my credit with Coutts, pray enter at some length into the question of Whitman's poems.

1. See L 1989.
2. See L 2095.
3. That is, the printing of the letter B on the title.
4. A banking house in London and Edinburgh.

2099. *To Janet Ross*

560 Zattere Venice March 20 1893

My dear Janet

Madge & I came here Saturday. We are going to Bari tomorrow, & on Thursday hope to reach Leucaspide.

I have written nearly all of that wretched Conferenza.[1] But it seems so ridiculous to read it in English. Don't you think you could manage for me, to get it translated into Italian & read for me? I would willingly pay the translator.

Do try & arrange this! Or if they really want me to do the absurd thing, will you try to have my day changed to April 19?

You see, if we come up from Leucaspide, I should like to show Madge places on the way. And supposing we stay six days at Leucaspide (23–29), this would only give us 11 days to spend between it & Florence. There is Salerno Paestum Amalfi Naples Rome Orvieto on the way!

It is very beastly of me to ask you to do this for me. But I know Biagi[2] is in Rome; & I am not acquainted with anyone personally who manages the lectures.

Ernesto Masi,[3] I suppose, is the man to go to.

Do, there's a dear, strike one or the other bargain for me. I should be so grateful. And telegraph to Leucaspide—or write. If the lecture is to be translated, I will send it up registered immediately. It is a regular skunk of a Conferenza I have produced.

Yours ever affecty

J A Symonds

The wine had not come before I left. I had to go off in a hurry, over-worked, very much worried by a disagreeable business[.]
P.S. I should like a little Caratello of the same wine sent to me here. About 100 litres. Can you do it?

---

1. See L 2071.

2. Guido Biagi: see L 1869.

3. Ernesto Masi (1837–1908), prolific writer on art and literature, editor of collections of plays, and historian of Italian life.

2100. *To Janet Ross*

[Leucaspide] March 24 1893

My dear Janet

We came here last night, & I found your letter. Thank you so very much.

I send the Ms of my Lecture to Sign Bruschi,[1] as you recommended.

But would it not be better to have it sent registered to London to be type written? It would come back in about a week. I hope a week—or perhaps 10 days!

In case you think this would do, I enclose a letter to the people who work for me. I do not like to think of you copying it out.

If it is too long, whoever reads must cut out at his discretion. I always put as much stuff as I can into the writing, trusting to the moment to omit.

I have no time to tell you about first impressions of Leucaspide, because I have been working at this thing.

The Senatore[2] is better again, but frail I fear.

Sir Arthur Gordon[3] & his sister in law Lady G—are here—& his dr.

We stopped at Bari & went to see Bitonto[4] (in a garden of lovely flowering fruit trees).

It is cold & horribly dry here.

Yr most aff

JAS.

Miss Dickens'[5] address is at the foot of my letter to her.

If Nencioni does not translate, do you know Signora Fortini Santarelli?[6] She did a lot of my Renaissance for Le Monnier.

---

1. Domenico Bruschi (1840–1910), Italian artist, executed many decorations in churches and palazzi in Rome and in Umbria; worked in England from 1862 to 1868, and from 1880 taught at the Academy of Fine Arts in Rome.

2. Sir James Lacaita. See L 1879.

3. Arthur Hamilton Gordon: see L 2003. His sister-in-law was Carolina Emilia Mary (d. 1909), daughter of Sir John Herschel (1792–1871) and wife of the second son

of the 4th Earl of Aberdeen, Alexander Hamilton Gordon (1817–90), whom she married in 1852. His daughter was Rachel-Nevil, born July 13, 1869.

4. Bari della Puglie, formerly Tearo di Bari, a city in Apulia in southern Italy on the Adriatic. About 10 miles from Bari is Bitonto, a town producing olive oil and famed for its Romaneseque cathedral (built 1175–1200).

5. His London typist; her address is in L 2101. We have not been able to trace Symonds' letter to her.

6. Enrico Nencioni (1836–96), Italian literary critic and poet; translated works of Browning, Tennyson, Swinburne, and others; wrote *Medaglioni* (1883) and *Saggi Critici di Letterature Inglese* (2 vols., 1897). Sofia Fortini-Santarelli (?–?) translated *The Renaissance in Italy: The Fine Arts* in 1879.

2101. *To Janet Ross*

Leucaspide March 24. [1893]

My dear Janet

I wrote you a very hurried line today, thanking you for what you had done about the Lecture, & suggesting that it might be sent to London to be type-written—unless that could be done at Florence.

The excellent Senatore[1] has given me his library & a little bedroom close to it, on the terreno [ground floor] opening upon the lemon terrazzo where the violets are all in bloom. He is all kindness & hospitality.

There is something extremely fine in the broad sweep of view from this height—that exquisite curve of the bay toward Metaponte with the silver shimmer of light along its margin—& then the olive trees along the coast, &, nearer, dotted over the green of the young corn with sombre shadows. I feel already that I could learn to love it.

I wish you & Lina[2] were here instead of these Gordons.[3] Sir Arthur is a good fellow, I doubt not, but unsympathetic to the place. And Lady Gordon (who was a dr of Sir John Herschell, & whom I have known more or less for years) is not an amiable personality. She seemed even in her days of youth a beauty to be permanently discontented with her lot in life.

Don Eugenio & Don Enrico[4] lunched today, & then left for Manduria, not to return till after Easter. I think both of them were rather bored by the excessively English tone of the Gordons.

I have been already into two of the Gravina:[5] one of them at a distance from the house, where Sir James is rebuilding a masseria [large farm], is a very picturesque & interesting place. All the grey rocks are bloomed over with blue-grey rosemary. But there are few signs of flowers & the earth is like iron. They say that the drought of the season has been most injurious to the country. They had no Feby rains, & hardly any last autumn.

On the Adriatic coast I did not notice so much dryness. And never had I seen anything to equal the orchards between Bari & Bitanto. Fortunately I drove out in an open carriage by a road different from the tramway; & here in a more protected situation the almonds & peaches in bloom mixed with the olives were magnificent.

In case anything happened to the first letter I wrote & gave to Angelo [Fusato] to post, I repeat Miss Dickens' address. Typewriting Establishment, 3 Tavistock St. Wellington St. Strand, London W. C. I wrote a letter to her wh I enclosed in yours.

Everyr aff JAS.

---

1. Sir James Lacaita. See L 1879.
2. Lina Duff-Gordon; see L 1882.
3. See L 2100 to Janet Ross.
4. Don Eugenio Arno: Sir James Lacaita's nephew, lived at Manduria in the heel of Italy, west of Brindisi. For a description of a visit paid to him see Janet Ross, *The Fourth Generation* (1912), pp. 234 ff. We have not been able to identify Don Enrico.
5. An area in Puglia, about 30 miles west of Bari in southeastern Italy, surrounded by deep gorges and known for its cave churches. See Janet Ross, *Land of Manfred,* pp. 98 ff.

2102. *To Janet Ross*

Leucaspide March 25 [1893]

My dear Janet

I am sure that you will be interested to know the little events here. So, before I go to bed, I shall write a few notes.

First of all, in answer to your letter about the lecture,[1] I shall of course be willing to pay handsomely for the translation; & in fact, what I receive from the society, I will divide with my coadjutors. I mean that there is sufficient there to satisfy all claims, as I do not want to profit for myself.

Now I must begin by saying that I have danced the Pizzica,[2] with what applause I dare not tell you. It satisfied my English awkwardness. I think Madge stirred the Pizzica up this morning. But at all events it came off tonight. The people have heavy hearts, however. All their crops are ruined by the drought. The olives have been nothing—& you know what that means here. Then the young crops, beans etc, are dying in the fields. But the Guardiano, Vito Anton,[3] & Isabella, & the kitchen boy, & one of the musicians also came from Massafra were admirable. Miss [Rachel-Nevil] Gordon danced well. Lady Gordon was led out. Madge looked pretty, but rather romped about the place. Sir Arthur [Gordon][4] turned round like a hop-pole. Angelo [Fusato] could not endure the "critica", & ran away. I tried to skip in a "froc," & felt very stiff. How I envied the scullion-boy's beautiful toes!!

I have been out walking all the day. In the morning through the fields of olives westward for three hours. In the afternoon I went to Mater Gratia,[5] & made friends with the funny old man who lives there & saw a party of three contadini [peasants]—mother & daughter & sposo [bridegroom]—paying their devotios, to what purpose I could only guess, at the rustic shrine. It seemed to me a little living bit plucked out of old Greek life. So like something in (A visit to the Nymphs or Arcadian Artemis) in Alciphron[6] or Longus.[7] There is a dell in that Gravina,[8] where the asphodels are in full bloom, & the spring seems to have come.

I am already in love with the place. But I wish that you were bossing it instead of Sir Arthur G. He behaves rather too much as though Sir James' guests were his on-hangers. And this makes one inclined to be brutal to him, which I must admit he bears well. So we shall shake down.

I am afraid that our old friend the Senatore[9] is very near to failing. He likes his friends about him, & he takes thought for everybody in the most affectionate & charming way. But he is fatigued; & I think that the presence of guests would be bad for him, were it not compensated by the pleasure he takes in being kind to others & hearing movement in his neighborhood. He has a very good nurse from Florence. Probably you sent her.

March 29. Some days have elapsed since I wrote the last. And now I have seen more, & lived into far more, of Leucaspide. I have walked for 2 hrs up the Gravina, have walked to Statte & all over it, have walked to the Tavola del Paladino[10] & the Gravina di S. Giovanni, have driven into Taranto & seen the Tesoro[11] (such as it is) in the Duomo, have driven to Messapa & gone about the towers & the ravines thereof.

I am chock-full of Leucaspide & its natural beauties.

Lord & Lady Wantage[12] have been added to the party; & that is enough to say that the party has become most sociably pleasant.

In these days I have come to like Lady Gordon (née Herschel) more than I ever did before. I am bound to respect Sir Arthur; but I cannot yet say that I am drawn toward him. He is a fearful fidget. But he is a cousin of yours, & perhaps you will tell me, when we meet at last, that I do not understand him. Then I promise to be penitent.

Madge is having a "high old time." She will tell you all about it in her young enthusiastic style, wh is so different from my dried almonds & withered figs of experience.

I hear that Lina, Mme Villari, Gino,[13] are all at Venice. I hope, before we get to Florence, they will all be back again.

Recommend me to the Padrone. Yr affectionate friend

J A Symonds

They are killing the new-born lambs I hear.

---

1. To be delivered in Florence in April. See L 2071.

2. In her *The Land of Manfred* (1889), pp. 153–54, Mrs. Ross describes this dance, which she performed at one of Sir James Lacaita's parties. The dance tells a love story in pantomime: the man dances around his coquettish partner until she suddenly throws one arm above her head and darts away, the male in pursuit.

3. Sir James Lacaita's guard.

4. See L 2003.

5. A rock chapel near Leucaspide; described in Ross, *Fourth Generation* (1912), p. 219.

6. Greek writer, 2nd century A.D., of a series of imaginary letters supposedly written by lower-class Athenians of the 4th century B.C.; describes manners and social conditions of the time.

7. Flourished probably end of 2nd century A.D.; Greek romancer and sophist; author of the pastoral romance *Daphnis and Chloe*.

8. See L 2101.

9. Sir James Lacaita, the "Senatore," died January 4, 1895.

10. A huge slab of stone ca. 2 miles from Leucaspide. According to the peasants, the Paladins spread their feasts on this rock to celebrate their victories over the pagans.

11. The treasure. In *Land of Manfred*, p. 139, Janet Ross describes it:
There are a quantity of MSS . . . in the Municipal Palace of 1334, 1367, 1370, 1477, etc., all stuffed pell-mell into a chest of drawers in one of the clerks' rooms. I was kindly permitted to see them, but it would have demanded many days' labour to unroll them and read the contents . . . ; they ought to be sorted and arranged.

12. Robert James Loyd-Lindsay, 1st Baron Wantage (1832–1901), an M. P. (1865–85); served as A.D.C. in the Crimea; extra equerry to Prince of Wales; finance secretary to War Office; married (1858) Harriet Sarah Jones-Loyd (1837–1920), whose surname of Loyd he assumed to precede "Lindsay." Lady Harriet published a *Memoir* of her husband (1907).

13. Lina Duff-Gordon and Mrs. Pasquale Villari (see L 1297); Gino is unidentified.

2103. *To Alfred Lord Douglas*[1]

Leucaspide, Paraceto. March 30, 1893

My dear Bosie,

As you do not care to be called Lord Alfred, I shall call you by what you say your friends call you.

Your letter from that awful place (it must be awful if it is like its name) reached me today. I am staying here with an old friend Sir James Lacaita. It is a wonderful place, and the country is Magna Graecia untouched by all the centuries. The ground is called after a cavalry troop of noble Palatine youths, raised during the war with Pyrrhus, who are called the Leucaspides or White Shields. But the weather is awfully cold, and we had what my daughter calls 'a colony of cold English' in the house. Lord and Lady Wantage,[2] Sir Arthur Gordon and his daughter, a Lady Gordon (*nee* Herschel),[3] all Coutts Lindsays[4] and Aberdeens.[5] They are very nice, of course, but they won't catch on to the people and the customs of this wild country. Such shepherds! Like young fauns.

I daresay it is rather dreadful for you at Klein Schmalkalden.[6] But you'll shake down. You can't be always pampered in the Savoy [Club]. It was very pleasant for Oscar [Wilde] pampering you, I doubt not. I wish you would come and see how I can make you comfortable, and feed your soul on honey of sweet-bitter thoughts—in Italy—in Switzerland—it is all the same.

I wonder what you thought about Kains-Jackson.[7] He rather took me aback when I first met him. But he is a very good fellow, I think, and has a lot of enthusiasm. I wish all people who feel as deeply as he does, and had his courage and his brains, could be also attractive by their manners and appearance. This would help much.

We are going into Taranto tomorrow to see a Passion procession go by torchlight through the town and along the seashore. I mean to spend the night there with my daughter and my faithful friend and servant Angelo [Fusato]. We shall then part from the 'Old Glory' and make our way by Metapaitum [Metapontum?] to Paestum, and then Naples.

If you write, send to the address below, and believe me affectionately yours,

J. A. Symonds
560 Zattere
Venezia

P.S. If I see any nice photograph upon my way, I will send it you.

1. Lord Alfred Douglas (1870–1945), editor of the periodical *The Spirit Lamp,* published in 1893 Symonds' "To Leander" in Vol. III (February), 29; Symonds' prose sketch, "Beethoven's Concerto in E Dur" (probably the "Emperor" Concerto in E-flat major) in Vol. IV (May), 2–3; and Symonds' "From the Arabic," a poem, in Vol. IV (June), 100. In March 1893, Douglas was only 23 years old; he had met Wilde in 1891, approximately 1½ years before. Thus gossip about Wilde and Douglas must already have been extensive. Douglas published, 1914, *Oscar Wilde and Myself.*
2. See L 2102.
3. See L 2100.
4. Sir Coutts Lindsay (1824–1913), 2nd Bart., and his wife Caroline (née Fitzroy). Sir Coutts Lindsay was a lieutenant colonel during the Crimean War.
5. The family of John Campbell Hamilton-Gordon (1847–1934), 7th Earl and 1st Marquess of Aberdeen. There were 3 sons and a daughter.
6. Schmalkalden, a summer-resort town in Prussia in a district also called Schmalkalden, in Thuringia, 11 miles north of Meiningen.
7. See L 1887.

2104. *To Janet Ross*

Salerno, April 3, 1893.

My dear Janet,

We came from Taranto yesterday and saw Paestum to-day. I am anxious about Catherine. Last Friday came a telegram to say she was down at Venice with gastric fever. I have had daily telegrams since and hope the attack is quite a light one.

The last days at Leucaspide were very pleasant. We all planted olive trees on Friday morning. The Senatore[1] seemed to fluctuate in health. But his spirits were wonderful. He brightened in society and told the most charming stories. My anxiety about my wife prevented me from going to Oria or Manduria. But I drove with Madge to Luperano and Pulsano.

It is very good of you to have engaged Nencioni[2] for the reading of my lecture. He shall certainly, as you suggest, have a copy of the *Renaissance.* I read the *Land of Manfred*[3] again on my journey and find it admirable on the spot. It is only two full of various information, and suffers perhaps a little by want of composition—I mean throwing into relief and subordination. I am too tired to write more.

Your affectionate

J.A.S.

1. Sir James Lacaita. See L 1879.

2. Professor Nencioni (see L 2100), agreed to read Symonds' lecture scheduled for April in Florence. Mrs. Ross engaged a Signora Falorsi as translator.

3. Janet Ross' travel book (1889).

2105. To Dr. J. W. Wallace

Naples April 10. 1893

Dear Mr Wallace

I have just arrived here from Taranto, & found your letter of the 3rd March, wh has been wandering after me from Davos to Venice & thence to Naples.

I do not think it probably that I omitted to return any of Traubel's[1] letters. I was careful to do them up in packets & send them by the hand of a servant to the post.

However, it is possible that some may have been omitted. If so, on my return to Davos, I will look for them in the drawer which I reserved for these communications.

My little book on Whitman[2] ought soon to be out. I wish to send a copy to yourself & one to Dr Johnston. But as yet I have not heard from the publisher regarding its appearance.

Believe me to be most sincerely yours

John Addington Symonds

1. See L 1728.

2. The work was published on April 19, 1893, the day of Symonds' death.

2106. To Janet Ross

Albergo d' Italia Roma April 14. 1893

My dear Janet

It is a good thing that I did not attempt to give my lecture at Florence; for I had been laid up with a bad cold & sorethroat. On Wednesday I was

23. *Symonds' last letter: To Catherine Symonds written on his deathbed.*

quite incapable of speaking. Madge & Angelo [Fusato] are both ill with the same sort of cold; & I hear of this kind of thing in all quarters.

Catherine has been in bed at Venice ever since she got there on the 28th of March. It is typhoid, but of a mild kind. She has Lotta & her Swiss maid & a nurse. So she is well looked after. But of course it is a great nuisance.

I wonder whether it would suit you if Madge & I & Angelo were to come to Poggio [Gherardo] on Monday or Tuesday next week? I do not really want to see the Feste here, though the Tournament tempts.

I am so stupid that I can think of nothing. So goodbye.

Your affectionate friend

J.A.S.

2107. *To Mrs. John Addington Symonds*[1]

My dearest Catherine[2]

Show this at once to him

There is something I ought to tell you, and being ill at Rome I take this occasion. If I do not see you again in this life you remember that I made H F Brown depositary of my printed books. I wish that legacy to cover all Mss Diaries Letters & other matters found in my books cupboard, with the exception of business papers. I do this because I have written things you could not like to read, but which I have always felt justified and useful for society.[3] Brown will consult & publish nothing without your consent.[4]

Ever yours

J A Symonds

You are ill at Venice & I have fallen here.
Rome April 19/93
No time for more.

I want to write all I have to say
 cannot talk at all
The Doctor[5] particularly wants to see it
Se ho qualche cosa che bisogno l'amo da piri . . . perdere[?]

---

1. On April 19, 1893, Margaret Symonds, attending her father during what became his last (but brief) illness in Rome, wrote her sister Katharine describing their father's

death on that day from respiratory complications. It is now owned by Margaret's daughter, Dame Janet Vaughan.

2. This note is part of the Bristol University collection of Symonds materials, but exists also in a copy made by Mrs. Symonds for Henry Graham Dakyns. Included in the Dakyns collection, the copy is accompanied by the following note from Mrs. Symonds:

6. Sussex Place [London]

Nov 2 [1893]

Dearest Graham

These were his last written words in pencil—hardly legible—wh they gave me when I reached Rome that morning. You see how the great question was supreme in his mind to the very last. Are we right in being cowardly & suppressing it? I am glad we have Henry's [Sidgwick's] wisdom for *final* reference. I trust Horatio fully & want to help, but hinder him as you know. I think if I write a very short preface embodying part of this letter, it will make his position clear to the outside world (not his friends, I mean) but critics & relations.

I go tomorrow. Goodbye. My dear love to you both. I am so glad I saw you——

Henry Sidgwick followed the course of Brown's editing with great diligence, and Mrs. Symonds published the letter, complete except for the fourth sentence, in her brief preface to Brown's *Biography,* and took occasion to express her satisfaction with Brown's handling of the materials at hand.

The Davos Courier noted Symonds' death in a two-columned, block-edged, front-page notice on April 22:

Death of
Mr. John Addington Symonds.
——++——

The sad and unexpected news, which was received here on Wednesday, of the death, at Rome, of Mr. John Addington Symonds, will be heard everywhere with feelings of sincere regret, not only by those who have been acquainted with his genial disposition and enjoyed the rich current of his conversation, but by that larger world who, in the absence of personal intercourse, have found their attraction in his writings. Of his position in the world of letters there will be much no doubt to be said in other quarters. It concerns us just now only to deplore the irreparable loss to Davos of one who for fourteen years past has been the most prominent member of its society, who has taken the lead in everything that might conduce to its welfare, and who has found a greater interest than this in extending to his Swiss neighbours all that sympathy and a large generosity can do. There may seem a fitness in his having breathed his last in the capital of the country which has filled his thoughts for so many years and inspired the charm of so much of his writings, but we may be permitted to wish that his body might rest with his eldest daughter in the place where his memory will always be retained with affection, and among the people he loved so well.

In the library of Balliol College, Oxford, is a letter by Mrs. Symonds addressed on Aug. 12, 1893, to Benjamin Jowett, who wrote Symonds' epitaph. The epitaph, essentially the same as Jowett wrote it, but with a few minor revisions suggested by Mrs. Symonds in this letter, reads thus:

INFRA JACET

JOHANNES ADDINGTON SYMONDS

VIR LUMINIBUS INGENII MULTIS

ET INDUSTRIA SINGULARI,

CUJUS ANIMUS

INFIRMO LICET IN CORPORE

LITERARUM ET HISTORIÆ STUDIO ARDEBAT.

BRISTOLII NATUS V. OCT. MDCCCXL.

REQUIEVIT IN CHRISTO XIX AP. MDCCCXCIII.

———

AVE CARISSIME

NEMO TE MAGIS IN CORDE AMICOS FOVEBAT

NEC IN SIMPLICES ET INDOCTOS BENEVOLENTIOR ERAT.

(Here lies John Addington Symonds, a man of singular industry and of many flashes of genius, whose spirit, though lodged in a frail body, was ardent in the study of letters and history. Born in Bristol, 5 October 1840, and gone to rest in Christ, 19 April 1893.

Farewell, my dearest friend. No one in his heart sustained his friends more than you did, nor was more benevolent to the simple and unlearned.)

And below is Symonds's own translation of Cleanthes's hymn—

> Lead thou me, God, Law, Reason, Motion, Life,
> All names for Thee alike are vain and hollow:
> Lead me, for I will follow without strife,
> Or if I strive, still must I blindly follow!

Symonds was buried on Saturday, April 22, in the English Cemetery in Rome.

In his will, dated Oct. 14, 1882, Symonds gave copyright interest in his published works and all his manuscripts and unpublished writings, whether in print or not, to H. F. Brown; gave his letters and, for all practical purposes, the remainder of his possessions and income to his wife; and gave £8,000 to each of his daughters upon her reaching the age of 21. The executors were his wife, Charles Henry Cave (his nephew), Robert Henry Otter (who had married Isabella Gamble, his cousin), and Henry Napier Abbott of Bristol (see L 787). The will was executed by probate Aug. 4, 1893, in Switzerland.

3. The papers willed to Brown of course included the as yet only partially published autobiography and other papers, the latter now lost or destroyed (see L 972), which Brown willed to the London Library.

4. This caused Brown some difficulties when he prepared the biography (1895) and the *Letters and Papers* (1923).

5. Axel Munthe (1857–1949), Swedish physician and author; practiced in Paris and Rome; wrote *Red Cross and Iron Cross* (1916) and *The Story of San Michele* (1929).

Appendix

2108 (365a).[1] *To Mrs. Alfred Tennyson*[2]

[Freshwater] Nov: 25 1864

Dear Mrs Tennyson

I must write to thank you from my wife & from myself for your great kindness to us. You have truly given what Mr Jowett wished for us—a happy recollection, to be connected with a great event in our lives.—If you have not seen the portrait I enclose, you may perhaps value it. It has never been sold, but my father has the plate, & I chanced to have this copy in my writing case.

Believe us both to be yours truly—

J. A. Symonds.

---

1. This letter comes between Ls 365 and 366.
2. Alfred Tennyson, later (1884) Lord Tennyson (1809–92), on June 13, 1850, married Emily (?–1896), daughter of Henry Sellwood of Berkshire.

2109 (859a).[1] *To Mrs. Alfred Tennyson*

Clifton Hill House
Bristol
Nov 2 1872

My dear Mrs Tennyson

I am sorry you should have had the trouble to thank me for sending you my little book:[2] though it is a pleasure to me to receive a letter from you. I could not do otherwise than send you the book—not hoping you would read it,—but as a proof of the memory I have of your courtesy & kindness to me this spring at Farringford. Mr Dakyns will be pleased to receive your message. He is happy in his marriage; but the drudgery of a master's work in a big school—a sort of workshop for elaborating brains—tries his health much. He has a delicacy both of perception & of intellect which is not exactly adapted to the rough work of education en masse.

With many thanks to you for your kind messages to my wife & myself I am yours most sincerely

J. A. Symonds—

The week of the wedding[3] at Freshwater this Spring has left a charming Idyll in many minds.

---

1. This letter should follow L 859.
2. *An Introduction to the Study of Dante* (1872).
3. Of Annie Russell and Charles Petar. See L 829.

2110 (893a).[1] *To Dawsonne Strong*[2]

[April, 1873]

& call them trumpery imitations of willows, I know not. To me they are purely beautiful & unlike any other tree on earth.—Everything here is Greek. The poetry of Theocritus was written in Sicilian scenery like this. Almost every flower has a Greek legend. The sound in the pines, the sea, the shadows on the hills, the pools of water overgrown with ferns & starry clear, the echoes, the sound of sheep dogs, the little cottages pale pink against the greyness of their olive gardens—all is Greek, Idyllic, pagan, placid, beautiful, & full of light & form. It only needs some of the divine youths & maidens of Hellenic dreams—some Narcissus bending over the pool some Galatea hiding full of smiles from the Cyclops, some Adonis wounded & wild wailing Aphrodite, some Thyrsis piping in the noontide heat, some slumbering Pan, some Hyacinth bewept by Phoebus. These dreams fancy has to conjure up.—I have already bored you with so much description. Please give our best love to Aunt Charlotte[3] & Agnes,[4] & believe me to be yr aff Cousin

J A Symonds.

---

1. We conjecture that this fragment follows L 893.

846

3. Charlotte Symonds Strong, Symonds' aunt, his father's sister and Dawsonne's mother.

4. Symonds' cousin, Charlotte Symonds Strong's daughter and Dawsonne's sister.

2111 (1138a).[1] *To* La Rassegna Settimanale

[Davos, ca. March 1, 1879][2]

Ai Direttori[3]

Il Professore A. d'Ancona[4] nel suo libro intitolato « La poesia popolare italiana » ha pubblicato una Canzone antica la quale ci presenta, tanto nella forma generale quanto nei particolari, una coincidenza più che accidentale con due *ballate* inglesi o piuttosto scozzesi. Ecco la Canzone come venne dettata al d'Ancona da un cantore del contado pisano (op. cit. p. 106).

>Dov'eri 'ersera a cena,
>Caro mio figlio, savio e gentil?
>>Mi fai morire
>>>Ohimè!
>>Dov'eri 'ersera a cena,
>>Gentile mio cavalier?
>Ero dalla mi' dama;
>>Mio core stà male,
>>Che male mi stà!
>>Ero dalla mi' dama;
>>'L mio core che se ne và.
>Che ti diènno da cena . . .
>Gentile mio cavalier! . .
>Un'anguilletta arrosto,
>>Cara mia madre;
>>Mio core stà male,
>>Che male mi stà!
>Un'anguilletta arrosto,
>'L mio core che se ne va.

L'antichità di questa canzone vien provata da un canto del « Cieco fiorentino » stampato nel 1629 a Verona, che ne riporta i due primi versetti. Altre versioni veneziane e lombarde e leccesi della medesima canzone attestano la sua popolarità. Nella versione comasca si sviluppa tutta la tragedia. Il giovine è andato alla casa della sua dama; la perfida gli ha dato un'anguilla avvelenata da mangiare.

          L'avì mangiada tutta,
          Figliuol mio caro, fiorito e gentil?
          L'avì mangiata tutta?
              Non n'hô mangiâ che mezza:
          Signôra mama, mio core stâ mal!
          Non n' hô mangiâ che mezza:
              Ohimè, ch'io moro, ohimè!
          Coss'avi fà dell'altra mezza? etc.
              L'hô dada alla cagnòla: etc.
          Cossa avì fâ della cagnola? etc.
              L'è morta drè la strada: etc.

Alla fine del racconto il giovine fa il suo testamento. Ne citerò solamente l'ultima stanza:

          Cossa lassò alla vostra dama,
          Figliuol mio car, fiorito e gentil,
          Cossa lassè alla vostra dama?
              La forca da impiccarla,
          Signôra mama, mio core sta mal!
          La forca da impiccarla:
              Ohimè ch'io moro, ohimè!

Mi faccio adesso a confrontare queste versioni italiane colle due canzoni scozzesi. La prima si trova nella collezione americana Child (English and Scottish Ballads, Boston. 1857, vol. 2º p. 248). Comincia così: « O where hae ye been, Lord Randal, my son? » * Trascriverò una traduzione fatta da me, acciocchè i lettori italiani possano più facilmente intendere come esattamente corrispondano fra loro le versioni inglesi ed italiane di quest'antichissima canzone:

          Dove sei stato, Lord Randal, figliuolo mio,
          Dove sei stato, bel giovinotto mio?
          Sono stato al bosco: fammi il letto, madre, presto;
          Sono stanco della caccia, e vorrei coricarmi.

          Dove eri a cena, Lord Randal? etc.
          Ero dalla mia dama; fammi etc.

          Cosa ebbì da cena? etc.
          Ebbi un'auguilla cotta nel brodo, etc.

          (manca una stanza)

Cosa hanno fatto di mastini tuoi? etc.
Gonfiarono e poi morirono, etc.

Temo che sia tu avvelenato! etc.
O sì! sono avvelenato, etc.

Nell' altro esemplare (op. cit. p. 245) il giovane fa il suo testamento. Avendo lasciato la sua casa al padre, la sua cassa d'oro alla sorella, e il suo cavallo al fratello, slancia contro la sua perfida innamorata questa maledizione:

« Cosa lascerai alla tua dama? etc.
» La forca e la corda per impiccarla! »

In questa seconda versione della Ballata, il giovane risponde a sua madre:

Fammi il letto, madre, presto;
Perchè sto male al cuore, e vorrei coricarmi.**

In tutte le due ripetesi il ritornello come nelle versioni italiane.

Come ognuno s'accorgerà, noi abbiamo un fatto di grandissima importanza storica in questa corrispondenza fra le letterature volgari di nazioni tanto disgiunte al giorno di oggi, e tanto lontane ora dalla loro culla comune. Bisogna aggiungere che simili composizioni liriche sullo stesso argomento si ritrovano nelle raccolte di poesie popolari tedesche, svedesi e francesi. Sarebbe forse questo poemetto dell'*Anguilla* l' ultimo resto d'una *Saga* indo-germanica?

Disgraziatamente la canzone dell'*Anguilla* è quasi un fenomeno isolato nella storia della poesia popolare italiana; e sebbene le sue corrispondenze colle canzoni settentrionali disopra citate siano tanto precise, non si può trarre conseguenze sicure da un solo fatto. Abbondantemente ricche di canti erotici, rispetti, strambotti, stornelli, etc., le raccolte recentemente fatte con somma e lodabilissima industria in tutte le provincie del Regno, sono finora scarsissime di canti narrativi. Lo scopo principale dunque di questa mia lettera si è di destare gli studiosi italiani alla ricerca di cotali canti.

Che non tralascino veruno sforzo per rinvenire i monumenti d'una poesia orale che va perdendosi ogni giorno di più in più, e per spigolarne ogni menomissimo brano. Le storiette siciliane in prosa raccolte poco tempo fa,[5] hanno già recato frutti di non poca importanza alla scienza della mitologia comparativa. Ma si desidera finora una più ricca collezione di canzoni narrative italiane simili a quelle che si chiamano *Ballads* dai popoli settentrionali.* Che l'Italia non sia del tutto priva di questo genere di poesia volgare, puossi dedurre dalla canzone dell'*Anguilla*.

Devot. John Addington Symonds.[6]

* « O where hae ye been, Lord Randal, my son?
   O where hae ye been, my handsome young man? »
« I hae been to the wild wood; mother, make my bed soon,
   For I'm weary wi' hunting, and fain wad lie doun. »
« Where gat ye your dinner, Lord Randal? etc.
   I dined wi' my true-love; etc.
   What gat ye to your dinner, etc.
   I got eels boiled in broo, etc.
What became of your bloodhounds? etc.
   O they swell'd and they died, etc.
   O I fear ye are poisoned! etc.
   O yes! I am poisoned, etc.
** Ecco i versetti inglesi:
   What will ye leave to your true-love? etc.
   My tow and the halter for to hang on yon tole.
         Mither, mak my bed sune,
   For I'm sick at the heart and I fain wad lie down.

---

1. This follows L 1138.
2. Published March 9, 1879, pp. 193–94.
3. Following is a translation of the body of this letter:
To the Editors:
   Professor A. d'Ancona, in his book entitled *Italian Folk Poetry,* has published an old canzone which displays, both in its general outline and in its details, a more than accidental resemblance to two English (or rather "Scottish") ballads. Here is the canzone as sung for d'Ancona (op. cit., p. 106) by a singer from the region around Pisa:

> Where were you for dinner last evening
> My son so dear, so noble and wise?
>   You will be my death
>   Alas!
> Where were ye for dinner last evening
> My noble cavalier?
> I was with my lady love:
>
> My heart is sick,
> How sick I am!
>
> I was with my lady love;
> Ah, the state of my heart!
>
> What did they give you for dinner . . .
> My noble cavalier!
> A roasted eel,
>   Dear Mother:

> My heart is sick,
> How sick I am!
> A roasted eel.
> Ah, the state of my heart.

The antiquity of this song is proven by a song of the "Blind Florentine," printed in 1629 at Verona, which contains the first two verses. Other Venetian and Lombard and Lecco versions of the same song attest to its popularity. In the version from Lake Como the whole tragedy is developed. The young man has gone to his lady's house; in her perfidy she has given him a poisoned eel to eat.

> And did you eat it all,
> My dear young son, so handsome and noble?
> And did you eat it all?
> I ate not more than half:
> Mother, my heart is sick!
> I ate not more than half:
> Alas, I am dying, alas!
> What did you do with the other half? etc.
> I gave it to my hound: etc.
> What did you do with the hound? etc.
> He is lying dead on the road: etc.

At the end of the narrative the young man makes his will. I shall cite only the final stanza:

> What will you leave to your lady love,
> My dear young son, so handsome and noble,
> What will you leave to your lady love?
> The gallows to hang her on,
> Mother, my heart is sick!
> The gallows to hang her on:
> Alas, I am dying, alas!

I turn now to a comparison of these Italian versions with two Scottish ballads. The first is found in the collection of the American scholar Child. . . . It begins: "O where etc."

I shall transcribe here a translation I have made in order that Italian readers may understand how exact are the correspondences between the English and Italian versions of this old song:

. . . .

In the other variant (op. cit., p. 245) the young man makes his will. Having left his house to his father, his golden robe to his sister, his horse to his brother, he hurls this malediction against his perfidious beloved:

. . . .

In the second version of the ballad, the young man replies to his mother:

. . . .

In both versions the refrain is repeated as in the Italian versions.

As everyone will perceive, we have a fact of the utmost historical importance in this correspondence between the folk literatures of nations so far apart today, and so distant now from their common cradle. One must add that similar lyric compositions on the same theme are found in collections of German, French, and Swedish folk poetry. In this little poem of *The Eel* is perhaps the last remnant of an Indo-Germanic Saga.

Unfortunately, the song of *The Eel* is almost an isolated phenomenon in the history of Italian folk poetry; and although its correspondences with the Northern songs cited above are so precise, one cannot safely draw conclusions from one isolated fact. Abundantly rich in erotic songs, *rispetti, strambotti, stornelli,* etc., the collections recently made with the utmost praiseworthy industry throughout the regions of the kingdom, are extremely barren of narrative songs. The principal endeavor of this letter, then, is to stimulate Italian scholars to search for such songs.

They ought not to forego any effort at rediscovering the monuments of an oral poetry that is every day becoming more and more lost to us, nor at gleaning every grain, however tiny. The little Sicilian prose tales that were collected a short time ago[5] have already yielded fruits of no small importance to the science of comparative mythology. But at present there is still a need for a richer collection of Italian narrative songs similar to those that are called *Ballads* by the peoples of the North. That Italy is not wholly lacking in this genre of folk poetry may be deduced from the canzone of *The Eel*.

4. Alessandro d'Ancona (1835–1914), Italian critic, journalist, and scholar, best known for his *Origini del teatro in Italia* (1877).

5. *Novelline (Cinque) Populari Siciliana, publicata da G. Pitrè* (1878).

6. 1878. Symonds refers to this letter and its contents in *The Renaissance in Italy: Italian Literature,* Chap. IV, where he says it brought forth only a Tuscan version of "Donna Lombarda."

2112 (1309a).[1] *To Robert Baker Girdlestone*[2]

Am Hof. Davos Platz Dec 20 1882

My dear Girdlestone

It is a great pleasure to hear from you; & to answer your letter is assuredly more a pleasure than a pain in any sense to me. I do not correspond much. But my heart warms toward you, when I think of the happy hours we used to spend together here! You belong to the heroic period of Davos in my remembrance. Things have changed here much. Personally, upon a sober reckoning, I ought to say they have improved. I have a very fairly comfortable house of my own, with plenty of room, & all my family around me, withdrawn from the pernicious influences of hotel gossip. The place itself, owing to my agitation last winter, is making sanitary experiments, wh prove good will, & may lead to good results. But successive years do not render the exile, isolation & abnormal circumstances of life here easier. I find that a certain glow & exhileration generated by the climate & the combat with inexorable malady, tends to fade out; while the sterner aspects of our lot make themselves more felt. This is very natural. To carve out of the conditions some life of wh a man may not be wholly ashamed, is my business. One sad dispiriting circumstance is the shifting state of the population. We lose many friends by death. None come who are not impatient to leave & be free of their imprisonment. Those who revisit us, groan on taking up a heavy chain. You will understand that all this, becoming ever more obvious, defining itself more & more exactly as the novelty of the situation merges into commonplace, implies much that is depressing to my wife & myself.

I was extremely sorry not to be able to see you at Clifton in June. Great demands were made upon my time by relations, by business, & by my sister's [Charlotte's] friends who were also my old friends. The climate of England affected my very unfavorably. I was ill & anxious & depressed by the conviction that life in England was hopeless for me. This made me make less efforts than I should have liked to make. As it was, I made far too many. [Drs.] Clark & Williams[3] ordered me out of England at a day's notice, & when I got back to Davos I had to spend 3 months of the most absolute invalid life.

You will excuse me. Your kind letter shews you have excused me.

I am sorry to hear bad news of your wife. A hint about spinal trouble is very grave. Nothing but absolute supine rest can be recommended. But I need not say that to a physiologist!

Conceive how much I live out of the world! I have not even heard of Shelley's letters.[4] I must write to get the no of the Edinburgh.[5] Probably, some neglect of mine in the quarter of Mr Garnett has caused me to be passed over in the list of Shelley's biographers & to lose the privately printed volume. How careful we ought to be, even on the vulgarest score of self-interest, to repay small attentions! My own wandering & sickly life has made me a sinner. I am too apt to consecrate my little strength to literary work; & to leave officia alone.

I get about 4 hours of mental vigour in the day. The rest I spend in out-door exercise, casual society, & listening to my wife's reading aloud of books wh interest us.

I shall, on your recommendation, send for Wallace's book,[6] to get her to read it to me. We go through a good deal of English reading in 2 hours per diem.

My own work at present is upon the Elizn Drama, considered in its totality as a national display. I feel the subject to be a fairly good one for my special faculties. But it has been much worked over. Doing it here, quite quite alone, I fear lest I should not keep to the right lines of study & presentment. But a man can only do his best, & leave the rest to God who in one way or the other rules all. We cannot do without that great generalization, to unify our efforts & consecrate our labours. Man must function. Following his bias in sincerity, man may dare to speak of God.

Christian Palmy came in at this point, & hearing I am writing to you, he begged me to send you his remembrances. My wife joins me in the best wishes to yourself & Mrs Girdlestone for the coming year.

Ever yours

J A Symonds

What a very very strange thing is human life! Trite saying indeed, but in its triteness tragic with intensity.

---

1. This follows L 1309.
2. See L 1139a.
3. For Dr. Clark see Ls 908 and 1028; for Dr. Williams see L 1279.
4. *Select Letters of Shelley,* with an Introduction by Richard Garnett (1882). Richard Garnett (1835–1906), English librarian in the British Museum and author of works on librarianship and verse, as well as several volumes in the "Great Writers" series; also published *Relics of Shelley* (1862).
5. "Shelley and Mary," *The Edinburgh Review,* CLVII (1882), 472–507, by Henry Reeve (1813–95), editor (1855–95) of that journal.
6. Probably Alfred Russel Wallace's (1823–1913), *Miracles and Modern Spiritualism* (1875).

2. An Additional Undatable Letter

2113. *To Unknown*

[place and date uncertain]

It is very late. You know how I go on talking when the night wears forward. And I have only my pen to talk by.

I want to talk still. You say that, when I first saw you at Venice, you had a notion of me— "So different to what I am." I wonder what you thought! That does not matter. You know me now. And you know how much I care for [you . . . ms. cut off].

So goodnight. There remains so much upon the heart unsaid, which the pen cannot communicate. Goodnight. It is late, & I think I see you, alone perhaps, in your room by the big fireplace. Goodnight!

Yours JAS.

List of Sources of Letters
Volume III

(All references are to locations of manuscripts except where printed sources are indicated.)

Letters	Sources
1448	Colby College Collection.
1449	Bristol University.
1450	Dakyns Collection.
1451	Bodleian Library.
1452	Bristol University.
1453	Printed, *Biography,* pp. 398–99.
1454	Brotherton Collection—University of Leeds.
1455	Printed, *Biography,* p. 399.
1456	Bristol University.
1457	British Museum.
1458	Berg Collection—New York Public Library.
1459	Bristol University.
1460	Printed, *L & P,* p. 173.
1461	Brewster Collection; pr. in part, *Biography,* pp. 399–400.
1462	Bristol University.
1463	Printed, *Biography,* pp. 400–01.
1464	Printed, *Biography,* pp. 401–02.
1465–66	Bristol University.
1467	Yale University.
1468	Printed, *L & P,* pp. 173–74.
1469	Bristol University.
1470	Printed, *L & P,* p. 174.
1471	Bristol University.

1472	Printed, *Biography*, pp. 402–03.
1473	Berg Collection—New York Public Library.
1474	Bristol University.
1475	Printed, *Biography*, p. 403.
1476	Printed, *Biography*, pp. 403–04.
1477	Printed, *L & P*, pp. 174–75.
1478	Boston Public Library.
1479	Printed, *L & P*, pp. 176–77.
1480	Printed, *L & P*, pp. 177–78.
1481	Boston Public Library.
1482	Printed, *L & P*, pp. 178–79.
1483	Printed, *L & P*, pp. 179–80.
1484	University of Pennsylvania.
1485	Bristol University.
1486	Printed, William Sharp, *Selected Writings*, ed. Mrs. William Sharp (2 vols., 1912); II: *Studies and Appreciations*, pp. 423–24.
1487	Printed, *Biography*, pp. 404–05.
1488	Printed, *L & P*, pp. 180–81.
1489	Bristol University.
1490	University of Pennsylvania.
1491	Printed, *L & P*, pp. 181–82.
1492	Printed, *L & P*, pp. 182–83.
1493	Printed, *Academy*, no. 700 (Oct. 3, 1885), 223.
1494–95	Bristol University.
1496	Printed, *L & P*, pp. 183–85.
1497	Printed, *L & P*, pp. 185–86.
1498	Boston Public Library.
1499	Quentin Keynes Collection.
1500	Printed, *L & P*, pp. 186–87.
1501	Printed, *Biography*, p. 405.
1502–03	Cambridge University.
1504	Typescript, Arthur Symons, "A Study of John Addington Symonds," Princeton University Library.
1505	Printed, *L & P*, p. 187.
1506	Typescript, KF, Bristol University.
1507	Grosskurth Collection.
1508	Typescript, Arthur Symons, *op. cit.*, Princeton University Library.
1509	Printed, *L & P*, pp. 187–88.
1510	Typescript, KF, Bristol University.
1511	Dakyns Collection.
1512	British Museum.
1513–14	Bristol University.
1515	Printed, *Biography*, pp. 405–07.
1516	Typescript, Arthur Symons, *op. cit.*, Princeton University Library.
1517	Bristol University.
1518	Dakyns Collection.
1519	Bristol University.

1520	Yale University.
1521	Bristol University.
1522	Yale University; printed, *Biography*, pp. 407–08.
1523	Printed, *Biography*, pp. 408–09.
1524	Grosskurth Collection.
1525	Bristol University.
1526	Dakyns Collection.
1527	Printed, *Biography*, pp. 409–10.
1528–29	Typescript, Arthur Symons, *op. cit.*, Princeton University Library.
1530	Bristol University.
1531	Central Library, Manchester, England.
1532	Printed, *L & P*, pp. 188–89.
1533	Typescript, KF, Bristol University.
1534	Bristol University.
1535	Printed, *L & P*, pp. 189–90.
1536	Berg Collection—New York Public Library.
1537	Columbia University.
1538	Printed, *L & P*, pp. 190–91.
1539	Bristol University
1540	Bristol University, pr. in part, *Biography*, p. 115.
1541	Printed, *L & P*, pp. 191–92.
1542	Cambridge University.
1543	Typescript, Arthur Symons, *op. cit.*, Princeton University Library.
1544	Bristol University.
1545	Henry E. Huntington Library Collection.
1546	Typescript, KF, Bristol University.
1547	Brotherton Collection—University of Leeds.
1548	Typescript, Arthur Symons, *op. cit.*, Princeton University Library.
1549	Typescript, KF, Bristol University.
1550	Typescript, Arthur Symons, *op. cit.*, Princeton University Library.
1551	Murray Collection.
1552	Bristol University.
1553–54	Cambridge University.
1555	Brotherton Collection—University of Leeds.
1556	Cambridge University.
1557	Typescript, KF, Bristol University.
1558	Printed, *Biography*, pp. 410–12.
1559	Boston Public Library.
1560	Typescript, KF, Bristol University.
1561–62	Bristol University.
1563	Printed, *Biography*, pp. 412–13.
1564	Printed, *Biography*, pp. 193–94.
1565	Brotherton Collection—University of Leeds.
1566	Balliol College Library.
1567	Printed, *L & P*, pp. 194–95.
1568	Printed, *Biography*, pp. 414–15.
1569	Brotherton Collection—University of Leeds.

1570	Bristol University.
1571	Printed, *L & P*, p. 195.
1572	Bristol University.
1573	Brotherton Collection—University of Leeds.
1574	Bristol University.
1575	Dakyns Collection.
1576	Brotherton Collection—University of Leeds.
1577	Printed, *L & P*, pp. 195–96.
1578	Boston Public Library.
1579	Bristol University.
1580	Printed, *L & P*, pp. 196–97.
1581	Cambridge University.
1582	Printed, *L & P*, pp. 197–98.
1583	Bristol University.
1584	Dugdale Collection.
1585	Printed, *Biography*, pp. 415–18.
1586	Bristol University.
1587	Printed, *L & P*, p. 199.
1588	Printed, *L & P*, pp. 199–200.
1589–90	Bristol University.
1591	Printed, *Fortnightly Review*, XLVII (April 1, 1887), 613–15.
1592	Printed, *Biography*, p. 420.
1593	University of Texas.
1594	Printed, *Biography*, pp. 418–20.
1595	Bristol University.
1596	Bristol University; pr. in part, *OOP*, p. 282.
1597	Brotherton Collection—University of Leeds.
1598	Bristol University; pr. in part, *OOP*, pp. 283–84, 286.
1599	Bristol University; pr. in part, *OOP*, pp. 284–85.
1600	Printed, *Biography*, pp. 420–22.
1601	Brotherton Collection—University of Leeds.
1602	Bristol University.
1603	Bristol University; pr. in part, *OOP*, pp. 287–88.
1604	Dugdale Collection.
1605	Henry E. Huntington Library Collection.
1606	University of Texas.
1607	Yale University.
1608	Boston Public Library.
1609	Feinberg Collection.
1610	Boston Public Library.
1611	Yale University.
1612	Boston Public Library.
1613	Yale University.
1614	Dugdale Collection.
1615	Boston Public Library.
1616	Bristol University.
1617	Printed, *L & P*, pp. 200–01.

1618	Bristol University.
1619	Bristol University; printed, *OOP*, pp. 225–28.
1620	Bristol University.
1621	Printed, *Biography*, pp. 423–25.
1622	Printed, *L & P*, pp. 201–02.
1623	Printed, *Fortnightly Review*, XLVIII (September, 1887), 459–60.
1624	Dugdale Collection.
1625	Bristol University.
1626	Columbia University.
1627	University of Texas.
1628	Folger Collection.
1629	Dugdale Collection.
1630	Printed, *L & P*, pp. 202–03.
1631	Printed, *Biography*, p. 425.
1632	Printed, William Sloane Kennedy *Reminiscences of Walt Whitman* (1896), p. viii.
1633	Printed, *Biography*, p. 426.
1634	Wayne State University.
1635	Printed, *L & P*, pp. 203–04.
1636	British Museum.
1637	Cambridge University.
1638	Printed, *L & P*, p. 206.
1639	Printed, *L & P*, pp. 204–05.
1640	Printed, *Margot Asquith: An Autobiography* (4 vols., 1920–22), II, 65–66.
1641	Bristol University.
1642	Typescript, KF, Bristol University.
1643	Printed, *L & P*, pp. 206–07.
1644	Dugdale Collection.
1645	Dakyns Collection.
1646	Printed, *Biography*, pp. 426–27.
1647	Printed, *Biography*, pp. 427–29.
1648–49	Dugdale Collection.
1650	Printed, *Biography*, p. 429.
1651	Boston Public Library.
1652	Kay-Shuttleworth Collection.
1653	Printed, "Winter in the High Alps," *Pall Mall Gazette*, XLVIII (February 28, 1888), 1–2.
1654	Printed, *Biography*, pp. 429–30.
1655	British Museum.
1656	Printed, *L & P*, pp. 207–08.
1657	Boston Public Library.
1658	Printed, *Biography*, p. 432.
1659	Dakyns Collection.
1660–61	Boston Public Library.
1662	Printed, *Biography*, pp. 432–33.
1663	Timothy d'Arch Smith Collection.
1664	Printed, *Biography*, pp. 434–35.

1665	Printed, *Biography*, p. 434.
1666	Printed, *L & P*, pp. 208–09.
1667	Printed, *L & P*, p. 209.
1668	Printed, *L & P*, pp. 209–10.
1669	Printed, *Biography*, p. 435.
1670	Printed, *Biography*, pp. 435–36.
1671	Bristol University.
1672	Library of Congress.
1673	H. Walker Taylor, Jr., Collection.
1674	Fitzwilliam Museum, Cambridge University.
1675	Bristol University.
1676–77	Fitzwilliam Museum, Cambridge University.
1678	Dugdale Collection.
1679	Printed, "The Truth about Christopher Marlowe," *Pall Mall Gazette*, XLVIII (Dec. 17, 1888), 5.
1680	Bristol University; pr. in part, *Biography*, pp. 436–37.
1681–82	British Museum.
1683	Printed, "The Theft of a Raphael," *Pall Mall Gazette*, XLIX (January 3, 1889), 7.
1684	Fitzwilliam Museum, Cambridge University.
1685	Boston Public Library.
1686	Printed, *The Davos Courier* (January 26, 1889), p. 145.
1687	Bristol University.
1688	Printed, *The Davos Courier* (Jan. 26, 1889), p. 143.
1689	Bristol University.
1690	Printed, *L & P*, pp. 216–17.
1691	British Museum.
1692	Feinberg Collection.
1693	Berg Collection—New York Public Library.
1694	"Autobiography," London Library.
1695–96	Dakyns Collection.
1697	Printed, *Biography*, pp. 437–38; pr. in part, *L & P*, p. 217.
1698	Bristol University.
1699	Cambridge University.
1700	Bristol University.
1701	Henry E. Huntington Library Collection.
1702	Printed, *Biography*, pp. 438–39.
1703	Bristol University.
1704	Printed, *L & P*, pp. 217–18.
1705	Cambridge University.
1706	Typescript, Arthur Symons, *op. cit.*, Princeton University Library.
1707	Printed, *Biography*, pp. 439–40.
1708	Robert L. Peters Collection.
1709	Dakyns Collection.
1710	Robert L. Peters Collection.
1711	Printed, *Biography*, p. 440.
1712	Bristol University.

1713	Printed, *Biography*, p. 440.
1714	Printed, *Biography*, pp. 445–46.
1715	Printed, *L & P*, pp. 218–19.
1716	Bristol University.
1717	Dugdale Collection.
1718	Printed, *L & P*, pp. 219–21.
1719	Brewster Collection.
1720	Printed, *Biography*, pp. 447–48.
1721	Printed, *Biography*, pp. 448–49.
1722	Printed, *Biography*, p. 449.
1723	Printed, *Biography*, p. 450.
1724	Printed, *L & P*, pp. 224–25.
1725	Printed, "Preface," *E S & S*, ed. H. F. Brown (3rd ed., 1907).
1726	Printed, *L & P*, p. 225.
1727	Fitzwilliam Museum, Cambridge University.
1728	Feinberg Collection.
1729	Printed, *L & P*, p. 226.
1730	Dakyns Collection.
1731	Printed, *L & P*, pp. 226–27.
1732	Bristol University.
1733–34	Dakyns Collection.
1735	Balliol College Library.
1736	University of Texas.
1737	Bristol University.
1738	Fitzwilliam Museum, Cambridge University.
1739	Dakyns Collection.
1740	Timothy d'Arch Smith Collection.
1741–42	Brewster Collection.
1743	Bristol University.
1744	Brotherton Collection—University of Leeds.
1745	Printed, *H & P*, pp. 56–57.
1746	Printed, "Preface," *E S & S*, ed. H. F. Brown (3rd ed., 1907).
1747	Bristol University; pr. in part, *OOP*, p. 268.
1748	Bristol University.
1749–50	Brewster Collection.
1751	Printed, *L & P*, pp. 227–28.
1752	Printed, *L & P*, pp. 228–29.
1753	Bristol University; pr., *H & P*, pp. 57–58.
1754	Printed, *L & P*, pp. 229–30.
1755	Bristol University.
1756	Bristol University; pr. in part, *OOP*, pp. 204–05.
1757	Printed, *L & P*, p. 230.
1758	Bristol University; pr. in part, *OOP*, pp. 197, 255–56.
1759	Brotherton Collection—University of Leeds.
1760	Henry Huntington Library Collection.
1761	Feinberg Collection; pr. in part, *In Re Walt Whitman* (1893), p. 412.
1762	Printed, *OOP*, p. 247, note.

1763	Brewster Collection.
1764	Brotherton Collection—University of Leeds.
1765	Bristol University.
1766	Typescript, Arthur Symons, *op. cit.*, Princeton University Library.
1767–68	Robert L. Peters Collection.
1769	Magdalen College, Oxford.
1770	Brotherton Collection—University of Leeds.
1771	Typescript, Arthur Symons, *op. cit.*, Princeton University Library.
1772	Brewster Collection.
1773	Printed, *OOP*, pp. 208–09.
1774	Brewster Collection.
1775	Printed, *L & P*, pp. 230–31; pr. in part, *Biography*, pp. 450–51.
1776	Asquith, *op. cit.*, II, 66–68.
1777	Printed, *L & P*, pp. 231–32; pr. in part, "Preface," *E S & S*, ed. H. F. Brown (3rd ed., 1907).
1778	National Library of Scotland.
1779	Robert L. Peters Collection.
1780–81	Brewster Collection.
1782	Robert L. Peters Collection.
1783	Brotherton Collection—University of Leeds.
1784	Printed, Asquith, *op. cit.*, II, 63.
1785	National Library of Scotland.
1786	Brotherton Collection—University of Leeds.
1787	National Library of Scotland.
1788–90	Robert L. Peters Collection.
1791	Bristol University.
1792	Brotherton Collection—University of Leeds; pr. in part, *Biography*, p. 451.
1793	University of Texas.
1794	Printed, "Mr. J. A. Symonds's School Days," *Pall Mall Gazette*, L (May 27, 1890), 2.
1795	Printed, "Mr. J. A. Symonds and the 'Fortnightly Review,'" *Pall Mall Gazette*, L (June 13, 1890), 2.
1796	Brewster Collection.
1797	Brotherton Collection—University of Leeds.
1798	University of Texas.
1799	Printed, "Preface," *E S & S*, ed. H. F. Brown (3rd ed., 1907).
1800	Printed, *L & P*, pp. 238–39.
1801	Brewster Collection.
1802	Robert L. Peters Collection.
1803	Dugdale Collection.
1804	University of Texas.
1805	Printed, *Biography*, p. 452.
1806	Brewster Collection.
1807	Dakyns Collection.
1808	University of Chicago.
1809	Printed, *L & P*, p. 240.
1810	Brotherton Collection—University of Leeds.

1811	University of Texas.
1812	Printed, *Biography*, pp. 452–53; also pr., "Preface," *E S & S*, ed. H. F. Brown (3rd ed., 1907).
1813	University of Chicago.
1814	Feinberg Collection.
1815	University of Texas.
1816	Printed, "Preface," *E S & S*, ed. H. F. Brown (3rd ed., 1907).
1817	Robert L. Peters Collection.
1818	Printed, Babington, *Bibliography*, p. 50.
1819	University of Texas.
1820	Printed, Asquith, *op. cit.*, II, 63–65.
1821	Printed, *Biography*, pp. 453–54; also pr., "Preface," *E S & S*, ed. H. F. Brown (3rd ed., 1907).
1822	Feinberg Collection.
1823	British Museum.
1824	Brewster Collection.
1825	Printed, *OOP*, p. 255.
1826	Printed, "Preface," *E S & S*, ed. H. F. Brown (3rd ed., 1907).
1827	Brewster Collection.
1828	Printed, "Preface," *E S & S*, ed. H. F. Brown (3rd ed., 1907).
1829	Timothy d'Arch Smith Collection.
1830	Dugdale Collection.
1831	Dakyns Collection.
1832	Printed, *Biography*, p. 454.
1833	British Museum.
1834	Brewster Collection.
1835–36	University of Texas.
1837	Printed, Ernest Rhys, *Letters from Limbo* (1936), pp. 41–42.
1838	Printed, Maria Tuke Sainsbury, *Henry Scott Tuke: A Memoir* (1933), p. 106.
1839	University of Texas.
1840	Printed, *Biography*, p. 454; also pr., "Preface," *E S & S*, ed. H. F. Brown (3rd ed., 1907).
1841	Robert L. Peters Collection.
1842	Printed, *OOP*, pp. 260–61.
1843	Bristol University.
1844	Dugdale Collection.
1845–47	Brotherton Collection—University of Leeds.
1848	Bristol University; pr. in part, *Biography*, p. 447.
1849	Printed, *Biography*, pp. 455–56.
1850	Bristol University.
1851	Printed, *OOP*, pp. 210–11.
1852	Bristol University.
1853	Printed, *L & P*, pp. 240–41.
1854	Bristol University.
1855	Typescript, John Rylands Library, Manchester.
1856	Printed, *Biography*, pp. 458–59.

1857	Dakyns Collection.
1858	Bristol University.
1859	Printed, *L & P*, pp. 241–43.
1860	Bristol University.
1861	University of California, Los Angeles.
1862	Typescript, John Rylands Library, Manchester.
1863	Dakyns Collection.
1864	Bristol University; also pr. in part, Janet Ross, *The Fourth Generation* (1912), pp. 301–02.
1865	Dakyns Collection.
1865a	Bristol University.
1866	Brotherton Collection—University of Leeds.
1867	Feinberg Collection.
1868	Brotherton Collection—University of Leeds.
1869	Bristol University.
1870	Printed, *Biography*, pp. 456–57.
1871	Bristol University.
1872	Printed, *L & P*, p. 243.
1873	National Library, Florence.
1874	Feinberg—Wayne State University Collection.
1875	Printed, *L & P*, p. 244.
1876	University of Texas.
1877	Printed, *L & P*, pp. 244–45.
1878	Timothy d'Arch Smith Collection.
1879	Bristol University.
1880–81	National Library, Florence.
1882	Printed, *L & P*, pp. 245–46.
1883	National Library, Florence.
1884	Printed, *L & P*, p. 246.
1885	Feinberg Collection.
1886	National Library, Florence.
1887	Donald Weeks Collection.
1888	Bristol University.
1889	British Museum.
1890	National Library, Florence.
1891	Dakyns Collection.
1892–93	Bristol University.
1894–95	Dugdale Collection.
1896	Bristol University.
1897	Brotherton Collection—University of Leeds.
1898	Typescript, KF, Bristol University.
1899	Printed, *Biography*, pp. 460–61.
1900	National Library, Florence.
1901	Bristol University.
1902	Bristol University.
1903	Bristol University; pr. in part, *OOP*, pp. 197–98.
1904	Bristol University.

1905	Bristol University and pr. Ross, *op. cit.*, pp. 305–06.
1906	Printed, *L & P*, p. 247.
1907	Feinberg Collection.
1908	Bristol University.
1909	Dakyns Collection.
1910	Bristol University.
1911	Brotherton Collection—University of Leeds.
1912	Bristol University; pr. in part, *OOP*, p. 257.
1913	Printed, Asquith, *op. cit.*, II, 68–69.
1914	Bristol University.
1915	National Library, Florence.
1916	Bristol University; pr. in part, *OOP*, p. 257.
1917	Bristol University.
1918	National Library, Florence.
1919	Printed, *L & P*, pp. 247–48.
1920	Balliol College, Oxford University.
1921	Typescript, Bristol University.
1922	Bristol University; printed, Ross, *op. cit.*, pp. 307–08.
1923	Printed, *Biography*, pp. 466–68.
1924	Printed, *L & P*, pp. 248–49.
1925	Bristol University; pr., Ross, *op. cit.*, pp. 308–09.
1926	Bristol University.
1927	Typescript, Arthur Symons, *op. cit.*, Princeton University Library, p. 32.
1928	Bristol University; printed, Ross, *op. cit.*, p. 310.
1929	Bristol University; printed, Ross, *op. cit.*, pp. 311–12.
1930	Donald Weeks Collection.
1931	Printed, *L & P*, pp. 249–50, and *Biography*, pp. 468–69.
1932	National Library, Florence.
1933	Bristol University.
1933a	Compiled from Wilfred Austin Gill, *Edward Cracroft Lefroy: His Life and Poems* . . . (1897), pp. 45 and 21.
1934	Bristol University; printed, Ross, *op. cit.*, pp. 312–13.
1935	Printed, *Biography*, pp. 469–70.
1935a	Gill, *op. cit.*, compiled from pp. 22 and 45.
1936	Printed, "A Browning Puzzle," *Pall Mall Gazette*, LIII (Dec. 16, 1891), 2.
1937–38	National Library, Florence.
1939–40	Bristol University.
1941	Feinberg—Wayne State University Collection.
1942	A. & C. Black Collection.
1943	Typescript, London Library.
1944	A. & C. Black Collection.
1945	Donald Weeks Collection.
1946–47	Bristol University.
1948	Printed, *L & P*, p. 251.
1949	Printed, *L & P*, pp. 251–52.
1950	Dakyns Collection.
1951	Goodspeed Collection.

1952	Brotherton Collection—University of Leeds.
1953	Typescript, Feinberg Collection.
1954	Bristol University.
1955	National Library, Florence.
1956	Bristol University.
1957	Printed, *L & P*, pp. 252–53.
1958	Bristol University.
1959	Printed, *L & P*, pp. 253–55.
1960	British Museum.
1961–62	Feinberg Collection.
1963	Brotherton Collection—University of Leeds.
1964	Donald Weeks Collection.
1965	Printed, *L & P*, pp. 255–56.
1965a	Printed, Gill, *op. cit.,* pp. 45–46.
1966	Donald Weeks Collection.
1967	Bristol University.
1968	Typescript, Feinberg Collection.
1969	Cambridge University.
1970	Typescript, John Rylands Library, Manchester.
1971–72	Bristol University.
1973	Printed, *H & P*, pp. 71–72.
1974	Yale University.
1975	Donald Weeks Collection.
1976	Matthew Russell, comp., *Sonnets on the Sonnet: an Anthology* (1898), p. ix.
1977	Bristol University; pr. in part, Ross, *op. cit.,* p. 318.
1978	Bristol University.
1979	National Library, Florence.
1980	Bristol University.
1981	Printed, *OOP*, p. 204.
1982	Compiled from Roger Lhombreaud, *Arthur Symons: A Critical Biography* (1964), pp. 92–93; and typescript, Arthur Symons, *op. cit.,* Princeton University Library, p. 43.
1983	Bristol University.
1984	Typescript, KF, Bristol University.
1985	Bristol University.
1986	Printed, *L & P*, pp. 256–57.
1987	Printed, *L & P*, pp. 257–59.
1988	Donald Weeks Collection.
1989	Princeton University.
1990	Typescript, KF, Bristol University.
1991	National Library, Florence.
1992	Bristol University.
1993	Dakyns Collection.
1994	Printed, *L & P*, pp. 259–60.
1995	Bristol University.
1996	Typescript, KF, Bristol University.
1997–98	Bristol University.

1999	Dakyns Collection.
2000–01	Bristol University.
2002	Printed, *Biography*, p. 431.
2003	Bristol University.
2004	Donald Weeks Collection.
2005–06	Brewster Collection.
2007	Princeton University.
2008	Bristol University.
2009	Typescript, John Rylands Library, Manchester.
2010	Bristol University.
2011	Printed, *L & P*, pp. 260–62.
2012	Bristol University.
2013	Donald Weeks Collection.
2014	Feinberg—Wayne State University Collection.
2015	Printed, *L & P*, p. 262.
2016	Princeton University.
2017	Feinberg—Wayne State University Collection.
2018	Bristol University; pr. in part, *OOP*, pp. 228–29.
2019	Printed, *L & P*, pp. 262–64.
2020	Princeton University.
2021	Dame Janet Vaughn Collection.
2022	Fitzwilliam Museum, Cambridge University.
2023	Princeton University.
2024–25	Dakyns Collection.
2026	Bristol University.
2027	Printed, *OOP*, pp. 229–31.
2028	Dakyns Collection.
2029	Timothy d'Arch Smith Collection.
2030	Printed, *H & P*, pp. 112–13.
2031	Donald Weeks Collection.
2032	Typescript, KF, Bristol University.
2033	Printed, *L & P*, p. 264.
2034	Printed, *H & P*, pp. 113–15.
2035	Brewster Collection.
2036–37	Typescript, KF, Bristol University.
2038–43	Bristol University.
2044	Typescript, Arthur Symons, *op. cit.*, Princeton University Library.
2045	Princeton University.
2046	Bristol University.
2047	Printed, Charles Kains-Jackson, "John Addington Symonds," *The Quarto*, III (1896–97), 75–76.
2048	Bristol University.
2049	Bristol University.
2050	Princeton University.
2051–52	Bristol University.
2053	Feinberg Collection.
2054–55	Bristol University.

2056	Donald Weeks Collection.
2057	Goodspeed Collection.
2058	National Library, Florence.
2059	Bristol University.
2060	Printed, First Edition Club (1922).
2061	Princeton University.
2062	Typescript, KF, Bristol University.
2063	Reading University.
2064	Donald Weeks Collection.
2065	University of Pennsylvania.
2066	Dulan and Co., Lt., Cat. 165.
2067	Printed, *L & P*, p. 265.
2068	Donald Weeks Collection.
2069	Brotherton Collection—University of Leeds.
2070	Ohio Wesleyan.
2071	National Library, Florence.
2072	Sainsbury, *op. cit.*, pp. 106–07.
2073	Yale University. (Not in Symonds' hand.)
2074	Typescript, Feinberg Collection.
2075	Brotherton Collection—University of Leeds.
2076	Typescript, John Rylands Library, Manchester.
2077	Feinberg—Wayne State University Collection.
2078	Printed, *L & P*, pp. 265–66.
2079	Ohio Wesleyan.
2080	Typescript, John Rylands Library, Manchester.
2081	Typescript, Feinberg Collection.
2082	Typescript, John Rylands Library, Manchester.
2083–84	Typescript, Feinberg Collection.
2085	Sainsbury, *op. cit.*, p. 108.
2086	Printed, *Biography*, pp. 470–71.
2087	Typescript, KF, Bristol University.
2088	Ohio Wesleyan.
2089	Feinberg—Wayne State University Collection.
2090	Typescript, KF, Bristol University.
2091	Printed, *L & P*, p. 267, and *Biography*, p. 471.
2092	Printed, *L & P*, pp. 267–68.
2093	Bristol University.
2094	Feinberg—Wayne State University Collection.
2095	Brewster Collection.
2096	Cambridge University.
2097	Dakyns Collection.
2098	Brewster Collection.
2099–2101	Bristol University.
2102	Bristol University; printed, Ross, *op. cit.*, pp. 326–27.
2103	Printed, Rupert Croft-Cooke, *Bosie* (1963), pp. 77–78.
2104	Printed, Ross, *op. cit.*, p. 328.
2105	Feinberg—Wayne State University Collection.

2106–07	Bristol University.
2108–09	Tennyson Library, City of Lincoln.
2110	Bristol University.
2111	*La Rassegna Settimanale,* March 9, 1879, pp. 193–94.
2112	Feinberg Collection.
2113	Timothy d'Arch Smith Collection.

List of Recipients of Letters
Volume III

Listed below are the recipients of the letters written by Symonds from 1885 to 1893. The numbers refer to letters, not to pages.

Academy, The: 1493
Bainton, the Rev. George: 1634
Battersby, the Rev. Harford: 1671
Biagi, Guido: 1873, 1880–81, 1883, 1886, 1890, 1900, 1915, 1918, 1932, 1937–38, 1955, 1979, 1991, 2058, 2071
Black, A. & C. Co.: 1778, 1787, 1942, 1944
Blackwood, Alexander: 1687, 1689, 1698
Boyle, Mrs. Eleanor: 1507, 1524
Bronson, Mrs. Arthur: 1673
Brown, Horatio Forbes: 1455, 1460, 1464, 1468, 1472, 1475–77, 1479–80, 1482–83, 1488, 1491–92, 1496–97, 1500–01, 1505, 1509, 1515, 1527, 1532, 1535, 1538, 1541, 1558, 1563–64, 1567–68, 1571, 1577, 1580, 1582, 1587–88, 1617, 1621–22, 1630–31, 1633, 1635, 1638–39, 1643, 1646–47, 1650, 1654, 1656, 1658, 1664–67, 1669–70, 1690, 1697, 1702, 1707, 1711, 1713, 1715, 1720–21, 1723–26, 1729, 1731, 1746, 1751–52, 1754, 1757, 1775, 1777, 1799–1800, 1805, 1809, 1812, 1821, 1826, 1828, 1832, 1853, 1859, 1870, 1872, 1875, 1877, 1882, 1884, 1899, 1906, 1919, 1923–24, 1931, 1935, 1943, 1948–49, 1957, 1959, 1987, 1994, 2002, 2011, 2015, 2019, 2027, 2033, 2067, 2078, 2086, 2091
Browning, Sarina: 1672
Bruce, Henry Austin: 1458
Bunting, Percy William: 1808, 1813
Burton, Richard: 1499, 1818

Nicholson, John Gambril: 2060

Noel, Roden: 1592

Nutt, Albert Trübner: 1951

Paitson, Leonard W.: 1688

Pall Mall Gazette: 1653, 1679, 1683, 1794–95, 1936

Parkes, W. Kineton: 1749, 1772, 1774, 1780–81, 1796, 1827, 1834

Payn, James: 1663

Perry, T. S.: 1478, 1481, 1498, 1559, 1578, 1608, 1610, 1612, 1615, 1651, 1657, 1660–61, 1685

Rassegnale Settimanale, La: 2111

Rea, George: 1701

Rhys, Ernest: 1606, 1609, 1627, 1815, 1819, 1837

Richards, Samuel: 1708, 1710, 1767–68, 1779, 1782, 1788–90, 1802, 1817, 1841

Robinson, Mary: 1449, 1462, 1465, 1466, 1474, 1485, 1494, 1513, 1521, 1525, 1530, 1561, 1570, 1572, 1579, 1586, 1589, 1595

Ross, Janet: 1562, 1843, 1848, 1850, 1852, 1854, 1858, 1860, 1864, 1865a, 1869, 1871, 1879, 1892–93, 1896, 1901, 1905, 1914, 1921–22, 1925–26, 1928–29, 1933–34, 1946–47, 1954, 1958, 1967, 1971–72, 1977–78, 1980, 1998, 2026, 2038–39, 2041, 2048, 2051, 2055, 2093, 2099–2102, 2104, 2106

Russell, the Rev. Matthew: 1976

Rutson, Albert O.: 1489, 1495, 1519, 1616, 1618, 1620, 1743

Sayle, Charles Edward: 1502–03, 1542, 1553–54, 1556, 1581, 1637, 1699, 1705, 1763, 1969, 2096

Sharp, William: 1486

Sidgwick, Henry: 1453, 1463, 1470, 1487, 1523, 1585, 1594, 1600, 1662, 1668, 1704, 1718, 1840, 1849, 1965, 1986

Squire, William Barclay: 1674, 1677, 1682, 1684, 1691, 1727, 1738, 1740–42, 1801, 1806, 1823–24, 1827, 1833, 1861, 1889, 1956, 2005, 2022

Stevenson, Robert Louis: 1457, 1461, 1522, 1607, 1611, 2092

Sevenson, Mrs. Robert Louis: 1467, 1613

Stevenson, Mr. & Mrs. Robert Louis: 1520

Strong, Agnes: 1939

Strong, Dawsonne: 2110

Sykes, Mary Ann: 1517, 1539, 1700, 1773, 1940

Symonds, Mrs. John Addington: 2012, 2021, 2042, 2107

Symonds, Katharine: 1973, 2030, 2034

Symonds, Charlotte Mary and Margaret: 1583, 1596, 1598–99, 1625

Symonds, Margaret: 1452, 1459, 1590, 1603, 1619, 1716, 1732, 1745, 1747–48, 1753, 1755–56, 1758, 1762, 1765, 1825, 1842, 1851, 1888, 1902–04, 1908, 1910, 1912, 1916–17, 1981, 1983, 1985, 1990, 1992, 1995, 1997, 2000–01, 2003, 2010, 2018, 2027, 2040, 2043, 2046, 2049, 2052, 2054

Symons, Arthur: 1504, 1508, 1516, 1528–29, 1537, 1543, 1545, 1548, 1550, 1706, 1750, 1760, 1766, 1771, 1927, 1982, 2006, 2035, 2044

Tennant, Margot: 1640, 1776, 1784, 1820, 1913, 2057

Tennyson, Mrs. Alfred: 2108–09

Traubel, Horace: 1728, 1867, 1885, 1907, 1961–62, 2053

Tuke, Dr. Daniel Hack: 1878

Corrections and Additions to Volumes I and II

Following are all the corrections and additions of substance which have come to our attention in Volumes I and II of these letters. Not all errors are indicated. Obvious typographical or printer's errors, especially in Greek quotations for instance, are not indicated but have been placed in our own records for a possible second edition. Also, the sources of certain quotations which have not been identified remain for further searching.

Volume I

P. 9, caption 3: *For* 4 *read* 3.

    caption 4: *Delete:* 2 views *and* parentheses.

    caption 10: *Delete:* Two views of.

    caption 16: *Delete:* Two views of *and* The Meadow.

P. 35, last line: *For* Bertrand Dobell *read* Bertram Dobell.

P. 36, l.4: *For* J. C. Squire *read* William Barclay Squire.

P. 37, l.2: *For* Margaret *read* Katharine.

Pp. 45–46, Chronology for 1887, 1888, 1893: *See* Vol. II, pp. 21–22, and Vol. III, pp. 21–22.

P. 61, n.2: *For rasonnée read raisonnée.*

P. 68, n.2: *For* Randall's *read* Rendall's.

P. 73, n.5: *For* Putlochry *read* Pitlochry.

P. 87, n.5, l.2: *For* legende *read* légende.

P. 96, n.4: *For* the note *substitute:* Verdant Green, the country lad in *The Adventures of Mr. Verdant Green* (1853), called "A College Joke to Cure the Dumps," by Cuthbert Bede (the Rev. Edward Bradley,

1827–89). Green attends Brazenface College, Oxford, and after many vicissitudes passes his degree "with flying colours" and retires to the country after marrying an appropriately worshipful female from the appropriate social class.

P. 168, n.1: *For* Francois Peirre *read* François Pierre; *for* (1850) *read* (Pt. I: 2 vols., 1826–27; Pt. II, 1854; Pt. III, 1856).

P. 179, n.1, ¶2: "Composition" is incorrectly interpreted as the art of writing; here it means translation into Latin and Greek verse, as opposed to prose.

P. 184, n.11: *Substitute:* Possibly the hymn-tune of H. Wilson (1766–1824). *But see also* p. 206, n.23.

P. 187, n.5: *Substitute:* William Ewart Gladstone (1809–98) spoke in the House of Commons about two subjects: the recent purchases for the National Gallery (reported in *The Times* on Saturday, April 16) and the question of Italian liberation from Austria (reported in *The Times* on Tuesday, April 19). Symonds was probably interested in the latter. Gladstone's stand on Italy earned him the appointment, on June 20 when Palmerston became Prime Minister, of Chancellor of the Exchequer.

P. 193, n.4: *For* Hellmore *read* Helmore; *after* his *add* book of; *for* 1878 *read* published 1877, etc.

P. 213, n.1: *For* 1856–88 *read* 1843.

P. 219, n.2: *After* "As pants the hart" *transpose* see L 172 *and* by Mendelssohn.

P. 226, n.1: *For* the second of three *read* the first of two.

P. 264, n.2: *Substitute:* A reference to the celebration on Guy Fawkes Day, November 5, the day in 1605 on which the Gunpowder Plot, led by Guy Fawkes, failed.

P. 288, n.3: *For* Wendbury-on-Trym *read* Westbury-on-Trym.

P. 353, n.1: *For* Tricentennial *read* Triennial.

P. 386, n.2: *For* le read la.

P. 400, n.18: *Add:* The "Sorgte" which Belletti sang was probably the tarantella "Sorgete" from Rossini's *L'Assedio di Corinto* (1828).

P. 406, n.5: *Should read:* Félicité Robert de Lamennais (or La Mennais) 1782–1854), French priest and philosopher: *Essai sur l'indifférence en matière de religion* (4 vols., 1817–23).

P. 406, n.6: *For traduit read traduits.*

P. 441, n.4: *Substitute:* "His salt-box, tongs, and bones": Browning (speaking of Verdi and his operas) in "Bishop Blougram's Apology" (1855), l.384.

Pp. 484 ff.: Ls 331 and 332 *should follow* L 342; L 339 *should follow* L 336.

Pp. 496–98: Ls 346 and 347 *should change places.*

P. 518, n.2, l.6: *After* Christian *add:* (1856–1914).

P. 526, n.1: *For Precteussors read Predecessors.*

P. 546: The lines from Musset are as Symonds gives them, but *for* tout *read* tant.

P. 550, n.1: *After* originally *add:* in *The North British Review,* XLIX (Dec., 1868), 154–67, and in part *After Gazette add:* (See Babington pp. 202 and 204; Babington does not mention the original publication.)

P. 578, n.1: *Should read:* In Musset's poem *La Nuit de Mai* in the Muse's last speech to the poet: "Lorsque le pélican, lassé d'un long voyage. . . ." The pelican, symbolizing the poet, offers himself as a sacrificial banquet to his famished young.

P. 625, n.2: *For matress read mattress.*

P. 647, L 485, ¶2: *Add* une *after* avec.

P. 662, l.14: *For* Magré *read* Malgré.

P. 664, n.5: *Add:* See translation, p. 725, n.6.

P. 668, n.4: *Delete:* See L 495.

P. 674, n.1, l.4: *For the second* nice *read* mice.
　　　　　l.7: *For nice,* I wrote *read mice* I wrote.

P. 702, L 521, ¶4, l.2: *For* ébraulés *read* ébranlés.

P. 703, l.3: *For* fatigueé *read* fatiguée.

P. 716, 4 ll. from the bottom: *For* Belgain *read* Belgian.

P. 720, n.2: *For* we are stretching . . . come *read* We were sitting there on the church steps. We were not expecting anything. And then you came along. *For* Francois *read* François.

P. 721, L 541, l.2: *For* Grouville *read* Granville.

P. 724, l.3 of the verse: *For* ceil *read* ciel.

P. 725, n.6: *For* the translation *substitute:*
　　　"I suffer; it is to late; the world has grown old,
　　　　An immense hope has travelled across the earth;
　　　　In spite of ourselves we must raise our eyes to heaven!"

P. 735, n.2: *For* Decembre *read* Décembre.

P. 739, n.4: *For* L'Espair *read* L'Espoir.

P. 753, n.2: *Substitute:* To content oneself, almost, in all things.

P. 814, l.12: *For* bruissonière *read* buissonnière.

P. 842, n.5: *Add:* The source of the tag may be *Valentine et Orson,* a medieval French romance in which Orson, one of the heroes, is abandoned as a baby and brought up by a she-bear.

P. 846, l.14: *For* j'à *read* d'à.

Volume II

Illustrations: "Michael Field" is the pseudonym of both women called so, the upper left figure on the plate being Katherine Bradley and the lower left figure, Edith Cooper. On p. 9, Ill. 26: *for* Mower *read* Sower.

P. 64, l.1 after rule: *For* tennissima *read* tenuissima.

P. 70, n.8: *Add:* Mme. Vilda was the English stage-name for Marie Wilt (née Liebenthaler; 1833–91), Austrian soprano who sang in London in 1866–67 and again in 1874–75; became a great favorite in Vienna.

P. 122, n.2: *For* For Morley, see L 602, n.17 *substitute* John Rickards Mozley, see L 1511.

P. 123, n.1, l.a: *Add* colon after is and *delete* not quite as Symonds gives it:

P. 190, l.11 from bottom: *For* Oh, thy unjust heart! *read* O peace, my unjust heart!

P. 301, n.4: *Delete:* Either Frances . . . or, and *substitute* Possibly.

P. 306, n.5: *Add:* Mill had just died—on May 8, 1873.

Pp. 314, 5 ll. from bottom, 315, n.1, 317, n.3: *For* Toirray *in each instance read* Tairraz.

P. 338, l.9: *For* Comrade *read* couvade.

P. 393, n.2: *For* 389–90 *read* 543–44.

P. 406, n.1: *For* cousin. *substitute* cousin, Janet Elizabeth Kay-Shuttleworth (1843–1914).

P. 425, the poem in Italian: l.1: *For* Granto *read* Grato.
l.2: *For* damno *read* danno.
n.3: In every instance *for* Brovo *read* Bravo.

P. 455, n.5, l.1: *For* 1922 *read* 1912.

P. 478: *Add note:* 2. For Lewis Campbell, see L 963.

P. 479, n.2: *Substitute:* Samuel George Chetwynd Middlemore (1848–90), educated at Merton College, Oxford, and a friend of Gosse and Stevenson, whose fellow-member he was at the Savile Club.

P. 484, L 1060: Probably follows L 1068.

P. 491, n.7: Mrs. MacMorland's death date is 1917. Her husband's dates are 1839–93. They married in 1865.
n.9: *Substitute:* Unidentified; probably a visitor at Davos.

P. 498, L 1072: The original of this letter was in the collection of Dorothea Mary Benson, Baroness Charnwood (1876–1942) and is printed in full in her *Call Back Yesterday* (1937), pp. 243–45. Our version comes from *Biography* and the differences are these: In the two versions ¶1 is the same. Brown cuts from ¶2 all but the first sentence, the rest being a reference to an article in the *Lancet* (see L 1074, n.6). ¶3 is intact. The original ¶4, referring to a prior meeting of Middlemore (see note for p. 479 above) and ¶5, referring to Gosse's piece on Symonds' *Fine Arts* (see L 1069, n.4), are missing in our version. In ¶6, also absent from our version, Symonds asks for a gift of Gosse's poems in return for his *Sonnets of Michael Angelo and Companella.* ¶7 is intact (¶4 in our version). ¶8 concerns Swinburne's *A Note on Charlotte Brontë* (1877). ¶9 is the last ¶ in our version. ¶10 is a comment on the dreariness of Davos, and the last is a greeting to Mrs. Gosse.

P. 525, l.11: *Transfer* index 4 to l.12 *after* Czartoryski.
n.4: *Add:* We have not identified the cousins, his grandsons.

P. 531, n.1: *Delete:* See L 319.

P. 562, n.3: *Add:* Symonds must in any case be mistaken about the relationship: Edward Thurlow, 1st Baron Thurlow, died unmarried.

P. 568, L 1126, l.2: *For* Songs *read* Sonnets.

P. 572, n.2: *Substitute:* John Rickards Mozley. See L 1511.

P. 580, n.5: *Add:* See Appendix to Vol. III.

P. 585, l.3: *For* Francis North *read* Frederick North.

P. 606, n.1: *Add:* See L 1405 and addition to p. 930, n.2.

P. 611, bottom l.: *For* M[ichel] A[ngelo] *read* M[atthew] A[rnold].

P. 646, L 1192, l.2: *For* brave *read* broke.

P. 667, l.1: *For* 1926 *read* 1934.

P. 694, L 1230, n.1: *Add after* Hamilton: (1847–1908).

P. 703, n.9: *Substitute:* Stevenson and his wife had projected a series of supernatural stories. Mrs. Stevenson wrote "The Shadow on the Bed," which has not survived, and Stevenson wrote "Thrawn Janet," "The Body-Snatcher," and "The Merry Men." Other stories were planned, but were not written or have disappeared.

P. 707, n.5: *Add:* But the reference, also not reported in Babington, is probably to *The Magazine of Art,* ed. by W. E. Henley and published by Cassell. In a letter to Henley (Tusitala ed. of Stevenson's *Works,* 35 vols. [1924], XXXII, 77), Stevenson says Symonds will write about Vesalius and Botticelli's *Dante.* But Symonds never apparently did.

P. 717, n.4: *For* 1926 *read* 1934.

P. 723, n.1: *Delete:* 1867 *and substitute* ?.

P. 733, L 1261, n.4: *Add:* Mr. Ernest J. Mehew has sent us the following addition to this note:
"At this time Stevenson was interested in the Duke of Wellington. Early in 1882 Stevenson wrote to W. E. Henley [unpublished letter in National Library of Scotland]:
  You know nothing of Arthur [the Duke of Wellington]. I'll tell you one stage in the Via Dolorosa through which he kicked that idiot Falstaff George the IV. His Majesty, once more disobeying the Dook's orders, had granted to some creature an Irish peerage. "I observe," wrote Arthur (I quote from memory) "that your Majesty has been misinformed. *I shall reserve the* patent until I have an opportunity of learning your Majesty's pleasure upon it!!"

P. 746, l.2: *For* vanished *read* evanished.

P. 755, n.3: Dr. Williams' death date was 1912. *Delete:* became Physician Extraordinary to the Queen. This refers to his father, Dr. C. J. B. Williams.

P. 759, n.3: *Add:* It had appeared in *The Cornhill Magazine,* XLV (June, 1882), Pt. I: 676–95; XLVI (July, 1882), Pt. II: 56–73.

P. 760, n.6: *Add:* Symonds had the play in the privately printed ed. of 1880.

P. 780, n.10: *Substitute:* James Hinton (1822–75) was aural surgeon in London and author of philosophical works like *The Mystery of Pain* (1866); *Philosophy and Religion,* ed. by Caroline Haddon (selections from his manuscripts, 1881); *Selections from Manuscripts* (4 vols., 1870–74). Edith M. O. Ellis wrote about him (1910 and 1918), and Jane

Ellice Hopkins wrote his *Life and Letters* (1878). According to Havelock Ellis, some of his writings on sex were for a long time privately passed around in manuscripts.

n.11: *For* Harrell *read* Hurrell.

P. 795, n.3: *For* Sibylla *read* Sibella, and *for* ca. 1890 *read* 1886.

P. 813, last l.: *For* dévergardage *read* dévergondage.

P. 816 In the poem "Idle Charon," l.8: *For* ear *read* oar.

P. 844, n.1: *After* £100 *add:* in advance.

P. 861, n.2: *After* the first sentence *add:* She died in 1919.

P. 866, n.4: *For* Dr. John Beddoe: see Ls 753 and 1349 *substitute:* Dr. C. T. Williams, see L 1279.

P. 875, n.2: *For* Count Litta Pompeo *read* Count Pompeo Litta.

P. 877, n.3: *Add:* On pp. 66–68 in *Seventeenth Century Studies* Gosse claims to have discovered this separate comedy which he calls "Love's Graduate" and which he identifies as the work of Webster in *A Cure for a Cuckold.*

P. 880, n.1: *Substitute:* Dr. Lionel Edward Kay-Shuttleworth (1849–1900), brother of Ughtred Kay-Shuttleworth (see L 148); vice-consul at San Remo; treated Symonds and his daughter during typhoid scare, April 1884. See L 1388.

P. 897, n.4: *Add* death date: 1919.

P. 905, n.1: *Delete: Paron:* probably a local term, *and substitute: Paron,* captain or master (*padrone*) of a merchant ship or fishing boat. Piero, captain of the *Beppo,* a sailing boat trading between Venice and the Istrian coast, was a friend of Antonio Salin, Brown's gondolier.

P. 930, n.2: *Add:* This may have been the "old Col Pearson" mentioned in L 1156.

P. 956, n.3: *For* 1930 *read* 1903. *For* 1879 *read* 1880; *for Robert Macaire* (1884) *read Macaire* (1885).

Index
Volume III

This index is general rather than detailed. The roman numerals refer to volumes, the arabic to pages.

It has not been thought necessary to list every mention of members of Symonds' and Dakyns' families or places which Symonds visited; these latter can be identified through the Chronology. The emphasis is on items mentioned in Symonds' letters. Painters, composers, and writers are indexed, but their works usually are not.

Hyphenated names are indexed according to the last name. Within the index items, names of persons are abbreviated to initial letters. Since this is not a bibliography, Symonds' works are indexed as far as possible according to subject-matter; his poems, articles, books, translations, and reviews are identified by the letters p(s), art, b(s), tr(s), and rev(s) in parentheses, and authors or editors of works not by Symonds are also identified in parentheses. In general periodicals for which he wrote are omitted because they are listed in Babington.

462, 555, 556n; II, 148, 365 and n, 379, 396; III, 433

Agamemnon and Iphigeneia: III, 236

Agape: II, 68 and n

Age of the Despots, The (b): II, 340 and n, 373–74, 422, 451, 459, 615, 616n, 617; revs: 372n, 376–77 and ns, 378 and n

Agrippa: I, 435n

Aguilar, Emmanuel: I, 399, 400n

Aïdé, Charles Hamilton: II, 824, 825n; III, 724, 725n, 726, 729

Aitken, Sir William: II, 593, 594n

"Ajaccio" (art): I, 838, 839n

Alamannus, Johannes (Giovanni d'Alemagna): I, 424, 425n

Alaudae: I, 38; III, 548, 663

Alberti, Leon Battista: III, 407 and n, 437–39

Alboni, Marietta: I, 290 and n

Albutt, Dr. Clifford: II, 501, 502n

"Alcibiade fanciullo a scola": III, 517, 519n

Alcibiades: II, 28n, 34

Alcides (Hercules): I, 852 and n

Alciphron: III, 834, 835n

Alcuin: II, 729 and n

Aldworth: III, 743

Alessandro de Medici: II, 707; III, 638, 639n

Alexander VI (Pope): II, 467, 468n; III, 298–99

Alexander, Boyd Francis: II, 489, 491n

Alexander the Great: II, 145n

Alexander, William: II, 448 and n; III, 101n

Alford, Henry: I, 77, 78n, 103 and n

Alfredo (servant): III, 646, 647n

Alinari (publisher): III, 540–41 and n, 546, 781 and n, 785, 824

Allen, the Rev. Baylies: III, 261, 263n, 264

Alleyne, Forster McGeachy: I, 99n; II, 454, 456, 457n, 468; III, 37 and n

Alleyne, Mrs. Forster McGeachy: I, 97, 99n

Alleyne, Sarah Frances ("Fanny"): I, 33, 792n; II, 204, 204–05n, 354, 355n, 373, 415 and n, 517, 531–32, 594, 937, 943–44; III, 37 and n

"Alliteration and Assonance" (art): I, 420n

Alma-Tadema, Sir Lawrence: II, 174, 175n, 751, 753n, 965, 966n

Alps, the: II, 815, 855–56. *See also* all items under Davos and Swiss.

"Alps, Winter in the High" (ps): III, 235, 237n

"Am Hof": II, 674 and n, 768, 769 and n, 780, 782, 821, 833, 834n

"Amateur Immigrant" in *Pall Mall Gazette:* III, 47, 48n

Ames, Edward: I, 108, 109n

Ames, Reginald: I, 106, 107n, 109n

Amiel, Henri Frédéric: III, 51 and n, 56, 66, 67n, 109, 110n

Ammann, Johannes: III, 29, 30n, 406, 411, 503, 713

Anderson, Hans Christian: I, 391, 392n

Andrea del Sarto: II, 437, 439n

Angelini (Angiolini), Bartolommeo: III, 577, 578n, 590, 591n, 655, 800, 801n

Animi Figura (b of ps): II, 690, 691n, 692n, 697, 704n, 708n, 728, 729 and n, 732 and n, 734n, 737–38, 743, 752, 754, 759, 760–61, 764, 766, 865, 869, 881–82, 886n, 887, 893, 895, 926, 974; III, 93–94, 95n, 96, 238, 447, 451n. *See also Vagabunduli Libellus.*

Anteros: II, 97 and n

Antinous: II, 518, 519n, 522–23, 527, 531, 533, 534n, 538–39, 548

"Antinous" (art): II, 531, 532n, 545, 546n; II, (rev) 589 and 590n; III, 585, 627

"Antinous, The Lotus Garland of" (p): II, 118, 119n, 166, 524n, 535, 541

Apelles: I, 90

Aphrodite Pandemos: I, 677n, 697; II, 34, 35n, 218n, 653, 655

Aphrodite Urania: I, 677n; II, 218n, 653, 655

"Apoxyomenos" (Lysippus): II, 280–81, 404n

"Apoxyomenos" (Praxiteles): II, 531, 532n

Appleton, Charles Edward: II, 456, 457n

Appleton, William Sumner: II, 712, 713n

Aquila (Italy): I, 38; III, 617, 619, 620, 650

Arber, Edward: II, 781 and n

Archer, William: III, 550, 551n

Archivio Storico Italiano: II, 408, 409n

"Arden of Feversham": III, 101, 136, 154

Browning, Oscar: III, 165, 166n, 428, 430n

Browning, Robert: I, 35, 426, 512n, 532, 533n, 563n, 584, 774; II, 209n, 628, 706; III, 131, 132, (an evening with) 314–15n, 426; quoted: I, 411 [III, 875] 750, 751n, 764, 766n; "Aristophanes' Apology" (rev by S): II, 366, 367n, 368 and n; *Asolando*: III, 440 and n, 441; "Balaustian's Adventure": II, 266, 267n; "Cleon": II, 322; *Inn Album, The* (rev by S): II, 392n, 393 and n; III, 154n; *Jocoseria* (rev by S): III, 154n; *Red Cotton Night-Cap Country*: II, 306 and n; *Ring and the Book, The*: II, 27, 36, 37n, (S's rev of) 28n

Browning, Robert Weidemann Barrett: II, 927, 927–28n; III, 768, 770–71n

Browning, Sarina: III, 314, (an evening with) 314–15n

Bruce, Henry Austin, Lord Aberdare: III, 37n, 210

Bruce, Norah Napier: I, 741 and n

Bruce, Rachel Mary (Rachel Bruce Harcourt): II, 245 and n

Brugger, Edwin: III, 594, 595n, 603, 682–83 and n, 699 and ns, 721

Bruhns, Karl Christian: I, 110n

Brunnhofer, Hermann: III, 65, 67n, 75 and n

Bruno, Giordano: I, 32; III, 36, 38, 39 and n, 40n, 42, 59, 65, 74, 75, 87, 91, 107, 323, 386, 744

Brunton, Sir Thomas Lauder: III, 121 and n

Bruschi, Domenico: III, 831 and n

"Brutus, A Cinquecento" (art): II, 707, 708n

Bryce, James: I, 267n, 295, 296n; II, 456, 457n

Brydges, Samuel Egerton: I, 781, 782n

Buchanan, Dr. Robert and family: I, 187 and n, 202, 204n, 306, 331; II, 47

Buchanan, Robert Williams: I, 776 and n, 803, 840, 841n; II, 162 and n, 276n, 551, 552n; III, 107, 108n

Bucke, Dr. Richard Maurice: III, 262, 263n, 264, 344, 531n, 811, 812n, 820

Buckle, George: III, 314n

Budd, Dr. William: I, 418, 419n; II, 233, 234n

Bueccheler, Franz: II, 899, 900n

Bugiardini, Giuliano: III, 630, 631n, 633

Bullen, Arthur Henry: II, 845 and n; III, 136, 150, 154, 265, 266n, 284, 285n, 418

Buller, James Howard: I, 267n

Bulley, the Rev. Frederick: I, 371 and n, 542 and n

Bülow, Hans von: II, 334 and n

Bulpett, Captain: III, 576 and n

Bunney, John Wharlton: II, 771 and n, 781

Bunsen, Christian Karl Josias: I, 271, 272n

Bunting, Percy William: III, 476, 477n

Bunyan, John: II, 639

Buol family: II, 490, 518n, 538, 554, 726

Buol, Christian: I, 39; II, 518, 528, 538, 542–43, 546, 582, 633, 664, 666, 667n, 691, 726–28, 749, 754; III, 603, 604n

Buol, Florian: II, 518n; III, 214, 215n, 695, 709, 713

Buol Hotel (rates): II, 563–64, 820

Buol, Simeon: II, 666, 667n, 937

Buonarroti Archives: III, 560, 561n 570–71, 573, 578, 590, 613–14, 682 and n, 756, 783, 824

Buonarroti Genealogy: III, 638n, 654–56

Buonarroti, Lodovico Simoni (Michelangelo's father): 637, 638, 654–56, 687, 688n

Buonarroti, Michelangelo: *see* Michelangelo

Burckhardt, Jacob: II, 467, 468ns

Burke, John Bernard: I, 228n; II, 712

Burnand, Francis Cowley: II, 558, 559n

Burns, Robert (quoted): I, 159n, 206, 207n; III, 282 and n

Burr, Mr. and Mrs. Higford: II, 567, 568n; III, 660, 662n

Burroughs, John: I, 841 and n; III, 563–64n, 811, 812n

Burrows, Montagu: II, 534 and n

Burton, Frederic William: II, 339n

Burton, Lady Isabel: III, 516, 710

Burton, Richard: III, 81–82 and ns, 84, 90–91, 488n, 489n, 500–01 and n, 516, 516–17n, 691, 694, 695n, 710

Bush, Major Robert: I, 204, 206n

Butcher, Samuel Henry: II, 583, 585n

Butler, George: I, 152, 153n, 325n, 369, 535

Carré, Mrs. (mother of Arthur): I, 582, 667; II, 53

Carrington: *see* Cesaresco

Carrissimi, Giacomo: II, 636, 637n

Carter, Alice Bonham: I, 762n

Carter, Elinor Mary Bonham: I, 762n; II, 245 and n

Carter, Frances Maria Bonham: I, 762n

Carter, Hilary Bonham: I, 665, 666n, 762n

Carters, Bonham, the: I, 753n, 762n, 773, 843n

Casanova, Giovanni: III, 286, 287n

Casaubon, Isaac: II, 533, 534n

Case, Thomas: II, 170 and n, 171

Casentino: III, 619

Casper, J. Leopold: III, 694, 695n, 798, 799n

Cassell, John: 706, 707n

Cassell's Magazine: II, 707n

Cassone, Giacomo del: III, 824, 825n

Castagnolo: II, 385, 386n; III, 41

Castiglione, Baldassare: III, 708, 709n

Castle, Cecil E. J.: III, 748 and n

Castle Hill: I, 128, 129 and n, 135, 136, 140, 313, 326, 328n, 363

Castle Howard (York): III, 723–24, 726–29, 731, 735, 739, 741

Castle, R.: I, 106, 107n, 119

Cater, Frank: II, 666, 667n

Catholic Reaction, The (b): II, 966, 968; III, 36, 38, 42n, 48, 50, 51, 61, 65, 70–71, 74–75, 83, 85, 89, 105, 107–08, 112, 117, 119, 125, 126n, 128, 133, 140, 147, 150, 165, 188, 197

"Catholic Revival": *see Catholic Rection*

Cato: I, 112; II, 192n

Catullus: I, 256, 257, 332, 436; II, 641 and n; III, 100

Cavalcaselle, Giovanni B.: I, 514, 515n

Cavalieri, Tommaso: III, 570 and n, 655

Cave, Arthur Stephen (nephew): I, 50n; III, 388, 389, 391n, 414, 415n

Cave, Charles Daniel (brother-in-law): I, 50n, 194, 198, 201n, 206, 209n, 212, 265n, 319, 387, 389n, 415, 416, 417n, 483, 496n, 531, 754, 755n, 778; II, 48n, 73n, 140n, 257 and n, 289, 431, 738, 739, 819, 820n; III, 392, 393n, 652, 653n

Cave, Charles Henry (nephew): I, 50n, 287 and n

Cave, Daniel (father of S's brother-in-law): I, 265n

Cave, Daniel (brother of S's brother-in-law): I, 389 and n

Cave, Daniel Charles Addington (nephew): I, 50n, 241 and n, 266, 267n, 630; II, 254 and n, 257 and n; III, 62

Cave, Edith (sister): *see* Symonds, Edith Harriet

Cave, (Edith) Frances (niece): I, 50n; III, 73 and n, 604, 605n

Cave, John: II, 48n

Cave, Lewis William: II, 177 and n

Cave, Sir Stephen (brother of S's brother-in-law): I, 378 and n; II, 48n, 456, 457n, 459

Cave, Walter Frederic (nephew): I, 50n; III, 414, 415n

Cay, Amy: II, 220 and n; 254 and n, 424, 495n

Cay, Charles Hope: II, 43, 44n, 64 and n, 99, 100n, 216n

Cay, Mrs. Margaret Pirie: *see* Daykyns, Mrs. Margaret Cay

Cecil, William (Lord Burleigh): I, 222 and n

Cellini, Benevenuto: I, 434, 435n; II, ("Perseus") 769 and 770n and 796 and n; III, 158, 171–72 and n, 209, 281 and n, 364, 407 and n, 586, 687; *Autobiography* (tr by S): I, 36; III, 146, 158, 165, 173–74, 177, 178, 179, 182–84, 186, 188, 196, 207, 211, 214, 236, 248, (date of) 249n and 254–55 and 274, (revs of) 274 and 277n, 278, 281, 301, 312, 383, 394

Censors of Morals: III, 90–91

Century Guild Hobbyhorse, The (name of): III, 322

Cervantes, Miguel: I, 90

Cesaresco, Countess Evelyn Lillian (Corrington): III, 373, 374 and n

Chaffers, Thomas: III, 189, 190n

Chalet am Stein, the: II, 788, 956

Chancellor's Prize: II, 98n

Chandos, the Hon. Edward: I, 73 and n

Chapman, Dr. John: II, 482, 483n; III, 689, 690n

Chapman and Hall (publishers): I, 564 and n; III, 395, 462, 478, 479

Charles II (of England): III, 669

Charles V, Emperor: I, 265, 267n; III, 181

Chatterton, Thomas: I, 90, 318 and n, 386 and n; II, 103

"Chatterton Essays, The" (arts): I, 266, 267n

Chaucer, Geoffrey: I, 90, 167, 393, 846

Chavasse, Francis James: I, 322, 323n

Cheltenham Women's College: II, 128n, 176

Chenier, Audré: I, 386 and n

"Cherubino at the Scala" (art): II, 707, 708n

Chettle, Henry: II, 331, 332n

Chiabrera, Gabriello: III, 87

Chiara da Rimini, Beata: II, 702 and n

Chiavenna: III, 758–59; S's poem on: 759

Child, Mr. (American tobogganer): III, 288 and n, 337n

Chiswick Press: III, 478

Chivalry (Modern): III, 448, 483, 494

Cholmondeley, the Rev. Hugh Pitt: I, 203, 205n

Chopin, Frédéric: II, 26, 389

Christianity: II, 400–01

Chur: III, 695–96, 697–99

Church, R. W.: II, 498 and n; III, 180, 181n

Cialdini, Enrico (Duke of Gaeta): I, 593, 598n

Cicero: I, 96, 174, 188, 189n; II, 295, 958

Cicognara, Count Leopoldo: III, 283 and n

Cima, Giovanni Battista: I, 499, 500n

Cimabue, Giovanni: I, 123

Cimarosa, Domenico: II, 636, 637n; III, 214, 215n

Cino da Pistoia: II, 923, 924n

Clairmont, Claire: II, 652; III, 217–18

Clarac, Charles Othon, Comte de: I, 579, 580n

Clark, Dr. Andrew: II, 310, 311n, 449, 450n, 754, 755, 757; III, 853

Clark, Helen Annette Doxat: II, 781 and n

Clark, William George: I, 231, 232n

Clarke, H. M.: II, 350, 351n

Clayton, Emily Rosa: I, 76, 77n

Clayton, Louisa Maude: I, 76, 77n

Cleanthes (his prayer, tr by S): I, 723; II, 284, 284–85n; III, 841

Clement VII, Pope: III, 208, 210n, 638

Clevedon Court: I, 271, 272n, 273

Cleveland Street affair: III, 554, 555n

Clifford, Edward: II, 115, 116n, 132, 133n, 165n, 167n, 195 and n, 207, 334, 658, 741, 818, 944, 974, 976, 985–86; III, 681

Clifford, Mary: II, 116n, 204n; III, 681

Clifford, William Kingdom: II, 836, 837n

"Clifton and a Lad's Love" (art): III, 92 and n, 796, 797

Clifton Chronicle, The: I, 80, 91; II, 41, 42n, 43

Clifton College: I, 205n, 388n, 487–88, 550, 601n, 607n, 612n, 658n, 668n, 676, 742n, 810n, 833n, 846; II, 41, 42, 44n, 48n, 49, 51, 56, 61, 68n, 77n, 88n, 99n, 119n, (homosexuality at) 132 and 133n, 153, 265n, 631n, 639n; III, 828

Clifton Hill House: I, 35, 173, 185, 188, 189, 192, 198, 200, 329n, 373n, 589, 818, 819; II, 27, 35, 65, 141, 149, 152n, 153n, 181, 513, 517, (bonfire at) 638n, 639, 641, (disposal of) 646; III, 596

Cliftonian, The: II, 105n, 216 and n, 501 and n

Clive, Archer Anthony: I, 263 and n

Clive, Mrs. Caroline: I, 263 and n, 267; II, 437, 438n

Clive, Meysey and Lady Katherine: II, 437

Clough, Anne Jemimah (sister of A.H.C.): II, 85, 86n

Clough, Arthur Hugh: I, 32, 607, 669, 670, 691, 799, 845–47, 848n; II, 49 and n, (Palgrave on) 81 and 82n; *Amours de Voyage*: I, 773, 775n; II, 37, 89; *Bothie of Tober-na-Vuolich, The:* I, 355 and n, 764, 766n; *Dipsychus:* I, 803 and n, 821, 822n; II, 667 and n; quoted: III, 527 and n; "In a Gondola" quoted: III, 768, 771n; *Poems* (Palgrave ed.): I, 355 and n, 666n; *Poems and Prose Remains:* I, 665, 666n, 804, 806n, 809, 810n, 847; "Clough, Arthur Hugh" (art): I, 824, 838, 839n, 842 and n

Clough, Arthur Hugh (son of A.H.C.): I, 763, 766n, 793; II, 32, 33n, 184 and n, 192 and n, 245n, 401

Clough, Blanche Athena (daughter of A.H.C.): I, 763, 766n, 793, 801, 802n; II, 32 and n, 33n, 271 and n, 401

Clough, Blanche Smith (wife of A.H.C.): I, 29, 334, 665 and n, 669, 691, 741, 744, 745n, 748, 753n, 774n, 775n,

Courthope, Mary Scott: II, 701 and n
Courthope, William John: I, 760, 762n, 765, 773–74, 782, 803–04, 807, 819, 820n, 825, 826n; II, 28n, 47, 76, 334, 701 and n, 706; III, 99 and n, 104, 242, 276, 495
Cousin, Victor: I, 377, 378n, 385, 386n
Cowell, E. Byles: I, 701 and n
Cowley, Abraham: I, 90
Cox, George William: II, 683, 684n
Cox (police sergeant): III, 39, 40n
Craik, George L.: I, 314, 315n
Crawley, Richard: I, 825, 826n
Creighton, Mandell: II, 487, 488n, 691, 692n, 809 and n; III, 119, 120n, 256, 257n, 298–99
Creighton, Mrs. Mandell: II, 336, 337n, 530, 531n
"Crema, Crucifix of" (tragedy by S): II, 950, 951n, 955
"Cretan Idyll, The" (p): II, 405
Criminal Code (English) for Homosexuals: III, 710
Cripps, Arthur Shearly: III, 461, 463n
"Criticism, On Principles of" (art): III, 284
Croft, Lady Georgiana: III, 662 and n
Crookes, William: II, 365 and n
Crosbie, John Gustavus: I, 78–79, 80n
Cross, Alexander: I, 830, 832n; II, 31n
Cross, William C. F.: I, 830, 833n; II, 31n
Crossley, the Rev. Thomas: III, 54, 55n
Crowe, Sir Joseph Arthur: I, 514, 515n
Cullum, Gerry: III, 768, 771n
"Culture, Its Meaning and Its Uses" (art): III, 672n, 698, 699n
Cumming, Constance Frederica Gordon: III, 138
Cunningham, J. W.: I, 83, 84n
Currey, William Edmund: I, 67, 68n, 81, 98, 114, 134, 137, 220, 741
Curtis, Daniel: III, 375n, 761–62
Curtis, Mrs. Daniel (Ariana Wormeley): III 314n, 374, 375n, 406, 567 and n, 761–62, 768
Curtius, Márcus: I, 598n
Cust, Sir Lionel Henry: III, 384, 681 and n
Czartoryski, Prince Adam J.: II, 525 and n
Dakyns, Andrew: I, 388n; II, 825n
Dakyns, Arthur Lindsay: I, 388n; II, 823–24, 825n

Dakyns, Charles Smithies: II, 128 and n, 149 and n
Dakyns, Connie Gerrard: II, 128n, 149 and n
Dakyns, Elsie: II, 269, 270n
Dakyns, Frances: I, 388n; II, 823–24, 825n, 496 and n; III, 365, 366n
Dakyns, George Doherty: II, 200, 201n
Dakyns, Henry Graham: I, 29, 31, 38, 387, 388n, 458, 464, 478, 502, 506n, 511, 530, 545n, 547n, 601n, 633, 658n, 674n, 676, 677n, 684n, 698n, 701n, 704n, 747, 851n; II, 35, 40n, 44n, 51, 100n, 119n, 120n, 128 and n, 133n, 150 and n, 152, 157n, 158n, 161, 167n, 195n, 197n, 198n, 200n, 212n, 213, 216n, 219, 223n, 230n, 277n, 389, 489, 492, 598, 631n, 639n, 643; III, 195, 285–87, 304n, 305, 391–92 and n, 739, 845–46; at Haslemere: III, 741, 742n, 743–45; proposed as S's literary executor: II, 421–22, and as financial executor: II, 903n. See also Xenophon.
Dakyns, Henry Graham, Jr. (Bo): I, 388n; II, 332 and n, 424, 507, 508n, 528, 630, 746 and n, 790, 823–24; III, 349, 350n
Dakyns House, Clifton College: II, 190, 191n
Dakyns, Janine: I, 388n; II, 825n
Dakyns, Margaret Cay (Maggie): I, 388n; II, 44n, 193, 194n, 197n, 198n, 206n, 212n, 214n, 219–20, 222, 225, 232, 241, 247, 253–54, 262n, 274, 324, 509, 527; III, 105
Dakyns, Mrs. Peggy: I, 388n; II, 825n
Dakyns, Roche: I, 388n; II, 206 and n
Dakyns, Thomas Henry: I, 388n; II, 128n
Dale, G.: III, 30 and n
Dalhousie, Lady Edith: I, 184 and n
Dallas, Eneas Sweetland: I, 664n
Dalrymple, Charles: I, 110, 111n, 117, 121, 138, 140, 147, 154–55, 162, 184; III, 76, 750
Dalrymple, James Fergusson: I, 184 and n
d'Ancona, Alessandro: II, 549, 550n, 574 and n; III, 847, 850n, 852n
Daniel, Samuel: III, 101n
Danieli's: II, 807, 808n
D'Annunzio, Gabriele: II, 932, 933n
Dansey, Frances Milborough: I, 52 and n
Dante, Alighieri: I, 36, 105, 330, 380, 530, 616, 688, 689n, 726, 757, 777, 784,

Dobson, Austin: II, 953, 954n; III, 418, 421n
Dodsley, Robert: III, 154, 155n
Dolby, Charlotte Helen Sainton-: I, 155, 156n, 205n
Dolgoruki Villa: III, 758. *See also* Ekaterina, Princess Dolgorukaya.
Domenichino (Domenico Zampieri): III, 83, 84n
Donaldson, John William: I, 214 and n
Don Antonio: III, 343 and n, 708
Donatello: III, 50
Donne, John: II, 567
Donoghue, John: III, 556 and n
Donovan, Cornelius: I, 319 and n
Don Quixote: III, 286–87
Doré, Gustave: II, 437, 439n
Dossi, Dosso (Giovanni di Lutero): II, 511 and n, 593, 594n
Dostoyevsky, Teodor: I, 35; III, 35 and n, 66, 121
Douglas, Lord Alfred: I, 36; III, 837n
Douglas, Henry Pelham, Duke of Newcastle: III, 29, 30n
Douglas, Sally: I, 202, 204 and n
Douglas, Mrs. Stair: II, 430, 431n
Dowden, Edward: III, 195 and n, 197, 199 and n, 215–19
Doyle, Sir Francis Hastings: II, 456, 457n
Doyle, Peter: III, 819–20 and n, 825, 826n
Dreams (of S): II, 734–37
Drummond, William: I, 156, 158n; III, 161, 162n
Drury, Benjamin: I, 63 and n, 67, 80, 124, 185
Dryden, John: I, 90, 324
Dubois, Paul: II, 659, 660n
Du Camp, Maxime: II, 858 and n
Ducie, Lady Elizabeth Dutton Moreton (d. 1865): I, 473, 474n, 478, 501n
Ducie, Henry George Francis Moreton, 2nd Earl of (d. 1853): I, 474n
Ducie, Henry John Moreton, 3rd Earl of (d. 1921): I, 474n; II, 278, 279n, 281, 282n, 435; III, 392
Ducie, Lady Julia Langston Moreton (d. 1895) I, 474n; II, 430, 431n, 435, 460; III, 389 392, 739, 740n
Duckworth, Stella: III, 403n
Dudley, Charles: II, 932
Duff, Archibald Hay Gordon-: III, 722, 723n

Duff, Lachlan Gordon-: III, 722, 723n
Duff, Thomas Duff Gordon-: III, 157–58n, 280, 332, 334n
Duff, Mrs. Thomas Duff Gordon- (Pauline Emma Terrant): III, 157–58n, 722, 723n
Dugdale, Sir William: I, 116n
Duméril, Edélstand Pontas: II, 881, 882n
Dunn, T. W.: I, 847, 848n; II, 527, 528n
Dunster: III, 651, 652n, 796
Durm, Joseph: III, 703 and n, 706, 707
Dürer, Albrecht: I, 66 and n, 90, 334, 335n
Dutch humanists: II, 896
Dyce, Alexander: I, 784, 785n
Dyer, Stella: III, 763
Dyer, Willie: I, 39, 149, 150n, 218, 219n, 426 and n, 447n, 493n, 505, 603n, 831n, 832n; II, 56
"Dying Gaul, The" (replica of): II, 893–94, 894n
"Eel, The" (Italian ballad): III, 850–51
Easton, John: II, 149, 150n
Eaton, the Rev. John Richard: II, 503 and n
Ebulus: II, 450, 451n, 462, 463n
Eden, Sibyl Frances Grey: III, 763, 764n, 768
Education (of S) as a writer: III, 270–72
Edwards, Amelia B.: II, 314n
Edwards, Leighton Hope: I, 128 and n, 139
Edwards, Passinore: I, 184n
Egglestone, Mr.: II, 528
"Eiger and the Monk" (p): II, 161
Ekaterina, Princess Dolgorukaya: III, 516, 517n
Elgin Marbles: II, 605; III, 215
Eliot, George: I, 269n, 530 and n, 533n, 765, 766n, 787, 826n, 827 and n, 838, 840n, 842 and n; II, 26, 28n, 38, 39n, 151, 152n, 200, 201n, 243n, 417, 450–51 and n, 583, 585n, 961, 962n; III, 57
Eliot, Mrs. Gilbert: I, 537 and n
Elizabeth I: I, 222n, 230n
Elizabethan Dramatic Literature, S's studies in (arts): II, 814, 817, 915
Elizabethan Plays, "Mermaid Series": III, 136, 141
Elizabethan Plays, series projected: II, 844, 865

"Elizabethan and Victorian Poetry, A Comparison of" (art): III, 311, and n, 312, 371

"Elizabethan Songbooks" (art): III, 284n

Elkington, George Richard: II, 884n

Ella, John: II, 70 and n

Ellicott, Mr. and Mrs. Charles John: II, 70 and n

Ellicott, Rosalind: II, 70 and n

Elliot, Gilbert: I, 537 and n

Ellis, Havelock: I, 37, 38; III (on S as critic) 98 and 99n, 136, 141, 146, 458, 482, 691, 798, 808, 809n

Ellis, Mrs. Havelock: III, 695 and n

Ellis, Robinson: I, 256, 257n, 318, 332; III, 663, 664n

Elton, Charles Isaac: I, 168 and n

Elton, Mrs. F. B.: II, 270, 271n

Elton, Sergeant W. P.: II, 119n

Elvey, Sir George: I, 219n

Elvey, Stephen: I, 217, 219n

Elzevir (printers): II, 522, 523n

Empedocles: I, 633

Engel, Rosa: I, 406n, 414n, 417n, 418, 484, 498, 835 and n; II, 56, 158, 160 and n, 774–75

"English Men of Letters" series: I, 36; III, 32, 57, 58n, 198

English people and English life: III, 122, 389–90

"English Worthies" series: III, 31, 139

Ente (Society) Buonarroti, the: III, 654 and n

Enys (Cornwall): III, 739, 747

Enys, Mrs. Catherine: II, 455, 455–56n

Enyses, the: III, 395, 396n

"Epaminondas" (p): I, 138, 139n, 141

Epicureanism: II, 37

Erba, Giuseppe (friend of H. F. Brown): II, 571, 576n

Erdmann, Benno: II, 779, 780n

Eros: II, 35, 68 and n, 97, (in Plato) 358 and 359n

"Eros" (Praxitiles): II, 531, 532n

"Escorial, The" (p): I, 199 and n, 200, 239n, 246n, 248

Essays and Reviews: I, 32, 239n; Controversy over: I, 269, 270n, 276n, 284, 285n, 513n; Westminster Review art on: I, 271

Essays on a Liberal Education (ed. F. W. Farrar): I, 791, 792n

Essays Speculative and Suggestive (b): III, 255, 256n, 268, 276, 284, 312, 341, 350, 353, 365, 380, 382, 403, 421, 443, 444n, 448–49, 455, 457n, 458, 460–61, 466–68, 470, 472–73, 477–82, 486, 500, 511–13, 554–55; Whitman thanks S for: III, 484n; revs of: III, 490–91, 492 and n, 497–98, 501 and n, 502, 503n

Ethics, A Problem in Greek (b): I, 38, 792n; II, 211n, 881, 882n, 895–96, 934; III, 301–02, 436 and n, 448 and n, 488 and n, 489n, 515, 710, 749, 798, 799n, 808, 810, 813, 817, 821

Ethics, A Problem in Modern (b): I, 38, III, 302, 303n, 418–19, 478, 479n, 515, 519n, 520, 537, 544, 548, 551, 553–54, 579, 585–86 and n, 710, 755, 813, 814, 819 and n

Ettinger, Christian: III, 298

Etty, William: I, 206, 207n

Euclid: I, 62, 185

"Eudiades" (p): I, 38, 851n, 852; II, 29, 30n, 34, 56, 65–66n, 125n, 152n, 399–401, 405

"Euganean Hills, Among the" (art): III, 469n

Euripides: I, 588; II, 58, 101, 102ns, 143, 146, 166, 267, 277, 396, 571

"Euripides" (bust): II, 531, 532n

Eurystheus: III, 646, 647n

Evans, Emma: I, 313, 314n

Evans, Sir George de Lacy: I, family of: 327, 328n, 535, 536n

Evans, Sir John: I, family of: 327, 328n, 535, 536n

Evans, Lucy: I, 313, 314n

Evans, Mary Ann: see Eliot, George

Evelyn, John: I, 122 and n

Evolution, Doctrine of: II, 964, 969; III, 386

"Evolutionary Ideas, The Application of, to Literature and Art" (art): III, 255, 284

Ewart, John: I, 508n

Ewart, Joseph: I, 768, 769n

Ewart, Mary: I, 507, 508n, 550, 553, 727, 768

Ewart, William: I, 378n, 394, 394–95n, 508n, 618, 743, 768

"Exile, The" (p): I, 93, 94n, 98, 99n, 106

Eyre, Edward John: II, 490, 491n

Eyre, George Edward: I, 256, 258n, 592, 598

Fairweather, Mrs. Drinkwater: III, 791 and n

Falconer (photographer): II, 526

Falke, Jacob von: III, 66, 67n

Falmouth: III, 742, 743n, 746, 748

Falsori, Signora Ida: III, 801n, 838n

Faraday, Michael: I, 315

Farnese, Pier Luigi: II, 467, 468n

Farrar, the Rev. Frederic William: I, 108, 109n, 146, 792n

Farrer, Thomas Henry: 11, 456, 457n

Farrer, Lady William James: III, 626, 627n

Farringford: 11, 216 and n; III, 743, 845

Farrington, Margaret Vere: III, 646, 647n

Fattucci, Giovanni Francesco: III, 614 and n, 639 and n

Faust legend: II, 842, 930

Fay, Mrs. (a medium): II, 365 and **n**

Febo di Poggio: III, 570 and n, 578–79 and n, 638, 639n, 686, 687n

Fechter, Charles A.: I, 314, 315n, 389

Felsina Pittrice: III, 50n, 407 and n

Fergusson, Lady Dalrymple-: I, 155, 156n

Fergusson, Georgina Grace Buchanan: I, 162, 163n

Fergusson, Henriette: I, 157

Fergusson, Sir James: I, 110, 111n, 156

Fergusson, Mrs. James: I, 156, 157

Ferrari, Giuseppe: II, 600 and n

Ferriday, Mrs.: II, 795 and n

Feuerbach, Ludwig Andreas: I, 426 and n

Fichte, Johann Gottlieb: II, 504, 505n

"Ficino, Marsilio" (art): II, 547 and n, 551, 552n

Fielding, Henry: II, 289, 291

"Filelfo" (art): II, 547 and n

Finch, Henry Randolph: I, 69, 70n

Finch, Lady Louisa Elizabeth: I, 69, 70n

Fine Arts, The (b): II, 422, 451, 470, 472–73, 539, 578, 807

Fiorentino, Francesco: II, 538n

Firenzuola, Agnolo: II, 537, 538n, 558n

Fitzgerald, Edward: III, 385 and n

Fitzpatrick, Lady John Wilson: II, 471, 472n

Flaminius, Gaius: II, 633 and n

Flaubert, Gustave: III, 56

Flandrin, Hippolyte: II, 420 and n; III, 435, 456

Flaxman, John: II, 649 and n

Fletcher, John: III, 473

Florence (Italy): III, 41, 526, 578, 607, 620

"Florence and the Medici, Parts I and II" (arts): II, 448n

Flower, Edgar: III, 724, 725n, 726

"Flower o' the Thorn" (tr): II, 913, 914n

Folgore da San Gemignano: II, 697, 698n; III, 185, 186n

Forbes, Mrs. Alicia Wauchope: I, 57, 58n, 72, 73n, 145, 154–55, 293, 770, 772

Forbes, George: II, 353n

Forbes, James David: I, 30, 57, 58n, 72, 73n, 154, 293, 302n, 408 and n, 769–70 and n, 774n, 777

Forbes, William L.: II, 353n

Ford, Edmund Salwey: I, 323 and n

Ford, John: I, 488; quoted: II, 77 and n

Formes, Karl: I, 399 and n

Forrest, Catharine: I, 161, 162 and n

Forrest, James: I, 162n

Forrest, Violet: I, 161, 162 and n

Forster, Mr. and Mrs. Henry Brooks: I, 802 and n

Forsyth, Miss: II, 901, 902n

Fortini-Santarelli (translator): II, 539n; III, 541 and n, 831n

Fortnum, C. Drury E.: III, 633, 634n

Fortunato (servant): III, 654 and n, 662

Foster, Joseph: II, 932, 933n

Fowle, Thomas Welbank: I, 339 and n

Fowler, Thomas: II, 278, 279n, 294n, 330, 331n

Fox, Mr.: I, 450, 451n, 571, 572

Fox, Dr. E. Long: II, 309 and n

Fox, H. F.: II, 605, 606n

Fra Angelico: II, 923, 924n; III, 108

Fragilia Labilia (ps): II, 950, 951n; III, 69 and n, 114, 115n

"Fragmenta Litteraria": *see* "Miscellanies"

France, Anatole: III, 545n

France, Francis: I, 203, 205n

Francia (Francesco Railolinia): I, 399, 400n; II, 47, 48n

Francis I: III, 209

Franco, Niccoló: III, 145, 146n

Franco-Prussian War: II, 115n, 148n

Franklin, Lady Jane Griffin: I, 615n

Frari Library (Venice): II, 912 and n; III, 103

Fraticelli, Pietro: II, 111 and n

Frederick III, Emperor of Germany: II, 824–25n; III, 506, 507–08n

Frederick, Empress of Germany (Victoria, the English Princess Royal): I, 133n; II, 825n; III, 500, 501n, 521, 580, 763, 768–69, 771, 797, 804

Frederick the Great: III: 821

Freeman, Mrs. Edith: III, 228, 231n

Freeman, Edward Augustus: II, 860, 861n

Freeman Harold: III, 30 and n, 288 and n, 331, 334n, 341

Fremantle, William Henry: II, 456, 457n

Freshfield, Douglas William: III, 156n

Freud, Sigmund: I, 38

Frey, Karl: III, 615 and n, 630 and n

Friedrich, Charles Ludwig, Prince of Hesse: III, 763, 764n, 768, 769

"Friend Leaving England in September, To a" (p): II, 314 and n

Fritzinger, Warren: III, 531n, 563, 599, 601n, 666, 809, 811

Froude, James Anthony: I, 512, 513n, 537, 845 and n; II, 81, 498 and n

Fry, Lewis: I, 829, 831n

Fuller, Edith: III, 728, 729n, 760 and n

Furse, Katharine: see Symonds, Katharine

Fusato, Angelo: I, 39; II, 707n, 714, 714–15n, 822, 905: III, 26n, 38, 120, 124n, 125, 383–84, 515, 525, 528–29, 538, 569, 597 618, 624–25, 628–29, 646, 682, 705, 712, 715, 719–21, 724, 730, 735, 739, 741–42, 743, 745–46, 761, 768, 779, 781, 790–91, 815, 824, 834, 836, 839

Fusato, Mrs. Angelo (Maria): III, 591, 712, 761

Fusato, Giacomo: II, 911

Fusato, "Hop": II, 822, 823n; III, 38 and n

"Gabriel" (p): I, 38; II, 66n

Gainsborough, Lady Francis: II, 453, 454n

Gaisford Prize: I, 295, 296n, 393 and n

Gaisford, Thomas: I, 295, 296n

Gale, Norman Rowland: III, 795, 796n

Gale, William Henry: II, 31, 32n

Galilei, Galileo: I, 90; III, 91

Galton, the Rev. Arthur: III, 201, 202n, 205 and n, 220 and n, 275, 461, 462n, 471, 505, 506 and n, 510, 511n, 514, 515n, 566ns

Galton, Sir Francis: I, 36, 37, 536n; II,

317, 318–19n, 365, 387, 842 and n; III, 138, 813, 814n

Galuppi, Baldassare: II, 480, 481n; III, 319, 321n

Gamble, Dr. Harpur (uncle): I, 231 and n, 582 and n

Gamble, Isabella (later Otter) (cousin): II, 480, 481n, 489, 542, 629, 631n; III, 228, 231n

Gamble, Isobel Sykes (aunt): I, 231–32n

Gamble, John George (cousin): I, 136 and n, 186, 194, 209–10, 231 and n, 262, 297, 303, 307, 365, 402

Gardiner, Stephen: I, 120, 121n

Garibaldi, Giuseppe: I, 387, 388n, 635n; III, 693 and n

Garnett, Richard: II, 494; III, 216, 218n, 341, 853, 854n

Garnier, Charles: III, 656, 657n

Garrison, William Lloyd: I, 741 and n

Gaskell, Elizabeth Cleghorn: I, 106, 107n, 498 and n, 553, 561; II, 159n

Gassier, Édouard: I, 489 and n

Gaston de Foix: III, 827, 828n

"Gaudeamus Igitur": II, 903

Gautier Théophile: II, 154, 155n, 256, 257n, 266

Gawthorpe Hall: III, 591–92 and n

Gaye, Giovanni: III, 655, 657n

Geiger, Ludwig: II, 896, 897n

George, Arthur: II, 233n

George, the bookseller: III, 365

George, Duncan: II, 233n

George IV (of England): II, 732, 733n; III, 878

Gerard, John: II, 787 and n

Gherardi, Alessandro: III, 629, 631n

Gherardi family: III, 517

Ghose, Manomohan (1844–96): I, 518 and n

Ghose, Manomohan (1869–1924): III, 461, 462ns

Ghosts (Spiritualism): II, 361, 365, 392, 395

Giacomo della Porta: III, 584 and n

Gifford, Robert Francis, Baron: I, 479 and n; II, 62 and n

Gilbert, Sir John: III, 761, 762n

Gilbert, William Schwenck: II, 196n

Gilchrist, Herbert H.: III, 70n

Gilder, Richard Watson: II, 712, 713n

Gordon, Lady Lucie Duff-: III, 519–20 and n, 528

Gordon, Rachel-Nevil: III, 834, 836

Gordon, Urania Duff-: II, 499–500 and n

"Gorgo": I, 345, 346 and n, 355, 384

Goss, Sir John: I, 176, 178n

Gosse, Edmund: I, 29, 35, 37, 38; II, 381–82 and n, 392ns, 538; III, 31 and n, 136, 528, 544; on Donne and Campanella: II, 567–68 and n; on Vondel and on certain verse forms: II, 482, 483ns; on Sidney: III, 179, 180n, 182, 185; on Kipling and Stevenson: III, 664–65 and n; tr of Ibsen: III, 550, 551n, 557 and n; his life of his father: III, 550, and n; *Firdausi in Exile:* III, 430–31 and ns; *Gossip in a Library:* III, 668, 669n; *History of 18th Cent. Eng. Lit.:* III, 370–71; *King Eric:* II, 398 and n, 399, 403, 673, 817, 819; *New Poems:* II, 527n, 610, 611n, 613, 614n, 617 and n; *Northern Studies:* II, 585n, 589–90n, 612; *Raleigh:* III, 139, 140n, 161–62; *Secret of Narcisse:* III, 606, 607n; *Seventeenth Century Studies:* II, 876, 950, 953–54, 955n; "The Taming of Chimaera": III, 449–51; "The Unknown Lover": II, 523n; and the critics: III, 109, 109–10n; Oscar Wilde on: III, 188–89, 190n; and *Pall Mall Gazette:* III, 106; and *Punch* and *PMG:* III, 174, 175n, 182, 183n; and *The Quarterly Review:* III, 174–75

Gosse, Philip Henry: III, 551n

Gotti, Aurilio: III, 565, 566n, 567 and n, 614, 630, 655–56 and n, 703 and n

Goulburn, Edward Meyrick: I, 231, 232n

Gounod, Charles: I, 376n, 488, 489n

Gower, Lord Albert Leveson: I, 105n

Gower, Lord Francis Leveson: I, 305, 306n

Gower, Grace Emma Abdy: I, 105n

Gower, Lord Ronald: III, 244 and n, 598, 599n, 602, 606, 620, 623, 628, 629n, 650, 662, 713, 715, 719, 720, 723–24, 725n, 726, 728–29, 731, 732n, 775, 825, 826n

Gozzi, Carlo: II, 635, 636n; III, (and S's tr of memoirs) 277 and n, 281, 286, 301–02, 309, 310, 312, 319, 322, 325, 342, 353, 356, 362, 364, 367, 376–77, 381, 383, 394, 406, 410, 413, 527

Graeme, Alexander Malcolm: I, 124, 125n

Granville, Lord George Leveson-Gower: II, 281, 282n

Grath, H. W. M.: I, 402 and n

Graubünden (Grisons) District, Switzerland: II, 155–56, 558

Graubünden, A projected history of the: II, 657; III, 411, 443, 565, 679, 697, 711, 756. *See also* Planta, Peter Conradin von

"Graubünden, Bacchus in" (art): II, 665n

Gray, Thomas, memorial for: II, 948 and n, 953

Grazzini, Antonio Francisco: III, 560 and n

Grazzini, Reginaldo: III, 527, 528n

Greek Anthology: III, 228n

Greek Comradeship: II, 399–401; III, 458–59

"Greek Idyllic Poets" (art): I, 824, 825n

Greek (Platonic) love: II, 923; III, 365, 458, 664, 755; and Jowett: III, 345–47

"Greek Lyrical Poetry" (art): II, 244–45n

Greek Music: I, 469

Greek myth and religion: II, 683–84

Greek Poets, Studies of the, 1st series (b): I, 725n; II, 125n, 166n, 209n, 211n, 255n, 263n, 277n, 279–80, 282–83, 294, 298, 300–01, 307, 322, 322–23n, 396, 578, 615, 616n; 2nd series (b): II, 313, 374, 390, 391, 392, 395, 397, 402, 404, 407, 410, 413, 415–16, 417, 418n, 540; III, 673n; both series (bs): II, (rev of) 462n, 595 and n, 597, 683, 782, 787; III, 632, 683, 737; 3rd ed.: III, 750, 756–57, 804, 828, 829n

Greek, teaching and study of: III, 537, 544

"Greek Tragedy and Euripides" (art): II, 143, 144n, 166 and n

Green, Thomas Hill: I, 32, 33, 194n, 198n, 199 and n, 200, 211n, 223, 242, 244, 250 and n, 251, 253, 258, 263, 267, 278, 281, 315, 339n, 365, 396, 409, 410, 411 and n, 412–14, 415n, 416, 417n, 418–23, 441, 482–83, 488, 490, 538n, 579, 584, 633, 661, 672, 741, 767n; II, 127, 129, 139, 140 and n, 143, 150, 151n, 152, 154, 158, 169, 170, 245n, 253, 264–65 and n, 278, 284, 310–11, 336, 357–58, 402, 407, 417, 448, 460, 465, 477, 490, 496, 503, 516, 517ns, 525, 553, 554 and n, 555, 557, 579, 580n, 634, 677, 685, 695, 718, 735,

Herschel, Sir John: I, 536, 537n
Hertford Prize: I, 282 and n; II, 336, 337n
Hesiod: II, 85, 432n
Heyse, Paul Johann: I, 773, 774n
Heywood, Thomas: I, 488
"Heywood, Thomas, the Dramatic Works of" (art): II, 340 and n
Heyworth, George Frederick: I, 204n
Heyworth, James: I, 202, 203, 204n, 309, 311n; II, 47
Higginson, Florence Virginia: II, 471, 472n
Higginson, Thomas Wentworth: II, 713n
Hill, Alfred: I, 327, 329n
Hill, M. D.: I, 329n
Hillern, Wilhelmine von: II, 439, 440 and n, 441, 597 and n
Hinton, James: II, 778; III, 878–79
Hipwell, James: I, 429, 430n
Hoffman, Heinrich: I, 784, 785n
Hoffmann, E. T. A.: II, 629
Hogg, T. James: II, 494
Hohenstaufen, House of: II, 783; III, 618 and n
Holbein, Hans: I, 533n; II, 312, 313n; III, 736
Hold, Mr.: II, 941, 942n
Holland, Charlotte Dorothea Gifford: I, 478, 479n
Holland, Henry: II, 489, 491n
Hollyer, Frederick: I, 851 and n, 852n; II, 388–89; III, 213, 587
Holmes, Oliver Wendell: I, 795, 796n
Holsboer, W. J.: II, 728 and n
Holt, Henry, and Co.: III, 486, 487 and ns, 737
Holte, Mrs. Richard: I, 57, 58n, 124, 140
"Holy Grail, The," (art): III, 744, 745n
Homer: I, 90, 190, 377, 378n, 472n, 596, 597; II, 82, 300, 354; III, 101n, 271
Homosexual love and its benefits: III, 798–99, 808, 810–11
Homosexuality, cases of: III, 813, 816–17, 821
Homosexuality in *Michelangelo*: III, 679, 680n, 685–86, 687n
Homosexuals, penal codes for: III, 694
Hone, Evelyn Joseph: I, 171 and n
Hood, Thomas: I, 90, 190 and n
Hook, Dr. Walter Farquhar: I, 215 and n
Hope, Miss: I, 152 and n

Hopkins, Edward John: I, 183, 184n
Hopkins, John Larkin: I, 224 and n
Hopper, Miss Annie: I, 508n
Horace: I, 94, 95; II, 236, 432n; III, quoted: 482, 484n, 826, 827n
Horne, Herbert P.: III, 30 and n, 394 and n, 479, 582, 583n
Horner, Friedrich: III, 167 and n
Horner, Mrs. John Francis: III, 756, 757n
Horner, Susan and Joanna B.: II, 407, 408n
Horridge, Mr.: II, 515
Horsey, General William de: II, 714n; III, 768, 771n
Hotten, John Camden: I, 790, 792n
Howard, Lady Cecilia: *see* Roberts, Mrs. Charles Henry
Howard, Charles James ("Morpeth"): III, 725, 726n, 735, 736n
Howard, Frederick John, "old" Lord Carlisle: III, 724, 726n, 727
Howard, George James, 9th Earl of Carlisle: II, 417, 418n; III, 723, 725, 726 and n, 727–29, 731, 732n, 733–34, 742, 824, 825n
Howard, Mrs. George (Lady Rosalind): III, 728, 729n
Howard, Lord William: III, 736n
Howells, William Dean: II, 865, 866n, 915, 916n, 964; III, 109–10n, 166 and n, 197, 198n, (rev of S's *Catholic Reaction*) 291, 292n
Howlett, William Frederick: I, 830, 833n; II, 132 and n, 133 and n, 134, 200
Hubatsch, Oscar: II, 881, 882n
Huggard, Dr. W. R.: III, 596, 596–97n
Hughes, H. R.: I, 304, 305n
Hughes, Thomas: I, 268, 269n
Hughes, William: III, 472, 473n
Hugo, F. Victor: I, 405–06 and n, 838; III, 56, 57n, 257
Hullah, John Pyke: I, 251, 252n, 393 and n
Humanity as a religion: III, 588–89
Humbert, Prince of Piedmont: I, 806n
Hunt, William: I, 97, 99n, 207, 285n
Hunt, William Holman: I, 262 and n, 591, 592, 594, 597n, 599; II, 334, 335ns; III, 138 and n
Hussey, J.: I, 149, 150n
Huxley, Thomas Henry: I, 595; II, 453

Job: I, 506 and n
Johns Hopkins University, the: III, 64
Johnson, Lionel Pigot: III, 394 and n, 461, 463n, 471, 479, 510, 514, 515n, 582, 583n
Johnston, Dr. John: III, 530, 531n, 563, 563–64n, 653, 666, 792 and n, 806, 819–20
Joll, Mrs.: I, 334
Jommelli, Niccolò: III, 214, 215n
"Jonathan and David" (p): II, 198, 203, 204n
Jones, Cyril Edward Arengo-: II, 533, 534n
Jones, Sir Edward Burne-: II, 218 and n, 438, 439n, 453, 751
Jones, Henry Warren: I, 117 and n
Jonson, Ben: I, 343, 488, 671; III, 562
Jonson, Ben (b): III, 31, 32n, 50, 117, 119, 125, 128, 133, 136, 147, 150, 161, 165, 180, 181n, 188, (rev of) 188 and 190n
Jonson, Ben, Dramatic Works and Lyrics of, ed. by S(b): III, 125, 126n, 136
Jost (of Davos): III, 260
Jouffroy, Theodore Simon: I, 377, 378n
Jowett, Benjamin: I, 32, 33, 103 and n, 169, 172, 179n, 190, 210, 213, 219n, 225–26, 237, 239n, 240, 242, 247, 262–63, 270n, 274, 275, 277, 278, 279 and n, 280–81, 283, 285n, 291–92, 293n, 297, 311 and n, 312n, 315–16, 321, 322n, 323, 329n, 330, 332, 334, 365, 368, 369n, 375–77, 397, 427, 441–42, 443n, 462, 465, 469, 509, 512, (salary) 512 and 513n, 516n, 538, 550–51, 553, 558, 559n, 561, 562n, 568, 569n, 582, 590, 591n, 599, 601, 608, 629, 630 and n, 633 and n, 665, 668n, 670, 672, 730, 743, 744n, 745n, 767 and n; II, 25, 26, 28n, 34, 37, 38, 60, 94 and n, 100, 101, 111, 246, 264, 337, 402, 460, 625, 631, 640, 643, 646–47, 693, 695, 696, 698–99, 719, 751, 763, 764, 776, 829, 919, 929; III, 54, 81, 160, 165, 211, 247, 271, 309–12, 341, (and Greek love) 345–47 and 365 and 371 and 491, 537, 544, 609, 613, 618, 620, 623, 624n, 641, 845, (and S's epitaph) 840
Julian, the Apostate: I, 342

Julian School of Art, proposal to: III, 453–54 and n, 487
Juon, Anton: III, 378, 432 and n, 546–47, 549, 550n, 559
Justinian: I, 538n; III, 754 and n, 788, 817
Juvenal: I, 90, 108, 339n, 440, 441n; II, 118n; III, 81
Kane, Elisha Kent: I, 97, 99n
Kay, William: I, 326–27, 328n
Kean, Charles: II, 196n
Keats, John: I, 31, 386, 513n, 772; II, 529 and n, 981; III, 271; quoted: II, 92 and n, 984, 985n; III, 602 and n
Keble, John, III, 116 and n
Kegan, Paul Trench and Co. (publishers): II, 811n, 903, 913, 915; III, 737
Kempis, Thomas à: I, 800, 802n, 824
Kennedy, Margaret: I, 580n
Kennedy, William Sloane: III, 239, 240n, 242 and n, (on Whitman) 261–62, 262–63n, 263–65
Kerr, Russell James (1832–1910): III, 683n
Kerr, Russell James (1863–?): III, 683n
Kerslake, Thomas: I, 338 and n; II, 107n
Khayyam, Omar: *see* Omar Khayyan
Kibritzi Pasha: III, 524
"King Arthur, The History of" (art): I, 579, 580n
King, William, Lord Lovelace: II, 286, 287n
Kinglake, Alexander William: III, 537–38 and n, 660
Kinglake, Dr. John Hamilton: III, 604, 605n
Kingscote, Mrs. Emily Marie Curzon: I, 317, 318n
Kingscote, Sir Robert Nigel: I, 317, 318n
Kingsley, Charles: I, 223, 224n, 225 and n, 280, 764, 766n; II, 85, 86n, 88, 305, 306n
Kingsley, Fanny Grenfell: II, 88 and n
Kington, William Miles Nairn: I, 67, 68n
Kinsey, Matthew: II, 215, 216n
Kipling, Rudyard: I, 35, 36; III, 381, 409, 422–23, 518, 664–65
Kirkup, Seymour: I, 512, 513n; II, 249 and n, 251n, 266, 267n, 275, 276 and n
Kitchener, Francis Elliot: II, 79 and n, 81, 82n
Kitchin, George William: I, 215 and n

Lycidas of Ageanax: I, 187, 661

Lynch, Jeremiah: III, 602, 603n, 604, 605n

Lysippus: II, 280–81, 403, 404n; III, 623n

Lyska, Elizabeth: III, 411, 412n

Lytton, Edward Robert Bulwer- ("Owen Meredith"): II, 36n; III, 47, 48n

Mabuse, Jan: I, 161, 163n; III, 726n, 736

Macaulay, Thomas Babington: I, 637, 638n; II, 626, 627; III, 86 and n, 88 and n, 113

MacCarthy, D. F.: II, 572, 573n

MacColl, Dugald S.: III, 168 and 168–69n, 181, 182n

Maccoll, William: III, 28, 29n

McCosh, James: I, 817, 818n

Macdonald, George: I, 531 and n

Macfarren, John Alexander: I, 393 and n

Machiavelli, Niccolò: II, 233, 319, 321n, 771; III, 43 and n, 172

"Machiavelli" (art): II, 745, 746n, 767

Maclean, W. C.: I, 151 and n

MacLeod, Fiona: see Sharp, William

Macmillan (publisher): III, 740n

MacMorland, Bessie: III, 541–42 and n

MacMorland, Mrs. Elizabeth Macdonald: II, 489, 491n, 554, 564; III, 877

MacMorland, the Rev. John Peter: II, 491n, 515, 516n, 554; III, 877

Maecenas: I, 95

Magazine of Art: III, 878

Magdalen College (Oxford): I, 30, 186, 209, 227, 233, 243, 246, 266, 282, 317, 363, 365–67, 392, 442, 468n, 515n, 639, 651, 662; II, 690

Mahaffy, John Pentland: II, 683, 684n

"Mahomet" (p): I, 71 and n, 197

Maimonides: II, 978, 979n

Maitland, John Alexander Fuller-: III, 397 and n

Maitland, Thomas: II, 276n

Malcolm, William Rolle: I, 180 and n

Malet, Edward Baldwin: III, 187 and n

Mallock, William Hurrell: II, 778, 780n

Maloja: III, 125, 126n, 163–64

Malone, Edward: III, 473n

Malthus, Letitia: I, 390 and n, 393, 396, 476 and n; II, 56

Malvern: I, 291 and n, 342–43, 345–46, 353–54, 384–85, 398, 475, 477

Manin, Daniele: III, 200, 201n

Mansel, Henry Longueville: I, 231, 232n, 292, 293n, 314, 315n, 321, 322

Mansiello, Tommaso: II, 753, 754n

Manso, Giovanni Battista: III, 64 and n

Mansueti, Giovanni (Sebastiano Mainardi): I, 424, 425n

Mantegna, Andrea: I, 424, 425n; II, 334, 335n, 515, 516n, 922; III, 50

Mantovani, Dino: II, 939, 940n

"Manutti, The" (art): II, 745, 746n, 767

Many Moods (b of ps): II, 160n, 165n, 205n, 350n, 351–53, 512 and n, 515, 516n, 551, 553, (rev) 556 and 557n, 635n, 730

Manzoni, Alessandro: I, 638n

Map, Walter: III, 344, 345n

Marcello, Benedetto: II, 635, 636n

Marchisio, Barbara and Carlotta: I, 399, 400n

Marcus Aurelius: I, 763, 799n, 800, 824, 848; II, 143, 144n, 235, 236, 397, 666

Marden, Edward and James: I, 81 and n

Margarete Beatrice Fedora, Princess of Germany: III, 763, 764n, 768, 769

Maria, Princess Giovanelli: III, 525, 526n

Mariana, Juan: III, 172 and n

Marillier, Jacob F.: I, 93n

Marini, Giambattista: III, 69 and n, 70–71, 85, 87, 107

Marjoribanks, Sir John: II, 468, 469n, 859, 861n

Marks, the Rev. R.: II, 257 and n

Marlowe, Christopher: I, 488, 639, 671; II, 400; III, 128, 130n, 246, 322–23, 821; quoted: III, 535, 536n

Marriage, S's reminiscences of his: III, 178–79

Marshall, Alfred: I, 802 and n

Marshall, Dr. John: I, 829, 831n

Marshall, Roger: I, 253, 254n

Marshall, Walter: I, 711 and n

Marshall, Mrs. Walter: II, 431 and n

Marsham, Charles (the Earl of Romney): I, 247 and n

Marsham, Robert Bullock: I, 247n

Marston, John: I, 488

Marston, Philip Bourke: II, 886, 887n, 946, 947n

Martin, Charles: I, 354n

Martineau, Harriet: I, 250, 251n

Martini, Ferdinando: III, 703 and n

Marville, Mme.: II, 30 and n, 34, 39

Mary I: III, 552, 553n

Marylebone Cricket Club: I, 60 and n

Moritz, Neville: II, 536n
Morley, Guy: III, 643 and n
Morley, John: II, 456 and n, 498n, 609
and n, 611, 656, 657n, 701, 706, 707
and n; III, 31, 32n, 57, 58n, 643
Mornay, Philippe du Plessis: III, 80 and n
Morrell, Frederick Parker: II, 819, 820n
Morris, Lewis: II, 870, 871n
Morris, William: I, 826n, 847; II, 103,
151, 152n, 161, 429 and n
Moscardi, M.: I, 380
Moschus: I, 251, 252n, 257, 278 and n,
627n
Moseley, Henry Nottidge: I, 130 and n
Moulton, Louise Chandler: II, 584–85n
Mozart, Wolfgang Amadeus: I, 281, 299,
307, 368–69, 399, 476, 477n, 580n, 637
and n, 674n, 686n, 720n, 802n; II, 239,
419–20, 421, 507, 514; III, 214, 215n
Mozley, John Rickards: II, 44n, 100n, 121,
571; III, 105 and n, 114, 115n, 876–77
Mozley, Thomas: I, 830, 832n; II, 428
and n, 557, 558n, 560–61
Mücke, Heinrich: I, 93n
Mudie, Edward Charles: III, 251, 254n
Müller, Alfred: I, 253 and n
Müller, Karl: I, 675 and n
Müller, (Friedrich) Max: I, 362 and n; II,
46n, 51, 74 and n, 255 and n
Mullins (servant): II, 494, 512, 540, 549
Mullins, Joseph Denis: II, 966, 967n
Muncaster, Lord and Lady: II, 281, 282n
Munich: III, 80, 468–69, 470
"Munich, Modern German Art at" (art):
II, 775, 780n
Munkacsy, Mihály von: II, 751, 753n
Munro, Hector: III, 340n
Munthe, Dr. Axel: III, 839, 841n
Murano Glass and Murano Glass Com-
pany: II, 821 and n, 826, 827, 920
and n
Muratori, Lodovico Antonio: II, 328,
329n, 697, 698n; III, 208, 210n
Mure, William: I, 214 and n; II, 255
and n
Murillo, Bartolomé E.: I, 87 and n, 533n
Murphy, Arthur: I, 97, 99n
Murray, Alexander Henry: III, 580, 581n
Murray, John: I, 514–15n, 726 and n; II,
458 and n; III, 300 and n
Murray, Louisa Mary: I, 77n
Murray's Guidebooks: II, 289

Mürren, Switzerland: I, 406 and n, 407,
409, 417 and n, 484, 496, 819, 835n,
844; II, 79, 81, 155–57, 159, 161–62,
170, 240, 270, 774
Museo Buonarroti: see Buonarroti Archives
Music, effect of: I, (and St. Augustine)
453, 457; III, 676
"Music the Type and Measure for All Art,
Is?" (art): III, 266n, 284, 289
Musset, Alfred de: I, 511n, 550 and n, 578
and n, 584, 729; II, 35, 36n; 708;
quoted: I, 546, 547n, 724, 725n, 734,
735n, 736n; II, 123 and n, 261, 343
and n
Mutinelli, Fabio: III, 68 and n
Myers, Ernest James: II, 454, 455n, 456,
624, 625n
Myers, Frederick W. H.: I, 36, 253, 254n,
299, 387, 388n, 485, 666, 688, 782,
790, 792n, 794n; II, 81, 82n, 85, 88–
89, 117–18, 128n, 143, 167n, 189
and n, 190, 191n, 350n, 363, 365,
392, 450, 451n, 570, 583, 590, 591n,
624, 625n, 656, 657n, 680, 681n,
807, 808n; III, 99 and n, 671, 672n,
705
Myers, Mrs. F. W. H. (Eveleen Tennant):
III, 400, 401n, 409, 410n
"Mystery of Mysteries" (ps): II, 731
Nalder, Mrs.: I, 336, 366 and n
Napier, Miss: I, 741 and n
Napier, Col. Alexander: III, 411, 412n
Napoleon Bonaparte: I, 191, 275 and n,
277, 423
Narcissus: II, 418
"Narcissus' Flower" (p): III, 205 and n,
259 and n, 266, 292
Nardi, Jacopo: II, 319, 321n
Nash, Herbert: II, 308, 309
Nash, James Ezekiel (uncle): I, 51 and n,
(family of) 192 and 193n, 284, 285,
291, 297, 298n; II, 181 and n
Nash, James Palmer (cousin): I, 51 and n,
77, 84 and n, 88, 90, 129 and n, 133,
143, 284, 285, 298n, 312, 419, 422
Nash, Lucy (cousin): I, 217–18, 219n,
298n, 309 and n
Nash, Mary Susan Symonds (aunt): I, 88,
89n, 222, 298n
Nash, Spencer Hampden: II, 353n
"Nature Myths and Moral Allegories"
(art): III, 284

Parlagreco, Carlo: III, 685 and n, 694

Parmenides: I, 633, 738, 739n; III, 75 and n

Parr, Thomas Philip: I, 64 and n, 203, 205n

Pary, S.: III, 602, 603n, 604

Pascal, Blaise: II, 243n

Passerini, Luigi: III, 655, 656n

"Passion, On True and False" (p): III, 782–83

Paston, George: see Symonds, Emily Morse

Pater: Walter: I, 35, 847; II, 246, 273–74, 336, 388, 460, 500–01, 612 and n, 775; III, 99, 510, 511n, 635, 673 and n; on Sir Thomas Browne: III, 146 and n; *Appreciations:* III, 440; *Marius the Epicurean:* III, 41–42 and n, 43, 48; "School of Giorgione": III, 289; *Studies in the Hist. of the Ren.* and S's rev of: II, 273, 274n

Patmore, Coventry: I, 794, 795 and n; III, 451n

Patti, Adelina: I, 392 and n, 476, 477n; II, 70

Pattison, Mark: I, 270n; II, 359n, 360, 498n; III, 65, 66n

Paulssen, Antonius J.: III, 66, 67n

Payn, James: III, 307n

Payne, John: III, 807 and n

Payne, John Burnell: II, 83 and n

Pearson, Colonel: II, 605; III, 879

Pearson, Alfred Astley: II, 929, 930n; III, 226, 412, 674 and n

Pearson, Arthur C.: I, 280 and n

Pearson, Hugh: I, 280 and n, 287, 327, 329n, 332, 351, 401n, 466n, 514, 553; II, 431 and n, 455, 456, 581

Pearson, James Edward: II, 76, 77n, 235, 236n, 308–09, 355 and n, 424, 425n, 428 and n, 430, 431n, 435, 474

Peirce, Benjamin Osgood: III, 579, 579–80n, 586

Pellew, Henry Edward: II, 832, 834n

Pembroke, George Robert Charles Herbert, Lord: I, 353 and n, 354 n, 366n

Pembroke, Mary Herbert, Countess of: III, 139, 140n

"Penelope and Other Women of Homer" (art): II, 364, 365n

Penrith: III, 728, 741, 742

Pepys, Samuel: I, 122; II, 293; III, 371

Percival, John: I, 429, 430n, 612, 658,
666–701 and n, 704 and n, 742 and n, 830, 846; II, 47, 49, 68 and n, 76, 85, 86n, 97, 99 and n, 116n, 132 and n, 133–34 and n, 153, 194, 195n, 207, 209, 222, 264, 265n, 281, 328, 329n, 332, 352, 435, 456, 556, 557n, 558, 609 and n, 630, 631n, 639n; III, 501, 502n

Percival, Mrs. John: II, 68, 207, 208, 438

Percy, Bishop Thomas: I, 149

Périer (banker): III, 335 and n

Perini, Gherardo; III, 570 and n

Perino del Vaga: II, 114, 115n

Perkins, Charles Callahan: II, 713, 714n

Perry, T. S.: I, 36, 38; II, 834n, 887, 894, 895n, 915, 916n, 964, 969–70; III, 61, 62n, 65, 67n, 88–89n, 89, 196, 198n, 243, 252, 353, 554

Perry, Mrs. T. S. (Lila Cabot): II, 865, 866n, 914–16 and n, 986; III, 61, 197

Perugino, Il: I, 556n

Peter, Henry (Baron Brougham and Vaux): I, 281, 282n

Petrarch: I, 211, 380, 711, 777; III, quoted: 565, 566n

"Petrarch" (art): II, 893; III, 65

Pettigrew, Lizzie: I, 136

Pettigrew, Thomas Joseph: I, 137

Philemon (quoted): II, 532 and n

Philippson, Martin: III, 65, 67n, 202, 203n

Phillipotts, James Surtus: I, 336, 337n, 348, 456, 457n

Phillipps, James Orchard Halliwell-: II, 982, 983n

Phillips, Stephen: III, 461, 462n

Philostratus (quoted): II, 31 and n

Pierantonio: III, 655, 657n

Pindar: I, 90; II, 85, 267, 268n

Pinkerton, Percy E.: II, 932, 933n; III, 76 and n, 136, 138–39, 459, 460n, 526, 527n, 698, 699n, 700, 750, 782; S's rev of *Galeazzo*: III, 137n, 460n

Piombo, Sebastiano del: III, 630, 631n, 639, 655, 657n

Pirie, Alexander: II, 197 and n, 204, 205n, 206, 261, 262n; III, 304, 348, 349n, 391–92, 393n

Pirie, Arthur Lindsay: III, 388 and n

Pisani, Count Almorò: III, 525

Pisani, Countess Almorò: III 343n, 374, 375n, 383, 406, 449, 500, 519, 521–22, 524–25, 569, 576, 593, 689, 697, 702, 704, 708, 762–63, 768, 773, 779, 780n,

916

Scottish and Italian ballads: III, 847–52
"Sea Calls, The" (ps): II, 703n, 759
Sebright, Mrs. John George: II, 471, 472n
Seckendorf, Count: III, 763, 764n
Sedlatzek, Johann: I, 290 and n
Seeley, John (engineer): II, 785
Seeley, John Robert: I, 618n
Segni, Bernardo: II, 319, 321n
Sellajo, Lionardo: III, 614 and n
Sellar, William Young: II, 96 and n; III, 309, 310n
Semitecolo, Nocoló: I, 424, 425n
Senior, the Rev. Walter: I, 405, 406n
Sepoy Mutiny, the: I, 592, 598n
"Sequel, A" (p): III, 795, 796n
"Series on Self" (ps): II, 708 and n
Servetus, Michael: III, 39, 40n
Severn, Joseph: II, 981, 983n
Sex: *see* Censors of Morals; Chivalry (Modern); Comradeship; *Ethics, A Problem in Greek; Ethics, A Problem in Modern;* Greek Comradeship; Greek (Hellenic) Love; Homosexual love and its benefits; Homosexuality, Cases of; "Inverted Sexuality"; Homosexuality: Penal Codes; Sexual Inversion; Socialism and Sexual Inverts
Sexual Inversion: III, 753–54, 787–89, 797–99
Sexual Inversion (b with Havelock Ellis): I, 37; III, 691, 693–94, 709–11, 788–89, 789–90ns, 797–99, 804, 805n, 808, 809n, 816–18 and n, 820–21
Sforza, Gian Galeazzo: III, 184, 185n, 208, 209–10n, 212
Shairp, John Campbell: II, 372n, 461, 469, 469–70n, 473, 477
Shakespeare, William: I, 90, 134, 173, 174n, 201, 243, 244n, 354, 401, 434, 510, 511, 616, 623–24, 641, 646, 648, 795 and ns, 838, 839; II, 36, 56, 64, 82, 126, 276, 307; III, 81, 101n, 102, 438, 503, 821; quoted: I, 422 and n, 429, 430n, 441 and n, 679, 680n, 758, 759n, 821, 822n; II, 72, 73n, 275, 276n, 405 and n, 417, 418n; III, 589 and n, 708, 709n; problem of the *Sonnets:* I, 603–04 and n; II, 26, 472–73 and n, 708
Shakspere (spelling by S): II, 873
Shakspere's Predecessors (b): II, 656, 657n, 686, 782, 784, 787, 789, 791, 793, 795, 796n, 816n, 819n, 828, 833–34,

842–44, 846, 848, 854, 860, 865, 873, (pay for) 873–74, 888, 895, (rev by Vernon Lee) 889 and n, 915, 934; III, 36, 96, 97n, 101, 129, 136, 853
Shannon, Charles Hazelwood: III, 582, 583n
Sharp, William ("Fiona MacLeod"): II, 815 and n, 818, 825, 870, 871n, 952, 953n; III, 73, 74n
Sharp, Mrs. William: II, 815n
Shaw, Alexander: I, 71, 73n
"Sheepfold, The Song of the" (p): II, 137
Shelley, Jane Gibson: I, 252n, 330n; III, 216, 219n
Shelley, Percy Bysshe: I, 31, 36, 223–24 and n, 227, 251, 252n, 268, 328, 330n, 386, 449, 454, 478, 499, 500n, 546, 648, 811; II, 246, 423, 453–54, 494, 501, 507–08, 510, 533, 566–67, 572–73 and ns, 629, 651–52 and ns, 652–55, 847 and ns, 872–73 and n, 885; III, 28, 106, 247, 800, 853; quoted: II, 89 and n, 318; III, 651, 652n
Shelley (b): II, 498 and n, 508, 538, 548, 558, 561, 571, (revs) 571, 572, 573n, 579, 583, (rev of) 585n, 585–86, 670, (rev by James Thomson) 982, 983n; III, 198–99
"Shelleys" (books): II, 459, 461, 466, 470, 484
Sherrington, Helen Lemmens: I, 399, 400n; II, 70 and n
Shore, Arabella: I, 765, 766n
Shorthouse, Joseph Henry: II, 740, 741n
Shorting, Charles George: I, 186, 187n, 229, 232, 243, 282, 376, 378n; II, 56
Shrenk-Notzing, Baron Albert: III, 813, 814n
Shuttleworth, James Phillips Kay-: I, 251n, 523, 740; II, 92, 93n
Shuttleworth, Janet Elizabeth Kay-: I, 508n; II, 406, 569; III, 876
Shuttleworth, Lady Janet Kay-: I, 250, 251n, 360
Shuttleworth, Dr. Lionel Kay-: II, 878, 880n, 892, 904, 909, 919, 937, 943, 952; III, 37, 879
Shuttleworth, Ughtred Kay-: I, 535, 571, 572 and n, 704; II, 92, 93 and n
Sicilian prose tales: III, 852 and n
Sicily: II, 288–93; III, 846; brigandage in: II, 281, 282n, 288–89, 291

918

Smith, Sir William: I, 769, 773, 774n; II, 451–52, 457–58, 469, 507, 508n, 527, 528n, 539, 540n, 786, 787n
Smithson, Sir Hugh: II, 932, 933n
Smollet, Tobias: II, 625
Smythe, Percy E. F. W. (Lord Strangford): I, 220, 221n
Social Science, National Association for the Promotion of: II, 84, 85, 86n, 87
Socialism: III, 84–85
Socialism and sexual inverts: III, 808, 809n
Society of Authors: III, 689, 690n
Socrates: I, 251, 274, 630
Sodoma, Il (Bazzi, Giovanni): II, 438, 439n
Solly, Miss: I, 531, 677 and n
Solly, Dr. Samuel: I, 518, 519n
Solomon, Simeon: I, 852, 853n; II, 27, 28n, 43, 44n, 388–89, 389–90n; III, 394 and n, 399
Somerset, Lord Henry Richard Charles: II, 791 and n; III, 354 and n, 813
"Somersetshire House, Notes of a" (art): III, 92 and n
Somerville Hall: II, 979–80
Sommer, H. Oskar: III, 510, 511n
Sophocles: I, 77, 90, 125, 175, 748; II, 379, 438
Sotheby's: II, 645 and n
Southern Europe, Sketches and Studies in (b): II, 615, 616n; III, 737n
Southey, Robert: I, 90, 256, 258n, 365 and n
"South Seas" (p): III, 319–20
Souvestre, Emile: I, 114, 115n
Spartian: II, 527, 528n, 534
Spence, Mr.: III, 647, 648n
Spencer, Herbert, and Spencerism: II, 830, 837 and n
Spengler, Dr. Alexander: III, 52, 53n
Spenser, Edmund: I, 167, 200; III, 100, 101n, 139, 180, 181n, 394 and n; quoted: III, 121 and n
Spinoza, Baruch: I, 376, 401, 551, 738, 739n; II, 978 and n
Spiritualism: see Ghosts
Spiritualized Stocism: III, 219–20, 222
Spohr, Ludwig: I, 203, 204, 205n, 307–08, 309n, 393 and n, 520 and n, 522
Sports: Symonds Cup and Symonds

Shield: III, 288n, 332–33, 340, 353, 357–58
Spottiswoode (Eyre and Spottiswoode, printers): II, 404 and n, 406, 730, 731n
Spottiswoode, William: II, 412, 413n, 414
Springer, Anton: III, 656, 657n
Squire, William Barclay: I, 36; III, 316n, 318, 400, 681
Staël, Mme. Germaine de: I, 401, 402n
Stafford, William: II, 982, 983n
Stanhope, Philip Henry: I, 285n
Stanhope Prize: I, 285 and n, 295, 354
Stanley, Arthur Penrhyn: I, 68, 69n, 224 and n, 235, 238, 239, 278, 280, 281, 284, 285 and n, 292, 293n, 321, 330, 331, 332n, 333 and n, 525, 527, 528n, 539n
Stanley, Edward Henry, 15th Earl of Derby: II, 540, 540–41n
Stanley, Edward Lyulph (Lord Sheffield): I, 223, 224n, 239, 267n, 268n, 276, 277n, 282, 322, 363; II, 456 and n; III, 160 and n, 165
Stanton Harcourt Church: I, 236, 237n
Stead, William Thomas: III, 106, 107n
Steel, the Rev. Thomas Henry: I, 69, 70n, 92, 93n, 112, 114 and n
"Stella Maris" (ps): II, 672 and n, 882, 885, 893, 895, 913, 929, 940, 946, 963, 967, 973; III, (revs of) 25 and 26n, 96, 129, 130n, 238, 624 and n, 663
Stendhal (Henri Beyle): II, 325; III, 132 and n, 153, 154n, 547
Stephen, Leslie, I, 36; II, 129n, 209n, 456, 457n, 501, 659, 701–02, 759; III, 341 and n, 342, 396, 606, 652, 796, 812
Stephen, Mrs. Leslie: III, 390, 396, 403n, 404
Stephen, (Julius) Thoby: III, 414, 415n
Stephens, William Richard Wood: I, 180, 181n, 248, 251, 263, 268, 279, 283, 304n, 307–09, 316, 327, 340–41, 343, 345, 366, 399, 438 and n, 466, 475, 476n, 477, 727, 729, 735n
Sterchi, Herr (Swiss innkeeper): II, 76, 77n, 159 and n
Sterling, John: II, 640
Sterne, Laurence: I, 796 and n; Tristiam Shandy, II, 789
Stevens, Frederick Haller: II, 560, 562n
Stevenson, Robert Louis: I, 31, 35; II, 645n, 659, 664, 668, 690–91 and n,

702, 705, 708 and n, 712, 716–17, 721, 732, 741, 745–46 and n, 748, 750, 811, 861, 917, 921, 955; III, 80, 109, 142, 150, 267, 268n, 318, 518, 519n, 664–65, 828, 878–79; *Child's Garden of Verse:* III, 40, 41n, 46–48 and n; *Deacon Brodie:* II, 759, 760n; *Dr. Jekyll and Mr. Hyde:* III, 118, 119n, 120–21, 249; *Dynamiter, The:* III, 47, 48n; *Footnote to History, A:* III, 823 and n; *Master of Ballantrae:* III, 410–11; *Merry Men:* II, 759 and n; *New Arabian Nights:* II, 793, 794n; *Prince Otto:* II, 866; III, 118, 119n; "Talk and Talkers": II, 742, 743n; *Treasure Island:* II, 843 and n

Stevenson, Mrs. R. L.: II, 664, 702, 703, 746, 748, 750, 758, 759, 791, 821, 843, 917; III, 823 and n, 878

Stillman, William James: III, 706, 706–07n

Stillman, Mrs. William James: II, 792, 793n

Stillwell, James, John G., and Thomas: I, 317 and n, 327

Stoddard, Charles Warren: III, 76 and n, 799, 799–800n, 814 and n

Stone, Alfred: II, 164 and n

Stone, Edward James: I, 297, 298n

Storge: II, 68 and n

Stornelli: III, 169, 170n, (tr by S) 169–70

Storr, Francis: I, 67, 68n

Story, Julian: II, 751, 753n

Story, William Wetmore: I, 436, 437n, 438

Stowe, Harriet Beecher: II, 82, 83n

Stowell, Hugh: I, 231, 232n

Strachey, Constance (niece) (Mrs. Edward Strachey): III, 595 and n

Strachey, Sir Edward (brother-in-law): I, 30, 50n, 119, 120n, 124, 141, 171n, 172, 190, 201, 219–20n, 228 and n, 241, 264, 280, 306 and n, 307, 377, 390, 397, 562, 591 and n, 634, 635, 793n; II, 348, 561, 850, 925; III, 595, 652

Strachey, Edward, family: I, 50n, 219–20n; II, 850–51

Strachey, (Edith) Frances (niece): I, 50n, 220n; II, 850, 851 and n

Strachey, George Edward: I, 367 and n

Strachey, Henry (nephew): I, 50n, 220n; III, 187 and n, 559, 560n, 595 and n

Strachey, Lady Mary Isabella (sister): *see* Symonds, Mary Isabella

Strachey, Richard Charles: I, 207n

Strachey, (John) St. Loe (nephew): I, 50n, 220n, 228n, 591n; II, 484–85, (L to Whitman) 485–86 and n, 525, 568, 678, 679n, 690, 691n, 718, 720n, 764, 768, 769 and n, 770–71, 773, 781, 784, 790, 851, 878, 879; III, 62, 136, 187 and n

Stradanus, Jo.: III, 702, 703n, 743, 775, 775–76n, 781, 800; his *Dante,* "Intro." to by S: III, 765

Stratford-on-Avon: III, 724, 729

Straton (Strato) of Lampascus: III, 788, 789n

Straton (Strato) of Sardis: II, 965–66n

Strauss, David Friedrich: I, 533 and n

Strickland, Agnes: I, 120, 121n

Strickland, F. de Beauchamp: III, 412, 413n

Strong, Agnes (cousin): I, 629; II, 287, 288n, 292–93, 461 and n; III, 846

Strong, Charlotte Symonds (aunt): I, 131, 170, 180, 285n, 465n, 503, 585, 613 and n, 624, 629, 644, 762; III, 846; family of: I, 203

Strong, Clement Dawsonne (uncle): I, 285 and n, 465n; III, 640 and n

Strong, Clementina (cousin): I, 65n, 285n, 367 and n, 385, 386n, 443n, 447, 452, 465n, 468, 575, 586n, 613 and n, 623, 627, 644, 645n, 652

Strong, Dawsonne Melancthon (cousin): I, 89 and n, 189, 196, 208, 210, 285n, 465n, 586n, 652, 654

Strong, Herbert Augustus: I, 285 and n

Stuckey's Bank: II, 579, 580n

Stufa, the Marchese Lottaringo della: II, 385, 386n, 660; III, 156–57, 170, 633, 634n

"Style, Notes on" (art): III, 351, 352n, 455–56

Suidas: II, 331, 332n

Suetonius: II, 155n

Sully, James: II, 363n

Sulmona: III, 617, 618, 620

Summer, John Bird: I, 275, 276n, 280

Sutherland, family of 2nd Duke of: III, 813, 814n

Sutton Court: I, 141, 151, 286, 305, 306n,

312, 451, 561; II, 39, 47, 69, 222 and n, 679 and n; III, 247, 652, 803

Suvarov, Aleksandr Vasilyevitch: I, 648, 652n

Swayne, Dr. Joseph Griffiths: II, 149 and n

Swinburne, Algernon Charles: I, 35, 595, 663, 664n, 666, 680, 774, 776 and n, 803; II, 102–03, 141, 161, 162, 246, 251n, 253, 285, 363, 567, 872, 873n; III, 99, 101, 102n, 114, 129, (on Whitman) 257–58 and 259n, 262, 269, (on Charlotte Brontë) 877; *Bothwell:* II, 349, 351; *Chapman* and S's rev of: II, 366, 367n; *Erechtheus:* II, 394, 403, (rev by S) 396n; *Poems and Ballads:* I, 663, (rev by S) 664n; *Songs before Sunrise:* III, 257; *Study of Shakespeare:* II, 873; "Tombeau de T. Gautier, Le": II, 266, 267ns; *Tristram of Lyonesse:* II, (and S's rev) 760 and n, 762, 763n; "Walt Whitman in America, To": II, 180, 181n; *William Blake:* I, 791, 792n

Swiss Athletic Sports: II, 929, 932

"Swiss Athletic Sports" (art): III, 598, 599n, 603, 604n, 606, 607n, 627

Swiss government: III, 84–85

Swiss Highlands, Our Life in the (b with Margaret Symonds): I, 34; III, 633, 635, 640–41, 642, (photos for) 644–45 and n, 654, 658, 661, 664, 667, 670, 671, 676 and n, 680, 683, (rev by Symons) 690–91 and n, 697, 702, 734

Sykes, Sir Anthony Charles (cousin): I, 105n

Sykes, James: I, 328n, 409n

Sykes, Admiral John: I, 135 and n, 317n, 328n, 582, 583

Sykes, Mrs. Maria Henrietta Abdy (grandmother): I, 99, 106, 107n, 110n, 140, 238n, 313, 330n, 341 and n

Sykes, Mary Ann (aunt): I, 52, 53n, 59, 60, 86, 99, 106, 109, 112, 115, 119, 122, 128–29, 135–36, 140, 144, 148, 151, 158–59, 161, 167, 170, 187, 192, 194, 198, 201, 204, 206, 209, 212, 220, 225–26, 245–47, 253, 267, 273, 276, 280, 299, 300, 306, 311–12, 328, 333, 371, 374, 392, 394, 406–07, 411, 414, 416, 482, 492, 507, 522, 528, 552, 560, 582, 605, 629–30, 634, 637, 654, 727, 752, 754, 806, 807n; II, 48, 140n, 141,

602, 819–20; III, 52, 138, (moves to Oxford) 142–45, 186–87, 324

Sylva, Carmen, Queen of Roumania: II, 936

Sylvester Abend: III, 117

Symon, Adam Fitz-: II, 712

Symonds, Alfred Radford (uncle): I, 66 and n

Symonds, Mrs. Ann (aunt): I, 52 and n, 83, 141, 170, 171, 172, 175, 186, 212, 216, 222, 228, 235 and n, 247, 289, 313, 317, 362, 365, 367, 369, 393

Symonds, Annie (cousin): II, 378 and n

Symonds, (Janet) Catherine North (wife): I, 36–37, 39, 251n, 345n, 407, 408n, 414n, 480n, 485, 492n, 493n, 495, 496 and n, 497, 498–99, 501, 507, 508n, 512, 513n, 516 and n, 518, 520, 522, 527, 528, 532, 540, 541, 548, 550, 552, 553 and n, 554, 556, 560, 563 and n, 569, 571, 574, 578, 580 and n, 581, 583, 585–86, 588, 589, 598, 601, 605, 613, 615–19, 621–22, 623 and n, 624, 627, 629, 630, 632, 634, 637, 641–47, 651, 656, 669, 673, 679, 681, 691, 693, 699, 703, 712, 713n, 714, 727, 728, 739, 743–47, 749, 751–57, 760–63, 765, 768–69, 771, 774, 777, 786, 789, 794, 804, 806, 812, 815, 817, 823n, 828, 831, 848, 849, 852; II, 26, 34, 38, 40, 45, 47, 49, 51, 54, 58–59, 65, 76, 79, 84–85, 90–91, 92n, 92–93, 99, (article on Monte Generoso) 106, 107n, 108, 109, 113, 116, 118–19, 126, 129, 137 and n, 140–42, 146, 148, 151–52, 156, 161, 174, 187, 190, 192–93, 197, 204, 207, 208, 211, 219, 221–22, 232, 234, 240–41, 243–44, 246, 254, 268, 271, 274, 278, 324, 510, 513, 516, 517, 524, 532, 533, 629, 631, 639, (reaction to S's book on Dante) 679, 706, 709 and n, 710n, (dislike for Davos) 744, 810, 812, 820, 900, 904, 909, 913, 914, 917; III, 738, 775, 837, 839

Symonds, Charlotte Byron (Green) (sister): I, 29, 30, 49, 50–51n, 52, 99, 115, 130, 161, 184n, 209, 238, 241, 273, 305, 307, 351, 356n, 409, 412, 415–16, 419, 469, 485n, 502n, 508 and n, 516, 525n, 538, 583, 624, 630, 712, 713n, 719, 728, 744n, 754, 766n, 802, 806–07, 817; II, 47, 141, 151n, 152, 154, 168,

568, 568–69n; *Principles of Beauty:* I, 93n; *Versus and Miscellanies* (ed. by S): II, 141–42 and n, 152 and n, 184

Symonds, Joshua: I, 131, 132n; II, 681, 682n; III, 668–69

Symonds, Katharine (Furse) (daughter): I, 37, 606n; II, 370n, 390n, 391, 392n, 402, 503, 638n, 820, 907; III, 116, 117, 227, 402, 411, 626, 715; at school in Switzerland: 747 and n; visited by S in Lausanne: 750–51; advice to: 751–52, 839–40n

Symonds, Lotta: *see* Symonds, Charlotte Mary (daughter)

Symonds, Margaret (daughter): I, 34, 414n, 507n, 580n, 630n, 785n, 792n, 793 and n, 801; II, 28n, 38 and n, 41 and n, 163n, 176, 179n, 249, 293, 489, 900–04, 906–09, 911, 913–14, 917; III, 26–27, 31, 389–91, (advice from S) 402–05, 414–16, (advice about writing) 497–98, (advice about drawing) 513, (at Vescovana) 569, 580, 626, 681, 707, 720 and n, 824, 834–35, 839, 839–40n; *Days Spent on a Doge's Farm:* 702 and n, 766–67 and ns, 771, 772n; *see also Swiss Highlands, Our Life in the*

Symonds, Mary Isabella (Maribella) (Lady Strachey) (sister): I, 34, 49, 50n, 59, 63, 71, 76, 84, 86, 91, 95, 99, 104–05, 109, 110n, 121, 122 and n, 123–24, 128–29, 131, 141, 144, 170, 171n, 190, 220n, 222, 228 and n, 230, 241, 245, 248, 264, 266, 280, 289, 306 and n, 307, 313, 324–25, 365n, 367, 377, 390, 394, 397, 477, 479, 488, 591 and n, 601–02, 626, 629–30, 634, 637, 700, 752; II, 163n, 222n, 378–79, 471, 634, (death) 850, 853–54, 857, 859, 871, 879, 917

Symonds, Percy Horatio (cousin): I, 50n, 186, 187n; II, 738

Symonds, Samuel: II, 712 and n, 973; III, 78n, 89

Symonds, Lady Susan (aunt): I, 69, 70n

Symonds, William: II, 640, 641n

Symons, Arthur: I, 36; III, 96–98 and n, 101, 102 and n, 113–14, 115n, 128, 130n, 130–32 and n, 150, 152–53, 360–61, 432–33, 459, 691 and n, 693, 753 and n, 764–65, (rev of OLSH) 690 and n

Symons, Elizabeth: II, 712, 713n

Tacitus, Cornelius: I, 81, 125, 211; III, 505–06, 509

Tagliacozzo: III, 618 and n, 619

Taine, Hippolyte: I, 487 and n, 839, 840n

Tairraz, Jean: II, 95n, 302, 314, 315n, 317 and n, 320; III, 327

Tait, Archibald Campbell: I, 113, 114 and n, 122n

Tait, Walter James: I, 229, 230n, 274

Tallis, Thomas: I, 176 and n, 212 and n

Talmud, the: I, 784

Tardieu, A.: III, 694, 695n

Tarnowsky, B.: III, 694, 695n

Tasso, Bernardo: I, 809; III, 87 and n

Tasso, Torquato: II, 601, 602n, 632n; III, 36, 64, 65, 70–71, 74, 85, 86n, 100, 101n, 107

"Tasso" (art): III, 125

Tassoni, Alessandro: I, 809; III, 87

Tauchnitz, Baron Christian: I, 784, 785n; II, 364 and n, 810

Taxil, Leo: III, 694, 695n

Tay Bridge Incident: II, 619, 620n

Taylor (Bristol jeweler): I, 86, 87n, 126; II, 164 and n

Taylor, Jeremy: III, 271

Taylor Institution Galleries: I, 152, 153n, 225 and n; II, 502

Telesio, Bernardino: III, 75 and n

Temple, Frederick: I, 174, 175n, 231, 232n, 270n

Temple, Miss: II, 300, 301n

Tennant, Sir Charles: III, 250, 253n, 626, 730, 733–34, 742, 824

Tennant, (Emma Winsloe) Lady: III, 250, 252, 626, 734

Tennant, Mrs. Harold John (Helen Gordon-Duff): III, 593 and n

Tennant, Henry: I, 590n

Tennant, Margot: I, 36; III, 183 and n, 250, 253n, 279–80, 281–82, 283, 371–72, 441, 598, 602, 604, 626, 734, 736, 756, 757n, 775–76, 824

Tennyson, Alfred, Lord: I, 30, 31, 35, 90, 91n, 105, 106ns, 213, 233, 248, 287, 288n, 298, 330, 375, 376n, 386, 388n, 449–50, 480, 506 and n, 509–11, 512n, 513, 534, 566 and n, 567, 570, 591–98, 603–04, 673, 683–84, 698n, 708, 802, 803n, 808, 809n, 810–11, 825, 836, 839, 845 and n, 853; II, 139, 176, 177 and n, 313, 346, 446, 577, 703, 704n, 773;

924

III, 106, 107n, 114, 122n, 163, 164n, 183, 235, 250, 271, 341, 365, 440–41, 548, 609, 713 and n, 756, 757n; quoted: I, 90, 150 and n, 188, 189n, 266, 267n, 478n, 636 and n, 779, 780n; II, 100 and n, 425, 426n, 637, 638n, 906 and n, 923, 924n; III, 417 and n, 735, 736n, 743–45 and ns

"Tennyson, Recollections of Lord" (art): III, 762 and n, 784–85 and n

Tennyson, Mrs. Alfred: I, 30, 509, 510, 512, 615 and n, 666n; II, 216 and n; III, 745, 845n

Tennyson, Hallam, 2nd Lord: I, 510, 511n, 512, 545n, 650, 698n, 708n; III, 743–44, 784, 785n

Tennyson, Mrs. Hallam (Audry Boyle): III, 743, 745n, 785, 786n

Tennyson, Lionel: I, 510, 511n, 608, 609n, 614, 650

Terentianus Marus (quoted): II, 680, 681n; III, 799, 800n

"Terza Rima, Studies in" (ps): II, 183, 184n

Thackeray, Anne Isabella (Lady Ritchie): I, 220, 221n; II, 333 and n, 334, 335n, 346, 431

Thackeray, William Makepiece: I, 136 and n, 268, 269n; II, 209n, 229, 861

"Theism, Notes on" (art): III, 350

Theocritus: I, 251, 252n, 257, 260, 278 and n, 588, 628, 682, 684n, 698; II, 55; III, 82, 579, 580n, 846

"Theodore" (p): I, 39, 472, 473n

Thirlwall, Newell G.: I, 97, 99n

Thomas, Edith M.: II, 936 and n, 939, 954

Thomas, Gertrude: II, 180 and n

Thomas, Lewis William: I, 391, 392n

Thompson, Alice Christiana (later Meynell): II, 453, 454n

Thompson, Sir Henry: II, 85, 86n; III, 685–86 and n

Thompson, Henry Yates: I, 128, 134, 135n, 138, 249 and n; II, 757

Thompson, Mrs. Henry Yates: II, 339 and n, 757n

Thompson, Jacob: I, 266, 267n

Thompson, Dr. Reginald Edward: II, 384, 384–85n

Thomson, James ("B.V."): II, 583, 875,

876n, 883–84, 886, 980–82, 981n; III, 28, 359

Thoreau, Henry David (quoted): III, 598–99 and n

Thornycroft, Mrs. Mary: I, 344 and n

Thornycroft, William Hamo: II, 927 and n, 929, 954, 956–57, 961; III, 466, 555, 556n

"Thought, Priority of, to Language" (art): III, 350

"Thought, Progress of, in Our Time, The" (art): III, 236, 237n, 299

Thucydides: I, 90, 95, 267n, 290, 297; II, 293, 294n, 320

Thurlow, Edward, 1st Baron: III, 877

Thurlow, Thomas John Bruce, 5th Baron: II, 560, 562n

"Thusis, At a Jura Feast in": III, 683–84n

Thynn, Francis: II, 982, 983n

Tiberius: III, 506, 507

Ticknor, George: II, 896, 897n; III, 111, 112n

Tiepolo, Giovanni Battista: II, 810, 858; III, 582, 583n, 584ns, 628

"Tiepolo, On an Altar-Piece of" (art): II, 810, 811n; III, 582–83 and n, 584n

Tietjens, Mme. Therese: I, 206, 207n, 353n, 391, 392n, 399, 489; II, 70, 420 and n

Time, Italian reckoning of: III, 173

Timoleon: II, 284 and n

Timon of Athens: II, 649 and n

Tintoretto, Il (Robusti, Jacopo): II, 114 and n, 480, 481n, 810, 982

Tiraboschi, Girolamo: I, 379 and n, 380; II, 214, 215n, 227, 244, 245n, 336, 535, 537, 549; III, 152 and n

Tirindelli, Pier Adolfo: III, 763, 764n

Titian: I, 715 and n, 811, 814; II, 115n, 511; III, 376

Tivoli, Vitale de: II, 502, 503n

"Toady Tree, The" (p): I, 98, 99n

Toboggan (Bob Sled) Races (at Davos): II, 799, 800–02n; III, 29, 200, 287–88, 331–34, 342, 352–53, 357–58, 443

"Toboggin Race, An International" (art): II, 800–02n

Todhunter, John: II, 445, 446n, 651, 652n, 652–54

Tollemache, Lionel A.: I, 223, 224n; III, 65, 66n

Velasquez, Rodriguez: I, 533n, 542 and n
Veneroni, Giovanni: I, 369, 370n
Venetian Archives: II, 912 and n
"Venetian Medley" (p): II, 752, 753n, 765, 766n, 809
"Venetian Melancholy" (art): III, 781, 782n, 790, 794, 804
"Venetian Vilote" (p): II, 791n
Veneziano, Lorenzo: I, 424, 425n
Venice: II, 701, 706, 812, 814–15 and n, 817, 821–22, 906, 910–11, 913; III, 36–37, 41, 45, 47, 48–49, 110–11, 304–07, 372–78, 459, 465–66, 767–69, 772–73, 775–76
"Venice, Prayer of to her King" (tr by S): II, 863, 864
Venier, Lorenzo: II, 811, 812n
Venturi, Silvio: III, 810, 811n
Verdant Green: III, 873–74
Verdi, Giuseppe: I, 206; II, 437, 438n; III, 875
Verlaine, Paul: III, 571, 572n, 587, 588n; quoted: 677
Veronese, Paolo: I, 811; II, 242
Verrochio, Andrea del: III, 200, 201n
Verse capping: I, 173n
Vescovana: III, 519, 522, 569, 580, 689, 715, 719, 760, 771, 773, 776, 779
Vespasiano da Bisticci: II, 318, 320n
Vianelli (photographer): III, 790, 791n
Vickers, Randall William: I, 86, 87n, 116–17, 191
Vico, Giovanni Battista: III, 75
Victoria, Queen: I, 161, 163n, 762n; II, 91n
Viesseux, Giampietro: III, 614 and n
Vigny, Alfred de: I, 385, 386n
Vilda, Mme. (Marie Wilt): II, 70 and n; III, 876
Villa, Emily: II, 901, 902 and n, 906, 908n
Villani, Giovanni: II, 284, 285n, 479, 480n
Villari, Pasquale: I, 527–28, 529n, 530 and n; II, 385, 386n, 496, 771, 772n, 792, 807, 811, 845, 853, 887–88 and n, 898; III, 353, 406, 541, 611, 630, 654–56
Villari, Mrs. Pasquale: III, 835
Vilote, the Italian: II, 791, 839
Virgil: I, 94, 125, 131, 174, 216 and n, 223, 388, 441, 528n, 648, 689; II, 31n; III, 101n, 271, 523, 678
Visconti, Filippo Maria: III, 212, 213n

"Vista, A" (p): II, 520–21, 521n; *see also* "In Wanderstunden Geschrieben"
Vivarini, Antonio, Bartolommeo, and Alvise: I, 424, 425n, 499, 500n
Vizetelly, Henry Richard (publisher): III, 151, 154, 283
Volksbuch, the: I, 423 and n
Volpini, Salvatore: III, 707, 709n
Voltaire: II, 242 and n; "Voltarism": II, 35
Vondel, Joost van der: II, 482, 483n
Vosmaer, Carel: II, 536n
Waagen, Gustav Friedrich: I, 343 and n
Wagner, Richard: I, 334; II, 417, 474, 764, 968 and n; III, 592, 670
Wailes, William: I, 123, 124n, 146, 147n
Wait, Mr. and Mrs. William Killigrew: I, 204, 205n; II, 530, 531n
Waite, John: II, 175, 176n
"Waiting (Heart and Head Converse Together)" (p): III, 498 and n, 504 and n
Waldegrave, Frances Elizabeth, Countess: II, 385, 386n, 451, 452ns, 453
Waldegrave (-Leslie), George: I, 558, 559n
Waldstein, Charles: II, 574 and n
Wales, Prince of (later Edward VII): I, 216, 331; II, 90
Walker, Frederick: III, 736 and n
Walker, John Chesshyre: II, 177 and n
Walker, S. A.: II, 96 and n
Walker, Miss: II, 516 and n
Wall, Henry: II, 278, 279n, 294n
Wallace, Alfred Russel: III, 853, 854n
Wallace, Dr. J. W.: III, 563–64n, 666, 730, 731n, 733, 791, 792 and n, 809, 811, 812n
Wallace, William: II, 390, 391n
Wallace, Sir William: I, 157, 158n
Waller, Edmund: III, 100, 101n
Walsh, William P.: I, 237n
Walter of Lille: III, 344, 345n
Wantage, 1st Baron: *see* Lindsay, Robert James Loyd-
Warburton, the Rev. W. P.: II, 489, 491n
Ward, Genevieve (Mme. Guerrabella): I, 401, 402n
Ward, Mrs. Humphry: II, 517 and n, 892 and n
"Warning for Fair Women, A" (Anon.): III, 136, 137n

Herbert M. Schueller, from 1955–1968 chairman of the Department of English, Wayne State University, and twice acting associate dean of the College of Liberal Arts, Wayne State University, holds B.A. and M.A. degrees from the University of Minnesota and a Ph.D. degree from the University of Michigan. The author of numerous articles on literature, music, and aesthetics, he has translated several works on aesthetics from the German, has been editor of *Criticism—A Quarterly for Literature and the Arts*, and since 1963 has been editor of the *Journal of Aesthetics and Art Criticism*. He has received four ACLS travel grants: to Athens, Greece, Amsterdam, and Uppsala, Sweden, to attend the IVth, Vth, and VIth International Congresses for Aesthetics, and to England and Switzerland to gather Symonds materials.

Robert L. Peters is a well-known poet and a professor of English at the University of California at Irvine. His B.A., M.A. and Ph.D. degrees were all earned at the University of Wisconsin. He was the winner of the Hilberry Publication Prize with *The Crown of Apollo: Swinburne's Principles of Literature and Art* (Wayne State University Press, 1964). He is also the editor of *Victorians on Literature & Art* (Appleton Century Crofts, 1961) as well as numerous articles and essays. His volumes of poetry include *Songs for A Son* (W. W. Norton, Inc., 1967), *Pioneers of Modern Poetry* (with George Hitchcock, Kayak Press, 1967), and *The Sow's Head and Other Poems* (Wayne State University Press, 1968).

The manuscripts for Volumes I, II, and III were edited by Elvin T. Gidley and Alexander Brede. The volume set was designed by Richard Kinney. The text type face is Mergenthaler Linotype's Granjon designed by George W. Jones (1928–1931) based on a Garamond type of the late 16th century. The display face is Garamont also derived from type designed by Claude Garamond.

The book is printed on S. D. Warren's Olde Style Antique and bound in Columbia Mills' Riverside Chambray cloth. Manufactured in the United States of America.